THE YOUNG READER'S

COMPANION TO

AMERICAN

HISTORY

West Feb. 6

THE YOUNG READER'S COMPANION TO AMERICAN HISTORY

JOHN A. GARRATY

EDITOR

Houghton Mifflin Company

Boston   New York

For information about permission to reproduce selections
from this book, write to Permissions, Houghton Mifflin Company,
215 Park Avenue South, New York, New York 10003.

Library of Congress Cataloging-in-Publication Data

The young reader's companion to American history / John A. Garraty, editor.
    p.   cm.
   Includes index.
  ISBN 0-395-66920-0
   1. United States—History—Encyclopedias—Juvenile literature.
  I. Garraty, John Arthur, date.
  E174.Y68 1994
  973'.03—dc20
                                94-22759
                                CIP

Book design by Anne Chalmers

Printed in the United States of America

DOW 10 9 8 7 6 5 4 3 2 1

CONTENTS

MAPS AND TABLES

MAPS

TABLES

INTRODUCTION

Students often turn to the family library when faced with a homework assignment, or simply when they want to uncover the details or the significance of a particular event. But all too often the shelf of reference books is stacked with works that are dry, out of date, or assume too much background knowledge on the part of younger members of the family. Furthermore, most students are interested in subjects that are not always covered in conventional encyclopedias designed for adults.

The Young Reader's Companion to American History is meant to provide students with answers to questions about the American past that take into account the latest scholarship and are written with the special interests and capacities of such readers in mind. The volume is designed for readers age eleven and up, but this is only a rough gauge. The book will in fact capture the interest of precocious younger children and at the same time provide material sophisticated enough to benefit students throughout high school. An encyclopedia format has the advantage of permitting each reader to follow his or her own interests: younger readers may gravitate toward the entries on Pocahontas, the Minutemen, Harry Houdini, or the gold rushes, whereas older students might focus on Watergate, the Civil War, NATO, or *Brown* v. *Board of Education.* And if these articles are not challenging enough, there are pieces on Jeffersonian democracy, social legislation, and the antitrust movement—articles that may be passed over by younger readers but should appeal to the high school senior with an above-average interest in history, and, no doubt, to a parent or two.

Our main purpose, of course, has been to provide the young adult reader with the basics of American history, with articles about everything from abolitionism and the Alamo to the XYZ Affair and the Zenger trial. There are biographies of every president, as well as of other famous Americans, ranging from Samuel Adams, Louisa May Alcott, and Marian Anderson to Richard Wright, John Wayne, and Eli Whitney.

Like *The Reader's Companion to American History,* an encyclopedia for adults that inspired the creation of this volume, *The Young Reader's Companion* pays as much attention to social and cultural history as to political topics. There are articles on the history of poverty and homelessness, on affirmative action, libraries and museums, crime, painting and sculpture, police and fire departments, censorship, and the Sixties. Controversial issues such as birth control, abortion, drugs, and gun control are also covered, for these "adult" topics are ones that many children are deeply interested in, do not always understand, and will be hearing more and more about as time goes on.

The histories of minority groups and of women also figure prominently in the encyclopedia, both in separate articles devoted to their experiences and through the integration of women and minorities in discussions in which they were previously neglected. There is, for example, an article on women and work, but the history of women is also treated in the general articles on pioneer and frontier life, espionage, the labor movement, and in many other pieces.

Above all, as editor I have cast as wide a net as possible while trying to confine the book to a single volume. Where biographies are concerned, I have had to leave out some "famous" people in order to include less obviously important ones whose impact on America may not have been as strong, but whose lives are likely to be of greater interest to our audience. There is no biography of Adlai Stevenson, for example, but there are sketches of Muhammad Ali and Bob Dylan, who represent aspects of American life that also deserve mention. The biographical entries provide an estimation of the subjects' significance and achievements instead of simply factual accounts of their lives.

The encyclopedia is meant primarily as a reference tool, but it is my hope that it will also be read for pleasure. Although history as it is now taught in schools is no longer confined to political history, it will no doubt surprise a number of students to find the enormous range of subjects covered here that fall under the heading of history—the history of comic strips, toys and games, family life and childhood, scouting, fashion and style, radio and television, children's and young adult literature. We have given special emphasis to topics such as sports and popular music that many young people are particularly interested in.

Like its predecessor, *The Reader's Companion to American History*, *The Young Reader's Companion* is as much about ideas and opin-

ions as it is about facts. The articles attempt to assess the significance of each subject— not simply describe what happened but explain why it happened and what its importance was. And the articles accomplish this in a lively, straightforward way. They provide all the necessary dates and details needed for a homework assignment, but also explain why each topic is important for a complete understanding of American history.

The articles are easy to read, but writing that is easy to read is not always easy to write. Too often, books for young adults talk down to readers both in what they try to convey and in their choice of words to convey it. They either offer too little information about a topic, assuming that the reader will not be capable of understanding more, or they assume too much and thus fail to explain the topic adequately. Such books deliberately avoid "big" words, evidently failing to realize that the main way children expand their vocabularies is by grasping the meaning of new words from the context in which they occur. We have taken pains to ensure that the volume does not patronize our readers, whatever their age, and venture to assert that the parents of these children for whom the book is intended will also find the encyclopedia interesting and illuminating. As I see it, a clear, well-written article for the adult reader differs from a clear, well-written piece for the young adult only in that writing for young adults generally does not assume much background knowledge, is less abstract, draws conclusions more explicitly, and does its best to entertain and engage the reader as well as impart information.

Having said this, I am proud to point out that our contributors, some one hundred fifty in number, are an experienced and prestigious lot. About half are preeminent historians well known to readers of adult books, including winners of the Pulitzer Prize, National Book Award, and other honors. The other half are highly regarded children's book writers specializing in history, including numerous Newbery medalists and other award-winning authors. All have dedicated themselves to the task of writing first-rate history for young people and to presenting the past in a lively and vivid manner.

In closing I wish to express my deep appreciation to Borgna Brunner and the staff at Houghton Mifflin. Ms. Brunner, the senior editor responsible for the project, should properly be described as the book's coeditor. She contributed a number of the unsigned and signed articles, tracked down and commissioned authors to write many of the articles, critiqued and edited the entire work, and kept this complicated enterprise involving one hundred fifty contributors on course and (more remarkably) on schedule. Amy K. Smith, the editorial assistant on the project; Cecile Rhinehart Watters, one of the finest copyeditors I have ever come across; Manya S. Chylinski, the fact checker; and Margaret Anne Miles, the picture researcher, also merit special praise.

JOHN A. GARRATY
Sag Harbor, New York

THE YOUNG READER'S
COMPANION TO
AMERICAN
HISTORY

A

ABOLITIONIST MOVEMENT

The abolitionist movement began in small quiet ways among individuals who felt that slavery was wrong. The first antislavery document written in colonial America was presented in 1688 by four Quakers to their quarterly meeting at Philadelphia, asking, "Is

A portrait of William Lloyd Garrison, a passionate abolitionist. "On this subject," he proclaimed, "I do not wish to think, or speak, or write, with moderation . . . I will not excuse—I will not retreat a single inch—AND I WILL BE HEARD."

there any that would be handled in like manner—to be a slave for life?"

Early Black Abolitionists

More often, the people who spoke out against slavery were those who were most affected by it. On January 13, 1777, a group of enslaved blacks petitioned the state of Massachusetts, saying that to be "Deprived of Every Social Privilege of Every thing Requiset [requisite, or necessary] to Render Life tolable [tolerable] is far worse than Nonexistence."

The Free African Society founded in Philadelphia in 1787 by Absalom Jones, Richard Allen, and six other black men was the first black antislavery organization. By 1790 there were sixty thousand free blacks in the United States. They formed organizations, churches, and self-help groups and published pamphlets and newspapers. By 1830 there were about fifty black antislavery organizations in the country.

Blacks protested slavery in both word and deed. In 1829 David Walker, a free black living in Boston, published a pamphlet entitled in part, *Walker's Appeal . . . to the Coloured Citizens of the World . . . Expressly to Those of the United States.* Walker's militant message calling for blacks to fight oppression caused a stir in southern states.

Another method of rebelling against slavery was to run away. Many who did benefited from a network of secret escape routes and safe houses called the Underground Railroad. Fugitives were guided from the South to free territories and states in the North and the West, as well as Canada. Many people reached freedom and safety helped by blacks and sympathetic whites.

Sometimes a more desperate bid for freedom was made by blacks who led actual revolts against slavery. In 1800 Gabriel Prosser unsuccessfully attempted an insurrection. Denmark Vesey organized a revolt in 1822 that was exposed by an informer. The bloodiest uprising was led by Nat Turner in Virginia in 1831.

• •

For biographies of people active in the abolitionist movement, see the following entries:

Abolitionism as a Reform Movement

Eliminating slavery remained the focus of black leaders and organizations. But among many white abolitionists, antislavery activity in the years 1790–1815 was only one of a variety of reform movements in American life. There were religious movements, temperance societies (against drinking alcoholic beverages), prison reform groups, and organizations to help the mentally ill.

A number of white abolitionists during this period favored colonization—freeing slaves and sending them to live in Africa or the Caribbean, thus gradually ending slavery. Benjamin Lundy, a Quaker from New Jersey, was a major figure in the early abolitionist movement. In 1816 he organized the Union Humane Society in Ohio and in 1821 published a paper entitled *Genius of Universal Emancipation.* For two years Lundy toured the North speaking against slavery. William Lloyd Garrison, then a young editor, heard Lundy speak and joined his organization.

Garrisonian Abolitionism

Garrison became the editor of Lundy's paper in 1829. Several years later, however, growing impatient with the idea of colonization and gradually ending slavery, Garrison established his own paper, the *Liberator.* He and his followers demanded an immediate end to slavery. They disagreed with abolitionists who believed that slavery could be ended through political activities, such as getting abolitionist candidates elected to office.

The Garrisonians wanted not only to end slavery but also to end racism and sexism. Garrison insisted, over the objections of some of his colleagues, that women be allowed to fill leadership roles. White women, such as the writer Lydia Maria Child and the sisters Sarah and Angelina Grimké, along with black women, such as Sojourner Truth, Harriet Tubman, and Frances Harper, worked tirelessly for the movement. On the other hand, though the abolitionists hated slavery, many were not ready to accept blacks—or women—as equals.

The American Anti-Slavery Society, a national organization, was founded in 1833 by

Garrison's famous antislavery newspaper, the Liberator, was published from 1831 until the Civil War. The illustration behind the masthead shows a slave auction with a sign announcing the sale of "slaves, horses, and other cattle." It points out the inhumanity of the slave trade, implying that it looked upon slaves as no better than animals.

Garrison and others. As the wealth and power of the southern slaveholders grew and threatened to spread to new territories opening up in the West, abolitionists saw an urgent need to mount a strong national effort against the expansion of slavery. The organization distributed antislavery pamphlets and other literature. They sent speakers to villages and towns throughout the North and petitioned local governments to enact antislavery legislation. One of the most powerful weapons the abolitionists had were fugitives who, after escaping to freedom, lectured to white audiences about the horrors of slavery. Frederick Douglass, one of the most famous fugitives and black abolitionists, gave some five hundred speeches from 1855 to 1863.

By 1837 there were 1,346 antislavery organizations in the North and the West. Garrison, though, was again becoming impatient—this time with the efforts of the Anti-Slavery Society, which he felt was not militant enough and not committed to ending racism and sexism. He also continued to belittle the efforts to put abolitionists into political office. A number of the society's members felt that Garrison and his followers were too radical, and in 1840, the society split into two organizations.

Growing Violence and Final Victory

As the abolitionists' messages spread through an increasingly troubled and divided nation, violence against them grew. They were viewed by many Americans, both North and South, as dangerous troublemakers who were the cause of much of the national strife during the 1830s through the late 1850s. Southern members of Congress even managed to pass what was called the "gag rule" in 1836. Under this rule, congressmen were not allowed to debate the petitions opposing slavery submitted by abolitionists. The abolitionists became increasingly militant, and a few began to advocate violence themselves.

When John Brown, a white abolitionist, tried to stage a slave revolt at Harpers Ferry in 1859, there were other abolitionists who, like Brown, felt that slavery would never be eradicated through peaceful means. Unfortunately, they were correct, for slavery ended only after a bloody and horrible civil war.

Though they did not directly end slavery, sexism, or racism, the abolitionists greatly affected the course of events. It was the abolitionists who eventually convinced President Abraham Lincoln that the Civil War was being fought not just to save the Union but also to end slavery, and they influenced his decision to sign the Emancipation Proclamation in 1863.

The movement also left a body of important literature, including the slave narratives, which are stories by ex-slaves telling of their experiences, and works by Frederick Douglass, the abolitionist poet John Greenleaf Whittier, and the novelist Harriet Beecher Stowe, who wrote *Uncle Tom's Cabin*. Most important, the abolitionists were the conscience of a nation, forcing Americans to face the contradictions of a slave society within a country founded on the idea that all people are created free and equal.

The American Anti-Slavery Society disbanded in 1870, five years after the end of the Civil War and the passage of the Thirteenth Amendment to the Constitution, which abolished slavery in the United States.

See also African Americans: to 1865; Emancipation Proclamation and Thirteenth Amendment; Free-Soil Party; Gag Rule; Liberty Party; Slavery; Underground Railroad.

JOYCE HANSEN

ABORTION

Abortion is the termination of a pregnancy. When this happens on its own, or spontaneously, as it does in one in six pregnancies, it is called a miscarriage. Abortion can also be caused by someone using one of several medical techniques. About 1.6 million abortions are performed each year, 90 percent within the first twelve weeks of pregnancy. Among the safest of all medical procedures, they have less than a 1 percent complication rate, about the same as having tonsils removed.

Reasons for Abortion

Women have abortions for many different reasons. The most common are feeling too young or too old to be a mother; not being prepared to be a parent; already having the number of children one wants; needing to finish one's education; and not being able to afford to raise a child.

Some women decide to have abortions even though they really want to have a child because continuing their pregnancy threatens their health or their life or because they learn that their fetus has something seriously wrong with it. And women who are pregnant as a result of rape or incest may decide to have an abortion.

In every society women have had abortions, but not always legally. In the United States abortion became legal only in 1973 with the Supreme Court decision, *Roe* v. *Wade*. Before that, millions of illegal abortions were performed, but it was a dangerous and scary experience. About a thousand women died each year and hundreds of thousands of women became ill from illegal abortions, mostly because they were performed by untrained persons under unsterile conditions.

Antiabortionists

Abortion is the subject of tremendous political and ethical controversy. There is a strong movement (led primarily by the Catholic church and Christian fundamentalist churches) to make abortion illegal again. From the point of view of women's health, it is hard to understand this. But the antiabortion movement, or prolife movement, as its

Prochoice and antiabortion activists in 1989 protest side by side in Washington, D.C., outside the Supreme Court as they wait for a decision to be handed down. The prolife demonstrators (at left) include a Catholic priest and a protester displaying a poster of a fetus. At right, prochoice advocates hold signs urging the Supreme Court to "Keep abortion legal."

adherents call it, argues that abortion is immoral. It believes that human life begins at conception, that a fetus is an unborn baby, already a human being. Thus, they believe that abortion is murder.

While their ultimate goal is to make all abortion illegal, their immediate goal is to make it less available. They have persuaded Congress and state legislatures to pass laws restricting abortion. The most significant of these affect low-income women and teenagers. Because the Hyde Amendment of 1977 prohibits federal funding of abortions, Medicaid, the federal insurance program for poor people, cannot pay for them. Thirty-three

states have laws that require either that women under the age of eighteen have the consent of one or both parents or a judge in order to have an abortion or that the parents be notified in advance.

During the 1980s, part of the movement adopted the tactic of civil disobedience. There were 33,000 arrests at abortion and family planning clinics for attempting to block women's access to abortion services. And in the 1990s increasing numbers of antiabortionists turned to violence. Between 1984 and 1993, 1,285 abortion and family planning clinics reported violent incidents, and 6,000 experienced bomb threats, harassing calls, and picketing. Doctors, clinic workers, and their families have received death threats or had their homes picketed and their families stalked. In 1993 a doctor was murdered by a demonstrator at a clinic.

Prochoice Movement

In response a movement to defend abortion rights has developed. Called the prochoice movement, it believes that the decision to continue a pregnancy must belong to the woman herself.

There are several reasons offered to support this position: legal abortion is a matter of life or death for women; abortion is one of the most personal decisions a person makes; religious positions on abortion differ—accepting the view that abortion is murder because the fetus is a person violates our freedom of religion by imposing one religious belief on everyone; and if women are to be equal with men, they must have control over their bodies. The movement also appeals to ideas of social justice: restrictions on abortions fall disproportionately on low-income women, women of color, and very young women. In the 1990s, the prochoice movement talked more about reproductive health and rights, reflecting an understanding that abortion is linked to other aspects of women's lives.

Polls show that public opinion on abortion has remained relatively constant since legalization. About 70 percent of the people approve of abortion in at least some circumstances, and 78 percent believe that the government should not be involved in the abortion decision. Yet the antiabortion minority has made itself a powerful political force.

See also Birth Control; *Roe* v. *Wade*.

MARLENE GERBER FRIED

ABSTRACT EXPRESSIONISM

From the colonial period until World War II most American painters were powerfully influenced by European artistic trends. But in the 1940s and 1950s the most original movement in American art history, abstract expressionism, burst upon the scene. Also known as the New York school, abstract expressionist artists covered huge canvases with abstract shapes and broad bands of color. Their aim was to create a sense of powerful emotion without any reference to specific objects. "Action painters" among them stressed lines and shapes, spattering or dripping paint on the canvas. "Color field" abstract expressionists used great expanses of color, often a single shade. Included among the abstract expressionists are Willem de Kooning, Robert Motherwell, Franz Kline, Mark Rothko, Barnett Newman, Adolph Gottlieb, Arshile Gorky, and its most famous member, Jackson Pollock.

See also de Kooning, Willem; Painting and Sculpture; Pollock, Jackson.

ACHESON, DEAN

(1883–1971) *Lawyer and statesman.*

A graduate of Harvard and Yale, Acheson served as secretary of state under President Harry S. Truman (1949–53). He helped initiate the Truman Doctrine, which provided military aid to Greece and Turkey in 1947, and the Marshall Plan, which spent $12.4 billion for the economic recovery of Western Europe between 1947 and 1951. Acheson also negotiated American membership in the North Atlantic Treaty Organization in 1949.

Following an Acheson speech in January 1950 that placed South Korea outside America's defense zone in Asia, Republican opponents claimed he had invited the communist North Korean attack that launched the Korean War. He also angered critics by saying he would "not turn my back on Alger Hiss," a former associate accused of being a communist spy. The stalemate in the Korean War intensified criticism during the 1952 election when Republicans jeered at "Dean Acheson's college of cowardly communist containment."

In fact, Acheson was not at all soft in dealing with enemies. He pushed for a huge military buildup after 1950, including development of the hydrogen bomb. With a self-confidence bordering on arrogance, he stressed "negotiating from strength," which usually meant making no concessions. "There is no way to argue with a river," he once said of the Russians. "You can channel it; you can dam it up. But you can't argue with it." Thus Acheson focused on reconstructing Western Europe, integrating Japan and West Germany into the global capitalist economy, and building what historian Melvyn Leffler called a "preponderant power" to contain the Soviet Union and its allies.

After his retirement in 1953 Acheson wrote his best-selling memoirs, *Present at the Creation* (1969). He headed a diplomatic mission to Europe during the Cuban missile crisis in 1962 and helped persuade President Lyndon B. Johnson to deescalate the Vietnam War. The elegantly attired "Wise Man" even advised his old adversary President Richard M. Nixon before his death in 1971.

See also Cold War; Truman, Harry S.

J. GARRY CLIFFORD

ACLU
See American Civil Liberties Union.

ADAMS, ABIGAIL

(1744–1818)   *Wife and political adviser of President John Adams.*

Abigail Adams is famous partly because, against her wishes, her husband preserved her many letters after her death. She believed it unsuitable for a woman to have a public reputation and intended her letters for the eyes only of family and friends. She often apologized for her poor handwriting and errors in spelling and punctuation. She considered herself "uneducated" because she could not read Latin and Greek (though almost no American woman of that day was taught any foreign language). Yet her writing sparkles with warmth and wit.

While John Adams served the country at home and abroad, she managed their Massachusetts farm. Although her husband was proud of her, she did not like to have her business activities known. "Tho' I am very willing to relieve [*sic*] him from every care in my power, yet I think it has too much the appearance of weilding [*sic*] instead of sharing the Scepter," she wrote to a relative. And her concern was well founded.

When John Adams became president, his political critics called her "Mrs. President" and charged that Adams was "under the sovereignty of his wife." The first First Lady to live in the White House, she was glad to return to Massachusetts when Adams left the presidency.

Abigail Adams was the mother of five children. One of these, John Quincy Adams, followed in his father's footsteps, entering public service and becoming the nation's sixth president. His mother gave him plentiful advice as long as she lived. We know this to be so because he, too, carefully saved her letters.

A family friend wrote of Abigail Adams after her death, "She was possessed of the history of our country & of the great occurrences in it. She had a distinct view of our public men & measures & had her opinions which she was free to disclose but not eager to defend in public circles."

See also Adams, John; Adams, John Quincy.

LINDA GRANT DE PAUW

ADAMS, HENRY

(1838–1918)   *Historian and writer.*

Henry Adams belonged to one of America's most distinguished families. Both his great-grandfather, John Adams, and his grandfather, John Quincy Adams, were presidents of the United States. His father, Charles Francis Adams, was a prominent politician, diplomat, and historian. Born in Boston, Henry Adams graduated from Harvard in 1858. A short time later, he became personal secretary to his father, who was U.S. minister to Great Britain during the critical years of the American Civil War.

After returning to America in 1868, Adams taught medieval history at Harvard from 1870 to 1877. During his years as an assistant professor, he introduced the seminar method of teaching. In 1877, he moved to Washington, D.C., where, except for frequent foreign trips, he spent the rest of his life.

Adams wrote many scholarly essays, two novels, and a biography of Treasury Secretary Albert Gallatin. His reputation as a historian was firmly established with the publication of his nine-volume work *History of the United States during the Administrations of Jefferson and Madison* (1884–91).

His two most popular books were written when he was past sixty-five years of age. In his *Mont-Saint-Michel and Chartres* (privately printed, 1904; published, 1913), Adams praised the Middle Ages as a period of exquisite beauty and spiritual unity, very different from the turbulent times in which he felt he lived. The towering climax of Adams's writing career was his autobiography, *The Education of Henry Adams.* In this book he raises the question of whether human institutions, like the human body, are subject to aging and decay. He expresses concern that the production of power in modern society exceeds people's ability to control it. Adams gave friends copies of his privately printed autobiography in 1907, but this widely acclaimed classic was not published until shortly after his death in 1918.

See also Literature.

EDMUND LINDOP

ADAMS, JOHN

(1735–1826)   *American revolutionary leader, vice president (1789–97), and president of the United States (1797–1801).*

Adams was the son of a farmer and community leader who insisted that the boy prepare for Harvard College. After John's graduation in 1755 he taught school and trained for a career as a lawyer. Adams began his practice in 1758 in his hometown, Braintree, Massachusetts, where he also took an interest in politics. In 1765 he prepared Braintree's instructions to its representative opposing the Stamp Act, a statement that attracted wide attention in the colony. Adams also wrote a number of newspaper essays on politics, including *The Dissertation Concerning the Canon and Feudal Law,* which was republished by an influential admirer in London. By 1770, when Adams agreed to defend the

British soldiers who had committed the "Boston Massacre," he was a leading Patriot and ally of his second cousin Samuel Adams, who helped engineer his election by Boston voters to the Massachusetts legislature in 1771. Thereafter Adams emerged as one of the leading thinkers of the Revolution.

In 1774 the colony elected Adams to the Continental Congress, where he was a powerful supporter of independence, the author of *Thoughts on Government* (1776), and one of the committee that drafted the Declaration. He was also a key organizer of American military forces from 1775 to 1778, screening and selecting officers, raising and supplying troops, and finding financial support. Because he was so respected and deeply committed, Congress sent him on diplomatic missions to France, where he helped negotiate the alliance treaty of 1778, to the Netherlands, where he secured a major loan, and to Britain, where he headed the commission that negotiated the peace treaty of 1783 (Treaty of Paris). During the war he also drafted the Massachusetts Constitution of 1780, one of the models for the U.S. Constitution. While in Europe, Adams wrote *Defence of the Constitutions* (1787–88) of the American states, a major theoretical work.

Adams was elected in 1789 as the nation's first vice president, a position in which he served for eight years with frustration over his own limited authority and the divisive character of national politics. When President George Washington announced his retirement, Adams was elected to succeed him. But divisions over foreign policy intensified, and Adams's irritable temperament made matters worse. His greatest presidential achievement was to block the Federalist movement to bring the naval friction with France (the Quasi-War) into an all-out de-

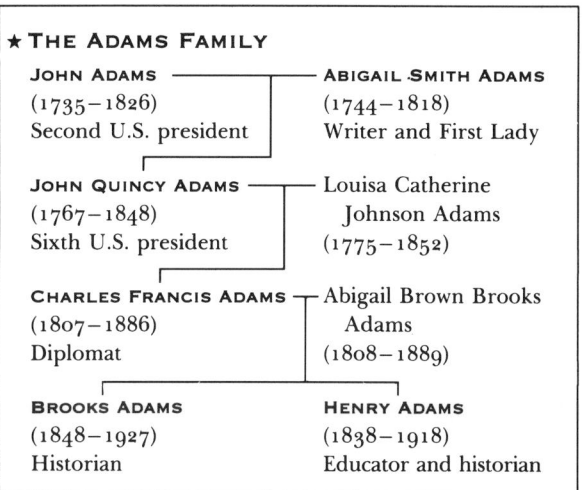

★ THE ADAMS FAMILY

JOHN ADAMS (1735–1826) Second U.S. president — ABIGAIL SMITH ADAMS (1744–1818) Writer and First Lady

JOHN QUINCY ADAMS (1767–1848) Sixth U.S. president — Louisa Catherine Johnson Adams (1775–1852)

CHARLES FRANCIS ADAMS (1807–1886) Diplomat — Abigail Brown Brooks Adams (1808–1889)

BROOKS ADAMS (1848–1927) Historian   HENRY ADAMS (1838–1918) Educator and historian

clared war. But Adams also signed the infamous Alien and Sedition Acts (1798), which limited civil liberties. When he ran for reelection in 1800, he was defeated by Thomas Jefferson, his former friend and revolutionary ally.

Thereafter, the sixty-five-year-old Adams retired with his wife, Abigail Smith Adams, to his farm in Braintree (now Quincy), where he gradually became resigned to his disappointments. In 1812 he resumed correspondence with Jefferson—a correspondence in which two of America's greatest and most learned intellectuals discussed political theory, history, literature, and natural science. In 1825 he was pleased by the election of his eldest son, John Quincy Adams, to the presidency. On July 4, 1826, fifty years to the day after the Declaration of Independence was adopted, both Adams and Jefferson died. Though Jefferson's death preceded his by a few hours, Adams's last words were "Thomas Jefferson still lives."

See also Adams, Abigail; Boston Massacre; Continental Congresses; Federalist Party; Paris, Treaty of (1783); Revolution; Stamp Act. *For events during Adams's administration, see* Alien and Sedition Acts; XYZ Affair.

RICHARD D. BROWN

ADAMS, JOHN QUINCY

(1767–1848) *Sixth president of the United States (1825–29).*

The son of President John Adams devoted his life to public service. Besides his term as president, he served in both houses of Congress, in many diplomatic posts, and as secretary of state. As secretary he negotiated the 1819 treaty in which Spain ceded Florida to the United States (the Adams-Onís Treaty) and drafted President James Monroe's famous Monroe Doctrine (1823).

In 1824 Adams ran for president. Being from Massachusetts he did well in New Eng-

John Quincy Adams served as a diplomat, congressman, senator, and secretary of state as well as the sixth president of the United States. He was considered one of the most experienced and intelligent of all American presidents.

land, but there were three other candidates, Andrew Jackson, Henry Clay, and William H. Crawford. No one obtained a majority in the electoral college, so the House of Representatives was to elect the president.

Andrew Jackson had the most popular as well as the most electoral votes, but the House chose Adams when Henry Clay persuaded the congressmen who had favored him to vote for Adams. When Adams then appointed Clay secretary of state, Jackson charged him with having won the election by a "corrupt bargain."

Adams was not a successful president. He believed in greatly expanding the functions of the federal government in such areas as road and canal construction, higher education, and scientific research. These were all worthwhile objectives, but radical for those times. Congress refused to support them. Adams also lacked the human touch. He was an extremely hard worker, rising normally at five in the morning, even in the dead of winter. When ordinary people failed to meet his standards, he considered them lazy loafers. Little wonder that when he ran for reelection in 1828, he was soundly defeated.

Unlike other presidents, Adams did not retire when his term ended. In 1831 he was elected to the House of Representatives (in keeping with his belief that all branches of the government were equally important). He was serving in the House when southern congressmen imposed the "gag rule" on Congress in 1836. Citizens opposed to slavery repeatedly sent petitions urging their congressmen to abolish or limit slavery. The southerners got a rule passed forbidding even the reading of these petitions. Adams fought this rule for years—it plainly violated the First Amendment right of free speech and citizens' right "to petition the government for a redress of grievances." He was ultimately successful in repealing the rule (1844), and many consider this his greatest achievement.

See also Adams-Onís Treaty; Corrupt Bargain; Gag Rule; Monroe Doctrine.

JOHN A. GARRATY

ADAMS, SAMUEL

(1722–1803) *American revolutionary political leader.*

The son of a Boston merchant and brewer, Adams was a 1740 graduate of Harvard College who, after failing as a brewer and newspaper publisher, found his true calling in politics. His contributions to the independence movement were many and varied. During the 1760s and 1770s he wrote political articles in the local newspapers, planned strategy, recruited talented men into the Patriot cause, including his second cousin and future president John Adams, and organized Boston's Sons of Liberty, which opposed the Stamp Act and other British taxes. He also led the Boston Committee of Correspondence, which promoted Massachusetts opposition to British government; and in 1773 he played a role in organizing the Boston Tea Party.

From 1774 through 1781 Adams represented Massachusetts in the Continental Congress, where he supported and signed the Declaration of Independence. In Congress, Adams was a workhorse who served on many committees. Later, he helped gain approval of the U.S. Constitution in Massachusetts, although he remained wary of a too-centralized government. He served as John Hancock's lieutenant governor from 1789 to 1793, when upon Hancock's death he became governor of Massachusetts. Ill-health forced his retirement in 1797.

Personally, Adams displayed great self-discipline and patience. "We cannot make events," he explained. "Our business is wisely to improve them." His personal tastes were simple; his clothes were so worn that his friends bought him a new suit in 1774 so that he would not embarrass Massachusetts when he went to Congress. His wife managed the family's household and budget. Joining with friends to sing psalms from the Bible was his favorite recreation. His son, a physician who served in the Revolutionary army, died in 1788 while Adams was working for the Constitution. He numbered Thomas Jefferson and Thomas Paine among his political friends. John Adams said he was born "a wedge of steel" to split the bonds between Britain and America.

See also Boston Tea Party; Committees of Correspondence; Constitution; Continental Congresses; Declaration of Independence; Revolution; Sons of Liberty.

RICHARD D. BROWN

ADAMS-ONÍS TREATY

This agreement, also known as the Transcontinental Treaty, was negotiated by Secretary of State John Quincy Adams and Luís de Onís, the Spanish minister to the United States, in 1819. Spain agreed to sell Florida to the United States for a mere $5 million. (Actually the money never left Spain. It was paid to Americans who had claims against the Spanish government.) Spain also accepted the American interpretation of the boundary between the Louisiana Purchase and Spanish Texas and gave up all claim to the Oregon region. Since the United States and Great Britain had agreed in 1818 to joint control of the Oregon country, this gave the United States clear title to land as far west as the Pacific Ocean.

See also Expansion, Territorial *and map on p. 288.*

ADDAMS, JANE

(1860–1935)   *Social reformer.*

Addams, the daughter of a prominent miller and banker, was born on September 6, 1860, in Cedarville, Illinois. A quiet, thoughtful child, she grew up wanting to help those who were less fortunate than she. Upon finishing her schooling at nearby Rockford Female Seminary, she toured Europe with a close friend, Ellen Gates Starr. Impressed by the work they saw being accomplished at Toynbee Hall, a settlement house in a poor section of London, the two young women returned to America determined to begin a similar project at home.

Chicago was by then a city of over a million people, three-fourths of whom were immigrants living in the shadow of the steel mills, stockyards, and factories. In 1889 Addams and Starr converted the decaying Hull Mansion on the city's West Side into a center where the area's Irish, Italian, German, Greek, and Russian residents could gather for social, cultur-

Jane Addams talking to neighborhood children near Hull-House in Chicago, a community center founded in 1889 that provided housing, education, medical assistance, and cultural events to recent immigrants and to the poor.

al, and educational events. Beginning with meeting rooms and a day-care center, Hull-House soon offered a kindergarten, a gymnasium, a library, an art gallery, and a theater. In time the project included thirteen buildings and covered an entire city block. The success of Hull-House can be explained in large part by Addams's ability to recruit talented and energetic people to carry on its work and to inspire wealthy and influential people to finance that work.

In 1917 Addams, a staunch pacifist, spoke out against America's involvement in World War I. This cost her some friends and supporters at the time, but along with her other antiwar activities, gained her the Nobel Peace Prize in 1931. The first American woman to win a Nobel, she gave her sixteen thousand dollars in prize money to the Women's International League for Peace and Freedom, an organization whose presidency she held from its founding in 1919 until her death in 1935.

Addams also helped found the American Civil Liberties Union in 1920. Over the years she wrote a number of books about her experiences and ideas. They included *Twenty Years at Hull-House* (1910), *Democracy and Social Ethics* (1902), and *Peace and Bread in Time of War* (1922).

See also Conscientious Objectors; Settlement House Movement.

For further reading: Linda Peavy and Ursula Smith, *Dreams into Deeds: Nine Women Who Dared* (New York: Scribner's, 1985).

LINDA PEAVY
URSULA SMITH

ADOLESCENCE
See Childhood and Adolescence.

ADVERTISING

Advertising is used to convey information about a product, service, or idea. About 50 trillion advertising messages are released yearly in the United States. On average, people see and hear three thousand of them each day.

Types of Advertising
Consumer product advertising is as old as the human impulse to buy, sell, and trade. In colonial America, carved images hanging above shop doors told customers where to find the goods they wanted. A shoe indicated a cobbler; a hat suggested a milliner. In 1704, a Boston newspaper solicited advertising from "Persons who have Houses, Lands, Tenements, Farms, Ships, Vessels, Goods, Wares or merchandise, &c to be Sold or Let; or Servants Run-Away, or Goods Stole or Lost"— the first newspaper ad. Then as now, newspapers concentrated on advertisements for local businesses and classified want ads. Advertising for soaps, soft drinks, and other products marketed on a nationwide basis began in the 1880s with the founding of magazines expressly designed to carry paid advertising, such as the *Ladies' Home Journal*.

With national advertising came advertising agencies. The first agent had appeared in 1841, selling newspaper space to advertisers and collecting a commission from the paper's owner. Later agents hired writers and artists to prepare sophisticated campaigns for their clients. Along with earning their commissions, these agents billed clients for their creative work. Since many agencies were located on New York City's Madison Avenue, "Madison Avenue" came to mean "advertising."

Today, advertising is a $125 billion annual business. Roughly two-thirds of that money goes into newspapers (America's leading advertising medium), television (the second biggest medium), magazines, and radio. The rest is spent on mailings sent directly to homes, billboard space, bus and subway placards, store displays, and so forth.

Political advertising began with nineteenth-century slogans, banners, and buttons, but only since 1952 has it dominated campaigns. Present-day candidates hire advertising professionals to help them use the media, particularly radio and television, to convey their messages to voters. Advertising expenses for candidates for Congress commonly reach millions of dollars.

Public service advertising promotes such worthwhile causes as recycling or the use of automobile seat belts. Much of it is paid for by government and business or is donated by ad agencies.

Institutional, professional, trade, and industrial advertising have specialized purposes and audiences. The National Dairy Council, for example, publicizes not one company's milk but milk in general. Drug companies advertise in journals read by doctors. A trade ad for a line of clothing is aimed at retail store owners. A steel company's industrial ad urges automakers to buy its products.

Benefits of Advertising

Besides benefiting the businesses they serve, institutional, professional, trade, and industrial advertising benefit consumers by encouraging the development of new and useful products. The utility of public service announcements is obvious. Political advertising helps inform voters.

Even ads whose primary goal is selling a product to consumers may fulfill a social function. Many power company ads offer tips on saving energy. A supermarket flier may urge shoppers to contribute food to the hungry or give information about good nutrition. Above all, consumer advertising offers information about products and prices. It increases the public demand for goods and services. That brings more business to the companies that provide them. More business may mean building new factories and hiring more workers, which can help the nation's economy to prosper.

Advertising has persuaded consumers to buy hundreds of safer, more convenient products, making America's standard of living among the highest in the world. Advertising also keeps newspapers, magazines, radio, and television financially within reach of most Americans. The sale of advertising space pays two-thirds of newspaper and magazine production costs and all the costs of commercial radio and television.

Finally, ads can be entertaining and provide a sort of cultural glue. Basketball fans thrill as Michael Jordan slam-dunks for Nike sneakers. People smile at the sight of an Oscar Mayer "Wienermobile." Sandals from Camel cigarettes, with the company name embossed on the soles, amuse beach-goers by leaving "Camel tracks" in the sand. Slogans like "Just do it," "Coke is it," and "Buckle up" are national catchphrases. Everyone knows the Energizer Bunny.

Criticisms of Advertising

Yet advertising has its critics. All advertising, including ads from trade and industrial groups, is expensive to produce, and its cost is passed on to consumers. Political advertising comes in for special criticism when candidates devote their advertising budgets to spreading damaging—often misleading—information about their opponents. This "negative campaigning" confuses the issues, making it difficult for voters to cast their ballots wisely. As for consumer product advertising, some critics complain that much of it tempts people to buy products that they can't afford—like $170 sneakers instead of $50 ones—or that are harmful—like cigarettes and alcohol. Although federal law keeps cigarette and hard liquor ads off radio and television, tobacco and alcohol companies indulge in what is called "backdoor advertising," spending millions of dollars a year to publicize their products through events like the Virginia Slims tennis tour.

Critics also denounce advertising that suggests that products can accomplish something beyond what they were designed to do: a man slaps on a certain after-shave lotion and gorgeous women surround him. Many advertisements promote over-the-counter vitamins, sleeping pills, or diet aids without pointing out that overusing any of them may be dangerous. Some ads lie indirectly, suggesting that one brand is superior to another, virtually identical brand. Others overstate a product's usefulness or safety. The Federal Trade Commission (FTC), which oversees the advertising industry, has rules aimed at keeping ads honest, but the rules are not always enforced.

A growing criticism of advertising is that there is simply too much of it—pounds of junk mail and newspaper inserts; dozens of fifteen- and thirty-second spots in each radio or television hour; endless-seeming pages of magazine ads; junk phone calls. Sports events are becoming huge commercials with athletes and arenas decked out in brand names and logos. And more advertising is on the way. At some fast-food restaurants, televisions hang over the counter. As customers await their orders, they see short news and entertainment features—and ads. Similar programming filled with ads is found in doctors' waiting rooms, airport lounges, amusement park ticket lines, theater lobbies, commuter rail stations, next to supermarket checkouts, and health club treadmills—anywhere there is a "captive" audience of people who have no choice but to see the ad. Other captives are the thousands of U.S. public school students exposed daily to Channel One television. Channel One, with its controversial two minutes of advertisements for every ten minutes of news, comes free to schools. Sometimes the television sets themselves are free. The company that produces Channel One earns $90 million a year in advertising revenues. Is this an informational boon for schools? Or advertising excess?

See also Federal Trade Commission. *For color illustrations, see insert following p. 20.*

For further reading: Ann E. Weiss, *The School on Madison Avenue: Advertising and What It Teaches* (New York: Dutton, 1979).

ANN E. WEISS

AFFIRMATIVE ACTION

Affirmative action programs attempt to counter the effects of past discrimination against certain groups of Americans—in particular, women, blacks, and members of other racial or ethnic minorities. Although the discrimination of earlier times extended into nearly every aspect of life, today's affirmative action addresses itself mainly to education and the workplace.

President Lyndon B. Johnson was the first to use the term *affirmative action*. In 1964, Johnson signed into law a historic civil rights act. The law prohibited racial segregation in state-supported schools, in such public facilities as hotels and restaurants, and in business.

It also outlawed discrimination based on gender, religion, or place of national origin. Before the law's passage, segregation and discrimination had been common, legally or by custom, throughout much of the country. Now people who believed that their civil rights were being violated for reasons of color, religion, ethnicity, or sex could seek relief in court. Every American would, theoretically at least, enjoy what the Fourteenth Amendment to the U.S. Constitution describes as "the equal protection of the laws."

Reasons for Programs

But President Johnson knew that the Civil Rights Act of 1964 could not, by itself, produce a truly just society. Even if federal, state, and local governments acted wholeheartedly to abolish all forms of discrimination—and no one thought that was likely to happen— the group discrimination suffered in the past would continue to handicap its victims. Blacks, compelled for generations to attend inferior segregated schools, would still be ill equipped to find good jobs or meet university entrance requirements. Working women, routinely passed over for promotion and pay raises, would still find it virtually impossible to move into executive positions. Ethnic Americans raised in non-English-speaking homes, or whose customs or looks made them seem "different," would continue to be held back by prejudice. For the new civil rights law to be effective, Johnson told the nation in 1965, it must be supplemented by affirmative action, programs designed to reach out to America's neglected groups and individuals and draw them into the educational and economic mainstream.

So affirmative action plans were written. Typically, each included integration guidelines and goals and timetables for meeting them. Colleges and universities that depended upon state or federal aid began reserving a certain number of places for female and minority-group applicants. Large businesses that had discriminated in the past were required to develop affirmative action recruitment and promotion plans. Companies seeking contracts with the federal government faced the same requirement.

Programs Criticized

Affirmative action has its critics. Among them was Allen Bakke, a white college graduate who applied to a California state medical school in 1973 and 1974. Twice denied admission to the school, Bakke discovered that his academic record was better and his test scores higher than those of several minority-group applicants who had been admitted. The reason: the university's affirmative action program called for enrolling a set number of minority students even if some of those enrolled were less qualified than some white applicants who were, like Bakke, turned away. Bakke sued the university, arguing that in favoring people of color, it had discriminated against him because he was white, thereby displaying the very sort of racial bias and *un*equal protection of the law illegal under the Civil Rights Act of 1964 and the Fourteenth Amendment. In 1978, the U.S. Supreme Court issued a split decision in the case. Calling the university's rigid race-based quota system unconstitutional, the Court ordered Bakke admitted to its medical school. Yet at the same time, the Court supported the concept of affirmative action, conceding the reality of past and present discrimination and acknowledging that something must be done to ensure racial (as well as sexual and ethnic) balance in American society.

Subsequent Supreme Court decisions have added to the confusion. One endorsed racial quotas for a formerly segregated police force. A 1980 ruling allowed the federal government to require that 10 percent of its public works projects go to minority businesses. But nine years later, the Court overturned a Virginia law with a similar public works requirement. Those two decisions, combined with a 1990 ruling that encouraged increased minority-group ownership of federally granted radio and television broadcast licenses, suggest that the Court regards the Fourteenth Amendment as being more binding upon the states than upon the U.S. government. That notion strikes many legal scholars as unconvincing.

The controversies surrounding affirmative action will not easily be resolved. Not only do affirmative action plans pit men against women and white Americans against Americans of other skin colors; they can also create conflict among minority groups. In 1993, for instance, a federal court was scheduled to consider a Hispanic student's challenge to his college's blacks-only scholarship program. Such a program does sound arbitrary, and many Americans are uneasy with the idea of quotas. But the question remains: by what other means can society overcome the wrongs of the past?

ANN E. WEISS

AFRICAN AMERICANS: TO 1865

Nearly all Africans brought to America came from a strip of western Africa stretching from the Senegal River to the southern boundary of Angola. The area was not more than 250 miles from the seacoast. Tales of white traders striking far into the interior in order to kidnap Africans to be sold as slaves are misleading. Perhaps more than half of the slaves had been captured in wars between Africans themselves, and possibly only one in six was a kidnap victim.

A group picture would show that most of the slaves were adult males, who had known limited freedom; they were pagans, aside from a few Muslims. About one in seven brought to the Americas was a child under fourteen years of age. Generally speaking, the slaves were the healthier people in Africa, fit for hard labor.

Carrying Africans for sale to white Americans became profitable when plantation agriculture developed. Growing tobacco, rice, and eventually cotton required many tasks done by hand. Increasing costs of white labor and prices for plantation-grown crops caused planters to turn to African labor. Africans were not only cheaper; they were easier to control as slaves, and they could be worked during their entire lifetime.

Making Africans slaves rather than hiring them as servants was justified by white planters' prejudice against their skin color (black suggesting evil), their non-Christian religion, and their level of culture, as the whites saw it. A false science of the time also proclaimed blacks to be inferior. Thus, colonists passed laws that made blacks property and a permanent class whose children belonged to the owner.

The African-American population grew rapidly in the eighteenth century. In 1700 blacks numbered about 28,000; seventy years later, about 460,000. By then they formed the highest proportion of the American population in their history. African Americans lived in all thirteen colonies, but mainly in the South. In the North they tended to live in cities and work as servants and artisans. New

The majority of slaves on large plantations worked in the fields. They labored long hours, six days a week, cultivating tobacco, rice, sugarcane, and cotton.

York City and Boston both had large African-American populations. A small number were free, but generally speaking white northerners at first shared southern notions justifying slavery.

Nature of Black Societies

Uprooted and brutalized, the first African Americans struggled to maintain a sense of identity and self-esteem. If they mingled with others from Africa, they often encountered an African culture different from their own in customs and languages, for they came from diverse groups. The continuing arrival of such newcomers worked against blacks' forging a sense of community. And the small proportion of women—about one in three—similarly made establishing a family life difficult.

The situation changed about 1725 when the number of African Americans born in this country exceeded the number born in Africa.

More native-born women, an adequate diet, and labor less severe than in the West Indies help explain the change. African Americans now had roots in America and more fellow blacks they could communicate with. Their sense of togetherness gathered strength after the foreign slave trade was banned in 1807 ending the arrival of new groups, after the westward migration in America erased some of the regional differences known on the Atlantic coast, and after the plantation system formed the way of life for the majority of African Americans.

Though born in America and exposed to white culture, blacks developed what some historians have called a slave community or African-American culture. How far this development extended is unclear, but African and American elements blended into a life apart from white culture. The blend took one form in music with work songs and spirituals. Dancing was popular; their dances, sometimes lasting for hours, originated in the Congo and elsewhere in Africa. Folk tales, proverbs, and other lore passed from generation to generation.

Marriage and the family took a separate course for African Americans. Usually prohibited from legally marrying in the Western fashion, couples often followed an African custom of jumping over a broom together, which served as the marriage ceremony. They honored the African taboo on marriage of cousins, unlike the practice common among some plantation owners who wanted to keep land together in the family. With permission of masters slave couples lived together in their own cabin. Slave marriages, contrary to once-popular belief, were often lasting, as was attested to after the Civil War when many of the freed people went searching for spouses they had been separated from through sales.

Slave owners often encouraged unions and allowed time for new mothers to rest and nurse their babies. After all, these children were a source of labor and profit for their owners. Babies' names could be reminders of the African heritage—"Cuffee," for example, meant a male born on a Friday. The sense of kinfolk was also expressed by naming babies for relatives. But the African-American family constantly suffered from the possibility of separation by sale or violence from white people.

Nineteenth-Century Changes
In the early nineteenth century the world of African Americans changed, both for better and for worse. Brutal treatment probably decreased and so did the proportion of babies born to parents of different races. A number of masters assigned slaves to supervisory positions. Some slaves worked for rewards; some were hired out and allowed to keep part of their wages; and some gained their freedom. States passed laws easing the severity of punishment and restricting masters' authority to discipline slaves.

New ideas about the master-slave relationship emerged. Many masters adopted an attitude like that of a father toward his slaves—an attitude called paternalism. This went hand in hand with the defense of or apology for slavery: blacks, being inferior, needed a "father" to look out for them. The leading southern politician, John C. Calhoun, in 1837 declared slavery to be a "positive good."

But from the early 1800s until the Civil War, the outlook for African Americans also took an unhappy turn. Whites guarded their slaves more carefully after Denmark Vesey's conspiracy for a rebellion in South Carolina in 1822 and Nat Turner's revolt in Virginia in 1831. They justified perpetuation of slavery on grounds of paternalism, the positive-good theory, Scripture, and racism. Free African Americans, North and South, usually lived in poverty; though dependent on whites, they were excluded from white society and its privileges. Only in New England (except in Connecticut) could they vote. Many states further west had laws restricting black freedom. Equality and freedom seemed very distant for African Americans who aspired to those ideals.

African Americans were important in the antislavery movement. They held conventions condemning slavery and colonization—schemes to free slaves but send them off to settle in places outside the United States. Henry Highland Garnet, a clergyman, created an uproar when in 1843 he urged blacks to revolt and kill their masters. Martin R. Delany, a physician, favored their returning to Africa. The most influential black leader before the Civil War was Frederick Douglass, an escaped slave who became a magnetic abolitionist orator and newspaper editor. During the Civil War nearly 190,000 African Americans served in Union military forces. Thus, by 1865 African Americans had contributed importantly to the freedom that came with the Thirteenth Amendment abolishing slavery in the United States.

See also Free Blacks before Emancipation; Slavery.

For further reading: Milton Meltzer, *The Black Americans: A History in Their Own Words* (New York: Crowell, 1984).

JAMES A. RAWLEY

AFRICAN AMERICANS: 1865–1877
See Civil War; Reconstruction.

AFRICAN AMERICANS: 1877–1945

The Thirteenth Amendment adopted after the Civil War abolished slavery, the Fourteenth made blacks citizens of the United States, and the Fifteenth gave them the right to vote. In the South new state constitutions guaranteed access to public schools and other facilities, though often on a segregated basis.

Post-Reconstruction Conditions

Conditions for southern blacks began to deteriorate, however, in the mid-1870s, when the former Confederates returned to power in the South; the Democratic Party, which had opposed Congressional Reconstruction, captured control of the House of Representatives; and northern Republicans lost interest in protecting the rights of southern blacks. By 1900, southern states had systematically deprived blacks of the right to vote and had made segregation legal.

Despite the emergence of a small middle class, most blacks were limited to menial jobs in the cities and to sharecropping in the countryside. White mobs increasingly sought to intimidate blacks, often through hideous lynchings. A Supreme Court decision, *Plessy v. Ferguson* (1896), legalized separate but equal treatment of the races. Thus, the federal government left southern whites alone to deal with their "Negro Problem." Booker T. Washington, the president of Tuskegee Institute in Alabama and the period's most influential black leader, urged blacks to remain in the South, accommodate themselves to discrimination, and work hard in the hope that white southerners would eventually accept them as equals.

Blacks fared a little better in the North. With the Republican and Democratic Parties evenly matched in many states, black votes could determine the outcome of elections, forcing white politicians to respond to black demands for better treatment. After the Supreme Court in 1883 declared the Civil Rights Act of 1875 unconstitutional, northern states passed their own civil rights laws. Although segregation persisted in many places, it was now against the law. Laws barring racial intermarriage were repealed as they were being reinstituted in the South, and the industrializing North provided blacks with better job and housing opportunities. Nevertheless, as late as 1900, almost 90 percent of the nation's blacks remained in the South, more than 80 percent of them in poor rural areas, where whites were most hostile to black aspirations. By contrast, the 10 percent in the North and 0.3 percent in the West were primarily urban.

Migration and Backlash

World War I seemed to bring prospects for change. Northern industry needed workers to replace those in the armed services and the immigrants who could not enter the country

ADVERTISING

(See article on page 13)

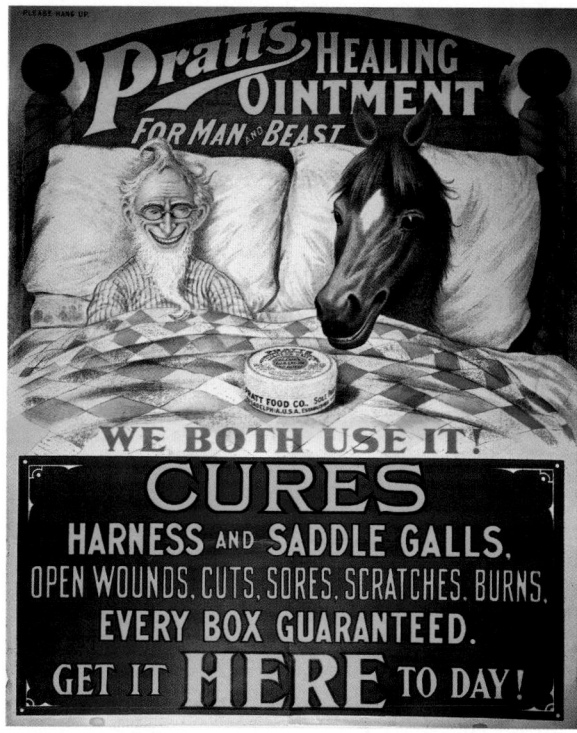

Pratts Healing Ointment (1885) was one of many such products that claimed to cure an astounding variety of ailments, until the government began to regulate the advertising of medicines.

This Hall's Hair Renewal advertisement from the late nineteenth century appealed to the vanity of women of all ages. It promised to prevent baldness and dandruff as well as eliminate grey hair.

Welch's grape juice, originally called "Dr. Welch's Unfermented Wine," was created by Dr. Thomas B. Welch, a dentist, in 1896. He was so against alcohol consumption that he hoped his concoction would someday replace the wine served during communion at his Methodist church. This ad promoted Welch's as the ideal nonalcoholic drink for a night out with the boys.

Lifebuoy used trade cards (c.1900) to advertise its soap. Lifebuoy later promoted its products in comic strips that featured "true 'B.O.' [body odor] experiences."

By 1914, when this Coca-Cola ad was printed, there were over five million square feet of painted walls advertising the soft drink.

Ads for toilet paper and other "unmentionables" took pains not to offend the sensibilities of potential customers. This 1920s ad for ScotTissue avoided discussing the product directly, focusing instead on "the atmosphere of elegance and refinement" surrounding it.

Pontiac advertised its pink convertible (1957) as a car for people who were sophisticated and "going places."

This 1959 General Motors refrigerator ad glorified the housewife by crowning her queen and vowing to save her money, space, and time in the domestic realm.

Summertime U.S.A. begins with U.S. KEDS...for everybody

Teens, tots, moms, pops, everybody loves U. S. Keds for lots of reasons. Keds look so nice. They feel so good. They wear so well. And kids will tell you Keds run faster.

The truth is genuine Keds are built over lasts that are scientifically shaped to fit active feet. Unlike ordinary sneakers, Keds are

made with shockproof arch cushions like this to absorb the jolts and jars of running and jumping. And Keds wear longer. Soles and uppers are permanently bonded together. You can keep them clean in your washing machine. Genuine Keds are easy to identify. Always look for the blue label.

US United States Rubber

"It was the only thing to do after the mule died."

Three years back, the Hinsleys of Dove, Missouri, had a tough decision to make. To buy a new mule. Or invest in a used bug. They weighed the two possibilities. First there was the problem of the bitter Ozark winters. Tough on a warm-blooded mule. Not so tough on an air-cooled VW. Then, what about the eating habits of

the two contenders? Hay vs. gasoline. As Mr. Hinsley puts it: "I get over eighty miles out of a dollar's worth of gas and I get where I want to go a lot quicker." Then there's the road leading to their cabin. Many a mule pulling a wagon and many a conventional automobile has spent many an hour stuck in the mud. Also, a mule needs a barn. A bug doesn't.

"It sets out there all day and the paint looks near as good as the day we got it." Finally, there was maintenance to think about. When a mule breaks down, there's only one thing to do. Shoot it. But if and when their bug breaks down, the Hinsleys have a Volkswagen dealer only two gallons away.

Viceroy's got the taste that's right!

VICEROY Filter Tip CIGARETTES

not too strong...not too light... Viceroy's got-the taste that's right!

Top: Keds employed the bandwagon approach, asking Americans to follow the leader and buy Keds sneakers (1959).

Middle left: Instead of touting its product with the usual exaggerated enthusiasm of advertising, Volkswagen attracted attention to its smallest car, the Bug (1960), with humor and disarming modesty.

Middle right: Viceroy strived for a manly, robust image in this 1963 ad by picturing hunters smoking Viceroy cigarettes in the great outdoors.

Left: McDonald's golden arches are instantly recognizable throughout the world, from Moscow to Miami. They first appeared at a hamburger stand opened by Maurice and Richard McDonald in San Bernardino, California, in 1948. The ready-to-go hamburgers sold for fifteen cents each.

Top left: The California Raisins, popular 1980s animated characters, performing "I Heard It Through the Grapevine." The television ad campaign was so popular that it not only increased the sales of raisins (not a particularly exciting product on their own) but led to the marketing of T-shirts, key chains, and other California Raisin paraphernalia.

Top right: In this 1990s television commercial, Ray Charles is surrounded by attractive women while he sings "Uh-huh!", a song inspired by the taste of Diet Pepsi. Pepsi uses a trio of reliable advertising strategies: celebrity, sex, and a memorable catch phrase.

HOW CAN WE ENCOURAGE OUR KIDS TO HAVE DREAMS THEN DENY THEM THE MEANS TO ACHIEVE THEM?

For nine-year-old Carolyn Michel, the dream is to become a doctor. For the United Negro College Fund, that's a dream too precious to let die.

For more than 50 years, we've been helping bright, deserving students get the education they need to turn their hopes into realities.

Please give generously. Your contribution could help someone like Carolyn make a contribution that benefits everyone. Call 1 800 332-UNCF.

UNITED NEGRO COLLEGE FUND
A mind is a terrible thing to waste.

Drew Barrymore, actress and one of the Guess? jeans models, exhibits how little of the product actually needs to be visible to capture the attention of a magazine reader.

Advertising is used not only to sell commercial products but also to aid social causes. This public-service advertisement for the United Negro College Fund features one of advertising's best-known campaign slogans, "A mind is a terrible thing to waste."

now. About 500,000 blacks headed north in the Great Migration of 1914–19. Many reported home, as did one migrant writing from Akron, Ohio, "I am making good." Economic conditions improved somewhat for those who remained behind as southern labor grew scarce. But the level of violence and discrimination remained high.

The influx of blacks in the North, however, eventually produced a backlash among whites. Republican Party dominance after 1894 diminished the need for black votes, and the growing numbers of black migrants combined with the many foreigners who had arrived before the war provided alarming competition for jobs and housing. Those blacks who went North thus initially found greater economic opportunity, but once the war was over they encountered the wrath of returning white veterans and new immigrants. Whites had already resorted to violence against blacks in earlier race riots, but far more frightening and bloody were the riots in communities such as East St. Louis, Illinois, in 1917, and Chicago in 1919. There were occasional riots in southern cities, but the most serious ones during these years were in the North.

These riots were only the most visible part of the North's assault on black rights. De facto segregation—that is, segregation by custom rather than law—once again became the norm. Schools became more separate and unequal, and blacks lost factory jobs and service positions as waiters, barbers, and caterers. Large-scale black ghettos emerged.

Black migration from the South slowed in the 1920s, but the persistent decline of the cotton economy, the lure of jobs in the North, and hopes for greater personal dignity kept the movement going until the Great Depression in the 1930s. After the depression began, blacks continued to leave the rural South, but until World War II the more likely destination was the region's own cities rather than those in the North.

Many blacks continued to embrace Booker T. Washington's philosophy of accommodation and self-help, which had been given further support by the founding of the Urban League in 1911. Others, particularly those among the growing black middle class in the North, embraced the demands for equal rights by W. E. B. Du Bois and the National Association for the Advancement of Colored People, the organization he helped found in 1910. Still others, especially among the urban lower classes, were drawn in the 1920s to Marcus Garvey's call for black pride and emigration from the United States to Africa. One major byproduct of the 1920s migration was the black literary and artistic flowering known as the Harlem Renaissance.

The New Deal and WW II
The election of President Franklin D. Roosevelt in 1932 proved to be a mixed blessing. In some ways his New Deal perpetuated racial discrimination: the Agricultural Adjustment Act favored white landowners rather than black tenants, the Civilian Conservation Corps camps and public housing projects were segregated, the new greenbelt towns of the period excluded blacks altogether, and the National Recovery Administration permitted lower wages in the South. But through its relatively color-blind relief activities, sensitivity to the opinions of selected black leaders, and the well-publicized efforts of key figures such as First Lady Eleanor Roosevelt and Secretary of the Interior Harold Ickes to promote racial justice, the New Deal brought northern blacks into the Democratic Party and paved the way for the expansion of the federal government's interest in protecting black rights.

After the beginning of World War II, large numbers of blacks again left the South for jobs in the factories and shipyards of the North and West; by 1950, the South contained only 68 percent of the nation's blacks as compared to the North's 28.2 percent and the West's 3.8 percent. Nevertheless, neither the New Deal nor World War II (which was fought by segregated armed forces) fundamentally altered the pattern of early-twentieth-century race relations. Despite a series of court suits, marches, sit-ins, bus and school boycotts, "Don't-Buy-Where-You-Can't-Work" campaigns, and rent strikes that produced occasional victories against discrimination, prospects for most blacks in the northern urban ghettos seemed little different from those facing their largely rural southern counterparts. Symptomatic were the race riots in Harlem, Detroit, and Mobile during World War II, though in the South blacks were still more likely to be victims of white violence than were northern blacks, who started riots out of frustration and anger over their treatment.

Still, by 1945, blacks once again had reason to believe that intervention by the federal government would, as during Reconstruction, bring meaningful improvement into their lives.

See also Du Bois, W. E. B.; Garvey, Marcus; Harlem Renaissance; Lynching; National Association for the Advancement of Colored People; *Plessy* v. *Ferguson;* Race Riots; Reconstruction; Roosevelt, Eleanor; Segregation; Washington, Booker T.

HOWARD N. RABINOWITZ

AFRICAN AMERICANS: SINCE WORLD WAR II

The years immediately after World War II saw much the same resistance to black progress as in earlier years. But President Harry S. Truman—though not entirely without prejudice himself—nevertheless realized and disapproved of the injustices suffered by blacks in the United States. He made some efforts to correct conditions, especially integrating the armed forces by executive order on July 26, 1948. There was a great outcry over his order and predictions of disaster to follow in military morale and proficiency. But Truman stood his ground, and the integration was a great success.

In the meantime, the National Association for the Advancement of Colored People (NAACP) was conducting its campaign in the courts to gain equality in education by attacking the notion of separate but equal facilities (the legal foundation of segregation, established in *Plessy* v. *Ferguson,* a case involving segregated transportation, in 1896). By the early 1950s, the campaign had reached the U.S. Supreme Court, which in May 1954 ruled in *Brown* v. *Board of Education* that separate black and white education was inherently unequal and unconstitutional. This landmark ruling established a legal precedent against segregation in all areas of American life.

Ruling Tested

The first major test of that precedent was the boycott by blacks of the segregated city buses that began in December 1955 in Montgomery, Alabama. It was sparked by Rosa Parks when she refused to give up her seat to a white man and was arrested. After more than a year, the boycott ended in success when the Supreme Court ruled that bus segregation was unconstitutional. A young Baptist minister in Montgomery, Martin Luther King, Jr., who believed in the principles of nonviolent protest, had emerged as an important leader during the boycott. He formed the Southern

Christian Leadership Conference (SCLC) and launched a campaign for voting rights with a Prayer Pilgrimage to Washington, D.C., in 1957.

It was spontaneous protests by southern black college students three years later that extended the civil rights movement into the 1960s. The student sit-in movement spread like wildfire across the South and led to the founding of the Student Non-Violent Coordinating Committee (SNCC).

March on Washington

By 1962, older civil rights organizations such as the NAACP had also launched nonviolent protests against segregation in the South. But the various organizations had different goals and tactics, and so attempts at cooperation did not always go well. By 1963, A. Philip Randolph, president of the first black labor union, the Brotherhood of Sleeping Car Porters, had come to fear that the movement would soon splinter and turn violent. He called for all the organizations to join together for a massive March on Washington for Jobs and Freedom whose primary purposes were to show unity and to pressure Congress to vote into law the civil rights bill that President John F. Kennedy had introduced. On August 28, 1963, more than 250,000 demonstrators, black and white, young and old, marched peacefully to the Lincoln Memorial. There Martin Luther King, Jr., riveted the crowd and gained international fame with his I Have a Dream speech.

President Kennedy did not live to see the civil rights bill enacted into law. The year after Kennedy's assassination, former vice president Lyndon B. Johnson, who had succeeded Kennedy to the presidency, signed the Civil Rights Act of 1964. The year after that, he signed the Voting Rights Act. With the passage of those two pieces of federal legislation,

the legal bases for equality were established throughout the land. The nonviolent civil rights movement in the South now lost steam.

Movement Changes

Meanwhile, in the summer of 1964, northern blacks rioted in several cities, showing that the conditions under which they lived had not been affected by the gains in the South. Northern urban blacks responded more readily to the black nationalism espoused by

A young black activist helps an older woman register to vote. Voter registration drives in the South were one of the primary goals of the civil rights movement. Poll taxes, literacy tests, and discriminatory voting laws kept the majority of black adults from the polls. Behind them, a poster announces, "Wake-up! Jim Crow is dead." Jim Crow laws were the laws in the South that segregated the races in public schools, trains, buses, restaurants, hotels, and other facilities.

Malcolm X, a minister of the Nation of Islam (Black Muslims), who advised meeting violence with violence and advocated black separatism and self-help. Malcolm X then left the Nation of Islam and tried to organize a new movement; but he was assassinated by Black Muslims while making a speech in Harlem in 1965.

The Student Non-Violent Coordinating Committee also gave up the notion of nonviolence, changed its name to the Student National Coordinating Committee, and called for "Black Power!" The Black Panther Party, whose major base was California, gained some attention but not many converts with its radical call for self-defense ("picking up the gun").

Martin Luther King, Jr., tried unsuccessfully to take his nonviolent crusade north, beginning his campaign in Chicago. Awarded the Nobel Peace Prize in 1964 for his commitment to nonviolence, he spoke out against growing U.S. involvement in the conflict in Vietnam but was criticized for getting involved in international affairs. King was assassinated in 1968 in Memphis, Tennessee, where he had traveled to support striking black sanitation workers.

Following King's assassination, Jesse Jackson, a young minister who had worked with King in the SCLC, rose to prominence nationally with his Operation PUSH (People United to Save Humanity) and his "rainbow coalition" of all races working together for equality of opportunity. During the 1970s he solidified his position as the nation's most prominent black leader and in 1984 and 1988 waged campaigns for the Democratic presidential nomination. Though he was successful in attracting millions of votes in the primaries and registered thousands of new black voters, he failed to win a sufficient number of delegates' votes.

New Middle Class

Jackson's prominence, however, would have been unheard of before the 1980s. It testified to the increased influence of blacks in American life. From the 1970s onward, many blacks benefited from the new legal and social climate to better their standard of living, and a new black middle class emerged. Hundreds of blacks were elected to state and local offices throughout the South and in cities nationwide.

At the same time, however, a black underclass marked by poverty, despair, drug use, and crime grew alarmingly. One of the reasons for its growth was the lack of positive role models as middle-class blacks took advantage of the end of segregation in many regions of the country and moved out of traditionally black neighborhoods. Though the nation has undergone a sea change in race relations, and African Americans have made great strides in just a few decades, the problems of racism and lack of opportunity for many black people remain to be solved.

See also Brown v. *Board of Education;* Civil Rights Movement; Jackson, Jesse; King, Martin Luther, Jr.; Malcolm X; Marches on Washington; National Association for the Advancement of Colored People; Parks, Rosa; Randolph, A. Philip; Southern Christian Leadership Conference; Student Non-Violent Coordinating Committee; Voting Rights Act of 1965.

JIM HASKINS

AGRICULTURE

The United States has a great deal of land that is well suited to agriculture. The natural conditions include a temperate climate, abundant water, and rich soils. These advantages, combined with the ease of people acquiring land, made the United States the most productive agricultural nation in the world.

A family harvesting red clover on a Wisconsin farm in 1895.

Colonial Farms

When the first English settlers arrived on the eastern seacoast in 1607, they found the Indians raising tobacco, corn, pumpkins, and other vegetables. The Europeans acquired plots of land from companies and individuals who had received large grants from the English king. Soon the settlers were raising corn, wheat, oats and other grains, as well as vegetables and fruit. Tobacco became a major crop in Maryland and Virginia, and by the 1690s rice was being grown in South Carolina. By the 1770s a few southern farmers were raising cotton for home use. Colonial farmers also raised poultry, pigs, cattle, and sheep.

There were some large estates of thousands of acres in colonial America, but most farms covered less than a hundred acres and were operated by family members. Tools were made of wood, with iron cutting edges. The ax, hoe, shovel, and fork were common hand tools. Farmers used wooden plows and planted grain, harvested it with a sickle, and threshed it with a flail, all by hand. People grew most of their own food and kept cows for milk and butter, chickens for eggs, and hogs for meat. Women spun and wove linen from the flax plant and wool from sheep for cloth, which they then sewed by hand into clothing and household linens. Thus, farm families were largely self-sufficient and also sold some commodities to people in the towns. They exported large quantities of wheat and tobacco to Europe and the West Indies.

Nineteenth-Century Developments

Between American independence in 1783 and the outbreak of the Civil War in 1861, farmers pushed into the fertile lands west of the Appalachian Mountains. By 1861 some had moved west of the Mississippi River into Iowa and East Texas. This westward expansion of agriculture was encouraged by people's desire to own their own land, by laws that made land acquisition easy, and by the growing foreign demand for American farm products, especially cotton and wheat.

By 1860 there were 2,044,077 farms in the United States. Corn was the major grain crop. It was used mainly for food for people and for livestock. The main cash crop of northern farmers was wheat, and they also grew oats, barley, flax, and rye. Horses, cattle, hogs, and poultry were found on most farms.

With the invention of the cotton gin in 1793, cotton emerged as the principal cash crop in the South. In 1859 the region produced over 5 million bales of cotton. Tobacco, however, continued to be important, as were rice and sugar. Slaves, who had been introduced into colonial America in 1619, provided much of the labor on cotton, rice, and sugar plantations before 1860.

Other farm machines appeared on the scene between 1800 and 1860. John Deere invented the steel plow in 1837, and Cyrus McCormick developed the horse-drawn reaper to harvest grain in the 1830s. A mechanical threshing machine was in use by 1850. There were also improved planters, drills, cultivators, and other horse-drawn machines.

Between 1860 and 1920 the number of farms in the United States increased to 6,448,000. Besides a greater number of farms in the South and Midwest, farmers and ranchers completed settling the region between the Mississippi River and the Pacific Coast. In much of the West, farmers depended on irrigation to produce crops.

The main patterns of American agricultural production were established by 1920. The corn belt extended from Ohio to eastern Nebraska. This was one of the richest agricultural regions in the world. The wheat belt reached from North and South Dakota south to West Texas. The Rocky Mountain and Pacific Coast states raised some wheat, but specialized in fruit and vegetables. In 1930 California marketed 32.8 million boxes of oranges. Fruit and vegetables were also raised in Florida and South Texas. Throughout the heart of the South, cotton, tobacco, rice, and sugarcane were the main commercial crops. In the Northeast, farmers produced dairy products, poultry, and fruits and vegetables. Farmers in all sections of the country raised livestock.

Modern Changes

American agriculture had changed only slowly before 1920 because farm production was governed by the speed and energy of horsepower. In the 1920s, however, the gasoline tractor began to bring dramatic change to American farming. Tractors provided power to plow, plant, cultivate, and harvest crops. In the 1930s the combine, a machine that harvested and threshed grain in one operation, came into general use; in the 1940s a mechanical cotton picker was introduced; and in the 1970s a tobacco harvester was perfected.

Farmers also began to use more chemical fertilizers in the 1940s, and they adopted insecticides to kill insects and herbicides to destroy weeds in the 1950s. Scientists developed better breeds of livestock and improved crop strains. Hybrid corn introduced in the 1930s yielded much better harvests than the older varieties. Average production of corn rose from 28 to 110 bushels per acre between 1940 and 1981. In 1949 the United States produced about a billion bushels of wheat and 212 million bushels of soybeans. By 1989 production of wheat had risen to 2 billion bushels and soybeans to 1.9 billion bushels.

The combination of modern machines and science had produced a tremendous increase in efficiency on individual farms and in total agricultural production. Other trends in late twentieth-century agriculture included raising chickens, turkeys, and hogs in confinement. Housed in special structures, they were fed balanced diets and brought to market in record time.

Farming Becomes Commercial

Whereas most farmers had been at least partially self-sufficient before the 1930s, agriculture after that gradually became a strictly commercial enterprise. Rather than producing their own food, farmers sold their crops and livestock and purchased food and other supplies. Electricity extended to farms after 1935 made possible electric lights, running water, and other conveniences. By the 1950s and 1960s farm families were living in much the same way as people in towns and cities.

Farming was the major way of making a living in America from 1607 to around 1900. In the twentieth century agriculture as an occupation was overtaken by industry, trade, finance, and services. But agriculture continued to be a vital part of the nation's economy. It provided an abundance of high-quality food, plus commodities for export.

By 1990 farmers made up only 2.5 percent of the total population. They operated 2.1 million farms, one-third the number that had existed in the 1920s. Their size and efficiency in the 1990s is seen in the fact that less than 500,000 farmers produced a great majority of the crops and livestock needed by all Americans. The diversity and productivity of American agriculture ranked first among the nations of the world.

See also Carver, George Washington; Chavez, Cesar; Dust Bowl; Farmers' Alliance; 4-H Clubs; Granger Movement; Homestead Act; McCormick, Cyrus Hall; Populism; Tobacco; Whitney, Eli.

GILBERT C. FITE

AIR FORCE

On a frosty morning, December 17, 1903, Orville Wright launched the Air Age by completing a flight that covered about half the length of a football field. Five years after that historic first flight the American army bought an airplane from the Wright brothers, and the U.S. Air Force was born.

Early in World War I (1914–18) European countries used airplanes to make scouting missions. (These took the place of hot air balloons armies had used earlier to spy on each other.) Soon the pilots on scouting missions began shooting pistols and shotguns at one another. After a year of warfare, planes were equipped with machine guns, and wild dogfights broke out in the skies over Europe. In 1916 a group of American volunteer pilots called the Lafayette Escadrille linked up with the French flying corps and began dueling with German planes. After America officially entered the war in 1917, the United States trained some ten thousand men to serve as pilots. Capt. Eddie Rickenbacker shot down twenty-two enemy planes to become America's leading fighter pilot.

After World War I America allowed its air force to shrink, angering a visionary general named Billy Mitchell. Mitchell claimed that bomb-equipped airplanes could destroy a battleship, an idea scoffed at by admirals. In 1921 Mitchell proved his theory by sinking a captured German battleship that had been towed to sea for use as a target. But even though he had been proved right, he was later court-martialed because he was so outspoken about his views on air power.

The Air Force in Wartime

Germany built a strong air force in the 1930s, and when World War II began in 1939, the country's swift-moving armies shocked military leaders around the world. Spearheading the German advances were sleek fighters and dive bombers. America entered World War II after the Japanese bombed Pearl Harbor on December 7, 1941. Before the end of the war the American air force grew to eighty thousand planes staffed by 2.5 million men and women. The American P-51 Mustang was considered by many experts to be the best all-around fighter aircraft of the war. The four-engine B-29, which carried up to twenty thousand pounds of bombs, was the world's mightiest bomber. On August 6, 1945, the frightening Nuclear Age began when a B-29 dropped a single atomic bomb on the Japanese city of Hiroshima, killing at least seventy thousand people.

During World War II the U.S. air command was a branch of the army. Then the National Security Act of 1947 made the air force a separate service. On October 14, 1947, air force pilot Chuck Yeager became the first man to fly faster than the speed of sound (660 mph). Yeager flew an experimental rocket-propelled plane called the X-1.

The Korean War (1950–53) featured the first jet-versus-jet aerial combat. The principal planes engaged over Korea were the U.S. Air Force's F-86 Saber jet against the Russian-built Mig 15. The two planes were about equal in speed and maneuverability, but American pilots were better trained. During the war the U.S. Air Force shot down 976 planes and lost 147. Air force planes also swept the enemy from the sky during the Vietnam War, fought in the late 1960s and early 1970s. Huge eight-engine B-52 bombers pounded enemy targets in Vietnam almost at will. But the Korean and the Vietnam conflicts proved that aerial supremacy alone cannot defeat a determined foe. Both wars dragged on despite the fact that the U.S. Air Force reigned supreme over the battlefields.

High-tech aircraft such as the F-15 and F-16 made their first combat appearances during the Persian Gulf War of 1990–91. These planes flew at better than twice the speed of sound. They fired laser-guided "smart bombs" that sought out and destroyed targets with pinpoint accuracy.

Makeup of the Air Force

The modern U.S. Air Force is a huge organization that employs 560,000 men and women and maintains 6,900 aircraft. It is divided into twelve commands, the most important of which are the Strategic Air Command, the Tactical Air Command, the Military Airlift Command, and the Air Force Space Command.

The Strategic Air Command (SAC) oversees the nation's heavy bombers, its land-based long-range missiles, and its early warning systems. The Tactical Air Command (TAC) runs the fighter force that protects American skies and clears the way for ground troops in wartime. The Military Airlift Command operates cargo-carrying airplanes such as the giant C-5 Galaxy, which can transport four hundred or more fully equipped troops nonstop across oceans. The super-secret Air Force Space Command coordinates the activities of space satellites.

The air force also administers the U.S. Air Force Academy at Colorado Springs, Colorado. Opened in 1955, the academy prepares young men and women for careers as air force officers.

See also Aviation.

For further reading: R. Conrad Stein, *Fighter Planes* (Chicago: Childrens Press, 1986).

R. CONRAD STEIN

AIRPLANES
See Aviation.

ALABAMA CLAIMS

During the Civil War the British government allowed a number of Confederate warships, among them the *Alabama,* to be built in British shipyards. These vessels then destroyed a large number of American merchant ships. Since Great Britain was a neutral nation, this was a violation of both British and international law. After the war the United States demanded compensation for the damage caused by these vessels. In 1871, Secretary of State Hamilton Fish negotiated an arbitration agreement with the British, and in 1872 the arbitrators awarded the United States $15 million in damages.

See also Civil War.

ALAMO

Beginning in 1821 large numbers of Americans, mostly from the southern states, settled in Texas, which was then a Mexican state. At first the Mexicans encouraged this migration. But the newcomers felt no loyalty to Mexico. They wanted Texas to become part of the United States. Many of the settlers owned slaves, who were employed in raising cotton. So in 1835, when Mexico abolished slavery, the Texans declared their independence. Mexico then sent troops to put down their rebellion.

In February 1836, an estimated 187 Texans commanded by William B. Travis were trapped in the Alamo, a fortified mission in

The Alamo was the site of a legendary battle in the war for Texas's independence from Mexico. The illustration depicts the final day of the thirteen-day siege (March 6, 1836), during which all the Texans, with the exception of women, children, and a slave, were killed. Their heroic resistance against the Mexicans led to the famous battle cry, "Remember the Alamo!"

San Antonio, by a force of more than four thousand soldiers commanded by Antonio López de Santa Anna, the president of Mexico. On March 6, after a bloody siege, the Mexicans broke into the mission and killed all the defenders. Among the dead were Davy Crockett and James Bowie. The heroic defense of the Alamo and its terrible ending inspired the famous battle cry: "Remember the Alamo!" Texans used it to great effect a month later when their army defeated the Mexicans and captured Santa Anna at the Battle of San Jacinto, thus winning the war.

See also Texas Revolution and Annexation.

ALASKA PURCHASE

The United States purchased Alaska from Russia shortly after the Civil War, in 1867. The area, twice the size of Texas, had been a Russian colony since the 1740s. But the Russian government was in need of money. The Russians also worried about the increasing numbers of Canadians and Americans settling along Alaska's southern border, who they thought posed a threat to the Russian territory. After long negotiations, William H. Seward, President Andrew Johnson's secretary of state, and Baron Edouard de Stoeckl, the Russian minister in Washington, agreed on a price of $7.2 million for this huge area.

Many congressmen had doubts about buying Alaska. They called the purchase "Seward's folly." Some raised objections simply because they disliked President Johnson. These were Reconstruction years after the Civil War when people were arguing bitterly over how to treat the South. Many thought Johnson was too hostile toward the freed slaves and too friendly toward ex-slaveholders. They were not inclined to support any-

thing he proposed. Still others believed that the deal was simply a waste of money, since Alaska then seemed no more than a gigantic wilderness of snow and ice. ("Seward's icebox" was another nickname for the area.) Nevertheless, on April 9, 1867, the treaty was ratified by the Senate by a vote of 37 to 2.

Of course, after the discovery of gold in Alaska in 1896, people realized that the purchase of Alaska had been a real bargain—comparable to the purchase of the Louisiana territory from France in 1803.

See also Expansion, Territorial.

ALCOHOL
See Prohibition and Temperance.

ALCOTT, LOUISA MAY

(1832–88) *Writer and women's rights advocate.*

Alcott was a hard-working professional writer who tried her hand at many styles of fiction. But it is for a handful of children's books that she was best known in her own day and is remembered now. Her *Little Women* is perhaps the most loved girls' book in American literature.

She was the daughter of Bronson Alcott, an eccentric philosopher whose unrealistic schemes kept him on the verge of bankruptcy. She, her three sisters, and her mother always had to work to keep the family fed. Louisa sewed, taught school, and became a servant and tried desperately to make extra money by writing. She turned out hundreds of stories, earning a few dollars apiece for them, but gained no reputation because many were written under pen names.

In 1862, during the Civil War, Alcott became a volunteer nurse in a military hospital.

Overwork and bad sanitation ruined her health permanently, but the experience gave her the material for her first successful book, *Hospital Sketches* (1863). When her publisher suggested that she write something for girls, she recalled her own childhood. The result was *Little Women* (1867), which was an immediate success with both young and old. The bittersweet tale of the four March girls, Jo, Meg, Beth, and Amy—clearly modeled on the author (Jo) and her three sisters—was followed by several sequels, *Little Men* (1871; based on her nephews), *Eight Cousins* (1874), and *Jo's Boys* (1886). Generations of young girls have identified particularly with the character of Jo, who wants passionately to be a writer and gets into constant trouble because of her impulsiveness and quick temper.

Alcott never took her writing for children seriously, preferring her adult novels. But the humor and pathos she brought to the re-creation of family memories in her juvenile fiction made it a lasting contribution to American literature.

Alcott was also active in the women's rights movement of the nineteenth century. She herself never married and insisted that women should be free to live an independent and dignified life of their own.

See also Literature, Children's and Young Adult.

For further reading: Norma Johnston, *Louisa May: The World and Works of Louisa May Alcott* (New York: Macmillan, 1991).

DENNIS WEPMAN

Horatio Alger wrote more than one hundred dime novels for boys, including the book from the Ragged Dick series pictured above, that popularized the "rags to riches" theme. The notion that through hard work, honesty, and virtue anyone can escape from the rags of poverty to the riches of success is an idea firmly planted in the American mind. Alger's own life was not so rosy. He frittered away the fortune he had made as a writer and died a poor man.

ALGER, HORATIO

(1834–99)   *Writer of boys' books.*

Although his books are regarded today as badly written, with clumsy and unbelievable plots and characters, Horatio Alger was one of the most popular American authors of the nineteenth century. In about 130 novels—selling over 20 million copies—Alger repeated almost exactly the same story. But readers loved the vigorous style and rapid pace of his novels. The philosophy underlying them had a strong influence on the American character and ideas about what it takes to be successful in life.

Alger was born in Massachusetts, the son of a Unitarian minister, and after graduating from Harvard he too was ordained. He served two years as a pastor and then moved to New York City to be a writer. His first successful publication, *Ragged Dick* (1867), established his typical plot: a poor street boy bravely saves someone's life and receives a rich reward. For the next thirty years Alger was to write variations on this rags-to-riches theme.

Alger became a patron of several orphanages and homes for runaway boys, contributing money and time to help them out. He was especially attached to the Newsboys' Lodging House, which he served as chaplain. In such places he learned about the life of the poor and homeless. He used that knowledge for the settings of his sentimental stories of poor children who, with a combination of courage, honesty, and good fortune, become rich. The title of his second successful novel, *Luck and Pluck* (1869), perfectly summarized the elements of the standard "Horatio Alger story." Alger the minister never completely gave up preaching, but the message he preached in his novels was the optimistic one that virtue and hard work are always rewarded with money.

Alger himself, however, reversed the plot of his books and went from riches to rags. Generous and impractical, he gave his money away freely. Although he had earned a large fortune by his writing, he had to move in with his married sister in 1898 and died almost penniless two years later.

See also Literature, Children's and Young Adult.

For further reading: Edwin P. Hoyt, *Horatio's Boys: The Life and Work of Horatio Alger, Jr.* (Lanham, Md.: Madison Books, 1983).

DENNIS WEPMAN

ALI, MUHAMMAD

(1942–)   *Professional boxer.*

Known as "The Greatest" for his dazzling boxing style, Muhammad Ali was the first boxer to win the world heavyweight title three times. The great-grandson of a slave, Ali was born in Louisville, Kentucky. He was originally named Cassius Clay, Jr.

With his powerful body and lightning-quick fists, Ali leaped into boxing prominence at the age of fourteen. In 1960 he won the national Golden Gloves championship, the Amateur Athletic Union championship, and an Olympic gold medal. That same year he turned professional.

After winning nineteen bouts, Ali captured the world heavyweight championship from Sonny Liston in 1964. Following the match, he announced that he had joined the Nation of Islam (Black Muslims), the same organization that Malcolm X had joined, and changed his name to Muhammad Ali.

Between 1965 and 1966, he defended his title seven times. In 1967, however, he was stripped of his title when he refused induction into the U.S. Army to serve in the Vietnam War. Ali claimed exemption from military service because of his religious beliefs. A few months later he was suspended by the World Boxing Association and sentenced to five years in jail for draft evasion. Ali was allowed to return to boxing in 1970, and his conviction was reversed by the U.S. Supreme Court the next year.

In 1974 he regained his world heavyweight title by knocking out George Forman. He then lost it in 1978 when he was beaten by Leon Spinks, but regained it again later that year. Other than Spinks, and Joe Frazier who beat Ali in 1971, the only other boxers to defeat him were Ken Norton (1973), Larry

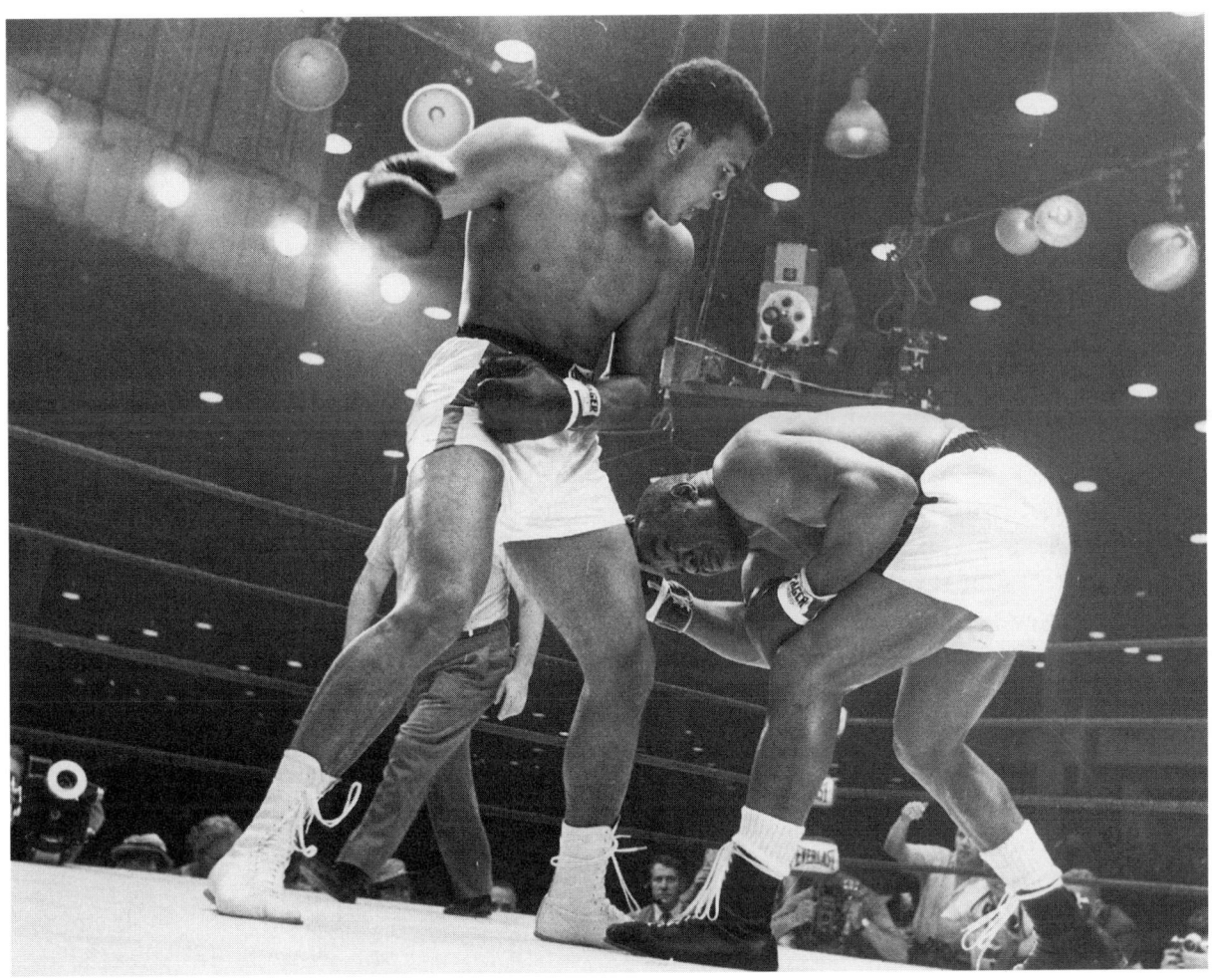

Sonny Liston, right, ducks in order to escape a blow from Muhammad Ali during the fifth round of the heavy-weight title fight in 1964. Ali won the championship two rounds later.

Holmes (1980), and Trevor Berbick (1981), after which Ali announced his retirement.

Ali liked to boast about his talent and tease his opponents by reciting playful poems before a match. He described his fighting style as "float like a butterfly, sting like a bee." He was perhaps the most famous sports figure in the world during the 1960s and 1970s. Although his health is declining, he still visits boxing training centers and encourages young boxers.

See also Boxing.

JOANN BIONDI

ALIEN AND SEDITION ACTS

Congress, which was controlled by the Federalists, passed the Alien and Sedition Acts in 1798, at a time when war with France threatened. Fear of French radical ideas that had been unleashed in the French Revolution, anger at the revelation that Talleyrand, the French foreign minister, had tried to bribe American negotiators seeking a peaceful settlement of the crisis with France, as well as suspicion that the opposition Democratic-Republican Party would side with France if war did break out led to these attacks on freedom of expression.

The laws increased from five to fourteen years the time foreigners had to live in the United States before they could apply for citizenship. They also gave the president the power to arrest and deport foreigners whom he considered "dangerous to the peace and safety of the United States." In addition, the Sedition Act made even criticism of the government illegal. Anyone who spoke or published "false, scandalous, and malicious" comments about government officials could be fined or imprisoned.

The restrictions on foreigners had little practical effect, but several pro-Democratic-Republican newspaper editors were tried and convicted under the Sedition Act. Even a member of the House of Representatives, Matthew Lyon of Vermont, was sentenced to four months in jail and fined a thousand dollars for criticizing the Sedition Act in a letter to a Vermont newspaper.

Fortunately the Democratic-Republican victory in the election of 1800 put an end to these attacks on freedom of speech and the press.

ALLEN, RICHARD

(1760–1831) *African-American religious leader and reformer.*

Born a slave in Philadelphia, Richard Allen, at about the age of eight, was sold with his family to a farmer in Delaware. Allen's master let him spend part of his time working for wages. By chopping wood and laboring in a brickyard, he was eventually able to purchase his freedom.

In 1777, Allen experienced a religious awakening and joined the Methodist church. Educating himself, he became a minister. At first he preached to racially mixed congregations, but growing increasingly concerned about racial discrimination in the church, he founded Bethel, a black Methodist church, in Philadelphia in 1794. It joined with other black congregations in 1816 to form the African Methodist Episcopal (A.M.E.) church, the first large independent black Protestant denomination. Chosen its first bishop, Allen worked to the end of his life to make this church a strong unifying force among African Americans.

Allen played an active role in many important causes. In 1792–93, when a terrible yellow fever epidemic struck Philadelphia, he helped organize blacks to care for and bury the victims of this disease, when many people, out of fear, refused to do so. He started schools for black youth and mutual aid societies to relieve needy African Americans of having to rely on the charity of white people. During the War of 1812, he helped recruit African Americans to aid in the defense of Philadelphia.

The cause to which Allen devoted the most attention was the elimination of racial discrimination. This former slave asserted that blacks, though treated unequally by the system under which they lived, were not inferior to other Americans. In stirring articles and impassioned sermons and speeches, Allen also lashed out repeatedly at the institution of slavery and the slave trade.

See also Abolitionist Movement; African Americans: to 1865; Free Blacks before Emancipation.

EDMUND LINDOP

AMENDMENTS, CONSTITUTIONAL
See Constitution.

AMERICA FIRST COMMITTEE

The America First Committee was founded in July 1940 by persons who hoped to keep the United States from getting involved in World War II, which had broken out in Europe a year earlier. Many America Firsters were isolationists—that is, they thought that what happened in other countries was of no concern to the United States. Some saw entering the war as a threat to the growing prosperity of the United States, which was just emerging from the Great Depression. Others feared that if the country went to war, the government would interfere with the operation of businesses and labor unions by regulating production and fixing prices. Still others joined simply because they disliked President Franklin D. Roosevelt. They believed that his policy of trying to help the Western nations fight Nazi Germany was likely to lead to a declaration of war.

The best-known America Firster was the famous Charles A. Lindbergh, the first person to fly an airplane alone across the Atlantic Ocean. Lindbergh was opposed to entering the war because he believed that the Germans would win it. At its height in 1941, the America First Committee had several hundred thousand members in some 450 chapters all over the country. But after the Japanese attacked Pearl Harbor on December 7, 1941, and Adolf Hitler declared war on the United States on December 11, the movement quickly collapsed.

AMERICAN CIVIL LIBERTIES UNION

The American Civil Liberties Union (ACLU) was founded in 1920 by a group alarmed by the way the government had arrested and jailed pacifists and other people who had opposed the military draft and various policies during World War I. Among its leading founders were the philosopher John Dewey, the settlement-house worker Jane Addams, and Professor Felix Frankfurter, later a Supreme Court justice. The founders were even more upset by the arrest and deportation of foreign-born radicals after the war without evidence that they had broken any law.

The policy of the ACLU is to support everyone's right of free speech and the press without regard for the person's particular views, liberal or conservative. This has meant on occasion taking positions that were disapproved of by a majority of Americans. The right of the Ku Klux Klan to organize demonstrations and parades attacking desegregation and the right of Nazi organizations to publish anti-Semitic statements—things that members of the ACLU dislike intensely—are supported along with the positions of liberal groups that ACLU members agree with wholeheartedly.

This does not mean that the ACLU supports violent *actions* of any kind, simply freedom of speech and thought.

See also Bill of Rights.

AMERICAN FEDERATION OF LABOR

The growth of industry after the Civil War led to the development of many craft unions. For a time in the 1880s a broader-based union, the Knights of Labor, flourished. But in 1886 a reaction set in after the Haymarket bombing tragedy. Because it occurred at a workers' rally in support of a strike, the bombing caused an illogical but powerful popular reaction against unions, and the Knights soon ceased to exist. Its place, however, was filled by the American Federation of Labor (AFL), a loose combination of national craft unions founded in December 1886. The AFL avoided politics and all noneconomic issues, concentrating instead on improving members' wages, hours, and working conditions. "Our organization does not consist of idealists," Adolph Strasser of the cigarmakers' union told a congressional committee. "I look first to cigars."

The president of the AFL from 1886 until his death in 1924 (with the exception of one year) was Samuel Gompers. Between 1886 and 1901 AFL membership grew from about 150,000 to more than a million. It made further gains during World War I, but declined during the postwar years. Under the New Deal it again expanded but lost influence to the Congress of Industrial Organizations (CIO), which enrolled workers in industry-wide unions rather than in separate crafts. It remained important, however, and in 1955 it merged with the CIO to form the AFL-CIO.

See also Congress of Industrial Organizations; Gompers, Samuel; Labor Movement.

AMERICAN PARTY
See Know-Nothing Party.

AMERICAN RED CROSS

When Swiss philanthropist Jean Henri Dunant founded the International Committee of the Red Cross in 1863, the volunteer social service agency was devoted exclusively to relief for the wounded in European wars and was limited to Swiss membership. He chose for its symbol the Swiss flag—a white cross on a red background—with its colors reversed. The following year, representatives from twelve nations met in Geneva to sign an agreement to care for sick and wounded soldiers from all countries. The United States, unwilling to become involved in European military affairs, did not sign the treaty.

It was not until eighteen years later, in 1881, that Clara Barton, a volunteer nurse in the American Civil War, founded the American Association of the Red Cross. She persuaded President Chester A. Arthur to sign the Geneva Convention treaty in 1882, making the United States the thirty-second member of the international body.

Under Barton's leadership, the American Red Cross broadened its range of services to include relief for victims of natural disasters. In 1889 it provided housing for people made homeless by the Johnstown, Pennsylvania, flood; in 1892 its volunteer members worked with famine victims in Russia; and in 1898 it helped the U.S. Army in Cuba during the Spanish-American War. Congress granted the organization a charter as the nation's official relief agency in 1900.

Clara Barton retired in 1904 and was replaced by Mabel Boardman, who used her own considerable wealth to support the organization. Boardman extended the services of the American Red Cross still further and unified its many independent groups into a network of local chapters with national headquarters in Washington, D.C.

Still supported by private contributions, the American Red Cross today has an annual budget of over $1 billion. Its 25,394 paid employees and 1.7 million volunteers operate 2,763 chapters and 57 blood centers. Besides its high-profile relief activities after natural disasters, it is active in organ, tissue, and bone marrow donations, operates a health education program, and provides services to the homeless.

DENNIS WEPMAN

AMERICAN REVOLUTION
See Revolution.

AMERICAN SYSTEM

The American System was a policy designed after the War of 1812 by Congressman Henry Clay of Kentucky. Clay hoped to speed economic growth in the new nation (and eventually win the presidency for himself) by forging an alliance between western farmers and eastern business and manufacturing interests. He called for a national bank and protective tariffs on imported manufactured products to please easterners, whose businesses would benefit from these measures. He proposed federally financed road and canal construction, what was known as "internal improvements," to win the backing of westerners, who badly needed better transportation facilities.

For a time the system seemed to work. In 1816 Congress created the Second Bank of the United States and imposed high tariffs on many goods imported from abroad that competed with eastern manufactured products. Large-scale road and canal building was also undertaken, though mostly by the states and by private companies. In the 1830s and 1840s, however, the growing opposition to slavery in the northern states and southerners' dislike of high tariffs on manufactured goods (they wanted imported goods to re-

main cheap because they relied on them) weakened the political appeal of Clay's system.

See also Clay, Henry.

AMISTAD CASE

In 1839 fifty-three African slaves were being transported by their Cuban owners on the ship *Amistad*. They broke loose from their chains, killed two crew members, and took command of the vessel. They ordered the captain to sail for Africa, but he fooled them by sailing a zigzag course northeastward off the coast of the United States. Eventually the *Amistad* was stopped by an American warship.

The slaves were then brought ashore and jailed. The government intended to ship them back to Cuba, but protests by American abolitionists, who pointed out that the international slave trade was illegal, won them a hearing in a federal court. The judge ruled that they were not guilty of mutiny because they had been illegally enslaved.

The case was appealed to the Supreme Court, where their lawyer, former president John Quincy Adams, successfully argued that since the slave trade was illegal, the blacks were not merely blameless but entitled to their freedom.

See also Slavery.

ANDERSON, MARIAN
(1902–93)   *Concert singer.*

Born in Philadelphia on February 17, 1902, Marian Anderson grew up singing in church choirs and dreaming of a career in music.

When she attempted to enroll in a local music school, however, the teenaged African American was told that "coloreds" were not accepted. Fortunately, sympathetic friends started a "Fund for Marian's Future," which allowed her to take private voice lessons.

In time Anderson's talent won out, and in the 1920s she was invited to sing at New York City's Carnegie Hall. Still not welcome in most concert halls of America, Anderson, like many other black performers, toured Europe, where she sang before royalty and won widespread acclaim. When she returned to America in 1935, a New York music critic called her "one of the great singers of our times," and Franklin and Eleanor Roosevelt received her at the White House. Over the next few years she sang before sell-out crowds in cities across the nation.

But Anderson's struggle was not over. In 1939 the Daughters of the American Revolution (DAR) canceled her scheduled concert in Washington, D.C.'s, Constitution Hall, which they owned. Their hall, they said, "could not be used by one of [her] race." In response, Eleanor Roosevelt resigned her membership in the DAR and arranged for Anderson to sing at the Lincoln Memorial. An audience of seventy-five thousand gathered for a nationally broadcast concert that made both musical and civil rights history.

In 1955, at age fifty-three, Marian Anderson broke still another barrier: she became the first black to sing with the New York Metropolitan Opera Company. Though she received a standing ovation, her voice was now past its prime, and she remarked, "I wish [this opportunity] had come earlier that I might have been able to bring more to it."

In 1962 President Lyndon B. Johnson awarded Anderson the Presidential Medal of Freedom, and shortly thereafter she retired. She lived quietly in Danbury, Connecticut, until her death on April 8, 1993.

See also African Americans; Music.

For further reading: Linda Peavy and Ursula Smith, *Dreams into Deeds: Nine Women Who Dared* (New York: Scribner's, 1985).

LINDA PEAVY
URSULA SMITH

In 1939 Marian Anderson, an acclaimed singer, was barred from performing in Constitution Hall in Washington, D.C., by the Daughters of the American Revolution because of her race. First Lady Eleanor Roosevelt resigned from the DAR in protest and arranged for Anderson to perform for an audience of seventy-five thousand at the Lincoln Memorial.

ANGLO-AMERICANS

Anglo-Americans are people who trace their ancestry to the British Isles. This was the primary group that accomplished the colonization of what became the original United States. People from England composed the majority of the Anglo-Americans, especially in the early years of colonial settlement. But beginning in the mid-eighteenth century, immigrants to America also came in large numbers from other parts of the United Kingdom: from Scotland; from Wales; and from the northern part of Ireland, the Scots-Irish. (Those from Catholic southern Ireland form their own ethnic group and have a very different history.)

Each group—English, Scottish, Welsh, and Scots-Irish—had its own characteristics, and the last three had historic reasons for disliking the dominant English. But they were united in having had the same monarch, speaking English (except for some Welsh and Highland Scots), professing a Protestant form of religion, and sharing a belief in individual advancement through hard work. Their descendants are sometimes called WASPS (from the initials of "white Anglo-Saxon Protestants").

Anglo-Americans led the young nation during the American Revolution. George Washington, Benjamin Franklin, Thomas Jefferson, and just about every other famous figure of the time were Anglo-Americans. Anglo-Americans also did more than any other people to shape early America. Our form of government is an adaptation of what the Founding Fathers had known under Great Britain's rule. Our legal system is based on English common law. The free enterprise economy evolved from British practices. And our literature—at least through the nineteenth century—was almost entirely written by Anglo-Americans.

Because the various Anglo-American groups composed the basic stock of what became American society, they did not suffer the prejudice and discrimination felt by many other immigrants. In fact, it was Anglo-Americans who did the discriminating. They became so quickly and thoroughly the American mainstream that it is hard to think of them as an ethnic group at all. Although emigrants from all over the world have made the United States a "nation of nations," the Anglo-American influence on our culture continues strong.

BENJAMIN MCARTHUR

ANTHONY, SUSAN B.

(1820–1906)   *Pioneer crusader for women's rights.*

Born in Adams, Massachusetts, Anthony spent her childhood on a farm in New York State. She was greatly influenced by her Quaker father who fought for the abolition of slavery. Family life centered around heated discussions in her home where great abolitionists such as Frederick Douglass came for dinner.

After teaching for three years, Anthony quit her job and devoted her life to the women's suffrage and antislavery movements. She encouraged women teachers to demand higher salaries, and her 1860 petition of the New York legislature led to the passage of laws granting women control over their wages and the guardianship of their children.

As a steadfast abolitionist, she worked with the American Anti-Slavery Society in New York from 1856 on and was often challenged by angry mobs at her meetings. During the Civil War Anthony organized the Women's National Loyal League to push for emancipation.

When the Fourteenth and Fifteenth Amendments to the Constitution were proposed to extend civil rights and the vote to

African-American men, Anthony demanded that the amendments also apply to women. When this failed, she petitioned for the right to vote as an American citizen. Although this too failed, and she was arrested and fined for voting illegally, it did not lessen her dedication to the cause.

In the years that followed, Anthony continued to campaign for women's suffrage while working with the National Woman Suffrage Association, which she organized in 1869, and later with the National American Woman Suffrage Association, serving as president from 1892 to 1900. In 1888 she organized the International Council of Women and in 1904, the International Woman Suffrage Alliance in Berlin, Germany. In collaboration with other women reformers, she published a weekly newspaper called the *Revolution* and a book, *The History of Woman Suffrage.*

At the time of her death, women were allowed to vote only in Wyoming, Utah, Colorado, Idaho, New Zealand, and Australia, but Anthony died certain that the next generation of women would win the vote, which they did when the Nineteenth Amendment was adopted in 1920.

See also Abolitionist Movement; Feminist Movement to 1919; Voting.

JOANN BIONDI

ANTICOMMUNISM

The term *anticommunism* describes the fear and suspicion in the United States aimed at followers of the Communist Party and sympathizers with the former Soviet Union. Periods of intense anticommunism are also called "red scares."

In 1919, after the Soviet revolution of 1917 and the end of World War I, fears of radicals in the United States led to hundreds of arrests and mass deportations of aliens suspected of being Communists.

Similar distrust and near-panic swept the country in the late 1940s and 1950s. As World War II ended, Americans became fearful of their former ally, the Soviet Union, as the Soviets swallowed up much of Eastern Europe as well as when it was disclosed that U.S. nuclear secrets had been passed to the Russians during the war. Then the Soviet Union learned how to make atomic bombs, and the Chinese government fell to Communists. Thousands of Americans died defending South Korea from invasion by Communist-dominated North Korea.

Many people, anxious over these events, suspected that Communist sympathizers in the U.S. government had helped them along. They feared that Communists might take over the United States, too—although at the height of its popularity in the 1940s, the American Communist Party had no more than eighty thousand members. By 1957, there were only ten thousand.

During these years, a few dozen leaders of the U.S. Communist Party were tried and convicted of advocating the overthrow of the U.S. government. It became clear later that the convictions violated their constitutional right to free speech. But often, actions taken to uproot Communism were not as clear-cut as prosecution in a court where the accused could at least answer the charges. Many Americans were found "guilty by association" because they once belonged to a left-wing group or had merely known a Communist.

In 1945, the Committee on Un-American Activities in the House of Representatives (HUAC) began questioning suspected and former Communists as well as people with no link to Communism; they were simply liberals. Those who refused to testify could be cited for contempt of Congress and sent to jail. From 1945 to 1957, the committee interviewed about three thousand people.

Witnesses were asked to name members of Communist front organizations, which were liberal groups with Communist ties. Many pleaded the Fifth Amendment against self-incrimination, which was their constitutional right but left the impression that they were guilty when they were in fact only trying to protect themselves and friends from unfair treatment.

In one of the committee's most notorious cases, a former State Department official, Alger Hiss, was accused by a confessed spy, Whittaker Chambers, of passing secret docu-

ments to the Soviets during the 1930s. The case was pursued by a congressman on the committee, Richard M. Nixon, which made the future president a national figure. Hiss went to prison for perjury in 1950 for his denial. A debate raged for years over whether he was really guilty. In 1992, a Russian historian, after searching the Soviet Union's KGB files, declared that Hiss had never been a spy for Russia.

The Senate's Internal Security Subcommittee also investigated the Foreign Service and suspected Communists in labor unions, schools, and other organizations. State legislatures, too, formed investigative committees.

Senator Joseph R. McCarthy, the country's most notorious anticommunist crusader, points to a map claiming to reveal areas under communist control in the United States. McCarthy typically used official-looking maps and fake evidence to lend an air of authority to his accusations, which were usually outright lies. His vicious and irresponsible attacks created an atmosphere of anticommunist hysteria and fear during the early 1950s.

Many ex-Communists testified before these committees about their past lives and named long lists of "fellow Communists." Just being named before a committee could ruin a person's career. Later some informers admitted they had lied in their testimony.

Some states required teachers and government employees to swear that they were not members of the Communist Party; those who refused lost their jobs. Congress demanded loyalty oaths from labor union officers, and unions themselves required that members sign such oaths. Employers directed employees to swear their loyalty. Thousands of Americans were investigated by the FBI as potential spies. Some foreign-born labor leaders were refused citizenship or deported.

The entertainment industry was especially hard hit. In 1950, some ex-FBI agents issued *Red Channels,* a book listing 151 actors, directors, and writers with "suspicious" associations. Those on this blacklist could not get jobs for many years.

There were some laughable incidents, too. In Indiana professional wrestlers were required to take a loyalty oath; in New York a woman got her marriage annulled on the grounds that her husband was a Communist.

Perhaps the most notorious case was that of Julius and Ethel Rosenberg, executed in 1953 for allegedly passing atomic secrets to the Russians during World War II. To the end they denied being spies, and the nation was deeply torn over the question of their guilt.

Senator Joseph R. McCarthy of Wisconsin was one of the most flamboyant of the anti-communists. He ruined many careers using his Senate subcommittee to conduct witch-hunts throughout the government. In 1954, he was discredited in the Army-McCarthy televised hearings, and soon after, the Senate censured him. That rebuke was a turning point. In the late 1950s, fears of Communist infiltration of America began to fade.

See also Cold War; McCarthy, Joseph R.; Miller, Arthur; Oppenheimer, J. Robert; *Rosenberg* Case.

REBECCA LARSEN

ANTIFEDERALISTS

After the Constitution was drafted at the Philadelphia Convention of 1787, it had to be ratified (approved) by the states before it could go into effect. The Antifederalists were people who disliked at least some aspects of the new document. Despite their name, Antifederalists were not opposed in principle to a central federal government. But they thought the Constitution as written would give the new United States *too much* power. In general, they preferred local governments, where people were more likely to know their representatives and where judges and elected officials could be counted upon to be familiar with the needs and desires of the average citizen.

This did not mean that the Antifederalists were more democratic than the Federalists, who strongly supported the new system. People who believe in local independence do not always favor equal rights for everyone in the neighborhood.

Antifederalists tended to be farmers, debtors, people who lived simply, often in the more rural areas of the various states. Yet many wealthy, sophisticated, and well-educated people adopted the Antifederalist position. Having fought a revolution to overthrow a powerful, sometimes tyrannical British government, many had a healthy suspicion of all "outside" authority, even one created by Americans like themselves.

The contests in some of the states about ratifying the Constitution were close and bitterly fought. In the end all accepted it. The agreement of the Federalists to add a Bill of Rights to the Constitution spelling out what the federal government could *not* do probably convinced most Antifederalists that the new system should be approved.

See also Constitution; Constitution, the Making of the.

ANTI-SALOON LEAGUE

The Anti-Saloon League was founded in Washington, D.C., in 1893. Unlike other groups opposed to the use of intoxicating beverages, it sought to influence both major parties, rather than back the relatively unimportant Prohibition Party. The organization was headed by Wayne Wheeler, a young graduate of Oberlin College. It recruited members through churches and other local institutions, lobbied actively in state legislatures, and during election campaigns quizzed candidates closely about their views on drinking before deciding whom to support.

The Anti-Saloon League had considerable effect on early-twentieth-century antiliquor legislation, especially in the southern states. It also played a large role in the drive for the Eighteenth Amendment to the Constitution, which in 1919 prohibited the manufacture and sale of alcohol in the United States. During the 1920s the League was active in encouraging the enforcement of Prohibition.

During these years the country divided into "drys," people who favored Prohibition, and "wets," who hoped to have the Eighteenth Amendment modified or repealed. When the Democrats nominated Alfred E. Smith, a "wet," for president in 1928, the League backed the "dry" Republican, Herbert

Hoover. It won that battle, but after the election of Franklin D. Roosevelt in 1932 and the ending of Prohibition a year later, it ceased to play an important role in American life.

See also Prohibition and Temperance.

ANTISLAVERY MOVEMENT
See Abolitionist Movement.

ANTITRUST MOVEMENT

Most Americans thought of themselves as free individuals during the nineteenth century and that as free individuals they had the right to run their companies as they wished. But between the end of the Civil War in 1865 and the end of the century, public opinion about the nature of such freedom began to change. As industries grew and combined into what were called "trusts," the problem of such monopolies became a matter of concern. For the free businessman, a trust was a sensible way to control some of the uncertainties of doing business. A trust might combine banking services, supplies of raw materials, the means of transportation to and from the factory, and a vast network of wholesalers.

To an individual citizen, this understanding of freedom seemed increasingly inadequate. Trusts might be efficient for the businessman, but they also served to eliminate competition. To a worker who had no choice but to accept low wages, to a retired employee with no pension, to a purchaser who had to pay more than a product seemed to be worth, such freedom for a businessman meant exploitation for everyone else. Public opinion came increasingly to support legislation that would prevent the formation of trusts or otherwise regulate large industries so that they could not use their great power to force out smaller companies, reduce wages, and raise prices. The assumption was that antitrust laws would restore fairness by preserving competition and thus benefit consumers with lower prices and more variety.

Antitrust Acts

The first legislation regulating trusts was the Sherman Antitrust Act (1890). It was a weak and vague law that forbade any business activities that seemed likely to monopolize trade. The courts interpreted it almost into meaninglessness, throwing out early cases against the whiskey and sugar trusts.

President Theodore Roosevelt (1901–09) was representative of many Americans when he distinguished between good trusts and bad trusts. The good trusts used their power efficiently, making possible lower prices, which they passed on to consumers. The bad ones forced competitors into bankruptcy, treated workers poorly, and kept the increased profits instead of lowering prices. Roosevelt added some force to the Sherman Act by having his attorney general file suit against the Northern Securities Company, a railroad combination. In 1904, the Supreme Court backed him up. It declared that the combination violated the Sherman Act and broke it up. The company's operations were not truly threatened, but many businessmen were indignant at what they thought of as government meddling with legitimate business practices. Essentially, the decision meant that there were some limitations on how businesses could combine. It remained unclear how severe these restrictions were and whether other administrations would follow similar guidelines.

Under Presidents William Howard Taft (1909–13) and Woodrow Wilson (1913–21),

the pace picked up. Taft enforced the Sherman Act vigorously. Wilson sponsored new legislation, the Federal Trade Commission Act and the Clayton Antitrust Act, which specifically prohibited companies from entering into pricing agreements that restricted trade, outlawed the common practice of having the same people sit on the boards of companies that were supposed to be competing with each other, and made it illegal for a firm to buy stock in its competitors' firms.

Even with such progressive reforms, court interpretations of the laws meant that antitrust pressures played only a small role in business practices until late in the New Deal. President Franklin D. Roosevelt appointed a sharp critic of antitrust, Thurman Arnold, to take charge. He reinvigorated government regulatory practices for about four years, but then the pressures of World War II intervened. No one wanted to irritate big business in the middle of a war when all-out production was so important.

Changes in Antitrust

Attitudes toward the antitrust laws went through a major change during the 1970s and 1980s. Most antitrust thought until then had been "structuralist"—that is, it focused on market structure and how businesses behaved. Then the focus changed and became oriented toward "price theory." If a business restricted its output and raised prices, it should be a target for legal attack; but if it merely expanded efficiently and kept prices reasonable, no one cared. It sounded a bit technical, but at its core, such thinking was merely the old idea that good trusts should be left alone and only bad ones prosecuted.

Antitrust activities became increasingly suspect because of two famous cases: one against the American Telephone and Telegraph Company (AT & T) and the other against International Business Machines (I B M), both filed in the late 1960s. The first, A T & T, ended by taking an efficient and even popular company and breaking it into many pieces, "fixing" something that was not broken and raising prices for customers in the process. The I B M case was finally dropped by the government. In a short time competition from other companies in America, Japan, and elsewhere proved far more effective than attacks by the Justice Department in reducing I B M's power. Antitrust legislation remains on the books, but now does little except curb the worst sorts of price-fixing agreements and provide some way of dealing with other types of antisocial business behavior.

R O B E R T   M.   C R U N D E N

A R A B   A M E R I C A N S

Discoveries by Arab scientists helped Columbus reach the New World—but not until the 1880s did Arabs themselves "discover America." At the 1876 Philadelphia Centennial Exposition, a few merchants from Jerusalem and other cities in Palestine and Lebanon found Americans eager to buy souvenirs from the Holy Land. This encouraged other Arabs to come to America, seeking better opportunities. Most were Christians from Mount Lebanon, who already knew something of the United States through the educational work of American missionaries.

Although poor, these immigrants wanted to be their own boss. Rather than working in factories, mines, or farms, they became peddlers, walking from house to house with packs of useful items. Soon they developed networks to help newcomers get started and go farther afield. By 1900 peddlers from Mount Lebanon could be found all over the United States.

In the beginning, most planned to return home eventually, but life in America proved too good to leave. Working hard, saving every penny possible, many peddlers managed both to send money home and to start small businesses such as stores, restaurants, and garment factories. Family members followed, and many courageous women came on their own. At first known as Syrians, or Turks because Mount Lebanon was in the Ottoman (Turkish) Empire, the immigrants began calling themselves Lebanese after Lebanon became a republic in 1926.

Muslims, who had earlier been reluctant to come to an unfamiliar Christian-dominated country, immigrated increasingly after World War I, along with some Druze, another religious sect in Lebanon. Because they wanted to practice their religion together, most Muslims preferred a settled life. In particular they were attracted to the automobile industry in and around Detroit, which has become the largest single Arab community in America.

Most Palestinians in the United States (presently around 120,000) immigrated following the creation of Israel in 1948 and the 1967 war. Many are well educated and successful in business and the professions. Recent immigrants from Syria and Iraq have come because of conditions in their home countries. A number of them were refugees from the bloody Iran-Iraq War of 1980–88. Like immigrants from Egypt and those who fled the 1975–90 war in Lebanon, they are largely students, professionals, and business people. In contrast, several thousand Yemeni immigrants are mostly workers in Detroit industry and California agriculture. With the Lebanese still the main component, Arab Americans now total between 2 and 3 million.

Arab immigrants have always taken pride in their hard work, strong family structure, and good citizenship. They have assimilated readily into American life while still retaining elements of Arab culture such as food (shish kebab, tabbouleh, falafel, pita bread), music, and religion. Many have become famous in entertainment (Casey Kasem, Paula Abdul, Jamie Farr, Marlo Thomas), medicine and science (pioneer heart surgeon Dr. Michael DeBakey, *Apollo* moon-landing geologist Farouk el-Baz), government and public service (Senate Majority Leader George Mitchell, Secretary of Health and Human Services Donna Shalala, White House correspondent Helen Thomas, consumer advocate Ralph Nader), writing (William Peter Blatty, *The Exorcist;* Callie Khouri, *Thelma and Louise;* literary and music critic Edward Said), and sports (football player Doug Flutie, race car driver Bobby Rahal), as well as many other fields.

Arab Americans sometimes feel discriminated against because of political problems in the Middle East, especially the Arab-Israeli conflict. Several Arab-American organizations work to provide information from their point of view, combat discrimination, increase cohesiveness within the community, and encourage participation in the political process.

For further reading: Brent Ashabranner, *An Ancient Heritage: The Arab-American Minority* (New York: HarperCollins, 1991); Elsa Marston Harik, *The Lebanese in America* (Minneapolis, Minn.: Lerner Books, 1987).

ELSA MARSTON HARIK

ARCHITECTURE

From its origins in simple homesteads through the skyscrapers and shopping malls of today, American architecture has reflected the diversity and creative energy, but also the restrictive aspects, of American life.

Architecture is an art form, but commercial concerns have played an unusually significant role in its history. Commercial buildings dominate the landscape of most cities, vying with one another to catch our attention. Architects compete among themselves for jobs and fame; and they compete with ordinary builders, who still produce the vast majority of new housing and commercial buildings.

Buildings in Early America

When the first European settlers arrived, the Native Americans had already developed their own architectural traditions: the pueblo, hogan, longhouse, and tipi call to mind the Indian way of life. Similarly, the colonial Spanish mission, the clapboard-sided New England dwelling, and the compact towns of the seventeenth century endure as romantic prototypes for new housing.

At the time of the Revolution the colonies still had no trained architects. Carpenters designed and built most structures, though gentlemen amateurs such as Thomas Jefferson often designed their own country estates. Both groups adapted the English fashion of neoclassicism (modeled on ancient Greek or Roman architecture), usually building in wood and simplifying the detailing in a style we now call Federal.

The early nineteenth century witnessed the rapid growth of cities. With them came banks, exchanges, public markets, and private commercial buildings. Filling in land along rivers and the seacoast provided plots for new warehouses, wharves, and residential districts. With this increased activity, dwellings and public buildings came to look more alike from one city to the next.

Jefferson designed not only his own home but the University of Virginia, the Virginia state capital, and the National Survey—a simple rectilinear scheme for dividing and selling public land. Influenced by European Enlightenment ideas, he believed that the right environment would encourage virtue in America's citizens. This widespread belief also led to important pre–Civil War reforms in such buildings as prisons, orphanages, mental hospitals, and the like, as well as the creation of spacious urban parks.

Changing Fashions

A distinctive American architectural fashion (later named the Shingle Style) emerged in the late-nineteenth-century suburbs. Houses became more individualized, combining diverse materials and ornament with a rambling floor plan. Technological advances allowed this fashion to spread rapidly, with inexpensive factory production of architectural decorations, the publication of "builders' guides" with many illustrations, and electric streetcars to carry commuters to jobs in the central cities. Stylistic differences also had other meanings. In the cities these decades produced crowded tenements, as well as elaborate museums, libraries, and mansions that resembled Renaissance palaces or medieval castles.

Urban business districts were being transformed by a major American innovation: the skyscraper. Beginning in the 1880s, architects and engineers in Chicago and New York began to experiment with new construction systems. Commercial buildings soon rose to ten, then twenty stories high. The concentration of these structures affected the economy, the experience, and the appearance of American downtown districts.

In other areas, business also sponsored new opportunities for architects. Movie houses, theaters, and department stores lured customers with dazzling lights and colorful ornament. In the Detroit area, the factory

was transformed into a sprawling industrial plant to house automobile assembly lines.

Soon people recognized the need to organize this fast-growing environment. New York's zoning regulations of 1916 controlled the height and use of commercial and apartment buildings. Other cities followed, and many suburbs excluded businesses, industry, and multifamily residences. Simultaneously, as urban commercial buildings grew larger in the 1920s, encompassing several blocks, they often included many different versions of similar activities.

Architectural modernism sought to simplify the plan and façades (or fronts) of buildings, supposedly basing them on their function rather than historic styles. During the 1930s American architectural schools embraced this idea. At the same time, under the impetus of Franklin D. Roosevelt's New Deal, the federal government produced a range of modern structures, including dams, offices, and housing projects.

Postwar Architecture

Large-scale development characterized all aspects of American architecture after World War II. Glass and steel skyscrapers epitomized the corporate world, and large concrete buildings brought together public services. The Urban Renewal Act of 1954 provided federal funds for acres of new luxury apartments, office buildings, and convention centers in downtown areas, replacing dilapidated older housing that was torn down.

While the majority of new suburban houses still featured historic styles, others adopted the simplified "ranch style." But whatever their look, most suburban houses were part of large, mass-produced tract developments, following the example of Levittown, New York. In 1956 Victor Gruen's vast mall at Southland, outside Minneapolis, first brought suburban shopping and social life together under one air-conditioned roof, with abundant parking all around. Soon entire new towns like Reston, Virginia, and Columbia, Maryland, featured a careful mixture of housing types and recreational facilities, all set in a protected natural environment.

In the 1970s a reaction set in. The preservation and reuse of historic buildings became a rallying cry in many communities. Critics blamed modern architecture for the disappearance of urban neighborhoods, the sterility of downtowns, and the problems of public housing. "Postmodern" skyscrapers and small shops featured an array of brightly colored, eye-catching decorations. Even "modern" buildings became more playful, animated, and unusual.

The postwar era brought celebrity to several American architects, the most famous being Frank Lloyd Wright. Beginning in the Midwest with his early-twentieth-century "prairie houses" and culminating with the Guggenheim Museum in New York (1959), Wright's long career encompassed virtually every region and building type, as well as continuous innovations in both technology and design.

Architecture will always have exceptional designers, of course. But it is also the world of ordinary buildings, the old as well as the new. To study the history of American architecture one has to take both factors into account.

See also Housing; Jefferson, Thomas; Levittowns; Pei, I. M.; Sullivan, Louis H.; Urban Growth; Wright, Frank Lloyd. *For color illustrations, see insert following p. 52.*

GWENDOLYN WRIGHT

ARMED FORCES
See Air Force; Army; Marine Corps; Navy.

ARMORY SHOW

In 1913 a group of American artists organized a large exhibition, held at the Sixty-ninth Regiment Armory in New York City. They considered themselves artistic radicals and hoped to educate the public about the latest trends in painting. To lend an international

Marcel Duchamp's cubist painting, Nude Descending a Staircase, *created a scandal at the Armory Show in 1913, offending conservative American tastes. One critic ridiculed the painting as "an explosion in a shingle factory," and an art magazine held a contest asking readers to find the nude on the staircase.*

aspect to the show they invited European painters, including Henri Matisse, Pablo Picasso, and other modernists, to participate.

The exhibition attracted huge crowds in New York and in Chicago and Boston, where it was later displayed. But the American artists failed to attract the notice they had expected. Their works were overshadowed by the far more unconventional canvases of the Europeans. Neither the public nor most American critics liked the European paintings. Many people were outraged by the distortions and garish colors of the European "madmen," or they wrote them off as deliberate spoofs. Marcel Duchamp's cubist canvas, *Nude Descending a Staircase,* seemed particularly outrageous. It was compared to "an explosion in a shingle factory" and dismissed as a scandalous joke.

Because of the attention the Europeans attracted, the American organizers of the Armory Show were practically ignored. Nevertheless, their show was an event of landmark proportions in the history of American art, for it did what they had hoped it would do. It introduced a huge audience to the kind of art that has dominated twentieth-century painting and sculpture.

See also Painting and Sculpture.

ARMSTRONG, LOUIS

(1898?–1971)   *Jazz musician.*

Virtually no documents exist mentioning Louis Armstrong before he was around eighteen years old, so much of his early life remains obscure. He was a child of the New Orleans slums. His mother and father were not married, and he grew up on his own or with relatives. An incident with a revolver in his early teens sent him to a home for black orphans, where he learned the basics of music. This upbringing scarred him permanently: he had no confidence in himself or his natural abilities.

Just as Armstrong was mastering the cornet in Storyville, a New Orleans district notorious for prostitution as well as a jazz center, the military authorities closed it down as part of a World War I clean-up. Armstrong then worked the cabaret boats that floated up the Mississippi River. In 1921, he moved to Chicago and began to make recordings. His hot New Orleans style became the standard that countless aspiring musicians, both black and white, imitated around the country. The recordings he made from 1925 to 1928, with pianist Earl "Fatha" Hines or the Hot Fives or the Hot Sevens as sidemen, represent him at his peak. "Basin Street Blues," "St. James Infirmary," and "Weather Bird" were among the works that became classics.

Being self-taught, Armstrong developed a bad embouchure, the position and use of the mouth in playing a wind instrument. It ruined his lips and prevented his continued greatness. He played more popular and less demanding pieces on national and world tours, radio and television shows, and numerous record albums. He took film roles, playing "himself" as entertainer, which critics thought reinforced unpleasant black stereotypes. He became noted for his appealing personality as much as for his playing. Armstrong persisted, though. He had earned the right to his success, even though the public valued his more trivial work and remained ignorant of his most important achievements.

See also Jazz; Music.

ROBERT M. CRUNDEN

ARMSTRONG, NEIL

(1930–) *Astronaut and first person to walk on the moon.*

Excited viewers throughout the world stared at television sets as a space capsule called the *Eagle* drifted toward the surface of the moon. Commanding the *Eagle* was Neil Armstrong. He was a gifted aviator who had received his pilot's license when he was only sixteen. During the Korean War (1950–53), he flew seventy-eight combat missions. He also flew a space mission in March 1966 aboard a two-man Gemini spacecraft.

Armstrong peered out the porthole as the *Eagle* plunged downward. The landing area was strewn with large boulders, any one of which could dangerously tilt the spacecraft. Burning precious fuel, Armstrong maneuvered the *Eagle* toward a flat surface. He was one of the world's best pilots, and it took all his skill to bring the craft down safely. Finally Armstrong radioed earth, "The *Eagle* has landed."

It was Sunday, July 20, 1969. Science fiction had come true. Earthlings had landed on the moon.

Four hours after landing, Armstrong and his copilot, Edwin "Buzz" Aldrin, prepared to leave the *Eagle*. Armstrong was scheduled to take the historic first step on the moon's surface. Television viewers saw a ghostly image of him on the bottom rung of the *Eagle*'s ladder. It was estimated that one of every four persons on earth was watching. Armstrong stepped off the ladder and said, "That's one small step for a man, one giant leap for mankind."

For more than two hours, he and Aldrin explored a tiny area of the moon. They gathered forty-one pounds of moon rocks and assembled a device to record "moonquakes."

After a safe flight home, Armstrong, Aldrin, and the third crew member, Michael Collins, who had remained in orbit around the moon during the walk, were greeted as heroes. But Armstrong shunned his role as a celebrity, preferring instead a quiet life with his family. In 1971 he resigned from the space program to become a professor at the University of Cincinnati.

See also Space Program.

R. CONRAD STEIN

ARMY

An army is a nation's primary land combat force. Armies are trained and equipped to defend home territory or to attack an enemy's territory. Over the centuries army weapons have evolved from spears and shields to rifles, machine guns, and tanks.

There were American soldiers before there was a United States. Riflemen from each of the thirteen colonies fought alongside British troops in the French and Indian War of 1754–63. The first true U.S. Army was formed on June 14, 1775, when the Continental Congress established it to fight against the British in the Revolutionary War (1775–83) and named George Washington its commander.

After the Revolution, Congress declared that "standing armies in time of peace are inconsistent with the principles of republican government." Thus, a pattern emerged that held true for the next hundred years. In peacetime the U.S. Army would dwindle in size, and then its ranks would swell when a war broke out. During the War of 1812 the army grew from 800 to 38,000 men, and it reached a strength of 115,000 in the Mexican War of 1846–48. Although there was some fighting on Canadian soil in the War of 1812, the Mexican War marked the first time the U.S. Army fought in lands far outside the nation's borders.

The First Draft

During the Civil War (1861–65), the Confederacy (made up of those states that had left the Union) passed in 1862 the first draft law in American history. The next year, the U.S. Congress followed suit, requiring all men aged twenty to forty-five to register for service in the Union forces. The draft was so hated that it sparked bloody riots in New York City that summer. During the war, the U.S. Army expanded from 16,000 men at the beginning to more than a million troops at the end. But afterward, once again, the army shrunk in size until the outbreak of the Spanish-American War in 1898, when the number of troops increased fivefold.

Throughout the 1800s cavalry forces made up the elite units of the American army. The horse soldiers fought in the Indian Wars in the West and led many of the charges during the Civil War. But machine guns and fast-firing artillery pieces, developed early in the twentieth century, doomed the proud cavalry. Because of the new weapons, a terrible trench warfare evolved in Europe during World War I (1914–18). The United States entered the conflict late, but in 1918 over 4.7 million American "doughboys" helped the Allies drive the German army back in the Meuse-Argonne region in France.

More than 8 million men and women served in the U.S. Army during World War II (1939–45). The army relied on tanks to spearhead advances. Airborne troops, dropping in parachutes or landing in gliders, assaulted key positions far behind enemy lines. D-day, the invasion of the European continent at Normandy, France, on June 6, 1944, was a combined air and sea assault. This was the largest single military operation in history. For the first time, heavy bombing of enemy targets in Europe and islands in the Pacific prepared the way for the advance of army troops.

Blacks had served with the U.S. Army in every war since the Revolution, but African-American troops were put in separate units. In 1948 President Harry S. Truman signed an executive order integrating all branches of the military service. Army Gen. Colin Powell, an African American, became the military's top officer in 1989 when he was appointed by President George Bush to head the Joint Chiefs of Staff.

The Army in the Cold War

Because of tensions with the Soviet Union during the cold war, membership in the army remained high after World War II. A military draft that lasted from 1948 to 1973 provided a steady supply of soldiers. The army sent 480,000 men to the Far East during the Korean War (1950–53). This war was disappointing for many army leaders because it ended in a frustrating stalemate rather than victory.

The Vietnam War ended similarly. American involvement in that country began in 1957 when the army sent military advisers to South Vietnam. The army reached its peak strength in 1969 when 365,000 soldiers served there. Hostilities ended in 1973, after the army had suffered 30,904 battle deaths. Many of the men who fought and died in Vietnam had been drafted. The war produced bitter feelings among young men who disagreed with the war's aims but were still required to serve in the military. During the Vietnam era thousands of young men escaped the draft by staying in school, thereby getting a deferment, or by fleeing the country. The United States ended the draft in 1973, and the army today is an all-volunteer force.

Throughout the cold war the army developed tactics to fit its new weapons. Troops rode in fully enclosed armored personnel carriers. Helicopters allowed soldiers to range swiftly over a foe's territory. Faster and more powerfully armed airplanes increased the efficiency of airborne troops. Fort Hood in Texas became the largest base for American armored troops, and Fort Bragg in North Carolina was the largest airborne base.

The latest high-technology army weapons were used in the Persian Gulf War fought in 1990–91. Rocket artillery delivered bombs far inside Iraqi territory. Sixty-ton tanks led the assault over the desert, and helicopters swiftly carried soldiers to the front. During the Gulf War, women for the first time served alongside men in combat regions. In World War II and later, they were confined to all-woman units and were kept in safer rear areas as much as possible.

The modern and highly mobile army is still very much in tune with its old theme song:

> Over hill, over dale,
> We will hit the dusty trail
> As those caissons go rolling along.

See also Conscription; Draft Riots; *and entries for individual wars, military leaders.*

R. CONRAD STEIN

ARNOLD, BENEDICT

(1741–1801)   Officer in the American Revolution and traitor.

As a boy, Arnold was high-spirited. When a constable ordered him to stop some prank, Arnold challenged him to a fistfight. At age fourteen, he ran away from home twice to fight in the French and Indian War. He learned to focus this energy as he grew older, building a simple apothecary shop (drugstore) into a lucrative trading company. When America declared its independence from Great Britain, he was among the first to organize a militia unit.

Eager for action, Arnold conceived a daring plan that resulted in the capture of Fort Ticonderoga and its valuable supplies in 1775. His command of the fleet on Lake Champlain in New York delayed a British advance from Canada the next year. He earned promotion to major general after his five hundred militiamen drove off two thousand British soldiers at Ridgefield, Connecticut, in 1777. He was wounded later that year during the important defeat of Gen. John Burgoyne in New York State.

Arnold had the strong support of George Washington, who recommended him for numerous promotions. Unfortunately, Arnold never felt he was given enough recognition for his achievements and complained publicly. Political enemies brought various charges against him, most of which were dismissed, but their criticism left him bitter.

In 1779 he began selling information concerning American troop movements to the British. When Washington appointed him commander of West Point (1780), he set about turning the fort over to the enemy. The scheme was discovered and Arnold and his family fled, eventually ending up in England. He lived there the rest of his life, distrusted by the British and despised by the Americans. A man less proud could have come down in history as one of our greatest patriot soldiers. Instead, his very name is synonymous with the ideas of deceit and betrayal.

See also Revolution.

JIM MURPHY

ARCHITECTURE
(See article on page 46)

*Anasazi cliff dwellings, Mesa Verde, Colorado
(thirteenth to fourteenth century).*

*Replicas of tipis.
Cascade Mountains, Washington.*

*Bottom left: Close-up of a log cabin,
showing the joint construction.
Bottom right: A log cabin in Tennessee.*

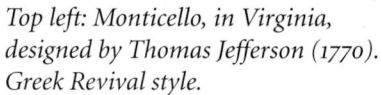

Top left: Monticello, in Virginia, designed by Thomas Jefferson (1770). Greek Revival style.

Top right: Massachusetts State House, Boston, designed by Charles Bulfinch (1795–98).

Left: Madewood Plantation, Louisiana (1840s). Greek Revival style.

Acorn Street on Beacon Hill, Boston (late nineteenth century).

Top left:
Empire State Building,
New York City (1930–31).

Top right:
Fallingwater,
or Kaufmann House,
Bear Run, Pennsylvania,
designed by Frank Lloyd
Wright (1936).

The interior of the Solomon
R. Guggenheim Museum,
New York City, designed
by Frank Lloyd Wright
(1956–59).

Top left: Seagram
Building, New York City,
designed by Ludwig Mies
Van Der Rohe (1956).

Top right:
John Hancock Building,
Boston, designed by
I. M. Pei (1973).

Spanish-style ranch house
in Florida.

ARTHUR, CHESTER A.

(1829–86) *Twenty-first president of the United States (1881–85).*

Arthur was nicknamed the "gentleman boss" because of his elegant clothing and his support of Roscoe Conkling's Republican political machine in New York. In 1871, President Ulysses S. Grant appointed Arthur, a lawyer, as Collector of the Port of New York. For seven years, he conscientiously supervised the collection of customs (fees paid for bringing foreign-made goods into the United States). His critics, however, complained that he added too many jobs to the payroll and filled them with Conkling's supporters. As a result, President Rutherford B. Hayes removed him from the post.

In 1880, Arthur backed Grant's campaign for the Republican nomination for an unprecedented third term as president. The party deadlocked, however, but finally compromised on the thirty-sixth ballot and chose James A. Garfield as its presidential candidate and Arthur as his running mate. The vice presidential nominee disagreed with Garfield's proposed civil service reform—to select the most qualified federal employees by competitive examinations. Arthur instead believed that government jobs should be awarded to loyal politicians, as was customary.

In 1881, President Garfield was assassinated and Arthur became president. Although the public expected the worst from the "gentleman boss," he gave the nation honest and effective government. Despite his earlier opposition to reform, he supported the Pendleton Act of 1883, which set up an independent civil service system. In doing so, he gave up the right to appoint politicians to fourteen thousand federal jobs. His administration vigorously prosecuted those involved in post office "star-route" frauds, which had overcharged the government for mail deliveries. In 1882, Arthur even vetoed a rivers and harbors bill that would have provided many jobs for politicians and their friends. Congress, however, overrode this veto.

Arthur is known as the father of the modern American navy because he scrapped the aging U.S. fleet, replacing outmoded wooden vessels with steel warships carrying the latest weapons. Retiring to New York after one term in office, Arthur died the next year of kidney disease.

BARBARA SILBERDICK FEINBERG

ARTICLES OF CONFEDERATION

This was the document that set up the first form of government of the United States. After more than a year of arguing about ideas for governing, the Continental Congress proposed the Articles of Confederation in November 1777. All thirteen states had ratified the Articles by March 1, 1781.

The Articles authorized a one-house Confederation Congress, in which each state, large or small, had one vote. There was no chief executive, such as the president, but Congress set up executive departments to handle the Confederation's business. The Confederation had no power over individual citizens and almost none over state governments. It had no way to raise the money it needed to finance itself or to solve national problems, except by asking the states for funds. And nothing could be done to fix the problems plaguing the Articles of Confederation because all thirteen states had to approve any amendments, or changes, to them. At least twice in the 1780s, for example, twelve states agreed to give the Confederation the power to impose a small tax on imported goods—but the thirteenth, Rhode Island, refused, and the amendment failed.

Under the Articles, nevertheless, the United States won the War for Independence and worked out a favorable peace treaty with Great Britain (the Treaty of Paris of 1783). The Confederation also established rules for governing the territory between the Allegheny Mountains and the Mississippi River that Britain gave the United States, and it invented the way that territories could be organized into new states equal to the original thirteen.

But the Confederation was too weak and too poor to solve the nation's problems. Its weakness led politicians who thought in national terms to call for a special meeting, or convention, to rework or replace the Articles of Confederation. In 1787, the Philadelphia Convention did just that, writing a new document, the Constitution of the United States. The weakness of the Articles helped persuade the people to adopt the Constitution. On October 10, 1788, the Confederation Congress voted that the Constitution would replace the Articles of Confederation on March 4, 1789, as the new charter of government for the United States.

See also Constitution, The Making of the.

RICHARD B. BERNSTEIN

ARTS

See Architecture; Dance; Literature; Music; Painting and Sculpture; Theater.

ASHCAN SCHOOL

The Ashcan school was the first important American art movement of the twentieth century. Its members painted in a realistic style, not very different from that of earlier American artists. But they focused on ordinary people going about their daily affairs and on city scenes that other people might have thought shabby or ugly, such as ashcans, crowded subways, and slums—thus the name they were given. They painted young women squeezing into the subway on their way to work, crowds at prize fights, dark streets below the elevated railways of early-twentieth-century Manhattan. The beauties of nature and formal portraits of rich businessmen, debutantes, and statesmen that most academic artists painted did not interest them.

The leading Ashcan artists, such as Robert Henri (pronounced *Hen*-rye) and John Sloan, were not social reformers. They did not want to *change* the aspects of the city they painted. Rather, they wished to capture the city's energy and vitality and the lives of its millions of anonymous people. Also called the New York Realists, they were much criticized for their "ugly" subject matter, but gradually came to be appreciated.

See also Painting and Sculpture.

ASIAN AMERICANS

The phrase *Asian Americans* is now used to describe all Asian immigrants and their American-born descendants. Once very small groups, they now number more than 7 million people—almost 3 percent of the population. The 1990 census recognized twenty-seven different peoples as Asian American. (The table gives the figures for the eight largest groups.)

GROUP	NUMBER
Chinese	1,643,621
Filipinos	1,403,624
Japanese	850,901
Asian Indians	814,538
Koreans	799,993
Vietnamese	610,904
Laotian/Hmong	239,000
Cambodian	210,724

Source: U.S. Census

Although many Asian Americans are very recent immigrants, some of these families have been in the United States for five or six generations.

Asian Americans before 1943
Before World War II, Chinese, Japanese, and Filipinos were the only Asian groups of any size in the United States. Chinese, who began to cross the Pacific in fairly large numbers in the 1850s, were the pioneer Asian immigrants. But there were never more than 125,000 here in the nineteenth century. Initially almost all were young men who mined for gold, built railroads, raised crops, and otherwise helped build up the Far West where most of them lived. But white workingmen, many of them European immigrants, complained that the Chinese workers lowered wages; they claimed that they were an alien people with nasty habits. We recognize this today as racism, but it seemed right at the time. Congress and several presidents therefore agreed that they should be kept out of the United States: a Chinese Exclusion Act was passed in 1882 and stayed in effect until 1943. This and other laws not only kept most Asians from coming to America but also barred those here from becoming citizens, voting, holding certain jobs, and, in some

states, owning farmland. (Chinese born in the United States had some of their rights protected by the Fourteenth Amendment to the Constitution, which guaranteed them citizenship.)

Soon after 1882 Japanese began to come, and as the Chinese population declined that of the Japanese grew. A strong movement developed in the Far West to exclude Japanese, too. But Japan, unlike China, was a rising power, and three American presidents—Theodore Roosevelt, William Howard Taft, and Woodrow Wilson—prevented the passage of federal anti-Japanese legislation. Instead they limited Japanese immigration through negotiations with Japan beginning with the Gentlemen's Agreement of 1907–08. These were broken in 1924 when Congress barred the immigration of Japanese—and all other Asians—as "aliens ineligible to citizenship." One Asian group, Filipinos, could continue to come even after 1924 because the courts ruled that since the Philippines were an American colony—which they remained until 1946—Filipinos were "American nationals": they could not be blocked from immigrating. But they could be barred from naturalization (becoming citizens) and were often discriminated against in other ways.

Changes after 1943
During World War II the United States put 120,000 Japanese—most of them native-born citizens—into concentration camps but began to treat Chinese and Filipinos, who were allies in the war against Japan, more equitably. The Chinese Exclusion Act was repealed in 1943, and by 1946 Chinese, Filipinos, and natives of India had been made eligible for naturalization. The last color bars to naturalization were dropped in 1952, and all nations were given at least token immigration quotas.

Despite these liberalizations, the fewer than 900,000 Asian Americans in 1960 constituted less than half of 1 percent of the American people.

Major changes in immigration law in 1965 made it easier for Asians to come to America, and U.S. involvement in the wars in Southeast Asia helped create millions of refugees, many of whom also came. By the 1980s 42 percent of all legal immigrants were coming from Asia.

Although Asian Americans have been favorably described as "model minorities," no simple stereotype is appropriate. Many Asian Americans today are well educated and upwardly mobile. But many others, particularly large numbers of those who came as refugees, are among the most economically disadvantaged groups in American society.

Despite its near universal use, the term *Asian American* is misleading. It encourages outsiders to regard these people as "all alike." If one imagines a comparable term, *European American*, being used to cover people from all the nations of Europe over the years, it is easy to see how inappropriate it is. A fourth- or fifth-generation middle-class college-educated Japanese American, for example, is no

A family of Chinese immigrants in California.

more like an uneducated, impoverished Hmong refugee than a fourth- or fifth-generation German American is like a recent Bosnian refugee. Asian Americans are at least as diverse as European Americans: no simple stereotype, however flattering, can even begin to describe them all.

See also Chinese Exclusion Act; Gentlemen's Agreement; Immigration; Japanese Americans, Internment of; Nativism.

For further reading: Harry H. L. Kitano and Roger Daniels, *Asian Americans: Emerging Minorities* (Englewood Cliffs, N.J.: Prentice Hall, 1989).

ROGER DANIELS

ASSASSINATIONS, PRESIDENTIAL

Four presidents of the United States have been assassinated. They were Abraham Lincoln, James A. Garfield, William McKinley, and John F. Kennedy. When assassination strikes down a president, millions of Americans mourn the death of the nation's leader. These brutal acts undoubtedly change the course of history.

Lincoln
In April 1865, as the Civil War was ending victoriously for the Union forces of the North, a small band of Southern conspirators sought revenge for the Confederacy's defeat. They plotted the murders of President Lincoln, Vice President Andrew Johnson, Secretary of State William H. Seward, and Gen. Ulysses S. Grant, commander of the Northern armies. Their leader was John Wilkes Booth, a well-known actor.

On the evening of April 14, President and Mrs. Lincoln attended a play, *Our American Cousin,* at Ford's Theatre in Washington, D.C. At about 10:15 P.M., Booth opened the

unguarded door to Lincoln's box. He aimed a pistol at the president's head, and a loud shot rang out. Then the assailant leapt from the box to the stage below. Entangling his right foot in a flag as he jumped, he fell awkwardly and broke his leg. Booth hobbled offstage and mounted a horse tethered behind the theater. Pursuing troops later caught him hiding in a Virginia barn. The barn was set afire and Booth was shot to death—whether by a soldier or by himself is uncertain.

Lincoln, whose brain had been pierced by the bullet, was carried across the street to a boardinghouse. Early the next morning, he died without ever regaining consciousness.

The other conspirators failed to assassinate Johnson and Grant. One of them slashed Seward several times with a knife, but the secretary of state recovered. Four of the conspirators were tried by a military commission and hanged; four others were given prison sentences.

Garfield
When James A. Garfield became president in 1881, he was frequently approached by persons wanting government jobs. A persistent job seeker was Charles J. Guiteau, a mentally unstable man who had failed at every type of work he had attempted. When he realized that the president would not give him a job, Guiteau purchased a pistol and awaited his chance. When he learned that the president would be leaving by train July 2 on vacation, he acted.

On that morning, Garfield was walking through the railroad depot when Guiteau shot him in the back. One bullet entered the president's body to the right of his spinal cord, and doctors were unable to remove it. Blood poisoning set in, followed by pneumonia. Garfield died on September 19, 1881, more than ten weeks after the shooting. Guiteau was convicted of murder and hanged.

McKinley

On September 6, 1901, President William McKinley was attending the Pan-American Exposition in Buffalo, New York. In the line of people waiting to shake hands with the president was Leon Czolgosz, whose right hand held a pistol hidden beneath a white cloth that looked like a bandage. Czolgosz, an unemployed mill worker, was an anarchist who believed that all governments should be destroyed and rulers struck down.

As Czolgosz approached McKinley, he fired two shots at the president, and one bullet entered his stomach. Doctors hunted in vain for the bullet, and McKinley died on September 14, apparently from gangrene poisoning. Czolgosz was found guilty of murder and put to death in the electric chair.

Kennedy

President and Mrs. John F. Kennedy were traveling with Texas Governor and Mrs. John Connally through the streets of Dallas in an open limousine on November 22, 1963. Just as the car passed a tall building known as the Texas School Book Depository, shots rang out. Kennedy was hit in the head and throat, and his car sped to the Parkland Memorial Hospital, where he died about half an hour later. Connally was also wounded but recovered.

Police arrested Lee Harvey Oswald, a former U.S. Marine, who had lived for a time in the Soviet Union and was an admirer of the Cuban dictator, Fidel Castro. He worked at the Texas Book Depository and owned the type of rifle that ballistic tests showed could have been used to kill the president. Two days after the murder, Oswald was being transferred from jail, an event being shown live on national television. Viewers watched in hor-

ror as Jack Ruby, a Dallas nightclub owner, lurched forward and shot Oswald to death.

A commission headed by Supreme Court Chief Justice Earl Warren investigated the president's murder. It concluded that the shots that killed Kennedy were fired by Oswald and that it appeared he had acted alone. The Warren Report, however, left a number of questions unanswered. Hundreds of books and articles appeared, questioning the report's conclusions and putting forth various conspiracy theories.

In 1979, a second commission, created by Congress, investigated the Kennedy assassination again. It concluded that conspirators possibly plotted Kennedy's murder and that there might have been a second gunman besides Oswald. No conspiracy theory, however, has ever been definitely proved.

Several other chief executives were targets of unsuccessful assassination attempts, including former President Theodore Roosevelt, President-elect Franklin D. Roosevelt, and Presidents Harry S. Truman, Gerald R. Ford, and Ronald Reagan. Andrew Jackson, in 1835, had the most miraculous escape. An insane man shot two correctly loaded pistols at Jackson from six feet away, but neither pistol discharged a bullet. Gun experts estimated that the chance of neither pistol firing was one in 125,000.

The assassinations of Lincoln and McKinley certainly were politically motivated. Lincoln was murdered by a proslavery Southerner intent on punishing the North for defeating the Confederacy, and McKinley was killed by an anarchist opposed to all rulers. Garfield was assassinated by a crazed office seeker for personal reasons, but the president's death had a political consequence, the establishment in 1883 of the national civil service system regulating appointments to gov-

Just hours after President John F. Kennedy was assassinated in Dallas, on November 22, 1963, Vice President Lyndon B. Johnson was sworn in as the next president aboard Air Force 1, the presidential plane that transported Kennedy's body to Washington. Johnson's wife Lady Bird is on his right; the president's widow, Jacqueline Kennedy, is on Johnson's left.

ernment jobs. The murder of Kennedy probably was politically motivated, although its precise reasons are still unknown.

For further reading: Edmund Lindop, *Assassinations That Shook America* (New York: Franklin Watts, 1992).

E D M U N D   L I N D O P

A S T A I R E ,   F R E D

(1899–1987)   *Dancer and film star.*

For generations of Americans, Fred Astaire was the symbol of elegance in motion. Wear-

ing his trademark top hat, white tie, and tails, he whirled across the Broadway stage, movie screens, and television sets. Astaire combined ballroom dancing with tap to create his memorable performances. A perfectionist, he rehearsed for weeks to make sure that his difficult routines looked easy and effortless. Because he worked so hard and worried so much, his sister, Adele, nicknamed him "Moaning Minnie." The pair, teamed since childhood in a dancing act, achieved fame in Broadway musical comedies during the 1920s. In 1932, when Adele retired to get married, Fred left for Hollywood.

A studio official wrote of Astaire's screen test: "Can't act. Slightly bald. Also dances." Nevertheless, audiences flocked to movie theaters to see him dance with Ginger Rogers in his second film, *Flying Down to Rio* (1933). Over the next six years, Astaire and Rogers starred in eight more movies, including *The Gay Divorcée, Top Hat, Swingtime,* and *Shall We Dance,* introducing songs by Cole Porter, Irving Berlin, Jerome Kern, George Gershwin, and others. Their last film together was *The Barkleys of Broadway* (1949).

In his thirty-three Hollywood musicals, Astaire danced with many other gifted leading ladies, such as Rita Hayworth, Judy Garland, and Audrey Hepburn. He was so talented that he made even a hat rack look graceful when he twirled with it in his arms in the film *Royal Wedding* (1951).

On television, Astaire starred in three outstanding programs with dancer Barrie Chase from 1958 to 1960 and went on to play many dramatic roles through the 1970s. He also made eight films as a featured actor, starting with *On the Beach* (1959) and ending with *Ghost Story* (1981). At age seventy-seven, he appeared in his last musical, *That's Entertainment Part II* (1976). Over his lifetime, he received numerous awards for his musical and dramatic performances.

See also Dance; Movies.

BARBARA SILBERDICK FEINBERG

ASTOR, JOHN JACOB

(1763–1848) *Businessman and real estate investor.*

Astor began life the son of a poor German butcher and died the richest man in America, thanks to the fur trade and the rapid growth of New York City. Born in Waldorf, Germany, Astor was twenty when he arrived in New York. He became a clerk to a fur trader, mastering the business quickly. Before long Astor was successfully operating on his own.

He began putting his profits into Manhattan real estate. Astor's strategy was to buy cheap land that lay far beyond the developed area of the city and then wait for the city's rapid growth to reach his lots. In 1803, for instance, he paid $25,000 for seventy acres located more than an hour's drive by horse-drawn carriage north of what were then the city's physical limits. By the 1870s the land was worth $20 million to the Astor family. Today, the area is known as Times Square.

Astor entered the trade with China in 1800 and earned large profits, often as much as $50,000 a voyage. In 1808 he established a company to exploit the newly acquired Louisiana Purchase and the Pacific Northwest. He built a trading post at the mouth of Oregon's Columbia River in 1811, naming it Astoria. This grand scheme fell apart when one of Astor's ships was lost at sea and the War of 1812 cost him the support of his allies in Canada. It was to prove Astor's one great defeat.

By the end of the 1820s Astor had a near monopoly of the American fur trade, but he was smart enough to realize that fashion and rising costs were making the trade much less profitable. He sold out all his fur interests and spent the last sixteen years of his life buying New York real estate.

When Astor died in 1848, he left an estimated $25 million, far more than any other American fortune of the day. Nearly all of it went to his son, but he earmarked $400,000 to establish the Astor Library, one of the three that would merge to form today's great New York Public Library.

JOHN STEELE GORDON

A T L A N T I C   C H A R T E R

The Atlantic Charter was drafted by President Franklin D. Roosevelt and Prime Minister Winston Churchill of Great Britain at a conference on the USS *Augusta* in August 1941, two years after the start of World War II. The charter declared that the United States and Great Britain recognized the rights of all people to choose their own form of government, and it guaranteed the right of all nations to trade freely with one another. It also called for international cooperation to promote economic development and social security. The object was to make sure that all the world's people "may live out their lives in freedom from fear and want." Roosevelt and Churchill also called for the disarmament of Germany and Italy after the war was won. In short they prepared a kind of blueprint for the postwar world.

See also World War II.

A T O M I C   E N E R G Y
See Nuclear Energy.

A T O M I C   W E A P O N S
See Manhattan Project; Nuclear Energy.

A T T U C K S ,   C R I S P U S

(c. 1723–70)   *Black colonial Patriot.*

A turning point in the growing conflict between England and the American colonies was a skirmish in front of the Customs House in Boston on March 5, 1770. Tensions had built up because of the oppressive Townshend Acts and the presence of several thousand Redcoats in the town. A crowd of Bostonians had gathered to taunt British soldiers guarding the Customs House. Someone in the crowd shouted, "Do not be afraid. They

dare not fire." The British did fire, however, and five of the Patriots were killed. Crispus Attucks, in the front of the crowd, was apparently the first to fall.

We do not know very much about this African American who lost his life protesting British policies. He seems to have been an escaped slave, probably part Native American or white (he was known to his neighbors in Boston as "the mulatto," a term for a person of mixed African and other ancestry), and is believed to have been a sailor. The *Boston Gazette,* in an ad placed by his owner seeking his return as a runaway slave in 1750, described him as "6 feet 2 inches high" with "short curl'd hair."

The incident, known as the Boston Massacre, was one of the first examples of protest against British rule and dramatized the claims for justice of the emerging nation. March 5 was honored in several towns and colonies, and the massacre and Crispus Attucks became symbols of American resistance. Attucks's name stands first on the list of martyrs carved on the Boston monument celebrating that tragic event.

See also Boston Massacre.

D E N N I S   W E P M A N

A U D U B O N ,   J O H N   J A M E S

(1785–1851)   *Artist and naturalist, famous for his paintings of birds.*

Born in Santo Domingo (now Haiti) and educated in France, Audubon became a specialist in the wildlife of the United States. The illegitimate son of a French sea captain, he was taken to France at the age of four and adopted by his father's family. He studied art in Paris in 1802–03 and the next year came to the United States to live.

Audubon was fascinated by birds even as a child and began sketching them in his early teens. When his father lost his money, young Audubon had to go to work and opened a small general store in the wilderness of Kentucky. Leaving a partner to take care of the business, he spent most of his time roaming the countryside looking for birds to draw. The shop went bankrupt in 1819, and Audubon made a bare living as a portrait painter and art teacher. But with the loyal support of his wife, who took a job to help support him and their two sons, he continued to devote most of his time to observing and painting birds.

He was unable to publish his work in the United States, and in 1826 he took his paintings to England, where they became very popular. His great series *The Birds of North America* (1827–38), a four-volume portfolio of 435 huge hand-colored engravings, contained 1,065 life-sized figures of birds. After returning to the United States in 1839, he traveled from Florida to Labrador in search of material and published three more collections of engravings. Nearly photographic in appearance, Audubon's art is sometimes wrong in detail but possesses a dramatic realism and vitality never previously achieved in nature painting. Audubon was not a scientific student of birds but an inspired artist who captured their spirit and their beauty.

See also Painting and Sculpture.

DENNIS WEPMAN

AUSTIN, STEPHEN F.

(1793–1836) *Colonizer of Texas.*

Born in Virginia, Austin moved with his family to Missouri when he was five years old. His wealthy father, Moses Austin, sent Ste-

phen to an academy in Connecticut and later to Transylvania University in Kentucky. Young Austin became a member of the Missouri territorial legislature in 1814 and a territorial judge in Arkansas in 1820.

After Moses Austin lost his wealth in the panic of 1819, he planned a new business venture—bringing American families into Spanish Texas and helping them establish settlements. He obtained permission from Spanish authorities to colonize three hundred American families in Texas but died before he could recruit the settlers. Carrying out his father's dying wish, Stephen Austin in 1822 founded the first authorized American community in Texas, at a site on the Brazos River. Mexico, which had gained its independence from Spain in 1821, approved of Austin's colonization plan.

During the next few years, thousands of American settlers, including many African-American slaves, streamed into Texas. When Mexico abolished slavery in 1828, Austin was chiefly responsible for a law whereby slaves could still be brought into Texas, technically as indentured servants. But slave children were to be freed at age fourteen. Austin proved to be an efficient administrator, maintaining friendly relations with the Mexican government, mapping the land, building schools, and promoting economic development.

In 1833, Austin journeyed to Mexico City with the colonists' petition for a separate state government. The Mexican government officials, fearing that he had become a revolutionary, imprisoned Austin for over a year. When he returned to Texas in 1835, the Americans there were determined to fight for their freedom. Austin took command of the Texan forces but soon left the army to seek recruits and financial support in the United States.

After Texas won its independence in 1836,

Austin ran for president of the new republic. He was defeated by Gen. Sam Houston, who appointed him secretary of state. A short time later, however, Austin died at the age of forty-three. Now called the "father of Texas," Austin was honored by having the republic's capital (now the state capital) named for him.

See also Texas Revolution and Annexation.

E D M U N D   L I N D O P

A U T O M O B I L E S

Few inventions in the past two centuries have had as great an impact on civilization as the automobile. In the United States there are over 100 million cars on the road, traveling more than 2 trillion miles a year. Much more convenient than trains, airplanes, or boats, they allow us to travel comfortably when and where we wish, and they make available a wide range of activities and facilities. The automobile has enormously increased the choice of where people can live and work.

The first machine that can be called an automobile—a self-propelled passenger vehicle—was a steam-driven carriage invented in Paris by Nicolas Joseph Cugnot in 1769. Its top speed was only two and a half miles an hour, it couldn't be effectively steered, and the engine was neither light nor powerful enough to be usable. It was the development of the internal combustion engine, powered by burning fuel inside the engine itself instead of in an external furnace, that made gasoline-powered automobiles possible. The application of this principle to a vehicle was first demonstrated by German engineer Niklaus August Otto in 1876. By the middle 1880s, practical automobiles were being marketed in Germany by Gottlieb Daimler and Carl Benz.

A 1920 Model T runabout. It sold for $550 and its maximum speed was forty miles per hour.

The Car Industry

The automobile industry grew very rapidly from the beginning. The first American model, the Duryea, went on sale in 1896, and in the next ten years hundreds of U.S. companies were manufacturing cars. In 1908, Henry Ford created his famous Model T. At $875, it was more expensive than some earlier cars, but through the development of the assembly-line technique of mass production, Ford was able to reduce its price and make cars affordable to the general public. The same year the Model T was introduced, William C. Durant founded General Motors, and that company and Ford, both located in Detroit, Michigan, dominated the world market until 1950.

The industry became the most important one in the American economy. It provided a major market for steel, glass, and plastics and spurred the growth of huge oil companies to provide gasoline. The mass use of automobiles made massive highway construction necessary. Since the 1980s, one of every six jobs in America has depended on the automobile industry; vehicle taxes, registration and license fees, and tolls represent a major source of government revenue.

But the United States lost its leadership in car manufacturing in the 1960s, when the more economical German Volkswagen and several Japanese automobiles began to compete with American models. During the next decade, fuel shortages further weakened the industry, and the federal government was forced to support it with subsidies. In 1950, the United States produced more than two-thirds of the world's automobiles; by 1980, its share had dropped to one-fifth.

The industry is now global. During the 1980s, many national and international mergers took place. Since 1990, some 20 percent of American brand-name cars have been manufactured abroad, and many foreign manufacturers have opened factories in the United States. However, although the number of automobile companies has shrunk, the output continues to grow. Fewer than ten thousand automobiles were manufactured worldwide in 1900; nearly 5 million are pro-

The Cadillac, such as the 1960 sedan above, was considered an American status symbol.

duced annually today. In North America, Western Europe, and Japan, there is one car to every two or three people.

Impact of Cars

The coming of the automobile age has greatly increased individual freedom, but improved mobility has come at a price. Cars are noisy, they pollute the air, they use up the world's limited resources of fuel; highway accidents take a terrible toll of lives. The industry and government alike have been trying since the 1960s to correct some of the problems created by the widespread use of automobiles. Legislation has been passed requiring mufflers to reduce the noise of engines, and mechanical changes have been made to limit the toxic emissions of gasoline. For increased safety, seat belts are now required by law in many states, and the use of air bags is growing.

Concern for the environment, fear of exhausting fuel supplies, and a desire for greater economy are leading automotive engineers to explore new methods of making motor vehicles more efficient. They are turning out more streamlined designs, replacing glass and steel with plastics and lighter metals, and seeking alternative sources of power, such as methanol, propane, and electricity. Automotive technology seems likely to change steadily in the future. But despite the problems automobiles create, their importance to our society remains constant.

See also Ford, Henry; Sit-Down Strikes.

DENNIS WEPMAN

AVIATION

During the nineteenth century, would-be aviators tried donning flappable wings or fly-

ing gliders from hilltops in attempts to achieve manned flight. In 1896, Octave Chanute, a civil engineer, supervised some two thousand celebrated glider flights near Lake Michigan conducted by his pilot, Augustus Moore Herring. Later, Herring tried unsuccessfully to power a glider with a small steam engine.

The Wright Brothers

In October 1900, the Wright brothers of Dayton, Ohio—Wilbur and Orville—began glider experiments from the dunes at Kitty Hawk, North Carolina. In 1901, Chanute came to watch. Impressed, he carried word of their flights to a meeting of the Aero Club of France. Some then ordered copies of the Wright glider.

During the winter of 1901–02, the Wrights returned home to construct a small, six-foot-long wind tunnel in their bicycle shop to observe the effects of wind on various wing shapes. (The tunnel is now on permanent display at the Air Force Museum in Dayton.) Next, they built a lightweight gasoline engine (since none was commercially available), and with this, the brothers, on December 17, 1903, became the first to achieve powered flight.

No in-flight photographs were released by the Wrights, and none appeared in news media even after the Wrights continued their flights at Dayton during the next several years. Their goal was not publicity. They attempted, at first unsuccessfully, to sell their design to the United States and even to foreign governments.

But the know-how now existed. Powered flights, and the founding of aircraft manufacturing firms soon followed. With Herring as partner, Glenn Curtiss, of Hammondsport, New York, established a second U.S. airplane company and flew his *June Bug* in 1908. That same year, Wilbur Wright startled Europe by flying for over two hours before a crowd at a French air meet.

In 1911, a Curtiss company pilot, Eugene Ely, landed an airplane on the deck of the U.S. Navy cruiser *Pennsylvania* and then took off again. But many in the navy could not foresee a sea-based role for military aircraft. One who did was the navy's assistant secretary, Franklin D. Roosevelt. Another, in Britain, was the first sea lord, Winston Churchill. In 1913, both took steps to give wings to their respective navies.

Industry's Growth

The American aviation industry was still small when the United States entered World War I in 1917. The auto industry, however, had grown large, and its leaders prevailed upon the Wilson administration to give them a chance to apply assembly-line production methods to aircraft manufacture. A Willys Overland executive took control of Curtiss, where the Curtiss-designed JN-4 (the famed "Jenny") was manufactured. Production of the British-designed DH-4 reconnaissance plane under Hudson, Packard, and National Cash Register management in Ohio, however, proved disastrous. In 1918, Glenn L. Martin and his chief engineer, Donald Douglas, were given the go-ahead to build America's first strategic bomber. It was not completed before the war's end, but afterward became the U.S. Army's standard bomber for over a decade.

During the 1920s, ex-army and young civilian pilots flew war-surplus craft at barnstorming flight exhibitions, and their accidents blunted public enthusiasm for flying. Charles A. Lindbergh's carefully planned solo flight across the Atlantic in 1927, however, signaled a new day. Mergers of fledgling air-

line companies quickly followed. By the mid-1930s, Americans were crossing the country in a Douglas DC-3 or flying the Pacific in a Martin China Clipper.

Military Uses

Although restricted by a 1922 treaty limiting naval armaments, a Pacific rivalry began as the United States and Japan built their first generation of aircraft carriers. In January 1929, U.S. naval aviators operated for the first time as a strategic air force, conducting a mock attack on Panama from the deck of the carrier *Saratoga*. Soon, Pan American Airways became America's chosen instrument to develop bases on Pacific islands to be used by the War Department as well as by commercial aviation. Japan also established air bases on islands under its jurisdiction. Japanese newspapers, at the time, even cited Pan American's route to the Far East as a military operation. On the evening before the first clipper was due to leave San Francisco for Honolulu, the FBI arrested two Japanese nationals in the plane's cockpit who were trying to miscalibrate directional finding equipment.

The American practice of developing a commercial airliner from a military design began before World War II when the wing design for the Boeing B-17 strategic bomber was utilized for transatlantic service by Pan American. In the era of piston-engine aircraft, Douglas had reigned as the nation's principal supplier of commercial transports, but after the war this changed.

As the Korean War and the cold war with the Soviet Union unfolded, the newly separate U.S. Air Force developed its first strategic jet bombers, the B-47 followed by the B-52. From the B-47 line, Boeing could more economically develop the first U.S. commercial jet—the 707—flown to Europe by Pan American on its inaugural flight October 26, 1958. Boeing thereafter retained its predominant position, utilizing the air force–funded, high-thrust "fanjet" to power its 747, and solidifying its role as supplier of fleets of 727 and 737 jets for regional carriers. Congress, however, called a halt in 1971 to Boeing's supersonic transport program, leaving this small niche in transatlantic air service to the British/French Concorde.

With all of this, public ground transportation, particularly rail service, began its decline. At first, new interstate highways cut through cities and carried middle- and upper-income Americans to the fast-growing suburbs. Air travelers thus gained ready though increasingly congested highway access to airports. Then, in 1973, the cutoff of oil supplies from the Mideast led to skyrocketing fuel costs. Next, airline deregulation in 1978 was followed by a consolidation of some lines and the extinction of others (most notably Eastern and Pan American). Labor unrest in the industry and public concern over safety and air and noise pollution followed.

The airlines turned to a hub system—feeding passengers to central points for transfer on less costly bookings to a final destination. But this, too, also compromised airline operating economics. Aviation had, indeed, changed the world in myriad ways both for better and in some ways for worse.

See also Air Force; Earhart, Amelia; Lindbergh, Charles A.; Wright, Orville and Wilbur.

WILLIAM WELLING

B

BACON'S REBELLION

Bacon's rebellion was a kind of civil war that erupted in the young colony of Virginia in 1676. Settlers in the western part of the colony were angry because the autocratic governor, Sir William Berkeley, refused to respond to their demands for help in driving the Indians off lands they hoped to make use of. For his part Berkeley considered the westerners "rabble of the basest sort" and "a giddy multitude." Berkeley had ruled Virginia for thirty years, and he and his local supporters, all well-established planters, were principally interested in lining their own pockets.

In the spring of 1676 westerners under the leadership of Nathaniel Bacon raised an informal five-hundred-man army, and after much confusion marched on the seat of government at Jamestown. After negotiations with Berkeley broke down, they burned the town to the ground. The governor was forced to flee across Chesapeake Bay to Virginia's Eastern Shore. The Baconites then plundered the plantations of Berkeley's leading supporters.

At this point, however, Bacon suddenly died of dysentery, probably caused by drinking polluted water. A little later a squadron of the Royal Navy arrived with enough English soldiers to restore order in the colony.

See also Colonial America.

BAKER, ELLA

(1903–86) *Civil rights activist.*

Ella Baker grew up in Littleton, North Carolina, where her preacher grandfather had built a church on land he had once worked as a slave. Ella remembered learning lessons about life while sitting next to her grandfather in his pulpit on Sunday mornings and hearing about the importance of education around the dinner table. She attended Shaw

Ella Baker at a news conference in 1968. Baker was one of the most militant of the civil rights leaders and particularly influential among younger activists and college students.

University in Raleigh, the state capital, and graduated in 1927.

She then went to live with her cousin in New York City where she hoped to earn enough money to go to graduate school, but the 1929 stock market crash dashed her hopes as the Great Depression swept across the country. Even with her college degree, Baker, as a black woman, was denied many jobs. She worked for a newspaper in Harlem in the early 1930s and got involved in some of the New Deal relief projects established by President Franklin D. Roosevelt.

In 1938 Baker joined the civil rights organization, the National Association for the Advancement of Colored People (NAACP), and became a field secretary—someone who travels and works for a group outside its headquarters. She organized African-Americans into campaigns to challenge segregation, lynching (mob violence against an individual), and other kinds of racial injustice. In 1946 she retired from her job to raise her niece at her home in New York City. But Baker continued her civil rights work and became president of the Manhattan branch of the NAACP in 1954.

After the Montgomery bus boycott in 1955–56, Baker was called back to the South to work with Martin Luther King, Jr., and other ministers who had formed the Southern Christian Leadership Conference (SCLC). In February 1960, groups of college students held a sit-in at lunch counters in Greensboro, North Carolina, to protest their policy of serving only whites. Baker and these young people then formed a grass-roots organization called the Student Non-Violent Coordinating Committee (SNCC). She left SCLC to work full time with the student movement, helping SNCC set up its headquarters in Atlanta. Baker was an invaluable ally for the students who helped launch Freedom Rides (integrating interstate buses in the South), voting rights campaigns, and other efforts.

This inspiring woman remained active into the 1980s. She worked for the liberation of Zimbabwe (formerly Rhodesia), against apartheid in South Africa, and in other campaigns for racial justice all over the globe. She once recalled that when she was a young girl, a boy called her an ugly name on the street in Norfolk. In anger she struck him across the face. Years later she told her fellow activists that she had learned from this experience that it was not enough just to hit someone in anger. What mattered was working with others against prejudice and hatred and promoting brotherhood and sisterhood among all people.

See also Civil Rights Movement; National Association for the Advancement of Colored People; Student Non-Violent Coordinating Committee.

CATHERINE CLINTON

BALANCHINE, GEORGE

(1904–83) *Ballet director and choreographer.*

Russian-born Balanchine brought his revolutionary vision of ballet to the United States and made this elegant art form a vital part of American culture.

Georgi Melitonovitch Balanchivadze, born in St. Petersburg, Russia, shortened his name to George Balanchine for easier pronunciation. He attended the Maryinsky Theater's School in St. Petersburg, soon performing in solo roles and choreographing, or creating, his own ballets.

In 1924, he met the director of the world-famous Ballets Russes company, Serge Diaghilev, who hired him as a ballet master and

Choreographer George Balanchine (left) arranges a group of ballet dancers during a rehearsal in the 1930s. Standing in the center is ballerina Vera Zorina, who appeared in a number of American films as well as on the stage. She and Balanchine later married.

choreographer. The dances Balanchine created for the company brought him international acclaim, and he went on to choreograph new ballets for other companies. But he did not find his true niche until he immigrated to the United States in 1933 and became cofounder of the School of American Ballet and a new company, the American Ballet.

In its early years, the company floundered because ballet was not popular. In 1948, the company became affiliated with New York's City Center for the arts and was renamed the New York City Ballet. It gradually achieved acclaim as audiences discovered the artistry of Balanchine's work.

Balanchine created over two hundred ballets as well as a brilliant new vision of the art. He drew on a centuries-old tradition of prescribed steps and movements but expanded it

into a more daring art form. Ballet had been a blend of dance, spectacular scenery, story telling, acting, and music, but Balanchine made dancing the most important element of the performance. Mr. B.—as his dancers called him—wanted to showcase the beauty and purity of the human body in motion. He called himself an "adherent of pure art, or art for art's sake." After his death, the New York City Ballet has continued to perform at Lincoln Center in New York City and on stages around the world.

See also Dance.

HARRIET SIGERMAN

BALDWIN, JAMES

(1924–87) *Author and civil rights advocate.*

Outraged by what he described as the "chronic disease of racism" in America, Baldwin was one of the country's most admired and influential authors. Born in New York City the eldest of nine children, Baldwin grew up in the slums of Harlem. At the age of fourteen he became a preacher and after graduating from high school decided to become a writer. He wrote about the experience of preaching in his first novel, *Go Tell It on the Mountain* (1953).

Fleeing racism in America, Baldwin moved to France in the late 1940s where he established his literary reputation. His novels *Giovanni's Room*, set in Paris, and *Another Country* deal with the hardships of homosexuals. Some of his other powerful works include collections of his essays, *Notes of a Native Son, Nobody Knows My Name,* and *The Fire Next Time,* and the novels *Tell Me How Long the Train's Been Gone,* and *If Beale Street Could Talk.* His book *Remember This House* combined his memoirs of the civil rights movement with biographies of Martin Luther King, Jr., Malcolm X, and Medgar Evers.

During his career, Baldwin focused his attention on civil rights issues, but his outlook on the future of race relations in America remained pessimistic. In 1986, the French government made him a commander of the Legion of Honor, France's highest civilian honor. Baldwin died in St. Paul de Vence, France.

See also African Americans; Civil Rights Movement; Literature.

JOANN BIONDI

BALLET
See Dance.

BALLINGER-PINCHOT CONTROVERSY

The Ballinger-Pinchot controversy was a dispute about the conservation of natural resources. It occurred in 1909 after Secretary of the Interior Richard A. Ballinger reassigned a million acres of public land, previously reserved for forest ranger stations, to the public domain. The land was therefore open to loggers and other private developers. This alarmed Gifford Pinchot, head of the Forestry Service, who was an enthusiastic conservationist. Pinchot criticized Ballinger's decision. More important, he charged that Ballinger had also improperly allowed vast coal-bearing tracts in Alaska to be exploited by mining companies. An investigation followed and Ballinger was proved innocent of any wrongdoing.

Pinchot nevertheless continued to attack Ballinger and his policies. He called the secre-

tary "the most effective opponent the conservation policies have yet had." President William Howard Taft then felt compelled to discharge Pinchot.

The controversy had an additional significance because Pinchot was a close friend of the former president Theodore Roosevelt, who was also an ardent conservationist. It was one of a number of reasons Roosevelt decided to run for president against Taft in 1912, even though they were members of the same party. Because the two men split the Republican vote, the Democrat Woodrow Wilson won.

See also Conservation and Environmental Movements.

BANK OF THE UNITED STATES

There were two Banks of the United States. One, proposed in 1791 by Alexander Hamilton, operated until its charter expired in 1811. The second, larger and more influential, was created in 1816. Both banks served as depositories for federal funds and provided loans for businessmen and other entrepreneurs. The Second Bank also acted as a check on inflation by compelling so-called wildcat banks to convert the paper money that they issued so recklessly into gold and silver.

Creating the First Bank triggered a controversy about its legality. The Constitution did not specifically grant Congress the power to create banks. But Hamilton convinced the legislators and President George Washington that the clause giving Congress the right to pass laws that were "necessary and proper" for carrying out powers specifically mentioned in the Constitution made the Bank Act constitutional. This interpretation was upheld by the Supreme Court in the case of *McCulloch* v. *Maryland* in 1819.

The Second Bank of the United States, under the presidency of Nicholas Biddle, roused the ire of state banks by restricting their lending practices. This made them operate conservatively and limited their profits. The Second Bank also alarmed many people because it was so large and powerful. President Andrew Jackson considered it a monopoly and therefore a threat to democracy. In 1832 Jackson vetoed a bill rechartering the bank. When he was elected to a second term by a large margin, he withdrew federal funds from the bank. After its federal charter expired in 1836 it soon passed out of existence.

BANNEKER, BENJAMIN

(1731–1806) *Astronomer, mathematician, and surveyor.*

The son of a former slave, Banneker was among the most influential African Americans of his time, although he lived his entire life on a small tobacco farm in Maryland. For a few winters he attended a country school, where he showed special talent in mathematics. He continued to study on his own for the rest of his life.

When he was twenty-one, Banneker designed and built a wooden striking clock, despite never having seen one. He carved every gear and wheel by hand with a jackknife. The clock was extremely accurate and ran for over fifty years.

Borrowing books from a neighbor, Banneker studied mathematics, astronomy, and surveying on his own. In 1791, he was chosen to assist the surveyor Andrew Ellicott in laying out the new capital city of Washington,

D.C. Banneker worked on the project for three months, helping to survey a parcel of land precisely ten miles square.

From 1791 to 1797, after teaching himself calculus and spherical trigonometry, Banneker published a series of almanacs containing weather predictions, calculations of tidal

A woodcut portrait of Benjamin Banneker, the first important African-American scientist, was featured on the cover of the 1795 edition of his almanac. The first edition of the almanac included an essay by a white abolitionist that described Banneker's considerable accomplishments as proof that "the powers of the mind are disconnected with the colour of the skin."

changes, and astronomical events. His work was supported by many people who wanted to abolish slavery. These abolitionists pointed to Banneker as living proof that people of African descent were not inferior to whites.

Banneker himself sent a copy of one of his almanacs to Thomas Jefferson (then secretary of state), who had expressed doubt about the mental capacities of black people. With the almanac, Banneker enclosed a letter, passionately calling on Jefferson to take up the antislavery cause. He reminded Jefferson that he had claimed in the Declaration of Independence that "all men are created equal." Banneker lamented the fate of his people living "under groaning captivity and cruel oppression."

Banneker lived his final years alone in a cabin on his farm, reading and doing mathematical calculations. His work earned him international recognition during his lifetime, and he is remembered today for his remarkable achievements as a self-taught scholar.

See also Abolitionist Movement; Free Blacks before Emancipation.

DEBORAH KENT

BARBARY WARS

For centuries pirates operating from ports in the Barbary states on the Mediterranean Sea—Morocco, Algeria, Tunis, and Tripoli—made a business of attacking merchant ships passing along their coasts. They seized cargoes and held the crews and passengers for ransom. The European nations to their north found it easier to pay money to the Barbary states for "protection" rather than to guard their ships or use their navies to fight the pirates.

Before the Revolution, American ships were protected by the British payments. Thereafter, the United States entered into treaties of its own with the Barbary states similar to those of the Europeans.

In 1801, however, when the pasha of Tripoli demanded larger annual payments, the newly elected president, Thomas Jefferson, refused. The pasha then declared war on the United States.

Jefferson sent a small fleet of warships to the Mediterranean under Commodore Edward Preble. The fleet had some success, but the frigate *Philadelphia* ran aground and was seized by the pirates. Then Lt. Stephen Decatur became a national hero by fighting his way aboard the *Philadelphia* at the head of a party of only ten sailors and setting the helpless ship afire.

The fighting (and the payment of tribute) ended in 1805. During the War of 1812, the dey of Algiers attempted to collect tribute again. But as soon as that war ended, another American fleet forced the dey to give up all claim to tribute, and U.S. ships suffered no further attacks.

BARNUM, PHINEAS T.

(1810–91)   *Showman and circus manager.*

A master of publicity with a keen sense of what the public would pay to see, P. T. Barnum is considered the father of modern showmanship and the inventor of the three-ring circus. He was also a self-confessed swindler, but he always gave his audience a good show and lived to become a respected businessman and public figure.

Barnum was born in Connecticut and began his business career as a shopkeeper, lottery-ticket salesman, and newspaper pub-

Phineas T. Barnum was already a wealthy and famous showman when he created "The Greatest Show on Earth" in the 1870s. A circus poster in 1897 features him and his younger partner, James A. Bailey.

lisher. He made his entry into show business at the age of twenty-five when he met Joice Heth, an elderly African American who claimed to be 160 years old and to have been George Washington's nurse. Barnum undoubtedly knew she was a fraud, but he saw the possibilities for profit and bought the rights to exhibit her as a curiosity. When the old lady died three years later (at the age of about 80, according to an autopsy), Barnum used his savings to purchase Scudder's American Museum in New York City. There he showed everything from jugglers, bearded ladies, and Siamese twins to trained fleas and rare birds. His "Great Model of Niagara Falls"

was only eighteen inches high, and his "Fee-jee Mermaid" was really a monkey's head attached to a fish's tail. But the public loved his shows and he made a fortune. Among his most popular attractions were the twenty-five-inch-tall Tom Thumb and the Swedish concert singer Jenny Lind.

In 1871 Barnum opened a circus in Brooklyn, New York, billed as "The Greatest Show on Earth." With James Bailey, an English circus owner who joined him as a partner in 1881, he developed a gigantic traveling spectacle, complete with aerialists, clowns, trained animals, and sideshows. Purchased in 1907 by the Ringling Brothers, Barnum's circus remains a national institution today. With his many humorous and sensational enterprises, Barnum gave a new face to American popular entertainment.

See also Circuses.

For further reading: Ann P. Tompert, *P. T. Barnum: The Greatest Showman on Earth* (New York: Macmillan, 1988).

DENNIS WEPMAN

BARTON, CLARA

(1821–1912)   *Founder of the American Red Cross.*

As a young girl, Clara Barton spent two years as nurse and companion to her brother David, who had been stricken with a serious illness. The experience stood the shy and lonely child in good stead later in life. Clara, who was also profoundly influenced by her father, overcame her timidity and grew into a woman possessed of humanitarian purpose, patriotism, and a love of the military.

After teaching for several years, Barton moved to Washington, D.C. There she secured an appointment to the U.S. Patent Office, becoming the first woman civil service

Clara Barton, photographed by Mathew Brady or one of his assistants. Founder of the American Red Cross, she began a lifetime of relief work during the Civil War.

appointee. During the next ten years she was active in volunteer work.

When the Civil War began in 1861, Barton immediately involved herself in providing aid to soldiers, because the lack of first-aid facilities was undermining the army's effectiveness. She advertised for donations, solicited volunteers, and established a private nursing and assistance corps independent of the government's Sanitary Commission. Barton, at the request of President Abraham Lincoln, also put together a system for locating missing soldiers.

After the war, when Barton was lecturing in Europe, she heard about the International Red Cross. From that point on, she was determined to establish the American Red Cross.

In 1881, she succeeded in doing so. For the next twenty-three years, she devoted herself to expanding the purpose and scope of the American Red Cross. It grew from a local Washington-based group to a national organization that, among other things, assists disaster victims with food, medicine, and shelter.

Barton retired in 1904 and spent the remainder of her long life in Glen Echo, Maryland. Her dedication and service made the American Red Cross a national symbol of humanitarianism.

See also American Red Cross.

For further reading: Clara Barton, *The Story of My Childhood* (Salem, N.H.: Ayer, 1980).

CHRISTINE A. LUNARDINI

BASEBALL

America's most distinctive spectator sport, baseball seems always to have lived more in myth than in history. Children had been playing versions of the game—known also as rounders, one o' cat, and base—for many years when, in 1845, some men in Manhattan organized the Knickerbocker Base Ball Club and wrote down the rules of the game they were playing. (Abner Doubleday, alas, had nothing to do with it.) Twenty years later dozens of baseball clubs in New York and Brooklyn, and their journalist friends, had made the "national pastime" more popular than cricket. New York had become the country's first baseball powerhouse.

Since the early clubs wanted to field winning teams, they became entertainment businesses looking for first-rate players who could attract paying crowds. The undefeated season of the nationally touring Cincinnati Red Stockings in 1869 paved the way for baseball's professionalization in the 1876 formation of the National League of Professional Base Ball *Clubs*. Although players had been employees of the clubs for years, the National League made this distinction formal. Baseball soon became more popular than all other sports.

Late-nineteenth-century baseball resembled the Gilded Age business world. Owners moved the clubs frequently, and rival leagues sprang up to compete for players and spectators. The National League either defeated its opponents outright or absorbed them into a structure of minor leagues. Not until 1901 was the National League forced to accept the American League, the only other surviving major league.

The Reserve Rule

Owners and leagues controlled the players through practices that combined elements of slavery—the infamous reserve rule—and freewheeling industrial capitalism: blacklisting, fines, salary caps, even using Pinkerton detectives to spy on the players. The reserve clause, begun in 1879 and eventually part of every player's contract, gave employers the right to "reserve" a player's services for the following year, and every subsequent year, unless he was traded, sold, or released.

Players fought the reserve rule, most notably when the Brotherhood of Professional Base Ball Players launched its own Players' League in 1890. When the players' financial backers sold them out to the National League, baseball owners ruled organized baseball virtually unchallenged for eighty-five years. The owners were helped by Supreme Court rulings that baseball was not interstate commerce and therefore could not be regulated by federal law.

In 1975 a labor arbitrator ruled that the reserve clause applied for only one year and

for the first time in nearly a century, players, as "free agents," could negotiate with any club they wished. Salaries quickly reached unheard-of levels. Owners retaliated in 1981 but were soundly defeated by a players' strike. Then in the late 1980s the owners conspired to limit salary offers to free agents. That was ruled illegal, and since then salaries have again taken off.

Baseball's Culture

Baseball was America's unquestioned national pastime until the late 1960s, when the combination of dominant pitching (which cut down the number of runs scored) and televised football games moved football ahead. But beginning with the superb 1975 World Series between the Boston Red Sox and the Cincinnati Reds, baseball began a comeback.

Baseball has been America's most popular sport for so long mainly because it has bridged some of the nation's cultural divisions. Though it originated among the respectable working class and sporting middle class, the game early on was part of the rowdy street life of saloon-based volunteer fire companies, militias, neighborhood gangs, and political factions.

The National League purposely appealed to middle-class audiences by requiring its teams to charge fifty cents and ban the sale of alcohol. The rival American Association appealed to immigrant and working-class audiences by charging a quarter and selling liquor.

Despite the outrage that greets baseball's occasional betting scandals (in 1865 and 1877 as well as the famous 1919 "Black Sox" scandal and the 1989 banishment of Pete Rose) the game has never been completely free of the sporting underworld of gambling and lowlife. Even though they have such disciplined athletic skills, ballplayers frequently behave badly off the field. Alongside the game's reputation as an upright, all-American pastime, its culture continues to have a whiff of the unrespectable.

Baseball has also reflected the past throughout much of its history. It celebrated craft excellence at just the time industrialists were establishing mass machine production. Although baseball's origins are urban, we still think of it as rural. While city populations swelled in the late nineteenth century and mass entertainment took root at places like Coney Island, urban baseball fans flocked to watch a game featuring individuals, surrounded by the green grass of ball*parks.*

Adult fans seek and remember their childhoods in the game. That is why they dislike the fact that men make money for playing baseball and why they usually prefer baseball's myth to history. It is also why fans identify so strongly with their home team. Baseball itself shows us home and away: danger abroad, the safety of "home." The owners have skillfully promoted their businesses by exploiting rivalries between cities and towns. The pompously named World Series, baseball's post-season showcase begun in 1903, effectively uses league loyalties as well.

The Media's Impact

Baseball's history has been closely linked to the development of the media. Sportswriters were some of the game's key early promoters. In the 1920s radio created a national audience for Babe Ruth's astonishing home run feats. When televised baseball concentrated spectators' attention on the major leagues in the 1950s and 1960s, most of the minor leagues collapsed. The largest source of income in the game, television has fueled and shaped the business of baseball. Indoor stadiums, Astroturf, divisions within leagues, playoffs, the

designated hitter, and nighttime World Series games all illustrate the power of television.

Blacks in Baseball

Baseball had never been a racially integrated sport, though a few blacks played in the major leagues in the early years. African-American players and entrepreneurs organized their own touring teams, and the 1920s saw the formation of Negro leagues. Some of the finest ballplayers ever played in these leagues, which peaked in popularity at the end of World War II.

The color barrier was broken in 1947 by the careful planning of Brooklyn Dodgers general manager Branch Rickey and the courage, self-control, and baseball skill of Jackie Robinson, whom Rickey invited to pioneer with his team. Robinson's talents and aggressiveness made him one of the best second basemen who has ever played the game.

Currently, baseball is integrated in that there are large numbers of African-American and Latin players; it is not unusual for a starting lineup to have a minority of whites. Still, the higher ranks—managers, general managers, owners—are almost completely white, and there are many fewer African-American catchers and pitchers than there are outfielders and first basemen.

See also DiMaggio, Joe; Mays, Willie; Rickey, Branch; Robinson, Jackie; Ruth, Babe; Sports, Spectator.

For further reading: Roger Kahn, *The Boys of Summer* (New York: Harper and Row, 1971); Lawrence S. Ritter, *The Glory of Their Times: The Story of Baseball's Early Years Told by the Men Who Played It* (New York: Macmillan, 1966).

WARREN GOLDSTEIN

BASKETBALL

In December 1891, Dr. James Naismith, a physical education instructor at the International Y M C A Training School in Springfield, Massachusetts, needed a new activity for his gym class. It was too cold for outdoor sports, and he wanted to offer his students an alternative to their usual indoor routine of calisthenics and gymnastics. Naismith had two wooden peach baskets nailed onto balcony railings on opposite sides of the gymnasium. Then he divided the students into two teams and handed them a soccer ball. He gave them a few rules that made throwing or shooting the ball into one of the baskets the object of the new game. Basketball was born.

James A. Naismith invented the game of basketball in 1891 to give men an indoor game to play between the end of the football season and the beginning of baseball in the spring. Above, Naismith holds a basketball and basket—the earliest hoop was a peach basket with the bottom removed.

Some of the first attempts at playing basketball were most irregular by modern standards. Naismith's first game with nine players on each side ended in a 1–0 final score. One early game played on the fields at Cornell University had as many as fifty players on each team. Scoring 20 points was usually more than enough to win games. Nowadays, teams have five players on each side, and many teams score over 100 points in almost every game.

Colleges and universities have had teams since the turn of the century, and rivalries within groups of schools have existed almost as long. For example, in 1901–02, the Ivy League was formed, with teams from Harvard, Cornell, Brown, Columbia, Princeton, Yale, and the University of Pennsylvania competing for a yearly championship. Over the years, a small group of teams have dominated the game, winning most of the intercollegiate competitions as well as individual games. The University of North Carolina's basketball squads have won a total of 1,570 games, the most ever. For almost a decade, the University of California at Los Angeles (U C L A) produced the best teams in college basketball, winning consecutive championships from 1967 to 1973.

Professional Teams Started

Most people believe that the first professional basketball team was formed in 1896 by a group of Y M C A basketball players from Trenton, New Jersey. They charged admission to people coming to watch their games. Any money not spent on rent for the gymnasium or equipment for the games was divided among the players. Businessmen soon recognized that these games could become profitable and began to sponsor contests among local teams to bring crowds to the gymnasiums. They also used other types of entertainment to sell tickets. Some set up games in dance halls and provided dancing before and after the contests. This drew complaints from players, who skidded on the slippery dance floors.

These early attempts to form professional basketball leagues did not last long, however. They were not well organized and failed at attracting enough fans to cover expenses. Finally, in 1925, the American Basketball League (ABL) was established. Its member teams were mainly drawn from the East Coast, with some in the Midwest. At the height of its popularity, the league was mentioned in the sports sections of most major newspapers. The ABL disbanded in 1931, when it ran into financial difficulties during the Great Depression. With the economy at a standstill, many people had barely enough money to buy food or pay their rent. They could not afford to attend basketball games.

The NBA Formed

Six years later, three large corporations (Firestone, Goodyear, and General Electric) banded together to form the National Basketball League (NBL). Each corporation had its own team in the league. It lasted from 1937 to 1950, when the NBL merged with the three-year-old Basketball Association of America to form the modern National Basketball Association (NBA). The NBA, unlike earlier leagues, had teams all over the country, including in such cities as Minneapolis, Denver, and Syracuse. In its early years, the NBA introduced new rules to the game. For example, in 1954, the league installed a twenty-four-second shot clock, giving a team only that much time to attempt a shot at the basket. This prevented teams from stalling and resulted in higher scoring and more exciting games.

The NBA remained the only professional basketball league until 1967, when a group of Californians organized the American Basketball Association (ABA). The ABA, hoping to gain support for basketball in new areas, organized teams in some cities that didn't have NBA teams. Three major changes made ABA games look very different from those of the NBA. The ABA used a red, white, and blue basketball, awarded three points for shots from farther than twenty-five feet away from the basket, and added six seconds (for a total of thirty) on the shot clock. The ABA's players, however, were not always as good or as well known as those in the NBA.

In 1976, the ABA merged with the NBA, once again making the NBA the only basketball league. In 1979, the NBA adopted the three-point rule for shots thrown twenty-three feet, nine inches or more away from the basket, but it did not accept the ABA's other changes. Since 1976, several small leagues have been formed, such as the Continental Basketball Association and the United States Basketball League, but none has offered the NBA serious competition. In fact, these leagues often give younger, unknown players a chance to improve their skills and gain the notice of NBA teams.

Great Players

No one is certain who is the greatest basketball player of all time. Many modern fans would say six-foot, six-inch guard Michael Jordan of the Chicago Bulls was the best ever. Since entering the NBA in 1984, Jordan has won a Rookie of the Year award and several Most Valuable Player awards, led the league in scoring for seven consecutive years, and as of 1993, led his team to three consecutive NBA championships. Others would say Kareem Abdul-Jabbar, who played for the Los Angeles

Lakers from 1975 to 1989, deserves that honor. This seven-foot, two-inch center is the NBA's all-time leading scorer. He was almost unstoppable, with his trademark "sky hook." More recent stars such as Boston Celtics sharpshooter Larry Bird, innovative Los Angeles Laker guard Magic Johnson, and powerful Phoenix Suns forward Charles Barkley can also be considered among the great players.

Yet another NBA star was Wilt Chamberlain, whose scoring record Abdul-Jabaar broke. Chamberlain, a seven-foot, one-inch center, completed basketball's greatest feat. On March 2, 1962, he scored 100 points in a game against the New York Knicks. Many NBA stars have scored 50 points in a game, and a few have scored 60, but none has come close to Chamberlain's accomplishment. In their own time, players like Bob Cousy and Bill Russell of the Boston Celtics were also considered to be outstanding.

Legendary basketball players such as these are honored in the Basketball Hall of Fame after they retire. Fittingly, this museum of basketball history is located in Springfield, Massachusetts, the game's birthplace.

See also Sports, Spectator.

For further reading: Jeremy R. Feinberg, *Reading the Sports Page* (New York: Macmillan, 1992); David Neft and Richard Cohen, *The Sports Encyclopedia of Basketball*, 4th ed. (New York: St. Martin's Press, 1991).

JEREMY R. FEINBERG

BAY OF PIGS INVASION

In 1959 revolutionary forces in Cuba led by Fidel Castro overthrew the existing government and entered into close relations with the Soviet Union. Castro was strongly anti-American, and he repressed local opposition to his government harshly. Thousands of anticommunist Cubans sought refuge in the United States.

President Dwight D. Eisenhower responded by breaking diplomatic relations with Cuba. He allowed the CIA to train about two thousand Cuban exiles in preparation for launching an invasion of Cuba from a base in Central America. The expectation was that once a beachhead had been seized, thousands of local Cubans would join in the fight to overthrow the Castro dictatorship.

When John F. Kennedy became president he learned of the plan and reluctantly agreed to go ahead with it. On April 17, 1961, the invaders landed at the Bay of Pigs on the south coast of Cuba. But no local Cubans came forward to join them. Since the United States did not provide air or naval support, the invaders were quickly pinned down by the Cuban army and forced to surrender.

After briefly denying knowledge of the invasion, the State Department admitted its involvement, and President Kennedy confessed that he should not have allowed the operation to go forward. However, he imposed an economic blockade on Cuba and apparently allowed the CIA to try to have Castro assassinated. All in all, the Bay of Pigs affair was a fiasco—a bad beginning for the Kennedy presidency.

See also Kennedy, John F.

BEECHER, CATHARINE

(1800–78) *Author and educator.*

Beecher accepted a great deal of responsibility at an early age, a characteristic that remained with her throughout her life. Her father, Lyman Beecher, was a Congregational minister, notable as a leader of the Second Great Awakening, a widespread religious revival of the nineteenth century. One of her sisters, Harriet Beecher Stowe, was the author of the famous antislavery novel, *Uncle Tom's Cabin.* Her mother died when Catharine was sixteen, and from then on, she took her seven brothers and sisters under her wing. Particularly close to her father, Catharine wrote a welcoming letter on behalf of all the children to their stepmother when Lyman Beecher remarried a year later in 1817.

After a brief stint at the Pierce School in Litchfield, Connecticut, Catharine started teaching in New London in 1821. In 1823, she and her sister Mary founded the Hartford Female Seminary. Addressing one of the burning issues of her day, Catharine took abolitionist Angelina Grimké to task for arguing her cause in public. Beecher objected to women being active in public affairs, including taking public stands on the issue of slavery. In 1837, Beecher expressed these views in *An Essay on Slavery and Abolition with Reference to the Duty of American Females.* She believed that women had a responsibility to become a moral force *within the home* and in that way influence society. She also believed deeply that the pressing issue that America needed to address was the number of children who failed to obtain any formal education.

Beecher's most influential book was *A Treatise on Domestic Economy for the Use of Young Ladies at Home and School* (1841), which went through several editions. In it, she offered advice to women on education, home management, and raising children. She was briefly engaged to a young mathematics professor from Yale who died four months after their engagement was announced in 1822. Thereafter, Beecher dedicated her life to teaching, writing, and working for the cause of education.

See also Education.

CHRISTINE A. LUNARDINI

BELL, ALEXANDER GRAHAM

(1847–1922)   *Inventor and teacher of the deaf.*

Alexander Bell (he adopted the middle name later) was born in Scotland, the second of three brothers. His father, Melville Bell, was famous on both sides of the Atlantic for his research on speech and hearing. His mother was deaf.

Alexander Graham Bell making the first phone call between Chicago and New York City, about two decades after he invented the telephone in 1876. When he died in 1922, people throughout North America were asked not to make phone calls during his burial so that the telephone lines would remain silent in tribute to the inventor.

In 1870, with the family sadly diminished by the recent deaths of a grandson and their oldest and youngest sons, the senior Bells decided to immigrate to Canada with their widowed daughter-in-law. Often ill with headaches, twenty-three-year-old "Aleck" agreed to join them. Bell's health improved in Canada, and before a year was out he found work as a teacher of the deaf, the profession he learned from his father and at which he excelled.

In 1872 a move to Boston provided Bell with opportunities to attend lectures on scientific topics and renewed his interest in telegraphy and the possibility of electrically transmitting the complex sounds of speech. Boston also brought Bell a new and gifted student. Deaf since childhood, Mabel Gardiner Hubbard was eighteen when they met. It was not long before the young people became fond of each other, and after overcoming some difficulties including the concern of their parents, they married.

Having combined his work with the deaf with experiments in transmitting sound, it was a twenty-nine-year-old Alexander Graham Bell who called out to his assistant, "Mr. Watson, come here. I need you!" Often quoted, these were the first sentences to be usefully carried by his primitive telephone. The year was 1876.

In 1887, Bell's reputation as an educator caused the father of a small deaf child to consult with him. Few remember that it was Bell's recommendation that brought together Helen Keller and her beloved teacher, Anne Sullivan. Many years later, Helen Keller's autobiography was dedicated to him.

Much of Bell's fame and, indeed, his fortune rested on his having invented, patented, and effectively promoted the first telephone. To this day, the name and bell-shaped logo of

the Bell Telephone Company recall his role in its founding. But Bell was a versatile as well as successful inventor. Among the many patents he held were those for a hydrofoil boat, an early iron lung, wax cylinders for recording machines, and a device that anticipated ultrasound (in 1881 Bell was called to Washington to assist, futilely, in the search for the assassin's bullet lodged in President James A. Garfield's dying body). Bell was influential in the development of both *Science* and *The National Geographic* magazines, the latter edited by his son-in-law, Gilbert Grosvenor, for many years.

Bell was expansive and generous by nature. Despite a tendency to become preoccupied with his work and idiosyncrasies that often kept him at his desk until four in the morning, Bell was very much a family man, enduringly devoted to Mabel. Although their two sons died in infancy, their daughters lived long successful lives that included parenthood. At the time of his death, at the age of eighty-five, Bell was actively engaged in aviation experiments.

See also Keller, Helen; Science and Technology.

JOAN W. BLOS

BENEDICT, RUTH

(1887–1948)   *Anthropologist and feminist.*

One of the most gifted women in anthropology, Benedict came by her insights the hard way. Her father was a promising young surgeon who died after catching a disease from a patient. Her mother never recovered from his death and made a family cult of mourning. Things became worse when Ruth caught the measles, which impaired her hearing. Shy and inarticulate, she grew up convinced that it was "a very terrible thing to be a woman."

All she wanted, she wrote in her diaries, was a husband to love, a quiet home, and children. She completed college more a poet than anything else and married chemist Stanley Benedict. Only when that marriage went sour did she turn to scholarship.

Professor Franz Boas was establishing anthropology as a new social science at Columbia University, and Benedict became his favorite assistant. Feeling rejected herself, she identified with nonconformists in all societies. This led her to wonder how societies decide what is and what is not "normal" behavior. Fascinated by the ideas of German philosopher Friedrich Nietzsche about "Apollonian" and "Dionysian" character types, she studied the Indian tribes of the American Southwest, such as the Zuñi and the Pima, which seemed dominated by these qualities. Each society had its own standard of conformity, and each excluded certain character types. An ecstatic, Dionysian culture might exclude someone who was calm and rational; a sober group of Apollonians might not tolerate religious ecstasy or drunkenness.

Benedict presented her insights most successfully in *Patterns of Culture* (1934), which became a standard text. It taught generations of students that all cultures have value but that all tend to exclude nonconformists. Democratic Americans should accept everyone and not merely demand conformity to current standards.

ROBERT M. CRUNDEN

BERLIN, IRVING

(1888–1989) *Songwriter.*

"Irving Berlin has no place in American music. He *is* American music," wrote one songwriter. Berlin's simple melodies with their sentimental and patriotic themes still please audiences today.

Berlin was born in Russia and grew up in poverty in New York City. While working as a singing waiter, he composed his first song "Marie of Sunny Italy" in 1907. Berlin, however, could neither read nor write music. He picked out tunes on a piano, memorized them, and paid others to write the notes down. Since Berlin could play only on the black notes, he bought a special piano that let him change musical keys with the shift of a lever.

In 1911, Berlin wrote his first hit song "Alexander's Ragtime Band"; his first musical comedy *Watch Your Step* came three years later. He claimed that he could produce as many as five songs a day, writing both the words and the music. In 1919, he established his own music publishing company and that same year wrote "A Pretty Girl Is Like a Melody." In 1920 he bought the Music Box Theater in order to stage his own shows.

Berlin's musical comedy scores contained many hit songs. During World War I, he was drafted into the army where he wrote *Yip Yip Yaphank* (1918). Its "Oh, How I Hate to Get Up in the Morning" reflected Berlin's own feelings about military life. Another song from the show, "God Bless America," became popular during World War II and won him a congressional medal in 1955. He donated the song's royalties to the Boy and Girl Scouts of America. Among his most outstanding shows are *As Thousands Cheer* (1933), introducing "Easter Parade"; *Annie Get Your Gun* (1946), with "There's No Business like Show Business"; and *Call Me Madam,* featuring "You're Just in Love."

Irving Berlin also wrote many film scores, including those for *Top Hat* (1935), *Follow the Fleet* (1936), *Carefree* (1938), and *Holiday Inn*

(1942). His most successful movie song was "White Christmas," a holiday standard.

See also Music.

BARBARA SILBERDICK FEINBERG

BERLIN BLOCKADE

After the end of World War II in Europe in 1945, Germany was divided into four zones, one occupied by the United States, one by the Soviet Union, one by Great Britain, one by

Residents of West Berlin wave to an approaching American plane during the Berlin airlift. Every day for almost ten months in 1948–49, American and British aircraft delivered essential supplies after Soviet leader Joseph Stalin cut off the West's ground access to the city. A Berlin clerk exclaimed, "Every two minutes a plane arrives from West Germany, loaded with food. . . . The sound of engines can be heard constantly in the air and is the most beautiful music to our ears."

France. The capital city of Berlin ended up deep in the Soviet zone and was itself divided into four sections in the same way. The three sectors controlled by the Western allies were like an island completely surrounded by a Soviet sea.

In 1948 the Western powers turned their separate German zones into the unified Republic of West Germany. The Soviets responded a few days later by closing all roads and rail lines connecting Berlin to the West. They argued, with some reason, that if West Germany was a separate country, Berlin was no longer its capital. If so, the Western allies had no right to control parts of the city.

The blockade of Berlin produced an international crisis of major importance. West Berliners were cut off from their usual deliveries of food, fuel, and other supplies from the West. After rejecting suggestions that he use troops to convoy supplies to Berlin by road, thus risking war, President Harry S. Truman decided to try to supply the Western-held sectors by air. This put the question of starting a new war on the Soviets' shoulders.

For nearly a year Allied planes shuttled back and forth 272,000 times, landing as often as once per minute to supply the tons of food and other supplies needed by 2 million Berliners. When finally convinced that their blockade could not force the Western powers to abandon Berlin, the Soviets ended it in May 1949.

See also Cold War.

BERNSTEIN, LEONARD

(1918–90)   *Conductor, composer, pianist, writer, and teacher.*

One day in 1943 the guest conductor of the New York Philharmonic Orchestra got sick, and the regular conductor was snowbound. The twenty-five-year-old Leonard Bernstein (pronounced *Burn*-stine) took over. The concert was broadcast on radio across the nation. The young man was a sensation and instantly famous.

Bernstein was lucky, no question of it, but there was more to it than that. His talents were formidable: he had a penetrating intelligence, and he was a brilliant pianist, a gifted composer, and a dynamic conductor. Able to explain complicated concepts in simple language, Bernstein had a gift for teaching as well as for music. He made his points with energy and humor. The conductor-composer became a regular television performer, which allowed him to reach an enormous audience.

He was born in Lawrence, Massachusetts. His father didn't want him to be a musician; he urged business as a career. But Lenny (as many called him) didn't listen to his father. He studied music at Harvard, at the Curtis Institute, and at Tanglewood, the summer home of the Boston Symphony.

His First Symphony, called *Jeremiah* (1944), was a predictor of the work to come. *Jeremiah* includes a melody chanted by every Jewish boy at his bar mitzvah. Much of his serious work, especially the oratorio *Kaddish* (1963; the name of the Jewish prayer for the dead) and *Chichester Psalms* (1965; based on liturgical music), was tied to religious themes. His *Mass* (1971) was written for the opening of the John F. Kennedy Center for the Performing Arts in Washington, D.C.

Bernstein also wrote the musicals *On the Town* (1944), *Wonderful Town* (1953), *Candide* (1956), and *West Side Story* (1957); a ballet, *Fancy Free* (1944); and the score for the movie *On the Waterfront*. He was conductor of the New York City Center Orchestra (1945–47) and a guest conductor with orchestras around the globe; in 1958, he became director of the New York Philharmonic.

America in the twentieth century developed music that would make any culture proud. It included blues, jazz, musical theater, and symphonic music. Bernstein tried them all. Besides that, he was a great communicator who dominated the American musical scene. Few were as talented; no one else was as versatile.

See also Music.

For further reading: Leonard Bernstein's Young People's Concerts, rev. ed. (New York: Doubleday Anchor, 1992).

JOY HAKIM

BERRY, CHUCK

(1926–   ) *Singer, guitarist, and songwriter.*

One of the greatest creative influences on blues, rock, and popular music, Berry is a legendary performer whose songs are still loved across America.

Berry began playing guitar when he was a teen in St. Louis. After a robbery attempt landed him in reform school, he worked in a factory and then as a hairdresser. In the early 1950s, married with two children, Berry began performing to supplement his income. By 1955 he had written several songs and traveled to Chicago to try to make it in the music industry. His break came when blues performer Muddy Waters heard him play. Waters was so impressed with Berry that he arranged a meeting with his record producer. Berry's song *Maybellene* became a big hit, and he catapulted to stardom.

In the mid-1950s, Berry proved to be an impressive artist on stage as well as in the recording studio, and fans clamored to see him. He followed *Maybellene* with *Roll Over*

Beethoven, which drew much acclaim. In the 1960s, the Beatles paid homage to Berry with their own song, *Beethoven.* John Lennon once declared, "If you tried to give rock 'n' roll another name, you might call it 'Chuck Berry.'" Another group that acknowledged his deep influence was the Rolling Stones.

Throughout the 1960s and 1970s, Berry was a rock idol known for his guitar playing, singing, and a dance called the duck walk, in which he gracefully pranced across the stage with his knees bent. Audiences howled with approval.

Some of Berry's songs include *Sweet Little Sixteen, Johnny B. Goode, Hail! Hail! Rock 'n' Roll,* and *School Days,* which complains about teachers: "Close your books/Get out of your seat/Down the hall/And into the street." In 1987, a film of Berry's sixtieth birthday concert, *Chuck Berry: Hail! Hail! Rock 'n' Roll,* documented his career and was praised by critics nationwide. Although no longer a young agile man, Berry still occasionally performs for his fans.

See also Rock Music.

JOANN BIONDI

BETHUNE, MARY McLEOD

(1875–1955)   *Educator and civil rights activist.*

Bethune, the daughter of former slaves, rose to become one of the most influential African-American women in twentieth-century America. Born near Mayesville, South Carolina, she started her professional life as a schoolteacher. In 1898, she married Albertus Bethune and a year later gave birth to a son.

In 1904, Bethune established a school for African-American women in Daytona Beach, Florida. With only six students—five girls and her son—and $1.50 in hand, she opened the school in a rented house. It flourished and gradually expanded to a twenty-acre campus with a student body of three hundred. The curriculum included vocational training as well as academic subjects. Bethune exhorted her students—and indeed all black women—to rise above racial discrimination and achieve "Self-Control, Self-Respect, Self-Reliance and Race Pride." In 1923, the school became coeducational and was later accredited as a junior college.

Meanwhile, Bethune expanded her own sights by joining several black women's organizations. Through this work, she developed

Mary McLeod Bethune, daughter of illiterate South Carolina sharecroppers who had once been slaves, was the only one of her seventeen brothers and sisters to attend school. Bethune became a leader in black education, a founder of black women's organizations, a civil rights leader, and an adviser to President Franklin D. Roosevelt.

a keen understanding of the needs of African Americans. She met Eleanor Roosevelt, wife of President Franklin D. Roosevelt, and became the First Lady's primary adviser on issues related to blacks.

During the 1930s, Bethune directed the Division of Negro Affairs within the National Youth Administration, which was part of the New Deal. She strove to expand educational and employment opportunities for blacks and worked to combat discrimination in government programs and agencies.

In later years, Bethune relinquished most of her organizational responsibilities but continued to crusade for equal rights. When she died in 1955, the African-American community lost a powerful and eloquent voice.

See also African Americans: Since World War II; Education.

For further reading: Malu Halasa, *Mary McLeod Bethune, Educator* (New York: Chelsea House, 1989).

HARRIET SIGERMAN

BIG-CITY BOSSES

Some of the most powerful political figures in American history never held a major political office. They were the local political leaders known as bosses. The typical boss held only a minor position in local government or no office at all. And yet, for most of the nineteenth century and part of the twentieth, these bosses wielded more real power than many governors, senators, and even some presidents.

The boss's power came from control of the local political party organization known as the machine. Whether Republican or Democratic, the local machine often held a stranglehold on the political life of the community. In many cities—and even some

THE "BRAINS"

Political cartoonist Thomas Nast's depiction of New York City's Boss Tweed, the most notorious of the big-city bosses. Nast shows Tweed as a fat politician with a money bag for brains. Tweed was furious with Nast's damaging cartoons: "I don't care a straw for newspaper articles. My constituents can't read, but they can't help seeing them damn pictures." He was right. Arrested for fraud, Tweed escaped from jail to Spain, where a police officer recognized him from one of Nast's cartoons and returned him to the United States.

states—the machine and the government were one and the same. And the boss ran the machine. In the mid-nineteenth century, for example, New York City was run by William Marcy "Boss" Tweed and his Democratic machine, and the Republican boss, Matthew Quay, controlled the political life of the entire state of Pennsylvania.

It was the machine that chose the party's candidates for office. "You may elect whichever candidate you please," granted one generous boss, "if you allow me to select the candidate." When there weren't enough real votes available to elect the candidates, some bosses were not above stuffing the ballot boxes with phony ones. A boss who controlled the vote in a city like New York or Chicago could affect the results not only of local elections but of state and national elections as well. When President Benjamin Harrison thanked Providence for his election in 1888, Matt Quay remarked that it wasn't God who deserved the credit: it was Quay and his fellow Republican bosses.

Many officeholders knew they owed their jobs to the bosses, and they paid their debt by allowing the boss to control *patronage*—the many jobs and profitable contracts at the disposal of the government. The bosses handed out these plums to their supporters and withheld them from their opponents. Patronage was the lifeblood of the boss's political power, just as his political power was the source of the patronage under their command.

Some cities had Democratic bosses, others Republican bosses, depending on which party machine was more powerful. Some cities had two bosses, one of each party, who battled for control. In other cities, rival bosses struck deals with each other and split the patronage between them.

Many of the old-time bosses were excellent administrators. In some respects, historians say, some cities were run more efficiently in the days of the bosses than they are today. But this efficiency was purchased at a very high price. Corruption was a fundamental part of the boss-machine system. Many of the bosses were simply thieves who operated on a grand scale, dipping into the city's budget to enrich themselves and their cronies. Virtually all of them took bribes or winked at the bribery of others in order to solidify their power. Matt Quay bragged that he had "approached the gates of the penitentiary" to elect Benjamin

Harrison. Other bosses actually did time inside. Despite their enormous power, many bosses were eventually exposed and punished.

Thomas Pendergast, the boss of Kansas City who gave Harry S. Truman his start in politics, was convicted of income tax evasion and sent to Leavenworth Prison. "Boss" Tweed and his machine were accused of stealing between $30 million and $200 million from the taxpayers of New York. Tweed was convicted of embezzlement and sent to prison three times. He eventually died there.

The power of political bosses was chipped away by a variety of factors. Citizens of many cities got tired of the rampant corruption and elected reformers to office. Civil service laws requiring candidates for jobs to pass tests and providing appointees with job security undermined the patronage system. So did other laws specifying that government contracts for construction projects like roads and buildings be awarded to the lowest bidder rather than to a "friend" of the boss. The introduction of primary elections took the power of choosing party candidates away from the bosses and gave it to the voters. And, perhaps most important, individual voters became more independent and less willing to cooperate with the machines. By the mid-twentieth century, the age of the big-city boss was over.

See also City Government; Corruption and Scandals in Government; Tweed Ring.

MICHAEL KRONENWETTER

BILL OF RIGHTS

The first ten amendments to the U.S. Constitution are known as the Bill of Rights. These amendments went into effect two years after the Constitution was adopted in 1789. No such list of rights was included in the original Constitution because most of the delegates to the Constitutional Convention felt it was not needed. Their chief goal, they reasoned, was to provide the framework for a strong national government. They believed it was unnecessary to guarantee rights that were already commonly accepted and included in many state constitutions.

Demand for a Bill of Rights

But when the Constitution was sent to the states for ratification (approval), both those who were opposed to it and those who wanted a bill of rights included argued that the Constitution was defective and incomplete. Prominent state leaders, such as George Mason and Patrick Henry of Virginia and Elbridge Gerry of Massachusetts, declared that they opposed the Constitution partly because it contained no bill of rights to protect the people against abuses by the new powerful central government, which the Constitution would create.

The demand for a bill of rights became a central issue in various state conventions called to ratify the Constitution. James Madison and other strong supporters of the document were concerned about the public clamor to reject it unless it contained provisions to protect personal liberties. Madison therefore promised that when the First Congress assembled, it would adopt a bill of rights. Only by making such a promise were the Constitution's supporters able to achieve ratification by narrow margins in closely divided states, such as New York and Virginia. Several of the state conventions that voted for the Constitution accompanied their ratification papers with written demands for adding a bill of rights.

Madison kept his promise. After he was elected to the House of Representatives, he proposed various amendments to his colleagues. The House acted favorably on seventeen, which were forwarded to the Senate. The two houses of Congress finally agreed on twelve amendments and submitted them to the states for ratification.

Two of the twelve amendments were not accepted by the states. They dealt with matters that had nothing to do with people's personal rights. The other ten were ratified by the necessary three-fourths of the states by December 15, 1791, thus making the Bill of Rights part of the Constitution.

Provisions of the Bill of Rights

In about four hundred words, the Bill of Rights provides Americans with fundamental liberties and protection against governmental acts of oppression. The First Amendment spells out many basic freedoms. It forbids the national government to establish a state religion or to favor one church more than others, and it assures individuals of the right to freely exercise their religious beliefs. The First Amendment also guarantees freedom of speech, the press, and the right of people to assemble, or meet together, peaceably. The Second Amendment grants the people the right to keep and bear arms (this amendment has been interpreted differently by those for and against gun control).

Several amendments protect individuals against wrongful actions by the national government. The Third Amendment prohibits the quartering of soldiers in people's houses. (Before the revolutionary war, British soldiers often were lodged in private homes, despite the opposition of the homeowners.) The Fourth Amendment makes unreasonable searches and seizures illegal. The Fifth Amendment prohibits double jeopardy (trying a person twice for the same offense) and prohibits forcing persons to testify against themselves in criminal cases. It also forbids depriving any person of life, liberty, or property without due process of law (fair and reasonable legal procedures), and it bans the taking of private property for public use without fair payment. The Sixth Amendment provides the right to a speedy and public trial, the right to confront one's accusers, and the right to have the assistance of a lawyer. The Seventh Amendment safeguards the

BILL OF RIGHTS

AMENDMENT I

Congress shall make no law respecting an establishment of religion, or prohibiting the free exercise thereof; or abridging the freedom of speech, or of the press; or the right of the people peaceably to assemble, and to petition the government for a redress of grievances.

AMENDMENT II

A well-regulated militia being necessary to the security of a free State, the right of the people to keep and bear arms shall not be infringed.

AMENDMENT III

No soldier shall, in time of peace, be quartered in any house without the consent of the owner, nor in time of war, but in a manner to be prescribed by law.

AMENDMENT IV

The right of the people to be secure in their persons, houses, papers, and effects, against unreasonable searches and seizures, shall not be violated, and no warrants shall issue upon probable cause, supported by oath or affirmation, and particularly describing the place to be searched, and the persons or things to be seized.

AMENDMENT V

No person shall be held to answer for a capital, or otherwise infamous crime, unless on a presentment or indictment of a grand jury, except in cases arising in the land or naval forces, or in the militia, when in actual service in time of war or public danger; nor shall any person be subject for the same offense to be twice put in jeopardy of life or limb; nor shall be compelled in any criminal case to be a witness against himself, nor be deprived of life, liberty, or property, without due process of law; nor shall private property be taken for public use without just compensation.

AMENDMENT VI

In all criminal prosecutions, the accused shall enjoy the right to a speedy and public trial, by an impartial jury of the State and district wherein the crime shall have been committed, which district shall have been previously ascertained by law, and to be informed of the nature and cause of the accusation; to be confronted with the witnesses against him; to have compulsory process for obtaining witnesses in his favor, and to have the assistance of counsel for his defense.

AMENDMENT VII

In suits at common law, where the value in controversy shall exceed twenty dollars, the right of trial by jury shall be preserved, and no fact tried by a jury shall be otherwise reexamined in any court of the United States, than according to the rules of the common law.

AMENDMENT VIII

Excessive bail shall not be required, nor excessive fines imposed, nor cruel and unusual punishments inflicted.

AMENDMENT IX

The enumeration in the Constitution, of certain rights, shall not be construed to deny or disparage others retained by the people.

AMENDMENT X

The powers not delegated to the United States by the Constitution, nor prohibited by it to the States, are reserved to the States respectively, or to the people.

right to trial by jury, and the Eighth Amendment prohibits excessive bail or fines and cruel or unusual punishment.

The Ninth Amendment says that the provision of certain rights in the Constitution does not deny other rights "retained by the people." For example, two rights not specifically mentioned in the Constitution are the right to take part in political activities and the right to privacy. The Tenth Amendment states that any powers not specifically delegated to the national government by the Constitution, or prohibited by it to the states, are reserved to the states or to the people.

The rights of the individual guaranteed in the first ten amendments are not unlimited. In general, a citizen's rights end whenever abuse of them harms other individuals or threatens public safety. Freedom of speech, for example, does not include the right to make false and malicious statements about someone orally (slander) or in writing (libel). Freedom of assembly does not permit people to gather in mobs that terrorize victims.

The Bill of Rights provides the legal basis on which individuals can challenge abusive governmental actions in courts of law. Sometimes these lawsuits are appealed through the court system all the way to the highest court in the land, the U.S. Supreme Court.

Extension to the States

In a case argued in 1833, the Supreme Court decreed that the first ten amendments guard against abuses by the *national* government but not against abuses by the *state* governments. This interpretation was first seriously challenged following the Civil War, when the Fourteenth Amendment was adopted in 1868. One provision of this amendment says, "Nor shall any State deprive any person of life, liberty, or property, without due process of law."

Nevertheless, for many years the Supreme Court stubbornly insisted that the Fourteenth Amendment did not extend the Bill of Rights to protect individuals against *state* offenses. Finally, in 1925, the Court began to reverse its position on this issue. In the case of *Gitlow* v. *New York,* the high Court proclaimed that freedom of speech and of the press are "among the fundamental personal rights and liberties protected by the due process clause of the Fourteenth Amendment from impairment by the states." Since 1925, the Supreme Court has ruled in many other cases that the Fourteenth Amendment's due process clause extends nearly all of the provisions in the Bill of Rights to state offenses.

History teaches that uncontrolled governmental powers can lead to the loss of the individual's freedom and the end of other personal rights. In the United States, the Bill of Rights has stood as the bulwark that protects Americans' precious liberties and perpetuates the democratic way of life.

See also Constitution; Constitution, The Making of the; Freedom of Speech; Freedom of the Press.

For further reading: Edmund Lindop, *The Bill of Rights and Landmark Cases* (New York: Franklin Watts, 1989).

E D M U N D   L I N D O P

B I R T H   C O N T R O L

For many centuries people—most often women—have attempted to avoid pregnancy by using devices or methods that prevented contact between a man's sperm and a woman's egg. Sometimes, when a woman found that she was already pregnant and did not want to be, she used methods that would end the pregnancy. Today, we refer to methods that avoid pregnancy as "birth control" or "contraception," and methods that end an already established pregnancy as "abortion."

Early Birth Control

Legalizing birth control in the United States was a long and difficult struggle. In 1915, Mary Ware Dennett founded the National Birth Control League, which sought to change restrictive birth control laws. For example, the Comstock Act of 1873 made it illegal to send any information or "appliances" (contraceptives) related to "preventing conception" through the mail.

While Dennett worked to change these laws, another activist, Margaret Sanger, broke them. Sanger ultimately became much better known for her efforts to legalize contraception and repeatedly rejected Dennett's invitations to work together. Sanger opposed a bill (supported by Dennett) that would have made birth control information and appliances accessible to everyone because she believed that only physicians should be able to dispense contraception. Dennett, in many ways a woman ahead of her time, recognized that a medical monopoly over contraception (a situation where only doctors could provide contraceptives) could restrict access to birth control, especially for poor people.

If Dennett and Sanger had been able to work together, birth control might have been legalized much earlier in the twentieth century. As it turned out, neither woman could get her own legislation passed, and the contraceptive clause of the Comstock Act was not fully stricken until 1970. Unmarried women in the United States did not gain legal access to birth control until 1972.

Although newer methods of birth control such as the oral contraceptive (the "pill"), the IUD (intrauterine device), and injectable contraceptives were not available to women born between 1901 and 1910, they still used birth control methods such as condoms and vaginal douches. Interestingly, these women had fewer children than any other group of women up until the 1980s, even though they relied upon methods now regarded as inconvenient and ineffective, *and* they did not have access to legal abortion. This suggests that factors other than the availability of contraceptives influence successful pregnancy prevention.

Newer Methods

Modern methods of birth control prevent the joining of egg and sperm, or "fertilization," in a variety of ways. Most methods are temporary and have a very short-term effect, but some are long-acting like the new contraceptive implant called NORPLANT, which lasts for up to five years. Some methods must be used at or around the time of sexual intercourse in order to be effective (like the male and female condoms, or spermicidal jellies, creams and foams), whereas other contraceptives are essentially "working" all the time (like the birth control pill, also called "oral contraceptive").

Fertility awareness methods of birth control—often called FAM or natural birth control—rely upon the fact that a woman is fertile only during a certain portion of every menstrual cycle. During her fertile periods, a woman who wants to avoid pregnancy either does not have sex or uses a barrier method of birth control. This approach can be highly effective, but it takes time to learn to read body signs with accuracy.

Surgical contraception, called "sterilization," is an operation that makes a woman or man *permanently* infertile or near-infertile by blocking or destroying the tubes inside the body that carry the sperm or the egg. The procedure is simpler and overall less risky for a man than for a woman. A sterilized man or woman can no longer produce a pregnancy by having sexual intercourse. (Because of modern techniques of so-called assisted reproduction, however, it *is* possible to retrieve an egg from a sterilized woman and join it with sperm *outside* the human body, sometimes resulting in fertilization.) Men or women should become sterilized only when they are sure that they no longer want to have children that are biologically their own.

Preventing Disease

There are many diseases and infections that can be transmitted or passed through sexual contact. The AIDS virus, genital warts, gonorrhea, and chlamydia are examples of these "sexually transmitted diseases." Because some of these diseases can lead to serious disability or even death, many people now believe that the ideal birth control method will not only prevent pregnancy but also help reduce the spread of these diseases.

Most so-called barrier methods of birth control, including condoms, diaphragms, and cervical caps, and chemical spermicides such as foams, creams, and jellies provide some protection against disease. But these methods may be less effective at preventing pregnancy, because they are more dependent upon proper use with each instance of sexual intercourse. In contrast, long-acting injectable contraceptives and implants—which are more effective at preventing pregnancy—provide no protection against sexually transmitted diseases. Using both kinds is probably the wisest course.

Researchers are trying to develop new contraceptives—and not just for women. More men now want to take responsibility for birth control and have asked that better

methods be developed for them as well. One new approach under investigation—the antifertility vaccine for women—has been particularly controversial, because it may affect the immune system in ways that are permanent and unpredictable. Many still feel that the ideal contraceptive has yet to be developed—something that is completely safe, easy to use, inexpensive, and not disruptive of lovemaking.

The availability of birth control has greatly changed the status of many modern women, freeing them of the fear of pregnancy. Birth control has made possible women's more effective participation in the work force because they have more control over whether and when to have children. Thus, they can more readily fit parenthood into a career. Although far from perfect, birth control has given women greater independence and control over their lives. Increasingly, men see birth control as their responsibility too, so the burden of avoiding unwanted pregnancies is not always just "the woman's job."

See also Abortion; Sanger, Margaret.

For further reading: The New Our Bodies, Ourselves (New York: Simon and Schuster, 1992).

JUDY NORSIGIAN

BLACK, HUGO

(1886–1971) *Associate justice, U.S. Supreme Court.*

Constitutional experts have hailed Black as "one of a handful of great judges in American history, second only to John Marshall in his impact on the Constitution."

Born in Alabama, Black practiced law in Birmingham. He was elected to the U.S. Senate in 1927 and became a strong supporter of

Franklin D. Roosevelt's New Deal. He was an aggressive Senate investigator of the economically powerful. In 1937, he became the first Roosevelt Supreme Court appointee.

Black had two primary constitutional goals. He knew the states often denied minorities their basic rights and felt that the federal government should not allow this. Thus he worked to find a constitutional way for people of any state to secure federal protection. This "nationalizing" of the Bill of Rights upgraded many people's rights and freedoms and played a major role in the civil rights movement. Black sought to expand freedom of speech and freedom of the press, convinced that their extension would create a more open and democratic society.

Black's judicial career went through two phases. Until 1953, his opinions were frequently liberal dissents from the Court's decisions. In 1952, however, he wrote a majority opinion challenging President Harry S. Truman's takeover of the country's steel mills, which had been shut down by striking workers. The decision was popular, reaffirming the separate and limited roles of all three branches of the federal government.

After Earl Warren became chief justice in 1953, Black's positions gained new support. His 1946 call for the "one-man, one-vote" principle in voting districts was now accepted by a majority of the Court. He also supported the criminal justice revolution and its extension of the principle of fair trial to everyone. To him equal justice was a birthright.

Critics charged that Black was making the Court an active agent of reform. But he believed that justices should not exercise personal judgment in constitutional cases. He especially denied that the Court could create new rights not written in the Constitution, such as privacy.

Black was a people's justice. His opinions were clear, not highly legalistic, and often moving in the concern they expressed for the people's welfare and the nation's principles.

See also Supreme Court.

PAUL L. MURPHY

BLACK CODES

The Black Codes were laws enacted in the southern states after the adoption of the Thirteenth Amendment abolishing slavery in 1865. Although blacks now possessed many rights they had not had under slavery—their marriages were legalized, for example, and blacks could testify in court and own some kinds of property—the codes sought to keep black people in a state as close as possible to slavery.

They differed in detail from state to state, but all were designed to force the blacks to continue working on farms and plantations. To begin with they could be employed *only* on farms or as household servants. In many states they were required to sign contracts to work for an entire year. If they quit before the end of the year, they received no wages for the work they had already done. If they violated any of the strict rules regulating their personal behavior, they could be fined or imprisoned. If a black could not pay a fine, he might be "hired out" (forced to work) for any white who would pay it. Preaching without a license, or "insulting" a white, or being a "vagrant" (meaning no more than "not working") were examples of illegal black behavior.

The Black Codes angered many northerners. Congress responded by passing the Civil Rights Act of 1866. This law declared that all blacks were citizens of the United States and outlawed many of the provisions of the codes.

See also Reconstruction.

BLACK HAWK

(1767–1838)   *Sauk warrior.*

Black Hawk was born near the site of the present-day city of Rock Island, Illinois. The Sauk and their ally, the Fox tribe, had migrated there from their previous homelands to the northeast. In 1804 a delegation from the Sauk people signed a treaty giving all their land east of the Mississippi to the United States. This treaty, however, allowed the Sauk to stay where they were until the federal government put the land up for sale, so at first there was no change. But Black Hawk never accepted the American claim. He viewed the whites as enemies and refused the alcohol that traders offered, seeing it as harmful to his people.

In 1831, white settlers from the East were clamoring for land in northwestern Illinois, and the federal government decided to exercise its rights under the old treaty. The Sauk and Fox withdrew to Iowa across the Mississippi River, but after a hard winter, Black Hawk decided to go back. He led a group of warriors and their families—some five hundred persons in all—back across the river and into the state of Illinois. The Black Hawk War of 1832 resulted when the federal army and the state militia tried to force them to return.

Black Hawk had hoped that his little group might receive help from other tribes in Illinois or even from the British in Canada, but

Black Hawk, Sauk Indian chief, resisted the westward expansion of white settlers, which led to the massacre of the Indians known as the Black Hawk War. In 1833 Black Hawk wrote his autobiography, a powerful story of the Indians' anguish at losing their homelands to whites.

he was disappointed. He was on the verge of giving up when soldiers who had discovered his camp ignored his signs for peace talks and fired on the Indians. Black Hawk won that battle, but a peaceful resolution of the conflict was now impossible. His group eluded capture for a summer, but most of its members were slaughtered by combined land and water forces as they attempted to cross back over the Mississippi.

Black Hawk survived and later dictated an autobiography to explain his actions to the American people. In it, he said he had given up his hostility toward whites. The Sauk were relocated many more times in the years to come. Their descendants live today mostly in Oklahoma.

See also Indian-White Relations.

THOMAS COLE

BLACK NATIONALISM BEFORE EMANCIPATION

Black nationalists argue that their people are so greatly outnumbered in America that they must unite to gain the strength needed to achieve freedom. Before emancipation, this goal of free blacks was established without knowledge of the efforts being made by slaves to achieve unity through their shared religious and artistic values. In fact, most free blacks never understood that the slaves' abilities in music, dance, and the telling of folk tales was a powerful argument against claims of white supremacy. Hence, the creativity that made possible slave successes in the arts was not taken into account when nationalists thought about how their people, once free, might contribute to the enrichment of all.

The Slaves' Contributions

Martin R. Delany, a journalist and physician, knew that Africans brought to America knowledge of rice, cotton, and tobacco cultivation. But he wrote only briefly on the subject and failed to connect it to the rewards of freedom that his people should have been given for the work they were doing that was enriching the nation. Thanks to him, however, such insights about Africans are being considered now more than a century after he wrote on the subject.

But his fellow nationalists did not recognize the slaves' skills in agriculture and in brickmaking, carpentry, and horsemanship, or their genius in the religious arts, especially the music of the spiritual. Nationalists also failed to respond to Frederick Douglass's argument that African values were responsible for the respect the young paid the old in the slave community. Here again was an instance of values that, after slavery, would be enriching to all Americans. Douglass also called attention to the mixture of joy and sadness that gave special weight to slave music, and he suggested that African influences could be felt in this realm as well. The African heritage was in important ways, therefore, the most creative foundation on which nationalists of later years would build.

Nationalists' Thought

No nationalists thought whites would permit blacks to form a political system of their own in America, nor did blacks think such a step would be to their benefit. In fact, most nationalists favored a degree of cooperation with whites who shared an interest in black liberation and favored white atonement for crimes committed against blacks. Moreover, such was the prejudice against their people that they thought real freedom would come only when the good name of the African motherland was restored in the world.

This was at the heart of David Walker's *Appeal to the Colored Citizens of the World*, published in Boston in 1829. In that fiery book, Walker attacked the love of money and ease that, he thought, had led Europeans to want to dominate others and, especially, people of color. But he did not believe that whites were by nature the enemies of blacks. Most nationalists of his time built on Walker's views and were more opposed to notions of racial superiority than any Americans before or since.

Typical of nationalists in this respect was Henry Highland Garnet, a great admirer of Walker's and a highly educated and moral man. Garnet thought white dislike of blacks stemmed from blacks having so long been on the bottom rung of life in America. As blacks rose from that lowly position, he thought, they would win growing respect and friendship from whites. Yet he knew as well as anyone that whites were responsible for the enslavement of blacks, that the efforts of his people had to be doubly strong for that reason.

These views Delany largely shared, but Delany believed that the problem of winning freedom was greater than Garnet realized. Delany was convinced that blacks would never have enough white friends in America to make real freedom possible. Their only hope, he thought, was for some blacks to leave America and build a powerful state that would win respect for his people everywhere. Still, he thought racial discrimination in every form should be fought as long as any blacks remained in America.

The government's abandonment of black rights during and after Reconstruction made it clear to nationalists that their people needed power to make self-reliance work. Frederick Douglass brilliantly argued this point of view: "No man can truly be free whose liberty is dependent upon . . . others, and has himself no means in his own hands for guarding, protecting, defending, and maintaining that liberty. . . . The law on the side of freedom is of great advantage only when there is power to make that law respected." Later black nationalist thought at its best, whether from W. E. B. Du Bois, Paul Robeson, or Malcolm X, largely developed from the tradition established by black nationalist thinkers before, and immediately following, the emancipation of the slaves.

See also African Americans: to 1865; Free Blacks before Emancipation; Slavery.

STERLING STUCKEY

BLACKWELL, ELIZABETH

(1821–1910)   *First woman to earn a medical degree in the United States.*

Blackwell was born in England and moved with her family to New York City when she was ten years old. The family home was always filled with books, music, and interesting friends discussing social issues. Elizabeth's father believed in the rights of women and encouraged his daughters to develop their minds fully. This was very unusual in the nineteenth century when women were expected only to stay at home and raise families. It was thought that education was not important for them. They were not allowed to vote, and almost all jobs, other than teaching, were closed to them.

Elizabeth Blackwell taught school for several years, but she yearned for something more. When a friend encouraged her to study medicine, she jumped at the challenge. No American woman had ever become a doctor before, and she was eager to be a pioneer. At first she studied on her own, reading everything she could find about the human body. But when she applied to medical schools, she was rejected time after time simply because she was a woman. Finally, in 1847, she was accepted by the Geneva Medical College in upstate New York.

During her training, Blackwell was ignored by many of her fellow students and professors. She graduated in 1849, however, and then went to London, England, for further studies. But when she looked for work in New York City, no clinic would hire her. To her sister she wrote that a woman doctor faces "a blank wall of social and professional antagonism . . . leaving her without support, respect, or professional counsel."

Blackwell was especially concerned with the plight of women and children living in poverty. With her sister Emily (who also became a doctor) she founded the New York Infirmary for Women and Children in 1857. She also established a medical school for women in New York.

In 1869, Blackwell returned to England, where she lived for the rest of her life. She founded another medical school for women and taught there. In later life she wrote several books on public health, promoting her philosophy that "prevention is better than cure."

See also Feminist Movement to 1919; Medicine.

DEBORAH KENT

BLAINE, JAMES G.

(1830–93)   *Member of Congress, secretary of state, and presidential candidate.*

Born in Pennsylvania, Blaine moved in his twenties to Augusta, Maine, where he edited a newspaper and took a lively interest in promoting the young Republican Party. An eloquent orator and effective campaigner, Blaine served first in the state legislature and was elected to the U.S. House of Representatives in 1862. Until 1876, he remained in the House, serving as its Speaker for six years and acquiring a national reputation as one of the foremost leaders in Congress.

Blaine, whose supporters called him the "plumed knight" because his political style resembled a knight heading into battle, was favored to win the Republican nomination for the presidency in 1876. His reputation, however, had been tarnished by a scandal that occurred while he was House Speaker; Blaine allegedly had used his political influence to help a railroad company keep a land grant, presumably in return for the privilege of selling the company's bonds and receiving large commissions. The Maine politician de-

nied these charges, but the Republican convention decided his nomination was too risky and instead ran Governor Rutherford B. Hayes of Ohio for president.

Continuing to bask in the political limelight, Blaine won a Senate seat in 1876 and again sought his party's nomination for the presidency in 1880. This time the Republicans chose Ohio Congressman James A. Garfield as their candidate. After his election, Garfield appointed Blaine secretary of state in 1881, but later that year the president was assassinated and Blaine resigned from the State Department.

Finally, on his third attempt, Blaine became the Republican presidential nominee in 1884. He narrowly lost the election to his Democratic opponent, Governor Grover Cleveland of New York; a change of six hundred votes in New York would have made Blaine president. During Benjamin Harrison's administration (1889–93), Blaine served again as secretary of state. He succeeded in improving relations with Latin America and organized the first Pan-American Conference in 1889.

EDMUND LINDOP

BLEEDING KANSAS

In 1854 Congress passed a law opening the land west of Missouri and Iowa to settlers. The law divided the region into two territories, Kansas and Nebraska, and provided that the settlers of each should be free to decide whether or not to allow slavery to exist in their territory. (This was called the doctrine of "popular sovereignty.") No one expected that slavery would be established in Nebraska. But since Kansas was immediately west of the slave state of Missouri, the future of slavery there was unclear. This resulted in a struggle between proslavery and antislavery settlers for control of that territory.

The conflict had both political and military aspects. On the political side, by the end of 1855 there were two governments in Kansas. One government, in the town of Lecompton, was run by proslavery Missourians. The other, in the town of Lawrence, was controlled by antislavery groups. Outsiders concerned about whether slavery was right or wrong tried to influence the situation. Proslavery "border ruffians" (so called because they were crude, violent men) from Missouri flocked into Kansas to vote in elections. The New England Emigrant Aid Society was founded to transport eastern antislavery settlers to the area.

Soon hotheads in both camps took up arms. In May 1856, eight hundred Missourians burned and looted Lawrence. Later in May, an abolitionist extremist, John Brown, together with six companions, invaded a small proslavery settlement on Pottawatomie Creek in the dead of night. They dragged five men from their beds and murdered them. By year's end some two hundred people had been killed in what was in effect a civil war in miniature—leading to the region's being called "Bleeding Kansas."

The antislavery voters in the state ultimately defeated the proslavery forces in 1858, and Kansas was admitted to the Union as a free state in 1861.

See also Kansas-Nebraska Act; Popular Sovereignty.

BLUE LAWS

State and local regulations making it illegal to do certain things on Sundays are popularly known as "blue laws." No one knows exactly where the name comes from, but the laws themselves date back from ancient times: the Bible has many references to activities that were forbidden on the Sabbath. The earliest colonists in America brought the laws with them from Europe. They varied greatly about what could and could not be done on Sundays. Many required church attendance; others made dancing, playing games, selling liquor, operating a store, going to the theater, or other forms of entertainment illegal.

Though many of these laws are still on the books, in recent years their numbers have declined. The ban on selling liquor on Sundays is still common, but compelling a business to close has become increasingly rare. Many blue laws have been repealed outright. Of those that remain, most are simply not enforced by the authorities.

BLUES

The blues is strongly emotional music with a forceful beat and chords that use what are

Leadbelly (Huddie Ledbetter) was an early blues singer and guitarist (1885–1949), who began performing at about age fifteen for fifty cents a night in Louisiana. He was jailed three times over the years, but eventually became a celebrated musician performing throughout the country and abroad.

called "blue notes." Often (but not always) blues lyrics build on a repeated first line capped by a closing line:

> Pretty mama, where have you been so long?
> Pretty mama, where have you been so long?
> You better get yourself back home where you belong. ⋆

The blues began as "field hollers," work songs, and spirituals sung by black people in the rural South around the end of the Civil War. By 1910 there were two main forms— the "country" and the "city" styles.

The simplest blues mode is just a singer with a guitar—the country blues. Blind Lemon Jefferson began performing that way in the streets and cheap bars of Dallas, Texas, around World War I. His songs were crude but effective, and for a while he made a decent living. But his personal life was tragic, and though he went to Chicago to record in the 1920s, his career slowly came apart. He froze to death on a Chicago street in 1930.

Still, Blind Lemon influenced many performers. The most famous was Huddie Ledbetter, better known as "Leadbelly." He joined Blind Lemon as a street musician in Dallas, but he committed murder and in 1918 was sentenced to thirty years in a Texas peniten-

tiary. He continued to sing behind bars until a pardon came in 1934. Leadbelly went on to a very successful career, even performing at Harvard University. His "Irene, Goodnight" became a best-selling song in the 1950s.

City blues performers generally did better than people like Blind Lemon or Leadbelly, though. The best example is W. C. Handy, a bandleader, songwriter, and publisher. He produced the first blues tunes that were smooth enough to sell in music stores, starting with "Memphis Blues" in 1912. "St. Louis Blues" followed a bit later; it is the world's most famous blues. Handy's music paved the way for a number of city blues musicians to find wider audiences and a better living.

"Ma" Rainey was one of them. With a flashy gown and a regular orchestra, she belted out the blues as headliner of a black vaudeville show traveling from town to town. Handy's music helped make her act even more popular, and she performed until the early 1930s. Late in her career she made a few records that are valuable collectors' items today. Her most famous song, "See See Rider," is almost sure to be performed at any blues festival.

In 1910 Bessie Smith was a lonely, abandoned girl from Chattanooga when she joined Ma Rainey's troupe. With Ma's help, Bessie learned to sing the blues better than anyone. Her voice was deep, rich, and strong enough to overpower the orchestra without a microphone. During the 1920s when the blues were most popular, she was a superstar. The average person's pay then was about $100 per month, but Bessie's income was $1,500 a week. She made over 160 recordings, resulting in sales of 10 million records before the depression of the 1930s. An especially great one is of Handy's "St. Louis Blues," which she recorded with the famous jazz trumpeter

---

⋆Anyone who knows a little about the piano can make up a simple blues song using the words above with flatted seventh chords. Start with three notes—middle C, E, and G. Now add a B-flat (the blue note) above the G. Play all four together as one chord 16 times, singing the first line above in the first 8 beats. Invent the tune yourself. Now make a new chord: C, E-flat (another blue note), F, and A. Play that one 8 times, while you sing the second line, going back to the first chord on the word "long" for 8 more beats. (During those nonsinging 8 beats, many blues performers like to say a word or two extra, like "Hear me talkin'.") Sing the final line with 8 beats of a chord made up of D, F, and G, and then return to the first chord at the "long" in "belong" for the last 8 beats.

Louis Armstrong. Bessie's success faded after 1929, when many people could no longer afford to see her shows or buy so many records. Her marriage broke up, and her heavy drinking began to hurt her performances. Perhaps her most haunting song comes from this period: "Nobody Knows You When You're Down and Out." An auto accident killed her in 1937.

Other important names in blues history are Leroy Carr, Muddy Waters (McKinley Morganfield), Ida Cox, Victoria Spivey, B. B. King, and many more. Although few performers specialize in the blues today, popular artists perform that style occasionally. For instance, one side of Elvis Presley's first hit record was "Hound Dog," a classic upbeat blues like the one described at the beginning.

See also Music.

For further reading: Peter Guralnick, *The Listener's Guide to the Blues* (New York: Facts on File, 1982).

JAN CHARLES HALUSKA

BLY, NELLIE

(c. 1865–1922)   *Investigative reporter.*

Elizabeth Cochrane, the girl who became a celebrity as the reporter Nellie Bly, was born in a small Pennsylvania town named for her mill-owning father. Before she was twenty years old, she obtained a job with the *Pittsburg-Dispatch,* and, with a pen name suggested by a Stephen Foster song, her meteoric career began.

As a novice reporter Nellie investigated working conditions in factories, wrote about divorce, and interviewed notable citizens. She also covered society events although she found them dull. A six-month visit to Mexico in 1886–87 resulted in the first of Nellie Bly's

Nellie Bly, an early woman reporter. Her most famous exploit involved her attempt in 1889 to beat the record of Phineas Fogg, the main character in Jules Verne's Around the World in Eighty Days. *Bly accomplished the feat in seventy-two days, six hours, eleven minutes, and fourteen seconds.*

three published books. Soon thereafter she moved to New York City and a job on Joseph Pulitzer's newspaper, the *New York World.*

Clever, courageous, and truthful, Nellie Bly wrote on subjects ranging from the care of the mentally ill to politics. She wrote entertainingly about her adventures, which ranged from auditioning as a dance-hall hostess to surviving the Blizzard of 1888.

In November 1889, a confident Nellie Bly began a highly publicized journey around the world, an adventure she reported along the way to an eager readership. With a monkey she acquired in Hong Kong (and had to defend against superstitious sailors during a stormy Pacific crossing), she returned to find herself famous. *Nelly Bly's Book: Around the World in 72 Days* and a forty-week lecture tour brought further fame.

In 1885, a chance meeting with a wealthy manufacturer more than twice her age led to marriage and an active partnership in Brooklyn's Iron Clad Manufacturing Company. As Mrs. Robert Seaman, Nellie Bly attempted to continue the business when her husband died eleven years later. Unfortunately, dishonest employees and poor management on her part brought it all to ruin. Nellie Bly's final years, which included an enforced stay in Paris during World War I, cannot have been very happy. It was only after her death that tributes from former colleagues recalled her early renown.

See also Magazines and Newspapers; Pulitzer, Joseph.

JOAN W. BLOS

BOONE, DANIEL

(1734–1820)   *Frontiersman and Kentucky pioneer.*

Daniel Boone is the most widely known of American frontiersmen. Motion pictures and television have depicted his life, and the hero in James Fenimore Cooper's Leatherstocking Tales is modeled on him.

Boone was born in Berks County, Pennsylvania. When he was sixteen his family moved to the Yadkin River valley, a frontier area in northwestern North Carolina. In 1755 the adventurous young man was working as a wagon driver with British general Edward Braddock, when Braddock's ill-fated expedition to Fort Duquesne (present-day Pittsburgh) was ambushed by Indians. In 1763 he and his brother Squire looked for lands in Florida, but they did not stay.

Boone's fame lies with his exploits in Kentucky. Although he traveled into eastern "Kentucke" (its original spelling) in 1767, his expedition of 1769–71 is most widely known. His party followed what was called the Warrior's Path across Cumberland Gap into "the dark and bloody ground," as Kentucky was known then. He remained behind when the rest of the party returned, not emerging from the wilderness until March 1771. He was enthusiastic about the beautiful land and its possibilities and vowed to return.

Boone, his family, and forty settlers started for Kentucky in 1773, but were turned back by Indians. In March 1775, however, he began hacking out the Wilderness Road into the region. Subsequently he built Boonesboro, one of several forts, or stations, in the area. Until 1778, during the American Revolution, he was active defending Boonesboro and other stations, surviving an ambush at Blue Licks, his capture by Shawnee Indians, and a siege of Boonesboro.

Boone was highly respected, and after moving to western Virginia in 1788, he served in the state legislature. He lost his Kentucky lands, however, and in September 1799 set out for Missouri where he lived the remainder of his life.

See also Pioneers and Frontier Life.

For further reading: Seamus Cavan, *Daniel Boone and the Opening of the Ohio Country* (New York: Chelsea House, 1991).

RICHARD A. BARTLETT

BOSSES, POLITICAL
See Big-City Bosses.

BOSTON MASSACRE

In 1768 the Massachusetts legislature sent a message to the legislatures of the other colonies arguing that the taxes Parliament had placed on tea, paint, glass, and other imported products by the Townshend Act of 1767 were unconstitutional and should not be paid. In response the British government stationed four thousand Redcoats in Boston to maintain order. This was a very large number of soldiers, considering that the population of Boston was only about sixteen thousand. It caused widespread resentment and over the following months led to many scuffles between the soldiers and citizens. Times were hard in Boston to begin with. The fact that the poorly paid soldiers often competed with Bostonians for jobs in their time off only increased local resentment.

The so-called Boston Massacre occurred on March 5, 1770. It erupted when a crowd began to jeer at a squad of Redcoats guarding the Custom House and pelted them with snowballs, some of them wrapped around rocks. After enduring this for a time, the soldiers panicked and fired into the crowd. Five Bostonians were killed, including Crispus Attucks, later said to be the first black man to die in the Revolution. To prevent further trouble, Governor Thomas Hutchinson withdrew the troops from the town, stationing them on an island in the harbor.

The soldiers were tried for murder, with John Adams, the Revolutionary leader and future president, representing them. (He believed that everyone—no matter how unpopular—was entitled to a fair trial.) They

This engraving of the Boston Massacre was done by Paul Revere. It shows a group of British soldiers firing at an unarmed crowd of colonists. The engraving was widely circulated and intensified the already strong anti-British feeling in the colonies.

were acquitted of murder charges, though two were convicted of lesser offenses. But Patriot leaders used the incident to stir up popular anger at the British. In England, Parliament repealed all the Townshend duties except the tax on tea.

See also Revolution: The War for Independence; Townshend Act.

BOSTON TEA PARTY

The Boston Tea Party was a protest by local Patriots against the Tea Act of 1773. Parliament had passed that law to help the British East India Company sell some of the 17 million pounds of tea it had in storage. By eliminating middlemen and reducing local British taxes, the act enabled the company to offer the tea for sale in America at very low prices. But, the three-penny-a-pound tax on tea imposed by the Townshend Act in 1767 was still in effect. Despite the low price, almost no colonist was willing to buy the tea. If they did, they'd have to pay the tax and that would involve acknowledging Parliament's right to tax them.

By late autumn the East India Company had shipped 500,000 pounds of tea to agents in the main colonial ports of Boston, New York, Philadelphia, and Charleston. Opposition was so strong to the tea coming in that in most ports it was impossible for the ships even to unload. They returned to England with the tea still in their holds.

But in Boston Governor Thomas Hutchinson refused to let the tea ship depart. On December 16, 1773, fearing that the governor would have the tea unloaded in the dark, a group of citizens led by Samuel Adams disguised themselves as Mohawk Indians, boarded the vessels, and tossed the tea chests overboard.

Indignation in Great Britain at this destruction of property resulted in Parliament's passage of the Coercive Acts, which in turn brought the colonists closer to revolution.

See also Coercive Acts; Revolution: The War for Independence.

BOURKE-WHITE, MARGARET

(1904–71)   *Photographer.*

Bourke-White is best remembered for her classic photo-essays on such topics as Ameri-

The Boston Tea Party took place at midnight on December 16, 1773. A group of colonists organized by Samuel Adams disguised themselves as Mohawk Indians, sneaked aboard ships owned by Britain's East India Tea Company, and dumped their cargoes of tea into Boston Harbor. The act was a protest against the British tea tax.

can and Soviet industry, the depression-ridden American South, and historic moments during World War II and the Korean War. She was *Fortune* magazine's first staff photographer and was on the masthead of *Life*'s first issue. A critic has called her "the most famous woman photojournalist of the twentieth century."

Bourke-White studied photography while attending Columbia University. She received a B.A. from Cornell in 1927 and then opened a studio in Cleveland. Her photographs of steelmaking led the publisher of *Life,* Henry Luce, to employ her. Luce taught her a lesson she never forgot: pictures should be beautiful, but they should also convey facts.

By all accounts, Bourke-White possessed "extraordinary courage." She was always determined to get "exactly the picture she wanted," often endlessly organizing, lighting, and posing her subjects to the point of their exasperation. She loved taking pictures from heights and flew B-17 bombing missions over Africa. When she asked to be sent to Korea, it was not to cover battles but to photograph the effects of the carnage on the Korean people.

In 1940 she quit *Life* to work for the New York liberal newspaper *PM*. The FBI then opened a file on her, and director J. Edgar Hoover placed her on a list of people to face "custodial detention" (arrest) in the event of a national emergency. When she later flew in a top-secret bomber for *Life,* ultraconservatives Senator William Jenner and newsman Westbrook Pegler protested. Bourke-White refuted these claims of disloyalty in an affidavit declassified in 1980.

Bourke-White published six books about her assignments and collaborated with her one-time husband, novelist Erskine Caldwell, on three others. In 1963, she published her autobiography, *Portrait of Myself.* In it, she

Margaret Bourke-White, shown photographing the New York skyline from the sixty-first floor of the Chrysler Building in 1934, documented the important events and people of her time. She photographed Mahatma Gandhi and India's independence movement, life under apartheid in South Africa, the American civil rights movement, and World War II. She shot some of the first photographs of those who survived the death camps of the Holocaust. A photo by Bourke-White is reproduced on page 397.

reflects on the extent to which the "impersonality of modern war has become stupendous, grotesque." She could only think "in terms of my own field," she writes, "how a photographer tries to help—how all the best photographers I know have tried to help by building up the pictorial files of history for the world to see."

See also Photography.

WILLIAM WELLING

BOXING

Human beings fight, but fighting and boxing are very different things. Boxing is a sport, where men battle with fists according to rules. A boxing match is not a fight in the sense of settling a grudge; it is an athletic event, if a brutal one.

The ancient Greeks and Romans developed the "manly art," as boxing came to be known. The sport was one event in the Greek Olympiad, and boxers became athletic heroes. The Romans too accorded great respect to champions, although the sport became increasingly brutal.

After the Romans, boxing died out, but during the seventeenth century, the sport was revived in England. During the eighteenth century, Broughton's Rules (named for the champion James Broughton) brought some order to the ring, and by late in the century, prizefighting was called the "National Sport" of England.

From 1775 to 1825, a series of champions — like Jewish boxer Daniel Mendoza, the American ex-slave Tom Molineaux, John Gully, who rose from debtors' prison to the championship and then to a seat in Parliament, and perhaps the greatest of them all, Tom Cribb — brought distinction to the ring. These working-class men were backed by rich aristocrats, so although prizefighting was illegal, matches took place without police interference.

Bare-knuckle rules did not change much until boxing with gloves under the Marquis of Queensbury rules became the norm at the end of the nineteenth century. Because pre-Queensbury fights were illegal, matches were held in isolated rural settings. A ring was set up in a meadow, with a "scratch" mark drawn in the center. The men (each with a "second,"

or helper, sitting in a corner) "toed the mark," and the fight began. Fighters could punch each other, and wrestling throws and holds were also allowed. Rounds had no time limit—each ended when a man went down, followed by half a minute of rest. Some fights lasted over a hundred rounds and more than two hours. When a man failed to continue, the fight was over.

In America, New York City became the center of boxing. From 1849 until the Civil War, a series of fights pitted Irish immigrants against each other, against English fighters, and against native-born Americans, and these ethnic combinations attracted tremendous interest. During these years, bare-knuckle fighting was perhaps the country's most popular sport.

The first great American championship fight pitted an Irish immigrant, James "Yankee" Sullivan, against American-born Tom Hyer in 1849. Both men were well-known gang leaders with loyal followings. Their fight was interpreted as a playing out of ethnic rivalry—native-born Americans against foreigners. Many Irish were immigrating to America, and discrimination against them was reaching a peak. As it turned out, the younger, taller, and stronger Hyer beat Sullivan in sixteen rounds.

For the next forty years boxing remained a sport that respectable men and women hated, but that many young working-class males took to be the epitome of manhood. By the late nineteenth century, however, more Americans—especially the middle class—became interested in sports. Boxing, football, and basketball appealed to growing numbers of fans. And with new rules (boxers now wore gloves, rounds were timed, the knockout became important), boxing became an acceptable spectator event. During this era modern weight classifications were established and record keeping became more systematic.

Boxing was slow to shed its outlaw image. John L. Sullivan, the greatest American sports hero of the late nineteenth century, was seen by many as a drunkard and braggart; the great Jack Johnson, who reigned as champion in the years just before World War I, was a proud black man who defied convention by marrying a white woman and defeating a series of "great white hopes"; Jack Dempsey dominated the 1920s with a fierce, punishing style. Joe Louis in the thirties and forties avoided Jack Johnson's controversial style but was still outspoken against white opponents with his fists; and Muhammad Ali in the sixties and seventies not only won the heavyweight championship three times but became known as a supporter of the civil rights movement and critic of the Vietnam War.

Boxing remains controversial. The sport has opened opportunities for various ethnic

Heavyweight boxing champion Joe Louis shown having just knocked out Germany's Max Schmeling in 1938. With anti-Nazi sentiment intensifying before the outbreak of World War II, Americans were especially elated at the defeat of Germany's champion.

groups—Irish, Jewish, Italian, African American, Hispanic, Asian. But it would be a mistake to see boxing as a grand arena of oppotunity. Most boxers make meager livings at best. Men often go into the sport because they have few good alternatives. And with its elemental violence many fighters end their boxing careers permanently brain-damaged. The American Medical Association has condemned the sport.

See also Ali, Muhammad; Louis, Joe; Sports, Spectator.

ELLIOTT J. GORN

BOY SCOUTS
See Scouting.

BRADFORD, WILLIAM

(1590–1657)   *Governor of Plymouth Colony and historian.*

As a young man living in the north of England, Bradford joined a church whose members disagreed so strongly with the practices of the Church of England that they formed their own congregation separate from the national church. In doing so, Bradford's group was in violation of the law. So they decided in 1609 to move their congregation to Holland, where they could worship more freely. After ten years, Bradford was one of a hundred Separatist emigrants who chose to relocate in America. Historians have given them the name of "Pilgrims."

In November 1620, the ship *Mayflower* landed near Cape Cod, part of present-day Massachusetts. The Pilgrims named their settlement "Plymouth" after the last town they had seen in England. Bradford was chosen governor, a post he held almost continually until 1656. As governor, Bradford believed that he had to maintain strict discipline in order to hold the little colony together. Once, for example, he punished some servants for playing games instead of working on Christmas Day. (The Pilgrims did not believe in observing Christmas as people do nowadays.)

Bradford wrote a history of the colony called *Of Plymouth Plantation*. The book describes the colonists' initial sufferings from disease and other hardships. The survivors relied on their religious faith for strength and on members of the nearby Wampanoag Indian tribe for advice on growing food. Bradford's history further relates how the Wampanoag leader, Massasoit, allied his people with the English. But the Pilgrims fought against other tribes in 1623, fearing that an Indian alliance might exterminate the white settlements.

Bradford began his history around 1630, as English families began arriving elsewhere in New England in great numbers. He wished to record the story of his particular community before it was overshadowed by others. He finished the work twenty years later with a list of the original *Mayflower* passengers so that future generations would remember the names and also, he hoped, the sacrifices and achievements of his generation.

See also Colonial America; Pilgrims.

THOMAS COLE

BRADLEY, OMAR

(1893–1981)   *U.S. Army general.*

Bradley, who was born in Clark, Missouri, graduated from West Point in 1915. He served as a captain in the northwestern U.S. during

World War I, later taught at West Point, and spent two years on the army general staff in Washington, D.C. In 1941, the year the United States entered World War II, Bradley, now a major general, headed the Infantry School at Fort Benning, Georgia.

In February 1943, Gen. George C. Marshall, the army chief of staff, appointed Bradley to serve under Gen. Dwight D. Eisenhower in North Africa. Bradley assumed control of the U.S. Second Corps in Tunisia, where he led American troops in the final campaign that swept North Africa clear of enemy forces. Later, as a corps commander under Gen. George S. Patton's Fifth Army, he helped achieve the conquest of Sicily.

Bradley was then given the difficult task of directing the First Army soldiers who landed on the beachheads of Normandy, France, on D-day (June 6, 1944). After his forces secured a firm foothold in France, other American armies joined his troops in the fight to liberate Western Europe from Nazi control and crush Adolf Hitler's war machine. From August 1, 1944, until the end of the war, Bradley commanded 1.2 million soldiers, the largest American army ever entrusted to a single general.

In 1948, Bradley became the first chairman of the Joint Chiefs of Staff and held this position during the Korean War (1950–53). Gen. Douglas MacArthur, commander of the U.N. forces in Korea, advocated expanding the conflict to include direct attacks on Communist China. Bradley agreed with President Harry S. Truman's decision to reject this advice and declared later in a famous statement that a fight with China would involve the United States "in the wrong war, at the wrong place, at the wrong time, and with the wrong enemy." When Truman finally fired MacArthur for continuing to oppose his policies

publicly, Bradley firmly supported Truman's action (which was very unpopular at the time). Civilian control of the military, the general pointed out, was a bedrock principle of American democracy.

Bradley was one of the most brilliant strategists and capable leaders in American military history. He was known as "the soldiers' general" because of his lack of arrogance, natural manner, and genuine concern for the welfare of the soldiers he commanded.

See also Army; Korean War; World War II.

EDMUND LINDOP

BRADY, MATHEW

(1823?–96) *Photographer.*

Brady early sought out the famous to pose for his daguerreotype camera. From his first New York gallery, he transported his cumbersome apparatus to Washington, D.C., to photograph the wives of James Madison and Alexander Hamilton, President James K. Polk, Daniel Webster, and John C. Calhoun, among others. In New York, Brady had his portraits copied as engravings and published. In 1851, he took some daguerreotypes to a world's fair in London. They brought him top awards. In 1853, as photographers adopted a new style of camera using glass negatives, "Mr. B," as he was widely known, moved uptown and installed a newly invented enlarging device in his gallery, which enabled him to produce pioneering large photographs.

In 1860 a new calling-card-size photograph came into vogue. Four photographs could be made in one sitting with a single four-lens camera. Brady that year photographed the as-yet-unnominated Republican candidate

Mathew Brady in 1861. His photographs of the Civil War and of prominent people made him one of America's most important documentary photographers. Brady was responsible for more than a third of the one hundred photos of Abraham Lincoln in existence. His photos are reproduced on pages 75, 215, 257, 362, 488, 497, and 560.

for president, Abraham Lincoln. The photograph was widely distributed in the campaign (a first). Later, Lincoln said that the Brady photograph helped elect him president. Photographs by "Brady of Broadway" soon became famous.

During the Civil War, Brady's cameras turned out a rising volume of popular political and military portraits. He also made arrangements to have negatives processed by

the thousands and then paid for and sent men in wagons to follow and photograph Union troops as the war progressed (another first). Most of our pictures of that war were taken by him or by others in his employ.

When the fighting ended, Brady thought the government would purchase and mount a visual record of the war. But it did not, and his career declined steeply. In 1873, he abandoned his New York gallery in the middle of the night to escape people to whom he owed money. He lived thereafter in Washington. Although people still came to his gallery, his popularity was over. When his wife died, he was forced to live with his nephew and dispersed his collection of glass negatives. A collector took possession of many, and Congress appropriated $25,000 to purchase others. About 1908, a tradesman bought ninety thousand more and tried to sell them to newspapers. When that failed, he wiped them clean and sold the glass—a terrible loss to future generations.

See also Photography.

WILLIAM WELLING

BRANDEIS, LOUIS D.

(1856–1941)   *Reformer and associate justice on the U.S. Supreme Court.*

Born in Louisville, Kentucky, Brandeis attended the Harvard Law School and then established a successful law firm in Boston. During the late nineteenth century, legal practice was changing. With the industrialization of the country, business owners needed advice from lawyers before they embarked on new ventures. A lawyer thus had to know not only the law but business as well. In this combination of abilities Brandeis excelled. He learned so much about his clients' businesses that they consulted him on business as well as legal matters.

Brandeis was also a Progressive, one of those reformers who, at the start of the twentieth century, tried to improve society by protecting workers, preserving natural resources, and opposing corruption in government. He is perhaps best known for the "Brandeis brief," a revolutionary new type of legal argument presented to courts that emphasized the facts of a case rather than abstract legal theory. He introduced this kind of brief in *Muller* v. *Oregon* (1908), in which he persuaded the Supreme Court to approve a law restricting the maximum working hours for women.

His reform work brought him to the attention of Woodrow Wilson, and when Wilson was elected president in 1912, Brandeis became one of his chief advisers. Then in 1916 Wilson named Brandeis to the Supreme Court, where he served for twenty-three years.

Brandeis affected the law in many areas, but perhaps the two most important are freedom of speech and privacy. In several cases decided in the 1920s, Brandeis developed a theory as to why speech must be protected. He argued that in a democracy, citizens have the responsibility to debate issues about what the government is doing. Sometimes these debates can be shrill, but the only way for a democracy to survive is for people to have complete freedom to express their views.

He also argued eloquently that each individual is entitled to a right to privacy. The most important of all rights, he said, is the right "to be let alone." Brandeis expressed these ideas in dissents—opinions that differed from those of a majority of the Court.

But they proved so powerful that they became the basis of modern ideas of free speech and privacy.

Brandeis University near Boston was named in his honor.

See also Supreme Court.

MELVIN I. UROFSKY

BROTHERHOOD OF SLEEPING CAR PORTERS

The Brotherhood of Sleeping Car Porters was a labor union of workers who served as waiters and attendants in the dining and sleeping cars of trains. Founded in 1925, it was the nation's first African-American union. The brotherhood eventually won a contract from the railroads, obtaining wage increases and job security for its members and a reduction in the number of work hours.

A. Philip Randolph, the president of the brotherhood, became the most important civil rights leader to emerge from the labor movement. Randolph was a tireless fighter for the rights of blacks. Under his leadership, the union became better known for its work in civil rights than in labor issues. Among many civil rights activities, Randolph proposed a March on Washington in 1941 to publicize the discrimination against blacks in hiring practices in the defense industry. To forestall the march, President Franklin D. Roosevelt created the Fair Employment Practices Committee to investigate charges of discrimination, and the march was canceled. Twenty years later Randolph and the brotherhood were in the forefront of the 1963 March on Washington.

See also Labor Movement; Marches on Washington: 1941, 1963; Randolph, A. Philip.

BROWN, JOHN

(1800–1859)   *Abolitionist.*

John Brown was born in Torrington, Connecticut, at a time when slavery of black people had been legal and commonplace in most of America, especially the southern states, for more than a hundred years. Most people sim-

John Brown, the fiery abolitionist who believed he was a messenger sent by God to destroy slavery. At the trial for his raid on Harpers Ferry he was convicted of treason, murder, and inciting insurrection. In his statement to the court he declared: "I believe that to have interfered as I have done . . . in behalf of His despised poor, I did no wrong, but right."

ply accepted this, but Brown's father taught him to believe that God had given all people the right to be free and that slavery was a sin. Brown became deeply religious and firmly opposed to slavery.

During the 1830s an antislavery movement known as abolition (to *abolish* slavery) grew strong in the northern states. But there were many people who favored slavery and were violently opposed to the abolitionists. In 1837, an abolitionist friend of Brown's was killed by a proslavery mob, and Brown vowed to devote his life to the destruction of slavery, asking his wife and sons to make the same vow. He became active in helping escaped slaves make their way to freedom and in trying to help free blacks gain a better life.

In 1854, Brown and his five sons and their families moved to the new territory of Kansas. Divided between pro- and antislavery settlers, it was racked by violence and bloodshed. Brown and his sons took part in this, murdering some proslavery men who had been responsible for attacks on abolitionists. Brown led battles against bands of proslavery marauders and became a symbol for abolitionists.

In 1857, Brown conceived a plan to lead a band of fighters into Virginia and take over part of its territory to form a new state for abolitionists and escaped slaves. On October 16, 1859, he and twenty-one men, both blacks and whites, seized the federal arsenal (a weapons storehouse) at the town of Harpers Ferry, Virginia. The government sent a company of marines to recapture the arsenal. In a battle, ten of Brown's men, including two of his sons, were killed, and Brown was wounded and captured.

Brown was tried for treason, found guilty, and on December 2, 1859, executed by hanging. To proslavery people he was a fanatical terrorist, but to those opposed to slavery he was a hero and freedom fighter.

See also Abolitionist Movement; Bleeding Kansas.

TOM MCGOWEN

BROWNSVILLE AFFAIR

In 1906 black soldiers from the Twenty-fifth U.S. Infantry, stationed at Fort Brown, Texas, became increasingly angered by the racial slurs and insults they received from the people of Brownsville. One night, in retaliation, a group of twelve soldiers fired their guns and one white civilian was killed. The soldiers then returned unobserved to Fort Brown.

An investigation was made, but no one could identify the soldiers other than that all were blacks. When none of the 167 soldiers in the three black companies of the regiment would confess or identify the rioters, President Theodore Roosevelt ordered that *all* of them be dishonorably discharged from the army. Even the six black soldiers who had won the nation's highest military medal for bravery, the Congressional Medal of Honor, were discharged.

Liberal northerners were outraged by Roosevelt's action, which was obviously unfair to all but a handful of the men. But he would not reverse his decision. In 1972, however, the secretary of the army officially cleared all the soldiers of guilt and changed their discharges from dishonorable to honorable.

BROWN V. BOARD OF EDUCATION

Throughout the first half of the twentieth century, separate public schools for black and white students were legal, provided that they were of equal quality. This "separate but equal" rule had been laid down by the Supreme Court in the case of *Plessy* v. *Ferguson* in 1896. In practice, however, schools for blacks in the South were overcrowded, the teachers poorly trained and underpaid, the school buildings ramshackle. "Separate but equal" was just a convenient argument for keeping white students in white schools where they received a much better education. It was an argument that sounded reasonable but was very clearly racist.

Beginning in the 1930s, lawyers for the National Association for the Advancement of Colored People (NAACP) gradually persuaded the Court to compel states to admit blacks to all-white law and technical schools if no decent schools for blacks existed. In 1950, when Texas attempted to create a separate law school for one black applicant, the Court decided that a one-person school simply could not provide an equal education. Texas was forced to admit the student to the all-white University of Texas law school.

In 1954 in the *Brown* case, the NAACP team, led by Thurgood Marshall, who later became the first black Supreme Court justice, argued that the mere fact of separating schoolchildren by race made equal education impossible. If everyone is equal, why bother to separate them from each other? Segregation, they insisted, did psychological damage to *all* students, white as well as black. This argument convinced the justices. Speaking for a unanimous Court, Chief Justice Earl Warren ruled that "separate educational facilities are inherently unequal."

The case did not end segregation outright. The Court soon had to lay down rules requiring that desegregation proceed "with all deliberate speed." But legal segregation had been ended.

See also Segregation.

BRYAN, WILLIAM JENNINGS

(1860–1925) *Statesman, orator, and political reformer.*

Raised on a farm in Illinois, Bryan moved to Nebraska as a young man. He was elected to Congress as a Democrat in 1890, a time of serious depression in the country. Bryan advocated the rights of farmers, who were among the hardest hit by the economic troubles.

Bryan was a brilliant speaker whose admirers called him "the boy orator of the Platte" (a river in Nebraska) and "the silver-tongued orator of the West." His famous "Cross of Gold" speech so thrilled the delegates at the 1896 Democratic National Convention that they nominated him for president. The new

William Jennings Bryan made three unsuccessful bids for the presidency on the Democratic ticket. He was nicknamed the Great Commoner because of his concern for the ordinary citizen.

Populist Party, another group supporting farmers, also chose him as their candidate.

Bryan waged what some historians have called "the most spectacular campaign in American history." In a time when long-distance travel was hard, Bryan swept back and forth across the country, speaking many times a day. He lost the election, but established himself as a major voice in American politics. He called for such reforms as imposing a national income tax and allowing women to vote. He also supported a constitutional amendment to make alcohol illegal. Bryan was nominated again in 1900 and in 1908, but lost both times.

In 1912, President Woodrow Wilson named Bryan secretary of state. A pacifist at heart, Bryan disliked the way America sometimes used its military power to dominate other nations. As secretary, he favored negotiation over force and arranged thirty "cooling-off" treaties to calm international disputes. In 1915, Bryan resigned as secretary to protest President Wilson's policies toward Germany, which he feared would lead the United States into World War I. Two years later he was proved right.

A devout Presbyterian, Bryan often spoke on behalf of fundamentalist Christianity. In 1925, he helped prosecute John Scopes, a Tennessee schoolteacher charged with teaching the theory of evolution, which was then illegal in that state. The theory of evolution maintains that human beings evolved from lower animals over millions of years. This is in contrast to creationism, the belief in the biblical account that God created Adam and Eve, and all humans are descended from them. Bryan took the stand himself as an expert on the Bible. He defended his belief in its literal truth against a mocking cross-examination by Scopes's lawyer, Clarence Darrow.

Ironically, Darrow and Bryan had often been allies in support of liberal causes in earlier years. Scopes was found guilty by the Tennessee jury. Five days after the trial ended, Bryan died of a heart attack.

See also Democratic Party; Populism; *Scopes* Trial.

MICHAEL KRONENWETTER

BUCHANAN, JAMES

(1791–1868) *Fifteenth president of the United States (1857–61).*

Despite a long career in politics and diplomacy, Buchanan, the nation's only bachelor president, was an ineffective leader. He lacked the forcefulness to prevent the South from leaving the Union.

Buchanan, who was a conservative Democrat, served in the House of Representatives (1821–31), the Senate (1835–45) and as minister to Russia (1832–34) and Great Britain (1853–56). He was President James K. Polk's secretary of state during the annexation of Texas (1845) and the Mexican War (1846–48).

In 1856, Buchanan won a three-way race for the presidency, winning out over John C. Frémont, candidate of the newly established Republican Party, and Millard Fillmore of the American Party. In an effort to bring unity to a nation bitterly divided over the issues of slavery and states' rights (whether a state's laws should prevail over national laws), he appointed both Northerners and Southerners to his cabinet. His policy of making concessions to the South and his narrow interpretation of his constitutional duties, however, only increased sectional tensions. He especially angered Northerners by endorsing the Lecompton constitution for the new state of Kansas, which would have allowed slavery in that state. They also resented him for supporting the Supreme Court's decision in the *Dred Scott* case (1857), which held that slaves brought to free soil were still their owners' property. His refusal to sponsor Northern economic legislation during the depression of 1857 did not improve matters.

When South Carolina, followed by other Southern states, finally withdrew from the Union after Abraham Lincoln's election in 1860, the usually cautious Buchanan denounced secession and kept control of federal installations in the South during the last few months of his term. He insisted, however, that the Constitution did not give him the power to deal further with the crisis.

In his last speech to Congress, Buchanan declared, "I at least meant well for my country." His policies, however, had further divided the nation and the Democratic Party, ensuring the election of Republican Abraham Lincoln and failing to prevent the coming of the Civil War.

See also Democratic Party. *For events during Buchanan's administration, see* Brown, John; *Dred Scott* Case; Secession.

BARBARA SILBERDICK FEINBERG

BUFFALO BILL
See Cody, Buffalo Bill

BUNCHE, RALPH

(1904–71) *Political scientist, international relations expert, and first African-American winner of the Nobel Peace Prize.*

Bunche won the prize for his work in bringing about an armistice between Israel and its

Middle East neighbors in the conflict over the issue of Palestine. It was the most important of several "firsts" that Bunche achieved in his life.

Bunche grew up in Albuquerque, New Mexico, and, after both his parents died within a few months of each other, in Los Angeles. He excelled in school despite racial prejudice and won a scholarship to the University of California. Then he was awarded a fellowship to Harvard University and in 1934, at the age of thirty, became the first black American to earn a Ph.D. in political science. While attending Harvard, he took time out from his studies to establish the first political science department at Howard University.

After studying in London and South Africa on a grant from the Social Research Council and working with Swedish sociologist Gunnar Myrdal on his landmark study of blacks in the United States, *An American Dilemma*, Bunche scored another first: in 1941, after the United States entered World War II, he became the first African American to hold a desk job in the U.S. State Department. He served as an adviser on dependent territories (countries or regions run by another nation).

After the war, Bunche helped organize the United Nations, one of whose divisions he served as director. He then headed the U.N. staff under Count Folke Bernadotte of Sweden, who was the mediator on the issue of the partitioning of Palestine between the Arabs and Jews living there. After Bernadotte was assassinated on September 17, 1948, Bunche took over his duties and managed to bring about the four armistice agreements necessary to end the fighting in Palestine.

Bunche served in the United Nations until his retirement in 1971. In poor health, he died six months later.

For further reading: Jim Haskins, *One More River to Cross: The Stories of Twelve Black Americans* (New York: Scholastic, 1992); Jim Haskins, *Ralph Bunche: A Most Reluctant Hero* (New York: Hawthorn Books, 1974).

JIM HASKINS

BURGER, WARREN

(1907–   )   *Chief justice of the U.S. Supreme Court.*

Born in St. Paul, Minnesota, Burger was the epitome of the self-made man. As a young man he sold insurance in the daytime and attended college and law school at night. He then practiced law in St. Paul for twenty years and got involved in Republican Party politics. In 1953 he joined the administration of President Dwight D. Eisenhower as an assistant attorney general.

Eisenhower named Burger to the Court of Appeals for the District of Columbia, the most important federal court in the country next to the Supreme Court. There he became known as a conservative who believed in strict construction of the Constitution. By this Burger meant that judges had to interpret the Constitution narrowly, following its exact wording, and not read their own views into the document. A speech he gave criticizing the criminal procedure decisions of the Supreme Court under Chief Justice Earl Warren brought him to the attention of President Richard M. Nixon. In 1969, Nixon named Burger chief justice to succeed Warren.

Many people expected the Burger Court to reverse many of the Warren Court decisions, but in fact the opposite occurred. The Court consolidated many of the earlier decisions, even in the area of criminal law, thus strengthening constitutional protection of people accused of crimes.

Burger himself wrote a number of important decisions regarding the First Amendment. In *Lemon* v. *Kurtzman* (1971) he set out the test of when government aid to religious schools could be approved. And though he and reporters did not get along well, he wrote several opinions supporting the rights of the press in covering trials.

All in all, Burger is not considered one of the better chief justices. Although he did a great deal to improve the administrative workings of the Court, he did not lead it, as John Marshall or Earl Warren had. Nor was he considered strong intellectually, and during his tenure the Court was dominated by the liberal William Brennan.

Burger retired in 1986 and devoted the next few years to leading the nation's bicentennial celebration of the adoption of the U.S. Constitution.

See also Supreme Court.

MELVIN I. UROFSKY

BURR, AARON

(1756–1836)   *Third vice president of the United States (1801–05).*

Burr was educated at Princeton and served in the Revolutionary War before becoming a lawyer. He entered politics as a New York State assemblyman in 1784 and was appointed state attorney general in 1789. In 1791 he was elected to the U.S. Senate.

In 1800, the Democratic-Republican Party nominated him to be Thomas Jefferson's vice president. Until the Twelfth Amendment to the Constitution changed the system in 1804, each elector voted for two candidates for president. The winner became president, and the runner-up, vice president. Jefferson and Burr tied because the Democratic-Republican electors gave one vote to each man. In these circumstances, the House of Representatives had to choose the president. It took

thirty-six ballots before Jefferson beat Burr, who became vice president.

Former secretary of the Treasury Alexander Hamilton, Burr's longtime rival in New York politics, had helped Jefferson win the election. He also engineered Burr's defeat in the 1804 race for governor of New York. When newspapers printed Hamilton's insulting comments about him, Burr felt that Hamilton had turned their political differences into a personal feud. He then challenged Hamilton to a duel. When they met in Weehawken, New Jersey, on July 11, 1804, Burr killed his opponent instead of wounding him, as was customary, and fled south to avoid charges.

For the next three years, Burr and Gen. James Wilkinson conspired to set up a new country by seizing territory west of the Appalachians, including land belonging to Mexico. Burr was leading a small group of armed men on a mysterious expedition down the Mississippi when Wilkinson betrayed him. Burr fled but was arrested in Alabama in 1807. Chief Justice John Marshall presided over his trial for treason, but he was acquitted for lack of evidence.

In 1808, Burr traveled to Europe in a vain attempt to interest foreign governments in his failed schemes. After returning to New York in 1812, he spent the rest of his life practicing law.

See also Hamilton, Alexander.

BARBARA SILBERDICK FEINBERG

BUSH, GEORGE

(1924–   )   *Forty-first president of the United States (1989–93).*

The high point of George Bush's presidency came in February 1991, when he announced victory in Operation Desert Storm, the Gulf War against Iraq. The war was fought after Iraq refused to withdraw from its occupation of Kuwait. Before and during the fighting, Bush explained his Iraq policy clearly, rallying the nation behind the war. His popularity soared. But the president was not always so deft at communicating his stand on public issues—one reason he lost his reelection bid the next year.

Born to wealth, his father a U.S. senator from Connecticut, Bush served in the navy during World War II, graduated from Yale, moved to Texas, and made a fortune in oil. He entered Republican party politics and was elected to the House of Representatives in 1966 and 1968. He voted as a moderate while demonstrating strong party loyalty. After he lost a race for the Senate in 1970, Republican presidents rewarded his loyalty with high-level jobs including ambassador to the United Nations and head of the CIA.

In 1980, Bush sought the Republican nomination for president, but lost to Ronald Reagan. He had rejected Reagan's ultraconservative positions, but when he became Reagan's vice president, he adopted those positions wholeheartedly. During their eight years in office, Bush's loyalty to President Reagan never wavered.

As president, Bush's strength lay in foreign affairs. In addition to Desert Storm, he ordered an invasion of Panama that resulted in that country's military strongman being captured and convicted on drug charges in American courts. Bush witnessed the collapse of communism in Eastern Europe and the breakup of the Soviet Union.

But on the domestic front, his administration drifted. He broke his campaign promise not to raise taxes. Once a supporter of civil rights legislation, he refused to sign an anti-discrimination measure into law. As the economy worsened, Bush expressed little concern for the poor and jobless while vetoing bills that would have raised wages, given family leave to workers, and offered health care tax breaks to the needy. He lost the 1992 election to Arkansas governor Bill Clinton.

See also Gulf War.

ANN E. WEISS

BYRD, RICHARD E.

(1888–1957) *Explorer and naval officer.*

A member of a distinguished Virginia family that produced two U.S. senators in the twentieth century, Richard E. Byrd became one of the world's most famous modern explorers. He graduated from the U.S. Naval Academy in 1912, served as a naval officer in World War I, and was promoted to the rank of rear admiral in 1930.

Byrd commanded an expedition to the Arctic in 1926. With co-pilot Floyd Bennett, he flew the first plane over the North Pole. For their achievement Byrd and Bennett each won the Congressional Medal of Honor. In 1927, a few weeks after Charles Lindbergh's famous solo flight, Byrd and three companions attempted a nonstop flight from New York to Paris, carrying the first transatlantic airmail. Bad weather forced their plane to crash-land on the coast of France.

In 1928, Byrd began his first expedition to Antarctica. He established his base, which he called Little America, on the Ross Ice Shelf near the Bay of Whales. While exploring the vast new territory, he made the first airplane flight over the South Pole in 1929.

The second Byrd Antarctic expedition, from 1933 to 1935, undertook many scientific research projects. To study weather conditions, Byrd lived alone for five months in a tiny hut and endured temperatures as low as −76°F. Fumes from a clogged chimney almost killed him before he was rescued by a tractor party. During his third trip to Antarctica, from 1939 to 1941, Byrd made flights that resulted in the discovery of five islands and some mountain ranges.

In 1946–47, Admiral Byrd commanded the largest Antarctic expedition in history, composed of more than four thousand persons and many ships and planes. The explorers made aerial maps of the continent's coastline and discovered an area equal in size to that of Germany and France. On his last visit to Antarctica in 1955–56, Byrd was in charge of Operation Deepfreeze, a project undertaken to provide scientific information for the Geophysical Year of 1957 and 1958.

EDMUND LINDOP

CABINET

Imagine yourself president of the United States. You face decisions on many complicated issues. Should a new space station be built? How can we improve our cities? Should taxes be raised?

Where will you get advice about these issues? One place will be your cabinet, made up of the secretaries of the various federal departments, the vice president, and other high-ranking officials. Since the time of George Washington, the cabinet has been the formal body that advises presidents about the affairs of the nation. Members of the cabinet are appointed by the president. They must be approved by the Senate, but the president can dismiss a cabinet official whenever he wishes.

Early Cabinets
The term *cabinet* was borrowed from England, where it referred to the king's close advisers. (The advisers met in small private rooms, which were called cabinets in those days; thus, the name.) Interestingly, the Founding Fathers said nothing about a cabinet in the Constitution. Congress created the Departments of Foreign Affairs (soon renamed State), War, and Treasury in 1789. Their heads, Thomas Jefferson at State, Henry Knox at War, and Alexander Hamilton at Treasury, along with Attorney General Edmund Randolph, formed the first cabinet. At the start Washington consulted individually

with these men, but beginning in 1791 he began calling them together to discuss important issues. No cabinet since has been as important an advisory body as Washington's. Nor has any cabinet had as influential a figure in it as Hamilton. Hamilton dominated the cabinet by earning Washington's trust and by suggesting important goals for the new government.

Washington's cabinet (like many later ones) witnessed strong disagreements among its members. Arguments between Jefferson and Hamilton over government policy greatly distressed Washington and finally drove Jefferson to resign. Washington's successor, John Adams, experienced a different problem. His cabinet members seemed more loyal to Hamilton than to him!

In the nineteenth century the cabinet's influence declined. Two major reasons explain this. First, presidents began to use cabinet appointments as a way to reward important political groups. Presidents often did not know well or completely trust some cabinet members. And second, presidents began looking to informal groups of friends for advice. Andrew Jackson had his "Kitchen Cabinet," Grover Cleveland his "Fishing Cabinet," Theodore Roosevelt his "Tennis Cabinet," Warren G. Harding his "Poker Cabinet," and Franklin D. Roosevelt his "Brain Trust."

Still, some presidents used their cabinets effectively. James K. Polk held around 350 cabinet meetings, more than any other one-term president. Abraham Lincoln surrounded himself with a strong-willed cabinet, which he often turned to for advice. But Lincoln never let his cabinet officials forget who was in charge. His vote was the only one that mattered.

The cabinet grew in size as more departments were created: the Department of Navy (1798), the Department of Interior (1849), the Post Office Department (1872), and the Department of Agriculture (1889). In the twentieth century the size and complexity of the federal government increased greatly. This meant the cabinet continued to grow, until today it contains fourteen departments (War and Navy were combined into Defense and the Post Office was removed). Since the mid-twentieth century the vice president has also been a regular member of the cabinet.

Cabinet Functions

Modern presidents have used their cabinets in different ways. Dwight D. Eisenhower and Gerald R. Ford probably tried the hardest to make their cabinets true councils of state. Ronald Reagan formed smaller councils within the cabinet to deal with specific issues. But various developments, including large White House staffs close to the president and the tendency of cabinet officials to place the good of their own department over the wider interests of the president, have made attempts to use the cabinet as Washington did very difficult.

The cabinet nevertheless continues to be important as a place where the president may try out ideas on a group reflecting many different interests. Cabinet officials now are chosen not only for their expertise but also as representatives of America's social diversity. Frances Perkins, Franklin Roosevelt's secretary of labor, was the first woman cabinet member. Robert Weaver, Lyndon B. Johnson's secretary of housing and urban development, was the first black. And Bill Clinton made a point of emphasizing that his cabinet would "look like America." To this end, he appointed both men and women, as well as members of several minority groups.

The cabinet also carries symbolic importance. Photographs of the president seated about the great cabinet table flanked by department heads (the secretary of state and secretary of treasury sit on the president's immediate right and left, indicating the seniority of their offices) reassure Americans that the president is consulting with wise representatives of the country.

Some prominent cabinet members in American history have included John Quincy Adams, William H. Seward, Dean Acheson, Henry Kissinger (all secretaries of state), Andrew Mellon (secretary of treasury), and Herbert Hoover (secretary of commerce).

BENJAMIN MCARTHUR

CALDER, ALEXANDER

(1898–1976)   *Artist and inventor of the mobile.*

Recognized internationally as a major twentieth-century artist, Calder was born in Lawnton (now part of Philadelphia), Pennsylvania. Preoccupied with abstract art, he once said that his primary subject matter was "the universe."

The son and grandson of sculptors, "Sandy" Calder was nine when his parents gave him his first tools and a room in their basement for a workshop. "Mother and father were all for my efforts to build things myself," he recalled in his autobiography. Using bits of trash, he constructed imaginative toys for himself and his sister.

A 1939 mobile by Alexander Calder, Lobster Trap and Fish Tail. *His works include paintings, tapestries, jewelry, sculpture, toys, and stage sets, but he is best known for his mobiles, an art form he invented.*

Following high school, Calder earned a degree in mechanical engineering at the Stevens Institute of Technology in Hoboken, New Jersey. Later, deciding to become an artist, he studied painting and drawing for three years at the Art Students League in New York. In the late 1920s, after moving to Paris and in need of a timepiece, he made his first wire sculpture—a sundial in the form of a rooster standing on one leg.

A roly-poly, baby-faced man with unruly hair and a wonderful sense of humor that permeates his art, Calder was enormously versatile. His works include paintings in oil and gouache, drawings, engravings, jewelry, tapestries, rugs, toys, stage sets, and sculpture in bronze, Plexiglas, wood, and wire. A miniature *Circus* of wire animals and toys that he started constructing in his twenties is on permanent display at the Whitney Museum of American Art in New York.

Combining his artistic and engineering skills, Calder in the 1930s created a refreshing new kind of sculpture dubbed "mobiles." Freeing sculpture from its base, he initiated what we now call "art in motion." His larger sculptures, which were motionless, he called "stabiles." Lionized in his lifetime—his remarkably original works were displayed in the world's most important museums—Calder divided his time between his homes and studios in Connecticut and France. Today Calder mobiles and stabiles dominate many city plazas and public buildings around the world.

See also Painting and Sculpture.

PATRICIA CONDON JOHNSTON

CALHOUN, JOHN C.

(1782–1850)   *Congressman, senator, cabinet member, and vice president (1825–32).*

Calhoun entered national politics in 1810 when South Carolina elected him to the first of three consecutive terms in the U.S. House of Representatives. As a young congressman, he was one of the War Hawks who helped maneuver the United States into war with Great Britain in 1812. During his years in the House, Calhoun was an ardent nationalist, who supported a high tariff and a national bank. He left the House in 1817 when President James Monroe appointed him secretary of war, a position he held until his election as vice president in 1824.

Calhoun served first under President John Quincy Adams. Four years later, when Andrew Jackson won the presidency, Calhoun was reelected to the vice presidency. By this time, however, his views had radically changed. No longer a fervid nationalist, he had become a strong champion of states' rights, low tariffs, and slavery.

In 1828, southerners were furious at Congress for passing the so-called Tariff of Abominations, which they claimed imposed high tariffs on goods imported by southerners in order to benefit northern manufacturers and farmers. To protest this tariff, Calhoun wrote the *South Carolina Exposition,* a paper stating that the new tariff law was unconstitutional and that every state had the right to declare such a law null and void within its borders—a principle called "nullification."

When another high tariff was adopted in 1832, South Carolina nullified it. Calhoun then resigned as vice president and was elected to the Senate from South Carolina. President Jackson threatened to enforce the tariff law with troops, but an armed clash was averted when Congress passed a compromise tariff measure.

Except for a brief period in 1844–45 when he was secretary of state, Calhoun served in the Senate for the rest of his life. For many years he was regarded as the chief spokesman for the South, and he vigorously defended slavery and a low tariff as necessary to sustain the southern economy.

See also Nullification Controversy; War Hawks.

EDMUND LINDOP

CALIFORNIA GOLD RUSH
See Gold Rushes.

CAMPAIGNS, PRESIDENTIAL
See Elections (table).

CANALS
See Erie Canal; Panama Canal.

CAPONE, AL
(1899–1947)   *Gangster.*

Alphonse Capone, the most notorious mobster in American history, was born in Naples, Italy, and grew up in Brooklyn, New York. He quit school after sixth grade to join a teenage street gang run by hoodlum Johnny Torrio. During those years a cut across his left cheek from ear to lip gave him the nickname "Scarface."

By 1919 Torrio had enlisted in a Chicago crime syndicate and needed a loyal henchman. He called Al Capone. Shortly afterward Torrio's boss was murdered—probably by Capone himself—and the two took over the operation. Then in 1925, as profits began to soar from the illegal liquor trade during Prohibition, Torrio retired.

Capone and his men now began a brutal war against rivals in the Chicago underworld that captured headlines nationwide. Although they used everything from baseball bats to hand grenades, their favorite weapon was the Thompson submachine gun, which could spray a hundred .45 caliber bullets with a single pull of the trigger. Contrary to popular belief, most gangsters avoided the tommy gun as too tricky to fire accurately, but Capone's killers were experts. When thugs dressed like police blasted the Moran gang to pieces with machine guns on St. Valentine's

Day 1929, other mobsters knew instantly who was responsible. "Only Capone kills like that," said one.

Thus Al Capone became lord of illegal alcohol, gambling, and prostitution in Chicago, building a personal fortune estimated at $100 million. He lived like a celebrity, arriving grandly at theaters and sporting events in his armored limousine and entertaining his guests, including city officials, lavishly.

But federal authorities, especially Eliot Ness's famous Untouchables, worked to convict him under the new income tax laws. He was sent to the Atlanta penitentiary in 1932 and then transferred to Alcatraz in 1934. An advanced case of venereal disease left him partially paralyzed, and in 1939 he was re-

Chicago gangster Al Capone (in all-white hat at left) leaving court at the conclusion of his 1931 trial. Because it was difficult to secure evidence against him for his many more serious crimes, he was charged with and convicted of income tax evasion. He served his prison sentence at Alcatraz, the country's most notorious high-security prison, situated on a rocky island in San Francisco Bay.

leased to a hospital in Baltimore. He spent the rest of his life as an invalid, shut up in his Miami Beach estate.

See also Crime.

JAN CHARLES HALUSKA

CARNEGIE, ANDREW

(1835–1919)   *Industrialist and philanthropist.*

During his long life Andrew Carnegie made a huge fortune and used it wisely to help others. His life as a boy in Scotland pushed him toward both getting and giving. His mother taught him to be thrifty and enterprising in the Scottish tradition. When his father, a weaver of wool cloth, was put out of work by weaving machines, the boy experienced the pain of being poor and therefore became impressed with the importance of making money. But because his idealistic father and uncles believed in and worked for liberty and justice for all people, young Andy also learned that there was more to life than acquiring riches. When he was twelve his family sought a better life in America, the land of promise for both material gain and social justice.

In the new land they got help from relatives and other Scots, who led them to Pittsburgh, Pennsylvania. That city had coal and iron nearby, as well as rivers and railroads for shipping goods to the rest of the nation. So it prospered as American industry boomed, and young Andrew rose with it.

As a bright, alert telegrapher Carnegie won the favor of Thomas A. Scott, a high official of the Pennsylvania Railroad. With Scott's help, Carnegie at twenty-four became superintendent of the western division. Backed by loans, advice, and influence from Scott, Car-

negie made money buying and selling stock, and by his thirties he was a rich investor and running several business enterprises. He was careful with the money he made, and so when a depression hit American business in the 1870s Carnegie was able to buy out firms that had gone heavily into debt.

At this time, the new Bessemer process was revolutionizing the making of steel. (It burned out impurities by forcing air through molten pig iron, thus producing five tons of steel in half an hour, whereas the old process took 350 hours to make fifty pounds.) Carnegie decided to concentrate all his money and time in that rising industry. He found and hired the best people in steel technology and plant management. Instead of selling stock in his enterprise, which would have given stockholders a voice in running it, he financed and enlarged it out of his own profits. And in running it he outsmarted all his rivals. He kept up with the latest technology, held down wages, drove his men and equipment hard, and used the accounting and coordinating techniques he had learned from the railroad. So he was able to undersell his competitors. By his sixties he dominated the American steel industry. In 1901 he sold out to a combination of bankers and investors for $250 million, a large sum even now, but a fabulous fortune in those days.

He had not forgotten his boyhood concern for social justice, however. Years before, he had publicly urged rich men to use their wealth for the welfare of their fellow human beings. The man who dies rich dies disgraced, he had written. In retirement as one of the world's richest men, he paid for thousands of library buildings throughout the United States, set up foundations for science, medicine, and education, built New York City's famous Carnegie Hall for music, and much more. By the time he died at eighty-three he had given away most of his riches. He did not die poor, but neither did he die disgraced.

ROBERT V. BRUCE

CARPETBAGGERS AND SCALAWAGS

These were names given to white Republicans in the southern states during the Reconstruction period. Carpetbaggers were northerners who came to the South after the Civil War. They were called carpetbaggers because many of them carried their possessions in a

Political cartoonist Thomas Nast's 1872 caricature of a carpetbagger after the Civil War. He is depicted as southerners saw him—a villainous Northerner, carrying carpetbags filled with his belongings and heading south to take advantage of the defeated Confederacy. The cartoon's legend read: "The bag in front of him, filled with others' faults, he always sees. The one filled with his own faults he never sees." In reality, carpetbaggers were ordinary businessmen, teachers, preachers, and the like.

bag made of carpeting. White southerners looked upon them as seedy, down-at-the-heel types. Actually many were respectable, well-educated, and fairly prosperous. Some came to teach and work with the recently freed slaves to help them get established in their new lives. Others were seeking business opportunities, such as buying up abandoned plantations and investing in railroads. Some became officeholders during the late 1860s and early 1870s, when the South was under military rule and the Republican Party controlled most public offices.

The scalawags were native southerners who supported the Republican administrations. Some did so merely to obtain political jobs. Others were small farmers who disliked the old planter class, whose members were nearly all Democrats. Some were Unionists who had opposed secession in 1861.

Most white southerners disliked both carpetbaggers and scalawags. They charged the former with being greedy invaders, the latter with being traitors, and all with being far too friendly toward blacks.

See also Reconstruction.

CARS
See Automobiles.

CARSON, RACHEL

(1907–64)   *Writer, environmentalist, and biologist.*

Growing up along the Allegheny River in Springdale, Pennsylvania, Carson developed from childhood a deep love for the birds and animals in the woodlands near her home. She loved books and writing as well and entered Pennsylvania College for Women (now Chatham College) as an English major. She later changed her field of study to biology, though she was warned that there would be little work for a "lady biologist."

After graduate study at Johns Hopkins University, she combined her talents as a writer with her scientific interests, publishing an article on sea creatures in the *Atlantic Monthly* in 1937. That article eventually led to the publication of three books—*Under the Sea Wind, The Sea around Us,* and *The Edge of the Sea.* Through these books—and a fourth, *A Sense of Wonder,* a book inspired by her ten-year-old nephew—Rachel Carson, now editor-in-chief of the Office of Information of the U.S. Fish and Wildlife Service, gave the American public a new way to look at nature.

In 1958, concerned about the widespread use of DDT, a chemical used to kill mosquitoes and other insects, she began to study its effects on fish, birds, and animals farther up the food chain. In 1962 she brought out *Silent Spring,* which described the "silence [that] lay over the fields and woods and marsh" after they had been sprayed with DDT. Although she was at first attacked as an "alarmist" and a "sentimental birdwatcher," Carson was later proved right when the U.S. government issued a report that supported her findings.

Rachel Carson died of breast cancer in 1964 without seeing the long-range results of her work, but sixteen years after her death President Jimmy Carter gave the presidential Medal of Freedom to the "lady biologist" who had helped launch the environmental movement in the United States.

See also Conservation and Environmental Movements.

For further reading: Linda Peavy and Ursula Smith, *Dreams into Deeds: Nine Women Who Dared* (New York: Scribner's, 1985).

LINDA PEAVY
URSULA SMITH

CARTER, JIMMY

(1924–   )   *Thirty-ninth president of the United States (1977–81).*

James Earl "Jimmy" Carter was the first candidate from the Deep South to be elected president since the Civil War. A nuclear submarine naval officer, Georgia peanut farmer, and businessman, Carter was part of the generation of southern politicians who emerged as a result of the civil rights movement.

In his single term as Georgia governor (1971–75), he gained little national attention. But when he ran for president in 1976, American voters were disgusted by the Watergate revelations of corruption, and they responded warmly to the smiling soft-spoken southerner who promised: "I'll never lie to you." His middle-of-the-road economic views, his support for civil rights, and his background as a deeply religious southerner helped him assemble a fragile coalition of traditional Democrats, blacks, and southern whites in order to narrowly defeat incumbent Gerald Ford with 50.1 percent of the vote.

His greatest achievements as president lay in foreign policy. In 1977, Carter persuaded the Congress to transfer control of the Panama Canal to the government of Panama. He played a major role in negotiating the Camp David accords, a peace agreement between Israel and Egypt signed in 1979, which was the first break in thirty years of conflict between the new nation of Israel and its Arab neighbors.

But events overseas also proved his undoing. In the aftermath of the 1973 oil embargo by Middle Eastern countries, Americans' wages had failed to keep pace with higher prices. The Soviet Union invaded Afghanistan, which led to heightened tensions with the United States. When Islamic revolutionaries in the once pro-American country of Iran seized the American embassy in the fall of 1979 and held fifty-two Americans hostage for more than a year, voters lost faith in Carter, and he went down to a smashing defeat at the hands of Ronald Reagan.

In 1986, Jimmy Carter founded the Carter Center of Emory University, a private organization devoted to settling international disputes and dealing with the health and social problems of the poor at home and abroad. In the years since his defeat he has become a highly admired and respected former president.

For events during Carter's administration, see Iran Hostage Crisis; Panama Canal.

DAN T. CARTER

CARVER, GEORGE WASHINGTON

(c. 1864–1943)   *Agricultural chemist and educator.*

An African-American scientist whose work revolutionized American agriculture, Carver helped bring prosperity to poor regions of the rural South by introducing new techniques to the farmers and new agricultural products to the world.

Born a slave in Missouri, Carver was orphaned as a child and raised in the household of Moses Carver, a German farmer to whom his parents had belonged. He was on his own from the age of thirteen, but managed to work his way through Simpson College in Iowa, where he was the second African American to be admitted, and Iowa State Agricultural College, where he was at first refused entrance because of his race. He earned an M.S. in agriculture there in 1896.

The year he graduated, Carver received an

George Washington Carver, botanist and teacher, working in his laboratory at Tuskegee Institute in Alabama.

invitation from the African-American educator Booker T. Washington to create an agriculture department at Tuskegee Institute in Alabama. "I cannot offer you money, position, or fame," Washington wrote Carver. "I offer you in their place: work—hard, hard work, the task of bringing a people from degradation, poverty, and waste to full manhood." Carver accepted the challenge and spent the rest of his life teaching and experimenting at Tuskegee.

Carver made many contributions to the theory and practice of crop rotation and soil conservation with his "school on wheels," a traveling classroom that introduced new equipment, techniques, and crops to local farmers. He discovered that peanuts and sweet potatoes both improved the soil and were better cash crops than the cotton that then dominated southern agriculture. He developed 75 new commercial products from pecans, more than 100 from sweet potatoes, and some 325 from peanuts. He took out a patent on only one of his findings, preferring that others benefit from his work. (A patent gives an inventor the exclusive right to make, use, or sell an invention. Others must pay the inventor a fee if they wish to use the invention.)

Carver left his savings to Tuskegee when he died. As a role model for African-American youth, he had an important influence on race relations as well as on agricultural research.

See also African Americans: 1877–1945; Agriculture.

For further reading: Carol Greene, *George Washington Carver: Scientist and Teacher* (Emeryville, Calif.: Children's Book Press, 1992).

DENNIS WEPMAN

CASSATT, MARY

(1844–1926)   *Artist.*

Cassatt was a pioneer in two ways: she was the only American to become a fully accepted member of the French impressionist art movement, and she was the first woman to become an important figure in modern art.

Born in Pittsburgh, the sister of Alexander Cassatt, the president of the Pennsylvania Railroad, Mary Cassatt studied at the Pennsylvania Academy of Fine Arts in Philadelphia. She was determined to pursue a career in the field, although few opportunities existed for women, and moved to Paris, the center of modern art, in 1866. As women were not admitted to the better art schools there, she worked alone in museums, copying classical paintings. But when she saw the work of Edgar Degas, one of the leaders of the new

and not-yet-accepted style of art later known as impressionism, she so admired it that she persuaded him to accept her as a student, the only one he ever had.

Cassatt worked and exhibited with the impressionists from 1877 to 1886, mastering their style of free, loose brushwork and natural light. She had her first solo show in Paris in 1893. A specialist in oil and pastel portraits of women with their children, she became known as "the painter and poet of the nursery." She also became an expert at etching and engraving and is now considered one of America's most important printmakers.

Beginning in the mid-1890s, Cassatt's style grew increasingly distinct from that of the impressionists. Always identifiably American in their clear, three-dimensional forms, her paintings and prints employed stronger, less delicate colors and sharper details. In her last years, as her eyesight began to fail, she painted less and devoted her efforts to promoting the impressionists in the United States, where she succeeded in placing many in important collections.

Mary Cassatt broke no new ground in art, but the strength and sensitivity of her work has earned her a place among the major artists of the turn of the century.

See also Painting and Sculpture.

For further reading: Susan E. Meyer, *Mary Cassatt* (New York: Abrams, 1990).

DENNIS WEPMAN

CATHER, WILLA

(1873–1947)   *Novelist, poet, and critic.*

Cather, the most famous writer about the last days of the midwestern frontier, created perceptive psychological stories of pioneer life.

Willa Cather wrote novels and stories capturing the spirit of pioneer life.

Her vivid descriptions of the land, her sensitive understanding of human personality, and her knowledge of history made her novels an important chronicle of the period.

Born in Virginia, Cather moved to Nebraska at the age of nine and spent her early life among the European immigrants who settled in that harsh new land. Her best-known novels reflect this background. Written with cool objectivity but great sympathy, they portray the emotional conflicts of their characters with powerful understated force.

In *O Pioneers!* (1913), *My Ántonia* (1918), and *A Lost Lady* (1923), all novels describing the struggles of women living on the frontier, Cather drew directly from her childhood experiences. In *The Song of the Lark* (1915) and *Lucy Greatheart* (1935), her characters escape from the prairie and make careers in music.

Cather won the Pulitzer Prize for *One of Ours* (1922), in which a discontented young man finds freedom from midwestern farm life as a soldier during World War I.

Cather herself left the Midwest after graduating from the University of Nebraska in 1895. She moved to Pittsburgh, Pennsylvania, where she taught high school and wrote newspaper articles and drama criticism. In 1906 she went to New York City to become managing editor of *McClure's* magazine. She held that position until 1912, after which she devoted herself entirely to her writing.

In her later novels and short stories, Cather explored other areas. She described the desert country of New Mexico in *Death Comes for the Archbishop* (1927) and early Quebec in *Shadows on the Rock* (1931), two historical novels about the struggles of Catholic churchmen on the frontier. In these, as in her work set in Nebraska, Cather provides moving accounts of human courage and dedication in the face of suffering.

See also Literature.

DENNIS WEPMAN

CATHOLIC CHURCH

The first permanent settlement in the United States was made by Spanish Catholics at St. Augustine, Florida, in 1565. This was forty-two years before the Jamestown colony was founded and fifty-five years before the Pilgrims landed on Plymouth Rock. Catholics have played an important role in American history ever since. Today, one in five Americans is a Catholic. With 57 million adherents, the Catholic church is by far the largest single denomination in the United States. (All Protestant sects combined total 79 million.)

Maryland was established as a Catholic colony in 1634 by Cecil Calvert, the second Lord Baltimore. Calvert was a Catholic, but members of that religion were a minority in his colony from the outset. Among those who disembarked from the *Ark* and the *Dove* were three Jesuit priests and sixteen "gentlemen-adventurers," as well as a host of servants, laborers, and artisans, most of whom were Protestants. Because of this, religious freedom was declared for all Christians (though not for Jews). Such tolerance lasted only until 1645 when Virginia adventurers sacked the colony. The Calverts regained control and then lost it again. By 1689 Protestants were in firm control and Catholics were severely oppressed.

To understand these religious conflicts one must go back to 1534, when the pope in Rome forbade Henry VIII of England to divorce Catherine of Aragon so that he could marry Anne Boleyn in hopes of obtaining a male heir. Henry then defied the pope and established his own Church of England, which permitted him to divorce. This launched two centuries of religious turmoil in England between Catholics and Protestants, both Anglicans (Church of England, or Episcopalians) and Puritans. Catholic churches, monasteries, and seminaries were seized or destroyed. Adherents of one religion were murdered by those of another. There was open warfare for control of the state. Charles I was beheaded, leading to the Commonwealth under Oliver Cromwell, a Puritan, in 1649. Anglicans returned to power in 1660 under Charles II.

Much of this turmoil was imported to America. Protestantism was dominant in the English colonies, especially Anglicans in Virginia and Puritans in New England, where a theocracy, or government by the church, was established. Catholics were a small minority in the English colonies. They were dominant, however, in the rest of the continent and South America. In what became the United States, Spanish Catholics settled Florida and the Southwest, what is now Mexico, Arizona, and California. A string of missions was established as the Spanish sought to convert Indians to Christianity. The French, spreading along the St. Lawrence River into the Great Lakes area and down the Mississippi River to New Orleans, also brought Catholicism to America.

Oppression of Catholics largely ceased with the American Revolution, which they wholeheartedly supported. Charles Carroll of Maryland, a Catholic, was a signer of the Declaration of Independence, a member of the First Continental Congress, and a "flaming patriot." Another Marylander of great influence in the postrevolutionary period was John Carroll, the first Catholic bishop in the United States. He founded the first Catholic college (Georgetown University in Washington) and the first seminary to train American priests. Catholic churches, or parishes, were controlled then by members, not the clergy. Carroll sought to limit the authority of the pope in Rome to spiritual matters. This was an effort to adapt Catholicism to the American ideals of individual liberty and the separation of church and state.

But the efforts to create a special American Catholicism foundered under an influx of immigrants from Europe. It began about 1820 and continued for a century. In large measure these immigrants were Catholic and brought with them the European traditions of the church, which attached greater importance to the pope and the clergy. Catholic immigration came in ethnic waves and in astonishing numbers. The first to come were the Irish, eventually 4.1 million of them. The Irish became dominant in American Catholicism, probably because they were English speaking. The German immigration was larger than the Irish, over 5 million, but only an estimated 30 percent of them were Catholic. Beginning in the 1880s, about 3.8 million Italian Catholics came to the United States, but around 2.1 million of them returned to Italy after saving some money. The ranks of Catholics in America were swelled by the arrival of more than 2 million Poles, nearly a million French-Canadians, and large numbers of Mexicans, Slovaks, Czechs, Lithuanians, and Ukrainians. America truly became the "melting pot of nations."

The vast number of Catholic immigrants led to outbreaks of anti-Catholicism marked by violence, including lynchings and arson. In May 1844, Philadelphia was the scene of religious rioting. Two Catholic churches were burned and thirteen people killed. In the 1850s the Know-Nothing Party and its anti-immigrant, anti-Catholic platform won control of several city and state governments. An issue in the election of 1884 was "rum, Romanism, and rebellion." Violent organizations such as the American Protective Association and the Ku Klux Klan carried on anti-Catholic campaigns well into the twentieth century. The doctrine of papal infallibility (which states that the pope cannot be wrong when speaking officially about Christian faith or morals), adopted by the First Vatican Council in 1870, plus what has been called the "Cult of the Papacy" (the great popularity of popes since the 1940s), encouraged Protestant fears that Rome controlled American Catholics politically.

Such fears were not laid to rest until 1960 when the Catholic John F. Kennedy, while running for president, told a group of Protestant ministers in Houston, "I do not accept the right of any ecclesiastical official to tell me what to do in the sphere of my public responsibility as an elected official." He was elected president by a narrow margin, becoming the first and so far only Catholic president. Catholics, however, are now routinely elected governors, senators, and representatives. The issue of separation of church and state is for the most part settled in America. The only area still hotly debated is the influence of the church on the issues of abortion and contraception, both of which the Catholic church strongly opposes. But the ideal of an American Catholic church envisioned by Bishop John Carroll has largely come to pass.

ROBERT A. LISTON

CATT, CARRIE CHAPMAN

(1859–1947)   *Woman suffragist and peace activist.*

Catt was one of the most important leaders in securing the right to vote for American women.

Carrie Lane was born in Ripon, Wisconsin, and moved with her family to a farm on the Iowa frontier when she was seven. After graduating from Iowa State College at Ames, she became superintendent of schools in Mason City—an unusual achievement at a time when women were expected to stay home and keep house. In 1885, she married Leo Chapman, a newspaper editor, and moved with him to San Francisco. The following year her husband died, leaving her to survive on her own.

As a struggling young widow, Carrie

Chapman quickly realized that women had little control over their lives and virtually no way to change their situation. Convinced that women could improve conditions for themselves if they were allowed to vote, Chapman devoted herself to the cause of woman suffrage. In 1890 she joined the National American Woman Suffrage Association (NAWSA), which sought to secure the vote for women nationwide. In the same year, she married George W. Catt, who shared her commitment to woman suffrage. She later wrote that he let her do the reforming for them both while he earned a living for them both.

An excellent public speaker and gifted organizer, Carrie Chapman Catt served as president of NAWSA from 1900 to 1904 and again from 1915 to 1920. She led dozens of local and statewide campaigns while striving for the ultimate goal of securing an amendment to the U.S. Constitution permitting women to vote. President Woodrow Wilson, at Catt's urging, finally backed the proposal, and Congress approved an amendment in 1919. The states ratified the Nineteenth Amendment on August 26, 1920, and the battle was won.

In 1920, Catt founded the League of Women Voters to help women participate effectively in the political process they were now part of. In the decades that followed, she turned her energy to the prevention of war. Until the end of her life she traveled widely, pleading eloquently for international understanding and world peace.

See also Feminist Movement to 1919; League of Women Voters; Voting.

DEBORAH KENT

CCC
See Civilian Conservation Corps.

CENSORSHIP

The year was 1977 and the Spanish people were lined up for blocks, waiting hours to vote for the first time in their history. One old gentleman said, "It is better now. We can speak." For forty years, to criticize Spain's dictator Francisco Franco or his actions meant arrest, imprisonment, torture, even death.

We Americans have been guaranteed the right to speak—and write—for over two hundred years. We take it for granted and find it hard to believe that a majority of people on earth do not have this right. Our freedom rests in the First Amendment to the Constitution, the first article of our Bill of Rights: "Congress shall make no law . . . abridging the freedom of speech, or of the press."

If these fourteen words give us great liberty, they also cause enormous problems, for obviously there are some limits to what can be said or written. A person cannot cry "Fire" in a crowded building when there is no fire; use the telephone or mails to send obscene or threatening messages; reveal military or other vital secrets.

No one seriously quarrels with these limits on our freedoms of speech and press. The problems arise when people try to add further limits—that is, to *censor* what is said or written so as to shape the knowledge and thoughts of others. Throughout American history, censors have sought to ban certain information or ideas on moral grounds. The battles have been fought in the courts of law and of public opinion.

The most famous censor in American history was Anthony Comstock. Through various organizations and as a special agent for the U.S. Post Office in 1865, he sought for

American censors during World War II inspecting mail. After reading the letters, they placed a censor's stamp on the envelope.

over half a century to ban "every obscene, lewd, lascivious, or filthy book, pamphlet, picture, paper, writing, print, or other publication of an indecent character." Comstock estimated he had convicted enough persons during his career to fill a passenger train of sixty-one coaches and had destroyed over 160 tons of obscene literature. He had a large following for a time, but eventually he became a subject of national ridicule. In commenting on his death in 1915, the *New Republic* said he had "conspicuously made an ass of himself"—a word that could not have been printed in Comstock's heyday.

America has had many groups seeking to censor what people read. Among the more famous was the Watch and Ward Society in Boston, founded in the 1880s. It sought for decades to regulate which books could be sold in the city. Being "banned in Boston" became an article of national scorn—and a sure way to sell books. Even today groups try to limit books available in public and school libraries, denouncing such classics as *Catcher in the Rye* and *Huckleberry Finn*. Librarians are under pressure to hide certain books on

obscure shelves or not stock them at all.

Most censorship today, as with librarians, is subtle, taking the form of "self-regulation." The film industry censors movies by deciding who may see them. First, such labels as G for General, R for Restricted, and X for Pornographic are affixed. Then these are further broken down into the age groups who may see the variously rated films. Television hires censors to rule on the content of programs. And "watchdog" groups exert pressure on advertisers not to sponsor programs they

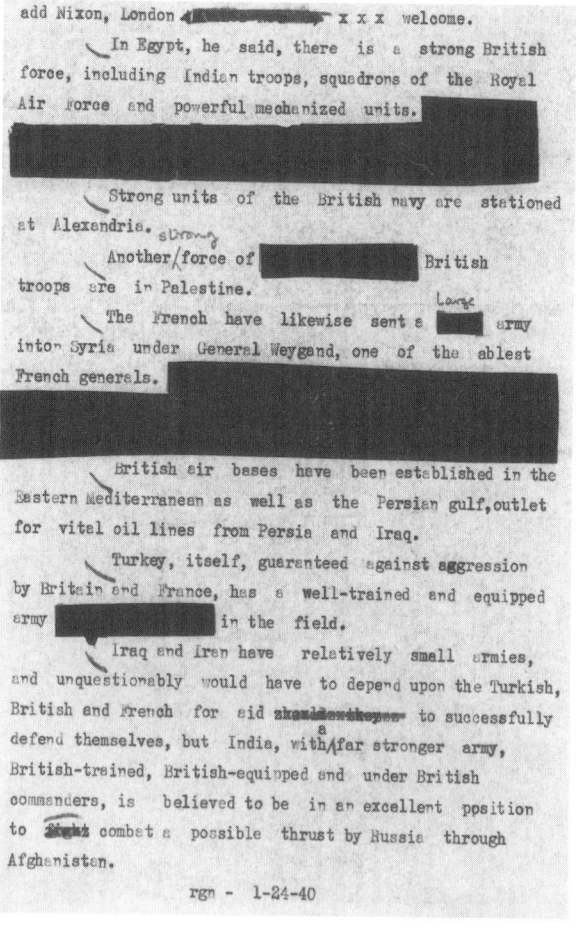

An example of a censored news dispatch from World War II. Passages from this release, sent by an American correspondent from London to his New York headquarters, have been removed with scissors.

believe are offensive. The recording and publishing industries, faced with the threat of organized boycotts (the refusal to buy a product), also censor themselves.

Critics of censorship argue that it interferes with the free flow of information and ideas that society depends upon for growth and sound decisions by its citizens. Advocates argue that some knowledge and ideas are harmful, especially to children. What an adult may understand may be confusing to a child, they say. Both arguments have merit. Some censorship is clearly necessary, as in the case of someone yelling "Fire" in a crowded theater. The problem, however, is twofold: what is to be censored and who is to do the censoring? In the 1960s, the U.S. Supreme Court tried to answer such questions by defining obscenity as something *utterly* without redeeming social importance and using other terms so vague as to make the definition meaningless. The best answer seems to be that there is no answer—except in the hearts and minds of the people.

There is another censorship problem in the United States: government secrecy. During World War II, it was necessary to keep information about troop movements, ship sailings, and battle plans from the enemy. Information was put into a secret code and then classified as top secret, secret, or confidential. Only persons with a security clearance had access to the information. This system continued during the cold war with the Soviet Union. Eventually it led to abuses. Even newspaper clippings and testimony given at public hearings have been classified. The system was used to hide merely embarrassing information and perhaps even illegal actions.

Critics have denounced the system of codes and classification as government by secrecy, which has led to a host of scandals such as Watergate and the Iran-contra affair. Numerous incidents, illegal or unwise, have been hidden from the public, even from members of Congress, through denials and outright lies. The bombing of Cambodia during the Vietnam War and the secret sale of weapons to Iran are examples. When such incidents were discovered, widespread distrust of national leaders and calls for more open government followed.

In 1966 Congress passed the Freedom of Information Act to give citizens access to classified information. The process it set up is cumbersome and expensive, however. The abuse of classification, censorship of information, and government by secrecy remain problems in a democratic nation.

See also Bill of Rights; Freedom of Speech; Freedom of the Press; Zenger Trial.

ROBERT A. LISTON

CENSUS

Every ten years the federal government makes a huge effort to locate, count, and gather information about every person who lives in the United States. This gigantic task is called a census of population. The United States is the first country in history that has taken a census from its very beginning as a nation. When the first census was taken in 1790, the final count showed that 3,929,214 people were living in the new nation. The 1990 census put the population of the United States at 249,632,692—an increase of almost a quarter of a billion people in two hundred years.

Reasons for the Census

A decennial (ten-year) census is required by the U.S. Constitution because the number of seats allotted to each state in the House of Representatives depends on the state's population. Seat allotments have changed many times throughout our nation's history as some states grew faster than others and people moved from state to state. As a result of the 1990 census, for example, a number of northern and northeastern states lost seats in the House of Representatives to the Sunbelt states of the South and West. New York lost three seats while California gained seven. An accurate census is crucial to our system of representative democracy.

Early censuses were little more than head counts to determine state populations. By the mid-nineteenth century, however, both government and the private sector realized that detailed information about America's rapidly expanding population was necessary to plan intelligently for growth and development. Census questions have changed from decade to decade, but some important ones now seek to determine every person's age, sex, education, occupation, income, employment status, race and ethnic background, and condition of housing.

Such questions are not asked on the census out of idle curiosity. We need to know how many children live in a certain area and how old they are so that schools can be built in the right places at the right times. We need to know what parts of the country are growing fastest in order to plan for roads, airports, hospitals, and water and power supplies. Information about areas of poverty and bad housing helps focus programs of government assistance where they are most needed. In a socially concerned nation, we need information about differences of income and education between men and women and between racial and ethnic groups.

American business and industry use cen-

sus information when deciding where to start new factories, how much demand there is likely to be for new products, where new television stations will reach the widest audiences, and thousands of similar questions. "Profiles" on almost seventy thousand U.S. communities can be drawn from census data. Figures on urban populations, age, income levels, and even traffic patterns help supermarkets, video stores, fast-food outlets like McDonald's and Wendy's, and hundreds of other businesses decide where to locate.

Growth of the Census
The first census in 1790 was a hit-and-miss effort carried out by sixteen federal marshals and two hundred assistants riding horseback. Today the Bureau of the Census, established in 1902, has almost nine thousand full-time professional employees. Its headquarters in the Washington, D.C., suburb of Suitland, Maryland, and its twelve regional offices throughout the country are staffed with statisticians, economists, demographers (population experts), geographers, cartographers (mapmakers), and computer specialists. The Census Bureau analyzes billions of pieces of information and issues hundreds of reports on its findings. To update the great ten-year census, many smaller censuses are regularly carried out on migration, birthrates, employment, and other topics.

But the greatest effort begins on April 1 of every year that ends in zero. That is the day the Census Bureau calls Census Day, when the decennial census taking begins. Questionnaires are mailed to tens of millions of households with instructions to complete them and mail them back. The bureau hopes to reach 95 percent of all people living in America through the mailing system. But almost 250,000 temporary workers have to go door-to-door to follow up on questionnaires not returned or to assist people in filling them out. A special effort is made to count homeless people and people who are away from home. In a nation the size of the United States, finding everyone is not possible, but census workers try to do the impossible.

The Bureau of the Census proudly and properly calls itself "Factfinder for the Nation."

For further reading: Melissa Ashabranner and Brent Ashabranner, *Counting America: The Story of the United States Census* (New York: G. P. Putnam's Sons, 1989).

BRENT ASHABRANNER

CENTRAL INTELLIGENCE AGENCY

During World War II the Office of Strategic Services (OSS) was created to conduct espionage and plan commandolike raids in enemy-held regions. In 1947, as part of the military reorganization involved in creating the cabinet-level Department of Defense, the OSS was replaced by the Central Intelligence Agency (CIA). The assignment of the CIA is to carry out spying activities in foreign countries (friendly as well as unfriendly) and to conduct secret operations in unfriendly nations aimed at thwarting actions deemed to be against the national interests of the United States.

Because of the strict secrecy of CIA missions, details of its actions are rarely made known outside the organization, even to members of Congress. Usually only actions that have gone badly come to public attention. Among the most notorious of these CIA

failures were the Bay of Pigs invasion of Cuba, the shooting down of the spy plane over the Soviet Union (the U-2 affair), and the Iran-contra affair involving the financing of Nicaraguan rebels, something Congress had specifically forbidden.

See also Espionage.

CHAPLIN, CHARLIE

(1889–1977)   *Actor and filmmaker.*

Charlie Chaplin was among the most brilliant comic actors in movie history. His character of the Little Tramp, which he developed into something both funny and pathetic, was internationally recognized and loved. The many films Chaplin made in Hollywood set the standard for film comedy for a quarter of a century.

Chaplin was born in London, England, to a poverty-stricken family of unsuccessful vaudeville performers and joined his parents' act at the age of five. In 1906 he became part of Fred Karno's popular music-hall troupe, with whom he appeared as a clown. While on tour with the company in the United States in 1913, he was invited by Hollywood filmmaker Mack Sennett to join Keystone, the leading comedy studio in America. Chaplin's first slapstick film with Keystone, *Making a Living,* was made in 1914, and the next year he created his gentleman-tramp routine in *Kid Auto Races at Venice.*

In his first four years in Hollywood, Chaplin's salary went from $175 to $10,000 a week, and in 1918 he signed a contract for $1 million a year. The next year he cofounded United Artists, with which he wrote, directed, produced, and composed the music for his films.

The feature-length movies he made during the 1920s and 1930s include such classics as *The Kid* (1921), *The Gold Rush* (1925), *City Lights* (1931), *Modern Times* (1936), and his first talking film, *The Great Dictator* (1940).

Chaplin's films became more serious in the 1940s and 1950s, and only the touching *Limelight* (1952) was a popular hit. Personal scandals and his refusal to become an American citizen brought him bad publicity. Because of this and his radical political beliefs, he was barred from returning to the United States after a trip to Europe. He moved to Switzerland in 1952.

Chaplin's reputation was rehabilitated in his last years. He was finally readmitted to the United States to receive a special award from the Motion Picture Academy in 1972. He won an Academy Award for the score of *Limelight* the following year. At his death, noted Italian filmmaker Federico Fellini described Chaplin as "a sort of Adam from whom we are all descended."

See also Movies.

DENNIS WEPMAN

Charlie Chaplin, left, and his sidekick Jackie Coogan in the 1921 silent movie The Kid. *It was the first feature film Chaplin directed.*

CHAUTAUQUA MOVEMENT

In 1874 a clergyman, John H. Vincent, who was in charge of Sunday schools for the Methodist church, organized a course for Sunday school teachers at Lake Chautauqua, one of the Finger Lakes in New York State. Besides religious instruction amid attractive country surroundings, the program included good meals, group singing around evening campfires, and other simple amusements. It was a great success, and in the following summers the idea was expanded. Courses in science, literature, and other subjects were included. Famous lecturers participated, including, over the years, six former presidents of the United States.

Eventually a magazine, the *Chautauquan*, was published, and Vincent's organization (and his many imitators) offered formal correspondence courses. There were also traveling chautauquas, tent shows that had little to do with adult education and moved from town to town like the circuses of the era. The movement peaked in the early 1900s but declined rapidly after World War I as the public became better educated and the new sources of entertainment—radio and the movies—became increasingly popular.

CHAVEZ, CESAR

(1927–93)   Leader of farm workers' union.

Chavez, who was born in Yuma, Arizona, moved to California with his family in 1939 where they worked as migrant laborers and participated in strikes to improve working conditions. He served in the navy in World War II.

Chavez was introduced to community organizing by Father Donald McDonnell, an activist Catholic priest, and Fred Ross, an organizer for the Community Service Organization, a group that fought for civil rights for Mexican Americans. Chavez served as its national director before resigning in 1962 to devote his energies to building a farm workers' union.

Chavez and the United Farm Workers (UFW) went on strike in Delano's grape fields in 1965, joining Filipino farm workers to protest their low pay and the use of pesticides in the fields. For the next five years Chavez used a variety of tactics to induce the grape growers to sign union contracts: they marched from Delano to Sacramento to publicize their struggle; Chavez fasted several times to dramatize his commitment to nonviolence and social justice; and the UFW organized a nationwide boycott of table grapes. Finally on July 29, 1970, twenty-six Delano growers signed union agreements, the first time in American history that agricultural corporations signed a contract with a farm workers' union.

After 1970 Chavez had to fight the Teamsters Union, which wanted to take over organizing farm workers. But after four years

United Farm Workers president Cesar Chavez (second from left) walks a picket line in Los Angeles. He devoted his life to improving conditions for migrant farm workers, who typically endured backbreaking work for miserable wages.

of struggle, during which two UFW workers were killed, the Teamsters lost their bid to replace the UFW. In 1974, Chavez supported the passage of the California Agricultural Labor Relations Act, the nation's first law to protect the farm workers' right to form unions. Unfortunately, its implementation was carried out by anti-union politicians, and growers were soon able to get around it.

Chavez called for an international grape boycott in 1984 to protest the careless use of pesticides, which harmed farm workers as well as consumers. He was still working to build the union when he died unexpectedly near Yuma, Arizona, in 1993.

Cesar Chavez devoted his life to the problems of America's poorest workers. His UFW and the movement, La Causa, succeeded in raising wages and improving working conditions for farm workers throughout the Southwest.

See also Agriculture; Hispanics; Labor Movement.

For further reading: James Terzian and Kathryn Cramer, *Mighty Hard Road: The Story of Cesar Chavez* (Garden City, N.Y.: Doubleday, 1970); Florence White, *Cesar Chavez, Man of Courage* (Champaign, Ill.: Garrard, 1973).

RICHARD GRISWOLD DEL CASTILLO

CHICANAS/CHICANOS
See Hispanics.

CHIEF JOSEPH
See Joseph (Chief Joseph).

CHILDHOOD AND ADOLESCENCE

Childhood and adolescence are now considered different stages of life, the first lasting until puberty, the latter to adulthood. But childhood and adolescence have meant different things at different times in American history. Nor has adolescence always been regarded as a distinct phase of life.

Childhood in the Colonies

Before 1800 in America childhood was always a key part of the life cycle, but adolescence was not. Adults regarded children as miniature adults, no different except in size, age, and experience. Once children could fend for themselves, as in doing chores or fixing a meal, they were defined as adults, thus eliminating the stage of adolescence. According to contemporary economic thinking, children also resembled adults in that they were a resource, a part of the labor supply just as older persons were, similar in their economic value to, say, seeds in agriculture, timber in house building, or tea in the colonial trade.

The first English settlements in North America, radiating out from Jamestown (1607) and the Chesapeake Bay, were especially dangerous for youngsters. Life expectancy was as low in Virginia and Maryland as any place in the British Empire. Between 1635 and 1699, about eighty thousand people arrived in Virginia, yet its population was only about sixty thousand in 1700. Maryland's experience was even worse. Most marriages were brief, and relatively few children were born. About half of them survived to adulthood. Diseases, such as dysentery, typhoid, and influenza, were common; people surviving to their twenties might live another twenty-five years.

Life for children in New England was less dangerous. Childhood diseases and other terrors existed, but the northern colonies always had more stable communities, and family life was much like that in England. But child welfare depended greatly on individual family circumstances; thus children of color had a harder life than white children. Social status mattered too.

In the 1700s colonial life became more settled everywhere. People now married earlier, had more children than before, and lived longer. Life was more secure. Still, public health was a great problem. Boston's epidemics of 1702, 1730, and 1752, for example, doubled the infant death rate of 30 per thousand; smallpox, yellow fever, respiratory diseases, fevers, and influenzas devastated children. Smallpox inoculation (variolation), tried first in 1721, eventually reduced deaths, however. West African children could not adapt biologically to their slave diet in America; they died at twice the rate of whites before age four.

Circumstances facing children as always reflected those of their families. Boys and girls on farms did chores; in the cities, they were put to work early too, either as apprentices to masters or as jacks-and-jills-of-all-trades. Indenture, or the binding of a child to a master outside the home who would teach him a trade, often prepared children for their adult roles, regardless of family wealth. Few children received any formal education, save in New England, where boys were taught reading and writing, but girls, only reading. In the later 1700s schooling became more available elsewhere, especially in wealthy families and among certain religious and ethnic groups.

Changes in the 1800s

Americans after 1800 increasingly came to believe in progress, in an infinite future, and they acted toward and thought of children in entirely new ways. They believed that everything in life grew and developed, including social systems, technologies, plants, animals, whole peoples, and individuals. Adults treated children as if they could be molded, as if particular social programs would change them for the better. Since no one really wanted to change the institutions of the new order, democratic market capitalism, reform meant changing the people in the existing social system. Americans knew that children could learn new things. Therefore future generations could keep up with material progress and thus make moral progress. Here was the secret to a better tomorrow.

Until the 1830s reformers based their crusades on the idea that children should be nurtured and protected as *individuals;* cities such as Boston, New York, and Baltimore created orphanages for such purposes. From the 1830s to the 1870s reformers created many institutions for juveniles intended to remake

children morally. As before, the cultivation of rigid habits was key, but now children were to be taught the standard of being an American, of belonging to a group called Americans, not merely that they were civilized individuals, as before. This was the age of the group and of conformity to its norms, not of the individual's conformity to the standards of civilized society. All child-saving institutions recognized children's emotional and intellectual development. No longer was pure rationality the sole goal, as in Thomas Jefferson's day. Reformers focused on the problems of adolescents, now seen as persons capable of violating middle-class moral standards. Thus reform of America's adolescents became crucial, and adolescence achieved recognition and legitimacy.

Modern Attitudes

Between the 1870s and the 1920s, notions and actions concerning childhood and adolescence became more pessimistic and more openly racist than ever before, as the offspring of former slaves and European peasants competed with the middle-class Anglo-Saxon majority. Usually the newcomers fared poorly in this contest; they suffered discrimination.

Most city children attended free if racially segregated public schools and lived in two-parent households through adolescence until they married. Their chances in life depended enormously on their social, economic, and ethnic backgrounds, with those belonging to stigmatized groups getting the least. Starting with Illinois in 1899, most states adopted the juvenile court system, which created a body of juvenile law and justice distinct from that of adult criminal law and put juveniles under the control of special judges, thus recognizing a difference between the child, the adolescent, and the adult. In rural areas, however,

This 1674 portrait, Mrs. Elizabeth Freake and Baby Mary, *shows a Boston mother and child. Children during the colonial period were viewed as miniature adults and were dressed accordingly.*

traditional institutions such as the family continued to guide the lives of children and adolescents.

Since the 1920s, as the economy has shifted from production to consumption, childhood, adolescence, and adulthood have been commonly regarded as entirely distinct periods of the life cycle. Children have been seen as needing protection by adults against physical as well as emotional dangers, such as disease, malnutrition, poverty, and abuse. Adolescents have been defined as persons who can study advanced subjects and hold paying jobs, but whose potential for violating social norms appears almost unlimited.

Since the 1950s, various groups in public life have competed with one another over how much they are owed by society to compensate for the harm society is said to have done to them. Those who succeed in portray-

ing themselves as the most victimized gain the greatest reparations; this has been just as true of child and adolescent welfare. Because adolescents can be more active than children, they have come into their own as a subculture, capable of great power as consumers in the economy. And there has been a children's rights movement, whose leaders have debated over the best techniques to redress the victimization of children, to right the wrongs done to them. Some argue, for example, that kids should be able to sue their own parents.

No better evidence of the vast differences between our colonial past and our contemporary culture could be cited than this, proving again that childhood and adolescence have meant different things at different times in American history.

See also Child Labor; Family Life; Games and Toys.

HAMILTON CRAVENS

CHILD LABOR

Today about 5 million young people fourteen to eighteen years old work some time during the year. Six out of every ten in the twelfth grade, and three out of every ten in the ninth grade, hold jobs. Thousands much younger, between the ages of seven and nine, also work. Some put in long hours for low pay, with harm to their schooling and their health.

What work do they do? They harvest food, stitch clothing in dreary factories, assemble cheap jewelry in trailer homes or tenements, or operate dangerous machines in restaurant kitchens and neighborhood stores. Across the country they serve fast-food meals from early morning till late at night.

A *Boston Globe* journalist who crisscrossed America to find out what's happening to young people who work reported that "often they are scalded and burned, sliced up by food machines, exposed to pesticides in the field and choking fumes in the factory. They fall and fracture their backs and break their arms and hands frequently delivering and picking up things for us. Sometimes they are left badly maimed or disfigured for life. Sometimes they are killed. Nearly all the time, they get tired, miss school and are ignored."

The *Globe* reporter concluded that America's children are among the nation's most widely exploited workers, and called this situation "a national shame."

Child Labor in Early Times

Of course, children have always worked. From the earliest times in human history, the very young did their share in the family, foraging for food, herding animals, raising crops, and doing household chores. When slavery developed in the ancient world, slave children were made to work as their masters wanted. (And they still are, for slavery continues to exist in some parts of the world.)

The use of child labor among whites in America began when European nations planted colonies on this continent. They shipped young boys and girls across the Atlantic and put them to work on farms and in households and shops. Often homeless children were picked up off city streets and sent to the colonies as workers. White immigrants of all ages wanting to escape poverty at home frequently came to America as indentured servants. Under the system of "indentured servitude," people signed contracts agreeing to work for someone for a certain number of years, usually seven to ten. They were not free to leave their jobs during that time. In return, their employers paid their fare across the Atlantic and provided room, board, cloth-

ing, and so on during the years the servants worked for them. Grown-ups who came to America as indentured servants usually had to put their children out as indentured servants also.

It was common, too, in colonial America for people to "apprentice" their children, especially boys, to craftsmen when they were ten to fourteen years of age. The system of apprenticeship was like the indenture system in some ways. Apprentices were expected to do much of the work the craftsmen needed done for a given number of years, usually until they were twenty-one. In return, they were

A young boy working in the coal mines, a notoriously dangerous profession. Before the first child-labor laws were enacted, employers frequently exploited children, working them long hours for low wages under deplorable conditions.

housed, fed, and clothed. But they were also taught the craft of their employer—who might be, for example, an ironworker, a silversmith, a candlemaker, a blacksmith, or a printer. All these skills were important in the years when jobs were performed and things were made in individual shops rather than factories. Working as an apprentice was how a young person was trained for his future occupation. Young girls, too, might be apprenticed, but much more often they were sent out to work as servants in someone else's home. There they learned skills they put to use when they established their own households or operated small businesses as dressmakers, milliners (hatmakers), innkeepers, dairy farmers, or other occupations.

The situation for most black children was very different. They were among the many millions of Africans brought to the New World in chains or were born in America to enslaved parents, becoming slaves themselves. In the North until the early nineteenth century and in the South until the Thirteenth Amendment ended slavery in 1865, they labored alongside adult slaves in the fields, the household, and the workshop. The relatively few who were children of free blacks followed much the same path as white children.

Child Labor under the Factory System

When manufacturing developed in the nineteenth century, little children went to work with their parents in the cotton mills of New England. By the 1830s half of the nation's textile workers were under ten years of age. They worked ten to twelve hours a day under dangerous, dirty conditions, earning twelve to twenty-five cents a day.

Most people did not give child labor a second thought. They believed that work was morally good and that "idleness" was sinful. Children not working in factories spent endless hours at farm chores the year round, milking cows, tending chickens, and weeding in vegetable gardens.

By the 1830s social reformers and labor unions were calling for laws requiring children working in factories or on farms to attend school for a set number of weeks or months each year, and to work no more than ten hours a day. Only a few such laws were adopted, and they were poorly enforced.

As production methods were modernized and tasks simplified, the skilled craftsmen were replaced by women and children, who worked for lower wages. In the 1880s mass emigration from southern and eastern Europe began. Huge numbers of immigrant children were put to work in sweatshops that sprang up in the slums of the large cities. In 1900 in New York City 100,000 children labored in sweatshops, as domestic servants, or as peddlers on the street. They worked as many as seventy hours a week for starvation wages. Soon a National Child Labor Committee was created by reformers hoping to do something about the evils of child labor. Investigative journalists (called "muckrakers") exposed these wrongs and helped arouse the country's conscience. Both the unions and reformers pressed the federal government for help, but employers usually fought their proposals.

Child Labor in Recent Times

Twice in the early 1900s Congress passed protective child labor laws, but the Supreme Court declared them unconstitutional. Not until 1938, during President Franklin D. Roosevelt's administration, was a Fair Labor Standards Act adopted. It sets standards for workers sixteen and over in most occupations and bars children from jobs that are oppressive or hazardous or harmful to their health and well-being. Young people fourteen and fifteen years of age are allowed to work only in a limited number of occupations and only outside of school hours. Today all fifty states also have laws regulating the employment of children.

Despite the laws (which are too often poorly administered and inadequately enforced) tens of thousands of violations are reported annually to federal and state labor departments. Employers in recent decades have been hiring more and more children to fill menial jobs at low wages. Young people continue to work too many hours, below the minimum wage, often at dangerous jobs, and at the cost of health and schooling.

For further reading: Milton Meltzer, *Cheap Raw Material: How Our Youngest Workers Are Exploited and Abused* (New York: Viking Penguin, 1994).

MILTON MELTZER

CHILDREN'S AND YOUNG ADULT LITERATURE
See Literature, Children's and Young Adult.

CHINESE EXCLUSION ACT

By the 1880s substantial numbers of Chinese, 90 percent of them men, were working in the

"WHAT SHALL WE DO WITH OUR BOYS?"

Nineteenth-century Chinese workers in the United States were often blamed for America's economic ills. This 1882 cartoon in Wasp *magazine reflects the fiercely anti-immigrant sentiments of the time. A many-limbed Chinese man with a sinister expression is featured furiously painting, sewing, hammering, and in general monopolizing the available jobs while American citizens stand idly about, jobless.*

West Coast states. Many of them had labored originally on the crews building the transcontinental railroads. After they began to compete in other fields with native-born workers, resentment against them grew. Labor claimed that the Asians were driving down wage rates because they had been accustomed to a lower standard of living and were willing to work for much less than Americans. Moreover, most did not learn English or adopt American customs. Nor did they seem interested in bringing their wives to the United States and settling permanently. There was also a strong racist bias against them, with some arguing that they posed a threat to "white racial purity."

In response to the mounting complaints, Congress passed the Chinese Exclusion Act of 1882. This law suspended Chinese immigration for ten years. It was renewed for another ten years in 1892, and in 1902, the ban was made permanent. Not until 1943 were very limited numbers of Chinese allowed to immigrate into the United States. The quota was raised considerably in the Immigration Act of 1965.

See also Immigration; Nativism; Racism.

CHISHOLM, SHIRLEY

(1924–) *Congresswoman and the first black woman to run for the presidential nomination of a major party.*

Born Shirley Anita St. Hill in Brooklyn, New York, Chisholm at the age of three was sent to live in Barbados, from which her parents had emigrated. When she was seven, she rejoined her parents in Brooklyn, where she attended Girls' High School and Brooklyn College. She received a master's degree in education from Columbia University.

Long interested in politics, she helped form the Unity Democratic Club in Brooklyn and in 1964 waged a successful campaign for a seat in the New York State Assembly. After two terms, she ran for Congress in 1968. Running against Republican James Farmer, a respected civil rights leader, she campaigned hard for the women's vote. Chisholm won more than twice Farmer's total, thus becoming the first black woman in the U.S. House of Representatives. In Congress, she focused on legislation to benefit education, women, and minorities.

Four years later Chisholm became the first black woman to mount a serious campaign to head the ticket of a major party. Campaigning as a "catalyst for change," she attracted considerable support from women's and black groups. But because she won few delegates in the primaries, she had little influence on the Democratic convention, which selected South Dakota senator George McGovern to face Republican incumbent Richard Nixon in the 1972 election.

Chisholm remained in Congress until 1982, stepping down in order to spend more time with her family. She has held teaching positions at Mount Holyoke and Spelman colleges and helped found the National Political Caucus of Black Women.

For further reading: Jim Haskins, *Fighting Shirley Chisholm* (New York: The Dial Press, 1975); Jim Haskins, *One More River to Cross: The Stories of Twelve Black Americans* (New York: Scholastic, 1992).

JIM HASKINS

CHRISTIAN SCIENCE

Christian Science was founded by Mary Baker Eddy in the nineteenth century. She suffered from a variety of ailments and in 1862 traveled to Portland, Maine, to receive treatment from a "healer," Phineas Parkhurst Quimby. After he effected a cure through massage, encouragement, and what he called "mental healing," she became his student and associate.

Shortly after Quimby's death in 1866, Mary Baker fell on an icy street. While confined to bed, she studied the Bible and became convinced that her life was in God and that God was the only life. From this revelation followed her healing: to the amazement of those around her, she dressed and walked out of the sickroom.

In 1875 she published *Science and Health,* which outlines her beliefs. In it she asserts that "all is mind and there is no matter," that death and sickness are only illusions, and that everything comes from God and is perfect. Healing, she said, comes from the true understanding of these doctrines. Thus, a sick person should seek this understanding through the help of what are called Christian Science practitioners rather than call on the medical profession.

This belief has subjected the church to much criticism, particularly when members have refused to obtain medical help for seriously ill children. Nevertheless, the church had grown to a membership of over 100,000 people when Eddy died in 1910, and it is still an important sect in American religion.

See also Eddy, Mary Baker.

CHURCH AND STATE, SEPARATION OF

The separation of church and state is a fundamental principle of American democracy. The Bill of Rights guarantees all citizens freedom of religion. Yet Americans have never agreed on how complete the separation between religion and government should be.

Church and State in History

During colonial times, church and state were one. In Puritan Massachusetts, only church members could vote or hold public office. Anyone who questioned the church's teaching was expelled from the colony, and Boston Quakers were executed for their beliefs as late as 1661. In most of the southern colonies, the Church of England was the official religion, established by law and supported with public taxes. Catholics, Jews, and Baptists faced whippings, fines, or imprisonment for practicing their religion. Only in Providence, Rhode Island, founded in 1636 by Roger Williams, a former Massachusetts minister, were all faiths tolerated. Williams called Providence his "lively experiment."

Gradually, the "experiment" was introduced elsewhere. On the eve of the American Revolution in 1775, most colonies welcomed members of all Protestant churches. Some also tolerated Catholics, Jews, and atheists (those who do not believe in God). But to the men who gathered in 1787 to write a constitution for the new United States, tolerance was not enough. It can become intolerance merely by passing a law. "The right of every man is to liberty—not toleration," said one. So the Constitution states that citizens may not be denied federal office because of their religious beliefs. Unsure that this provision was strong enough to assure freedom of conscience, the states demanded—and got—a Bill of Rights added to the Constitution. It consists of ten amendments. The first one prohibits Congress from either establishing an official religion or interfering with anyone's right to worship freely.

But although this prevented the *federal* government from favoring one religion over another, *state* governments could do so. New Jersey withheld full civil rights from non-Protestants until 1844. In New Hampshire, Catholics could not vote until 1851. Finally, in 1868, the Fourteenth Amendment to the Constitution was adopted. It forbids states to make laws that interfere with people's "liberty." Over time, the Supreme Court has ruled that the "liberty" of the Fourteenth Amendment includes the religious liberty of the First Amendment. Today, separation is written into state, as well as federal, law.

How Much Separation?

The separation, however, is not absolute. American money, for example, carries the motto "In God We Trust." According to the Pledge of Allegiance, we are "one nation, under God." Presidents and other officials take an oath to uphold the Constitution with their hand on the Bible. Public school children sing Christmas songs. Christmas itself is a federal holiday, and Good Friday is legally observed in some states. State and federal tax dollars help support schools and hospitals run by religious organizations. Governments further aid religious institutions by not taxing them. Strict separationists object to such government support for religion, noting that it tends to favor Christian religions over non-Christian ones, and large, rich churches with extensive school and hospital systems over smaller, poorer ones.

But other Americans see it differently and believe there should be less separation, not more. One of their goals is to reverse the 1962 Supreme Court decision that banned the reciting of Christian prayers in public schools. Another is to force schools to instruct students in creationism—the story of the earth's

beginning as told in the Bible—rather than the scientific theory of evolution. Some Americans see threats to religious freedom in such government acts as a court's ordering medical treatment for a child whose parents believe treatment is against the will of God, imposing state educational standards on parochial schools, or prosecuting religious leaders accused of endangering or defrauding their followers.

Separation and Public Policy

In separating church and state, the Founding Fathers sought not to restrict religious activity but to encourage it. "Religion," said James Madison, "flourishes in greater purity without than with the aid of government." Indeed, religion has always influenced American public life. Many nineteenth-century abolitionists embarked upon the struggle against slavery out of religious conviction. Religion motivated many who fought for laws to protect the rights of workers, the insane, the handicapped, and members of racial minorities. Most of today's antiabortion activists are inspired by their religious beliefs. So are many who oppose laws protecting the rights of homosexuals or who want to make the death penalty cover more types of crimes. So, of course, are those Americans on the other side who oppose capital punishment, or favor guaranteeing homosexuals their civil rights, or want to preserve a woman's right to have an abortion.

All this is as it should be. Moral issues cry out for moral discussion. But sometimes, rather than simply trying to convince others through discussion that their views are right, a few people want to transform their particular, Bible-based rules for living into laws enforced by state and national governments. When that happens, everyone's religious freedom is jeopardized. Only to the extent that our democracy looks to all its cathedrals, temples, and mosques, to its synagogues, churches, and meetinghouses, and to its non-believers as well—respecting and using the best that each has to offer—does the "lively experiment" succeed.

See also Bill of Rights; Constitution; Constitution, The Making of the; Scopes Trial; Williams, Roger.

For further reading: Ann E. Weiss, *God and Government: The Separation of Church and State* (Boston: Houghton Mifflin, 1982).

ANN E. WEISS

CHURCH OF JESUS CHRIST OF LATTER-DAY SAINTS
See Mormons.

CIA
See Central Intelligence Agency.

CIO
See Congress of Industrial Organizations.

CIRCUSES

Public entertainments with trained animals, skilled horseback riders, and acrobats, all performing in a circle surrounded by an audience, can be traced back more than two thousand years. Such shows were popular in ancient Rome, where athletic contests and chariot races were held in a ring (*circus* comes from the Latin word for "circle"). They also existed in the Far East. But the giant three-

Circus performers pose outside of the Barnum & Bailey three-ring circus in 1932.

Tightrope walkers performing with bicycles and a chair up on the high wire.

ring spectacle of the modern circus is an American invention dating only from the nineteenth century.

Early Circuses

Traveling bands of acrobats and jugglers were a common feature of popular entertainment in Europe in the Middle Ages. Credit for creating a ring show stationed in one place is usually given to Philip Astley, who began exhibiting animals, trick horseback riders, and tumblers in a ring near London in 1768. The first indoor circus in the United States was that of John Bill Ricketts, a noted English horseman who established a permanent show in a large building in Philadelphia in 1792. Most early American circuses, however, traveled from town to town and set up in open fields.

While European circuses generally continued to be indoor shows, American traveling circuses grew larger and more elaborate during the nineteenth century. In 1826, Nathan Home and Aaron Turner began to carry tents with their touring shows to provide their rural audiences with protection from the weather, and soon the canvas "big top" be-

came a regular part of American circuses.

Another distinctive feature of traveling circuses in the United States was a colorful parade, complete with costumed performers, brass bands, and animals in richly decorated wagons, marching through towns to advertise the show the day before it opened. The first circus parade took place in Albany, New York, in 1837. The invention in Massachusetts in 1855 of the calliope, a loud keyboard instrument made up of a set of steam-powered whistles, added to the excitement and fun of both the parade and the show itself. A calliope, patterned on locomotive whistles and especially devised for circuses and carnivals, can be heard up to twelve miles away.

Changing Attractions

The exhibition of wild animals had been a popular entertainment in America since colonial times. It is known that George Washington enjoyed attending such shows. In the 1860s, a New York State showman named Isaac A. Van Amburgh was the first to combine such shows with circus acts. Van Amburgh included trick horseback riders, acrobats, and clowns in his show of trained lions, tigers, bears, and elephants and so erased the line between animal show and circus in America.

The difference between European and American circuses became more distinct when U.S. showmen added a second ring in the 1870s, an innovation that never became popular in Europe. Later American circuses were to grow to three rings, and some have boasted as many as seven, all presenting individual acts at the same time.

The most famous circus manager in American history was Phineas T. Barnum, a popular showman who had made his reputation exhibiting curiosities in New York City. In

1871 he opened his "Greatest Show on Earth," the first to offer two rings (1873). This spectacle merged with the circus of James Bailey in 1881 to become Barnum & Bailey, surely the largest, if not the greatest, show on earth. Its big top, covering three rings by then, could seat up to twenty thousand spectators in 1882, and its giant elephant, Jumbo, was the best-known animal attraction in the world. Sixteen years after Barnum's death in 1891, the Greatest Show on Earth was acquired by the five Ringling brothers, America's leading family of circus owners. It was run separately from the Ringlings' own circus until 1919, when the two were merged into Ringling Bros. and Barnum & Bailey.

Circuses Today

In the twentieth century, American circuses have become more like those of Europe. The tradition of the traveling tent show has largely disappeared with the growth of big cities capable of supporting such productions. The number of traveling circuses in the United States has fallen from nearly a hundred in 1909 to about six today. Still the largest circus in the country, Ringling Bros. and Barnum & Bailey stopped using tents in 1956 after a tragic fire and now appears only in air-conditioned buildings in cities.

Circuses today are larger and more sensational than ever, and with the advent of television and international travel they reach a wider audience. But the spectacle of wild animals, skilled artists, and death-defying acts has lost none of its appeal for people of all ages worldwide.

See also Barnum, Phineas T.

DENNIS WEPMAN

CITIES
See Urban Growth.

CITY GOVERNMENT

During the past three hundred years, American cities have changed a great deal. Automobiles have replaced horses. Skyscrapers have replaced two-story buildings. City government has changed, too. By 1900 thousands of people were working for cities as fire fighters, police officers, and garbage collectors. City government had become a big business, spending billions of dollars each year.

In the 1600s and 1700s the few American cities were small and their governments did not do much. They fixed the price of bread and built marketplaces where farmers sold their vegetables and butchers sold their meat. They also tried to keep cattle from wandering through the streets and bought fire engines to put out fires. But there were no police forces, and cities did not build waterworks.

Growth of Governments

As cities grew larger in the 1800s, their governments spent more money and did more. They established police departments, built sewers, piped water to houses, founded libraries, and cleaned the streets. They also laid out giant parks. By the end of the 1800s American cities had some of the best parks and public libraries in the world, and their waterworks and sewer systems were among the largest anywhere. City governments laid hundreds of miles of pipes under the streets to bring water to factories, stores, and homes and to carry sewage away.

As city governments spent more money, however, taxes increased and some people complained. They said that their leaders were spending too much and stealing from the taxpayers. And some indeed were stealing. For example, in the late 1860s and early 1870s William Tweed was leader of the Democratic Party in New York City. He was known as "Boss Tweed" because people knew he was the boss of the men who ran the city. Boss Tweed built a courthouse. At first it was supposed to cost $150,000, but by the time it was finished, it had cost $14 million. Tweed and his friends had overcharged the city for constructing and furnishing the building. Because of his dishonesty, Boss Tweed was sent to jail.

Reform Efforts

Around the turn of the century, people known as reformers opposed leaders like Tweed. In order to make city governments more honest, they suggested that respectable business leaders govern cities. They also proposed a number of other changes to improve city government. Some wanted to give more power to mayors and less to city councils. The city council is the legislative branch of city government, similar to the national Congress or state legislatures. These reformers thought that most city council members were dishonest and should have less power.

Another group of reformers favored the city manager plan. Rather than the voters electing a mayor, the city council would hire a manager to run the government. He would be an expert in the field, having gone to school to learn how to govern cities. Hundreds of cities adopted this system and hired managers. But there were still problems—people still thought some city leaders were dishonest.

Modern Problems

By the 1920s many Americans were moving from the center of the city to houses on the edge of town. The new cities and villages they founded were known as suburbs. By the 1950s many older cities were surrounded by these suburbs, each with a separate government. The New York City area, for example, had hundreds of different city and village governments.

This caused problems for older cities like New York, Detroit, and Chicago. The wealthier people were moving out of these cities and buying homes in the suburbs, leaving mostly poor people behind. As a result, the cities became poorer, dirtier, and more run down.

During the 1950s and 1960s mayors in these older cities tried to rebuild them, an effort known as "urban renewal." Many new apartments and office towers were built. But the wealthier people continued to move to the suburbs, and many stores and factories moved as well.

By the 1970s and 1980s, the older cities were having trouble raising enough money to pay the police, fire fighters, and garbage collectors. They suffered a "fiscal crisis," which meant that they did not have enough money to operate. The state and federal governments had to help pay the bills for such cities as New York, Cleveland, and Detroit. At the end of the 1900s, many city governments continued to have money problems. Money had moved to the suburbs, leaving the older cities poorer and more troubled.

See also Big-City Bosses; Corruption and Scandals in Government; Fire Departments; Police Departments; Tweed Ring; Urban Growth.

JON C. TEAFORD

CIVIL DISOBEDIENCE

Civil disobedience involves publicly breaking the law in an effort to force change in government policy or legislation. The laws broken are usually civil, involving people's private rights as citizens, rather than criminal, dealing with felonies like theft or assault. Nonviolent confrontation is the object. For example, environmental activists trespass on private property hoping to stop a factory's careless disposal of wastes dangerous to people's health. Antiabortion demonstrators block public roadways to keep patients from enter-

ing abortion clinics. Homeless people take over the mayor's office to publicize their demand for more and better shelters.

Although civil disobedience is by definition peaceful, it sometimes provokes violent reactions. The police summoned to remove homeless demonstrators may handle them roughly. Antiabortionists and prochoice advocates have gotten into shoving matches outside many clinics. Environmental activists

The civil rights movement represented the most effective and large-scale use of civil disobedience in U.S. history. Here activists in 1960 conduct a nonviolent sit-in at an Atlanta, Georgia, whites-only lunch counter. Typically, a group would take seats at a counter, and the white management would order them to leave. They would refuse, and the police would haul them away, usually to jail. Immediately, more activists would take their places, and the protest would continue. One of these Atlanta protesters declared, "We'll stay all day if we have to, but we expect to get waited on before the day is over."

have been attacked by workers afraid of losing their jobs if antipollution laws take effect. Occasionally, demonstrators themselves lose control when under attack, and civil disobedience turns violent.

History of Civil Disobedience

Civil disobedience is nothing new in American life. In the early colonies, religious dissenters—Baptists, Quakers, Catholics, Jews, atheists, and others—who defied laws requiring them to worship in an officially established church were practicing what we would call civil disobedience. Some were exiled, whipped, imprisoned, or put to death, but their resistance eventually brought change. By the time of the American Revolution, religious toleration was nearly universal in the English colonies.

The Revolution itself started with civil disobedience aimed at getting England to stop imposing duties and taxes on the colonies. Many colonists avoided paying the duties and boycotted (refused to buy or use) English goods that carried even the smallest tax. In 1773, a group of Boston men dressed as Mohawk Indians swarmed onto three English ships anchored in Boston Harbor and dumped their taxed cargoes—tea—overboard. Yet not even this "Boston Tea Party" persuaded the English to lift the hated taxes. On April 19, 1775, peaceful protest erupted into revolution.

It was a Massachusetts writer, Henry David Thoreau, who formally defined civil disobedience. Thoreau was outraged when, in 1846, President James K. Polk ordered U.S. troops into Mexico, bringing on the Mexican War. Thoreau believed that the U.S. plan was to seize Mexican territory and carve it up into new American states in which slavery would

be permitted. Thoreau regarded slavery as evil. In 1848, having refused to pay a special war tax, Thoreau was briefly jailed. He wrote an essay, "Civil Disobedience," in which he argued that what is *legal*—as slavery was—is less important than what is *right*—as slavery is not. When "unjust laws exist," he asked, should we obey such laws blindly, obey them hoping for change, or disobey them? His answer: we should disobey nonviolently and be willing to suffer the consequences. Other war opponents and abolitionists (antislavery activists) joined Thoreau in committing or encouraging acts of civil disobedience. Many of the people who participated in later protest movements, like those in support of women's rights and those against unfair labor laws, resorted to similar tactics.

Thoreau's ideas also found a response outside the United States. In 1906, Mohandas K. Gandhi, a native of India then living in South Africa, read "Civil Disobedience" and decided upon nonviolent protest as the means by which he would seek to end English rule in his homeland. The mass demonstrations organized by Gandhi, along with the prison terms he served for his actions, claimed world attention and ended in 1948 with India's independence.

Civil Disobedience in Modern America

Inspired by Gandhi, a young black American minister, Martin Luther King, Jr., resolved to apply the Indian pacifist's methods to his goal of establishing racial justice in the United States. Though slavery had ended after the Civil War, law and custom kept most blacks and whites segregated in schools, neighborhoods, and public accommodations, such as theaters, stores, restaurants, and trains and buses. In the South, most blacks were not allowed to vote. In 1955, after Rosa Parks in Montgomery, Alabama, was arrested for refusing to move from the "white" section of a bus, King and others announced a boycott of the city's bus system. During the year-long protest, many boycotters lost their jobs or were mistreated by police. Some were beaten or jailed. But they stuck it out, and Montgomery finally integrated its buses.

During the next years, King and others led dozens of civil rights demonstrations. Their followers—white and black—"sat in" at segregated lunch counters whose owners refused to serve blacks, ignored laws and court orders designed to keep them from marching or registering to vote, and traveled at great personal risk (several were killed) through the South demanding change. The 1964 Civil Rights Act and the 1965 Voting Rights Act were the direct results of King's brand of civil disobedience.

Other examples of civil disobedience include conscientious objectors to the Vietnam War, many of whom went to prison rather than fight in that war, and Cesar Chavez, who fasted and led a national boycott of table grapes to gain recognition for a farm workers' union in California.

Civil disobedience continues today, but on a smaller scale. Environmentalists, antiabortionists, and the homeless are only some who practice it. Young men may protest when the United States attacks another nation, as it did Libya in 1986, Panama in 1989, and Iraq in 1991, by failing to register for the Selective Service. Men and women of all ages may refuse to pay that portion of their federal taxes that goes for military purposes. Some have lost their homes by doing so. Homosexual rights activists and people pushing government to do more to fight the disease AIDS are among those most intensely engaged in civil disobedience in the 1990s.

See also Boston Tea Party; Chavez, Cesar; Civil Rights Movement; Conscientious Objectors; Freedom Rides; King, Martin Luther, Jr.; Parks, Rosa; Student Non-Violent Coordinating Committee; Thoreau, Henry David.

For further reading: Ann E. Weiss, *We Will Be Heard: Dissent in the United States* (New York: Messner, 1972).

A N N   E.   W E I S S

CIVILIAN CONSERVATION CORPS

The Civilian Conservation Corps (CCC) was a New Deal public works program created by Congress in March 1933 in the midst of the Great Depression. It enrolled unemployed young men between the ages of eighteen and twenty-five and set them to work on reforestation, erosion control, and other conservation projects. They also built wildlife shelters, stocked rivers and lakes with fish, and constructed and maintained beaches, parks, and historic sites.

These projects were of great value in themselves; many of them are still in use today. But giving idle youths useful work to do and, as President Franklin D. Roosevelt said, keeping them "off the city street corners" was of equal importance, both for the men and for a nation suffering economic hardship and low morale.

The CCC was run by the army. The men marched to their assignments, addressed their leaders as "sir," and were subject to strict discipline. But the program was a popular one. By the time of its disbanding in 1942, nearly 3 million young men had served in the corps.

See also Conservation and Environmental Movements; New Deal.

CIVIL RIGHTS MOVEMENT

The phrase "civil rights movement" commonly refers to a period in the 1950s and 1960s when a number of organizations and individuals, black and white, successfully challenged legal segregation of the races. It is also called the interracial movement, the freedom fight, and the black struggle. The battle for racial equality has been a constant in our nation's history. It has been fought in the courts through lawsuits and in legislative bodies through political pressure. And it has been fought in the streets, using the power of nonviolent protests.

Slavery Years

When the American revolutionaries issued the Declaration of Independence in 1776, nearly one-fourth of the New World's population were slaves. Under the Constitution written after the Revolution, the institution of slavery was protected. In 1857, as the nation became increasingly divided over slavery, the Supreme Court ruled in a case called *Dred Scott* v. *Sanford* that blacks—slave or free—were not citizens. They were, the Court said, "subordinate and inferior beings, who had been subjugated by the dominant race, and whether emancipated or not, yet remained subject to their authority."

Within four years, however, the Civil War began, pitting northern states against states in the South that defended the right to own, buy, and sell other human beings. In January 1863, President Abraham Lincoln issued the Emancipation Proclamation, setting free all the slaves in the states at war with the United States. After the war ended, slavery was abolished by passage of the Thirteenth Amendment to the Constitution.

After Emancipation

The southern states, however, refused to make peace with the freed slaves. They introduced Black Codes, which were new versions of their old laws regulating slave behavior, aimed this time at free blacks, who found their lives controlled much as they had been before slavery ended. The white South was determined to keep blacks from exercising political power, acquiring economic wealth, or attaining education. Blacks were kept from voting by terror and by complicated rules that usually applied only to them. They were forbidden by law and custom from holding all but the most menial jobs. Black schools received less money than white schools, and black teachers were paid less. Blacks were kept separate from whites everywhere—at drinking fountains and in buses and restaurants. One city even made it illegal for blacks and whites to play checkers together. By 1900 many thought that blacks in the southern states were not much better off than before the Civil War.

In 1905, a university professor named W. E. B. Du Bois, angered at the condition of blacks, called together a conference in Niagara Falls, Canada, to draw up a list of goals for black America that included fighting for the right to vote and ending the system of segregation. Du Bois's 1909 Niagara Movement joined liberal whites who were also angered at racial conditions to form the National Association for the Advancement of Colored People (NAACP). The NAACP, organizing chapters across America, began legal attacks on racial separation.

The First and Second World Wars did much to accelerate black progress. Having served overseas and enjoyed freedoms they had never known in the United States, black soldiers returned home determined to seek

A fifty-four-mile civil rights march led by John Lewis (now a U.S. congressman) between Selma, Alabama, and the state's capital, Montgomery, in 1965. The marchers were protesting the discriminatory practices that prevented blacks from voting. Turned back once by state troopers who beat, gassed, and trampled them with horses, they were joined by thousands of others including Martin Luther King, Jr., two weeks later and withstood further brutal attacks to make the march. Viola Liuzzo, a white civil rights worker from the North, was fatally shot on this march. Five months later, Congress passed the Voting Rights Act.

freedom. Many white Americans found it harder to tolerate racial inequality at home while fighting Adolf Hitler's theories of racial purity abroad.

The NAACP then concentrated its legal attack on segregated schools. In 1954, the Supreme Court declared in *Brown* v. *Board of Education of Topeka* that segregated public education is unconstitutional. A year later the Court ruled that segregated schools must be integrated "with all deliberate speed."

The Court's failure to order immediate desegregation gave opponents of integration time to organize resistance. They passed laws designed to avoid desegregation, and they engaged in acts of terror aimed at intimidating southern blacks and their supporters. Bombings, beatings, and burnings increased across the South. Court action was costly and, as the 1954 *Brown* case showed, did not always produce immediate results. But in 1955 in Montgomery, Alabama, freedom fighters developed another weapon.

Modern Movement Born

On December 1, 1955, a black woman named Rosa Parks was arrested on a Montgomery bus for refusing to give up her seat to a white man. No one knew it at the time, but the modern civil rights movement had begun.

In response to Parks's arrest, community

This famous image showing police using attack dogs against peaceful demonstrators in Birmingham, Alabama (1963), appeared in newspapers and magazines across the country. Photographs capturing southern brutality became one of the most effective methods of stirring national sympathy for the civil rights movement.

leaders organized a one-day boycott in which no black person would ride the buses. The Montgomery Improvement Association was formed to support the boycott, and a new minister in Montgomery, Dr. Martin Luther King, Jr., was chosen as its leader. The boycott was so successful the first day that the community decided to continue it. It ended 381 days later! For more than a year, no black person rode a single bus in the entire city. At its successful conclusion, the boycott's new method of fighting segregation—nonviolent resistance—and its leader—Martin Luther King—were known all over the United States.

Across the South, the nonviolent method was employed to end other forms of segregation. In 1960, black college students used what were called "sit-in demonstrations" against segregated lunch counters. Students made purchases in a department store and then sought service at the store's lunch counter. When they were denied service, they remained seated until they were arrested or the lunch counters were integrated. By the end of 1960, thousands had participated in demonstrations, and lunch counters in many cities had been integrated.

In May 1961, integrated teams rode interstate buses on a journey called the "Freedom Ride" from Washington, D.C., through the South testing whether a recent Supreme Court decision ordering integrated facilities for interstate passengers was obeyed. In Alabama, Freedom Riders were met with violence as police stood by and watched mobs beat the riders and set the buses afire. When they reached Mississippi, all the riders were arrested and jailed. In spite of the violence, many more joined later rides, convincing the government that integration of transportation facilities had to be enforced.

The movement continued to grow, as more joined its organizations and demonstrations despite the dangers, including many young people of high school and college age.

In 1963, King led demonstrations against segregated facilities in Birmingham, Alabama. The world watched in horror as firemen turned powerful hoses on the demonstrators, some of them as young as six years old. More and more Americans became concerned about civil rights.

In August 1963, 250,000 citizens gathered at the Lincoln Memorial in Washington, D.C., to hear civil rights leaders speak of their plans for the movement. The most notable speech that day was made by King, who told a national television audience of his dream that black and white Americans would one day live together in peace. Before that day would come, however, much more work had to be done.

Many Freedom Riders who had served thirty days in Mississippi jails stayed on in the state to help Mississippi blacks register to vote. In 1964, they invited northern college students to join them for Freedom Summer. During the summer, one local volunteer and two civil rights workers—James Chaney, Michael Schwerner, and Andrew Goodman—were beaten to death and buried in a common grave. Over a thousand other civil rights workers were also beaten or arrested on trumped-up charges.

Pressures from the southern movement and its growing number of supporters forced Congress in 1964 to pass the Civil Rights Act, ending segregation in places of public accommodation, such as hotels and restaurants.

In 1965, the movement concentrated on winning the right to vote in Selma, Alabama. When peaceful marchers there were run down by police on horses and were beaten on national television, outrage—and anger at the denial of the right to vote in southern states—caused Congress to pass the 1965 Voting Rights Act, ensuring federal protection of this basic right.

After the 1964 and 1965 laws ended legal segregation, the civil rights movement turned its attention more and more toward economic inequality. King, the movement's most prominent spokesman, was assassinated in Memphis, Tennessee, in 1968 while helping striking garbage workers there fight for better working conditions. Despite his death, the movement continued with different leaders and different organizations, but with the same goals it has had since the United States began—eliminating barriers against people because of their race.

The modern movement for civil rights thus had succeeded in ending state-sponsored segregation and in passing laws forbidding discrimination. It did so by using methods protected by the same Constitution that had once protected slavery. The civil rights movement was a victory for ordinary women and men, most of them faceless and unknown. It was our democracy's finest hour.

See also African Americans: Since World War II; Black Codes; *Brown* v. *Board of Education;* Congress of Racial Equality; Du Bois, W. E. B.; Freedom Rides; King, Martin Luther, Jr.; Marches on Washington: 1941, 1963; National Association for the Advancement of Colored People; Niagara Movement; Parks, Rosa; Segregation; Slavery; Southern Christian Leadership Conference; Student Non-Violent Coordinating Committee; Voting Rights Act of 1965.

JULIAN BOND

CIVIL WAR

Shooting came in 1861 because Americans grew tired of shouting. The United States had existed for eighty-five years. Yet the nation was one of varying sections. A Mississippi cotton planter had little in common with a Massachusetts factory worker, or a Georgia store owner with an Indiana shopkeeper.

In the period 1820–60 slavery became the burning issue of the day. Most Southerners defended it as necessary to their agricultural way of life. Most Northerners opposed it as contrary to democracy. One stormy incident followed another. Late in 1860 Southern states began leaving the Union to secure their own independence. Northern states resisted the move in order to preserve the Union. Thus war came on April 12, 1861, when the South fired on the Union's Fort Sumter in the harbor of Charleston, South Carolina.

The Situation in 1861
The North faced a huge task. To pull the

South back into the Union, Federal armies would have to invade the extensive lands of the Southern Confederacy. Federals had also to shatter the will of the Southern people to resist.

There were three military zones in the South. The eastern theater extended from the Atlantic Ocean to the Appalachian Mountains; the western theater, from the opposite side of the mountains to the Mississippi River. The land beyond the river was the third, or Trans-Mississippi, theater. For the first three years of the war, operations in one theater had little connection with those elsewhere. It was as if three different wars were taking place at the same time.

For hundreds of years military leaders argued that an army should drive toward the enemy's key city. Once that city was captured, the country would fall. This "city strategy" continued in the Civil War. But the South was so large that not one but five city targets emerged: Vicksburg, Mississippi, and New Orleans, Louisiana, which together controlled most of the Mississippi River; Chattanooga, Tennessee, and Atlanta, Georgia, both transportation and supply centers deep in the South; and Richmond, Virginia, capital of the Confederacy and site of its only real industrial complex. Richmond's importance, plus the fact that is was only 110 miles from the Northern capital of Washington, made the eastern theater the focus of attention on both sides. It became the bloodiest arena of the war.

Federal authorities soon announced a naval blockade of the Southern coastline. It took many months, but the blockade proved to be one of the decisive Union movements of the war, hampering trade the Confederacy badly needed. Settling the issue on land took four years and dozens of battles.

Early Engagements: 1861–62

Two battles in the Trans-Mississippi in 1861 produced more bitterness than solution. Offsetting a Union defeat at Wilson's Creek, Missouri, in August was a federal success at Belmont, Missouri, in November. Things then remained quiet in the western theater for a while. In the East, a Northern effort to seize Richmond occurred in July. Green troops of North and South collided at Bull Run, a railroad junction in northern Virginia. Casualties in the day-long fight—over 4,400 men killed, wounded, and missing—shocked Americans who had expected a short, easy war.

But in 1862 the Civil War became bloody beyond anyone's imagination. Three days of fighting in March at Pea Ridge, Arkansas, cleared Missouri of Confederate forces and saved northern Arkansas for the Union. Earlier that year, on February 6, Northern general Ulysses S. Grant began a long campaign in the West. With a combined army-navy force, he captured the Confederacy's main defense of the Tennessee River at Fort Henry, Tennessee. Ten days later, his troops seized Fort Donelson, Tennessee, the South's major protection of the Cumberland River. At Fort Donelson, *U. S.* Grant's reply to the Confederate request for surrender terms brought him the nickname "*U*nconditional *S*urrender" Grant.

Tennessee's capital, Nashville, fell to Grant shortly thereafter. But as he advanced across the state, Southern forces launched desperate attacks at Shiloh on April 6–7. This first major battle in the western theater produced over 23,700 losses, including 4,000 dead. Other Union forces captured Island Number 10 in the Mississippi River and the important river towns of Memphis, Baton Rouge, and New Orleans.

By summer, all of Kentucky, half of Tennessee, and parts of Alabama, Mississippi, and Louisiana were in Union hands. Confederates fought back in August with the South's Army of Tennessee invading Kentucky. It was defeated on October 8 at the Battle of Perryville. The last weeks of 1862 saw Grant strike for the Confederate stronghold at Vicksburg, while another Union army gained a victory after three days of combat in the Battle of Stones River.

Eastern Theater: 1862

The second attempt to take Richmond, Virginia, had come with Union general George B. McClellan's Peninsular campaign of April–July 1862. McClellan had organized the largest army ever seen in the Western Hemisphere. His strategy was to transfer his 150,000 soldiers to the tip of the Virginia peninsula formed by the York and James rivers and then march due west through undefended country and seize the Southern capital.

Battles at Williamsburg and Seven Pines occurred in May 1862 during the Union advance. General Robert E. Lee took command of the Southern forces and counterattacked just outside Richmond. Union soldiers withstood furious assaults at Mechanicsville, Gaines' Mill, Savage Station, Glendale, and Malvern Hill. Although McClellan managed to avoid total defeat, Lee's blows sent the Union army reeling to the banks of the James River. Richmond for the moment was out of

The Union dead scattered on the Gettysburg battlefield (July 1–3, 1863), a crucial battle won by the North that started the gradual decline of the Confederate forces. The photo was taken by Timothy H. O'Sullivan, who named it "A Harvest of Death."

danger. Casualties in the Peninsular campaign were shockingly high: 20,000 Confederates, 16,500 federals.

Later that summer a second Union army under Gen. John Pope moved into northern Virginia. Lee detached troops under his principal lieutenant, Gen. Thomas J. "Stonewall" Jackson, to block this threat until the main Southern army could shift position. Jackson on August 9 successfully struck Pope's forces at Cedar Mountain. Then after Lee arrived, he and Jackson routed Pope's army on August 28–30 at the Second Battle of Bull Run.

Virginia was now clear of Union troops. Some European nations seemed on the verge of giving the Confederacy official recognition and aid. Another major Southern victory could win the war for the "Rebels." So Lee crossed the Potomac River and pushed into western Maryland. That movement ended at Antietam Creek on September 17, the bloodiest day in all of American history. Twelve hours of fighting resulted in 25,000 casualties. Four times as many Americans fell at Antietam as were lost on D-day in World War II.

Lee's army limped back to Virginia. President Abraham Lincoln then issued the Emancipation Proclamation, which, among other things, made ending slavery a major Union war goal. This also had the effect of making any nation coming to the aid of the South subject to a declaration of the war from the North.

In December, another Union attempt to take Richmond ended in disaster at Fredericksburg, Virginia. Gen. Ambrose Burnside, commanding the Army of the Potomac after McClellan's removal, attacked Lee's lines and lost 12,600 men. Confederate casualties were less than half that number. At one point in the lopsided battle, Lee observed, "It is well that war is so terrible; else we should grow too fond of it."

Campaigns of 1863

Confederate hopes of success plunged sharply in the 1863 campaigns. Grant's army in the West made a series of brilliantly executed marches and surrounded Vicksburg, Mississippi, the last major Southern fortress on the river. Unable to take Vicksburg by assault, Grant besieged it. Forty-seven days of hunger and disease wore down the defenders. On July 4, some 28,000 Confederates surrendered. This Union victory cut off the Trans-Mississippi area from the rest of the Confederacy.

A second major Union army drove toward the supply center of Chattanooga, Tennessee. It suffered a repulse in September after two days of combat at Chickamauga, Georgia, but in November, with Grant directing operations, it defeated the Confederates at Lookout Mountain and Missionary Ridge overlooking Chattanooga. The Southern army fled south into Georgia.

Earlier that year, Lee in the East had gained his greatest victory and suffered his worst defeat. In spring the federal army of the Potomac, now under Gen. Joseph Hooker, sought to get around Lee's flanks and trap him in a huge vise. Lee countered by striking each pincer in turn. The May 2–6 Battle of Chancellorsville cost Lee 13,000 soldiers but averted the capture of Richmond. Among the dead, however, was Lee's best general, the legendary "Stonewall" Jackson.

Lee's next move was bold but risky: a second invasion of the North, this time marching into Pennsylvania. The most famous battle of the war took place July 1–3, 1863, at Gettysburg. Gen. George G. Meade had been in command of the Federal troops only three days when the armies clashed. Lee attacked again and again but could not break the Union line. The 45,000 men killed, wounded, and captured at Gettysburg were a third of Lee's army. Both sides were too battered to do battle again that year.

Union Drive: 1864–65

The beginning of the end of the Confederacy was approaching in the spring of 1864 when fighting resumed. Grant came east as general in chief of all Union forces, and military operations in the two theaters were now coordinated. In the first week of May, Grant advanced into Virginia on a new campaign against Lee, and Gen. William Tecumseh Sherman and another Federal force moved south from Tennessee toward Atlanta.

Grant met bloody setbacks in his Virginia campaign. On May 5–6, Lee surprised the Union troops inside a tangled woodland known as the Wilderness. The Federals, though defeated, lunged southward again. Ten days of bitter conflict at Spotsylvania resulted only in longer casualty lists. Grant tried to get around the eastern flank of Lee's army in heavy fighting at the North Anna River and Cold Harbor. By early June, Grant had suffered 55,000 casualties and was no closer to Richmond than McClellan's Union forces had been two years earlier.

In mid-June Grant again swung widely to the east of Lee, crossed the James River, and struck out for the railroad and supply center of Petersburg, only twenty-five miles south of Richmond. Military blunders by the Federals enabled Petersburg's meager defenders to hold out until Lee arrived. Grant then turned again to siege warfare. Petersburg and approaches to Richmond were encircled by a vast network of entrenchments. Lee could not move without losing the cities. This per-

The ruins of Richmond, the Confederate capital.

mitted other Federal units to seize the agriculturally rich Shenandoah Valley. Yet it would take Grant nine months to break Petersburg's defenses.

During that time, in Georgia, Sherman's veteran army tightened a military noose around Atlanta. On September 2, Sherman telegraphed the War Department: "Atlanta is ours, and fairly won." That victory helped ensure Lincoln's reelection two months later.

Sherman was not content with this victory, however. He wanted to destroy the South's will to fight as well. After sending a third of his army back to Tennessee, he set fire to Atlanta and marched east to the Atlantic. His plan was to cut the Confederacy in two. On December 22, Sherman presented Savannah, on the coast, to Mr. Lincoln as a "Christmas gift."

What was left of the ragged Southern army had advanced into Tennessee with the hope of blocking the Union advance to the coast. But the force that Sherman had dispatched mangled the Confederates on November 30 at Franklin and on December 15–16 at Nashville.

Major Battles of the Civil War, 1861–65

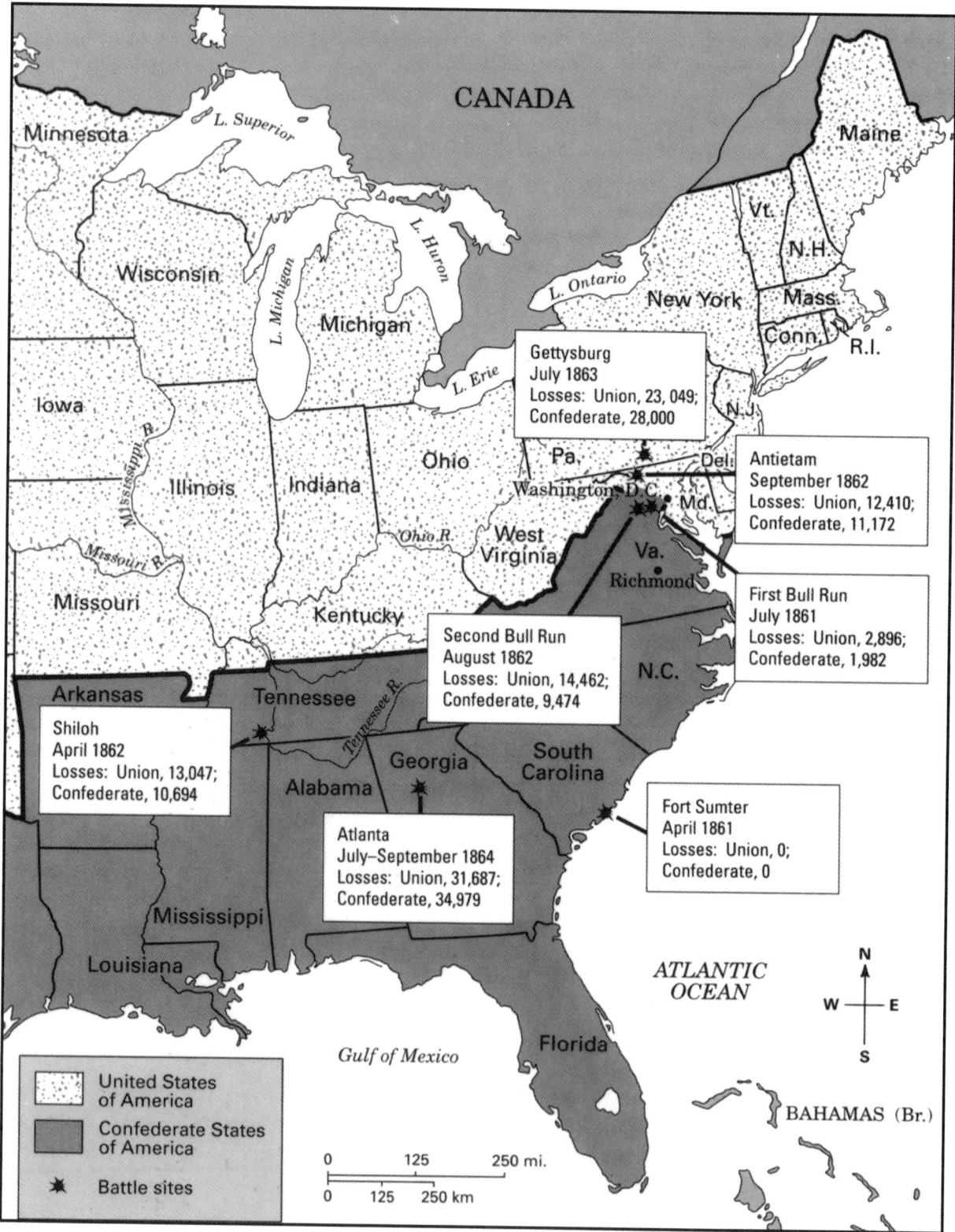

CANADA

Minnesota

L. Superior

Maine

Wisconsin

L. Michigan

L. Huron

Michigan

Vt.

N.H.

L. Ontario

New York

Mass.

Conn.

L. Erie

R.I.

Iowa

Gettysburg
July 1863
Losses: Union, 23, 049;
Confederate, 28,000

N.J.

Illinois

Indiana

Ohio

Pa.

Del.

Antietam
September 1862
Losses: Union, 12,410;
Confederate, 11,172

Washington, D.C.

Md.

Mississippi R.

Ohio R.

West
Virginia

Va.

Richmond

Missouri R.

Missouri

Kentucky

Second Bull Run
August 1862
Losses: Union, 14,462;
Confederate, 9,474

N.C.

First Bull Run
July 1861
Losses: Union, 2,896;
Confederate, 1,982

Arkansas

Tennessee

Tennessee R.

Shiloh
April 1862
Losses: Union, 13,047;
Confederate, 10,694

Georgia

South
Carolina

Alabama

Fort Sumter
April 1861
Losses: Union, 0;
Confederate, 0

Atlanta
July–September 1864
Losses: Union, 31,687;
Confederate, 34,979

Mississippi

ATLANTIC
OCEAN

N

W — E

S

Louisiana

Florida

BAHAMAS (Br.)

Gulf of Mexico

United States
of America

Confederate States
of America

Battle sites

0   125   250 mi.

0   125   250 km

The end came quickly in 1865. In February, Sherman marched north through the Carolinas, leaving a path of destruction behind him. Confederate resistance was by then too weak to offer more than token opposition.

Grant had spent the winter months spreading his lines around Petersburg. Lee had no choice but to extend his thin ranks to maintain a front. The Confederate position resembled a rubber band stretched to the limit when, late in March, Grant launched a series of assaults. On April 2, the Southern line snapped. Lee fell back to the west, and Union forces occupied Petersburg and Richmond.

Lee sought to get to a defensible point in the Virginia interior where he could link with the small army retreating in the face of Sherman's advance. But Grant's men marched hard and surrounded Lee's half-starved, half-naked forces at Appomattox Court House. On April 9, Lee met Grant under a flag of truce and surrendered. On April 26, the Confederate army in North Carolina surrendered to Sherman's forces at Durham Station.

The War's Results

Thus ended the bloodiest conflict in American history. Over 700,000 American soldiers and civilians had died, more than the number killed in all other American wars *combined*. A fourth of all Southern males perished from battle wounds and sickness; another fourth were crippled. If the Civil War were to occur today and casualties were in the same proportion to population, over 15 million Americans would die.

The loss of life was high for several reasons. Armies were very large in the Civil War, and more men fighting meant more men killed. Commanders continued the old-fashioned way of sending large numbers of soldiers charging across open fields, but in the face of weapons that had been vastly improved by the 1860s. The transition from the musket to the rifle, for example, gave the advantage in war to the defense for the first time. Disease also ravaged the armies. The science of medicine was still woefully undeveloped and the new germ theory of disease little understood if it were even known. For every man killed in action, two died behind the lines from infection and sickness.

The price was high, but the benefits were great. Slavery ceased to exist in America. The United States became a true nation rather than a confederation with a weak central government. Secession would never again threaten national unity. The war also gave a tremendous boost to America's industry. The United States in name became the United States in fact.

See also Alabama Claims; Confederate States of America; Copperheads; Emancipation Proclamation and Thirteenth Amendment; Gettysburg Address; Sanitary Commission; Secession; Slavery. *Also see biographies of the following Civil War figures:* Davis, Jefferson; Grant, Ulysses S.; Jackson, Thomas J. (Stonewall); Lee, Robert E.; Lincoln, Abraham; McClellan, George B.; Sherman, William Tecumseh.

For further reading: James I. Robertson, Jr., *Civil War! America Becomes One Nation* (New York: Knopf Books for Young Readers, 1992).

JAMES I. ROBERTSON, JR.

CLAY, HENRY

(1777–1852)   *Senator, congressman, and secretary of state.*

Clay was born in Virginia and moved to Kentucky in 1797. For over forty years he provided forceful leadership and wielded enormous influence in American politics. In 1806, the Kentucky legislature selected him to fill

Henry Clay (standing) was called the Great Compromiser because of his role in negotiating compromises over the issue of slavery. Speaker of the House of Representatives, he is pictured here urging the House to accept the Compromise of 1850, which divided new territory gained in the Mexican War into slave and free territory.

an unexpired term in the U.S. Senate, even though he had not yet reached the Senate's minimum age of thirty. In 1811, he was elected to the House of Representatives and was chosen its Speaker. Except for two brief periods, Clay remained House Speaker until 1825, longer than anyone else in the nineteenth century. Later, he returned to the Senate, serving from 1831 to 1842 and from 1849 to 1852. An eloquent orator with a cordial manner, he displayed a personal charm and magnetism that won him many friends in Congress.

A man who very much wanted to be president, Clay developed a plan called the "American System," which was designed to win support from all sections of the country. It called for high tariffs (duties, or taxes on imported goods) to protect eastern manufactures, federally financed roads to benefit the West, and improved navigation of southern rivers. Eastern textile mills would provide a domestic market for southern cotton and eastern factories would ship more products to the South, thus reducing the need for both southern exports and imports.

Clay made his first bid for the presidency in 1824. Since none of the four candidates had a majority of electoral votes, the election was thrown into the House of Representatives. Clay, who had finished fourth, asked his House friends to vote for John Quincy Adams rather than Andrew Jackson, who had won the most popular and electoral votes. Adams won and after taking office appointed Clay secretary of state. This caused the Jacksonians to charge that Adams and Clay had made a "corrupt bargain." In 1832 and 1844, Clay was the presidential candidate of the Whig Party but was again defeated, first by Jackson and later by James K. Polk.

Three times Clay applied his political skills to bring about concessions that temporarily reduced the ongoing tensions between the North and the South. In 1820, he played an important part in developing the Missouri Compromise. When South Carolinians attempted to nullify, or refuse to enforce in their state, the high tariff of 1832 and threatened to leave the Union, Clay led Congress to pass a new tariff bill that lowered duties. Later, he designed and argued strenuously for the Compromise of 1850, which was enacted and helped delay the Civil War for a decade. For his ceaseless efforts to settle differences peacefully, Clay earned the title of the "Great Compromiser."

See also American System; Compromise of 1850; Corrupt Bargain; Missouri Compromise; Nullification Controversy.

EDMUND LINDOP

CLEMENS, SAMUEL
See Twain, Mark.

CLEVELAND, GROVER

(1837–1908)   *Twenty-second and twenty-fourth president of the United States (1885–89, 1893–97).*

Cleveland was the first Democrat to occupy the White House after the Civil War and the only chief executive to serve two unconnected terms in office. He was also the first president to marry while in the White House (1886), giving the nation its youngest First Lady, twenty-two-year-old Frances Folsom.

Cleveland avoided military service during the Civil War by hiring a substitute, a legal practice at the time. He studied law and held a number of minor political posts in New York State before becoming mayor of Buffalo in 1881. His success in reforming the city's government led to his election as governor in 1882. His reputation as an honest and efficient leader made him an attractive candidate for president in 1884, and he defeated Republican James G. Blaine of Maine in a hard-fought campaign.

President Cleveland's efforts to limit government spending were unpopular. He vetoed costly pension bills for veterans and refused to approve many expensive local projects favored by Congress. He did sign the Interstate Commerce Act (1887), regulating railroads for the first time in the nation's history. He lost his bid for reelection in 1888 to Republican Benjamin Harrison. Though Cleveland received 90,000 more popular votes, Harrison won the most electoral votes. Four years later, however, Cleveland defeated Harrison and the Populist Party candidate, James B. Weaver.

Cleveland's second administration dis-

During the 1884 presidential campaign, gossip circulated that Democratic nominee Grover Cleveland had fathered an illegitimate child. This cartoon shows "Grover the Good" confronted with a weeping child and mother whose existence tarnished his clean image. Cleveland's enemies enjoyed taunting him with "Ma! Ma! Where's my pa?/ Gone to the White House/ Ha! Ha! Ha!" To the surprise of many, Cleveland admitted that the child was his. Rather than condemning him as immoral, the public admired his honesty.

pleased many groups. During the panic of 1893, his conservative economic policies angered Western farmers and miners and split his party. He antagonized workers by ordering federal troops to keep the railroads running during the nationwide Pullman strike of 1894. He offended sugar investors by withdrawing a treaty to annex Hawaii because he felt that the American planters in the islands had seized power from the Hawaiian monarchy illegally. His support for Venezuela in its boundary dispute with British Guiana was less controversial, however.

For events during Cleveland's administrations, see Coxey's Army; Dawes Severalty Act; Depressions and Recessions; Hawaii Annexation; Pullman Strike; Tenure of Office Act.

BARBARA SILBERDICK FEINBERG

CLINTON, BILL

(1946–) Forty-second president of the United States (1993–).

Born in Hope, Arkansas, three months after his father's accidental death, William Jefferson Blythe IV lived with his grandparents while his mother attended an out-of-state nursing school. His mother then rejoined her son and married again. As a teenager, he took his stepfather's name of Clinton.

In 1963, Clinton was selected as a delegate to the Boys' Nation model government program in Washington, D.C. There he met President John F. Kennedy, whose example fired his ambition. After college, Clinton was a Rhodes Scholar at Oxford University in England, where he protested American involvement in the Vietnam War. In a move that would haunt him later, he used legal but controversial means to avoid the army draft. Back in the United States, he graduated from Yale Law School and married fellow student Hillary Rodham.

Entering politics in Arkansas, Clinton became, in 1978, the nation's youngest governor. But his self-assertive style antagonized voters, costing him his job in 1980. The defeat sharpened his skills of persuasion and compromise. Elected governor four more times between 1982 and 1990, he relied upon those skills to reform his state's educational, health care, welfare, and environmental programs. He and his wife, a top lawyer, acted as a team.

Bill Clinton and Al Gore cheered by delegates after their acceptance speeches at the Democratic National Convention in 1992, a step on the road to their election as president and vice president of the United States.

In 1991, Clinton's fellow governors named him the country's most effective governor.

In 1992, Clinton won the Democratic nomination for president. With running mate Al Gore, he conducted an energetic campaign against incumbent George Bush, touring the nation by bus and holding lively question-and-answer sessions with voters in "town meetings." Although inexperienced in foreign affairs and attacked as a draft dodger and for aspects of his personal life, he won the election by promising change.

Clinton kept his promise, appointing record numbers of women and members of minority groups to high posts, reversing the antiabortion policies of past administrations, and becoming the first president to endorse handgun control, among other things. He named Hillary Rodham Clinton to head a task force charged with devising a universal health care plan that would cover all Americans. The president was criticized, however, for his occasional tendency to switch positions under pressure.

ANN E. WEISS

Buffalo Bill poses in a buckskin outfit next to his saddle. His Wild West Show featured enactments of stagecoach robberies, "Custer's Last Stand," and other colorful scenes from the American West that included plenty of Indians, cowboys, horses, and buffalo. The show toured for thirty years throughout the United States and Europe. England's Queen Victoria was a great fan.

CODY, BUFFALO BILL

(1846–1917)   *Showman and western hero.*

Between 1883 and 1912 thousands on both sides of the Atlantic Ocean attended Buffalo Bill's Wild West Show portraying the frontier American West.

William F. Cody was born near LeClaire, Iowa. At the age of fourteen young Bill became a Pony Express rider, making one of the longest of all the Pony Express rides—384 miles in just twenty-five hours. He occasionally scouted for the army until 1876. He also furnished buffalo meat for railroad workers, which was probably how he earned the nickname of "Buffalo Bill."

By 1869 Cody had married and settled down near North Platte, Nebraska. He fought in several Indian battles and served as a hunting guide for the Grand Duke Alexis of Russia. From these exploits, which were widely reported, Buffalo Bill became a celebrity. He was the hero of popular stories of the time, called "dime novels," and was soon appearing on stage in poorly written, poorly acted "shoot-em-ups," which critics hated but audiences loved.

In 1882 Buffalo Bill planned an "Old Glory Blowout" to celebrate the Fourth of July in North Platte. Part spectacle, part rodeo, and part circus, it was a big success. Cody went on the road with a similar Wild West Show from 1883 to 1912. In time it included splendidly dressed Indians and cowboys, and buffalo, elk, and burros with packs. Annie Oakley, a sharpshooter, and an Indian attack on a stagecoach were among the acts. An orator with a thunderous voice announced the horseraces, shootings acts, military exhibitions, riding and horse acts, and dramatic spectacles that constituted the show. Clowns entertained the audience between acts and a thirty-six-piece band supplied continuity. After he stopped touring, Buffalo Bill appeared in movies and with the Sells-Floto Circus until his death in 1917. He and his show had made the legends of the Wild West a part of American mythology.

For further reading: Augusta Stevenson, *Buffalo Bill: Frontier Daredevil* (New York: Macmillan, 1991).

RICHARD A. BARTLETT

COERCIVE ACTS

These laws were passed by Parliament in 1774 after news of the Boston Tea Party reached London. Colonists had tossed a shipment of tea into the harbor rather than admit it into the country and pay a hated Tea Tax on it.

The Coercive Acts were designed specifically to punish the people of Boston regardless of whether they had been involved in the destruction of the tea. One of these laws, the Boston Port Act, closed the town's harbor to all shipping until the East India Company and the British customs office had been paid for the tea. Another, the Administration of Justice Act, provided for transferring local cases to English courts if the governor of Massachusetts believed an accused person was likely to be acquitted by a local jury no matter what the evidence against him. The Massachusetts Government Act revised the colony's charter: it weakened the power of the town meetings by which towns governed themselves, increased the authority of the royal governor, and changed many offices that had been filled by elections to posts appointed by the governor or the king. A fourth law, the Quartering Act, applied to all the colonies. It provided that British soldiers could be housed in private homes or other buildings without the permission of the owners.

The colonists in Massachusetts and elsewhere called the Coercive Acts the Intolerable Acts. The very names make clear why they were such a significant step toward the Revolution: the British decided to deal with the Tea Party crisis through coercion, or force, and the colonists found the arbitrary use of force intolerable.

See also Boston Tea Party; Revolution.

COLD WAR

The fierce rivalry between the United States and the Soviet Union that began with the end of World War II in 1945 and lasted until the early 1990s is known as the cold war. Although the conflict sometimes threatened to flare into "hot" fighting between the two superpowers, it never did.

The tensions began back in 1917, when Russia became the Union of Soviet Socialist Republics (USSR), a communist nation in which all property—land, housing, business, and industry—was owned and managed by the state. Most Americans were devoted to capitalism—free enterprise and private property—and saw communism as a threat to their basic values. The tension also had political roots. The United States is a democracy. The Soviet Union was a dictatorship, its people lacking any tradition of self-rule.

But with the coming of World War II, these differences were put aside. In June 1941, Germany invaded Soviet territory and began inflicting terrible damage. In December, America entered the war when Japan attacked Pearl Harbor and Germany declared war on the United States. For over three years, the United States and the Soviet Union fought as allies alongside England, France, and other nations. By February 1945, victory was in sight, and the Allied leaders met to plan the postwar world. Among the plans: split Germany into East Germany (administered by the Soviet Union) and West Germany (administered by the United States, England, and France) and allow democratic elections in the Eastern European countries formerly occupied by Germany.

The Cold War Begins

The Soviet Union, however, went back on its promise to hold free elections and imposed communist dictatorships on Poland, Hungary, Czechoslovakia, and other countries along its border. The Soviets may have regarded this "Eastern bloc" of nations as a shield against future invasions from the West, but American leaders suspected it was the first step in an aggressive Soviet policy aimed at establishing communism worldwide. That suspicion strengthened in 1948, when the Soviets broke another promise: to guarantee the West's right to control its part of Berlin, the former German capital, which was now deep inside East Germany. Hoping to starve the United States and its Allies out of West Berlin, the Soviets established a ground blockade around the city. The Allies countered by flying in food and supplies for ten months. When the Soviets finally abandoned the blockade on May 17, 1949, America claimed a victory in what many were already calling the cold war.

Superpower Strife

With cold war battle lines drawn, hostilities deepened. To each side, the other's political and economic system seemed wrong, even evil, and each was convinced that the other was bent on dominating the whole world. America's goal became trying to contain Soviet communism within Eastern Europe. Under the Truman Doctrine, U.S. aid did enable the governments of Greece and Turkey to defeat communist revolutionaries. Next, the Marshall Plan provided $12 billion for rebuilding the war-torn Western European democracies and keeping them as American allies. In 1949, those democracies, along with the United States and Canada, formed the North Atlantic Treaty Organization (NATO). Each member agreed to oppose any communist threat to the others. The Southeast Asia Treaty Organization (SEATO) safeguarded the Pacific in the same way. In Africa, Latin America, and the Middle East, too, the United States lined up allies.

In 1949, Soviet scientists successfully tested

an atomic bomb, ending America's monopoly on such weapons. A costly, dangerous arms race started, with each side trying to build more deadly weapons than the other side. That same year, communists seized power in China. In 1959, Fidel Castro established a communist government in Cuba, just ninety miles from the United States. In April 1961, an American-backed attempt to overthrow Castro by invading Cuba at the Bay of Pigs failed miserably—one of the country's most humiliating cold war defeats. Months later, tension shifted back to Berlin, where the Soviets were constructing a massive wall to seal off East Berlin from the rest of the city. For almost thirty years, the Berlin Wall stood as a symbol of the cold war.

America and the Soviet Union never met in direct combat, but at times, the cold war turned hot. In 1950, North Korea, armed by the Soviet Union and reinforced by Chinese communist troops, invaded noncommunist South Korea. The United States came to South Korea's aid, believing that if it fell to communism, so would other nations in the region, tumbling one by one like a row of dominoes. Fighting lasted until 1953, when the two Koreas returned to their prewar borders. Between 1964 and 1973, the "domino theory" led U.S. officials to send Americans to fight with the forces of South Vietnam in their losing battle against Soviet-backed North Vietnam. About 100,000 Americans died in Korea and Vietnam.

The two superpowers came closest to war with each other in October 1962, when the Soviets were observed building nuclear missile sites in Cuba. President John F. Kennedy warned the Soviets to stop—or face military attack. After six tense days, ships carrying nuclear warheads to Cuba reversed course and headed home. The most dangerous point of the cold war, the moment at which it most nearly exploded into World War III—nuclear holocaust—had passed.

An End to the Cold War

By the mid-1960s, the cold war was thawing. True, there was the war in Vietnam, and the United States and the Soviet Union continued to compete with each other in every possible area, especially in science and technology. Even sports events like the Olympic Games became contests to see whose athletes could bring home the most winning medals. But a new spirit of cooperation was stirring. American and Soviet diplomats sought to slow down the nuclear arms race, negotiating eight weapons-control treaties between 1963 and 1992. In 1972, President Richard M. Nixon traveled to China to meet with that nation's communist rulers and start working toward friendlier relations. East and West undertook cultural and student exchanges, so that their people could learn more about each other. Their leaders signed trade agreements and launched joint space missions.

The cold war finally ended when the Soviet bloc began to break up. During the fall of 1989, one Eastern European nation after another rejected its communist government and proclaimed itself independent. In November, the Berlin Wall was torn down, and East and West German soldiers and civilians joined in the joyful demolition. Within the year, the two Germanies reunited under one Western-style government. In December 1991, the Soviet Union itself broke apart into several independent republics, each hoping to establish a democratic system and a capitalist economy. Americans declared they had won the cold war.

Really, both sides were victors. Freed from their pervasive competition and a terrifying nuclear arms race, the two nations could turn their attention to their needs at home and cooperate on world affairs. Yet problems remained. People in the former Soviet Union faced an economy that no longer provided the food and products they needed. They had no experience with democracy, and learning how self-government works promised to be a challenge. In parts of the country, and in several former Eastern bloc nations, fighting erupted between people of different ethnic and religious backgrounds. Another cold war legacy: the nuclear weapons that once had belonged to the Soviet Union now became the property of several of the new republics, making international arms negotiations more difficult.

See also Anticommunism; Bay of Pigs Invasion; Berlin Blockade; Cuban Missile Crisis; Kennan, George; Korean War; Marshall Plan; North Atlantic Treaty Organization; Potsdam Conference; Truman Doctrine; U-2 Affair; Vietnam War; Yalta Conference.

ANN E. WEISS

COLLEGES
See Education: Universities and Colleges.

COLONIAL AMERICA

The development of the English colonies in North America was part of a vast movement of people from western Europe to what they thought of as a New World. Of course it was "new" to them only because they knew nothing about it. It had been home to Native American peoples for thousands of years.

Like most other European colonists the English settled in North America for many reasons, such as adventure, economic gain, and religious freedom. Between 1607 and 1733 thirteen permanent English colonies were established along the Atlantic Coast. These developed into three groups—Virginia, Mary-land, North and South Carolina, and Georgia in the South; Massachusetts, Connecticut, Rhode Island, and New Hampshire in the North, known collectively as New England; and the so-called Middle Colonies, New York, New Jersey, Pennsylvania, and Delaware.

Many people from other parts of the world settled in these English-controlled colonies. For example, by the end of the colonial period there were Dutch and Portuguese in New York, Swedes in New Jersey, German-speaking settlers in Pennsylvania, and Scotch-Irish in the valleys and foothills of the southern Appalachian mountains. The largest non-English ethnic group in the English colonies was composed of black Africans, taken to America by force and sold as slaves.

All the colonies were founded by private groups operating under royal charters. Most evolved into royal colonies—headed by a governor appointed by the king, but with legislatures made up of locally elected colonists—or proprietary colonies, where the founder controlled the distribution and sale of land and appointed the governor. All, of course, were subject to the laws of Parliament and edicts of the king.

Economies
Agriculture was the main activity in all the colonies. In the South the chief crops were tobacco, rice, and indigo, a blue dye. These were in great demand in England and could be easily exchanged for the manufactured goods the colonists needed. In the northern colonies the main crops, wheat, rye, and other grains, were easily available in England. So colonists developed a complicated trading pattern in these grains, fish, and products like furs and lumber that could be sold in southern Europe and the West Indies. Shipbuilding and shipping became important industries in

American Colonies in the Early Eighteenth Century

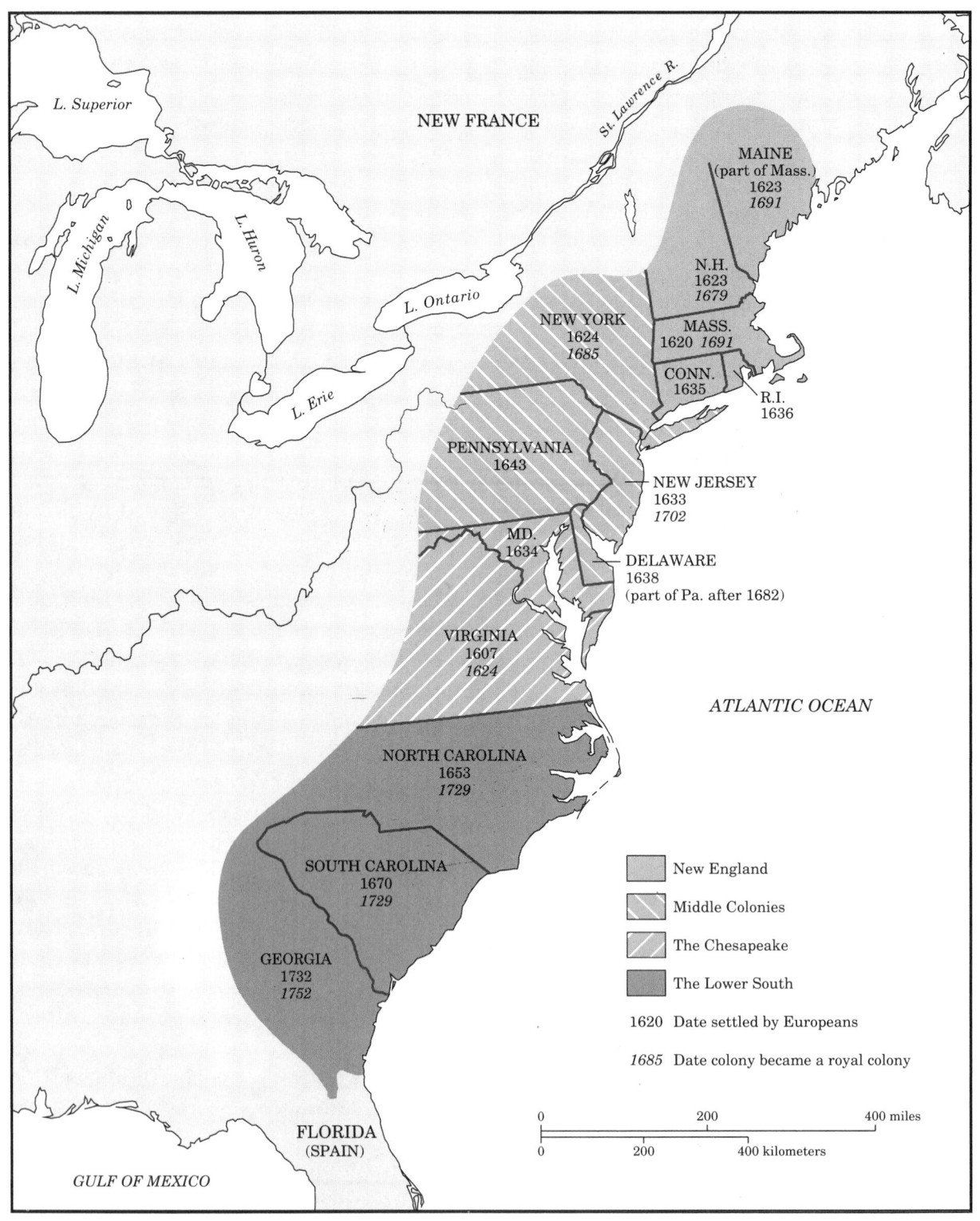

L. Superior

NEW FRANCE

St. Lawrence R.

L. Michigan

L. Huron

MAINE
(part of Mass.)
1623
1691

N.H.
1623
1679

L. Ontario

NEW YORK
1624
1685

MASS.
1620 *1691*

CONN.
1635

L. Erie

R.I.
1636

PENNSYLVANIA
1643

NEW JERSEY
1633
1702

MD.
1634

DELAWARE
1638
(part of Pa. after 1682)

VIRGINIA
1607
1624

ATLANTIC OCEAN

NORTH CAROLINA
1653
1729

SOUTH CAROLINA
1670
1729

GEORGIA
1732
1752

FLORIDA
(SPAIN)

GULF OF MEXICO

New England

Middle Colonies

The Chesapeake

The Lower South

1620   Date settled by Europeans

1685   Date colony became a royal colony

0   200   400 miles

0   200   400 kilometers

all the northern coast towns. These economic differences caused different kinds of societies to evolve in the North and the South. There were few towns in the South, and the political and social leaders tended to be large planters who lived on plantations worked by numbers of slaves. In the North most farms were quite small. Towns developed and the people who dominated colonial life were mostly merchants.

To regulate colonial trade in ways that encouraged American economic activity and at the same time protected English interests, Parliament passed laws known as the Navigation Acts that regulated colonial foreign commerce. These laws banned the sale to foreign nations of colonial products needed in England and encouraged the building of English and colonial ships in order to strengthen the navy and control the flow of goods to and from the colonies.

Reasons for Immigrating

The principal difference between life in America and England for ordinary people was that in England land was scarce and therefore expensive; labor was abundant and therefore cheap. The reverse was true in the colonies. Poor people in England and other parts of Europe naturally found this situation a powerful magnet drawing them to the New World. Since many lacked the money to pay for passage to America, a system known as indentured servitude developed. A male immigrant, for example, would agree to work for a person who paid his passage for a period of time, usually five to seven years. When his time was up he was given a suit of clothes, a gun, and a few tools, and was free to seek his fortune. Usually he headed west to take over some land on the frontier and build a farm of his own. This system speeded western development and provided an opportunity for en-

COLONIAL POPULATION ESTIMATES (IN ROUND NUMBERS)

Year	Population
1610	350
1620	2,300
1630	4,600
1640	26,600
1650	50,400
1660	75,100
1670	111,900
1680	151,500
1690	210,400
1700	250,900
1710	331,700
1720	466,200
1730	629,400
1740	905,600
1750	1,170,800
1760	1,593,600
1770	2,148,100
1780	2,780,400

ergetic young settlers to improve themselves. So long as life remained hard in England, thousands volunteered to sign on as indentured servants.

In the late 1600s, however, economic conditions improved in England and fewer people were willing to migrate. This resulted in the importation of many more slaves. Since slaves, and their children, became a permanent labor force that never became free to compete with their masters, this further encouraged the dominance of large planters in the southern colonies. While all the colonies contained slaves, slave labor was much less important in the North than in the South.

As the colonies grew in size and wealth, numerous new problems arose. One was repeated conflict with the Indians, who naturally resented the seizure of more and more of their lands as white settlers moved westward. Another was conflict with the French in Canada, who had set up posts in western New York and Pennsylvania, and with the Spanish in Florida, who claimed lands the English considered parts of Georgia and South Carolina. Several wars with the French and Spanish colonies in America erupted, most of them related to larger wars in Europe. These culminated with the French and Indian War, which raged from 1756 to 1763. The English victory in that conflict greatly expanded the size of England's possessions in North America, but led indirectly to the American Revolution and the end of the colonial period of American history.

JOHN A. GARRATY

COLUMBIAN EXCHANGE

The term *Columbian Exchange* was coined by Alfred Crosby in his book of that title. It refers to the ways in which the arrival of Europeans in the Western Hemisphere beginning with Columbus's first voyage in 1492 affected both the Europeans and the Indians with whom they came in contact.

Each society absorbed a great deal from the other, including things they grew and manufactured, their ideas, and even their diseases. Examples include foods like potatoes and Indian corn, which were soon being grown in Europe, and European wheat, which Indians were soon cultivating. The Indians acquired horses as well as guns, steel knives, and other metal products previously unknown to them. The Europeans learned how to build and use birchbark canoes, and became familiar with the advantages of moccasins and leather clothes, which were far more durable when living in the tangled for-

ests of the New World than the clothes they had brought with them.

Most important, perhaps, was the exchange of diseases. Syphilis seems to have been a mild disease among Indians, but Europeans, who had never been exposed to it, had no resistance to it. When they contracted syphilis, it was a serious matter. On the other hand, European diseases like measles, which European adults rarely died from, killed tens of thousands of Indians. Most historians believe that far more Indians died of European diseases than were killed in wars with the European invaders.

COLUMBUS, CHRISTOPHER

(1451–1506)   *Sailor and explorer.*

Columbus, who was born in Genoa, Italy, became a sailor and trader in the Mediterranean region. First in Portugal and then in Spain, he tried to interest the rulers of those countries in sponsoring a voyage west across the Atlantic Ocean to reach Japan and the Indies in Asia. Previously, European explorers and traders like Marco Polo had to make a difficult, months-long trip across the Eurasian continent in order to reach the Far East with its spices, silks, and gold, which were in great demand in Europe. Columbus, like a number of educated people of the time, believed that the world was round, not flat as many others thought. He was convinced that by traveling west across the unknown ocean, he would find a new, easier route to the East Indies and Japan. He miscalculated the distance, however, thinking the globe was much smaller than it actually is.

King Ferdinand and Queen Isabella of Spain turned Columbus down twice before deciding to take a chance on this persistent

A 1519 oil portrait of Christopher Columbus by Sebastiano del Piombo, painted after the explorer's death.

dreamer. They gave him three ships and the title of Admiral of the Ocean Sea; they promised him and his heirs the right to govern the lands he discovered and any riches they contained. The *Nina*, the *Pinta*, and the *Santa María* left the Canary Islands off the coast of Africa on September 9, 1492. A month later his crew, frightened by their voyage into unknown regions, nearly mutinied. But Columbus talked them into continuing, and on October 12, they sighted land, probably an island in the Bahamas, which Columbus named San Salvador.

The inhabitants of the island were Arawaks, a gentle people who wore no clothing and had no weapons apart from spears for fishing. Convinced that he had reached the East Indies, Columbus called the natives Indians, a name that stuck. Columbus then sailed on, landing on Cuba and Hispaniola (now Haiti and the Dominican Republic). After establishing a fort there, he sailed home to a triumphant welcome.

Next Ferdinand and Isabella gave him seventeen ships and twelve hundred men to colonize the islands on a second voyage (1493–96). Unfortunately, Columbus and his men were misled by some gold jewelry worn by the Arawaks into thinking that there were huge amounts of gold on Hispaniola. When the natives couldn't produce this gold, the Spaniards forced them to labor in mines. If the natives resisted, they were killed—often with incredible cruelty—or sent to Spain as slaves. Within a few months, 50,000 native people had died. The Spaniards worked many of them to death. Others were murdered or died from European diseases for which they had no immunity. To spare their children such a brutal fate, mothers sometimes killed their infants with poison made from melons. After fifty years, the Arawaks, who had probably numbered about 300,000 when Columbus arrived, had been completely wiped out.

Columbus tried on his second trip to establish a colony on Hispaniola. But it fell into disorder, and when he returned on a third voyage (1498–1500), he found much strife and illness on the island. Word of this reached Spain, and his enemies there sent men to arrest him. He was carried back in chains to face charges of wrongdoing by the Crown. After managing to regain the respect of the monarchs, he was allowed to make a fourth voyage (1502–04), though he lost his title of Admiral of the Ocean Sea and the right to govern the islands.

On his last trip, he explored Central America but lost his ships and was marooned on Jamaica for a year before being rescued. He died in a monastery in Spain two years later, never fully realizing he had discovered a New World. He and his heirs were deprived of their promised rewards by King Ferdinand, who decided to keep the riches of this New World for himself and Spain.

In 1892, on the 400th anniversary of his first landing, the Columbian Exposition (a world's fair) was held in Chicago and October 12 became a national holiday—Columbus Day. As the 500th anniversary approached in 1992, however, many groups, especially Native Americans, argued that Columbus Day honors not the discoverer of America but a man whose deeds led to the wiping out of whole populations and their cultures. What is more, they pointed out, America didn't need to be "discovered." Millions of people had lived here for centuries before the Europeans came.

See also Exploration of North America.

For further reading: Barbara Brenner, *If You Were There in 1492* (Toronto: Bradbury, 1991); Steve Dodge, *Christopher Columbus and the First Voyages to the New World* (New York: Chelsea House, 1991); Steve Lowe, ed., *The Log of Christopher Columbus: The First Voyage, Spring, Summer, and Fall, 1492* (New York: Philomel Books, 1992).

WARREN GOLDSTEIN

COMICS

A comic strip is a series of cartoons that tell a story. Comics have roots that run as far back as prehistoric cave drawings and ancient Egyptian tomb paintings, but the comic strip as we know it today first appeared in American newspapers about a hundred years ago.

The earliest true strip, one that possessed a permanent cast of characters and speech printed inside the pictures, was Rudolph Dirks's *The Katzenjammer Kids,* which first appeared in the *New York Sunday Journal* on December 12, 1897. A broad slapstick series set on a tropical island, *The Katzenjammer Kids* is about two mischievous little boys, Hans and Fritz, and the endless tricks they play on the grown-ups they live with.

The new form was called "comics," or "funnies," because almost all the early strips

The first frame of a 1923 Krazy Kat comic shows Offissa Pupp, the local police officer, attempting yet again to force Ignatz Mouse to stop tormenting Krazy Kat.

were humorous. The first continuous story told in comics was Winsor McKay's imaginative and beautifully drawn *Little Nemo in Slumberland,* about a little boy's weird dreams. A wild, often hilarious fantasy strip, it began in 1905. Bud Fisher's *Mutt and Jeff* appeared in 1907 as a daily illustrated joke featuring the tall, beanpole-thin Mr. Mutt and his short, bewhiskered sidekick, Jeff, a pair whose dialogue was like that of a stage comedy team.

The animal strip *Krazy Kat,* which some historians consider the greatest cartoon series of all time, was created by George Herriman in 1913. It was a collection of strange stories about a female cat named Krazy, who was in love with a malicious mouse named Ignatz who continually threw bricks at her. Krazy would interpret these attacks as marks of affection, but Offissa Pupp, a dog serving as the local policeman, tried constantly to protect her by arresting Ignatz. *Krazy Kat* continued until 1944.

The golden age of comics began with the development of special companies, which bought the rights to popular strips or commissioned the creation of new ones and sold them to newspapers all over the country, a practice called syndication. King Features Syndicate, the first and still the largest of these businesses, was founded in 1911. Once syndicated, a strip may outlive its creator. When a writer or artist retires or dies, the syndicate may simply hire someone else to continue it.

By 1920, comics had developed in several ways. Many new strips were far from "comic." Family strips, some with stories that went on for years, appeared. Sometimes the characters are fixed at one age for the life of the strip. The people in Gus Edson's popular feature *The Gumps,* for example, were no older

Lois Lane, Superman's girlfriend, eventually ended up with her own comic book. This 1962 edition features Lois who, having grown tired of waiting for Superman to propose, has married Lex Luthor, the superhero's archenemy. Superman, left out in the cold, jealously spies on this scene of domestic bliss.

when the strip ended in 1949 than when it began in 1917. In others, the cast ages normally. In *Gasoline Alley,* created by Frank King in 1919, the character of Skeezix appeared as an infant in 1921 and is now a grandfather.

After World War I, action and adventure became increasingly popular in the comics. The first extended story about a woman, *Winnie Winkle,* was started by Martin Bannerman in 1920. It still recounts its ageless heroine's adventures. *Little Orphan Annie,* by

Charles Schulz's comic strip, Peanuts, *which features Charlie Brown, always down on his luck, and whose most frequent comment on life is "Sigh." His dog, Snoopy, no ordinary pet, fancies himself a World War I pilot and rarely has time for his owner.*

Harold Gray, began her long career of surviving perils and hardships in 1924, and Burne Hogarth originated *Tarzan,* based on Edgar Rice Burroughs's jungle novels, in 1929. *Joe Palooka,* Ham Fisher's story of a gentle boxing champion, began in 1930, followed the next year by Chester Gould's often violent detective strip *Dick Tracy.* The year 1934 saw the start of Alex Raymond's science-fiction story *Flash Gordon* and one of the most popular of all adventure strips, Milt Caniff's *Terry and the Pirates.*

New humor strips appeared during this period, although less frequently than in the early days. Among the most successful was Chic Young's still popular *Blondie* (1930), a domestic series about a "normal" suburban family, Dagwood and Blondie Bumstead, their two children, and their dogs, Daisy and her pups. A very different humor strip, Al Capp's broad hillbilly satire *Li'l Abner,* was created in 1934. It related the adventures of its simple young hero, Abner Yokum, and his incredibly ignorant Mammy, Pappy, and friends.

But only after the end of World War II in the mid-1940s did the national mood really

Jules Feiffer's strip Feiffer *is a cross between an editorial cartoon and a comic.*

lighten. Walt Kelly created *Pogo,* a witty, often sharply satirical strip about a possum and his Okefenokee Swamp friends, in 1949. The next year two of the most popular strips ever drawn were created, Charles Schulz's *Peanuts* and Mort Walker's army spoof *Beetle Bailey.* Both are now published in more than two thousand newspapers worldwide. But adventure and romantic strips declined in number and readership during the 1950s, and by 1960 there were twice as many humor features as story strips in American newspapers. For stronger stuff, fans turned to comic books.

Comic books began as collections of newspaper strips reprinted in booklets and given away as advertising. The first, *Funnies on Parade,* came out in 1933. The first with original material followed two years later. The era of superheroes began in 1938 with the appearance of Superman, created by Jerry Siegel and Joe Schuster, in *Action Comics.* Comic books eventually became so violent and gory that critics protested, and in 1954 the industry required its members to adopt a Comics Code. During the 1960s and 1970s, however, "adult" comics emerged. They dealt defiantly with drugs, sex, and social protest.

The expression of serious ideas in "comic" form has become well established. Jules Feiffer, who started drawing cartoons in 1956, is now an influential social and political critic. Garry Trudeau's *Doonesbury* (see p. 862 for illustration), begun in 1970, was the first comic strip to win the Pulitzer Prize. That Trudeau's strip is meant as serious commentary on current events and trends is reflected in the fact that some newspapers run *Doonesbury* on the editorial page rather than in the comics section. Art Spiegelman's *Maus* retold the tragic history of the Nazi concentration camps during World War II.

Some characters in popular strips, like Jim Davis's cynical cat Garfield and Schulz's *Peanuts* characters, appear on television and on many commercial products. Comic strips have always reflected the tastes and interests of their times. In recent years, they have dealt with many contemporary issues. Blondie Bumstead started her own business in 1990, and Superman announced plans to get married in 1991. There are now "comics" about the problems of single parents, racial discrimination, and poverty. In less than a century, comic strips have progressed from crude visual jokes to an art form of great variety and depth. They have become one of America's most popular cultural exports around the world and a multimillion-dollar industry at home.

For further reading: Ron Goulart, ed., *Encyclopedia of American Comics* (New York: Facts on File, 1990).

DENNIS WEPMAN

COMMITTEES OF CORRESPONDENCE

These committees were informal organizations of colonial leaders seeking to keep in touch with similar groups in other colonies. The new British taxes and restrictions imposed during the 1760s and 1770s alarmed the colonists. They wanted to communicate with one another in order to arrive at common policies. Among the most important crises leading to the development of the committees was Parliament's passage of the Stamp Act in 1765 and the Townshend duties in 1767.

At first the committees were thought to be temporary—necessary responses to particular problems. But in 1773 nearly all the colonial legislatures joined in establishing permanent committees of correspondence. The committees can be seen as the earliest form of intercolonial government, a predecessor of the First Continental Congress.

See also Revolution.

COMMON SENSE

Even though fighting had already begun between British troops and colonial militiamen, in January 1776 most Americans probably still hoped for a settlement of their conflicts with the British that would allow them to remain part of the British Empire. But Thomas Paine's pamphlet *Common Sense,* which was published that month, convinced many Americans that they would have to make a total break with what they had considered their mother country. Thus, it was a major cause of the American Revolution. Indeed, it is no coincidence that *Common Sense* was followed within a few months by the Declaration of Independence.

Where earlier critics had blamed Parliament or the king's advisers for the British policies they disliked, Paine put the blame directly on King George III. He called George a "Royal Brute," and he denounced the very idea of monarchy as tyrannical. According to Paine, people had a right to govern themselves, and this was the time to exercise that right. "We have it in our power to begin the world again," he declared. "Ye that dare oppose not only tyranny but the tyrant, stand forth!"

Common Sense had a truly enormous impact on public opinion. Half a million copies were sold, about one for every six people in the land. The historian Bernard Bailyn, the leading authority on the pamphlets of the period, has described it as by far the most influ-

ential, and one of the most brilliant ever penned in the English language.

See also Paine, Thomas; Revolution: The War for Independence.

COMMUNISM
See Anticommunism; Cold War.

COMPROMISE OF 1850

The Compromise of 1850 decided how the territory obtained from Mexico after the Mexican War was to be divided and governed. In particular, the question of whether slavery should be permitted in the new lands caused a sharp division in Congress between pro- and antislavery forces. The debate in the Senate was particularly dramatic because it marked the last important appearances in public affairs of the great congressional leaders of the previous generation, Senators Henry Clay of Kentucky, Daniel Webster of Mas-

The Compromise of 1850

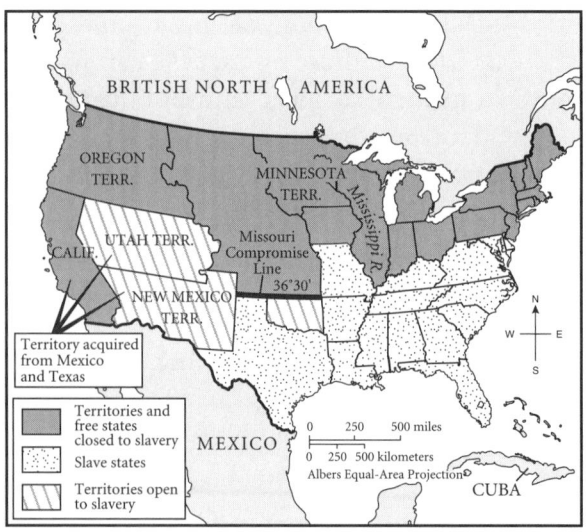

BRITISH NORTH AMERICA

OREGON TERR.

MINNESOTA TERR.

CALIF. UTAH TERR.

Missouri Compromise Line 36°30'

Mississippi R.

NEW MEXICO TERR.

Territory acquired from Mexico and Texas

MEXICO

Territories and free states closed to slavery

Slave states

Territories open to slavery

0   250   500 miles
0   250 500 kilometers
Albers Equal-Area Projection

CUBA

N
W   E
S

sachusetts, and John C. Calhoun of South Carolina.

Clay advanced the basic elements of the compromise. California, expanding rapidly because of the recent discovery of gold, was to be admitted to the Union at once as a free state. The rest of the Southwest would be given a territorial government, but the question of slavery in the region would be left to the people who settled there. A disputed boundary between what is now New Mexico and Texas was to be settled in New Mexico's favor, but in return the United States would assume the state debt of Texas. In addition, the slave trade (not slavery itself) was to be forbidden in the District of Columbia, and a fugitive slave law would be passed making it easier for southerners to regain slaves who had escaped to the free states.

Webster backed Clay's plan as the best way to persuade the southern states not to secede from the Union, something they were threatening to do. Calhoun, representing the extreme proslavery position, demanded that Congress should cease trying to limit slavery in the western territories. When it proved impossible to pass a single bill covering all the elements of the compromise, Senator Stephen A. Douglas engineered the passage of each of its parts in separate bills. The adoption of the compromise seemed at the time to solve for good the problem of slavery in the western territories. This did not prove to be the case.

See also Calhoun, John C.; Clay, Henry; Douglas, Stephen A.; Webster, Daniel.

COMPROMISE OF 1877

The 1876 presidential campaign between Rutherford B. Hayes, the Republican candidate, and Samuel J. Tilden, the Democrat, was ex-

tremely close. On election day Tilden received more popular votes and carried the electoral college by a small margin.

However, Republicans controlled the election machinery in Florida, South Carolina, and Louisiana and they threw out enough Democratic votes to make those states appear to have gone to Hayes. Together with a technicality affecting one electoral vote in Oregon, the changes would make Hayes president by an electoral vote of 185 to 184. Thus when the electors met to cast their votes, rival delegations from these states presented themselves.

To settle this disputed election, Congress appointed a fifteen-member commission made up of seven Democrats, seven Republicans, and one "independent" to decide which electoral votes to count. The independent, Supreme Court Justice Joseph P. Bradley, voted in each case for the Republican electors, thus making Hayes president.

To persuade Tilden and the Democrats to accept the decision, Hayes and his congressional supporters agreed to remove the last federal troops from the South, which they had occupied since the Civil War. Thus the compromise put an end to Reconstruction. In effect, it allowed southern whites to resume their domination of southern society and politics. It resulted in strict racial segregation and the near-total disfranchisement (loss of the right to vote) of southern blacks.

See also Hayes, Rutherford B.; Reconstruction.

CONFEDERATE STATES OF AMERICA

The election in 1860 of Abraham Lincoln as president of the United States was the last straw for the South. For forty years North-

THE CONFEDERATE STATES OF AMERICA

State	Seceded from Union	Readmitted to Union[*]
South Carolina	Dec. 20, 1860	July 9, 1868
Mississippi	Jan. 9, 1861	Feb. 23, 1870
Florida	Jan. 10, 1861	June 25, 1868
Alabama	Jan. 11, 1861	July 13, 1868
Georgia	Jan. 19, 1861	July 15, 1870[†]
Louisiana	Jan. 26, 1861	July 9, 1868
Texas	March 2, 1861	March 30, 1870
Virginia	April 17, 1861	Jan. 26, 1870
Arkansas	May 6, 1861	June 22, 1868
North Carolina	May 20, 1861	July 4, 1868
Tennessee	June 8, 1861	July 24, 1866

[*]Date of readmission to representation in U.S. House of Representatives.

[†]Second readmission date. First date was July 21, 1868, but the representatives were unseated until March 5, 1869.

NOTE: Four other slave states—Delaware, Kentucky, Maryland, and Missouri—remained in the Union.

South disagreements over slavery were compounded by debates over states' rights, different interpretations of the Constitution, and competition between Southern agricultural interests and Northern industrialism. The federal government seemed to be powerless as frictions increased between the two sections. Southern leaders viewed the new Republican Party as an army of abolitionists bent on shaping America to their own mold. When Republican candidate Lincoln won the 1860 race, the Southern states decided that they had to leave the Union to preserve the country as they felt the Founding Fathers had intended it to be.

Founding the Confederacy

On December 20, 1860, South Carolina passed an ordinance of secession and left the Union. Six other states—Mississippi, Florida, Alabama, Georgia, Louisiana, and Texas—quickly followed suit. Delegates from those states met in Montgomery, Alabama, and, on February 4, 1861, established the Confederate States of America. Jefferson Davis of Mississippi and Alexander H. Stephens of Georgia became president and vice president, respectively.

In April, following the Confederate bombardment of the federal garrison at Fort Sumter, South Carolina, and Lincoln's subsequent call for Union troops to put down this "rebellion," the states of Virginia, Tennessee, Arkansas, and North Carolina joined the Southern nation. This brought the total number of Confederate states to eleven. (The Southern battle flag had thirteen stars because Confederate officials considered Kentucky and Missouri to be member states. Yet neither withdrew from the Union.)

Since Southerners were attempting to preserve what they felt were traditional American values, the Confederate Constitution was strikingly similar to the U.S. Constitution. The Southern document differed in only a few ways: it recognized all aspects of states' rights and the legality of slavery; the president was to serve a single six-year term; and the power of the states was superior to that of the central government at the capital in Richmond, Virginia. This preference for allowing eleven separate states to have more authority than would be the case in a federation was a major weakness of the Confederacy.

The South's population was outnumbered four to one by the North. Its agricultural output was not equal in value to Northern industrial production. Thus, in the Civil War the South could not match the Union man for man and blow for blow. On the other hand, the South for the most part fought on the defensive rather than invading the North. This did not require as many soldiers; moreover, Confederates were maneuvering on familiar ground, and their supply lines were shorter, their movements easier. Most important, the South could win this war by simply not losing. As long as the Confederacy existed—as long as the Union was not united—the Southern nation had what it wanted.

The New Nation's Problems

At first, President Davis as commander in chief divided the Confederacy into eight military departments. Each had its own troops and responsibilities; none had any strong links with the others. Such loose command and lack of concentration had disastrous results, for in trying to defend everything, Confederate forces barely defended anything. The South did manage to wage a number of notable defensive campaigns, particularly those involving the protection of Richmond. Yet the story of the four-year struggle is that of a nation whose borders slowly, steadily crumbled until at the end only Virginia and North Carolina remained.

Defeat in war often produces unreal thoughts in the minds of the losers. Southerners in the postwar years created the myth of an honorable and glorious "Lost Cause." According to its image, a united South maintained a solid front but in the end lost the fight to overwhelming numbers of Northern men and matériel. Such was not the case. The Confederacy was born in an atmosphere of war and it died from that war. It did so in large part because of many internal problems it failed to solve.

At no time did the Confederate government secure as many men for the armies as were needed. The early flush of patriotism

waned quickly. This caused the Confederate Congress to pass America's first conscription act, whereby men were drafted into service. But conscription was so unfairly enforced that it created far more hard feelings than any spirit of cooperation.

Because the South was a farming region, it was never able to manufacture the many weapons of war necessary to win the contest with the North. But staple crops such as cotton and tobacco had always been the mainstay of the South. Switching over to growing more foodstuffs needed in time of war required more effort and sacrifice than the new nation could afford. Furthermore, the large numbers of men in the armies drastically reduced the number of farmers and planters behind the lines. All through the war, also, federal armies occupied more and more vital croplands. As the sphere of Union control increased, Confederate farmland decreased. Fewer acres fed fewer people.

The shortages of food soon made hunger a terrible reality in large sections of the Confederacy. The shortages in turn produced gal-

Confederate soldiers of the Third Georgia Infantry. Two were half brothers and became casualties of the war in July 1862.

loping inflation throughout the land. In 1861 bacon was twelve cents per pound; three years later it was twelve dollars per pound—when it could be found. In the same period, the price of tea jumped from one to twenty-two dollars per pound.

Railroads played a very important role in the Civil War, moving both troops and supplies from place to place. Southern lines were inadequate at the start. The war took such a terrible toll on what railroads there were that officials adopted the policy of removing the rails and rolling stock from lesser-used railroads and transplanting them to more important lines.

It is appropriate that Rhett Butler, the leading male character in Margaret Mitchell's famous war novel, *Gone with the Wind,* was a speculator and black marketeer. Corruption abounded inside the Southern nation. A few individuals made enormous profits while the Confederacy and its citizens wasted away.

At the same time, much internal strife marked Southern conduct in wartime. A "one for all and all for one" patriotism did not exist. Unionists quarreled with secessionists; bad blood continued between upper and lower classes; mountain folk and Tidewater residents made little effort at cooperation; governors and other strong believers in the rights of the states clashed almost daily with Confederate authorities who knew that only a strong central government could carry the South to victory.

Civil war destroyed the Old South. The antebellum Cotton Kingdom, slavery, strong beliefs in states' rights, total dependence on agriculture—all disappeared in the fire and smoke of war. For a century thereafter, the South would wage a new struggle of trying to catch up with the rest of the Union without

losing its identity in the process. That it has succeeded on both counts gives the South today a proud and unique place in the United States of America.

See also Civil War; Davis, Jefferson; Secession.

JAMES I. ROBERTSON, JR.

CONFEDERATION, ARTICLES OF
See Articles of Confederation.

CONGRESS
See House of Representatives; Senate.

CONGRESSES, CONTINENTAL
See Continental Congresses.

CONGRESS OF INDUSTRIAL ORGANIZATIONS

From the time of its founding in 1886, the American Federation of Labor (AFL) was an organization of particular craftsmen, such as carpenters, machinists, and printers. Unskilled workers, like ditch diggers and busboys in restaurants, and blacks, even those with particular skills, were excluded by the AFL. Large manufacturing companies often employed members of several different unions. United action by workers was therefore very difficult to arrange.

After the New Deal National Recovery Act of 1933 gave all workers the right to join unions and bargain collectively with their employers, the disadvantages of separate trade unions became more obvious. In 1935 a group of trade union leaders headed by John L. Lewis, Sidney Hillman, and David

Dubinsky formed the Committee for Industrial Organization. They intended, as the name indicated, to organize workers by entire industries, such as automobiles, steel, and textiles, rather than by particular skilled trades. In 1936 the AFL expelled the committee, which in 1938 became the Congress of Industrial Organizations (CIO). John L. Lewis was its first president.

The CIO proved far more aggressive in fighting for higher wages and better working conditions than the AFL. Its most effective tactic was the sit-down strike, in which workers occupied their factories and refused to leave until their demands were met. By 1943 the CIO had more than 5 million members and had proved capable of winning important gains. Finally, in 1955, the AFL and the CIO merged into a single superunion.

See also AFL; Labor Movement; Lewis, John L.

CONGRESS OF RACIAL EQUALITY

The Congress of Racial Equality (CORE), an organization of predominantly northern white reformers seeking to improve race relations in the United States, was founded in 1942. It became prominent in 1955 when its members worked to support the campaign led by Martin Luther King, Jr., to end bus segregation in Montgomery, Alabama. From then on it attracted large numbers of black members.

In doing so it became increasingly more militant. To integrate lunch counters in southern drugstores and department stores that refused to serve black customers, CORE supported nonviolent "sit-ins." Groups of blacks took seats at the lunch counters and refused to leave, even when subjected to abuse by whites or threatened with arrest. The group also organized "Freedom Rides" to test the effectiveness of a 1960 Supreme Court decision that prohibited segregation in public areas that served interstate travelers. Busloads of blacks and their white supporters traveled through the region, demanding to be allowed to use public facilities. They met with great resistance, even brutality, but persisted.

In 1961 CORE moved from directly fighting segregation to helping organize voter registration drives among southern blacks. Southern states had kept blacks from voting by claiming that they could not meet the standards of literacy required by law. Members of CORE persuaded educated black citizens to go to the registration centers and instituted lawsuits when white officials refused to register them.

What had been almost exclusively a white organization seeking racial integration became by the mid-1960s solidly black, often urging racial separation rather than integration.

See also Civil Rights Movement; Freedom Rides.

CONSCIENTIOUS OBJECTORS

Men and women have resisted the call to violent action from the time of the Revolution down through the wars of the twentieth century. They have invented a hundred quiet or dramatic ways to protest war and express their conviction that peaceful solutions to conflicts are possible. And when the government has not recognized their right to stand by their conscience, they have been jailed, flogged, deported, even murdered.

The term *conscientious objector* (CO for

short) did not come into use until World War I. Before then, COs were called "nonresistants." That term comes from the words of Jesus, opposing the use of violence. People have refused to participate in war for a number of reasons—religious, moral, and political—and the degree of refusal varies. Absolute pacifists will not cooperate with any preparation for war, let alone war itself. Other pacifists will accept some kind of service as long as they are not forced to fight. Still others are willing to fight in "just wars," but not in wars they believe to be "unjust."

Opposition to war on religious grounds is truly ancient. Taoism, born in China in the sixth century B.C., stressed love, moderation, and a nonviolent way of life. Although the Old Testament is full of battles, some of the Hebrew prophets anticipated the ethic of nonviolent resistance. The Jewish sect of the Essenes rejected violence as a matter of principle.

In the Sermon on the Mount, Jesus developed the ethic of nonviolence and love for one's enemies, saying "Blessed are the peacemakers for they shall be called the children of God." The early Christians were probably the first individuals to renounce participation in war unconditionally. Many soldiers left the Roman army after being converted to Christianity. In the fourth century, the classic Christian idea of the "just war" was developed by Saint Augustine.

Pacifism in America

Many immigrants—from the earliest days of white settlement—came to America to escape conscription (being drafted) in their homeland. Some were pacifists by conviction, and others were weary of the many wars in the Old World.

The Quakers were among the first to bring pacifism to the colonies. They stood against all wars and often suffered for their beliefs. Many went to jail for conscientious objection during the colonial wars. William Penn and John Woolman were two of the best-known Quakers who stood for peaceable negotiation of all differences. Several other "peace churches"—the Moravians, the Mennonites, the Brethren, the Dunkers, the Shakers, the Amish—took literally the biblical injunctions to "resist not evil" and "Thou shalt not kill."

During the American Revolution pacifists were often denounced as traitors, and the states punished them by fines, confiscation of property, or imprisonment. In 1815 the first American pacifist organization was formed in New York, and in 1828 a national organization, the American Peace Society, was founded. In 1838 the abolitionist William Lloyd Garrison with others founded the New England Non-Resistance Society.

In 1846 Henry David Thoreau was briefly jailed for refusing to pay taxes in support of the Mexican War. His powerful essay, "Civil Disobedience," urged COs to carry their nonviolent protests far enough to correct injustices. A year later Elihu Burritt created the League of Universal Brotherhood, the first nonreligious peace group to organize internationally. Burritt pioneered many techniques—taking a peace pledge, mass demonstrations, strikes—to rally people against war.

When the Civil War began, many COs joined the Union forces, placing their hatred of slavery above their pacifist convictions. Other members of peace groups, north and south, stood by their principles. They hid to avoid being drafted or were jailed.

Nearly fifty new peace groups appeared around the turn of the century, but their efforts failed to prevent the outbreak of World War I in 1914. When the United States entered the war in 1917, most pacifists from the peace churches were exempted from combat, but had to perform noncombatant service. Those who refused suffered long prison terms. The treatment of COs was a little more humane in World War II. About 50,000 were assigned to noncombatant duty, and another 12,000 were sent to public service camps. But six thousand went to prison rather than take any part in the draft process.

Protests against the Vietnam War

In 1954 the United States assumed the burden of defending South Vietnam from guerrilla forces sent in by North Vietnam. From then until 1975, 2.8 million U.S. troops were sent to Vietnam, and 58,000 Americans and about 2 million Vietnamese died. It proved to be America's most disastrous military adventure.

Late in 1964 massive bombing assaults on Vietnam and the growing casualty list galvanized Americans into opposition to the war. Major demonstrations took place in many cities and on college campuses, with protesters issuing "an appeal to the American conscience" that urged an immediate cease-fire and the withdrawal of U.S. troops. The antiwar movement brought together people of many differing political views who agreed only on the need to get America out of Vietnam—traditional pacifists, peace church members, liberals, and conservatives.

Beginning in the fall of 1965, many burned their draft cards as an act of defiance, and soon a federal law made it a crime to destroy the cards. Then came street demonstrations, sit-ins, speak-outs, teach-ins—all intended to rally popular protest against the war. A group of men who had served in the war, some of whom had earned medals for their bravery, came to feel that the war was wrong and organized the Vietnam Veterans against

the War. A number of them even returned their medals to the government.

Draft-age men in ever-greater numbers came to pacifist groups to seek advice on how to avoid induction. By the time the war ended, nearly 100,000 young men had refused military duty by going into hiding or fleeing the country. Another 170,000 did alternative service, and a good many resisters served prison terms. When the long war ended, most peace activists hoped that the United States had learned from the agony of Vietnam that the use of military power to counter social and political change in another nation is wrong.

See also Conscription; Draft Riots of 1863; Kent State Incident; Quakers; Shakers. *And see biographies of the following pacifists:* Addams, Jane; Day, Dorothy; Debs, Eugene V.; Garrison, William Lloyd; Goldman, Emma; King, Martin Luther, Jr.; Penn, William; Thoreau, Henry David.

For further reading: Milton Meltzer, *Ain't Gonna Study War No More: The Story of America's Peace-Seekers* (New York: Harper & Row, 1985).

MILTON MELTZER

CONSCRIPTION

Today the armed forces of the United States—the army, navy, air force, Marines, and coast guard—are all-volunteer services. For various reasons, men and women elect to serve in the military, either for a short time or as a career.

It was not always so. Through much of American history, men, never women, were *conscripted*, or *drafted*—that is, they were required (some would say forced) to serve in the military, fight for their country, and perhaps die for it.

Conscription was first used in the Civil War by both the South and the North. It was a disaster. Men were accustomed to serving with their friends and neighbors in state militias, the forerunners of today's National Guard. They usually enlisted or volunteered for a few months or a year and then went home. At times, this left both the Union and the Confederate armies strapped for men on the eve of a battle. Conscripting men to fight seemed a solution to both sides. But no one liked it, for the men were inducted into the regular army or served in other states' militias rather than with their friends. It also seemed to many to be the action of a tyrannical government.

Worse, draftees could hire substitutes for three hundred dollars in the North and an agreed-upon price in the South. The rich hired the poor to go to war for them. The substitutes often deserted and sold themselves over and over to other draftees. In the South the hiring price became so high that some ordinary soldiers earned more money than their officers. The abuses of Civil War conscription led to draft riots in New York City in 1863. More than a hundred people were killed before troops were brought in to restore order—troops that were badly needed at the Battle of Gettysburg going on at the same time.

Conscription was imposed again in 1917 for World War I and in 1940 for World War II. It now worked much better because the mistakes of the Civil War were not repeated. No hiring of substitutes was allowed. A person could be deferred only for a specific reason, such as poor health or because he had a special skill needed on the home front. Drafting was done by local civilians, who served on Selective Service Boards. Almost 3 million men were drafted in World War I and over 10 million in World War II. There was not much public opposition to these wars, so the draft seemed reasonable.

Secretary of War Newton D. Baker, blindfolded, draws the first draft number for World War I in 1918. Seventy-two percent of the 3.5 million troops who fought in this war came into the army through compulsory enrollment, called conscription, *or the* draft.

The Korean War, 1950–1953, again brought conscription problems. Men who had served in World War II were exempted, unless they had joined the National Guard or reserves units. Many had and thus were called to duty once again. But with so many men ineligible, it became difficult to find enough to be conscripted. Husbands and fathers were called, along with men as old as 35 and as young as 18½. About 1.5 million men were drafted.

Military conscription once again worked poorly with the escalation of the war in Vietnam in 1965. Millions of people considered the war unjust and unnecessary. There were widespread protests and riots over the war and the drafting of men to fight in it. Many burned their draft cards or refused to serve. Thousands fled the country, many to Canada, to evade the draft. (After the war, they were pardoned and allowed to return.)

Fueling the resistance was the gross unfairness of the draft. Men with high draft numbers chosen by lottery—thus men likely to be called up first—could avoid it by joining the National Guard or reserve units. Most of these units were not brought into the war. Men could gain deferments by going to college or graduate school. Thus, the war in Vietnam was fought, aside from regular enlisted troops, predominantly by men who were poor, undereducated, or black. The basic unfairness of this was not lost on anyone, and it left deep scars on the nation. Draft evasion was still a political issue in 1988, because it was reported that Vice President Dan Quayle had joined the National Guard, and in 1992, because President Bill Clinton was said to have used influence to evade conscription. That both were elected suggests that Americans no longer consider draft evasion during the Vietnam War very important.

Conscription ended in America in 1973. It seems unlikely to be revived because modern, high-tech warfare demands the highly skilled and trained people that an all-volunteer military can best provide.

See also Draft Riots of 1863.

R O B E R T A. L I S T O N

C O N S E R V A T I O N   A N D   E N V I R O N M E N T A L   M O V E M E N T S

The word *conservation,* which derives from the idea of saving or conserving, was specifically applied to nature in 1907 by President Theodore Roosevelt's chief forester, Gifford Pinchot. A major political movement followed that, by the 1960s, had broadened and transformed into what we know today as "environmentalism." But the history of concern for the environment goes well back into America's past.

In many ways the original native inhabitants of North America were sophisticated conservationists. They understood its most basic concept: excessive human demands on nature will eventually backfire. Without restraint and respect, both civilization and the environment on which it depends will suffer. Building on this idea, Native Americans frequently made animals, plants, and even places like mountains the subject of religious worship. The land itself was sacred. But the European colonists who replaced the Native Americans lacked this reverential attitude. To them nature was something to be feared, conquered, and turned into profit.

Early Conservation Efforts

Up until the middle of the nineteenth century only a few Americans questioned the wisdom of exploiting the environment. But the disappearance of valuable resources, particularly forests, topsoil, and populations of animals such as the buffalo gradually caused second thoughts. American anxiety increased in 1890 when the U.S. Census declared that the "frontier," or unbroken western wilderness, no longer existed. The nation had grown up, filled in its borders, and prospered, but not without major environmental damage.

Conservation was the effort to repair this damage and create a long-term, sustainable relationship between civilization and nature. Chief Forester Pinchot advocated efficient care in the cutting of forests so there would be lumber for tomorrow's needs. During Roosevelt's presidency (1901–09) millions of acres of timberland in the West were protected as "national forests." Pinchot, along with John Wesley Powell, also championed the wise use of America's rivers, a movement that led to such major federal environmental engineering projects as Hoover Dam (authorized in 1928) and the Tennessee Valley Authority (1933). In the Midwest a "Dust Bowl" resulted in the 1930s from careless farming methods and prolonged drought. The Soil Conservation Service (1935) was one federal response to this disaster.

Meanwhile conservationists interested in the beauty rather than the utility of nature campaigned for "national parks" and the preservation idea. Yellowstone National Park, established in Wyoming in 1872, was the first one in the world and perhaps the best idea our civilization ever had. John Muir helped create Yosemite National Park in California in 1890. Two years later he founded the Sierra Club, the nation's most famous citizen conservation organization, to defend parks and wilderness.

Ecology: A New Science

In the early twentieth century Aldo Leopold, among others, started a new kind of natural science called "ecology." Ecologists study the interrelationships between living creatures and their environment. The research revealed nature to be a complex and delicate system that is capable of being destroyed by humans. One consequence of this idea was the extraordinary attention paid to a book published in 1962—*Silent Spring* by Rachel Carson. She revealed the effects of pesticides, or chemicals intended to kill certain insects, on the entire ecosystem, including the birds that eat the insects, whatever eats the birds, and so on until, ultimately, the occupants of the tops of the food chains such as humans are reached.

Aiding Carson in her crusade to respect the balances and limits of nature were dramatic photographs of Earth from space. Environmentalists such as David Brower of the Sierra Club and Paul Ehrlich, a population biologist, argued that our planet is like a spaceship—limited in its resources, absolutely essential to life, and capable of being disrupted by the growth of human numbers and human demands. The National Environmental Policy Act of 1970, featuring the requirement of an environmental impact statement for actions potentially harmful to nature, was a major result of this kind of thinking. So was the Endangered Species Act of 1973, which recognized the right of non-human life forms to a share of the environment.

Although the American environmental movement achieved much in the 1960s and 1970s, some people were disappointed with the speed of the reforms. These "radical environmentalists" wanted to protect nature for its own sake and not just because it served human interests. They felt that nature should be included in society's ethical or moral ideal. Greenpeace (1969) and Earth First! (1980) are the best-known radical environmental organizations. Some of their members support civil disobedience on behalf of the environment, and others advocate violent resistance to nature's exploiters and destroyers. If the present political and economic system fails to advance environmental causes rapidly enough, we can expect to see more support for radical environmentalism in the coming century.

Recently, American environmentalism has taken on a global dimension. People realize that our nation is not an island but, instead, part of physical and biological systems that encompass the whole earth. Many hoped that the Earth Summit, organized by the United Nations and held in 1992 in Brazil, would mark the start of a new, sustainable relationship between people and nature. But major obstacles existed in the continuing growth of human population and the seemingly unending human appetite for material growth. In his book *Earth in the Balance* (1992) Vice President Al Gore warned that effective environmental protection would require massive commitments of time, money, and effort. Those who questioned these costs could be reminded that our very survival was ultimately at stake. The environment, it seems likely, will be at the top of the agendas for political reform in the coming century.

See also Ballinger-Pinchot Controversy; Carson, Rachel; Civilian Conservation Corps; Dust Bowl; Gore, Al; Roosevelt, Theodore; Tennessee Valley Authority.

RODERICK FRAZIER NASH

CONSTITUTION, THE MAKING OF THE

The Constitution of the United States was written by fifty-five politicians from twelve of the original thirteen states (Rhode Island refused to send delegates) at the Philadelphia Convention (also known as the Federal Convention and the Constitutional Convention). The convention met in the State House (now called Independence Hall) in Philadelphia, Pennsylvania, from May 25 to September 17, 1787. Once the convention made the proposed Constitution public, the people of twelve states (all but Rhode Island) elected conventions to ratify, or approve, the docu-

Scene at the Signing of the Constitution of the United States, *by Howard Chandler Christy. Thirty-nine delegates assembled in Philadelphia to sign their names to the document.*

ment. Eleven of these conventions, which met in late 1787 and through 1788, voted to adopt the Constitution, and it became the nation's form of government on March 4, 1789. The institutions it established—the Congress, the Presidency, and the Supreme Court—took shape during the rest of that year. North Carolina accepted the Constitution in late 1789, and Rhode Island adopted it in 1790.

Federal Convention Called

Before the Constitution, the United States governed itself under the Articles of Confederation (1781). The one-house Confederation Congress had no way to raise the money it needed to finance itself, to solve disputes between the states, or to defend American interests from foreign nations. Because the Confederation was too weak and too poor to solve the nation's problems, national politicians—such as George Washington of Virginia, Benjamin Franklin of Pennsylvania, Alexander Hamilton of New York, James Madison of Virginia, and James Wilson of Pennsylvania—realized that something had to be done. Two interstate conferences (in 1785 at Mount Vernon, Virginia, and in 1786 at Annapolis, Maryland) urged that the Articles be revised or replaced. The result was the Federal Convention.

The delegates who attended the convention's meetings fell into five groups. Washington and Franklin were *national symbols* who staked their great reputations on the convention's success. Madison, Hamilton, and Wilson were some of the *theorists of government* who put their learning and ideas at the convention's service. Roger Sherman of Connecticut, William Livingston of New Jersey, John Dickinson of Delaware, John Rutledge of South Carolina, and George Mason of Vir-

ginia were among the *senior statesmen* who brought their experience and their ability to arrange compromises. Luther Martin of Maryland, William Paterson of New Jersey, Elbridge Gerry of Massachusetts, Charles C. Pinckney of South Carolina, and John Lansing, Jr., and Robert Yates of New York were *voices of local interests,* who spoke for the hopes, desires, and fears of "the folks back home." And most delegates—men like John Blair of Virginia, Nicholas Gilman of New Hampshire, and William Few of Georgia—were *quiet men* who became the raw material of consensus and compromise.

Some important politicians could not or would not attend the convention. John Adams of Massachusetts was American minister to Great Britain, Thomas Jefferson of Virginia was American minister to France, and John Jay of New York was the Confederation's secretary for foreign affairs. Patrick Henry of Virginia stayed home, explaining later that he "smelled a rat."

The Convention at Work

The delegates scrapped the idea of rewriting the Articles of Confederation and started from scratch. They even wrote special rules to guide how they would argue about what to do and how to do it. They worked behind closed doors because they did not want to be pressured by public opinion. Nobody objected at the time, because "the public's right to know" was not a major theme in 1787. Nor were official minutes kept. We know much about what went on in the convention because some delegates—notably Madison—kept diaries of the debates.

The men drew on the world's political wisdom and on such American experiments in government as the state constitutions of the 1770s and 1780s. They based their work on

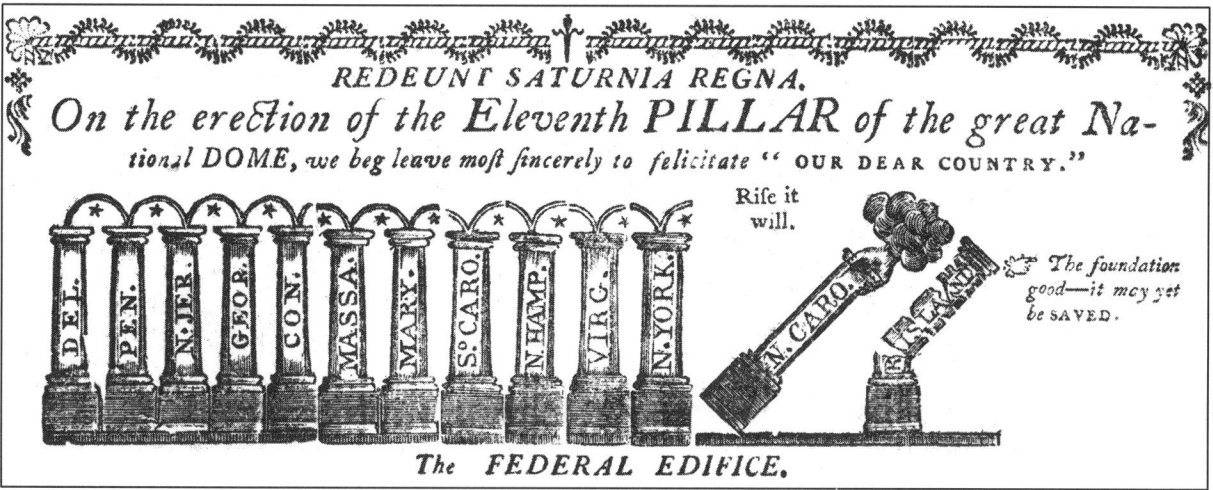

This cartoon was published after New York became the eleventh state to ratify, or approve, the Constitution in July 1788. The eleven standing columns, each representing a state, make up the country, while North Carolina, on the right, teeters unsteadily and Rhode Island seems ready to crumble. North Carolina finally ratified in November 1789, and Rhode Island followed in 1790.

the Virginia Plan, written by Madison and proposed by Virginia's governor, Edmund Randolph. The Virginia Plan provided for a national government of three branches—legislative, executive, and judicial. The large states backed the Virginia Plan. The small states rallied behind William Paterson's New Jersey Plan, which would have preserved the Confederation's structure of equal representation for all states regardless of population but would have given Congress more power. The convention rejected the New Jersey Plan but changed the Virginia Plan to satisfy small-state delegates who insisted that each state have an equal voice in at least one branch of the national legislature, or Congress.

The delegates often had to reach such compromises on which a majority could agree. This one is famous as the Great, or Connecticut, Compromise: the people of each state are represented by population in the House of Representatives, and each state elects two members of the Senate. The "three-fifths" compromise is another famous one that settled the question of whether slaves should be counted or not. Three-fifths of each state's total number of slaves would be counted for purposes of representation in the House and taxation.

Ratifying the Constitution

Most—but not all—of the delegates backed the Constitution. Some walked out, and three of the most important delegates—Randolph, Gerry, and Mason—refused to sign it. These opponents believed that the proposed government would be too strong to respect the power of the states or the liberties of the individuals.

The convention could not impose the Constitution on the American people. The document had to be ratified by the people of at least nine of the thirteen states before it went into effect. Between September 1787 and July 1788 the struggle for ratification took place. The Constitution's supporters called themselves *Federalists;* its opponents were called *Antifederalists* (even though they did not like the name). The ratification controversy was the first "great national discussion"; it took place in the nation's newspapers and magazines as well as in the formal debates of the ratifying conventions, which were open to the people. For the first time in history, a free people conducted a wide-ranging argument on how they wished to govern themselves. *The Federalist,* a series of eighty-five essays written by Hamilton, Madison, and Jay to explain and defend the Constitution, was part of that argument and has become a classic of political theory and constitutional law.

The Federalists helped make the Constitution's victory certain by promising to amend it by adding a bill of rights. Madison led this effort in the First Congress, and the Bill of Rights, proposed by Congress in 1789, became the first ten amendments in 1791.

The making of the Constitution was a political process. The politicians of the period invented that process one step at a time, with no guarantees that it, or the Constitution it produced, would work. That is how the Constitution continues to work today. It sets up the framework within which "We the People" live our lives and govern ourselves, but how we do that is up to us.

See also Antifederalists; Articles of Confederation; Bill of Rights; Constitution; Federalist Papers.

RICHARD B. BERNSTEIN

CONSTITUTION

The Constitution drafted by a convention of state delegates meeting in Philadelphia in 1787 has provided the framework of the government of the United States for over two hundred years. Only twenty-seven amendments have been added to that Constitution. The first ten—which make up the Bill of Rights—were ratified in 1791 soon after it went into effect.

Basic Framework

The Constitution was based on federalism, a system in which power is shared between a central government of a confederation and the governments of the separate states forming it. Under the earlier Articles of Confederation the Continental Congress provided the central government, but its powers were greatly restricted. It did not have the authority to tax or to regulate commerce. There was no executive branch or federal courts.

In ratifying the new Constitution the states gave to the federal government important powers—including those of taxation and control over foreign and interstate commerce—previously denied under the Articles of Confederation. At the same time, the states, or the people, retained all powers not delegated to the national government. The Tenth Amendment (1791) states this specifically.

The Constitution divides the powers of the national government among legislative, executive, and judicial branches. It also creates a number of checks and balances to prevent any single branch from becoming too powerful. The Senate must confirm major presidential appointments and ratify treaties. The president can approve or veto bills passed by Congress, but Congress may override the president's veto. The president is the commander in chief of the armed forces of the United States, but Congress has the power to declare war. Although it is not specifically stated in the Constitution, the Supreme Court early interpreted the document as authorizing judicial review—the Court's power to review acts of Congress to decide if they are constitutional.

In creating a two-house legislature the Constitution specifies that representation in the House of Representatives be based on population and that members be popularly elected. Membership in the Senate rests on the equality of states regardless of their size or population. Each state legislature was to elect two senators, though with adoption of the Seventeenth Amendment in 1913, senators became popularly elected. In both houses of Congress voting is by individual members, not by state delegations as under the earlier Articles of Confederation.

Electoral System

The electoral system for choosing the president and the vice president of the United States was one of the most original features of the Constitution. Fearful of allowing direct popular election of the president, the Constitutional Convention created the electoral college for indirect election. Presidential electors were to be chosen by whatever method each state legislature determined—by the legislature or by the people. The electors chosen met in their respective states. Each cast votes for two persons, at least one of whom could not be a resident of an elector's own state. When the returns from all states were counted, the candidate with a majority of the electoral votes became president. The candidate receiving the second highest number of electoral votes was elected vice president.

The number of representatives and senators a state is entitled to have in Congress determines each state's vote in the electoral college. The apportionment of electoral votes thus reflects the population-based membership of the House and the equality of states in the Senate. If no candidate receives a majority

of electoral votes, the election is decided by the House of Representatives with each state delegation having one vote.

In the election of 1800 the contest of political parties resulted in every elector who voted for Thomas Jefferson also voting for Aaron Burr, the Jeffersonian candidate for vice president. This tie in the electoral vote sent the election to the House of Representatives, where thirty-six ballots were taken before Jefferson was elected president. To avoid this situation in the future, the Twelfth Amendment (1804) was ratified prior to the next presidential election. It provided for the separate election of the president and the vice president.

Some Amendments

No further amendments were added to the Constitution until after the Civil War. The Thirteenth Amendment (1865) abolished slavery. The Fourteenth Amendment (1868) expanded the protection of civil liberties. The Fifteenth Amendment (1870) provided that the right to vote could not be denied or abridged because of race, color, or previous condition of servitude. In 1920, the Nineteenth Amendment ordered that the right to vote not be denied or abridged on account of sex. Continuing the expansion of the suffrage, the Twenty-fourth Amendment (1964) outlawed the payment of any tax as a condition for voting. The Twenty-sixth Amendment (1971) extended the suffrage to eighteen-year-olds.

Interpreting the Constitution

The Constitution contains a long list of the specific lawmaking powers of Congress and also grants authority "to make all laws which shall be necessary and proper to carry into execution the foregoing powers" (Article I, Section 8). How this should be interpreted early became a matter of dispute. When Alexander Hamilton proposed that Congress charter a national bank, for example, Jefferson objected that Congress had no power to do so because the Constitution did not specifically authorize Congress to charter banks. But Hamilton insisted that the "necessary and proper" clause implied ample authority. President George Washington accepted Hamilton's reasoning and signed the bill to charter the Bank of the United States, but the controversy continued.

The Supreme Court in the case of *McCulloch* v. *Maryland* (1819) settled the argument between "strict construction" and "loose construction" of the Constitution. Writing the opinion of a unanimous Court, Chief Justice John Marshall asserted the authority of Congress to make all laws necessary and proper to carry out its specified powers, so long as they were not specifically prohibited by the Constitution. Marshall's decision was the Court's most important pronouncement on the supremacy of the national government. It provided the elasticity to enable Congress to expand the scope of legislation as the country grew and the world changed over the course of two centuries. The interstate commerce power of Congress long provided a major basis for a wide range of legislation. By the time the Supreme Court in 1937 sustained the Social Security Act, the Hamiltonian view that Congress could tax and spend for the "general welfare" had become widely accepted.

The interpretation of the Constitution continues to evolve through the rulings of the Supreme Court of the United States.

See also Bill of Rights; Constitution, The Making of the.

NOBLE E. CUNNINGHAM, JR.

CONSTITUTIONAL CONVENTION
See Constitution, The Making of the.

CONSTITUTIONAL UNION PARTY

The Constitutional Union Party was founded in May 1860 as a result of the sectional split of the Democratic and Republican Parties and the growing threat of civil war, as southern states talked increasingly of secession, or leaving the Union. The party's members, mostly former Whigs and Know-Nothings, sought simply to sweep the issue of slavery in the western territories under the rug, not taking a direct stand on it one way or the other. They would, said their presidential candidate, John Bell of Tennessee, recognize "no political principle other than the Constitution of the country, the union of the states, and the enforcement of the laws."

Like Bell, most Constitutional Unionists came from the states on the border between North and South. In the election Bell received almost 600,000 popular votes and 39 electoral votes. He carried only the border slave states of Tennessee, Kentucky, and Virginia. These states contained large numbers of voters who were devoted as much to the Union as to slavery. And this was the region where, if war erupted, the fighting was almost sure to be concentrated. Thus, these voters were still hoping to find a way to settle the slavery issue that would involve neither abandoning the Union nor fighting a civil war.

See also Civil War.

CONTINENTAL CONGRESSES

In June 1774, after Parliament passed the Coercive Acts punishing Massachusetts for the Boston Tea Party, Massachusetts called for a meeting of all the colonies to decide how to react. This First Continental Congress, which met in Philadelphia from September 5 to October 26, consisted of delegates from all the colonies except Georgia. It was more like a committee than an elected legislature. It urged each colony to form a militia and called for a colonywide boycott (refusal to buy) of British goods.

The Second Congress was a better organized body, a kind of revolutionary central government. It met in Philadelphia the following May in order to coordinate the military effort that had begun the previous month with the Battles of Lexington and Concord. Among the members of the Congress were Benjamin Franklin, Patrick Henry, Thomas Jefferson, John Adams, George Washington, Samuel Adams, and John Hancock, who was chosen president. The Congress raised a Continental army, appointed Washington its commander in chief, and then called upon the newly formed state governments to raise troops and supplies for it. In July 1776 the group drafted and adopted the Declaration of Independence.

The Congress continued to function as a combined legislative and executive branch until the adoption of the Articles of Confederation in 1781, which provided a formal frame of government for the United States of America.

See also Revolution.

CONTRACEPTION
See Birth Control.

CONVENTIONS
See Constitution, The Making of the; Party Conventions; Seneca Falls Convention.

COOLIDGE, CALVIN

(1872–1933) *Thirtieth president of the United States (1923–29).*

A solemn and aloof vice president, Coolidge unexpectedly became the nation's leader on August 2, 1923, upon the death of President Warren G. Harding. He was sworn into office by the light of a kerosene lamp at his father's farmhouse in Vermont.

An undistinguished politician, Coolidge had served in a number of state and local posts. He first attracted national attention in 1919 when as governor of Massachusetts he issued a short statement about a lengthy Boston police strike: "There is no right to strike against the public safety by anybody, anywhere, any time." Actually, he had delayed calling out the state militia to end the strike, but his much publicized comment won him a second term as governor and led the Republicans to nominate him for vice president in 1920.

Coolidge was a man of few words and even fewer deeds. He worked four hours a day at most, less than any other president. He would receive callers at the White House and then take extended afternoon naps. After the scandals of the Harding era, however, the American people apparently approved of his inactivity for they elected him president in his own right in 1924.

In a typically brief comment, "Silent Cal" explained his hands-off approach to governing by saying, "The business of America is business." He believed that the economy could take care of itself without government interference, and he vetoed bills to regulate industry. Ignoring warnings of a possible stock market crash, he urged Americans to continue to buy stocks. He also showed little interest in foreign affairs.

At the end of his term, Coolidge simply announced, "I do not choose to run for president in 1928." He retired to a small town in Massachusetts where he spent his last years writing his autobiography and a daily newspaper column.

BARBARA SILBERDICK FEINBERG

COOPER, JAMES FENIMORE

(1789–1851)   *Novelist.*

The first major author to use American themes in fiction, Cooper created sea stories and frontier romances that did more than any other writer's work to establish truly American characters in literature. His books were among the first American novels to gain an international audience and to define the personality of the new nation for European readers.

Cooper grew up in Cooperstown, New York, on his father's estate at the edge of the wilderness, where he came to know the local Native Americans. After three years at Yale University, he joined the navy in 1806 and served until his father's death five years later. In 1820, while living as a country gentleman on his wife's farm, he published an unsuccessful first novel in the style of the British novels then popular in America.

His second effort, *The Spy,* published the next year, was a romantic adventure of the revolutionary war. It has been called "the first living American novel." Because of its great popularity, he decided to become a professional author. In 1822 he wrote *The Pilot,* regarded as the first modern American sea novel. The following year he began his most famous series, the Leatherstocking Tales, with *The Pioneers.*

The five novels of frontier life in this series tell the story of Natty Bumppo, a pioneer who lived among the Native Americans. They trace the life of their hero, known as Leatherstocking, till his death at ninety, and include *The Last of the Mohicans* (1826), *The Prairie* (1827), *The Pathfinder* (1840), and *The Deerslayer* (1841). In them Cooper created the romantic image of the Noble Red Man and that of the heroic pioneer who has gained wisdom by living close to nature.

Cooper also wrote travel books, social and political criticism, and a history of the U.S. Navy, but it is for his sea stories and his frontier novels that he is best remembered. Although some critics consider his plots unrealistic and his prose awkward, Cooper had a vigorous imagination and a sense of drama that have given his novels a permanent place in American literature.

See also Literature.

DENNIS WEPMAN

COPLAND, AARON

(1900–90)   *Composer and conductor.*

Americans have always made music—in the fields, in wagons heading west, on whaling boats, and in church. But it wasn't until the beginning of the twentieth century that composers took that singing and fiddling and stomping and turned it into music that could hold its own in concert halls around the world. Of those who first tried, two names stand out: one is Charles Ives, the other Aaron Copland. It took a long time before most listeners understood what Ives was up to. Copland's acceptance was astonishingly quick (astonishing in the world of serious music, that is).

Copland was born just as the century began, to a Jewish family living in Brooklyn,

New York, on a street that he described as "drab." It was an unlikely environment for an aspiring musician. "Music was the last thing anyone would have connected with it," he said. Copland went to public school, and his older sister taught him to play piano. He soon knew that he wanted to be a composer, and he sent away for a mail-order course in musical harmony.

At age twenty-one Copland went off to Paris and that changed his life. He found a great teacher, Nadia Boulanger, who taught him musical composition and introduced him to the best of modern music. When Copland returned to America in 1924, he was ready to take America's popular music—especially jazz and folk songs—and incorporate it into symphonic compositions. His best-known works include ballets, *Billy the Kid* (1938), *Rodeo* (1942), and *Appalachian Spring* (1944); two works for high school musicians, *The Second Hurricane* (1937) and *An Outdoor Overture* (1938); the orchestral *El Salon Mexico* (1936) and Third Symphony (1946); an opera, *The Tender Land* (1954); a work for narrator and chorus, *Lincoln Portrait* (1942); the film score for *Our Town* (1940); the twelve-tone composition *Connotations for Orchestra* (1962); and, perhaps most performed of all, *Fanfare for the Common Man* (1942).

It was not only as a composer that Copland led American music in new directions but also as a teacher, writer, and conductor. He brought a youthful spirit to all his endeavors; it gladdened his colleagues and inspired his music. His life came close to spanning the century. His music helped define it.

See also Ives, Charles; Music.

For further reading: Aaron Copland, *What to Listen for in Music* (New York: McGraw-Hill, 1988).

JOY HAKIM

COPLEY, JOHN SINGLETON
(1738–1815)   *Painter.*

The son of immigrant Irish parents, Copley became America's first major artist. Growing up in colonial Boston where his widowed mother operated a tobacco shop on Long Wharf, young Copley was a studious boy who preferred staying indoors drawing pictures to the rough-and-tumble of the waterfront. He was ten when his mother married a London-trained engraver and painter named Peter Pelham who introduced him to oil paints and English engravings. At fifteen, after Pelham had died leaving the family nearly penniless, Copley set himself up as a portrait painter.

Portraits were much in demand by moneyed Bostonians before the advent of photography, and Copley, whose realistic and perceptive portraits were soon the best produced in America, prospered. Becoming a rich man, he married Susanna Clarke, the daughter of a wealthy East India Company agent, and purchased a twenty-acre farm on the west side of Beacon Hill. Hard-working and prolific, Copley in 1771 traveled to New York where he painted thirty-seven portraits in six months. Three years later, on the eve of the American Revolution, he sailed for Europe to study and copy paintings by the old masters in Italy, Germany, and Holland.

Copley never returned to America, largely because his wife's family were Loyalists who in 1775 fled to England. His father-in-law, Richard Clarke, had been the merchant who was to receive the tea that provoked the Boston Tea Party. Beginning a promising career as a portrait artist in London, Copley went on to paint grand historical paintings that were widely acclaimed.

The artist was never accepted into London society, however, and he grew increasingly

John Singleon Copley's painting Watson and the Shark *(1778) features Brook Watson, a young boy pursued by a shark while boatmen attempt to rescue him. The painting, based on an actual event, was commissioned by Watson himself, who lost a leg to the shark.*

bad-tempered and quarrelsome as he grew older. His painting suffered, and he borrowed heavily to keep up his large house in London's fashionable George Street. He is best remembered today for his American portraits, especially one of Paul Revere.

See also Painting and Sculpture.

For further reading: James T. Flexner, *The Double Adventure of John Singleton Copley* (Boston: Little, Brown, 1969).

PATRICIA CONDON JOHNSTON

COPPERHEADS

The Copperheads were northern Democrats who were opposed to the Civil War. The name did not refer to the poisonous snake. Rather, in the past many Democrats had distrusted paper money because it lacked the real value of metal coins and could be printed at will in large amounts, which would cause inflation. To make their point, they sometimes wore copper pennies around their necks.

Copperheads disapproved of freeing the slaves and opposed all measures in support of the war. In politics they hoped to win control of Congress and then seek a negotiated peace with the Confederacy.

The most troublesome Copperhead from the point of view of the Lincoln administration was Clement L. Vallandigham of Ohio. In 1863 he was jailed by the military for making a speech calling for a negotiated peace. The president, however, had him released and then exiled him to the Confederacy. From there, he went to Canada by ship and later in the war returned to Ohio.

Copperhead strength declined after the northern victories in the Battles of Gettysburg and Vicksburg in 1863. But Copperheads continued their unconditional opposition to the war. They even objected to the Democratic presidential candidate in 1864, Gen. George B. McClellan, because he refused to call for an immediate peace.

See also Civil War.

CORE
See Congress of Racial Equality.

CORRUPT BARGAIN

In 1824 there were four candidates for president: Andrew Jackson, John Quincy Adams, Henry Clay, and William H. Crawford. No one of them obtained a majority in the electoral college, which was needed for election. Jackson had 99 electoral votes, Adams 84, Crawford 41, and Clay 37. In such cases the Constitution provided that the House of Representatives choose the president from among the three leading candidates, with each state delegation having a single vote. Clay was therefore eliminated.

Andrew Jackson believed that since he had received the largest number of electoral votes and also more popular votes than any of the others, he had a moral right to be chosen president. But Clay, who was Speaker of the House, had great influence on many of its members. He used that influence in favor of Adams, who was elected president.

When Adams then appointed Clay secretary of state, Jackson was furious. He charged that Adams and Clay had made a "corrupt bargain." The fact that every previous president since Thomas Jefferson had served as secretary of state before being elected president suggested to Jackson that Adams had agreed to support Clay as his successor.

CORRUPTION AND SCANDALS IN GOVERNMENT

"Corruption" means rottenness. Political corruption, or graft, occurs whenever government officials abuse their power by putting their own interests above those of the people as a whole. Some of the most common forms of political corruption are:

- *Bribery:* Government officials take money or a favor for using their position to do something for the person offering the bribe. Examples include a legislator who accepts money for voting a certain way or a police officer who agrees to let a suspect go in return for a payoff.
- *Extortion:* Officials use the power of their office to force citizens to pay them money. An example would be a city building inspector who threatens to condemn an apartment building, whether it's safe or not, unless given a payoff by the owner.
- *Kickbacks:* Government employees or

businesses with contracts from the government pay, or "kick back," part of their earnings to the officials who arranged for them to get the job or the contract.

♦ *Election fraud:* Results of an election are changed by bribing voters, miscounting votes, or stuffing ballot boxes with phony votes.

Famous Scandals

Virtually every form of graft was common during much of the nineteenth century. At that time, the local political party organizations known as "machines" controlled the governments of most cities and many states. The corruption was encouraged by the patronage system that put large numbers of jobs under the control of whichever machine—Democratic or Republican—was in power and the "boss" who ran it. It was commonplace for people to "purchase" government jobs by paying money to the machine. "Bagmen" working for the boss bought the votes of state legislators, getting them to pass laws favoring the boss's friends and business partners.

The most notorious of the big-city machines was New York's Tammany Hall Democratic organization run by William "Boss" Tweed in the 1860s and 1870s. When Tweed's bagman was asked whether it was "proper" for him to bribe the New York state legislature, he responded that "every legislature is bought more or less." Exposed by the *New York Times,* the extravagant corruption of the so-called Tweed Ring produced a wave of reform that resulted in a more honest Democratic government in New York. Tweed himself was sent to prison.

The pattern seen in the Tweed Ring scandal was typical. There have often been waves of corruption and reform, sometimes involving state and local governments, and sometimes reaching high up into the federal government. The Republican administration of President Ulysses S. Grant (1869–77), for example, was troubled by many accusations of corruption. In the 1920s, two important members of President Warren G. Harding's Republican administration were forced to resign for taking bribes. Charles Forbes, head of the Veterans' Bureau, was convicted of taking money in return for awarding contracts to construct veterans' hospitals. In what came to be known as the "Teapot Dome Scandal," Secretary of the Interior Albert Fall was convicted of taking bribes to award leases to drill for oil on federal lands in Wyoming. Lesser scandals involved members of the Truman (Democratic) and Eisenhower (Republican) administrations in the late 1940s and 1950s.

After the presidential election of 1960, which was very close, some Republicans charged that election frauds in Texas and Illinois allowed the Democratic ticket of John F. Kennedy and Lyndon B. Johnson to win those states. The charges were never proved, however. In 1972, burglars working for the reelection committee of the Republican president, Richard M. Nixon, were caught breaking into Democratic campaign headquarters in the Watergate apartment building in Washington, D.C. The investigation that resulted exposed widespread corruption in the Nixon administration, and the president was forced to resign. He is the only president to resign in disgrace.

The executive branch is not the only level of government where corruption has occurred. Judges have sometimes been found to have accepted bribes, and scandals have often rocked Congress as well. Individual senators and representatives have been caught accepting bribes or abusing their office for personal gain. In the late 1970s, an F B I operation known as "Abscam" sent agents posing as Arab sheiks to offer bribes to lawmakers. Several House members and at least one senator took the money. In the early 1990s, accusations that members routinely misused the House of Representatives' private check-cashing service and post office outraged many Americans. The so-called House bank was closed, and several representatives involved in the scandal decided not to run for reelection.

Less Obvious Corruption

Graft has never been entirely absent from the American political system and probably never will be. Greed for money and power will always attract some people, and some officials will always give in to temptation. But stricter ethics laws, like those passed after the Watergate scandal, have made it less likely that that sort of out-and-out corruption will occur again. More troubling today is the less obvious corruption that results because of the importance of money in modern political campaigns. Politicians need enormous amounts to run for office. This gives the individuals and big organizations willing to contribute large sums to candidates great influence with those who win.

In the early 1990s, a number of senators were accused of using their influence to interfere with a government investigation of a savings and loan operator named Charles Keating. Keating's company had failed and cost the government—and taxpayers—billions of dollars. The government was investigating to see whether Keating had defrauded his investors. Several senators who had received large contributions from Keating had talked to federal investigators about the case. A Sen-

ate ethics committee found that at least one had tried to discourage them from continuing the investigation. Keating was eventually sent to prison, and the senator was reprimanded by the Senate. Although the Senate found no "corrupt intent" on the part of the senator, it decided that he had been wrong to mix his fund-raising activities with his official duties. Critics charge that this kind of confusion goes on all the time.

The Keating scandal shows that, in the long run, the corrupting influence of money in political campaigns may be even more dangerous to the public good than the more old-fashioned kinds of graft.

See also Big-City Bosses; Iran-Contra Affair; Teapot Dome Affair; Tweed Ring; Watergate.

For further reading: Michael Kronenwetter, *The Threat from Within* (New York: Franklin Watts, 1986).

MICHAEL KRONENWETTER

COUNTRY MUSIC

Country music is a blend of many forms of popular American music, including ballads, folk songs, blues, bluegrass, western swing, Cajun, cowboy/western, jazz, rock, and Tin Pan Alley. It has evolved from a simple kind of rural recreation into a highly profitable commercial industry with fans worldwide, particularly throughout Europe, Australia, and Japan. Its acceptance by this broad audience came because it slowly absorbed the different sounds of music in America.

Early Development

Its origins lay in folk songs identified with the southern mountain regions. Since its early recording artists were usually untrained mu-

Patsy Cline was one of the first women in country music to gain a national reputation. She died tragically young in a plane crash.

sicians from rural America, country music was often called "hillbilly music."

The first known country music recording was made in 1922 with A. C. "Eck" Robertson, a fiddling cowboy from Amarillo, Texas, and Henry Gilliland, a fiddler from Altus, Oklahoma. The fiddle, or violin, was the popular instrument in rural America and for many years was the instrument most often identified with country music. Its popularity slowly gave way to the guitar, however.

The most significant recording sessions in country music history took place in Bristol,

Tennessee, during July and August 1927 on the Victor Records label. Jimmie Rodgers, a former railroad worker from Mississippi, quickly attracted national attention. His yodeling and distinctive guitar style, both of which are still copied by country musicians, made him the first superstar and most influential figure in country music and earned him the title "the Father of Country Music."

The other influential recording session that summer was with the Carter family, who came from the Virginia mountains. Sara and A.P. were husband and wife and Maybelle was a cousin of Sara's. The women sang and played the guitar, autoharp, and banjo. Their guitar style, significantly different from Rodgers's, is also copied by country musicians; the popularity of the autoharp resulted from their influence; and many of their songs are still being sung. June Carter, daughter of Maybelle, is the wife of Johnny Cash and continues the family musical tradition.

Other Styles

In later decades other singers and musicians from the South created new sounds in country music. They have included Bill Monroe, "the Father of Bluegrass"; Hank Williams, singer and songwriter, whose lyrics are masterpieces of emotion and mood; and Merle Travis, whose inventive finger-picking guitar style influenced Chet Atkins and generations of guitar players. Elvis Presley and others involved in the birth of rock had strong southern country music backgrounds.

Country music is not limited to the South, though. Many influential country musicians were born west of the Mississippi River. In 1935, Gene Autry starred in the first singing cowboy movie and was soon followed by Tex Ritter, Roy Rogers, and others. Western singers such as the Sons of the Pioneers developed musical sounds still being imitated by groups such as Riders in the Sky. These cowboy singers helped popularize the western clothes, hats, and boots worn by many country music entertainers. The use of drums, horns, and electrical and amplified instruments in country music came from the influence and popularity of Bob Wills ("the Daddy of Western Swing") and His Texas Playboys.

Nashville and New Stars
On November 28, 1925, radio station WSM, in Nashville, Tennessee, broadcast the "WSM Barn Dance" under the direction of George D. Hay. Two years later he renamed the show "Grand Ole Opry," and by the end of the 1930s, it had become the most important outlet for country music in the world. In the 1950s, Nashville, now called "the Home of Country Music," became the center for recording studios. An entertainment park, Opryland, was built to house larger facilities for the "Grand Ole Opry" show and to attract fans from around the world. But in the 1990s, Branson, Missouri, with numerous country music theaters and live shows, emerged as competition with Nashville for international fan appeal.

For many years country music gave poorer working-class people the chance to rise economically. Each superstar gained recognition for distinctive musical sounds and a particular theme that ran through his or her songs. Johnny Cash sang about prison and railroad life; Loretta Lynn, the daughter of a coal miner, attracted new fans with songs about the problems women and housewives confront; Conway Twitty, a 1950s rock musician, became one of the early "crossover" singers in the 1960s and brought a modified rock sound to country music; and Willie Nelson in the

1970s directed attention to music from Austin, Texas, appealing to a wide variety of listeners. In the 1990s, Garth Brooks from Oklahoma emerged as a superstar with fans of all ages throughout the world by singing a wide range of songs from cowboy to rock. He personifies the dynamic diversity and future of country music.

See also Music.

GUY LOGSDON

COURTS
See Supreme Court.

COWBOYS

People all over the world like to dress, walk, and talk the way they think American cowboys did in the heyday of the Wild West. For more than a hundred years, the cowboy has been portrayed in song and story as a colorful folk hero on horseback—a man of few words who sits tall in the saddle, who never complains, who shoots straight, and whose horse always comes when he whistles.

In real life, an old-time trail-driving cowboy usually rode a horse owned by his employer. He seldom carried a gun. He was paid to herd cows, and he spent his time rounding up cattle, branding calves, and driving the herds to market.

The cowboy trade began in Mexico more than four hundred years ago, when Spanish settlers brought the first domesticated horses and cattle to North America. Since the cattle roamed about freely, Spanish ranchers taught the local Indians to ride horses and handle cattle on the open range. Those Indian cow herders were called *vaqueros*, from the Spanish word *vaca*, for "cow." They became experts at snaring a running steer with a braided rawhide rope, called *la reata*. Over the years *la reata*—"the lariat"—became the cowboy's most important tool.

Vaqueros drove the first herds of cattle north into Texas. By the time of the American Civil War, millions of hardy long-horned cattle were running wild all over the Texas plains. New methods of meatpacking and refrigeration had created a profitable market for beef in the cities of the North and East, but there were no railroads linking Texas with the rest of the country. The only way to get the cattle to market was to put them on the trail and drive them hundreds of miles to the nearest railroad.

Texas ranchers built up their herds by cap-turing wild longhorns, branding them as their own, and setting them loose to graze until they were ready for market. Then they were rounded up and driven in large herds to railroad towns in Kansas, where they were loaded aboard freight cars and shipped to meat-packing plants in Kansas City and Chicago. As the demand for beef grew, the cattle-raising industry spread northward from Texas. Soon a vast tract of cattle country stretched from Colorado up through Wyoming, Montana, and the Dakotas.

At the heart of this booming cattle industry was the hardworking cowboy. An expert rider and skilled roper, he knew how to doctor an ailing cow or find a lost calf, how to calm a restless herd in the middle of the

Cowboys gather around a campfire for storytelling in Matador, Texas.

night, how to head off a thousand stamped-ing longhorns. He might be kicked by a horse, trampled in a stampede, drowned dur-ing a river crossing, or caught on the open prairie in the midst of an electrical storm. Probably more cowboys were killed by light-ning than by outlaws or Indians.

Most cowboys were very young men, in their late teens or early twenties. Except for some cooks and trail bosses, there were few men as old as thirty on the trail. A large num-ber of cowboys were black or Mexican. After the Civil War, thousands of freed slaves found work as professional cowhands. Mexican cowboys, descendants of the vaqueros, were common in southern Texas, where many ranches were still owned by old Spanish fam-ilies.

It took two or three months to drive a herd from Texas to railroad shipping points in Kansas, and twice that long to deliver cattle to ranches on the northern plains. Men who took part in the great trail drives of the 1860s, 1870s, and 1880s talked about the experience for the rest of their lives. Bawling and bellow-ing, the longhorns tramped along dusty trails in herds that numbered a thousand or more. Cowboys on horseback rode behind and be-side and in front of the herd, singing to the cattle as they drove them along. On a trail drive, a cowboy might spend eighteen hours a day in the saddle. At night he slept in his bedroll on the ground.

Out on the range, a cowboy wore practical working clothes—a collarless flannel pull-over shirt and heavy-duty woolen pants. Le-vis didn't become popular until the 1890s, and at first they were dyed brown rather than blue. Gradually a distinctive cowboy outfit appeared. Cowboy boots had pointed toes so a rider could easily slip his foot into the stir-rup, thin soles to give him the feel of the

stirrup, and high heels to grip the stirrup firmly. Seatless leather leggings called chaps protected a cowboy's legs while he was riding through thickets or brush. A wide-brimmed hat shielded his face from low-lying branch-es, shaded his eyes from the sun, and kept rain from running down his neck. A ban-danna protected his neck from sunburn. During roundups and trail drives it could be pulled over his face as a dust mask and, in cold weather, tied over his head to keep his ears warm.

Working cowboys rarely carried a gun. Herding cattle on horseback with a loaded pistol hanging from your hip or a rifle strapped to your saddle was dangerous and uncomfortable. On roundups and trail drives, cowboys stashed their firearms in the supply wagon or back at the bunkhouse. And though every cowboy owned a saddle, he did not always own a horse. Horses were supplied by the ranch or trail outfit a man worked for. If he had his own horse, he kept it with the ranch's common pool of horses as long as he was employed there.

The American cowboy came into his own in Texas during the late 1860s. By the 1890s, barbed-wire fences put up by homesteaders and ranchers all across the western plains had put an end to the open range. Meanwhile a network of railroad tracks had reached cen-tral Texas, making long trail drives unneces-sary. The last herd was driven north to Kan-sas in 1896. Men on horseback still drove herds of cattle, but only from their fenced pastures to railroad loading pens a few miles away. The era of the open-range cowboy had lasted less than thirty years. Altogether, per-haps twenty-five or thirty thousand men and boys had gone up the trail. By the time the last trail was closed, those cowboys had cap-tured the imagination of the world.

Today's cowboy works with fine breeds of thoroughbred cattle instead of the half-wild longhorn. He drives from pasture to pasture in a pickup truck, hauling his horse behind him in a trailer to ride in places where the truck can't go. Sometimes he flies over the grazing herds at the controls of a helicopter. But he still moves herds of cattle from place to place, ropes steers, brands calves, and doctors ailing animals. His work still demands daring and skill, and like his legendary predecessors, he still takes pride in being a cowboy.

See also Pioneers and Frontier Life.

For further reading: Russell Freedman, *Cowboys of the Wild West* (New York: Clarion Books, 1985).

RUSSELL FREEDMAN

COXEY'S ARMY

During the economic depression of the 1890s, Jacob Coxey, an Ohio businessman, attempted to call attention to the plight of unemployed workers by organizing an "army" of jobless men and marching with them to Washington, D.C., to demand relief. Coxey also drafted a plan for ending the depression. He proposed that the federal government provide the money for local communities to hire idle men and put them to work building much-needed roads.

Coxey's army set out from Massillon, Ohio, in March 1894. They arrived in Washington on April 30, some 500 strong. But Coxey and two of his associates were immediately arrested for trespassing on the grounds of the Capitol. The rest of his army was driven off by the police. A number of other groups from places as far away as the state of Washington set out during the same period, sometimes forcing the railroads to allow them to travel in empty freight cars.

Those who reached Washington, D.C.—about 1,200 men—were also roughly treated.

The publicity the armies attracted as they passed through the country, however, won them much public support. And the harsh reception they received in the capital added to the sympathy for their cause. Coxey did not succeed in getting his plan adopted, but he had made clear to the government the seriousness of unemployment.

See also Depressions and Recessions.

CRANE, STEPHEN

(1871–1900) *Writer.*

A pioneer of realistic fiction, Crane broke new ground with his novels and short stories. He focused on subjects that had never been written about honestly before. His spare, graphic style and psychological penetration had a major influence on twentieth-century American literature.

Crane was born in New Jersey, the son of a Methodist minister who died when the boy was eight years old. He spent a year at Syracuse University but left at the age of eighteen for New York, where he made a bare living as a free-lance newspaper writer. Living in the poorest part of the city, he composed what is considered the first American realistic novel, *Maggie: A Girl of the Streets* (1893). No publisher would take this tale of a girl from the slums who sinks to prostitution, and Crane had it printed himself.

Maggie sold only a hundred copies but was admired by important critics who helped Crane publish his next book commercially. *The Red Badge of Courage* (1895), a tale of a young Civil War soldier's first encounter with danger in a battle, was an instant success. At the age of twenty-five, and with no experience of combat, Crane had entered the mind of his terrified hero with such insight, and reported it with such clarity, that the book has become a classic.

Although his masterpiece earned him little money, it brought him better newspaper assignments. He traveled widely and in 1898 reported the Spanish-American War. In 1897, on his way to cover the Cuban rebellion that led to that war, Crane was shipwrecked off the coast of Florida and spent thirty hours adrift. The resulting story, "The Open Boat," described by one critic as "the finest short story in English," reflects his dark view of humans as helpless beings in a hostile universe.

Broken in health after that ordeal, Crane went to England, where he became friends with many successful writers but found it hard to make a living himself. He wrote feverishly until his death at the age of twenty-eight.

See also Literature.

DENNIS WEPMAN

CRAZY HORSE

(c. 1842–77)   *Sioux military leader.*

Born near Bear Butte, in what is now South Dakota, Crazy Horse was the son of an Oglala medicine man and a Brulé woman. As a youth he was known as Curly. After proving himself in battle, he acquired the name Crazy Horse, which may also have been his father's name.

In a fight at Platte Bridge on the Oregon Trail, July 25, 1865, he encountered U.S. soldiers for the first time. Later that summer he was one of Red Cloud's guerrilla fighters who resisted the building of forts along the Boze-

man Trail. During this period he became a keen observer of the army's cavalry tactics, and later he made good use of what he had learned.

In December 1866, when the Sioux and Cheyenne combined to attack Fort Phil Kearny, Crazy Horse led a group of warriors. Serving as a decoy, they lured Lt. Col. W. J. Fetterman and eighty soldiers into an ambush now known as the Fetterman Massacre. No soldiers survived.

To force the Plains Indians onto reservations, the government in 1876 sent three separate military columns against them. Crazy Horse and his warriors played a leading role in blocking the advance of Gen. George Crook's column at Rosebud Creek. A few days later, June 25, he was with Sitting Bull at the Battle of Little Bighorn. When Lt. Col. George Armstrong Custer attacked with one battalion, Crazy Horse and Gall, a chief of the Hunkpapa Sioux, used a pincers assault against the outnumbered troopers, and none of them survived.

After a winter of flight and starvation, Crazy Horse brought his followers to Fort Robinson to surrender and await assignment to a promised reservation. On September 5, 1877, military authorities arrested Crazy Horse with the intention of placing him in prison. When he was brought to the Fort Robinson guardhouse, he struggled with his guards. One of them stabbed him fatally.

In the years that have followed, Crazy Horse has become an almost mythical figure of the Plains Indian wars.

See also Custer, George Armstrong; Indian Reservations; Indian-White Relations.

For further reading: Jim Razzi, *Custer and Crazy Horse* (New York: Scholastic, 1989).

DEE BROWN

CRIME

On September 26, 1872, three men, believed to include the notorious Jesse and Frank James, rode up on horseback to the gate of a fair in Kansas City, attended by about ten thousand people. The bandits shot at a ticket seller, but hit a small girl, shattering her leg, and escaped with about a thousand dollars.

In reporting the crime, the *Kansas City Times* called it "so diabolically daring and so utterly in contempt of fear that we are bound to admire it and revere its perpetrators." Two days later the *Times* rhapsodized: "It is as though three bandits had come to us . . . with the halo of medieval chivalry upon their garments and shown us how the things were done that poets sing of. Nowhere else in the United States or in the civilized world, probably, could this thing have been done."

This incident illustrates that violent crime is nothing new in America, and also how our attitudes toward it have changed. Were such a crime to occur today, it would be greeted with outrage, demands for better police protection, and calls for stricter gun control laws. Most likely a fund would be started to care for the little girl who was shot. The *Times* report also suggests how we have glorified criminals. The likes of Jesse James, Billy the Kid, Al Capone, John Dillinger, Baby Face Nelson, and Bonnie and Clyde have been the subject of more books and movies than most of our presidents.

Crime is an act forbidden by public law, such as murder or robbery. It is also failure to perform an act commanded by public law, such as paying taxes or caring for one's children. There are several types of crime. A *capital crime,* such as murder and treason, is one for which the death penalty may be imposed. A *felony* is a serious crime punished by a sentence of more than a year in prison. Examples are rape, aggravated assault, robbery, burglary, and larceny. A *misdemeanor* is a less serious crime punished by fines or jail terms of less than a year. Examples are drunkenness, disorderly conduct, small thefts, and trespassing. A *civil crime* is one committed not against persons or property but against society and government, such as sedition, perjury, contempt of court, and election fraud. Many people divide crime into two categories: *violent crime,* such as murder, rape, assault, arson, and manslaughter, which causes injury or the threat of injury to a person; and *white-collar crime,* which poses no threat of physical injury. Examples are embezzlement, forgery, and bribery. (It is called "white-collar crime" because it is usually committed by executives or office workers, who customarily wear suits and shirts with white collars.)

There have been three periods of great lawlessness in America: after the Civil War, after World War I, and following the war in Vietnam. Thousands of movies and television shows have been made about the "Wild West." In the years following the Civil War as the population expanded westward, the frontier was marked by an absence of law and police forces. Citizens armed themselves for protection against bandits such as the James brothers and the Dalton gang. The period was also marked by mobs, called vigilantes, who took the law into their own hands to punish suspected criminals, usually by lynching (killing someone without a trial first). These years also witnessed great lawlessness in the South during Reconstruction. Vigilantes, most commonly the Ku Klux Klan, abounded.

The 1920s and 1930s, following the First World War and coinciding with Prohibition (which banned the sale of alcoholic beverages), were marked by organized gangs, usually called mobs or bootleggers. These men illegally imported and sold liquor and then fought among themselves for control of supplies and territories. It remains the greatest period of violent crimes in American history. The most famous of the mobsters was Al Capone in Chicago. The hard economic times of the 1930s also saw a sharp rise in bank robberies and other forms of banditry and violence. Criminals such as John Dillinger, Baby Face Nelson, and Bonnie and Clyde became the stuff of legends.

The 1970s, 1980s, and early 1990s, following the war in Vietnam, have been marked by a sharp rise in the illicit use of narcotics, especially heroin and cocaine. The importation and sale of these drugs have resulted in an increase in crime and violence. Use of drugs has led to *street crime,* as addicts seek money to buy narcotics. An alarming feature has been the increase in juvenile crime, with persons as young as fourteen and fifteen committing murders and robberies to obtain money or drugs. As in the "Wild West" and "Roaring Twenties," gangs fight and kill for control of territories and the illegal but profitable activities therein. Street and gang violence, however, has not been the only crime on the rise. All three of the major periods of crime have been marked by a higher incidence of white-collar crime in the business world and increased political unrest that sometimes led to riots, arson, and looting.

The roots of crime in America appear to lie in war, economic hard times, and inequitable distribution of wealth. Other causes frequently cited are racial, ethnic, religious, and gender prejudice; unemployment and poverty leading to hopelessness and desperation; poor housing and run-down neighborhoods; inadequate education and lack of opportunity; breakdown of the family and the moral values taught there; easy access to weapons, particularly handguns; and the frequent depiction of crime and violence in movies and on television, often bringing fame or notoriety to criminals.

These various theories about the causes of crime have led to four, sharply different approaches to preventing crime. One advocates a "get tough" policy with more police on the streets and harsher penalties to deter crime. A second policy recommends guidance, especially for juveniles, and treatment for drug and alcohol addiction. A third approach suggests that improved education and more jobs will prevent crime. A fourth believes greater attention to family values and personal morality will provide the best answer. Perhaps the solution to the crime problem lies in adoption of all four approaches.

See also Capone, Al; Corruption and Scandals in Government; Drugs; Guns and Gun Control; James, Jesse; Lynching; Prisons.

ROBERT A. LISTON

CROCKETT, DAVY

(1786–1836)   *Frontiersman and Tennessee politician.*

Crockett's life is best told by separating the respectable politician *David* from the boisterous, half-mythical frontier folk hero, *Davy.*

David Crockett was born in Tennessee. He took part in the Indian war against the Creeks in 1813–14 and later fought with Andrew Jackson in Florida. After returning to Tennessee, he served three terms in Congress but broke with President Jackson and was defeated in 1835. Late that year he left for

Texas and was among those killed defending the Alamo when it fell to the Mexicans in March 1836.

Crockett's congressional record was not outstanding, nor is there any reason he should be honored more than any other of the Alamo's defenders. Yet movies and a television series have been made about him, and he has come to seem equal in frontier skills to Daniel Boone. These dramas are about the other Crockett, *Davy.* This came about because Crockett really was a colorful figure whose tall stories attracted journalists. The many books about Davy Crockett, the "ring-tailed roarer" from Tennessee, sold well, including a fictional biography that appeared in 1833.

Here is an example of his tall tales. In a

Davy Crockett, dressed in buckskin and his coonskin hat, helps defend the Alamo. Crockett served several terms as a congressman, but then suffered several defeats. Disgusted with politics, he supposedly declared, "You can all go to hell and I'm going to Texas." Crockett did go to Texas, where he fought in the Battle of the Alamo and lost his life, along with the other defenders.

shooting match with Mike Fink, a legendary Mississippi River boatman, Crockett announced his target: "Do you see that cat sitting on the top rail of your potato patch, about 150 yards off?" he asked Fink. "If he ever hears again, I'll be shot if it shant be without ears." Then, as Crockett told the story, he "blazed away, and I'll bet you a horse, the ball [bullet] cut off both the old tom cat's ears close to his head, and shaved the hair clean across the skull, as slick as if I'd done it with a razor, and the critter never stirred, nor knew he'd lost his ears till he tried to scratch 'em."

Written in western lingo, these tall tales all claimed to narrate the true adventures of the "half-horse half-alligator" frontiersman, Davy Crockett.

See also Alamo; Pioneers and Frontier Life.

For further reading: Elizabeth Mosely Robards, *Davy Crockett, Hero of the Wild Frontier* (New York: Chelsea House, 1991).

RICHARD A. BARTLETT

CUBAN MISSILE CRISIS

In 1962, about a year after the Bay of Pigs affair, Soviet premier Nikita Khrushchev began to move military equipment and large numbers of technicians into Cuba, which was ruled by his ally, Fidel Castro. Photographs taken by American reconnaissance planes soon revealed that launching pads capable of firing Soviet guided missiles at the United States were under construction there. In a television address to the American people, President Kennedy called this action "deliberately provocative and unjustified." He ordered American warships to stop all Soviet ships headed for Cuba and search them. If they contained any offensive weapons, they were to be sent back. He called on Khrushchev to remove all the Soviet offensive weapons already in Cuba and warned him that if any nuclear attack was made on the United States, he would launch an all-out atomic attack on Russia. After some hesitation, Khrushchev agreed to withdraw the missiles and dismantle the bases. Kennedy then lifted his order to stop Soviet vessels.

Kennedy may have risked too much by his bold policy. He had no hard evidence that the Soviets were planning an atomic attack on the United States, and in any case they already had missiles capable of striking the United States on their own soil in Siberia. But Kennedy's action ended concerns that he lacked decisiveness and made his "toughness" apparent to Khrushchev.

See also Cold War.

CUMBERLAND ROAD
See National Road.

CUSTER, GEORGE ARMSTRONG

(1839–76)   *Civil War cavalry commander and Indian fighter.*

Born in New Rumley, Ohio, Custer graduated from West Point in 1861 and was sent immediately to duty in the Civil War. His boldness in battle as a cavalry leader brought rapid promotions. At twenty-three he was the youngest officer in the Union army holding the brevet, or temporary, rank of brigadier general.

During the war, Custer married Elizabeth Bacon, and throughout the postwar years she accompanied him on assignments to forts in the West. With the permanent rank of lieutenant colonel he was soon leading the Seventh Cavalry in skirmishes against the Plains Indians. In 1867, after being charged with cruelty to his men, leaving his troops without permission in order to visit his wife, and other military misdeeds, he was suspended from command. The following year Gen. Philip Sheridan returned him to duty and ordered him to attack a Cheyenne village in Indian Territory. This action brought him praise but also criticism for failing to search for a missing unit that had been ambushed by Indians.

Custer's expedition into the Black Hills in 1874, in violation of the treaty of 1868, led to

George Armstrong Custer, photographed by Mathew Brady or one of his assistants.

discovery of gold there but also to trouble with the northern Plains tribes. The Black Hills was sacred land to the Indians. They were bitterly opposed to the numerous gold seekers and settlers who then invaded their territory.

In 1876 the Seventh Cavalry joined a large military campaign. Its purpose was to force all the Plains tribes onto reservations. After marching into Montana, Custer was ordered to search out Chief Sitting Bull's camp along the Little Bighorn River, but the plan called for him to await arrival of additional forces before attacking. Custer apparently had verbal permission, however, to use his own judg-

ment upon sighting the Indians. After dividing his regiment into three widely separated battalions, Custer attacked with about 250 men. What followed is now known as "Custer's Last Stand." He and all of his men were killed.

In the years since, Custer has become a legendary figure, mostly through his widow's efforts to perpetuate and glorify his name. In real life he was a brave but extremely reckless cavalryman, admired by some and severely criticized by others.

See also Crazy Horse; Indian-White Relations; Sitting Bull.

DEE BROWN

D

DANCE

From the earliest days, Americans have used dancing to express their values and beliefs, to entertain, even to convey religious awe. Native Americans performed ritual dances in prayers to their deities, and the Shakers, a religious sect, danced exuberantly to express their piety. Even the Puritans, who disapproved of dancing, could not prevent colonists from dancing for pleasure. Early theatrical groups also incorporated clogs, jigs, acrobatics, and pantomine in their spectacles.

Early American Dancing

American theatrical dance emerged as a native art form only in the 1890s. Before that, Americans adapted forms of dance from other countries and cultures. African slaves, for example, brought their tribal dances to the New World and passed them down to their children.

In 1735, the first known "ballet" performed in America was a pantomime arranged by Henry Holt, an English dancing master in Charleston. But ballets during the early years were simply minor aspects of other forms of entertainment, like circuses or operettas, not the lavish productions they are today. The first well-known American dancer, John Durang, was also an actor, acrobat, rope dancer, and blackface comic.

As the nation prospered, more people patronized the arts, and new American dancers emerged. In 1837, two ballerinas, trained by a former dancer with the Paris Opéra de Ballet, made their debut in Philadelphia: Augusta Maywood and Mary Ann Lee. Both had long and distinguished careers.

In contrast to classical ballet—a dance form that appealed to those seeking culture—minstrel shows attracted audiences

Denise Pons and Geoffrey Rhue of the Boston Ballet performing in The Nutcracker, *the most popular ballet regularly staged in the United States.*

who craved more homespun entertainment. Tap dancing and comic skits were important parts of minstrel shows. Tap dancing, a blend of African-American and northern European dance steps, also found a home in musical theater. Perhaps the most celebrated tap dancer was Bill "Bojangles" Robinson (1878–1949), who tapped his way across theater and nightclub stages and onto the silver screen.

In the late nineteenth century, theatrical spectacles encompassing ballet, melodramatic plots, and lavish stage effects competed with more popular forms of dance, such as music hall dancing. In the 1880s, vaudeville, a blend of pantomime, dialogue, acting, singing, acrobatics, and stage dancing, captured Americans' fancy.

Modern Dance

By the early twentieth century, Americans were questioning traditional values and beliefs, and in the dance world, people like Isadora Duncan (1878–1927) gave artistic expression to these new ways of thinking. Duncan, a one-woman revolution, rejected ballet's rigid movements and tried to recapture the flowing, expressive movements of ancient forms of dance. She drew inspiration from sculpture and the natural world. But her revealing poses and costumes shocked American audiences, who regarded her work as immoral, and she found greater support among Europeans.

Her belief in the beauty and purity of free, flowing movement paved the way for other dancers and choreographers—those who design dances for specific pieces of music—who wished to express their artistic vision through dance. Ruth St. Denis (1877–1968) adopted a fluid and expressive form of dancing, drawing on mystical traditions from India and the Orient. In 1915, she and her part-

ner, Ted Shawn, formed the Denishawn company and school to train dancers in a variety of forms, from classical ballet to ethnic dance.

One of St. Denis's pupils, Martha Graham (1894–1991), was another maverick who wanted to infuse dance with more spontaneity and expressiveness. She wished, she said, to "chart the graph of the heart" through her dance. The Martha Graham Dance Company, which she founded in the 1920s, still dazzles audiences today.

Throughout the 1950s and 1960s, more modern dance companies emerged. The Alvin Ailey Dance Theatre, for example, founded in 1957 by Alvin Ailey (1931–89), has captured the vitality of African-American culture on stages around the world. Other influential modern companies include those led by Paul Taylor, Merce Cunningham, Twyla Tharp, and Mark Morris. These and other dance groups draw large audiences, and new American companies are born every few years.

Ballet and Musicals

No professional American ballet company existed until 1935, when Russian-born George Balanchine, formerly with the Ballets Russes, cofounded the American Ballet Company. After a shaky start, the company, renamed the New York City Ballet in 1948, enjoyed critical and popular acclaim. Like Duncan and Graham, Balanchine strove to capture the beauty of the human body in motion by doing away with elaborate plots and spectacle and showcasing graceful movement as an art in itself. His luminous vision of ballet continues to inspire dancers, choreographers, and audiences. The other major ballet company is American Ballet Theater, founded in 1940 by Lucia Chase and Richard Pleasant. Its dancers perform the great Russian classics as well as more contemporary works.

Twentieth-century Americans have swayed to the catchy rhythms of another form of theatrical dance—the Broadway musical. Producer Florenz Ziegfeld (1867–1932) launched Broadway dancing by introducing a chorus line of lavishly costumed women set against dazzling backdrops. Although the women did not dance, they paraded down grand staircases, giving a sense of movement to the stage.

During the Great Depression, Americans found escape in the movies and musicals such as *42nd Street*. Busby Berkeley's (1885–1976) kaleidoscopic choreography made dancers, when viewed from afar, resemble human flowers as they lay in a circle and moved their arms and legs in unison to the music. Berkeley paved the way for other talented choreographers, such as Agnes de Mille (1905–93). Her choreography for *Oklahoma!*, a musical that opened in 1943, launched a new era in Broadway show dance: dancing became central rather than incidental to the action. Others, such as Bob Fosse (1927–87) and Jerome Robbins (1918–   ), followed in her footsteps, turning the Broadway stage into a magical tableau of sleek, jazzy, high-energy dancing.

See also Astaire, Fred; Balanchine, George; Duncan, Isadora; Graham, Martha; Movies; Theater; Ziegfeld, Florenz.

HARRIET SIGERMAN

DARROW, CLARENCE

(1857–1938)   *Attorney.*

Darrow was the most famous defense lawyer in American history, but he never graduated from law school. In the nineteenth century,

people didn't need a college degree to practice law. They only had to pass an examination, which Darrow did when he was twenty-one years old.

Darrow began his legal career working for big corporations, but the heartless way many companies treated their workers troubled him. In 1894, he was working for the Chicago and Northwestern Railroad when the workers went on strike. The company appealed to the courts, who declared the strike illegal and jailed the railroad workers' union leader Eugene V. Debs when he refused to order the men back to work. Outraged, Darrow quit his job and went to Debs's defense. From that time on, he was famous as a legal champion of the underdog.

Darrow often took clients no other prominent lawyer would defend: black people charged with crimes against whites; poor workers battling wealthy employers; political rebels denied their civil rights. He believed that every defendant deserved a good defense, no matter how unpopular he or she might be.

Darrow opposed all kinds of prejudice, injustice, and cruelty. Most of all, he hated the death penalty. During his career he defended over a hundred people facing the death penalty, and not one was ever executed. Near the end of his career, he took on the most unpopular clients he'd ever had, just to save them from the hangman. Richard Loeb and Nathan Leopold were spoiled, rich young men who had murdered a fourteen-year-old boy for the "thrill" of it. Darrow made an impassioned two-day plea to spare their lives. The judge was so moved he sentenced them to life in prison.

The most famous of all Darrow's cases was the so-called Monkey Trial in 1925. He defended a teacher named John Scopes, who was accused of breaking a Tennessee law against teaching the theory of evolution, which states that all human beings evolved from lower animals over millions of years. A famous politician, William Jennings Bryan, served as prosecutor. Bryan took the stand to defend creationism, the belief in the biblical account that God created Adam and Eve, and all humans are descended from them. Darrow made a biting cross-examination of Bryan, challenging his belief in the literal truth of the Bible. The trial received so much attention, parts of it were broadcast over the radio. Scopes was convicted, but Darrow's plea for freedom of thought inspired people throughout the country.

See also Scopes Trial.

MICHAEL KRONENWETTER

DAVIS, JEFFERSON

(1808–89)   *American statesman and president of the Confederate States of America.*

Born in Kentucky, Davis received an excellent education at Transylvania University and the U.S. Military Academy. Gallant service in the Mexican War only increased his love for the military, but he left the army, became a prosperous Mississippi planter, and embarked on a successful political career. In steady fashion he served as a U.S. congressman, secretary of war, and U.S. senator. By 1860, he was the South's leading statesman.

Davis's election as president of the new Confederate States of America in 1861 was an honor he accepted only with reluctance. (He really wanted to be a general and lead an army into battle.) Tall, thin, gray-haired, with all the bearing of the aristocrat he was, Davis spoke well in public and was honest to

Jefferson Davis, president of the Confederacy, and his wife, Varina Howell Davis. Jefferson remained a Confederate to the end, refusing to take the oath of loyalty to the Union that would have restored his U.S. citizenship. Congress, however, again made him a citizen in 1978, almost ninety years after his death.

a fault. He would not compromise on a point if he felt he was correct.

The four years Davis spent as Confederate president were a personal disaster. He was a dedicated patriot, but he could not inspire others with his own devotion to the Southern cause. Personality flaws marred his effectiveness. Aloof, impatient, and quarrelsome, he proved to be a poor administrator. He was a slow worker and sadly unable to delegate authority to others. Ill health that included migraine headaches, neuralgia, and boils plagued Davis during much of the war. Blind in one eye, he so severely strained the other that for a time there were fears of his losing all vision.

Davis was imprisoned by the federal government for two years after the war. This produced a turnabout both in him and in the feelings of the Southern people toward him. He became more outgoing and likable; the South by then regarded him as a living martyr. Davis spent his last twenty years making speeches, writing his memoirs, and basking in a glow of affection he never knew during the Civil War. He is buried in Hollywood Cemetery in Richmond, Virginia.

In his last public address, Davis urged a large Southern audience to "lay aside all rancor, all bitter sectional feeling, and to take your places in the ranks of . . . a reunited country."

See also Civil War; Confederate States of America.

JAMES I. ROBERTSON, JR.

DAWES PLAN

During World War I the United States lent about $10 billion to its European Allies. After the war was won, the Allies required the defeated Germans to pay them $33 billion in reparations, money to repair the damage caused by the war. Germany claimed that this was far more than it could possibly pay, and in 1921 it defaulted, or stopped paying, on its debt. France and Belgium then seized the Ruhr, an important German industrial region. The German economy then collapsed and runaway inflation followed.

The Allies claimed that they could not pay their debts to the United States unless the Germans paid the reparations to them. America was therefore deeply interested in finding a solution to the problem. The result

was the creation of an international commission, headed by Charles G. Dawes, director of the U.S. Bureau of the Budget. In 1924 the commission agreed to reduce the amount of reparations to be paid by Germany and stretch out the time for repayment. The United States also lent Germany more money so that it could stabilize its currency and stop inflation. Germany then began paying the Allies $250 million a year, which enabled the Allies to begin paying their debts to the United States.

That fall Dawes was elected vice president of the United States, and the next year he was awarded the Nobel Peace Prize for his work on the commission. Actually the new system worked only as long as American bankers continued to make loans to Germany. America was lending money to Germany that Germany was passing on to the Allies and the Allies to America. It would probably have been better simply to have written off the original Allied debts.

See also World War I.

DAWES SEVERALTY ACT

After the Civil War the rapid advance of white settlers into the Great Plains put great pressure on the Indians of that region. Bitter warfare followed, which inevitably resulted in the destruction of many tribes. This led white reformers to demand that to end the bloodshed, the Indians should be "assimilated." They should be persuaded to give up their traditional way of life, adopt white culture, and settle down on family farms.

Congress responded by passing the Dawes Severalty Act of 1887. Lands held by Indian tribes in common were to be divided into individual family "allotments" of 160 acres. The

Indian families could not sell these allotments for twenty-five years. (This restriction was intended to prevent white speculators from tricking the Indians into selling their property for less than it was worth before they had time to adjust to their new way of life.) The Dawes Act also provided money for educating and training Indians. Those who accepted the new system and adopted what the law called "the habits of civilized life" were granted American citizenship.

The Dawes Act was well meant, but a disastrous failure. It further undermined Indian culture and did not do much to help the Indians adjust to white culture. It did nothing to encourage the white majority to accept Indians as equal members of American society. And it actually speeded the loss of Indian-owned land. After allotments were made, land left over was offered for public sale. In 1887 Indians controlled 138 million acres. When the allotment policy was abandoned in 1934 only 52 million acres were still in Indian hands.

See also Indian-White Relations.

DAY, DOROTHY

(1897–1980) *Journalist, peace activist, and founder of the Catholic Worker movement.*

Day combined traditional Catholic faith with a deep commitment to social justice and the cause of peace. After leaving college in 1916, Day worked on a number of socialist and antiwar newspapers in New York City. She was determined to use her writing gifts on behalf of the poor. A turning point in her life came when she joined the Roman Catholic church in 1927.

Day found a way to combine her religious and social beliefs. The solution came in 1932 when she met the French-born philosopher Peter Maurin. With him she launched the *Catholic Worker* in 1933. Originally a newspaper, and then a broad-based movement of communities across the country, the Catholic Worker movement supported workers, the unemployed, and the down-and-out during the depression of the 1930s. Because of her strong criticism of social injustice, some people accused Day of promoting communism. But her position was based on her understanding of the Bible and her Catholic faith. As she said, "The mystery of the poor is that they are Jesus, and what we do for them we do for him."

This position led her to establish what she called houses of hospitality to shelter the homeless and feed the hungry. At the same time, Day opposed all wars and was repeatedly jailed for her protests on behalf of peace, civil rights, and other causes. Although her opposition to war drew criticism at the time, in her later years she was widely admired as a heroic and holy woman who left a deep impact on the American Catholic church.

See also Conscientious Objectors.

For further reading: Jim Forest, *Love Is the Measure: A Biography of Dorothy Day* (Maryknoll, N.Y.: Orbis Books, 1993).

ROBERT ELLSBERG

D-DAY

From the time the United States entered World War II in December 1941, plans for an invasion of the European continent from bases in Great Britain were being prepared. Finally, in June 1944, American and British forces along with other Allied troops of many nations commanded by Gen. Dwight D. Eisenhower were ready to launch an all-out invasion of Nazi-occupied Normandy, in northern France, the first step in the final attack on German forces in Europe.

On June 6, D-day, a vast fleet of warships and landing craft crossed the English Channel, supported by bombers. They were headed for five beaches along the coast of the French province of Normandy. American troops landed at code-named Omaha and Utah Beaches, British forces at Sword, Gold, and Juno Beaches. At the same time American airborne units were parachuted behind the enemy defenses. It was the largest and most complicated operation of its kind in history.

The Germans fought fiercely and the Allies suffered heavy casualties, but by the end of the day the five beachheads were firmly established. Within a few days more than 300,000 troops were ashore, and thousands of tanks and other vehicles along with many tons of ammunition and other supplies were coming ashore in a steady stream. Technical innovations helped make all this possible: the invention of landing craft capable of carrying tanks, the construction of an entire prefabricated port to replace the ports destroyed by the Nazis, and the use of PLUTO, a flexible, ever-advancing pipeline for gasoline.

A month later the Allied armies on the Continent numbered more than a million, and thereafter the defeat of the Axis powers was only a matter of time.

See also World War II.

DEBS, EUGENE V.

(1855–1926) *Labor organizer and socialist.*

Debs was the preeminent leader of American socialism in the early twentieth century. His first labor activity was as secretary of the local lodge of the Brotherhood of Locomotive Firemen in his home state of Indiana. By 1881, he had become the union's national secretary, a tireless organizer, and a popular elected official.

Most railroad workers' unions were divided by crafts (engineers, firemen, brakemen), and Debs decided they would have a better chance of improving their wages and working conditions if they came together in one large industrial (industrywide) union. He quit the brotherhood and began organizing the American Railway Union.

He led that union in a national strike against the Pullman Company of Chicago in 1894 but lost when the U.S. government backed the railroad owners and used federal troops to break the strike. Debs and other leaders were jailed. When he finished his six-month sentence, a special train carried him to a rally of more than 100,000 supporters.

By then Debs had concluded that the government and the corporations together were so powerful that workers had to seek control of the government through the ballot. The answer was socialism: in Debs's words, "The collective ownership and control of industry and its democratic management in the interest of all the people."

Debs ran as the Socialist Party candidate for president five times between 1900 and 1920. In 1912, he received his highest total—6 percent of the vote. Despite his defeats, Debs was a tireless organizer for the party and one of the most eloquent public speakers in the country.

Because he publicly opposed U.S. involvement in World War I, Debs was imprisoned for nearly three years (1919–21). From his cell he again ran for president—and received nearly a million votes. At his sentencing Debs

Eugene Debs delivering an antiwar speech in 1918. Debs ran for president five times between 1900 and 1920 on the Socialist Party ticket.

had declared: "Your honor, . . . while there is a lower class, I am in it; while there is a criminal element, I am of it; while there is a soul in prison, I am not free."

See also Conscientious Objectors; Labor Movement; Pullman Strike.

WARREN GOLDSTEIN

DECLARATION OF INDEPENDENCE

The Revolutionary War was more than a year old before Congress declared independence from Great Britain. But after the Battles of Lexington and Concord in April 1775, inde-

pendence was probably inevitable. Congress then organized the Continental army and named George Washington commander in chief, but it did not formally break away from the British Empire. In 1776, however, the enormous popularity of Thomas Paine's pamphlet *Common Sense,* which attacked King George III as a tyrant and murderer for sending soldiers against his own subjects, encouraged Congress to make the final break.

In June 1776 Richard Henry Lee of Virginia introduced a resolution stating "that these United Colonies are, and of right ought to be, free and independent States." Congress then appointed a committee to draw up a statement explaining why the colonies were justified in wanting to be free of English rule. The

John Trumbull's painting of the signing of the Declaration of Independence, which took place in Independence Hall, Philadelphia, on July 4, 1776. The painting depicts forty-seven of the fifty-six men who signed the document.

1. George Wythe, Virginia
2. William Whipple, New Hampshire
3. Josiah Bartlett, New Hampshire
4. Benjamin Harrison, Virginia
5. Thomas Lynch, South Carolina
6. Richard Henry Lee, Virginia
7. Samuel Adams, Massachusetts
*8. George Clinton, New York
9. William Paca, Maryland
10. Samuel Chase, Maryland
11. Lewis Morris, New York
12. William Floyd, New York

13. Arthur Middleton, South Carolina
14. Thomas Heyward, Jr., South Carolina
15. Charles Carroll, Maryland
16. George Walton, Georgia
17. Robert Morris, Pennsylvania
*18. Thomas Willing, Pennsylvania
19. Benjamin Rush, Pennsylvania
20. Elbridge Gerry, Massachusetts
21. Robert Treat Paine, Massachusetts
22. Abraham Clark, New Jersey
23. Stephen Hopkins, Rhode Island
24. William Ellery, Rhode Island

25. George Clymer, Pennsylvania
26. William Hooper, North Carolina
27. Joseph Hewes, North Carolina
28. James Willson, Pennsylvania
29. Francis Hopkinson, New Jersey
30. John Adams, Massachusetts
31. Roger Sherman, Connecticut
*32. Robert R. Livingston, New York
33. Thomas Jefferson, Virginia
34. Benjamin Franklin, Pennsylvania
35. Richard Stockton, New Jersey
36. Francis Lewis, New York

37. John Witherspoon, New Jersey
38. Samuel Huntington, Connecticut
39. William Williams, Connecticut
40. Oliver Wolcott, Connecticut
41. John Hancock, Massachusetts
*42. Charles Thomson, Secretary,
     Pennsylvania
43. George Read, Delaware
*44. John Dickinson, Pennsylvania
45. Edward Rutledge, South Carolina
46. Thomas McKean, Delaware
47. Philip Livingston, New York

There were 56 signers of the Declaration of Independence. The painting portrays only 47. The 5 men whose names are starred were not signers. The portraits of the following 14 do not appear in the painting.

Matthew Thornton, New Hampshire
John Hart, New Jersey
John Morton, Pennsylvania
James Smith, Pennsylvania

George Taylor, Pennsylvania
George Ross, Pennsylvania
Caesar Rodney, Delaware
Thomas Stone, Maryland

Thomas Nelson, Jr., Virginia
Francis Lightfoot Lee, Virginia
Carter Braxton, Virginia
John Penn, North Carolina

Button Gwinnett, Georgia
Lyman Hall, Georgia

committee consisted of Thomas Jefferson of Virginia, Benjamin Franklin of Pennsylvania, John Adams of Massachusetts, Robert R. Livingston of New York, and Roger Sherman of Connecticut. Jefferson wrote most of the statement, which we know as the Declaration of Independence.

Jefferson began by stating the purpose of the document: to explain why the colonies were declaring themselves independent. "All men are created equal," he wrote, and have God-given rights to "life, liberty, and the pursuit of happiness." Governments existed to protect these rights, and any government that failed to do so could be changed or even abolished by the people. They could then create a new government. In other words, the people possessed the right of revolution.

Jefferson then presented a long list of examples showing how King George III had repeatedly violated the rights of the colonies, his object being, Jefferson claimed, "the establishment of an absolute Tyranny over these states." The indictment was somewhat exaggerated: the British Parliament was responsible for many of the actions for which Jefferson blamed the king personally. For instance, it was Parliament that adopted legislation to tax the colonies and to restrict their trade "with all parts of the world."

Jefferson deliberately used emotional language. His purpose was to persuade "a candid world" that the Americans were justified in throwing off British rule. He described the military actions in New England, the burning of Norfolk, Virginia, and the bombardment of Charleston, South Carolina, by the Royal Navy by saying that the king had "ravaged our coasts, burnt our towns, and destroyed the lives of our people."

Jefferson showed his draft to Adams and Franklin who made a few changes. The full committee accepted these and forwarded the draft to Congress. Congress made a few more changes and then adopted it on July 4, 1776.

On July 8, the Declaration was read aloud at the Philadelphia Statehouse to a large crowd of people. The next day Gen. George Washington and his troops heard it read in New York City.

Nowadays, few people are familiar with the detailed charges Jefferson made in arguing that King George III was a tyrant. But the first part of the Declaration, his explanation of why the people had a right to revolt, has become a classic statement of the belief that governments can justly exercise their powers only with the consent of the governed. Whenever any government acts against the interest of its citizens, they have the right to overturn it.

In later years, John Adams pointed out that the ideas expressed in the Declaration were not original. Jefferson freely admitted that this was so. "I did not consider it . . . my charge to invent new ideas, but to place before mankind the common sense of the subject," he wrote. The Declaration was, he added, "an expression of the American mind."

Jefferson's powerful expression of the "common sense" principles underlying the American Revolution has inspired popular resistance to tyranny all over the world ever since. The French Revolution of 1789, the Russian Revolution of 1917, and dozens of other popular movements on every continent have been inspired at least to some degree by the American example, and their participants often quote Jefferson's words when justifying their own striving for freedom.

See also Revolution.

LINDA GRANT DE PAUW

DEFENSE
See Air Force; Army; Marine Corps; Navy.

DE KOONING, WILLEM
(1904–   ) *Painter.*

De Kooning was a founder of the American movement in painting called abstract expressionism. When he arrived in the United States in 1926, de Kooning had already had eight years of training at the Rotterdam Academy of Fine Arts and Techniques. He had also acquainted himself with the works of the great early modernists, including his countryman, Piet Mondrian.

A highly original artist, de Kooning surprised New York in his first one-man show in 1948 with his bold black and white abstractions painted with enamel house paints and filled with freely sweeping strokes. Subsequent works were marked by de Kooning's ability to organize large paintings in which hints of organic forms, such as parts of the human body, were interwoven with animated abstract areas, enlivened with swiftly moving, thickly painted strokes. Along with Jackson Pollock, whom he had known since the early 1940s, de Kooning was soon to be regarded as a pioneer of a new painterly language, sometimes described as *gestural* or *informal.*

In 1953, de Kooning startled his appreciative audience by showing a group of paintings called *Woman.* In these heavily brushed paintings, the vague allusions to the human body seen in earlier works were made specific. Rather fierce, these women reminded many of primitive goddesses of frightening intensity. Thereafter, de Kooning's spirited brush moved to capture ideas of figures, landscapes, and urban New York, abstracting greatly but always carrying the feeling of his subjects.

De Kooning never wanted to be limited by any established idea of what painting should be. He felt free to paint specific subjects, such as the sea and the sand near his studio on Long Island or fishermen and swimmers. But he felt equally free to use the abstract painting language inherited from early modernists in order to suggest states of mind or general feelings. He is now regarded as an American old master of abstract expressionism.

See also Abstract Expressionism; Painting and Sculpture.

DORE ASHTON

DEMILLE, CECIL B.
(1881–1959) *Film director and producer.*

DeMille was the man most responsible for establishing Hollywood as the film capital of the United States and for creating the image of the industry. His spectacular productions and publicity stunts became synonymous with extravagance and glamour.

DeMille came by his interest in the theater naturally. The son of a successful Broadway playwright, he left military school at the age of seventeen to study acting at the American Academy of Dramatic Arts in New York. He had a modest career on the stage and tried his hand at writing and directing plays while he was in his twenties. In 1913 he accepted the job of director general with a new motion picture company formed by vaudeville producer Jesse Lasky and his brother-in-law Samuel Goldfish (who later changed his name to Goldwyn). Their first film, *The Squaw Man,* appealed to a more sophisticated audience than the work of most other studios and was a big success. His 1917 historical drama about Joan of Arc, *Joan the Woman,* established his reputation for the large-scale costume productions that were to become his specialty.

With a keen eye for what the movie audience wanted, DeMille made patriotic films during World War I. As social customs began to change during the early 1920s, he reflected the new trends, making witty movies about married life. When the public was shocked by Hollywood scandals, he kept up with popular taste by making his first religious epic, *The Ten Commandments* (1923). DeMille opened his own studio, DeMille Productions, in 1925, but in 1932, he returned to Lasky's company, now called Paramount Pictures. He remained with Paramount throughout the rest of his career. His last film was an even more spectacular version of *The Ten Commandments,* made in 1956.

Famous for his flamboyant style and special effects, DeMille made over seventy films. Although they were seldom admired by critics, who considered him more a showman than an artist, they were almost all very popular with the public.

See also Movies.

D E N N I S   W E P M A N

D E M O C R A T I C   P A R T Y

The Democratic Party is the oldest existing political party in the United States. Its origins, unlike those of the Republican Party, are hazy. Present-day Democrats like to trace their history back to the Democratic-Republican Party founded in the 1790s by Thomas Jefferson and others to challenge the policies of President John Adams. Actually, that party soon disintegrated. Only after 1824, when some of its former members rallied behind the presidential candidacy of Tennessee senator Andrew Jackson, did the modern Democratic Party begin taking shape.

Jacksonian Democrats

Organizing and campaigning on the local, state, and national levels, Jackson and his backers won the White House in 1828. In 1832, Jackson was nominated for reelection at the party's first national convention.

Andrew Jackson, born to immigrant parents and raised in humble circumstances, typified the new Democratic spirit. He was a veteran of the American Revolution and hero of the War of 1812 and was ruthlessly dedicated to westward expansion at the expense of Native Americans. A lawyer and politician, a land speculator, and eventually a slaveholding plantation owner, Jackson was a self-made man, and as such, he demanded voting rights for all white males. (At the time, some states still limited the franchise to white males who owned property.) Suspicious of powerful centralized government, he believed states should run their own affairs free of federal interference.

Jackson's enthusiasm for states' rights, his scorn of wealth and privilege, and his racial views appealed strongly to small farmers, workers, and white southern landowners. Other Democrats followed his lead, and they lost the White House only twice between 1828 and 1856. But between 1860 and 1908, they *won* it only twice.

Civil War Issues

Their troubles began over slavery. In 1860, Democrats split on the issue, nominating two presidential candidates, one for slavery and one more or less against it. Both lost to Abraham Lincoln, candidate of the new Republican Party, which was opposed to the expansion of slavery into the western territories.

Eleven largely Democratic southern states seceded from the Union, and the Civil War began. In 1864, Lincoln, anticipating Union victory and reconciliation with the South, chose a pro-Union southern Democrat, Andrew Johnson, as his vice president. Then Lincoln was assassinated.

As president, Johnson failed to resolve the differences between a triumphant Republican Congress and a defeated Democratic South. To punish the South for seceding, Congress placed it under military rule. Determined to become the new majority party, Republicans accused Democrats of disloyalty to the Union. In 1868, Republicans in Congress impeached Johnson, charging him with "high crimes and misdemeanors" and putting him on trial in the Senate. The charges were narrowly dismissed, and Johnson served out his term. But except in the "Solid South," his party had been devastated. There, white Democrats used their influence to strip former slaves of their newfound civil rights.

Gradually, the party recovered, reinvigorated by support from growing numbers of immigrants and laborers in the urban North. Democrats gained seats in Congress and elected Grover Cleveland president in 1884 and 1892. In 1912, a split in the Republican Party sent Democrat Woodrow Wilson to the White House and gave him majorities in both houses of Congress.

Centralizing Government

Wilson believed in using the power of the federal government to improve life for ordinary citizens. He signed prolabor legislation, initiated federal aid to education, and established the Federal Trade Commission to promote fair business practices. As commander in chief during the First World War, he guid-

ed the country through its first full-scale involvement in international conflict.

If Wilson did much to centralize government, the next Democrat to occupy the White House, Franklin D. Roosevelt, did more. When Roosevelt was elected in 1932, the country was in a terrible economic depression. Businesses and banks had failed, leaving millions without jobs or savings. Promising Americans a "New Deal," Roosevelt asked Congress for laws to better regulate banking and business, create jobs for the unemployed, and provide such social benefits as unemployment insurance, aid to dependent children, and retirement pensions. Congress obliged.

Although many in the business community strongly criticized the New Deal as excessive "big government," Roosevelt's programs made the Democratic Party enormously pop-

The first representation of the Democratic Party emblem as the donkey appeared in this cartoon by Thomas Nast. The word "Copperhead" on the side of the donkey referred to a branch of the party during the Civil War.

sular among most other groups including, for the first time, blacks. During his second term, Roosevelt began mobilizing the country for World War II. He was reelected for third and fourth terms in 1940 and 1944. Roosevelt died in office just before the war ended, and the new president, Harry S. Truman, presided over the victory.

Domestically, Truman's "Fair Deal" programs echoed Roosevelt's New Deal. His backing of civil rights legislation cost the Democrats much of their white southern support, and the party split in the 1948 election. The southern states formed the States' Rights Party, popularly called the Dixiecrats. Although they received thirty-nine electoral votes, Truman won the election in an upset victory. In 1950, seeking to stop the spread of communism in Asia, Truman sent U.S. troops along with servicemen from other United Nations countries to help anti-Communist South Korea fend off an invasion by Communist North Korea. His later inability to extricate America from the fighting was one reason Democrats lost the White House in 1952. Another was the Republican charge in the midst of a red scare that Democrats generally were "soft on communism."

Liberal Policies

Democratic presidents since Truman have pursued the party's liberal social goals. John F. Kennedy, elected in 1960 and assassinated in 1963, saw much of his "New Frontier" program blocked in Congress by Republicans and conservative Democrats. Kennedy's successor, Lyndon B. Johnson, called upon lawmakers to honor the slain president's memory with a commitment to social change. The historic Civil Rights Act of 1964, which outlawed discrimination based on race, sex, religion, or national origin, and the Voting Rights Act of 1965, which made it easier for

blacks and others to exercise their right to vote, were the result. Other Johnson "Great Society" programs provided health insurance to the needy (Medicaid) and elderly (Medicare) and increased federal aid to education and the arts. Elected in a landslide over an extremely conservative Republican in 1964, Johnson became entangled, as Truman had, in a far-off war against communism. Public opposition to the Vietnam War helped produce Democratic defeats in 1968 and 1972. Democrat Jimmy Carter was elected president in 1976 in the wake of the Republican Watergate scandal but lost four years later.

During the 1980 campaign, Republicans attacked not only Carter but Democratic policies since the New Deal. Democrats had enacted hundreds of social programs, they said, encouraging Americans to depend upon welfare and bloating the federal bureaucracy. They accused Democrats of overemphasizing minority rights at the expense of white middle-class voters, wasting taxpayers' money, and increasing the federal deficit from $602 billion to $907 billion during the Carter years alone. Much of the country agreed. Republicans took the White House in 1980, 1984, and 1988.

But as the 1990s began, attitudes changed somewhat. The economy was poor, unemployment high, social welfare programs strained, and racial tensions growing. The deficit hit $3.5 *trillion*. Suddenly, the kind of aspirations that had fueled the New Deal and the Fair Deal, the New Frontier and the Great Society, looked better to many Americans. In 1992 they chose the Democratic governor of Arkansas, Bill Clinton, as their forty-second president.

See also Jacksonian Democracy; Party Conventions. *And see biographies of Democratic presidents listed in table under the entry* Presidents.

A N N   E .   W E I S S

DEPRESSIONS AND RECESSIONS

The U.S. economy, like all economies, is subject to the business cycle. This is simply the alternation between periods of increasing production and employment, called booms, and periods when production declines and unemployment rises, known as depressions. The basic causes of the business cycle are hotly disputed among economists.

In the colonial and early national periods, the great majority of Americans lived on farms and produced most of the goods they needed at home. They lived largely outside what economists call the "cash economy" and thus were not greatly affected by fluctuations of the business cycle. It was only when the country began to industrialize in the nineteenth century, and more and more Americans worked for wages, that the business cycle began to affect the daily lives of millions of citizens.

Bank Panics and Depressions

The first major depression in this country began when a banking panic ended the boom of the mid-1830s. Banking panics—when depositors, fearing bank failure, rush to withdraw their money—were a common feature of the nineteenth- and early-twentieth-century American economy and they marked the beginning of each new depression. The reason they were so common was that the country lacked a central bank, which regulates the money supply and loans regular banks cash if the demand for it suddenly rises.

The contraction that started in 1837 was quite severe and lasted until 1843. The price of cotton fell by almost half on the New Orleans market, and sales of public lands on the frontier fell from 20 million acres in 1836 to only 3.5 million in 1838. New York City saw demonstrations protesting unemployment, and one Wall Street speculator lamented that the fortunes that had been built up during the mid-1830s "have melted like the snows before an April sun."

Prosperity finally returned and it wasn't until another panic swept the country in 1857 that depression again gripped the economy. Depression also struck in 1873 and in 1893. This last was exceptionally severe because the economy was now fully industrialized, and most Americans worked in the cash economy. In 1860 there had been four people working on farms for every one working in a factory. But by 1890 the ratio had dropped to two to one. And farmers were specializing more and more in one or two crops, selling them on the open market for cash.

The gross national product (the total value of all the goods and services produced by the people of the country in a given period of time, usually a year) fell by almost 12 percent in the depression of the early 1890s while unemployment rose from 3 percent in 1892 to 18.4 percent in 1894. Many unemployed joined "armies" to press for relief. The most famous of these, Coxey's army, disbanded only when its leaders were arrested on the steps of the Capitol in Washington, D.C.

The economy recovered beginning in 1896 and began a rapid expansion that made it the largest and richest in the world. In 1907 a new sharp financial panic finally convinced the country that a central bank was indispensable to a modern economy, and the Federal Reserve was established in 1913.

The aftermath of World War I caused a severe but short-lived depression in 1920–21, but the rest of the decade was prosperous as American industry expanded. This prosperity did not extend to the agricultural segment of the economy, however. The rapid spread of the automobile and the tractor in the 1910s

The despair of the jobless during the Great Depression of the 1930s.

and 1920s caused the number of horses and mules in the country to fall dramatically. Much of the land that had been used to grow fodder and feed grains for them was converted to growing food for humans, causing prices to drop sharply as the supply increased and inflicting widespread distress on rural areas.

The Great Depression

In 1928 the Federal Reserve raised interest rates three times in order to hold down inflation and the speculation that increasingly characterized Wall Street activity. This caused the economy as a whole to slow, but the speculation in the stock market continued unabated until the crash of October 1929 ended it abruptly.

The stock market crash did not cause the Great Depression that followed it and was itself, in fact, only an effect of the slowdown in the economy. Instead, three decisions by the federal government over the next few years converted what had begun as an ordinary downturn in the business cycle into an economic calamity far worse than any the country had known before.

First, although the economy was already

slowing and speculation on Wall Street had ended, the Federal Reserve did not lower interest rates from their high levels in the late 1920s. It continued to fight inflation while the country began the greatest deflation in its history. In effect, the Federal Reserve kept treating the patient for fever long after he had begun to freeze to death.

Second, Congress passed and President Herbert Hoover signed the Smoot-Hawley Tariff, the largest tariff increase in the nation's history. This devastated foreign trade as other countries increased their own tariffs in retaliation. In 1929 the country exported $5.2 billion worth of goods, in 1932 only $1.6 billion.

Third, the federal government tried to balance its budget by sharply raising taxes even as the depression continued to tighten.

By 1933, 25 percent of the work force was unemployed and the gross national product was cut nearly in half. For the next eight years, the New Deal tried to bring relief to those out of work and bring a return of prosperity. But it was only the outbreak of the Second World War that finally ended the Great Depression.

In 1937, the economy, which had slowly been improving since it hit bottom in 1933, suddenly dipped again. As the country was already in a depression, economists called this new downturn a *recession,* a term that has been used to refer to every economic downturn since.

Because the government learned the lessons of the Great Depression, and because government spending on social programs has steadily risen as a percentage of gross national product since the New Deal began, these postwar downturns have been far milder and caused far less distress than the depression of the 1930s.

Indeed, today the word *depression* belongs to the 1930s and is often capitalized to emphasize its unique status.

See also Coxey's Army; New Deal; Unemployment.

JOHN STEELE GORDON

DESEGREGATION
See African Americans: Since World War II; Civil Rights Movement; Segregation.

DEWEY, GEORGE
(1837–1917)   *Spanish-American War naval commander.*

Born in Montpelier, Vermont, Dewey entered the U.S. Naval Academy at seventeen, graduating in 1858. Three years later the Civil War began, and Lieutenant Dewey became second in command of the warship *Mississippi.* He was in several battles, and his commanding officer praised his calmness in times of danger.

For many years after the war, few new navy ships were built, promotions were slow, and many officers left the service. Dewey, however, felt there was always a chance for action. In 1897, now a commodore (the rank just below admiral), Dewey was appointed commander of the American Asian Squadron, stationed at Hong Kong, China. On April 25, 1898, war was declared between the United States and Spain. Dewey received orders to take his squadron to the Spanish-owned Philippine Islands and attack the Spanish fleet guarding the Cavite naval base at Manila Bay.

Dewey had six fighting ships, but there were nine major Spanish warships and a number of lesser ones in Manila Bay. There were also shore fortresses with large cannons, and the entrance to the bay was reported to be strewn with explosive mines. Nevertheless, Dewey ordered his squadron straight into the bay shortly after midnight on April 30. No mines were encountered and only a few shells were fired from the fortifications, none hitting any of his ships. When the Spanish ships became visible, Dewey gave the order to begin firing. The Spaniards seemed caught by surprise and unable to respond. By noon, the Battle of Manila Bay was over, with eight Spanish ships and several fortresses destroyed. Not one American seaman had been killed.

Dewey's victory captured the Philippines, which became an important American military base in the Far East. He was hailed as a hero throughout the United States. The government awarded him the special rank of admiral of the navy, which no other American naval officer has ever held. He served as an adviser to the navy until his death.

See also Philippines, Acquisition of; Spanish-American War.

For further reading: Alden R. Carter, The Spanish-American War: Imperial Ambitions (New York: Franklin Watts, 1991).

TOM McGOWEN

DEWEY, JOHN

(1859–1953)   Educator and philosopher.

John Dewey grew up in small-town Vermont, in a rigidly Congregationalist, middle-class home. He remained a deeply religious idealist into his twenties. Depressed by an early effort at teaching, he studied philosophy and psychology at the new Johns Hopkins University (1882–84). He then taught at the University of Michigan (1884–94) before moving to the University of Chicago (1894–1904).

The Chicago years were most fruitful for Dewey's ideas about education. Under the influence of William James's *Principles of Psychology* (1890), he moved away from idealism toward a scientific materialism. This meant a stress on the study of people and problems under laboratory conditions without reliance on religious or philosophical ideas. He abandoned his religious faith. Using the University of Chicago's famous Laboratory School, Dewey experimented with teaching methods that soon revolutionized many American classrooms. In two pamphlets, "The School and Society" (1899) and "The Child and the Curriculum" (1902), he advocated relating what is taught to the interests and experience of students.

He also stressed the importance of democracy and equality in schooling. He wanted to get away from lecturing, memorization, and passive obedience. He thought that students should solve real-life problems and prepare for jobs in society.

After moving to Columbia University, Dewey soon became the most influential philosopher of his generation. He applied the pragmatism of William James to schools and then to social problems. This meant always looking at the practical consequences of an act: what difference in behavior would an idea make in school or in society? He also became one of the most prominent liberal intellectuals. In a long series of books, especially *Reconstruction in Philosophy* (1920), he was highly critical of previous philosophical thought. He argued that the task of the philosopher is similar to the tasks of the educator and social reformer: solve the real problems of society to make it a better place for all citizens.

See also Education; James, William.

ROBERT M. CRUNDEN

DICKINSON, EMILY

(1830–86) *Poet.*

Dickinson was born in the middle of a chilly December in Amherst, a town in northwestern Massachusetts. She wrote the best compositions in school (Amherst Academy), was known as a wit, and was called "Socrates" by her girlfriends. She loved her school and boasted of its "big studies," which she listed: "Mental Philosophy, Geology, Latin, and Botany." Her favorite was botany.

Dickinson spent a year at college—Mount Holyoke Female Seminary, as it was then called. But she had studied much the same things at the academy and was given to severe colds; so her father thought it better for her to be at home. Of the next several years she wrote, "My Lexicon [dictionary] was my only companion." This was not quite true. She had plenty of friends. When she was eighteen, she wrote, "Amherst is alive with fun this winter."

But she was a born poet. As her friends drifted away or married, she became more and more absorbed in her work, to the point of excluding almost everything else except family and household chores. They called her "The Myth" in town. She wrote and wrote, bound up many of her poems in little packets, but never published them. Her name was not attached to the eight or ten of her poems that were printed in newspapers, mainly through the kindness of friends. Her poetry had none of the qualities—lilting rhythms, tinkling rhymes, easy "message"—that publishers were looking for at the time.

When, five years after her death, a small collection of Dickinson's poems was finally published, a reviewer called them "barbaric." But they were a great popular success, going through eleven reprintings in two years. Rumors about this remarkable "recluse" in Amherst began to spread. It was not until the 1950s, however, that the complete *Poems* (1,775 of them) and the complete *Letters* (1,046) gave the world a full view of her enormous creative power. Books and critical essays began to flow from the presses and are still coming out in a steady stream. Dickinson is now recognized the world over as a major figure.

See also Literature.

RICHARD B. SEWALL

DIMAGGIO, JOE

(1914–) *Baseball player.*

One of the most popular of all American athletes, DiMaggio has become a legendary hero. The eighth of nine children, he was born into a family of Italian immigrants and brought up in San Francisco. Joe, who had to work to help support the family, showed an unusual aptitude for baseball while still a child. He began his professional career playing for the San Francisco Seals of the Pacific Coast League. At the age of eighteen, he gained fame by hitting safely in sixty-one consecutive games and batting .340. As a consequence, he was sought by a number of major league teams, finally signing with the New York Yankees.

DiMaggio made his debut as a Yankee in 1936, batting .323, driving in 125 runs, and getting 206 hits in only 138 games. More phenomenally successful years followed. His greatest season was that of 1941, the year of his record-breaking 56-game hitting streak during which he got 91 hits in 223 times at bat, for an average of .408. His batting average for the entire season was .357.

Because of a recurring heel ailment, DiMaggio retired from baseball in 1951, when he was only thirty-seven years old. Since then his name has remained before the public as a television personality and as the husband of the actress Marilyn Monroe, to whom he was married for a short time. He will always be remembered as a baseball great, a powerful hitter as well as a superb outfielder—an incomparably graceful and elegant athlete who led the Yankees to ten American League pennants. He was, not surprisingly, elected to the baseball Hall of Fame in 1955.

See also Baseball.

HOWARD GREENFELD

DISCOVERY OF AMERICA, EUROPEAN
See Exploration of North America.

DISNEY, WALT

(1901–66)   *Animated cartoon producer and amusement park developer.*

A pioneer in animation and an influential figure in the history of motion pictures, Walt Disney helped shape the tastes of the nation. He made many important contributions to the filming technique of cartoons, introduc-

Joe DiMaggio, nicknamed "Joltin' Joe" and the "Yankee Clipper," batting during a 1951 game.

ing sound and color as well as a cast of beloved cartoon characters known throughout the world. The most honored filmmaker in Hollywood history, he won a record thirty-one Academy Awards.

Disney spent his childhood on a farm in Missouri, where he came to know and love animals, and at the age of eight moved to Kansas City. There he studied art through correspondence courses, and in 1919 he became a commercial illustrator. Fascinated by the new field of animation, he began to make primitive advertising cartoons, to be shown in local movie theaters as commercials are now shown on television. In 1922 he opened a cartoon studio with the artist Ub Iwerks. The business did not succeed, and the next year he went to Hollywood, already the center of the film industry. In partnership with his brother Roy, and with Iwerks doing most of his drawing, Disney made a bare living as an independent producer of short cartoons.

It was with *Steamboat Willie*, which introduced Mickey Mouse in 1928, that Disney became famous. The first cartoon to use sound, it was a sensation. Mickey, his squeaky voice provided by Disney himself, appeared in over a hundred short cartoon features in the next ten years and became an international star. Like many of Disney's other characters, Mickey was adapted to comic strips and comic books with great success. Images from Disney's cartoons have been used on thousands of products, from toys to clothing, worldwide.

In his series of shorts called *Silly Symphonies*, made from 1929 through the 1930s, Disney matched motion to a prerecorded musical sound track. His *Flowers and Trees* (1932) was the first animated cartoon made in color. The mischievous, ill-tempered Donald Duck was introduced in 1934, replacing the overly

Walt Disney boards a plane with his creation, Mickey Mouse, on their way to the 1933 World's Fair in Chicago. Flight attendant Izola Readle poses with them.

sweet Mickey Mouse in the public's affections.

That same year, against everybody's advice, Disney began production of the world's first feature-length animated film, *Snow White*. Released in 1937, *Snow White* grossed $8 million its first year and remained the film industry's biggest money-maker for several more. *Fantasia* (1940) illustrated classical music with cartoon sequences, and the next year Disney made the first film to combine animation with live action, *The Reluctant Dragon*.

Walt Disney Productions began making wildlife documentaries in 1948 and two years later produced its first live-action film featuring a human cast. Disney, dedicated to wholesome entertainment for the "family market," pioneered made-for-television films and developed his own television channel.

In 1957, he opened a giant entertainment park, Disneyland, in California. The most successful amusement complex in history, it reflects the same slick techniques and upbeat philosophy as his films. The formula has been repeated in Disneyworld (Florida), EuroDisney (France), and elsewhere since his death. Although Disney's work has been criticized for sentimentality and shallow optimism, his personal style and imagination exerted a major influence on the popular culture of the twentieth century.

See also Movies.

For further reading: Maxine P. Fisher, *The Walt Disney Story* (New York: Franklin Watts, 1988).

DENNIS WEPMAN

DIVORCE

Few colonists divorced in the seventeenth century, but New England Puritans, unlike the English who permitted only legal separations, held that marriage was a civil contract that could, under certain circumstances, be ended by law. Divorces were granted for several reasons, including adultery (unfaithfulness to one's spouse), long absence, and cruelty. Divorce laws and procedures did not, however, treat men and women equally. For example, women were far more likely to be accused of adultery than were men.

Although rare in the northern colonies, divorce was at least possible. In the South, only legal separations were permitted, which meant that though they were separated, neither party had the right to remarry. In both the North and the South, most people frowned on divorce, feeling that marriage should be for life. Nevertheless, some did divorce and others simply deserted their mates.

During and after the American Revolution, divorce laws and procedures changed in ways that helped women. In the revolutionary era, wives found courts more willing to hear complaints about their husbands' adultery, and in the early nineteenth century, women could bring suits on the grounds of drunkenness and an expanded legal definition of what constituted matrimonial cruelty. Ultimately, judges began accepting the idea of "mental cruelty" as a sufficient reason for divorce. Although men sometimes made use of this cause, women were its chief beneficiaries. By 1929, 44 percent of divorces granted to women (who received two-thirds of all divorces) were on the ground of cruelty.

Changing Divorce Rates

In the half century after 1880, the number of divorces rose rapidly, a sign that men and women had higher expectations about marriage. The rising rate prompted a debate on the subject of divorce. On one side were people who saw no reason for divorce laws standing in the way of individual freedom and happiness; on the other were those who saw in divorce a sign of social disorder and female "selfishness." This debate took shape in the 1920s and has continued until the present day.

During the Great Depression of the 1930s when millions of Americans were without work, the divorce rate slowed temporarily, but the numbers rose steadily in the late 1930s and soared during World War II (1941–45). Divorces reached an all-time high in 1946 and then declined before leveling off in the 1950s and the early 1960s.

Beginning in the mid-1960s, the divorce rate began to rise again for several reasons. More and more people came to expect greater personal satisfaction in marriage and saw no reason to settle for less. Increasing numbers of married women entered the work force and thus could support themselves. The rebirth of feminism meant that women came to see themselves not just as wives but as independent persons in their own right. Legally, there was a shift toward consensual divorce, in which both parties can simply agree to a divorce rather than one person having to sue the other. And no-fault divorce became common in almost every state: neither the husband nor the wife has to "prove" the other is to blame for the breakdown of the marriage.

Unexpected Results

These factors all made marital stability more difficult to maintain and brought changes that few people had foreseen. For example, although no-fault divorce seemed like a good idea, it has had unexpected and troubling consequences for women and children. Based on the idea that husbands and wives will face life after divorce as more or less equals—thus ignoring the fact that women usually earn considerably less money than men—no-fault divorce has left many women and their children in a difficult position. While men's standard of living usually rises in the first years following divorce, women's and children's fall. This situation occurs because too often fathers fail to pay for their children's economic support. Sad to say, many of these same men for whatever reason have little personal contact with their children as well. (Recently, states have passed laws designed to force divorced fathers to help support their children.)

Women also face problems after divorce because frequently they have been out of the job market for years and find it hard to compete with men. In contrast, most divorcing husbands take with them their education, job training, professional certification, good business name, or other advantages that come to men in America's labor market. In short, the no-fault revolution has all too often made losers of women and children. This situation will change only when alimony and child support awards are based on an attempt to achieve some measure of equality in the living standards of divorced men and women—or, better yet, when women, whether married or single, are treated the same in the labor market. There must also be more widespread recognition of how important *both* mothers and fathers are to their children, financially and emotionally. When divorce occurs, every effort must be made to ensure that children continue to have sustained contact with both parents.

See also Family Life; Marriage.

ROBERT L. GRISWOLD

DIX, DOROTHEA

(1802–87)   *Crusader for the mentally ill.*

Dorothea Dix overcame an unhappy childhood resulting from an absent father and a chronically ill mother. She left home at the age of twelve to live with her grandmother in Boston and was determined to get an education. A good student herself, Dorothea opened a school for young children at the age of fourteen. Over the next decade, she repeated her initial success, operating several other schools and teaching as well as furthering her own education. Ill health curtailed her teaching in 1828, and she turned to writing and voluntary work.

An invitation to conduct a Sunday school class for women in the East Cambridge jail in 1841 proved to be a turning point in Dix's life. Appalled at the horrendous conditions endured by the inmates, whose only "crime" usually was mental illness, Dix began an intensive study of the plight of the mentally ill in Massachusetts. Over the next eighteen months, she visited every almshouse and asylum in the state, constantly finding evidence of the neglect and cruelty that characterized treatment in these facilities. In 1843, after a tough battle with the Massachusetts legislature, she was able to secure provisions for upgrading the care in the Worcester asylum.

After that success, Dix broadened the scope of her investigations to other states, traveling tirelessly through rough country under often primitive conditions. She initiated innumerable petitions demanding improved care for the suffering people she found. Eventually her name and reputation as a champion of the mentally ill and an advocate for the reform of mental facilities throughout the country became well known not only in America but abroad as well. She spent several years in England and Scotland lobbying for her cause before returning home in 1856.

During the Civil War, Dix was appointed superintendent of army nurses and threw herself into that endeavor with as much fervor as she had into her fight for the mentally ill. But her insistence on controlling all aspects of nursing and medical facilities created conflicts that made her tenure a difficult one. She nevertheless continued as administrator until 1866, when she returned once again to her work as an investigator, this time in the South.

Old age finally caught up with Dix, and she was unable to maintain her previous demanding schedule. But she had already established a legacy that lived long after her death in 1887. Her work had forced society to face up to its obligation to treat the mentally ill responsibly and humanely.

See also Medicine; Mental Health.

CHRISTINE A. LUNARDINI

DOLLAR DIPLOMACY

Dollar diplomacy was a term used by President William Howard Taft to describe his policy of trying to advance American interests in the countries of Latin America and the Far East by means of investments and other forms of economic power. The policy was a response to the public's growing dislike of America's taking over another country as a colony and of its using military force to control areas considered vital to American interests. Taft argued that economic penetration would both protect American interests in the small underdeveloped nations of the Caribbean region and also improve the standard of living of their people.

Examples of dollar diplomacy in action include the purchase of the foreign debt of Honduras from British bankers in 1909 and American management of the Nicaraguan customs service in 1911 after Nicaragua had defaulted (stopped paying) on its foreign debt. The policy was also employed in Asia in 1910 to obtain a share of the international financing of railroads in China and Manchuria for American banks.

Dollar diplomacy alarmed the governments of most Latin American nations and only rarely benefited the people of the lands involved. When President Woodrow Wilson succeeded Taft in 1913 he repudiated dollar diplomacy as a national policy. But he did not succeed in ending American investments and American economic influence in the under-developed regions of the world.

DOUGLAS, STEPHEN A.

(1813–61)   *Political leader.*

Born in Vermont, Douglas moved to Illinois in 1833, where he practiced law and entered politics. After serving in various state offices, he was elected to the U.S. House of Representatives in 1843 and to the Senate in 1847, a position he held for the rest of his brief life.

Douglas, who ardently favored the expansion of the United States, supported the annexation of Texas, the acquisition of Oregon, and the Mexican War. A fiery speaker with strong convictions, this prominent Democrat — who was only five feet, four inches tall — acquired the nickname of the "Little Giant."

In 1854, Douglas pushed through Congress the Kansas-Nebraska Act. This law permitted the actual settlers of Kansas and Nebraska to decide whether their territories would join the Union as free or slave states — a principle Douglas called "popular sovereignty." The act repealed the 1820 Missouri Compromise, which had banned slavery in land north of 36°30' latitude. Angering antislavery Whigs, Democrats, and Free-Soilers, the Kansas-Nebraska Act led to the formation of the Republican Party. It also contributed to Douglas's failure to win the Democratic presidential nomination in 1856.

When Douglas ran for reelection to the Senate in 1858, he and Abraham Lincoln, his Republican opponent, engaged in a famous series of debates about slavery and its future expansion into the territories. Douglas won the election, but Lincoln acquired national prominence from the debates.

The Democratic Party was so deeply divided by the slavery issue in the 1860 presidential campaign that the northern Democrats nominated Douglas for president, and the southern Democrats ran John C. Breckinridge of Kentucky. The Republican candidate, Lincoln, won the election; Douglas finished second in the popular vote but captured only twelve electoral votes.

After Lincoln's election, Douglas worked strenuously but unsuccessfully to find some compromise that might prevent war between the North and the South. After hostilities began in April 1861, however, he loyally pledged his support to the Union cause just before his death.

See also Compromise of 1850; Freeport Doctrine; Kansas-Nebraska Act; Missouri Compromise; Popular Sovereignty.

EDMUND LINDOP

DOUGLASS, FREDERICK

(1818–95)   *Abolitionist, writer, and orator.*

Douglass was the most important African-American leader of the nineteenth century. Born Frederick Augustus Washington Bailey on Maryland's Eastern Shore, he was the son of a slave woman and probably her white master. Upon his escape from slavery at age twenty, he adopted the name of the hero in Sir Walter Scott's *The Lady of the Lake.* Douglass immortalized his years as a slave in *Narrative of the Life of Frederick Douglass, an American Slave* (1845). This and two later autobiographies, *My Bondage and My Freedom* (1855) and *The Life and Times of Frederick*

Douglass (1881), are among his greatest contributions to American culture. They are classics of American autobiography, as well as major sources for understanding the antislavery movement.

Douglass's life as a reformer ranged from his work as an abolitionist lecturer in the early 1840s to his attacks on Jim Crow laws and lynching in the 1890s. For sixteen years he edited an influential black newspaper and achieved international fame as an orator and

Frederick Douglass's voice was one of the most eloquent raised against slavery and racism. At an Independence Day speech in 1852, he charged his startled listeners and the nation with hypocrisy: "What, to the American slave, is your Fourth of July? I answer: a day that reveals to him, more than all other days . . . the gross injustice and cruelty to which he is the constant victim. To him, your celebration is a sham; your boasted liberty, an unholy license; your national greatness, swelling vanity; your sounds of rejoicing are empty and heartless."

writer of great skill and power. In thousands of speeches and editorials, he argued against slavery and racism, and provided a voice of hope for his people in a time when, for many, it appeared that slavery might never be destroyed. Douglass also joined antislavery political parties in the 1850s and preached his own brand of American ideals. He believed, as did most black abolitionists, that all the liberties guaranteed in the U.S. Constitution were the birthright of African Americans. In the 1850s he broke away from the strictly moralist brand of abolitionism advocated by William Lloyd Garrison. Douglass supported the early women's rights movement and gave direct assistance to John Brown's conspiracy that led to the raid on Harpers Ferry in 1859.

In his writings, Douglass was a master of irony. For example, in a famous Fourth of July speech to a white audience in 1852, he declared: "This Fourth of July is *yours,* not *mine. You* may rejoice, *I* must mourn." Then he accused his unsuspecting audience in Rochester, New York, of mockery for inviting him to speak. He compared his situation to that of the children of Israel in Psalm 137, who were forced to sit down "by the rivers of Babylon," there to "sing the Lord's song in a strange land." For the ways that racism has caused the deepest contradictions in American history, few better sources of insight exist than Douglass's speeches. And for understanding prejudice, there are few better starting points than his timeless definition of racism as a "diseased imagination."

Douglass welcomed the Civil War in 1861 as a moral crusade against slavery. During the war he labored for the Union cause and emancipation. He recruited black troops and was an adviser to President Abraham Lincoln. He viewed the Union victory as a political and moral rebirth of America, based on the ideal of racial equality. Some of his hopes were dashed during Reconstruction (1870s) and the Gilded Age (1880s), when many of the hard-won rights gained after emancipation were taken away in the South. But he continued to travel widely to lecture on racial issues, national politics, and women's rights.

In the 1870s Douglass moved to Washington, D.C., where he edited a newspaper and became president of the Freedman's Bank, an unsuccessful attempt to provide money and land for the freed slaves. During these years, his leadership became more symbolic than activist. As a loyal spokesman for the Republican Party, Douglass was appointed marshal (1877–81) and recorder of deeds (1881–86) for the District of Columbia, and U.S. chargé d'affaires for Santo Domingo and minister to Haiti (1889–91).

Brilliant, heroic, and complex, Douglass became a symbol of his age and a unique voice for humanism and social justice. His life and thought speak profoundly to the meaning of being black in America, as well as to the human calling to resist oppression and transcend the boundaries of race.

See also Abolitionist Movement; African Americans: 1877–1945; Emancipation Proclamation and Thirteenth Amendment; Reconstruction.

For further reading: Douglas T. Miller, *Frederick Douglass and the Fight for Freedom* (New York: Facts on File, 1988).

D A V I D   W.   B L I G H T

D R A F T
See Conscription.

D R A F T   R I O T S   O F   1863

In March 1863, in the middle of the Civil War, Congress passed a Conscription Act making men between the ages of twenty and forty-five subject to being drafted into the army. This law triggered riots in a number of Northern cities. The worst of these occurred in July 1863 in New York City. The rioting there began with an attack on the building where the draft lottery was taking place. For four days, during which more than a hundred people were killed and large sections of the city set afire, the fighting raged. Troops had to be called in before peace could be restored.

Most of the rioters were poor Irish laborers. They particularly objected to a provision in the Conscription Act allowing men to gain exemption from the draft by paying $300, roughly equal to what an unskilled laborer earned in a year. They were also angered by Abraham Lincoln's Emancipation Proclamation. The idea that they would be forced by the draft to risk their lives to free blacks who would then compete with them for jobs seemed to them doubly unjust.

A large percentage of the people who were killed and injured during the New York riot were black. The rioters even burned a Colored Orphan Asylum to the ground. The innocent blacks were thus scapegoats, victims of racial prejudice and the rioters' anger at being forced into what they saw as "a rich man's war and a poor man's fight."

See also Civil War.

D R E D   S C O T T   C A S E

In 1834 Dr. John Emerson, a Missouri army surgeon, was assigned to a post in Illinois. Later he served in Wisconsin Territory. Then, in 1838, he returned to Missouri. Dr. Emerson was accompanied during this period by a slave, Dred Scott, and Scott's wife, Harriet.

Dred Scott, a slave, was taken by his master from Missouri, a slave state, to reside in a free territory where slavery was prohibited. Scott later filed a lawsuit claiming that because he had lived on free soil, he was entitled to his freedom. The Supreme Court, however, in a highly controversial 1857 decision, disagreed. Furious debate followed between pro- and antislavery factions, contributing ultimately to the Civil War, which began four years later.

Eight years later, after Emerson's death, Scott and his wife sued for their liberty, claiming that since Illinois was a free state and since slavery had been banned in Wisconsin Territory by the Missouri Compromise of 1820, having lived in both places, they were entitled to their freedom.

With the help of friendly white lawyers, the Scotts' case was fought all the way to the Supreme Court. In 1857, in a complicated decision, written by Chief Justice Roger B. Taney, the Court ruled in *Dred Scott* v. *Sanford* that the Scotts could not sue in a federal court because blacks were not citizens of the United States. This decision, while questionable, was enough to settle the case. But Taney also declared that even if a black could be a citizen, residence in Wisconsin Territory would not have freed the Scotts because the Missouri Compromise of 1820, which had banned slavery in that area, was unconstitutional.

Most southerners were delighted with Taney's decision. But it greatly angered many northerners. Taney's argument meant that there was no way that slavery could be kept out of a territory before it became a state. If *Congress* could not ban slavery in a territory, surely a mere territorial legislature could not keep a settler who owned slaves from bringing them into a territory with him.

The decision increased ill-feeling between northerners, even those who were not in favor of abolishing slavery where it already existed, and southerners, even those who did not own slaves. It was a major step in the direction of civil war.

See also Slavery; Taney, Roger B.

DRUGS

A drug is a chemical that changes a person's physical or mental condition. Drugs can be swallowed, inhaled, injected, or absorbed through the skin. They are often classified by what they are used for. *Medicines* are used to cure illnesses or lessen their effects. *Recreational drugs* are taken for pleasure or other nonmedical reasons.

The Effects of Drugs

Both medicines and recreational drugs can have unwanted "side effects"—effects that are different from what is intended. Someone, for example, might take aspirin to ease a headache, but the aspirin might also cause the person to have an upset stomach. The side effects of drugs like heroin or cocaine can be far more dangerous, particularly if a person is especially sensitive to the drug or takes too much of it. Certain drugs, even some recreational drugs people take to make them feel good, can make the user nervous, depressed, angry, or frightened. Some produce conditions similar to serious mental illnesses.

Many drugs are addictive (habit-forming). Users find they need more and more of the drug to get the desired effect. Eventually, they need large quantities just to feel comfortable.

Addiction can be physical or psychological. In the case of physical addiction, the body itself becomes dependent on the drug and can't function without it. For addicts, sudden withdrawal from a drug like heroin can produce a physical shock strong enough to make them seriously ill or it can even kill them. In psychological addiction, the craving for the drug gets so strong, the person can't bear to give it up. Marijuana is an example of a drug that is not physically addictive, but can sometimes become psychologically addictive. Either kind can destroy a person's life. For the most strongly addicted, nothing matters— not family, friends, or job—except getting more of the drug.

Most drugs that are addictive or have serious side effects are regulated by law. Of these, there are four main kinds. *Narcotics,* like morphine and heroin, reduce pain and give an exaggerated sense of well-being. *Stimulants,* like amphetamines, spark the nervous system to produce a feeling of energy or excitement. *Depressants,* like the barbiturates in sleeping pills, soothe users or make them drowsy. *Hallucinogens,* like LSD, cause users to have fantastic visions, or hallucinations.

Some drugs—like crack, a chemically purified, very potent form of cocaine—have no medical use. They are always illegal. Others, like the pain-killer morphine, are medicines when prescribed by a doctor, but are illegal under other circumstances. Most dangerous drugs are regulated in the United States. And yet, the two most often abused drugs—tobacco and alcohol—are available to adults without restrictions and are even advertised.

Drug Use and Abuse

"Drug abuse" can mean either using an illegal drug or using a legal drug improperly. People abuse drugs for different reasons. Some do so because those around them are, and they want to be one of the crowd. Others experiment out of a sense of curiosity or adventure. Still others feel depressed and unhappy and turn to drugs to feel better. Others, for whatever reason they started, are addicted and can't help themselves.

Drug use—and abuse—is nothing new. The ancient Sumerians used the narcotic opium more than six thousand years ago. Cannabis, the plant from which marijuana and hashish are produced, was grown in Asia at least five thousand years ago. When Europeans first arrived in the New World, they found some Indians in North America using mescaline and other hallucinogens, and some South American Indians chewing coca leaves, the raw material of cocaine. The Native Americans also introduced the Europeans to tobacco, which they often used in connection with religious and social rites.

Opium was once an important and legal commodity in international trade. In the eighteenth and nineteenth centuries, opium grown in British colonies was exported to China. The Chinese government became alarmed by the growing number of addicts. When it tried to ban the drug in 1839 and 1856, however, England went to war to keep the trade in opium flowing. The legal trade was finally ended early in the twentieth century, but an illegal trade in the drug continues even today.

Modern Drug Abuse

It was in 1914 that the U.S. government first banned the nonmedical use of drugs like heroin and cocaine. Until then, such drugs were used openly by many Americans. Smoking marijuana was a common activity in parts of the Southwest, for example. Small amounts of cocaine had even been available in popular products like patent medicines, wine, and Coca-Cola (it was removed from Coca-Cola in 1900). The even more common drug alcohol was banned for a time by the Eighteenth Amendment and the Volstead Act of 1919. Prohibition, as this era was called, ended with the repeal of the Eighteenth Amendment in 1933, and alcohol once again became legal.

Laws reduced drug abuse, but failed to end it. Some people continued to abuse recreational drugs, and many became addicted to barbiturates and stimulants prescribed for them by careless doctors. Whenever there was a war, some soldiers came home addicted to the morphine they'd been given for the injuries they had suffered.

Abuse of drugs other than alcohol was not considered a major national problem, however, until the 1960s. In that decade, the use of recreational drugs soared among a rebellious generation of young Americans protesting racism, the war in Vietnam, and what they saw as a society that was too conventional and too wrapped up in acquiring material things. A new "hippie culture" emerged at the time, with men like Timothy Leary and others encouraging people to experiment with marijuana, L S D, and other drugs to "expand" their minds. The "flower children" of the sixties glorified drug use, some describing it as a spiritual experience, others as part of a hip subculture of "sex, drugs, and rock 'n' roll."

Illicit drug use kept rising until the early 1980s, when a study showed that 69 percent of all Americans between eighteen and twenty-five had used illegal drugs at least once. Since then, drug use has dropped. Even so, 26 million Americans—roughly 13 percent of everyone over twelve years of age—reported in 1990 having used an illicit drug in the past year. About 24 percent of high school seniors had used marijuana or hashish, and 3.5 percent had tried cocaine (1.5 percent in the more powerful form of crack).

Although fewer people use illicit drugs today, more are becoming addicted. This is because the drugs have changed. Marijuana, cocaine, and heroin are sold in more highly concentrated—and dangerous—forms than ever before. And new and even more addictive drugs are being developed all the time.

Drug abuse is a costly social, medical, and law enforcement problem. Americans spend between $40 billion and $50 billion on illegal drugs each year, and almost twice that much on alcohol and tobacco. The health problems caused by drugs cost many billions more. Thousands of Americans become seriously ill or die from drug overdoses or side effects each year. Many thousands more die from cancer, heart disease, or other problems caused by cigarette smoking. Drinking, too, takes a high toll among people who suffer from alcoholism.

High crime rates are also closely related to the use of drugs. Those addicted to illegal drugs turn to robbery or violence to get the money they need to buy the drugs they crave.

And a high proportion of traffic accidents and violent crimes are caused by people under the influence of alcohol.

Because the costs are so high—to individuals, to families, and to society at large—teachers, government officials, and doctors conduct educational campaigns to persuade people to give up drugs—or better yet, not to start using them in the first place.

See also Anti-Saloon League; Crime; Nation, Carrie; Prohibition and Temperance; Sixties, The; Tobacco.

For further reading: Michael Kronenwetter, *Drugs in America* (New York: Messner, 1990).

MICHAEL KRONENWETTER

DU BOIS, W. E. B.

(1868–1963) *Writer, scholar, and civil rights leader.*

A crusader for the modern African American movement, William Edward Burghardt Du Bois believed that blacks should cultivate their own values and forcefully demand, rather than patiently wait for, racial equality.

Born in Massachusetts of Dutch, French, and African heritage, Du Bois received a bachelor's degree from Fisk University and a master's and doctorate from Harvard. He taught sociology, economics, and history at Wilberforce College, the University of Pennsylvania, and Atlanta University.

In 1909, Du Bois was one of the founders of the National Association for the Advancement of Colored People (NAACP) and served as the organization's director of publications and editor of its magazine, *Crisis.* Believing the organization should take a more aggressive and intellectual stance, Du Bois grew impatient with the NAACP and left in 1934. He was publicly opposed to the views of civil rights leader Booker T. Washington, who felt that blacks should concentrate on acquiring

W. E. B. Du Bois was a historian, civil rights activist, and the most important black intellectual of his time. He urged blacks not to accept an inferior status in American society: "We are cowards and jackasses if . . . we do not marshal every ounce of our brain and brawn to fight . . . against the forces of hell in our own land."

technical rather than intellectual skills in order to gain social equality.

Following World War II, Du Bois joined the worldwide peace movement and advocated socialism. In 1959 he was awarded the Lenin Peace Prize. In 1961 he joined the American Communist Party and emigrated from the United States to Ghana, where he died in 1961. Although considered a national hero for his civil rights work, Du Bois received a great deal of criticism because of his affiliation with the Communist Party.

Among Du Bois's finest works are *The Philadelphia Negro: A Social Study* and *Souls of Black Folk.* Du Bois is credited with coining the term *the talented tenth,* referring to educated and gifted blacks who he believed have a responsibility to promote racial equality.

See also African Americans: Since World War II; Civil Rights Movement; National Association for the Advancement of Colored People.

JOANN BIONDI

DULLES, JOHN FOSTER

(1888–1959) *Secretary of state under President Dwight D. Eisenhower from 1953 to 1959.*

Dulles was the son of a Presbyterian minister. His brother, Allen Dulles, served as director of the Central Intelligence Agency (C I A).

After graduating from Princeton University and studying law at the Sorbonne and George Washington University, Dulles joined a Wall Street firm specializing in international law. His uncle, Robert Lansing, secretary of state under Woodrow Wilson, won the young lawyer many diplomatic assignments. At the Versailles peace conference after World War I, Dulles was a member of the commission to set penalties for Germany and fought against heavy reparations. Later he worked with international church groups trying to prevent World War II and served on the U.S. delegation that helped establish the United Nations. At first, he was conciliatory toward the Soviet Union, but gradually his opinions hardened.

Although he had worked for Democrats, Dulles was a Republican, and in 1949 the governor of New York appointed him to serve out the term of an ailing U.S. senator. When Dulles ran for the seat that same year, he lost to a Democrat. Although he had criticized

President Harry S. Truman in the campaign, Dulles later served Truman as a consultant. In 1951, Dulles negotiated the final peace treaty with Japan.

In 1953 the newly elected president Dwight D. Eisenhower appointed Dulles secretary of state. Although Eisenhower favored a thaw in U.S. relations with the Soviets, Dulles insisted there could be no negotiations until the Russians showed good faith.

Dulles used threats of "massive retaliation" with nuclear weapons in his dealings with the Russians. Many called his policies "brinkmanship." This term was coined after Dulles told the press: "The ability to get to the verge without getting into the war is the necessary art. . . . If you are scared to go to the brink, you are lost." He claimed that he went to the brink during the Korean War and when Chinese Communists threatened to invade Taiwan, the island where the Chinese government deposed by the Communists in 1948–49 was in exile. Other Eisenhower officials, however, disputed this.

Dulles negotiated important alliances with non-Communist nations including the Organization of American States and the Southeast Asia Treaty Organization. All told, he committed the United States to defend more than forty nations.

See also Cold War; Eisenhower, Dwight D.

REBECCA LARSEN

DUNCAN, ISADORA

(1878–1927) *Dancer.*

Isadora Duncan was a one-woman revolution. She devoted her life to creating new dances that expressed the beauty of nature and the mysteries of the human spirit.

Duncan's upbringing prepared her for

such a life. Born in San Francisco, she acquired a love of poetry, music, and nature from her mother, a free spirit who rejected conventional morality. At ten, Isadora left school to teach dancing and educated herself through extensive reading. Over the next several years, she danced and acted with traveling theater companies, but soon discovered that she preferred to perform solo.

Duncan wanted to recapture the flowing, expressive movements that once characterized the art of dance. She studied sculpture and experimented with new forms of move-

Isadora Duncan was a pioneer of modern dance who was influenced, in part, by the traditions of ancient Greece. She often danced outdoors, barefoot, and costumed in flowing tunics. She epitomized the expression "free spirit."

ment. Rejecting the rigid steps of ballet, she believed that all movement originates in the solar plexus—a network of nerves in the abdomen—rather than at the base of the spine. She looked to the rhythm of music to inspire her as she moved, lithe and graceful in her flowing robes. Duncan sought inspiration from Greek mythology and from American poet Walt Whitman, who celebrated the ecstasies of the human spirit. But most American audiences rejected her daring forms of dance, and were shocked by her love affairs and her bearing children out of wedlock.

In 1900, Duncan made her London debut and for the rest of her life performed mainly in Europe, where she also established dance schools. Audiences there applauded her dances, and artists embraced her as a kindred spirit.

Duncan died as dramatically as she lived. On September 14, 1927, stepping into an open sports car in the seaside resort of Nice, France, she merrily called out to nearby friends, "Good-bye, my friends. I am going to glory!" As the car pulled away from the curb, her long, fringed scarf caught in the spokes of the spinning rear wheel and broke her neck. In her intense life, Duncan had profoundly influenced other dancers and choreographers and ushered in a bold new era of artistic expression.

See also Dance.

For further reading: Ruth Kozody, *Isadora Duncan* (New York: Chelsea House, 1988).

HARRIET SIGERMAN

DUST BOWL

The Dust Bowl is the name given to the western section of the Great Plains during the Great Depression of the 1930s. This region,

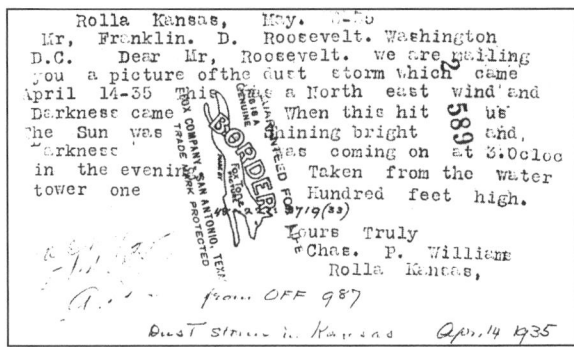

A postcard from Charles P. Williams, citizen of Kansas, sent to President Franklin D. Roosevelt in May 1935. The card bears a photograph of the immense black dust storm that struck without warning in Rolla, Kansas, in April that year.

running roughly from central North Dakota to the Texas panhandle and west to the Rocky Mountains, suffered during the mid-1930s from a severe shortage of rainfall. In its natural state the plains were covered by tough, deeply rooted grasses that held the soil in place in wet years and dry. Most early settlers had raised cattle in the area, which grazed on these grasses. But during World War I high agricultural prices and the availability of efficient farm machinery had led farmers to plow up millions of acres of grass and plant wheat and other grains.

These crops flourish in wet years. But during the drought of the 1930s the plants shriveled and died, and there was nothing left to hold the soil in place. The high winds of summer swept up the topsoil, and clouds of dust, "black blizzards," filled the sky. Then, when the winds subsided and rain finally came, what was left of the fertile soil was washed off into gullies, the land left barren.

Between 1934 and 1937 thousands of farmers in the region had no income at all and lost their homes and land. Some Dust Bowl states lost more than half their population, as farm families moved away to seek work elsewhere. John Steinbeck's novel *The Grapes of Wrath* describes the fate of one such family who sought to make a new life picking fruits and vegetables on California farms.

New Deal agencies worked to restore the region by encouraging those who remained to plant grasses, trees, and drought-resistant varieties of grain. The government also paid farmers to take land not well suited to agriculture out of production and return it to its natural state.

See also Agriculture.

DYLAN, BOB

(1941–) *Musician.*

Dylan's somber songs about the need for social change sparked a folk music revival during the 1960s and 1970s and left a lasting influence on many types of music in the decades that followed.

Born Robert Allen Zimmerman in Duluth, Minnesota, he changed his name to Dylan in honor of his favorite poet, Dylan Thomas, while attending the University of Minnesota. A self-taught musician, Dylan began performing in small coffeehouses while still in college. In 1961 he moved to New York City with two goals in mind: to meet his musical idol, the legendary folk singer Woody Guthrie, and to break into the recording industry.

Although he had no formal training and a voice that many considered to be shrill and unappealing, Dylan was determined to bring his soulful songs to the world. He met Guthrie shortly after he arrived and within three years had produced four albums. His folk, rock, and blues style was full of poetic messages that encouraged listeners to fight social injustice and quickly established him as one of the most popular folk and rock singers in the world. He was considered by many to be the most eloquent songwriter of the era—the voice of the sixties.

During the late 1960s and early 1970s, the appeal of folk music faded and Dylan crossed over to rock where he also left an influential mark. He traded his acoustic guitar for an electric one and his music grew more upbeat and modern. Music critics complained that he had lost his appeal, but Dylan's fans disagreed. Among the many musicians who say that they were influenced by his music are Mick Jagger and Bruce Springsteen. Former president Jimmy Carter used a passage from one of Dylan's songs in his inaugural address.

Some of Dylan's most popular songs include *The Times They Are a-Changin', Just Like a Woman, Like a Rolling Stone,* and *Blowin' in the Wind.* In 1988, Dylan was inducted into the Rock and Roll Hall of Fame.

See also Music; Rock Music; Sixties, The.

JOANN BIONDI

EAKINS, THOMAS

(1844–1916)   *Painter, photographer, and teacher.*

Ahead of his time and unappreciated in his own era, Eakins was the first American painter to base his art on scientific inquiry. Born in Philadelphia, where his father taught penmanship, Tom Eakins grew up among artists and thinkers. Following high school, he studied drawing at the Pennsylvania Academy of Fine Arts and dissected bodies in anatomy classes at Jefferson Medical School. He wrote: "One dissects simply to increase his knowledge of how beautiful objects are put together [so] that he may be able to imitate them."

After completing his training as a painter at the École des Beaux-Arts in Paris, Eakins returned to Philadelphia and his childhood home, where he lived for the rest of his life. In 1875 his realistic painting titled *The Gross Clinic*—showing the respected Dr. Samuel Gross performing surgery—shocked, even sickened polite society. Although it was rejected for the next year's centennial exposition in Philadelphia, it was later purchased for two hundred dollars by the Jefferson Medical College. Today considered a masterpiece, it is Eakins's most famous painting. (For illustration, see color insert following page 628.)

While teaching at the Pennsylvania Academy of Art, where he was professor of anatomy, Eakins in the 1880s made an experimental series of photographs of the human body and animals in motion that led ultimately to the invention of the motion picture camera. This accomplishment went unnoticed. Soon afterward, the artist was fired from his post for removing the loin cloth from a male model in a women's drawing class in order to demonstrate the origin of a muscle.

"My honors," wrote Eakins, "are misunderstanding, persecution and neglect." A conscientious man, striving always for accuracy, he painted people in their everyday lives exactly as he saw them to be, not as they might wish to be seen. Only in truth did he find beauty. Despite his early rejection, Eakins has since been judged a landmark painter in the history of American art.

See also Painting and Sculpture.

PATRICIA CONDON JOHNSTON

EARHART, AMELIA

(1897–1937)   *Aviator.*

Earhart's public career lasted only from 1928 to 1937, but she used her fame to promote two causes: the advancement of commercial aviation and the advancement of women.

She was born in Kansas, on July 24, 1897. She played lots of active games and sports as a child, which was unusual for girls at the time. Instead of going to college, she served as a nurse's aide in Toronto during World War I, where she developed a passion for flying. She received her pilot's license in 1921.

Amelia Earhart in her plane waving good-bye before her flight around the world in 1937. Before leaving she wrote to her husband explaining her reasons for the trip: "Please know I am quite aware of the hazards. I want to do it because I want to do it. Women must try to do things as men have tried. When they fail, their failure must be but a challenge to others." It was to be her last flight; she disappeared somewhere over the Pacific Ocean.

In 1928, while working at a settlement house in Boston, Earhart jumped at the chance to become the first woman to fly the Atlantic. Although only a passenger who kept the log (or in her words, "a sack of potatoes"), she became an overnight celebrity. With her short, tousled hair and trim, athletic build, she was an attractive role model for young women. In May 1932 she flew the Atlantic again, this time solo, just as Charles Lindbergh had done in 1927. This was a first for women, and it made her a national heroine.

In 1931 Earhart married George Palmer Putnam, a New York publisher who had helped to organize her 1928 flight. As her manager, he was an enormous asset to her career. In 1935 Earhart made the first solo flight from Hawaii to California. Then in 1937 she decided to try to fly around the world at the equator. During the longest leg, a 2,556-mile stretch from New Guinea to a tiny speck in mid-Pacific called Howland Island, Earhart and her navigator, Fred Noonan, disappeared on July 2.

The circumstances of Earhart's "popping off" (her matter-of-fact phrase) have been a source of speculation ever since. Was she on a pre–World War II spy mission for President Franklin D. Roosevelt? Did she land on a desert island and later become a Japanese prisoner of war? Despite all the guesses, it is most probable that her plane ran out of fuel somewhere near Howland Island and sank quickly. But given the aviator's hold on the popular imagination, Amelia Earhart still intrigues—and inspires—us today.

See also Aviation.

For further reading: Susan Sloate, *Amelia Earhart, Challenging the Skies* (New York: Fawcett Columbine, 1990).

SUSAN WARE

EASTERN EUROPEANS IN AMERICA

Of all of the immigrant groups in America, Eastern Europeans are among the least visible and most poorly understood. Calling them a "group" is in itself misleading because they come from many countries, speak different languages, and practice different religions, as the accompanying table of the present-day Eastern European countries shows. In addition, the Eastern European countries have been home to various minority groups, such as Jews, Gypsies, and Germans.

Because of the many differences, it is impossible to make statements that are true for all the national groups that have emigrated from Eastern Europe to the United States. There are, however, certain characteristics and historical experiences that most of these people share.

By far the greatest number of Eastern Europeans came to America between about 1880 and 1914. Most came for financial reasons. Eastern Europe had a traditional agricultural economy ruled by a land-owning aristocracy, which offered little opportunity for material advancement. Others came for political reasons or to avoid being drafted into military service, for Eastern Europe then was divided among the German, Austro-Hungarian, Russian, and Turkish empires, all of which had

authoritarian governments and large armies. Still others were members of minority groups who came to escape religious or cultural restrictions or persecution.

The numbers coming decreased sharply after World War I because of the United States' restrictive immigration policies and the lessening of economic opportunities during the Great Depression. Then World War II and the rise of communism in Eastern Europe effectively ended emigration from those countries.

EASTERN EUROPEANS IN AMERICA

Country*	Language Group	Traditional Majority Religious Affiliation
Albania	Albanian	Muslim
Belarus	Slavic	Orthodox
Bosnia-Herzegovina	Slavic	Muslim
Bulgaria	Slavic	Orthodox
Croatia	Slavic	Catholic
Czech Republic	Slavic	Catholic/ Protestant
Estonia	Finno-Ugric	Protestant
Hungary	Finno-Ugric	Catholic
Latvia	Baltic	Protestant
Lithuania	Baltic	Catholic
Macedonia†	Slavic	Orthodox
Moldova	Romance	Orthodox
Poland	Slavic	Catholic
Romania	Romance	Orthodox
Russia	Slavic	Othodox
Slovakia	Slavic	Catholic
Slovenia	Slavic	Catholic
Ukraine	Slavic	Orthodox
Yugoslavia	Slavic	Orthodox

* Jews, Gypsies, and other ethnic and religious minorities often made up a large percentage of the émigrés from the countries listed above.

† A former part of Yugoslavia

Between 1820 and 1940 about 6 million people came to the United States from Eastern Europe. Most of them had little education and many were unskilled. They had to take whatever employment they could find. Their early years in America were marked by struggle and often brutal exploitation. The men frequently had to take jobs as manual laborers, and women and children would work in clothing factories, which had such terrible working conditions they were called "sweatshops."

Generally, the economic hardships they suffered pushed many of them toward the liberal economic policies of the Democratic Party. But with the growth of labor unions and higher levels of education, Eastern European Americans eventually came to enjoy higher standards of living and moved into a wider range of professions. Then their social conservatism, based on traditional cultural and religious values, as well as their greater affluence and their opposition to communism, made them more likely to vote for Republican candidates.

Because of the communist domination of Eastern Europe, with the resulting restrictions on travel and communication, Eastern European Americans were cut off from their countries of origin to a greater extent than other ethnic Americans. But the fall of communism resulted in a new wave of immigration and provided renewed avenues of contact between the various countries and America.

Famous Americans of Eastern European origin include the writers Vladimir Nabokov and Isaac Asimov (Russia), the chairman of the Joint Chiefs of Staff, Gen. John Shalikashvili and Representative Dan Rostenkowski (Poland), the social commentator Andrei Codrescu (Romania), the tennis champions Martina Navratilova (Czech Republic) and Vitas Gerulaitis (Lithuania), the inventor Nikola Tesla (Croatia, of Serbian parents), the film stars Bela Lugosi and Zsa Zsa Gabor (Hungary), and the comedian John Belushi (Albania).

See also Immigration; Jews in America.

WALTER PETROVITZ

EASTMAN, GEORGE

(1854–1932) *Photographic inventor and manufacturer.*

Born at Waterville, New York, Eastman transformed photography from a laborious and costly art into an easy, inexpensive hobby enjoyed by millions. While working at a Rochester bank, he purchased a bulky wet plate apparatus, read everything he could about photography, and began experimenting with dry plate emulsions.

Wet plate photography required the use of a fragile glass negative that was dampened in a special solution and exposed in the camera while still wet. Eastman's first invention was an improved process for preparing easier-to-use dry plates, and in 1880 he established the Eastman Dry Plate Company with a partner, Henry A. Strong. In 1884 he replaced awkward glass plates altogether with a paper-backed roll film. Four years later, he introduced the hand-held Kodak camera, which produced round pictures two and a half inches in diameter. In 1889, providing the foundation for an entirely new industry—moving pictures—Eastman invented celluloid film.

During the next decade, Eastman became an industrial giant. To lessen his competition, he bought out many rivals, acquired the rights to their products from others, and made exclusive contracts with his dealers. By

1928, the year the company perfected color photography for motion pictures, Eastman Kodak was the largest manufacturer of photographic supplies in the world, producing everything needed by amateur, commercial, scientific, and motion picture photographers.

Eastman's phenomenal success was rooted in continuing research, efficient manufacturing methods, and a loyal labor force. He was one of the first American manufacturers to employ full-time research chemists; he pioneered large-scale production at low costs for a world market; and he introduced profit-sharing and stock-option plans for employees.

Eastman, who was a big-game hunter and fond of growing orchids, never married. His philanthropies, including bequests, totaled more than $75 million. His primary beneficiary was the University of Rochester, to which he contributed $35 million for the Eastman Theater, the School of Music, the School of Medicine and Dentistry, and the College for Women.

See also Photography.

PATRICIA CONDON JOHNSTON

EDDY, MARY BAKER

(1821–1910)   *Founder of the Christian Science religion.*

Born near Concord, New Hampshire, young Mary attended school irregularly because of poor health. Her first husband died six months after they were married, and because she was often sick, she asked another family to take care of her little boy. Her second marriage ended in divorce, and her third husband died in 1882, five years after their marriage.

Eddy's health improved in 1862, when she was treated by Phineas Parkhurst Quimby of Portland, Maine, who claimed that a person's mind could often overcome sickness. Quimby wrote out his ideas on keeping well, and Eddy copied them. When he died she began teaching them. In 1875 she published *Science and Health,* the handbook of the Christian Science movement, which made Quimby's teachings a religion. Slowly revising these teachings and linking them to parts of the Bible, Eddy reprinted her book 381 times. If members of her church felt sick, she told them to consult not medical doctors but the special healing practitioners who had been trained in her teachings.

Eddy was a good teacher and a good businesswoman. Those taking her classes to be-

A portrait of Mary Baker Eddy, founder of the Christian Science church.

come healing practitioners paid $300, making her the highest paid teacher of her time. She worked hard at organizing the Church of Christ (Scientist), which was chartered in 1877. She inspired loyalty in her followers, but repeatedly clipped the wings of possible rivals. Realizing that publicity would help her church grow, Eddy started a monthly paper in 1883, a weekly one in 1898, and a daily newspaper, the *Christian Science Monitor,* in 1908. A shrewd and powerful spiritual leader, she was one of the most famous women in America during the last twenty years of her life. Eddy always retained control of her church, which had 100,000 members at the time of her death.

See also Christian Science.

For further reading: Ernest Sutherland Bates and John V. Dittemore, *Mary Baker Eddy: The Truth and the Tradition* (New York: Alfred A. Knopf, 1932).

OLIVE HOOGENBOOM

EDISON, THOMAS A.

(1847–1931) *Inventor.*

During his own time and afterward, people have seen Edison's life as a fine example of American ideals. Born in a small Ohio town, he became hard of hearing as a boy. His father's business declined, and the family lost its home. He had little schooling. But he

Thomas A. Edison demonstrates one of his many inventions, the phonograph, at the National Academy of Science in 1878. The photo was taken by Mathew Brady.

showed grit and enterprise in peddling candy and newspapers to railroad passengers. He also set up a small lab in a baggage car, where he tinkered with electrical experiments. So he fitted into two enduring American ideals: the spunky, ambitious country boy and the bright young inventor.

Young Tom Edison went deeper into electricity. Every station had its telegraph office, where he found that despite being hard of hearing he could hear the clicking of the receivers. He became an expert operator, wandering from place to place like most telegraphers in that day. Only he had to move on even oftener because of his habit of upsetting people with practical jokes.

In 1868 Edison arrived in Boston, a center of American science and technology, where he decided to become a full-time inventor. A year later he went to New York City because it offered greater opportunities to make money. There and in New Jersey over the next twenty years he astonished the world with his important inventions, more than any other one person before or since. His "quadruplex telegraph" carried two messages each way on a single wire. His "carbon-button transmitter" made the telephone much more efficient. Most famous and fundamental were his inventions of phonograph recording and electric lighting, along with the whole system of making and distributing electricity. He took out hundreds more patents, though some were mainly the creations of people who worked for him.

One of his most influential ideas was that of setting up what he called an "invention factory" in Menlo Park, New Jersey, in 1876. It was a pioneering model of an independent, self-supporting research and development center, staffed with brilliant technicians and trained scientists. In some ways it foreshad-owed the great corporation research labs of our time, like those of the General Electric and American Telephone & Telegraph companies. The Menlo Park laboratory was not part of a particular industry, but it brought whole new industries into being. Edison was hailed as "the Wizard of Menlo Park."

Edison unwisely squandered much of his time in later years by running some of the new enterprises he had created. He was not as good a businessman as he was an inventor, and his inventive imagination declined as he got older. So after the 1880s he came up with no more really fundamental inventions, though his team did much to develop motion pictures. Still, his earlier achievements have made him a unique figure in American legend. His work provided a bridge between the world in which he was born and the world in which all of us now live.

See also Science and Technology.

R O B E R T   V.   B R U C E

EDUCATION: ELEMENTARY AND HIGH SCHOOL

Education has always been rooted in a particular society at a particular time. Before 1800 American education fit into a mercantilist age. Mercantilism was the economic system of the day; among other features, it looked upon the individual as a resource of the community, no less than other more material assets like timber or gold.

Colonial Schools
New England's schools were the most numerous in North America. The Puritans were

strong believers in education and followed the English example of grammar schools. Massachusetts's first educational law (1642) made heads of households responsible for instructing their children to read. The second (1647) required towns of fifty families to provide a teacher of reading and writing in a common school. Towns of one hundred families had to establish a Latin grammar school, where classical languages (Greek, Latin) and advanced mathematics (algebra and geometry) were taught and students were prepared for entrance to college. Connecticut (1650), Plymouth (1671), and New Hampshire (1689) passed similar laws. How much these laws were enforced is unclear. But New England's literacy rate of 95 percent was the highest in the English-speaking world. After 1692, Massachusetts's compulsory attendance laws were repealed, and local officials could bind out poor children as indentured servants.

In the 1700s the New England schools tended to be poorer than in the 1600s. Elsewhere this pattern was reversed, with education improving as time went on, but within a private rather than a public context. In the Middle Atlantic area, there were parochial schools, as in New Amsterdam (1638). But only in 1721, long after the Dutch left, was a free school founded in New York City. In Pennsylvania the Quakers founded numerous elementary schools, almost all of them private. Throughout the region, masters often required apprentices to take classes to learn to read; larger towns had evening schools for them.

Throughout the South, the plantation, not the town, was the unit of settlement. The resulting dispersal of population made establishment of schools on the northern pattern impossible except in the region's one town, Charleston, South Carolina, which had private schools for rich planters' sons. Private education, through tutors or academies, was the southern pattern throughout the eighteenth century.

After the Revolution, Thomas Jefferson and Benjamin Rush, a Philadelphia physician and social reformer, proposed similar statewide free public educational systems ranging from elementary schools to state universities. The goals of both were to create good citizens. But if Rush and Jefferson foreshadowed modern elementary and secondary education, they also underlined its lack of interest in the arts and in learning for its own sake.

Impact of Democracy

Not surprisingly, in the age of democracy, public education became closely related to it. Before the Civil War the growing free public schools in the northern and midwestern states were supposed to make good citizens and good workers out of their pupils, male and female, white and nonwhite, native-born and immigrant. Until the 1830s district schools attempted to teach every individual. Students were not placed in grades; once a pupil had memorized everything in one text and could recite it all, he or she moved on to the next text. Beyond the elementary schools, academies prepared boys for college, a profession, or a technical field and girls for motherhood and domesticity. Most were private institutions.

From the 1830s to the 1870s the new graded public elementary schools sought to teach democracy, Christianity, and patriotism as well as the three R's as preparation for citizenship and an occupation. The school year's length varied from 60 to 180 days throughout the North and Midwest, with farm areas having the shortest year. School was not compulsory, and most children left by the fifth grade.

Nineteenth-century schoolchildren on their best behavior in front of their teacher and the photographer of this picture.

During Reconstruction (1865–77) in the South after the Civil War, free graded public schools came to these states for the first time. But even as late as 1900 very few southern schools were open more than 90 days a year, funding per pupil was much less than outside the region, and there were great differences between funding for white and nonwhite schools.

Changing Goals

The era of the 1870s to the 1920s saw many new developments in education. This was an age of top-down organization and centralization in all aspects of life and of progressive education, the attempt to make the schools adapt to the needs of the emerging urban-industrial order. The mid-nineteenth-century democratic ideology was thus repudiated in several ways. All states organized public school systems, from kindergarten to graduate or professional school, arranged in a pyramid, to produce trained citizens who would fit into their proper niches in society. In elementary education, there were new pressures on urban schools in the North and West to train immigrant and nonwhite children. In the South, the public school system became racially segregated. There was also enormous pressure to segregate children according to ethnicity, gender, and religion on the premise that different groups had inherently different mental abilities.

This was also the era when public high schools got under way. In 1890 there were about 200,000 high school pupils; in 1920, more than ten times that number. In the new high schools, there were commonly two curricula, one for college-bound pupils, the other for those not so destined. There were also different courses for boys and girls and for whites and nonwhites, all in harmony with the social expectations of the community that sponsored the schools and paid for them.

Schools in the 1900s

From the 1920s to the 1950s, public education underwent yet another series of changes. The curriculum covered new areas, such as music, the arts, and athletics. It aimed to produce the well-rounded citizen—progressive education's "life adjustment" purpose. The importance of a high school diploma for getting a job increased dramatically. High schools for African-American pupils were founded, and members of other minority groups—Asian Americans and Jews, for example—began to attend high school in record numbers. Pupils from all backgrounds were taught to be proud of their common American national identity. The nation's schools emerged from the Great Depression and World War II need-ing more resources—teachers, buildings, supplies, and money. The average yearly ex-penditure per pupil increased from $88 in 1940 to $341 in 1958.

Since 1950 schools have been taking on more burdens of social reform. Progressive education's emphasis on life adjustment rath-er than academic merit was attacked in the 1950s and 1960s, especially after the Soviets sent up the first artificial satellite, *Sputnik* (1957). Congress then enacted the National Defense Education Act (1958), a loan pro-gram to attract teachers into fields deemed crucial to national security. Almost simulta-neously a clamor arose for assisting children at risk; many became concerned that the edu-cational system was oppressing poor and nonwhite children. In 1954 the Supreme Court ruled in *Brown* v. *Board of Education* that separate school facilities for blacks and whites were inherently unequal and therefore violated the Fourteenth Amendment to the U.S. Constitution. School desegregation, the Court's remedy, still proceeds slowly. In the 1960s federal aid to education continued. Head Start (1965), a preschool program, and the Elementary and Secondary Education Act (1965) were both targeted at providing assis-tance to disadvantaged children.

A new individualism and a new commit-ment to decentralization and private market forces has challenged public education in re-cent years, however. In the 1980s and 1990s critics called on schools both to improve the self-esteem of children and to make sure that they actually learn their subjects. Other crit-ics called for private schools to compete with public schools to improve education.

See also McGuffey's *Reader.*

HAMILTON CRAVENS

EDUCATION: UNIVERSITIES AND COLLEGES

America's system of higher education is the envy of the world. Our universities have pro-duced more Nobel Prize winners than those of any other nation. At the same time, more high school graduates get to attend college here than they do in other countries.

What is the difference between a college and a university? These two words are often used interchangeably, but in fact the two are different. Suppose you want to become a vet-erinarian. You might go first to a college for your undergraduate study. But for specific training in veterinary science you would have to go to a university that has a graduate school in that field. At a university professors not only teach; they also do research in order to discover new knowledge, whether the field is law, physics, engineering, history, or litera-ture.

America's Early Colleges
The Puritans were barely settled in America when they founded Harvard College in 1636 as a school to train ministers. Other early col-leges were also founded for religious purpos-es, such as William and Mary (1693), Yale (1701), and Princeton (1746). In college every student studied the same subjects, mostly an-cient languages (one had to know Greek and Latin even *before* entering), with a smattering of other subjects thrown in. Students attend-ed chapel each day, and if they misbehaved they received a flogging or had their ears boxed.

The American Revolution disrupted col-lege activities. Some campuses were taken over by troops for part of the war. These col-leges had trained a number of America's top revolutionary leaders: Thomas Jefferson studied at William and Mary, Alexander Hamilton at King's College (now Columbia University), and James Madison at Princeton.

Following the war the democratic spirit encouraged by the Revolution led to an expansion of colleges. State governments from Vermont to Georgia established their own public universities. One of these, the University of Virginia, was a favorite project of Thomas Jefferson's: he planned the curriculum (the course of study) and designed the buildings and grounds. It remains among the most beautiful campuses in America.

The Spread of Colleges

As the nation grew in the first half of the nineteenth century, small colleges—often started by religious denominations—were planted throughout the Midwest. These schools often lacked money for adequate books or buildings and frequently had few students. They existed because of their founders' confidence in their communities' future and in the importance of education. The classical curricula of these colleges did not attempt to provide what we today call job-related skills. Instead, courses were intended to "discipline the mind" and thus make one a better person.

The second half of the nineteenth century brought several important advances. In 1862 Congress passed the Morrill Land Grant Act, which helped states establish colleges designed to improve agricultural and mechanical education. This development pointed out how colleges were moving away from the old practice of having students memorize and recite passages of ancient languages to teaching them more practical subjects. In addition, the "elective system" begun at Harvard offered students the chance to choose their own classes (which is the practice at virtually all

colleges now). Finally, Johns Hopkins University (1876) introduced from Germany the idea of graduate education leading to the Ph.D. degree. These developments shaped the modern college and university.

Twentieth-Century Developments

The years around the beginning of the twentieth century saw women entering higher education in substantial numbers. Previously, most colleges had taught only men. But following the lead of Oberlin College (which admitted the first women in 1837) more and more schools became coeducational, and opportunities for women in many fields began to open. Women's colleges such as Vassar and Smith were also founded. In recent years the situation has so changed that now more women than men enroll in college.

World War II had an important impact on universities. First, the national government sponsored war-related university research on such things as radar and the atomic bomb. A high level of government funding for research has continued to the present. Also, when the war ended in 1945 Congress passed the G.I. bill, which supplied money for veterans to go to college. The flood of new students ushered in the biggest expansion of higher education in history, which continued through the 1960s. Junior and community colleges, which are inexpensive and available to most people, have in recent decades become an important part of higher education.

The 1960s also brought political demonstrations to campuses. Civil rights and anti–Vietnam War protests erupted at many schools, leading in one case to a tragic shooting of four Kent State University (Ohio) students in 1970.

America's ever-more complex economy has made a college degree increasingly important to career success. But college should mean more than just job training. It provides important social and leadership opportunities for young people and broadens one's understanding of life.

See also G.I. Bill; Kent State Incident; Morrill Land Grant Act; Student Non-Violent Coordinating Committee; Students for a Democratic Society.

BENJAMIN MCARTHUR

EDUCATION, WOMEN'S

In colonial times, girls were usually educated at home, where they learned to perform household tasks and, occasionally, to read. Girls who were apprentices in others' homes received training in housework and sometimes learned "to read the English tongue." Some girls attended New England's primary schools or "dame schools"—small schools for young children that were run by women in their homes. Reading and writing were taught separately, and few girls learned writing or arithmetic.

Because colonial women had so little formal schooling, their literacy, or ability to read or write, lagged behind that of men. At the end of the colonial era, less than half the women in New England could sign their names on wills, compared to 80 percent of the men. An unknown number of women probably learned to read but not to write.

Admission into Schools
After the American Revolution, there were

In 1837, Oberlin College in Ohio became the first college to enroll women. Shown here is Oberlin's graduating class of 1855, which included a black woman.

several advances that improved women's education. In the early nineteenth century, many girls and boys went to public primary schools, called "common schools." These were mainly one-room schools in which students learned reading, writing, and arithmetic. Typically, boys and girls sat in separate sections of the classroom. Some youngsters went to school for only a few years or for only a few months a year. Older girls from well-off families might attend "female academies," modeled on private secondary schools for boys. Academies, which first appeared in the late eighteenth century, offered a combination of primary and secondary schooling, plus religious training and what were called "accomplishments," such as drawing and embroidery.

A small number of young women in the early nineteenth century enrolled in female seminaries, which required examinations for admission and offered the kind of subjects taught at male colleges, such as Latin, Greek, and science. Emma Willard, for instance, opened Troy Seminary in New York State in 1821, and Mary Lyon founded Mount Holyoke Seminary in Massachusetts in 1837. Graduates of female seminaries often became teachers. By the end of the century, a majority of the nation's teachers were women.

Girls also began to attend public high schools. The first of these for girls opened in Worcester, Massachusetts, in 1824. High schools tested applicants for admission, gave regular examinations, and provided a two-to-four-year course of study. Around 1850, separate high schools for boys and girls gave way to less costly coeducational high schools. The proportion of school-age youngsters who attended secondary school, public or private, surged from 2 percent in 1870 to 17 percent in 1920. From 1870 on, the majority of high school graduates were girls. Many became teachers or worked in offices.

Higher Education for Women

The rise of secondary schooling for women led to demands for college education. The first women college students had been accepted in 1837 at Oberlin College in Ohio. They enrolled in a special "female department" and received special degrees. After the Civil War, an era of college founding began. Excluded from the older colleges for men, such as Harvard, Yale, and Brown, some women attended new women's colleges such as Vassar, founded in 1865. Others went to "coordinate" colleges for women at men's universities, such as Barnard College (1889) at Columbia. Some enrolled in coeducational colleges, such as Swarthmore (1864) or Stanford (1885).

Most women students, however, attended coeducational state universities, fostered by the Morrill Land Grant Act of 1862, which was designed to help states finance the founding of colleges. By 1870, eight state universities in the West and Midwest admitted women. Black institutions founded after the Civil War were also open to women. By 1900, over one hundred coeducational colleges and universities had been founded in the United States.

As higher education expanded, so did the proportion of women among college students. By 1910, when 5 percent of college-age people attended college, 40 percent of them were women. After graduation, some women attended law, medical, or other graduate schools. Most women graduates who worked became teachers. After 1920, as college enrollments rose again, the proportion of women among college students fell for several decades.

Then during the 1960s, the number of women college students doubled, and their educational opportunities increased. In the 1970s, many colleges once reserved for men began to admit women, and military academies, such as West Point, admitted them, too. The growth of state university systems and community colleges also increased women's enrollment. In the 1980s, women became a majority of college students.

Issues concerning women's education that have arisen since the 1970s include how boys and girls are depicted in textbooks and treated in classrooms, funding of programs for girls' and women's athletics, and debate over the advantages of single-sex versus coeducational schools.

See also Feminist Movement; Morrill Land Grant Act.

NANCY WOLOCH

EDWARDS, JONATHAN

(1703–58) *Minister and theologian.*

Edwards attempted no less than a revolution in theology and church practices in colonial New England. He believed that the churches there had forgotten their roots and become too comfortable. He challenged them first by emphasizing the difference between Christians who had been "born again"—that is, transformed in spirit—and those who merely went to church. He argued furthermore that God alone chose whom to save, or admit to heaven, and then changed that person's life and behavior accordingly. These had been the central assumptions of Calvinism, the religion that the Puritans had brought over with them from England in the previous century and to which Edwards gave renewed vitality.

In his congregation at Northampton, Massachusetts, such a doctrine led to great anxiety among worshipers. They longed for salvation and searched their hearts for signs that God had selected them. Edwards sometimes played on his listeners' fears of being sent to hell, as in a sermon he delivered on eternal punishment, "Sinners in the Hands of an Angry God." "Hell," he thundered, is "a bottomless pit, full of the fire of wrath, that you are held over."

In 1735, strained to the breaking point, members of the church at Northampton found release from their fears in a wave of emotional religious conversions. Such scenes became common in colonial America during the "Great Awakening" of the 1740s, when traveling preachers stirred up large crowds. Edwards, however, accomplished the same feat at home.

In another return to the old ways, Edwards tightened standards for church membership. He insisted that only those who could testify to being saved should receive communion, for instance. He offended important members of the community in this way, and in 1750 he was forced to resign. He then served as a missionary for a number of years before being named president of the College of New Jersey (present-day Princeton University). This post would have given him a greater chance than ever to influence American religion. But soon after accepting the position, he died from the effects of a smallpox vaccination.

See also Colonial America; Great Awakening; Puritans.

THOMAS COLE

EIGHTEENTH AMENDMENT
See Prohibition and Temperance.

EINSTEIN, ALBERT

(1879–1955)   *Scientist.*

When Albert Einstein was a boy in Germany, some people thought he was "backward" and wouldn't amount to much. As a young man of twenty-five he was an ordinary office worker, with apparently not much of a future.

But Einstein was tremendously interested in physics—the science that tries to explain why things happen, from a bolt of lightning to the birth of a star—and he worked hard at it in his spare time. In 1905, at age twenty-six, he published three articles presenting some of his ideas and discoveries in a science magazine. They created great excitement among

Albert Einstein writes out the equation for the density of the Milky Way on a blackboard at the Mt. Wilson Observatory in California in 1931.

scientists, for they opened up three brand-new paths in physics (in time, they led to such things as sound movies and nuclear energy). One of the articles presented the now-famous equation $E = mc^2$, which showed that energy (light and heat) and mass (matter) are actually the same, and led to an understanding of where the energy of a radioactive element comes from.

Over the next twenty-eight years Einstein did other important scientific work and received many honors and awards. He also became known as a crusader against war. While he was traveling in America in 1933, the political party known as the Nazis took over Germany. The Nazis hated Einstein because he was Jewish, and so it was not safe for him to return home. He eventually settled in America, becoming an American citizen and working at the Institute for Advanced Studies at Princeton University.

In 1939 Einstein sent a letter to President Franklin D. Roosevelt, telling him of the possibility of making an atomic bomb and warning that German physicists were working in that direction. He urged that America develop such a bomb as protection. Roosevelt approved, and many scientists were put to work on the Manhattan Project, which was charged with building the new weapon. Germany surrendered before the project was completed, but two atomic bombs were dropped on Japan in August 1945 (at Hiroshima and Nagasaki). That ended World War II. But the extent of the deaths and destruction horrified Einstein. He became active in a movement to form a world government to control nuclear weapons.

In 1952, the new nation of Israel invited Einstein to be its president. He declined because, he said, he was not worthy and it would interfere with his work. He continued his scientific projects at Princeton University until his death.

See also Manhattan Project; Science and Technology.

For further reading: Mae Blacker Freeman, *The Story of Albert Einstein* (New York: Random House, 1958).

TOM MCGOWEN

EISENHOWER, DWIGHT D.

(1890–1969)   *Thirty-fourth president of the United States (1953–61) and supreme commander of Allied forces in Europe during World War II.*

Born in Texas and raised in Kansas, Eisenhower was one of six sons in a working-class family. In 1915 he graduated from the U.S. Military Academy at West Point and began an army career.

Eisenhower rose quickly through the ranks. Nicknamed "Ike," he had a knack for getting people to work together. As Allied commander in Europe in World War II, he planned successful assaults on North Africa, Sicily, and Italy. On D-day, June 6, 1944, he directed the invasion of occupied France, and in May 1945, the German army surrendered.

As a war hero, Eisenhower was urged to run for president in 1948. But he held back from politics at first and became president of Columbia University. In 1950, he returned to the military to command NATO, the North Atlantic Treaty Organization forces in Europe. Finally, in 1952 he agreed to run for president and was elected as a Republican. Boosted by his popularity, Republicans took control of Congress. Although plagued by ill health, including a heart attack in 1955, he was reelected in 1956.

Early on as president, Eisenhower negotiated an end to the Korean War. Although he opposed the growing influence of the Rus-

sians in Eastern Europe during the cold war, he objected to using force to stop them and disliked the idea of threatening "massive retaliation" with nuclear weapons in moments of crisis. He tried to arrange an atomic test ban with the Russians, but when a U.S. U-2 plane (a "spy" plane) was shot down over the Soviet Union, arms talks broke down.

During his administration, the role of the CIA, the Central Intelligence Agency, grew. Eisenhower authorized schemes to overthrow governments in Guatemala, Iran, and Cuba. But in 1956, he was furious when the British and French invaded Egypt to try to regain control of the Suez Canal, and he demanded a cease-fire. He also declined to help the French fight their war in Vietnam.

Although many view him as a president who did little about social reform, others note he did not reverse the policies of the New Deal and the Fair Deal launched by his predecessors. He balanced the federal budget and held inflation in check. He was also criticized for not publicly condemning Senator Joseph R. McCarthy's wild accusations about Communist plots in the United States. Although the president privately objected to McCarthy, he was afraid of alienating old-guard Republicans by taking strong action.

Eisenhower found racism distasteful but was slow to push for civil rights reform. In 1954 the Supreme Court in *Brown* v. *Board of Education* held that segregation of blacks and whites in schools was unconstitutional. When Governor Orval Faubus of Arkansas refused to obey a court order integrating the Little Rock high school, Eisenhower sent troops to escort black children to the white school. He did so reluctantly, however, for he believed that the Court had set back race relations with its ruling.

Eisenhower spent much of his second term

resisting demands for more military spending. After the Russians launched *Sputnik,* the first artificial satellite, Democrats and Republicans said he was tolerating a technological gap that put the United States behind the Russians in military strength. But Eisenhower had intelligence reports indicating that the United States was ahead. On leaving office he made a famous speech in which he warned the nation against the growing influence of the "military-industrial complex."

See also D-day; Dulles, John Foster; North Atlantic Treaty Organization; World War II. *For events during Eisenhower's administration, see* Anticommunism; *Brown* v. *Board of Education*; Cold War; *Rosenberg* Case; U-2 Affair.

REBECCA LARSEN

Gen. Dwight D. Eisenhower (left of center) was supreme commander of Allied forces in Europe during World War II. Here he is seen speaking to his troops just before D-day, June 6, 1944, when his men invaded Nazi-occupied Normandy, France.

ELECTIONS, PRESIDENTIAL

| Year | States in Union | Candidates | Parties | Popular Vote | | Electoral Vote |
				Total votes	%	
1789	11	**George Washington** (Va.)	No party designations	—	—	69
		John Adams (Mass.)		—	—	34
		Others		—	—	35
1792	15	**George Washington** (Va.)	No party designations	—	—	132
		John Adams (Mass.)		—	—	77
		George Clinton (N.Y.)		—	—	50
		Thomas Jefferson (Va.)		—	—	4
		Aaron Burr (N.Y.)		—	—	1
1796	16	**John Adams** (Mass.)	Federalist	—	—	71
		Thomas Jefferson (Va.)	Democratic-Republican	—	—	68
		Thomas Pinckney (S.C.)	Federalist	—	—	59
		Aaron Burr (N.Y.)	Democratic-Republican	—	—	30
		Other		—	—	48
1800	16	**Thomas Jefferson** (Va.)	Democratic-Republican	—	—	73
		Aaron Burr (N.Y)	Democratic-Republican	—	—	73
		John Adams (Mass.)	Federalist	—	—	65
		Charles C. Pinckney (S.C.)	Federalist	—	—	64
		John Jay (N.Y.)	Federalist	—	—	1
1804	17	**Thomas Jefferson** (Va.)	Democratic-Republican	—	—	162
		and George Clinton (N.Y.)		—	—	162
		Charles C. Pinckney (S.C.)	Federalist	—	—	14
		and Rufus King (N.Y.)		—	—	14
1808	17	**James Madison** (Va.)	Democratic-Republican	—	—	122
		and George Clinton (N.Y)		—	—	113
		Charles C. Pinckney (S.C.)	Federalist	—	—	47
		and Rufus King (N.Y.)		—	—	47
		George Clinton (N.Y.)	Democratic-Republican	—	—	6
1812	18	**James Madison** (Va.)	Democratic-Republican	—	—	128
		and Elbridge Gerry (Mass.)		—	—	131
		DeWitt Clinton (N.Y.)	Federalist	—	—	89
		and Jared Ingersoll (Pa.)		—	—	86
1816	19	**James Monroe** (Va.)	Democratic-Republican	—	—	183
		and Daniel Tompkins (N.Y.)		—	—	183
		Rufus King (N.Y.)	Federalist	—	—	34
		and John Howard (Md.)		—	—	22
1820	24	**James Monroe** (Va.)	Democratic-Republican	—	—	231
		and Daniel Tompkins (N.Y.)		—	—	218
		John Quincy Adams (Mass.)	Democratic-Republican	—	—	1

Year	States in Union	Candidates	Parties	Popular Vote Total votes	%	Electoral Vote
1824	24	**John Quincy Adams** (Mass.)	Democratic-Republican	113,122	30.92	84
		Andrew Jackson (Tenn.)	Democratic-Republican	151,271	41.34	99
		William H. Crawford (Ga.)	Democratic-Republican	40,856	11.17	41
		Henry Clay (Ky.)	Democratic-Republican	47,531	12.99	37
		Other		13,053	3.57	—

(As no candidate received a majority of electoral votes, the election was decided by the House of Representatives. John C. Calhoun ran unopposed for and was elected as vice president.)

Year	States in Union	Candidates	Parties	Popular Vote Total votes	%	Electoral Vote
1828	24	**Andrew Jackson** (Tenn.)	Democratic	642,553	55.97	178
		and John C. Calhoun (S.C.)				171
		John Quincy Adams (Mass.)	National-Republican	500,897	43.63	83
		and Richard Rush (Pa.)				83
		Other		4,568	0.40	—
1832	24	**Andew Jackson** (Tenn.)	Democratic	701,780	54.23	219
		and Martin Van Buren (N.Y.)				189
		Henry Clay (Ky.)	National-Republican	484,205	37.42	49
		and John Sergeant (Pa.)				49
		John Floyd (Va.)	Independent	N/A	N/A	11
		and Henry Lee (Mass.)				11
		William Wirt (Md.)	Anti-Masonic	100,715	7.78	7
		and Amos Ellmaker (Pa.)				7
		Other		7,273	0.56	—
1836	26	**Martin Van Buren** (N.Y.)	Democratic	764,176	50.83	170
		and Richard M. Johnson (Ky.)				147
		William H. Harrison (Ohio)	Whig	550,816	36.63	73
		Hugh L. White (Tenn.)	Whig	146,107	9.72	26
		Daniel Webster (Mass.)	Whig	41,201	2.74	14
		W. P. Mangum (N.C.)	Independent	N/A		11
		Other		1,234	0.08	—
1840	26	**William H. Harrison** (Ohio)	Whig	1,275,390	52.88	234
		and John Tyler (Va.)				
		Martin Van Buren (N.Y.)	Democratic	1,128,854	46.81	60
		James G. Birney (N.Y.)	Liberty	6,797	0.28	—
		Other		767	0.03	—
1844	26	**James K. Polk** (Tenn.)	Democratic	1,339,494	49.54	170
		and George M. Dallas (Pa.)				
		Henry Clay (Ky.)	Whig	1,300,004	48.08	105
		and Theodore Frelinghuysen (N.J)				
		James G. Birney (N.Y.)	Liberty	62,103	2.30	—
		Other		2,058	0.08	—
1848	30	**Zachary Taylor** (La.)	Whig	1,361,393	47.28	163
		and Millard Fillmore (N.Y.)				
		Lewis Cass (Mich.)	Democratic	1,223,460	42.49	127
		and William O. Butler (Ky.)				
		Martin Van Buren (N.Y.)	Free-Soil	291,501	10.12	—
		and Charles Francis Adams (Mass.)				
		Other		2,830	0.10	—

Year	States in Union	Candidates	Parties	Popular Vote		Electoral Vote
				Total votes	%	
1852	31	**Franklin Pierce** (N.H.) and William King (Ala.)	Democratic	1,607,510	50.84	254
		Winfield Scott (Va.) and William A. Graham (N.C.)	Whig	1,386,942	43.87	42
		John P. Hale (N.H.) and George Washington Julian (Ind.)	Free-Soil	155,210	4.91	—
		Other		12,168	0.38	—
1856	31	**James Buchanan** (Pa.) and John C. Breckinridge (Ky.)	Democratic	1,836,072	45.28	174
		John C. Frémont (Calif.) and William L. Dayton (N.J.)	Republican	1,342,345	33.11	114
		Millard Fillmore (N.Y.) and Andrew J. Donelson (Tenn.)	American (Know-Nothing)	873,053	21.53	8
		Other		3,177	0.08	—
1860	33	**Abraham Lincoln** (Ill.) and Hannibal Hamlin (Maine)	Republican	1,865,908	39.82	180
		Stephen A. Douglas (Ill.) and Herschel V. Johnson (Ga.)	Democratic	1,380,202	29.46	12
		John C. Breckinridge (Ky.) and Joseph Lane (Oreg.)	Southern Democratic	848,019	18.09	72
		John Bell (Tenn.) and Edward Everett (Mass.)	Constitutional Union	590,901	12.61	39
		Other		531	0.01	—
1864	36	**Abraham Lincoln** (Ill.) and Andrew Johnson (Tenn.)	Republican	2,218,388	55.02	212
		George B. McClellan (N.Y.) and George Pendleton (Ohio)	Democratic	1,812,807	44.96	21
		Other		692	0.02	—
1868	37	**Ulysses S. Grant** (Ohio) and Schuyler Colfax (Ind.)	Republican	3,013,650	52.66	214
		Horatio Seymour (N.Y) and Francis P. Blair (Mo.)	Democratic	2,708,744	47.3	80
		Other		46	—	—
1872	37	**Ulysses S. Grant** (Ohio) and Henry Wilson (Mass.)	Republican	3,598,235	55.63	286
		Horace Greeley (N.Y.) and Benjamin Gratz Brown (Mo.)	Democratic, Liberal Republican	2,834,761	43.83	
		Charles O'Conor (N.Y.) and John Quincy Adams II (Mass.)	"Straight" Democratic	18,602	0.29	—
		Other		16,081	0.25	—
		(Greeley died shortly after the popular election and before the meeting of the presidential electors. The electors supporting him divided their 66 votes among minor candidates.)				
1876	38	**Rutherford B. Hayes** (Ohio) and William A. Wheeler (N.Y)	Republican	4,034,311	47.95	185
		Samuel J. Tilden (N.Y.) and Thomas Hendrix (Ind.)	Democratic	4,288,546	50.97	184
		Peter Cooper (N.Y.)	Greenback	75,973	0.90	—
		Other		14,271	0.17	—

Year	States in Union	Candidates	Parties	Popular Vote Total votes	%	Electoral Vote
1880	38	**James A. Garfield** (Ohio) and Chester A. Arthur (N.Y.)	Republican	4,446,158	48.27	214
		Winfield S. Hancock (Pa.) and William English (Ind.)	Democratic	4,444,260	48.25	155
		James B. Weaver (Iowa) and Benjamin J. Chambers (Tex.)	Greenback-Labor	305,997	3.32	—
		Other		14,005	0.15	—
1884	38	**Grover Cleveland** (N.Y.) and Thomas A. Hendricks (Ind.)	Democratic	4,874,621	48.50	219
		James G. Blaine (Maine) and John A. Logan (Ill.)	Republican	4,848,936	48.25	182
		Benjamin F. Butler (Mass.)	Greenback-Labor	175,096	1.74	—
		John P. St. John (Kans.)	Prohibition	147,482	1.47	—
		Other		3,619	0.04	—
1888	38	**Benjamin Harrison** (Ind.) and Levi. P. Morton (N.Y.)	Republican	5,443,892	47.82	233
		Grover Cleveland (N.Y.) and Allen G. Thurman (Ohio)	Democratic	5,534,488	48.62	168
		Clinton B. Fisk (N.J.)	Prohibition	249,813	2.19	—
		Alson J. Streeter (Ill.)	Union Labor	146,602	1.29	—
		Other		8,519	0.07	—
1892	44	**Grover Cleveland** (N.Y.) and Adlai E. Stevenson (Ill.)	Democratic	5,551,883	46.05	277
		Benjamin Harrison (Ind.) and Whitelaw Reid (N.Y.)	Republican	5,179,244	42.96	145
		James B. Weaver (Iowa) and James G. Field (Va.)	Populist	1,024,280	8.50	22
		John Bidwell (Calif.)	Prohibition	270,770	2.25	—
		Other		29,920	0.25	—
1896	45	**William McKinley** (Ohio) and Garret Hobart (Va.)	Republican	7,108,480	51.01	271
		William Jennings Bryan (Nebr.) and Arthur Sewall (Maine)	Democratic Democratic	6,511,495	46.73	176 149
		William Jennings Bryan (endorsed) and Thomas E. Watson (Ga.)	Populist			—
		John M. Palmer (Ill.)	National Democratic	133,435	0.96	—
		Joshua Levering (Md.)	Prohibition	125,072	0.90	—
		Other		57,256	0.41	—
1900	45	**William McKinley** (Ohio) and Theodore Roosevelt (N.Y.)	Republican	7,218,039	51.67	292
		William Jennings Bryan (Nebr.) and Adlai E. Stevenson (Ill.)	Democratic, Populist	6,358,345	45.51	155
		John C. Woolley (Ill.)	Prohibition	209,004	1.50	—
		Eugene V. Debs (Ind.)	Socialist	86,935	0.62	—
		Other		98,147	0.70	—

Year	States in Union	Candidates	Parties	Popular Vote Total votes	%	Electoral Vote
1904	45	**Theodore Roosevelt** (N.Y.) and Charles Fairbanks (Ind.)	Republican	7,626,593	56.41	336
		Alton B. Parker (N.Y.) and Henry G. Davis (W.Va.)	Democratic	5,082,898	37.60	140
		Eugene V. Debs (Ind.)	Socialist	402,489	2.98	—
		Silas C. Swallow (Pa.)	Prohibition	258,596	1.91	—
		Other		148,388	1.10	—
1908	46	**William H. Taft** (Ohio) and James Sherman (N.Y.)	Republican	7,676,258	51.58	321
		William Jennings Bryan (Nebr.) and John W. Kern (Ind.)	Democratic	6,406,801	43.05	162
		Eugene V. Debs (Ind.)	Socialist	420,380	2.82	—
		Eugene W. Chafin (Ill.)	Prohibition	252,821	1.70	—
		Other		126,474	0.85	—
1912	48	**Woodrow Wilson** (N.J) and Thomas Marshall (Ind.)	Democratic	6,293,152	41.84	435
		Theodore Roosevelt (N.Y.) and Hiram Johnson (Calif.)	Progressive	4,119,207	27.39	88
		William Howard Taft (Ohio) and James Sherman (N.Y.)	Republican	3,486,333	23.18	8
		Eugene V. Debs (Ind.)	Socialist	900,369	5.99	—
		Other		241,902	1.61	—
1916	48	**Woodrow Wilson** (N.J.) and Thomas Marshall (Ind.)	Democratic	9,126,300	49.24	277
		Charles Evans Hughes (N.Y.) and Charles W. Fairbanks (Ind.)	Republican	8,546,789	46.11	254
		A. L. Benson (N.Y.)	Socialist	589,924	3.18	—
		James Hanly (Ind.)	Prohibition	221,030	1.19	—
		Other		50,979	0.28	—
1920	48	**Warren G. Harding** (Ohio) and Calvin Coolidge (Mass.)	Republican	16,133,314	60.30	404
		James M. Cox (Ohio) and Franklin D. Roosevelt (N.Y.)	Democratic	9,140,884	34.17	127
		Eugene V. Debs (Ind.)	Socialist	913,664	3.42	—
		Parley P. Christensen (Utah)	Farmer Labor	264,540	0.99	—
		Other		301,384	1.13	—
1924	48	**Calvin Coolidge** (Mass.) and Charles Dawes (Ohio)	Republican	15,717,553	54.00	382
		John W. Davis (N.Y.) and Charles W. Bryan (Nebr.)	Democratic	8,386,169	28.84	136
		Robert M. La Follette (Wis.) and Burton K. Wheeler (Mont.)	Progressive	4,814,050	16.56	13
		Other		158,187	0.55	—

Year	States in Union	Candidates	Parties	Popular Vote Total votes	%	Electoral Vote
28	48	**Herbert C. Hoover** (Calif.) and Charles Curtis (Kans.)	Republican	21,411,991	58.20	444
		Alfred E. Smith (N.Y.) and Joseph Robison (Ariz.)	Democratic	15,000,185	40.77	87
		Norman M. Thomas (N.Y.)	Socialist	266,453	0.72	—
		William Foster (Ill.)	Communist	48,170	0.13	—
		Other		63,565	0.17	—
1932	48	**Franklin D. Roosevelt** (N.Y.) and John Nance Garner (Tex.)	Democratic	22,825,016	57.42	472
		Herbert C. Hoover (Calif..) and Charles Curtis (Kans.)	Republican	15,758,397	39.64	59
		Norman M. Thomas (N.Y.)	Socialist	883,990	2.22	—
		William Foster (Ill.)	Communist	102,221	0.26	—
		Other		179,758	0.45	—
1936	48	**Franklin D. Roosevelt** (N.Y.) and John Nance Garner (Tex.)	Democratic	27,747,636	60.79	523
		Alfred M. Landon (Kans.) and Frank Knox (Ill.)	Republican	16,679,543	36.54	8
		William Lemke (N.Dak.)	Union	892,492	1.96	—
		Norman M. Thomas (N.Y)	Socialist	187,785	0.41	—
		Other		134,874	0.30	—
1940	48	**Franklin D. Roosevelt** (N.Y) and Henry A. Wallace (Iowa)	Democratic	27,263,448	54.70	449
		Wendell L. Willkie (Ind.) and Charles NcNary (Oreg.)	Republican	22,336,260	44.82	82
		Norman M. Thomas (N.Y)	Socialist	116,827	0.23	—
		Roger W. Babson (Mass.)	Prohibition	58,685	0.12	—
		Other		65,223	0.13	—
1944	48	**Franklin D. Roosevelt** (N.Y.) and Harry S. Truman (Mo.)	Democratic	25,611,936	53.39	432
		Thomas E. Dewey (N.Y.) and John W. Bricker (Ohio)	Republican	22,013,372	45.89	99
		Norman Thomas (N.Y.)	Socialist	79,100	0.16	—
		Claude A. Watson (Calif.)	Prohibition	74,733	0.16	—
		Other		195,778	0.41	—
1948	48	**Harry S. Truman** (Mo.) and Alben Barkley (Ky.)	Democratic	24,105,587	49.51	303
		Thomas E. Dewey (N.Y.) and Earl Warren (Calif.)	Republican	21,970,017	45.12	189
		J. Strom Thurmond (S.C.) and Fielding Wright (Miss.)	State's Rights Democratic	1,169,134	2.40	39
		Henry A. Wallace (Iowa) and Glen Taylor (Idaho)	Progressive	1,157,057	2.38	—
		Other		290,647	0.60	—

| Year | States in Union | Candidates | Parties | Popular Vote | | Electoral Vote |
				Total votes	%	
1952	48	**Dwight D. Eisenhower** (Kans.) and Richard M. Nixon (Calif.)	Republican	33,936,137	55.13	442
		Adlai E. Stevenson (Ill.) and John Sparkman (Ala.)	Democratic	27,314,649	44.38	89
		Vincent Hallinan (Calif.)	Progressive	140,416	0.23	—
		Stuart Hamblen (Calif.)	Prohibition	73,413	0.12	—
		Other		86,503	0.14	—
1956	48	**Dwight D. Eisenhower** (Kans.) and Richard M. Nixon (Calif.)	Republican	35,585,245	57.37	457
		Adlai E. Stevenson (Ill.) and Estes Kefauver (Tenn.)	Democratic	26,030,172	41.97	73
		T. Coleman Andrews (Va.)	Constitution States' Rights	108,055	0.17	—
		Eric Hass (N.Y.)	Socialist Labor	44,300	0.07	—
		Other		257,600	0.42	
1960	50	**John F. Kennedy** (Mass.) and Lyndon Johnson (Tex.)	Democratic	34,221,344	49.72	303
		Richard M. Nixon (Calif.) and Henry Cabot Lodge (Mass.)	Republican	34,106,671	49.55	219
		Eric Hass (N.Y.)	Socialist Labor	47,522	0.07	—
		Other		337,175	0.48	—
		Unpledged (Miss.)		116,248	0.17	—
1964	50	**Lyndon B. Johnson** (Tex.) and Hubert H. Humphrey (Minn.)	Democratic	43,126,584	61.05	486
		Barry M. Goldwater (Ariz.) and William Miller (N.Y.)	Republican	27,177,838	38.47	52
		Eric Hass (N.Y.)	Socialist Labor	45,187	0.06	—
		Clifton DeBerry (N.Y.)	Socialist Workers	32,701	0.05	—
		Other		258,794	0.37	—
1968	50	**Richard M. Nixon** (Calif.) and Spiro T. Agnew (Md.)	Republican	31,785,148	43.42	301
		Hubert H. Humphrey (Minn.) and Edmund Muskie (Maine)	Democratic	31,274,503	42.72	191
		George C. Wallace (Ala.) and Curtis LeMay (Ohio)	American Independent	9,901,151	13.53	46
		Henning A. Blomen (Mass.)	Socialist Labor	52,591	0.07	—
		Other		189,977	0.20	—
72	50	**Richard M. Nixon** (Calif.) and Spiro T. Agnew (Md.)	Republican	47,170,179	60.69	520
		George S. McGovern (S. Dak.) and R. Sargent Shriver (Md.)	Democratic	29,171,791	37.53	17
		John G. Schmitz (Calif.)	American	1,090,673	1.40	—
		Benjamin Spock (Conn.)	People's	78,751	0.10	—
		Other		216,196	0.28	—

Year	States in Union	Candidates	Parties	Popular Vote Total votes	%	Electoral Vote
1976	50	**Jimmy Carter** (Ga.) and Walter Mondale (Minn.)	Democratic	40,830,763	50.06	297
		Gerald R. Ford (Mich.) and Robert Dole (Kans.)	Republican	39,147,793	48.00	240
		Eugene McCarthy (Minn.)	Independent	756,691	0.93	—
		Roger MacBride (Va.)	Libertarian	173,011	0.21	—
		Other		647,631	0.79	—
1980	50	**Ronald Reagan** (Calif.) and George Bush (Tex.)	Republican	43,901,812	50.75	489
		Jimmy Carter (Ga.) and Walter Mondale (Minn.)	Democratic	35,483,820	41.02	49
		John B. Anderson (Ill.) and Patrick J. Lucey (Wis.)	Independent	5,719,722	6.61	—
		Ed Clark (Calif.)	Libertarian	921,188	1.06	—
		Other		486,754	0.56	—
1984	50	**Ronald Reagan** (Calif.) and George Bush (Tex.)	Republican	54,450,603	58.78	525
		Walter Mondale (Minn.) and Geraldine Ferraro (N.Y.)	Democratic	37,573,671	40.56	13
		David Bergland (Calif.)	Libertarian	227,949	0.25	—
		Other		570,343	0.61	—
1988	50	**George Bush** (Tex.) and Dan Quayle (Ind.)	Republican	48,881,011	53.37	426
		Michael Dukakis (Mass.) and Lloyd Bentsen (Tex.)	Democratic	41,828,350	45.67	111
		Ron Paul (Tex.)	Libertarian	431,499	0.47	—
		Lenora Fulani (N.Y.)	New Alliance	218,159	0.24	—
		Other			0.25	—
1992	50	**Bill Clinton** (Ark.) and Al Gore, Jr. (Tenn.)	Democratic	43,688,671	42.97	370
		George Bush (Tex.) and Dan Quayle (Ind.)	Republican	38,109,410	37.49	168
		Ross Perot (Tex.) and James B. Stockdale (Calif.)	Independent	19,089,432	18.78	—
		Andre Marrou (Tex.)	Libertarian	278,528	00.27	—
		Other		494,633	00.49	—

ELECTORAL COLLEGE

The electoral college is the method established by the Constitution for electing the president and vice president. Each state has as many electors as it has senators and representatives in Congress. Originally the state legislatures decided how their electors were chosen. Its electors then met and each voted for two persons, at least one of whom had to be from another state. The votes of the electors of all the states were then counted. The person receiving the most votes became president, with the runner-up becoming vice president.

The reason this complicated system was

adopted rather than everyone in all the states voting directly for a president and vice president was that the young nation was large and communication slow and expensive. The Founding Fathers thought that most ordinary people would know very little about worthy candidates outside their own state, whereas the electors would. Therefore this indirect system of election was employed.

As soon as political parties developed, the original system proved unworkable. In 1800 the winning Democratic-Republican Party nominees, Thomas Jefferson and Aaron Burr, received the same number of votes. The electors had intended Jefferson to be president and Burr vice president, but only after a long political battle was Jefferson declared presi-

dent. In 1804 the Twelfth Amendment was adopted requiring that the electors vote separately for the two top offices.

Nowadays, voters appear to cast ballots directly for the candidates for president and vice president of their choice. But in fact, they are voting for blocks of electors. Technically electors are not legally bound to vote for their party's candidates, but it would be political death for any who did not.

ELLINGTON, DUKE

(1899–1974)   *Composer and bandleader.*

Born Edward Kennedy Ellington, but given the nickname "Duke" as a teenager because

Duke Ellington at the piano with his band in 1945.

of his regal bearing, Ellington grew up to become our most important composer of black music. Although some critics think of him mainly as a gifted arranger of the ideas of others, he remains an important role model for young talented blacks.

Ellington was a product of the black elite in Washington, D.C. His father served as coachman and butler in a wealthy home, and the boy acquired his elegant manner from this environment. His mother, who was the daughter of a police captain, kept a puritanical home; Ellington revered her and outwardly conformed to her expectations. Musically, he studied in the European tradition; the black elite disliked jazz and most popular music. He did not take discipline well, dropped out of high school, and remained largely self-taught. His lack of formal education would always be a problem.

Performing music was one of the few ways blacks could earn a respectable living in the 1920s. Dance music, largely independent of jazz, was all the rage, and Ellington learned how to play it by listening to successful bands and piano rolls. (These were rolls that were inserted into mechanical player pianos, which when turned on produced piano music without someone at the keyboard.) By early 1927, he was directing his own orchestra and integrating white dances and black jazz rhythms into a popular style. Late that year he opened at the Cotton Club, an important nightclub in Harlem, and built a band that made him famous.

"Black and Tan Fantasy" (1927) was Ellington's first mature work, and for the next two decades he wrote many important shorter works, helping to make jazz a serious cultural subject. Despite the Great Depression, World War II, and the collapse of big band music afterward, he kept going until his death in 1974.

His late effort to write classical music was a failure, but that did not tarnish his earlier achievements.

See also Jazz; Music.

ROBERT M. CRUNDEN

ELLISON, RALPH

(1914–94) *Essayist and novelist.*

Ralph Ellison has had an extraordinary influence on literature by and about white and black Americans. He was reared by his widowed mother in Oklahoma between World War I and the Great Depression. Named after Ralph Waldo Emerson, the nineteenth-century writer, he was educated as a humanist and musician at Tuskegee Institute, founded by Booker T. Washington, who looked upon industrial training and racial compromise as the keys to economic self-determination and social development for black people. This complex cultural background inspired Ellison to celebrate both his African-American and his national cultural heritages. Thus, even before meeting his mentor Richard Wright, the black novelist, in Harlem in 1937, Ellison had absorbed the idea of cultural pluralism and its rich oral forms, especially the blues, jazz, and black speech.

Wryly calling himself a "college dropout" because he did not finish Tuskegee, Ellison nevertheless realized his boyhood dream of becoming a man of many talents and achievements, rising from shoeshine boy to Albert Schweitzer Professor of the Humanities at New York University. On the strength of a single novel, *Invisible Man* (1952), two collections of essays, *Shadow and Act* (1964) and *Going to the Territory* (1986), and nearly two dozen stories, Ellison has won respect as a major author. His most significant articles sparkle with bittersweet humor and wisdom. His best stories, "Flying Home" and "King of the Bingo Game," are superb blends of dream fantasy and black folklore. They anticipate the laughing-to-keep-from-crying truths of *Invisible Man.* In a poll by *Book Week,* it was judged "the most distinguished single work" published in America between 1945 and 1965. The title of the novel refers to the inability or unwillingness of many white Americans to see and respect black people as individual human beings and as citizens with equal civil rights.

Like *Invisible Man, Shadow and Act* has become a standard text for studying African-American folk and formal art. Eight sections from a second novel begun in 1953 have been published in journals. The best of these is "And Hickman Arrives."

See also Literature; Wright, Richard.

BERNARD W. BELL

EMANCIPATION PROCLAMATION AND THIRTEENTH AMENDMENT

Although Abraham Lincoln's administration accepted the challenge of civil war not to abolish slavery but to preserve the Union, the emancipation of slaves soon became a means of winning the war and the abolition of slavery became a goal.

Lincoln abhorred slavery. But at the beginning of the Civil War he assured Southern whites that he had no intention of interfering with the institution. For one thing, he was bound by the U.S. Constitution, which protected slavery in any state where the citizens wanted it. As commander in chief of the Union army, Lincoln, a Republican, also worried about the support of those Northern Democrats who were proslavery and the four slave states that lay along the border between the North and the South. These groups, despite their belief in slavery, supported the North's war to preserve the Union. They might have turned against it if Lincoln and his party had made a move against slavery in the first year of the war.

But the president's role as commander in chief cut two ways. If it restrained him from alienating people who were for both slavery and the Union, it also empowered him to seize enemy property used to wage war against the United States—and slaves were the Southerners' most conspicuous such property. They raised food and cotton for the Southern war effort, worked in munitions factories, and served as teamsters and laborers in the army. Thousands of them also voted with their feet for freedom by escaping to Union lines. Some Northern commanders gave them shelter and protection, but others returned them to masters who could prove their loyalty to the United States. In March 1862 Congress enacted a new article of war forbidding army officers to return fugitive slaves to their masters.

A New War Aim

By the summer of 1862 most Republicans, including Lincoln, had become convinced that a war against the slaveholders' rebellion must become a war against slavery itself. As Union armies suffered reverses, the argument that emancipation was a military necessity also became increasingly attractive. It would weaken the Confederacy and correspondingly strengthen the Union by siphoning off part

The Emancipation Proclamation (1863) was a military order issued by President Abraham Lincoln (third from left) abolishing slavery in the Confederate states during the Civil War. The engraving records the first reading of the proclamation before the cabinet. Three years later, the Thirteenth Amendment legally ended all slavery, giving constitutional backing to the declaration that "neither slavery nor involuntary servitude . . . shall exist within the United States."

of the Southern labor force and adding this manpower to the Northern side. In July 1862 Congress enacted two laws intended to do just that: a confiscation act that freed slaves of persons who were engaged in rebellion against the United States, and a militia act that authorized the president to use freed slaves in the army in any capacity he saw fit— even as soldiers.

By this time Lincoln had decided on an even more dramatic move: a proclamation freeing all slaves in states waging war against the Union. At the suggestion of Secretary of State William H. Seward, he delayed announcement of the proclamation until the Union won a military victory that would back it up and demonstrate its practicality. Lincoln used the delay to help prepare conservative opinion for what was coming. In a letter to the journalist Horace Greeley, published in the *New York Tribune* on August 22, 1862, the president repeated that his "paramount object in the struggle *is* to save the Union, and is *not* either to save or destroy slavery." If he could accomplish his objective by freeing all, some, or none of the slaves, he said, that was what he would do. Lincoln, however, had already decided to free some slaves and was in effect warning potential opponents of the Emancipation Proclamation that they must accept it as a necessary measure to save the Union.

Emancipation Comes

Five days after the Union victory in the Battle of Antietam on September 17, 1862, Lincoln issued a preliminary proclamation warning that in all states still in rebellion on January 1, 1863, he would declare their slaves "then, thenceforward, and forever free." January 1 came, and with it the final proclamation, which committed the Union government and army to the liberation of slaves in rebellious states "as an act of justice, warranted by the Constitution, upon military necessity."

The proclamation exempted the border states and parts of the Confederacy already occupied by Union forces because they were not then in rebellion against the United States. Without further steps, therefore, slavery might have survived the war in some areas. Moreover, Lincoln and the Republican leaders recognized that because the Emancipation Proclamation was a war measure, it might not be constitutionally valid once the war was over. So they committed themselves to securing a constitutional amendment to abolish the institution.

The overwhelmingly Republican Senate passed the Thirteenth Amendment by more than the necessary two-thirds majority on April 8, 1864. But not until January 31, 1865, did enough Democrats in the House of Representatives abstain from voting or vote for the amendment to pass it by a bare two-thirds. By December 18, 1865, the necessary three-fourths of the states had ratified the Thirteenth Amendment, which declared that forever after "neither slavery nor involuntary servitude . . . shall exist within the United States."

See also Civil War; Slavery.

For further reading: James M. McPherson, Marching Toward Freedom: Blacks in the Civil War 1861-1865 (New York: Facts on File, 1991).

JAMES M. MCPHERSON

EMBARGO ACT OF 1807

During the war between France and Great Britain that followed the French Revolution in the late 1700s, the demand in Europe for American goods soared. American producers and shipowners profited greatly. But both the French and the British attempted to keep each other from obtaining American products. In doing so their navies caused much damage to American ships and sailors. In a process called *impressment,* British warships took crewmen off American vessels and forced them to serve in the British navy. The British claimed that they were impressing only English-born sailors, but in practice they frequently took American citizens. Both the French and the British navies also stopped American merchant ships on the high seas and seized or destroyed any cargo they believed was headed for the enemy's port. Between 1803 and 1807 the two warring powers seized more than seven hundred American vessels.

The United States at this point lacked a navy powerful enough to protect its merchant ships. President Thomas Jefferson therefore persuaded Congress to pass the Embargo Act of 1807. The law prohibited *all* exports from the United States in order to deprive France and England of American products and to eliminate any reason for them to seize American merchant ships. Foreign ships could bring cargoes to American ports, but since the law compelled them to return empty, few did so.

The Embargo Act was bitterly resented by American merchants and shippers. Prices fell, and seamen were thrown out of work. The entire American economy was depressed. Traders soon found ways to evade the law, the most effective being to smuggle goods into Canada. Early in 1809 Congress replaced it with the Nonintercourse Act, which banned trade only with Great Britain and France.

See also Impressment Controversy.

EMERSON, RALPH WALDO

(1803–82)   *Philosopher, essayist, poet, and orator.*

Emerson, who lived most of his life in Concord, Massachusetts, challenged others with his ideas. In his day many people thought that Americans could not write or think as well as Europeans could. But Emerson believed that Americans could succeed at anything they attempted. He urged his countrymen to stop copying European ways of doing things—to create their own art and do their own thinking.

Emerson was convinced that if people thought for themselves and did not worry about the opinions of others, they would be successful. He was the leader of a group of New Englanders, the transcendentalists, who believed that one's ideas are more important than anything else. In an age when Americans were interested in material things like making money and building factories, transcendentalists encouraged people to focus on living good lives by listening to their own thoughts.

Emerson was a good speaker and presented many of his ideas in lectures before large audiences. These talks were later collected and published in essay form. His first book,

Nature (1836), explains that all that a man needs to meet life's challenges can be found within himself. "The American Scholar" (1837) calls for learning through personal experience. In those days students learned primarily by memorizing facts, but Emerson encouraged activities like field trips to help children learn by personal observation. "The Divinity School Address" (1838) suggests that a good life can best be lived by relying on personal opinion rather than the beliefs or teachings of others. He also wrote poetry that conveys his ideas.

Though Emerson traveled widely and met many of the great thinkers of his day, it is his own thinking that has most forcefully shaped American ideas on the importance of living independent and moral lives.

See also Literature.

DAVID C. SMITH

ENVIRONMENTAL MOVEMENTS
See Conservation and Environmental Movements.

EPIDEMICS

When a disease comes swiftly to a defenseless population, and great numbers of people sicken and many die, it is called an epidemic. The cause is usually what is termed a *pathogen*—a virus (such as the cause of smallpox and AIDS), a bacterium (such as the cause of plague and cholera), or a protozoan (such as the cause of malaria).

The defenselessness of the affected people is essentially due to the absence of individual and collective immunity. When a person is exposed to a pathogen in the environment, the body manufactures what is called an antibody, which will fight the pathogen if the person is ever infected with it. These antibodies together with specialized white blood cells make up humans' immune systems. Thus, if a pathogen is new to humans, they will not have acquired an immunity to it. That pathogen may have come from out of the blue: for example, it may be carried by an animal newly brought in contact with humans after its natural environment has been disturbed. Or the pathogen may be "new" in terms of immunity because it has changed (mutated) in character; it has become a new strain. The successive epidemics of influenza (flu) are caused by viruses that have undergone this kind of change. Finally, there are some pathogens to which humans cannot, under any circumstances, mount an effective immune defense. Rabies is an example; HIV (the human immunodeficiency virus), responsible for causing AIDS, is another.

Epidemics among Indians

Very little is known about the kinds of diseases and epidemics suffered by Native Americans before the coming of Christopher Columbus. Ancient skeletons reveal few clues, but judging from the accounts of Aztecs, Incas, Mayas, and early explorers, it seems that the New World was a fairly healthy place before the arrival of Europeans. There evidently was no malaria, smallpox, tuberculosis, plague, or cholera. These and other diseases came into the Americas as "stowaways" in the bodies of European explorers, missionaries, and colonists, and their African slaves. The yellow fever virus probably came within the body of its host mosquito and/or was carried by humans or animals.

The nonimmune Native Americans were

so susceptible to these infections that they suffered frequent epidemics that brought them to the brink of extinction. Even diseases like measles and chickenpox, which were relatively harmless to Europeans, were highly dangerous to Indians, who had no immunity to them. In many cases, the rapid intrusion into tribal lands by white colonists was so successful because the Indians, weakened by smallpox in particular, were unable to mount an effective resistance.

Other American Epidemics

Smallpox, a viral disease now eradicated by a vaccination program, caused lethal epidemics in the American colonies from the 1600s until the early 1800s when a vaccine became available. Smallpox epidemics in 1677 and 1721 brought Boston to near collapse. "It was a very dying time," one diarist recorded. In 1775, during the Revolutionary War, a smallpox epidemic forced Gen. Horatio Gates to stop fighting for five weeks when half his troops came down with the disease.

Many American epidemics were caused by what we now consider to be exotic tropical diseases. Until the early 1940s, for example, malaria was *the* American disease. When Columbus and later explorers came from the then highly malarious Europe and the slaves came from the still malarious Africa, they were bitten by American mosquitoes that were capable of transmitting the malaria parasites carried by the humans. The colony of Jamestown, founded in 1607, was almost wiped out in 1608 because of what is believed to have been an epidemic of malaria. By 1633 malaria had spread as far north as Plymouth and Rhode Island. Even as late as the Civil War years, malaria attacked one-half of the Union troops annually.

From the seventeenth to the nineteenth

centuries North America was ravaged by epidemics of another "tropical" disease, yellow fever—a frequently fatal virus infection also transmitted by mosquitoes. Yellow fever struck New York City in the 1690s, and in 1793 a yellow fever epidemic in Philadelphia is estimated to have killed a tenth of that city's population.

Twentieth-Century Developments

The great discoveries of the twentieth century in microbiology, immunology, chemotherapy, and genetics have not freed us of epidemics. The 1918 global epidemic (pandemic) of influenza killed over 20 million people, 500,000 in the United States alone. "New" diseases have appeared—Legionnaires' and Lyme disease and AIDS, which is now so entrenched as to be of epidemic proportions. "Old" diseases thought to be disappearing, such as tuberculosis, have returned in drug-resistant forms. As recently as 1991, there was an epidemic in Peru of cholera, the most feared disease of the nineteenth century, which last struck the United States in the 1830s.

Some of the old methods of dealing with epidemics are no longer used. Quarantine—isolating sick people—was one such measure. There is a period of days, or months, between the time a person becomes infected and the time when the symptoms of a disease first appear; this is known as the incubation period. When people traveled by ship in the past, the long sea voyages would fall within the incubation period of most epidemic diseases; anyone infected would show symptoms of an illness by journey's end and could be stopped from landing and thus spreading a disease in the United States. Most visitors and immigrants now, however, come to our country by air or by simply walking or driving across the border. The speed of modern travel makes quarantine ineffective.

The most efficient way of preventing many epidemic diseases is immunization. America led the way in developing a vaccine to prevent people from getting polio, for example. Measles, too, could be eradicated because there is a good vaccine available. The current problem is that cuts in public health budgets have reduced vaccination programs that could reach all children. This is a shortsighted policy and should be changed in the future.

See also Medicine.

R O B E R T   S.   D E S O W I T Z

E Q U A L   R I G H T S   A M E N D M E N T

In 1923 the National Woman's Party drafted an amendment to the U.S. Constitution that would guarantee equal rights for women. Nothing came of it at the time, but the revival of the feminist movement in the 1960s led

Feminist leaders Betty Friedan (right) and Gloria Steinem (center) sign an oversize telegram in 1977 urging President Jimmy Carter to support the Equal Rights Amendment.

to increased interest in an Equal Rights Amendment (E R A). In 1972, after considerable debate, Congress approved an amendment that read: "Equality of rights under the law shall not be denied or abridged by the United States or any State on account of sex."

Polls showed that a solid majority of Americans favored the E R A, and it was quickly ratified (approved) by thirty states. But the additional eight states needed to make the three-fourths majority required for adoption proved difficult to obtain. Numerous objections were raised. Some opposed it because they believed it would make existing social legislation that protected women workers unconstitutional. Others feared it would result in women being drafted into the army. When the deadline set by Congress for ratification passed in 1982, the amendment died.

See also Feminist Movement since 1919.

E R I E   C A N A L

Settlement of the land west of the Appalachian Mountains in the early nineteenth century made the need for cheap transportation between that area and eastern markets urgent. Roads were relatively easy to build, but moving bulky farm products over the mountains by horse and wagon was impractical. Goods could be floated down the Mississippi River and its tributaries to New Orleans, and carried from there by ship to ports in the eastern states or Europe. But a direct east-west water route would have obvious advantages, and that required the construction of a canal.

The only possible route through the mountains was in central New York State between the Hudson River at Albany and Buffalo on Lake Erie. In 1817 Canal Commissioner DeWitt Clinton, a former U.S. senator and mayor of New York City, persuaded the state legislature to authorize construction of the Erie Canal. He promised the lawmakers that the canal would "create the greatest inland trade ever witnessed."

This promise was kept. When completed in 1825 the canal was 363 miles long, far more than ten times the length of any canal in the nation. Its entire cost, $7 million, was quickly recovered in tolls, and soon it was earning the state a profit of about $3 million a year.

E S P I O N A G E

Espionage is the use of spies to collect information. It is conducted with great secrecy both to hide what the spy is gathering and to protect the spy, who usually is breaking the laws of the country whose secrets he or she is seeking.

Washington as Spymaster

American espionage played an especially important role in the Revolution, the Civil War, World War II, and the cold war. It began with George Washington, who was one of our best spymasters. He had a knack for running espionage operations, but he had to learn his skills by trial and error. In September 1776, he sent Nathan Hale behind the British lines to discover when and where they planned to attack New York City. Hale's mission failed, and he was captured and hanged. Americans still remember his words spoken before his death: "I only regret that I have but one life to lose for my country." General Washington, however, learned from this disaster, and three months later, his skillful use of John Honeyman to spy on the Hessian troops in Trenton, New Jersey, contributed to the important American victory there.

In 1778, Washington picked Nathan Hale's friend, Benjamin Tallmadge, to control the war's most famous espionage group. His "Culper Net" in New York City alerted Washington to British plans and movements. Tallmadge's espionage experience made him a key player in thwarting Benedict Arnold's treasonous plan to surrender West Point to the British.

Civil War Spies

Civil War espionage included the exploits of two female spies. Early in the war, a Confederate spy in Washington, Rose Greenhow, reported on Union preparations before the First Battle of Bull Run. The Confederate commander, Gen. P. G. T. Beauregard, probably too generously, gave her credit for making his victory possible. She continued to spy until she was arrested, jailed, and then deported to the South, where she was paid $2,500 for her spying.

In Richmond, the Confederate capital, Elizabeth van Lew ran a spy net for the North, which Gen. Ulysses S. Grant's intelligence chief said provided the "greater portion" of the intelligence received during the campaign in Virginia that won the war. Afterward, Grant tried unsuccessfully to get Congress to reimburse her for the money she had spent spying. Later, as president, he appointed her postmistress of Richmond.

Espionage in WWII

During World War II, the Office of Strategic Services (OSS) became our first truly national intelligence organization. It conducted espionage, special operations in support of guerrillas and resistance movements behind ene-my lines, and other intelligence activities. Its espionage provided information on bombing targets in Germany, the German rocket program, and troop movements to support Allied armies in Europe; similar espionage was conducted against the Japanese in China and Southeast Asia.

There are many World War II espionage stories. One illustrates the value of double agents, persons supposedly working for one side who actually work for the other. William Sebold, a German-born American citizen, was blackmailed by German intelligence to spy for them. Pretending to go along, he reported his situation to American officials. He became a double agent for the FBI and pro-

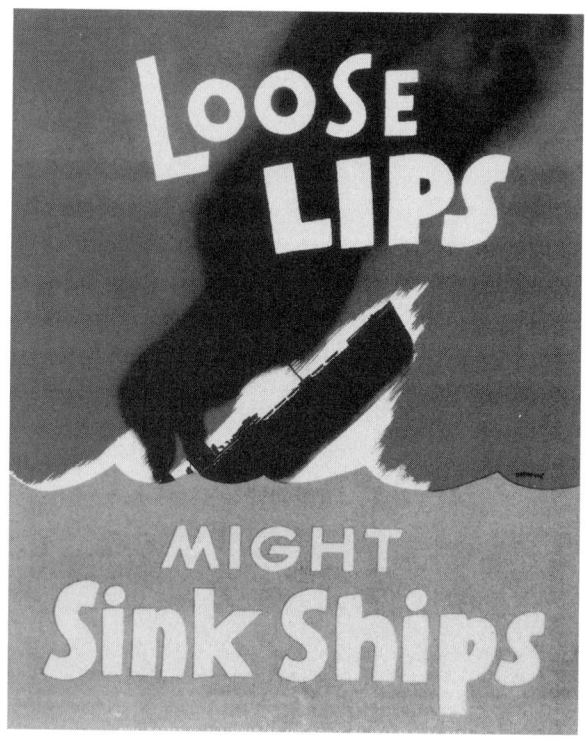

A World War II poster cautioning citizens to beware of spies: "Loose lips might sink ships," the posters read. And they were right. For many months before an enemy code was broken, Allied ships were sunk at an alarming rate in the North Atlantic.

vided enough information for them to arrest virtually all German spies in the United States.

Another case involved Soviet efforts to obtain U.S. secrets on the atomic bomb. The Soviets learned enough to help them build their bomb, but eventually their spies were caught. Two of them, Julius and Ethel Rosenberg, became the only two Americans ever to be executed for espionage in peacetime.

Postwar Intelligence

The cold war was a conflict that was fought not by armies but by diplomacy, intelligence, and other peacetime means. The communists and the free world conducted espionage against each other. In the United States, the Central Intelligence Agency (CIA) replaced the OSS and masterminded most of America's cold war espionage. The cold war came closest to becoming a real, "hot" war during the 1962 Cuban missile crisis, when the Russians tried to install nuclear missiles in Cuba. Two espionage cases were important to the peaceful ending of that crisis. Colonel Oleg Penkovsky, a Soviet intelligence officer working secretly for the CIA and British intelligence, reported vital information on Soviet plans. A French intelligence officer, Philippe Thyraud de Vosjoli, gave the CIA early warning that Soviet nuclear weapons probably were in Cuba. His story was told in the novel and movie *Topaz.*

Aerial photography and other intelligence also played an important role in the Cuban missile crisis. In fact, in modern times, using secret agents has become a smaller part of intelligence activity than it used to be. Much information now is collected by aerial and satellite photography, by the interception of radio and other electronic signals, and by other modern technologies. Many contemporary intelligence questions, however, do not lend themselves to this kind of technical collection. They may concern the explosion of ethnic and religious hatreds or terrorism. Often, such questions can be answered only by highly skilled, well-placed spies.

See also Arnold, Benedict; Central Intelligence Agency; Cuban Missile Crisis; *Rosenberg* Case.

EDMUND R. THOMPSON

ETHNICITY AND RACE
See African Americans; Anglo-Americans; Arab Americans; Asian Americans; Eastern Europeans in America; German Americans; Greek Americans; Hispanics; Irish Americans; Italian Americans; Jews in America; Scandinavian Americans.

EXECUTIVE BRANCH
See Presidency.

EXPANSION, TERRITORIAL

Central to the American experience has been the country's growth from a collection of colonial settlements hugging the Atlantic shore into the fourth largest nation on earth. The story of America's expansion includes many tales of the pioneers' heroism and reflects the great vision of the nation's leaders. But it also includes the tragic account of how the native Indians were driven from their land.

Continental Expansion
American territorial growth continued the British Empire's expansion in North America during the colonial period. The settling of huge land grants (given by English kings to

Westward Expansion of the Continental United States

Map labels: Line of Treaty with Great Britain, 1846; CANADA; Convention with Great Britain, 1818; From Great Britain, 1842; From Great Britain, 1818; From Great Britain, 1842; Columbia R.; Lake Superior; Lake Michigan; Lake Huron; Lake Ontario; OREGON TERRITORY, 1846; Line of Adams-Onís Treaty with Spain, 1819; LOUISIANA PURCHASE, 1803; Mississippi R.; L. Erie; Great Salt Lake; Missouri R.; MEXICAN CESSION, 1848; UNITED STATES IN 1783; ATLANTIC OCEAN; Colorado R.; Arkansas R.; ORIGINAL THIRTEEN STATES; Line of Treaty of Guadalupe Hidalgo with Mexico, 1848; Ohio R.; Gila R.; GADSDEN PURCHASE, 1853; Red R.; PACIFIC OCEAN; Pinckney's Treaty with Spain, 1795; FLORIDA CESSION, 1819 (from Spain by Adams-Onís Treaty); ANNEXATION OF TEXAS, 1845; 1810 1813; Rio Grande; Gulf of Mexico; MEXICO; present-day state boundaries; 0 100 200 300 400 500 miles; 0 100 200 300 400 500 kilometers; Albers Equal-Area Projection

their favorites) was made easier by the absence of serious geographic obstacles. Even the Appalachian Mountains proved not to be a great hindrance to people moving west. More serious was the resistance of the native peoples. But they were repeatedly weakened by disease, divided among themselves, and overwhelmed by the weapons and sheer number of the European colonists.

Why did the Anglo-American settlers constantly desire more territory? First, one must remember that most of them were farmers whose wealth depended on land. Moreover, land became less fertile after years of cultivation, especially in the South where tobacco and then cotton depleted the soil. So settlers would move on, seeking fresh land to farm. Second, new territory could have strategic

importance in England's competition with rivals such as Spain and France. The colony of Georgia, for example, was established in part to protect English settlers in the Carolinas from the Spanish in Florida.

The peace treaty ending the American Revolution (1783) extended the new United States to the Mississippi River. A few years later, concerned that Spain might close the mouth of the river to American trade, President Thomas Jefferson sought to buy New Orleans. Instead, France (which had obtained the land from Spain) offered to sell at a rock-bottom price almost a million square miles between the Mississippi and the Rocky Mountains. Virtually overnight the 1803 Louisiana Purchase doubled America's size. Moreover, the 1819 Adams-Onís Treaty between the United States and Spain added Florida to the national domain.

The various Indian tribes whose land this really was had not been consulted about the sale or about the steady movement of whites onto their eastern lands. After unsuccessful and halfhearted attempts to keep whites off of land that the United States had agreed would belong to the Indians, the federal government decided in the 1830s to move almost all eastern Indians beyond the Mississippi to Indian Territory (present-day Oklahoma). Through treaties, forced sales, and ultimately military force, Indians were relocated on

lands that were thought at the time to be safely beyond the desire of white settlers.

But by the 1840s many Americans were listening to people like John L. O'Sullivan, a writer and editor who proclaimed it the nation's "manifest destiny" to occupy all the land from the Atlantic to the Pacific. Doing so involved several complications, however. First, annexing Texas (which had won its independence from Mexico in 1836) reawakened the issue of slavery between the North and South. The Civil War (1861–65) probably would not have happened without the conflicts surrounding the question of whether

TERRITORIAL EXPANSION OF THE UNITED STATES

Territory	Date Acquired	Square Miles	How Acquired
Original states and territories	1783	888,685	Treaty with Great Britain
Louisiana Purchase	1803	827,192	Purchase from France
Florida	1819	72,003	Treaty with Spain
Texas	1845	390,143	Annexation of independent nation
Oregon	1846	285,580	Treaty with Great Britain
Mexican Cession	1848	529,017	Conquest from Mexico
Gadsden Purchase	1853	29,640	Purchase from Mexico
Alaska	1867	589,757	Purchase from Russia
Hawaii	1898	6,450	Annexation of independent nation
The Philippines	1899	115,600	Conquest from Spain (granted independence in 1946)
Puerto Rico	1899	3,435	Conquest from Spain
Guam	1899	212	Conquest from Spain
American Samoa	1900	76	Treaty with Germany and Great Britain
Panama Canal Zone	1904	553	Treaty with Panama (returned to Panama by treaty in 1978)
Corn Islands	1914	4	Treaty with Nicaragua (returned to Nicaragua by treaty in 1971)
Virgin Islands	1917	133	Purchase from Denmark
Pacific Islands Trust (Micronesia)	1947	8,489	Trusteeship under United Nations (some granted independence)
All others (Midway, Wake, and other islands)		42	

slavery should be allowed to expand into new territories.

Second, much of the Northwest was claimed by the British and all the Southwest was owned by Mexico. England recognized that Oregon Territory (which was being flooded by Americans traveling the Oregon Trail in the 1840s) could not be held much longer, and in 1846 it agreed to America's owning it. But Mexico was less willing to surrender what amounted to half its national territory. When the United States annexed Texas in 1845, a border dispute with Mexico soon erupted into war (1846–48). Although many Americans felt that it was wrong to fight Mexico, the United States easily defeated its southern neighbor. The Treaty of Guadalupe Hidalgo in 1848 added California plus Utah and New Mexico Territories to the nation, as well as extending Texas's southern border. The Gadsden Purchase of another, smaller parcel from Mexico in 1853 completed the United States' acquisitions in the Southwest.

Third, even with foreign claims settled, the U.S. government had to deal with native tribes west of the Mississippi, some of whom were ready to fight in defense of their land. The most famous Indian wars of our history—with the Sioux, Cheyenne, Nez Percé, Comanche, and Apache among others—followed white expansion into the West, ending only in the late 1880s.

By the middle of the nineteenth century America was three times larger than it had been at independence. The purchase of Alaska from Russia in 1867 added millions more acres and brought to a close the growth of the nation on the North American continent.

Overseas Expansion

To some early leaders, neither the Pacific Ocean nor the Gulf of Mexico marked the limits of American growth. Throughout the first half of the nineteenth century government officials discussed buying Cuba, valued for its strategic Caribbean location. In addition, many southerners thought Cuban sugar and tobacco plantations would strengthen slavery's future. There was also talk as early as the 1850s about acquiring the Hawaiian Islands, which had become an important harbor in Pacific seagoing trade.

But it was not until the end of the century that America seriously pursued overseas territory. Influenced by Europe's scramble for colonies in Africa and Asia, the United States began to find the idea of colonies attractive. In 1898 came both the annexation of Hawaii and the Spanish-American War, which was fought to free Cuba from Spain. Its victory gave America the largest addition of overseas territory it has known: the Philippines, Puerto Rico, and Guam. Oddly, though Cuba had been the main reason for the war, it did not become an American possession.

Why not Cuba? The answer involves America's uneasiness about the idea of empire. Many people believed that since republican America had always advocated independence for all peoples it would be a betrayal of principle to establish colonies. This group got as a condition for supporting the war the promise that Cuba would be given its independence. These "anti-imperialists," however, could not prevent the United States from annexing the Philippines. Nor could they prevent the greatest champion of American expansion, President Theodore Roosevelt, from encouraging a Panamanian revolt against Colombia, which led to American acquisition of the Panama Canal Zone in 1904.

Despite this fling with overseas expansion at the turn of the century, America has added few possessions since then (only some islands in the Pacific and Caribbean). Even victories in the two world wars led America not to annex territory but to encourage European powers to end colonialism. The United States granted the Philippines independence in 1946, and in 1999 the Canal Zone will be returned to Panama. Not often in history does one witness a great power willingly surrender territory. America in the twentieth century is one of the few exceptions.

See also Adams-Onís Treaty; Alaska Purchase; Gadsden Purchase; Hawaii Annexation; Indian Reservations; Indian-White Relations; Louisiana Purchase; Manifest Destiny; Mexican War; Oregon Trail; Panama Canal; Philippines, Acquisition of; Puerto Rico, Acquisition of; Spanish-American War; Texas Revolution and Annexation.

B E N J A M I N   M C A R T H U R

EXPLORATION OF NORTH AMERICA

All the early adventurers sailing west across the stormy waters of the North Atlantic— whether Irish monks in the sixth century, Norsemen two to four hundred years later, or fishermen from French Normandy—were curious about what lay beyond the western horizon. Some settled in Iceland and Greenland, and probably a few landed on the shores of North America. But Europeans in those very early years paid little attention to what they found.

In the fourteenth, fifteenth, and sixteenth centuries, however, increased trade and a growing demand for spices from the East led the emerging nation-states of Europe to search for an all-water route to the Indies (as lands in the Far East were called). They wanted to avoid the months-long dangerous journey to the East across the huge land mass and mountains of Europe and Asia. Most sailor-

navigators believed that the best way to go via the sea was to sail south around the bottom tip of Africa and then bear east across the Indian Ocean. But Christopher Columbus, convinced along with some others that the world was round and believing that it was much smaller than it actually is, thought that a shorter way lay in sailing west. In 1492 he made the first of four voyages to the New World, and soon dozens of other men followed.

Spanish Explorations

The Spanish established early settlements on the islands of the Caribbean Sea. And in 1513, one of them, Juan Ponce de León, became the first European to explore what was to become part of the United States. He landed on the Saint Johns River near present-day Jacksonville and then sailed along the Florida coast to Pensacola Bay. Other conquistadors, as these Spanish explorers were known, got as far north as Cape Fear in North Carolina. In 1528 Pánfilo de Narváez led an ill-fated expedition up the coast of west Florida. Narváez and some of his four hundred men were killed by Indians. But survivors built boats, determined to reach Spanish settlements in Mexico by sailing along the shores of the Gulf of Mexico. When they were shipwrecked in Galveston Bay, they set out on an overland trek. By the time they were rescued in 1536, only four Spaniards and a black slave named Esteban remained alive.

Their exaggerated stories of what they had seen resulted in two more exploring expeditions. The first was led by Hernando de Soto. He and his men landed in 1539 on the west coast of Florida. For the next four years these conquistadors explored much of today's southeastern United States from the Atlantic to east Texas before floating down the Missis-

An engraving showing Christopher Columbus arriving on an island in the Bahamas on October 12, 1492. It was the first land in the Americas that he encountered, and he named it San Salvador; its exact location is still disputed. His three famous ships are pictured—the Niña, *the* Pinta, *and the* Santa María.

sippi and skirting the Gulf of Mexico to return to the Spanish settlements in Mexico.

The second expedition was led by Francisco Vásquez de Coronado. In April 1540, with about two thousand men, he marched up the western portion of Mexico into present-day New Mexico and Arizona. In northwest New Mexico, Coronado came upon the Zuni pueblo (a type of Indian village), which he at first believed to be one of the mythical Seven Cities of Cibola thought to contain fabulous amounts of gold. Disappointed by its poverty, Coronado sent an expedition west. Its members were the first white men to gaze down upon the Colorado River from the rim of the Grand Canyon. Coronado wintered near what is now Albuquerque and in the spring traveled northeast into Kansas in search of a village called Quivera. It proved more of a disappointment than the Zuni pueblo had been. In April 1542, the conquistadors returned to Mexico.

As a result of the de Soto and Coronado expeditions, the Spanish had gained a fairly good knowledge of the lower half of the present United States. In the next 250 years the Spanish learned still more, advancing up the Pacific Coast to Vancouver Island and exploring much of the Great Plains, the southern Rockies, and the Great Basin.

Discoveries by Others
In contrast to the Spanish, the French were interested in the lands bordering the North Atlantic. Beginning as early as 1603 under the leadership of Samuel de Champlain, French adventurers followed rivers and lakes from the St. Lawrence south to the mouth of the Mississippi and west to the prairies beyond the Great Lakes. Some of the explorers' names—Jean Nicolet, Father Louis Hennepin, Father Marquette, Louis Joliet, Sieur de La Salle—are well known today. La Salle reached the mouth of the Mississippi from Canada in April 1682 and gave Louisiana its name. Two other Frenchmen, Pierre Radisson and Sieur des Groseilliers, probably explored west of the Mississippi. By the 1680s the French had a good knowledge of much of the interior of North America.

European Explorations of America

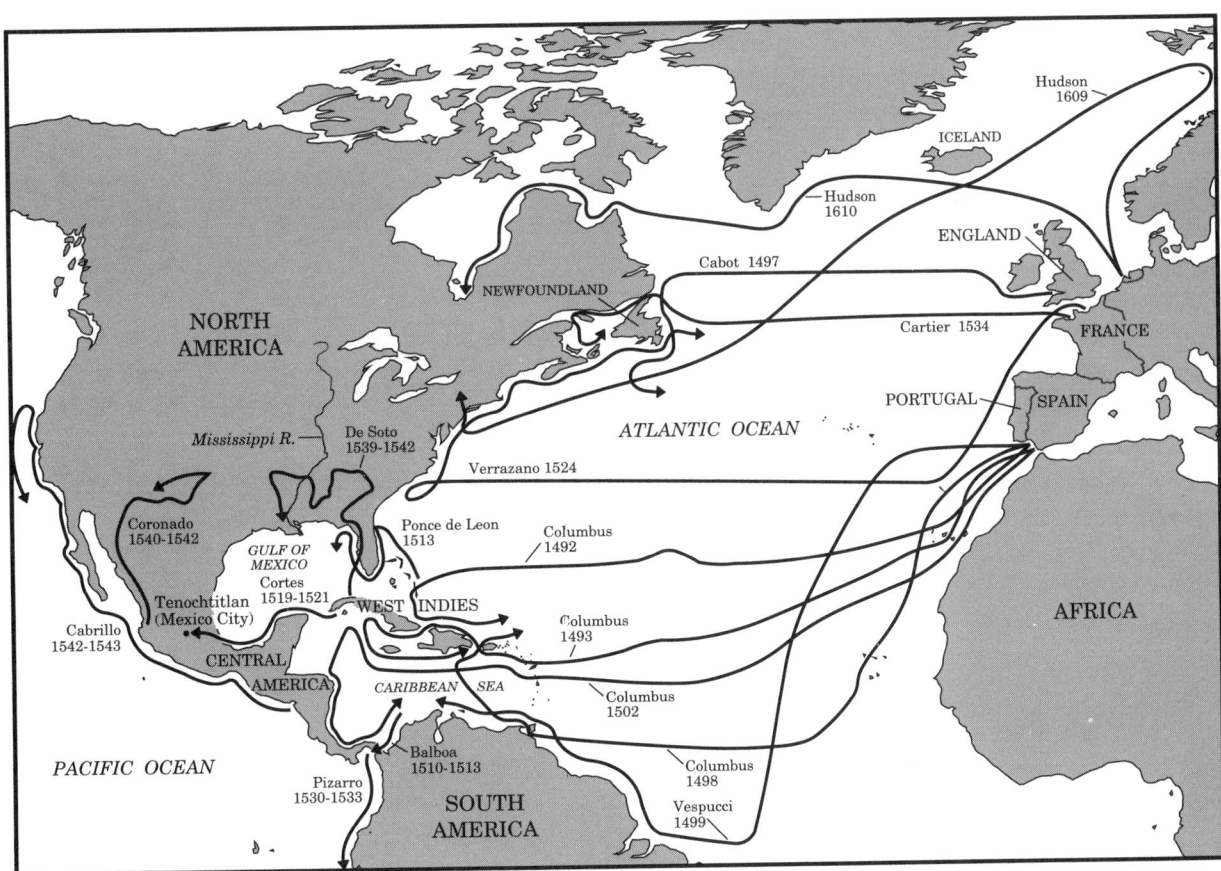

English explorations began with the voyage of John Cabot, who in 1497 reached Cape Breton Island at the entrance to the Gulf of St. Lawrence. In 1509 Cabot's son Sebastian reached Cape Hatteras off the North Carolina coast. The Englishman Henry Hudson, employed by the Dutch, in 1609 explored Chesapeake Bay, Delaware Bay, and the Hudson River. Sailing for the English in 1610 he discovered Hudson Bay. Within a few years after England had established settlements at Jamestown, Plymouth, and other sites on the Atlantic Coast, the colonists or others from England were probing the wilderness along the Appalachian Mountains. Much of the colonial knowledge of the regions to their west came from fur traders and settlers or speculators searching for new lands.

Northwest of Canada lay Alaska, first reached by Russia's Vitus Bering and Aleksandr Chirikov in 1741. Two British captains, James Cook in 1778 and George Vancouver in 1791, surveyed part of Alaska's coast. Robert Campbell and Alexander Murray, employees of the Hudson's Bay Company, had explored the Yukon by 1847, but much of the vast Alaskan interior remained unknown territory until gold seekers descended on the region in the 1890s.

By the 1770s the outlines of North America were known to most educated people, but the details of the interior had yet to be identified. In Canada Alexander Mackenzie in 1793 completed the first transcontinental journey to the Pacific north of Mexico. The American captain Robert Gray discovered the mouth of the Columbia River in 1791. Meriwether Lewis and William Clark, from 1804 to 1806, voyaged up the Missouri River, crossed the Rocky Mountains, and made their way down the Clearwater, Snake, and Columbia rivers to the Pacific Ocean. Zebulon Pike discovered the peak that bears his name and explored the southern Great Plains. The Pacific Railroad Surveys of 1853–56 and the Great Surveys of 1867–78 examined scientifically much of the western United States. By the close of the American frontier in 1890 almost all of North America had been explored.

See also Columbus, Christopher; Frémont, John C.; Lewis and Clark Expedition; Sacajawea.

RICHARD A. BARTLETT

F

FAIR DEAL

After his unexpected victory in the presidential election of 1948, Harry S. Truman gave the name Fair Deal to his administration's program for the next four years. He called it the Fair Deal because he saw it as an extension of Franklin D. Roosevelt's New Deal. Both before and after the election he proposed a large number of reform measures, such as having the government take responsibility for maintaining full employment, increasing the minimum wage, and extending economic aid to farmers. He also called for expanding the Social Security system and instituting national health insurance, federal aid to education, slum clearance projects, and various measures aimed at ending racial discrimination, such as an antilynching law and a law prohibiting racial discrimination in employment.

Few Fair Deal reforms were enacted into law because of the opposition of Republican and conservative Democratic congressmen. The minimum wage was raised, however, and Social Security was extended to an additional 10 million people.

See also Truman, Harry S.

FAMILY LIFE

The family, as generations of Americans came to know it, has consisted of a married mother and father and their two or three children. But over the centuries it has taken different forms for different groups, and changes in recent decades have created millions of households that do not fit the familiar pattern. The differences are striking, but so is the persistence of some kind of family life for so long and in so many cultures.

Most scholars agree that the family, which is probably our oldest social institution, developed out of the need for food, sex, and nurture of the young.

American Indian Families

A glance at the oldest known American family arrangements, those of American Indians, indicates the varied forms they could take in a group's efforts to stay alive and together. The Shoshone, for example, were a hunting people who lived on high desert plateaus in the West. Since a lot of the barren land was needed to feed and clothe very few people, large groups could not live together. As the young reached maturity, they had to go off in search of food, but they returned for tribal get-togethers, where new marriages and new families were formed. If there were more girls than boys, one boy might marry two or more girls. If there were more boys than girls, a girl might marry several boys. For their particular culture, the simple one-man–one-woman household did not work.

In tribes that began to raise domestic animals, women could help care for the livestock and so add to the family wealth. Since food could be stored and existence was less chancy, women also had time to make objects that could be traded. As the home became a center of industry and training for the young, family ties were strengthened.

The discovery of farming further enhanced the importance of women and children, who could help work the land. When the Shoshone moved south and came upon land more suitable for crops, women could tend them while the men went hunting. When a man married, he was taken into his wife's household and the land could be kept in the family, a very important consideration for all farmers, to whom land means wealth.

Colonial Families

The Europeans who came to America in pre-Revolution times had little in common with the natives they found, yet there were similarities. All members of these hardworking farm families contributed to their self-contained household economy, not only tilling the fields, but making virtually all their own clothes, furniture, candles, drugs, and much else. Men headed this enterprise; children were treated like small adults and expected to do their share.

With never enough hands to do all the work and early death common in some of the colonies, people were expected to marry young and produce big families. Cotton Mather, the powerful New England clergyman, had sixteen children—and outlived all but one of them. Since sex was considered sinful outside of marriage, if a husband or wife died, the survivor was expected to re-marry promptly.

Black Families

The colonial example influenced and helped sustain the less strict frontier farm families of the nineteenth century. But there was one group of Americans to whom the rules did not apply—America's slaves. These people, at the mercy of their owners, had their families torn apart when a parent or child was sold. On many plantations, slave girls were subject to the attentions of the white master and his sons, and the mulatto children of such unions became slaves without fathers.

Slaves were not allowed to marry legally, but some held their own private ceremonies anyway. After they were freed, ex-slaves could be seen traveling through the South looking for the mates they had been separated from when their owners sold them.

Despite the cruelties, black families, usually headed by the husband, did survive. But the institution of slavery itself, the trauma of sudden freedom followed by many years of oppression, the mass movement of blacks north during and after both world wars, and continued discrimination in employment and education had devastating effects on black family life. Today, America's inner cities are filled with households run by women alone.

Modern Families

The coming of industry and the growth of big cities revolutionized the American family. On the farm, with its ample space, there was room for grandparents, parents, children, and often uncles, aunts, and cousins. Each person contributed to the running of household and farm. But the new factories drew individuals out of the home, and the city tenements where many now lived were barely big enough for parents and their children. So young people went off to find jobs of their own, and contacts among relatives became less close.

Groups like the Mormons and the Amish have tried to safeguard their special ways of life from outside influences with some success. And in recent years an influx of immigrants faced with a shortage of affordable housing has increased dramatically the number of people living in households with other relatives—a return to something resembling the big farm families.

In the twentieth century, the importance of the once self-reliant family was also lessened by government programs to help the needy, the sick, the aged. Americans began to count less on the kindness of relatives and more on government offices. And legislatures and courts have further reduced the powers of the male head of household by upholding legal rights for women and children.

In the past few decades the conventional husband-wife-children family group has also been shaken by the sexual revolution. The arrival of the birth-control pill, the legalization and frequency of abortion, the increase in divorces, the flood of women into the work force, the influence of feminism, and sexual permissiveness have broken what had been a strong tie between sex and marriage. A new openness of homosexual relations is also reflected in the shape of some households. Today in cities like New York, Chicago, and San Francisco, married couples living with their own children make up only a minority.

Changes continue to come fast. But if history is a guide, the family, broadly defined, will adapt and endure, even if in forms that would have stunned our ancestors.

See also Childhood and Adolescence; Divorce; Marriage.

ELAINE AND WALTER GOODMAN

FARMERS' ALLIANCE

During the Civil War western farmers had borrowed heavily in order to expand their production of food. But after the war de-

mand for their crops slackened. Prices fell and a severe agricultural depression followed. One result was the spontaneous formation of farmers' clubs, which came to combine into what were called *alliances.*

The first important Farmers' Alliance sprang up in Texas in the late 1870s. During the next decade it spread steadily through the southern states and north into Kansas and the Dakotas. A smaller Northern Alliance developed in the plains states at about the same time.

All these organizations formed cooperatives. They pooled their money and resources in order to purchase fertilizer, farm machinery, and other necessities in bulk quantities, thereby getting them more cheaply. Many published local newspapers. But they were unable to force banks to lower their interest rates or railroads to lower their freight charges. This led the alliances to seek government help. Some called for what became known as the "subtreasury" plan, whereby the government would lend money to farmers, secured by crops held in storage because prices were so low. Others favored the coinage of silver in order to increase the amount of money in circulation.

To get these reforms enacted, they became involved in politics. In 1890 they backed candidates for state and local offices. A number of southern governors won election because of alliance support. Eight southern legislatures had pro-alliance majorities. Encouraged by these gains, the major alliances joined in 1892 to form the People's, or Populist, Party.

See also People's Party; Populism.

FARMING
See Agriculture.

FASHION AND STYLE

Over the centuries of American development, farmers and workers usually wore simple, cheap clothing. In contrast, the upper and middle classes wore expensive clothing—often by well-known designers, many of whom lived in Paris.

Early Fashions

In the 1700s women wore floor-length dresses held out from the body on each side by whalebone extenders known as panniers. They also often wore elaborate white wigs and heavy makeup. When Napoleon Bonaparte became emperor of France in 1804, a more natural look came into vogue. Women abandoned wigs and heavy makeup and wore simple gowns with a high waistline gathered under the bosom. This fashion came to be known as empire style.

This style was followed in about 1820 by a return to a bell-shaped skirt held out from the body by starched crinoline (horsehair) petticoats. By the mid-1850s a bent steel cage-like contraption known as a hoop had replaced the petticoats. In the 1870s the hoop was abandoned for a dress style focused on a flat front and an artificially enlarged backside. This latter feature was attained by wearing a small hooped bustle under the skirt. During all these years women also wore boned and laced corsets. In the nineteenth century corsets were laced as tightly as possible, to produce the eighteen-inch waistline then very popular.

In the early nineteenth century, the Industrial Revolution and the rise of a capitalist economy produced the simple dark business suit for men which they have worn ever since. This sober garb was in keeping with their new work role outside the home making

money in business and professions. At the same time, women continued to wear variations on older fashions. They did so both to signify home and family stability in the face of the startling new economic order and also to display through elaborate dress the status of their husbands.

The rising popularity of exercise and sports late in the century, as well as doctors' warnings that tight-laced corsets could damage a woman's internal organs, brought a healthy female body into vogue. This look replaced the thin, pale appearance that had been fashionable for women earlier. For a time during the mid-nineteenth century, in fact, to be fat was even stylish, as a number of hefty stage actresses gained great popularity.

As women began to enter business and the professions toward the end of the century, they began to wear on the job dark suits with long black skirts and shirtwaist blouses modeled on men's shirts. The rise of a dress reform movement, whose leaders advocated simplified dress and a healthy body look, hastened these changes. By the early twentieth century the tight-laced corset was being abandoned. The new fashionable look was exemplified by the athletic "Gibson girl." She was a fictionalized figure in popular drawings by New York artist Charles Dana Gibson.

Twentieth-Century Trends

Simplified dress for women has remained popular throughout the twentieth century, especially after short skirts came into vogue in the 1920s. Yet the economic and class factors that had previously affected fashion remained strong. Many women still tried to show their class status through dress and appearance. For example, as sports became a popular form of upper-class leisure in the 1920s, tanned skin became fashionable. (In

A group of women in 1922, sporting the latest style in bathing suits, are confronted by two policewomen who reprimand them for their skimpy beach wear. For additional illustrations, see insert following p. 308.

previous centuries a darkened appearance had a negative identification with people of color and lower-class farmers who worked out of doors, so women went to a great deal of trouble to keep their complexions white.) In addition, the rise of a commercial culture based on the sale of goods through advertising encouraged the increased use of makeup. (Makeup earlier had been identified with prostitution.) Large cosmetic companies like Helena Rubinstein's depended on convincing women that they had to wear makeup to be beautiful. Such advertising brought huge sales.

In the twentieth century the fashionable beauty look has especially been identified with youth. This trend culminated in the 1960s vogue of the model, Twiggy, whose thinness made her seem like a little girl. The rebelliousness of young people during those years, evident in the popularity of protest music and demonstrations against the Vietnam War, extended to the clothes they wore. Blue jeans, miniskirts, bell-bottomed pants, and bright tie-dyed fabrics replaced the more conservative styles of their parents. Some men began to wear their hair long.

But dangerous dictates of fashion exemplified in earlier years by overly tight corsets did not entirely disappear. One beauty ideal came to be that of thinness, and to attain it, too many young women starved themselves and became prey to the life-threatening illnesses of anorexia nervosa and bulimia. And, by the 1980s, surgical techniques to reshape the body in accord with a near-unattainable ideal of perfection had been devised. These included face lifts, liposuction (the surgical removal of body fat deposits), and implants to enlarge the size of breasts.

Nevertheless, most women—influenced by the real lives they lived, by their increasing participation in the professions or the work force generally, and by the feminist movement—insisted on simply being themselves and dressing in comfortable, attractive clothes.

See also illustrations in insert following p. 308.

LOIS W. BANNER

FAULKNER, WILLIAM

(1897–1962) *Writer.*

The works of great writers need more than an everyday effort from readers. When readers first turn to a novel by William Faulkner, they may feel they are at the edge of an impenetrable forest. But if they persist, they will master Faulkner's prose. They find they are able to follow his difficult and beautiful sentences that wind their way into the human soul.

Faulkner imagined a world with all its furnishings, both material and spiritual. He called it Yoknapatawpha County, and he gave it a population of 15,511 people, some white, some black, some Native American. They come from all walks of life. They are dirt farmers and aristocrats, generals and trappers, the educated and the ignorant. Most

have been born into a South almost destroyed by the Civil War and its aftermath.

From William Faulkner's vivid—sometimes exasperating—language spring his characters. From his profound knowledge of the American past comes the power and fascination of his stories. Over these often tragic, occasionally comic, tales of suffering and courage, of folly and violence, of love and hatred, his compassion casts a light that makes us see that what we call ordinary life is not ordinary at all.

William Faulkner is called a regional writer. Yet it was because he understood the South and southerners so deeply, with such a luminous and clear-eyed vision, that he transcended that one part of America and saw into the hearts of people everywhere.

Because of that, and because of the singular imagination out of which his novels grew, Faulkner was awarded the Nobel Prize for literature in 1949.

Among his best-known works are *The Sound and the Fury, As I Lay Dying,* and *Absalom, Absalom!* But a good place to start is with his short stories. The young reader can't do better than to begin with "Spotted Horses."

See also Literature.

PAULA FOX

FBI
See Federal Bureau of Investigation.

FEDERAL BUREAU OF INVESTIGATION

In 1908 a new branch of the Department of Justice, the Federal Bureau of Investigation (FBI), was created. Its function was to search for criminals who had broken federal laws.

During World War I the bureau investigated draft resisters, violators of the Espionage Act of 1917, foreign-born radicals, and anyone who seemed a threat to national security. During the postwar red scare FBI agents conducted raids and arrested many people without a shred of evidence that they had broken the law.

For this reason in 1924 the FBI was reorganized and a new director, J. Edgar Hoover, was appointed. Hoover proved to be an excellent manager. He made sure in these early years that his G-men did not engage in illegal activities such as wire tapping in their efforts to track down lawbreakers. Many notorious criminals, such as John Dillinger and "Machine Gun" Kelly, were brought to justice by the FBI.

With the passage of time, however, Hoover assumed more power than the law provided. During World War II and the cold war the FBI greatly expanded its search for "security risks," often invading the privacy and violating other rights of innocent people. Hoover collected embarrassing evidence about the private lives of many members of Congress and other government officials, and no president dared fire him. Only after he died in 1972 was the bureau again reformed.

See also Hoover, J. Edgar.

FEDERAL COMMUNICATIONS COMMISSION

The Federal Communications Commission (FCC) is one of many government bodies created by Congress to supervise various aspects of the economy. The FCC was established in 1934. It consists of seven members, chosen by the president with the consent of the Senate, each of whom serves for seven years.

Originally the FCC oversaw the telephone and radio industries. When television developed after World War II, it was added to the commission's responsibilities. It assigns broadcasting frequencies and awards licenses to the companies that operate these stations. It can also revoke a license if it sees fit. Its primary responsibility is to protect the "public interest," but how to define what that interest is is sometimes difficult. In the 1980s the FCC's powers were reduced by President Ronald Reagan's policy of limiting government regulation.

FEDERAL CONVENTION
See Constitution, The Making of the.

FEDERALIST PAPERS

When the U.S. Constitution was written by the Philadelphia Convention of 1787, Article VII provided that the new charter had to be ratified (approved) by specially chosen conventions in at least nine of the thirteen states before it could go into effect. In many of the states the conventions approved the document by large margins. But in some, many citizens thought the Constitution made the new central government too powerful. They feared that it would seriously limit their liberties and ability to manage their own affairs. These people, known as Antifederalists, were particularly numerous in New York. Of the sixty-five members of the New York convention, a solid majority, forty-six, had serious doubts about ratification.

It was extremely important that New York approve the Constitution because without it the Union would be divided in two. To persuade these Antifederalist delegates to support it, Alexander Hamilton, James Madison, and John Jay, writing under the pen name "Publius," produced eighty-five essays describing the advantages of the Constitution and responding to the criticisms raised by its opponents. These were published in the newspapers and later in book form.

The New York convention finally ratified the Constitution by a small margin. Historians do not think the Federalist Papers accounted for this as much as the fact that by the time the delegates voted, ten other states had ratified it. A negative vote would have left New York isolated. But the brilliance of Publius's defense and explanations of the Constitution have made the Papers seem almost a part of the document itself.

See also Constitution, The Making of the.

FEDERALIST PARTY

When the United States of America came into existence with the ratification of the Constitution and the inauguration of George Washington in 1789, no one expected that a two-party political system was about to be born. President Washington particularly disliked parties, which he called "factions." But by the early 1790s new issues had caused sharp differences of opinion among leaders who had all been solid supporters of the new government during the debates over the ratification of the Constitution. Two political parties soon developed, the Federalist Party, headed by Alexander Hamilton, and the Democratic-Republican Party, headed by Thomas Jefferson and James Madison.

The chief domestic policies favored by the Federalist Party were Secretary of the Treasury Hamilton's financial reforms and espe-cially his plan to establish the Bank of the United States. The party also favored a pro-British foreign policy over one sympathetic to France, which was then in the midst of its bloody revolution.

The Federalists were dominant during Washington's two terms, though he never identified himself with any party. In 1796 Federalist John Adams was elected president. But in 1798 the Federalists pushed through Congress two unpopular laws, the Alien Act and the Sedition Act. As a result, Adams was defeated when he ran for a second term in 1800. Thomas Jefferson became president and his Democratic-Republican Party remained in control of the presidency for the next forty years.

FEDERAL THEATRE PROJECT

The Federal Theatre Project was one of the more imaginative New Deal efforts to deal with the unemployment problem during the Great Depression of the 1930s. It was created in 1935 as part of the Works Project Administration. Its primary assignment was to provide jobs for unemployed actors, playwrights, directors, and stagehands. In doing so, however, it also sought to provide first-class theatrical entertainment for the public.

The Federal Theatre Project was headed by Hallie Flanagan of Vassar College. Besides putting on standard performances of the classics, she focused on experimenting with new theatrical techniques and on plays that dealt with current social and economic problems. *Carmen Jones,* for example, was a musical in which the music came from Bizet's nineteenth-century French opera *Carmen.* But all the actors were blacks engaged in activities typical of modern black life. The bull-fighter of *Carmen* became a boxer in *Carmen Jones*.

These policies were controversial, and in 1939 the project was abolished by Congress. During its brief existence, however, about 30 million people attended its various productions.

See also New Deal.

FEDERAL TRADE COMMISSION

The Federal Trade Commission (FTC) is one of many government bodies created by Congress to supervise various aspects of the economy. It was established in 1914 to deal with problems resulting from the development of large semimonopolistic corporations. It consists of five members (no more than three from any one political party) chosen by the president with the consent of the Senate. Each commissioner's term of appointment is seven years.

The act declared "that unfair methods of competition in commerce are hereby declared unlawful." It did not define "unfair," but when the FTC "had reason to believe" that unfair methods were being employed it could compel accused persons and corporations to make their records available and it could issue "cease and desist" orders. The culprits still had the right to appeal the orders to the courts, but the commission greatly strengthened national antitrust policy.

FEDERAL WRITERS' PROJECT

The Federal Writers' Project (FWP) was created in 1935 as part of the Work Projects Ad-

ministration, the New Deal agency designed to provide jobs for unemployed workers during the Great Depression. Many novelists and poets were supported by the project, although no one was employed specifically to write fiction. In addition to professional writers, the project provided work for many unemployed teachers and librarians.

Probably the most important of the hundreds of publications produced by the FWP were guides to states and regions, describing their geography and recounting their history. These works are still widely used. Other significant projects included a 150-volume Life in America series and various collections of American folklore.

In addition FWP workers conducted interviews with about two thousand former slaves. The recollections of these elderly blacks, which would otherwise have been lost forever, are an extremely valuable source of information about race relations and the experiences of the newly freed people in the Reconstruction era.

Although some people objected to the government providing any form of employment other than physical labor, the FWP won wide support. It was continued until 1943, when the wartime demand for labor put an end to the unemployment problem.

See also New Deal.

FEMINIST MOVEMENT TO 1919

In modern America, the feminist movement is often associated with the 1960s resurgence of the women's movement. Historically, however, there have always been women who could rightfully be referred to as feminists, although what they were called and their numbers have fluctuated with the times.

Women's Status in the Early Republic

The founding of the United States was not an event that helped women as such. Abigail Adams implored her husband, John, to "remember the ladies" as he and the other Founding Fathers were framing the Constitution. But there were only a few Abigail Adamses, and they generally held their positions of privilege primarily through their husbands. By and large, women in the early Republic (1775–1825) were second-class citizens.

Paradoxically, at the same time women were also necessary partners in the establishment of a thriving nation. Without women working alongside their fathers, husbands, sons, and brothers, the country would not have developed as it did, with a large core of family farms supporting a growing network of commerce and industry gradually moving

A women's suffrage march, displaying a banner that proclaims President Woodrow Wilson's support. The president was at first reluctant to back women's voting rights, but after acknowledging their important contributions during World War I, he lent his support.

from east to west. But it was not until the Age of Expansion in the early to mid-nineteenth century that a self-aware women's movement began to take shape in the United States.

First Reform Efforts

As the country prospered, more and more women were able and willing to engage in various forms of voluntary work. Their concerns ranged from aid for widows, orphans, and the poor to education, temperance, and religion. In addition, slavery became a critical issue. As time went on, many women activists became abolitionists. Women like Lucretia Mott dedicated years to seeking the abolition of slavery.

Abolition, in fact, helped create the women's movement. Ironically, it was not because abolitionists recognized the parallels in the lack of rights for slaves and women. It was because so many male abolitionists failed to see the parallels. For instance, when American women delegates to an international abolition conference in London in 1840 were refused seating, their male colleagues did not rise to support them. The incident sent a signal that women could not ignore.

In 1848, Mott and Elizabeth Cady Stanton, who had become friends in London, issued an invitation to women to meet in Seneca Falls, New York, to discuss their status. The Women's Rights Conference of 1848 largely shaped the women's movement in the United States even into the twentieth century. A Declaration of the Rights of Women, written by Stanton and purposely modeled after the Declaration of Independence, listed demands for full and equal citizenship. One of the demands, the right to vote, was almost an afterthought and not immediately considered a key issue. Indeed, many at the conference disagreed with its inclusion, arguing that the

right to vote for women was unnecessary.

Seeking the Vote

It quickly became clear, however, that without the vote, most of the other demands for equality could not be secured. In a democracy, the vote is the equalizer that gives power to common citizens to protect and ensure their rights and freedoms. Women needed that minimum power before other rights could be obtained. Thus, the quest for suffrage became the primary focus for feminists from the 1850s to 1919.

As in any movement, not all feminists agreed with that focus, especially as industrialization increasingly changed the face of America. Many women believed that issues such as working conditions, wages, and child labor were more direct and pressing concerns affecting far greater numbers of women than whether or not they could vote. But the working-class women most directly affected by work-related issues had neither the time nor the means to organize and take up even their own social causes. Middle-class women reformers were convinced that with the vote, women could remedy a whole range of social ills affecting not only women but society in general. Susan B. Anthony, for example, was most sympathetic to the harsh lives led by women forced by their economic situation to work long hours for meager wages outside of the home. In her view, the best thing she could do for women in all circumstances was to help secure for them the power to make changes. Like Anthony, most feminists put their efforts into the suffrage cause.

The suffrage movement finally succeeded for two reasons: first, because countless thousands of women spent nearly seventy years persuading, through a variety of means, local, state, and federal governments that women were entitled to vote and, second, because outstanding leaders rose to the occasion. Stanton and Anthony, her long-time colleague and friend, organized the suffrage

• •

Many women contributed in different ways to the early feminist movement. Some worked directly within groups dedicated to seeking women's equality. Others wrote important books and articles on the subject. Still others showed through the example of their own lives what women could achieve. See the following biographies in this book:

ADAMS, ABIGAIL

ALCOTT, LOUISA MAY

ANTHONY, SUSAN B.

BLACKWELL, ELIZABETH

CATT, CARRIE CHAPMAN

DIX, DOROTHEA

FULLER, MARGARET

GILMAN, CHARLOTTE PERKINS

GOLDMAN, EMMA

GRIMKÉ, ANGELINA AND SARAH

HAMILTON, ALICE

MITCHELL, MARIA

MOTT, LUCRETIA

PAUL, ALICE

RANKIN, JEANNETTE

SANGER, MARGARET

STANTON, ELIZABETH CADY

TRUTH, SOJOURNER

TUBMAN, HARRIET

WELLS-BARNETT, IDA

WOODHULL, VICTORIA

WRIGHT, FRANCES

movement. Anthony spent most of her adult life traveling the country, speaking, raising funds, and popularizing the idea of woman suffrage. She proved to be more than equal to

an often thankless job. Through her monumental efforts, the National American Woman Suffrage Association (NAWSA) was born.

At first, the suffrage battle was fought on the state and local levels, with thousands of campaigns waged in an effort to influence legislators to change state constitutions. By 1910, only six states had granted women the right to vote. Then NAWSA, now under the leadership of Carrie Chapman Catt, continued to press for suffrage in other states, especially some of the larger eastern ones. A few years later, a second organization, the National Woman's Party, under the leadership of its founder, Alice Paul, focused its efforts on securing a federal suffrage amendment.

Because of the strong efforts of both suffrage groups, President Woodrow Wilson, noting the crucial contributions made by women during World War I, eventually declared woman suffrage to be an emergency war measure. Congress finally passed a suffrage amendment on June 4, 1919. The Nineteenth Amendment was ratified by the states in 1920, in time for women to vote in the presidential election that year. With the passage of the amendment, the first stage of feminists' efforts to gain equality drew to a close.

See also Abolitionist Movement; Married Women's Property Acts; National Woman's Party; Seneca Falls Convention; Voting.

CHRISTINE A. LUNARDINI

FEMINIST MOVEMENT SINCE 1919

When women got the vote, many feminists believed they had won equality. Former suffragists created the League of Women Voters in 1920 to educate the new voters. One explained, "The crusade was over. . . . We went back to a hundred different causes and tasks that we'd been putting off."

The ERA Proposed

The bipartisan League worked for good government and laws protecting working women and children, but a few militant feminists wanted more. The courts had repeatedly found that the Fourteenth Amendment did not guarantee full rights to women. So Alice Paul formed the small National Woman's Party (NWP), proposing an Equal Rights Amendment (ERA) to wipe away discriminatory laws—federal, state, and local. A few sympathetic congressmen introduced the ERA in 1923.

Yet organized feminism declined. The NWP kept lobbying, but membership dwindled. Only because of women's industrial work during World War II did the ERA garner bipartisan backing in 1943. Even without a feminist movement, the bill gained support in the 1950s; but unions opposed the ERA because it would do away with laws protecting only women. The NWP and many professional women's groups wanted to do just that, arguing that such legislation kept women in inferior jobs and out of competition for better ones.

In the 1960 election, Republicans endorsed the ERA, but Democrats ignored the issue. President John F. Kennedy chose a union woman, Esther Peterson, as his assistant secretary of labor. To distract attention from the ERA, she formed the Presidential Commission on the Status of Women to study women's place in society and to show that progress was emerging gradually. Because of cold war competition with communism, Kennedy wanted to assure the free world that under democracy women had legal rights but also responsibilities in the home. Such messages

filled the commission's report, *American Women* (1963), concluding that "a constitutional amendment need not *now* be sought."

President Lyndon B. Johnson persuaded Congress to pass the Civil Rights Act in 1964. Southern politicians tried but failed to defeat it by adding "sex" along with "race, color, religion, and national origin" to Title VII as a factor against which employers could not discriminate. Gender equality thus became part of a federal law. The Civil Rights Act set up the Equal Employment Opportunities Commission (EEOC) to enforce the law; but its director considered the gender clause "a fluke" and did nothing to help women. Feminists were not yet involved.

Founding of NOW

By 1964, thirty-two states had set up commissions on the status of women; and others followed. Representatives, many of them women, met in national conventions annually. One was Betty Friedan, whose book, *The Feminine Mystique* (1963), exposed society's limitations on women. She and some state commissioners, including some men, disliked the EEOC's failure to prohibit segregated "Help Wanted–Male" and "–Female" classified ads offering well-paying sales and management positions to men and low-paying secretarial and domestic work to women. In 1966, they formed the National Organization for Women (NOW).

The 1960s was a decade of reform movements, all depending on the activism of women, old and young. Many had been moved by feminist books by Simone de Beauvoir (translated from the French in 1952), Eleanor Flexner (1959), and Doris Lessing (1962). The spirit of activism attracted many women wanting change to the "new feminism." Many joined NOW, hoping to expand its focus to include all aspects of women's status. The organization's egalitarian feminists crusaded for the ERA; but others wanted even more, declaring, "We believe that true partnership between the sexes demands a different concept of marriage, an equitable sharing of the responsibilities of home and children and of the economic burdens of their support." They also called for recognition of "the economic and social values of homemaking and child care." A target for change was "the false image of women now prevalent in the mass media and in the texts, ceremonies, laws and practices of our major social institutions ... church, state, college, factory or office which ... foster in women self-denigration, dependence, and evasion of responsibility, undermine their confidence in their own abilities and foster a contempt for women." By 1974, NOW had over seven hundred chapters in the United States and nine other nations.

NOW was reformist, not revolutionary, and worked within the political system and the "establishment." It forced the EEOC to consider women's concerns. It instigated lawsuits to force equality in some corporations and educational institutions. One case ended the airlines' practice of firing stewardesses when they married, became pregnant, or turned thirty-two. Now men joined women as "flight attendants."

Many women, however, considered NOW far too liberal; and the new movement fragmented. When NOW's 1967 convention called for "the right of women to control their own reproductive lives" with birth control and even abortion, some members resigned. In 1969, these more moderate feminists formed the Women's Equity Action League (WEAL) to promote female participation in politics and government. The League wanted to cor-rect administrative, educational, and legal inequalities in a "conservative" way. Its *Washington Report* provided news to help feminists lobby for new laws. In 1968, moderate feminists formed smaller pressure groups like Federally Employed Women (FEW) and Human Rights for Women to provide legal services. Only in the ERA did all feminists find common ground.

Radical Feminism

Simultaneously, a radical feminism began on a grass-roots level. Women's Liberation groups rejected the gradualist approach. They called NOW and WEAL conventional, "elitist," "bourgeois feminists." Whereas NOW wanted "to get women into positions of power," Ti-Grace Atkinson, a radical, said women should "get rid of positions of power." Younger, countercultural radical feminists proposed reforms through newsletters and meetings. Some were activists from New Left movements like the Students for a Democratic Society, who rejected the male chauvinism they had experienced there. Some tried demonstrations and street theater tactics to make their points. New York Radical Women led a torchlight march to Arlington National Cemetery in 1968 to stage the "Burial of Traditional Womanhood." Kathy Amatnick changed her last name to Sarachild to deny patriarchy, the father's supremacy. Some feminists declared their identity and rights as "lesbian separatists."

New York radicals Ellen Willis and Shulamith Firestone founded the Redstockings in 1969, claiming "that criticism of women—even any one woman—was ... 'blaming the victim.'" They called all women "an oppressed class" because of "sexism." Radical feminists created branches with diverse names in many cities—the Furies in Wash-

Left: Puritans wore plain, somber-colored clothing. Men's attire featured large, squared collars, and bonnets and aprons were common among the women.
Right: American military uniforms during the revolutionary war.

Captain Samuel Chandler and his wife posed for these portraits dressed in upper-class colonial attire (c.1780).

Left: A late-nineteenth-century family portrait featuring Victorian dress.
Right: This advertisement shows clothing typical of the late nineteenth century. Women wore hoop skirts, long full skirts shaped by a circular steel frame. The man on the left wears a stovepipe hat.

Left: Bustles were popular during the 1860s and 1870s. Some were made of cork or down, while others were baskets made from wood, steel, or whalebone. Bustles were tied to the waist and pleated skirts were worn over them.
Right: A caricature of a bustle (1872), which evolved from the hoop skirt.

Top left: A Winnebago Indian shirt (c.1880) made of wool with silk and velvet ribbons. Elaborate designs were created by sewing glass beads on the fabric.

Top right: An Arapaho Indian dress (c.1890) made of buckskin and decorated with feathers, leather fringe, and brightly colored designs.

Left: The Gibson girl (1890–1910) was the creation of illustrator Charles Dana Gibson. Tall and athletic, the Gibson girl wore starched blouses, and long skirts over a small bustle. The style was a departure from the constricting and fussy clothing that characterized the preceding generation of women's fashions.

Right: The flapper style, popular in the 1920s, was associated with female independence and unconventional behavior. Ironically, however, most women had to diet stringently to achieve the boyish figures best suited to the style. Flappers bobbed their hair and wore short skirts, stockings rolled at the knees, and heeled shoes.

Left: The bobby soxer style worn by teenagers in the 1950s featured cashmere sweaters, headbands, bobby socks and saddle shoes, and flared skirts—the most famous of which was the poodle skirt.

Bottom left: The Afro hairstyle, as worn by rock guitarist Jimi Hendrix. Afros were first popularized in the 1960s and 1970s by African-American civil rights activists. Hendrix completes his psychedelic look with a flamboyant jacket and fringed boots.

Bottom right: In the 1970s Women's Wear Daily *coined the term "hot pants" to describe the very brief, fitted shorts that were stylish for a short time. They were an outgrowth of the 1960s miniskirt. This model's outfit is accessorized with white vinyl boots and a headband.*

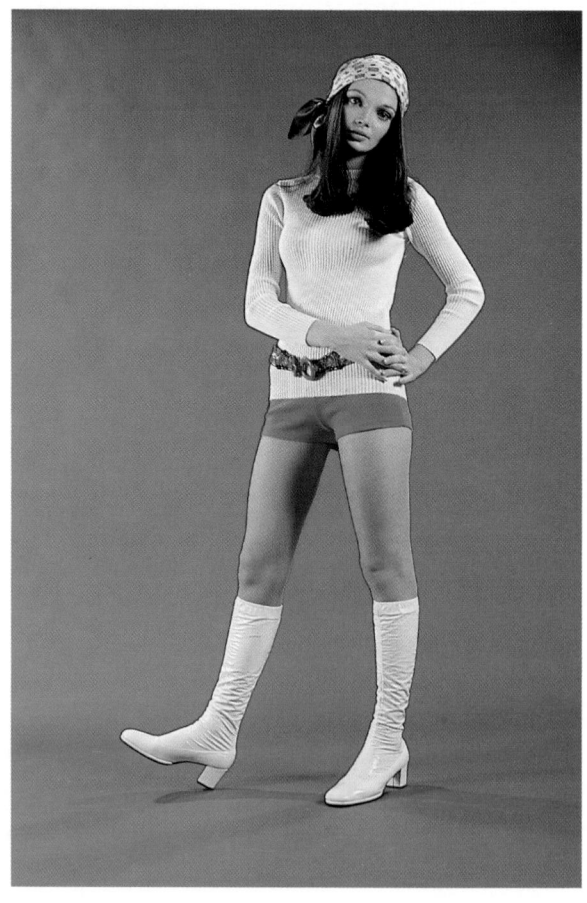

A 1974 photo of a march by the National Organization for Women in Atlantic City, New Jersey. On the left of the banner is N O W's *symbol.*

ington, D.C., Bread and Roses and Cell 16 in Boston. The Women's International Terrorist Conspiracy from Hell (WITCH) engaged in "zap" actions, dressing as witches to protest in places like Wall Street. Some rejected any leadership, calling for systems that let all speak equally. Some called on women "to isolate themselves from men in order to come to terms with what it means to be female." Many women organized "Consciousness-Raising" groups, small-group discussions of private problems, asserting that "the personal is political." Robin Morgan collected radical writings in *Sisterhood Is Powerful* (1970). Kate Millett's *Sexual Politics* (1970) pioneered in feminist literary and cultural criticism. Shulamith Firestone's *The Dialectic of Sex* (1970) argued for separation of sex and procreation.

Radicals joined in abortion rights marches and national meetings; but their most publi-cized events took place at the 1968 and 1969 Miss America pageants. Accusing the winner of selling her body along with consumer goods, protesters carried signs: "Cattle Parades Are Degrading to Human Beings," "Can Make-Up Cover Up the Wounds of Our Oppression?" and "No More Beauty Standards—Everyone Is Beautiful." The media created the myth that these feminists burned their bras. They only tossed symbols of women's "oppression" and "enslavement"— girdles, high heels, curlers, make-up, dish-cloths, copies of *Ladies' Home Journal* and *Playboy*—into "freedom trash cans."

Successes and Failures
On August 26, 1970, the fiftieth anniversary of the adoption of the women's suffrage amendment, tens of thousands across the nation joined the Women's Strike for Equality, pro-

claiming "the end of millenniums of oppression." More actions followed. Secretaries organized Nine to Five. Feminists "liberated" male-only restaurants and bars. Women journalists won admission to press clubs that had been limited to men. Others protested ads stereotyping women as "servants and sex objects." Law, medical, and other professional schools were opened to a fairer share of female students. *Ms.* magazine, founded in 1972, became a national feminist forum for such issues; and its editor Gloria Steinem emerged as an important feminist spokesperson, generally receiving more positive media coverage than other activists.

Since the 1960s, major changes have taken place in legislatures, courts, and public and private life, thanks to pressure from all sorts of feminists. Other changes, like the 1973 Supreme Court decision in *Roe* v. *Wade* legalizing abortion, occurred apart from activism. Yet fragmentation of feminism slowed change in the "Me Decade" of the 1970s and the era of "New Traditionalism" in the 1980s. The very successes sparked an antifeminism described by Susan Faludi in *Backlash: The Undeclared War against Women* (1991). Labels like "libber" and "feminist" became negative. Although the ERA passed Congress in 1973 and was approved by many states and First Lady Betty Ford flew an ERA flag at the White House, Phyllis Schlafly's Stop ERA crusade and other political reactionaries prevented the required two-thirds of the states from approving it. Even with a deadline extended to 1981, the ERA died and has not come before Congress since. Nevertheless, anticipating the ERA, the Pentagon opened up many military jobs to women.

By the 1990s, many women had internalized feminist ideals even if they did not call themselves feminists or join organizations—

that is, these ideals had become a normal part of the way they saw themselves and their lives. They simply assumed they would have careers, share domestic arrangements equally with their mates, not be shut out of places or activities because of their gender. A host of feminist groups continued to crusade for diverse causes—for women's health and against sexual harassment. Some women have reached new heights. Hillary Rodham Clinton redefined the role of First Lady as an equal partner in the White House. Ruth Bader Ginsburg, a 1960s feminist activist, joined the U.S. Supreme Court. Although the recent "feminization of poverty" cannot be denied, women hold unprecedented power in business, government, education, and the professions.

See also Equal Rights Amendment; League of Women Voters; National Organization for Women; National Woman's Party; *Roe* v. *Wade. Also see biographies of the following feminists:* Earhart, Amelia; Friedan, Betty; Ginsburg, Ruth Bader; Paul, Alice; Rankin, Jeannette; Steinem, Gloria.

BLANCHE LINDEN-WARD

FIFTEENTH AMENDMENT
See Voting.

FILLMORE, MILLARD
(1800–74)   *Thirteenth president of the United States (1850-53).*

Millard Fillmore overcame his poverty-stricken upbringing and limited education to have a successful if undistinguished political career.

In 1828, he was elected to the New York State Assembly for the first of three terms. He then served in the U.S. House of Representatives from 1833 to 1843. During the heated debates in Congress over slavery, Fillmore quietly allied himself with the moderate Whig Party leader Henry Clay. He lost a race for the governorship of New York in 1844, but in 1848, with help from Clay, he was chosen as running mate for the Whig Party's presidential nominee, Gen. Zachary Taylor, a Mexican War hero and Southern slave owner, who won the election.

In July 1850, when Taylor died after a brief illness, Fillmore became president. Unlike Taylor, he gave full support to Daniel Webster's and Henry Clay's struggle to secure passage of the Compromise of 1850 designed to resolve sectional differences over slavery. Among other features, the measure admitted California to the Union as a free state and applied the principle of popular sovereignty—letting local voters decide whether or not to permit slavery—to other newly acquired territories. It also contained stricter requirements for the return of runaway slaves from the North.

With uncharacteristic firmness and decisiveness, Fillmore signed the Compromise bills, a move intended to decrease sectional tensions. He weakened the already divided Whig Party by removing those members who opposed the law from federal posts. His actions, however, helped postpone the Civil War for another eleven years. Fillmore is also remembered for sending Commodore Matthew Perry to Japan in 1852 to open that Asian nation to trade with the West.

In the 1856 presidential election, Fillmore was rejected by the Whigs but became the candidate of the anti-immigrant Know-Nothing Party. After losing the election, he

retired from politics. He helped found the University of Buffalo before he died in 1874.

See also Know-Nothing Party; Nativism; Whig Party. *For events during Fillmore's administration, see* Compromise of 1850; Fugitive Slave Law.

BARBARA SILBERDICK FEINBERG

FILM
See Movies.

FIRE DEPARTMENTS

The firefighters of the 1700s and early 1800s were volunteers—ordinary citizens who had other jobs and were not paid to fight fires. The earliest fire engines were water-pumping carts. Volunteers would pull a cart to the fire and then pour buckets of water into the cart. Other volunteers stood on either side of the cart and pushed a pump handle up and down, which forced the water from the cart through a hose and onto the fire.

The volunteers were formed into fire companies that were much like clubs. The men were often a little rowdy. They not only fought fires but sat around the fire stations drinking, telling stories, and picking fights with other companies. When a building caught fire, the companies fought over which one would put it out. Some volunteers even cut the hoses of other companies so they could not fight fires. Many people began to complain about the unruly fire companies.

In the 1850s the steam-powered fire engine was invented. Since a few men could operate the steam pumpers, cities no longer needed so many volunteers to pump water by hand. The largest cities replaced the volunteers with a smaller number of paid firefighters. By the late 1800s all large American cities had professionals, and only in small towns and the country were there still volunteer fire companies. (Some still exist.)

Americans demanded further improvement of the fire departments after a number of terrible fires occurred. For example, in 1871 a great fire swept through Chicago. It destroyed the homes of 100,000 people, and the city's largest stores, hotels, theaters, and office buildings were burned to the ground. To stop such destruction, cities installed fire alarm boxes at street corners to make sure fires were quickly reported and firefighters arrived before the fires could spread. These alarm boxes were connected by telegraph lines to the fire stations. If there was a fire, one could run to the alarm box and notify the fire station simply by turning a handle on the box. By 1900 over 750 cities had such fire warning systems. In 1872 Boston's fire department bought the first boat designed to fight fires. During the late 1800s other cities bought fireboats as well. Cities also improved the training of their firefighters. Departments held contests to see which firefighters could harness horses and drive to a fire the fastest.

During the 1900s fire departments continued to buy new and improved equipment. Fire trucks replaced horses, allowing firefighters to arrive at blazes faster than ever. By the second half of the 1900s there were no longer any great fires burning whole cities like the Chicago fire of 1871. Firefighters were able to put out fires before they spread.

See also Triangle Shirtwaist Fire.

JON C. TEAFORD

FIRST AMENDMENT
See Bill of Rights; Freedom of Speech; Freedom of the Press.

FIRST LADIES

For social purposes, the presidency has always been regarded as a two-person position and the president's wife has been accorded unusual respect. In a nation still getting used to not having a king and a royal court, people referred to Martha Dandridge Custis Washington (1789–97) as "Lady Washington," a style that soon vanished. But some people, still infatuated with royalty, would use the word *queen* to describe the president's lady. For instance, Harriet Lane, a niece of James

Martha Custis Washington, wife of President George Washington, the first of the First Ladies, was often referred to as Lady Washington. The term First Lady *was not used regularly until after the Civil War.*

Buchanan, who served as his hostess (1857–61) because he was a bachelor, was labeled by some writers "our Democratic queen." Frequently also the president's wife was known as "Mrs. President" or as the "Presidentress."

The phrase "First Lady" was apparently first used in 1870 by a newspaperwoman referring to Martha Washington and Ulysses S. Grant's wife, Julia Dent Grant (1869–77). It came into general use after it was applied to Lucy Ware Webb Hayes (1877–81), wife of Rutherford B. Hayes. Most holders of the title—including Jacqueline Bouvier Kennedy (1961–63), wife of John F. Kennedy—have deplored its use as inappropriate in a republic. Still, it has been a convenient term, especially since newspaper and magazine illustrations have made the faces of the president's wife and family familiar to the public. Although the First Lady legally is only a private citizen who happens to be married to the president, she can be a powerful person. What the limits of her power may be has never been tested in the courts. Hillary Rodham Clinton (1993–) in her position as head of President Bill Clinton's task force on health-care reform has brought national attention to the subject.

The wives of presidents, nevertheless, have always been influential. Martha Washington helped establish the aristocratic tone of the first president's administration. Abigail Smith Adams (1797–1801) did not shrink from making policy suggestions to her husband, John, setting a precedent for all First Ladies since. Dolley Payne Madison (who served as hostess for Thomas Jefferson, a widower, and then for her husband, James Madison, 1801–17) was expert at turning social events to her husband's political advantage. Sarah Childress Polk (1845–49) was no less a politician than her husband, James K. Polk. Edith Carow Roosevelt (1901–09)

Hillary Rodham Clinton, wife of President Bill Clinton, is the country's forty-second First Lady. Here she addresses a meeting of the American Medical Association on health-care reform.

helped as Theodore Roosevelt's wife to make the White House a national monument. Edith Galt Wilson (1913–21) performed so many presidential duties after Woodrow Wilson suffered a massive stroke that she has been called the "First Woman President." Eleanor Roosevelt Roosevelt (1933–45), independently of Franklin D. Roosevelt, was famously active in labor, civil rights, and anti-poverty causes. Bess Wallace Truman (1945–53) was called "the Boss" by President Harry S. Truman in tribute to her place in his life. Betty Bloomer Ford (1974–77), who said she influenced her husband, Gerald R. Ford, through "pillow talk," broke fresh ground in going public about her operation for breast cancer and, after Ford left office, her drinking problem. Nancy Davis Reagan (1981–89) was widely known to have influenced the selection of some of Ronald Reagan's chief aides and to have set some of the dates on which he performed official duties.

Varied Images

The images projected by the First Ladies have been varied. George Bush's wife, Barbara Pierce Bush (1989–93), for instance, whose book about the White House dog, Millie, delighted readers, had a comfortable grandmotherly manner. The youthful elegance of Jacqueline Kennedy was a notable asset to her husband, as was Grover Cleveland's young bride, Frances Folsom (1886–89; 1893–97). Frequently the First Lady served as a lightning rod for the president, drawing criticism from opponents who were reluctant to attack him directly. For instance, Abraham Lincoln's wife, Mary Todd Lincoln (1861–65), was denounced for her heavy personal spending during the Civil War. Nancy Davis Reagan was criticized for buying expensive china for the White House, even though it was needed. Rosalynn Smith Carter (1977–81) drew frowns for sitting in on Jimmy Carter's cabinet meetings.

In general, the prominence and functions of the First Lady have followed the development of women's rights. In the nineteenth century, when all wives were expected to limit themselves to domestic matters, presidential wives stayed out of the limelight. But in the twentieth century they have increasingly played a more visible role in presidential administrations, which has attracted criticism that reflects a lingering suspicion of independent women. With staffs of their own, however, First Ladies today constitute a separate, although not independent, base of power in the White House. The extensive services they perform led Betty Ford and Rosalynn Carter to maintain that the office of First Lady ought to be a paid position.

See also Adams, Abigail; Roosevelt, Eleanor.

HENRY F. GRAFF

FITZGERALD, ELLA

(1918–   )   *Jazz singer.*

Born in Newport News, Virginia, and orphaned at an early age, Fitzgerald was raised in an orphanage in Yonkers, New York. A performance at the popular amateur night at Harlem's Apollo Theater in 1934 led to her discovery at the age of sixteen. The next year, she began singing with the Chick Webb Orchestra. Known for her improvisation, she used her voice like a musical instrument, leaving the melody of a song and returning to it in intricate melodic patterns. Fitzgerald's reputation was based on her ability as a "scat" singer who replaced the lyrics of a song with syllables more appropriate to her complex melodic improvisations.

After Chick Webb's death in 1939, Fitzgerald took over the leadership of his band until she started her solo career in 1942. In 1946, she began a long association with jazz promoter Norman Granz, who founded the Jazz at the Philharmonic concerts in Los Angeles. This professional relationship continued into the 1970s. In 1956, when Granz founded his own company, Verve Records, Fitzgerald joined him, recording many jazz and popular songs that appealed to a wide audience in the United States and abroad.

From 1948 to 1952 Fitzgerald sang in a small group led by her husband, bassist Ray Brown. Later in the 1950s and throughout the following decade, she appeared at jazz festivals throughout the world with such notable musicians as Count Basie, Duke Ellington, and Oscar Peterson. From 1953 to 1970 she was consistently voted the outstanding female jazz vocalist in *Down Beat* magazine's annual poll of its readers.

In 1971, Fitzgerald underwent eye surgery and had to reduce her performing and recording schedule somewhat. But she recovered quickly and appeared with the Boston Pops Orchestra in 1972. This concert led to engagements with most of the major symphony orchestras in the United States. She also made numerous television appearances in the 1970s and received a Grammy Award in 1980.

Fitzgerald is best known for her performances of songs with light or upbeat lyrics. Unsurpassed as an improviser and scat singer, she has influenced numerous contemporary popular singers with her vocal agility and interpretive grace.

See also Jazz; Music.

For further reading: Carolyn Wyman, *Ella Fitzgerald, Jazz Singer Supreme* (New York: Franklin Watts, 1993).

BARBARA L. TISCHLER

FITZGERALD, F. SCOTT

(1896–1940)   *Author.*

As if to make up for the shabby treatment he received during his lifetime, modern critics have been kind to Scott Fitzgerald. The attention he enjoys is out of proportion to the work he left behind. His reputation rests largely on one masterly novel, *The Great Gatsby* (1925), and a handful of short stories. American literature would be the less without them, but they lack the power of the work of his contemporaries, Ernest Hemingway and William Faulkner.

Among a talented generation of writers of the 1920s, Fitzgerald had perhaps the greatest natural gift, and he seemed blessed with every advantage: a good family, an excellent education, the profile of a matinee idol, and great personal charm. He married a beautiful, talented woman, Zelda Sayre, and quickly

The novelist F. Scott Fitzgerald with his wife, Zelda, and daughter, Scottie, in Paris. Their life-style became a symbol of the Jazz Age, which was characterized by wild parties, too much bathtub gin, and various other forms of excess. Nevertheless, he wrote several excellent novels, including his masterpiece, The Great Gatsby.

produced a best-seller, *This Side of Paradise* (1920), a novel of "flaming youth." With the profits from that book, he and Zelda moved to New York City, where they embarked upon a life as frantic and reckless as the lives portrayed in his fiction. In story after story he chronicled the Roaring Twenties, and the money rolled in.

Flushed with success, the Fitzgeralds moved to France and joined the hard-drinking, rootless colony of American and British writers and artists living there. Fitzgerald was torn between his wish to be a serious artist and his need to support his madcap life. He lost the battle. His drinking got out of control, and Zelda began to show alarming signs of mental illness.

After the Wall Street crash of 1929, the Fitzgeralds returned to the United States. The Roaring Twenties were finished and so were the Fitzgeralds. Zelda was placed in a mental hospital, and Scott struggled to earn a living in Hollywood. When he died of a heart attack in 1940, World War II had begun. The excesses of the Jazz Age, which Fitzgerald had taken so seriously, now seemed silly.

In his fine novel, *The Great Gatsby,* Fitzgerald brilliantly analyzed the forces of money and greed that were corrupting the American Dream. The spectacle of a man destroyed by the very society he exposed has proved irresistible to later writers. His story has been retold in a torrent of memoirs, biographies, critical studies, films, and plays. Fitzgerald's life has become a more powerful symbol of his times than anything he devised for his fictions.

See also Literature.

CHARLES BOHNER

FOOTBALL

The origins of American football can be traced to Europe in the Middle Ages when men, women, and children played a very rough game that historians call "folk football." When one village played folk football against another village a mile or two away, each side tried to kick, carry, or throw the ball through the doors of the other side's church. The contest was so wild that it often resembled a riot. But in the middle of the nine-teenth century, British schoolboys and university students agreed on rules that made this game safer and more orderly. The modern games of soccer, rugby, and American football all developed from these nineteenth-century rules.

Some historians say that the first game of American intercollegiate football was played on November 6, 1869, when Rutgers University defeated Princeton by a score of 6–4. That contest, however, was really a game of soccer. American football actually grew from a game of rugby played on May 15, 1874. On that day a Canadian team from McGill University in Montreal battled a team from Harvard to a scoreless tie. As Yale and other schools took up the game, the rules of rugby were modified by Walter Camp and others. Instead of continuous play, for instance, American football stops and starts as the offensive team tries repeatedly for a "first down." Another striking difference is the elaborate equipment worn by modern football players.

Success Brings Problems

By the end of the nineteenth century, American football, now very different from soccer and rugby, had become the most popular intercollegiate sport. Tens of thousands of students and alumni turned out to cheer their teams to victory. The "football weekend" became a part of collegiate life. But there were problems, too. Faculties and administrations struggled with students for control of the game, which had become very violent. Competition was so intense that many players were injured and some even killed. A number of schools dropped the sport; others decided that reform was needed. Led by President Henry MacCracken of New York University, a group of educators

The Stanford University football team of 1902 pose with their cheerleaders.

met in the winter of 1905–06 and formed the National Collegiate Athletic Association.

The NCAA's rules reduced the level of on-the-field violence, but they failed to solve another serious problem that continues to plague colleges and universities: how to be sure that student-athletes are really students as well as athletes. After decades of discussion, no one has the answer to that problem. Various reforms, like requiring players to make a minimum score on the Scholastic Aptitude Tests, have been ineffective. Still, only some people are bothered by the fact that many players merely pretend to be students. What matters for most is the excitement of the contest. In the twenties and thirties, collegians like Harold "Red" Grange of Illinois were heroes to millions who never went to college, and sports fans today continue to idolize great athletes.

For many years, professional football was less popular than the amateur game. The National Football League, founded in 1920, did not attract much attention until after World War II. One reason for the sport's postwar surge in popularity was that the owners decided to end racial segregation. In 1946, two African Americans—Kenny Washington and Woody Strode—joined the Los Angeles Rams. By the eighties, one-third of the entire NFL was composed of African-American players, many of whom were real stars. It is, however, still difficult for a black player to become his team's quarterback. Many suspect that the position is reserved for white players.

Television's Effect
In the sixties, television transformed the way that most fans experience football. Thousands wrap themselves in coats and scarves and cheer their team from the stands, but most spectators follow cold-weather games while seated before television sets in the com-

fort of their homes. Two men arranged for the happy marriage between network television and professional football: Roone Arledge, who worked for ABC television, and Alvin "Pete" Rozelle, the NFL's commissioner. The millions of dollars that television pays for the right to broadcast games makes the NFL's owners and players immensely wealthy; the millions of viewers who watch NFL football make corporate executives eager to buy spots for their advertisements. Networks now sign billion-dollar contracts with the NFL, and companies like IBM and General Motors pay more than $500,000 for a thirty-second Super Bowl commercial.

The huge sums of money available because of television changed the collegiate game, too. For many years, the NCAA signed lucrative contracts with the television networks and distributed the money among its member institutions. Some universities thought that they might do better financially if they made their own economic arrangements with the networks. The University of Georgia and several other schools sued the NCAA. In 1984, the Supreme Court ended the NCAA's monopoly and ruled that each school has the right to negotiate its own television contract.

The result of this decision was that the financial rewards of success have become greater than ever. Since success in intercollegiate sports is measured by the won-lost ratio, coaches are under tremendous pressure to produce winners. Many have been tempted to give scholarships to gifted athletes who are barely able to read and write. Many young athletes have been tempted to take anabolic steroids in order to gain the strength needed to win scholarships, become stars, and increase their chances for a career in the NFL. No one seems to have the answer to these problems.

In many regions, especially in the South, high school football also attracts tens of thousands of enthusiastic spectators. The interscholastic game has become as competitive as the collegiate and professional games. High school coaches, too, have begun to feel the pressure to win at almost any cost. Some have started to recruit promising athletes from outside their districts and to "red shirt"—that is, encourage athletes to spend an extra year in school in order to gain size and strength.

Despite the continual controversy over big-time sports, fans still scramble for season tickets to NCAA games, and the Super Bowl has become an important part of American culture. Football has never been played as well as it is today. For most fans, this—not the abuses of the sport—is what really counts.

See also Sports, Spectator.

ALLEN GUTTMANN

FORD, GERALD R.

(1913–) *Thirty-eighth president of the United States (1974–77).*

Ford, the first vice president to be appointed to the office, was the only one to succeed to the presidency because a president resigned. Raised in Grand Rapids, Michigan, Ford was a football star at the University of Michigan. He received a law degree at Yale and served in the navy during World War II. After returning to Grand Rapids, he ran for the House of Representatives in 1948 on the Republican ticket.

In the House, he became an expert on

defense and a fiscal conservative, voting against many antipoverty bills proposed by President Lyndon B. Johnson. Respected for his integrity, Ford served on the Warren Commission, which investigated the assassination of President John F. Kennedy in 1963. He was elected House minority leader in 1965.

Ford, a loyal party man, staunchly supported President Richard M. Nixon in the Watergate crisis when Nixon was accused of involvement in the burglary of the Democratic headquarters and its cover-up. Possibly because of this, Nixon appointed Ford to succeed Vice President Spiro Agnew when Agnew had to resign to avoid facing criminal charges.

When Nixon himself resigned, Ford became president on August 9, 1974. In his first speech to the nation, he reassured his fellow citizens: "Our long national nightmare is over. Our Constitution works. Our great republic is a government of laws and not of men." But a month later, he pardoned Nixon for any charges that might arise from the Watergate affair, an action that aroused a storm of nationwide protest.

As president, Ford faced the problems of inflation, recession, and unemployment. He was criticized for failing to develop a national energy policy. He vetoed dozens of spending bills but worked to improve relations with the Soviet Union and China. He won the 1976 Republican nomination for president, beating Ronald Reagan in a hard-fought campaign. But he lost the election to Jimmy Carter, the Democratic candidate.

See also Watergate.

For further reading: Sallie Randolph, *Gerald R. Ford, President* (New York: Walker and Company, 1987).

REBECCA LARSEN

FORD, HENRY

(1863–1947)   *Industrialist.*

Henry Ford did not invent the automobile. Instead, he developed ways to manufacture them so cheaply that he could sell them at prices the average wage earner could afford. As a result, Ford, perhaps more than any other single individual, invented the twentieth century.

Ford was born on a farm near Dearborn, Michigan. From his earliest days he displayed a marked mechanical aptitude, and all his life he delighted in working with machinery. In 1879 he went to work as an apprentice in a machine shop in Detroit while repairing watches at night to make ends meet.

In the early 1890s Ford began experimenting with the new internal combustion engine and in 1896 produced his first car, built by hand in the garage of his rented house. In 1903 he established the Ford Motor Company with $28,000 in capital provided by his partners. Successful from the first, the company became even more so when the famous Model T was introduced in 1908.

As Henry Ford continued to develop his ideas for making inexpensive cars—he introduced the assembly-line principle in 1913—the price of the Model T dropped steadily. In 1908 the company made 10,607 and sold them for $850 apiece. In 1917 it manufactured 730,041 Model T's, priced at $360 each. Originally owning only a quarter of the company, Ford by 1920 was the sole owner of one of the largest industrial enterprises on earth. By 1927, when the last of more than 15 million Model T's was produced, the company had not only distributed millions in earnings to its shareholders but still had nearly $700 million in profits in the bank, along with billions more invested in plant and equipment. Hen-

Henry Ford and his son Edsel pose in a Model F car in Detroit in 1905.

ry Ford became one of the richest men in the world.

In 1914, when factory workers were averaging about eleven dollars a week in pay, Ford announced that his workers would be paid five dollars for an eight-hour day. His purpose was not only to motivate his workers to endure the drudgery of the assembly line but also to bring their earnings up to where they could afford to buy his automobiles. The policy made Ford famous around the world, and it seemed for a time that he might have a political career.

Although he had been an industrial revolutionary, Ford became set in his ways in his later years. He refused to make changes in his production system, his automobiles, or his labor policies even when the need was clear. Finally, plummeting sales left him no choice but to shut down production of the Model T and retool to produce the new Model A. The other automobile companies, especially General Motors, took advantage of Ford's troubles, and his company never regained its place as the world's largest manufacturer of automobiles.

Henry Ford was a mechanical genius. But he was otherwise ignorant, narrow, and bigoted. He published many ugly anti-Semitic articles and fought unionization in every way he could, including hiring a private police force to intimidate the workers. Nor would Ford allow modern management methods to interfere with his autocratic ways. By the mid-1930s the company was deeply divided, and no one was really in charge. A decade later the Ford Motor Company, once the greatest engine of wealth creation in the American economy, was losing a million dollars a day and was on the brink of ruin.

In 1945, his family finally forced Ford to hand over control to his grandson, Henry Ford II, who rebuilt the company into the modern giant it is today. Two years later, Henry Ford died.

See also Automobiles.

JOHN STEELE GORDON

FOUR FREEDOMS

After the outbreak of World War II in 1939 and the rapid conquest of most of the western European democracies by the Nazis, concern about the future of free institutions increased rapidly in the United States. On the other hand, fear that the United States would become involved in the fighting also increased.

President Franklin D. Roosevelt was pulled in both directions by these contradictory attitudes, but by January 1941 he had decided to spell out his views on what freedom mean and why it is worth defending. In his annual State of the Union message to Congress he listed four "essential human freedoms" that must be guaranteed if a peaceful world order was to be restored and maintained. These were freedom of speech, freedom of religion, freedom from want, and freedom from fear of armed attack. Although he did not ask Congress to enter the war in order to safeguard these freedoms, he made it clear that the United States must do everything it could to prevent Germany from winning the war.

See also World War II.

4-H CLUBS

The 4-H Clubs are an organization of educational groups dedicated to practical learning through experience. The 4-H program was founded in the United States in 1900 by the Department of Agriculture to teach good farming techniques and home economics practices to rural youth. Its name, which was made official in 1924, derives from the members' vow: "I pledge my Head to clearer thinking, my Heart to greater loyalty, my Hands to larger service, and my Health to better living for my Club, my Community, my Country, and my World." The clubs' emblem is a four-leaf clover with an "H" on each leaf.

Originally open to people between the ages of nine and nineteen, membership has been extended in some states to those from five to twenty-one, and the program now includes activities in both rural and urban areas throughout the United States and its territories. In 1931 Canada organized a 4-H movement, and the idea has spread to some eighty other countries. The National 4-H Council in Chevy Chase, Maryland, sponsors international activities, including a youth exchange program.

Since the formation of the national Cooperative Extension Service in 1914, state universities and the U.S. Department of Agriculture have shared the sponsorship of the "learn-by-doing" programs of the 4-H Clubs. The National 4-H Service Committee, headquartered in Chicago, and the National 4-H Club Foundation, in Washington, D.C., are voluntary organizations which coordinate private support for local branches.

Now numbering over 5 million members in more than three thousand counties in the United States, the 4-H Clubs provide instruction in many subjects. In rural areas young people are trained in farming methods, livestock breeding, and the use of agricultural equipment; in cities and suburbs, they are taught automotive safety, electrical work, indoor gardening, and lawn maintenance. Instruction is offered in cooking, sewing, and housekeeping. Principles of self-reliance and respect for the environment and the community are stressed in all 4-H Club activities.

DENNIS WEPMAN

FOURTEEN POINTS

When President Woodrow Wilson asked Congress to declare war on Germany in April 1917, thus entering World War I, he insisted that the object was not to punish Germany. Instead, America's aims should be to obtain "peace and justice" and make the world "safe for democracy." In other words, he was suggesting that neither side was solely responsible for the war and that the only peace that would last would be one that was fair to both sides.

Then, in January 1918, he explained what he meant by a fair peace more specifically in a speech to Congress. His proposal had fourteen parts, or points. Many of these involved readjustments of the boundaries of European

nations so that most people could live under governments of their own choosing. Point XIII, for example, ran: "An independent Polish state should be erected which should include the territories inhabited by indisputably Polish populations." More generally the points called for an end to secret treaties, freedom of the seas in war as well as in peacetime, an end to restrictions on international trade, the drastic reduction of armaments, the management of colonies in ways that protected the interests of local peoples, and finally, the creation of "a general association of nations . . . for the purpose of affording mutual guarantees of political independence and territorial integrity to great and small states alike."

Some of these humane terms were achieved by the Versailles treaty ending the war, but many were not. This disappointed millions of liberals and led to much bitterness in the 1920s and 1930s.

See also Wilson, Woodrow; World War I.

FRANKFURTER, FELIX

(1882–1965)   *Associate justice, U.S. Supreme Court.*

Born in Vienna, Austria, Frankfurter immigrated to New York in 1894. Upon graduating from the Harvard Law School in 1906, he joined the U.S. attorney's office in New York, in part because, being Jewish, he had not received a job offer from any leading private law firm. Thus he began a lifetime of public service at all levels of government, which culminated in his becoming the first foreign-born American to serve on the Supreme Court.

Frankfurter taught at the Harvard Law School for twenty-five years beginning in 1914. Throughout this period he took part in the public debates of the day, including opposition to the red scare and suppression of civil liberties of political radicals in 1919–20. In 1927 he attacked the fairness of the Massachusetts trial that convicted two poor immigrant anarchists, Nicola Sacco and Bartolomeo Vanzetti, of murdering a payroll clerk. (They were executed.)

By 1933 Frankfurter had become a trusted adviser to Franklin D. Roosevelt, and he was one of the major architects of Roosevelt's New Deal. Roosevelt named Frankfurter to the Supreme Court in 1939 to succeed Benjamin Cardozo. Although there was some anti-Semitic opposition, the appointment was generally well received.

Frankfurter and other Roosevelt-appointed justices agreed that the increasing number of laws to regulate the economy being passed by Congress and many state legislatures was constitutional. They therefore reversed many previous decisions that had struck down such laws, saying that the Court should defer to the elected representatives of the people. These justices, however, began to disagree sharply about the role the Court should play in safeguarding the rights of unpopular minorities, especially in regard to such issues as freedom of speech and religion and criminal justice. Frankfurter disappointed many of his admirers by emphasizing his belief that the Court should also defer to legislatures in these areas, even when lawmakers restricted the civil liberties of individuals. In this view he was strongly challenged by Hugo Black, William O. Douglas, and others who thought the Court should play a more active role in protecting minorities and monitoring the fairness of the political process.

After suffering a stroke in 1962, Frankfurter resigned from the Court and died three years later.

See also Supreme Court.

SANFORD LEVINSON

FRANKLIN, BENJAMIN

(1706–90)   *Writer, scientist, inventor, politician, and diplomat.*

From printer's apprentice to world-famous scientist and a Founding Father of the new American nation, Franklin was one of America's first and most successful self-made men. His forthright character, inquisitive mind,

Benjamin Franklin at a printing press. He was apprenticed to his printer brother at age twelve, soon began writing essays, and went on to launch a newspaper and an almanac. But writing and publishing were only two of his remarkable talents. Franklin distinguished himself as a scientist, inventor, philosopher, politician, and diplomat.

ready wit, and driving energy served him well in whatever he chose to do. Born in Boston, he was the fifteenth of seventeen children of Josiah, a candlemaker (Josiah married twice). Although he had only two years of schooling, Franklin made himself into one of the most learned men of his century. He began work in his father's trade, but unhappy with it, he apprenticed himself to a brother who was a printer.

At seventeen Franklin left Boston to work as a printer in Philadelphia. There he founded a weekly newspaper, the *Philadelphia Gazette,* and a general store. He proved to be an adaptable and crafty businessman. At twenty-four, he married Deborah Read, a cheerful and hard-working woman who was of great help to him in his business. His *Gazette* became the best paper in the colonies, brightened by his humor and satire. He invented the character of Poor Richard, whose appearance for twenty-five years in *Poor Richard's Almanack* made it a national and international favorite.

Business was only a means for Franklin to reach other goals. He believed strongly in improving himself and just as much in improving the community. In Philadelphia he launched many social projects, including the first circulating library, a street cleaning system, a fire brigade, a police force, free elementary schools, a city hospital, and the University of Pennsylvania. He also advocated better education for women to prepare them for a more independent life.

At the same time, Franklin's curious mind was busy with scientific projects. He earned international fame and respect among scientists for his electrical experiments and for his many inventions, including the lightning rod, the Franklin stove, and the flexible catheter. But politics was already dominating his life.

He served the colony of Pennsylvania in several offices and the British government as postmaster general. His diplomatic career began with his negotiating Indian treaties and extended to London, England, where for ten years he served as Pennsylvania's agent. As the independence movement for the colonies developed, he spoke before Parliament, defending America's positions.

Home again when the Revolution broke out, Franklin served in the Continental Congress, taking on several tasks in defense and foreign affairs. He was on the committee for which Thomas Jefferson drafted the Declaration of Independence. When over seventy, he was sent to Paris to negotiate the treaty of alliance with France and later to make peace with Great Britain after the Revolution. In his last years he helped draft the Constitution of the new Republic and worked for its ratification by the states. Franklin died at the age of eighty-four, leaving behind a great heritage to his country.

See also Constitution, The Making of the; Continental Congresses; Declaration of Independence; Paris, Treaty of (1783); Revolution.

For further reading: Milton Meltzer, *Benjamin Franklin: The New American* (New York: Franklin Watts, 1988).

MILTON MELTZER

FREE BLACKS BEFORE EMANCIPATION

In 1860, half a million free people of African descent resided in the United States. They made up less than 2 percent of the nation's population and about 9 percent of all blacks. But they were important far beyond their numbers. They played a pivotal role in society during slave times and set precedents for both race relations and relations among black people when slavery ended. Their status and treatment were indications of what was to come after emancipation. Often the laws, attitudes, and institutions that victimized free blacks during the slave years—denial of the right to vote or hold office, segregation, and various forms of debt peonage—became the dominant modes of racial oppression after slavery ended. Similarly, their years of liberty influenced the pattern of black life after slavery. Many became leaders in black society. For example, nearly half of the twenty-two black men who served in Congress between 1869 and 1900 had been free before the Civil War.

Although free blacks have been described as more black than free, they were not all alike. By the nineteenth century three distinctive groups had emerged: one in the northern free states, a second in the Upper South, and a third in the Lower South. Each had its own economic and social characteristics. These differences, in turn, made for different relations with whites and slaves and, most important, distinctive modes of social behavior.

The North

In large measure, the northern free blacks— about half of the nation's total—were a product of the emancipations that followed the American Revolution. Before they were freed, they had lived mostly in the cities, were black in color, and unskilled in occupation. Northern free blacks followed the same pattern, becoming more urban and unskilled during the antebellum years, as they increasingly migrated to cities and found themselves pushed out of artisan trades by European immigrants.

Nevertheless, postrevolutionary emancipation allowed blacks certain rights. Because the abolition of slavery freed northern whites from the fear of slave revolts, they did not look upon every gathering of black people as the beginning of an insurrection. They allowed blacks to travel freely, organize their own institutions, publish newspapers, and petition and protest. Black men and women transformed these liberties into a powerful organizational and political tradition. From Richard Allen to Frederick Douglass, their primary mode of social action was organizing to protect themselves from the difficulties of living in a white world and to demand an end to slavery.

The Upper South

The free blacks in the Upper South were the product of two patterns of manumissions (someone releasing an individual he owns from slavery). The first and most important was the result of masters influenced by the ideology of the American Revolution: "all men are created equal." The second originated in personal relations between master and slave, an owner deciding to free someone simply because he or she was a favorite. The first produced a population that was largely rural and black in color. The second, to the extent it was selective (masters choosing whom they would free), produced a free black population that was more skilled and lighter in color than that of the North.

Skills and close ties with slave owners allowed Upper South free blacks to enjoy a higher economic standing than those in the North, but the presence of slavery severely limited their opportunities for political activism. Slaveholders, concerned that free blacks would stir up unrest among their slaves, not only prevented blacks from voting, sitting on juries, and testifying in court but also barred them from traveling without permission and holding meetings without the supervision of whites. No black newspapers were published and no black conventions met in the South. There were no southern free blacks like Allen or Douglass. Black churches, schools, and fraternal societies were fragile organizations, often forced to meet secretly.

The Lower South

The tendency toward economic advancement at the expense of political activism was present in an even more exaggerated form in the Lower South, particularly the port cities of Charleston, South Carolina, Mobile, Alabama, and New Orleans, Louisiana. Almost all free blacks in these areas were drawn from the small group of privileged slaves who had lived in close contact with their owners. Often they were the children of white masters. As a result, former slaves were overwhelmingly urban and light-skinned; they were called "free people of color."

Although comparatively few in number, they were far more skilled than free blacks in the Upper South. In some places, like Charleston and New Orleans, over three-quarters of the free men of color practiced skilled crafts, and they monopolized some trades. A handful of wealthy free people of color purchased slaves themselves and moved into the planter class. Still, they were denied the vote, could not hold public office, and allowed a political voice only through their white patrons. Their own organizations remained private, exclusive, and often shadowy, especially in comparison to the robust public institutions created by black people in the North. They dared not attack slavery or racial inequality publicly, lest they become identified with the slave. Rather, they saw

themselves—and increasingly came to be seen by whites—as a third caste, distinct from both free whites and enslaved blacks.

See also African Americans: to 1865; Allen, Richard; Banneker, Benjamin; Douglass, Frederick; Truth, Sojourner; Tubman, Harriet.

IRA BERLIN

FREEDMEN'S BUREAU

In March 1865, during the last stages of the Civil War, Congress established the Bureau of Refugees, Freedmen, and Abandoned Lands, commonly known as the Freedmen's Bureau. The purpose of the law was to provide food, housing, education, and medical care for freed blacks in areas of the Confederacy controlled by the U.S. Army. The law also authorized the bureau to distribute "abandoned" land to black families. The bureau, made part of the War Department, was headed by Gen. Oliver O. Howard.

After the war ended, the Freedmen's Bureau had the additional responsibility of protecting the blacks against exploitation by their former masters throughout the South. Aside from providing food and other assistance to homeless and destitute ex-slaves, the bureau, aided by northern private charitable organizations, set up nearly three thousand schools and a substantial number of colleges and teacher training institutions for the former slaves. It was, however, unable to obtain congressional support for turning over the property of former Confederates to black families.

In 1869 Congress put an end to all the bureau's activities other than education. Instead, it passed a Civil Rights Act that made blacks U.S. citizens and forbade the states to restrict the freedmen's civil rights. This policy was further confirmed by the Fourteenth Amendment to the Constitution.

See also Reconstruction.

FREEDOM OF SPEECH

Freedom of speech is the right to voice an opinion, no matter how unpopular, unpatriotic, misguided, or obnoxious it may sound. Freedom of speech is closely linked to freedom of the press. Both are protected by the First Amendment to the U.S. Constitution. Each is essential to democratic political liberty.

Origins of Freedom of Speech

Americans have not always enjoyed freedom of speech as we know it. Seventeenth-century colonists who criticized the English king or his New World governors or dissented from a colony's established (official) religion might be fined, jailed, or exiled. But slowly, laws restricting free speech were relaxed. By the 1770s, when the Revolution began, most Americans felt that people had the right to express their opinions freely. So certain were the Founding Fathers that freedom of speech is an unquestionable right of citizenship that they decided it was unnecessary to provide for it specifically in the Constitution they wrote in 1789.

That decision troubled the state lawmakers who had to ratify (approve) the Constitution before it could take effect. After some debate, they agreed to ratify, but only on condition that the document be amended to guarantee freedom of speech and other individual liberties. It was. According to the First Amendment of the Bill of Rights adopted in 1791, "Congress shall make no law . . . abridging the freedom of speech."

Yet seven years later Congress did exactly that. The Alien and Sedition Acts of 1798 made it illegal to "print, utter, or publish" anything critical of the government or its president, John Adams. These laws—which represented an attempt by Adams and his supporters to silence their political opponents—led to several arrests and convictions, including that of a congressman. After Adams lost the 1800 election, the laws expired. Not until this century did freedom of speech reemerge as an important legal issue.

A Clear and Present Danger?

In 1917, the United States entered World War I. Seeking to ensure wartime patriotism and loyalty, Congress made it a crime to criticize the United States, its government, Constitution, flag, or armed forces. Congress also made it illegal to urge men to resist being drafted into the army.

Two years later, Charles Schenck, a man convicted of the last offense, appealed his case to the Supreme Court, which decides whether laws are valid under the Constitution. Schenck argued that the law under which he had been convicted was invalid because it violated his First Amendment right to express his antidraft convictions freely. The Court disagreed, upholding Schenck's conviction. Since the United States had been at war when Schenck urged draft resistance, wrote Justice Oliver Wendell Holmes, his words had posed a "clear and present [immediate] danger" to the nation.

Although this decision was a defeat for free speech, Holmes's "clear and present danger" standard later became the basis for *extending* Americans' First Amendment rights. That is because Holmes implied that had the country not been at war, Schenck's protest *would* have been legal.

.

In fact, the Court eventually decided that the danger must be clearer and even more immediate than Holmes had suggested in order to justify free speech restrictions. During World War II, for example, the Court upheld the right of Americans to criticize the government and its war policies. And though the Court ruled in 1951 that the First Amendment does not protect someone who advocates the violent overthrow of the U.S. government, it reversed itself just six years later. The 1957 ruling held that only if a call to rebellion is accompanied by the urging of a specific lawless action, such as assassinating the president, may it be forbidden. Decisions related to religious preaching established free speech rights even for those whose words may annoy or offend others.

During the 1960s and 1970s, the Court continued to broaden First Amendment protections. In cases involving activists in the civil rights movement and people protesting U.S. involvement in the Vietnam War, the justices repeatedly found in favor of the dissenters. As they saw it, verbal dissent, however provocative, is less dangerous to democracy than restricting speech would be. Even protest actions like burning the American flag or tearing up a copy of the Constitution amount to "symbolic speech" and are therefore protected under the First Amendment, the Court has ruled.

Free Speech Issues Today

The American right to freedom of speech is not absolute. Slandering someone—saying untrue or damaging things about him or her—can be a punishable offense. Inciting someone to commit murder, assault, arson, or other crimes is itself a crime. And some First Amendment issues remain unresolved. For instance, to what extent is so-called hate speech protected by the Constitution? Is it permissible to shout insults at members of particular ethnic groups? To express unflattering opinions about supposed racial characteristics in a classroom or during a public debate? What about advertising and free speech? Do cigarette companies have a First Amendment right to promote their potentially deadly products to children and teenagers? Can a television station or other media outlet refuse to accept certain kinds of political or commercial messages or be forced to accept them?

See also Alien and Sedition Acts; Bill of Rights; Freedom of the Press.

For further reading: Ann E. Weiss, *We Will Be Heard: Dissent in the United States* (New York: Messner, 1972).

ANN E. WEISS

FREEDOM OF THE PRESS

Freedom of the press has been treasured by Americans since before the American Revolution. In 1735, a German immigrant named John Peter Zenger was put on trial for printing a harsh attack on the governor of the colony of New York. Zenger's attorney, Andrew Hamilton, argued that what Zenger had published was true. He pleaded with the jury to lay a "noble foundation for securing to ourselves, our posterity and our neighbors . . . the liberty, both of exposing and opposing arbitrary power by speaking and writing truth." The jury did just that. By acquitting Zenger, it established the principle of press freedom that has stood as a foundation of our liberties ever since.

The men who wrote the U.S. Constitution were keenly aware of the vital role the press had played in their revolution against the British government. What's more, they were suspicious of *any* government, even the one they were creating themselves. They believed that people in a democracy would need an uninhibited press, not merely to describe events but also to keep the government honest. It would be up to the press to criticize the government and to expose the inevitable mistakes and occasional corruptions of public officials. For that reason, they made sure that press freedom was guaranteed by the First Amendment to the Constitution. In a real sense, then, the right of freedom of the press is not for the benefit of journalists but for the good of the people.

Limitations on Press Freedom

The general principle of press freedom applies to all media. Yet the federal government places certain restrictions on radio and television stations that it cannot legally place on newspapers, books, and other printed material. Disk jockeys, for example, are not allowed to use very vulgar or obscene language. Television stations are required to devote a certain amount of time to educational programming. Defenders of absolute press freedom argue that these special restrictions are unconstitutional. So far, however, the courts have upheld them, on the ground that since the airwaves over which the stations broadcast belong to the public, the stations can be licensed and regulated.

Even the print media are not free to publish anything at all with no risk of consequences. The Supreme Court has established three major exceptions to the press's constitutional right to publish whatever it wants. The first is libel: a lie that deliberately damages a person's reputation. Anyone who publishes a libelous statement can be sued for damages, although the courts have made it hard for anyone already in the public eye to win a suit for libel.

The second limitation on press freedom forbids obscenity, or what is sometimes called hard-core pornography. The courts have trouble defining the difference between what is obscene and what is merely sexy. Although Supreme Court Justice Potter Stewart couldn't explain exactly what makes pornography pornographic, he still insisted that, "I know it when I see it."

Finally, the press is not free to publish anything that creates what Justice Oliver Wendell Holmes called a "clear and present danger," either to individuals or to society. Examples might be a published call to murder a public official or to blow up a government building.

Attacks on Press Freedom

Even the First Amendment has not been powerful enough to protect the press in all circumstances. As early as 1798, the Federalists who controlled Congress passed the Sedition Act, which made it a crime to publish anything that criticized the government. Several journalists were actually thrown into prison under the act; when Thomas Jefferson became president he pardoned them.

The rights of the press have come under attack many times since, particularly in times of national crisis. During World War I, for example, the federal government shut down several German-language American newspapers and jailed some of their editors. During the Vietnam War, the government tried to prevent the *New York Times* from publishing a secret government report known as the Pentagon Papers. In that case, the U.S. Supreme Court ruled that such "prior restraint" (or censorship in advance) was almost never acceptable.

But even when such efforts to censor the press fail, they can have what is called a "chilling" effect, causing some journalists to be more cautious. Hoping to avoid greater censorship by the government, the press often censors itself.

See also Bill of Rights; Freedom of Speech; Pentagon Papers; *Zenger* Trial.

For further reading: Nat Hentoff, *The First Freedom: The Tumultuous History of Free Speech in America* (New York: Delacorte, 1988).

MICHAEL KRONENWETTER

FREEDOM RIDES

Southern resistance to desegregation even after the Supreme Court declared it illegal in *Brown* v. *Board of Education* and other cases led various civil rights groups to move actively to compel southern whites to obey the law. In May 1961 black and white members of the Congress of Racial Equality (CORE) chartered two buses and traveled through the South to test the effectiveness of a 1960 Supreme Court decision that prohibited racial

In May 1961, an interracial group of Freedom Riders traveled through the South on interstate buses to test the enforcement of a federal desegregation law in the bathrooms, waiting rooms, and restaurants of bus terminals. Southern racists reacted violently. In Alabama a white mob attacked the Freedom Riders, setting their bus on fire and beating the passengers as they escaped the burning vehicle. Here injured Freedom Riders survey their charred bus.

segregation in bus station restrooms, waiting rooms, and restaurants.

In Anniston, Alabama, one of these buses was set on fire. Later, in Birmingham and again in Montgomery, Alabama, the Freedom Riders were assaulted and badly beaten while police looked on. But news of these attacks spurred about a thousand other opponents of segregation to tour the South during that summer. Many of these riders deliberately sought to be arrested by local authorities in order to test segregationist laws in the courts. The movement greatly speeded the desegregation of public facilities in the South.

See also Civil Rights Movement

FREEPORT DOCTRINE

In July 1858, Abraham Lincoln, the Republican candidate for U.S. senator from Illinois, challenged his Democratic opponent Senator Stephen A. Douglas, to a series of seven debates on the issues of the campaign. These Lincoln-Douglas debates were both of enormous historical importance and outstanding examples of political oratory. The physical appearance and conflicting styles of the two candidates helped voters distinguish between them. Lincoln was tall, thin, and deliberate, Douglas short, plump, and dynamic. More important, they discussed the vital issues of the day intelligently and at length.

The best known of these debates occurred on August 27 in the town of Freeport, in the northwestern part of Illinois. Douglas had repeatedly argued in favor of popular sovereignty—that the future of slavery in the western territories should be left to the actual settlers. At Freeport, Lincoln asked him how

they could do so now that the Supreme Court in the *Dred Scott* case had decided that slave owners had the right to bring their slaves anywhere.

Douglas answered with what became known as the Freeport Doctrine. The white settlers of a territory, he argued, could keep out slaves merely by doing nothing. If the territorial legislature refused to pass local laws keeping black people in bondage, slaves could simply walk away and a so-called owner would have no legal way to restrain them. "Slavery cannot exist . . . unless it is supported by local police regulations," he said.

Douglas's argument probably won him the senatorial election. But it killed any chance of his winning southern support in his campaign for the Democratic presidential nomination in 1860.

See also Douglas, Stephen A.; Lincoln, Abraham; Popular Sovereignty.

FREE-SOIL PARTY

The Free-Soil Party was formed in 1848 by abolitionist supporters of the former Liberty Party and the "Barnburner" wing of the Democratic Party. The Barnburners were radicals, so named because they were said to be willing to "burn down the barn to get rid of the rats." They refused to back the Democratic presidential candidate, Lewis Cass, in part because he had failed to support President Martin Van Buren's bid for renomination at the 1844 Democratic convention.

The Free-Soil Party platform did not call for the abolition of slavery. But it did call for banning slavery from all of the territories. Since Lewis Cass favored popular sovereignty, the policy of leaving the future of slavery in the territories to the people who settled there, neither the abolitionists nor the Barnburners could stomach him.

The party nominated Martin Van Buren for president and Charles Francis Adams, a son of John Quincy Adams, for vice president. They polled fewer than 300,000 votes. The party did elect twelve congressmen, however. It fielded candidates again in 1852 and then passed out of existence. The vast majority of its supporters shifted to the new Republican Party.

See also Abolitionist Movement.

FRÉMONT, JOHN C.

(1813–90) *Explorer, military officer, and political leader.*

Born in Savannah, Georgia, Frémont was the son of a French immigrant father and an American mother. Because he made extensive explorations of the American West and produced accurate maps of that region, he became widely known as "The Pathfinder."

Frémont's career as an explorer began shortly after 1838 when he was commissioned a second lieutenant in the U.S. Army Corps of Topographical Engineers. In 1841, he married Jessie Benton, the daughter of Missouri senator Thomas Hart Benton. She became an author and helped her husband write reports on Indian tribes, western mountain passes, weather and soil conditions, and their adventures on the trail.

Frémont's first major expedition occurred in 1842, when he explored the Oregon Trail as far as Wyoming, with Kit Carson serving as his guide. His second expedition, in 1843–44, pushed farther west, reaching the Columbia River and then moving southward through Nevada and over the mountains into California. On his third expedition, in 1845–47, Fré-

mont helped free California from Mexican rule. Reports of his exciting achievements made The Pathfinder a national hero.

When California became a state in 1850, Frémont was elected to serve as one of its first U.S. senators. In 1856, the newly formed Republican Party nominated him for president. Since the party was opposed to the extension of slavery, Frémont's name was not on the ballot in southern states. But he still ran a strong race: he lost the presidency to Democrat James Buchanan by only sixty electoral votes.

When the Civil War began in 1861, President Abraham Lincoln gave Frémont command of the Union forces in St. Louis, Missouri, with the rank of major general. Without consulting the president, Frémont ordered the confiscation of property owned by Missouri slaveholders and the release of their slaves. Lincoln was angry at Frémont for taking this action and transferred him to western Virginia. Later, Frémont served from 1878 to 1883 as territorial governor of Arizona.

See also Republican Party.

EDMUND LINDOP

FRENCH AND INDIAN WAR
See Seven Years' War.

FRIEDAN, BETTY

(1921–) *Feminist, author, and activist.*

After distinguishing herself academically and working as a reporter, Betty Friedan (pronounced Free-*dan*) put a halt to her ambitions and chose a role widely considered the ideal for middle-class women in the 1950s: she married, left her full-time job, and became a housewife in the suburbs. But although Friedan believed in the "feminine mystique"—the notion that becoming the perfect wife and mother was the key to happiness—life as a suburban housewife struck her as empty.

Friedan began interviewing other women and discovered that a great many were also disillusioned. They wondered why men were encouraged to pursue creativity, power, wealth, and intellect, whereas women, no matter how smart or talented, were expected to be content with the narrow world of the household. In 1963 Friedan published *The Feminine Mystique,* which identified "the problem without a name." It opens with this passage:

> The problem lay buried, unspoken, for many years in the minds of American women. It was a strange stirring, a sense of dissatisfaction, a yearning that women suffered in the middle of the twentieth century in the United States. Each suburban wife struggled with it alone. As she made the beds, shopped for groceries, matched her slipcover material, ate peanut butter sandwiches with her children . . . lay beside her husband at night—she was afraid to ask even of herself the silent question—"Is this all?"

The book struck a chord with women everywhere and became an instant bestseller. So influential was *The Feminine Mystique* that it is credited with sparking the second wave of the feminist movement. The first wave had focused on gaining women the right to vote. But after women's suffrage was achieved in 1920, the movement lost its momentum. Four decades later, *The Feminine Mystique* again jarred women awake to the inequality between the sexes.

Friedan became one of the women's rights movement's chief activists. In 1966 she helped found the National Organization for Women

(NOW), the largest mainstream women's rights group in the country, and became its first president. She led NOW in the fight for the Equal Rights Amendment and for legalized abortion.

Friedan revised some of her earlier views in *The Second Stage* (1981), arguing that she had underestimated the value of the family. The book made her unpopular with more radical feminists. In *The Fountain of Age* (1993) she discusses age discrimination, a problem common among older women. In all her work Friedan has fought against the confining roles imposed upon women, urging them to pursue the more challenging and gratifying lives that have long been the privilege of men.

See also Feminist Movement since 1919; National Organization for Women.

B O R G N A   B R U N N E R

F R O N T I E R   L I F E
See Pioneers and Frontier Life.

F R O S T ,   R O B E R T
(1874–1963)   *Poet.*

For many years regarded as "the dean of American poets," Robert Frost was more specifically the voice of New England. His deceptively simple poems, written in blank verse or with traditional rhymes and metrical form, are easily understood. They capture the natural rhythm of direct speech, yet convey powerful feelings and often complex and subtle ideas.

The son of a newspaper editor whose family had been New Englanders for nine generations, Frost was born in San Francisco but moved to Massachusetts when his father died in 1885. An indifferent student, he dropped out of college after a few months and lived by odd jobs for several years. From an early age he wrote poetry, but it was seldom accepted for publication. In 1894 his family persuaded him to try college again, and he spent two unproductive years at Harvard studying classics. Then his grandfather bought him a farm in New Hampshire, where he made a bare living while still writing poems in his spare time.

In 1912 Frost sold his farm and went to England with his wife and two children in hopes of finding a wider audience for his poetry. In London he was encouraged by other poets, including the American Ezra Pound, and published his first collection, *A Boy's Will*, in 1913. Though it sold poorly, it was well reviewed. His second collection, published the next year, was more popular, and he returned to the United States in 1915 an established poet.

For the rest of his life he farmed, occasionally taught, and continued to write, earning Pulitzer Prizes in 1924, 1930, 1936, and 1942. His lyrics, character studies, and dramatic monologues always contain the same economic language, dry New England flavor, and controlled emotion that characterize his earliest work. His unusual combination of simplicity and philosophical depth brought him both critical and popular success. Such memorable poems as "Birches," "The Road Not Taken," and "Stopping by Woods on a Snowy Evening" have become classics in American literature.

See also Literature.

For further reading: Lucas Longo, *Robert Frost: 20th Century Modern American Poet Laureate* (Charlottesville, N.Y.: Sam-Har Press, 1972).

DENNIS WEPMAN

FTC
See Federal Trade Commission.

FUGITIVE SLAVE LAW

Although the word *slave* does not appear in the Constitution, that document included a provision for recapturing fugitives. Article IV stated that a "person held to Service or Labour in one State . . . escaping into another . . . shall be delivered up on Claim of the Party to whom such Service or Labour shall be due." Congress put teeth in this provision by passing the Fugitive Slave Act of 1793.

When opposition to slavery began to increase in the North in the mid-nineteenth century, however, many northern state legislatures passed personal liberty laws that made it difficult for slave owners to obtain the return of escaped slaves. Therefore, as part of the Compromise of 1850, Congress passed a law designed to prevent northern governments from making the recovery of slaves difficult. Under this law a professional slave catcher bearing only a sworn statement by the supposed owner could cause a black person in the North to be arrested and after a simple hearing carried south into slavery. A black—even if wrongly held to be a fugitive slave—could not testify in his or her own defense. "In no trial or hearing," the law went on, "shall the testimony of such alleged fugitive be admitted in evidence." Federal officials could even force private citizens who were personally opposed to slavery to "aid and assist in the . . . execution of this law" by helping to hunt down suspected fugitives.

The obviously unfair aspects of this law turned many northerners into abolitionists.

See also Slavery.

FULLER, MARGARET

(1810–50)   *Author and feminist.*

The dominant memory that Margaret Fuller retained of her childhood was that it was filled with "glooms and terrors." She was the first of Mary and Timothy Fuller's nine children. Her father, disappointed that she was not a boy, nevertheless insisted on her receiving a rigorous masculine education from the time she was a toddler. Thus, she grew up intellectually mature beyond her years, but having to cope with a child's sensibilities and emotions.

Fuller left home in Cambridgeport, Massachusetts, to attend school in Groton, Connecticut, and Cambridge, thereafter supporting herself as a teacher. Attracted to the philosophy of transcendentalism, Fuller was a member of a New England transcendentalist group, which held what were called "Conversations," or discussions on philosophy, reform, religion, and the human condition. From 1840 to 1842 she also edited Ralph Waldo Emerson's radical literary magazine, *The Dial.*

In 1844, Fuller moved to New York to pursue a writing career. The next year, she published *Woman in the Nineteenth Century,* which is a classic discussion of American feminism. Fuller wrote on and off as a critic and contributor for the *New York Tribune,* and in 1846 the newspaper sent her to Europe as its foreign correspondent, an extraordinary position for a woman then.

While in Rome, Fuller entered into a relationship with Giovanni Ossoli, a member of the nobility. A son was born in 1848, the same year the two became active in the Italian revolution. When Rome fell to invading French troops in 1849, Ossoli and Fuller, fearing persecution, fled to Florence and then boarded a ship bound for the United States. The couple may have been married before leaving Italy. Fuller carried with her a manuscript she planned to publish, but tragically they never reached America. On July 19, 1850, their ship broke up in a storm off Fire Island, New York. Fuller, Ossoli, and their son all drowned.

See also Feminist Movement to 1919.

CHRISTINE A. LUNARDINI

FULTON, ROBERT

(1765–1815)   *Engineer.*

Although Fulton is often said to have invented the steamboat, he actually did not. Rather he designed and built the first commercially successful one. Indeed, Fulton's genius lay not in original ideas but in putting the ideas of others to practical use.

Fulton, born in New Britain, Pennsylvania, early showed a marked mechanical and artistic aptitude. He learned the art of gunsmithing before being apprenticed to a Philadelphia jeweler. In 1785 he went into business for himself as a "miniature painter and hair worker" (today we would say wig maker). He set off for England in 1786 to study art, but soon abandoned it for engineering.

After moving to France, Fulton submitted plans in 1797 for a submarine by which, he argued, France could overcome Britain's naval supremacy. He built the *Nautilus* in 1800, and it worked better than previous attempts, although many of its features were borrowed from the earlier work of David Bushnell. But France rejected the idea.

Fulton then turned his energies to steamboats, and with financing from Robert Livingston, the American minister to Paris, he built one in 1803 that operated on the Seine River. The following year the British government invited him to return and experiment there. The British soon lost interest, however, and Fulton returned to the United States.

Livingston had also returned by that time, and the pair ordered a boat to be powered by a twenty-eight-horsepower Watt steam engine. It was launched on August 9, 1807. On August 17 the boat traveled from New York City to Albany in thirty-two hours, far faster than sailing vessels could make the trip.

The vessel, now remembered as the *Cler-* *mont*, was rebuilt the following year. Fulton and Livingston built several other steamboats for the Hudson River as well as ferries to connect Manhattan with New Jersey and Long Island. Fulton also designed the first steamboat to operate on the Mississippi River.

His last major project was a floating fortress for New York Harbor. It was launched shortly before the end of the War of 1812, but never saw action.

See also Science and Technology.

JOHN STEELE GORDON

A replica of Robert Fulton's famous steamboat, the Clermont. *Fulton did not invent the steamboat, but he improved upon earlier models and built the first commercially successful one.*

G

GADSDEN PURCHASE

In 1853 the American minister to Mexico, James Gadsden, negotiated a treaty with Mexico in which Mexico sold a strip of land south of the Gila River along the southern boundary of what is now Arizona and New Mexico to the United States for $10 million. Several complicated issues were involved, but the most significant by far was the interest of American railroad promoters, one of whom was Gadsden himself. The area offered a relatively easy passage through the Rocky Mountains. Some decades after the purchase the Southern Pacific Railroad was built through the region.

The treaty, ratified in 1854, was the last acquisition of land to become part of the continental United States.

See also Expansion, Territorial; *and map on p. 288.*

GAG RULE

During the 1830s and 1840s, northern abolitionist groups deluged Congress with large numbers of antislavery petitions, in particular petitions calling for the abolition of slavery in the District of Columbia, where Congress had the constitutional authority to do so. No one could question their right to petition Congress, since the First Amendment to the Constitution plainly guarantees "the right of the people . . . to petition the Government for a redress of grievances."

For some years both houses of Congress simply voted to reject these petitions. But southern members of the House of Representatives became increasingly angry. They felt (with some reason) that the petitioners were more interested in annoying and shaming slaveholders than in actually trying to change the representatives' minds. In 1836 they persuaded a majority of the House to adopt a *gag rule*. Thereafter all petitions critical of slavery were automatically "laid on the table." That is, they were discarded without debate and without a vote.

The gag rule outraged John Quincy Adams, who served in the House for many years after his term as president. He persisted in submitting antislavery petitions by the dozens. "I hold the [gag] resolution to be a direct violation of the Constitution," he said. Finally, this obviously correct argument carried the day. In 1844, the gag rule was repealed.

See also Abolitionist Movement; Adams, John Quincy; Bill of Rights.

GAMES AND TOYS

Games and toys existed in ancient Egypt as long ago as 1570 B.C. They have always reflected the attitudes of adults toward the role of children as well as society's social customs, current events, and manufacturing ability.

Native Americans such as Eskimo boys owned small harpoons and future Indian braves had little bows with which they could learn to shoot as their fathers did. One of the earliest surviving toys brought by Europeans to this country is a wooden doll that William Penn carried to Pennsylvania in 1699.

Colonial life was hard. Children worked and devoted themselves to religion at an early age, leaving little time for play. But by the late eighteenth century there was more leisure time, and they occupied themselves with hoops, stilts, balls, tops, and whistles, mostly imported from Europe. But between 1820 and 1870 the Northeast and Mid-Atlantic states were industrializing. The techniques for producing goods, including toys, in mass quantities were being developed.

Materials Used

Early makers of wooden toys included William Tower of Massachusetts who manufactured sand toys, which taught the child about mechanization, and the Charles M. Crandall family in Pennsylvania, who produced interlocking alphabet blocks in the form of figures, thus combining amusement and instruction. American manufacturers excelled in cast iron, a material ideally suited for mass production. The molten material was poured into metal molds, and when hardened the finished toys were painted by hand. Companies like J. and E. Stevens of Connecticut produced stationary (still) and mechanical (movable) banks, guns, and bell toys.

Another material widely used for playthings during this era was paper. Around 1858 the firm of McLoughlin Brothers was the leading publisher of games, blocks, books, and dolls printed with color lithography. Board games using dice or cards to move counters were expected to be educational.

Many featured maps and were based on history and geography or provided religious or moral instruction.

Other toys were cut or stamped out from thin sheets of steel, covered with tin, soldered together, and painted or stenciled by hand; these were produced in the 1840s. Connecticut firms manufactured tin-plate toys using motors made by clockmaking firms to create some of the first mechanical playthings in America. Another new material that was popular about 1850 was vulcanized rubber, invented by Charles Goodyear. Still other companies made air balls (squeak toys, which when squeezed blew air out through a whistle) and the first all-rubber dolls.

Turn-of-the-Century Toys

The golden age of toy manufacture in America was from about 1870 to 1920 when, with new mass production techniques, large quantities of toys could be cheaply made, and more money was available to spend on luxuries. Transportation toys such as horse-drawn carts, carriages, and wagons, steam-driven and electric trains, and cars, trucks, and firefighting equipment were popular. This is not surprising given the transportation advances of those years: railways were expanding rapidly by the 1860s, and automobiles originated in the late 1800s.

Optical toys that demonstrated the latest scientific principles were popular family entertainment. These included kaleidoscopes containing pieces of colored glass that when rotated fell into patterns reflected by mirrors; zoetropes, which produced a moving picture show on paper; and magic lanterns, the forerunners of the modern slide projector. Lead soldiers and wooden dollhouses covered with lithographed paper were preferred miniature toys for boys and girls. Important manufacturers during this period included Lionel, Milton Bradley, Hubley, and Bliss.

A decrease in the birthrate and the rise of the kindergarten movement after the turn of the century caused people to pay more attention to children after World War I. The Fisher-Price Company's wooden animals that made a noise when pulled were highly popular with very young children. An emphasis on toys imitating adult activities resulted in all kinds of "housekeeping" equipment, including miniature washing and sewing machines, refrigerators, stoves, ironing boards, brooms, and carpet sweepers. Construction toys like A. C. Gilbert's erector set, reflecting the new interest in skyscrapers, imitated the framework of structural steel buildings.

With the widespread use of radio, the telegraph, and the telephone, news traveled fast. Manufacturers found an eager market for games and toys reflecting the events of the day such as Teddy Roosevelt's African safari and Charles Lindbergh's flight across the Atlantic. Movies, radio shows, and comics also inspired toys. Major companies like Louis Marx produced inexpensive tin-plate wind-up characters representing Popeye, Mickey Mouse, L'il Abner, and Amos and Andy.

Post–World War II Toys

The post-1940s cold war society produced truckloads of hi-tech toys made of plastic and vinyl, and increases in disposable income prompted a burst of consumerism. Girls trained to believe in the importance of learning to be attractive, good mothers, and efficient housewives were given Mattel's Barbie doll with accessories, Kenner's ovens, and Milton Bradley's shopping games. Boys' games centered on defeating enemies and conquering frontiers in the Wild West, outer space, or behind the iron curtain. Their

world was peopled with cowboys and Indians, astronauts and aliens from space, and G.I. Joes and Russian spies. With the end of the arms race in the 1990s, the "enemy" became more generalized, appearing in electronic form in home video games like Atari, Pac-Man, and Sega.

See also Childhood and Adolescence; Family Life.

For further reading: Linda Baker, *Modern Toys, 1930–1980* (Paducah, Ky.: Collector Books, 1991).

JEAN M. BURKS

GARFIELD, JAMES A.

(1831–81)   *Twentieth president of the United States (1881).*

Garfield was the last president to be born in a log cabin and from such humble beginnings, worked his way through Williams College to become a teacher and preacher. During the Civil War, he fought for the Union, seeing action at Shiloh and Chickamauga.

In 1863, Garfield was elected to Congress as a Republican, representing a district in Ohio, and served for the next seventeen years. He was respected as a morally upright and capable leader despite being linked to the Crédit Mobilier scandal of 1873. (He had accepted a bribe of $329 to grant favors to a company completing construction of the nation's first transcontinental railroad.) In 1874, he became Speaker of the House of Representatives, the most powerful post in Congress.

Although Garfield was elected to the Senate in 1880, he never took his seat. Instead, he became the Republican Party's compromise presidential nominee on the thirty-sixth ballot, breaking a deadlock among three other candidates. He defeated his Democratic opponent, Winfield Scott Hancock, by only

9,464 popular votes. His mother, who attended the inauguration, was the first woman to see her son sworn in as president.

Garfield was expected to remove a number of government jobs from the control of politicians by setting up a professional civil service. He had already managed to outmaneuver Senator Roscoe Conkling of New York, a political boss, by naming his archrival to an important government post. On July 2, 1881, however, Charles J. Guiteau, a supporter of Conkling, shot the president in a Washington train station, seriously wounding him. Since Congress was not then in session, members of the cabinet debated whether Vice President Chester A. Arthur should serve as acting president or be sworn in as president. They had not solved the problem by the time Garfield died on September 19. He had been president for only 200 days.

BARBARA SILBERDICK FEINBERG

GARRISON, WILLIAM LLOYD

(1805–79) *Abolitionist leader and journalist.*

Born into a poor family in Newburyport, Massachusetts, Garrison was apprenticed to a printer at the age of thirteen. After learning the printing trade, he became a competent journalist and editor. In 1828, he met Benjamin Lundy, a Quaker and outspoken advocate of the abolition of slavery. Garrison became an ardent abolitionist and helped Lundy write and edit an antislavery newspaper. His articles attacking slave traders led to a libel lawsuit that he lost in court, and he was jailed for seven months.

In 1831, Garrison began publishing the *Liberator* in Boston. It became the leading abolitionist newspaper and at times aroused violent reaction from people who claimed that the abolitionists were fanatics intent on destroying the Union over the issue of freeing the slaves. In Boston, once, an angry mob put a rope around Garrison's neck and threatened to lynch him.

Despite his fierce denunciation of slavery, Garrison was a pacifist who believed that the emancipation of African Americans should be accomplished by nonviolent means. Declaring that slavery was a sin in God's sight, he appealed to the conscience of Americans to put an end to this degrading institution. He helped found the American Anti-Slavery Society in 1833, but his insistence that women be equal participants in the society caused a division among its male members. Garrison felt that the North should secede from the Union because it permitted slavery and called for adopting a doctrine of "No Union with Slaveholders." In 1854 he publicly burned a copy of the U.S. Constitution, proclaiming, "So perish all compromises with tyranny!"

After the Civil War began, it became evident that large numbers of Northerners considered freeing the slaves a major war aim, and he fully supported the Northern cause in spite of his pacifism. In 1865, when the Thirteenth Amendment abolished slavery, Garrison rejoiced that his long-sought goal had finally been achieved. He then ceased publication of the *Liberator* and resigned from the American Anti-Slavery Society.

See also Abolitionist Movement.

EDMUND LINDOP

GARVEY, MARCUS

(1887–1940) *Black nationalist.*

Garvey was born and reared in Jamaica, a British colony in the West Indies. Although he received some elementary education, his

appreciation for reading and writing was primarily a result of his attending Sunday school and his reading books owned by his father. At the age of fourteen Garvey left school and became an apprentice to a local printer.

As Garvey grew older he became increasingly concerned about the poor living conditions that prevailed in Jamaica. He moved to Kingston, Jamaica's capital city, where he participated in debates, organized and supported worker strikes, and joined political reform groups. In 1909, he began to travel in foreign countries, earning a living by working at odd jobs. He was disturbed by the poor conditions of workers in the countries he visited.

After returning to Jamaica in 1914, Garvey founded the Universal Negro Improvement and Conservation Association and African Communities' League, popularly referred to as the UNIA. Its primary purpose was to form a United States of Africa for peoples of African descent. Garvey believed blacks needed their own nation in order to gain the respect of the world. The UNIA attracted a large following in the United States and abroad.

The UNIA's strongest branch was in New York City, which became its headquarters in 1917. A weekly paper, the *Negro World*, was established there and served as the UNIA's voice. Garvey also founded several companies owned and run by blacks, including the Black Star Steamship Line.

Garvey had many critics who mounted campaigns against the UNIA. They attacked his Black Star shipping company on the ground that Garvey had used it to cheat stockholders. In 1922 he was arrested, tried, and convicted. He was imprisoned in New York in 1923 and later transferred to the Atlanta penitentiary. Garvey's prison sentence was commuted by President Calvin Coolidge on November 18, 1927. He was then deported

Marcus Garvey, founder of the Universal Negro Improvement Association, promoted black pride and advocated a black nationalist "back to Africa" policy. Garvey was a charismatic speaker and exhibited a flair for the dramatic, often wearing a plumed hat and braided uniform, and traveling by limousine.

from the United States as an undesirable alien.

After leaving the United States, Garvey spent most of his time traveling between Jamaica and London. He continued his work with the UNIA and founded the School of African Philosophy in Toronto. Today, Garvey is best remembered for his back-to-Africa movement and for the slogan "Africa for the Africans."

See also African Americans: 1877–1945.

LAYN SAINT-LOUIS

GENTLEMEN'S AGREEMENT

The Chinese Exclusion Act of 1882 did not put an end to the migration of all Asians to the United States or to West Coast prejudice against Asian immigration. In the early 1900s slowly increasing numbers of Japanese and Korean laborers came to California. Local resentment of the willingness of the newcomers to work for low wages resulted in discrimination. The worst example of this occurred in 1906 when the San Francisco school board began segregating Asian children by sending them to a separate school.

The Japanese government protested this act to President Theodore Roosevelt. He responded by inviting the school board and the mayor of San Francisco to Washington and persuading them to end segregation. In return Roosevelt promised that no more Japanese laborers would be coming to America. He accomplished this by entering into the Gentlemen's Agreement with the Japanese government in 1907. The United States did not officially exclude Japanese immigrants. But Japan promised not to issue passports to laborers intending to come to the United States.

See also Chinese Exclusion Act; Immigration.

GEORGE, HENRY

(1839–97) *Economist and social reformer.*

As a sixteen-year-old youth, Henry George sailed to India and Australia from Philadelphia, the city of his birth. He returned the next year and worked for a short time as a newspaper typesetter. Then he set out for California, took part in the gold rush in British Columbia, Canada, in 1859, and held a series of newspaper jobs in San Francisco. George was distressed by the abject poverty he had seen in India and the greedy land grabbing going on in California. On a trip to New York City in 1869, he was troubled by the sharp contrast between the lives of the wealthy few and the huge mass of poor workers.

George decided to investigate a serious economic problem that plagued the United States after the Civil War: he wanted to learn why the Industrial Revolution, which was constantly generating new machinery for producing wealth, seemed unable to raise the living standards of millions of people. He concluded that the chief reason for this unfortunate situation was that many property owners kept their land unused while waiting for a rise in its value. To solve this problem, George urged that a "single tax" be imposed on land value—a tax based not on *existing* value but on *potential* value if the land were developed and used efficiently. There then would be no profit in keeping land unused and undeveloped. George believed that using land to its fullest extent would help promote widespread prosperity.

George first expressed his theories in 1871 in a pamphlet called *Our Land and Land Policy*. His masterpiece, *Progress and Poverty* (1879), became a very important book. It sold more than 3 million copies and influenced thinking about the uneven distribution of wealth, both in the United States and abroad. Single-tax movements sprang up, and George became a popular speaker throughout the country and in the British Isles. He ran for mayor of New York City in 1886. He drew more votes than Theodore Roosevelt, the Republican candidate, but narrowly lost to Abram S. Hewitt, the Democratic nominee. When the champion of the single tax died,

about 100,000 Americans filed past his casket in New York City to pay tribute to him.

EDMUND LINDOP

GERMAN AMERICANS

The first Germans to migrate to America were the so-called Pennsylvania Dutch, who arrived in the 1680s. Many of their descendants still maintain their distinctive rural way of life. By 1760 more than half the people of Pennsylvania were of German origin.

After 1815 hundreds of thousands more Germans came to America. Most were small farmers forced off their land by the competition of more efficient producers, or artisans displaced by unskilled workers in the new factories, turning out more cheaply the objects they had made by hand. A number of German liberals came to America in the 1850s to escape persecution in their native land.

Many German immigrants settled in the West where land was cheap. Most were Catholics, and they tended to join the Democratic Party. Though that was the party of slavery in the nineteenth century, most Germans supported the Union during the Civil War. Their best-known political leader was Carl Schurz, who immigrated in 1852. Schurz rose to the rank of brigadier general in the Union army and later served in the Senate and as secretary of the interior. Among important German business leaders was Jacob Schiff, who came to America in 1865 and later headed the banking house of Kuhn, Loeb & Co.

Late in the century many German-speaking Jews immigrated to the United States, most of them settling in the cities. Some of this group were anarchists, which caused many people to turn against all the newcom-

ers. These hostile feelings peaked during and after World War I when the United States fought Germany. The teaching of German was banned in many schools, and symphony orchestras refused to play music by German composers. People with German names were frequently persecuted even though nearly all of them were loyal citizens.

During World War II, however, this did not occur, in part because most Americans of German background were outspoken enemies of the Nazis. Many distinguished German Jews managed to escape to America during the war, among them the physicist Albert Einstein. All told, about 7 million Germans have immigrated to America. In general they have adjusted easily to American ways and have contributed much to the nation's culture.

See also Immigration.

JOHN A. GARRATY

GERONIMO

(182?–1909)   *Native American warrior and leader.*

For a thousand years the Apache Indians freely roamed the American Southwest. The Chiricahua Apache group often camped beside the Gila River in present-day Arizona. Sometime in the 1820s a baby was born there named Goyakla, meaning "One Who Yawns." The yawning child would become famous by his Spanish nickname, Geronimo.

When Mexican soldiers murdered his first wife and three small children in 1858, Geronimo vowed revenge. Through the 1860s he led many bloody raiding parties into Mexico. Then in the 1870s American miners and ranchers began claiming Apache lands. The U.S. government expected the Apaches to

A 1907 photograph of the Apache Indian chief Geronimo by Edward Curtis. Mexican soldiers killed his mother, wife, and three small children. Later, the U.S. government forced his people to live on a barren reservation away from their homeland. Geronimo dedicated his life to fighting these two enemies. His legendary resistance is reflected in the famous battle cry used by generations of American soldiers: "Geronimo!"

On May 17, 1885, Geronimo and over one hundred other Chiricahuas fled the Turkey Creek Reservation. They dashed southward, stealing horses and killing dozens of settlers. To capture Geronimo, Gen. Nelson Miles assembled five thousand soldiers. Although he eluded them for months, Geronimo finally surrendered in September 1886. "I will quit the warpath," he promised, "and live in peace hereafter." The last of the Apache wars had ended.

For eight years Geronimo was imprisoned at Fort Pickens, Florida, and Mount Vernon Barracks, Alabama. In 1893 the government transferred the Chiricahua Apaches to the grassy plains around Fort Sill, Oklahoma. At national expositions, such as the St. Louis World's Fair in 1904, Geronimo sold autographed pictures of himself. In 1905 the old Apache rode in President Theodore Roosevelt's inaugural parade. Americans marveled at the stories of Geronimo's bravery and fighting spirit. By the time of his death in 1909, he had become a national folk hero.

See also Indian-White Relations.

For further reading: Zachary Kent, *The Story of Geronimo* (Chicago: Childrens Press, 1989).

ZACHARY KENT

adopt the white man's way of life on reservations. The Chiricahua Apaches were crowded onto the dry, treeless plains of Arizona's San Carlos Reservation. Geronimo refused to accept this treatment, and in 1877 and 1881 he led other Chiricahua Apaches south into the Sierra Madre mountains. On both occasions Gen. George Crook chased down Geronimo and his followers and forced them to surrender.

GERRYMANDER

This term was coined in Massachusetts in 1812, during the administration of Governor Elbridge Gerry, a Jeffersonian Democratic-Republican. That party had a majority in the state legislature. To improve the party's chances in an upcoming election, they redrew the boundaries of the districts from which the members of the legislature were elected in ways designed to give their party an

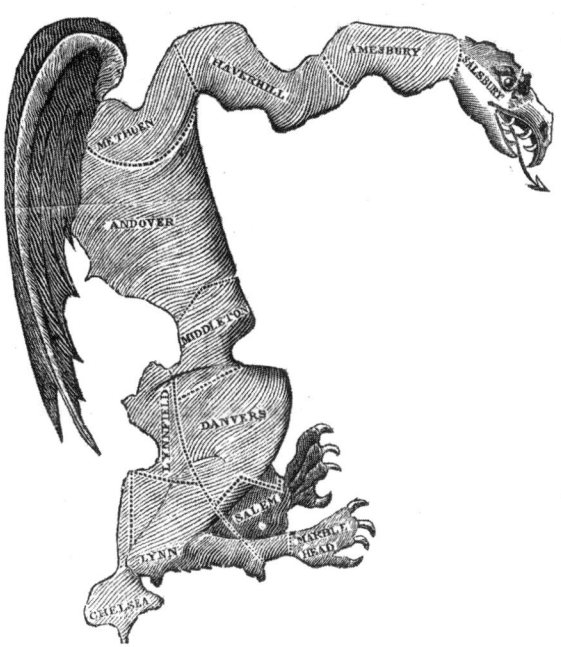

The original cartoon of a gerrymander. *The term was a combination of Massachusetts governor Elbridge Gerry's last name and the word* salamander, *which is what an electoral district in the state looked like after politicians in his party had redrawn it to their political advantage in 1812. Ironically, Gerry had nothing to do with it.*

advantage. This was done, for example, either by splitting regions where opposition Federalists were concentrated or by getting as many Federalists as possible into a single district.

As a result, many of the new districts had highly irregular shapes. Commenting on this, a Federalist newspaper published a cartoon making the district look like a salamander. The cartoonist called it a "gerry-mander," and the political tactic of manipulating district boundaries has ever since been known as *gerrymandering* (although Governor Gerry himself actually had had nothing to do with it).

In recent years, the courts have tended to

declare the practice illegal, except in cases where the purpose is to make sure that particular minorities obtain a fair percentage of seats in lawmaking bodies.

GERSHWIN, GEORGE

(1898–1937)   *Composer.*

Gershwin's music transformed blues and jazz rhythms of the 1920s and 1930s into popular songs, show tunes, movie scores, and symphonic pieces that still delight audiences today.

The son of Russian immigrants, Gershwin left high school at age fifteen to work as a pianist for a music publisher. Six years later, in 1919, he composed the hit song "Swanee" and his first musical comedy score, *La La Lucille*. With his talented older brother, Ira, as his lyricist, Gershwin went on to write many successful shows, including *Lady Be Good* (1924), *Oh Kay!* (1926), and *Girl Crazy* (1930), with such timeless songs as "Embraceable You," "S'Wonderful," and "I Got Rhythm." *Of Thee I Sing* (1931), which spoofed presidential campaigns, became the first Broadway musical to win a Pulitzer Prize. To keep up with their busy schedule, the Gershwins sometimes took tunes discarded from one show and rewrote them for new productions.

As a serious composer, George Gershwin introduced jazz and blues to symphonic music with his *Rhapsody in Blue* (1924). Having forgotten about the assignment, he dashed it off at the last minute, but he always worked best under the pressure of deadlines. At the *Rhapsody*'s premiere, he performed the piano solo himself. He enjoyed playing his own works in public and for family and friends at parties. Among his other concert pieces is *An American in Paris* (1928), written during one of his many trips to Europe. It turned French taxi horns into jazz instruments. Gershwin's memorable *Porgy and Bess* (1935), a folk opera about southern blacks, made use of authentic African-American rhythms he had heard in South Carolina.

In Hollywood, the Gershwin brothers wrote four film scores, featuring such classic songs as "They All Laughed," "A Foggy Day," and "Love Is Here to Stay." George did not like California as much as Ira did. He was making plans to return to New York to work on new projects when he died of a brain tumor at age thirty-eight.

See also Music.

BARBARA SILBERDICK FEINBERG

GETTY, JOHN PAUL

(1892–1976)   *Oil company executive.*

Regarded as the richest American of his time, J. Paul Getty was born to wealth but increased his fortunes enormously during his long lifetime. The son of a Minneapolis lawyer who bought a small Oklahoma oil company in 1902, he attended Oxford University in England and two American universities, working summers in his father's oil fields. After graduating he went into business drilling for oil in new locations and made his first million at the age of twenty-three. He inherited his father's oil business, valued at $15 million, in 1930.

Although many great American fortunes were lost during the Depression, Getty's grew much larger. Taking advantage of the unusual amount of cash he had available when money was scarce, he bought controlling interests in many other oil companies during the early 1930s, acquiring control of the Tidewater,

Skelly, and Mission corporations and creating an important network of domestic and overseas operations. By continued shrewd investments, he added agriculture, chemical plants, and gold, uranium, and copper mines to his enterprises. By the 1950s, the value of his holdings was estimated at over $1 billion.

Getty was known for both the splendor of his life-style and his often petty personal cheapness. He lived in a sixteenth-century manor house, Sutton Place, with seventy-three rooms, near London, England, and gave parties said to cost millions of dollars. But he installed pay telephones in his home and was careful about small expenses. His main extravagance was collecting art. In 1954 he built the Getty Museum on his estate in Malibu, California, to house his collection of Greek and Roman antiquities. When he died, he left the museum more than $700 million with which it has acquired many valuable Renaissance paintings and built an important collection of French decorative art and furniture. The value of the endowment has now grown to over $3 billion, making it the richest museum in the world.

DENNIS WEPMAN

GETTYSBURG ADDRESS

This speech was given by President Abraham Lincoln on November 19, 1863, at a ceremony dedicating the cemetery where soldiers killed at the Battle of Gettysburg on July 1–3 were buried. The main speaker on that occasion was Edward Everett, a former secretary of state and governor of Massachusetts, and a famous orator. Lincoln's far more famous remarks are brief enough to be quoted in full:

The opening of the Gettysburg Address in Abraham Lincoln's handwriting. Lincoln wrote six copies of the address; five are known to survive.

Four score and seven years ago our fathers brought forth on this continent, a new nation, conceived in liberty, and dedicated to the proposition that all men are created equal.

Now we are engaged in a great civil war, testing whether that nation or any nation so conceived and so dedicated, can long endure. We are met on a great battle-field of that war. We have come to dedicate a portion of that field, as a final resting place for those who here gave their lives that that nation might live. It is altogether fitting and proper that we should do this.

But, in a larger sense, we can not dedicate—we can not consecrate—we can not hallow—this ground. The brave men, living and dead, who struggled here, have consecrated it, far above our poor power to add or detract. The world will little note, nor long remember what we say here, but it can never forget what they did here. It is for us the living, rather, to be dedicated here to the unfinished work which they who fought here have thus far so nobly advanced. It is rather for us to be here dedicated to the great task remaining before us—that from these honored dead we take increased devotion to that cause for which they gave the last full measure of devotion—that we here highly resolve that these dead shall not have died in vain—that this nation, under God, shall have a new birth of freedom—and that government of the people, by the people, for the people, shall not perish from the earth.

There is no truth to the story that Lincoln wrote the address on the back of an envelope while riding to Gettysburg on a train from Washington. He planned it carefully and revised the text more than once. But because he spoke so briefly and so simply on this solemn occasion, the original reaction of some to the speech was unfavorable. Before long, however, its greatness was widely recognized. In these few words he summarized the reasons for fighting the Civil War: to guarantee that the principles outlined in the Declaration of Independence, individual freedom and democracy, would "not perish from the earth."

See also Civil War; Lincoln, Abraham.

GHETTOS

Urban ghettos—places of concentrated and nearly exclusive African-American residential and institutional life—are relatively recent creations. Until the twentieth century, the black population of the United States had been overwhelmingly located in the South. Southern cities, consequently, had the largest African-American populations, but nowhere did they develop what could be called "ghettos." Scattered neighborhoods still sprinkled with white residents housed most of the black urban dwellers. True ghettos emerged in two stages, the first between 1880 and 1930, and a second extending from 1940 to at least 1970.

Forming of Ghettos

After 1880, the movement of blacks from farms to cities and from the South to the North and West sparked the rapid growth of concentrated black neighborhoods. The demand for unskilled labor in northern cities around World War I particularly lured African-American migrants. The Great Migration of southern blacks that brought hundreds of thousands to the North in the war years (1914–18) continued through the 1920s.

World War II, the mechanization of southern agriculture, and a postwar economic boom later provided even stronger incentives for movement. Between 1940 and 1970 nearly 5 million blacks left the South; where 77 percent of all blacks lived in the South on the eve of World War II, only 53 percent did so thirty years later. This regional shift accompanied black urbanization. In 1880 only 12.9 percent of African Americans lived in cities; by 1950 a majority did, and by 1960 blacks were more highly urbanized than whites.

Economic limitations and cultural factors were partly responsible for blacks having to live in the same areas. But white hostility was the main reason. Racially restrictive covenants (contracts that prohibited the sale of property to blacks), banks that refused to make mortgage loans to blacks, and white protests and violence when a black tried to move into a "white" neighborhood restrained the freedom of blacks to live where they wished. By the late 1920s, well-defined ghettos such as Chicago's South Side "Black Belt"

and New York's Harlem dotted the cities. Other ghettos, such as Chicago's West Side and New York's Bedford-Stuyvesant, developed later. Smaller cities developed their black neighborhoods more slowly.

Beginning in the 1930s, the federal government contributed to the forming of ghettos. It supported discriminatory practices by the Federal Housing Administration (F H A) and, in the 1950s and 1960s, its slum clearance, urban renewal, public housing, and highway construction programs all encouraged whites to move to the suburbs. Those same programs practically guaranteed that blacks would remain locked in economically weakened central cities.

Paradoxically, the federal government also took steps to overcome racial barriers. The U.S. Supreme Court ruled in 1948 that restrictive covenants could not be enforced, and in 1962 President John F. Kennedy issued an executive order that partially banned discrimination in federally supported housing programs. The Civil Rights Act of 1964 and the Fair Housing Act of 1968 made racial discrimination in virtually all housing illegal, but by that time neighborhood patterns had been set.

Impact of Ghettos

The creation of substantial segregated urban black communities gave rise to new economic, social, political, and intellectual forces within those communities. Most visible, particularly to outsiders, have been the concentrated poverty, crime, and violence that have erupted into riots periodically from the 1960s into the 1990s. Members of the growing black middle class often fled the grim conditions in the poorest areas, further weakening those neighborhoods and leaving them even more exposed to high unemployment, the activities of drug dealers, and an escalating cycle of destructive violence.

On the other hand, ghettos have led to increased black power movements and creativity. The New York ghetto made possible the Harlem Renaissance, the literary and artistic flowering among black New York society in the 1920s. Ideologically, movements for self-help, race pride, and black nationalism found a natural home in the ghettos. The militant "New Negro" of the World War I era, Marcus Garvey's Universal Negro Improvement Association, and black newspapers such as the *Chicago Defender* and the *Pittsburgh Courier* were all nourished by concentrated bases of black people. Churches, fraternal groups, labor unions, and civil rights organizations drew on similar support and helped advance the civil rights revolution of the 1950s and 1960s. Most notably, the ghettos have provided a political base for a growing number of black officeholders, including representatives in Congress, mayors, and others at the local level. None of this, however, has succeeded in resolving the difficult problems that called forth protest in the first place.

The "ghetto" concept has also been used to describe the experience of European ethnics—such as Jews, the Irish, and Italians—as they crowded the industrial centers of the Northeast and Midwest in the era of mass immigration (1880–1920), as well as more recent concentrations of Hispanics and Asians. The degree of racial isolation, however, the historical record of restriction, and the relative permanence of the barriers facing African Americans all argue that the ghettos of white ethnics, Hispanics, and Asians were fundamentally different from those that remain associated with urban black America.

See also African Americans; Black Nationalism; Harlem Renaissance; Housing; Racism; Segregation.

For further reading: Alex Kotlowitz, *There Are No Children Here: The Story of Two Boys Growing Up in the Other America* (New York: Doubleday, 1991).

ARNOLD R. HIRSCH

G.I. BILL

During World War II, while American soldiers and sailors were risking their lives on distant battlefields, millions of civilian workers were earning excellent wages and living safely at home. In an effort to compensate servicemen and servicewomen for their sacrifices, in 1944 Congress passed the Servicemen's Adjustment Act, commonly known as the G.I. bill. Besides funding the construction of veterans' hospitals and making low-interest loans available to veterans seeking to buy homes or start new businesses, the law gave those who wished to attend college, a vocational training school, or other educational institution money to cover their tuition and living expenses. Later the law was extended to cover veterans of the Korean War.

Because of the G.I. bill the percentage of college graduates increased more rapidly between 1945 and 1950 than at any period before or since. By 1956 nearly 10 million veterans had taken advantage of the law's various educational provisions. By 1962, when the loan provision was ended, these and other veterans had received insured loans amounting to more than $50 billion.

GILMAN, CHARLOTTE PERKINS

(1860–1935)   *Feminist and author.*

A leading spokesperson for the women's rights movement at the turn of the century,

Gilman was one of the most influential writers and speakers of her time. Born into a prominent New England family of intellectuals, she learned firsthand of the financial oppression of women. She was raised by an overworked mother when her father abandoned the family. Although twice married, Gilman had to support herself for much of her life at a time when women were excluded from most well-paying jobs. In her many books, articles, poems, and lectures, she spoke out eloquently against the economic dependence of women. The noted suffragist Carrie Chapman Catt described her as "the most original and challenging mind which the movement produced."

Her best-known book, *Women and Economics,* published in 1898, established Gilman as a major theorist of feminism. From 1909 to 1916 she edited and wrote the *Forerunner,* a monthly magazine devoted to equal rights for women. In it she published her most important novel, *Herland,* a fantasy about a feminist utopia, in which she continued her attack on "domestic enslavement" and the submissive role imposed on women in our society.

Gilman did not see herself as a writer of fiction, and her novels and stories are essentially dramatizations of her feminist ideas. Nevertheless her autobiographical short story "The Yellow Wallpaper" (1892) has become a classic. A fictionalized account of a nervous breakdown she suffered, it is a terrifying narrative of an overprotected woman's decline into insanity. In symbolic form, the story movingly presents Gilman's lifelong protest against the enforced idleness and dependence of middle-class women.

See also Feminist Movement to 1919; Literature.

DENNIS WEPMAN

GINSBERG, ALLEN

(1926–)   *Poet.*

Ginsberg was a key figure in the "Beat generation" of American writers, which emerged in the 1950s. These men and women rejected the customs and values of the society around them. Their work also frequently reflected the "beat" of jazz music.

Allen Ginsberg grew up in Paterson, New Jersey, where his father taught high school English. His mother, an ardent communist, died in a psychiatric hospital. Ginsberg later

The beat poet Allen Ginsberg in 1967, perched above a crowd, chanting a poem. His most famous poem, Howl, *adopted the rhythms and spontaneity of ordinary speech and chronicled a crazed dream world of drugs and outcasts. From Ginsberg's perspective this was more desirable than the stuffy world of strait-laced America, obsessed with manners and money.*

mourned her in his moving poem "Kaddish" (1959).

After graduating from Columbia University in 1948, Ginsberg shipped out on merchant vessels, mopped floors in a cafeteria, and years later, had a successful stint as a market researcher. While working at these jobs, he read and wrote poetry. His first published work, a long poem entitled *Howl*, appeared in 1956. *Howl* is a cry of outrage against post–World War II American society, which Ginsberg felt was obsessed with money, machinery, and war. He celebrated rebellion through drugs, drink, homosexuality, and the Buddhist religion.

During the 1960s, he read his poetry on college campuses across the country. Ginsberg became an important symbol for young people who were distressed over the war in Vietnam and disenchanted with society in general. But his travels in India deepened Ginsberg's understanding of Buddhism, and his poems increasingly reflected a love for all living things. In the 1970s, his work earned wider recognition for its literary value. *Fall of America* won the National Book Award in 1974. Eventually the rebel poet became a professor of English at Brooklyn College.

In his poetry, Ginsberg used long, flowing lines with the rhythms of everyday speech. "America," considered one of his best works, ends with the lines:

> It's true I don't want to join the Army or turn lathes in precision parts factories, I'm nearsighted and psychopathic anyway.
> America I'm putting my queer shoulder to the wheel.

See also Literature.

DEBORAH KENT

GINSBURG, RUTH BADER

(1933–   ) *Supreme Court justice.*

In 1960 Supreme Court Justice Felix Frankfurter was asked to consider hiring Ruth Bader Ginsburg as one of his law clerks. Her qualifications were first-rate: she had attended both Harvard and Columbia law schools and served on the law review of both, an honor that normally guaranteed a student a distinguished career in law. She had tied for first place in her graduating class, and, as an undergraduate classmate put it, she was "scary smart." Justice Frankfurter, however, refused to interview her, acknowledging that he was just not ready to hire a woman. Three decades later, this woman deemed unsuitable as a law clerk for the Supreme Court became one of its nine justices.

Since childhood Ginsburg had been told that females should not, and could not, excel in areas slated for men. As a girl she was discouraged from becoming a lawyer, and while attending Harvard Law School a dean questioned why she and the handful of other women students were taking up classroom space traditionally reserved for men. And despite her place at the top of her law school class, not a single law firm would hire her upon graduation. She later wrote that to work as a lawyer in the fifties and "to be a woman, a Jew, and a mother to boot—that combination was a bit too much."

Eventually Ginsburg became a clerk for a U.S. district judge and taught law, becoming the first female tenured professor at Columbia School of Law. She then became a judge on the U.S. Court of Appeals, a position she held until President Bill Clinton appointed her to the Supreme Court in 1993, making her the second woman to serve on the nation's highest court.

Much of the impressive legal career that earned Ginsburg's appointment to the Court involved sex discrimination cases. She argued six such cases before the Supreme Court, winning five, each significantly advancing women's legal rights. Ginsburg opposed laws that treated men and women differently, even if these laws benefited women: "It is not *women's* liberation," she once explained, "it is women's *and men's* liberation" that she was after.

Ginsburg is known for her independent thinking. Although a strong advocate of women's rights, her opinions have sometimes angered feminists; a pioneering liberal, she has not been afraid to express conservative views. Her independence and integrity continued to surface during her early tenure on the Supreme Court.

See also Supreme Court.

BORGNA BRUNNER

GIRL SCOUTS
See Scouting.

GLENN, JOHN

(1921–   )   *Astronaut and senator.*

"The view is tremendous, it is a beautiful— a beautiful sight." John Glenn spoke those words on February 20, 1962, from a space capsule called *Friendship 7.* He was more than one hundred miles above the earth, flying at speeds greater than seventeen thousand miles per hour. Excited Americans crowded around television sets, following every detail of his flight.

Early in Glenn's mission the spacecraft's automatic pilot system malfunctioned, forc-

ing him to steer the ship manually. This was not an overwhelming problem for Glenn. He had been a marine pilot in World War II and in Korea, and was regarded as one of the country's finest aviators. A far greater danger emerged when *Friendship 7's* heat shield jarred loose. Loss of the heat shield could have caused the spacecraft to burn up like a meteor as soon as it encountered earth's atmosphere. But Glenn's skillful flying allowed him to splash down safely in the Caribbean Sea. His mission had lasted four hours and fifty-five minutes. He had completed three earth orbits, witnessed four sunsets, and traveled a total of 75,679 miles. As the first American astronaut to achieve earth orbit, he became an instant American hero.

Astronaut John Glenn poses in front of the space capsule Friendship 7 *in 1962, after becoming the first American to orbit the earth.*

In 1974 Glenn, who was born in Ohio, was elected senator by the people of that state. He drafted the 1978 Nuclear Nonproliferation Act, which prohibited the overseas sale of equipment that could be used to make atomic bombs. In 1983 he announced he was a candidate for president. But he withdrew after he failed to win any of the primary races he entered.

Despite his years as a politician, most Americans still think of Glenn first as a space pioneer. Manned space flight was new in 1962. The entire country felt a sense of wonder as Glenn made an eight-minute dash the length of the United States and said, "I can see the whole state of Florida laid out just like a map. It's beautiful."

See also Space Program.

R. CONRAD STEIN

Emma Goldman, anarchist and feminist, was the most famous rebel of her time.

GOLDMAN, EMMA

(1869–1940)   *Political activist and lecturer.*

Goldman was one of the fieriest political and social rebels to sweep through American history. For many years, she fought for a better life for all people. She was born in Kovno, Lithuania, to Orthodox Jewish parents. Her childhood was plagued by poverty and religious persecution. These harsh conditions, along with her early exposure to radical ideas that challenged prevailing notions of how people should live and work, converted Goldman into a rebel.

In 1885, Goldman immigrated to the United States. In New York City, a breeding ground of new ideas, her true life began, she said. By day she worked in a garment factory and in the evenings attended political meetings and made speeches. Goldman had become an anarchist, and she met leading exponents of anarchism, including Alexander Berkman, her lover and lifelong friend.

Goldman defined anarchism as "the spirit of revolt, in whatever form, against everything that hinders human growth." She opposed centrally organized governments, organized religion, private property, and traditional morality. She envisioned a society composed of small local communities in which people shared resources and freely expressed their opinions, no matter how unpopular.

She gave impassioned speeches across the nation to promote her views. From 1906 to 1917, she published *Mother Earth,* a journal of anarchist ideas and other unconventional views. She urged women to use birth control—a practice that was then against the law. Three times, "Red Emma," as she was called, was imprisoned for her beliefs.

In 1919, the U.S. government deported Goldman, Berkman, and other immigrant radicals to Russia on suspicion that they were planning to overthrow the government. Disillusioned by the new Communist regime, Goldman and Berkman moved to Germany and then France. Barred from returning to the United States, she supported Spanish anarchists in their political struggles. She died in 1940 during a visit to Canada. Courageous and uncompromising, she had devoted her life to the fight for social justice.

For further reading: David Waldstreicher, *Emma Goldman* (New York: Chelsea House, 1990).

HARRIET SIGERMAN

GOLD RUSHES

Gold had been mined in North Carolina in 1799 and in Georgia in 1828, but the amounts were small compared with the tremendous deposits discovered in America's West.

The famous California gold rush began in January 1848, when a nugget no bigger than a dime was found in the Sacramento valley on land owned by a Swiss immigrant, John Sutter. Sutter's workmen quit their jobs, headed for the hills, and found more gold. News of their finds reached San Francisco, which was a small town at that time. Doctors, lawyers, soldiers, sailors, bakers, blacksmiths, laborers—even the mayor and the sheriff—set out to prospect for gold. Many were successful and hit pay dirt. By the end of 1848, the mania called "gold fever" had infected people up and down the West Coast. It reached South America and crossed the Pacific to Hawaii, Australia, and Asia. Thou-

sands crowded aboard ships that carried fortune seekers to California's shores.

Not many Americans living east of the Mississippi River joined the great gold rush during 1848. Newspaper stories about successful miners sounded like tall tales, and people were skeptical. In 1849, however, after receiving reports and seeing samples of gold from the West Coast, President James K. Polk told the nation that California's earth truly held fabulous riches. As a result of the president's pronouncement, a raging epidemic of gold fever spread throughout the United States. Ships carried the news to Europe and motivated many there to travel to the Wild West.

Getting to the West

Thousands, called "forty-niners," rushed to California. Going by sea seemed easier and safer than trudging through wilderness and over mountains. Easterners living near the Atlantic Ocean chose to voyage around the southern tip of South America, even though it was a fifteen-thousand-mile trip that took at least six months and sometimes a year. (The Panama Canal cutting through Central America hadn't been built yet.) There were well-run, seaworthy vessels for those who could afford to pay the price. But broken-down fishing boats, merchant ships, any dirty old tub that could float, set sail crammed with passengers. Bad food and putrid water resulted in sickness. Rounding Cape Horn at the tip of South America in rough waters caused countless shipwrecks.

People who wanted to avoid the long Cape Horn voyage tried shorter routes that were supposed to take no more than six weeks. They sailed to the east coast of Panama, Nicaragua, or Mexico. Then they made their way across country to the Pacific Coast, where

A gold prospector in Alaska.

they boarded another ship to San Francisco. Here, too, filth, foul food, and cramped space on ships caused much suffering. Disease, terrifying terrain, and unfriendly natives made the overland trips ordeals for many travelers. Upon reaching Pacific Coast ports, gold seekers frequently had to wait for months before they found space on a vessel sailing north to California.

While people in the East clamored to board ships, those in the Midwest chose overland routes. St. Joseph, Missouri, Independence, Missouri, and other frontier towns were jumping-off points where fortune seekers could stock up on supplies before starting a two-thousand-mile journey that might take five months. Farmers hitched oxen and mules to family wagons. Groups formed companies to pay expenses and help one another while crossing the country. City people who had never faced the wilderness were ill prepared for the incredible hardships they had to endure. They forded rivers, climbed mountains, and crossed deserts. During 1849 the dread disease, cholera, caused an appalling number of deaths among overland travelers.

Life at the Mines

At least a quarter of a million people migrated to California during the first five years of the gold rush (1848–53). The majority of miners were men. When they arrived at the diggings they faced hard physical labor. A few found enough gold to become wealthy, but most were lucky if they covered their expenses. More merchants than miners struck it rich because the needs of the migrants had created a huge market.

Some women went west, too, with their families or on their own. A few were looking for gold, but most made a living providing services to the miners. They took in laundry and operated rooming houses, stores, and small restaurants in the little settlements that sprang up near the mine sites.

These sites were scattered along the western slopes of the Sierra Nevada. *Lode deposits* were located in quartz veins deep in the ground. *Placer deposits* consisted of gold dust, flakes, and nuggets scattered through the sand and gravel of mountain streams. During the early days of the gold rush, men were able to uncover buried treasure with picks and shovels. *Panning* in rivers and streams was another technique individuals used. But the loose gold in riverbeds and the placer deposits were soon exhausted. The easier methods gave way to the expensive machinery needed to extract riches deep in the earth. The time of the lone miner had passed, and big corporations took over the work. Nevertheless, gold seekers kept coming to California throughout the 1850s.

Later Rushes

Disappointed miners continued to search throughout the West for a rich strike. Some went to the Fraser River of British Columbia. Others tried their luck in Idaho, Montana, Colorado, and Arizona. The most sensational finds were in Nevada, where, in 1859, prospectors discovered the Comstock lode, consisting of both gold and silver. A heavy migration was soon under way and within a few months mountainsides were covered with staked-out claims, chiefly by veterans of the California gold rush. Equipment and supplies were carried over the Sierra Nevada for exorbitant prices, and Virginia City, Nevada, became a famous Wild West mining town.

In the late 1890s thousands of American gold seekers rushed to newly discovered gold fields in the Canadian Klondike. Long lines of prospectors climbed almost impassable mountains in the upper Yukon Territory. Men suffered from freezing weather, lack of provisions, and exhaustion. In 1898 word spread that the beach at Nome, Alaska, was laced with gold. Shores there and along the Bering Sea were quickly overrun with men and women competing for space, but only a few found the precious metal.

Gold rushes drew not only fortune hunters but merchants, bankers, farmers, artists, and writers to the American West. As a result of the rushes, sparsely populated territories were quickly settled, wagon roads and railroads were constructed, and new towns and cities sprang up. The West's economy boomed, and small towns like San Francisco,

California, Denver, Colorado, and Helena, Montana, became thriving cities. Gold rushes stimulated the growth of businesses and helped make the United States a rich nation.

See also Pioneers and Frontier Life.

For further reading: Rhoda Blumberg, *The Great American Gold Rush* (New York: Bradbury Press, 1989).

RHODA BLUMBERG

GOLF

Introduced in the United States in the 1890s by Scotland-born John Reid, golf for much of the past century deserved its reputation as a rich man's sport. Some of the wealthiest Americans took up golf in that decade. One of them, William K. Vanderbilt, commissioned the first professionally designed U.S. course, Shinnecock Hills, at Southampton, Long Island. Early golf clubs excluded all but wealthy white Christians, and most people gave the sport little attention. Theodore Roosevelt even warned President William Howard Taft, who liked to play, that the game was politically hazardous—"Golf is fatal," he wrote.

Golf first attracted favorable attention from the public in 1913, when an unknown American, Francis Ouimet, took the U.S. Open title away from two British champions. Later that decade and through the 1920s, Walter Hagen brought professional golf into the limelight as he won tournaments, played nationwide exhibitions, and, like other celebrities, earned large sums from product endorsements.

But American amateur Bobby Jones was golf's superstar of the era. From 1923 to 1930 he won thirteen national titles in the United

States and Great Britain, including in 1930 the Grand Slam—the American Open and Amateur and the British Open and Amateur tournaments—a feat that has never been repeated. The gentlemanly Jones drew huge crowds and public adoration. The combination of his achievements and the dramatic growth of country clubs made golf the premier businessman's sport, a kind of "outdoor office."

But it took Arnold Palmer and television to make golf the truly popular sport it has become. Palmer won televised tournaments throughout the 1960s in exciting, come-from-behind fashion and, unlike his predecessors, showing the emotion he felt. With Palmer as a telegenic hero, television poured money into professional golf, and purses exploded for both men and women, from a total of less than $2 million in 1960 to more than $30 million by 1987. Currently golf is played by more people than ever, but the exclusive tradition remains. Not until 1992 did the Shinnecock Hills Club admit an African-American member.

See also Sports.

WARREN GOLDSTEIN

GOMPERS, SAMUEL

(1850–1924)   *Labor leader.*

Gompers was born in London, the son of a poor cigar maker. He left school at the age of ten to work for a shoemaker and a short time later learned his father's trade. When Gompers was thirteen, his family moved to New York City, where he found a job in a cigar factory. He soon joined the Cigarmakers Union and became its president in 1877.

Many labor leaders, including Gompers, believed that unions would be stronger if they worked together in a national union. In 1886, twenty-five trade unions throughout the United States joined to form the American Federation of Labor (AFL), with Gompers as president. The AFL members were skilled workers, organized into separate units, each covering a particular craft.

As AFL president, Gompers worked hard to get rid of the injunctions (court orders) sought by businesses to curb strikes, and he campaigned vigorously for the Clayton Antitrust Act of 1914 that came to be known as labor's "Magna Carta." During World War I, President Woodrow Wilson appointed Gompers to the Council on National Defense, where he helped mobilize labor support for the war. By 1920, the AFL had more than 4 million members.

Considering himself a practical man, Gompers repudiated radical ideas and was interested mainly in securing day-to-day gains for federation members. He opposed both socialism and a separate labor political party. He believed that instead labor should work within the capitalist economy and the two-party political system to improve wages, hours, and working conditions. His conservative views earned him the title of "Labor Statesman." Except for the year 1895, Gompers headed the AFL until his death, serving in that position for thirty-seven years.

In 1955, the AFL, which had represented only skilled workers organized by crafts, and the Congress of Industrial Organizations (CIO), representing both skilled and unskilled workers by industries, merged to form the AFL-CIO.

See also American Federation of Labor; Congress of Industrial Organizations; Labor Movement.

EDMUND LINDOP

GOODMAN, BENNY

(1909–1986) *Clarinetist, composer, and jazz bandleader.*

Goodman was born in Chicago, Illinois. After early musical training at his neighborhood synagogue and Hull-House, the Chicago settlement, he made his performing debut at the age of twelve at the Central Park Theater. As a high school student, Goodman played New Orleans–style jazz with other young musicians.

After playing on a Lake Michigan excursion boat, Goodman joined Ben Pollack's band and performed in Los Angeles, Chicago, and New York in the 1920s. He then established himself as New York's leading freelance clarinetist, playing in orchestras, on the radio, and in *Strike Up the Band* and *Girl Crazy,* popular musicals composed by George Gershwin.

Goodman put together a big band that played popular tunes in a swing style in 1934. He worked closely with Fletcher Henderson, who arranged many pieces for him. In 1935, Goodman organized a trio with Gene Krupa and Teddy Wilson, a year later adding Lionel Hampton to the group. Goodman excelled as leader of a big band, as a soloist, and as a member of a small group because of the precision of his playing. His big band's 1935 performance at the Palomar Ballroom in Los Angeles was broadcast nationwide and is often credited with beginning the swing era.

Even as the "King of Swing" achieved success as a jazz musician, he established a reputation as an interpreter of works in the classical clarinet repertory, including compositions by Mozart, Weber, and Stravinsky. He commissioned pieces by such important composers as Béla Bartók, Paul Hindemith, and Aaron Copland.

With the transition from swing to be-bop and other jazz styles, Goodman used big orchestras only for tours. His most innovative work continued to be with small ensembles. From the 1950s through the 1970s, he toured internationally as a goodwill ambassador for the United States, and in 1982 he was recognized for his achievements at the Kennedy Center.

Goodman was a technically extraordinary performer whose abilities transcended any one musical style. Another significant contribution was his bringing together black and white musicians in his performing groups at a time when segregation prevailed in the musical world. He was the first major bandleader to do so.

See also Jazz; Music.

BARBARA L. TISCHLER

GOOD NEIGHBOR POLICY

Beginning with the Monroe Doctrine of 1823, U.S. policy toward the nations of Latin America—especially the small states of Central America and the Caribbean region—was fundamentally one-sided. However well meaning, it was deeply influenced by the fact that the United States was enormously richer and more powerful than any of its neighbors. To some extent this is still the case, but since the late 1920s the United States has officially adopted a Good Neighbor policy. The term was first used by President-elect Herbert Hoover in 1928. On a goodwill tour of Latin America shortly after his election he promised to "maintain ... the relations of good neighbors" with the nations of the area. Franklin D. Roosevelt used the same term in his 1933 inaugural address (and thus got more credit for it).

Important examples of the practical application of the Good Neighbor policy include the withdrawal of U.S. Marines from Nicaragua, Haiti, and the Dominican Republic during the 1930s, the granting of economic aid to many Latin American nations during World War II, the mutual defense pact of Rio de Janeiro of 1947, and the creation of the Organization of American States in 1948.

Self-interest, however, has remained the basic policy of the United States. During the cold war this usually meant supporting reactionary Latin American dictatorships on the ground that these governments preserved "stability" and were a bulwark against communism.

See also Monroe Doctrine; Roosevelt Corollary.

GORE, AL, JR.

(1948–)   *Vice president of the United States.*

Although Gore was born in Washington D.C., he considers Tennessee his home. His father, Albert A. Gore, Sr., was a longtime representative and senator from that state.

The younger Gore attended schools in Carthage, Tennessee, and Washington, D.C. After graduating from Harvard in 1961, he studied at Vanderbilt University's School of Religion and School of Law. From 1969 until 1971 he served with the U.S. Army in Vietnam. Upon returning to Tennessee he was involved in real estate in Carthage and then worked as a reporter in Nashville.

Gore won election on the Democratic ticket to the U.S. House of Representatives in 1976 and served four terms. In 1984 he was elected senator from Tennessee and was re-elected in 1990. In 1988 Gore campaigned unsuccessfully for the Democratic presidential nomination. Four years later, Bill Clinton chose him as his running mate and the two were elected.

A turning point in Gore's outlook on life was the near death of his young son who was struck by an automobile in 1989 but later recovered. It made him appreciate the value of life, which he extended to the world around him. Since then Gore's dedication to the environment, which he has studied for twenty years, has grown. He was the Senate's leading authority on environmental matters until his election to the vice presidency, and he still works on these issues for the Clinton administration. His award-winning book *Earth in the Balance: Ecology and the Human Spirit* (1992) outlines the severity of the problem and suggests ways the crisis can be resolved.

For further reading: Hank Hillin, *Al Gore, Jr.: His Life and Career* (New York: Birch Lane Press, 1992).

RICHARD A. BARTLETT

GRAHAM, BILLY

(1918–)   *Preacher and evangelist.*

Billy Graham claims to have preached in person to more people than anyone else in history. His evangelistic crusades around the world, his television appearances and radio broadcasts, his friendships with world leaders, and his unofficial role as spokesman for America's evangelicals made him one of the most recognized religious figures of the twentieth century.

William Franklin Graham, born near Charlotte, North Carolina, went to a revival service in 1934 and there experienced a religious conversion that shaped the direction of

Billy Graham delivering a sermon. His evangelistic crusades throughout the world and his television appearances have made him one of the most recognized religious figures of his time.

his life. He began preaching while still in college and in 1939 was ordained a Southern Baptist. In 1946, having graduated from Wheaton College three years earlier, Graham joined the staff of Youth for Christ and later became, for a time, president of Northwestern Schools in Minneapolis, all the while continuing his evangelistic campaigns.

A successful Los Angeles campaign in 1949 brought Graham national attention, in no small measure because the newspaper publisher William Randolph Hearst, impressed with the young evangelist's preaching and his anticommunist rhetoric, instructed his papers to "puff Graham." From Los Angeles,

Graham took his crusades around the country and the world, thereby gaining international renown.

Throughout his career, Graham's appeal lay in his forceful preaching of a simple, homespun message: repent of your sins, accept Christ as savior, and you shall be saved. Behind that simple message, however, stood a sophisticated organization, the Billy Graham Evangelistic Association, which provided extensive advance work and a follow-up program for converts. Even though he pioneered the use of television for religious purposes, Graham has always shied away from the label "televangelist." During the

1980s, when other television preachers were embroiled in sensational scandals, Graham maintained a spotless reputation. Throughout a career that spanned more than half a century few people have questioned his integrity.

RANDALL BALMER

GRAHAM, MARTHA

(1894–1991)   *Dancer, choreographer.*

For over sixty years, the Martha Graham Dance Company has electrified audiences around the world with its founder's dance creations. Graham was a maverick who introduced a style of dance more spontaneous than classical ballet. In her choreography—

Martha Graham performing in Letter to the World, *which she choreographed in 1940. An emotionally charged work, the dance is based on the life and poetry of Emily Dickinson.*

the process of planning dance steps for a piece of music—Graham aspired, in her words, to "chart the graph of the heart." She regarded dancing as an "affirmation of life."

Graham was born in Allegheny, Pennsylvania. When she was fourteen, her family moved to southern California, where she enrolled in dance school. She then joined the Denishawn Company, the only major group that did not perform classical ballet.

In 1923, Graham struck out on her own. She taught dance in New York City and formed a small company of women dancers. By 1938, she had added males and went on to choreograph over 180 ballets for her group, the Martha Graham Dance Company.

Graham explored many ideas through the dances she created. In the 1930s, during the Great Depression, she choreographed dances that celebrated the American spirit. *Two Primitive Canticles, Primitive Mysteries,* and *Ceremonials* expressed the cultural traditions of Native Americans. The lyrical *Appalachian Spring* portrayed the strength and spirit of the pioneers, and *Letter to the World* dramatized the life and poetry of Emily Dickinson. In later years, Graham created dances that explored the myths of the ancient Greeks and Hebrews. *Cave of the Heart, Night Journey, Errand into the Maze, Phaedra,* and *Clytemnestra* vividly dramatized these ancient stories.

To the end of her long life, Graham, a slender, lithe woman with the majestic bearing of an eagle in flight, continued to create new dances, raising American dancing to new heights of expression.

See also Dance.

For further reading: Walter Terry, *Frontiers of Dance: The Life of Martha Graham* (New York: Crowell, 1975).

HARRIET SIGERMAN

GRANGER MOVEMENT

In 1867 Oliver H. Kelley, a clerk in the U.S. Bureau of Agriculture, founded the National Grange of the Patrons of Husbandry. At first the Granges were mostly social clubs. But during the depression of the early 1870s the movement began to focus on the economic problems of farmers.

The prices of wheat and other farm products were falling much faster than the cost of farm machinery and other things that farmers had to buy. Farmers who had borrowed heavily during the Civil War, when prices of farm products were high, were hard pressed to pay off these loans when prices fell. Moreover, in the Middle West, where the movement was strongest, most districts were served by only one railroad. Lack of competition enabled the lines to charge relatively high prices for transporting farm products to eastern markets. Many of the Granges were able to cut costs by forming cooperatives and buying fertilizer and other supplies at wholesale prices. But there was no easy way to pay off their debts or to persuade a railroad monopoly to reduce its rates.

For solving these problems, the Grangers turned to the state governments. By the mid-1870s many Granger candidates were running for office, and almost overnight, they won control of many state legislatures. Laws regulating railroad rates and the charges of grain storage companies followed. At its height at this time, the Grange clubs had more than 850,000 members.

In the 1880s economic conditions improved. Membership in the Grange fell steeply. It became what it had been originally, a primarily social and cultural organization.

See also Agriculture.

GRANT, ULYSSES S.

(1822–85)   Eighteenth president of the United States (1869–77) and Civil War general.

Grant, a West Point graduate, fought in the Mexican War (1846–48). In 1854, he resigned from the army but proved ill suited to civilian life. After failing in farming and business ventures, he rejoined the army when the Civil War broke out.

During the war, Grant's troops captured Forts Henry and Donelson in Tennessee in 1862, the Union's first victory, but they suf-

Ulysses S. Grant, photographed by Mathew Brady, during the Civil War. A war hero who served as supreme commander of the Union armies as well as president of the United States for two terms, Grant nevertheless went bankrupt in the last years of his life as the result of bad investments. He struggled against a painful form of cancer in order to finish writing his memoirs so that his family would not be penniless after his death.

fered heavy losses at the Battle of Shiloh. The next year, Grant was made a major general in the Union army after he captured the important city of Vicksburg, Mississippi. His successes in the West brought him promotion to lieutenant general.

Grant, a talented strategist, was chosen by President Abraham Lincoln to command all the Union armies in 1864. Unlike his cautious predecessors, he threw all the Union might against the Confederacy. He sent Gen. William Tecumseh Sherman to attack Atlanta and march across Georgia to the sea. He himself in the Wilderness campaign relentlessly attacked Gen. Robert E. Lee's army in Virginia. After a lengthy siege at Petersburg and a series of bloody battles, he forced Lee to surrender in April 1865. Because Grant respected his enemy, his surrender terms were generous. Later, he was honored with the rank of general of the army, a post previously held only by George Washington.

After the war, Grant, a Republican, won two terms as president. Although he was personally honest, he was a poor judge of men and trusted a number of corrupt officials to help run the government. For example, his private secretary Orville Babcock was involved with the Whiskey Ring, which sold alcoholic beverages for personal profit, and Secretary of War William W. Belknap made a fortune selling trading rights to Indian posts. Grant's foreign policy included the peaceful settlement of Civil War disputes with Britain and an unsuccessful attempt to annex Santo Domingo.

After he left office, Grant lost his savings in an investment swindle and fell ill with cancer. To pay his debts and provide an income for his family, he spent the last months of his life writing his *Personal Memoirs.* Published by author Mark Twain after Grant's death, the book is considered a classic of American literature.

See also Civil War. *For events during Grant's administration, see Alabama* Claims; Corruption and Scandals in Government; Tweed Ring.

BARBARA SILBERDICK FEINBERG

GREAT AWAKENING

As the colonies expanded and prospered in the early eighteenth century, people tended to be less concerned with religion and more with taking advantage of business opportunities and the land's rich natural resources. At the same time, people from different parts of Europe brought their local varieties of Christianity with them. It became extremely difficult for the already established churches to control religious practices. Church attendance declined steeply in many districts.

This situation changed quite suddenly in the late 1730s, after a young English clergyman named George Whitefield arrived in the new colony of Georgia. Whitefield was a remarkable preacher with a dramatic style and an urge to spread a new religious message. Traveling through the colonies from Charleston in the South to Boston in New England, he preached a message that was both frightening and reassuring. People were mostly sinners, Whitefield would announce. If they did not repent and reform, they were sure to go to hell, the horrors of which he described in vivid detail. If they did see the light and change their ways, however, eternal life in heaven would be theirs. To get to heaven no one need be a learned expert on theology or philosophy; what was needed was total submission to God's power, to be what would today be called "born again."

People by the tens of thousands flocked to hear Whitefield preach. Both his message and his brilliance as an orator attracted them, and a wave of religious emotionalism spread through the colonies in his wake.

Soon other preachers began to imitate Whitefield. Many were men without congregations of their own, often little educated and lacking in his talents. Local ministers who had opened their churches to Whitefield because of his religious enthusiasm and his ability to attract an audience were often shocked by the crude and extravagant sermons of these "itinerants." But often their excited parishioners were impressed. After Whitefield or one of his many imitators had preached, they found the routine sermons of their regular pastor dull by comparison. Many churches then split into "Old Light" and "New Light" factions. Anglicans and Congregationalist churches lost ground to Baptists and Methodists.

The Great Awakening lasted until the 1760s. Despite the conflicts it inspired, it was ultimately a force for religious toleration. It also encouraged democracy by stressing that it was possible for each individual to achieve salvation on his or her own. The Awakening was an early sign of American nationalism because it was the first movement to spread throughout the colonies.

See also Colonial America.

GREAT DEPRESSION
See Depressions and Recessions.

GREAT RAILROAD STRIKE OF 1877
See Railroad Strike of 1877.

GREAT SOCIETY

President Lyndon B. Johnson gave the name "Great Society" to his reform program in a speech during his campaign for reelection in May 1964. Having become president originally only because President John F. Kennedy had been assassinated, he was eager to develop an ambitious program that would assure him a place among the nation's great presidents.

After his landslide victory in 1964 Johnson pushed through Congress the largest body of social and economic legislation since Franklin D. Roosevelt's New Deal of the 1930s. New civil rights acts outlawed racial segregation and job discrimination. The Medicare and Medicaid programs provided medical insurance for persons over sixty-five and for the poor of all ages. The Department of Housing and Urban Development (HUD) was established. Federal aid to education, both at the school and college levels, was expanded.

The keystone to the Great Society was what Johnson called the "War on Poverty." The Economic Opportunity Act of 1964 developed a food stamp program that enabled poor people to obtain surplus produce. The Job Corps provided training for young people without special skills. Project Head Start offered preschool education for poor children.

The civil rights and medical insurance elements in the Great Society were permanent reforms of enormous importance. In practice, however, they were hard to enforce and difficult to run efficiently. And by inevitably failing to live up to Johnson's grandiose expectations, his War on Poverty disappointed many liberals and enabled conservatives to claim that it was a waste of money.

See also Johnson, Lyndon B.

GREEK AMERICANS

In 1763, when Florida passed from Spanish into British hands, Andrew Turnbull, a Scottish physician who was married to the daughter of a wealthy Greek merchant in London, secured a royal land grant seventy-five miles south of Saint Augustine. He named it New Smyrna, after the birthplace of his wife. Turnbull then recruited four hundred Greek men and women, and soon thereafter, the first generation of Greek immigrants was established in America.

Over the years, more followed, but by far the largest Greek migration to America occurred between 1890 and 1920. The original intent of many of these immigrants was to earn money in America and then return to their poor villages in Greece to enjoy a comfortable life. Only a few, however, did return. Most remained in America, learned the language, found work, married, educated their children, and prospered in various business endeavors.

The second generation achieved a respectable status in their communities. Many graduated from colleges and universities and became teachers, doctors, lawyers, scientists, and businessmen. Quite a few entered the political arena and were elected mayors, state representatives, governors, and members of Congress. In 1988 Governor Michael Dukakis of Massachusetts was the Democratic nominee for president.

A large number of Greek Americans have gained fame in the sciences: Dr. George Papanicolaou is responsible for the "Pap smear," a test designed to detect cervical cancer; Dr. George Kotzias, a neurologist, discovered L-dopa, a drug used to treat Parkinson's disease; Dr. Michael Dertouzos directs the Computer Science Laboratory at M.I.T.; Dr. Matina Horner was president of Radcliffe College.

In the arts, Greek Americans have been particularly prominent: soprano Maria Callas, Oscar winner Olympia Dukakis, directors Elia Kazan and John Cassavetes, actor Telly Savalas, and many others. Theodoros Stamos and William Baziotis are important modern painters.

Today, there are almost 2 million Greek Americans in the United States. Greek Orthodox churches have sprouted throughout the nation, all guided by the Greek Archdiocese in New York.

THEODORE VRETTOS

GREENBACK PARTY

During the Civil War the federal government issued about $450 million in paper money that was not backed by gold or silver. It had to do so because it was unable to borrow or collect through taxes enough money to meet its greatly increased wartime expenses. These bills were popularly known as "greenbacks" because they were printed with green ink to distinguish them from the regular "yellowback" currency.

This inflation of the amount of money in circulation caused prices to rise. In addition, people were reluctant to accept greenbacks in payment for goods and services. Therefore, after the war the government sought to withdraw the greenbacks from circulation. This could be done by continuing to accept them in payment of taxes and not using them to pay government bills.

But reducing the amount of money in circulation at a time when the country was growing caused prices to fall. This hurt anyone who owed a fixed amount of money. A farmer who had to pay off a thousand-dollar mortgage was hard hit when the price of the wheat he grew fell from a dollar a bushel to fifty cents.

Falling prices explain the rise of the Greenback Party, which was founded in 1876. It called for *increasing* the amount of greenbacks rather than retiring them from circulation. Two years later the Greenback Party attracted many industrial workers as well as hard-pressed farmers. It polled nearly a million votes and elected fourteen congressmen and many more local officials. The return of good times in the 1880s, however, caused the party to lose most of its popular appeal.

GRIFFITH, D. W.

(1875–1948)   *Motion picture director.*

Griffith originated some of the most important techniques in the newly born motion picture industry and helped turn movies into an art form. His pioneering ideas influenced generations of filmmakers throughout the world.

Born to a poor family in rural Kentucky, Griffith had little formal education. He began his career as a stage actor and tried writing plays to supplement his income. He was not very successful in either field, and in 1907 he went to New York, then the center of the film industry, to write scripts for movies. He sold some to the Edison Film Company and the Biograph Company and acted in films for both. When an opening for a director appeared at Biograph, he took the job.

From 1908 to 1913, Griffith made more than four hundred films, mostly one reel long

and lasting about twelve minutes. During his five years at Biograph, he introduced many new techniques. Among his innovations were the flashback, the close-up, the long shot, the fade-out and fade-in in which the screen darkens or lightens to indicate the end or the beginning of a scene, and cross-cutting, the switching back and forth of scenes to convey the idea of different actions taking place at the same time.

In 1915, Griffith independently produced his most famous picture, *Birth of a Nation,* the longest American film yet made. Running over three hours, this story of post–Civil War racial conflict was a great commercial success. It was technically advanced but socially offensive and angered many by its sympathetic portrayal of the Ku Klux Klan. In response to the criticism it provoked, he made *Intolerance* (1916), a plea for racial and social justice by which he was clearly trying to atone for the crude racism of *Birth of a Nation.*

Griffith developed such stars as Mary Pickford, the Gish sisters, and Lionel Barrymore, but he could not adjust to the introduction of sound or to the economics of the big studios. He retired in 1931 and died seventeen years later in relative obscurity. Today he is recognized as the father of modern motion pictures.

See also Movies.

DENNIS WEPMAN

GRIMKÉ, ANGELINA
GRIMKÉ, SARAH

(Angelina: 1805–79; Sarah: 1792–1873)
Abolitionists and advocates of women's rights.

Born in Charleston, South Carolina, Angelina and Sarah Grimké grew up in the slave-owning household of their father, Judge John Faucheraud Grimké. They learned early that even though a master might treat his own slaves well, slavery rested on the idea that *people could be owned*. This, in itself, was a frightening idea and, because it was supported by the law, cruelty and injustice often went unpunished.

In 1832 Angelina moved north to the Quaker city of Philadelphia where Sarah soon joined her. Wishing to work for the antislavery movement, the sisters faced an unexpected and difficult problem. It appeared that many persons, including some abolitionists, believed that it was wrong for women to give public lectures or to travel about alone. Fighting for the right to speak their minds turned the Grimké sisters into strong feminists; later they became effective and well-known speakers in favor of abolition. The year 1836 saw the publication of *An Appeal to the Christian Women of the South* by Angelina Grimké and *An Epistle to the Clergy of the Southern States* by Sarah Grimké; two years later Sarah Grimké published *Letters on the Equality of the Sexes and the Condition of Women*. Although they later downplayed their feminist beliefs in order to emphasize their abolitionist convictions, their early struggles and these several publications show that the Grimkés understood that freedom for slaves and extended rights for women really were twin causes.

In 1838 Angelina married Theodore D. Weld, a prominent abolitionist. Among the friends who attended the wedding as guests were a number of former slaves and free Negroes. As Quakers, the couple welcomed the opportunity to compose their own marriage vows. After Angelina's marriage Sarah Grimké, who remained single, lived with her sister and brother-in-law, and helped to take care

of their children. This was not an uncommon arrangement in the mid-nineteenth century and when the Welds decided to give up touring and speaking to open a small boarding school, Sarah stayed on to help with the teaching. It is true that there were times when Angelina complained that Sarah's assistance had turned into interference and Sarah suffered hurt feelings. But the sisters were able to recover from their quarrels and to turn their energies to the work they loved and shared. At one time, for example, they arranged to have several racially mixed nephews live with them in the North so that the boys—at least one of whom went on to prestigious achievements as a lawyer, biographer, academician and crusader for civil rights—would be sure to have the good education they would be barred from in the South.

Although the Grimké sisters' efforts were not well recognized in their own time, later generations have come to appreciate their good and courageous work.

See also Abolitionist Movement; Feminist Movement to 1919.

JOAN W. BLOS

GULF OF TONKIN RESOLUTION

During the early 1960s the fighting in Vietnam took place almost entirely in South Vietnam. By the summer of 1964, Communist South Vietnamese, the Vietcong, drawing upon North Vietnamese supplies, controlled roughly half of the country. Early that August President Lyndon B. Johnson suddenly informed congressional leaders that two North Vietnamese gunboats in the Gulf of Tonkin had fired at the *Maddox*, an American destroyer. He described the attack as "open aggression on the high seas" and for the first time in the war authorized air strikes on North Vietnamese targets. He also asked the Senate to adopt a resolution empowering him to repel "any armed attack against the forces of the United States and to prevent further aggression."

Only two votes were cast in the Senate against the Gulf of Tonkin Resolution. It later became clear, however, that Johnson had greatly exaggerated the seriousness of the incident. The *Maddox* may not have been far enough offshore to be in international waters, and in any case it was conducting electronic reconnaissance of territory clearly under Communist control. Many senators felt that the president had deliberately misled them in order to justify his further escalation of the war. In 1970 the Gulf of Tonkin Resolution was terminated.

See also Vietnam War.

GULF WAR

In August 1990 troops of President Saddam Hussein of Iraq overran without warning the tiny kingdom of Kuwait. Saddam then massed his troops along the border of Saudi Arabia. Since with Kuwait Iraq controlled about a quarter of the world's oil, adding that of Saudi Arabia, whose army was far smaller than his own, would enable Saddam to set the world price of oil.

To prevent this from happening, President George Bush mobilized the United States and a number of European and Middle Eastern nations to send with U.N. approval troops and military supplies to defend Saudi Arabia. A powerful army that included half a million Americans was rapidly deployed under the command of Gen. H. Norman Schwarzkopf. In November the United Nations authorized it to expel the Iraqis from Kuwait by force if Saddam did not pull out voluntarily by January 15, 1991.

When Saddam failed to do so, the United States launched an all-out air attack on Iraqi forces in Kuwait and on military and strategic targets in Iraq itself. A month of these attacks reduced much of Iraq to rubble and inflicted heavy casualties on the Iraqi troops in Kuwait. When Saddam still refused to withdraw from Kuwait, Schwarzkopf ordered infantry and tank forces to attack. In three days this army liberated Kuwait. Uncounted thousands of Iraqi soldiers were killed, wounded, or captured. More than four thousand tanks, along with much military equipment, were destroyed.

To save the remnants of his army, Saddam finally agreed to pay reparations to Kuwait and permit destruction of his ability to manufacture missiles and atomic weapons. Everyone expected him to be driven from power by his own people, but this did not occur.

GUNS AND GUN CONTROL

The origins of the gun are unknown, but some form of metal tube propelling a missile by means of an explosive charge was common in Europe as early as 1350. Mechanical firing mechanisms, lit by a match, date from the fifteenth century, and a hundred years later self-igniting firearms useful in warfare were developed.

Guns in U.S. History

The construction and use of guns lie deep in

American history, with its pioneer tradition of independence and self-sufficiency. The Pilgrims brought muskets with them from England, many so heavy they had to be fired resting on a fork placed in the ground. They used them to hunt for game and protect themselves against Indians.

Skilled gunsmiths were necessary to survival in colonial days, and Americans made important contributions to gun design. The famous Kentucky rifle, developed in the 1740s, played a major part in the American Revolution. The Colt .45 revolver (with a barrel opening .45 inches in diameter), designed by Samuel Colt in the 1830s, was widely used in the Civil War and on the western frontier. Other important nineteenth-century American gun designers and producers were the Remington Arms Company, the Springfield Armory, and the Winchester Repeating Arms Company.

Drive for Gun Control

Many Americans have considered it both a right and a responsibility to keep guns to protect themselves and defend their country. The Second Amendment to the Constitution, added in 1791, guarantees "that the right of the people to keep and bear arms shall not be infringed." But the increased level of violent crime during the twentieth century has alarmed many people and prompted a demand for legislation to limit the sale and possession of firearms, especially handguns. Polls taken in the early 1990s revealed that the public is behind the passage of such laws by nearly nine to one. Estimates made in 1993 placed the number of privately owned firearms in the United States at from 200 million to 400 million. Yet America is the only industrial nation in the world with no effective handgun legislation.

Half the states already have laws requiring some sort of investigation of the background of gun purchasers or waiting periods before they can buy guns. In 1968 the national government passed a Federal Gun Control Act limiting interstate commerce in firearms and making the sale of guns to minors, known criminals, and drug addicts illegal.

Pressure for further gun control on a national level was spurred by the 1981 shooting of President Ronald Reagan and his press secretary, James Brady, and led to the passage of the "Brady bill" in Congress. This law requires background checks on handgun purchasers in all states and a waiting period of five business days before a purchaser could take possession of a gun. When a man killed five California schoolchildren with a semiautomatic rifle in 1989, the federal government banned the import of most foreign-made assault rifles.

Gun Control Debate

Opponents to gun control, including the 3 million members of the National Rifle Association (NRA), assert that such legislation is an infringement of the Second Amendment's guarantee of the right of Americans to bear arms and that it would have no impact on reducing or preventing gun-related violence. Criminals would find ways to buy or steal guns, they argue, and legal restrictions would affect only the law-abiding who want guns for protection or hunting. The NRA has been extremely effective in preventing the passage of antigun legislation. In 1986 it successfully pressured Congress to relax some of the restrictions included in the Federal Gun Control Act.

Supporters of the Brady bill, such as Handgun Control Inc. headed by Brady's wife, Sarah, hope that it will open the door to even stronger measures covering more than just handguns and retail sales. They contend that the Second Amendment was prompted by the eighteenth-century need for state militias and does not refer to private ownership of firearms. The Handgun Control organization calls for a national ban on all semiautomatic assault weapons, limits on multiple purchases of guns, careful background checks (including fingerprinting) in private as well as retail gun sales, and tighter control of federal licenses to sell guns. Other organizations demand safety regulations covering unlocked and loaded weapons, a parental responsibility law for the use of weapons by minors, national hospital rules regarding the reporting of firearm fatalities, and even a total ban on all handgun sales.

State and local gun laws are very different from place to place. Among the strictest are those of California, which has a fifteen-day waiting period for the purchase of all firearms, retail and private. Virginia limits buyers to one handgun a month, and other states provide severe punishment for illegal possession or use of guns. With repeated government promises to "get tough on crime" in the 1990s, it seems likely that strict national gun control laws will follow.

For further reading: Helen Strahinich, *Guns in America* (New York: Walker and Company, 1992).

D E N N I S W E P M A N

G U T H R I E , W O O D Y

(1912–67) *Folksinger and songwriter.*

Guthrie wrote over a thousand songs in the 1930s and 1940s, including such popular tunes as "This Land Is Your Land," "So Long, It's Been Good to Know You," and "Put Your Finger in the Air." Often using humor and vivid language, he wrote songs that documented the depressed Dust Bowl decade of the thirties and problems confronted by migrant agricultural workers. He also turned out charming children's songs, peace and war songs, cowboy and hobo songs, union and work songs, and love songs. All of them make people feel good and take pride in themselves.

Guthrie wrote novels, short stories, newspaper columns, magazine articles, and hundreds of letters. Words flowed from his pen as easily as speech from his mouth. He also drew hundreds of illustrations for his songs and books and, when he needed money, worked as a sign painter. In the 1940s he recorded songs for the Library of Congress, R C A Victor, and other, smaller companies. But most of his output is preserved on Folkways Records, now owned by the Smithsonian Institution.

Guthrie was born and reared in Okemah, Oklahoma. His parents were prosperous until Huntington's disease altered his mother's behavior and tore the family apart. When he was fourteen, she was committed to a mental asylum. His father suffered severe burns in an accident and was taken to Pampa, Texas, to live with his sister while recuperating. In his autobiographical novel *Bound for Glory*, Guthrie tells how these experiences taught him compassion and shaped his desire to travel. He spent much time in his early years tramping the roads and byways of America.

In 1937 he moved to California and became involved in leftist activities there. He then went to New York City in late 1939 where he met and worked with Alan Lomax, Pete Seeger, and others who were part of the social protest song movement of those years. Guthrie believed that songs could inspire people to change social conditions.

Woody Guthrie was a songwriter with a special empathy for the poor, the downtrodden, and just ordinary folk. He said "I hate a song that makes you think you're not any good. . . . I'm out to fight those kinds of songs to my very last breath of air and my last drop of blood. I'm out to sing songs that prove to you that this is your world. . . . no matter how hard it's run you down or rolled over you, no matter what color, what size you are. . . . I'm out to sing the songs that make you take pride in yourself and in your work."

Like his mother, Guthrie suffered from Huntington's disease and was hospitalized for the last fifteen years of his life. Nevertheless, the music he had written influenced many songwriters and singers who came along later, such as Bob Dylan and Bruce Springsteen. His songs have become a valued part of America's musical heritage. As one critic said, they are "a national possession, like Yellowstone and Yosemite." The contemporary folksinger, Arlo Guthrie, is his son.

See also Music.

For further reading: Henrietta Yurchenco, *A Mighty Hard Road: The Woody Guthrie Story* (New York: McGraw-Hill, 1973).

GUY LOGSDON

GYMNASTICS

Gymnastics today is a sport of aerial complexity, grace, and drama. Large audiences fill arenas to marvel at world-class athletes seldom out of their teens. But the sport has not always had such entertainment value.

Origin of Gymnastics

American gymnastics traces its origin to the work of the German educational reformer Friedrich Ludwig Jahn (1778–1852). Jahn founded the Turner societies, or *Turnverein,* to combine German culture and national pride with a program of physical strengthening through gymnastics, which then included exercises resembling calisthenics. A number of American educators studied with Jahn and brought his ideas and system to this country.

German Turner societies were also deeply involved in trying to establish democracy in their country. When they, and others, failed to do so in the German Revolution of 1848, many immigrated to the United States, bringing their faith in democracy, socialism, and gymnastics with them. One of these immigrants, Friedrich Hecker, established a gymnasium in Cincinnati in 1849 to promote "rational training, both physical and social." In the decade before the Civil War, Turner societies began to hold annual meetings of gymnasts from all over the country.

During the same years, other reformers promoted gymnastics in order to make sure that Americans—who were increasingly becoming city dwellers—were getting enough exercise. Dr. Dioclesian Lewis, for example, developed what he called "New Gymnastics" to combat "the prevalence of pale faces, undeveloped and distorted bodies, and nervous debility." Inspired by Lewis and other advocates of physical education, cities and private groups built gymnasiums in Boston, Chicago, and New York, among other places, in the decades around the Civil War.

Gymnastics became a central part of the movement for "muscular Christianity" in the United States in the third quarter of the nineteenth century. The Young Men's Christian Association, or YMCA, which had come to the United States from England in the early 1850s, began after the Civil War to build gymnasiums and hire physical directors all over the country. Although most gymnastics were intended for men, Lewis's system included women, and the Young Women's Christian Association (YWCA) started offering gymnastic instruction in the 1870s.

Popularity Eclipsed

The late-nineteenth-century boom in organized competitive sports like baseball pushed gymnastics into the background. Increasingly, physical educators focused on the importance of play (rather than exercise) in the development of children. College students flocked to big intercollegiate sporting events, and basketball (invented at the YMCA training school in Springfield, Massachusetts, in 1891) quickly became the premier gymnasium sport throughout the United States for both men and women.

After World War I, physical education became thoroughly integrated into America's public schools, but principally through intercollegiate sports such as football, basketball, baseball, and track and field. Gymnastics remained a relatively minor sport. Given the prejudices of the day against women participating in sports, this was probably why it was one of the few open to girls and women.

Renewed Interest

Not until the 1972 Munich Olympics did gymnastics make a comeback among the public. That year, the inherent drama of the games (and the tragedy of the murder of Israeli athletes by terrorists), combined with remarkable individual performances and superb television coverage, focused world attention for several evenings on a tiny Soviet gymnast. Olga Korbut's pixy charm and astonishing feats on the bars made her an instant international celebrity. Almost overnight, Korbut's performance transformed the image of gymnastics, particularly as performed by women and girls. At the 1976 Olympics in Montreal, however, Korbut was overshadowed by the even smaller and younger Romanian Nadia Comanici, whose perfect scores won gold medals and the admiration of millions.

No longer principally a series of conditioning exercises, gymnastics had become drama and art, a sport designed for audiences and incorporating elements of circuslike acrobatics as well as dance. Because their governments paid for extensive training programs, Eastern Europeans before the fall of communism dominated the international sport for some years. Spurred by their performances in the Olympics, American gymnastics organizations started a push to train a new generation of athletes in the United States. In a few years, girls' gymnastics in particular became extremely popular, with highly organized high school competitions throughout the country.

The new American training, helped by the former Romanian Olympic coach Bela Karolyi, paid off at the 1984 Olympics in Los Angeles, when Mary Lou Retton became the first American gymnast in Olympic history, male or female, to win the all-around championship. Her flawless performances, including a perfect 10 on the final event of the competition—a routine now known as the "Retton Vault"—along with her appealing personality, helped usher in the New Gymnastics. Girls now used strength, flexibility, and daring to create the "wow" factor in their routines.

Like other world-class sports, top-flight competitive gymnastics requires tremendous physical endurance and discipline beginning at a very young age. Many observers now worry about the possible harmful physical and emotional effects of such intense training for very young girls.

See also Olympic Games.

For further reading: Herma Silverstein, *Mary Lou Retton and the New Gymnasts* (New York: Franklin Watts, 1985).

WARREN GOLDSTEIN

H

HAMILTON, ALEXANDER

(1755–1804)   Aide to Gen. George Washington, delegate to the Constitutional Convention, and secretary of the treasury.

At a time when family connections counted for almost everything in determining one's future, Hamilton's early circumstances put him at a disadvantage. As a foster child living with his mother's family in the Danish colony of St. Croix (part of the modern-day Virgin Islands), young Alexander combined talent and diligence in order to rise in the world. He clerked in a merchant house, training himself in business and finance along the way.

Friends and family supported the gifted young man by sending Hamilton to New York in 1772 to pursue his education at King's College (now Columbia). As a student he read widely in history and political science and became caught up in Revolutionary politics. It would be his life's work to apply the knowledge he had gained from study and experience in finance and government to practical questions of making the United States work.

Hamilton joined the Continental army in 1776 and soon came to the notice of General Washington, who asked him to become an aide on his personal staff. The staff served as a "family" of officers who wrote letters, conveyed orders, and negotiated with friends and foes on behalf of the commander in chief. After the War for Independence was won, Hamilton became a lawyer and kept his hand in politics by pamphlet-writing and public service. He also helped found a Society for Promoting the Manumission (freeing) of Slaves in New York.

Hamilton had witnessed the inefficiency of the Continental Congress at first hand during the war. From studying the defects of the existing national government, he concluded that in order to hold the Union together, the states must give up some of their powers to the federal government so that it could defend the nation's borders, settle disputes between the states, and promote the national good. Hamilton and his allies supported the Constitution agreed upon in Philadelphia in 1787 as a way to achieve the necessary reforms. Hamilton, James Madison, and John Jay collaborated on the Federalist Papers, a series of essays that urged approval of the proposed Constitution.

As Washington's secretary of the treasury in the first cabinet, Hamilton worked to secure the reputation of the new nation as a trustworthy borrower. He proposed measures to reassure holders of bonds and other debts of the federal and state governments that they would receive their money back with interest. He also sought to establish steady tax revenues so that the new government could pay off these debts.

Hamilton set out next to stimulate economic growth by asking Congress to create a national bank. Secretary of State Thomas

Jefferson led the opposition to the bank, protesting that the federal government had no such authority, but Hamilton won the argument. He persuaded President Washington to interpret the Constitution so as to widen rather than restrict the powers of Congress. Hamilton and Jefferson differed on foreign affairs, too: Hamilton advocated a pro-British policy, whereas Jefferson favored the French.

Hamilton attacked Aaron Burr in print when the latter ran for governor of New York in 1804. Burr challenged him to a duel, and Hamilton was killed.

See also Bank of the United States; Burr, Aaron; Federalist Papers; Federalist Party; Revolution.

THOMAS COLE

Alice Hamilton, physician and social reformer, was the first woman on the faculty of Harvard Medical School. Her medical contributions focused on protecting the health of workers. As a reformer she worked on behalf of women's rights, child labor reform, and the peace movement. Hamilton remained professionally active until she was eighty and in her nineties was an outspoken critic of the U.S. involvement in Vietnam.

HAMILTON, ALICE

(1869–1970)   *Social reformer and pioneer in the field of industrial medicine.*

Hamilton grew up amid privilege and comfort on her family's estate near Fort Wayne, Indiana. As a young woman, she overrode her family's objections and earned a medical degreefrom the University of Michigan in 1893. She spent the next four years in study at hospitals in the United States and Germany.

In 1897, Hamilton moved to Chicago, where she worked at Hull-House, a settlement house in one of the city's poorest neighborhoods. Appalled by the poverty and disease she saw around her, she vowed to leave behind some "definite achievement, something really lasting for the better." In 1910 she combined her interest in science with her concern for social justice, conducting Illinois's first investigation into the dangers of lead poisoning in the workplace. Her com-

pelling report led the state to enact a law requiring safety measures in factories where lead was used.

The following year, Hamilton became an investigator with the U.S. Bureau of Labor. Her work exposed conditions that led to disease in the lead, rubber, and munitions industries. After World War I she became the first woman to teach at the Harvard School of Medicine. In 1925 she gathered the product of her years of research in *Industrial Poisons in the United States.* After she retired from teaching in 1935, Hamilton continued to write on industrial medicine. She also remained active politically. She protested Mc-

Carthyism in the early 1950s and the war in Vietnam in the 1960s.

Hamilton's groundbreaking work awakened Americans to the hazards of toxic chemicals and helped improve safety standards in many industries. Yet throughout her long life, she remained modest about her achievements. When she was eighty-eight, she remarked simply, "For me the satisfaction is that things are better now, and I had some part in it."

DEBORAH KENT

HAMILTON, EDITH

(1867–1963) *Educator and author of books about ancient Greece and Rome.*

Hamilton grew up in Fort Wayne, Indiana, the eldest of five children. The Hamiltons were a close-knit family, fond of books and witty conversation. (Her sister was the reformer Alice Hamilton.) When Edith was seven, her father began to teach her Latin. She had a gift for languages and quickly mastered Greek, French, and German as well.

The collapse of her father's business convinced Hamilton that she needed a means to support herself, and she determined to become a teacher. In 1891 she entered Bryn Mawr College in Pennsylvania, where she continued her study of Greek and Latin. After receiving her B.A. in 1894, she studied for a year in Germany.

In 1896, Edith Hamilton became headmistress of the newly founded Bryn Mawr School in Baltimore, a college preparatory program for girls. At first she was overwhelmed by her responsibilities, but she soon won the respect of her students. Always sternly demanding, she tried to instill them with the ideals she found in her study of ancient Greece and Rome.

After retiring in 1922, Hamilton settled in New York, where she launched her second career. She published her first article, a piece on ancient Greek drama, in 1927. In 1930, Hamilton won national fame with her first full-length book, *The Greek Way.* It was followed by *The Roman Way* in 1932 and *Prophets of Israel* in 1936. Scholars grumbled that Hamilton's work was sometimes inaccurate. But the listing of facts were not her main concern. She saw ancient cultures as a wellspring of values for modern people to live by.

In 1943 Hamilton moved to Washington, D.C., where she continued to write into her nineties. She received honorary degrees from several universities and was elected to the American Academy of Arts and Letters in 1957. She was especially moved when the people of Greece expressed their appreciation of her work by making her an honorary citizen of Athens.

DEBORAH KENT

HANCOCK, JOHN

(1737–93) *Merchant and American revolutionary political leader.*

Although best known for his bold signature on the Declaration of Independence, Hancock's historical importance rests chiefly on his leadership in Massachusetts from 1774 until his death in 1793. The son of a Congregational minister, young Hancock, after his father's premature death, was adopted by his childless uncle, Thomas Hancock, a wealthy Boston merchant. His uncle put him through Harvard, sent him to London, and made the young man his partner and heir. When Thomas Hancock died in 1764, John became one of Boston's richest men.

Hancock's public career began with his

A portrait of John Hancock by John Singleton Copley.

election as a Boston selectman in 1765. When one of his ships was seized for smuggling in 1768, Hancock stood up as a champion of resistance to British tyranny and gained election to the Massachusetts legislature. Later, when the legislature transformed itself into a revolutionary Provincial Congress in 1774, Hancock was elected its president. The next year Massachusetts sent Hancock to the Continental Congress, and it was as president of that body that he signed the Declaration.

The most famous signature in American history— John Hancock's on the Declaration of Independence.

Later in the war he served the American cause at state and national levels and helped supply the army and build a navy.

In 1780 Massachusetts voters elected him their first governor, and thereafter he was reelected whenever he chose to run. But Hancock hated making unpopular decisions, and he bowed out of politics during the state's financial and political crisis of 1785–87, when Shays' Rebellion, a farmer-debtor uprising, shook Massachusetts to its foundations. After the rebels were defeated, however, Hancock returned to the governorship, where he urged conciliation, pardoned rebels, and donated part of his salary to the state treasury. In 1788 Hancock played a key role in leading the state convention to approve the U.S. Constitution with the addition of the Bill of Rights. Hancock, who had no children, was generous with his money throughout his life and popular when he died. His name has entered the American language as another term for "signature" because of the way he signed the Declaration of Independence—his name is twice the size of the other signatures.

See also Constitution; Constitution, The Making of the; Continental Congresses; Declaration of Independence; Revolution; Shays' Rebellion.

RICHARD D. BROWN

HARDING, WARREN G.

(1865–1923)   *Twenty-ninth president of the United States (1921–23).*

Harding campaigned for a "return to normalcy" after World War I ended, yet his presidency ushered in an era that was anything but normal. Not since Ulysses S. Grant's administration was political corruption in Washington so widespread.

Harding, a former Ohio newspaper editor,

Warren G. Harding preparing to throw out the first ball in a 1922 baseball game. Many historians regard Harding as the country's worst president. Not only was he ineffectual and ill-equipped to lead the country, but his administration was ridden with scandals.

was elected to the U.S. Senate in 1914. As senator, he accomplished little, but he was well liked and loyal to his party. His reputation as a speaker at Republican Party gatherings as well as his striking good looks further boosted his career. When the Republican National Convention of 1920 was deadlocked, he was nominated as a compromise candidate for president, described as the "best of the second-raters."

Aware of his shortcomings, President Harding appointed some of the nation's most capable men to office, such as Herbert Hoo-

ver as secretary of commerce, Charles Evans Hughes as secretary of state, and Andrew Mellon as secretary of the treasury. "Normalcy" for Harding meant business prosperity and economical government. Corporate taxes were cut, and a high tariff was enacted to protect business from foreign competition. Harding signed the Budgeting and Accounting Act (1921) to streamline government procedures and vetoed the veterans bonus bill (1922), thus denying benefits to those who had fought in World War I. Under Harding, the United States did not join the League of Nations. Instead, his administration protected American overseas interests by holding the Washington Disarmament Conference of 1921–22 and signing the Naval Arms Limitation Treaty.

The Harding administration was rocked by scandals. For example, Secretary of the Interior Albert B. Fall took bribes to lease naval oil reserves at Teapot Dome to private oil companies, and Director of the Veterans' Bureau Charles R. Forbes sold off medical supplies for personal profit. Even Attorney General Harry M. Daugherty was accused of illegal activities. Harding, a personally honest but inept president, never learned the full extent of the corruption that plagued his administration. Deeply disturbed by what little he did know, he took sick while traveling from Alaska to California and died in San Francisco.

See also Corruption and Scandals in Government; Teapot Dome Affair.

BARBARA SILBERDICK FEINBERG

HARLAN, JOHN MARSHALL

(1833–1911)   *Associate justice, U.S. Supreme Court.*

Educated in Kentucky at Centre College and Transylvania University, Harlan joined the Kentucky bar in 1853. Upon the collapse of the Whig Party in the 1850s, Harlan became a member of the Know-Nothing Party, whose principal platform was opposition to immigration and, in Kentucky, vigorous support of white supremacy. He was elected to serve as a county judge in 1858.

Because Kentucky lay along the border between North and South, it was divided over the issue of slavery. Thus, it was an important decision for the slave-owning Harlan to join the Union army when the Civil War broke out in 1861. Returning to Kentucky in 1863 after his father's death, Harlan was elected state attorney general as a Constitutional Unionist (the successor to the Whig Party). By the end of the war, Harlan belonged to the Republican Party. He twice ran, unsuccessfully, as the Republican candidate for governor of Kentucky.

President Rutherford B. Hayes appointed Harlan, a key supporter, to the Supreme Court in 1877. Harlan's lasting fame as a justice comes from two dissents he wrote in cases involving the newly added Thirteenth and Fourteenth Amendments to the Constitution. In the *Civil Rights Cases* (1883), the Court struck down the Civil Rights Act of 1875 as beyond Congress's power. Harlan, writing for himself alone, denounced the decision, saying that racial discrimination was a "badge and incident of slavery" that was well within the power of Congress to prohibit. In *Plessy* v. *Ferguson,* a seven-justice majority upheld racial segregation in Louisiana. Again, Harlan was the lone dissenter, saying that the Court was in effect accepting the maintenance of a racial caste system in the country. The Constitution, Harlan wrote, is "color-blind."

Harlan stands as an example of the capacity for remarkable moral growth and insight. The opinions of this former slaveholder regarding the meaning of racial justice continue to be studied and admired more than three-quarters of a century after his death.

See also Plessy v. *Ferguson;* Supreme Court.

SANFORD LEVINSON

HARLEM RENAISSANCE

Between 1910 and 1930 Harlem, a white middle-class neighborhood in New York City, was transformed by a flood of black newcomers into the largest concentration of black people in the world. Most of these people were poor, and much of the area was a slum. But Harlem also attracted large numbers of ambitious and talented black writers, musicians, and artists. These people made the community a thriving intellectual and cultural center. They produced the Harlem Renaissance.

Black-owned and managed theaters, clubs, magazines, and newspapers flourished. Surrounded by people like themselves and relatively free from the unreasoning prejudices of white society, poets like Langston Hughes, actors like Canada Lee, and writers like Zora Neale Hurston and Richard Wright felt free —able to employ their creative energies as they wished.

One result of the Harlem Renaissance was to interest white intellectuals in black literature, music, and painting. It also became a force for racial harmony. Because black writers described the harsh side of ghetto life so realistically, some black critics feared their works would impede the development of interracial understanding. But this was not the case, for the most part. For the artists themselves, as Langston Hughes once explained, the Harlem Renaissance was an "expression of our individual dark-skinned selves."

See also Literature; Music; Painting and Sculpture.

HARRIS, JOEL CHANDLER

(1848–1908) *Humorist and southern local-color writer.*

Harris, the creator of Uncle Remus, one of the most popular characters in young peo-ple's literature, was born in rural Georgia. As a boy he got a job setting type for a small newspaper published on a plantation, and there he had the opportunity to read widely in the owner's excellent library. More important, he got to know the slaves who worked on the plantation and listened to the African and African-American animal legends they told. From these humorous tales he drew the dialect narratives he later wrote in the voice of his fictitious storyteller, the old slave, Uncle Remus.

After fifteen years as a reporter and editor for various Georgia newspapers, Harris was asked to write an African-American dialect piece for the *Atlanta Constitution* in 1879. The first Uncle Remus animal story was so popular that he went on retelling the plantation fables he remembered from his youth and the next year published a collection, *Uncle Remus: His Songs and His Sayings.* A great success, it was followed by seven additional collections between 1888 and 1918. The books became international favorites and have been translated into twenty-seven foreign languages.

In the Uncle Remus stories, animals are given human personalities. The trickster Brer (brother) Rabbit, the cruel Brer Fox and Brer Bear, and other animals engage in various conflicts, but the weaker "creeturs" always end up outwitting their stronger opponents.

Harris also wrote "serious" short stories and novels with a southern background. The title story of *Mingo and Other Stories in Black and White* (1884) tells of a slave who remains loyal to his ruined mistress after the Civil War. Other tales recount the problems of freed slaves and whites trying to adjust to the changed life in the South. But it was his subtly wise Uncle Remus stories, with their optimistic message of the ultimate triumph of the weak, that have survived as an important and beloved part of American literature.

See also Literature, Children's and Young Adult.

DENNIS WEPMAN

HARRISON, BENJAMIN

(1833–1901) *Twenty-third president of the United States (1889–93).*

Harrison was the grandson of President William Henry Harrison and spent his childhood on his grandfather's farm in Ohio. During the Civil War, he fought for the Union under William Tecumseh Sherman and saw more combat than his famous Indian-fighting grandparent ever did.

Despite an aloof and forbidding personality, Harrison became a successful lawyer and respected Republican politician in Indiana. He lost a race for governor in 1876 but won a seat in the Senate four years later. In 1888, the Republican Party made him their presidential candidate. He campaigned from the front porch of his home in Indianapolis, giving short speeches to his supporters. The Democratic candidate, President Grover Cleveland, won the popular vote by a very narrow margin, but Harrison carried states with more electoral votes and won the election.

President Harrison reduced the surplus in the Treasury with help from the "Billion-Dollar Congress" (so called because it spent such large amounts of money). He signed laws permitting for expensive river and harbor construction projects, generous veterans' benefits, and the building of a large modern navy. He also approved the Sherman Antitrust Act (1890), intended to encourage business competition. He modified the McKinley Tariff, which had imposed very high fees on foreign-made goods coming into the United States, by negotiating with other nations for mutual reductions of the rates.

Harrison also took a personal interest in foreign policy. He successfully sponsored the first Pan-American Conference (1889) in an effort to improve relations with Latin America and brought the Pacific island of Samoa under American protection. He was, however, unable to persuade the Senate to approve the annexation of Hawaii, and he failed in an effort to secure a naval base in Haiti.

Before he left office, Harrison had Thomas A. Edison's new electric lights installed in the White House and ordered American flags to be displayed on all public buildings. He lost the 1892 presidential election to Grover Cleveland and retired to Indiana to practice law. Before his death, Harrison ably defended Venezuela in its boundary dispute with Great Britain (1898–99).

See also Antitrust Movement.

BARBARA SILBERDICK FEINBERG

HARRISON, WILLIAM HENRY

(1773–1841) *Ninth president of the United States (March 4–April 4, 1841).*

Harrison is remembered more as an Indian fighter than as president because he died only a month after his inauguration.

Harrison, whose father signed the Declaration of Independence, was raised in comfort on a Virginia plantation. He joined the army in 1791 and was an aide to Gen. "Mad Anthony" Wayne during the Battle of Fallen Timbers (1794) against the Indians, which opened the old Northwest Territory to white settlement. In 1798, he became secretary of

The top portion of a campaign poster for William Henry Harrison's 1840 run for the presidency, the first campaign to rely heavily on slogans and advertising. The poster portrays him as a simple farmer outside his humble log cabin, with a barrel of hard cider on the ground, meant to show that he was just an ordinary, rough-and-tough hard-drinking man. Ironically, this "log cabin and hard cider" candidate was in fact from a wealthy background. Harrison won by a landslide, but died a month after his inauguration.

the Northwest Territory and a year later, the territory's first delegate to Congress.

One of his duties as governor of the Indiana Territory (1800–12) was to defend the frontier. In 1809, the great Shawnee Chief Tecumseh organized many tribes into a confederation to resist federal seizure of Indian lands. In 1811, Harrison was leading an army of a thousand men into the wilderness to wipe out Indian villages when Tecumseh's braves attacked his encampment at the Tippecanoe River, just before dawn. After two and a half hours of heavy fighting, they were driven off. Although the confederation was shattered, Indian resistance in the region did not end until Harrison defeated Tecumseh and his British allies at the Battle of the Thames in southern Canada during the War of 1812.

After the war Harrison settled in Ohio, serving in the House of Representatives (1816–19), the Senate (1825–28), and as minister to Colombia (1830). In 1840, the Whig Party nominated him as their presidential candidate, with John Tyler as his running mate. Despite Harrison's upper-class background, the campaign presented him as a frontiersman of humble origins. His campaign slogan "Tippecanoe and Tyler too" reminded voters of his record as an Indian fighter. He defeated Democrat Martin Van Buren to win the election.

Harrison asked Senator Daniel Webster, famous for his oratory, to help him with his inaugural address. Webster, knowing Harrison's fondness for ancient history and long-winded speeches, boasted that he shortened it by killing "seventeen Roman proconsuls as dead as smelts." Nevertheless, it was the longest inauguration speech ever given. After delivering it in a cold driving rain, Harrison developed pneumonia and died a month later, the first president to die in office.

See also Indian-White Relations; Tecumseh; War of 1812.

BARBARA SILBERDICK FEINBERG

HARTFORD CONVENTION OF 1814

The outbreak of the War of 1812 between the United States and Great Britain severely damaged America's foreign commerce because the British navy swiftly blockaded American seaports. The New England states opposed the war because their prosperity depended on overseas trade, especially trade with the British. The governor of Massachusetts, for example, called it an "Unhappy War," and the Massachusetts legislature described it as "impolitic, improper, and unjust." Some New England states refused to supply state militia units for the army, and merchants continued to trade with the enemy by smuggling goods across the Canadian border.

One result of the unpopularity of the war in the region was to enable the Federalist Party to make a strong comeback. By 1814 extremists were even talking of seceding from the Union. That December representatives of all the New England states met at Hartford, Connecticut, to decide what to do. A proposal to leave the Union and form a New England Confederacy was discussed, but a majority was not ready for such a drastic step. Instead the convention asserted that if the federal government violated the Constitution, a state had a right to "interpose its authority" and refuse to obey. In addition, the delegates proposed some constitutional amendments, including one requiring that Congress have a two-thirds majority in order to declare war.

All this came to nothing because by the time the convention acted, news had reached America that a treaty of peace had been negotiated at Ghent in Holland. This good news discredited the Hartford Convention and dealt a final blow to the Federalist Party, which now appeared to have been unpatriotic.

See also War of 1812.

HAWAII ANNEXATION

Americans first became interested in the Hawaiian Islands in the 1820s when sea captains stopped there for supplies on the way to China. Soon thereafter came missionaries who

Queen Liliuokalani, the last ruler of Hawaii, was a strong nationalist who led a "Hawaii for the Hawaiians" movement. She resisted the political and economic dominance of American settlers on the island, but was overthrown by them in 1893.

wanted to convert the local people to Christianity. The children of these early missionaries often grew wealthy raising sugar, which flourished there. In the period after the Civil War American economic interests in the islands increased steadily.

The native Hawaiians were governed by a monarchy, but the Americans had always exerted great influence on the royal government. In 1891, however, a new ruler, Queen Liliuokalani, came to the throne. When she tried to reduce the power of the American sugar planters, they staged a coup. With the help of U.S. Marines from the cruiser *Boston*, the planters declared Hawaii a republic with

Sanford B. Dole, a prominent planter, as president.

Early in 1893 this government negotiated a treaty of annexation with the administration of President Benjamin Harrison, a Republican. But on March 4, the newly elected Democratic president, Grover Cleveland, took office. He disapproved of the way the planters had taken over the islands and withdrew the treaty of annexation. This only delayed annexation, however, because the Americans had firm control of Hawaii and Cleveland was unwilling to use force to overthrow them. Finally, after the Spanish-American War in 1898, Congress annexed the islands by joint resolution.

See also Expansion, Territorial.

HAWTHORNE, NATHANIEL

(1804–64) *Novelist and short-story writer.*

Hawthorne was born in Salem, Massachusetts. His ancestors included a judge who had presided at the famous Salem witchcraft trials of the seventeenth century. His childhood was lonely and unhappy. His father was lost at sea and his mother mourned him for the rest of her life. Not until Hawthorne went to Bowdoin College in Maine did he find friends. One of them was Franklin Pierce, a future president of the United States.

Hawthorne's first books did not attract much attention. He made his living writing children's books under the name Peter Parley. His friend Pierce helped by getting him a job in the Boston Customs House. After his marriage to Sophia Peabody, Hawthorne settled in Concord in 1842, but he did not like Ralph Waldo Emerson and the other famous New

Englanders who lived there. They were optimists who believed in transcendentalism, a philosophy that Hawthorne thought was superficial.

Hawthorne next moved to western Massachusetts and vowed to make a living as a serious writer. The result was his masterpiece, *The Scarlet Letter* (1850), a tragic story of love and guilt set in seventeenth-century New England. He followed this with two equally successful novels, *The House of the Seven Gables* (1851) and *The Blithedale Romance* (1852).

When his friend Pierce became president in 1853, he appointed Hawthorne the American consul in Liverpool. He stayed in England four years and then spent two more years touring the Continent with his family. During this trip he wrote *The Marble Faun* (1860), a novel about conflicts between American and Italian morality.

Hawthorne died in 1864 as the Civil War was coming to a close. He was pessimistic about the effects of this great conflict on America. He was both a gifted artist and a profound thinker. The power of the past in everyone's life is the great lesson that emerges from his books.

See also Literature.

THOMAS FLEMING

HAYES, RUTHERFORD B.

(1822–93) *Nineteenth president of the United States (1877–81).*

Hayes, an incorruptible man devoted to public causes, won the most controversial presidential election in American history. An Ohio Republican, he was educated at Kenyon College and Harvard Law School. He served with a volunteer regiment during the Civil War and was wounded in action. In 1865, he won a seat in the U.S. House of Representatives even though he had refused to leave his military unit to campaign for office. Elected governor of Ohio in 1867, he served three terms and then became the Republican candidate for president in the election of 1876.

Hayes was convinced he had lost to Democrat Samuel J. Tilden, who received the most popular votes. Election returns, however, were challenged in three southern states, and enough electoral votes were involved to decide the election. The House of Representatives appointed a commission to investigate charges of voting fraud and violence and declare the winner. Meanwhile, Republicans negotiated a compromise, offering southern Democrats in exchange for the disputed votes a cabinet seat, federally financed improvements in their states, and the withdrawal of the remaining federal troops occupying the South after the war. Just three days before the presidential inauguration, Congress accepted the commission's decision to award the election to Hayes.

As president, Hayes fulfilled the compromise agreements. He conducted a morally upright administration in contrast to the corruption that had marked the presidency of Ulysses S. Grant, his predecessor. He was careful to make appointments on the basis of ability rather than political loyalty. For example, he discharged future president Chester A. Arthur from a political post because he suspected him of using his office to benefit friends. Hayes also defended the executive branch from congressional attempts to name his appointees and to force him to sign bills with provisions canceling voting rights for the newly freed blacks. He and his wife refused to serve alcoholic beverages to guests in the White House, which earned her the nickname "Lemonade Lucy."

Hayes kept a pledge he had made to retire after one term and devoted the rest of his life to various reform projects, including the National Prison Association in 1883.

See also Compromise of 1877. *For events during Hayes's administration, see* Greenback Party; Railroad Strike of 1877; Reconstruction.

BARBARA SILBERDICK FEINBERG

HAYMARKET BOMBING

During the spring of 1886 American labor unions made a determined effort to obtain the eight-hour work day. Many thousands went out on strike. In Chicago, a center of the movement, about eighty thousand workers struck. On May 3 trouble broke out around the factory of the McCormick Harvester Company. Police were called in and when the crowd did not break up, they opened fire, killing four men.

To protest the police action, a local radical group organized a demonstration to take place at Haymarket Square the next evening. When the police attempted to break up this gathering, someone threw a bomb in their midst. Eight officers were killed, and when their comrades fired into the crowd, there were many more casualties.

No one ever knew who threw the bomb. But the anarchists who had planned the meeting were arrested and charged with murder. Although there was no evidence that they had done anything except organize a protest meeting, a perfectly legal action, most were convicted. Four were hanged; the rest were sentenced to life in prison. The affair also dealt a heavy and undeserved blow to the strikers and the entire labor movement.

The eight-hour-day campaign collapsed and union membership fell steeply.

See also Labor Movement.

HAYNES, LEMUEL

(1753–1833)   *African-American clergyman.*

Born the illegitimate son of an African slave father and a white mother at Hartford, Connecticut, Haynes was bound from infancy to age twenty-one as a servant in the David Rose family of Granville, Massachusetts. His master and mistress, who were active Christians, treated Lemuel like one of their own children. He gained access to a local gentleman's library at age seventeen and so educated himself beyond the basic level. Upon gaining his freedom in 1774, he continued to live with the Rose family until he joined Gen. George Washington's army at the siege of Boston in 1775. In 1776 he also served in the American garrison at Fort Ticonderoga.

The Revolution fired Haynes's imagination

A painted tray showing Lemuel Haynes, the first ordained black minister in the United States, preaching from his pulpit.

and led him to write a long patriotic poem, "The Battle of Lexington," in 1775, and a lengthy antislavery essay, "Liberty Further Extended," in 1776. The next year he began to deliver sermons in Granville when there was no regular clergyman available, and soon after he decided to become a minister himself. After training with two nearby clergymen in 1779 and 1780, he became the first ordained black minister in the United States and was installed at a new parish in Granville. Five years later he accepted the pulpit at Torrington, Connecticut, where he stayed for three years before moving on to the Congregational church at West Rutland, Vermont.

Haynes served at West Rutland from 1788 to 1818, and it was here that he gained fame as the author of *Universal Salvation, a very ancient doctrine* (1805), a satirical attack on the Universalist ideas of Hosea Ballou, a preacher who claimed that all people would go to heaven and that there was no hell. Haynes's pamphlet went through seventy editions (1805–70) and was popular among orthodox Christians as a defense of the ideas of heaven and hell and divine judgment in the afterlife.

A man of keen wit and great piety, Haynes was invited to preach before large audiences at New Haven and Fairfield, Connecticut, in 1814. But a few years later he was dismissed from West Rutland because of divisions in the church and rising racial prejudice. He finished his career at a small parish in Manchester, Vermont. Haynes married Elizabeth Babbit, a white woman, in 1783, and they had two girls and two boys.

RICHARD D. BROWN

HEALTH
See Epidemics; Medicine.

HEARST, WILLIAM RANDOLPH
(1863–1951)   *Journalist.*

This wealthy Californian, son of a successful miner, was expelled from Harvard University for playing pranks. He worked briefly for Joseph Pulitzer's *New York World* before spending more than $8 million of his family's money running a paper in San Francisco and then challenging Pulitzer with his *New York Journal.* Because they competed for a comic strip, *The Yellow Kid*, the *World* and the *Journal* were put down as "the yellow press."

But poor people in the cities liked the papers. The many pictures and bold headlines were easy to understand. Hearst favored labor unions, higher taxes on the rich, and more government services. He praised the Irish and German immigrants, condemned British influence in American affairs, and spread fear about the increasing Asian immigration.

Hearst cheered when Cuban rebels took up arms against the Spanish and praised the U.S. declaration of war against Spain in 1898. More than a million copies of the *Journal* were sold each day at the height of the crisis. Hearst ordered a reporter to scuttle a ship in the Suez Canal to stop the Spanish fleet from reaching the Philippines, then owned by Spain. In his mind, a publisher and a president had an equal right to act in a national crisis. Fortunately this scheme failed.

Hearst wanted to run for president on the Democratic ticket, but his radical ideas alienated many. His papers spoke lightly about political assassinations, and when President William McKinley was shot and killed in 1901, Hearst was blamed. He was twice elected to the House of Representatives from New York City (1903–07), but he never persuaded enough voters to trust him with a higher office.

Hearst overexpanded in the 1920s and spent recklessly on himself. In 1937 he lost control of his business. He had to sell two-thirds of his art collection and stop construction on San Simeon, his estate in California. Marion Davies, with whom he had a long love affair, lent him a million dollars to weather the crisis. Of the forty-two papers that Hearst had bought or established, only seventeen remained by 1940. He had by now become extremely conservative in his politics. His newspapers did not try to be fair and were held in contempt by many journalists. Hearst increasingly lost touch with workers, especially as he attacked Franklin D. Roosevelt's New Deal.

The 1941 film *Citizen Kane* was partly based on Hearst's life. The movie made him seem far more unhappy than he was, but it showed, accurately, that Hearst no longer understood the public.

See also Magazines and Newspapers.

THOMAS C. LEONARD

HEMINGWAY, ERNEST

(1899–1961)   *Author.*

By the time Hemingway received the Nobel Prize for literature in 1954, he was the most famous living author in America and, perhaps, in the world. People who had never read a line of his work were acquainted with his legend. Photographs of him with safari guides, bullfighters, and army colonels appeared in the popular press. His weathered face, encircled with a bristly crew cut and a grizzled beard, was as widely recognized as

Ernest Hemingway's reputation as a sportsman and adventurer became almost as important as his literary career. Here he is seen on safari.

that of any movie star. His career demonstrated that a man could be both an author and an adventurer.

Hemingway served as an ambulance driver in World War I and returned to his hometown of Oak Park, Illinois, a hero, having been badly wounded in Italy. Rather than going to college as his doctor father and society mother wanted, Ernest returned to Europe, where he worked in Paris as a foreign correspondent to the *Toronto Star*. Reporting, however, was only a means to an end. He wanted to be a great writer, and throughout his life he subordinated everything to that grand ambition.

During the 1920s in Paris, Hemingway married the first of four wives, lived an unconventional life among the writers and artists he met there, and began to write stories in a deceptively simple and understated style unmistakably his own. In time his clipped, jagged rhythms were imitated by countless writers of detective stories, spy novels, and gangster films.

With the appearance of his novel *The Sun Also Rises* (1926), an account of American and British people living aimlessly in Europe, Hemingway became known as the voice of the "Lost Generation." This was the label bestowed by the American writer Gertrude Stein upon the young people whose faith in the future and in the values of their parents had been destroyed by the horrors of World War I. Hemingway's claim to that title was strengthened by his first popular success, *A Farewell to Arms* (1929). It drew on his war experiences and expressed his belief that in a world stripped of traditional values, the first duty of a man is personal courage, a duty that must be met with grace and dignity.

As his fame increased, Hemingway's books seemed to his readers to reflect a carefully cultivated image of Ernest Hemingway, sportsman-adventurer. His obsession with violent death drew him to bullfighting and big-game hunting, which he explored in two book-length essays, *Death in the Afternoon* (1932) and *Green Hills of Africa* (1935). He covered the Spanish civil war in 1936–37 as a newspaper correspondent, and out of that experience came the novel *For Whom the Bell Tolls* (1940). Films based on that and other novels and stories further increased his fame.

After World War II, in which he characteristically sought danger by advancing across France with the American infantry, Hemingway began to drink heavily and his work suffered accordingly. A short novel, *The Old Man and the Sea* (1952), rekindled the faith of his admirers, but he recognized, as did his public, that his powers were on the wane. Ill and depressed, he committed suicide in 1961 by shooting himself.

Several works he left unpublished have ap-peared since his death, but the only one that has not diminished his reputation is *A Moveable Feast* (1964), his memoir of Paris in the 1920s. A flood of scholarly writing has altered his public image, revealing sides of his character that were all too human. But his place as one of the prose masters of twentieth-century literature is secure.

See also Literature.

CHARLES BOHNER

HENRY, JOSEPH

(1797–1878)   Physicist and first director and secretary of the Smithsonian Institution.

When Henry was born in Albany, New York, in 1797, the United States was on the verge of an era of westward expansion and would soon develop communication, transportation, and manufacturing facilities that would join East and West. In 1878, when he died, the country held a prominent place among industrialized nations. His achievements in the physical sciences had contributed to that progress. He helped make our technological age possible.

Henry at fourteen read a book on physics written for young people. Finding it fascinating, he decided to devote himself to the study of this field. While training at the Albany Institute, he showed so much ability that he was made a professor of "natural philosophy" (physics) at the Albany Academy in 1826. In 1832 he was appointed professor at Princeton University, a remarkable achievement for a thirty-five-year-old man.

Henry was excited by the possibilities of electricity and magnetism. He discovered how to transform magnetism into electricity and constructed an electromagnet that could lift one and a half tons. He also built the first electric motor in 1829. By elaborating the principle of long-distance electric current transmission through magnetism, Henry invented the electric telegraph.

In 1846, Congress established the Smithsonian Institution in Washington and named Henry its first secretary and director. He increased its funding by the government, encouraged original investigations, established a publication program, and started a system of international exchanges of scientific information.

Involvement in the administration of science changed the direction of Henry's career. But in later years he did much to pioneer the study of weather prediction. He put science in the service of the Union in the Civil War. The boy who first thrilled to the appeal of a juvenile science book matured into one of the scientific giants of his age.

See also Science and Technology.

For further reading: Thomas Coulson, *Joseph Henry: His Life and Work* (Princeton, N.J.: Princeton University Press, 1950).

E D W A R D   L U R I E

H E N R Y ,   P A T R I C K

(1736–99)   *American Revolution leader.*

Henry was one of the greatest orators in American history. Like that other famous Virginian, Thomas Jefferson, he was a lawyer. But where Jefferson excelled in writing persuasive explanations of why the colonies should resist British oppression, Henry excelled in public debate. In a speech in the Virginia House of Burgesses attacking the Stamp Act in 1765, he denounced King George III, comparing him to tyrants of past ages. In the

A portrait of Patrick Henry commemorates the 1775 speech in which he called for a revolution against Britain: "Gentlemen may cry peace, peace—but there is no peace. The war is actually begun! . . . Why stand we here idle? . . . Is life so dear, or peace so sweet, as to be purchased at the price of chains and slavery? Forbid it, Almighty God! I know not what course others may take, but as for me, give me liberty or give me death!"

following years he was constantly critical of British policy. Calling for armed resistance to Great Britain in 1775, he ended his speech with the famous line, "I know not what course others may take, but as for me, give me liberty or give me death!" After the Revolution broke out, Henry served two terms as governor of Virginia.

When the war ended, Henry, surprisingly, favored restoring the property of those who had remained loyal to England. And in an even more surprising stand, he opposed giving much power to the new central government. He considered it proper for the individual colonies to create a close alliance to throw off British rule, but wrong for the free states to surrender much of their newly won liberty to the United States.

Henry was elected to the Constitutional Convention that met in Philadelphia in 1787, but refused to attend. He bitterly criticized the Constitution drafted at the convention. Even the preamble to the Constitution, beginning "We the people . . . ," offended him. According to Henry it should have read "We the *states* . . ." He demanded that the liberties won in the Revolution be protected against possible violation by the central government. Largely because of criticisms by people like Henry, the first ten amendments that make up the Bill of Rights were added to the Constitution. Thus satisfied, he became a firm supporter of the new government.

See also Antifederalists; Bill of Rights; Revolution.

JOHN A. GARRATY

HIGHER EDUCATION
See Education: Universities and Colleges.

HIROSHIMA
See Nuclear Energy.

HISPANICS

The United States is a country of immigrants. Except for American Indians, every American citizen either came here from another country or is descended from people who did so. Until well into the twentieth century, most immigrants came involuntarily as slaves from Africa or as people from Europe looking for a better way of life. The Europeans came first from England and northern Europe and then from the southern and eastern parts of the Continent.

Hispanics are part of this overall immigrant picture. Except for the Mexicans who were incorporated into the United States as a result of the Mexican War in 1848, nearly all have arrived in the twentieth century. These Hispanics continue to immigrate because they can get here easily (Mexicans, for example, merely by crossing the Rio Grande) and because they continue to face economic hardship, political oppression, and underdevelopment in their native lands.

Within the Hispanic-American population, the term *Latino/Latina* is often used to emphasize an exclusive cultural link to Latin America rather than to Spain; *Mexican American* is often used in the Southwest to indicate an American of Mexican descent; and *Chicano/Chicana* (a term popularized in the sixties) is often used by the youth to indicate opposition to acculturation.

According to census statistics, the United States has the seventh largest "Hispanic" population in the world, exceeded only by Mexico, Spain, Argentina, Colombia, Peru, and Venezuela. There are about 25 million Hispanic Americans in the United States, not counting somewhere between 4 and 10 million "undocumented" people—those who live in the country illegally. Nearly three-quarters of the Hispanic Americans live in the southern and western states. The largest groups, mostly Mexicans, live in California and Texas. Another group made up of Cubans and people from other Caribbean islands inhabits Florida, and another, principally people from Puerto Rico, lives in the big cities of the Northeast.

Contrary to common belief, most Hispanic Americans are not farm workers and do not live in rural areas. Rather, they are heavily concentrated in cities. For example, Los Angeles contains the fourth largest Spanish-speaking population in the world, exceeded only by Mexico City, Barcelona, and Madrid. Miami is heavily Cuban in atmosphere, language, and culture. It is often referred to as "Little Cuba." San Antonio, Texas, has been bilingual and bicultural since its beginnings in the eighteenth century.

Overall, Hispanic Americans are the fastest-growing ethnic group in the United States. If present trends continue, by the middle of the twenty-first century almost half the people of the United States will be able to speak Spanish. Multilingualism is already transforming the Southwest and making important inroads in Miami and New York. But the Hispanic Americans, the varied people of all Latin America, are not merely changing the United States. They are enriching the nation, making it a country where everyone can be both ethnic and American.

See also Immigration.

R I C H A R D   A .   G A R C I A

H O C K E Y

Unlike many other professional sports, hockey was not born in the United States. British soldiers stationed in Canada around 1860 passed the time playing a game called "shinny" with sticks and a ball. In the winter, the soldiers moved onto the frozen lakes and rivers, and the game took off from there.

In 1860, people started to play with a puck instead of a ball, and in 1879, the first set of rules were written at McGill University in Montreal. Six years later, the first amateur hockey organization was formed, and in 1892, the governor of Canada, Lord Stanley, donated an award to be given to the best team in Canada—the Stanley Cup. Since 1927, the Stanley Cup has been awarded to the winner of the National Hockey League (N H L) play-offs.

The first professional league was the National Hockey Association, formed in 1910 from Canadian teams. It became the N H L in 1917. In 1924, the Boston Bruins became the first American team in the league. From 1942 to 1967, only six teams played in the N H L: the Bruins, Montreal Canadiens, Toronto Maple Leafs, New York Rangers, Chicago Blackhawks, and Detroit Red Wings. These teams are sometimes called "the Original Six." Today there are twenty-six teams, including the two newest, the Florida Panthers and the Mighty Ducks of Anaheim, California.

Most people agree that Wayne Gretzky is the greatest hockey player ever. The all-time leading scorer in N H L history, Gretzky also holds dozens of other N H L records. He is a nine-time Most Valuable Player and a nine-time leading scorer. It is no surprise that his nickname is "the Great One."

But the N H L has had many other stars in its history. Gordie Howe was the N H L's leading scorer until Gretzky broke his record. He played in the N H L for a record twenty-six seasons, beginning in 1946. Boston's Bobby Orr was the game's greatest defense man. He was named the league's best defense man eight years in a row from 1968 to 1975. Terry Sawchuk was a dominant goal tender in the 1950s and 1960s. His N H L records for wins (435) and shutouts (103) still stand. Mario Lemieux, who stars for Pittsburgh, has been called "the next Gretzky." The league's rookie of the year in 1985, Lemieux has led the league in scoring four times and has been MVP twice.

There is much debate over the greatest team of all time. Hockey historians usually look at a team's record over a number of years to determine which is the best ever. The Montreal Canadiens from 1955 to 1960 won a record five Stanley Cups in a row. From 1975 to 1979 the Canadiens had another great team, nicknamed "the Flying Frenchmen." This team had the best single season win-loss record in history. Perhaps the best expansion team ever was the 1979–83 New York Islanders. They were only the second expansion team to win the Stanley Cup and went on to win four straight championships.

The greatest, most exciting individual team in hockey never played in the NHL. In 1980, the U.S. Olympic hockey team stunned the nation and the world by winning the gold medal. To do so, the team had to beat much stronger squads from Finland and the former Soviet Union. Many players from that team went on to careers in the NHL.

See also Olympic Games; Sports, Spectator.

For further reading: Jeremy R. Feinberg, *Reading the Sports Page* (New York: Macmillan, 1992).

JEREMY R. FEINBERG
ALEX OBERWEGER

HOLIDAYS

Americans celebrate many holidays, from Valentine's Day to Mother's Day to Halloween, but the United States has no national holidays as such. Instead there are ten federal holidays, designated by the president and approved by Congress.

Strictly speaking, the federal holidays apply only to the District of Columbia and federal employees in other places. Each state has the authority to establish its own holidays and the dates on which they are observed. But to avoid confusion most states adopt the same basic holidays as the federal government.

In 1971, Congress created several three-day weekends by proclaiming that Presidents' Day, Memorial Day, and Columbus Day would henceforth be observed on Mondays regardless of their actual dates. On these and other federal holidays, government offices, banks, and schools are closed throughout the country. There are no mail deliveries, and most businesses give their employees the day off. But not retail stores: except for Thanksgiving and Christmas, the federal holidays have become an excuse for stores everywhere to stage special sales.

The holiday year begins with *New Year's Day* (January 1), which people throughout the western world have celebrated since the time of Julius Caesar. The English essayist Charles Lamb called it "everyone's second birthday." Among America's contributions to the holiday are the making of New Year's resolutions, the Mummers' Parade in Philadelphia (mummers are people who wear masks or disguises for fun), and the Rose Bowl football game in Pasadena, California.

The newest federal holiday is *Martin Luther King, Jr., Day* (the third Monday in January). It honors the memory of the African-American fighter for social justice and Nobel Peace Prize winner, who was assassinated in 1968. Proclaimed a federal holiday in 1983, it was endorsed by the last of the fifty states in 1994.

Presidents' Day (the third Monday in February) commemorates George Washington

The Fourth of July, 1961, celebrated in a Chicago neighborhood.

and Abraham Lincoln, both of whom were born in February: Washington on the twenty-second, Lincoln on the twelfth. The two used to be separate holidays before they were combined, and Lincoln's Birthday is still separate in many states (although not in the nine southern states that fought against the North in the Civil War).

Memorial Day (the last Monday in May) was established to honor the soldiers who died in the Civil War and was originally known as Decoration Day because of the flowers that people put on soldiers' graves. Today the meaning of the holiday has broadened to include American soldiers who died in all wars. On a lighter level, Memorial Day has come to signal the unofficial beginning of summer.

Independence Day (the Fourth of July) celebrates the signing of America's Declaration of Independence from Great Britain on July 4, 1776. One of the nation's happiest holidays, the Fourth of July has long been marked by parades, family picnics, and spectacular fireworks displays.

Labor Day (the first Monday in September) was the idea of Peter J. McGuire, a pioneer labor union leader, who argued in 1882 that the nation's workers deserved to be honored as much as its soldiers. Labor Day became a federal holiday in 1894. Today its union connections are often forgotten, and Labor Day is thought of simply as the last holiday of the summer.

Columbus Day (the second Monday in October) was formerly celebrated on October 12, the day in 1492 when the Italian explorer, Christopher Columbus, first sighted land in the Americas. Observed as a state holiday for many years, and a favorite of Italian Americans, Columbus Day did not become a federal holiday until 1968.

Veterans' Day (November 11) began life as Armistice Day because it commemorated the signing of the armistice that ended the fighting in World War I on November 11, 1918. After World War II and the Korean War, the name of the holiday was changed to honor the men and women who have fought in all of America's wars.

Thanksgiving Day (the fourth Thursday in November) was first observed in 1621 by the Pilgrim settlers of Plymouth, Massachusetts. The Pilgrims celebrated the survival of their colony with a feast, and feasting has been at the center of Thanksgiving Day celebrations ever since. In 1863 President Abraham Lincoln established the official date for the holiday as the last Thursday in November. Then, in 1941, Congress changed it to the fourth Thursday in the month to allow more shopping time between Thanksgiving and Christmas.

America's holiday year ends with *Christmas Day* (December 25), the age-old Christian feast that commemorates the birth of Jesus. In America, Christmas has also become a time for gift giving, decorating homes, stores, and streets, family get-togethers, and holiday parties. Among the uniquely American contributions to Christmas is the image of a fat, jolly Santa Claus, which was created

The first drawing of Santa Claus as we know him—with his large belly, white beard, fur jacket, and cap. Political cartoonist Thomas Nast created this version of the good-natured, roly-poly figure in 1890, and the image has stuck ever since.

by the nineteenth-century cartoonist Thomas Nast.

JAMES CROSS GIBLIN

HOLMES, OLIVER WENDELL, JR.

(1841–1935)   *Associate justice, U.S. Supreme Court.*

The son of an important Boston family, Holmes from an early age was brought into contact with leading New England thinkers, who inspired him to achieve great things intellectually. His most formative experience, though, was probably his service in the Civil War following graduation from Harvard in 1861. Holmes was wounded three times, and he developed a harsh, unsentimental view of life. He believed that human societies would always be marked by conflicts. He was convinced, moreover, that people had relatively little control over their lives, that pure chance often determines their destiny in life.

After graduating in 1866 from the Harvard Law School, Holmes briefly practiced law. He then devoted the next ten years to writing the lectures that brought him lasting fame in 1881 when he delivered them under the title *The Common Law.* In them he emphasized his belief that laws are based not on abstract principles or objective reasoning—what Holmes labeled "logic"—but instead on what people, responding to their experiences, think is necessary to achieve important social goals.

Holmes was appointed in 1882 to the Supreme Judicial Court of Massachusetts after teaching briefly at Harvard. Then in 1902 President Theodore Roosevelt named him to the U.S. Supreme Court, where he served for thirty years. Holmes was one of the most important legal figures of his time even though he was often in the minority on the Court. He emphasized the duty of the Court to defer to decisions made by elected legislatures who reflect the wishes of the majority of people. Political progressives cited Holmes's views, and many ultimately became settled law—though not until after his death when President Franklin D. Roosevelt appointed Felix Frankfurter and others who had been inspired by Holmes to the Court.

At the same time, however, Holmes became a major architect of the modern law of freedom of speech and the use of the First Amendment to safeguard the rights of unpopular minorities even against the wishes of the majority. He believed that ideas should be tested in the "marketplace of ideas." The "best test of truth," he wrote, is the ability of an idea to survive competition with other ideas. Again, many of his most important arguments were made in dissenting opinions, which led his supporters to term him "The Great Dissenter." But his views were written into law after his death, and they basically remain the foundation of current law.

See also Supreme Court.

SANFORD LEVINSON

HOLOCAUST, U.S. RESPONSE TO

By the time the United States entered World War II in 1941, Adolf Hitler's Nazis, who had come to power in 1933, ruled Germany and most of Europe. They believed Jews responsible for almost everything they disapproved of in the world and set out to destroy them all.

First, they passed legislation that made life increasingly difficult for Jews. Then they forced them into ghettos and concentration camps throughout Europe, where hundreds of thousands died of starvation, disease, slave labor, or outright murder.

In 1941, the Nazis devised their plan for the mass murder of all the Jews of Europe, which they called "the Final Solution." They built death camps for that purpose and constructed gas chambers in which Jews were gassed to death. They were also worked, starved, or tortured to death. By the time the war ended in 1945, they had killed 6 million of Europe's 8 million Jews. This was the period of the Holocaust.

Help Refused

The American public learned only a few details about what was going on from newspaper articles, usually printed in the back pages. The first *New York Times* story appeared on page ten. But government officials knew. Nevertheless, the United States did nearly nothing to help the Jews of Europe during the Holocaust. In fact, even when it could have helped, often it did not. Immigration laws, for example, gradually became stricter, so that fewer and fewer Jews from any country could enter the United States.

In 1938 President Franklin D. Roosevelt initiated a conference of thirty-two nations in Evian, France, to deal with the over 600,000 people—585,000 of whom were Jews or mar-

ried to Jews—who wanted to flee the Nazis. With the exception of the tiny countries of the Netherlands and Denmark, almost no changes in policy regarding immigration or the plight of refugees were made by America or any other nation.

In May 1942 a report from Nazi-occupied Poland detailed mass murders of Jews. Only one U.S. newspaper reported it. And in August of that year the American consulate in Switzerland forwarded a telegram to the U.S. State Department. Written by a leading Jew, it warned of Nazi plans for Jewish extermination. The telegram was not made public until months later, and even then it received little

A photograph by Margaret Bourke-White of the survivors of the Buchenwald concentration camp in April 1945 on the day of their release.

attention. The State Department asked the consulate not to pass on news from such sources again.

Bulgaria and Romania in early 1943 offered to cooperate in the removal of 100,000 Jews to a safe place chosen by the Allies. Led by the United States and Britain, the offer was turned down.

Great Britain and America held another conference in Bermuda in April 1943 to discuss "the refugee problem." The two countries knew the "problem" was really the extermination of the Jews, but both agreed that Jews were not to be mentioned by name. Although the Bermuda Conference was responsible for saving 630 refugees one year later, that was all it accomplished.

In June 1944, detailed information from two escapees described the horrifying conditions and mass killings in Auschwitz, Poland, the largest of the death camps. German industrial plants only five miles away had been bombed. Auschwitz had accidentally been bombed in that raid, but little damage was done. The Allies now were asked to bomb the railway lines leading to the camp, which would have slowed down the murders for a while. Since Germany was losing the war by then, that would have saved thousands of lives. Both America and England refused. The United States said that the planes were needed elsewhere, that bombing would be of little help, and that it might make things even worse. The truth is the State and War Departments had decided months before that rescue was not part of their job. Approximately 2 million people—by far the greatest number of them Jewish—were murdered in Auschwitz.

Inadequate Measures

Although the American public knew little about the extermination, most American Jews were informed of it through Jewish news agencies. They held several mass meetings and demonstrations demanding government action. The American Jewish organizations, however, were divided among themselves. Their disagreements with one another prevented them from effectively informing the public about the mass murders and from pressuring the government to take action.

President Roosevelt did create the War Refugee Board in January 1944. Its purpose was to rescue as many victims of the Nazis as possible and to slow down the extermination plan. But the State Department gave it no support, even often opposing its work, and the government gave it insufficient funding. Even so, it still managed to save the lives of over 200,000 Jews and 20,000 non-Jews during the few short months of its existence.

The Reasons

America did not act to help the Jews for several reasons. First, anti-Semitism played a role. During the 1930s, pro-Nazi groups had large followings. During the war, surveys found that 56 percent of Americans believed Jews "had too much power"; 24 percent saw them as "a menace to America." Second, the economy was weak and unemployment very high during the 1930s; the public would not accept thousands of new immigrants. Third, many well-meaning people simply could not believe that horrors of this magnitude were actually taking place. Fourth, during World War I stories of German atrocities in Belgium had made headlines and turned out to be false; no one wanted to be fooled again. Fifth, until 1943 America and its Allies were almost losing the war, and all power had to be directed to winning. After that, the official response was that the best solution to the murder of the Jews was "the earliest possible victory over the Germans"—except by then the Final Solution had left few Jews alive.

See also Jews in America; World War II.

For further reading: Milton Meltzer, *Never to Forget: The Jews of the Holocaust* (New York: Harper & Row, 1976); Barbara Rogasky, *Smoke and Ashes: The Story of the Holocaust* (New York: Holiday House, 1988).

BARBARA ROGASKY

HOMELESSNESS
See Poverty and Homelessness.

HOMER, WINSLOW

(1836–1910)   *Artist.*

Homer, who is widely regarded today as one of America's greatest painters, began his career as an illustrator for newspapers and magazines. When the Civil War broke out in 1861, *Harper's Weekly* sent him to the Virginia front with the Army of the Potomac. He drew realistic sketches of Union soldiers on duty or relaxing behind the lines. After the war he developed many of these drawings into oil paintings.

"If a man wants to be an artist," Homer once said, "he should paint the life around him." During the 1870s he followed his own advice, painting lively pictures of active young women and of children at play or helping with farm chores. By 1875 he was selling enough paintings to be able to give up his illustration work.

Deciding he needed a change of scene, Homer sailed to England in 1881 and settled in a fishing village on the North Sea. There he found the artistic theme that would concern him for the rest of his life: people struggling against the forces of nature, especially the sea.

Upon his return to America in 1883, Homer moved to Prout's Neck, Maine, where his older brother, Charles, had a home. The artist converted a stable on the property into a studio and spent most of his time there, painting the sea in all its moods.

During the 1890s, Homer turned his attention to watercolors. In a fresh, spontaneous style he portrayed trappers riding the rapids of northern rivers and sponge fishers at work in the warm, sunny Caribbean. "In the future, I will live by my watercolors," he predicted, and art critics agree that they rank with his finest works.

An extremely private man, Homer never married and refused suggestions that he write his autobiography. He continued to paint almost until the end of his life and died in his studio at Prout's Neck. Today, his paintings of soldiers, children, and the sea can be seen in art museums throughout the United States.

See also Painting and Sculpture.

JAMES CROSS GIBLIN

HOMESTEAD ACT

This law was one of the indirect results of the outbreak of the Civil War. Before the war the southern states had regularly blocked passage of bills in Congress offering free land to persons willing to live on and develop it. Southerners reasoned that such measures would encourage settlement of the West by independent small farmers rather than by the owners of slaves. In 1856 John C. Frémont, presidential candidate of the new Republican Party, had campaigned on the slogan: "Free Land, Free Soil, Frémont."

After the southern states left the Union, the remaining congressmen easily passed the Homestead Act of 1862. The law granted 160 acres of unoccupied government land to any adult or younger head of a family willing to live on it for five years. Fifteen thousand people had claimed land under this law by the end of the war. Tens of thousands more did so over the following years. The law is still in effect and numerous claims are filed under it every year.

The Homestead Act did not mean that large numbers of poor or unemployed city dwellers got a new start by moving west and becoming independent farmers, as many hoped they would. Farming is a skill that not many city people possess. The cost of moving, building a house, clearing and fencing land, and purchasing seed and fertilizer was another considerable barrier. So was the fact that on the Great Plains, small-scale agriculture was and is uneconomical.

HOMESTEAD STRIKE

The Homestead strike of 1892 was a clash between the Carnegie Steel Company in Pennsylvania, one of the most powerful American corporations, and the Amalgamated Association of Iron and Steel Workers, one of the nation's largest and best organized labor unions. The union represented highly skilled workers who had won large pay increases in 1889. Andrew Carnegie, the major owner of the company, believed they were resisting more efficient methods of making steel. He was determined to break the union.

Carnegie's plant manager, Henry Clay Frick, took charge of the operation. He demanded work changes to increase production. In July, after the union refused to agree,

he discharged the entire force. He then employed three hundred Pinkerton guards to occupy the plant. But when this private police force approached Homestead by a barge on the Monongahela River, they were met by thousands of armed strikers. For an entire day a miniature war raged on the banks of the river. Nine strikers and seven Pinkertons were killed and many more were injured. In the end the Pinkertons surrendered and were forced to withdraw.

A few days later, however, the governor of Pennsylvania sent eight thousand militiamen to Homestead to prevent the strikers from blocking access to the plant. Frick then brought in strike breakers and resumed production. By November the union had been crushed. Steel soon became a nonunion industry, and it remained so until the 1930s.

See also Carnegie, Andrew; Labor Movement; Pinkertons.

HOOVER, HERBERT

(1874–1964) Thirty-first president of the United States (1929–33).

Hoover was known as the "Great Humanitarian," but he was unable to ease the suffering that resulted from the Great Depression, the worst economic collapse in American history.

During World War I, Hoover, a professional engineer and self-made millionaire, supervised volunteers who were helping refugees in Belgium. In 1917, he was named U.S. food administrator, charged with keeping civilians and fighting men fed. Then he managed postwar relief efforts in Europe and served as secretary of commerce under Presidents Warren G. Harding and Calvin Coolidge.

In 1928, Republican Hoover soundly defeated Democratic Al Smith, winning forty of

President Herbert Hoover fishing for trout. He served as president from 1929 to 1933 as the worst depression in the nation's history gathered force.

the forty-eight states to become president. A year later, the Great Depression caused widespread business closings and unemployment. Hoover urged private charities to help the needy because he did not think the federal government should hand out benefits, but the charities soon ran out of money. He also asked for cooperation from businesses and workers to save jobs. Faced with hardship and despair, he tried to boost morale by insisting that "We have now passed the worst . . . and shall rapidly recover."

In 1932, when the depression worsened, Hoover set up the Reconstruction Finance Corporation (RFC) to loan money to failing banks and railroads. When, however, fifteen thousand desperate veterans camped out in Washington, D.C., after a march on the capital to demand relief, Hoover had the army forcibly remove them. By then the makeshift shacks where many jobless Americans lived were nicknamed "Hoovervilles." In foreign affairs, his efforts to help troubled European economies came too late, as did his protests over Japan's invasion of China.

In the 1932 presidential election, Hoover lost all but six states to Franklin D. Roosevelt. He organized European aid programs after World War II and headed two commissions to reorganize the executive branch in 1947 and 1953.

See also Depressions and Recessions; Reconstruction Finance Corporation.

BARBARA SILBERDICK FEINBERG

HOOVER, J. EDGAR

(1895–1972)   *Director of the Federal Bureau of Investigation.*

The son and grandson of federal employees, John Edgar Hoover after graduating from law school went to work in the alien radicals section of the Department of Justice in July 1917.

During World War I and the immediate postwar years, Hoover played a major role in identifying and deporting foreign-born radicals, most notably in planning and executing the dragnet raids of January 1920 (the so-called Palmer Raids, named after Attorney General A. Mitchell Palmer). Hoover's administrative abilities and lack of responsibility for the scandals that had occurred under his superiors, bureau director William Burns and Attorney General Harry Daugherty, led the new attorney general, Harlan Fiske Stone, to appoint Hoover director of the F B I in May 1924. The appointment was part of reforms intended to end the political cronyism and abuses of power that had gone on in the bureau.

Sensitive to the heightened concerns that followed the revelations of bureau abuses, Hoover raised the standards for bureau agents to emphasize the F B I's professionalism. A new image of the agent as "G-man"— efficient, scientific, free of politics—was forged. Hoover further capitalized on the concerns of the 1930s about gangsters and then of World War II about spies. He had many powerful supporters in the Congress, the media, and the general public. His sophisticated public relations efforts and his success in limiting public access to sensitive F B I records soon combined with post-1945 concerns about Communist "subversion" to create a powerful, independent agency.

After Hoover's death in 1972, public revelations of how President Richard M. Nixon misused the federal intelligence agencies for political purposes led Congress and the press to investigate. It was discovered that under Hoover's direction the F B I had massively, at times illegally, monitored the personal and political activities of thousands of citizens. His controversial behavior brought about legislative and executive reforms to ensure that future F B I investigations are lawful and properly authorized.

See also Federal Bureau of Investigation.

ATHAN G. THEOHARIS

HORSE RACING

Horse racing began and flourished in America as an English import. It was organized and patronized mostly by men during colo-

nial days. Gambling provided much of the excitement.

Generally frowned on by northern colonists as contributing to idleness and corruption, horse racing was most popular among the wealthy classes (known as the gentry) in the middle states, particularly New York, and especially in the South. The great southern planters wagered enormous sums on races, proving their "honor" by being willing to risk bankruptcy. Thoroughbred racing, in which horses raced a mile or more around a circular track, was the first really organized sport in the colonies.

After the Revolution, several races pitting northern against southern horses became America's first nationwide sport spectacle. The "Race of the Century" was held on Long Island's Union Course in 1823 between the northern champion Eclipse and Sir Henry of the South. The purse was twenty thousand dollars, and seventy thousand spectators watched Eclipse win.

Following the Civil War, wealthy sportsmen opened luxurious racetracks with elegant clubhouses and dining rooms. Some of the country's most famous racecourses date from these years: Monmouth Park in New Jersey and Pimlico in Baltimore (both in 1870), Churchill Downs in Louisville (1875), and Jerome Park in Westchester County, New York (1866). Horse racing soon became a part of upper-class life. Rich patrons founded the Jockey Club in 1894 and established the first national rules and standards for officials and jockeys.

Though only the rich could own a stable of horses, commercial racing has always depended on popular attendance. It is still the thrill of gambling that draws most spectators to the track. Nowadays many states raise millions of dollars by operating off-track betting parlors where people can bet on races legally. Today's horse racing fans follow the efforts of trainers, jockeys, and thoroughbreds to win the elusive "Triple Crown"—the Preakness, the Belmont Stakes, and the most famous race of all, the Kentucky Derby.

See also Sports, Spectator.

WARREN GOLDSTEIN

HOUDINI, HARRY

(1874–1926)   *Magician.*

A sensational performer known for his daring feats of freeing himself from handcuffs, ropes, and chains, Houdini was considered one of the greatest showmen of all time.

Born Ehrich Weiss in Budapest, Hungary, Houdini was the son of a rabbi who immigrated to the United States and settled in Appleton, Wisconsin, in 1874. Fascinated by magic and the circus, young Ehrich became a trapeze artist in New York City at the age of eight in order to earn money for his family. Shortly after, he worked in vaudeville shows and created a magic act with his brother. He took the stage name Houdini from a French magician, Jean Robert-Houdin. In 1894 he married, and his wife, Bessie, became his stage assistant.

Throughout the early 1900s, Houdini astounded audiences throughout the world with his death-defying escape acts. In one feat, he was shackled with chains and locked inside a roped box that was dropped into water. In another he was hung from the air upside down in a straitjacket and freed himself in less than a minute. Other acts included being tied in ropes and escaping from coffins, milk cans, and prison cells.

Houdini's extraordinary escape acts were successful because of his great strength and

Harry Houdini, the magician and escape artist, prepares to jump into Boston's Charles River in 1906 after he has been bound up in chains.

agility, and his remarkable skill at manipulating locks. He also starred in silent movies. Later in life he crusaded against performers who claimed to have supernatural powers such as mind readers and fortunetellers. Houdini exposed these people as fakes in his book *Miracle Mongers and Their Methods.*

He died in Detroit, Michigan, from complications relating to a stomach injury. Before he died, Houdini told his wife that he would try to visit her as a spirit after his death, but according to Bessie, this never happened.

JOANN BIONDI

HOUSE OF REPRESENTATIVES

The U.S. House of Representatives is one of the two houses of Congress, the lawmaking branch of the federal government. The other is the Senate. (For specific differences between the two houses and the reasons for them, see entry in this book on the Senate.)

The more people in a state, the more representatives it sends to Congress. When the House first convened in 1789, it had 65 members, each representing approximately 30,000 people. Today, there are 435 representatives. Fifty-two are from California, the country's most populous state. Each California representative is elected from one of the state's fifty-two *voting districts* and represents over 500,000 people. The seven least-populated states had one representative apiece in 1993.

Article 1, Section 2, of the U.S. Constitution defines the House. Its chief officer is the Speaker, elected from among its membership. House members must be at least twenty-five years old and have been U.S. citizens for seven years. They are elected to serve for only two years. This provision is aimed at keeping representatives familiar with the concerns of ordinary voters. Their presumed familiarity is the reason the Constitution gives the House the sole power to originate federal tax legislation. The House has other special duties. For example, it may *impeach*—bring charges against—government officials suspected of misconduct in office and investigate problems or alleged wrongdoing in public life. But its primary responsibility is lawmaking.

The Committee System

To enact legislation, the modern House relies upon the committee system it began developing in the early 1800s. Before then, bills were debated by the full House, with each member speaking for as long as he liked. Discussion frequently gave way to shouting matches, even fistfights. "Such a gang . . . makes one shudder," one English visitor commented. No wonder senators looked down upon the "lower house." As the country grew and governing became more complex, representatives found it impossible to inform themselves fully about all the bills before them. The Speaker began appointing a committee to examine each proposal and report back to members. Soon there were 350 committees! Representatives agreed to replace them with a limited number of *standing* (permanent) *committees*, each responsible for examining bills in a particular area: Ways and Means for tax bills, Appropriations for spending proposals, and so on.

Today, the House has 22 standing committees divided into 140 subcommittees. Most representatives serve on two committees and five subcommittees. Whichever political party, Democratic or Republican, holds the majority of House seats has a majority on each committee or subcommittee. Committee chairs are also members of the majority party.

It is at the subcommittee level that most real legislative work is done. About 10,000 bills are introduced during each session of Congress—sessions begin in the January of odd-numbered years—but only around 650 become law. Each bill is assigned a number and sent to the appropriate committee. If committee members oppose a bill outright, they *table* (kill) it. Otherwise, they discuss it, offering changes and amendments. A bill that wins committee approval goes to the Rules Committee. If members of that committee dislike the bill, they deny it a "rule," a denial that usually kills it. If they favor the bill, they issue a rule, stating how much time will be allowed for House debate and how amendments may be added and send it to the House for discussion and a vote. Bills face a somewhat similar process in the Senate.

When both houses have acted on similar bills, those bills, or *acts,* go to a conference committee. That committee, composed of both senators and representatives, tries to work out any differences between the two acts, making them identical in every detail. If a single act comes out of the conference committee and both houses pass it, it goes to the president. His signature makes it law. If the president *vetoes* (refuses to sign) the act, however, it can become law only if it is passed again—not by a simple majority this time, but by a two-thirds margin in each house. This sharing of power between the executive and legislative branches is part of the system of checks and balances written into the Constitution.

Role of the Speaker

The first Speaker of the House, Frederick Muhlenberg of Pennsylvania, performed the formal duties of the office, running meetings, calling members to order, recognizing those who wished to speak, and appointing committees. To such tasks, a later Speaker, Henry Clay of Kentucky, added partisan political leadership. Clay served as Speaker for eight years between 1811 and 1825, marshaling con-

A scene on the floor of the House of Representatives in 1857.

gressional support for the War of 1812 and thwarting the 1824 presidential hopes of Andrew Jackson. Jackson was one of three candidates for president that year, and when no clear winner emerged in the general election, the contest, as specified in the Constitution, went to the House for a decision. Speaker Clay used his influence to round up enough anti-Jackson votes to cost him the election.

Other forceful House Speakers have included Thomas Reed of Maine (who served 1889–91 and 1895–99) and Joseph Cannon of Illinois (1903–11). In 1890, Reed, arguing that overly long House floor debates were interfering with actual lawmaking, proposed strengthening the Speaker's authority to cut off discussion. Reed had the votes he needed to pass his proposal. But his opponents, although outnumbered, knew that if all of them left the House chamber, there would be no *quorum*—the minimum number of representatives required for a valid vote. They began slipping out. When Reed spotted them, he ordered that the House doors be locked. Defiantly, some hid behind curtains and under desks, only to be dragged out and counted as present. Reed's Rules passed.

The powers these rules gave the Speaker were subsequently used by Joseph Cannon to cut off debate on any legislation he personally opposed. In 1910, House members rebelled against the autocratic "Czar" Cannon and handed much of the debate-limiting power over to the Rules Committee. In 1975, concluding that that committee was arbitrarily blocking needed legislation, the House changed its rules again, stripping the Rules Committee of some of its authority and returning it to the Speaker.

The House Today

The House has changed a great deal since 1789. Then it was all-white and all-male. The first black representative was elected in 1870 and the first woman in 1916. In the 1992 elections, a record forty-eight women won House seats and there were over three dozen black members.

Other changes have been less positive. Many voters complain that House members are out of touch with the country, more concerned with being reelected and with their salaries ($129,500 a year in 1993; $166,200 for the Speaker) and privileges (free office space, travel and staff allowances, free postage for campaign mailings, among other things) than with the needs of everyday citizens. Some suggest curbing representatives' power by limiting the number of terms they can serve. Other proposed reforms include cutting salaries and congressional staffs, and forcing candidates for House seats to rely more upon campaign contributions from individual voters and less upon those from large wealthy business, trade, or professional groups.

See also Gag Rule; Senate. *And see biographies of the following representatives:* Blaine, James G.; Clay, Henry; Stevens, Thaddeus.

ANN E. WEISS

HOUSING

The building of housing is a central part of American economic history. It involves land development, financing, construction techniques, and the skills of countless people. The design and use of housing is also part of American social and cultural history, revealing patterns of family life and the conditions under which people live—how much space,

A photograph of the interior of a tenement house by the well-known documentary photographer Lewis Hine shows a mother and her six children living in a tiny room. Originally meant to provide "light, air, and health" for the working class, tenements were cramped and overcrowded apartment buildings, lacking adequate light, ventilation, and plumbing. For additional illustrations related to housing, see insert following page 52.

light, and air a family has. The home has always been a workplace for women, and its design tells us much about housework and child rearing, just as the design of a factory reveals much about a worker's daily routine.

Both single-family houses and multifamily complexes function as part of larger environments. Access to parks and schools, freedom from noise and pollution are aspects of good housing. Piped water, gas and electric lines, sewers, paved streets, and garbage collection also affect the healthfulness and quality of housing. These services were extended to an increasing number of Americans from 1850 on. They made possible indoor sinks, toilets,

and bathtubs, gas stoves, electric lights, central heating, and refrigeration. Historians find that dwellings themselves offer the best evidence of how people used to live. Other sources include building and zoning laws, building permits, deeds, insurance maps, and mortgage lending records. Builders' pattern books of house plans and trade journals are also useful.

American Housing Styles

The history of North American housing begins with Native American dwellings—tipis, pueblos, and longhouses. Colonizers brought British, French, Dutch, and Spanish dwelling forms and construction techniques with them, although at first they often received help from Native Americans in building basic shelter. These European house forms evolved into the heavy timber-framed houses of New England, the Dutch gable houses of New Amsterdam (present-day New York), and the courtyard adobes of the Southwest. Slaves sometimes re-created house forms, or parts of them, from Africa or the Caribbean. Then in the nineteenth century, immigrants from other parts of Europe introduced German, Irish, Polish, and Swedish house and farmstead forms, which created further housing diversity.

Early in the nineteenth century, an American style began to develop first in the brick row houses of eastern cities and then in the wooden Greek Revival houses created by country builders in New England. With the popularity of early carpenters' pattern books, these modest, well-proportioned homes were copied widely. Later styles included Gothic, Italianate, and Queen Anne. Most American cities and towns retain some examples.

By the 1840s, writers such as Andrew Jackson Downing and Catharine Beecher were producing illustrated books about model single-family houses, usually rural or suburban cottages with a garden to be tended by a housewife. From the 1870s to the turn of the century, advocates of women's rights such as Melusina Peirce and Charlotte Perkins Gilman criticized the housewife's role as too isolated and called for kitchenless houses or apartment hotels with child care and community restaurants, freeing women for other activities.

Apartments: Poor versus Rich

In the industrial cities, pervasive misery filled the tenements typical of workers' housing from 1870 to 1930. At first the word *tenement* meant simply a subdivided and sublet property; but it came to mean an apartment building, often on a very narrow lot, with four families or more per floor, sharing sinks on the landings, and privies (toilets) in the basement. Windowless rooms were common. In these cramped units lived whole families—grandparents, parents, children, in-laws, and cousins, sometimes boarders to help pay the rent. Reformers attacked these unhealthful, crowded tenements and campaigned to improve their light, air, and plumbing.

The second half of the nineteenth century also saw the building of comfortable apartment houses for middle-class and wealthy families. The earliest of these were nicknamed "French flats" to distinguish them from tenements. They were succeeded by residential hotels (with dining rooms and maid service) and then by apartment houses of both plain and lavish construction. Apartments became more common by the beginning of the twentieth century, but they were never as popular as single-family houses.

Coming of Suburbia

Beginning in the mid-nineteenth century, the development of streetcar lines that provided transportation out from the centers of cities led to triple-deckers in Boston and other kinds of small multifamily buildings as well as individual houses. Inexpensive bungalows and mail-order houses became popular. (Sears and Aladdin were two famous brands in the suburbs.) In the 1920s, Better Homes in America, Inc., an association of bankers, builders, realtors, and manufacturers, promoted home building and home ownership in cooperation with the Department of Commerce.

During the Great Depression and World War II in the thirties and forties, the federal government increased its support for private suburban housing. The G.I. mortgage for war veterans made mortgage payments a suburban single-family house cheaper than rent on an urban apartment. Unfortunately, federal policy also supported racial and sex discrimination in mortgage lending. As a result, most government support for housing went to white, male-headed families. In addition, the largest subsidies went to the families with the largest tax deductions, not the families most in need of assistance. The government also encouraged the development of suburbs by providing funds for road building, so that people living outside the city could easily drive to work in downtown areas. Road building destroyed many African-American and Latino neighborhoods, making housing conditions worse for minority families.

Public Housing

One alternative was public housing. Under the leadership of Catherine Bauer and Edith Elmer Wood, two housing specialists, the Wagner-Steagall Act, passed in 1937, created the U.S. Housing Authority. But public housing projects after World War II were often placed in urban locations thought undesirable. A Boston project was located on the site of a former garbage dump, for example. Design and construction standards were often poor.

By 1980 only a tiny proportion of American housing was publicly owned, compared with countries like France or Denmark, where as much as a third might be. Today the older housing projects in the United States often need extensive renovation. In 1980, the Reagan administration cut federal assistance to housing for poor families, and this con-

tributed to the rise in homelessness, a major problem across the country.

The history of housing in the United States can only be described as uneven. As a nation, we have been reluctant to establish shelter as a right of all citizens. And we tolerate homeless families living in the streets, families with children. The goal of affordable housing for all Americans is yet to be realized.

See also Architecture; Ghettos; G.I. Bill; Homestead Act; Levittowns; Poverty and Homelessness; Urban Growth. *For illustrations, see insert following page 52.*

DOLORES HAYDEN

HOUSTON, SAM

(1793–1863) *Soldier and politician.*

Many think of Sam Houston as the original Texan—tall, flamboyant, and ornery. Yet Houston was not typical of his breed. Unlike many white Texans of his day, he displayed an unusual familiarity and sympathy with American Indians and, as the Civil War approached, an unpopular devotion to national unity. Both qualities emerged early in his career. As a youth in eastern Tennessee Houston ran away and lived with the Cherokee. During the War of 1812, he came to the attention of Gen. Andrew Jackson. Later, as a supporter of "Old Hickory," Houston served in Congress and as Tennessee's governor. In later years, Houston followed Jackson's example of insisting to fellow Southerners that the Union be preserved. After the collapse of his marriage in 1829, Houston resigned the governorship and again chose to live among the Cherokee.

Although it is not clear whether Houston, as some charged, journeyed to Texas in 1832 to promote rebellion, he did quickly become involved in the protest against Texas's Mexican rulers. When the Texas Revolution began in 1835, the rebel government named Houston commander of its army. After the massacre of Texan fighters at the Alamo in March 1836, a small force led by Houston retreated across Texas. At San Jacinto, on April 21, his men won Texas's independence by surprising and destroying a Mexican army.

During his terms as president of the Republic of Texas (1836–38, 1841–44), Houston reduced government spending and discouraged warfare upon Indians. Many Texans were disappointed when the United States at first refused to admit Texas to the Union, but Houston played a clever diplomatic game. He flirted with England and France, hoping either that they would protect Texan independence against an unhappy Mexico or that Americans' worries about European meddling in the Southwest would lead them to reconsider annexation. Finally, in 1844, President John Tyler moved to make Texas part of the American nation.

As a U.S. senator (1846–59) Houston distinguished himself by his efforts to preserve the Union. The annexation of Texas and the war with Mexico had increased disagreements over the future of slavery in any territory America acquired. Though a slave owner himself, Houston—more than other southern senators—supported compromise measures designed to calm both sides in the bitter debate. He generally opposed measures that would unnecessarily anger Yankees.

Increasingly unpopular with other southern Democrats, even in Texas, Houston lost his Senate seat. He managed to win the governorship in 1859, but events soon moved beyond his control. Shortly after Abraham Lincoln's election in 1860, a convention met to take Texas out of the Union. Despite Houston's opposition, voters backed this move. Though he could accept Texas once again being independent, Houston opposed joining the southern Confederacy. The convention drove him from office, ending his career.

See also Texas Revolution and Annexation.

PATRICK G. WILLIAMS

Sam Houston, a soldier and politician, was a colorful public figure. He was tall and rugged, and had a reputation for courage enhanced by the fact that he had grown up among the Cherokee as a boy.

HOWELLS, WILLIAM DEAN

(1837–1920)   *Literary critic, author, and editor.*

Howells's career began when he wrote a campaign biography of Abraham Lincoln in 1860. Lincoln then appointed Howells U.S. consul to Venice, Italy, where Howells lived from 1861 to 1865. After returning to the United

States, he became assistant editor (1866–71) and then editor-in-chief (1871–81) of the *Atlantic Monthly,* the most important literary magazine in America at that time. He later joined the editorial staff of *Harper's,* writing a popular column for a number of years.

Howells published his views on literature in *Criticism and Fiction* (1891). At a time when many people enjoyed reading stories with unrealistic characters and sentimental plots, Howells encouraged authors to write realistically. Literary characters should act like ordinary people, he said, and should have the same kind of reasons for their actions as people in real life do. Howells also believed that literature should teach readers how to live their lives and should focus on positive things.

Howells wrote the kind of novels he encouraged others to write. Although he also wrote travel books, autobiography, poems, and drama, he is best known for his fiction. His stories present ordinary characters facing difficult choices or situations. *The Rise of Silas Lapham* (1885), Howells's best-known novel, for example, describes the pressures on a businessman and his family to do things they should not do in order to become successful in business and society.

By the end of his career, Howells was one of the most important literary figures in America. He was president of the American Academy of Arts and Letters from 1908 to 1920. He was close friends with many writers of his day including Henry James and Mark Twain. Howells promoted female authors like Sarah Orne Jewett and Emily Dickinson, and he encouraged a new generation of novelists, such as Theodore Dreiser, Hamlin Garland, Stephen Crane, and Frank Norris.

See also Literature.

DAVID C. SMITH

HUGHES, CHARLES EVANS

(1862–1948)   *Chief justice, U.S. Supreme Court.*

Hughes, a native of Glen Falls, New York, was educated at Madison University (now Colgate), Brown, and the Columbia Law School. After practicing law for twenty years, he entered public life as an active Republican participant in New York State reform politics. In 1906, Hughes was elected governor of New York and was reelected in 1908.

Upon nomination by President William Howard Taft and easy confirmation by the Senate, Hughes joined the Supreme Court in 1910. One of his significant opinions was *Bailey* v. *Alabama* (1911), which found unconstitutional Alabama labor regulations that in effect reinstituted a form of slavery. Because of his generally progressive political views, Hughes left the Court in 1916 to challenge the reelection of Woodrow Wilson. After an extremely close loss, Hughes returned to the private practice of law, though he remained active in public affairs. He courageously supported the right of several socialists who had been elected to the New York legislature to take their seats.

In 1921 Hughes returned to Washington as secretary of state in the administration of President Warren G. Harding, serving also under Harding's successor, Calvin Coolidge. He resigned in 1925 and once again resumed the practice of law, with time out for brief service on the International Court of Justice. President Herbert Hoover named him in 1930 to succeed William Howard Taft as the eleventh chief justice of the United States. This time Hughes's nomination was quite controversial, because some senators believed that he was too committed to the views of the corporations who had been his major clients as a lawyer.

During Hughes's tenure, the Court was bitterly divided in regard to the constitutionality of many of the new economic regulations being passed by Congress and state legislatures in response to the Great Depression that began in 1929. In *Home Building & Loan Assn.* v. *Blaisdell* (1934), Hughes wrote for a five-justice majority upholding a Minnesota law offering relief to persons who could not afford to pay the mortgages on their homes. But conservatives were able, sometimes with the support of Hughes, to strike down major components of President Franklin D. Roosevelt's New Deal, finding them beyond the power of the national government. As a result, Roosevelt, following his triumphant reelection in 1936, sought authority from Congress to "pack" the Supreme Court by increasing its membership. Before the Senate rejected the plan, however, the Court upheld, in 5–4 decisions that Hughes wrote, several majority state and federal regulatory laws (the sort of thing Roosevelt wanted). This so-called Revolution of 1937 constitutes one of the most important moments in all American legal thinking, as the Court ratified a far more active role for government in regulating the economy.

Hughes also wrote several important decisions protecting the civil liberties of political and racial minorities. He resigned from the Court in 1941.

See also Supreme Court.

SANFORD LEVINSON

HUGHES, LANGSTON

(1902–67)   *Poet.*

When Langston Hughes died at the age of sixty-five, he was known worldwide as the poet of his people. He was among the earliest African-American writers to re-create black speech and music in literature. He used the beat of jazz and the wail of the blues to express his basic theme—freedom.

Born in Joplin, Missouri, Hughes was raised in Kansas by his mother and grandmother. From childhood on, he worked at many odd jobs. During his high school years in Cleveland, Ohio, an English teacher opened the world of poetry to him, and soon he tried writing poems himself. By the time he was seventeen, his work was so extraordinary that W. E. B. Du Bois began to publish his poems in his magazine, the *Crisis*.

A 1932 portrait of poet and novelist Langston Hughes by photographer Edward Weston. Hughes's writing explored the realities of being black in America and sought to be an "expression of our individual dark-skinned selves."

Hughes dropped out after a year at Columbia College, but later graduated from Lincoln University in Pennsylvania. In the years between, he worked on freighters bound for Africa and Europe, all the while writing his poems. Back in New York in 1924, he became a central figure in the cultural flowering among black artists known as the Harlem Renaissance. It was now that he decided to become the first black writer to make a living solely by his craft. His great talents carried him beyond poetry to short stories, novels, plays, history, autobiography, children's books, opera, and films. But despite his fame, he often suffered financial troubles.

A warm and generous spirit, Hughes made his Harlem home a meeting place for black writers and artists. During the harsh years of the thirties, he was a political activist, often speaking out against poverty and discrimination. Later, in the McCarthy years when many people were being unfairly persecuted for their beliefs, Hughes was hounded for his liberal views. But despite such pressures, he continued to illuminate the lives of African Americans and to help his fellow writers, black and white, American or not. At the memorial service held after his death, friends read some of his poems, and then a jazz trio played a blues song he had requested: "Do Nothing till You Hear from Me." The world continues to hear from him, through the many works of art he created.

See also Harlem Renaissance; Literature.

For further reading: Milton Meltzer, *Langston Hughes: A Biography* (New York: Crowell, 1968).

MILTON MELTZER

HULL-HOUSE
See Settlement House Movement.

HUNDRED DAYS

When Franklin D. Roosevelt became president on March 4, 1933, the Great Depression was at its worst. More than 13 million workers were jobless and most of the nation's banks had either failed or been forced to suspend operations.

But then the president delivered his famous "the only thing we have to fear is fear itself" inaugural address and called Congress into special session to deal with the emergency. In the hundred days between March 9 and June 16, a mass of legislation revived the national spirit and set the country on the long road to economic recovery.

Actually, aside from an emergency banking act approving what Roosevelt had already done to restore confidence in the banking system and the creation of the Civilian Conservation Corps on March 31, all the key measures of the hundred days were passed between May 12 and June 16, a mere thirty-six days.

They included the Federal Emergency Relief Act providing money to help the jobless and the Agricultural Adjustment Act, a plan for raising farm prices by paying growers to take land out of production (both on May 12); the creation of the Tennessee Valley Authority (May 18); the Federal Securities Act regulating the issuance of stock and the management of the stock exchange (May 27); and on June 16, in a burst of activity before Congress adjourned, the creation of the Home Owners Loan Corporation and the Federal Deposit Insurance Corporation (FDIC), and the passage of the National Industrial Recovery Act.

See also New Deal.

HURSTON, ZORA NEALE

(1891?–1960)   Folklorist, anthropologist, and novelist.

Hurston was a major African-American woman writer during the Harlem Renaissance, a rebirth of black art and race consciousness in the 1920s and 1930s. She was born poor and grew up in all-black Eatonville, Florida. The memory of her dying mother's advice to "jump at de sun" and to tell the world the truth about the lives of black people inspired her to become a prizewinning writer, folklorist, and anthropologist.

Hard work, intelligence, imagination, and determination enabled Hurston to overcome the obstacles of race, sex, and class in her path. She studied at Morgan Academy, Howard University, Barnard College, and Columbia University, where Dr. Franz Boas, a famous anthropologist, was her mentor. With the aid of a Guggenheim Fellowship in 1936, Hurston conducted folklore research in the Deep South, Bahamas, Haiti, and Jamaica. She also won literary contests and prizes sponsored by the *Crisis* and *Opportunity,* the journals of the NAACP and the Urban League, the major national civil rights organizations. But she died in penniless obscurity.

The reassessment of her literary achievements began in 1971 with novelist Alice Walker's acknowledgment of Hurston as a literary ancestor in "Looking for Zora." Hurston's books include two pioneering collections of folklore (*Mules and Men,* 1935, and *Tell My Horse,* 1938), which provide valuable details on hoodoo and voodoo, blends of African and European religious systems in North America. In addition, Hurston published four romances and novels (*Jonah's Gourd Vine,* 1934; *Their Eyes Were Watching God,* 1937; *Moses, Man of the Mountain,* 1939; and *Seraph on the Suwanee,* 1948), an autobiography (*Dust Tracks on a Road,* 1942), and a play (*Mule Bone,* published in 1991) coauthored with Langston Hughes. Her most celebrated book is *Their Eyes Were Watching God.*

See also Harlem Renaissance; Literature.

BERNARD W. BELL

HUTCHINSON, ANNE

(1591–1643)   Religious dissenter.

When Anne Hutchinson began challenging religious orthodoxy in New England in 1635, she was taking a stand for her own religious beliefs that few men and even fewer women have dared to do. But the elder statesmen of the Massachusetts Bay Colony might have been less shocked if they had known Hutchinson's family history.

Anne Marbury was born in Alford, England. Her father, Francis Marbury, an Anglican minister, and her mother, Bridget Dryden, had thirteen children of which Anne was the second oldest. The children had access to their father's library and were educated by their parents. That education and her father's example shaped Anne's life. Twice, Francis Marbury, an independent thinker, had been "silenced" by the Anglican church for questioning its tenets. ("Silence" was the equivalent of being suspended by the church from participation.)

Anne married William Hutchinson, a successful merchant, when she was twenty-one. The couple had fifteen children, the last of whom was born in the New World, where Anne and William moved in 1634. They had immigrated with a group of Puritans to the Massachusetts Bay Colony. They arrived in

Anne Hutchinson, the Puritan religious leader, speaking out about her controversial religious beliefs at her trial in Boston in the 1630s. She was banished from the community and moved with her family to what became Rhode Island.

the midst of a raging political and religious struggle. Anne began to hold meetings in her home, advocating her belief that people could be saved regardless of their failings, that salvation was a gift from God to his elect—a belief that was opposed by Puritan ministers. She stood trial three times for her heresy, once before the Bay Colony's General Court and twice before the Church of Boston. In 1637 she was convicted and excommunicated by the church.

Banished from the Bay Colony, Hutchinson went with her family in 1638 to Aquidneck (Rhode Island), where her husband,

William, died. After that, Anne and six of her children settled in what is now New York State. But ill fortune followed them, and in 1643, she and all but one daughter were slain by local Indians. Anne Hutchinson's insistence on pursuing her own religious beliefs would in the next century be validated by the First Amendment to the U.S. Constitution, guaranteeing religious freedom to all Americans.

See also Colonial America; Puritans.

CHRISTINE A. LUNARDINI

HUTCHINSON, THOMAS

(1711–80)   *Colonial governor and historian.*

Hutchinson, who came from a well-to-do merchant family, took his Harvard degree at sixteen. Starting in 1737, he became involved in Massachusetts politics, serving as a selectman of Boston and as one of the town's legislative representatives, ultimately becoming Speaker. Hutchinson attended six Indian conferences and was a major figure in the Albany Congress of 1754, where delegates from seven colonies debated and eventually drafted a plan of colonial union.

Unfortunately, Hutchinson could never resist the temptation to hold numerous high public offices, all at the same time, which led some to envy and even hate him. He became judge of the Suffolk County Probate Court and a judge of the Inferior Court of Common Pleas. By the late 1760s, he had been promoted to the Superior Court of Judicature while retaining the Probate Court seat and taking the lieutenant governor's position as well as a seat on the Governor's Council. In his spare moments, he wrote a three-volume *History of Massachusetts Bay.*

When the first tremors of the drive for American independence began in 1763, Hutchinson found supporting the king and the Parliament natural and proper, although he opposed the Stamp Act taxes of 1765. That same year a violent Boston mob gutted his home and destroyed its contents.

After that, Hutchinson became less and less able to understand the political forces operating in Massachusetts and his own inability to control them, even with the support of the English authorities. As the violence escalated, culminating in the Boston Massacre (1770) and the Boston Tea Party (1773), Hutchinson, who was appointed governor in 1771, tried vainly to find a compromise. He hoped to accommodate both England's insistence on obedience and the independence movement's increasing resistance to London's policies, especially taxation.

Replaced as governor by Gen. Thomas Gage in 1774, Hutchinson sailed to England. Ignored, bitter, and homesick, he died there in 1780.

See also Revolution.

HILLER B. ZOBEL

HYDROGEN BOMB
See Nuclear Energy.

I

~

IMMIGRATION

From colonial times to the present day America has been a land of new beginnings for millions of people from other countries and a haven for persons persecuted for their religious or political beliefs. No less a Founding Father than George Washington said, "The bosom of America is open . . . to the oppressed and persecuted of all Nations and Religions." The Statue of Liberty bears the words of Emma Lazarus's poem, "Give me your tired, your poor/Your huddled masses yearning to breathe free." This was a welcome message to the 12 million immigrants who arrived at New York Harbor's Ellis Island between 1892 and 1924, its heyday as an immigrant processing center. Today 100 million Americans, 40 percent of our population, trace their ancestry to someone who passed through Ellis Island.

Before he became president, John F. Kennedy wrote a book entitled *A Nation of Immigrants* in which he endorsed a liberal immigration policy for the United States. Immigration, he wrote, "infused the nation with a commitment to far horizons, and thereby kept the pioneer spirit of American life, the spirit of equality and hope, always alive and strong."

Immigration's role in shaping the national character of the United States is beyond dispute. The ideas of human rights, representative democracy, and justice on which the

American Constitution is based were brought to this country by immigrants from England. Our religions (except the Native American religions) were brought by immigrants. Our traditions of religious freedom, tolerance, and separation of church and state were fostered by immigrants who had suffered religious persecution in other countries. Successive waves of immigrants have contributed to their new homeland their cultural values and traditions, their food and music, and most important, their determination to make a good life for themselves and their families.

For almost a hundred years after the Revolution immigration to America was unrestricted. Anyone who could buy a boat ticket could come here to live. During that period at least 80 percent of all immigrants came from England, Scotland, Ireland, Germany, and a few other western and northern European countries. But not all immigrants to America came willingly. Before federal law in 1808 barred their importation, over 500,000 enslaved persons had been brought from Africa in forced immigration. In human terms the roots of the United States are in both Europe and Africa.

Controversy over Immigration
Despite its fundamental importance, immigration has always been one of the most controversial and emotional issues in American life. From the beginning, opposition to immigration has stemmed from doubts about the

An immigrant family gazes at the Statue of Liberty across New York City Harbor.

capacity of the American culture and economy to absorb newcomers and from fear of the competition they might bring to the labor market. Even in the colonial period such a prominent figure as Benjamin Franklin asked, why should German immigrants "be suffered to swarm into our Settlements and, by herding together, establish their Language and Manners to the exclusion of ours?" The Know-Nothings, a political party of the 1850s, resented the growth of immigration, particularly of Roman Catholics. They advocated denying the rights of free-born Americans to all immigrants, even those from England and other European countries. In the mid-nineteenth century the American Protective Association was formed to protest increasing Irish immigration to American cities.

In 1882 Congress passed the infamous Chinese Exclusion Act, which was the first piece of U.S. immigration legislation to exclude a national group. In 1917 Congress established an "Asiatic Barred Zone," which halted almost all immigration to the United States from China, Japan, India, and other Asian countries. The Congressional Quota Act of 1921 and the National Origins Act of 1924 put severe limits on emigration from Italy, Russia, and other countries of southern and eastern Europe, as well as from Africa. The purpose of these highly discriminatory laws was to preserve the "ethnic balance" of the United States as it was at that time: a substantial majority of Americans could trace their ancestry to England, Scotland, Germany, and other western and northern European countries.

After World War II many Americans began to question the racism and ethnic prejudice that had become a part of U.S. immigration policy. In 1965 Congress passed a law that stated that no person could be refused immigrant status to the United States because of race, nationality, or religion. The law also stated that preference in issuing immigrant visas was to be shown to (1) persons who had close relatives living in the United States—family reunification—and (2) persons with occupational skills that would be useful in the United States. The landmark 1965 act remains the basis for present immigration law.

The annual limit on immigration, determined by Congress, is presently 700,000, but there are many exceptions to the ceiling—minor children and parents of legal immigrants already residing in the United States, for example, and refugees—persons who have fled their homeland because of political or religious persecution.

Changing Sources of Immigration

Throughout the nineteenth century and much of the twentieth, 80 percent of all immigration to the United States came from Europe, and only 8 percent from Asia and Latin America. After World War II emigration from Europe decreased sharply because of prosperity in western and northern Europe and restrictions on emigration from communist countries in eastern Europe. At the same time, the 1965 law and an outpouring of refugees after the Vietnam War greatly increased emigration from Asia. Latin American emigration increased because of the poverty and political disturbances there. By the 1980s European immigration to the United States had shrunk to just 13 percent of the total, and Asian and Latin American immigration made up 80 percent. In only a few

LEADING SOURCES OF IMMIGRANTS TO THE UNITED STATES

1820–1975		1976–1986	
Country of Origin	Numbers (approx.)	Country of Origin	Numbers (approx.)
Germany	6.9 million	Mexico	720,000
Italy	5.2 million	Vietnam	425,000
Ireland	4.7 million	Philippines	379,000
Austria-Hungary	4.3 million	Korea	363,000
Canada	4.0 million	China/Taiwan	331,000
Soviet Union/Russia	3.3 million	Cuba	258,000
England	3.1 million	Dominican Republic	211,000
Mexico	1.9 million	Jamaica	200,000
West Indies	1.4 million	United Kingdom	150,000
Sweden	1.2 million	Canada	129,000

years the pattern of worldwide immigration to America had turned upside down.

At present, immigration is as controversial as it has ever been in our history. Those who would sharply restrict immigration fear that large-scale Asian and Latin American immigration will further fragment our society and increase competition for jobs in an already depressed labor market. Immigration proponents argue that today's immigrants come to America for the reason that immigrants have always come: to make a better life for themselves and their children. They point out that Asian and Latin American immigrants bring qualities that have always been admired by Americans: a willingness to work hard, a desire for education for their children, and strong and supportive family networks. Both opponents and proponents of immigration, however, express concern about the large numbers of illegal immigrants, mostly crossing the Mexican border, who are burdening some U.S. cities.

Almost certainly the controversy over immigration will continue. And almost certainly, too, many Americans will agree with anthropologist Ashley Montagu who wrote in *The American Way of Life,* "There can be little doubt that a great part of the vitality which is so characteristic of the American scene is due to the static generated by so many different cultural charges."

See also Alien and Sedition Acts; Chinese Exclusion Act; Immigration Restriction League; Know-Nothing Party; Nativism; Settlement House Movement.

For further reading: Brent Ashabranner, *Still a Nation of Immigrants* (New York: Cobblehill Books/Dutton, 1993).

BRENT ASHABRANNER

IMMIGRATION RESTRICTION LEAGUE

In the 1880s and 1890s the number of so-called new immigrants to the United States from southern and eastern Europe increased rapidly. Most of these newcomers were poor and uneducated. Many were peasant farmers in their native lands and were unfamiliar with city life. When they crowded into city slums in America, where living conditions were already unhealthy and crime rates high, they made things even worse.

Earlier immigrants had had similar experiences, but these new immigrants were so numerous that they seemed to many native-born Americans less adaptable, and "inferior" to the poor Irish and German immigrants of the 1840s and 1850s. In 1894 a group of people in Boston founded the Immigration Restriction League. Its purpose was to find a way to limit the new immigration without discriminating directly against people from any particular country or region. Their "solution" was to require newcomers to display the ability to read. Any language, not necessarily English, would do.

Such a literacy test would keep out many of the "inferior" types considered "undesirable" by people who supported the League. Congress passed a literacy bill in 1897, but President Grover Cleveland vetoed it on the ground that it was a "radical departure" from the American policy of free immigration. In 1913 a similar bill was vetoed by President William Howard Taft, but in 1917 another literacy bill was passed by Congress over Woodrow Wilson's veto.

See also Immigration.

IMPEACHMENT

The Constitution provides a method for removing federal officeholders who have committed "Treason, Bribery, or other high Crimes and Misdemeanors" from office before their terms have ended. The process has two parts of which impeachment is the first.

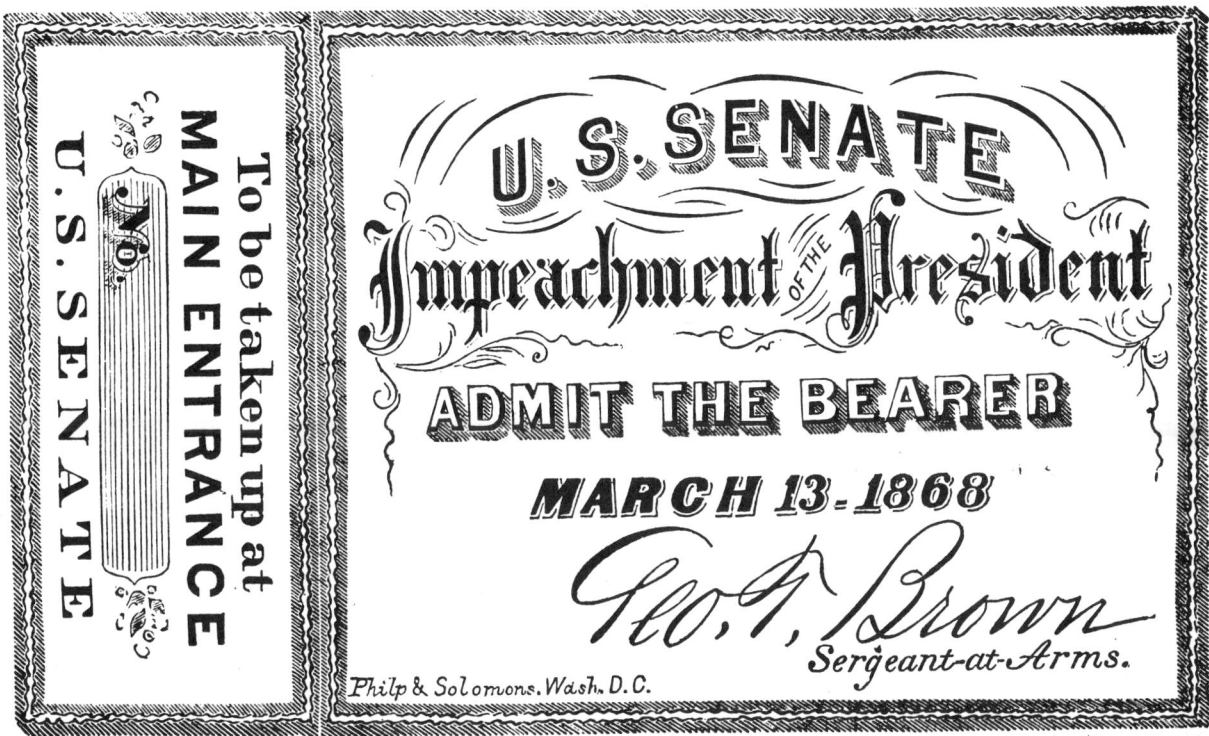

A ticket to the impeachment hearings of President Andrew Johnson in 1868. He was the only president ever impeached, but he was not convicted—the U.S. Senate failed by one vote to secure the two-thirds majority needed for conviction. He served out the remaining term of his presidency.

The House of Representatives makes the accusation, or formal charge. This is known as the "articles of impeachment." Only a majority vote is required to impeach an officeholder. Then a committee of the House acts as the prosecutor in a trial held before the Senate, which acts as judge and jury. A two-thirds vote of the Senate is required to convict the impeached person.

The only president who has actually been impeached was Andrew Johnson, who was charged with having violated the Tenure of Office Act in 1868. He was acquitted. In 1974 President Richard M. Nixon avoided being impeached on charges related to his role in the Watergate break-in by resigning.

IMPERIALISM
See Expansion, Territorial.

IMPRESSMENT CONTROVERSY

The impressment controversy plagued the relations of the United States and Great Britain between the Revolution and the War of 1812. Under British law the captain of a warship had the right to force any British subject to serve on his vessel in an emergency. This was called the right of impressment. For example, if a frigate of the Royal Navy lost several seamen in a battle with an enemy vessel, the captain could stop any British or neutral merchant vessel on the high seas, line up its crew, and make up for his losses by taking any of its sailors whom he thought were British-born.

The difficulty with this practice from the American point of view was that American and British sailors spoke the same language, and short-handed British captains seldom tried to distinguish between them. In addition, many British-born men had emigrated and become naturalized American citizens. But Great Britain did not recognize the right of its subjects to become citizens of another nation. "Once an Englishman, always an Englishman" was the British rule. As a result between 1803 and 1812 at least five thousand sailors were impressed while serving on American ships. A large majority of these men were American citizens. In 1807 H.M.S. *Leopard* actually seized four supposed "deserters" from an American warship, an action that led Congress to pass the Embargo Act. Impressment was a major cause of the War of 1812.

See also War of 1812.

INDEPENDENT TREASURY

After President Andrew Jackson vetoed the bill extending the charter of the Second Bank of the United States in 1832, he ordered his secretary of the treasury to withdraw the $9.8 million the government had on deposit in the Bank. This was accomplished by using the money to pay the government's bills and depositing money the government received in taxes and from the sale of land in state-chartered banks.

By 1836 the government's money was in about ninety banks. But critics complained that these "pet" banks had been chosen because they supported Jackson's Democratic Party. After the Bank of the United States lost influence over their policies, other state banks began to lend money recklessly. This caused inflation and led to the eventual collapse of many of these institutions during the panic of 1837. As a result, in 1840 Congress passed the Independent Treasury Act. Under this law government revenues were removed from all banks and kept in "subtreasuries" (government-owned vaults) until needed. This law was repealed in 1841, but reenacted in 1846. It remained in force until the creation of the national banking system in 1863.

See also Bank of the United States.

INDIAN RESERVATIONS

In 1638 the Puritans established a twelve-hundred-acre reservation for the Quinnipiac tribe near New Haven, Connecticut. With a magistrate (agent) in charge, many "praying Indians" of New England lived there under laws and religion dictated by the Puritans. ("Praying Indians" was the name given to those who adopted the Christian religion.) The Puritans pursued this policy in much of the seventeenth century, but it gave way to a widespread colonial system of separating Indians and whites through treaties. Colonial governments negotiated with Indian nations to create territories for each.

Reservation System

After the Revolution, the United States also established reserves and territories for Native Americans, with modern reservations emerging in the middle of the nineteenth century. The United States created them to end Indian ownership of millions of acres of land and to "save" Indians from extermination. Ranchers, farmers, merchants, miners, and others called for reservations in order to remove tribes from land containing gold, silver, timber, or oil, and from rich farmland.

Reformers wanted reservations in order to teach Indians to farm and to value property.

They also hoped to isolate Native Americans from liquor, gambling, and disease. Reformers sought to "civilize" Indians through education, particularly vocational training. They wanted to Christianize them and destroy their native religions. Although reformers saw reservations as an alternative to killing Indians, they were willing to war against Indian nations to force them onto the reservations. The objectives of reservations, they said, were to "teach their children how to read and write: teach them the art of peace; teach them the truths of Christianity." Reformers believed that as the older Indians died off, their children would abandon the old ways.

The Bureau of Indian Affairs of the Department of Interior ran the reservations. The secretary of the interior and the commissioner of Indian affairs worked through superintendents and agents. These officials carried out Indian policies set by congressional laws and federal court decisions. But many Indians could not speak or read English, and they did not understand the laws. Moreover, white men often made reservation rules that were contradictory to Indian laws. Reservations divided tribes into pro- and antiwhite groups. Agents hired proreservation Indians to serve as policemen. These police punished Indians who refused to obey the rules or who left their reservation.

The reservation system was intended to be temporary, a way to assimilate Indians into white society. To this end, the Bureau of Indian Affairs took native children from their families and sent them to boarding schools, where they were forced to give up their native languages, cultures, and identities. Whites often destroyed native economies, too, and agents insisted that men and women become farmers, ranchers, and wage earners, whether they wanted to or not.

RESERVATIONS WITH LARGEST NUMBER OF AMERICAN INDIANS
(1990 CENSUS POPULATIONS OVER 4,000)

Reservations	Population
Navajo and Trust Lands (Ariz., N.M., and Utah)	143,405
Pine Ridge and Trust Lands (Nev. and S.D.)	11,182
Fort Apache (Ariz.)	9,825
Gila River (Ariz.)	9,116
Papago (Ariz.)	8,480
Rosebud and Trust Lands (S.D.)	8,043
San Carlos (Ariz.)	7,110
Zuni Pueblo (Ariz. and N.M.)	7,073
Hopi and Trust Lands (Ariz.)	7,061
Blackfeet (Mont.)	7,025
Turtle Mountain and Trust Lands (N.D. and S.D.)	6,772
Yakima and Trust Lands (Wash.)	6,307
Osage (Okla.)	6,161
Fort Peck (Mont.)	5,782
Wind River (Wyo.)	5,676
Eastern Cherokee (N.C.)	5,388
Flathead (Mont.)	5,130
Cheyenne River (S.D.)	5,100
Standing Rock (N.D. and S.D.)	4,870
Crow and Trust Lands (Mont.)	4,724

Source: Department of Commerce, Bureau of the Census.

Unhappy Results
Poverty, despair, and disease resulted from the system because reservations lacked sufficient food, medicine, education, employment, housing, and sanitation. Large numbers of Indians died, particularly infants and children. On the Yakima Reservation in the state of Washington, the infant mortality rate was 4 to 11 times greater than it was for whites between 1926 and 1931. On the same reservation in 1930, deaths caused by pneumonia among Indians were 285 times greater than those among whites.

In 1887 the government passed the Dawes Severalty Act, also called the General Allotment Act, which divided reservation lands into parcels of 160, 80, and 40 acres, and allotted them to individual Indians who would renounce their tribal holdings. The government then offered for public sale the land left over after the allotments were made. This program destroyed many reservations, and Indians lost millions of acres.

The situation became so grim that in the 1920s, reformers published a report strongly criticizing Indian policy. The result was the Wheeler-Howard Act of 1934, which reestablished tribal groups, lands, and self-government. In the 1950s the government announced that some tribes would no longer be recognized as tribal groups. The government also relocated thousands of Indians from reservations to urban areas.

In the 1960s, however, many tribes took control of their own affairs. They have fought hard in the years since to control their resources, education, health, government, and employment conditions. Reservations still provide Indians with land bases. They remain the home of groups who preserve their identities as Native Americans, with diverse cultures, societies, and languages.

See also Dawes Severalty Act; Indian–White Relations.

CLIFFORD E. TRAFZER

INDIAN SOCIETIES AND CULTURES

Common themes link most Indian cultures, including the sacredness of the earth, respect for the dead, and the importance of spiritual things and of kinship and family. Still, there is no one type of Native American. The great diversity among them has resulted from thousands of years of varied cultural, linguistic, political, and religious experiences. Tribal societies and cultures have changed over time, but there is also continuity between present-day Native Americans and those of the past.

The Southwest
The Southwest is the home of Pueblo, Apache, Navajo, Ute, Yuman, Tohono O'odham (Papago), Pima, and other tribes. The pueblo-dwellers are a diverse people, descendants of ancient Anasazi farmers who lived in the region long before the arrival of Christopher Columbus and the Spanish invasion. Most Pueblo people live in adobe villages along the Rio Grande and its tributaries, although the Ácoma, Laguna, Zuni, and Hopi tribes live away from the river. They are farmers who retain their early spiritual beliefs. The Spanish introduced Catholicism, so the religion of the pueblo-dwellers is a mixture of native and Christian beliefs. The Pueblos are noted today for their pottery, silver jewelry, and traditional ceremonies.

The Pueblo people are surrounded by Athabascan-speaking neighbors who call themselves Diné (The People). Diné are best known as the Navajos and Apaches. Before the arrival of the Spanish, they lived in tipis and brush-and-skin houses called wickiups. They were independent bands, who hunted and gathered. Some of the Diné raided the pueblo-dwellers and later the Spanish, seizing crops and animals. After the Spanish introduced the horse into the New World around 1600, Navajos and Apaches became skilled riders. Although some Apaches raised corn, squash, and beans, far more Navajos farmed. In fact, the word *navaju* means "those who till the soil." Still, Navajos also

Hopi girls outside of pueblos, the stone or adobe communal houses where they lived. Their distinctive hairstyles indicate they are unmarried.

raided Pueblos and Spaniards, carrying off herds of horses, cattle, and sheep.

In 1680 the Pueblo people rose in a successful rebellion against Spanish oppression, but Pueblo rule of their own land ended in the 1700s when the Spanish reconquered them. The Apaches and Navajos fought against the Latinos and Anglos of New Mexico until the last half of the nineteenth century. Today the various bands of Apaches and Navajos still maintain their traditional language, religion, and literature. They share this distinction with other tribes in the Southwest that are less well known.

The Southeast

Like the pueblo-dwellers, the village-dwellers of the southeastern United States depended largely on agriculture. Many Indians in this region were greatly influenced by the ancient Mississippian culture that flourished prior to the arrival of Columbus. The people lived in villages, growing corn, squash, and beans. Their lives included a rich ceremonial calendar of feasts and rituals. The major tribes included the Tuscaroras, Lumbees, Cherokees, Choctaws, Chickasaws, Creeks, and Seminoles, and there were numerous smaller tribes. Europeans strongly influenced these southeastern Indians, especially those of mixed white and Indian blood. Some of them purchased plantations and slaves or operated saw and grist mills. The Cherokees devised their own written language, publishing a newspaper and books in it.

In the 1830s and 1840s, the United States forced many Indians out of the Southeast. Most of these tribes were compelled to mi-

grate to Indian Territory (present-day Oklahoma) along what is called the Trail of Tears
for the suffering it caused. Although their descendants have often adopted white ways,
they still hold many traditional cultural values.

The Northeast

This is also true of northeastern Indians. Pri-
or to white contact, northeastern, or woodland Indians, as they are also called, lived in
small bands. Women planted corn, squash,
and beans and gathered wild vegetables and
fruits; men fished and hunted. Women had

*Medicine Crow, a Crow chief, during an 1880 visit to
Washington, D.C. Medicine Crow wears a Plains-
style war shirt that commemorates his battles against
the Teton Sioux and the Blackfeet.*

*A Potawatomi couple around 1890. Originally from
the area around Lake Michigan, the Potawatomis
were forced onto reservations in Kansas.*

a great deal of power within their families,
clans, and bands. Among the Iroquois, wom-
en selected the chiefs, and family lineages
were traced through the mother.

During the 1600s and 1700s, most woodland Indians participated in the fur trade and
acquired manufactured goods, which made
them dependent on whites. Many of these
tribes fought against the United States during
the French and Indian War and the American
Revolution. Afterward, the U.S. government
removed most woodland tribes across the
Mississippi River. Today, their descendants
live in Kansas and Oklahoma.

The Great Plains

When the government moved the eastern tribes west, they met the tribes of the Great Plains. Mandans, Hidatsas, and Pawnees lived in huge earthen lodges and raised corn, squash, beans, and sunflowers. They also hunted buffalo. Other Plains tribes such as the Kiowas, Comanches, Cheyennes, Arapahos, and Sioux lived almost exclusively on the buffalo. The meat provided food, and the skins, clothing and shelter. Many of these tribes' ceremonies—Sun Dance, Morning Star, Okipa—are still performed today. The horse changed the Plains culture, permitting people to travel long distances and fight effectively. Many Plains Indians bitterly resisted white settlement on their lands, but all were forced eventually onto reservations run by the Bureau of Indian Affairs.

The Northwest

This was true of every region of the country, including the Pacific and inland Northwest. Traditionally, northwestern Indians lived in

An Assiniboin youth on horseback next to a painted tipi. Tipis were widely used by most of the Great Plains peoples. They could be quickly assembled and taken down and were easy to transport over long distances.

large extended families. Salmon, wild game, roots, and berries made up their diet. On the coast of Washington and Oregon, the Coos, Alsea, Siletz, Tillamook, Chinook, Chehalis, Quinault, Makah, Klallum, and other Indians harvested large quantities of food from the sea. They also developed the arts of wood carving, painting, canoe making, and masking. The coastal people of Alaska and Canada carved elaborate totem poles.

The northwestern peoples developed a rich religious complex of song, story, and ceremony—including one known as the potlatch. These were ceremonial feasts at which the host distributed many lavish gifts to guests. Potlatches were and still are common among the Yakima, Palouse, Wanapum, Walla Walla, Nez Percé, Coeur d'Alene, Spokane, Okanogan, Wenatchi, and others of the inland Northwest. In addition to salmon, these people ate fruits, vegetables, and game. They too adopted the horse culture, traveling to the Great Plains to hunt buffalo. They lived in large mat lodges and skin tipis. Like their neighbors, the United States confined them to reservations, many of which exist today.

A totem pole from a Northwest Coast tribe. Totem poles are carved wooden posts bearing the owner's crests or family history. This example dramatically depicts bird and animal spirit guardians. The word to-tem is from the central Algonquian language and means "family" or "clan."

California

California had the largest native population of any region. The tribes included the Karook, Hupa, Pomo, Miwok, Maidu, Yokuts, Paiute, Chumash, Luiseño, Quechan, and Kumeyaay. The people spoke many languages and resided in the desert, on mountains, in valleys, or along the coast. Their foods included grains, roots, berries, fish, and game. They observed various religions, but nearly all were influenced by Spanish Catholic missionaries. The Spaniards conquered the land, built ranching and farming enterprises, and often enslaved the Indians, destroying much of their culture.

After 1848 miners in the gold rush all but exterminated these native people. Between 1800 and 1900, in fact, the population of California's Indians fell from 260,000 to about 20,000. They have spent the twentieth century recovering from the devastation. Like Native Americans in every region of the United States, the Indians of California have faced a history of disease, death, religious oppression, forced removal from their homes, and economic deprivation. Yet, they have survived and are working with great determination and courage for a better future.

CLIFFORD E. TRAFZER

Indian Cultures of North America

INDIAN-WHITE RELATIONS

Suspicion and hostility have often characterized Indian-white relations in North America. Most early Europeans believed Indians to be culturally, racially, and morally inferior to whites. Noting the obvious differences between themselves and the Europeans, many Indians saw no reason to give up their traditional ways. Greed, nationalistic rivalries, and bad faith on the part of many often led to violence. The resulting conflicts resulted in the near destruction of the Indians.

Early Pressures by Whites

Warfare between Europeans and Indians was common throughout the sixteenth, seventeenth, and eighteenth centuries. The European nations colonizing the New World exploited existing rivalries between the tribes, pitting one Indian group against another. Spanish explorers and soldiers, who seized control of Mexico and the Southwest, wanted to use Indian labor in their mines and on their ranches. Along the Atlantic coast, early English colonists were especially interested in occupying land. In Canada and Louisiana, the French, who came to the New World in fewer numbers, were more successful in forging military and trade alliances with the various tribes.

Following the French and Indian War (1756–63), the French were forced to abandon their North American possessions. The British government, in an effort to reduce the violence between its colonists and the Indians, forbade settlement west of the Appalachian Mountains. But many whites ignored this law. Most Indians living east of the Mississippi River thus perceived the colonists to be a greater threat than the British. Consequently, most Indian tribes sided with Great Britain during the American Revolution (1775–83).

Upon securing its independence, the U.S. government demanded that Indians sell their land and allow whites to move west. Several tribes refused and again supported the British during the War of 1812. The United States became even more insistent that the Indians give way to white settlers. During the 1820s and 1830s, several eastern tribes were forced to move west of the Mississippi River, a migration often accompanied by severe hardships. The Cherokee Indians, for example, were forced to march west during the winter months, traveling without adequate food or clothing on what came to be called the Trail of Tears.

White Expansion in the West

During the 1840s, the United States acquired Texas, California, and the Southwest. The focus of Indian-white relations thus shifted from the eastern woodlands and prairies to the western plains and deserts. The federal government demanded that the Indians move to reservations. Many tribes rejected this solution, fearing that this would force them to give up their homelands and change their way of living. On the reservations, corruption and the government's failure to carry out all its treaty promises often caused great suffering and bitterness. Warfare often resulted, with that in Texas, New Mexico, California, Oregon, and Washington especially common.

During the Civil War, several of the tribes that had previously been removed to the Indian Territory (present-day Oklahoma) opposed the Union. Other Indian groups in Minnesota, Colorado, and New Mexico also resisted federal authority during these years. With the Regular Army having to fight against the Confederacy, less-disciplined vol-

Government officials meet with Sac, Fox, and Kansa chiefs in the 1860s to discuss the surrender of more Indian land west of the Mississippi.

unteer forces bore the brunt of the campaigning against Indians. The number and intensity of white-Indian conflicts increased, culminating in the massacre of several hundred Indians at Sand Creek, Colorado (November 29, 1864), by volunteer troops under the command of Col. John M. Chivington.

With tensions resulting from Civil War encounters already high, railroad expansion, new mining ventures, the destruction of the buffalo (a vital staple of Indian life), and competing demands for western land only added to the pressures. The government was determined that all Indians should accept reservation life. But the Cheyenne, Sioux, Comanche, Kiowa, Apache, Arapaho, and some Nez Percé Indians continued to fight to maintain their tribal integrity and independence. The U.S. Army found it difficult to bring these groups to battle. In hopes of trapping the Indians, army columns would often converge upon their villages from several directions. Although the Indians frequently eluded the army, they would lose their horses, lodges, and food supplies in the process. Equally devastating to the Indians were long, grueling chases that frequently took place during the winter.

U.S. Indian Policies after 1880

With the exceptions of clashes at Wounded Knee, South Dakota (1890–91 and 1973), armed Indian resistance had ended by the early 1880s. To this point, the United States had dealt with the tribes almost as separate nations. But in a crucial departure from past tradition, Congress in 1887 enacted the Dawes General Allotment Act, which distributed reservation property to individual Indians. It also enabled the federal government to sell off "surplus" lands to white settlers, greatly reducing the amount of property under Indian control. The tribes continued to lose authority over their members, but U.S. citizenship was finally granted to all Indians in 1924.

During the presidency of Franklin D. Roosevelt (1933–45), the federal government tried to restore power to the tribes. Commissioner of Indian Affairs John Collier sponsored the Indian Reorganization Act of 1934, which returned some land to tribal ownership. Collier also sought to recognize Indian self-determination, religion, and culture. But Collier's policies were reversed after the Second World War. In an effort to terminate the tribes and assimilate Indians into the larger American society, Congress encouraged individuals to leave the reservations.

Adjustment to nonreservation life proved difficult, however, and tribal loyalties remained strong. During the 1960s and 1970s, federal authorities again emphasized Indian self-determination and tribal influence. Support for Indian education, health care, and job training was increased as part of President Lyndon B. Johnson's Great Society programs, aimed at eliminating chronic poverty and inequality.

The increased spending, however, failed to resolve deep-seated problems on the reservations. Many Indians determined to take more direct control over their lives. Two spectacular examples of this increased activism and militancy came in November 1969, when Indians occupied Alcatraz Island in San Francisco Bay after the United States closed its prison there, and 1973, when for two and a half months an armed Indian group occupied Wounded Knee, South Dakota. Other Indians resorted to legal challenges, winning some grievance claims over old treaty violations and court recognition of tribal sovereignty. Distrust and bitterness caused by hundreds of years of Indian-white rivalry and the inconsistent policies of the U.S. government have not been forgotten.

See also Custer, George Armstrong; Dawes Severalty Act; Pocahontas; Reservations; Sacajawea; Trail of Tears; Wounded Knee Massacre. *And see biographies of the following Indian leaders:* Black Hawk; Crazy Horse; Geronimo; Joseph (Chief Joseph); Philip (King Philip); Pontiac; Sitting Bull; Tecumseh.

ROBERT WOOSTER

INDUSTRIAL REVOLUTION

The Industrial Revolution was marked by the application of machinery and mechanical power to the production of goods. Instead, for example, of thread being spun and cloth woven by hand, after the start of the Industrial Revolution both spinning and weaving were accomplished by machines driven by water power or steam.

The Industrial Revolution began in England in the last half of the eighteenth century. It reached the United States in 1790 when Samuel Slater, who was familiar with English developments, opened a small factory in which spinning machines driven by water power produced cotton thread. Slater quickly expanded his operations and other manufacturers copied his methods. During the War of 1812 English goods could not be imported and these early companies flourished. Soon manufacturers were installing power looms and turning out cotton cloth as well as thread. Eventually many other products were being produced by machines.

The Industrial Revolution made possible large-scale production and greatly reduced the cost of making almost everything. It affected workers, however, in contradictory ways. It made them far more efficient producers, but it lessened the importance of skills, weakened individual workers' bargaining power, and gave them less control over their lives. The first textile mills employed young women who looked upon the work as a way to earn money and escape routine farm work before settling down to married life. But as the pace of production was speeded up by competition and the introduction of more powerful machinery, adult males, especially immigrants, performed more of the work. Their employers often exploited them by requiring long hours of work and paying extremely low wages. This, in turn, led eventually to the growth of labor unions.

By the outbreak of the Civil War, the United States had become an important producer of manufactured goods. By the end of the nineteenth century, it was the largest such producer in the world.

INDUSTRIAL WORKERS OF THE WORLD

In 1905 radical labor leaders Eugene V. Debs, Daniel De Leon, and William "Wild Bill" Haywood formed a new union, the Industrial Workers of the World (IWW). The IWW was known popularly as the Wobblies. Its leaders believed in confronting employers with the combined power of "one big union." Their main idea was to try to organize workers by industries, such as mining or textile manufacturing, rather than by particular crafts, such as carpentry, printing, or bricklaying. The IWW favored striking and even sabotaging plant facilities rather than getting what it wanted by peaceful negotiation.

Ultimately the union hoped to destroy free enterprise capitalism and replace it with some kind of public ownership of the means of production. Its constitution stated: "A struggle must go on until the workers of the world . . . take possession of the earth and the machinery of production and abolish the wage system."

In the years before World War I the IWW was involved in bitter strikes of miners in Colorado, lumberjacks in the Pacific Northwest, and textile workers in Lawrence, Massachusetts, and Paterson, New Jersey. It was much in advance of its time in organizing women, blacks, and recent immigrants, types the American Federation of Labor paid little attention to. During the war many IWW members were jailed on charges of having tried to sabotage war production. The IWW never had more than 150,000 members at any one time and it declined swiftly in the 1920s.

See also Labor Movement.

INDUSTRY

See Automobiles; Industrial Revolution; Labor Movement; Lowell System; Tobacco.

INTEGRATION
See Civil Rights Movement; African Americans: Since World War II.

INVENTIONS
See Science and Technology.

IRAN-CONTRA AFFAIR

In 1979 revolutionary elements in Nicaragua known as the Sandinistas overthrew the dictatorship of Anastasio Somosa. With Russian support, the Sandinistas then set up a pro-Communist government. President Ronald Reagan sought to drive the Sandinistas from power by backing what was known as the *contras* (Spanish for "against"). In 1981 Congress voted to supply the contras with weapons, but the fighting dragged on inconclusively.

In 1984 fear that American troops would become involved led Congress to adopt the Boland Amendment banning further military aid to the contras. The Reagan administration, disturbed by the amendment, sought indirect means of helping the contras.

This effort led to a change in American policy—not in Nicaragua but in Iran! Despite American dislike of Iran because it had held American diplomats captive during the 1979–80 hostage crisis, Reagan in 1986 authorized the secret sale of arms to Iran. He did so in hopes that Iran would then persuade terrorists in Lebanon to release some Americans they were holding as hostages.

The deal was arranged by Lt. Col. Oliver North, an administration official. But with $12 million of the money paid by Iran for the weapons, North bought other weapons and shipped them secretly to the Nicaraguan con-

Marine Lt. Col. Oliver North testifying before a Senate committee during the Iran-contra affair.

tras in violation of the Boland Amendment. This became known in November 1986.

The resulting scandal caused North's superior, national security adviser Adm. John Poindexter, to resign. North was fired and a special prosecutor was appointed to investigate the affair. More than the deal with unpopular Iran was involved. The violation of the Boland Amendment, an act of Congress, was clearly illegal. President Reagan claimed that he knew nothing of this evasion of the Boland Amendment, but if that was the case, then he was certainly guilty of negligence.

IRAN HOSTAGE CRISIS

In the years after World War II the United States had supplied large numbers of planes along with other weapons to Iran. Much of the money received for these arms was used to pay for oil imported from Iran. Mohammad Reza Pahlavi, the shah of Iran, was an extremely unpopular ruler. In 1977 bloody riots protesting his rule broke out in Tehran, the capital of Iran. When his troops refused to fire at the rioters, the shah was forced to flee for his life. A popular religious leader, the Ayatollah Khomeini, took over the government.

Khomeini hated the United States because it had supplied arms to the shah. He called America "the great Satan." In November 1979 an Iranian mob seized the American embassy in Tehran, took the staff hostage, and demanded that the United States return the shah to Iran so that he could be tried for treason. This the United States refused to do. As a result fifty-two hostages remained prisoners in the Tehran embassy for months.

In April 1980, President Jimmy Carter sent U.S. Marine commandos on a daring helicopter raid to try to free the hostages. The raid was a fiasco. The helicopters landed at night southeast of Tehran, but in the confusion several of them crashed and the raid had to be called off. Finally, after war had broken out between Iran and Iraq and Carter had been defeated by Ronald Reagan in the 1980 presidential election, Iran agreed to release the hostages.

IRISH AMERICANS

When John Fitzgerald Kennedy was elected president in 1960, he fulfilled the dreams of generations of Irish Americans. Although Irish Americans were always active in American politics, they were never able to reach the nation's highest office until Kennedy's election. He was the first Irish American, and also the first Roman Catholic, to be elected president.

Irish Americans are one of the nation's largest ethnic groups. Over 40 million citizens trace their roots to Ireland, which is more than eight times the current population of Ireland and Northern Ireland. The earliest Irish immigrants came during the colonial era, before 1776, but the largest group arrived between the 1840s and the 1920s. The Irish potato famine of the 1840s forced over a million men and women to leave Ireland to escape hunger and disease. They settled in cities and towns up and down the East Coast, from Boston and New York to Savannah, Georgia, with some moving inland to Chicago and farther west to the mountain states. Irish immigrants also came in large numbers during the 1950s and 1960s, and again in the 1980s.

While some spoke the Irish language when they arrived, most Irish immigrants spoke English. This was a great advantage that many other immigrants did not have. It meant that they could work and attend school in the United States without having to learn a new language first.

In the mid-1800s, Irish Americans faced strong discrimination in the United States and could get only the lowliest jobs. Signs reading "No Irish Need Apply" appeared in the windows of shops and factories. The Irish, however, eventually found work in police and fire departments, on canals and railroads, as domestic servants, and in politics and education. They also fought valiantly on both sides of the Civil War. New York's famous Fighting 69th Regiment was composed primarily of Irish immigrants. This tradition of service in the military and law enforcement continues to this day.

Irish Americans rose to great prominence in the Roman Catholic church and built many schools, from local parish school systems to large universities. The "Fighting Irish" football team of Notre Dame no longer speaks with Irish brogues, but their nickname recalls the school's founders.

Besides President Kennedy and his family, some famous Irish Americans include Charles Carroll, a signer of the Declaration of Independence; Commodore John Barry, revolutionary war naval commander; James Hoban, architect of the White House; Governor Alfred E. Smith of New York, the first Roman Catholic to run for president (1928); Jimmy Cagney, film star; Grace Kelly, film star and princess of Monaco; Eugene O'Neill, Nobel Prize–winning playwright; Thomas P. "Tip" O'Neill, longtime Speaker of the House of Representatives; President Ronald Reagan; and Father Andrew Greeley, priest, author, and sociologist.

MARGARET M. WATERS

ITALIAN AMERICANS

Over 12 million Italian Americans live in the United States today, representing one of the largest and most influential ethnic groups in the country—one in every twenty Americans is a descendant of Italian Americans. Like that of many other immigrant groups, their story is one of hard work and perseverance in the pursuit of a better life.

Some of the earliest Italians to settle in this country came from the more prosperous parts of northern Italy during pre-Revolutionary times. Many of them opened schools and academies for art, music, writing, and dance. Others were hired by the colonists to create the art and architecture of early buildings.

From the early 1800s to the early 1900s, a massive number of Italians from the poor southern regions of Italy immigrated to America. Most arrived unable to read and almost penniless. Many changed their names to more American-sounding ones. For the most part they settled in large northern cities, although a few established wineries and farms in rural areas. By 1930 there were almost 2 million Italian Americans in the United States.

During World War II, more than a million Italian Americans fought in the armed services; thirteen received the congressional Medal of Honor. From the 1940s onward, more and more Italian Americans began to move into prestigious positions in society. Having overcome a negative image owing to the Mafia (an Italian secret society associated with crime), Italian Americans are now in the forefront of politics, education, business, sports, and culture.

Some of the more prominent Italian Americans include Mother Cabrini, a missionary who was the first American to be canonized by the Roman Catholic church; Enrico Fermi, winner of a Nobel Prize for physics; Frank Sinatra, singer and movie star; Joe DiMaggio, Hall of Fame baseball player; Lee Iacocca, highly successful business executive; A. Bartlett Giamatti, former president of Yale University and baseball commissioner; Antonin Scalia, Supreme Court justice; Geraldine Ferraro, the first woman candidate of a major party for the vice presidency of the United States; and Mario Cuomo, governor of New York State.

JOANN BIONDI

I V E S ,   C H A R L E S

(1874–1954)   *Composer.*

When Ives was born in Connecticut near the end of the nineteenth century, it was understood that serious music had rules and forms that had been established by the great European composers. By the time Ives died many of those old rules had been blown away. It was Ives, as much as any other American, who set the dynamite charges. He heard music everywhere: in revival hymns, in off-key singing, in children's shouts, in fire engine whistles, in factory bells, in city street noise. He took all those sounds and made music of them.

Before Ives, American composers tried to sound like Beethoven or Mozart. Ives used some ideas from the European masters, but, since he talked like an American, he thought he should compose like one. He included bits of American barn dance tunes, hymns, speeches, and popular songs in his music. His compositions are complex and sophisticated (although today they often don't seem so), and they anticipated much of the new music of the twentieth century.

It took a long time for most people to understand what Ives was doing. It took longer for them to take him seriously. His Third Symphony (called the *Camp Meeting*), which was completed in 1904, was not performed until 1946; it was awarded a Pulitzer Prize in 1947 and was finally recorded in 1950.

When Ives began using quarter tones in his compositions, one of his many innovations, he gave the orchestra an extra set of notes to use. It was like putting new colors on an artist's palette. Today quarter tones are commonly used.

Being ahead of your time isn't easy. Because Ives needed to earn a living, he entered the field of insurance and, eventually, became president of the largest insurance company in the world. A pioneer in that field, too, he came up with the idea of estate planning. Few people have been creators in both the world of business and the world of the arts. Ives was exceptional.

The best way to understand a composer is to listen to his music. Start with "Putnam's Camp," part of a composition called *Three Places in New England.* It is narrative music that tells the story of a Fourth of July celebration during the revolutionary war.

See also Music.

J O Y   H A K I M

I W W
See Industrial Workers of the World.

JACKSON, ANDREW

(1767–1845)   *Seventh president of the United States (1829–37).*

Andrew Jackson was the first man to achieve the American dream of a boy born in a log cabin rising to the White House. As president, he acted as a defender of the common man against the moneyed aristocracy. Of Irish Protestant stock, Jackson grew up in South Carolina. When only thirteen, he served in the revolutionary war, coming out of it a tough fighter and a passionate patriot.

At seventeen, Jackson began to study law and established a practice three years later. Soon he was made public prosecutor in wilderness territory that would become the state of Tennessee. There the hotheaded young lawyer fought the first of many duels to come, some bloody and deadly. Like most of the frontier elite, he speculated in land and got rich quickly. At twenty-one he began adding to his income by buying and selling slaves. Eventually he owned 150 and was one of Tennessee's largest planters.

When Indians in the region took up arms to resist the white settlers who were invading their lands, Jackson built a reputation as a fierce Indian fighter. During these years, he led raids on the tribes of the southeastern frontier, destroying their towns, slaughtering many, and forcing them to sign treaties on his harsh terms.

Andrew Jackson's rise in politics was swift.

Andrew Jackson, the first American president from a humble background, was nicknamed "Old Hickory" because of his reputation for toughness, and later "the common man's president," because he favored the ordinary citizen over the privileged and wealthy.

At twenty-one, he was elected Tennessee's first congressman. Then he briefly held a seat in the U.S. Senate until leaving it to become a judge on Tennessee's highest court. At thirty-five he became a major general in the state militia. The War of 1812 gave Jackson a chance to display abilities far beyond what peacetime pursuits had offered. When his troops defeated the British in the Battle of New Orleans, the victory restored national pride and made him a popular hero.

Jackson ran for president in 1824 and won the most popular votes. But because he did not receive the required majority of electoral college votes, the decision went to the House of Representatives. There John Quincy Adams was elected after Speaker of the House Henry Clay threw his support to him. When Adams named Clay his secretary of state, Jackson charged that the two men had struck a "corrupt bargain." Jackson then formed a new party, the Democrats, and built a political machine that won him the White House in 1828. He served two terms, often relying for advice on what was called his "Kitchen Cabinet," a group of close friends. Like other politicians, he used job appointments—patronage—to win and hold support for his policies and his party. To gain his goals, he often appealed to the public over the head of Congress.

Jackson's administration was marked by a considerable expansion of presidential power. He vetoed more bills than all earlier presidents together. He opposed federal spending on highways and canals and refused to renew the charter of the Bank of the United States, which he thought favored the rich over the ordinary citizen. When South Carolina threatened to nullify (not obey) a federal law, he warned he would use the army to enforce respect for national authority, and the state backed down. During his terms, Indian removal to land west of the Mississippi was speeded up. When Jackson's followers took part in riots against African Americans and abolitionists, the president praised the mobs, denounced the antislavery movement, and

called for censorship laws to stop the spread of the movement's materials.

After leaving the White House, Jackson retired to Nashville and his elegant mansion, the Hermitage (which is still preserved as a museum). He died in Tennessee at the age of seventy-eight.

See also Corrupt Bargain; Democratic Party; Electoral College; Indian-White Relations; Jacksonian Democracy; War of 1812. *For events during Jackson's administration, see* Alamo; Bank of the United States; Black Hawk; Nullification Controversy; Texas Revolution and Annexation; Webster-Hayne Debate; Whig Party.

MILTON MELTZER

JACKSON, JESSE

(1941–   )   *Civil rights leader and twice candidate for the Democratic presidential nomination.*

Born in Greenville, South Carolina, Jackson was in college in the North in 1960 when the student sit-in campaign against segregation began in the South. Influenced by the nonviolent philosophy of Dr. Martin Luther King, Jr., he decided to become a minister and joined King's Southern Christian Leadership Conference (SCLC) in the early 1960s. He was given responsibility for Operation Breadbasket, an SCLC effort to carry the civil rights movement to Chicago, where Jackson was attending a seminary. He led a number of successful boycotts of businesses that did not hire blacks. An eloquent speaker, Jackson urged his fellow blacks to believe "I *am* somebody" and rose to prominence in Chicago's black community.

Following King's assassination in 1968, Jackson broke with the SCLC and started his own organization in Chicago, Operation

Jesse Jackson—clergyman, civil rights leader, and politician—at a political rally in Los Angeles's "Little Tokyo" during his 1984 run for the presidency.

PUSH (People United to Save Humanity), a "rainbow coalition" of people of all races. Jackson and PUSH soon achieved national recognition. The following year he entered electoral politics with a failed campaign against incumbent Chicago mayor Richard J. Daley.

In 1984 and again in 1988, Jackson waged unsuccessful campaigns for the Democratic presidential nomination, although he did succeed in garnering millions of votes in the primaries and attracted thousands of new black voters to the registration rolls. His failure was due in large measure to white racism, but his lack of experience in elective office, questions about the finances of Operation PUSH, and misgivings about his tendency to self-promotion also played a role.

In 1992, Jackson moved to Washington, D.C., and won his first elective office as "shadow senator" from the District of Columbia, an unpaid lobbyist position. (Washington does not have representation in the legislative branch of government.) In this position, he has lobbied for statehood for the district and continued to keep his name in the news by speaking out on a variety of national and international issues.

See also Civil Rights Movement.

JIM HASKINS

JACKSON, THOMAS J. ("STONEWALL")

(1824–63)   Confederate general.

Jackson, who became one of the most famous generals in military history, grew up as an orphan in the mountains of what is now West Virginia. He was a struggling student who graduated from West Point more through sheer determination than intellectual ability. This illustrated one of his favorite mottoes: "You may be whatever you resolve to be."

Jackson won three promotions for bravery in the Mexican War. He left the army in 1851 and for ten years was a professor of physics and artillery at the Virginia Military Institute. His many strange habits caused VMI cadets to view him as a character.

His diet consisted of the plainest of food; he spoke only when necessary; he walked in extremely long strides and, whenever riding, seemed always on the verge of falling off his horse. A poor teacher who demanded complete obedience in class, Jackson was not the kind of man whom cadets or fellow faculty would have thought had seeds of greatness inside his makeup.

When Jackson entered the Confederate army in 1861, he was not impressive in appearance. Of above average height at five feet ten inches, he had blue eyes, brown hair, a beard, and enormous hands and feet. He paid little attention to his uniform and was an awkward horseman. Duty he demanded. Jackson had no hesitation in placing even friends under arrest for failure to obey orders to the letter.

Jackson acquired the nickname "Stonewall" at the First Battle of Bull Run, July 21, 1861. There he stood fast—"like a stone wall," it was said—against a strong federal attack. The nickname proved inappropriate, howev-er. His genius lay in secret swift marches, attacks at unexpected places, and heavy assaults intended to destroy rather than merely defeat the enemy.

He demonstrated these traits in all his major battles: the 1862 Shenandoah Valley campaign, Gaines' Mill, Cedar Mountain, Second Bull Run, Fredericksburg, and Chancellorsville. Jackson was a deeply religious man who prayed constantly and gave to God the credit for every success.

On May 2, 1863, at Chancellorsville, Jackson was accidentally shot by his own troops. The amputation of his left arm led to pneumonia, and he died on May 10. His passing was the greatest individual loss suffered by the Confederacy during the war.

See also Civil War.

JAMES I. ROBERTSON, JR.

JACKSONIAN DEMOCRACY

Jacksonian Democracy is the name given to the democratic movements that arose in the 1820s and dramatically changed American politics in the 1830s and 1840s. The largest and most famous of these movements elected Andrew Jackson to the White House in 1828 and laid the foundation for the modern Democratic Party. But Jackson and his supporters also drew their strength from related groups that demanded wider political rights and power for ordinary citizens (defined at that time as white men). With its successes, Jacksonian Democracy made the American political system more open and shattered the property-based elitism that had survived after the American Revolution.

Roots of Jacksonian Democracy

Jacksonian Democracy originated in the social and economic changes that followed the War of 1812. In the northern states, improvements in transportation and the beginnings of the Industrial Revolution turned what had been minor seaports and sleepy villages into bustling commercial centers. In the South, the success of the cotton economy brought the spread of plantation slavery. In the West, the forced removal of Indian tribes opened up fresh lands for cultivation by planters and small farmers.

The speed of these developments was amazing to the generation that lived through them, much as the rise of computer technology and space-age travel has amazed older Americans today. But along with that amazement came awareness that the changes were benefiting some more than others, and writers and politicians began demanding that the nation's political institutions be made more democratic.

In the North, the pressure for change came mostly from workers, small farmers, and small businessmen who thought they lacked sufficient power in local and national affairs. In the South, poorer farmers and smaller planters were in the forefront of the democratic movements, and in the West, migrants who were eager to gain land at cheap prices took the lead. All of them believed that if the political system were open to men like themselves, their interests would be protected and the country would live up to its ideals of equality.

These democratic protests triumphed in a number of ways in the decade after 1815. Most notably, state property requirements for voting were eliminated so that by the late 1820s, almost all adult white men could vote. But even then, the administration of President John Quincy Adams struck many as undemocratic. For one thing, Adams had been elected president in 1824 even though he got fewer popular votes than his rival, the famous Tennessee general Andrew Jackson. Moreover, in office, Adams appeared to many to favor the privileged classes, especially those centered in his native New England. Playing upon the variety of popular resentments that had arisen, Jackson presented himself as a Man of the People and defeated Adams handily in their rematch in 1828.

Jackson in Office

As president, Jackson did even more to raise his standing as a democratic leader. In vetoing a bill extending the charter of the Second Bank of the United States, the most powerful bank in the country, he declared that the nation's economic affairs should not be in the hands of a small group of wealthy men. By backing different measures in favor of land reform, he and his followers stood up for small farmers. When South Carolina's leaders threatened to reject a federal tariff law in the name of states' rights, Jackson threatened to use force if necessary to ensure that the Union and its democratic laws would not be trampled upon. At the height of his power, Jackson had so thoroughly combined the themes of equality and nationalism that his admirers thought his name was synonymous with democracy itself.

Of course, not every American agreed. Jackson's political opponents claimed that, in pushing his policies, he had exceeded the limits on presidential power as stipulated in the Constitution. To these men (known from the mid-1830s on as Whigs) Jackson was not a democrat but a tyrant—King Andrew I, some called him.

Still other Americans had different reasons to consider Jacksonian Democracy as undemocratic. In his desire to open western lands to white settlers, Jackson pursued an aggressive, and at times murderous Indian removal policy, which made him a devil in the Indians' eyes. And Jackson was no friend to the emerging abolitionist movement or to the millions of black southerners held in bondage. Himself a major plantation owner, Jackson never thought that democracy and slavery were incompatible. Moreover, he and his supporters knew that agitation over the slavery issue would threaten the stability of their national political coalition. Thus, Jackson denounced antislavery crusaders. It was, rather, among the lower and middling classes of white male citizens—men suspicious of the power of privileged, monied wealth—that Jackson had his greatest appeal.

Effects on Politics

By the time Jackson left office in 1837, that appeal had permanently altered American political life. His supporters, allied under the banner of the Democratic Party, introduced a more sophisticated form of professional party politics, eventually imitated by their opponents. Mass voting and party participation by the expanded electorate rose sharply to levels considerably higher than those of today. By gathering under him a wide array of democratic discontent, Jackson had made democracy the centerpiece of American politics. From then on, politicians would no longer dare proclaim themselves a special, elevated caste, men of superior breeding, virtue, and enlightenment; no matter what their views, they would have to accept the principle of equal rights, to persuade the voters that they, not their opponents, were common men who had the interests of the sovereign people at heart.

Indeed, the great irony of Jacksonian Democracy was that by enshrining democracy, the Jacksonians helped prepare the way for the political debates that broke up their national coalition and led to the Civil War. After

1840, expansion into western territories made it increasingly difficult to suppress the slavery issue. Southern Jacksonians, looking to protect slavery's expansion, effectively won control of the national Democratic Party. Northern Jacksonians, offended at the southerners' control and increasingly disgusted by slavery, fought back where they could or, failing that, moved off into antislavery politics. In the 1850s, what had once been the Jacksonian Democratic Party had become a stronghold of proslavery southerners allied with northerners who were willing to appease the South at almost any cost. Antislavery northern Jacksonians flocked to the new Republican Party, viewing it as an extension of their old democratic cause.

The dissolution of the Jacksonian movement was an important step on the road to civil war. Yet Jacksonian Democracy left an important legacy. The modern Democratic Party, which after many changes reemerged in the twentieth century as a major vehicle of reform, descends from the Jacksonian movement. And the democratic ideal, now expanded far beyond what it was in the 1820s and 1830s, remains a challenge. Each generation of Americans must define for themselves the limits and the as yet untested possibilities of equal rights.

See also Jackson, Andrew.

SEAN WILENTZ

JAMES, HENRY

(1843–1916)   *Novelist, critic, and essayist.*

James's father, Henry James, Sr., was a noted theologian and philosopher, and his older brother, William James, was a well-known philosopher and psychologist.

Though James was born in New York City,

he lived most of his life abroad. His father wanted him to learn about people in other countries. He sent him to England, Switzerland, and France to visit libraries, museums, theaters, and other cultural attractions.

James never married, and he devoted his life to writing. He wrote stories dealing with a variety of topics, including *The Turn of the Screw* (1898), about a haunted house. Most of his books, however, deal with Americans trying to adjust to European life or Europeans trying to adjust to American life. *Daisy Miller* (1878) explores an American girl's failure to understand what her European friends expect of her. *The Portrait of a Lady* (1881), one of his best-known novels, relates the experiences of Isabel Archer, an American girl who travels to England and then to the Continent. In her innocence she rejects the proposal of a rich American whom the story suggests could make her happy and marries a man who makes her very unhappy.

James brought a new level of sophistication to American writing. In most of his stories, the main characters are rich and smart, and they focus on the kind of things, such as conversation and manners, that interest such people. In "The Art of Fiction" (1884) he encourages writers to describe life realistically and examine how people think and why they act the way they do. James influenced a number of other writers to write the same way.

See also Literature.

DAVID C. SMITH

JAMES, JESSE

(1847–82) *Western outlaw and legendary American Robin Hood.*

More than twenty-five motion pictures, scores of books, and hundreds of articles have been written about the lives of Jesse James and his brother, Frank. Since almost all of them contain a mixture of historical truth, folklore, and legend, the true Jesse James is hard to portray. One thing is indisputable, though: he was a robber and murderer.

Jesse James was born on a farm in northwestern Missouri to the Reverend Robert James and his wife, Zerelda. His father died in California during the gold rush and his mother remarried. The family was pro-South in a violent, politically unstable region. When the Civil War came, Frank James joined William Quantrill's guerrillas, a gang that robbed and murdered civilians and plundered and burned down whole towns in Missouri in the name of the Confederacy. Jesse appears to have waited until 1863 or 1864 to join a similar group, "Bloody Bill" Anderson's gang. Jesse was present at the "Centralia Massacre" when twenty-five unarmed Union soldiers were shot in cold blood.

After the war the brothers formed an outlaw gang that specialized in bank robberies, although they also robbed trains and stagecoaches. Their bloodiest bank robbery took place in 1876 at Northfield, Minnesota. Another group of outlaws, the Younger gang, had joined them for this caper. Three men were killed and the Youngers captured, but the James brothers got away. Five years later, after they had murdered two more men, a reward was placed on Jesse's and Frank's heads. On April 3, 1882, Jesse was shot dead by Robert Ford, a new member of his gang, apparently for the reward money. (Frank James was never convicted and died a free man in 1915.)

In part because railroads and banks were so hated in those years, the legend grew that Jesse James was an American Robin Hood who stole from the rich and gave to the poor.

In reality, James was just an outlaw—and a bloody one, at that.

RICHARD A. BARTLETT

JAMES, WILLIAM

(1842–1910) *Professor and philosopher.*

William James was the son of Henry James, Sr., and the older brother of novelist Henry James, Jr. He grew up in a home of intellectual enthusiasms and educational whims. His father never had a career, having inherited enough money to live a life of leisure. William early on developed acute symptoms of depression as he worried about his future. Should he become an artist, a doctor, or a teacher or, like his father, simply enjoy life?

Study in Germany finally led to a career at Harvard, where he studied medicine and then became an instructor. He taught comparative anatomy, physiology, and hygiene before moving into psychology. Here he made his major contribution: his book *The Principles of Psychology* (1890). This massive tome, known as "James," was also published in an abridged student edition known as "Jimmy." Between them these books remade the discipline. Once largely religious, idealistic, and metaphysical, psychology became a scientific and materialistic field of study.

James later explored philosophy and religion. He proclaimed himself a "radical empiricist" in the British tradition, stressing common sense and experience, especially in *Pragmatism* (1907). This work argued that most philosophical disputes were meaningless because it made no practical difference which side won. A pragmatist always looked at results, asking what effects a given idea might have. Truth in such a context was relative. A true idea could be verified scientifi-

cally and would make a real difference in behavior.

James applied pragmatic methods to religion in *The Varieties of Religious Experience* (1902). He was at pains to defend the validity of religious faith in a world overly impressed by science. God was real, he insisted, because God created real effects. Belief in God made a difference in human actions.

James's ideas had a great influence on artists, writers, and social scientists as well as those working in his own fields.

ROBERT M. CRUNDEN

JAPANESE AMERICANS, INTERNMENT OF

In 1942, early in the war between the United States and Japan, the U.S. Army rounded up all Japanese Americans living in the far western United States and exiled them to ten desolate desert camps surrounded with barbed wire and armed guards. These camps were officially named "relocation centers," but President Franklin D. Roosevelt, who signed the February 19, 1942, executive order, called them "concentration camps." Of the 120,000 persons imprisoned in them more than two-thirds were native-born American citizens, called "Nisei," and the majority (64 percent) were women and children. Some were kept imprisoned for almost four years, and many lost their homes, farms, or businesses.

An Apology
Forty years later, in 1982, a presidential commission reported that these innocent people were imprisoned not for "military necessity" but because of

> race prejudice, war hysteria, and a failure of political leadership. Widespread ignorance of

Japanese Americans contributed to a policy conceived in haste and executed in an atmosphere of fear and anger at Japan. A grave injustice was done to American citizens and resident aliens of Japanese ancestry who, without individual review or any probative evidence against them, were excluded, removed, and detained by the United States during World War II.

As a result of that report Congress enacted the Civil Liberties Act of 1988, which made an unprecedented governmental apology and awarded $20,000, tax-free, to each of the more than sixty thousand survivors of America's concentration camps. (No such apology has ever been given either to American Indians, the victims of massive dislocations, or to enslaved African Americans or their descendants.)

The camps that the American government set up were not places of torture nor was deliberate cruelty generally practiced, although in three camps one or more Japanese Americans were shot to death by their guards. Nevertheless, American citizens were deprived of their freedom merely on the basis of where their parents had been born and where they lived. Most of the few thousand Japanese Americans living east of California were left in nervous liberty throughout the war. Even more surprising, in retrospect, is the fact that the relatively large Japanese-American population of the Territory of Hawaii, where the war started and where every third person was Japanese, was not imprisoned.

The government did make special efforts to create a life as "normal" as possible for the more than forty thousand children who were imprisoned. School systems were created, from pre-school through high school, and teachers were hired for them. These teachers had special problems, however. It was difficult to teach young Americans about the Constitution and the Bill of Rights while their own government was keeping them behind barbed wire.

Some Prisoners Released

The government soon released some Japanese Americans from the camps. As early as the summer of 1942 several thousand were freed to help harvest crops in the interior states, and in the fall hundreds of college students were allowed to leave to attend inland colleges.

Others were recruited that same year to serve in intelligence units of the U.S. Army if they had ability in the Japanese language. Later the army allowed Japanese Americans to volunteer for service in what became the 442d Regimental Combat Team, an all-Japanese unit with mostly white officers, which fought in Italy, France, and Germany. In 1944, the government reinstituted the draft for Japanese Americans, including some still in concentration camps. Altogether some twenty-five thousand, including about one hundred women, entered the army; most served in segregated units and many did so with distinction. The 442d, in fact, became the most decorated unit in American military history. Its men won 18,431 individual decorations including a Congressional Medal of Honor, 47 Distinguished Service Crosses, 350 Silver Stars, 810 Bronze Stars, and more than 3,600 Purple Hearts.

In 1943 the government began to resettle many families in interior and eastern states. But there were still more than fifty thousand persons in the camps when the war ended. The last prisoners were not released until March 1946.

Although many persons believed that the internment was unconstitutional, the U.S. Supreme Court, in three cases decided in 1943 and 1944, upheld the government's action. In

Japanese Americans, most of them native-born American citizens, arriving under guard at the Santa Anita Assembly Center outside Los Angeles in April, 1942. They were later sent to what the U.S. government called "relocation centers," in which some were imprisoned for over three years.

the most important case, six justices approved the forcible removal of native-born U.S. citizen Fred Korematsu from California to a "relocation center." Three justices, however, dissented. The most telling protest was by Justice Frank Murphy who called it "a legalization of racism."

The incarceration of the Japanese Americans is a grim reminder that in times of crisis even democratic governments can violate the rights of those held to be different.

See also Asian Americans; World War II.

For further reading: Yoshiko Uchida, *Journey to Topaz: A Story of the Japanese-American Evacuation* (Berkeley, Calif.: Creative Arts, 1985).

ROGER DANIELS

JAY, JOHN

(1745–1829)   *Statesman, diplomat, and first chief justice of the United States (1789–95).*

Jay, who was born in New York City, graduated from King's College (now Columbia) (1763) and became a lawyer (1768).

In 1774 and 1775, as a New York delegate at both Continental Congresses, Jay argued that the colonies should settle their differences with Great Britain peacefully. But when Congress declared American independence in 1776, he became a firm supporter of the American cause.

Jay was the major author of the New York Constitution (1777), a model for the U.S. Constitution. In 1782–83, he, John Adams, and Benjamin Franklin negotiated the American peace treaty with Great Britain. The Treaty of Paris recognized American independence and gave the United States all territory between the Allegheny Mountains and the Mississippi River.

From 1784 to 1789, Jay was the Confederation's secretary for foreign affairs. He urged that the Articles of Confederation be replaced, saying, "Let Congress legislate; let others execute; let others judge." In 1787–88 he along with Alexander Hamilton and James Madison wrote the Federalist Papers, essays supporting the Constitution. Jay also helped persuade delegates at the New York convention to ratify, or approve it.

In 1789, President Washington named Jay chief justice of the United States. As chief justice, he spent most of his time traveling from state to state to preside over federal circuit courts, which helped establish popular support for the new government. His most important Supreme Court decision, *Chisholm* v. *Georgia* (1793), held that citizens of one state or foreign country could sue another state in federal court; it was overturned by the Eleventh Amendment.

In 1794, Washington sent Jay to London to negotiate a new treaty with Great Britain. The Jay Treaty angered many Americans because it seemed to be too friendly toward the British, but it settled many issues between the

countries. Returning to America in 1795, Jay discovered that he had been elected governor of New York, and he resigned from the Supreme Court. He served as governor until 1801. John Jay did as much as any American to establish national unity, constitutional government, and federal judicial power.

See also Constitution; Federalist Papers; Jay's Treaty; Paris, Treaty of (1783); Supreme Court.

RICHARD B. BERNSTEIN

JAY'S TREATY

In 1794 President George Washington sent Chief Justice John Jay to London to try to settle a number of conflicts between the United States and Great Britain. The United States wanted to secure the removal of all British troops from American territory in the West and to get the British navy to stop interfering with American merchant ships on the high seas. It also sought payment to American shippers for property seized in the British West Indies and for slaves taken off ships during the Revolution.

Jay did persuade the British to evacuate their forts in the West and to pay compensation for goods and vessels seized. They also opened ports in their colonies in Asia to American vessels. But they did not agree to pay for the slaves they had freed. They also refused to abandon the so-called Rule of 1756, which limited the right of neutrals to trade with nations whose ports were closed to them in peacetime. This rule was bitterly resented by American merchants whose cargoes headed for French and other European ports were often being seized by British warships.

Many Americans considered Jay's Treaty humiliating to the United States. But Washington felt that its benefits outweighed its disadvantages. He submitted it to the Senate where it was ratified after a long debate.

See also Jay, John.

JAZZ

Jazz is essentially a mixture of black musical styles that grew up along the Mississippi River and its tributaries during the years 1890–1917. The word *jazz* was apparently used for the first time in 1917 to refer to this music, a hot, fast-paced Dixieland style with an ad-

mixture of slow blues derived from traditional black funeral music. During the early 1920s, the most creative jazz was played in Chicago cabarets that had close connections to the gangster community, which was then getting rich by selling liquor, which was illegal because of Prohibition. New York City became an important center of jazz about 1928 and remained so, despite competition from the West Coast as well as the older centers.

But the most important city for early jazz development was New Orleans. There the black community was the most advanced in

Jazz trumpeter Louis Armstrong (rear center) plays with King Oliver's Band. An original style of music developed by black Americans in the early twentieth century, jazz influenced many of the forms of popular music that followed.

the nation in terms of skills and social position. There were many free blacks in New Orleans before the Civil War, and they were relatively well treated. Some became competent musicians. Many aspired to cultural advancement, and music was an obvious career track. A large class of mulattoes subsequently produced a disproportionate number of talented jazz artists.

Sources of Jazz

The sources of jazz were many. Dance music was especially popular in the white community, and many blacks made a good living playing for white parties. Military music was popular, and the two-step march meshed easily with many dance tunes. Soldiers from military bands discharged after service in the Spanish-American War often sold their instruments, so poor black children could readily find cornets and trombones at low prices; early jazz bands often featured military instrumentation. They added banjos and drums, which they could make themselves, and pianos they could use in saloons.

From minstrel shows and cakewalks—those nineteenth-century efforts to recapture the customs of pre–Civil War days—jazz inherited a tradition of audience participation, of musicians mugging or conducting brief solo routines. It inherited as well a tradition of "ragging" the music. The usual two-step always stressed the first beat. Ragtime pianists stressed the second, creating an effect of syncopation. By the 1890s, ragtime was all the rage, spreading from saloons to middle-class parlors via both printed scores and pianola rolls. Scott Joplin's "Maple Leaf Rag" (1899) became the best known.

From their African heritage, black musicians adapted the famous "blue notes." Africans traditionally played notes that could not easily be played in Western music; they sounded wrong, slightly off pitch. A human voice could produce such a note, but a properly tuned piano could not. Jazz musicians soon prided themselves on their ability to hit these "wrong," or blue notes, often sliding from one of these to a note that sounded "proper." They also varied their sounds with "dirty" notes, distortions that could alter customary sounds. The plumbing device used to mute trumpets became the most famous way to produce dirty notes, along with wire brushes on drums or bits of felt or wood stuffed into pianos. Other "odd" sounds, from field workers' hollars (field workers' songs) to merchants' cries to children's songs, became part of the music as well.

Later Development

Jazz developed many styles. It included the rural blues, usually male, of Blind Lemon Jefferson and Robert Johnson. It included the urban blues, usually female, of Ma Rainey and Bessie Smith. During the 1930s, such stars as Benny Goodman, Duke Ellington, and Ella Fitzgerald emerged. So did the big bands, which bleached and homogenized the music for white audiences to dance to. Resenting this, blacks developed the style known as "bop" or "bebop." Led by Charlie Parker, Thelonious Monk, and Dizzy Gillespie, they deliberately altered their harmonics so that white musicians would be unable to steal their achievements.

After World War II, such figures as Miles Davis and John Coltrane carried innovations even further, making them the most creative of all American musicians during the 1950s. After that, jazz diffused into both popular and classical idioms. Some players assimilated rock music while others rediscovered Bach.

Jazz has proved one of the most important of American exports. The French, especially, greatly admired a figure like Louis Armstrong and gladly offered steady work to such musicians as Sidney Bechet. Many European composers incorporated jazz devices in their own work: Claude Debussy in his "Golliwog's Cakewalk," Igor Stravinsky in *A Soldier's Tale*, Maurice Ravel in the "Blues" movement of his *Violin Sonata*, and Darius Milhaud in *The Creation of the World*.

See also Armstrong, Louis; Blues; Ellington, Duke; Fitzgerald, Ella; Goodman, Benny; Music.

ROBERT M. CRUNDEN

JEFFERSON, THOMAS

(1743–1826)   Third president of the United States (1801–09).

Most Americans remember Thomas Jefferson for writing the Declaration of Independence in 1776. The lanky, freckle-faced redhead was only thirty-three at the time. The next fifty years, filled with successes and failures, testified to his brilliant but complex and contradictory personality.

Jefferson was born in Virginia, the largest and most populous of Britain's American colonies. His parents owned extensive plantations worked by many slaves. At seventeen the boy was sent to the College of William and Mary in Williamsburg, where he was befriended by some of the leading figures in the colonial capital. After college he studied law for five years under George Wythe, a prominent lawyer, and then opened his own practice.

Jefferson was soon drawn into the rising movement for American independence. He was elected to the House of Burgesses, the Virginia legislature, in 1769. He served in the

Thomas Jefferson's gravestone bears the inscription he composed himself: "Author of the Declaration of American Independence, Of the Statute of Virginia for Religious Freedom, and Father of the University of Virginia." He was unduly modest in listing his accomplishments, failing to mention his roles as lawyer, educator, architect, scientist, writer, statesman, and third president of the United States.

House for six years while practicing law and managing his farms. At this time, he began his lifelong project of designing and building his home at Monticello, a landmark in American architecture. In 1772 he married Martha Wayles Shelton, a young and wealthy widow. After bearing four daughters, she died in childbirth in 1782. Jefferson never remarried.

His talent as a writer (he was not a good speaker) brought Jefferson many assignments in the legislature, drafting statements of colonial rights and reforms in Virginia's laws. The colony sent him as a delegate to the Continental Congress in Philadelphia in 1775 and 1776, where he made his debut on the national stage by writing the Declaration of Independence.

During his long political career Jefferson served as governor of Virginia (1779–81), U.S. minister to France (1785–89), secretary of state in George Washington's cabinet (1790–93), vice president under John Adams (1797–1801), and finally his two terms as president. He and James Madison were leaders in the Democratic-Republican Party (forerunner of today's Democratic Party), which developed in opposition to Alexander Hamilton's Federalists.

Jefferson's principles and actions could sometimes be at odds. He authorized the Louisiana Purchase in 1803, for example, in spite of the fact that it was not clear that the federal government had the power to make such a purchase. This shifted the balance of power between the central government and the states, which went against Jefferson's belief in strong states' rights. He was ahead of many in his time in perceiving and publicly declaring slavery to be evil. But he did not believe blacks and whites were equal, and he continued to own and use the services of slaves to maintain his aristocratic way of living.

Thomas Jefferson once told a friend, "If you're never idle, you'll be surprised at what you may accomplish." True to his words, he excelled in many fields: as scientist, diplomat, architect, agriculturist, and educator. He founded and designed the buildings and curriculum for the University of Virginia. He drafted the ground-breaking Statute of Virginia for Religious Freedom. These last two accomplishments, along with the Declaration, were the achievements he was proudest

of: they were the ones he directed should be engraved on his tombstone at Monticello.

But he is remembered best for his eloquent words—his pleas for freedom of speech, the press, and religion; his defense of democracy and majority rule, and even the right of revolution; and above all for his everlasting phrase, the right to "life, liberty, and the pursuit of happiness."

See also Declaration of Independence; Jeffersonian Democracy; Revolution; Virginia and Kentucky Resolutions. For events during Jefferson's administration, see Barbary Wars; Embargo Act of 1807; Impressment Controversy; Lewis and Clark Expedition; Louisiana Purchase; Marbury v. Madison.

For further reading: Milton Meltzer, Thomas Jefferson: The Revolutionary Aristocrat (New York: Franklin Watts, 1991).

MILTON MELTZER

JEFFERSONIAN DEMOCRACY

The inauguration of Thomas Jefferson as the third president of the United States in 1801 put an end to many policies of Presidents George Washington and John Adams and replaced them with what we call Jeffersonian Democracy.

As Washington's secretary of state, Jefferson had opposed Secretary of the Treasury Alexander Hamilton's economic policies, which favored financial and manufacturing interests and strengthened the national government at the expense of the states. During Adams's presidency, Vice President Jefferson was alarmed by the Alien and Sedition Acts, which restricted freedom of speech, assembly, and the press. Under the administrations of both Washington and Adams, Jefferson also feared that the rituals of the presidency resembled the monarchies of Europe.

Jefferson in the election of 1800 told the voters that he wanted to put the federal government on a more republican course. His belief in the virtues of an agrarian republic consisting mostly of independent farmers won wide support in a nation of farmers. The Democratic Republicans, or simply Republicans—as Jefferson's supporters called themselves—also found favor among artisans and workers in towns and cities, where Jefferson's opposition to an aristocracy of privilege gained him the reputation of being a man of the people. The Jeffersonian Republicans were opposed by banking, manufacturing, and commercial interests because they preferred Hamilton's vision of an industrial America. Being a slaveholder who nevertheless opposed the institution of slavery, Jefferson won support from both slaveholders and opponents of slavery. His party, however, did not include freeing the slaves in its democratic program.

Jefferson's Principles

The roots of Jeffersonian Democracy are to be found in the concept of natural laws that Jefferson expounded in the Declaration of Independence. There he emphasized "the sufficiency of human reason for the care of human affairs" and stressed that "the will of the majority, the Natural law of every society, is the only sure guardian of the rights of man." This faith in the people was basic to the creed Jefferson argued for in the election of 1800 and carried out as president. He wanted to keep the government close to the people. "I am not for transferring all the powers of the States to the general government, and all those of that government to the Executive branch," he wrote. He promised a government that would practice economy, reduce military expenditures, and begin paying off the national debt. He also reaffirmed his support of the Bill of Rights.

Jefferson restated these principles in his inaugural address on March 4, 1801. In that concise explanation of Jeffersonian Democracy, he affirmed his commitment to an "absolute acquiescence in the decisions of the majority" as a vital principle of republicanism. He added that the will of the majority to be rightful must be fair. "The minority possess their equal rights, which equal laws must protect, and to violate would be oppression," he declared.

Jefferson promised "equal and exact justice to all men, of whatever state or persuasion, religious or political," and pledged to protect civil liberties. He also vowed to respect the rights of states. Jefferson favored having a strong militia for defense, but stressed the supremacy of civil over military authority, as well as economy in public expenditures, the payment of debts, and the encouragement of agriculture and its "handmaid" commerce. Though an agrarian republic was Jefferson's ideal, he recognized the need for commerce as well.

Actions as President

With the support of a majority in Congress, Jefferson as president carried out his promises. He reduced government expenditures, cut taxes, and set about paying off the national debt. He also reduced the size of the army, navy, and diplomatic establishment abroad.

Sometimes, however, he had to modify these policies. The chance to purchase the Louisiana territory from France, for example, meant he had to slow down his schedule for paying off the debt. It also posed a challenge to another of his principles, the strict reading of the Constitution (government can do only what the Constitution specifically says it can do). Nothing in it actually authorized the government to make such a purchase. Renewed war in Europe, and England's and France's interference with American shipping and commerce that followed, led to his imposing an embargo (ban) on foreign trade and to new military expenditures, too. In administering the Embargo Act of 1807, however, the federal government interfered more with individual rights than Jefferson wanted, and the embargo was repealed before he left office.

Jefferson reduced the more ceremonial aspects of the presidency. He began by simply walking to his inauguration rather than riding in a fancy coach. One reporter noted that his dress was that of an ordinary citizen, "without any distinctive badge of office." That was a sharp contrast to Washington and Adams, who had dressed elegantly and even worn swords at their inaugurations. Instead of appearing in person to deliver an annual address to Congress, as had his predecessors, President Jefferson sent a written message to be read by a clerk. He also eliminated formal presidential receptions and modified the European rules of diplomatic etiquette.

When he retired in 1809, Jefferson left a legacy of faith in the people and a widening popular participation in government that shaped the future course of American democracy.

See also Jefferson, Thomas.

NOBLE E. CUNNINGHAM, JR.

JEWS IN AMERICA

The first Jewish community in America was established in 1654, when twenty-three refugees of Spanish and Portuguese origin, traveling from Recife, Brazil, landed at the Dutch colonial port of New Amsterdam. Although they were permitted to remain there, they were not warmly welcomed by the Dutch governor, Peter Stuyvesant, who did not like Jews. Calling them "a deceitful race," he refused to grant them the rights given to other citizens and would not permit them to build a synagogue. In 1664, when the town was captured by the English and its name changed to New York, the Jews were granted full rights of citizenship and religious freedom.

Within a short time, other Jews seeking economic advancement arrived in Rhode Island (Newport was for a time the second largest Jewish community in North America) and in the Delaware valley. By 1700, between two and three hundred Jews had settled in the American colonies, and by 1776, with the establishment of communities in Philadelphia, Charleston, and Savannah, the number of Jews reached approximately two thousand. These new settlers sided enthusiastically with the movement for American independence. They enjoyed the benefits of the new Constitution, which guaranteed separation of church and state, and they were made to feel part of a new and exciting nation.

Jews in the Nineteenth Century

The Jewish population steadily increased throughout the nineteenth century. The early immigrants sent encouraging reports to their friends and families back home, urging them to leave behind the economic hard times and religious persecution that limited their opportunities in Europe and join them in the New World. Many, especially those from German-speaking countries, responded. In 1820, there were about 4,000 Jews in the United States; by the eve of the Civil War in 1860, there were some 150,000, more than 40,000 of whom had settled in New York City; and in

1880, the number had increased to just over 250,000.

Many of these new immigrants chose not to remain in the cities along the East Coast. Some migrated to the Midwest, and others at the time of the gold rush traveled to California. Wherever they went, most Jews fitted easily into American society, becoming business leaders, bankers, physicians, soldiers, and politicians. Beginning in the middle of the century, with the rise of Reform Judaism, many abandoned strict Jewish rules of diet and dress and simplified centuries-old rituals. This liberalization brought them even closer to the customs of the society to which they now belonged.

A Changing Population

Starting in 1881, all of this changed. A wave of pogroms (anti-Jewish massacres) and anti-Semitic legislation throughout Russia and eastern Europe set off the greatest migration of Jews in history. From then until 1924, more than 2.5 million frightened, desperate refugees arrived in the United States. In almost every way they differed from the Jewish immigrants who had preceded them and who had now assimilated. They spoke little or no English; the language of most was Yiddish. They were Orthodox Jews, who observed the strict customs dictated by many centuries of tradition. Most of them had little education and were extremely poor.

The large majority of these immigrants settled in New York City, where they crowded into tenements in the Lower East Side. Most found work in the sweatshops of the clothing industry, spending long hours cutting and sewing for very low wages. But they learned quickly and in a remarkably short time improved their lot. They became involved with and later, under the guidance of Samuel

Gompers, led the labor movement, organizing strikes that gained better working conditions and higher wages for all workers.

Before long, these Jews began to move from the Lower East Side to more prosperous parts of the city. Many sent their children to the best schools and universities, enabling them to become doctors and lawyers, businesspeople and department store owners, book and newspaper publishers. Among the Jews who made notable contributions to American society during this period were two justices of the Supreme Court, Louis Brandeis and Felix Frankfurter; the newspaper publishers Adolph Ochs and Arthur Hays Sulzberger (of the *New York Times*), and Joseph Pulitzer; pioneers of the radio and movie industries David Sarnoff, Louis B. Mayer, and Samuel Goldwyn; the popular composers George Gershwin, Irving Berlin, and Jerome Kern; and the owners of the department stores Sears, Roebuck and Company as well as R. H. Macy. In 1880, in a nation of 50 million people, there had been fewer than 300,000 Jews. In 1920, the population of the United States had grown to 115 million, of whom 4.5 million were Jews.

In the 1920s, however, the situation once again changed. At the end of the First World War, anti-immigrant and anti-Jewish sentiment spread across the United States. As a result, legislation limiting the number of foreigners allowed to settle in the country was enacted, and the era of mass immigration came to an end.

There have been two later, considerably smaller, waves of Jewish immigration, brought about by the rise of Adolf Hitler in Germany in the 1930s. Between 1933 and the beginning of the Second World War in 1939, 157,000 Jews fled Nazi persecution and arrived in the United States. These new immigrants, for the most part distinguished artists, writers, scientists, and teachers, among them Albert Einstein, the composer Kurt Weill, the conductor Bruno Walter, and the movie director Billy Wilder, added immeasurably to the intellectual wealth of their new home. They were followed after the war by 100,000 survivors of Nazi concentration camps and, later, thousands of refugees from the former Soviet Union.

From the time of their arrival in the United States, Jews have often met with an enormous amount of anti-Semitism. They have been excluded from neighborhoods, clubs, and many universities, and have all too frequently been denied employment because of their religious origins. The obstacles and hostility they have faced—and continue to face, somewhat more subtly—make their achievements and success all the more remarkable.

See also Holocaust, American Response to.

HOWARD GREENFELD

JIM CROW LAWS
See Segregation.

JOHNS, JASPER

(1930–   )   *Painter.*

After a stint in the U.S. Army, Johns settled in New York where he soon began producing startling paintings of flags, targets, numbers, and letter types. He declared that such objects were things the mind already knows and therefore gave him room to work with painting as a means to express other qualities.

By 1958, when he had his first one-man exhibition, Johns had established his emphasis on the puzzles presented by real objects appearing in the unreal contexts of painting. He had also begun to make three-dimensional replicas of such objects as flashlights and light bulbs, challenging his viewers to see the subtle differences between the commercial product and an almost exact copy, modified by the artist. Among his most celebrated acts was the casting of two beer cans in bronze, which he then painted to look precisely like ordinary beer cans.

Johns was deliberately criticizing the more romantic movement of painting that had immediately preceded him—abstract expressionist, gestural painting. He raised questions concerning the meaning of painting by basing his own on direct experiences with the ordinary things of daily life, using objects such as cups, spoons, rulers, and maps as subjects. His viewers were meant to question the very nature of painting itself.

The artist's interest in paradox, ambiguity, and the challenging of accepted ideas has been expressed both in small works and in vast, mural-like paintings to which he has sometimes attached real objects such as rulers, cups, and chairs. These perplexing de-partures from conventional painting have brought him worldwide attention.

See also Painting and Sculpture.

DORE ASHTON

JOHNSON, ANDREW

(1808–75)   *Seventeenth president of the United States (1865–69).*

Johnson was the only president to be impeached—that is, to be officially charged with misconduct by the House of Representatives. Politics brought glory and dishonor to this impoverished and uneducated Ten-

Andrew Johnson was vice president of the United States for only a few weeks before Abraham Lincoln was assassinated and he succeeded him as president.

nessee tailor whose wife taught him to read and write. Johnson, a southern Democrat, served in the U.S. House of Representatives for ten years (1843–53) before winning two terms as governor of Tennessee (1853–57). In 1857, he was elected to the U.S. Senate, where he sponsored measures to help ordinary people.

When the South seceded in 1860–61, Johnson was the only Southern senator to remain loyal to the Union. His refusal to go with the Confederacy made him a hero in the North. In 1862, President Abraham Lincoln appointed him military governor of Tennessee, and in 1864, he was elected vice president for Lincoln's second term.

When Lincoln was assassinated on April 14, 1865, and died the next morning, Johnson suddenly became president. Despite his hatred of secession, he favored moderate policies for Reconstruction—the readmittance of the southern states into the Union. Johnson was more concerned about helping whites in the southern states than the welfare of the ex-slaves. As a result, ex-Confederates soon won control in their states and set up "Black Codes," designed to deny the former slaves their basic rights. Radical Republicans in Congress responded with laws to help the freedpeople, but Johnson vetoed many of these measures and failed to enforce the rest.

In 1867, the Radicals struck back at the president by placing the South under military rule. They also passed the Tenure of Office Act to restrict his power to dismiss government officeholders without the approval of the Senate. To test the law's constitutionality, Johnson fired Radical Republican sympathizer Secretary of War Edwin M. Stanton without Senate approval and defied the Senate's order to reinstate him. In 1868, the U.S. House of Representatives impeached the president by a vote of 126–47, charging him with violating the act. He was put on trial before the Senate, which fell one vote short of the two-thirds majority needed to remove him from office.

Despite Johnson's many battles with Congress, his administration was able to gain its approval for the purchase of Alaska from Russia in 1867. After he left office, he reentered the Senate in 1875 but died five months later. In time, his impeachment was seen as unjust.

See also Civil War. *For events during Johnson's administration, see* Alaska Purchase; Black Codes; Freedmen's Bureau; Granger Movement; Impeachment; Reconstruction; Tenure of Office Act.

BARBARA SILBERDICK FEINBERG

JOHNSON, JAMES WELDON

(1871–1938) *Journalist and black spokesman.*

The son of a free black and a mother from the Bahamas, Johnson grew up chiefly in Jacksonville, Florida. His father was headwaiter at a luxury hotel and his mother a schoolteacher, and they were able to provide him with a stable childhood. His parents valued books and education and encouraged their son to be ambitious. Studying mostly with idealistic white teachers from New England, Johnson adopted the religious and moral values associated with puritanism.

After graduation from Atlanta University in 1894, Johnson served briefly as the principal of a black high school. Seeing no future in that field, he switched to law and found a white sponsor. But in a scene that makes for poignant reading in his book *Along This Way* (1933), he recounts the prejudices he faced when applying for admission to the bar. He finally passed, but he knew that as a black in the South he had no future in law either.

Music had always filled his home, and Weldon's father often visited New York. Upon his return, he would quote dialogue from plays and sing tunes from shows he had seen. James's brother, J. Rosamond, was trained at the New England Conservatory of Music in Boston and then went to New York, with James following. Together with playwright Bob Cole, they formed the successful team of Cole and Johnson Brothers; their biggest hit was "The Maiden with the Dreamy Eyes," written for singer Anna Held (Mrs. Florenz Ziegfeld). Many others followed.

Johnson went on to write *The Autobiography of an Ex-Colored Man* (1912) and to edit *The Book of American Negro Poetry* (1922) and, with his brother, *The Book of American Negro Spirituals* (1925). He wrote "You're All Right, Teddy" and other tunes for Theodore Roosevelt's 1904 presidential campaign and won several minor diplomatic posts as a reward. His best-known work is *Black Manhattan* (1930), the first significant study of the Harlem Renaissance, a cultural flowering among black writers, artists, and musicians in New York City in the 1920s and early 1930s.

See also African Americans; Harlem Renaissance; Literature; Music.

ROBERT M. CRUNDEN

JOHNSON, LYNDON B.

(1908–73) *Thirty-sixth president of the United States (1963–69).*

Born and raised in the hill country of West Texas, Johnson attended a one-room school until the ninth grade. A bright student who hated homework, he graduated from high school when he was fifteen and then worked for three years before enrolling in Southwest Texas State Teachers College. He graduated in 1930 and then taught school in Houston. In 1934 he married Claudia Taylor whom everyone called "Lady Bird."

Fascinated by politics, Johnson won election to Congress in 1937. It was the age of the New Deal, and he worked hard for programs that would help the poor people he'd grown up among. A man of tremendous energy—and even greater ambition—Johnson became first a powerful congressman, then a powerful senator, and finally Senate majority leader. Even a heart attack hardly slowed him down. He campaigned for the Democratic presidential nomination in 1960 but lost to Senator John F. Kennedy. He then agreed to become Kennedy's running mate. They won a close election, thanks in part to a tight victory in Texas. Critics charged Johnson's Texas cronies with voting fraud, but that was never proved.

When Kennedy was assassinated in 1963, Johnson became president. His presidency was marked by success at home and tragic failure abroad. Using his enormous political skills, he persuaded Congress to pass the most extensive program of social reforms since the New Deal of the 1930s. He was launching, he declared, a War on Poverty in order to make the United States the Great Society it was meant to be. Johnson also persuaded Congress to enact civil rights legislation that did more than any other programs before or since to end segregation and promote the welfare of African Americans.

Johnson was elected president in his own right by a landslide in 1964. But his popularity dropped dramatically because of the war in Vietnam. America had become involved in Vietnam under Presidents Dwight D. Eisenhower and Kennedy, but Johnson dramatically escalated America's role, sending almost half a million troops to Southeast Asia. At first most citizens supported the war, but opposition became widespread as thousands of Americans were killed or injured in the fighting. Realizing that his candidacy for reelection would further divide the country, Johnson withdrew from the 1968 presidential race and retired to his ranch in Texas.

For events during Johnson's administration, see Civil Rights Movement; Great Society; Medicare and Medicaid; Vietnam War; Voting Rights Act of 1965.

MICHAEL KRONENWETTER

JONES, JOHN PAUL

(1747–92)   *Naval officer.*

John Paul Jones was the first great hero of the American navy. At the time of his birth in Scotland, his name was John Paul. He went to sea when he was twelve years old, and by 1769 he was the commander of a merchant ship sailing between British ports and the West Indies. In 1773, the crew of his ship mutinied, and John Paul thrust his sword through the ringleader. Fearing that he might be arrested for murder, he fled to Virginia and changed his name to John Paul Jones.

Shortly after the Revolutionary War began, Jones was commissioned a lieutenant in the newly organized Continental navy. As commander of the *Providence,* he captured sixteen enemy ships in 1776 and was promoted to the rank of captain. The following year, he was given command of the *Ranger* and carried out raids on British shipping in the Irish Sea.

In 1779, Jones remodeled an old merchant ship as a fighting vessel and named it *Bonhomme Richard* (which means Good Man Richard) in honor of Benjamin Franklin's *Poor Richard's Almanack.* On September 23, the ship, leading a small squadron of American vessels, met a large British force in the North Sea. One of the most famous sea battles in history followed.

The *Serapis,* the leading ship of the British convoy, was larger and better armed than the *Bonhomme Richard.* Jones maneuvered his ship alongside the *Serapis* until the two vessels were so close that their rigging became entangled. With the ships lashed together, the *Bonhomme Richard* sustained heavy damages. But when the British commander asked if the Americans wanted to surrender, Jones is said to have replied, "I have not yet begun to fight!" After nearly four hours of intense battling, Jones captured the *Serapis.* But the *Bonhomme Richard* was so badly damaged that it sank two days later.

Following the war, Jones served briefly as a

John Paul Jones, naval hero of the American Revolution, commanded the ship Bonhomme Richard *("the good man Richard"), which had been renamed after Benjamin Franklin's* Poor Richard's Almanack.

rear admiral in the Russian navy in a war against Turkey. He died in Paris, and in 1905 what was believed to be Jones's casket was returned to the United States and buried in the chapel of the U.S. Naval Academy.

See also Navy; Revolution: The War for Independence.

EDMUND LINDOP

JONES, MARY HARRIS (MOTHER JONES)

(1837–1930)   *Social reformer and union organizer.*

After her husband and children died in an epidemic, Mary Jones devoted her life to fighting for better conditions for working Americans, especially coal miners. A white-haired older woman, she looked like a sweet grandmother but didn't sound like one. She was an exciting speaker famous for pronouncements like "Pray for the dead and fight like hell for the living!" Working people called her "Mother" Jones to express their respect and love for her.

She was an important organizer for the coal miners' union, the United Mine Workers of America (founded 1890). Miners worked under dangerous conditions, often for little pay. Their families were sometimes forced to live in company-owned towns ruled by one man—the mine superintendent. The union tried to persuade or, if necessary, force the mine owners to treat their workers fairly.

A colorful figure, Mother Jones skillfully drew public attention to the miners' cause, especially during strikes. She delivered rousing speeches, organized marches and picketing, spoke to reporters, and urged Congress to pass better laws.

Mother Jones's physical courage was legendary. Once in West Virginia she walked up to a gunman hired by a coal company to oppose striking miners. He was pointing his rifle at her. Mother Jones put her hand on the muzzle and said, "Shoot an old woman if you dare!"

She also worked passionately to end child labor. In 1903 she organized a week-long protest march of child mill workers. As the children marched along, everyone could see that they were missing arms and fingers, resulting from accidents on their jobs. Newspapers across the country reported on the march, and it increased public awareness that children ought to go to school instead of working in factories twelve to fifteen hours a day.

Politically, Mother Jones was a democratic

Mother Jones was a champion of coal miners and their families, who called her "the miner's angel." Her grandmotherly appearance was in sharp contrast to her courage and militant views.

socialist at first. Then in 1916 she became a Democrat and supported Woodrow Wilson for president.

Mother Jones had no permanent home, but traveled wherever there was "a good fight against wrong." Strangely enough, she held traditional beliefs about women. She believed that other women should work only at home, and she opposed woman suffrage (the right of women to vote).

See also Labor Movement.

PRISCILLA LONG

JOSEPH (CHIEF JOSEPH)

(1840?–1904)   *Native American leader.*

The real name of the man who was known as Chief Joseph was Hinmahtooyahlatkekt, which means "Thunder rolling on the mountaintops." He and his people were called Nez Percé Indians by the U.S. government, but to themselves they were Nimipu—"we people." (French trappers had named them Nez Percés, meaning "pierced noses," because some of them had pieces of seashell in their noses as decorations.)

The Nimipu lived where the states of Oregon, Idaho, and Washington now come together. In 1855, the U.S. government asked them to sell most of their lands for American settlers to live on, and to stay on a reservation—a large area that they were assured would be theirs only, forever. The Nimipu agreed.

In 1863, however, the government began urging them to sell part of their reservation, too, and live in a much smaller area. Many Nimipu agreed to this also, but about eight hundred of them, led by Chief Joseph and other chiefs, refused. For years, government officials who dealt with Indian affairs kept insisting they sell, and finally, in 1877, they were told they had no choice. Army troops were sent to force them to move to the smaller area.

But the little band of Nimipu fought to stay free. When violence broke out between them and whites, Joseph and the others decided they must leave their homeland and try to find freedom in Montana or Canada. They began a long, hard journey through the mountains, but were pursued by U.S. troops. For three months the Nimipu worked their way north, cleverly evading capture by the soldiers and fighting them off in several bat-

tles. The American commanders came to respect Joseph, regarding him as a brilliant general.

But finally, the Nimipu were surrounded
near the Canadian border where they had
stopped to rest. There was a bitter battle in
which more than sixty U.S. soldiers and
twenty-one Nimipu were killed or wounded,
but the Nimipu were unable to break away.
When Joseph saw that the situation was
hopeless, he met with the American commanders Col. Nelson Miles and Gen. Oliver
Howard, and surrendered.

Most of his people were eventually
brought to what is now the Nez Percé reservation in Idaho, where Chief Joseph also
wished to go. But federal authorities, fearful
of his influence over his tribe, sent him instead to a reservation in the state of Washington, where he spent the rest of his life.

See also Indian-White Relations.

TOM McGOWEN

*Chief Joseph led the Nez Percés on an extraordinary
flight from U.S. Army soldiers, but they were forced to
surrender just a few miles from the Canadian border
where they would have been free. His famous surrender speech concludes: "I want time to look for my children and see how many of them I can find. Maybe I
shall find them among the dead. Hear me, my chiefs, I
am tired; my heart is sick and sad. From where the
sun now stands, I will fight no more."*

JOURNALISM
See Magazines and Newspapers.

JUDAISM
See Jews.

JUDICIARY BRANCH
See Supreme Court.

JUNGLE, THE

In 1906 the reformer Upton Sinclair published *The Jungle,* a story about the exploitation of immigrant workers and their families
in Chicago. Living in the city, he argued, was
like living in a jungle, dangerous and brutal.
The main character, Jurgis Rudkus, is a Lith-
uanian who works in a meat-packing plant.
The book describes in horrible detail the
filthy conditions under which cattle were
butchered and prepared for market at that
time.

But Sinclair was not mainly interested in

exposing conditions in the stockyards. He was a socialist; his purpose was to attack capitalism by describing how the system was injuring the poor and ignorant working people of Chicago. Most readers, however, including President Theodore Roosevelt, were shocked by his account of the meat-packing business. Roosevelt ordered an investigation and urged Congress to act. The result was passage of meat inspection legislation and the Pure Food and Drug Act of 1906.

Sinclair benefited from all the publicity because *The Jungle* became a best-seller. But he was amused by the way readers interpreted his attack on capitalism. "I aimed at the public's heart," he explained, "and by accident hit it in the stomach."

See also Pure Food and Drug Act.

K

KANSAS-NEBRASKA ACT

In January 1854 Senator Stephen A. Douglas of Illinois introduced a bill organizing the region west of Iowa and Missouri as Nebraska Territory. He did so because he was interested in the possible construction of a transcontinental railroad through the region and because settlers were beginning to migrate there. The bill seemed routine, similar to ones that had to be drafted every time a new frontier region was opened to settlement.

But since the Missouri Compromise of 1820 had banned slavery in this region, southern congressmen objected. The bill would leave the slave state of Missouri surrounded on three sides by free territory. This would

The Kansas-Nebraska Act

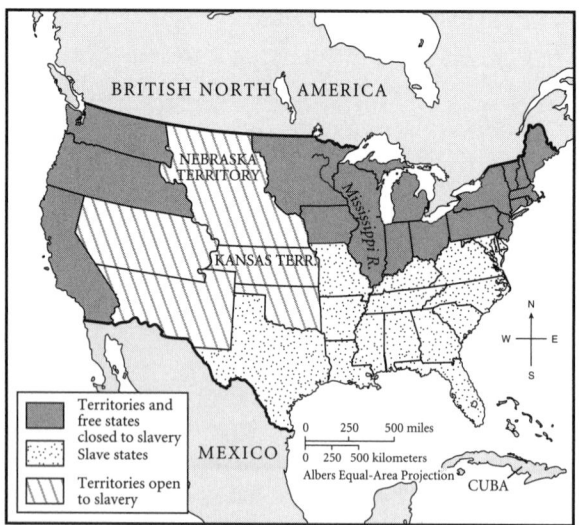

BRITISH NORTH AMERICA

NEBRASKA TERRITORY

KANSAS TERR.

Mississippi R.

N
W E
S

MEXICO

Territories and free states closed to slavery

Slave states

Territories open to slavery

0   250   500 miles
0 250 500 kilometers
Albers Equal-Area Projection   CUBA

464

make it easier for Missouri slaves to run away, and slave owners would be reluctant to move to Missouri.

Douglas met the southerners' objections by redrafting the bill. It now divided the region into two territories, Nebraska, west of Iowa, and Kansas, west of Missouri. More important, the bill declared the ban on slavery in the Missouri Compromise "inoperative and void." The settlers of the new territories, according to the doctrine of popular sovereignty, were to be "perfectly free to form and regulate their domestic institutions in their own way."

The bill passed in this form. It resulted in the long and bitter struggle between pro- and antislavery forces to control the government of Kansas Territory that we know as "Bleeding Kansas." It was thus a major stride along the path that led to the Civil War.

See also Bleeding Kansas; Popular Sovereignty.

KELLER, HELEN

(1880–1968) *Author, lecturer, and crusader for the handicapped.*

Keller, though blind and deaf herself, became an eloquent spokesperson for the disabled. Her courage, intelligence, and dedication to the welfare of others, despite her own handicaps, were an inspiration to people everywhere.

Keller, born in Alabama, contracted what was probably scarlet fever at the age of nine-

Helen Keller (left) communicates with her teacher Anne Sullivan by feeling the vibrations of her lips.

teen months and lost both her sight and her hearing. For five years she could communicate only with screams of pain or anger, and her parents were told she should be put in an institution. But through the Perkins Institute for the Blind in Boston they found a teacher, Anne Mansfield Sullivan, who succeeded in teaching the girl not only to understand language but also to read and write. With the help of Sullivan, who communicated lectures to her by spelling the words into the girl's hand in a manual alphabet-code, Keller graduated with honors from Radcliffe College.

Keller never learned to speak very clearly, but she wrote beautifully. Her first book, *The Story of My Life,* remains a classic account of triumph over adversity. (The film *The Miracle Worker* is based on the first part of this book. It is a moving portrayal of how Sullivan managed to reach through to the young Helen and make her aware of language.) She went on to write other books of autobiography, philosophy, and poetry, and she lectured widely.

Keller's main work was in fund-raising for the handicapped. The fame she earned for having overcome her own disabilities, accompanied by her great personal charm, brought her the friendship of such million-aires as Andrew Carnegie, Henry Ford, and John D. Rockefeller. She succeeded in obtaining large sums for the American Foundation for the Blind, which she served as an adviser. The foundation honored her by naming its overseas division Helen Keller International.

In her long life of service to others, Helen Keller was responsible for many changes in the treatment of the handicapped and for a deeper understanding of their needs. Her name remains a symbol for the strength and willpower to overcome personal handicaps.

For further reading: Dennis Wepman, *Helen Keller* (New York: Chelsea House, 1987).

D E N N I S   W E P M A N

K E L L O G G - B R I A N D   P A C T

This treaty was originally proposed by French foreign minister Aristide Briand in 1927. It provided that France and the United States agree never to go to war with each other. Secretary of State Frank B. Kellogg was unwilling to sign the agreement, which would have included an additional commitment to go to France's defense if another nation attacked it. But it was difficult to object to a treaty outlawing war. Kellogg therefore suggested that all the nations of the world be invited to sign the treaty. In August 1927 the revised treaty, condemning "recourse to war for the solution of international controversies," was signed by representatives of France, the United States, Germany, Great Britain, Japan, Italy, Belgium, Poland, Czechoslovakia, and half a dozen other nations.

The treaty was no more than an expression of good intentions. It said nothing about how it was to be enforced. It also contained the statement, "every nation is free at all times to defend its territory from attack," which made its peaceful promises meaningless.

Briand had already been awarded a Nobel Peace Prize for his design of the Locarno Pact, an earlier international agreement. Kellogg was awarded a Nobel in 1929 for his work on this one. But by 1941 all the nations that signed the Kellogg-Briand Pact were again at war.

K E N N A N ,   G E O R G E

(1904–   )   *Diplomat and historian.*

Joining the Foreign Service in 1925, George Kennan served in Central and Eastern Europe at the time of the rise of Adolf Hitler in Germany and Joseph Stalin's consolidation of power in the Soviet Union. Kennan became increasingly critical of the making of American foreign policy during these years. He disapproved of the way President Franklin D. Roosevelt dealt with Eastern Europe and the way in which President Harry S. Truman dealt with the founding of the United Nations and his attitude toward the Soviet Union during the early years of the cold war, which followed World War II. Roosevelt seemed too trusting of Soviet intentions; Truman seemed to be both too rude and too hostile.

Two documents he wrote made Kennan's reputation: a so-called long telegram he sent from Moscow in 1946 and an anonymously published article, "The Sources of Soviet Conduct" (1947; he signed it simply "X"). He warned the West against being naive about Soviet intentions after the war, but insisted that Stalin had legitimate reasons for annexing lands on his western frontier. Kennan advocated what came to be called a policy of containment. America could not impose democracy on Eastern Europe (which was mostly occupied by Russia) and should not try, he said. Rather, the West should work to contain the Soviets within their present borders and prevent them from expanding into still more states in Eastern Europe. Either neutral or pro-Soviet governments in such countries were inevitable, since these countries were so vulnerable to Soviet power. Time would soften the situation, he thought, and make war unnecessary.

Kennan soon saw his ideas applied more broadly than he had intended. He left the Foreign Service to write history and policy statements. His brief *American Diplomacy, 1900–1950* (1951) became a popular text, and his *Memoirs* (1967, 1972) had a broad impact. Two volumes he wrote on Soviet-American relations from 1917 to 1920, *Russia Leaves the War* (1956) and *The Decision to Intervene* (1958), became works most useful to scholars.

See also Cold War.

ROBERT M. CRUNDEN

KENNEDY, JOHN F.

(1917–63)   *Thirty-fifth president of the United States (1961–63).*

Kennedy was born to a wealthy, ambitious, Irish-American family active in Massachusetts Democratic politics. After graduating from Harvard, Kennedy joined the navy and became a World War II hero. He served in Congress before becoming the youngest man, and the first Roman Catholic, elected president.

Kennedy's promise of a "New Frontier" and his inaugural call to service—"Ask not what your country can do for you; ask what you can do for your country"—embodied the spirit of idealism that characterized his brief presidency. Yet after his death at the hand of presumed assassin Lee Harvey Oswald, some wondered how much he had actually accomplished.

Two months into office, Kennedy established the Peace Corps, putting young Americans to work helping people around the world. Other successes included his pledge (fulfilled in 1969) to land an American on the moon; his handling of the Cuban missile cri-

President John F. Kennedy (right) consults with Robert F. Kennedy, who served as U.S. attorney general in his brother's administration. Three generations of Kennedys have exerted an influence over American politics.

sis, during which he narrowly averted a threatened nuclear showdown with the Soviet Union; and completion of a partial nuclear test ban treaty with the Soviets. At the same time that Kennedy's optimism and vigor were revitalizing politics, he, his glamorous wife, Jacqueline, and their two young children were making the White House a livelier place. Mrs. Kennedy redecorated the mansion, and entertained writers, artists, and musicians.

But the administration suffered disappointments as well. Kennedy authorized a disastrous U.S.-led invasion of communist Cuba and aided the anticommunist, but corrupt, government of South Vietnam. Little of his New Frontier program became law, and he was slow to support the black civil rights movement.

Kennedy's assassination in Dallas on November 22, 1963, stunned the nation. What would he have accomplished if his presidency had not been cut so short? Would he have extricated the country from Vietnam, saving thousands of American lives? Would he have persuaded Congress to pass civil rights laws and other social legislation as his successor, Lyndon B. Johnson, did? The questions—and the debates they have inspired—are part of the Kennedy legacy.

For events during Kennedy's administration, see Bay of Pigs Invasion; Civil Rights Movement; Peace Corps; Space Program; Vietnam War.

ANN E. WEISS

KENT STATE INCIDENT

As the Vietnam War dragged on, antiwar demonstrations in the United States grew in size and intensity. This was especially true on college campuses. In 1969 President Rich-

ard M. Nixon began gradually to reduce American forces in Vietnam. He called his policy "Vietnamization," building up the South Vietnamese army so that it could defend the country without the help of American troops. Then, late in April 1970, Nixon suddenly reversed himself. He announced an invasion of Vietnam's neutral neighbor, Cambodia, where he claimed communist units were gathering. He dispatched American troops to destroy these forces, which he said were "poised like a dagger threatening the South Vietnamese capital, Saigon."

The invasion of Cambodia led to protests all over the country. At Kent State University in Ohio, one such protest led to tragedy. Kent State students demonstrated, broke windows, even set fire to the building housing the local Reserve Officers' Training Corps (ROTC). When the governor sent nine hundred National Guardsmen to control the situation, the students rained stones on them. Finally, on May 4, the nervous Guardsmen opened fire, killing four students and wounding a number of others. Two of the students who were shot were not even protesting the war; they were struck while crossing the campus on the way to class.

There was a great public outcry over the episode, with further protests spreading across the nation. At Jackson State University, a black college in Mississippi, a similar incident occurred ten days later. During a protest there, police and state highway patrolmen fired indiscriminately into a dormitory, killing two students and wounding nine others. The subsequent lack of national outrage over that killing contrasted with the anger over the Kent State deaths, embittering many in the black community.

See also Vietnam War.

This Pulitzer Prize–winning image shows a woman kneeling in anguish beside one of the slain students during the demonstration at Kent State University on May 4, 1970. Taken by a fellow student, the photograph became a symbol of the social upheaval of the time.

KEROUAC, JACK

(1922–69)   Author.

Kerouac was born in Lowell, Massachusetts, to a middle-class family of French-Canadian origin. He first demonstrated an unusual gift for writing while in high school, but it was his skill as an athlete that won him a football scholarship to Columbia University in New York in 1940.

He remained at Columbia for less than a year. The restlessness that characterized his life manifested itself early, and he spent several years wandering through the United States and Mexico. For short periods of time, he served in the Merchant Marine and worked at various odd jobs, including that of a forest-fire lookout. Throughout this period he con-

tinued to write, and in 1950 his first novel, *The Town and the City,* was published to critical if not popular acclaim.

Immediately following its publication, he began work on his second novel, *On the Road,* which, though written in only three weeks, was not published until 1957. This disorganized, sprawling, energetic work, based on his own experiences, tells the story of several characters, eager to experience everything, who travel across country in search of personal truth and find at least temporary fulfillment in sex, drugs, and fast driving. Though it received mixed reviews from the critics—some found it brilliant while others complained that it was hopelessly confused and infantile—the book was a best-seller. Kerouac became a celebrity. Along with his friends William Burroughs and Allen Ginsberg, he was recognized as one of the most important voices of the "beat generation." Beats challenged the status quo (the way things are), questioning authority and society's attitudes toward sex, experimenting with drugs, and drifting from job to job, town to town, and experience to experience.

Unlike his friends, however, Kerouac did not feel comfortable with his fame. He wrote several other books, but none equaled the success of *On the Road*. Suffering from depression, he turned to drink. He died at the age of forty-seven, of an alcohol-related sickness.

See also Literature.

HOWARD GREENFELD

KEY, FRANCIS SCOTT

(1779–1843) *Lawyer and author of our national anthem, "The Star-Spangled Banner."*

Key was born in Maryland and became a well-known lawyer in Georgetown and later Washington, in the District of Columbia (D.C.) As a hobby Key wrote hymns and poems. The verses he wrote during the War of 1812 later became our national anthem.

In 1814 the British landed a force in southern Maryland, marched overland defeated an American army sent to stop them, captured Washington, and burned some public buildings, including the president's house. While returning to their ships, the British arrested Dr. William Beanes of Upper Marlboro, Maryland, and took him with them. Friends of Dr. Beanes appealed to Key to try to rescue the physician. With Col. John S. Skinner, the U.S. government's agent for the exchange of prisoners, Key visited a British warship and received a promise from the commanding general that Dr. Beanes would be released.

Before this could take place, however, the Americans would have to wait on a neutral ship while the British forces carried out attacks on Baltimore. On a ship anchored eight miles below Fort McHenry, Key, Skinner, and Beanes listened to the British bombardment of the fort throughout a day and a night. Fearful that the fort had surrendered, Key looked toward it with a spyglass as soon as it was light on the morning of September 14, 1814. He was delighted to see that the American flag still flew over the fort.

Filled with joy and relief, Key began to write a poem on the back of a letter in his pocket: "Oh say can you see by the dawn's early light, What so proudly we hail'd at the twilight's last gleaming." After the British released the Americans, Key checked into a Baltimore hotel where he finished writing his poem. It was taken to a printer and published under the title "Defense of Fort M'Henry."

In a short time the poem was being sung to the tune of an old British drinking song. Later it became known under the title "The Star-Spangled Banner." Over the years it gradually became popular and was sung at various public ceremonies. But it did not become the official national anthem of the United States until 1931.

As for Key, he never took his poems seriously and a collection of them was not published until after his death. He continued to devote himself to the law and to his family. In 1830 he moved from Georgetown to Washington, where as the U.S. Attorney for the District of Columbia he did important legal work.

HAROLD D. LANGLEY

KING, BILLIE JEAN

(1943–   ) *Tennis player and crusader for women's equality in sports.*

Born in Long Beach, California, King fell in love with the game of tennis when she was eleven years old. Despite painful knee and foot injuries, she achieved top ranking in her sport and was the first woman athlete to earn more than $100,000 in a single year.

Between 1960 and 1979, she ranked among the top ten tennis players in the United States sixteen times and was the number one player seven times. At Wimbledon, the most prestigious tennis competition in the world, her skillful and determined playing earned her twenty championship titles in singles and doubles. For twenty years the number of her Wimbledon championships was an all-time record.

In 1973, Bobby Riggs, a professional tennis player and self-proclaimed male chauvinist who had made disparaging remarks about women's tennis, and women in general, for that matter, challenged King to compete in a match. The much-publicized televised game was called the "Battle of the Sexes," and men and women around the world cheered for their favorite. King not only won but ran the middle-aged Riggs into the ground. Women's sports advocates were thrilled.

King's match with Riggs inspired her to continue her fight for the rights of all women athletes. She pushed relentlessly to increase the amount of money women athletes are paid and helped create a separate women's tennis tour that gives women athletes the prestige and respect they deserve. In 1974 she was one of the founders and the first president of the Women's Tennis Association, and in the late 1970s she co-founded *Women's Sports* magazine. Although King retired from competitive tennis in 1984, she continues to work to improve the status of women in sports.

See also Sports, Spectator.

JOANN BIONDI

KING, ERNEST

(1878–1956) *Admiral and World War II leader.*

Ernest King was born and grew up in Ohio, where he never saw the ocean. Yet he became the most powerful naval leader in world history. In 1897 King was accepted as a midshipman at the U.S. Naval Academy and four years later graduated with honors. During World War I he worked on the staff of Adm. Henry Mayo, who commanded the American Atlantic fleet. After the war he served on various naval vessels, ranging from submarines to aircraft carriers. Convinced that naval aviation had a promising future, he learned to fly in 1928 at the age of forty-nine.

When America entered World War II, President Franklin D. Roosevelt made King the top-ranking member of the Combined Chiefs of Staff. This position required him to work with admirals from Great Britain. The British urged Roosevelt to pursue a policy of defeating Germany first and then concentrating military might on Japan. King disagreed with the British. He saw Japan as an offensive threat and wanted to send the bulk of American ships to the Pacific. During arguments with British officers, King often became abrasive and insulting. Even his countrymen were annoyed by his temper flareups. Gen. Dwight D. Eisenhower once wrote, "Admiral King is an arbitrary, stubborn type with too much brain and a tendency to bullying his juniors."

Still, no one doubted King's intellect or his commitment to victory. At King's prodding, most American ships served in the Pacific despite the wishes of the British. As the war continued, the American navy grew to possess more ships than all the other navies in the world combined. King, as chief of naval operations, presided over this immense fleet. The naval historian Samuel Eliot Morison said, "No officer on either side or in any armed service had so complete a strategic view of the war as King's."

See also Navy; World War II.

R. CONRAD STEIN

KING, MARTIN LUTHER, JR.

(1929–68) *Civil rights leader.*

Son of a southern Baptist preacher, King also pursued a career in the ministry, but finding his father's brand of faith too emotionally charged, he determined to appeal to the intellect. While in seminary school, he read the works of the writer Henry David Thoreau and Mahatma Gandhi, leader of the movement to free India from British rule. Both men advocated nonviolent resistance to overcome injustices. This led King to hope that the black church, long a black power base, could be used as a vehicle for gaining greater equality for black Americans.

King was catapulted into the civil rights movement when, as the new minister of Dexter Avenue Baptist Church in Montgomery, Alabama, he reluctantly accepted the leadership of the Montgomery Improvement Association. This group had formed in response to the arrest of Mrs. Rosa Parks for refusing to give up her seat on a bus to a white man. After the success of a year-long bus boycott, conducted in accordance with the principles

of nonviolent protest King had studied, he sought to build on its momentum by organizing southern ministers in the Southern Christian Leadership Conference (SCLC).

Highly articulate and possessed of an unshakable belief that there is a basic core of decency in Americans that could be appealed to through stirring rhetoric and nonviolent protests, King became the best-known civil rights leader in the nation, and his organization one of the best funded. His fame and success invited not only jealousy from other civil rights leaders but also a concerted campaign of harassment and intimidation on the part of FBI director J. Edgar Hoover, who used evidence of King's marital infidelities in an attempt to blackmail him.

Although a flawed human being, King was a charismatic leader whose speeches are among the most famous documents of twentieth-century American history. Perhaps his finest hour came on the steps of the Lincoln Memorial in Washington, D.C., on the occasion of the August 28, 1963, March on Washington. There he eloquently articulated his dream that Americans of all races would one day live in harmony: "It is a dream deeply rooted in the American dream that one day this nation will rise up and live out the true meaning ot its creed—we hold these truths to be self-evident, that all men are created equal." The I Have a Dream speech did more than any other public address to establish him as a moral leader of the nation.

King took his cause to Chicago, where he was dismayed to learn that traditional nonviolent tactics did not work in many areas where segregation existed in practice if not in law. Nevertheless, King was awarded the 1964 Nobel Peace Prize for his efforts to bring about nonviolent solutions to violence-laden problems. (He was the second African American to win the prize.)

Martin Luther King, Jr. (second from right), on the march from Selma to Montgomery, Alabama, one of the most famous protests of the civil rights movement. His wife, Coretta Scott King, is to the far right and Ralph Abernathy, another key leader of the Southern Christian Leadership Conference, is at the far left.

Having achieved international stature, King spoke out against U.S. involvement in the Vietnam War and was widely criticized for his stance, even by some supporters of his civil rights work. He was feeling discouraged and exhausted when he traveled to Memphis, Tennessee, to support a strike by black sanitation workers. There he was assassinated on April 4, 1968, at the age of thirty-nine. A lone gunman, James Earl Ray, confessed to killing King. Theories still abound that Ray did not act alone, but no conspiracy has ever been proved.

In 1984, President Ronald Reagan signed a bill making King's birthday a legal holiday. King is the only American not a president to be so honored.

See also Civil Rights Movement; Southern Christian Leadership Conference.

For further reading: Jim Haskins, *I Have a Dream: The Life and Words of Martin Luther King, Jr.* (Brookfield, Conn.: The Millbrook Press, 1992); Jim Haskins, *The Life and Death of Martin Luther King, Jr.* (New York: Beech Tree Books, 1992).

JIM HASKINS

KING PHILIP
See Philip (King Philip).

KISSINGER, HENRY A.

(1923–) *Statesman.*

This German-born Jewish refugee received his Ph.D. in 1954 from Harvard, where he taught until his appointment as President Richard M. Nixon's national security affairs adviser in 1969. As the country's most visible diplomat for the next eight years, Kissinger played many roles: theorist, negotiator, cabinet officer, bureaucratic infighter, public spokesman, policymaker. "I've always acted alone," he once said. "Americans admire the cowboy leading the caravan alone astride his horse."

Kissinger's secret trip to China in 1971 led to the reopening of relations between Washington and Beijing. He shared the Nobel Peace Prize for negotiating an end to the Vietnam War in 1973. Charming, thoughtful, and vain, Kissinger pursued détente with the Soviet Union. He achieved nuclear arms limitation agreements and expanded trade and played the Russians and Chinese against one another in what he termed "triangular diplomacy." He sought a geopolitical equilibrium that would contain the Soviet Union and China and curb radical revolution. Kissinger's shuttle diplomacy brought about an armistice between the Israelis and Arabs after their October war of 1973. He helped to end the Chilean government of Salvador Allende that same year.

Kissinger's tenure as secretary of state (1973–77) was marred by the Watergate scandal, which led to Nixon's resignation as president; the reestablishment of strong congressional influence over foreign policy; the fall of Cambodia and South Vietnam to communism; crises in Africa; and a souring of détente. Critics on the left compared Kissinger to another German émigré, "Dr. Strangelove," the movie character of that name who blows up the world, but conservative critics thought him too "soft" on communism.

Since leaving government in 1977, Kissinger has taught at Georgetown University, written his memoirs, and formed Kissinger Associates, a consulting firm that advises governments and corporations.

See also Nixon, Richard M.

J. GARRY CLIFFORD

Henry Kissinger, a celebrated as well as controversial diplomat, shakes hands with Foreign Minister Zhou Enlai of the People's Republic of China in 1972. Kissinger was instrumental in opening relations with China, which had ceased in 1949 when Chinese communists took over the country.

KNIGHTS OF LABOR

The development of labor unions after the Civil War went hand in hand with the development of corporations and other large business organizations. One of the most important unions was the Knights of Labor, founded in 1869 by garment workers in Philadelphia. As in most earlier unions, the leaders were not themselves workingmen but reformers interested in such matters as socialism, consumers' cooperatives, and land reform. Terence V. Powderly, who became grand master workman of the Knights in 1879, was opposed to strikes. He thought economic change could best be brought about by education rather than by dickering with employers about wages and working conditions.

The Knights were unusual for that time in admitting immigrants, women, unskilled laborers, and even—in segregated chapters—blacks. They also broke free from the common practice of organizing workers by particular trades. The eight-hour day became a major Knights' demand. Because of these policies, the union expanded rapidly. Some local branches made spectacular gains by striking, despite Powderly's objections to this tactic. Their success attracted more recruits. The Knights grew from 42,000 members in 1882 to more than 700,000 in 1886.

Such rapid expansion led to disorganization and ultimately to the Knights' collapse. An unsuccessful railroad strike against a major trunk line in 1886 was crushed. Support of a general strike in Chicago that led (through no fault of the Knights) to the Haymarket bombing turned the public against the union. It soon ceased to be a major force in the labor movement.

See also Labor Movement.

KNOW-NOTHING PARTY

The American Party was popularly known as the Know-Nothing Party because its members would reply "I know nothing" when questioned about the organization. It rose and fell in a brief period in the 1850s. The main issues attracting voters to the party were dislike of immigrants and Catholics and the social problems resulting from the recent influx of thousands of Irish and German immigrants into the towns and cities of the nation. Since the major parties tried to avoid taking positions on these controversial questions, people who considered them important, mostly native-born Protestants, flocked to the organization. In 1854 Philadelphia elected a Know-Nothing mayor, and more than forty Know-Nothing candidates won seats in the U.S. House of Representatives.

The controversy over the future of slavery in Kansas and the other territories led to the collapse of the Know-Nothing Party. In 1856,

after the Know-Nothing Party nominating convention put a plank supporting the Kansas-Nebraska Act in its platform—which was favored by proslavery people—most of its northern members shifted to another new organization, the Republican Party. The Know-Nothing presidential candidate in 1856, Millard Fillmore, carried only one state, Maryland.

See also Immigration.

KOREAN WAR

This war, which lasted from June 25, 1950, to July 27, 1953, involved the United States and fifteen other members of the United Nations (U.N.) who helped South Korea turn back an invasion from North Korea. This was the first limited war fought by the United States in the nuclear age.

At the end of World War II, the Korean Peninsula was divided on a line along the 38th parallel (which is one of the lines drawn on maps and used to indicate geographical positions). American troops were stationed to the south and Soviet forces to the north. Although the United Nations tried to hold free elections for the whole country, only South Korea cooperated, becoming the Republic of Korea (R O K). The Communists established a separate government in North Korea. In June 1950, North Korean troops crossed the parallel and quickly swept down to Seoul, South Korea's capital.

The War Starts
President Harry S. Truman immediately called for an emergency meeting of the U.N. Security Council. The council asked U.N.

The Korean War

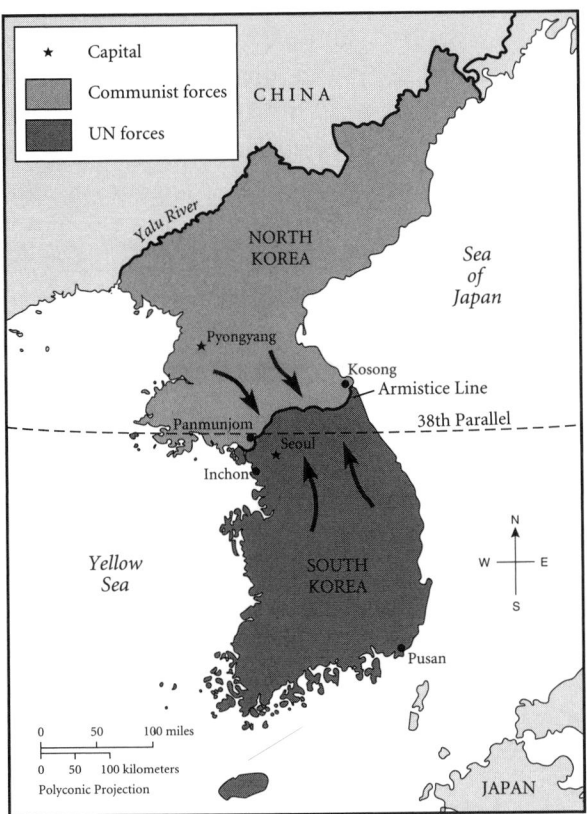

members to condemn North Korea's invasion and assist South Korea. Acting in support of the U.N. resolution, Truman ordered the U.S. armed services into action, under the leadership of Gen. Douglas MacArthur, commander of U.S. forces in the Far East.

Throughout the summer, American and ROK troops held on to the port of Pusan at the southern tip of the peninsula as North Koreans repeatedly tried to drive them into the sea. Despite U.N. air strikes against the enemy, the combined ground forces suffered heavy losses while awaiting the arrival of reinforcements. By September 15, MacArthur was ready to relieve them. He launched a daring landing at the port of Inchon, which was farther north close to Seoul and behind ene-

my lines. Treacherous tides and the absence of beaches made this a risky undertaking, but MacArthur's troops succeeded in cutting off enemy supply lines. The North Koreans were routed, and Seoul was recaptured.

Originally, the U.N. troops were engaged only in a "police action," to defend South Korea against aggression. Now as the enemy retreated across the 38th parallel, President Truman got U.N. approval to pursue them, and the mission was broadened to reuniting Korea. On October 7, U.N. troops moved into enemy territory, despite warnings that this might bring the Communist Chinese into the war. (China is located immediately north of Korea.) On the fifteenth, Truman flew to Wake Island in the Pacific to meet with General MacArthur, who assured him that the Chinese would not become involved. By October 19, U.N. forces had taken Pyongyang, the capital of North Korea.

Chinese Enter the War

Chinese armies, however, were already sneaking into North Korea, and in late October they launched a successful surprise attack against ROK troops near the Yalu River, bordering on China. Underestimating their strength, MacArthur opened an offensive on November 24, boldly declaring that his troops would be "home by Christmas." Two days later, however, massive Chinese attacks drove his men into a hasty retreat down the peninsula. The enemy retook Seoul on January 4, and it wasn't until mid-January that a counteroffensive could be undertaken.

MacArthur blamed the rout on Truman's refusal to let him bomb supply bases on the Chinese side of the Yalu River. The president, however, was determined to fight only a limited war, restricted to the Korean Peninsula and to the use of conventional (nonnuclear) weapons. He felt that if Chinese bases were attacked, American bases all over Asia would become vulnerable to enemy air strikes and that it could set off World War III. MacArthur, on the other hand, believed that the war should be fought without limitations until it was won. He continued to criticize Truman's policies publicly.

After the Chinese had entered the war, Truman revived the original U.N. mission—to restore and protect the Republic of Korea. In March 1951, as U.N. troops approached the 38th parallel once more, the president called for talks to end the war. MacArthur, however, demanded that the enemy surrender, insisting, "There is no substitute for victory." When he had his forces set up battle lines just north of the 38th parallel, an exasperated Truman dismissed him on April 11 for defying presidential orders. (The president under our Constitution is commander in chief of the military services. A general must obey him, just as a private must obey a sergeant and so on up the line.) Truman appointed Matthew B. Ridgway as MacArthur's replacement. Eleven days later, the Chinese opened a new offensive, but the American Eighth Army held its ground. The fighting then dragged on with no major gains by either side.

Peace Talks Begin

On June 23, the Soviet U.N. delegate proposed talks to bring about a cease-fire. Starting at Kaesong on July 10, they were suspended three times and were later moved to Panmunjom. Negotiators spent the next two years arguing about boundaries and debating the fate of Communist prisoners of war who did not wish to be exchanged. Sporadic fighting continued around the 38th parallel as the Communists tried unsuccessfully to break through U.N. lines. During that time, Dwight D. Eisenhower became president and Soviet leader Joseph Stalin died.

A cease-fire was finally signed on July 27, 1953, calling for mutual troop withdrawals, an exchange of those prisoners who wished to be returned, and the establishment of a two-and-a-half-mile-wide buffer zone on either side of the 38th parallel. The agreement brought an uneasy peace to the Korean Peninsula at a cost of 54,200 American lives and 103,284 wounded. Of the other U.N. participants, 3,094 were killed and 415,004 South Koreans died.

See also Cold War; MacArthur, Douglas; Truman, Harry S.

For further reading: Tom McGowen, *The Korean War* (New York: Franklin Watts, 1992).

BARBARA SILBERDICK FEINBERG

KROC, RAY

(1902–84)   *Restaurant chain developer.*

When Kroc founded the McDonald's Corporation in 1955, he created the world's largest restaurant chain. With his organizational skills and innovative marketing techniques, he became the leader of the fast-food industry and elevated it in both respectability and scale.

Born in Chicago, Kroc dropped out of school at the age of fifteen and lied about his age to become a Red Cross ambulance driver in World War I. After the war he worked as a jazz pianist but gave it up for a job as a paper-cup salesman. In 1937 he took on milkshake mixers as a sideline. These contacts with the food service industry prepared him for his successful career as a restaurant developer.

In 1954 Kroc noticed that a small drive-in hamburger restaurant in California needed eight of his mixers. Curious about its high volume of business, he learned that two brothers, Richard and Maurice McDonald, had developed an assembly-line method of preparing their food. He persuaded the McDonalds to let him sell franchises—the authorization to use their name and system. So successful were his franchise sales that in 1961 he bought their entire business, including the name, for $2.7 million. Eleven years later he franchised his two-thousandth McDonald's restaurant. Today there are more than ten thousand, and the company symbol—the twin "golden arches" that form the initial letter of the name—is seen all over the world.

Kroc maintained careful control over McDonald's, enforcing his motto, "Quality, Service, Cleanliness." He prohibited the installation of juke boxes and cigarette machines to prevent his restaurants from becoming hangouts and to keep each McDonald's a "dignified, clean place with a wholesome atmosphere." Kroc insisted that his licensees fly the American flag when possible and engage in community service.

In 1969 he established the Kroc Foundation to combat arthritis, diabetes, and multiple sclerosis, and three years later he gave $7.5 million to Chicago charities. In 1974 he began building Ronald McDonald Houses at children's hospitals across the country. These give the families of seriously ill children a nearby place to stay while their child is in the hospital.

DENNIS WEPMAN

KU KLUX KLAN

The Ku Klux Klan is America's oldest white supremacy organization. White supremacy is the mistaken idea that white people are a superior race. For more than a century, the Klan's trademarks—white robes and hoods, and the burning cross—have been symbols of racial hatred, bigotry, and fear.

The First Klan

The Ku Klux Klan was founded by six Confederate veterans in the little town of Pulaski, Tennessee. The Civil War had just ended, and the former soldiers were bored. Gathered around a fire on Christmas Eve 1865, they decided to form a social club.

Klan membership was secret, so members could break laws without being caught. They held ceremonies in which they called each other by titles like "Ghoul" and "Grand Cyclops." They dressed up in white sheets and hoods and rode about the countryside on horseback frightening people, especially the recently freed slaves. Their ghostlike appearance was meant to symbolize the spirits of dead Confederate soldiers. After a while, Klan activities became more violent. Klansmen dragged blacks from their homes, beat them, and sometimes burned their houses to the ground.

The Klan was mostly a local problem until the U.S. Congress passed the Reconstruction Acts of 1867. These were laws designed to protect the rights of the freed slaves and to punish the states that had seceded from the Union.

Most white southerners hated the acts, which greatly limited those who wouldn't swear loyalty to the United States. The Klan, under its new leader, a dashing ex-Confederate general named Nathan Bedford Forrest, took the lead in resisting Reconstruction. A Klan convention in Nashville, Tennessee, issued a declaration swearing to oppose "equality for Negroes" and maintain "the supremacy of the White Race." Young whites flocked to the group, swelling its membership to 500,000.

The Klan launched vicious attacks against freed blacks, scalawags, and carpetbaggers throughout the South. ("Scalawags" were white southerners who supported the Union and Reconstruction; "carpetbaggers" were northerners who came South to help educate the former slaves or to seek their own fortunes.) Hidden behind their hoods, Klansmen rampaged through the countryside, terrorizing their enemies, black and white alike, burning huge crosses on their victims' lawns, and lynching (murdering) those who committed what they considered "crimes" against the South. Within a few years, Klan lynchings numbered in the thousands.

The federal government declared the Klan illegal in 1871, and Forrest made a show of disbanding the organization. But the Klan's campaign of terror continued until Reconstruction came to an end in 1877. After that, the Klan seemed to disappear.

The Second Klan

In 1915, William J. Simmons, a life insurance salesman, launched a new version of the Ku Klux Klan. Simmons thought of the Klan as a business venture. He charged people ten dol-

White robes and hoods and a burning cross are the chilling features of a Ku Klux Klan rally. This meeting of the "Invisible Empire," as the Klan is also called, took place in 1950 in Jacksonville, Florida.

lars to join, and then sold them robes and hoods—and life insurance! Simmons proclaimed the Klan the champion of "Americanism, Christianity, and white supremacy." He expanded the old Klan's list of enemies to include Jews, Catholics, immigrants, and labor unions.

The original Klan had been confined to the South, but Simmons's group had branches as far north as Maine and as far west as California. At its peak, it claimed to have more than 5 million members. Its huge membership gave it great political influence: it virtually controlled the state government of Indiana, for example. In 1924, the Klan was a major reason the Democratic Party did not nominate Alfred E. Smith, a Catholic, for president.

Simmons's Klan collapsed in 1925, after D. C. Stephenson, one of its leaders, was convicted of killing a young woman. Stephenson testified against other Klan leaders, revealing so many financial and other misdeeds that most Klan members quit in disgust.

The Modern Klan

The Klan appeared again in the 1960s. At that time, the civil rights movement was battling to end legal segregation (separation of the races) in the South. Again, the Klan led a fight to preserve white supremacy. At least a thousand acts of violence resulted. Once again, Klan crosses blazed across the South, and black people who dared to stand up for their rights were threatened, attacked, or killed by marauding Klansmen.

Instead of helping to preserve segregation, however, the Klan's terrorism built sympathy for the civil rights movement. After reaching a high of about fifty thousand in the mid-1960s, Klan membership dwindled once again.

Over twenty small Klan groups are still active today, with a membership of under six thousand. There are also more than 150 other hate groups, including the Aryan Nation, the White Aryan Resistance, the Skinheads, and many small groups of neo-Nazis, who follow the teachings of the late German dictator Adolf Hitler.

See also Racism.

For further reading: Fred J. Cook, *The Ku Klux Klan: America's Recurring Nightmare* (New York: Messner, 1989).

MICHAEL KRONENWETTER

L

LABOR MOVEMENT

Labor movements are the way working people try to protect themselves from unfair treatment by employers. In America the first workers to grasp the idea that in unity there is strength were the journeymen who were employed on a wage basis by master craftsmen in the late colonial period. The earliest recorded strike occurred in 1768 when New York tailors protested a wage cut. In 1794 Philadelphia shoemakers formed the first permanent union—the Federal Society of Journeymen Cordwainers. From then on, many craft unions developed in the cities. Union members published lists of prices for their work, defended their trades against half-trained or cheap labor, and demanded a shorter workday.

Early Growth

These local organizations were the building blocks for a larger movement. Beginning in Philadelphia with the Mechanics' Union of Trade Associations in 1827, craft unions within a single city often united. And with the formation of the International Typographical Union in 1852, national unions brought into a single organization locals of the same trade.

Although the factory system was springing up during these years, industrial workers played only a small role in trade union development. Those factory workers who did participate were mostly craft workers whose oc-cupations had migrated into the factories. In the nineteenth century, trade unionism was mainly a movement of skilled workers.

The early labor movement was, however, inspired by more than the immediate job interests of its craft members. Workers also had a conception of the just society deriving from the republican ideals of the American Revolution—social equality, an independent and virtuous citizenship, the dignity of honest labor. Under the banner of equal rights, a labor reform movement got started in the 1830s and reached its peak with the Knights of Labor fifty years later. Labor reformers might seem to have been at odds with the aims of trade unions. They wanted a "cooperative commonwealth" rather than higher wages and appealed broadly to all "producers" rather than merely to wage earners. They emphasized education and politics rather than strikes and labor market control. But contemporaries saw no contradiction: trade unionism tended to workers' immediate needs; labor reform, to their higher hopes.

The AFL Organized

During the 1880s, however, those goals came into conflict. Despite its reform rhetoric, the Knights of Labor attracted large numbers of workers who saw it as a way to advance their job interests. The Knights began to organize along industrial lines and carry on strikes, thereby encroaching on the turf of the national trade unions. The unions struck back in 1886 by forming the American Federation of Labor (AFL) under the leadership of Samuel Gompers. Invoked to defend the old order, the new federation actually marked a decisive break with the past, for it denied that labor reform would help working people struggling to survive in a maturing industrial order. Gompers preached the doctrine of "pure-and-simple unionism." Only by organizing along job lines and concentrating on concrete job goals would a worker be "furnished with the weapons which shall secure his industrial emancipation."

The AFL lay claim to all workers regardless of skill, race, nationality, or gender. But the national unions that had created the AFL covered only the skilled trades. Almost at once, therefore, the labor movement encountered this dilemma: how to square theory against contrary realities? As technological change began to undermine the craft system of production, unions like those of the miners and clothing workers adopted a more inclusive membership. But most craft unions either refused to admit less skilled workers or made little headway among them. And since skill lines tended to reflect racial, ethnic, and gender divisions, the trade union movement took on a racist and sexist coloration as well. In 1902, blacks made up scarcely 3 percent of

A May Day parade in New York City in 1946. May 1st is celebrated in many parts of the world as a day honoring workers and unions.

total membership, most of them segregated in Jim Crow locals. In the case of women and eastern European immigrants, a similar contradiction prevailed—they were welcome in theory, but excluded or segregated in practice.

In politics, pure-and-simple unionism meant keeping the government at arm's length. Working people should rely on themselves, said Gompers, not on government to better their lives. In the Progressive Era after 1900, protective legislation won by middle-class reformers called this into question. In these years, too, the courts increasingly hamstrung trade union activities. In a Bill of Grievances (1906), the AFL called on the major parties to curb the antiunion courts and, to back up its demands, pledged that it would campaign regardless of party for candidates who responded and seek to defeat those who did not. This nonpartisan politics produced some modest results from the Democratic Wilson administration. But when the Republicans came into power in the 1920s, the unions lost political leverage, and as their economic power waned and membership shrank, they became inactive.

Movement Renewed

It took the Great Depression of the 1930s to revive the labor movement. The discontent of industrial workers, combined with New Deal collective-bargaining legislation, reopened the possibility of organizing the great mass-production industries like steel and auto manufacturing. When the craft-dominated AFL failed to respond, John L. Lewis of the miners' union broke away in 1935. He gave crucial aid to the emerging industrial unions in auto, rubber, steel, and other basic industries and in 1938 established a rival labor federation, the Congress of Industrial Organiza-

tions (CIO). By the end of World War II, some 12 million workers belonged to unions, and collective bargaining had taken hold in the industrial economy.

In 1955 the rival federations reunited. The AFL-CIO was visible proof of the fact that nothing fundamental had changed. In politics, nonpartisanship was amended, but not broken, by the alliance with the Democratic Party that had begun during the New Deal. Gompers's nonpartisan logic still prevailed: too much was at stake for organized labor to waste political capital on the kind of independent labor party that existed in Europe. The central purpose remained as always to advance the economic and job interests of the union membership. Collective bargaining worked well, more than tripling weekly earnings in manufacturing between 1945 and 1970, gaining for union members security against old age, illness, and unemployment, and strengthening their right to fair treatment in the workplace. But if the benefits were great and they went to more people, unions never covered more than a third of America's wage earners and were unavailable to those working in the low-wage, secondary labor market.

Recent Decline

Beginning in the 1970s, new competitive forces swept through the heavily unionized industries, set off by deregulation in communications and transportation, by nonunionized firms in meat packing, mining, and construction, and by waves of well-made foreign goods entering the automobile, steel, and electronics markets. Plant closings hurt many unions, and in collective bargaining they had to give back some of their earlier gains. With the election of President Ronald Reagan in 1980, there came to office an antiunion administration the likes of which had not been seen since the Harding era in the 1920s. Between 1975 and 1985, union membership fell by 5 million. By 1990, only 17 percent of American workers were organized, half the proportion after World War II.

The chances for a union revival are unclear. The labor movement has shown itself in the past to be resilient in the face of great economic change. And, as compared to the old AFL, organized labor is today much more diverse and broadly based: 40 percent of its members are white-collar workers, 30 percent are women, and blacks belong in proportionately larger numbers than whites. In the meantime, labor's weakness has been strongly felt in politics, where the downtrodden have lost their strongest champion. With collective bargaining in retreat, an unprecedented decline in living standards set in for working Americans after 1980, and the division of income became increasingly skewed in favor of the wealthy. The recent decline of the labor movement has, unquestionably, made for a less socially just nation.

See also American Federation of Labor; Congress of Industrial Organizations; Haymarket Bombing; Homestead Strike; Industrial Workers of the World; Knights of Labor; National Labor Relations Act; Pullman Strike; Railroad Strike of 1877; Sit-Down Strikes; Strikes; Taft-Hartley Act; Triangle Shirtwaist Fire; Women's Trade Union League. *Also see biographies of the following labor leaders:* Chavez, Cesar; Debs, Eugene V.; Gompers, Samuel; Jones, Mary Harris (Mother Jones); Lewis, John L.; Randolph, A. Philip.

DAVID BRODY

LANGE, DOROTHEA

(1895–1965)   *Photographer.*

Lange is best known for her pictorial record of rural Americans who were victims of the Great Depression in the 1930s. Her photos

Migrant Mother, *Dorothea Lange's most famous documentary photograph taken during the Great Depression. Lange's own notes about the 1936 photo read as follows: "Migrant agricultural worker's family. Seven hungry children. Mother age 32. Father is native Californian. Destitute in pea pickers' camp, Nipomo, California, because of the failure of the early pea crop. These people had just sold their tires in order to buy food. Of the 2,500 people in this camp most of them were destitute."*

such as the well-known *Migrant Mother* became widely known symbols in their time, and today they are seen as classic examples of documentary photography—that is, pictures that show ordinary life as people are living it rather than subjects posed in a studio.

The grandchild of German immigrants who had settled in Hoboken, New Jersey, Lange was struck by polio at seven, which left her permanently lame. Not long after, her father deserted the family. After high school Lange decided to become a photographer and persuaded Arnold Genthe, a New York City master photographer, to take her on as an apprentice.

At twenty-three Lange went to San Francisco and opened a portrait studio. Soon she married Maynard Dixon, a painter of the western wilderness, and had two sons. When the Great Depression began, she turned from making studio portraits of the rich to photographing the jobless on city streets. Her photos were quickly recognized as moving images of Americans in deep trouble—in bread lines, picket lines, communes, or wandering homeless on the nation's highways. Next she combined her talents with those of economist Paul Taylor (whom she married after divorcing Dixon) to document in words and pictures the migrant families flooding into California to seek work on the farms. Their reports influenced the federal government's decision to provide decent camp housing for the migrants.

In 1935 a federal agency concerned with farm problems hired Lange to record rural life throughout the country. For four years she captured on film how life was changing for the poor, both black and white. Her picture stories pioneered a new kind of journalism. During and after World War II, her powerful images continued to reveal how people lived and worked in war plants, in the internment camps holding Japanese Americans, and in places as far apart as Utah, Ireland, and Asia.

Lange died of cancer at the age of seventy, but not before preparing the prints for an exhibit of her life's work at the Museum of Modern Art in New York.

See also Photography.

For further reading: Milton Meltzer, *Dorothea Lange: Life Through the Camera* (New York: Viking, 1985).

MILTON MELTZER

LATINAS/LATINOS
See Hispanics.

LATTER-DAY SAINTS
See Mormons.

LAWRENCE, JACOB
(1917–) *Artist.*

Regarded as the foremost African-American painter in the country, Jacob Lawrence has for over fifty years ignored popular fashions in art. His distinctive work combines a vivid style with a powerful sense of social issues and the ability to make the tragic history of his race come alive. Regarded as "a sophisticated primitive painter," he is especially famous for his many series on single subjects, such as one person's life or a historical event. The simple, striking designs, natural figures, and pure colors in his work make his dramatic pictorial storytelling powerful and moving.

Lawrence was born in New Jersey, and his family moved to Harlem when he was thirteen. His education in art began at a settlement house where he went after school while his mother was at work. He dropped out of high school at the age of sixteen but continued studying art, both at the federally funded Harlem Art Workshop and by himself in the museums of New York City. Before he was twenty, he was producing excellent scenes of street life in Harlem that revealed his talent for honest, straightforward treatment of his subjects in flat simplified forms and primary colors.

In 1936 Lawrence began the first of his series. In forty-one paintings he recounted the story of Toussaint L'Ouverture, the black liberator of Haiti. In the next three years he created long series on the great opponents of slavery Frederick Douglass, Harriet Tubman, and John Brown. *The Migration of the Negro* (1940–41) portrays the mass movement of southern African Americans to the North in search of jobs during and after World War I. Its sixty images made him nationally famous. The series was reproduced in magazines and purchased by two major museums, each taking half.

In the years since then, Lawrence has continued to do important work as a painter and teacher. His many paintings are powerful visual commentaries on the blacks' struggle against hardship and oppression.

See also Painting and Sculpture, *and illustration in color insert following page 628.*

DENNIS WEPMAN

LEAGUE OF NATIONS
See Versailles Treaty and League of Nations.

LEAGUE OF WOMEN VOTERS

In 1920, after the passage of the Nineteenth Amendment guaranteeing women the right to vote, leaders of the women's movement founded the League of Women Voters. They hoped the League would help make women an influential force in national politics. Some leaders, such as Carrie Chapman Catt, who was a former president of the National American Woman Suffrage Association, thought women could best exercise influence by working within the established political parties. Others favored founding a new Women's

Carrie Chapman Catt (center) was a founder of the League of Women Voters, which sought to make women full participants in the political process.

Party. Still others thought the League should seek to influence public opinion by means of nonpartisan campaigns of information. This last position was the one finally adopted by the League. In the 1920s it opposed an Equal Rights Amendment to the Constitution and instead supported policies aimed at benefiting all citizens, not just women. In recent years, for example, the League has sponsored televised debates between the presidential candidates of the major parties.

See also Feminist Movement since 1919; Voting.

LEE, ROBERT E.

(1807–70)   *General in chief of the Confederate armies.*

Lee was born into a famous Virginia family, which included two signers of the Declaration of Independence. After graduating second at West Point, he distinguished himself in the Mexican War (1846–48). The commander of the U.S. Army called him "the greatest military genius in America."

When civil war seemed unavoidable, he found his loyalties divided. He disliked slavery, calling it "a moral and political evil," and worked to preserve the Union. "I take great pride in my country," he wrote in 1861. "I can anticipate no greater calamity . . . than a dissolution of the Union."

On the other hand, he objected to a federal government that could force states to act in ways their people opposed. He was offered command of the Union army, but turned it down to become general of Virginia's forces, explaining, "I cannot raise my hand against my birthplace."

Throughout the war, Lee's troops were usually outnumbered and undersupplied, yet

Robert E. Lee photographed by Mathew Brady in 1865 at his home in Richmond, Virginia. General Lee, commander of the Confederate forces during the Civil War, was respected on both sides of the conflict for his military brilliance and personal integrity. None other than Union commander Ulysses S. Grant had this to say about meeting Lee at the surrender of the Confederate army: "What General Lee's feelings were I do not know. . . . He was a man of much dignity. . . . I felt like anything rather than rejoicing at the downfall of a foe who had fought so long and valiantly, and had suffered so much for a cause."

he never doubted their ability. He became a master at motivating his soldiers and maneuvering them to confuse his opponents. When he spotted a weakness in enemy defenses, he struck with lightning speed. Such tactics earned him stunning victories at Manassas, the Seven Days' Battles, and Chancellorsville.

But Lee's single-mindedness proved a liability. At Antietam and Gettysburg, he underestimated his enemy and lost thousands of men needlessly. Finally, his army exhausted and out of ammunition, he surrendered to Ulysses S. Grant at Appomattox, April 9, 1865.

After hostilities ended, Lee rarely spoke about the Civil War. He accepted the fate of the Confederacy with the same dignity with which he had led his army. "Recollect that we form but one country *now*," he told an angry Southerner. "Abandon all these local animosities, and make your sons Americans."

See also Civil War; Confederate States of America.

JIM MURPHY

LEGISLATURE
See House of Representatives; Senate.

LEND-LEASE ACT

During the period between the outbreak of World War II in September 1939 and American entry into the war in December 1941 the United States moved from a policy of strict neutrality to one of open support of the Allies. First Congress approved the sale of arms to the Allies on a "cash and carry" basis: that is, they could buy American arms only if they paid for them on the spot. This limit was imposed to prevent the possibility that if Americans lent money to the Allies so that they could buy arms, the United States might be drawn into the war in order to make sure that the Allies won and would be able to repay the loans.

Then in May 1940 President Franklin D. Roosevelt exchanged fifty American destroyers for six British naval bases in the Caribbean Sea. The destroyers helped the British protect ships bringing supplies across the Atlantic Ocean against the attacks of German U-boats. By early 1941, however, the British no longer had enough cash to pay for all the supplies they were carrying from America. Rather than suggest lending them the money, which would have caused bitter arguments in Congress and the press, Roosevelt developed his "Lend-Lease" plan. He asked Congress for authority to "sell, lend, lease, exchange, or transfer" war matériel to any nation whose defense he considered essential to the defense of the United States. The Lend-Lease Act of March 1941 appropriated $7 billion for this purpose.

At first most of the money was used to supply arms for the British. But after the Nazi invasion of Russia in June 1941, Lend-Lease was also supplied to the Soviets. After the United States entered the war as a result of the Japanese attack on Pearl Harbor, Lend-Lease was supplied in ever-larger amounts to all the Allied nations. By the time the program came to an end in August 1945, more than $50 billion had been distributed.

L'ENFANT, PIERRE

(1754–1825)   *Architect.*

An accomplished soldier, engineer, and architect, L'Enfant is most remembered for his plan for Washington, D.C., which many consider to be among the most architecturally well designed cities in the world.

Born and educated in Paris, France, L'Enfant volunteered to fight in the American Revolution in 1776. As an army captain he was wounded, captured, and then released in Charleston, South Carolina, in 1782. In 1784 he settled in New York City where he began a career as an architect. Three years later he planned the conversion of the old city hall building into Federal Hall, the temporary seat of the new government.

In 1791 President George Washington commissioned him to design the new capital in Washington. L'Enfant, a creative genius with a bad temperament, put his artistic talents to work and designed a city with radiating streets, formal parks, broad boulevards, and prominent public buildings, much like Versailles, then the French capital. Although his project was well regarded, L'Enfant was unable to stay within the planned budget and angered government officials with his haughty attitude. He was dismissed in 1794.

In the years that followed, L'Enfant was hired to plan an industrial city in New Jersey, improve Fort Washington, and build a house in Philadelphia. He was dismissed from these projects as well, and all the plans fell through.

L'Enfant spent the last years of his life trying to collect payment from the U.S. government for the work he started in Washington. He had to live off the charity of friends and died a bitter and penniless man. In 1901, however, his Washington plan was revived and his original design implemented. In 1909 L'Enfant's remains were moved to Arlington Cemetery, which overlooks the city he designed.

See also Architecture.

JOANN BIONDI

LEVITTOWNS

During World War II there was little money and less labor available for building private homes. Building materials were also scarce, and relatively few new families were being formed because so many young men were off fighting the Germans and the Japanese.

When the war ended, all this changed swiftly. Returning servicemen and servicewomen were eager to establish the homes and families they had dreamed of during the war. In 1946 the marriage rate soared, and the birthrate followed soon thereafter. Couples with growing families were eager to have homes of their own, preferably outside large cities where there was plenty of fresh air and room for small children to play. Low-interest government mortgage loans and income tax deductions for the interest charged on these loans were available. The result was an enormous boom in home construction.

William Levitt's firm, Levitt and Sons, was quick to take advantage of the demand for housing. During the war Levitt had received government contracts to build homes for war workers. The company developed new construction methods that cut costs and shortened the time it took to build houses. The postwar boom enabled it to apply these techniques on a huge scale.

The simply designed houses were built by crews, each performing one job in a twenty-seven-step construction process and using prefabricated material. At the peak of production, over thirty houses were built per day.

The first Levittown sprang up in Hempstead, a suburb of New York City, between 1947 and 1951. In all 17,500 homes were built, complete with community swimming pools, playgrounds, and landscaped house plots. Levitt then built a second Levittown in Pennsylvania, and in the 1960s, a third in New Jersey. Other builders, large and small, soon adopted many of Levitt's methods.

See also Housing.

A 1949 aerial photo of one of three Levittowns in the United States, this one on Long Island in New York. Each house was a carbon copy of the others. Levittowns have been applauded because they provided cheap housing for the middle class and solved a housing shortage, but criticized by others because of their lack of personality and their numbing suburban sameness.

LEWIS, JOHN L.

(1880–1969)   *Labor leader.*

John L. Lewis was one of the most powerful, aggressive, and controversial figures in the history of the labor movement. Born in Iowa, the son of a Welsh coal miner, he left school after the seventh grade to help support his family by working in the mines. As a young man, he became involved in improving the miners' conditions through their union. He held various positions in the United Mine Workers (UMW) and in 1920 became its president, a position he held for forty years. The UMW in 1920 was the largest union within the American Federation of Labor (AFL).

Lewis's long career as a labor leader was marked by frequent conflicts with union opponents and politicians. In 1935, when the AFL refused to end its policy of organizing only skilled workers according to particular trades, such as butchers or printers, Lewis helped create a new labor organization that included all the workers in entire industries.

Called the Committee for Industrial Organization, it later became the Congress of Industrial Organizations (CIO). As head of the CIO, Lewis helped unionize mass-production industries, such as automobile and steel manufacturing.

When Franklin D. Roosevelt became president in 1933, Lewis at first supported him. But in 1940, when FDR was running for a third term, Lewis accused the president of deserting the labor movement and urged workers to vote against him. After Roosevelt was reelected, Lewis resigned as CIO president in protest. Two years later he took the UMW out of the CIO.

Often Lewis was criticized for what seemed to be ruthless, even unpatriotic practices. During World War II, several times he ordered coal miners to strike, although strikes were prohibited. These work delays in an industry vital to the war effort triggered a great deal of anger, but Lewis replied that his actions had provided coal miners with higher wages, better working conditions, increased medical care, and other benefits. With his large body, shaggy hair, thick eyebrows, and growling voice, Lewis was often described as "the roaring lion of labor."

See also American Federation of Labor; Congress of Industrial Organizations; Labor Movement.

For further reading: Melvyn Dubofsky and Warren Van Tine, *John L. Lewis: A Biography* (New York: Harper & Row, 1983).

E DMUND L INDOP

L EWIS , S INCLAIR

(1885–1951)   *Novelist and social critic.*

Lewis was born in Sauk Centre, Minnesota. His father was a stern, hardworking doctor. After writing several mediocre novels, Lewis

hit his stride in *Main Street*. Published in 1920, it mocked the dullness and prejudices of small-town American life. World War I had exposed millions of Americans to big-city styles and European sophistication, and readers loved it. Lewis's next book, *Babbitt* (1922), was a savagely critical portrait of a profit-hungry, narrow-minded, small-town businesssman. It was even more popular.

In 1925, Lewis revealed his admiration for the heroic side of the American dream. *Arrowsmith,* written with bacteriologist Paul de Kruif, is the story of a brilliant researcher who struggles against corruption in the medical profession and the temptations of irresponsible women. The novel won the Pulitzer Prize, but Lewis rejected it, causing a sensation. The Pulitzer judges had awarded the prize to *Main Street* in 1920, but Columbia University's trustees had refused to confirm their choice. Lewis, a lifelong foe of censorship, said the trustees were a menace to American literature.

For his next novel, Lewis went back to social criticism. *Elmer Gantry* (1927) was a hostile portrait of a scheming hypocritical evangelist. In *Dodsworth* (1929), Lewis portrayed a different kind of American businessman. Sam Dodsworth finds a new kind of life in Europe. He divorces his frivolous spendthrift wife and marries a serious woman, who inspires him to launch a new business building inexpensive well-designed homes. The novel won Lewis the Nobel Prize in 1930. In his acceptance speech he praised such realist writers as Theodore Dreiser and William Faulkner and attacked other writers for being afraid to tell the whole truth about American life.

For the next twenty years, Lewis continued to write novels about problems in American society. But he seldom achieved the razor-edge precision and breadth of his early work. Today he is best known for having invented Babbitt, whose name became a synonym for a narrowness and greed that Americans would just as soon disown.

See also Literature.

THOMAS FLEMING

LEWIS AND CLARK EXPEDITION

In 1803 President Thomas Jefferson sent two soldiers, Capt. Meriwether Lewis and Lt. William Clark, to explore the Louisiana Purchase and the land westward to the Pacific Ocean. The object was to locate and map the best routes through the Rocky Mountains and collect data on the climate, natural resources, and plant and animal life of the area. He also told Lewis and Clark to assure the Indians they met that the people of the United States were their "friends and protectors."

In May 1804 the party, some fifty in number, set out from St. Louis. They proceeded up the Missouri River to what is now North Dakota, where they built a fort and passed the winter. In the spring, having hired Sacajawea, an Indian woman, and her French Canadian husband, to act as guides and translators, they crossed through the Rockies and traveled down the Salmon, Snake, and Columbia rivers to the Pacific. After spending the winter of 1805 there, they recrossed the mountains, this time by separate routes, and proceeded down the Missouri together to St. Louis, which they reached in late September 1806.

Among their many achievements, Lewis and Clark located several passes through the mountains and established friendly relations with many Indian tribes, trading American

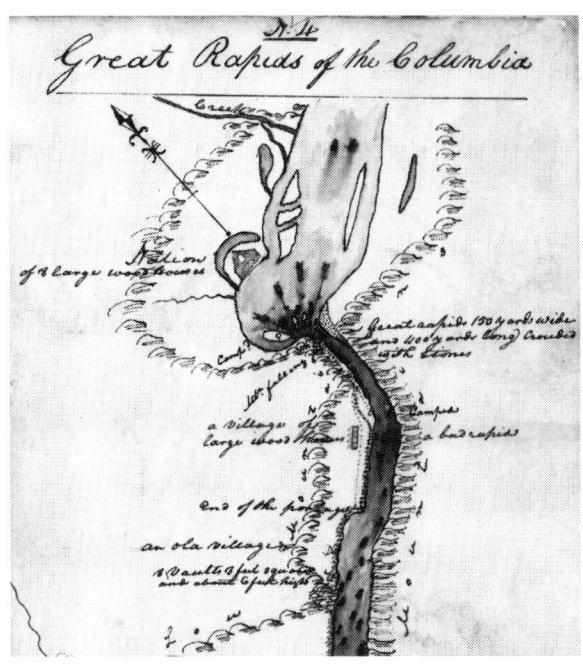

A detail from a map of the Columbia River rapids sketched by William Clark in his 1805 journal. Clark, and his partner Meriwether Lewis, commissioned to explore the uncharted wilderness of the Louisiana Purchase, made detailed notes and maps of the geography, wildlife, and inhabitants they encountered on their two-year expedition. For a map of their route, see the Louisiana Purchase map on p. 507.

flags, medals, and other gifts for examples of Indian art and culture. They also brought back careful maps and much of the scientific information Jefferson had requested. The expedition marked the beginning, for better and for worse, of white penetration of the Great West.

See also Louisiana Purchase, *which includes a map of the expedition's route;* Sacajawea.

LIBERTY LEAGUE

In August 1934 a group of conservative business and political leaders, including such prominent Democrats as John W. Davis, the

Democratic candidate for president in 1924 and John J. Rascob, a former national chairman of the party, formed the American Liberty League. The founders believed that the entire New Deal program was socialistic, a waste of money, and unconstitutional. They created the League in order to raise money to support anti–New Deal candidates for office and to publish pamphlets attacking President Franklin D. Roosevelt and his policies.

A former supporter of Roosevelt, ex-governor Alfred E. Smith of New York, became active in the Liberty League, but his aggressive personal attacks on Roosevelt had little effect. Despite the expenditure of considerable amounts of money, the League failed to influence public opinion. The landslide Democratic victories in the election of 1936 put an end to its activities.

him again four years later. Although he received only 62,000 votes, 16,000 of them were cast by antislavery New York Whigs. Since the Democratic candidate, James K. Polk, carried New York by only 5,000 votes, the Liberty Party total prevented the Whig candidate, Henry Clay, from carrying the state. Had he received New York's thirty-six electoral votes, Clay would have been elected president.

In the 1848 presidential election, abolitionist votes were again important. Supporters of the Liberty Party joined this time with sympathetic Democrats to form the more moderate Free-Soil Party. Their candidate, Martin Van Buren, polled about 300,000 votes on a platform committed to keeping slavery out of the western territories.

See also Abolitionist Movement.

LIBERTY PARTY

The Liberty Party was a tiny but enormously significant political organization devoted to the abolition of slavery. It was created in 1840 after a split in the abolitionist movement between the followers of William Lloyd Garrison, who opposed any involvement in politics because the United States tolerated the existence of slavery, and the group influenced by the Reverend Theodore D. Weld, who favored trying to persuade voters to stop tolerating it. Weld was in favor of "immediate" emancipation of the slaves, he said, but "gradually achieved."

The "gradualists" formed the Liberty Party and in 1840 nominated for president James G. Birney, a former Kentucky slaveholder, who had turned against slavery. Birney received only about 7,000 votes. The party nominated

LIBRARIES AND MUSEUMS

Libraries are assemblies of books, manuscripts, periodicals, and other sources of information; museums conserve and display collections of objects—historical, scientific, natural, and artistic. American libraries and museums serve many purposes and many publics. But during the past 150 years, they have become notable for their numbers, their size, the conveniences they have devised, and their concern with providing good service to those who use them.

Libraries
About the time of the American Revolution most libraries belonged either to private persons or to colleges. A few served groups who subscribed much as they would for a newspaper or magazine. Young clerks and artisans,

merchants, mechanics, and lawyers paid for the privilege of consulting books and charging them out. Libraries claimed to aid self-improvement, and free citizens were expected to be literate. But not until seventy-five years after the Revolution did government support public libraries. And not until the late nineteenth century, and the gifts of Andrew Carnegie, an industrialist millionaire, did they really multiply. Carnegie gave millions of dollars for library buildings throughout the United States, on condition that local communities support them through tax revenues.

During the twentieth century special libraries developed for children, for the blind, for the performing arts, and for foreign language speakers. Mobile libraries traveled to rural areas, and branch libraries served city neighborhoods. Meanwhile, wealthy collectors of rare books and manuscripts established their own institutions for scholarly research, and college and university libraries developed into some of the largest collections in the world. The Library of Congress in Washington, relatively small in size until the 1880s, is now the biggest library in the world.

Visitors at the Metropolitan Museum of Art in New York City around 1909 gazing at Emmanuel Leutze's famous painting, Washington Crossing the Delaware.

American libraries focus on written materials, but for the past fifty years they have tried to apply and compete with new technologies, ranging from photography, slides, films, and recordings to computers, videotapes, and laser disks. Although periodically threatened by tax cuts and by censors, they remain important settings for self-advancement and recreation in thousands of towns and cities.

Museums

Museums have almost as long a history in America as libraries. Again, the period of the Revolution was important, when for patriotic and scientific reasons several were established. Painter Charles Willson Peale's American Museum was founded in 1784 as an object lesson, he said, in "the harmony of the universe." It featured paintings, natural specimens, and curiosities like mastodon bones and historic relics.

In the next few decades commercial museums, run for profit as well as for enlightenment, multiplied. The most successful was P. T. Barnum's American Museum in New York City, an enormously popular mixture of genuine scientific specimens, suspicious historic mementoes, and certifiable fakes. With brass bands, fast-talking barkers, and other hoopla, Barnum drew thousands to his sign-covered building on Broadway.

After the Civil War, American museums of art, history, and science began to assume more serious features. Usually located on college campuses or in large cities, many were founded by philanthropists concerned about civic dignity, public education, and popular morals and tastes. Institutions like Boston's Museum of Fine Arts, New York's Metropolitan Museum of Art and American Museum of Natural History, and the Art Institute of Chicago blended private and public support.

Often state and city taxes paid for buildings and land, but collections were financed by private benefactors.

By the early twentieth century, many urban museum buildings had become large and elegant, and their collections began to fill with rare expensive pieces imported from abroad. Between the two world wars some museums became more specialized, featuring modern, medieval, or Far Eastern art, for example, or serving specific groups like children. Some devoted themselves to American history, as in the restored or reconstructed settings of Williamsburg, Virginia, and Dearborn, Michigan. Historic houses and shrines attracted thousands as automobile tourism grew.

Educational programs increased as well. Most major museums featured lecture programs, formed close connections with public school systems, hosted concerts and story hours, published books on their collections, and offered conducted tours of their galleries.

After World War II museum expansion was even more dramatic. Federal support, blockbuster exhibitions, generous gifts, dramatic purchases, and new startling structures gave American museums a hold on popular attention. Attendance surpassed even sports spectatorship. Glamorous museum shops and elaborate advertising attracted many new visitors, and interactive videos, orientation films, and recorded tours supplemented the exhibitions themselves. Like libraries, many museums welcomed new technology even though they also felt threatened by it. And, like libraries, museums had to deal with diminishing levels of tax support as well as critics of their sometimes controversial exhibits.

See also Barnum, Phineas T.; Carnegie, Andrew.

NEIL HARRIS

LINCOLN, ABRAHAM

(1809–65)   *Sixteenth president of the United States (1861–65).*

Born in a log cabin with one window and a dirt floor, Lincoln grew up swinging an ax on pioneer homesteads in Kentucky, Indiana, and Illinois. His formal schooling amounted to less than one year. Mostly he educated himself, borrowing books from his backwoods neighbors. When he came of age he settled in New Salem, Illinois, where he worked at all sorts of jobs, ranging from part-time postmaster to self-taught surveyor. In 1834 he was elected to the Illinois state legislature. Meanwhile he studied law on his own. After passing his bar exams, he moved to Springfield, the new state capital, and became a prosperous attorney and an influential figure in state politics.

Lincoln had always regarded slavery as a "monstrous injustice." He believed that if it was confined to those states where it already existed, it would gradually die a "natural death." When Congress passed the bitterly contested Kansas-Nebraska Act in 1854, he began to speak out against the spread of slavery to the vast new territories that were opening up in the West. The act let the settlers themselves decide whether a new territory would allow slavery or not. His debates on this issue with Stephen A. Douglas in the 1858 race for the U.S. Senate captured the nation's attention. He lost that election but in 1860 became the Republican nominee for president and was elected. Within five weeks of his inauguration, eleven slave-holding states had left the Union and the Civil War had begun.

Lincoln is best known as the Great Emancipator, the man who freed the slaves. Yet he did not enter the Civil War with that idea in mind. "My paramount object in this struggle *is* to save the Union," he said in 1862, "and

Abraham Lincoln photographed about 1864 by either Mathew Brady or A. Berger. This portrait was the model for the image of Lincoln that appears on the five-dollar bill.

is *not* either to save or destroy slavery." As the war dragged on at a terrible cost of lives, Lincoln changed his mind. He decided that freeing the slaves in the rebel states could cripple the Confederacy and hasten the end of the war. Emancipation became a Union war objective. On New Year's Day, 1863, as he signed the Emancipation Proclamation, Lincoln said, "If my name ever goes into history, it will be for this act."

Lincoln's wartime policies, which included emancipation, aroused so much opposition, the president himself doubted that he would be returned to office for a second term. But as the election of 1864 approached, Union armies began at last to win decisive victories. It was clear that the end of the war was in sight, and Lincoln was reelected easily. In his second inaugural address, he called "this mighty scourge of war" a terrible retribution, a punishment for allowing human bondage to flourish on the nation's soil. A month later, on April 14, 1865, five days after Robert E. Lee surrendered at Appomattox, Abraham Lincoln was shot by an assassin's bullet and died the next day. John Wilkes Booth, an actor and Southern sympathizer, shot him as he sat in a box at Ford's Theatre in Washington, D.C., attending a performance of *Our American Cousin*.

Abraham Lincoln was known for his personal warmth and rollicking sense of humor, but he was also a melancholy man whose frequent black moods puzzled those who knew him best. He spoke with a backwoods drawl and was unschooled, yet he became an eloquent public speaker and great writer. Lincoln's finest phrases—particularly those of the Gettysburg Address and his inaugural addresses—still ring in our ears. Frederick Douglass, the fiery black abolitionist writer and editor who had grown up as a slave, said this about Lincoln: "His greatest mission was to accomplish two things: first, to save his country from dismemberment and ruin; and, second, to free his country from the great crime of slavery."

See also Presidency; Republican Party. *For events during Lincoln's administration, see* Civil War; Confederate States of America; Copperheads; Draft Riots of 1863; Emancipation Proclamation and Thirteenth Amendment; Gettysburg Address; Homestead Act; Morrill Land Grant Act; Secession; Wade-Davis Bill.

For further reading: Russell Freedman, *Lincoln: A Photobiography* (New York: Clarion Books, 1987).

RUSSELL FREEDMAN

LINCOLN-DOUGLAS DEBATES
See Freeport Doctrine.

LINDBERGH, CHARLES A.

(1902–74) *Aviator who made the first solo flight across the Atlantic Ocean.*

Lindbergh was born in Detroit, Michigan, and grew up on a farm near Little Falls, Minnesota. He began flying as a stunt pilot in the early years of aviation, thrilling people at carnivals by putting a plane through daring loops and rolls.

In 1919 a New York millionaire offered a $25,000 prize to any pilot who could fly from New York to Paris, France. With the help of some St. Louis businessmen, Lindbergh bought a single-engine airplane, which

Charles Lindbergh and his wife, the writer Anne Morrow Lindbergh, photographed in 1931 in front of their plane, Sirius. *One of the many expeditions they flew together, this trip took them from New York to China.*

he named the *Spirit of St. Louis.* On May 20, 1927, he took off from Roosevelt Field near New York City and headed for Paris.

Alone, flying at 102 miles per hour, he looked down at the forbidding Atlantic Ocean. "I'm struck by my arrogance in attempting such a flight," he later wrote. "I'm giving up a continent, and heading out to sea in the most fragile vehicle ever devised by man." In the middle of the Atlantic, ice formed on his wings, and he struggled to stay aloft. Night fell, and the constant throb of the engine made him dangerously drowsy. But the next day Lindbergh saw a rocky coast. Ireland!

After a flight that lasted 33½ hours Lindbergh landed at Paris. He was the first aviator to cross the Atlantic Ocean alone. His feat electrified the world. Newspapers hailed him as the "Lone Eagle" and "Lucky Lindy," and an adoring public showered him with praise.

Although Lindbergh sought privacy, he could not escape the limelight. He married Anne Morrow, a talented writer and daughter of diplomat Dwight Morrow. In 1932 the Lindberghs' twenty-month-old son was kidnapped and later found dead. After a sensational court trial that ended in the conviction and execution of an unemployed carpenter named Bruno Hauptmann, the couple moved to Europe to escape the publicity surrounding the crime.

When World War II broke out in Europe, Lindbergh became an active isolationist, urging Americans to stay out of the conflict. Many people condemned him as being disloyal to America, though when the United States did enter the war, he flew fifty combat missions in the Pacific and advised the air force on aviation matters.

Lindbergh was without question the most celebrated American hero of the 1920s. He will always be remembered as one of aviation's boldest pioneers.

See also Aviation.

For further reading: R. Conrad Stein, *The Story of the "Spirit of St. Louis"* (Chicago: Childrens Press, 1984).

R. CONRAD STEIN

LITERATURE

Literature is the name we give to writings that last a long time—writings that remain exciting and enlarging long after those who composed them have died. If one thinks about how hard it is—in a letter or even in a conversation—to convey in words something that really interests or startles another person, then we have an inkling of how difficult it is to write compellingly for people who have no personal connection to the world in which the writer lives. This is the challenge taken up in all serious writing: to reduce the imaginative space that separates one person from another, and to introduce into the mind of the reader the feelings and thoughts that are fiercely alive in the mind of the writer.

To perform this magic, one has to master the language into which one is born. This means to get beyond the automatic phrases and expressions that control most of what we say or think and invent new ways of expressing our thoughts. It means to use old words in fresh ways. Every writer gifted in this way has the ability to surprise—as when Herman Melville, who produced what is perhaps the greatest of all American novels, *Moby-Dick* (1851), describes how, to a shivering sailor, the sky on a freezing night seems like "a steel-blue cymbal, that might ring, could you smite it," and the sea-air feels so cold that "any man could have undergone amputation with great ease, and helped to take up the arteries himself." Reading these words a century and a half after Melville wrote them, one *feels* the bitter cold as if one were actually exposed to it. Countless efforts to find new ways of describing the world have been undertaken in the three and a half centuries since English-speaking people first settled in what became the United States. But only a handful have survived as works that can still make us feel vividly the experience of what it meant to be alive in a time very different from our own. Even fewer have been able to shake our assumptions about what is important in life. Those works that have managed to do these difficult things constitute our national literature.

Early Literary Forms

The literature of every country, of course, reflects the social and political development of the society that is both its source and its subject. In the case of America, this literary history is brief. Until the early nineteenth century, the American literary imagination expressed itself not so much in written as in spoken form; and the kinds of writing we think of today as literary—poems, plays, and especially novels—were very scarce. Early America was the scene of intense religious and political controversies, a place where sermons and speeches were public performances to which people flocked not only for information but also for entertainment. The most powerful writers were, therefore, not poets and playwrights but ministers like Jonathan Edwards, who was famous for his vivid descriptions of sin and hell, or politicians like Benjamin Franklin and Thomas Jefferson, who used their rhetorical gifts on behalf of the cause of American independence.

So until the Revolution, educated people in the colonies who had a taste for what was called belles-lettres (literature that was nonreligious and amusing rather than pious and improving), had to be content with the latest productions by fashionable English writers. But suddenly, Americans found themselves citizens of a new country, yet practitioners of an old language. More gradually, they became aware of the unique scale and drama of their own national experience—of their continental expansion driven by the allure of enormous natural resources, by land hunger and the pressures of immigration, and by sheer greed, as well as by the exalted motives of various truth-seekers and visionaries.

Finding an *American* Literature

As the culture moved westward (a process recorded in the first American fictional work of epic ambition, the Leatherstocking tales of James Fenimore Cooper), it came into conflict with the old European powers that still had a stake in the New World, as well as with the indigenous peoples, the Indians, whom some of the conquerors admired even as they crushed them. It was in these expansive years that the American literary imagination broke free from the forms and standards of previous writings in English. "We have listened too long to the courtly muses of Europe," declared Ralph Waldo Emerson in 1837, and, with what the poet Walt Whitman called a "barbaric yawp," American writers began to express new pride in their swaggering young nation.

Soon they were producing rollicking poems in which they proclaimed, "I know I am deathless . . . I know I am august . . . I skirt sierras, my palm over continents." At the same time, our novelists took up directly—as if inhibiting social forms could be dissolved by the imagination—such subjects as dreams and unsanctioned lusts (in the works of

Edgar Allan Poe and Nathaniel Hawthorne), the basic existential questions that human beings face when they find themselves staring at death (a continual theme in Melville), and (in such works as Harriet Beecher Stowe's famous 1852 best-seller, *Uncle Tom's Cabin*) the truth they could not ignore—that they were building their nation on the backs of an enslaved people who had been brought against their will from Africa to do the country's dirty work.

This was the birth of modern American literature, which ever since has been both a celebration of the possibilities of democracy and a relentless attack on the hypocrisy, self-deception, and exploitation that are too often concealed in the platitudes with which we decorate our daily lives. From Stowe to Theodore Dreiser and Ernest Hemingway to more recent novelists like Bernard Malamud and Toni Morrison, American writers have always brought into view the realities we would prefer not to see: the cruelties of slavery, poverty, and the bitter legacies of both for the children of the enslaved and the poor.

Two Purposes

This has been the dual work of our national literature—to furnish and continually revive the sense that Americans, who come from all over the world and have only a brief shared history, nevertheless possess a common destiny. The great twentieth-century African-American writer, Richard Wright, whose works, especially *Native Son* (1940) and *Black Boy* (1945), are searing chronicles of what it means to be born black in a white man's country, put it this way when he looked back upon his own first discovery of the literary tradition to which he wished to add his name: "These writers" (he named Theodore Dreiser, Edgar Lee Masters, H. L. Mencken,

For biographies of poets, playwrights, and novelists see the following entries (nonfiction writers can be found through the index):

ALCOTT, LOUISA MAY
BALDWIN, JAMES
BEECHER, CATHARINE
CATHER, WILLA
COOPER, JAMES FENIMORE
CRANE, STEPHEN
DICKINSON, EMILY
ELLISON, RALPH
EMERSON, RALPH WALDO
FAULKNER, WILLIAM
FITZGERALD, F. SCOTT
FROST, ROBERT
GILMAN, CHARLOTTE PERKINS
GINSBERG, ALLEN
HAWTHORNE, NATHANIEL
HEMINGWAY, ERNEST
HUGHES, LANGSTON
HURSTON, ZORA NEALE
JAMES, HENRY
KEROUAC, JACK
LEWIS, SINCLAIR
LONDON, JACK
MELVILLE, HERMAN
MILLER, ARTHUR
MORRISON, TONI
O'NEILL, EUGENE
POE, EDGAR ALLEN
POUND, EZRA
SALINGER, J.D.
STEIN, GERTRUDE
STEINBECK, JOHN
STOWE, HARRIET BEECHER
THOREAU, HENRY DAVID
TWAIN, MARK
WALKER, ALICE
WRIGHT, RICHARD

Sherwood Anderson, and Sinclair Lewis, but many other lists would serve as well) "seemed to feel that America could be shaped nearer to the hearts of those who lived in it."

To achieve its purpose of disclosing the shortfall between the promise and reality of American life, our literature has recorded—as in F. Scott Fitzgerald's wonderful novel *The Great Gatsby* (1925)—the pettiness and vulgarity that are the dark underside of the American dream. American women, from the poet Emily Dickinson (1830–86), through the novelist Edith Wharton (1862–1937) and beyond, have written with a mixture of irony, humor, and rage about what it means to be a woman in a country that puts a premium on youth and power. And writers of both genders and all colors have been explosively angry, not uncommonly producing most of their work in a burst of youthful energy and then living out the rest of their lives in silence (one thinks, for instance, of J. D. Salinger, author of the 1951 classic, *The Catcher in the Rye*).

Yet every American writer who has lasted beyond his or her own time has, in one way or another, overcome this bitterness and has remained devoted, as Whitman put it, to "comprehending and effusing for the men and women of the States, what is universal, native, common to all." America, in this sense, *is* its literature—because our books are the place where the paradoxical democratic hope of diversity within unity has been most beautifully realized. If this democratic hope should prove mortal in the world, it will, at least, have been preserved by our writers, who have devoted their lives to imagining and reimagining it without end.

See also biographies of individual writers.

ANDREW DELBANCO

LITERATURE, CHILDREN'S AND YOUNG ADULT

American literature for young people dates back to the first settlements in colonial Massachusetts, but the early books were meant to instruct rather than entertain. An example is *New England Primer,* an alphabet book published in 1691, which begins "In Adam's fall/ We sinned all."

Instruction continued to be the chief purpose of American children's books in the eighteenth and nineteenth centuries. Martha Finley in the 1800s wrote a series of stories about a pious little girl named Elsie Dinsmore who used tears and fainting spells to bring grown-up sinners to their senses. Probably the best-known nineteenth-century writer of instructive stories was Horatio Alger, who took his young heroes from poverty to riches in a string of novels beginning with *Ragged Dick* (1867).

Meanwhile, other authors adopted a livelier and more enjoyable approach in their books. Clement Clark Moore's story poem *A Visit from St. Nicholas,* which is better known today as *The Night before Christmas,* was popular with children from the time of its first publication in 1822. Nathaniel Hawthorne retold the stories of the ancient Greek gods and heroes in *Tanglewood Tales for Boys and Girls* (1853). Louisa May Alcott's *Little Women* (1869) set a new standard for stories of family life. Joel Chandler Harris drew on the tales about Brer Rabbit that he had heard Georgia slaves tell when he wrote *Nights with Uncle Remus* (1883). And the rollicking adventures and realistic characterizations in Mark Twain's *Adventures of Tom Sawyer* (1876) and *Adventures of Huckleberry Finn* (1884) attracted thousands of enthusiastic young readers.

Rise in Importance

Children's literature in America grew in importance after the First World War. At that time publishers launched the first separate children's book departments and libraries established children's book rooms, staffed by specially trained librarians. New authors and illustrators came to the fore, and there was a vast increase in the number of children's books published.

Memorable titles from the 1920s include Wanda Gag's delightful picture book, *Millions of Cats* (1928), Will James's western novel, *Smoky, the Cowhorse* (1927), and Hendrik Willem Van Loon's imaginative history *The Story of Mankind* (1921). The latter was the first winner of the John Newbery Medal, named after an eighteenth-century English publisher of children's books. Awarded annually by the Association of Library Services to Children, a division of the American Library Association, the Newbery honors the previous year's "most distinguished contribution to American literature for children."

Children's literature flourished in the 1930s despite the economic downturn that accompanied the Great Depression. Laura Ingalls Wilder's *Little House in the Big Woods* (1932) was the first of a series that captured the flavor of pioneer life in the Midwest. Munro Leaf's *The Story of Ferdinand* (1937), more popularly known as *Ferdinand the Bull,* projected a pacifist theme as it told the story of a flower-loving young bull. Dr. Seuss (Theodor Seuss Geisel) began his long and distinguished career as a writer for children with *And to Think That I Saw It on Mulberry Street,* also published in 1937.

In response to the great variety of picture books that were now being published, the Randolph Caldecott Medal for distinguished children's book illustration was established in 1938. Named for a famous nineteenth-century British illustrator, the Caldecott, like the Newbery, is awarded annually. The first winner was Dorothy P. Lathrop for her picture book, *Animals of the Bible.*

Owing to paper shortages, there was a decline in overall children's book production during the Second World War. But the Little Golden Books, which offered quality children's literature at a low price, proved an instant success when they were introduced in 1944. The war years also saw the publication of such outstanding books as Esther Forbes's Newbery-winning novel of the American Revolution *Johnny Tremain* (1943) and Robert McCloskey's charming picture book *Make Way for Ducklings* (also 1943).

Postwar Trends

The postwar years were marked by an economic boom and a middle-class exodus to the suburbs. This was reflected in a string of bland children's books set in suburban locales. Still, some titles stood out. E. B. White created a memorable animal fantasy in *Charlotte's Web* (1952), and the African-American poet Gwendolyn Brooks caught the rhythms of the inner city in her collection *Bronzeville Boys and Girls* (1956). J. D. Salinger's adult novel *The Catcher in the Rye* (1951) was taken up by a host of teenagers who sympathized with its young hero's revolt against the "phoniness" of contemporary life.

The turbulent 1960s and early 1970s shook up all segments of American society including the field of children's literature. Hitherto taboo subjects like menstruation and homosexuality were explored in such novels for young adults as *Are You There, God? It's Me, Margaret* by Judy Blume (1970) and *I'll Get There, It Better Be Worth the Trip* by John Donovan (1969). The nation's minorities asserted themselves, and strong new African-American, Hispanic-American, and Chinese-American authors like Virginia Hamilton, Nicholasa Mohr, and Laurence Yep made their debuts on the juvenile literary scene.

Outstanding picture books of the period included Ezra Jack Keats's *The Snowy Day* (1962), Arnold Lobel's *Frog and Toad Are Friends* (1970), and Maurice Sendak's *Where the Wild Things Are* (1963). The monsters in Sendak's book alarmed some adults, who thought they were too frightening for children, but the book won the 1964 Caldecott Medal.

In the 1980s, the pendulum swung back toward more traditional material as exemplified by two Newbery winners of that decade—Patricia MacLachlan's sensitive story of a pioneer family, *Sarah, Plain and Tall* (1985) and Russell Freedman's *Lincoln: A Photobiography* (1987). But by the end of the 1980s and into the 1990s a new interest in the multicultural fabric of American society was making itself felt. It was evident in picture books like *Tree of Cranes* (1991) by the Japanese-American author-artist Allen Say and young adult novels like *Somewhere in the Darkness* (1992) by the African-American writer Walter Dean Myers.

As part of the trend toward computerization, some writers and illustrators in the 1990s began to experiment with interactive children's books. It's too soon to tell how great an impact these ventures will have on American children's literature in the future. It is safe to say, however, that children's and young adult books—like the other arts—will continue to mirror the shifting currents in American life as the nation approaches and enters the twenty-first century.

See also Alcott, Louisa May; Alger, Horatio; Harris, Joel

Chandler; Hawthorne, Nathaniel; McGuffey's *Reader;* Salinger, J. D.; Twain, Mark.

JAMES CROSS GIBLIN

LONDON, JACK
(1876–1916)   *Author.*

London wrote some of America's most beloved adventure novels based on his experiences as a seaman, world traveler, and rancher. Born in San Francisco, he grew up in Oakland, California. As a child, he sold newspapers to help support his family, and in his spare time, he read constantly. At age fourteen, he left school to work in a cannery. For several years, he held tough laboring jobs including serving on the crew of a ship that sailed to Japan in 1893. After that, he became a hobo, even once serving thirty days in jail in New York for being a tramp. Early on, he became a heavy drinker.

In 1895, he went to high school and then college but quickly dropped out. He believed in socialism as a way of fighting injustice and ran unsuccessfully for local office in California on the Socialist ticket. All the while, he wrote stories based on a diary of his travels but sold few of them. After a failed gold-panning expedition to Alaska, he settled down to writing seriously. In 1900, his first book, *The Son of the Wolf,* was published.

He went on to produce hundreds of articles and short stories and more than fifty books, including such classics as *The Call of the Wild, White Fang,* and *The Sea-Wolf.* His most beloved book, *The Call of the Wild* (1903), like many of his novels, was partly based on people he met and adventures he had in his travels. It was the story of a dog stolen from his home and abused as a sledge dog in the Klondike. London's writing was often stylistically awkward and filled with clichés. But he filled his tales with lots of action, strong characters, and colorful images that kept readers turning pages.

London also served as a war correspondent in Mexico and the Far East. Although he was one of America's most highly paid writers, he was often in financial trouble because he did not know how to manage money.

In 1905, London provoked a scandal by divorcing his first wife to marry Charmian Kittredge. Together they bought a ranch near Sonoma, California, and built a sailing vessel, the *Snark,* to cruise the South Pacific. He was often ill during their travels but used their adventures in his novels.

After returning home, the couple built a magnificent twenty-six-room mansion that they called Wolf House, on their ranch. But in August 1913, as the Londons were preparing to move in, the house burned down. The cause of the fire was never determined. London's health declined further, and he died at age forty. A park and museum on his ranch keep his memory alive.

See also Literature.

REBECCA LARSEN

LONG, HUEY

(1893–1935)   *Governor of Louisiana (1928–32) and U.S. senator (1932–35).*

Huey Long had two political careers, both of them extraordinary. The first was in his native Louisiana and the second in national politics.

In Louisiana Long rose from modest beginnings to become the most powerful governor in the history of the state. Capitalizing on widespread discontent with the existing political establishment, he developed a strong popular following and used it to build a power structure through which he dominated the entire state government. He used his power to build bridges, roads, hospitals, and schools and to shift some of the tax burden to corporations. But he also accumulated power for its own sake. To many Louisianans, he was known simply as "the Kingfish." To others, he was a tyrannical "dictator."

In 1932, Long resigned the governorship to enter the U.S. Senate, which he used principally to advance his growing national ambitions. At first, he supported President Franklin D. Roosevelt. But by the middle of 1933, he had broken with the president and struck out on his own. His bold but unrealistic Share-Our-Wealth Plan promised a radical redistribution of wealth: the government would tax large fortunes heavily and use the money to guarantee everyone a minimum annual income of $2,500. By 1935, he had launched a national political organization (the Share-Our-Wealth Society) and was talking openly of running for president the next year.

But Long never had a chance to demonstrate his national potential. In September 1935, he returned to Baton Rouge, Louisiana's capital, to supervise a special session of the state legislature (which he continued to control as completely while serving in the Senate as he had while governor). As he walked down a corridor in the state capitol, the son-in-law of one of his political opponents stepped from behind a pillar and shot him. Long died several days later, at age forty-two.

ALAN BRINKLEY

LOS ANGELES RIOTS
See Race Riots.

LOUIS, JOE

(1914–81)   *Boxer.*

Louis reigned as heavyweight boxing champion of the world from 1937 through 1949. Because he was born in Alabama to sharecropper parents, Louis's story is often told as the classic American tale of a poor youth rising to wealth and fame through hard work and determination. It was much more complicated than that.

Louis was a quiet man—he always said that he let his fists do the talking. Twenty-five successful title defenses in twelve years made his fists very articulate indeed. But Louis's career was more than the sum of his fights. Whether he liked it or not, he became a symbol for African Americans everywhere.

In an age when law and custom kept America's blacks rigidly segregated, Louis not only had the respect of many whites but worked in a field that allowed direct confrontation with them. In the depths of the Great Depression of the 1930s, Louis gave hope to black people first by defeating white opponents (he won the title from James J. Braddock in 1937) and then by "representing his people," as contemporaries put it, with pride and dignity. Still champion during the Second World War, Louis enlisted in the army and publicly supported the war effort. His victory over the German champion Max Schmeling in 1938 had been interpreted by many as a symbolic victory of American democracy over Nazi authoritarianism. But though proud of their champion, it was not lost on blacks that American democracy did

Joe Louis in 1938, a year after he became the heavyweight boxing champion of the world. He held the title for twelve years. Out of seventy-one professional fights, Louis was defeated only three times.

not prevent them from being segregated, lynched, and otherwise oppressed.

It would be wrong to interpret Louis's career as evidence that America had opened the doors of opportunity to black people; the 1930s and 1940s were filled with poverty and brutal racist laws. But Louis did help gain some grudging respect from racist whites, and he created immense pride among African Americans. When he left boxing in the 1950s, his skills and his personal fortunes declining, the image of Joe Louis, the greatest fighter in the world, a black man who could beat anyone, remained. Perhaps the feeling he gave black people—that victories *could* sometimes be won against heavy odds—

helped keep the faith for those who, during the coming decades, would lead the greatest American mass movement of the twentieth century, the civil rights movement.

See also Boxing.

Elliott J. Gorn

Louisiana Purchase

When pioneers began to settle the land west of the Appalachian Mountains in the 1790s, they quickly discovered that the only way to get bulky farm products to market was by floating them on rafts down the Mississippi River to New Orleans. There they were loaded onto boats bound for eastern cities and Europe. In 1795 Spain, which owned New Or-leans, gave Americans the right to deposit their farm goods in the city. But in 1800 Spain turned the city over to France. This alarmed President Thomas Jefferson, who feared that the French ruler, Napoleon Bonaparte, might cancel the right. He therefore instructed the American minister to France, Robert R. Livingston, to try to purchase New Orleans. He also sent his friend James Monroe to France to assist Livingston with the negotiations.

Napoleon had originally intended to use the New Orleans region to feed his West Indian sugar plantations. But having failed to suppress a revolution in Haiti and facing a costly war with England, he decided to sell not merely New Orleans but all of Louisiana, the territory between the Mississippi River and the Rocky Mountains, to the United States.

The Louisiana Purchase

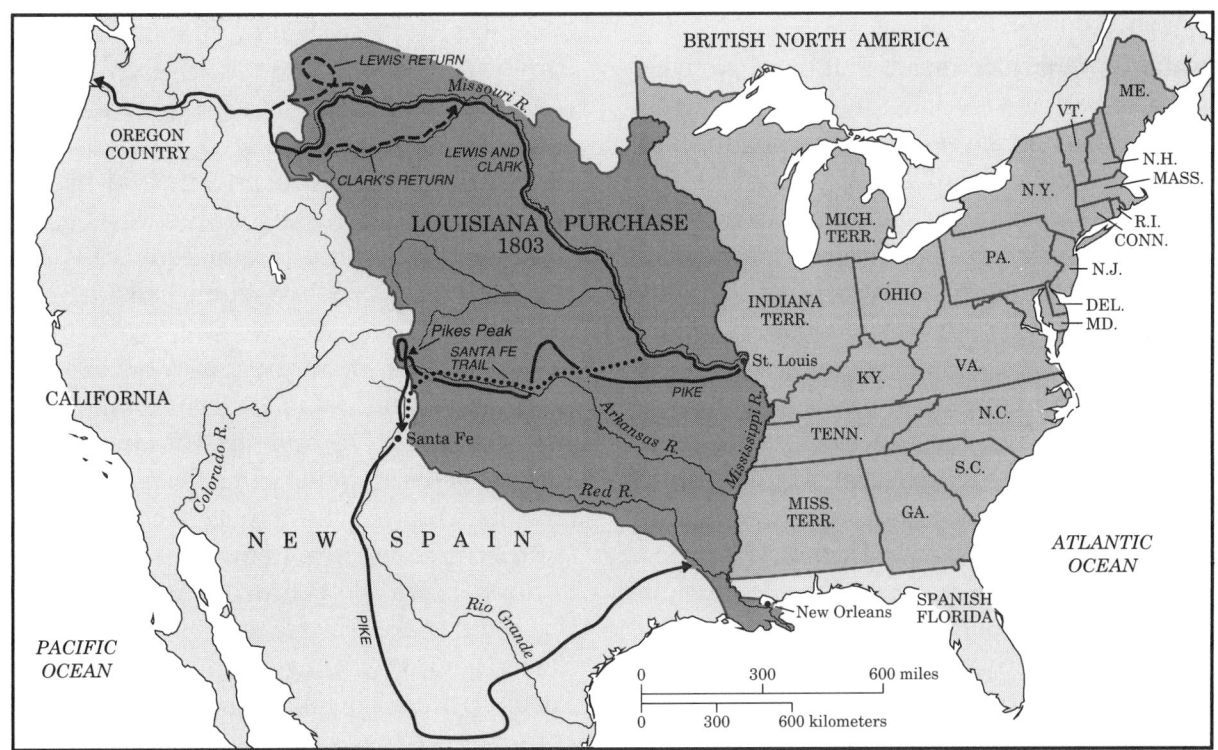

After some negotiation, Livingston and Monroe bought this vast area for 60 million francs, about $15 million. Although the exact size of the territory was unknown then, it came to about 828,000 square miles and doubled the size of the United States overnight. The Senate approved the purchase on October 20, 1803, and settlers began moving into the territory immediately. Eventually, the region was carved into thirteen states. When Livingston had asked the French foreign minister about the boundaries, he replied, "I can give you no direction. You have made a noble bargain . . . and I suppose you will make the most of it."

See also Expansion, Territorial.

LOWELL SYSTEM

The spinning and weaving machines of the early New England factories were driven by water power, which meant that they had to be located beside waterfalls or rapidly moving streams. Since such sites were seldom located in or near cities, labor usually had to be imported from surrounding farms. When the Boston Manufacturing Company constructed its textile mill on the Merrimack River, in Massachusetts in 1823, it had to build an entire town, named Lowell after its founder, Francis Cabot Lowell.

Most of the workers who flocked to Lowell were young unmarried farm women. They were housed in company-owned and supervised boardinghouses. No alcoholic beverages were allowed, a strict 10:00 P.M. curfew was enforced, even card playing was prohibited. This Lowell system was designed to reassure the workers and their parents that they would be properly chaperoned and cared for.

The restrictions were expected by respectable women of that time. They earned only two or three dollars a week, but most were able to save a good deal of this.

Most of the women did not intend to remain factory workers. Going to Lowell was viewed as an experience, a kind of education. Life there was similar to life in a late-nineteenth-century women's college dormitory. They published a magazine and organized sewing circles and debating societies. The Lowell system lasted only until the 1840s. Then competition led to lower wages and less attractive working conditions. Women could find better jobs as clerks and schoolteachers. The textile machines were then tended mostly by European immigrants.

LUCE, HENRY

(1898–1967)   *Journalist and publisher.*

Luce was born in China and educated in America. He was taunted as a "mish kid" because he was the son of a Presbyterian missionary. His classmates at boarding school and Yale laughed at his poverty and his announced ambition to change the world.

Luce's answer after graduation was *Time* (1923), a magazine first published out of a garage. *Time* was a new idea in American journalism—a brisk summary of the week's news. Luce's business partner then died unexpectedly, leaving him the sole owner. He wisely spent money hiring more reporters and starting yet more magazines. *Fortune* (1930), a magazine about business, and *Architectural Forum* (1934) proved that lively writing could make dry, technical subjects exciting. *Life* (1936) was suggested by Clare Booth Luce, his wife. This magazine used the camera to tell stories and was the first successful example of weekly photojournalism. *Sports Illustrated* (1954) was the last magazine developed under his leadership. Luce also published books and did innovative work in radio, movie newsreels, and television.

Luce often hired journalists who did not agree with him, although what they reported rarely got into his magazines. He was loyal to the Republican Party, but he was also committed to social change such as the civil rights movement. Luce exerted his greatest influence in the area of U.S. policy toward China. Probably because of his missionary background in that country, he refused to accept the Chinese Revolution of 1949. His attitude was not balanced by an opposing force in the American media. He helped to close minds in the 1950s and 1960s about establishing relations with the world's largest nation.

Theodore H. White, a reporter who lost his job with *Time* when he disagreed with Luce about China, saw that this publisher wanted to remake the world in America's image. Still, White said, "It was exhilarating to be working for a man who could discuss, all at the same time, the Bible, Confucius and the itchy gossip and color which sells readers on a magazine."

See also Magazines and Newspapers.

THOMAS C. LEONARD

LYCEUMS

In 1826 Josiah Holbrook, a Connecticut teacher and lecturer, founded an adult education program he called a lyceum in Millbury, Massachusetts. The lyceum was a kind of self-improvement society, based on an institution already functioning in Great Britain. It provided lectures and concerts, presented plays, and organized discussion groups and debates for the community. It also worked to improve local schools.

The lyceum idea caught on in America quickly. A National American Lyceum was set up to coordinate the local groups. Soon there were more than a thousand lyceums in various parts of the nation. Daniel Webster, Ralph Waldo Emerson, and other prominent writers and statesmen lectured on the lyceum circuit, as did many important artists and scientists. The movement served the needs of a rural society, where local cultural and educational opportunities were rare. Later institutions such as Cooper Union in New York and the Lowell Institute in Boston were originally lyceums. After the Civil War, the lyceums began to peter out, but they were soon replaced by the chautauqua movement.

LYNCHING

Lynching is murdering without a trial a person accused of a crime. Sometimes the so-called crime was no more than doing or believing something the accusers did not like. Lynchings were carried out by mobs who often hanged their victims.

The word most likely comes from the name of a man, Charles Lynch, who was a justice of the peace and a planter in Virginia in the 1700s. During the revolutionary war, Lynch and his neighbors punished suspected thieves and British sympathizers by whipping them.

As far back as the colonial era and into the 1800s, groups of men called vigilantes patrolled the frontier regions of the country. Vigilantes were not legally formed groups. Rather, they were men who took it upon themselves to police territories far from towns with systems of government and courts of law. Vigilantes in the West, for example, tracked down suspected horse thieves, cattle rustlers, and other criminals. Because their victims did not receive a fair trial, too often they punished innocent people. Such an incident happened in 1763, when German settlers killed a peaceful group of Conestoga Indians near Lancaster, Pennsylvania, during the French and Indian War. *Some* Indians were hostile, so the whites considered *all* Indians their enemy.

Lynching after the Civil War

Vigilantism grew into terrorism directed primarily against southern blacks after the Civil War. Former Confederates were determined that African Americans remain in an inferior economic and social position. Lynching and other forms of physical violence were used to keep the black population under white control. Over 2,500 lynchings, mostly of blacks, occurred during this period, primarily in Mississippi, Alabama, Georgia, and Louisiana.

Lynchings were directed mostly against black men, although some women and children were lynched also. Victims were accused of murder, robbery, rape of white women, or "insolence." Often charges based on a mere rumor resulted in a mob hanging an innocent person.

In 1892, 255 people were lynched. The lynching that year of a black postman, Thomas Moss, in Memphis, Tennessee, caused two African-American women to devote their lives to combating such violence. Mary Church Terrell and Ida B. Wells-Barnett were friends of Moss's. When Terrell read about his lynching in Wells's newspaper, *Free Speech,* she contacted a friend, Frederick Douglass,

the famous abolitionist. They went to the White House together to urge President Benjamin Harrison to speak out against antiblack violence, but he refused. Wells published a booklet, *Southern Horror: Lynch Law in All Its Phases,* to make the public aware of racial violence.

Lynching in the Twentieth Century

Lynching continued into the twentieth century, with over 1,000 black lynchings taking place before 1914. Incidents spread to the Midwest. The onset of World War I in 1914 caused many blacks to leave the South, drawn by jobs available in the North because of the war. This exodus brought them hope and also new problems as they crowded into northern cities. Although the reported cases of lynching decreased to 38 in 1917 and 52 in 1918, antiblack rioting increased in Georgia, Texas, North Carolina, South Carolina, Illinois, and Ohio.

The National Association for the Advancement of Colored People (NAACP) started campaigning in 1919 to get Congress to pass an antilynching bill and extend equal protection under the law for African Americans. The Dyer Anti-Lynching Bill passed the House of Representatives in 1921 but was defeated in the Senate. Other bills introduced then and in 1935 and 1940 were also defeated. The NAACP also published a report, *Thirty Years of Lynching in the United States, 1889–1918,* and held meetings throughout the country to protest this crime.

In 1930 a group of white middle-class women, the Association of Southern Women for the Prevention of Lynching (ASWPL), spoke out against the practice. Black women's organizations, who also campaigned against lynching, were disappointed when the ASWPL refused to support federal anti-

LYNCHING

lynching legislation, saying it would only anger southerners who would view it as an infringement on states' rights.

It is estimated that 4,736 southern blacks were murdered between 1880 and 1930. Although lynching finally decreased after World War II, it never entirely disappeared. In 1947 a black man accused of murdering a cab driver was lynched in South Carolina, and shortly after that, another black man barely escaped lynching in North Carolina. Emmett Till, a black teenage boy accused of flirting with a white woman, was lynched in 1955 in Mis-

sissippi. In 1964 three young workers in the civil rights movement, black and white, were lynched in Philadelphia, Mississippi.

Although crimes of hate are, unfortunately, still a reality of American life, wholesale lynching has ended. The civil rights legislation of the 1960s provides equal protection under the law for all.

See also African Americans; Ku Klux Klan; Wells-Barnett, Ida B.

JOYCE HANSEN

MacArthur, Douglas

(1880–1964) *World War II and Korean War general.*

MacArthur was born in Little Rock, Arkansas, the son of a famous general. He graduated from the U.S. Military Academy in 1903, with one of the best scholastic records in the academy's history. In 1918, during the First

Gen. Douglas MacArthur (in front seat of jeep), commander in chief of U.N. forces in Korea, 1951. He publicly and persistently criticized President Harry S. Truman's policy to limit the war, which led to his dismissal later that year for insubordination.

World War he was made a brigadier general. MacArthur received many medals for bravery and was highly respected by his men.

In the years after the war, MacArthur served in several important positions. In July 1941, he was appointed commander of American forces in the Far East. Five months later war began between the United States and Japan. During the next four years, forces under MacArthur's command gradually pushed the Japanese out of islands in the South Pacific area. MacArthur was often criticized for taking too much credit, but he was made a general of the army, the highest army rank, and was named supreme commander of the entire Pacific area at the war's end.

From 1945 to 1950, MacArthur was in charge of the Allied occupation of Japan. He managed to instill ideas of democracy into the Japanese way of life and became greatly admired by the Japanese people.

In 1950, the Republic of South Korea was invaded by Communist North Korea. MacArthur was appointed commander of the U.N. force put together to help defend South Korea. He devised a clever surprise assault that pushed the North Koreans back into their own territory. China, however, entered the war on North Korea's side and inflicted defeats on the U.N. troops. MacArthur wanted to bomb China, but U.N. and U.S. leaders refused, fearing this could cause World War III. When MacArthur continued to publicly criticize U.S. leadership, President Harry S.

Truman removed him from command on April 11, 1951.

MacArthur returned to the United States and was generally welcomed as a hero. He made a speech to Congress, and parades were held in his honor in many cities. But he was a controversial figure, some people regarding him as a military genius and others as a self-seeking "glory-hog." In 1952 he was made a top executive of a large corporation and spent the remaining years of his life living quietly in New York City.

See also Korean War; Truman, Harry S.; World War II.

For further reading: Tom McGowen, *The Korean War* (New York: Franklin Watts, 1992).

TOM MCGOWEN

MACHINE POLITICS
See Big-City Bosses.

MADISON, JAMES

(1751–1836) *Fourth president of the United States (1809–17).*

As a young man growing up on his family's plantation, James Madison was physically small, shy, and often sick, so that he found his greatest pleasure in study. At college in Princeton, New Jersey, Madison learned two valuable lessons. His exposure there to people from other parts of America besides his native Virginia persuaded him that the colonies could and should unite. Second, the fact that the College of New Jersey was a Presbyterian school made him a defender of religious toleration back home in Virginia, where the Anglican church was still established by law. He did not know what career to pursue after he finished college, but the American Revolu-

tion ended his indecision. He would serve his country through participation in government. Madison's first significant political achievement was a resolution in Virginia's Declaration of Rights in 1776 that guaranteed freedom of conscience in religion.

During the War for Independence, James Madison and Thomas Jefferson became fast friends on the basis of their common interests in science and philosophy as well as their commitment to the cause of independence. In the Continental Congress, Madison also joined a circle of nationalists who agreed with Robert Morris, the superintendent of finance, that the central government needed increased powers in order to pay its debts and finance the war effort. He pondered how to balance the former colonies' fears of tyranny with the need of the central government for money and authority to do its job. At the Constitutional Convention in 1787 Madison argued that "we, the people" could create a national government as well as state governments. He believed that the United States was not merely a creation of the states but a reflection of Americans being all one people. Out of his studies came the idea that forms the basis for the U.S. government today. Madison also authored the Bill of Rights, which spells out the limits to the power of government.

He collaborated with Alexander Hamilton in writing the Federalist Papers in defense of the Constitution in the effort to get it ratified (approved) by the states. But he broke with Hamilton and the Federalists in the new Congress to join Jefferson in a new party, the Democratic-Republicans. He feared that the Federalists had gone too far in claiming power for the central government.

As president, Madison led the country into the War of 1812 against Britain. The difficulties of making war once again convinced him of the need for a strong national government and led him to modify his beliefs. In 1815 he proposed to Congress a national bank and a system of tariffs, measures that had been the cornerstones of Hamilton's old plan.

James Madison outlived almost all the other Founders of the American Republic. His prestige grew in his old age, and travelers would stop by his Virginia home to pay respects and ask his opinion about the future of the United States. All his life, Madison worried that the institution of slavery would someday lead the Union to disaster. But despite his misgivings, he failed to free his own slaves in his will.

See also Bill of Rights; Constitution; Federalist Papers. *For events during Madison's administration, see* Hartford Convention of 1814; Impressment Controversy; Tecumseh; War Hawks; War of 1812.

THOMAS COLE

MAGAZINES AND NEWSPAPERS

In 1992 U.S. Marines were sent to the African nation of Somalia to stop armed gangs from interfering with the distribution of food meant for the starving people there. When the Marines landed on a beach in full battle gear, they were greeted by a crowd of American reporters who had arrived ahead of them. Military leaders were not too happy to have them there. Such aggressiveness in covering the news, as well as governmental displeasure at what is reported, has long been a hallmark of journalism in America.

Newspapers

The first newspaper on this continent was published in Boston in 1689, a one-page affair

that was quickly suppressed, because all news reporting had to be "authorized" by colonial governments. The issue came to a head in 1735 at the trial of John Peter Zenger, who had printed an attack on William Cosby, a corrupt governor of New York. Zenger was charged with criminal libel. At his trial he was eloquently defended by Andrew Hamilton, a man largely forgotten to history. His defense of press freedom induced the jury to find Zenger not guilty. Thus was freedom of the press secured on these shores, and it was ultimately written into the Bill of Rights as the First Amendment to the Constitution.

For a century, newspapers and magazines took little advantage of this freedom. They acted largely as propaganda organs for various political parties and factions, presenting only their side of a story. The first real newspaper in America was the *New York Herald,* established in 1835 by James Gordon Bennett. He sought to gather and report news fairly, rather than print only personal opinions. The *Herald* was quickly followed by the *New York Tribune* under Horace Greeley, the *New York Times* under Henry Jarvis Raymond, the *Chicago Tribune* by Joseph Medill, and a little later the *New York Sun* under Charles Anderson Dana, all great names in American journalism. These giants created the newspaper as we know it today, pioneering in the use of correspondents at home and abroad, briefer, simpler writing, and illustrations of the news first with engravings and then with photographs.

Two other men had enormous impact on journalism, Joseph Pulitzer of the *New York World* and William Randolph Hearst of the *New York Journal.* Beginning around the turn of the twentieth century, these men waged a circulation war by offering lurid sensationalism in their pages. The term *yellow journal-*

ism was used to describe such reportage. It came from the colored comics that Hearst first published. Both editors sought to make news as well as report it. Historians agree that Hearst's reporting helped bring on the Spanish-American War by presenting overly dramatic stories slanted against the Spanish in Cuba, which aroused war fever among the American public.

The past influences newspapers today. As with John Peter Zenger, editors perform a watchdog role by exposing wrongdoing in government and society. They also seek to uncover and report as much of the news as possible so as to keep the public informed. There also exists a segment of the press, such as tabloids sold in supermarkets, that is devoted to lurid reporting of crime, gossip, and other sensations.

Today more people learn the news from television than from newspapers. The number of papers has shrunk drastically until only a handful of cities have more than one newspaper publisher. Most of these feel an added responsibility to report events fairly and to offer thoughtful analysis, restricting opinions to the editorial pages. The decline in major newspapers, however, has led to a rise in smaller suburban dailies and weeklies.

Magazines

The magazine, published weekly, monthly, or quarterly, seeks to provide deeper coverage and analysis of events than newspapers or to provide news and features of special interest to its readers. The first magazine was published in this country in 1741 in Philadelphia, by either Benjamin Franklin or Andrew Bradford. Their first editions came out three days apart. These and other early magazines, all of them short-lived, mostly copied material from British publications.

The first truly American magazines—that is, ones in which American authors wrote about American topics—were *Harper's* in 1850 and *Atlantic Monthly* in 1857. Both exist today. Other important early magazines were *Leslie's, Godey's Lady's Book,* and *Youth's Companion.* A magazine of great influence on American history was the *Liberator,* published by William Lloyd Garrison. It fostered the abolitionist movement to end slavery. All of these magazines set a precedent by publishing the fiction and prose of America's finest writers. By reporting on American culture, they encouraged pride in this country's arts.

The first half of the twentieth century was the heyday of the mass-circulation magazine. These publications became fixtures in American homes for generations, offering entertainment, good writing, and interesting information, as well as shaping public opinion on important issues. Subscribers looked forward to receiving their copies of such magazines as the *Saturday Evening Post, Time* and *Life, Reader's Digest, Ladies' Home Journal, Good Housekeeping, Ebony, Grit, True Confessions, Esquire, Parents', Vogue, Better Homes and Gardens, True, Sports Afield, Popular Mechanics,* and *Boys' Life.*

Many of these titles have disappeared from the magazine racks, although some are still published and a few, such as the *Post* and *Life,* have been brought back as new publications. The decline in mass-circulation magazines was caused by the high costs of printing and the loss of advertising revenues to television. On the other hand, while the number of mass-circulation magazines has declined, the total of all publications has increased radically. There are an estimated 22,000 magazines published in the United States today—some say 60,000 if newsletters are counted. Most are smaller specialized magazines appealing to a particular interest, industry, or occupation. The list also includes numerous state, city, and regional magazines, as well as those published as supplements in Sunday newspapers.

See also Freedom of the Press; Muckrakers; *Poor Richard's Almanac;* Zenger Trial. *And see biographies of the following editors and journalists:* Bly, Nellie; Hearst, William Randolph; Howells, William Dean; Luce, Henry; Mencken, H. L.; Nast, Thomas; Pulitzer, Joseph; Steffens, Lincoln; Wallace, DeWitt; Wells-Barnett, Ida.

ROBERT A. LISTON

MALCOLM X

(1925–65)　*Black leader.*

He was born Malcolm Little in Omaha, Nebraska, the son of a Baptist preacher. After threats from the Ku Klux Klan, the Reverend Little moved his wife and eight children to Lansing, Michigan, but faced similar danger there. Though murdered by a group of whites called the Black Legionaries, Malcolm's father was judged to have committed suicide. Thus, his death benefit was denied the family. Shortly thereafter, when Malcolm was taken from his mother and placed in a foster home, she experienced a nervous breakdown from which she never recovered.

Even at that difficult time, Malcolm earned a reputation as an above-average student. For a while he aspired to become a lawyer, but he received little encouragement from his teachers. He dropped out of school after the eighth grade and headed for a life of crime in Detroit. He straightened his hair and became known, because of its color, as "Detroit Red." In due course, he moved to Boston, and at age twenty-one, he was sentenced to prison from eight to ten years for burglary.

While in prison, Malcolm studied the teachings of Elijah Muhammad, the leader of the Nation of Islam, popularly known as the Black Muslims. Elijah Muhammad believed that whites would never permit blacks to live in peace in America, that blacks, if they were to know freedom, must free themselves. Inspired by Elijah Muhammad, Malcolm decided to change his life drastically and began preparing to assist other blacks suffering from injustice. Acquiring knowledge together with the belief that sober living is essential to a good life became important to him. Malcolm now discarded his last name on the ground that it was given to his family after their African name was stolen and, as *X* suggests, forever lost. He believed that blacks must learn to love themselves or they would never be respected as a people.

After serving six years in prison, Malcolm was released and in time became the minister of the Nation of Islam's Temple No. 7 in Harlem. His fiery indictments of racism and his belief in self-defense for his people inspired admiration as well as fear far beyond the black community of New York. But he grew restless as the Nation of Islam failed to join in the civil rights struggles of the sixties. Eventually Malcolm became convinced that Elijah Muhammad was dishonest and corrupt, a point of view that is discussed in detail in his widely read and influential book, *The Autobiography of Malcolm X.*

Malcolm's concerns about Elijah Muhammad occurred at a time when he was himself gaining in stature in even the most respected civil rights circles. Meanwhile, it was widely thought that Elijah Muhammad was becoming jealous of Malcolm's influence with black people.

Malcolm was suspended from the Nation of Islam in December 1963 after he asserted

Malcolm X addressing a Black Muslim rally in 1961. He symbolized black self-respect and militant defiance. At one point he called himself "the angriest black man in America."

that President John F. Kennedy's assassination in November amounted to "the chickens coming home to roost," implying that white society got what it deserved, given the great number of blacks murdered by whites who went unpunished. A few months later, he left the organization, traveled to Mecca, and discovered that orthodox Muslims preach equality of the races. Back in America, however, he remained convinced that blacks must rely mainly on themselves for freedom. In some ways he became more radical than in his Black Muslim days. He was assassinated by a Black Muslim at a rally of his newly formed Organization of Afro-American Unity on February 21, 1965.

See also African Americans: Since World War II; Civil Rights Movement.

For further reading: Malcolm X, *The Autobiography of Malcolm X* (New York: Ballantine, 1987).

STERLING STUCKEY

MANHATTAN PROJECT

Shortly after the outbreak of World War II in Europe, Albert Einstein and other scientists warned President Franklin D. Roosevelt that there was reason to think that German scientists were working on a bomb of a power far beyond that of any known explosive. Roosevelt heeded their argument and agreed to support research on atomic energy at a number of universities. University of Chicago physicists produced the first chain reaction in December 1942. In May 1943, the Manhattan Project, a branch of the Army Corps of Engineers, was established. Its purpose was to design and manufacture atomic bombs. Plants to manufacture the necessary nuclear materials were built at Oak Ridge, Tennessee, and Hanford, Washington. The design for the bombs was created in a government laboratory in Los Alamos, New Mexico, under the direction of J. Robert Oppenheimer. Gen. Leslie R. Groves supervised the project for the army.

The first test atomic explosion took place in the desert at Alamogordo, New Mexico, on July 16, 1945. Less than a month later, on August 6, the bomber *Enola Gay* dropped an atomic bomb with the power of twenty thousand tons of T N T on the Japanese city of Hiroshima. A second bomb (the only other one then in existence), dropped on Nagasaki on August 9, led to the Japanese surrender on August 14.

See also Nuclear Energy; Oppenheimer, J. Robert; World War II.

MANIFEST DESTINY

The term *manifest destiny* dates from the 1840s. It refers to the popular belief that the United States and the virtues of American democratic institutions were sure to dominate the entire North American continent. The key word in the expression was *manifest,* in the sense of "obvious." That the nation would expand westward had been clear for two hundred years. Many colonial charters described the boundaries of the new settlements as running "from sea to sea," though no one had a clear idea of how far away the

Pacific Ocean was. But in the 1840s expansion seemed inevitable and limitless. John L. O'Sullivan, an editor and writer, made the now-famous prediction that it was "our manifest destiny to overspread the continent." His prediction was fulfilled in short order: Texas was annexed in 1845 and the United States acquired California and the Southwest from Mexico in 1848.

Manifest destiny was a reflection of the energy of a young and prosperous nation with an expanding population. It also reflected American disregard of the interests and needs of the Indians and other people whose land this was in the first place but who happened to stand in the way of the expansion of the nation. It was certainly a major cause of the Mexican War and of the crushing of the Plains Indians after the Civil War.

Although the country added little new territory after 1848, the urge to do so did not disappear. Before the Civil War, many southerners hoped to absorb Cuba and Central America. Movements to annex Santo Domingo, Hawaii, Alaska, and, of course, Puerto Rico and the Philippines followed. Many of the later expansionists lacked the naive faith in the inherent superiority of the American way of life that was characteristic of the 1840s. Imperialism, an urge to conquer and "improve backward" people and places, was never again wholly accepted by the American public.

See also Expansion, Territorial.

MANN, HORACE

(1796–1859)   *Reformer and educator.*

American culture went through a broad experience of reform in a variety of fields between about 1830 and 1861, when the Civil War began. Horace Mann was the most prominent educator in this larger picture. The product of a rigidly religious and moralistic home, he was educated at Brown University. Rejecting revivalistic religion, he decided to become a reformer who would spend his energies improving society.

Mann began with alcohol. Although moderate in his personal habits, he often went to extremes in his public positions. He decided that the prohibition of alcohol would empty the jails and poorhouses and move society toward perfection. He worked next to reform treatment of the insane, the blind, and those in debt and to improve the situation of American blacks.

By the middle 1830s, Mann was settling into his most famous role as advocate of universal public schooling. In 1837, he won an official if powerless position in Massachusetts that enabled him to investigate schooling and recommend legal remedies for deficiencies. He found that many towns took better care of their farm animals than their children. Schoolrooms were shabby places with scarcely more equipment than a few chairs, desks, and a water dipper. Many lacked even outhouses in a time before indoor plumbing. Teachers were untrained and badly paid.

Impoverished farmers resisted taxation for schools; they also wanted their children to stay home and work during harvest. Wealthy citizens who educated their children privately also wanted no additional tax burden. Despite this resistance, Mann worked to improve learning conditions, teacher training, and public attitudes. He made a major impact on education in Massachusetts, and through its example, in the nation.

See also Education.

ROBERT M. CRUNDEN

MARBURY V. MADISON

This Supreme Court case established the power of the Court to overturn acts of Congress that violate the Constitution. It was important because the Constitution does not specifically grant that power to the Court. The case established the principle that the Constitution means what the Supreme Court says it means.

On the night of March 3, 1801, during his last hours as president, John Adams signed a number of commissions appointing justices of the peace for the District of Columbia. All of his appointees were loyal members of Adams's Federalist Party. Most of the commissions were delivered to the new justices, but a few were not. When the new president, Thomas Jefferson, discovered the undelivered commissions, he ordered his secretary of state, James Madison, not to deliver them. He then appointed loyal members of his own Democratic-Republican Party to the offices.

One of Adams's choices, William Marbury, asked the Supreme Court to issue an order demanding that he receive his commission. The case put Chief Justice John Marshall in a difficult position. If Marshall issued the order, the new administration would surely ignore it, and that would undermine the authority of the Court. But if Marshall denied the order, he would be seen as caving in before the power of the president. He escaped this dilemma by declaring that he could not issue the order because the law authorizing the Court to do so was in violation of the Constitution.

The decision marked the first time the Supreme Court declared a law passed by Congress as unconstitutional and established the supremacy of the Constitution over the laws passed by Congress.

See also Supreme Court.

MARCHES ON WASHINGTON: 1941, 1963

Twice in American history, more than twenty years apart, a March on Washington was planned. Each march attempted to dramatize the rights of black Americans to political and economic equality.

The first march was proposed in 1941 by A. Philip Randolph, president of the Brotherhood of Sleeping Car Porters, the nation's first African-American union. Blacks had received few benefits from the New Deal programs of the 1930s, even though they were among those suffering the most from the

Martin Luther King before a crowd of over 200,000 nonviolent protesters at the 1963 March on Washington, where he delivered his famous I Have a Dream speech.

Great Depression. Racial discrimination also excluded them from the most important area of job growth in the early 1940s, the defense jobs that were created as America prepared for the possibility of war. One employer flatly stated that as far as these new job opportunities were concerned, the "Negro will be considered only as janitors and in other similar capacities."

When President Franklin D. Roosevelt showed little interest in helping to end these injustices, Randolph planned a March on Washington that would bring fifty thousand protesters to the capital. Wanting to avoid the bad publicity such a march would generate, Roosevelt issued Executive Order 8802 in June 1941, forbidding discrimination by defense contractors and establishing the Fair Employment Practices Committee to investigate charges of racial discrimination. With this victory, Randolph canceled the march.

Two decades later, in 1963, Randolph and other black leaders again felt a March on Washington was needed to focus national attention on the plight of blacks. This second march was designed specifically to advocate passage of the civil rights bill, which would outlaw segregation in public facilities and end racial discrimination in employment and education.

President John F. Kennedy showed as little enthusiasm for the march as had Roosevelt twenty years earlier, but this time the march took place. It was a spectacular success. On August 28, 1963, more than 200,000 black and white Americans participated in a day of speeches, songs, and prayers led by a celebrated array of clergymen, civil rights leaders, politicians, and entertainers. The Reverend Dr. Martin Luther King gave his I Have a Dream speech, the most famous of his career. "I have a dream," he said, "that one day this nation will rise up and live out the true meaning of its creed—we hold these truths to be self-evident, that all men are created equal." Both Marches on Washington represented an affirmation of hope, a belief in the democratic process, and a faith in the capacity of blacks and whites to work together for racial equality.

See also Civil Rights Movement; Randolph, A. Philip.

MARÍN, LUIS MUÑOZ
See Muñoz Marín, Luis.

MARINE CORPS

The U.S. Marine Corps is the amphibious branch of the American armed forces. ("Amphibious" means it operates on both land and sea.) Marines are specially trained to travel in ships and land on beaches in small craft and helicopters to assault the enemy. The Marine Corps consists of three divisions and three air wings. Each division is roughly the size of an army division, or about 19,000 men. The top officer is a general called the commandant of the marines.

When the marines sing "From the Halls of Montezuma to the shores of Tripoli," the opening line of their famous hymn, they are referring to two of the many wars they have fought in. Montezuma recalls the Mexican War of 1846–48, and Tripoli refers to an action against the Barbary pirates in North Africa in 1805. In their long history the marines have made three hundred landings.

The Early Marine Corps
The Marine Corps was born on November

A smiling marine with his bayonet held firmly rides backward on a snarling wildcat. This recruiting poster was meant to attract prospective marines with the promise of foreign travel and exotic adventures.

10, 1775, when the Continental Congress established it to fight in the Revolutionary War. The marines participated in battles against the British at Trenton and Morristown, New Jersey, and Brandywine, Pennsylvania. In a conflict that lasted from 1801 to 1805, the marines battled the Barbary pirates, who had been raiding American shipping in the Mediterranean Sea. The War of 1812 against Great Britain was primarily a sea war, and the marines served on ships as musketmen. In the Mexican War of 1846–48, marines landed on the Gulf coast of Mexico and fought along with army troops as far inland as Mexico City.

Marines played only a minimal role in the American Civil War, but they were at the forefront of the Spanish-American War in 1898. Marines were the first troops to land both in Cuba and in the Philippines. In the early 1900s marines were frequently used to protect American interests in the Caribbean region. They were sent into Cuba in 1906 and into Nicaragua in 1912 and again in 1926. Marines gained fame in World War I at the Battle of Belleau Wood in France, where they helped drive an entrenched German force out of a forested area near the Marne River.

Marines in World War II and After

The Marine Corps, with its specialty in amphibious landings, spearheaded the many island assaults in the Pacific theater during World War II. The islands of Guadalcanal (1942), Tarawa (1943), Saipan (1944), Iwo Jima (1945), and Okinawa (1945) were scenes of terrible battles with the Japanese. On Tarawa, marine landing boats were unable to cross a coral reef that ringed the island, and the men were forced to wade to the beaches in the face of withering machine-gun fire. A sailor watching the landing through binoculars wrote, "Those poor guys plodding in chest high water and getting shot down. I tried not to look, but I couldn't turn away. The horror of it hypnotized me. If I get to be a hundred years old, I'll always remember." The marines lost about a thousand men during the four-day Battle of Tarawa. When they stormed the beaches of Iwo Jima, they encountered 20,000 Japanese troops, all of whom were prepared to die rather than yield the island. On Iwo Jima the marines lost some 6,000 men. Navy Adm. Chester Nimitz said of their performance, "Uncommon valor was a common virtue."

In the Korean War, marines helped U.N. forces defend the Pusan Perimeter against the hard-driving North Korean army. They then took the offensive by landing at Inchon near the South Korean capital of Seoul. In a bitter winter campaign the Marine Corps was forced back in a fighting retreat by Chinese troops at the Chosin Reservoir in North Korea.

Marines were the first U.S. ground forces deployed in the Vietnam War. Elements of the Third Marine Division landed there in 1965 and saw continuous action until 1971. In 1968 the marines fought bloody battles in the city of Hue and at the marine base at Khe Sanh.

In the Persian Gulf War of 1990–91, marines fought a key tank battle against the Iraqi army. In 1993 they were sent to the African nation of Somalia in an attempt to end the civil war that was preventing international relief agencies from bringing food to the starving people in that country.

Marines, who consider themselves an elite branch of the armed forces, take pride in their ability to carry out difficult and dangerous assignments at a moment's notice. Their motto is "Semper Fidelis" (Always Faithful).

See also entries for individual wars.

R. CONRAD STEIN

MARRIAGE

The Europeans who came to settle in the American colonies understood marriage very differently than we do today. A man and a woman did not marry because they were "in love." Although they expected to come to love each other in time, most meant by this a sort of mutual respect and affection, not a passionate or romantic love.

Couples married for practical reasons. A man and a woman might be considered a good match because their families owned adjoining plots of land that could be combined into a farm, or because both families were prominent in their town, or because the woman was considered a hard worker and thus a good wife for a farmer. Their fathers often negotiated over money, property, and even household goods and tools before giving consent for their children to marry. When a woman married she lost the right to own property or to enter into legal contracts; according to the law all property, and even their children, belonged to the husband.

In New England during the seventeenth century, marriage and family were understood as a major source of stability and order for society, and took place within a tight network of family, community, and church control. In the South, controls were weaker, and there were four times as many men as women, making it very difficult for men to marry. Throughout the colonies, marriages did not last very long—not because of divorce, which was rare, but because of death. Half of all marriages ended within seven years because one of the partners died.

Changing Concepts of Marriage

By the mid-eighteenth century, the idea of marriage was changing. Couples began to call each other by first names or terms of endearment in letters, instead of "Sir" or "Madam," as they had in the previous century. By the middle of the Victorian era (roughly 1830–1900) most Americans believed marriage should be based on romantic love and followed elaborate rituals of courtship. This is the time when many of the wedding customs of today were developed. Once married, men and women were expected to follow very

strict gender roles (ideas about what it is proper for each sex to do). Historians have called this model "separate spheres," for men were expected to master the public sphere— the world of the economy—and women to care for the private sphere—the world of home and family.

Despite the new belief in romantic love, not all people could marry whomever they wished. Slaves had to have their owners' permission to marry, and their marriages were not recognized as legally binding. But most men and women held in slavery did marry, either in the church or by a simple ceremony such as jumping over a broomstick. About one out of six marriages between slaves was broken by the sale of the husband or wife. This happened so often, in fact, that one preacher married members of his community with the words "until death or distance do you part."

In the early decades of the twentieth century, a sexual revolution took place. The practice of "dating" was invented, and in general young men and women had more romantic and sexual experience before marriage. Changing courtship practices led to new ideas about marriage, shifting the ideal to "companionate marriage," in which couples were bound together by love and sexual attraction, and individual fulfillment was more important than concepts of duty.

Impact of World Events

During the Great Depression of the 1930s, fewer people could afford to marry and have families. The marriage rate dropped 13 percent between 1930 and 1932, and by the end of the decade the average age at marriage had risen from 24.3 to 26.7 for men and from 21.3 to 23.3 for women.

World War II brought economic recovery

but also uncertainty about the future—and for both reasons, the marriage rate boomed. Between 1940 and 1942, one thousand servicemen and their brides married each day. But marriage rates stayed high even after the war ended in 1945 and through the 1950s people got married at younger and younger ages. By 1959, 47 percent of all brides were under nineteen. The ideal marriage in postwar America was thought to be centered around children and devoted to "togetherness," and according to a 1957 poll, only 9 percent of Americans thought that a single person could be happy.

At the same time, this celebration of marriage masked many tensions over men's and women's roles within marriage, and as the women's movement developed in the 1960s and 1970s, feminists began to criticize the institution. A second twentieth-century sexual revolution and the invention of the birth-control pill weakened the connection between sex and marriage. Average age at marriage began to rise again, and the divorce rate soared.

"Living together" without being married became commonplace. Households made up of two unrelated persons of the opposite sex tripled between 1970 and 1980 and rose another 14 percent between 1981 and 1982. This prompted the U.S. Census Bureau to coin the term POSSLQ (persons of the opposite sex sharing living quarters). More recently, gay and lesbian couples have begun to seek the right to legal marriage.

The ideal and practice of marriage has changed dramatically over America's history, but marriage remains a central institution in our society.

See also Birth Control; Childhood and Adolescence; Divorce; Family Life.

BETH BAILEY

MARRIED WOMEN'S PROPERTY ACTS

Until the middle of the nineteenth century, when a woman married, control of all the property she owned passed to her husband. Married women could not buy or sell property, enter into contracts, sue or be sued, even make their own wills. Gradually, beginning in the decades just before the Civil War, the states passed laws removing these restrictions. The first such law, passed by Mississippi in 1839, guaranteed women the right to receive income from their property and protected their property from being seized in payment of their husbands' debts. But it left husbands in control of their wives' property.

In the 1850s the women's rights leader Susan B. Anthony conducted a campaign to persuade the New York legislature to reform the property and divorce laws. That effort failed. But in 1860 the New York legislature, pressured by women such as Anthony's associate, Elizabeth Cady Stanton, enacted a comprehensive Married Women's Property Act that gave married women the power to own, buy, and sell property and to keep whatever money they earned. Other long-denied rights were also granted.

Similar measures were enacted by most states after the Civil War. By the 1890s, a historic shift had taken place. Some states had even given adult women the right to vote.

See also Feminist Movement to 1919.

MARSHALL, GEORGE C.

(1880–1959)   *U.S. Army general, secretary of state, and secretary of defense.*

Born the son of a Pennsylvania coal-mine operator, Marshall graduated from the Virginia Military Institute in 1901 and received a commission in the U.S. Army. During World War I, he helped prepare some of the major offensive campaigns in France. After the war, he served at various military posts and quickly rose through the ranks until he became chief of staff of the army in 1939.

Marshall was responsible for overall strategic military planning during World War II and for increasing the size of the American army and air force from 200,000 to more than 8.3 million troops. Impressed by Marshall's ability to field a huge, well-equipped fighting force and plot successful military operations, Prime Minister Winston Churchill of Great Britain hailed Marshall as "the true organizer of victory."

Shortly after Marshall retired from the army in November 1945, President Harry S. Truman sent him to China on an unsuccessful mission to try to end the civil war between the Communists and Nationalists. He was named secretary of state in 1947, at a time when the countries of Europe were on the brink of economic collapse because of the devastation caused by World War II. Millions were homeless and threatened with starvation. In a historic speech at Harvard University on June 5, 1947, Marshall proposed a dramatic plan providing American financial aid to restore the European economy. Called the "Marshall Plan" by the press, this bold proposal was adopted by Congress in 1948 and went into effect as the European Recovery Program. It stimulated the speedy rebuilding of Western Europe, alleviating the terrible distress in the region and stabilizing the economy, which helped check the spread of communism from the Soviet Union.

In 1949, Marshall resigned as secretary of state, but in 1950 he returned to the cabinet as secretary of defense and served one year. This

remarkable soldier-statesman, who had devoted nearly a half century to military and civilian public service, received the Nobel Peace Prize in 1953.

See also Army; Marshall Plan; World War II.

EDMUND LINDOP

MARSHALL, JOHN

(1755–1835)   *Chief justice, U.S. Supreme Court.*

Marshall, a Virginian, participated in the American Revolution and developed strong beliefs in the importance of political union of the colonies as well as independence from

John Marshall served as chief justice of the Supreme Court for thirty-four years. Although he had little schooling and had studied law for only six weeks, he became one of the country's most influential and distinguished jurists.

Britain. After the war, Marshall practiced law and participated in Virginia state politics. He strongly defended the new Constitution of the United States in the Virginia ratifying convention that approved the document.

For financial reasons, Marshall was reluctant to accept a variety of offers to take part in the new government established by the Constitution, though he did agree to President John Adams's request to go to France as part of a diplomatic mission. On his return, he accepted former president George Washington's urgings to run for Congress. He served in the House of Representatives for six months in 1799–1800, before being selected by Adams to serve as his secretary of state. Just before leaving the presidency in 1801, Adams named Marshall as the fourth chief justice of the United States, a position in which Marshall achieved lasting fame.

Marshall's most famous opinion was also one of his first, *Marbury* v. *Madison* (1803). There Marshall held, first, that the Constitution was the supreme law of the land and, second, that the Supreme Court, as a court of law, was authorized to invalidate any laws passed by Congress that violated the Constitution. This power of "judicial review" is a major feature of the American constitutional system. In *Fletcher* v. *Peck* (1810), striking down a Georgia law, Marshall extended this principle to include state laws.

Although most famous for *Marbury*, Marshall's most important opinion may well have been *McCulloch* v. *Maryland* (1819). In a sweeping and magisterial decision, Marshall in effect dismissed the arguments of James Madison, Thomas Jefferson, and others that the United States rested on a legal compact entered into by the states of the union. Instead, he argued that the basis of the United States was popular sovereignty, an agreement

of the national "we the people" cited in the preamble to the Constitution. Moreover, he ruled that the new government established by the people had very wide-ranging powers and that Congress could pass almost any legislation that it believed was convenient for achieving the ends of government. Finally, he struck down as a violation of the Constitution an attempt by Maryland to tax the Bank of the United States established by Congress.

Many other opinions defended the claims of national authority against assertions of state power. In addition to nationalism, another of Marshall's central values was protection of private property, and a number of decisions attempted to safeguard property rights against state regulation. Somewhat surprisingly, given his values, he ruled in *Barron* v. *Baltimore* (1833) that the protections of the Bill of Rights applied only to the national government and not to the states.

One of Marshall's most notable achievements as chief justice was establishing the practice of a single "opinion of the Court," instead of continuing the practice, as in Great Britain, of having each justice issue a separate opinion in every case. Few judges wrote dissents from his opinions, and in turn only once in his thirty-four-year tenure did Marshall dissent from an opinion of the Court in a constitutional law case.

See also Marbury v. *Madison;* Supreme Court.

SANFORD LEVINSON

MARSHALL, THURGOOD

(1908–93)   *Associate justice, U.S. Supreme Court.*

Born in Baltimore, Maryland, Marshall graduated from Lincoln University in 1930. As an African American, he was barred from attending the University of Maryland Law School, his first choice. After graduating first in his class in 1933 from the Howard University Law School (a university devoted to education for blacks), Marshall committed himself to overcoming the many legal barriers blocking African Americans from full participation in American society.

As the director of the Legal Defense and Educational Fund of the National Association for the Advancement of Colored People

Thurgood Marshall (center) walks down the steps of the Supreme Court on May 17, 1954, with fellow lawyers George E. C. Hayes (left) and James M. Nabrit (right) after winning Brown v. Board of Education, *the landmark case that ended segregation in public schools. The Supreme Court unanimously ruled "that in the field of public education the doctrine of 'separate but equal' has no place." Thirteen years later, Marshall himself was appointed to the Supreme Court.*

(NAACP), he challenged racial discrimination in such areas as transportation, criminal justice, and elections. Marshall won twenty-nine cases in the U.S. Supreme Court and many hundreds of cases in lower courts. Undoubtedly his most famous case was *Brown v. Board of Education,* which in 1954 struck down as unconstitutional the assignment of African Americans to racially separate public schools. *Brown* was quickly extended to all sorts of governmental practices that separated Americans by race.

President John F. Kennedy nominated Marshall in 1961 to the U.S. Court of Appeals for the Second Circuit. He was confirmed by the Senate only after a vigorous fight with southern senators angry at his role in challenging segregation. Four years later President Lyndon B. Johnson named Marshall solicitor general of the United States, the chief lawyer for the country with primary responsibility for presenting its arguments to the Supreme Court. Marshall was the first African American to be named to that position. Two years later, in 1967, Johnson named Marshall as the first African-American member of the Supreme Court itself, on which he served until his retirement in 1991.

On the Court, Marshall was very sensitive to issues of racial justice, and he vigorously supported the constitutionality of affirmative action, the use of racial categories to benefit minorities. He was also extremely concerned about the opportunities open to poor Americans of all races.

The conservative shift of the Supreme Court that began with Chief Justice Earl Warren's replacement by Warren Burger in 1969 meant that many of Marshall's most important opinions were dissents (meaning the opinion he handed down differed from what the majority of the Court decided). For example, the Court in 1973 examined in *San Antonio Independent School District* v. *Rodriguez* the fact that children living in rich communities tended to have much more spent on their education than did children living in poor communities. The five-justice majority upheld this as constitutional under the equal protection clause of the Fourteenth Amendment. Marshall, joined by three other justices, wrote a powerful dissent suggesting that the Court was in effect tolerating the consignment of poor children to second-class citizenship.

Another great passion of Marshall's was his opposition to the death penalty, which he felt was imposed almost invariably on persons without financial resources adequate for purchasing a first-rate legal defense.

See also Brown v. Board of Education; Supreme Court.

SANFORD LEVINSON

MARSHALL PLAN

After the end of World War II, most of the European nations were in desperate need of economic aid. In some, Communist Parties made large gains. This alarmed the Truman administration and led to the decision to provide massive assistance to all the European nations willing to accept it. The plan was named for Secretary of State George C. Marshall, who presented it in a speech at Harvard University in June 1947.

The real enemy of freedom and democracy was not so much communism as hunger and poverty, Marshall explained. Eliminating these blights would restore "the confidence of the European people in the economic future." The United States was ready to help, if the Europeans would cooperate.

Sixteen nations from western Europe responded by creating the Committee for European Economic Cooperation. The Soviet Union, however, was suspicious of American motives and refused to join. It also kept the nations along its western border out of the plan and engineered a revolution in Czechoslovakia that prevented that country from participating. Congress appropriated more than $13 billion for the program, which was an immediate success. By 1951 western Europe was experiencing a major economic boom.

Whether the United States created the Marshall Plan for altruistic or selfish reasons is not clear—probably both. Concern for the suffering of its allies and the desire to check communism and stimulate the American economy were involved.

MATHER, COTTON

(1663–1728) *Minister, historian, and writer.*

Cotton Mather was born into a family of preachers in the colony of Massachusetts. Both his grandfathers had emigrated from England as part of the "Great Migration" of Puritans in the 1630s and had led congregations in the New World. His father, Increase Mather, combined spiritual and political authority as the leading preacher in Boston as well as the most important spokesman for the colony in London. Cotton Mather never attained his father's level of influence either at home or abroad. He is, however, better known to later generations because he published a large body of writings on many topics, ranging from religion to everyday affairs.

Cotton Mather's prestige suffered along with his father's as a result of the Salem witch trials of 1692. Neither one expressed at first

A portrait of Cotton Mather in 1727. A prominent Puritan minister, Mather is often remembered for his part in the Salem witchcraft trials. Mather claimed "not only that there are witches, but that good men (as well as others) may possibly have their lives shortened by such evil instruments of Satan."

any doubts about the procedures used to convict suspected witches. The lack of criticism by the Mathers bolstered the hysteria that continued until nineteen persons had been hanged. Cotton even wrote *The Wonders of the Invisible World,* a history of witchcraft that seemed to justify the actions of the court at Salem.

Mather continued to write and preach afterward, but without the attentive and respectful audience that his father had enjoyed. His history of New England, *Magnalia Christi Americana* (Latin for "the great works of Christ in America"), was published in London in 1702, but met with indifference from English critics. For his audience at home, Mather tried to reconcile the Puritan heritage of New England with new religious and philosophical ideas coming out of Europe. He stressed "doing good" as a practical basis of religious faith. He also dabbled in science and, in 1722, boldly came out in favor of the use of the new smallpox vaccine during an outbreak of that disease in Boston.

See also Puritans.

THOMAS COLE

MAYER, LOUIS B.

(1885–1957)   *Motion picture producer.*

As head of production for Metro-Goldwyn-Mayer Studios, Mayer was known as "the King of Hollywood." He was president of the Association of Motion Picture Producers for six years and unquestionably the most influential man in the industry.

Mayer immigrated to Canada from his native Russia at the age of three. The son of a scrap dealer, he went to work for his father at the age of fourteen and had little formal education. In 1907, while running his father's office in Boston, he bought a small theater in nearby Haverhill and began to show films, then a new form of entertainment. The venture was so successful that he soon controlled a chain of theaters throughout the Northeast. When D. W. Griffith finished his picture *Birth of a Nation,* Mayer acquired exclusive New England distribution rights.

Determined to have a hand in all aspects of the industry, Mayer went to Hollywood in 1918 to produce films. His production company and Metro Pictures, his distribution agency, merged with Goldwyn Pictures in 1924 to become Metro-Goldwyn-Mayer, the biggest film company in history, controlling worldwide production, distribution, and exhibition of its films. Mayer was its vice president in charge of production for twenty-seven years.

Mayer became a legend for the absolute power he wielded. He was personally responsible for creating MGM's stable of stars, including Greta Garbo, Spencer Tracy, Judy Garland, Clark Gable, and the Marx Brothers. He imposed his taste for lavish but wholesome films on his studio, promising, "I will only make pictures that I won't be ashamed to have my children see." A shrewd businessman, he kept MGM profitable even during the Great Depression, when other studios were losing money. For years he was the highest paid executive in America.

But when public taste turned away from the warm, sentimental entertainment he preferred, Mayer refused to adapt. In 1951 he was forced to resign from MGM. He vowed he would continue to make "decent, wholesome pictures" elsewhere, but he died, a bitter man, six years later, without having made another motion picture.

See also Movies.

DENNIS WEPMAN

MAYFLOWER COMPACT

When the Pilgrims left England on the *Mayflower* in September 1620 they were headed for a point near the mouth of the Hudson River, in what was then the northern part of the colony of Virginia. But they were driven off course by storms during the crossing and reached land north of their destination and outside the boundaries of Virginia. Unwilling to remain longer at sea in the dead of winter,

they decided to settle where they were, at what is now the town of Plymouth, Massachusetts.

Some of the Pilgrims felt that since they were outside the jurisdiction of Virginia, this liberated them from all control by anyone. To restrain these people, the Pilgrims before going ashore drafted and signed the Mayflower Compact, an agreement as to how they were to be governed. "In the presence of God and one another," the document ran, we "combine ourselves together into a civil Body Politick and by virtue hereof do enact ... such just and equal laws as shall be thought ... for the general Good." Every adult male was required to sign this compact before going ashore. The compact was the only frame of government of Plymouth until it was absorbed into the Massachusetts Bay Colony in 1691.

See also Pilgrims.

MAYS, WILLIE

(1931–   ) *Baseball player with the New York Giants (1951–57), San Francisco Giants (1958–71), and New York Mets (1972–73).*

One of the finest baseball players ever to play the game, Willie Mays could do everything in baseball brilliantly, except pitch. A slugging outfielder with speed (he led his league in stolen bases three years running), he ranks third on the all-time home run list (660).

Born to a black working-class family in Birmingham, Alabama, Mays played outfield for the Birmingham Black Barons while he was still in high school. The New York Giants signed him to a minor league contract in 1950, and the following year he was the Rookie of the Year in center field as the Giants won the pennant.

Most observers insist that however impressive, statistics alone cannot capture the essence of Willie Mays. He played baseball with a zest and enthusiasm that set him apart from other stars (with the exception of Jackie Robinson). Fans delighted in the sight of Mays running out from under his cap, whether pursuing an outfield fly or tearing around the bases. Mays's obvious joy in the game, as well as his astonishing skills, made him the most popular player in baseball in the 1950s and 1960s.

According to his manager, Leo Durocher, no one matched him in "the five things you look for in a player": hitting, hitting with power, fielding, throwing, and base running. Mays combined outstanding athletic gifts with an unerring baseball intelligence on the bases and in the field.

Willie Mays entered major league baseball just four years after Jackie Robinson had broken the color barrier. He was so attractive to fans—white and black—that he solidified the right of African Americans to play in the majors. The sportswriter Grantland Rice pointed out that Mays was "the kid everybody likes." Mays himself once said, "I don't make history. I catch fly balls." In fact he did both.

See also Baseball; Sports, Spectator.

For further reading: Willie Mays and Charles Einstein, *Born to Play Ball* (New York: G. B. Putnam's Sons, 1955).

W A R R E N   G O L D S T E I N

M C C A R T H Y ,   J O S E P H   R .

(1908–57) *U.S. senator and anticommunist crusader.*

On February 9, 1950, a Republican senator from Wisconsin gave a speech to the Wom-an's Club of Wheeling, West Virginia. In it, he declared that there were "205 known Communists" working for the U.S. State Department. That speech stunned the country. At that time, many Americans believed that the Communist-ruled Soviet Union was determined to take over the world and that American Communists were a part of that effort.

The senator's name was Joseph McCarthy, but everyone called him Joe. He had been elected in 1946, soon, he claimed, after serving as a tailgunner in World War II. He had been almost unknown outside Wisconsin, but the Wheeling speech changed that, making him famous overnight. Thriving on the attention, Joe McCarthy continued giving speeches denouncing the Communists that he said were in the government. Sometimes he waved in the air what he claimed was a list of these "agents." But he never let anyone else read it.

Meanwhile, a massive national campaign began to root out "Communists," particularly from government, the universities, and the arts. Anyone accused of being a Communist sympathizer was likely to be fired. Those who "confessed" and gave the names of other "Communists" were spared. Many innocent people were accused, and some named other innocent people just to save themselves. Others, who actually did hold Communist views, betrayed their friends, although there were some who refused to do this, even when it meant losing their jobs or going to prison.

For a time, merely holding an unpopular political opinion was enough to get the person treated like a criminal. Because McCarthy was the loudest voice in this anticommunist campaign (often called "the red scare"), this atmosphere of fear and accusation became known as "McCarthyism." McCarthy's tactics were characterized by flimsy evidence

Senator Joseph R. McCarthy assumes a typically combative, finger-pointing pose in February 1954. One journalist described him as "a screamer, a political thug, a master of the mob, an exploiter of popular fears."

or none at all, outrageous distortions of the facts, and a melodramatic style of presenting accusations. He also would declare people "guilty by association"—that is, they were "guilty" simply because they knew someone or joined a group others thought suspicious, not because they themselves had done anything wrong.

McCarthy eventually went too far. He launched a Senate committee investigation to prove that there were Communists in the U.S. Army. The committee's hearings were televised, and it soon became obvious to the nation that McCarthy was unfair and irresponsible. In December 1954, the U.S. Senate voted to "censure" him for his tactics, publicly disgracing him. McCarthy died of cancer and alcoholism in 1957.

See also Anticommunism.

MICHAEL KRONENWETTER

MCCLELLAN, GEORGE B.

(1826–85)   *Civil War general.*

McClellan, who was born in Philadelphia, was one of the brightest students in the U.S. Military Academy class of 1846. After graduating at age twenty, he fought in the war against Mexico and was eventually made a captain. But in 1857 he suddenly quit the army and became a highly paid business executive.

Four years later the Civil War began. Because of his military experience McClellan was made a major general of the Union forces. McClellan led a small army to victory in one of the first battles and was hailed as a hero throughout the North. When the main Union army suffered a bad defeat at the Battle of Bull Run, McClellan was called to take over its command.

McClellan did an excellent job of improving the army and rebuilding its confidence and became greatly admired by soldiers and most Northern citizens. They called him "the young Napoleon," after the French military genius Napoleon Bonaparte. McClellan enjoyed this admiration, even to the point of seeming to feel that he was the only person who could save the Union.

But McClellan was extremely cautious about risking his army in battle. He always claimed to be greatly outnumbered by enemy forces, which was not true. As time dragged on and he failed to engage the enemy, Northern leaders began to suspect he did not really want to fight the Confederate army at all. Some even wondered if he secretly supported the South!

After a number of months, McClellan finally led his troops against the Confederate capital of Richmond, Virginia, but was forced to retreat. When Confederate Gen. Robert E.

Lee invaded the North in 1862, McClellan fought him at the Battle of Antietam. If McClellan had made one final attack, he might have ended the war then. But he moved too slowly and cautiously and let the Southerners retreat without pursuing them. Because of this, President Abraham Lincoln removed him from command.

McClellan, however, was still popular with many people, and in 1864 the Democratic Party, some members of which wanted to stop the war, made him its candidate for U.S. president. He was defeated by Lincoln, who won a second term and led the Union to victory.

After the war, McClellan traveled, continued in business, and served as governor of New Jersey from 1878 to 1881.

See also Civil War.

TOM MCGOWEN

MCCLINTOCK, BARBARA

(1902–92) *Scientist and winner of the 1983 Nobel Prize in medicine.*

McClintock once said that she became committed very early to "the kinds of things girls were not supposed to do." Her parents encouraged this independence and self-reliance. Thus, when the young Barbara became fascinated with science, she was undeterred by the fact that few women in the early 1900s became research scientists.

McClintock enrolled in Cornell University in 1919 where she studied cytology and genetics. *Cytology* is the study of the cell's structure; *genetics* is the study of inheritance. Cells make up every living thing—people, plants, and animals—and every cell contains bodies called *chromosomes*. They look like short

threads under a microscope, and they carry *genes*. Genes determine the characteristics of all living things. The color of our eyes and hair, for example, and the shape of our nose are decided by the genes passed on to us by our parents.

Over the years, McClintock became famous for her ability to "read" cells under a microscope. She regularly saw things in their structure that others missed. When asked once how she did this, she replied, "Well, you know, when I look at a cell, I get down *in* that cell and look around." By "looking around," McClintock, in 1931, along with her student, Harriet Creighton, provided conclusive evidence for the chromosomal basis of genetics, which established her reputation. But this was only preliminary to her major discovery over the next six years that genes are not, as everyone had thought, static, or permanently situated, in their arrangement on the chromosome.

McClintock studied cells by growing corn and observing successive generations. She kept records of the cells of each generation so that she would know what the next generation had inherited. When a new ear of corn contained a kernel different in color or shape from the others, she set about trying to find out why. Her great insight was that genes sometimes move around on the chromosome, and this can change inheritance. She called this process "transposition"; it's popularly known as "jumping genes."

McClintock's discovery met with disbelief—even scorn—by other scientists, for her conclusion flew in the face of what they believed. Moreover, she was a woman in a profession dominated by men, many of whom were prejudiced against women working in their field. Her acceptance was also hampered by her approach to science and by her personality. Unlike most geneticists, she insisted on the importance of their having a feel for the organism as a whole. Highly intelligent and quick herself, she was impatient with those who could not follow her reasoning. Thus, she remained isolated, with her work ignored, for many years.

Nevertheless, in the 1970s, other researchers began to confirm the mechanism she had uncovered. She was vindicated finally in 1983 when she was awarded the Nobel Prize in medicine at the age of eighty-one.

See also Science and Technology.

For further reading: Joan Dash, *The Triumph of Discovery: Women Scientists Who Won the Nobel Prize* (Englewood Cliffs, N.J.: Messner, 1990); Mary Kittredge, *Barbara McClintock* (New York: Chelsea House, 1991).

CECILE RHINEHART WATTERS

MCCORMICK, CYRUS HALL

(1809–84) *Inventor, businessman, and philanthropist.*

Growing up on a Virginia farm, McCormick became interested in machines that would lighten farm labor. In 1831, at age twenty-two, he built a mechanical reaper for harvesting grain. This horse-drawn machine had knives that moved back and forth to cut wheat and other grains. During the next few years he improved his reaper and demonstrated it on local farms. He obtained a patent on the machine in 1834.

McCormick established a factory to manufacture the reaper in Chicago in 1847. He picked that city because it was close to the nation's main grain-growing areas of Ohio, Indiana, and Illinois. By 1856 his factory was producing forty reapers a day. The demand

for the machine was so great that he became a millionaire.

In the 1860s and 1870s McCormick continued to improve his reaper. He added a device that would automatically bind the grain into sheaves, tied at first with wire and after 1881 with twine. Despite competition from other farm machine manufacturers, McCormick developed the largest market for reapers in the United States. He also sold his machines in foreign countries. He was an ambitious, aggressive, and determined man who combined inventive genius with a keen sense for business and successful sales methods to achieve leadership in his field.

McCormick's reaper greatly reduced the amount of farm labor needed in grain production. It took twenty hours of labor to harvest an acre of wheat in 1830. In 1895, the time needed when the reaper was used was less than an hour.

McCormick gave much of his wealth to Presbyterian schools and seminaries. One of them, the McCormick Theological Seminary, was named for him.

See also Agriculture; Science and Technology.

GILBERT C. FITE

MCGUFFEY'S *READERS*

In 1836 William Holmes McGuffey, the president of Cincinnati College, began publishing a series of elementary school readers that probably had a greater influence on the education of American children than the work of any other writer. Between 1836 and 1857 he and his brother Alexander published six graded *Eclectic Readers*. The books contained material on many subjects of interest to chil-

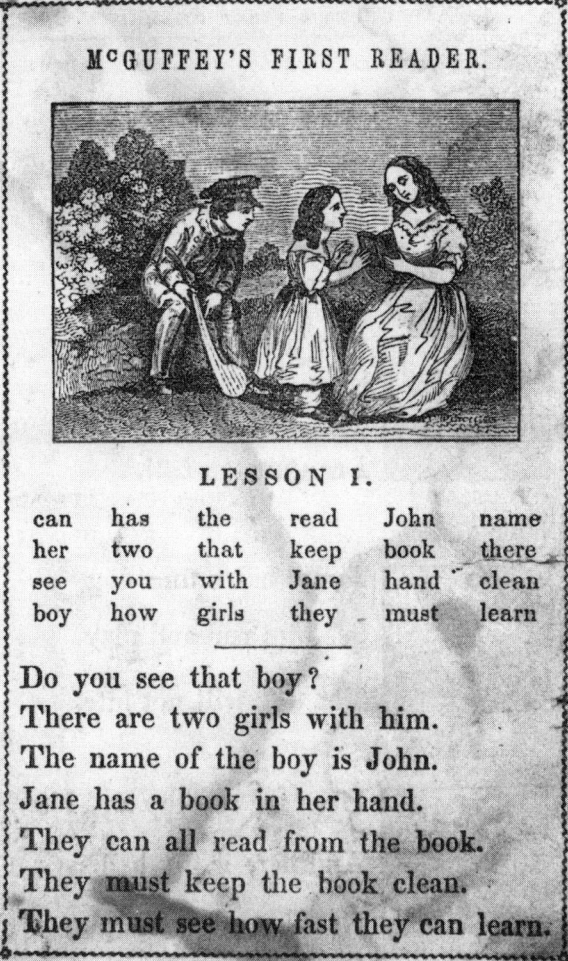

Lesson 1 from McGuffey's 1836 First Reader. McGuffey's Readers were the primers for American schoolchildren for almost a century. The Readers were meant to teach not only reading but lessons in good behavior. Note how this lesson cautions children that "they must keep the book clean" and that "they must see how fast they can learn."

dren. All stressed the religious and moral values dominant at the time—honesty, piety, hard work, respect for one's elders, and the like.

The original volumes sold about 7 million copies, but that was only the beginning. Ever-larger printings and revised editions, prepared after McGuffey died in 1873 by seven later editors, brought the total sold to more than 120 million by 1920.

See also Education: Elementary and High School.

MCKINLEY, WILLIAM

(1843–1901)   *Twenty-fifth president of the United States (1897–1901).*

Born and brought up in Ohio, McKinley, a bright eighteen-year-old, enlisted in the Civil War as a private and soon was promoted to sergeant in charge of commissary. He was so good at feeding soldiers that he was made an officer. His commander, future president Rutherford B. Hayes, became a friend, guide, and role model. After the war, McKinley studied law and in 1867 he began working as a lawyer. He then married Ida Saxton. Her health was not good, and as a result he was an especially tender and caring husband.

McKinley served in Congress from 1877 to 1891 except for one term. He became the champion of the protective tariff, which kept foreign-manufactured goods from selling at cheaper prices than American-made goods. He was the main author of the McKinley Tariff of 1890, which also included trade agreements designed to increase the sale of American products in other countries.

After he was elected governor of Ohio in 1891 and 1893, McKinley easily won the Republican nomination for president in 1896. Badly divided by the depression following the panic of 1893, the Democrats favored inflation by coining more silver dollars. But McKinley thought that free silver, as it was called, would delay prosperity and wanted all the money backed by gold in the U.S. Treasury. Most of the people agreed with him, and he won the election.

When McKinley became president, Cuba

was fighting for its independence from Spain. The bloody war made many Americans want to help Cuba, and McKinley in 1898 reluctantly led the nation into the Spanish-American War. Victory in that war made the nation a colonial power with territories and responsibilities in the Caribbean and the Pacific. Almost immediately the United States suppressed a revolt in the Philippines, one of its new territories.

McKinley's leadership in the Spanish-American War increased the power and prestige of the presidency, and he was easily elected to a second term. Shortly after it began, however, he was shot by an assassin while attending the Pan-American Exposition at Buffalo, New York, and died eight days later.

For events during McKinley's administration, see Hawaii Annexation; Open Door Policy; Panama Canal; Philippines, Acquisition of; Platt Amendment; Spanish-American War.

For further reading: Margaret Leech, *In the Days of McKinley* (New York: Harper & Brothers, 1959).

ARI HOOGENBOOM

MEAD, MARGARET

(1901–78)   *Anthropologist.*

Most noted for her studies of so-called primitive cultures, Mead was an outspoken and controversial figure in the field of anthropology. She challenged rigid popular beliefs regarding gender roles, sexuality, marriage, and cultural values.

Anthropologist Margaret Mead on a field trip to Bali, Indonesia, in 1957.

Born in Philadelphia, Margaret Mead was the daughter of an economics professor and a sociologist. From 1925 to 1926 she conducted research on the South Pacific island of Samoa on the transition of native girls from adolescence to adulthood and in 1928 published *Coming of Age in Samoa.* She received her Ph.D. in anthropology from Columbia University in 1929 and in the decade that followed made research trips to the Admiralty Islands, New Guinea, and Bali.

Mead served as a curator of the American Museum of Natural History in New York from 1926 until her death and as a professor of anthropology at Columbia University. Her many publications include *Growing up in New Guinea, Sex and Temperament in Three Primitive Societies, Male and Female,* and *The Family,* as well as the autobiographical *Blackberry Winter: My Earlier Years* and *Letters from the Field, 1925–1975.*

Although some anthropologists have criticized her research methods and challenged the accuracy of her conclusions, Mead was a respected pioneer in her field. She paved the way for innovative research and explored the effect that cultural conditioning has on the individual's behavior and beliefs. She was also an activist in public affairs. She served on national public health councils and spoke out in favor of civil liberties, women's liberation, population control, and ecological awareness. In 1979 Mead was posthumously awarded the Presidential Medal of Freedom, the most prestigious civilian honor in the United States.

JOANN BIONDI

MEDIA

See Magazines and Newspapers; Radio and Television.

MEDICARE AND MEDICAID

In January 1965, after his landslide victory in the 1964 election, President Lyndon B. Johnson proposed a compulsory hospital insurance plan, financed through the Social Security system, for persons over the age of sixty-five. The government's role in Medicare was, however, strictly financial. Patients obtained treatment directly from hospitals and physicians; the government then paid the bills. This meant that the government had almost no control over the cost of medical care, which rose during the 1970s and 1980s far more rapidly than the general cost of living. In 1984 the government fixed rates for specific treatments, but many doctors then refused to accept Medicare patients. By the early 1990s it was clear that changes in the system would have to be made.

When Congress enacted Medicare, it also created Medicaid, a similar program for poor people of all ages who could not afford medical insurance or were unemployed and thus not covered by a company plan. As with Medicare, those covered by Medicaid obtain treatment directly from doctors and hospitals and the fees are paid by the program.

Although added to the 1965 legislation almost as an afterthought, Medicaid has assumed enormous importance in the nation's public welfare system. Millions of people who would otherwise have to depend on private charity or go untreated benefit from it. As with Medicare, however, there has been no effective way to control the cost of Medicaid. In addition, part of its cost is paid by the individual states. Since the states vary in how generously they support the program, care is better in some states than in others.

See also Medicine.

MEDICINE

When people from Europe first began coming to America to start colonies, health care was very poor. Experienced doctors could recognize symptoms of many diseases, but they did not know the causes and their treatments were generally useless. About all they could do well was to take care of minor injuries, set broken bones, and amputate (cut off) injured arms or legs. Sick people were usually cared for within the family by a mother or grandmother, using homemade remedies. Most "doctors" in early times were ministers of churches. It was felt that the care of the sick was one of their duties, for many believed in those days that illness was a punishment from God.

Becoming a Doctor

The first real doctors in America came from Europe, where they had studied at medical schools. An American who wanted to become a doctor either had to study in Europe or serve as an apprentice (student assistant) to a trained doctor. Almost anyone, however, whether they had actually studied medicine or not, could call himself or herself a doctor. There were "doctors" who only set broken bones or only sold medicines along with tea, sugar, and the like. Thus, a "doctor" often was also a grocer, a carpenter, a barber, or some other occupation.

There were no hospitals in the colonies until 1751, when Benjamin Franklin and others founded one in Philadelphia. A few years later, in 1765, the first American medical school opened. By the time of the American Revolution, there were about 3,500 to 4,000 doctors in the colonies, most of them in the larger towns. These doctors did simple surgery (such as cutting open boils) and gave their patients medicines they had made themselves. The chief way of treating patients for any disease at this time was making them bleed for a while or giving them a drug that made them sweat. It was thought that this helped the body get rid of whatever substance was causing the illness. But of course, this was not of much use in most cases.

Early Operations

Some doctors learned useful things just by trying them. Up until 1809, no doctor anywhere would do an operation that required cutting open a person's stomach area, for it was believed that this would cause death. Then, a backwoods Kentucky doctor, Ephraim McDowell, decided to cut out a tumor that was growing in the stomach area of one of his patients. He knew that she would certainly die from the tumor and thought that she might not die from the operation (if she had, he would have been hanged for murder). He operated, and the woman lived. Thus, he proved that such operations could be done.

But operations of any sort were horrible torture for those who had to have them, for there was no way to keep people from feeling the pain of the cutting. Then a Georgia doctor named Crawford W. Long noticed that fumes of a chemical liquid called ether would put people into a sleepy state in which they felt no pain. In 1842 he used ether on a patient during surgery, and the man felt nothing. Because Dr. Long did not announce his discovery until 1848, the credit for first using ether was given for a long time to William T. G. Morton, a Boston dentist who used it publicly in 1846. At any rate, the news of ether quickly spread, and the blessing of surgery without pain came into the world.

By the end of the first half of the nineteenth century there were forty-two medical schools in the United States, and health care slowly began to improve. Doctors stopped bleeding people as a treatment, and became more aware of the need for cleanliness. But the causes of disease and infection were still unknown, and in the Civil War more soldiers died of disease and infection than were killed in combat. There was a gigantic step forward when the work of French scientist Louis Pasteur in the late 1800s showed that many diseases are caused by bacteria (germs), and American doctors began putting this knowledge to use. Operations were still risky, but with the discovery of X rays, in Germany in 1895, and the new system of sterilizing instruments to kill bacteria, surgery had become safer and more common by the beginning of the twentieth century. American health care in general, however, was still rather second-rate compared to that in Europe.

Twentieth-Century Medicine

Around 1900, the expansion of science, technology, and business in America had a tremendous effect on health care. Until World War I (1914–18), most doctors were still making their own medicines for each patient or having them specially made by a druggist. But during the war, businesses began to produce medicines in large quantities. Their laboratory research improved existing medicines and created valuable new ones. By the middle of the century, many of the diseases that had troubled the world for hundreds of years, such as cholera and smallpox, were gone from America.

From the 1940s on, American science and technology sparked an explosion of new treatments, new methods of surgery, and new ideas. Improved production methods made it possible to turn out the newly discovered an-

tibiotic penicillin in huge batches, so that millions of people could be treated for infectious diseases. Vaccines were produced that ended epidemics of the dreaded disease polio. An American surgeon was the first to do open-heart surgery, in which the patient's heart is temporarily stopped, and a machine takes over the work of circulating the blood during an operation. American doctors performed the first organ transplant, putting a new kidney in a patient's body. And an American surgeon was first to replace a diseased heart with an artificial mechanical one, which had been invented by an American doctor.

Also changing was the way doctors work. For generations, most American doctors had been "general practitioners," taking care of every kind of ailment from a broken bone to cancer. They often went to their patients' homes to give treatment, which was known as a "house call." But by the 1950s there was so much to know about each kind of disease or condition that many doctors became specialists, dealing with only one kind of illness or one part of the body. And nearly all doctors stopped making house calls. Still another major change is that there are now many more women doctors than there were at the beginning of the twentieth century.

Although many health problems were solved or brought under control in the twentieth century, some new illnesses, such as Lyme disease and Legionnaires' disease, have appeared. And millions of lives are threatened by A I D S (acquired immune deficiency syndrome), a terrible incurable disease. Another health problem to be solved includes the high cost of modern medicine. It can do wonderful things, but it has become increasingly expensive, and so the cost of health insurance has climbed, too. Many people find they cannot afford it and have to go without, leaving them wondering how they will pay for medical care if they fall ill. This has become one of the major problems facing the nation, and government leaders, doctors, and the general public alike are all searching hard for a solution.

See also Abortion; Birth Control; Blackwell, Elizabeth; Epidemics; Medicare and Medicaid; Mental Health; Salk, Jonas; Sanitary Commission.

TOM MCGOWEN

MELLON, ANDREW

(1855–1937)   *Financier and secretary of the treasury (1921–32).*

Born in Pittsburgh, Pennsylvania, Mellon left college in 1872 to start a lumber business. Shortly thereafter, he entered his father's bank and in 1902 became its president. As a financier, he showed exceptional ability to back promising businesses and eventually built a business empire that included such enterprises as the Aluminum Company of America and the Gulf Oil Corporation. By 1920 he was immensely wealthy and a recognized master of transactions in venture capital, a term indicating investment in new or fresh enterprises.

Mellon entered politics by supporting the conservative wing of Pennsylvania's Republican Party. Through its influence he was appointed secretary of the treasury by President Warren G. Harding. In office, he led a successful attack on progressive income taxes, arguing that higher rates for larger incomes penalized the successful and discouraged enterprise. In addition, he brought business methods to federal finance, substantially reduced the national debt, and introduced a new paper money, better designed and smaller in size.

In the 1920s, despite his frail and retiring appearance, Mellon became a media hero widely regarded as the greatest secretary of the treasury since Alexander Hamilton. The Great Depression, however, undercut his theory of prosperity and undermined his prestige. In 1932 he served briefly as ambassador to Great Britain and then retired from government service. Among his numerous philanthropies were donations to establish the National Gallery of Art.

Two quite different views of Mellon exist today. One sees him as a business genius contributing much to America's economic and cultural development; the other as a ruthless wielder of business power who widened the gap between rich and poor and helped produce the Great Depression. The latter view was long dominant, but conservatism in the 1980s resurrected Mellon as one of its prophets and heroes.

ELLIS W. HAWLEY

MELVILLE, HERMAN

(1819–91)   *Author.*

Melville led a roving life as a young man, which in retrospect seems an ideal preparation for the writing of his masterpiece, *Moby-Dick* (1851), the celebrated novel of whaling. Thrown back on his own resources by the early death of his father, Melville tried life as a farmer, a bank manager, and a schoolteacher, and hated all three. Then, at twenty, he made the decision that shaped his life—he went to sea as a cabin boy. Two years later, in 1841, he shipped on the whaler *Acushnet* out of New Bedford, Massachusetts, determined, he said, to "sail forbidden seas and land on barbarous coasts."

Discovering that he had a knack for narrative and a gift for language, Melville came to realize that his future lay not in hunting whales but in spinning yarns for landlubbers about romantic and often imaginary adventures in faraway places. He jumped ship in the Marquesas Islands in the South Pacific and for a time lived among cannibals, an experience that provided materials for his first novel, *Typee* (1846). Four more books followed in rapid succession, and at thirty he found himself with a popular following of readers clamoring for more romances of the sea.

But Melville was not content with a career as a popular novelist. He was by nature a seeker, a yearner, and he longed to be taken seriously as a man of letters. A decade after his decision to go to sea, he reversed course. He settled in western Massachusetts with his family, made friends with another ambitious young writer, his neighbor Nathaniel Hawthorne, and set out to write a book that would distill everything he had learned while sailing about the world. The result was *Moby-Dick*. The novel is, on the surface, an account of Captain Ahab's obsessive search for the White Whale that caused him to lose a leg on an earlier voyage. But the novel resembles its seagoing author's duffle bag: it's stuffed to overflowing with Melville's imaginings and speculations about human beings and their lives. It's a kind of voyage into uncharted waters. No one comes away from it untouched. The novel—perhaps it should be called an epic—has informed, fascinated, amused, and exasperated generations of readers, and there is no sign of its losing its magic.

Moby-Dick, unluckily for Melville, was a masterpiece for which the world was unpre-

A 1930 pen-and-ink drawing by Rockwell Kent for Herman Melville's novel Moby-Dick. *The illustration is of Captain Ahab, who fanatically pursues the white whale Moby-Dick. The whale severed Ahab's leg in an encounter and he now walks with a wooden peg. For Ahab, Moby-Dick is the embodiment of all evil: "He piled upon the whale's white hump the sum of all the general rage and hate felt by his whole race from Adam down."*

pared. Readers who had enjoyed his less complicated adventure tales did not like it. The poems and short stories he wrote later in hopes of recapturing his readers were also commercial failures. Two of these, "Bartleby the Scrivener" and "Benito Cereno," rank among the best an American has written.

Melville outlived his fame by forty years, earning his living as a customs inspector on the New York City docks. Not until the 1920s did readers and writers discover to their astonishment that what seemed to them the complex problems of modern existence had been powerfully explored by a distinguished literary ancestor decades earlier.

See also Literature.

CHARLES BOHNER

MENCKEN, H. L.

(1880–1956) *Journalist, critic, and essayist, known as "the sage of Baltimore."*

Mencken was born in Baltimore, and lived there his entire life. He worked as a reporter or editor with the *Baltimore Sun* newspaper for almost fifty years. From 1908 until 1923, he also coedited the *Smart Set*, a popular magazine known for its biting humor. In 1924, he helped found the most important literary magazine of the time, the *American Mercury*.

Although he never went beyond high school, Mencken had a great influence on American culture. His magazines gave voice to exciting new writers like the novelist Theodore Dreiser, the short-story writer Sherwood Anderson, and the poet Edgar Lee Masters. His essays gleefully attacked the smugness and hypocrisy he saw in every corner of American life.

Mencken was brilliant but intolerant. He bragged about *not* being fair. His ideas, he wrote, were "fixed and invariable"—and he expressed them with an often cruel wit. Distrustful of organized religion, he scoffed at the American South and Midwest as "the Bible belt." Scholars refer to the middle class as the "bourgeoisie," but Mencken called it the "booboisie." Deeply suspicious of democracy, he thought it was foolish to leave political decisions to ordinary citizens who knew little about economics or world affairs.

Mencken delighted in controversy. He seemed determined to disagree with (and offend) everyone. Mencken's attacks on the comfortable traditions of American culture pleased liberals and angered conservatives. But Mencken himself was very conservative politically. He distrusted big government and despised the New Deal policies of President Franklin D. Roosevelt. This angered the same liberals who hailed him as a hero when he wrote about cultural issues.

Mencken was fascinated by the way the English language was spoken in the United States. His massive study *The American Language* was the first major work on the subject, and it is still considered the most important. Mencken's many other books include three autobiographies—*Happy Days, Newspaper Days,* and *Heathen Days*—and six volumes of essays, which he frankly entitled *Prejudices.*

MICHAEL KRONENWETTER

MENTAL HEALTH

Mental health, a phrase coined in the twentieth century, has two related but different meanings: (1) the science of restoring healthy functioning to individuals who are having troubles of an emotional or intellectual kind and providing care for them; and (2) the science of developing and maintaining healthy, satisfying, and effective emotional attitudes and intellectual abilities in work, play, and relations with others. People who are specially trained to work in the field of mental health and mental illness are psychiatrists (medical specialists), psychoanalysts (who may or may not have been medically trained), psychologists, social workers, psychiatric nurses, and school counselors.

Mental illness has been present in all cultures and countries throughout history, but it is hard to define because it can reveal itself in a number of different ways. The *symptoms* of mental illness include strange behaviors and actions, extreme or distressing emotional experiences, odd and persistent thoughts and beliefs, and mental blocks that interfere with thinking and acting. But it is important to distinguish carefully between mentally ill persons and those who simply behave in ways that are different from others in their communities.

Historic Background

Words such as *insane, crazy,* and *lunatic* have long been used in Western societies to describe individuals whose behavior contradicted social standards and expectations and to separate them from the rest of the population—who were called *normal.* Because so little was known about mental illness, and its symptoms were so frightening, superstitions abounded. Neglect and brutal treatment of the mentally ill was commonplace. It was not until the middle of the eighteenth century that a more compassionate view of the mentally ill developed.

Early workers in the field of mental illness include the following:

♦ Benjamin Rush (1745–1813) is considered to be the first American psychiatrist. In addition to being a physician and teacher of medicine, he was politically active and signed the Declaration of Independence. Although his understanding of the causes of mental illness seems strange today, as do his treatments, he is remembered for writing America's first psychiatric textbook.

♦ Dorothea Dix (1802–87), the first Ameri-can crusader on behalf of the mentally ill, campaigned extensively for more humane treatment for them. Some of the hospitals she established are still in existence.

♦ Clifford Beers (1876–1943), a man who was hospitalized with a difficult mental illness and recovered, wrote a book called *The Mind That Found Itself.* Published in 1908, the book made a lasting impression. Beers and others began the mental hygiene movement, which focused national attention on the problems of the mentally ill and society's responsibility to help them.

♦ Anna Freud (1895–1982), Austrian child psychoanalyst and daughter of Sigmund Freud, and Leo Kanner (1894–1981), a child psychiatrist from Baltimore, were significant pioneers in the study and treatment of children's mental problems.

Early in the twentieth century three lines of thought evolved concerning the understanding and care of the mentally ill. One was scientific psychological research. The Austrian Sigmund Freud (1856–1939) and the American Adolf Meyer (1866–1950) were among the first physicians to demonstrate that the symptoms of mental illness are expressions of unconscious meanings and mental conflicts. Another important discovery by these men and their coworkers was the finding that disturbing childhood experiences can lead to the later development of a mental illness.

A second development was scientific biological research. In 1913 it was found that the microorganism that causes syphilis was present in the brain tissue of certain severely mentally ill patients, which made it possible to treat that specific psychosis. With continued research into the biological causes of mental illness, specific causes for other mental disorders have been found.

A third line of thought concerned psychosocial theory and research. Studies of family life and social and economic influences have shown that these everyday factors can have profound effects upon human beings. Similarly, traumatic events such as wars, the Holocaust, discrimination, or natural disasters can cause mental illness.

Mental Illness and the Young

The study of the mental life of children has a short history. It was not until the early 1900s that intelligence testing was developed in response to concerns about children with learning difficulties. Later, child mental health clinics were created. These child guidance clinics helped children who were having difficulties with learning, discipline, and social relationships. Nowadays, much of this effort has been taken on by social agencies and public school systems.

Most young people have troubled and uncomfortable feelings at one time or another, but they are usually able to handle them and get on with their lives. Some, though, get stuck with distressing and disabling emotions. After a while these feelings interfere with their ability to play, to enjoy their friends, and to learn. They do not feel good about themselves. Help is probably needed when a young person starts to withdraw, becomes cranky and irritable, loses friends, does not do well at school, cuts classes, insists that "I don't care about all these troubles," experiments repeatedly with drugs or alcohol, worries that something terrible is happening, is sexually promiscuous, or thinks of solving problems by running away, injuring oneself, or committing suicide. Sometimes the body expresses an emotional disturbance through such physical symptoms as headache, stomachache, or shortness of breath.

How an individual of any age manages such thoughts and feelings makes the difference between being mentally healthy or in need of help. People are often surprised to discover that just talking with a trusted person can be extremely useful. This person may be a parent or other adult relative, a friend, or a professional such as a doctor, teacher, school counselor, minister, priest, or rabbi. Paradoxically, it is a sign of mental health as well as of mental strength and courage to recognize that a problem exists and to do something about it.

See also Dix, Dorothea; Medicine.

PETER BLOS, JR., M.D.

MEXICAN AMERICANS
See Hispanics.

MEXICAN WAR

The issue of slavery lay behind the United States' war with Mexico in 1846–48. In the 1820s the Mexican republic had opened the rich lands of Texas, which was then a province of Mexico, to American immigrants. Many southerners moved in with their slaves to cultivate cotton. Soon after Mexico tried to abolish slavery in 1829, these Texans fought a war to set up an independent republic and asked for annexation to the United States. But abolitionists in the North opposed adding Texas to the Union. They feared the vast area would be carved up into several slave states, giving more power to the South. Although the Mexican government threatened war if annexation went through, Congress

This lithograph shows the Battle of Buena Vista, which resulted in the defeat of the Mexican army under Gen. Santa Anna in 1847 by U.S. forces led by Gen. Zachary Taylor.

approved it in 1845, and Mexico broke off diplomatic relations with the United States.

In January 1846 President James K. Polk ordered Gen. Zachary Taylor to move U.S. troops to the Texas-Mexican border, hoping to provoke the Mexicans into attacking the Americans. Meanwhile Polk drafted a message asking Congress for a declaration of war upon Mexico. When news came that American and Mexican troops had skirmished along the Rio Grande, the president declared that a state of war existed.

Polk's Democratic majority in Congress allowed only two hours to debate the war bill, stampeding the representatives into hasty action. Many in Congress who were against the war in the end voted aye. Some said they gave

in to Polk's demand because they feared being charged with treason. Congressman Abraham Lincoln of Illinois declared that Polk's sending an army into Mexican territory and building a fort there violated the Constitution. Other congressmen, like Joshua Giddings of Ohio, refused to vote for supplies for the men. Giddings told the House, "This war is waged against an unoffending people, without just or adequate cause, for the purposes of conquest, with the design to extend slavery, in violation of the Constitution, against the dictates of humanity . . . and the precepts of the religion we profess."

But when the newspapers announced that American blood had been shed by Mexicans, thousands of men responded to the call for volunteers. Press and public believed this war would be "short and sweet." Until the volunteers arrived, the regular army of 7,200 men did the fighting. The West Point officers thought the volunteers an undisciplined lot, but many of them, hunters on the frontier, were superb marksmen. Not all enlisted for love of flag; some signed up for a cash bonus and deserted easily.

The basic strategy of the Americans was a triple thrust against Mexico: to defeat the small Mexican forces in New Mexico and California and occupy the region; to seize that part of Mexico south of the Rio Grande; and then to drive south to Mexico City, capture the capital, and force a treaty on American terms. The navy blockaded Mexican ports.

President Polk wanted a short war for two reasons: one, to avoid heavy casualties, which would reduce popular enthusiasm for the war; and two, to avoid building the prestige of the two leading generals—Winfield Scott and Zachary Taylor—who happened to be members of the opposition Whig Party. He feared that either one might run for the presidency in the 1848 elections.

The Mexican army was in large part poorly trained and equipped. A great gulf separated these men of the poorer classes from their upper-class officers. In overall command was General Santa Anna, whom Mexican historians have called "a sly schemer . . . whose soul was sheer vanity and ambition." He wanted to rule Mexico and stop the liberal movement in the country.

In September 1846 General Taylor's forces captured Monterey after a four-day battle. In February 1847 he defeated Santa Anna at the Battle of Buena Vista. As news of the death toll from battle wounds and disease trickled to the states, it fueled a growing anger against the war, especially in New England. In Massachusetts, Henry David Thoreau went to jail rather than pay taxes to support a government that sanctioned slavery and was now fighting a war to extend it. Abolitionists and church groups who all along had opposed the war now spoke to more receptive ears.

In March 1847, General Scott—in the first large-scale amphibious (sea and land) assault in U.S. military history—landed 10,000 troops near the fortress of Vera Cruz and forced its surrender. Then Scott moved toward the enemy capital, beating the Mexicans in a series of battles that climaxed on September 14 with his capture of Mexico City.

With its armies defeated and its capital occupied, Mexico had no choice but to agree to American terms. Early in 1848 the Treaty of Guadalupe Hidalgo was signed. Under this agreement the United States acquired territory known as the Mexican Cession: 850,000 square miles, about one-third of Mexico's land. Mexicans who lived in the ceded areas became eligible for American citizenship, and the United States paid $15 million for the land.

The United States had grown enormously through its aggression. Ulysses S. Grant, who served in Mexico as a young officer, called it the most disgraceful war the country ever fought. The dissent expressed during the war revealed the sectional conflicts that had begun to strain the bonds of union and to break apart both major parties. Thirteen years after the Mexican War ended, the Civil War began.

See also Expansion, Territorial; Polk, James K.; Taylor, Zachary; Texas Revolution and Annexation.

For further reading: Milton Meltzer, *Bound for the Rio Grande: The Mexican Struggle, 1845–85* (New York: Knopf, 1974).

MILTON MELTZER

MILITARY

See Air Force; Army; Marine Corps; Navy.

MILLER, ARTHUR

(1915–) *Playwright.*

Arthur Miller is considered to be one of America's greatest living dramatists. By writing about life during the depression, prejudices against Jews, family tragedies, and the plight of hardworking citizens, Miller has helped his audiences and readers understand that many of the real heroes in life are common people.

Born in New York City, Miller as a youth suffered through the hard economic times of the Great Depression of the 1930s and was heavily influenced by those years. After reading Fyodor Dostoyevsky's novel *The Brothers Karamazov,* he decided to become a writer. His first successful play, *All My Sons,* was a tragic story about a father who indirectly causes the death of his son in the aftermath of World War II. The play was made into a movie, and Miller began to attract recognition as a serious writer.

What is probably his most famous play, *Death of a Salesman,* won the Pulitzer Prize for drama in 1949 and established him as one of the best playwrights in America. The play dramatizes the disappointment and regret a traveling salesman feels about his ordinary life.

Miller's play *The Crucible,* a tale about the seventeenth-century Salem witch trials, is a parable attacking Senator Joseph R. McCarthy's public hounding of Americans whom he accused of favoring communism during the 1950s. *The Crucible* demonstrated that what was being done to the people accused of having communist affiliations was the same thing that was done to the Salem women accused of being witches. The play reflected Miller's lifelong interest in social and political issues.

During the 1950s Miller was married to movie actress Marilyn Monroe. A character in his play *After the Fall* was supposedly modeled after her.

Miller's plays and movies are still performed throughout the world. His work is highly valued for its sensitive portrayals of ordinary human beings.

See also Theater.

JOANN BIONDI

MINUTEMEN

The name *Minutemen* was coined on the eve of the American Revolution in Massachusetts. In 1774 the Massachusetts militia had been reorganized in an effort to get rid of Loyalists opposed to independence. Besides establishing a regular militia, revolutionary leaders set up regiments of men ready "on a minute's notice" to take up arms in an emergency. After the First Continental Congress passed a resolution urging people to take up arms to protect their rights, these regiments began to gather and train in towns and villages, first in Massachusetts and then in other colonies. They called themselves "Minutemen."

When the first battle of the Revolution was fought at Lexington, Massachusetts, in April 1775, the Americans who were killed were all Minutemen. The Minutemen were soon absorbed into the Continental army, but throughout the Revolution whenever British

A woodcut of a Minuteman of the American Revolution.

troops invaded a region, patriotic local citizens took up arms in a similar manner to oppose them.

See also Revolution: The War for Independence.

MIRANDA V. ARIZONA

Miranda v. *Arizona*, a Supreme Court case decided in 1966, ensures the rights of individuals suspected of crimes. The Court ruled that before police can question suspects, they have to be informed of the following: that they have the right to remain silent, that anything they say can be used against them in court, and that they have the right to the presence of an attorney; if they cannot afford to hire an attorney, one will be appointed by the court. A statement obtained by the police without following these rules is inadmissible in court as evidence.

The Supreme Court reached this decision after an extensive review of actual police interrogation practices. The justices discovered that intimidation and outright physical abuse were common methods of obtaining confessions. The decision was hailed by many as a victory for the rights of the individual and protected citizens against the possibility of police brutality and illegally obtained evidence. Others, however, felt it placed too many restrictions on the police and interfered with law enforcement.

See also Bill of Rights.

MISSOURI COMPROMISE

As the nation expanded westward in the early nineteenth century, a balance between free and slave states was maintained. After Ohio became a free state in 1803, Louisiana was admitted with slavery in 1812. Between 1816 and 1819 Indiana and Illinois became free states, Mississippi and Alabama slave. In 1820 there were twenty-two states in the Union, eleven slave and eleven free. Such a balance was of great importance in Congress where it would affect the outcome of votes in the Senate bearing on slavery issues—neither side wanted the other to have more votes.

The balance threatened to be tipped, however, when the residents of Missouri Territory applied for statehood in 1817. The greater part

The Missouri Compromise

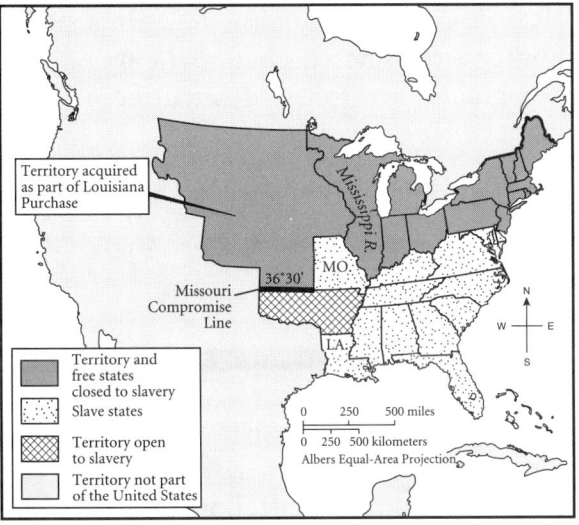

Territory acquired as part of Louisiana Purchase

Missouri Compromise Line

36°30'

MO.

LA.

N
W   E
S

Territory and free states closed to slavery

Slave states

Territory open to slavery

Territory not part of the United States

0   250   500 miles
0   250 500 kilometers
Albers Equal-Area Projection

of Missouri was directly west of free territory, but most of the settlers were southerners, many of them slave owners. It would surely become a slave state. But northern congressmen objected, and a bitter debate resulted that delayed action through 1818 and 1819 and into 1820. Finally a compromise was reached. Missouri was admitted with slavery and Maine, until then part of Massachusetts, became a separate free state. In addition a far more important part of the compromise provided that slavery should be "forever prohibited" in all the rest of the Louisiana Purchase territory north of the southern boundary of Missouri (36°30' north latitude). Slavery would be permitted south of that line.

Many southerners disliked the compromise because it established the principle that Congress could make laws regarding slavery, a position they disagreed with strongly, feeling that decisions about slavery should be up to individual states only. Northerners, on the other hand, were not happy that slavery was to be allowed to expand into the territories at all, even only south of the compromise line.

Nevertheless, the compromise held for over thirty years until it was repealed by the Kansas-Nebraska Act in 1854, which substituted popular sovereignty, or local choice, in deciding whether a new state would be free or slave.

See also Kansas-Nebraska Act; Slavery.

MITCHELL, MARIA

(1818–89)   *Astronomer.*

Mitchell was one of ten children born on the island of Nantucket, Massachusetts, to William and Lydia Mitchell, members of the Society of Friends, or Quakers. Her father loved science, a passion he passed on to his daughter. When she was a young girl, she helped him chart the stars from their "widow's walk"—a balcony built on housetops and so named because wives of sailors at sea would watch there for their husband's ship on the horizon. When she was twelve, Maria witnessed an eclipse, which whetted her appetite for astronomy.

Mitchell was an excellent student, and, in 1835, she ran her own school for a year before being appointed librarian of the Nantucket Atheneum. She used her father's telescope in his observatory on top of the bank where he worked and in October 1847, she discovered a new comet. In honor of her discovery, she was awarded a gold medal by the king of Denmark.

The following year, in 1848 Mitchell became the first woman elected to the American Academy of Arts and Sciences (the next woman member wasn't elected until 1943!), and in 1850 she was elected to the American Association for the Advancement of Science. Although a world-renowned scientist, as a woman she had few opportunities to pursue her scholarly interests. She toured Europe in

Astronomer and professor Maria Mitchell (seated) in the observatory at Vassar College.

1857–58, where she met with European scientists impressed by her research. Upon her return home a committee of women presented her with a five-inch telescope. In 1865 she was offered a teaching post at the newly founded Vassar College for women in Poughkeepsie, New York. The college was equipped with a twelve-inch telescope (the third largest in the country).

Mitchell was a strong advocate of women's rights. In 1873 she was a founder of the Association for the Advancement of Women. In 1869 and again in 1877 she headed expeditions of her women students to observe solar eclipses. Many of her pupils followed in her footsteps and became scientists or teachers. Continuing her astronomical observations and publications well into her sixties, she retired from Vassar in 1888.

After her death, Vassar alumnae and others raised funds to support the Maria Mitchell Association of Nantucket. It maintains her home there, which is open to the public, and keeps alive her spirit of scientific achievement.

See also Science and Technology.

CATHERINE CLINTON

MOLLY MAGUIRES

In the decade after the Civil War Irish-American coal miners in northeastern Pennsylvania founded a secret organization, the Molly Maguires. The name was taken from a radical organization prominent in Ireland in the 1840s, headed by a woman, one Molly Maguire. The miners' efforts to organize a union were resisted by the mine owners, who were backed by the police and local officials. The Molly Maguires eventually turned to violence, even murder, in an effort to intimidate the owners. In 1875 they managed to form a union and called a strike. The owners turned to the Pinkerton detective agency for help in breaking the strike, and the Pinkertons managed to infiltrate one of their agents, James McParlan, into the union. He revealed to the authorities the details of a number of murders and other crimes committed by the Molly Maguires. In 1877, twenty of the Mollies were convicted of murder and hanged. The secret society and the union were destroyed.

The Molly Maguire affair is an extreme example of the class conflict fairly common in late-nineteenth-century America. The rapid industrialization of the nation had produced much new wealth, but from the point of view of ordinary workers, far too much of it fell into the hands of what critics called the robber barons, the owners and managers of great corporations, most of whom had little sympathy for unions. That the Molly Maguires had just grievances is beyond dispute. That some of them were criminals is equally clear. Thus, whether they should be seen as brutal terrorists or martyred heroes of the struggle to unionize the American labor force is still a subject of debate among historians.

See also Labor Movement.

MONROE DOCTRINE

The principles of U.S. foreign policy known as the Monroe Doctrine were announced by President James Monroe in his annual message to Congress in December 1823. In making the pronouncement, Monroe was responding to two different situations.

European Nations Warned
The first concern was a threatened Russian expansion southward along the northwest coast of North America from what is now Alaska. In July 1823 Secretary of State John Quincy Adams told the Russian minister to the United States that the American continents were no longer open for any new European colonization. He indicated that the United States would oppose any Russian expansion in North America. In his message of December 2, 1823, President Monroe proclaimed that "the American continents, by the free and independent condition which they have assumed and maintain, are henceforth not to be considered as subjects for further colonization by any European power."

The second and the stronger influence on Monroe's message of 1823 was the situation in Central and South America. There the threat of European intervention to put down colonial revolts against Spanish rule was more pressing than the danger of Russian expansion in North America. In March 1822 President Monroe had announced his intention to recognize the new republics of Central and South America. Congress strongly supported the action. The people of the United States had great sympathy for the revolutionists of Latin America. They saw them as following the example of the American Revolution against British rule.

In his message to Congress, Monroe declared that the United States would regard any European intervention to suppress the newly independent states as dangerous to the peace and safety of the United States. He said that it would indicate "an unfriendly disposition toward the United States." But while warning against European intervention in the new republics of Latin America, Monroe promised that the United States would not interfere with existing European colonies in the Western Hemisphere. He also reaffirmed the policy of the United States not to become involved in the affairs of Europe.

When he made his announcement, Monroe refrained from joining Great Britain in a joint declaration against intervention in Latin America. The British had proposed that such a declaration renounce any intention of annexing territory. This would have included Cuba and Texas, which many Americans expected to become part of the United States someday.

Meanwhile, Great Britain pressured France not to intervene in Latin America to help Spain. This reduced the impact of Monroe's announcement. Interest in trade with Latin America, more than in republican government, motivated Britain.

Later Applications

The Monroe Doctrine became one of the most influential principles of American foreign policy. It was given new life in the 1840s by President James K. Polk when he reasserted the doctrine to forestall any British colonization in California. American presidents again invoked the Monroe Doctrine in the 1890s, and President Theodore Roosevelt expanded it in 1904 in "the Roosevelt Corollary."

Roosevelt's actions resulted from European threats to intervene in Latin America to collect debts owed them. In his annual message of 1904, Roosevelt announced, "We continue steadily to insist on the application of the Monroe Doctrine to the Western Hemisphere." European nations would not be permitted to use force to collect debts from Latin American nations. If intervening was necessary, the United States would be the one to do it. In other words, the United States would act as an international police power in the Western Hemisphere. Under Roosevelt's "big stick" policy, the United States took over the administration of the customs service and management of debts payments in Santo Domingo in the Caribbean.

In the 1930s President Franklin D. Roosevelt sought to change the image of the United States in Latin America created by the earlier Roosevelt Corollary to the Monroe Doctrine. He introduced a Good Neighbor policy and renounced a right to intervene in Cuban affairs that had earlier been asserted by Congress.

Following World War II the United States sought to replace the Monroe Doctrine with an inter-American system. When the United States intervened in the Dominican Republic in 1965, President Lyndon B. Johnson acted with the approval of the Organization of American States and did not invoke the Monroe Doctrine.

Under President Ronald Reagan, Secretary of Defense Caspar Weinberger redefined the Monroe Doctrine, when he declared in 1984 that "there should be no interference, no sponsorship of any kind of military activity in this hemisphere by countries in other hemispheres."

President George Bush did not invoke the Monroe Doctrine when he intervened in Panama to arrest the dictator Manuel Noriega in 1989. But the roots of his action may be traced back to 1823.

See also Good Neighbor Policy; Roosevelt Corollary.

NOBLE E. CUNNINGHAM, JR.

MONROE, JAMES

(1758–1831)   Fifth president of the United States (1817–25).

In 1776, at the age of eighteen, Monroe left the College of William and Mary in Virginia to enlist in the Continental army. He fought under George Washington in the fierce engagements of 1776 and was severely wounded at the Battle of Trenton. He spent the winter of 1777–78 at Valley Forge, and later returned home to read law under Thomas Jefferson, then governor of Virginia.

After the Revolution, Monroe served in the Continental Congress. Although he favored changes in the weak Confederation that had been set up by the Congress, he opposed ratification (approval) of the Constitution that was proposed to correct it. Monroe approved the basic structure of the new government but wanted more republican provisions, such as the direct popular election of the president and senators. He also urged that a bill of rights be added to the Constitution prior to ratification.

Monroe's opposition to the Constitution did not prevent his election to the U.S. Senate. He soon joined with Rep. James Madison in supporting Secretary of State Jefferson's opposition to Alexander Hamilton, the secretary of the treasury. He helped organize the Jeffersonian Republican Party, and when Jefferson became president, he sent Monroe to France on a mission to purchase the Louisiana territory in 1803. Later Jefferson appointed Monroe minister to Great Britain.

During the presidential election of 1808, Monroe had a falling out with Madison, but after Madison was elected, Jefferson promoted a reconciliation. In 1811 President Madison named Monroe secretary of state.

Succeeding Madison as president in 1817, Monroe served two terms. His presidency was characterized by the temporary decline of national political parties and the ill feelings and battles that went with them. The "era of good feelings," as it was called, was not without conflict, however. The issue of admitting Missouri as a slave state in 1820 ignited a controversy over slavery that threatened the existence of the Union. (Its admission would upset the balance between free and slave states.) Although settled by compromise, the crisis revealed underlying tensions between North and South that would only worsen later.

Monroe's presidency is remembered especially for the Monroe Doctrine, warning European nations to stay out of the Western Hemisphere. His policies relating to Latin America had a lasting influence on U.S. foreign policy.

See also Constitution, The Making of the; Louisiana Purchase; Revolution. *For events during Monroe's administra-*tion, see Adams-Onís Treaty; American System; Erie Canal; Missouri Compromise; Monroe Doctrine; National Road.

NOBLE E. CUNNINGHAM, JR.

MONROE, MARILYN

(1926–62)   *Movie actress.*

A strikingly beautiful woman with platinum blond hair, wide blue eyes, and a baby soft voice, Monroe was also an accomplished actress whose sexy movie star image was, and still is, idolized throughout the world.

Born to a single mother who suffered from mental illness, Monroe, originally named Norma Jean Baker, spent an unhappy childhood shuffled from orphanages to foster homes. After a failed teenage marriage, she began modeling, sometimes in the nude, and acting in poor-quality movies. Her big break came in 1950 when she appeared in the films *All About Eve* and *The Asphalt Jungle.* Soon after, she skyrocketed to fame. In 1953 she starred in *Gentlemen Prefer Blondes* and *How to Marry a Millionaire,* films that firmly established her as a "sex goddess." Her fame grew steadily thereafter.

In 1954 Monroe married baseball hero Joe DiMaggio, but the marriage ended a year later. In 1956 she married playwright Arthur Miller; they divorced in 1960. Monroe's later films included *The Seven Year Itch, Bus Stop, The Prince and the Showgirl, Some Like It Hot, Let's Make Love,* and *The Misfits.* All of them brought her critical recognition for her acting abilities as well as her beauty.

Although Monroe's movies grossed millions of dollars, and her fame surpassed that of most of her contemporaries, her personal life was far from successful. She used alcohol and drugs to dull the pain of her unhappi-

Marilyn Monroe, perhaps the most glamorous and eternally fascinating of American movie stars. Although intelligent, talented, and hard-working, she could not transcend her image as a sex goddess.

ness and loneliness. Her death, due to an overdose of sleeping pills, was ruled a possible suicide. Following her death, rumors—never confirmed—persisted about her possible romantic involvement with both President John F. Kennedy and his brother Senator Robert F. Kennedy. Many years later, innumerable books about her legend by such writers as Norman Mailer and Gloria Steinem were still being published.

See also Movies.

JOANN BIONDI

MOON LANDING
See Space Program.

MORGAN, J. P.

(1837–1913)   *Banker and art collector.*

J. P. Morgan's company was the most important force in American finance in the quarter century before World War I. In those years the American economy became the largest and most powerful in the world and corporations of national scope developed.

John Pierpont Morgan was born in Hartford, Connecticut, into a wealthy family. In 1854, his father, Junius Spencer Morgan, became a partner of George Peabody's banking house in London and took over the firm when Peabody retired, renaming it J. S. Morgan and Co.

Thus from his earliest days Morgan was exposed to two elements that were to dominate and characterize his life: international banking at the highest levels and the conviction held by his father and Peabody that personal integrity was indispensable to success in that field. Late in life Morgan was asked by a congressional committee if wealth was the basis of commercial credit. "No sir," he replied, "the first thing is character. . . . A man I do not trust could not get money from me on all the bonds in Christendom."

After completing his education at the University at Göttingen, Germany, in 1857, Morgan went to work on Wall Street. In 1862 he opened his own firm and in 1871 joined forces with the Drexel firm of Philadelphia. The new firm, Drexel, Morgan and Co., opened its offices at the corner of Wall and Broad streets, where the headquarters of the Morgan Bank have been ever since.

American railroads expanded rapidly after the Civil War, but their profitability declined as rate wars and competitive overbuilding increased. Frequent mergers and bankruptcies often gave railroads very complex corporate structures. Morgan did much to reorganize and rationalize the railroad system in the 1880s and 1890s, including the Baltimore and Ohio, the Chesapeake and Ohio, and the Erie lines, among others.

Morgan's success as a banker came from his formidable physical presence and dominating personality as well as from his expertise and creativity. He looked and acted like a man of supreme authority and wisdom, and most people took this at face value. In 1890, when his father died, he took over J. S. Morgan and Co. in London and renamed it J. P. Morgan and Company, changing the name of the New York firm as well.

He began to collect art, an interest that soon became an inspired mania. By the time of his death his collection was the largest in private hands the world has ever known and included paintings, drawings, jewelry, ceramics, sculpture, and manuscripts. Today, nearly all of Morgan's collection can be found at the Morgan Library and Metropolitan Museum in New York and at the Wadsworth Atheneum in Hartford.

As industrial companies came to dominate the American economy, it was the firm of J. P. Morgan and Company that financed many of them, including General Electric and International Harvester. In 1901 Morgan was instrumental in creating U.S. Steel, the largest corporate enterprise in the world at the time.

By the turn of the century Morgan had become the very symbol of Wall Street, the man the financial community looked to for leadership. In 1907, when a banking panic threatened to spin out of control, Morgan took command, rallied the other bankers, and restored confidence. This panic led to the creation of the Federal Reserve System in 1913, the same year Morgan died in Rome, Italy.

See also Robber Barons.

JOHN STEELE GORDON

MORMONS

In 1820 near Palmyra in western New York, a young man named Joseph Smith experienced a revelation. As he described it, "Two personages whose brightness and glory defy all description" appeared before him. "One of them spake unto me . . . and said, pointing to the other: 'This is my Beloved Son. Hear Him!'"

From this revelation has stemmed one of the largest, most active churches in the United States, the Church of Jesus Christ of Latter-day Saints, also known as the Mormon church. It now has over 4 million members and is still growing rapidly in America and many other parts of the world.

Mormon Beliefs

The term *Mormon* stems from another of Smith's revelations, this one in 1827. The angel Moroni appeared, he said, and led him to some hidden golden plates inscribed in "reformed Egyptian" hieroglyphics, as well as a set of "seer stones" that enabled him to read the plates. Smith published the translation in 1830 as the *Book of Mormon*.

The book is said to be an account of the wanderings of some people who lived in America before Columbus arrived. The Jaredites of the House of Israel left the Tower of Babel and crossed to America in remarkable barges to build great cities and civilizations. But they were ultimately destroyed in wars until only Mormon and his son, Moroni, were left. These two men buried their golden plates in the year 421. The *Book of Mormon* declares that Jesus Christ had visited the Western Hemisphere upon his ascension to heaven. After Smith translated the plates, an angel swept them away.

The *Book of Mormon* is *not* the Mormon Bible. It is looked upon as a supplement to the King James version of the Christian Bible. Latter-day Saints believe that God reveals many "great and important things" at various times. Smith is considered a prophet like

those of old, as is his successor, Brigham Young. Mormons accept most of the traditional Christian beliefs—God, Christ as his son, the Holy Trinity, the Virgin Birth, and the existence of heaven and hell. They baptize by immersion in water, confirm believers, and partake of Holy Communion, using bread and water. Religious scholars have a difficult time classifying Mormonism. It has been too long-lasting and grown too large to be called a cult, yet Mormons insist they are not Protestants.

Joseph Smith claimed that his judgment was infallible because he had had direct conversations with God. The end of the world was near, he said, and it was the duty of Mormons to found a new society, a "new Zion," that would be a proper place for the Messiah upon his return. Belief that they were a "chosen people" had tremendous appeal, and the ranks of Mormons grew rapidly. Whole Protestant congregations converted to Mormonism.

The Move Westward

Smith led the Mormons in the search for their Zion, or "New Jerusalem," first to Kirtland, Ohio, near Cleveland and then to Independence, Missouri. There they met with violence over their belief that they were a chosen people, their practice of polygamy (the Mormons permitted a man to have several wives at the same time), and their antislavery attitude. Even the governor of Missouri said that the Mormons "must be exterminated or driven out." In one grisly episode eighteen Mormon children who had hidden in a blacksmith shop were slain.

The Mormons and Smith next moved to Nauvoo on the Mississippi River in Illinois, and within five years the group had transformed a mosquito-infested bog into a pros-

A Mormon household around 1868. This family practiced polygamy, which was part of the Mormon religion at that time. The husband is seated in the doorway; his wives and children surround him.

perous town. But the harassment and violence continued. Smith and his brother Hyrum were arrested, jailed, and then murdered by a mob in 1844. His successor, Brigham Young, led the Mormons farther westward, and in 1847 they settled near the Great Salt Lake in Utah, "land nobody wanted." Now the violence took another turn. Hearing reports that a non-Mormon, or "Gentile" army was on its way to Utah to quell what the U.S. government called a "Mormon rebellion," the Mormons armed themselves and in 1857 fell on a wagon train of innocent people, massacring all but eighteen children.

Eventually the violence subsided, however, and with their strong belief in hard work, thrift, community service, education, and virtuous living (they neither smoke nor drink alcohol), the Mormons prospered, literally "making the desert bloom." But Utah was not admitted to statehood until 1896, and only after the church outlawed polygamy. A network of forty thousand volunteer missionaries, usually young people, continue to seek and gain converts, spreading the church far beyond its New Zion in Utah.

See also Smith, Joseph; Young, Brigham.

ROBERT A. LISTON

MORRILL LAND GRANT ACT

Before the Civil War there were a number of economic measures popular in the North that had been blocked by the opposition of southern congressmen. These were enacted into law after the war began.

One of these laws was the Morrill Land Grant Act of 1862. This law granted to each state thirty thousand acres of public land for each of its senators and representatives. The land was to be sold and the money invested in a "perpetual fund." The interest earned by the funds was to be used to support at least one college "where the leading object shall be . . . to teach such branches of learning as are related to agriculture and mechanic arts."

Over the years more than 17 million acres worth about $7 million were dispensed under the Morrill Act. Eastern states where public land was not available received land on the frontier. In some cases the states used the money to support existing institutions; Cornell University and the University of Michigan are outstanding examples. But more than seventy new "land grant" colleges were founded. Together they laid the basis for higher education throughout the Midwest and West.

In addition to teaching courses in such subjects as agricultural methods, home economics, and engineering, and stimulating agricultural research, all these institutions also offered regular academic subjects. And (perhaps because the law was passed in wartime) all were required to provide work on "military tactics." This led eventually to the establishment of the Reserve Officers' Training Corps (ROTC).

See also Education: Universities and Colleges.

MORRIS, ROBERT

(1734–1806)   *Financier of the American Revolution.*

Morris (no relation to the politically powerful Morris family of New York) made his fortune as a merchant in Philadelphia. He came late to revolutionary politics, supporting the Patriot cause only after the Battles of Lexington and Concord in 1775. He soon rose to prominence and was a member of the Pennsylvania delegation to the Second Continental Congress. Although he hesitated to sign the Declaration of Independence until late in the summer of 1776, he was a useful member of the infant government of the United States.

Morris used his connections as a merchant to obtain military supplies for the Continental army. He worked hard for the country but made sure that he, as the middleman of these transactions, earned some profit as well. His political enemies made much of this, and Morris, denying any wrongdoing, opened his books for inspection. But the mere appearance of improperly mixing public and private good led to his defeat in the congressional election of 1779.

After returning to the Pennsylvania Assembly in 1780, Morris became superintendent of finance for the United States in 1781. The government at the time needed new loans to carry on the war, but had no revenue to pay off the old ones. After the war ended, Morris resigned in 1784 because he could do nothing either to reduce the national debt or to guarantee that the country would have the means of paying it. His frustrations with the government established by the Articles of Confederation made him a natural political ally of Alexander Hamilton and the Federalists.

Sad to say, Morris died in poverty. He invested in western lands in the 1790s and went bankrupt when their value fell sharply. After a time in debtors' prison, he finished his days in obscurity.

See also Continental Congresses; Federalist Party; Revolution.

THOMAS COLE

MORRISON, TONI

(1931–)   *Novelist.*

Morrison grew up in a lively working-class neighborhood in Loraine, Ohio. She credits her parents and grandparents with giving her a passionate appreciation for African-American history and culture. Her childhood was filled with the black songs, ghost stories, and superstitious lore found in her fiction.

Although she is one of America's premiere novelists, Morrison didn't become a published writer until she was almost forty years old. She was working as an editor at Random House when she published *The Bluest Eye*. It is the story of Pecola Breedlove, a young black girl who longs for blue eyes. Pecola thinks that since everyone considers Shirley Temple to be an ideal little girl, her own blackness makes her ugly and unlovable. Morrison's next novel, *Sula*, focuses on the complex relationship between two black women. Both books helped establish Morrison as a powerful writer, but it was her third novel, *Song of Solomon*, that made her famous. The story of Milkman Dead searching for his cultural roots, struck a resonant chord with the reading public, and it won the National Book Critics Circle Award. In 1981 with much promotional fanfare, Morrison published the best-seller *Tar Baby*. A love story

Toni Morrison, winner of the 1993 Nobel Prize in Literature, remarked that fiction "should have something in it that enlightens; something in it that opens the door and points the way. Something in it that suggests what the conflicts are, what the problems are. But it need not solve these problems because it is not a case study, it is not a recipe."

set in the Caribbean, it is full of allusions to African-American folklore.

Most critics consider Morrison's Pulitzer Prize–winning fifth novel, *Beloved*, to be her finest book so far. The main character, Sethe, an escaped slave woman, is haunted by the ghost of the infant daughter she murdered years ago. Sethe felt that death was better for the child than a misery-filled life as a slave. Morrison powerfully evokes the cruelty of slavery that led Sethe to this horrible decision. Morrison's most recent book, *Jazz*, conjures up the passionate world of Harlem's jazz generation.

In 1984 Toni Morrison left her editing job at Random House after fostering the careers of many prominent black writers. She currently teaches college English courses and, through her fiction, continues to spellbind readers all over the world. In 1993, she won the Nobel Prize for literature.

See also Literature.

LAURIE LINDOP

MORSE, SAMUEL F. B.

(1791–1872)   *Artist, nativist, and inventor of the telegraph.*

Morse grew up in Massachusetts, the son of a Protestant minister, and studied painting in England. He returned to the United States in 1815 hoping to interest Americans in his paintings of historical subjects. But there was little demand in America for history painting, and he turned reluctantly to portraits. Although many of Morse's works are now admired, few Americans bought his work and he was often close to poverty.

During a visit to Rome in 1829, a soldier knocked Morse down when he failed to kneel before a Catholic procession. This created in him an intense hatred of Catholics. When Morse returned to the United States, he wrote a series of newspaper articles charging that the Catholic nations of Europe sought to overthrow American democracy by sending Catholic immigrants to take control of the country. Morse's articles helped create an anti-immigrant movement that would persist for generations.

Morse's 1829 voyage to Europe also led to his invention of the electric telegraph. Dur-

Samuel F. B. Morse at age seventy-five. He was a painter and inventor whose great achievement was the invention of the telegraph. The first words he transmitted on the telegraph were "What hath God wrought!" He also had a significant influence on American photography, teaching Mathew Brady and others the daguerreotype process. Brady (or one of his assistants) honored his teacher in return by taking this photograph of him.

ing his trip home, Morse talked to a scientist who convinced him that electrical current could be used for communication. Morse abandoned his artistic career and devoted his full attention to the project. Once he had perfected the telegraph, Morse persuaded Congress to finance construction of a line from Washington to Baltimore, and on May 24, 1844, he sent the first message: "What hath God wrought!" A decade after the first line opened, twenty-three thousand miles of telegraph cable crisscrossed the country, revolutionizing communications.

At his death, few remembered Morse for anything but the telegraph. But his contributions to American art, politics, and science made him one of the more versatile figures in the nation's history.

See also Nativism; Painting and Sculpture; Science and Technology.

TYLER ANBINDER

MOTHER JONES
See Jones, Mary Harris (Mother Jones).

MOTT, LUCRETIA

(1793–1880)   *Quaker minister, abolitionist, and women's rights activist.*

Growing up on the island of Nantucket, Massachusetts, Lucretia Coffin could not help but notice that the women in her mother's generation were strong, responsible, independent women who raised their families, took care of day-to-day matters, and often ran small businesses as well. Nantucket was a whaling community, and most men, like her father, Thomas Coffin, a sea captain in the China trade, were away for months or years at a time. Lucretia's mother, Anna, ran a shop and still managed to care for her seven children. Thus, Lucretia grew up aware of women's abilities and unwilling to accept the inequalities that implied they were weak or incompetent.

The road that led to her later career as a women's rights activist wound first through some years as a teacher, minister, and ardent abolitionist. In 1811, Lucretia married James Mott, a fellow teacher who later became a

manufacturer. Throughout their long marriage, James consistently supported Lucretia in all her endeavors, often traveling with her as she toured the country speaking on behalf of abolitionism and women's rights. The Motts had six children. When their first son, Thomas, died in 1817, Lucretia turned to her Quaker religion for solace and in time, became a minister.

Long before she met the famed abolitionist William Lloyd Garrison in 1831, Mott had come to the conclusion that slavery was wrong. She began working with Garrison, and it was, ironically, through her work as an abolitionist that she finally turned to the issue of women's rights as a full-time pursuit. In 1840, Mott traveled to London with the American Anti-Slavery Society, only to discover that women abolitionists were not allowed in the main meeting hall. To be discriminated against by other abolitionists profoundly affected her.

In 1848, Mott and fellow abolitionist Elizabeth Cady Stanton, with whom she had become friends in London, organized the first Women's Rights Convention in Seneca Falls, New York. The document issued by the convention, a Declaration of the Rights of Women, patterned after the Declaration of Independence, listed the group's goals. Mott continued the struggle afterward, making hundreds of speeches and publishing a book, *Discourse on Women,* in 1850, which called for women's suffrage and equal educational and economic opportunities.

In 1864, Mott was a cofounder of Swarthmore College, a coeducational institution. She worked for black suffrage after the Civil War and was elected head of the American Equal Rights Association in 1866. Often called upon to act as peacemaker when her fellow activists quarreled over methods or goals (a not infrequent occurrence), Mott worked unstintingly until her death in 1880 for the reforms she believed in.

See also Abolitionist Movement; Feminist Movement to 1919; Seneca Falls Convention.

CHRISTINE A. LUNARDINI

MOVIES

The exact birthday and birthplace of the movies are unclear. Some say the art form began in New Jersey in 1888 with Thomas A. Edison's invention of the Kinetograph and the Kinetoscope, forerunners of the motion picture camera and projector. Others credit the Lumière brothers, who first presented movies to a paying audience in the basement of a Paris café in 1895. In any case, many pioneers in Europe and the United States contributed to the emergence of the motion picture industry at the turn of the century.

The earliest films were less than a minute long and showed scenes of real life. The effect

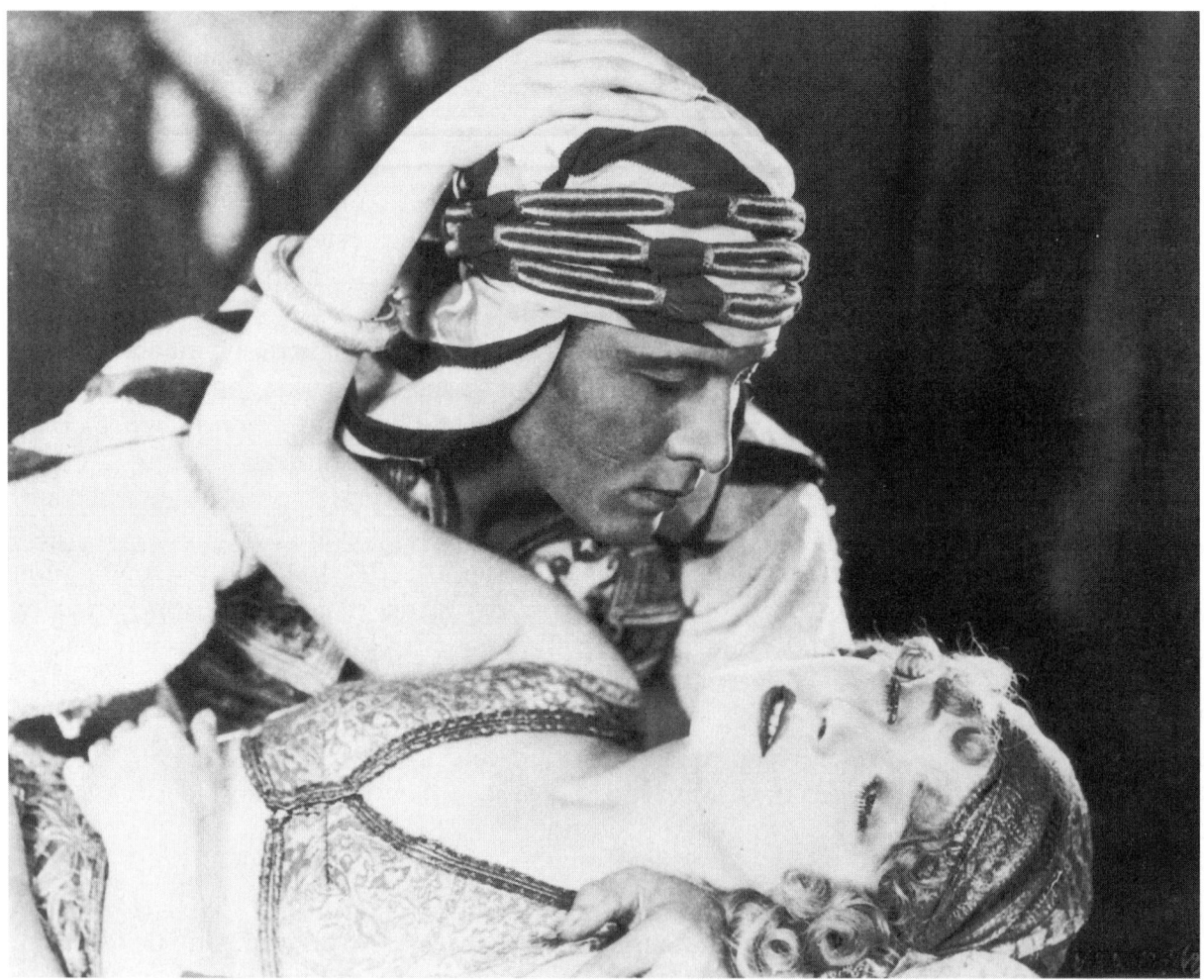

Rudolph Valentino, silent film star, in his typical role as a romantic desert sheik.

was sensational. Edison's first film was of a sneeze, and the audience marveled at it. A scene showing two people kissing nearly caused a riot, and when a locomotive flickered across the screen in 1896, the viewers screamed in terror. Soon the possibilities for storytelling in the new medium became apparent. In France, Georges Méliès, a stage magician, created the first science-fiction movie, *A Trip to the Moon,* in 1902. The next year *The Great Train Robbery,* made by Edwin S. Porter for the Edison Company in New York, had a fully developed plot with bandits, a chase scene, and a climactic shoot-out.

Edison, the first leader of the industry, fought to protect his patent rights. (A patent gives an inventor the exclusive right to an in-vention. Anyone who wants to use it must pay the inventor a fee.) When such rival companies as Vitagraph and Biograph formed in competition, he sued them, setting off a ten-year period of court battles. The so-called patent wars lasted from 1898 to 1908, when the nine biggest studios merged to form a monopoly called the Motion Picture Patents Company.

The Growth of Movies

After the breaking up of the monopoly by the courts a few years later, independent producers flourished. Programs of five or six one-reel films, lasting about ten minutes each, were shown in theaters called nickelodeons (they cost a nickel to get in) all over the coun-

Charlie Chaplin, wedged in the gears of a machine in a famous scene from Modern Times *(1936).*

try. Longer features followed, and splendid "picture palaces" were built to show them. D. W. Griffith's three-hour Civil War epic *Birth of a Nation* (1915) used many of the motion picture techniques employed today. Film comedy was developed at the same time by such early masters as Buster Keaton and Charlie Chaplin. Other stars such as Douglas Fairbanks and Mary Pickford became idolized by moviegoers.

The power of movies to influence thought and behavior as well as to entertain became evident during World War I. Producers turned out many patriotic films to support the war effort (nearly two hundred between 1914 and 1918), and movies became a major medium of propaganda. The number of motion picture theaters in the United States grew from ten thousand in 1910 to over twenty thousand in 1920. Movie fan magazines sprang up, beginning with *Photoplay* in 1912. During that decade, the industry moved westward, establishing its headquarters in Hollywood, California, with the founding there of the leading production companies, Fox, Paramount, and Universal.

The growing influence of the movies began to raise moral issues in the 1920s. The sometimes scandalous personal lives of the stars and the themes of crime and sex in the films aroused public protest. In 1922 the major studios hired Will G. Hays, the U.S. postmaster-general, to establish moral standards for the industry. Hays created a code forbidding films to show sexually explicit scenes, glorify crime, or use obscene language. The Hays Code, accepted by the industry in 1934, continued in force until 1968, when it was replaced by the present system of rating films G, PG, PG-13, R, and NC-17 (originally X) to indicate the maturity level of the audience.

The need for self-censorship in motion pictures was partly a result of the increasing technical sophistication of the medium. The 1920s saw the arrival of sound in films. In the Warner Brothers production *The Jazz Singer* (1927), phonograph disks were synchronized with the action to allow the star Al Jolson to sing and speak a few lines of dialogue. The following year Warner produced the first complete "talkie," *Lights of New York,* and a system of creating a soundtrack as part of the film itself was soon developed. By 1930 the era of the silent film was over.

The 1930s became the Golden Age of Hollywood movies. The stock market crash of 1929 and the Great Depression that followed created a need for escapist mass entertainment, and such glamorous stars as Greta Garbo, Marlene Dietrich, Bette Davis, Cary Grant, Gary Cooper, and Clark Gable provid-

Orson Welles starred in and directed Citizen Kane *(1941), one of the all-time masterpieces of film.*

ed it. Hollywood films were popular all over the world and created the international image of what America was like. Nevertheless, the hard times hurt the industry, and ticket sales fell during the decade. It was not until the Second World War that motion picture audiences returned to their former size.

Hollywood's Decline

Although the public was starved for entertainment at the end of the war in 1945, the profits of the U.S. motion picture industry began to decline. There were several reasons for this. Other countries began to provide serious competition, with excellent films coming in from Italy, England, Sweden, and Japan. During the postwar red scare, the House of Representatives Committee on Un-American Activities held hearings from 1948 to 1954, charging that Communists had infiltrated the industry. As a result, much of Hollywood's best talent was blacklisted and prevented from working. European countries, to help their own film industries, passed quota laws against importing American movies.

But the greatest blow to industry profits was the rise of television. Movie attendance fell from an all-time peak of nearly 100 million tickets a week in 1946 to below 20 million in 1968. Hollywood tried everything to win its audience back. It offered 3-D, stereophonic sound, Smell-O-Vision (with various odors released from theater seats), and wider screens. It also offered a greater range of subjects and styles to appeal to a new, better educated public. Nothing succeeded. Making a film became so costly (in 1992 it averaged nearly $20 million) that studios became increasingly reluctant to make any that did not conform to a safe formula guaranteed to appeal to a huge audience. Competition from television and videocassettes increasingly un-

dermined the theater market. In 1992, ticket sales hit a twelve-year low, down for the fourth year in a row.

The industry is still vital, however, as it enters its second century. Its technical range expands yearly, with digital technology providing new special effects unimagined a few years ago. And although television and the VCR have taken much of the audience from movie theaters, most of the material produced for those media comes from motion picture studios. Movies have progressed in a relatively few years from the crude novelty seen in nickelodeons to a highly sophisticated art form, probably the most influential one our society has ever seen.

See also Astaire, Fred; Chaplin, Charlie; DeMille, Cecil B.; Disney, Walt; Edison, Thomas A.; Griffith, D. W.; Mayer, Louis B.; Monroe, Marilyn; Sinatra, Frank; Wayne, John; Welles, Orson.

For further reading: Nigel Hunter, *Movies* (Madison, N.J.: Raintree Steck-Vaughan, 1990).

DENNIS WEPMAN

MUCKRAKERS

In the early twentieth century, a group of journalists concentrated on exposing the corruption and greed they saw everywhere in American society. They were nicknamed *muckrakers* by President Theodore Roosevelt, who borrowed the term from English writer John Bunyan's book, *Pilgrim's Progress*. The book included a character with a "muck-rake in his hand" who would rather rake the filth at his feet than look upward toward the more noble things in life. Roosevelt recognized the muckrakers' beneficial role in pointing out the need for reform, but he did not want them to go too far in "raking the muck," and thereby stirring up dissatisfaction among the public. Roosevelt meant *muckrakers* as a derogatory name, but instead it became a term of pride among journalists and their readers who felt that there was an enormous amount of muck in American society that badly needed to be cleaned up.

Most of the muckrakers' articles focused on business and political corruption, such as Ida Tarbell's series on the Standard Oil Company that exposed the greed of big business, Lincoln Steffens's investigations of scandals in city and state politics, and Upton Sinclair's exposé of unhealthy practices in the meat-packing industry. Other subjects examined by the muckrakers included the exploitation of child labor, slum conditions, and racial discrimination. From 1902 to 1912, over a thousand such articles were published. They heightened moral indignation among middle-class Americans over the corruption of big business and politicians, and contributed to the progressive reform movement that swept America in the early part of the century.

See also Jungle, The; Magazines and Newspapers; Steffens, Lincoln.

MUGWUMPS

The mugwumps were a group of Republicans in the late nineteenth century who were unhappy with the leaders of their party, whom they considered political hacks. Since most mugwumps lived in large eastern and midwestern cities such as Boston, New York, and Chicago, they were also alarmed by the corruption of big-city political machines. They particularly disliked the spoils system of awarding government jobs to faithful party workers without regard for their abilities. They were given the name "mugwump" (an old slang word for "kingpin" or "Indian chief") in 1884 when they refused to support the Republican presidential candidate, James G. Blaine. He had been involved in a scandal involving improper use of political influence, and, as a biographer put it, he "became wealthy without visible means of income." Instead the mugwumps supported the Democratic candidate, Grover Cleveland.

Since many mugwumps were what would today be called "opinion makers," and since the election was extremely close, they may well have supplied the votes that gave the victory to Cleveland. A shift of only six hundred votes in New York State, for example, would have given the state's electoral votes to Blaine and with it the presidency.

The mugwumps were never an organized political group, and very few of them were ever politicians or officeholders. Most Republican politicians who opposed Blaine's nomination nevertheless voted for him because of party loyalty.

MUÑOZ MARÍN, LUIS

(1898–1980)   *Governor of Puerto Rico (1948–64) and writer.*

Muñoz Marín inherited the mantle of fame from his father, Luis Muñoz Rivera, who was known as the "George Washington of Puerto Rico." He had secured self-rule from Spain in 1896, and after Puerto Rico was annexed by the United States following the Spanish-American War in 1898, he helped pass the 1917 Jones Act in the American Congress that gave Puerto Ricans U.S. citizenship.

Since Marín's father was U.S. resident commissioner to Congress in the early 1900s, Luis grew up in New York and Washington, D.C. Immersed in U.S. culture, Puerto Rican politics, and Puerto Rican ideas, Marín reflected the central dilemmas of Puerto Ricans in his life: the questions of dual identity and of independence.

As a young man, Marín lived for a while in New York's Greenwich Village where he wrote poetry, articles, and essays and founded a literary journal, achieving intellectual recognition in Latin America and the United States. In 1931, he returned with his family to Puerto Rico. He quickly entered politics and was elected to the territorial senate.

Marín became good friends with President Franklin D. Roosevelt, who at Marín's urging established the Puerto Rico Reconstruction

Puerto Rican governor Luis Muñoz Marín at a press conference in Washington, D.C., in 1954. He had led the campaign for Puerto Rican self-government, which had been achieved two years earlier, in 1952.

Administration to lay the base for the island's economic revolution. In 1938 he founded the Popular Democratic Party aimed at achieving progressive measures in a country where politics had always benefited the rich. Through his political and intellectual work, Marín learned that he could be both American and Puerto Rican, be at the center of power and still stay close to the base of power—the people.

Consequently, from 1940 through 1964, he was a central political figure in Puerto Rico. In 1940, he was instrumental in passing twenty-two New Deal–like bills aimed at changing the lives of Puerto Ricans dramatically. After fighting for an amendment to the Jones Act allowing Puerto Ricans to elect their own governor and giving women the right to vote, he became the first elected governor of Puerto Rico in 1948. In 1952, under his leadership, the people of the island voted overwhelmingly to approve a measure granting Puerto Rico commonwealth status, a relationship similar to Canada's relationship with Great Britain.

During his years of leadership, Marín turned Puerto Rico from the "poorhouse of the Caribbean" into the "economic showcase of the Caribbean."

See also Puerto Rico, Acquisition of.

RICHARD A. GARCIA

MURROW, EDWARD R.

(1908–65) *Broadcast journalist.*

"This . . . is London." With these words the newscaster Edward R. Murrow began his broadcasts to the United States from war-torn London in 1940 and 1941. In the background listeners could hear the thudding of bombs and the fearful wailing of sirens. Murrow delivered his broadcasts standing on the roof of a London office building while German bombers pounded the city. He was one of the first radio newsmen to make dramatic on-the-scene reports from the battlefronts, bringing the sights and sounds of war directly into people's homes. President Franklin D. Roosevelt said of his World War II service, "Ed Murrow has lived in the war since its beginning [and] . . . has kept faith with the truth-loving people of the world."

Murrow was born near Greensboro, North Carolina, and graduated from the State College of Washington. He joined the Columbia Broadcasting System (CBS) in 1935. After the war he continued delivering the news for radio networks and soon branched into television. His radio program "Hear It Now" appeared on television as "See It Now" in 1951. From 1953 to 1960 he hosted a popular interview show called "Person to Person."

Murrow stirred the conscience of the nation with two memorable television reports. In a 1954 "See It Now" segment he attacked Joseph R. McCarthy, a U.S. senator who grabbed headlines by wildly accusing prominent Americans of being Communists. In 1960 he produced a documentary called "Harvest of Shame," which revealed the miserable conditions suffered by American migrant farm workers.

In 1961 President John F. Kennedy appointed Murrow to head the U.S. Information Agency, a position he held until 1964, a year before his death. Murrow, a heavy smoker who was usually seen on television puffing a cigarette, died of lung cancer at age fifty-seven. He was the most famous newscaster of his era. Reporter Les Brown of the *New York Times* called him "broadcasting's supreme journalist, whose verbal gifts and superb de-

livery were matched by his humaneness and high professional standards."

See also Radio and Television

R. CONRAD STEIN

MUSEUMS
See Libraries and Museums.

MUSIC

In the United States, a variety of musical styles have been created from Native American, European, African, Asian, and Caribbean influences. The Spanish explorers and settlers in the sixteenth century heard the music of Native Americans in the Caribbean region. The Spanish did not always understand what they were hearing, and they sometimes described this music as "savage." Nevertheless, their writings tell us that music was an important part of everyday life in the New World.

Early American Music
In the seventeenth century, English settlers brought religious music with them in the form of psalms, poems of praise from the Old Testament. Unlike the Anglican settlers who became the planter elite of the southern colonies, the New Englanders viewed their music not as art but as a part of religious life. For the Puritans who wanted to keep their worship free of the ceremony of the Church of England, the words of the psalms were more important than the melodies. Worshipers chanted the psalms rather than actually singing them. But over time, it became difficult to

remember the chants, and, by the beginning of the eighteenth century, some ministers encouraged the writing of religious music and the teaching of musical notation in singing schools. These schools were forerunners of New England choral societies that sang both religious and secular music. Musical instruments remained forbidden in Congregational churches until the nineteenth century.

Americans expressed their feelings about the Revolution in song as well as in pamphlets and cartoons. When British soldiers taunted Americans with a song, the colonials used the same melody with new words to mock the British in turn. Thus, "Yankee Doodle" was born. William Billings, a Boston tanner, wrote an anthem, "Chester," that declared that New Englanders would never submit to British tyranny.

After the Revolution, musical life thrived in cities, as prohibitions against instrumental music in churches were relaxed. Many immigrant musicians, such as Johann Christian Gottlieb Graupner in Boston, composed, performed, taught, and published music. He helped found the Handel and Haydn Society in Boston in 1815. This group is still active.

Outside the large cities, musical activity continued to be centered in churches, and composers wrote religious music for local audiences. But in spite of their popularity in New England, many reformers thought that popular expressions of enthusiastic religious feeling were undignified. They argued that only the "best" European music could inspire true devotional feeling.

In the early nineteenth century, composers and promoters of American music wanted their country to have a music of its own. But they did not have a clear idea of what such music should sound like. Their works often reminded listeners of music written in Eu-

rope. Only occasionally did a composer incorporate the folk or popular music of his own country into music for the concert hall.

Folk Traditions

Nevertheless, there were many folk and popular traditions that contributed to the American musical mosaic. Native Americans used music in their religion and in preparation for war. African Americans, most of whom lived in slavery, created a music that was rooted in the African tradition of call and response singing in which a leader told a story and the rest of the singers sang a chorus. The spread of Christianity among slaves contributed to the creation of spirituals that mixed biblical images with the idea of freedom. On many plantations, there were song leaders, fiddlers, and banjo players who were extraordinary performers, but their music was almost never considered an art or their music making an occupation.

Among white settlers, music was used to chronicle the events of family and community, and story-telling ballads from England were passed down from generation to generation. Cowboys sang to pass the time, and immigrants brought their songs and dances with them. In most cases, writers about music ignored these songs because they thought they were inferior to European concert music.

The Late 1800s

The Civil War saw an increase in musical creativity. There were songs about Abraham Lincoln, popular generals, famous battles, and mothers and sweethearts left behind. Songs by composers like Stephen Foster reached middle-class households as the publication of piano-vocal sheet music became an important business. Foster's "Jeanie with the Light Brown Hair" found a place next to the hymnbooks on the upright piano in many households. Minstrel shows also provided popular entertainment, with the players, both black and white, performing in black face in traveling troupes. The most famous song to come from the minstrel shows was "Dixie," written by Dan Emmett, a performer from Ohio.

The growth of the United States as an economic power after the Civil War generated capital that could be invested in culture. The first symphony orchestra, the New York Philharmonic (founded in 1842) was joined by the New York Symphony in 1878, the Boston Symphony in 1881, the Chicago Symphony in 1891, and the Philadelphia Orchestra in 1900. During these years the United States celebrated democracy and progress with massive events that included music. In 1869, Boston bandmaster Patrick Sarsfield Gilmore staged the Great National Peace Jubilee and Music Festival, which attracted President Ulysses S. Grant, a huge orchestra and chorus, and bells and cannon firing live ammunition triggered by a switch at the conductor's podium. American accomplishment was the theme of the Philadelphia Centennial Exhibition of 1876, which featured a "Centennial Hymn" composed by John Knowles Paine, the most respected concert music composer of his day and the first professor of music at Harvard University.

As much as cultural reformers encouraged Americans to listen to classical European music, popular music could not be ignored. Workers in the labor movement used familiar songs to create new music. The Industrial Workers of the World published *The Little Red Song Book* that included songs by and about Joe Hill, a famous leader of the organization.

Birth of Blues, Jazz

African-American music had distinct country and city flavors. In the country, it took the form of work songs, field hollers, spirituals, and songs that were the forerunners of the blues. The main instrument of the blues was the human voice, which could be imitated by a guitar or harmonica, both of which could play pitches that fell in between those of Western musical scales. These came to be called "blue" notes. In cities such as New Orleans, black marching bands performed the syncopated (off the beat) rhythms of early jazz at funerals and festivals such as Mardi Gras. Composers Scott Joplin and Charles Lamb wrote popular piano pieces, and the cakewalk, a dance performed to music in "ragged time," was all the rage in black neighborhoods.

Early in the twentieth century, the center of jazz shifted from New Orleans to Chicago, Kansas City, and New York. Groups such as Jelly Roll Morton's Red Hot Peppers and King Oliver's Creole Jazz Band, which included the young Louis Armstrong, recorded in a style that included improvisation by all the players at once.

Twentieth-Century Changes

In elite musical circles, World War I sparked a debate over culture versus patriotism. For many critics, the best music was presumed to come from Germany. But patriotism demanded "one hundred percent Americanism," and in some cities this meant that orchestras could play little or no German music, though most of the music on orchestral programs, most of the conductors, and most of the players were German. Boston Symphony conductor Karl Muck was deported to Germany because he was suspected of disloyalty. But the war did provide an opportunity for orchestras to play more music by American composers.

After World War I, American and European composers took an active interest in jazz and incorporated some of its sounds into their compositions. In 1924, the Paul Whiteman Orchestra in New York performed George Gershwin's "Rhapsody in Blue," an example of what came to be called "symphonic jazz." Other composers, such as Jerome Kern, Irving Berlin, and Sigmund Romberg, wrote popular songs and scores for the musical theater.

In the 1920s, the popularity of jazz increased, and the blues singing of Mamie Smith, Ma Rainey, Bessie Smith, and other black female artists was preserved on so-called race records, as was the stride piano playing of James P. Johnson and the boogie-woogie of such performers as Pine Top Smith. In addition to early recordings, radio brought music into millions of homes.

The 1930s and 1940s was the age of swing. Orchestras under Fletcher Henderson, Benny Goodman, Duke Ellington, and many others played carefully arranged compositions that featured improvisation only in the solos. Frank Sinatra, Sarah Vaughan, Ella Fitzgerald, and others were popular singers. During World War II, orchestra leader Glenn Miller toured with his Army Air Force Band, and entertained the troops until his death in a plane crash.

During the Depression and the war, many songwriters developed an interest in the history of the American people. Folk singers Woody Guthrie and Huddie Ledbetter ("Leadbelly") created songs that talked about hard times and the need to fight fascism. In the concert hall, composers such as Aaron Copland incorporated everyday tunes into symphonic pieces with titles like *Billy the Kid,*

Rodeo, and *Appalachian Spring.* The music of the cowboy, the blues, and songs of workers' conflicts found their way into concert works that sounded identifiably American.

After World War II, many composers experimented with new sounds, some of which critics said were not "music" at all. Harry Partch invented instruments to create sounds that could not be made by traditional ones. John Cage organized notes and rhythm patterns randomly and even created a musical work with nothing but silence! Electronic music composers Mario Davidofsky and Vladimir Ussachevsky created music in synthesizers and made the stop watch and tape recorder part of musical performances. Synthesized sound has become part of everyday life, from rock concerts to commercials. In the concert hall, Leonard Bernstein brought classical music to millions on television in his Young People's Concerts, and Pierre Boulez programmed more challenging modern music.

New Jazz and Rock

As swing bands grew bigger and less creative, young musicians grew bored with the form. A number of black musicians created be-bop, the best-known performers being Charlie Parker, Dizzy Gillespie, Max Roach, and Curly Russell. In the early 1950s, a new group including Miles Davis and Thelonious Monk introduced "cool" jazz, which was quieter and more detached. And then rock 'n' roll emerged.

Rock music grew out of blues and African-American music. It was young people's music, its lyrics often expressing rebellion against parents, schools, and other voices of authority. Performers like Elvis Presley in the 1950s and Jim Morrison a decade later were popular as much for their rebellious images as for their music. Teenagers listened to rock on the radio, on records, and in live concerts that grew in size and scope to become major events. In spite of its detractors, rock has remained a constantly changing aspect of American and international musical culture.

Starting in the early 1960s, Americans heard cover versions of songs by Chuck Berry and other blues and rock artists performed by a group from Liverpool, England. These records were similar to many that teenagers had enjoyed for nearly a decade. Soon, however, the Beatles began performing their own music, much of it composed by John Lennon and Paul McCartney, and the "British invasion" in music, fashion, and style was under way. Along with the Rolling Stones, the Dave Clark Five, and other groups, the Beatles took this country by storm. To their sounds were added those of American groups like the Byrds and performers Janis Joplin and Jimi Hendrix who redefined musical virtuosity. For a brief period rock and folk music were part of a culture of protest. The civil rights, anti–Vietnam War, and feminist movements inspired their own songs. The social commentary of Bob Dylan, Joan Baez, Pete Seeger, Tom Paxton, and James Brown addressed issues important to many people.

The 1970s and 1980s saw the emergence of musical minimalism, a style that relies extensively on repetition. Philip Glass and Steve Reich are major minimalist composers. They and performance artists such as Laurie Anderson perform and record music that blurs generic boundaries. Often called "crossover" music, it sometimes uses the instruments and tonal effects of Tibetan and Japanese cultures.

American music reaches small audiences on college campuses, millions of fans in festivals or on the radio, and almost everyone in the supermarket. Efforts to censor and label popular music reflect a continuing debate over what is proper in art. Central to this debate is the realization that music is important and that what we hear can affect what we think and who we are.

See also Blues; Country Music; Jazz; Rock Music. *And see biographies of the following composers, musicians, and singers:* Anderson, Marian; Armstrong, Louis; Berlin, Irving; Bernstein, Leonard; Berry, Chuck; Copland, Aaron; Dylan, Bob; Ellington, Duke; Fitzgerald, Ella; Gershwin, George; Goodman, Benny; Guthrie, Woody; Porter, Cole; Presley, Elvis; Robeson, Paul; Sinatra, Frank.

BARBARA L. TISCHLER

N

NAACP

See National Association for the Advancement of Colored People.

NADER, RALPH

(1934–   )   *Consumer activist.*

Nader is one of the few Americans credited with inventing an entire social movement. He has been so effective, and the citizens' movement he founded so strong, that many believe Nader has made a more powerful impact on American life than some presidents.

Reared in Connecticut by immigrant parents, Nader graduated from Princeton University and Harvard Law School. In 1963, at the age of twenty-nine, he left his private law practice, packed one suitcase, and hitchhiked to Washington, D.C.

Upon checking into the Y M C A , Nader "walked across the street and had a hot dog, my last." After researching what was in that hot dog, he began a campaign against the meat-packing industry. He then founded what would become one of the most influential political forces in American history—a nationwide movement for consumer rights.

In 1965 Nader wrote *Unsafe at Any Speed*, attacking General Motors for producing the Corvair automobile, which Nader said was dangerously flawed. The company fought back by spying on Nader's personal life, hop-

Ralph Nader in 1979 demanding that General Motors fix safety defects in some of its cars. Nader, with the help of volunteers called "Nader's Raiders," has led reform efforts ranging from environmental issues and auto safety concerns to the rights of the disabled, insurance regulation, tax reform, and public health measures.

ing to discredit him, but found nothing. When this came out, GM's embarrassing public apology made Nader a national hero. Soon young "Nader's Raiders" began crusading for auto safety, environmental protections, an end to nuclear power, rights for the disabled, public health care, tax reform, and, especially, citizen control of government.

Having outlasted six presidencies and a dozen Congresses, Nader says, "The essence of the citizens' movement is persistence." Over the decades he has helped pass dozens of consumer safety and environmental protection laws. But his key legacy may be the belief that ordinary people can—and must—make a difference.

"The most important office in America for anyone to achieve is full-time citizen," he says. Nader has virtually defined that most exalted position.

HARVEY WASSERMAN

NARCOTICS
See Drugs.

NAST, THOMAS

(1840–1902)   *Political cartoonist and illustrator.*

Regarded as the father of American political cartooning, Nast was a skillful artist and a vigorous commentator on the affairs of his time. His work influenced both public opinion and the art of editorial cartooning.

Nast is credited with bringing about important political reforms through his caricatures of public figures and his biting satire. Some of his images have become established in the American imagination. He invented the elephant used to represent the Republican Party, popularized the emblem of the donkey for the Democrats, created the modern form of Uncle Sam, and first drew the jolly rotund figure we know as Santa Claus.

Born in Germany, Nast came to the United States when he was six. He attended public

Thomas Nast was among the most influential political cartoonists in American history. Among his many memorable images is his invention of Uncle Sam as a symbol of America. He is seen here disgruntled and riding on the back of "Congress," which is moving at a snail's pace on the issues before it. Other cartoons by Nast are featured on pp. 87, 126, 395, 702, and 829.

schools and the American Academy of Design in New York City. At the age of fifteen he got a job as a staff artist with *Frank Leslie's Illustrated News.* In 1862 he was hired by *Harper's Weekly* to draw scenes of the Civil War. At *Harper's* he increasingly turned from news illustration to cartooning, and his work was so effective that Abraham Lincoln called him "our best recruiting sergeant."

Nast was a moralist who supported the values of the American family and crusaded against alcohol abuse. He attacked political graft as well as discrimination against African

Americans, Native Americans, and Chinese. His scathing cartoons published from 1859 to 1861 were influential in bringing down the corrupt Democratic Party organization under "Boss" Tweed in New York City.

Nast's cartoons were woodblock engravings, and the introduction of photographic reproduction in the 1880s made his technique obsolete. His popularity diminished, and he lost his money through bad investments. President Theodore Roosevelt, a long-time fan of his, gave him a job as consul to Ecuador in 1902, but the tropical climate and unsanitary conditions of that country were too much for the sixty-two-year-old cartoonist. He died of yellow fever there shortly after his arrival.

DENNIS WEPMAN

NATION, CARRY

(1846–1911)   *Radical temperance advocate.*

Carry Moore was born in Gerrard County, Kentucky, the oldest of six children. Her mother, who was mentally ill for many years, had unpredictable mood swings. At times she smothered Carry with affection; at other times she turned on her in fits of violence. Throughout her troubled childhood, Carry found solace in her deep Christian faith.

When she was twenty Carry married Dr. Charles Gloyd, who had boarded in the Moore household. Within two years he died of severe alcoholism; his death was to have a profound impact on Carry's life. After teaching for four years in Missouri, she married David Nation, who worked off and on as a lawyer, newspaper editor, and minister. The marriage was not a happy one, and the Nations moved frequently as David drifted from job to job.

In 1889 the Nations settled in Medicine Lodge, Kansas, where Carry joined the Woman's Christian Temperance Union (WCTU). Convinced that drink caused most of society's ills, she visited local saloons, where she prayed, sang hymns, and begged the patrons to give up alcoholic spirits. When these efforts failed, she resorted to more direct methods. Wielding a brick or hatchet, she would enter a tavern and smash the tables, chairs, and bar to pieces. These "hatchetations," as she called them, closed dozens of Kansas saloons.

Carry Nation made sensational news in the press, and her reputation swept the country. At times she was beaten by outraged saloon keepers, and more than once she landed in jail. In 1901 her husband divorced her, and

Carry Nation, the staunch temperance leader, wielding a hatchet and a Bible—the one to smash saloons and bottles of liquor, the other to help her deliver her message about the demon alcohol.

she traveled east to deliver a series of lectures for the temperance movement. Though she performed fewer "hatchetations," she remained dedicated to the cause. On one occasion she disrupted a session of the U.S. Senate, shouting from the gallery until she was forcibly removed.

In 1910, Carry Nation was severely beaten by a tavern keeper in Montana. She never fully recovered and died six months later in an Arkansas hospital.

See also Prohibition and Temperance.

DEBORAH KENT

NATIONAL ASSOCIATION FOR THE ADVANCEMENT OF COLORED PEOPLE

The National Association for the Advancement of Colored People (NAACP) was founded in 1910 to combat racial discrimination. Its original members were sixty prominent black and white liberals, including the black leader W. E. B. Du Bois, the social worker Jane Addams, the philosopher John Dewey, and the novelist William Dean Howells.

The NAACP objected to the conservative views of Booker T. Washington, who believed that blacks should accept segregation and concentrate on improving their lives outside the mainstream of American society. The objective of the NAACP was full racial equality and its strategy was "litigation, legislation, and education." By educating the public through such magazines as Du Bois's *The Crisis,* it sought to demonstrate that the "separate but equal" doctrine of segregation was anything but equal: it condemned blacks to second-class citizenship. The organization backed legislation to abolish discriminatory Jim Crow laws, fought voting practices that

The first edition of The Crisis, *the journal of the NAACP, which was edited by W. E. B. Du Bois.*

kept blacks from the polls, and supported antilynching laws. In the courts, the NAACP worked to demonstrate that segregation was unconstitutional. The most famous NAACP-sponsored case, *Brown* v. *Board of Education of Topeka,* ended separate public schooling for blacks and whites. The case was argued by NAACP lawyer Thurgood Marshall, later to become the first black Supreme Court justice.

Made up primarily of progressive whites in its early days, the NAACP eventually gained a predominantly black membership. In recent years it has directed its energies to the problems of poverty and hopelessness faced by inner-city blacks.

See also African Americans.

A 1917 march down Fifth Avenue in New York City sponsored by the NAACP to urge the passage of laws against lynching.

NATIONALISM

See Black Nationalism before Emancipation; Nativism.

NATIONAL LABOR RELATIONS ACT

When the Supreme Court declared the National Industrial Recovery Act unconstitutional in 1935, the protections afforded by that law to workers ceased to exist. This caused Congress to pass the National Labor Relations Act. The law restored to workers the right to bargain collectively (that is, through a union rather than individually) and forbade employers to interfere with union organizers seeking to enlist workers in their factories. It also created a National Labor Relations Board (NLRB), which was charged with supervising factory elections to determine whether a majority of the workers wanted a union to represent them. The NLRB was also given the power to stop unfair labor practices by employers. It could hold investigations and act as a mediator to settle disputes and prevent strikes.

The National Labor Relations Act (popularly known as the Wagner Act after its principal sponsor, Senator Robert F. Wagner of New York) was one of the most important New Deal reforms. It was somewhat modified by the Taft-Hartley Act of 1947, which weakened the powers of the NLRB and required it to investigate charges of unfair practices against unions as well as employers. But the NLRB permanently changed the way employers dealt with their workers, greatly reduced the number of strikes, and made unions an important political force in both local and national elections.

See also Labor Movement; New Deal.

NATIONAL MONUMENTS

Thousands of Americans each year visit one of the nation's many memorials. Families and young people on senior class trips tour Washington, D.C., where most of the monuments are located. Many visit two other attractions that lie outside Washington. Following are some of the most frequently visited monuments in the United States.

Washington Monument

The monument honoring George Washington, located at one end of the Mall in Washington, D.C., was the first memorial to be built in the city. Privately funded at first, its construction ran into problems, including at one point a group of disgruntled citizens trying to take over the building and claim it as their own!

The Washington National Monument Society started fund-raising for the memorial in

The cornerstone for the Washington Monument was laid on July 4, 1848, with the same trowel George Washington had used to lay the cornerstone for the Capitol building in 1793.

1833. The design by Robert Mills called for an obelisk, an ancient Egyptian form, which starts as a four-sided tower and gradually tapers to a pyramid at the top. Many persons and groups around the world donated money and building blocks for the structure, until 1854 when Pope Pius IX contributed a marble block from a temple in Rome. The Know-Nothings, a radical anti-Catholic political party, stole the block and then broke into the Society's office and declared themselves in possession of the monument. Donations from the public and construction thereupon came to a halt. It was not until twenty years later, in 1876, that Congress voted to finish the memorial with public funds. It was completed in 1884 and opened to the public four years later.

The obelisk is 555 feet tall, and by agreement through the years the tallest structure in Washington. Its hollow interior is lined with many memorial stones of historic interest. Visitors can take an elevator to the top, or more hardy souls can climb the 898 steps.

Lincoln Memorial

Facing the Washington Monument at the other end of the Mall is the handsome Lincoln Memorial. This white marble building, 188 feet long and 118 feet wide, was designed by Henry Bacon. It is surrounded by thirty-six Doric columns, one for each state in the Union when Lincoln was president. Two side sections of the building contain tablets bearing the Gettysburg Address and Lincoln's second inaugural address.

In the central section, an immense statue of a seated Lincoln by Daniel Chester French gazes out through the open front to the wide sweep of steps leading up and into the building. These steps have been the site of some historic events. Marian Anderson, the black contralto, gave a concert here when she was denied use of Constitution Hall in Washington because of her race. And Martin Luther King, Jr., delivered his famous I Have a Dream speech from these steps at the 1963 March on Washington.

The cornerstone for the building was laid on February 12, 1915, and the memorial was dedicated on May 30, 1922.

Jefferson Memorial

Completing the group of monuments to presidents is the memorial to Thomas Jefferson located on the banks of the Tidal Basin near the Potomac River. When in the early 1930s John Russell Pope, Otto R. Eggers, and Daniel P. Higgins submitted their design for the monument, there was some grumbling about building a "Roman temple in twentieth-century Washington." But the classic architecture was fitting, given Jefferson's own love for the Palladian style, which he used in buildings he designed.

The monument's rotunda, the central round section, is formed by white marble walls ninety-six feet high. It is topped by a dome and circled by an interior walk and exterior colonnade. The memorial room at the center is dominated by Rudulph Evans's full-length nineteen-foot bronze statue of Jefferson standing in thought. Surrounding it are sixteen white marble columns and panels on which are carved selections from Jefferson's writings: the Declaration of Independence, the Virginia Statute of Religious Freedom, and other quotations on the importance of individual freedom and education for all citizens.

President Franklin D. Roosevelt broke ground for the memorial in 1938, and it was dedicated on April 13, 1943, the two hundredth anniversary of Jefferson's birth.

Vietnam Veterans' Memorial

Reflecting the controversy over the Vietnam War itself was the controversy over the design for the memorial to those killed in that war. Located in a park on the Mall in Washington, it is a unique war memorial. Built into the ground, so that one descends an incline when viewing it, the monument is a 493½-foot-long V-shaped wall of polished black granite, ten feet high at the center tapering to eight inches at the ends. The names of over 58,000 men and women killed or missing in Vietnam are engraved on it.

The country had been bitterly divided over the war when it was fought in 1965–73. Some thought it was worth fighting to keep Vietnam from becoming a communist nation;

The Vietnam Veterans' Memorial, the most visited monument in Washington. Some objected to the Wall's being made of black granite, thinking white marble more suitable. But it was pointed out that the names to be inscribed would show up better on black, especially in sunlight.

others thought the governing of Vietnam was none of our business and in any case not worth the increasingly terrible cost in American and Vietnamese lives. The war became so divisive and emotions ran so high that when it finally ended and the veterans returned home, Americans simply wanted to forget the war and get on with their lives.

Jan C. Scruggs, a veteran, disagreed. He believed the dead should be remembered, that a memorial would honor them and help heal the lingering bitterness over the war. Thus, he campaigned for a memorial to bear the names of the dead and missing. A nationwide competition was held, with the winning design submitted by Maya Ying Lin, a twenty-one-year-old architectural student at Yale.

Many objected strongly to her design: they wanted a more traditional statue of soldiers, flags, and weapons, and they wanted it above ground level, not below. But the entire project was designed to make the viewer *think*—about war and its cost, something a simple traditional statue could not do. After months of sometimes bitter argument, a compromise was reached. A statue and a flag were added a short distance away, and the Wall was built as designed. (Another statue, honoring the nurses who served in Vietnam, was erected nearby in 1993.)

Dedicated on November 13, 1982, the memorial has been everything Jan Scruggs hoped for. Veterans meet there to embrace and remember those they served with. Thousands visit it to look for and run their fingers over the names of friends and loved ones; to reflect on and weep over the sheer numbers of the dead; and to leave objects at the foot of the wall under a specific name like offerings on an altar: flags, flowers, canteens, army boots, objects only the donor knows the significance of (these are collected and preserved in the Smithsonian Institution; they run into the thousands now).

Statue of Liberty

Greeting immigrants and travelers in New York Harbor for generations has been France's gift to the United States, the Statue of Liberty. Frenchman Édouard de Laboulaye in 1865 conceived the idea of his country sponsoring the statue and presenting it to the United States in honor of both nations' commitment to liberty. The French raised $400,000 for the 151-foot statue. It was carved by sculptor Frédéric Auguste Bartholdi, who used his mother's face as a model.

The statue was shipped to America in 214 crates and reassembled on an 89-foot base on Bedloe's Island (now Liberty Island) near Ellis Island, the arrival point for European immigrants in those years. Dedicated on Octo-

The millions visiting the Statue of Liberty, combined with the effects of water, led to its deterioration over the years. It was closed to the public in 1984 for repairs and reopened in 1986 for the centennial celebration of its erection.

ber 28, 1886, it has inspired millions ever since. A famous poem by Emma Lazarus is carved on the base of the statue. Its final lines read:

> "Give me your tired, your poor,
> Your huddled masses yearning to breathe free,
> The wretched refuse of your teeming shore.
> Send these, the homeless, tempest-tost to me,
> I lift my lamp beside the golden door!"

On Mount Rushmore, South Dakota, the likenesses of (left to right) Presidents Washington, Jefferson, Theodore Roosevelt, and Lincoln were cut from granite with drills and dynamite.

Mount Rushmore

Carved on a granite cliff in the Black Hills of South Dakota are the heads of four of our presidents—George Washington, Thomas Jefferson, Abraham Lincoln, and Theodore Roosevelt. The figures, which are taller than the Great Pyramid of Egypt, are the largest of any statue in the world. The heads are scaled as if the men were 465 feet tall—the head of Washington alone is as high as a five-story building.

Gutzon Borglum, an American sculptor born in Idaho, designed and supervised most of the work on the carving under a commission from the state of South Dakota. He started the figures in 1927, but the group was still unfinished when he died early in 1941. His son, Lincoln, completed it the same year.

CECILE RHINEHART WATTERS

NATIONAL ORGANIZATION FOR WOMEN

In 1966 writer Betty Friedan and other feminist leaders founded the National Organization for Women (NOW). Its objective was "to take action to bring women into full participation in the mainstream of American society now, assuming all the privileges and responsibilities thereof in truly equal partnership with men." The group supported abortion rights and fought against sex discrimination in education and employment, calling for equal pay for equal work (in 1963 a woman earned an average of sixty-three cents for every dollar a man doing similar work earned). Much of the organization's energies went to campaigning for the Equal Rights Amendment (ERA), which gained much public support but was ultimately defeated. As the largest women's rights group in America, NOW has had great influence on issues affecting women's lives.

See also Feminist Movement since 1919; Friedan, Betty.

NATIONAL RECOVERY ACT

During the Great Depression manufacturers cut prices sharply as demand for their products declined. But sales of nearly everything still lagged. This law created the National Recovery Administration (NRA), a New Deal agency designed to stimulate the stagnant economy. The law authorized manufacturers in every field to draw up codes of "fair business practices" for their industry. This meant that they could agree to limit production and fix the prices of their products. This had been illegal under existing antitrust laws. In addition, Section 7a of the act required the codes to limit the hours of labor and set minimum wage rates for the industry and to guarantee to workers the right to form unions and to bargain collectively with them. Cooperating businesses, even small stores, were entitled to display the NRA symbol, a blue eagle, and the phrase "We Do Our Part."

The system got off to a good start; most industries quickly developed codes. But it did

The "Blue Eagle" of the National Recovery Administration was awarded to companies that agreed to accept codes that regulated wages, hours, and working conditions.

not work as well as people had hoped. The large producers in each industry tended to control the writing of the codes in ways that benefited them. They also resented being supervised by NRA officials and having to deal with their workers through the labor organizations, which expanded rapidly as a result of the law. Dissatisfaction with the code system mounted.

The end came in 1935 when the Supreme Court declared the Industrial Recovery Act unconstitutional.

See also New Deal.

NATIONAL ROAD

As people moved west during the early nineteenth century, the need for improved means of east-west transportation became more and more pressing. Because road building was expensive, local communities and the individual states had difficulty keeping up with the demand. The federal government had the resources to meet this need, but whether it was constitutional for the central government to build roads was debatable. On a practical level, many people in the developed sections of the country opposed federal construction because they already had roads and were worried about the cost. The only important federal road project before the Civil War was the National Road.

The road was originally authorized in 1806. It was scheduled to run from Cumberland, Maryland, to Wheeling, Virginia, but construction did not begin until after the War of 1812. The road reached Wheeling in 1818 and was extended to Columbus, Ohio, in 1833 and Vandalia, Illinois, in 1850. Present-day U.S. 40 follows the path blazed by the National Road.

NATIONAL WOMAN'S PARTY

This organization developed out of a split among American feminists after the ratification in 1920 of the amendment giving women the right to vote. Radical feminists, led by Alice Paul, who founded the party, made total equality for women their goal. They felt that women should be treated exactly the same as men. They should, for example, be drafted into the armed forces in time of war.

In 1923 the Woman's Party began a campaign for an Equal Rights Amendment to the Constitution, drafted by Paul. The party even considered legislation protecting women wrong. Laws, such as those limiting the

hours women could work, benefited and protected women, but they were still discriminatory laws because they were based on the differences between men and women. If women were treated truly equally, it was argued, they wouldn't need protective laws. On the other hand, women known as social feminists opposed the Equal Rights Amendment precisely because they feared it would make unconstitutional legislation providing special benefits to women and children, such as child labor laws. They were convinced that given the conditions of the day special protections were indeed needed by women.

The Equal Rights Amendment never made much progress before World War II, and the National Woman's Party remained quite small. It had only about ten thousand members. But it attracted much attention and kept the issue of truly equal rights for women before the public.

See also Equal Rights Amendment; Feminist Movement since 1919; Paul, Alice.

NATIVE AMERICANS
See Indian Reservations; Indian Societies and Cultures; Indian-White Relations.

NATIVISM

The United States has always claimed to be a place where foreign victims of cruelty and poverty are welcome. Yet anti-immigrant sentiment—known as nativism—has existed throughout most of the nation's history.

In the seventeenth and eighteenth centuries, the colonists welcomed immigrants because their labor was needed. But America's outlook toward immigration changed after the Revolution. Members of the Federalist Party, realizing that most immigrants supported their opponents, tried to limit immigrants' political activity by passing the Alien Acts in 1798. These laws limited freedom of speech and placed other restrictions on immigrants who had not yet become citizens.

In the 1830s, nativists focused their attention on the increasing number of Catholic immigrants. Many American Protestants believed that these immigrants did not have enough education or voting experience to become good American citizens.

Nativists also found strong support among industrial workers, who complained that immigrants drove down wages. They would work for less pay than those born in the United States. Employers often used immigrants to replace strikers, which deepened the workers' hatred of the newcomers. But employers, too, were prejudiced. Many help-wanted advertisements included the statement: "No Irish Need Apply."

The Know-Nothings

Anti-immigrant sentiment soon entered politics. Nativism reached a peak in 1854 with the rise of the Know-Nothing Party. This secret organization, which wanted to limit the political power of Catholics and immigrants by restricting their voting, got its name from its members' promise to reply, "I know nothing" if asked about the group.

By the end of 1855, more than 1 million Americans had joined the Know-Nothings. The party won political races in a dozen states and elected more than a hundred congressmen, as well as the mayors of Boston, Philadelphia, Chicago, and San Francisco. Disagreements among Know-Nothings over the slavery issue, however, led many northern members to switch to the new Republican Party. Consequently, the Know-Nothings' 1856 presidential candidate, Millard Fillmore, carried only one state, an embarrassing performance that killed the party.

Fear of Radicalism

By the late nineteenth century, fear of foreign radicals had replaced anti-Catholicism as the cornerstone of nativism. Many believed that immigrants brought European radicalism with them, and they blamed the newcomers for the violent strikes of the period. The role immigrants played in the communist, socialist, and anarchist movements also helped convince some Americans that radicals from abroad might soon take over the United States.

The first laws to restrict immigration had affected only Asians. Congress prohibited immigration from China in 1882, and President Theodore Roosevelt in 1908 concluded a "gentlemen's agreement" with Japan that excluded immigrants from that country. But soon efforts to restrict non-Asian immigrants became popular as well. Great Britain, Germany, and Scandinavia had provided most of America's immigrants in the nineteenth century, but by 1900 a majority were coming from Russia, Poland, Hungary, and Italy. Many Americans—believing that these immigrants lacked the intelligence and motivation that supposedly characterized northwestern Europeans—began pushing for immigration restriction.

The aftermath of World War I intensified nativism. Fear of foreign radicals, especially communists, reached epidemic proportions and resulted in the red scare of 1919–20. Many immigrants were arrested and deported even though they had not broken any law. Labor unions, concerned like earlier workers about wages, called for immigration restriction as

Anti-immigrant sentiment, known as nativism, is shown in Frank Beard's 1885 cartoon. Here the halls of liberty are guarded from a repulsive group of low-lifes—identified as dangerous anarchists, nihilists, communists, socialists, and dynamiters—who have crawled out of the sewers of Italy, Russia, and Germany, just visible in the distance.

well. Finally, many feared that millions would flock to America from war-torn Europe and spoil the United States' postwar prosperity.

Quotas Set

Congress responded to these pressures by passing the National Origins Act (1924), which reflected prevailing prejudices by setting immigration quotas that blatantly discriminated against southern and eastern Europeans. For example, the law permitted 65,721 immigrants from Great Britain annually, but only 5,802 from Italy and 2,712 from the Soviet Union. Asians were almost completely excluded. The movement to strictly limit immigration, started nearly a century earlier, had achieved its goal.

It is difficult to determine the extent to which nativism still exists in America. Congress in 1965 eliminated the quotas that had favored those from northwestern Europe, and organized nativist groups have no great following. Yet polls taken in the early 1990s indicated that most Americans, worried about growing unemployment and changes in the makeup of the population, thought that immigration should be further restricted. Violence against immigrants, especially Asian Americans, also suggests that nativism persists. Whatever the case, it is clear that though the world thinks of the United States as a nation of immigrants, nativist movements have enjoyed surprising success throughout the country's history.

See also Alien and Sedition Acts; Anticommunism; Chinese Exclusion Act; Fillmore, Millard; Gentlemen's Agreement; Immigration; Immigration Restriction League; Know-Nothing Party; Morse, Samuel F. B.

TYLER ANBINDER

NATO
See North Atlantic Treaty Organization.

NAVY

As far back as 3000 B.C. the Egyptian nation supported a navy. In ancient times the primary warship was a galley driven by oarsmen. Later naval vessels were powered by sail and armed with cannons.

The American navy can trace its beginnings to the year 1632 when the people of the Massachusetts Bay Colony built a vessel to battle the pirates operating off their coast. The first true U.S. navy was established in 1775 when the Continental Congress appropriated money to convert a few merchant vessels into combat ships. A famous sea battle fought during the revolutionary war (1775–83) pitted a British ship, the *Serapis,* against the American *Bonhomme Richard* commanded by John Paul Jones. During the height of battle the British captain shouted to Jones, asking him if he wished to surrender. Although Jones's ship was severely damaged (and later sank), he shouted back, "I have not yet begun to fight," and proceeded to defeat and capture the *Serapis.*

The Early Navy
In 1794 the United States built a new fleet designed to fight the Barbary pirates of North America, who were preying on American shipping. One of the vessels created was a forty-four-gun frigate called the *Constitution.*

The *Constitution* engaged in battles with the Barbary pirates in 1803 and 1804, and eight years later fought against the British in the War of 1812. American sailors claimed that during a battle with a British warship, enemy cannon balls bounced harmlessly off the *Constitution*'s thick oak sides. Ever since then the ship has been called *Old Ironsides.* It is now docked permanently in Boston Harbor, where thousands of people visit it every year.

In the early 1800s world navies gradually shifted from sail to steam as a source of power. In 1814 the American inventor Robert Fulton built the world's first steam-powered warship, a vessel he called a "floating battery." The U.S. Navy then led the world in steam-powered vessels.

The most important "first" achieved by American naval forces came in the waters off Hampton Roads, Virginia, during the Civil War. In March 1862 two steam-powered ships covered with iron plating engaged in a thundering gun duel. Although they exchanged cannon fire for five hours, the Union's *Monitor* and the Confederacy's *Virginia* (called the *Merrimack* before the South captured it from the Union and renamed it) were unable to damage each other. The clash between these ironclads demonstrated the toughness of armored ships, and other nations were forced to change from wooden to ironclad vessels.

The Navy in the Twentieth Century
During the Spanish-American War of 1898 the American navy defeated a badly outclassed Spanish navy in engagements off Cuba and the Philippines. In 1907 President Theodore Roosevelt ordered the "Great White Fleet," a flotilla of America's finest war vessels painted a gleaming white, on a fourteen-month world cruise. The Great White Fleet advertised to other nations that

Male and female naval reservists gather in New York City around 1917.

the United States was now a world-class sea power.

In World War I the U.S. Navy helped the British clear the Atlantic Ocean of German submarines and planted mines in the North Sea to tie up German shipping. It also transported more than 2 million soldiers to Europe. Between World War I and World War II the United States did important pioneering work with aircraft carriers. America's first carrier, the *Langley,* was converted to aircraft use in 1922.

World War II began for the United States on December 7, 1941, with Japan's devastating raid on the American naval base at Pearl Harbor in Hawaii. Japanese bombers sank or damaged America's most powerful battleships during the assault, but the navy's aircraft carriers were untouched because they

were at sea that day. The great turning point of the Pacific war came in June 1942 when Japanese and American aircraft carriers clashed near Midway Island. The Japanese lost four of their best carriers at Midway, and they were never able to recover from the blow. Although the capture of Japanese bases on the islands of the Pacific was accomplished by army and marine units, all were transported and protected by navy warships and planes. By the end of World War II the American fleet had more ships than all the other navies in the world combined.

In 1954 the U.S. Navy commissioned the *Nautilus,* the world's first nuclear-powered submarine. Its nuclear engines allowed the *Nautilus* to stay underwater for months at a time. The driving force behind the nuclear submarine program was Adm. Hyman Rickover, who envisioned an entirely nuclear fleet. The *Enterprise,* commissioned in 1961, was the first nuclear-powered aircraft carrier.

In the 1960s guided missiles replaced guns as the main armament on American surface ships. Nuclear submarines now carried long-range ballistic missiles, which could be fired when the vessel was submerged.

The U.S. Navy had lesser but important roles in the Korean, Vietnam, and Persian Gulf wars. Its aircraft carriers served as bases for planes attacking enemy positions.

See also Dewey, George; Fulton, Robert; Jones, John Paul; Pearl Harbor, Attack on; *and entries for individual wars.*

R. CONRAD STEIN

NEUTRALITY ACTS

The series of conflicts that occurred in Europe between 1935 and the outbreak of World War II in 1939 led to the passage in the United States of three laws intended to keep America out of these conflicts. The cause was isolationism, a widespread feeling that the United States should stay out of European affairs, and especially should not have fought in World War I. The laws failed to achieve their purpose because conditions in the 1930s were far different from what they had been in 1914–17.

The first Neutrality Act, passed after Italy invaded Ethiopia in 1935, gave the president the power to ban the export of arms to any warring nation and advised American citizens not to travel on ships owned by countries at war. The Neutrality Act of 1936 prohibited Americans from lending money to nations at war. The third act, passed in 1937 during the Spanish civil war, forbade the sale of arms in civil wars and made travel on belligerent vessels by American citizens illegal.

After World War II broke out in 1939 following the German invasion of Poland, American public opinion changed. Neutrality remained the objective, but making sure that the aggressors did not win became more important. In November 1939 a new neutrality act allowed the sale of arms to all the participants on a cash and carry basis. Again, the lawmakers were refighting World War I, when loans to the Allies were thought to have led to America entering the conflict. Though "cash and carry" treated both sides alike, in practice it favored the Allies, since their powerful navies prevented German and Italian merchant ships from getting to America to pick up cargoes.

See also World War II.

NEW DEAL

Franklin D. Roosevelt accepted the Democratic nomination for president in 1932 by promising "a new deal for the American peo-

ple." The phrase became the popular label for his administration (1933–45) and its many domestic achievements.

Programs of the First Term

Roosevelt and the Democrats won a substantial victory in 1932, largely because of the then almost four-year-old economic crisis of the Great Depression. As a result, Roosevelt had unusual influence over Congress in the opening months of his presidency. The celebrated "first hundred days" of the new administration produced a federal program to protect American farmers from the uncertainties of the market through subsidies and production controls (the Agricultural Adjustment Ad-

A cartoon entitled "New Deal Remedies" features Franklin D. Roosevelt as the doctor paying a house call on an ailing Uncle Sam. The president has prescribed an assortment of New Deal "medicines." A large bottle of the National Recovery Administration (NRA) is part of the cure, but doses of the Civilian Conservation Corps (CCC), the Public Works Administration (PWA), and other agencies are also prescribed. Nurse Congress stands watch.

ministration; AAA). It created a new federal regulatory agency to oversee the stock market (the Securities and Exchange Commission); a reform of the banking system that included a system of insurance for deposits (the Federal Deposit Insurance Corporation); and a series of relief measures to aid some of the approximately 15 million unemployed Americans (among them the Civilian Conservation Corps, the Federal Emergency Relief Administration, and the Civil Works Administration). The early New Deal also began an unprecedented experiment in flood control, public power, and regional planning (the Tennessee Valley Authority).

The National Industrial Recovery Act, perhaps the most important single measure of the first hundred days, contained a guarantee to workers of the right of collective bargaining and helped spur major union organizing drives in many industries. It created a substantial federal public works program (the Public Works Administration). Most importantly, but least successfully, it established the National Recovery Administration (NRA), which attempted to stabilize prices and wages through cooperative "code authorities" involving government, business, and labor. These and other early initiatives created broad popular support for the Roosevelt administration and halted the rapid unraveling of the financial system. They did not, however, end, or even significantly soften, the Great Depression. Several crucial New Deal programs—among them the NRA and the AAA—were declared unconstitutional by the Supreme Court.

In the spring of 1935, responding to the setbacks by the Court and the approach of the 1936 elections, the administration proposed (or endorsed) several important new initiatives. The National Labor Relations Act,

also known as the Wagner Act, revived and strengthened government guarantees of collective bargaining between unions and employers. New relief programs—above all, the Works Progress Administration—created hundreds of thousands of jobs for the unemployed. And the Social Security Act established a system of old-age pensions, unemployment insurance, and welfare benefits for such vulnerable groups as dependent children and the handicapped. It served as the basis of the American welfare system through the remainder of the century.

Events after 1936
Roosevelt's landslide reelection in 1936 produced large Democratic majorities in both houses of Congress. Even so, the administration encountered a long series of frustrations in its second term, partly as a result of the president's political errors. Early in 1937, he proposed a "reform" of the judiciary designed to stop the string of reverses his programs had been suffering in the Supreme Court. He asked Congress to expand the number of justices so he could appoint members sympathetic to his ideas and hence tip the ideological balance of the Court. The "Court-packing plan," as it was known, did lasting political damage to Roosevelt and was finally defeated in Congress. (Roosevelt was soon able to change the composition of the Court anyway as conservative justices resigned and he appointed more liberal ones.)

The biggest domestic event of Roosevelt's second term, however, was the severe recession that began in the fall of 1937 and continued through most of 1938. It was caused in part by the administration's efforts to balance the budget by reducing federal spending. The New Deal responded in two ways. First, New Dealers publicly attacked monopoly power, which many liberals believed was the cause of the recession. More significantly, Roosevelt abandoned his efforts to balance the budget and launched a $5 billion spending program in the spring of 1938 whose purpose was to increase mass purchasing power. The program set an important precedent for using government spending as an antidote to recessions.

The last major domestic achievement of the Roosevelt administration was the passage in 1938 of the Fair Labor Standards Act, which established a national minimum wage and set limits on hours of work. By the end of the year, the New Deal had effectively come to an end. Roosevelt himself went on to win an unprecedented third term in 1940, and a fourth in 1944, and to lead the nation through a great world war. But his domestic reform efforts no longer generated broad congressional or popular support. By 1939, he was turning his attention increasingly to the international crises that would dominate the last five years of his life.

The New Deal's Effects

In retrospect, the New Deal has often seemed as significant for the things it did not do as for the things it achieved. It did not end the Great Depression and its massive unemployment; only the enormous public and private spending for World War II finally did that. The New Deal did not end poverty or effect any significant redistribution of wealth. Nor did it do much to address some of the principal domestic issues of the postwar era, among them the problems of racial and sexual inequality.

Even so, the achievements of the Roosevelt administration rank among the most important of any presidency in American history. The New Deal created a series of new state in-stitutions that greatly, and permanently, expanded the role of the federal government in American life. The government was now committed to providing at least some assistance to the poor and unemployed; to protecting the rights of labor unions; to stabilizing the banking system; to building low-income housing; to regulating the financial markets; to subsidizing agricultural production; and to doing many other things that had not previously been federal responsibilities.

The New Deal produced a new political coalition that sustained the Democrats as the majority party in national politics for more than a generation after its own end. And the Roosevelt administration generated a set of political ideas—known to later generations as New Deal liberalism—that remained a source of inspiration and controversy for decades and that helped shape the next great experiment in liberal reform, the Great Society of the 1960s.

See also Civilian Conservation Corps; Depressions and Recessions; Federal Theatre Project; Federal Writers' Project; Hundred Days; National Labor Relations Act; National Recovery Act; Public Works Administration; Reconstruction Finance Corporation; Roosevelt, Franklin D.; Tennessee Valley Authority; Works Progress Administration.

ALAN BRINKLEY

NEW FREEDOM

Woodrow Wilson called the platform on which he ran for president in 1912 the New Freedom. By "freedom" he meant freeing society from the power of special interests, such as monopolistic corporations. He believed that these corporations, commonly called "trusts," should be broken up by strengthening the Sherman Antitrust Act of 1890. The separate, smaller companies in each industry would then compete with one another. Competition would lead to lower prices and more efficient methods of production. In addition, Wilson said, the federal government should establish fair rules fixing the ways companies should conduct their affairs and fine heavily those that did not obey the rules. "If America is not to have free enterprise," Wilson said, "then she can have freedom of no sort whatever."

This point of view was in direct conflict with third-party candidate Theodore Roosevelt's "New Nationalism"—his argument that large corporations should not be broken up because they were efficient. Instead they should be subject to strict regulation by the government.

Wilson won the election and persuaded Congress to pass a tougher antitrust law, the Clayton Act of 1914. In the same year, however, he also approved the creation of the Federal Trade Commission, an agency that resembled what Roosevelt had proposed.

See also Antitrust Movement; Federal Trade Commission; New Nationalism; Wilson, Woodrow.

NEW FRONTIER

The New Frontier was the legislative program advanced by President John F. Kennedy in campaigning for president in 1960. His aim, he said, was "to get the country moving again." He argued that the New Frontier would put an end to the series of minor recessions that had plagued the Eisenhower administration and at the same time extend the social reforms of the New Deal.

After his election he asked Congress to provide more federal aid to education, to guarantee decent medical care for older people, and to undertake a more extensive urban renewal program. He also recommended a higher minimum wage and larger and more extensive Social Security benefits.

Aside from raising the dollar-an-hour minimum wage by twenty-five cents and authorizing relatively modest expenditures on middle-class housing and mass transit programs, Congress did little to put these New Frontier proposals into effect. Discouraged, Kennedy early in 1963 tried a new approach. He suggested that the economy could be revived by deliberately running the government at a deficit. If tax rates were reduced without cutting back on government expenditures, people would have more money to spend and would buy more goods and services. This would encourage manufacturers to expand output. The general increase in economic activity would mean that the lower tax rates would actually bring more money into the Treasury.

This too failed to win congressional approval. But after Kennedy was assassinated in November 1963, the new president, Lyndon B. Johnson, persuaded Congress to enact much of the New Frontier program.

See also Kennedy, John F.

NEW NATIONALISM

Theodore Roosevelt gave the name "New Nationalism" to the platform on which he ran for president in 1912. Actually he first used the term in a speech at Osawatomie, Kansas, in 1910. Despite his reputation as a "trust-buster," Roosevelt believed that large corporations were an essential element in industrial society. Instead of trying to break them up ("bust the trusts"), the government should establish rules of fair competition and make sure that the corporations obeyed them. This meant regulating their activities closely. Furthermore, Roosevelt argued, the complicated modern economy required centralized management. In a democratic society this could best be supplied by the federal government. Management in this sense also made necessary an expanded national program of social legislation.

When he failed to win the Republican presidential nomination in 1912 Roosevelt founded the Progressive Party and campaigned hard for the New Nationalism. The Democratic candidate, Woodrow Wilson, used the contrasting slogan, New Freedom, to characterize his policy of breaking up large corporations in order to restore competition. Wilson won the election, but Roosevelt was correct in arguing that big corporations had become an essential part of modern life. Even Wilson accepted the need for federal regulation of big business when he signed the Federal Trade Commission Act of 1914.

See also Antitrust Movement; Federal Trade Commission; New Freedom; Roosevelt, Theodore.

NEW SOUTH

The defeat of the South in the Civil War completely disrupted the region's economy. The abolition of slavery revolutionized the way labor was employed and paid for and undermined the plantation system. Combined with the destruction of so many homes, workshops, and other property and the battered condition of roads and railroads, this slowed southern economic growth to a crawl. The production of the South's principal crop, cotton, did not reach the level of 1860 for twenty years. The output of tobacco and sugar took still longer to recover.

This situation led a number of southern business leaders and journalists to call for the creation of a New South. The region should try to diversify its economy. Farmers should grow many different crops, not just cotton and the other old standbys. And they ought to make use of fertilizers and the most up-to-date farming methods. Above all, the South should industrialize. This would mean forgetting about the past, especially the hatreds resulting from the bloody Civil War.

The best known of the advocates of the New South was Henry W. Grady, editor of the *Atlanta Constitution.* "The old South rested everything on slavery and agriculture," Grady said in a speech in New York City in 1886. "The new South [needs] . . . a diversified industry that meets the complex needs of this complex age." Northerners should be encouraged to move south and invest their savings in southern mines and factories.

NEWSPAPERS
See Magazines and Newspapers.

NIAGARA MOVEMENT

By the beginning of the twentieth century, many black leaders had become dissatisfied with the policies of Booker T. Washington, the most prominent spokesman for American blacks. Washington had urged black people to accept segregation, the denial of the right to vote, and other aspects of American racism and concentrate on improving themselves by working hard within the system. The most prominent of the anti-Washington blacks was W. E. B. Du Bois, who directly attacked Washington and his ideas in *The Souls of Black Folk* (1903).

The Niagara movement began when Du

Members of the Niagara movement, posed against a backdrop of Niagara Falls. Its leader, W. E. B. Du Bois, is in the center of the second row in the white hat. The 1905 meeting of the movement took place at Niagara Falls, but on the Canadian side since no hotel on the American side would allow blacks to register.

Bois and other black militants met at Niagara Falls, Canada, in July 1905. (They had to go across the border to Canada because no hotel in Niagara Falls, New York, would allow blacks to register.) They prepared a list of objectives that attacked every aspect of white racism: they called for an end to segregation in all public facilities; equal economic opportunities for blacks, including admission to all-white trade unions; the unrestricted right to vote in every state; and fair treatment in the courts.

The Niagara movement attracted little public attention. But in 1909 Du Bois joined with a number of white liberals to found the National Association for the Advancement of Colored People (NAACP), whose objectives closely resembled those of the Niagara group.

See also Du Bois, W. E. B.; National Association for the Advancement of Colored People.

NIMITZ, CHESTER

(1885–1966)   *World War II admiral.*

Born in Fredericksburg, Texas, Chester Nimitz received an appointment to the U.S. Naval Academy at the age of fifteen. During the next four decades of his service in the navy he became known as an officer with a keen mind, sound judgment, and a calm disposition. By 1938 he had reached the rank of rear admiral.

On December 7, 1941, the U.S. Pacific Fleet was badly damaged by the Japanese "sneak attack" on the naval base at Pearl Harbor, Hawaii. To Nimitz's surprise, he was appointed new commander of the fleet, with the rank of full admiral, over more than twenty-five other admirals who had been above him.

Because all its battleships had been put out of action at Pearl Harbor, the Pacific Fleet could not launch a major attack to strike back at Japan. But Nimitz acted quickly to do what he could. Using aircraft carriers, cruisers, destroyers, and submarines, he organized small fleets, called task forces, to raid Japanese bases and harass the movement of Japanese troops by sea. In 1942, when the Japanese sent a strong force to capture the American naval base of Midway Island, Nimitz learned of their plan. He put together two special task forces and set them in position to catch the Japanese by surprise. The American forces won the Battle of Midway, and the victory turned the Pacific war in America's favor.

Nimitz helped devise the island-hopping

strategy of attacking and capturing key Japanese island bases, which enabled American forces to move steadily closer to Japan and bring it under air attack. In 1944 he was promoted to fleet admiral, a rank specially created by the U.S. Congress.

When the war ended in September of 1945, Nimitz was appointed chief of naval operations in Washington, D.C. He later served on the American delegation to the United Nations. For the last seventeen years of his life he lived on the Treasure Island Naval Base in San Francisco Bay, within sight of the Pacific Ocean where he had served his country so well.

See also World War II.

TOM MCGOWEN

NINETEENTH AMENDMENT
See Voting.

NIXON, RICHARD M.

(1913–94)   *Thirty-seventh president of the United States (1969–74).*

Nixon was the only president to resign from office in disgrace. A native Californian, he worked his way through college and law school. After serving in the navy in World War II, he was elected to Congress as a Republican in 1946 and became a member of the House Un-American Activities Committee. His work investigating Alger Hiss, accused of spying for the Soviets, won him national attention and a Senate seat in 1950. During his campaigns, Nixon earned the nickname "Tricky Dick" because of his unscrupulous tactics. For example, he unfairly

suggested that his opponents were Communist sympathizers.

Nixon was presidential candidate Dwight D. Eisenhower's running mate in 1952. After his nomination, he was accused of receiving secret campaign contributions, which he put to personal use. He defended himself in an emotional televised address, during which he disclosed his finances, even mentioning the gift of a puppy named Checkers (thus, this was called the "Checkers speech").

As Eisenhower's vice president for two terms, Nixon was often a kind of troubleshooter. In one famous case, he more than held his own against Soviet leader Nikita S. Khrushchev during a "kitchen debate" about the merits of capitalism versus communism in Moscow in 1959 (so called because it took place in a model kitchen that was part of a trade show).

Nixon narrowly lost the 1960 presidential election to John F. Kennedy. This was the first campaign to feature televised debates between the candidates. It was generally agreed that Kennedy bested him by appearing as a young, vigorous challenger in contrast to Nixon's less appealing image. Nixon also lost the California governor's race in 1962 and then withdrew from politics to practice law.

Nevertheless, in 1968, he was again nominated for president and defeated Democrat Hubert H. Humphrey. During the campaign, Nixon claimed to have a plan for ending the unpopular Vietnam War, but once in office, he failed to do so. Despite gradually withdrawing U.S. troops, the president actually extended the war into North Vietnam and neutral Cambodia, leading to an increased number of antiwar demonstrations. After National Guard troops tragically shot several students demonstrating at Kent State University in 1970, Nixon met with protesters at the

Lincoln Memorial but failed to win them over.

Nixon, however, did succeed in changing American foreign policy. Despite his reputation as a strong anticommunist, he became the first president to visit Red China (1971–72), easing two decades of mutual distrust. He also signed an arms-reduction treaty with Soviet leaders in Moscow (1972).

After overpowering George S. McGovern in the 1972 presidential race, Nixon was soon disgraced by the Watergate scandal—a pre-election break-in at Democratic National Headquarters in the Watergate complex, a group of apartment and office buildings. The burglars had been hired by Nixon's Committee to Reelect the President (CREEP) to plant eavesdropping equipment. Nixon deliberately lied in order to protect the aides who had directed the burglary. He argued with Congress and the courts over his right as president to withhold information from them when they sought to investigate the incident. In July 1974, the House Judiciary Committee prepared to charge him with (1) obstructing justice by using the Central Intelligence Agency to block the FBI's investigation of Watergate; (2) abusing his powers by ordering the FBI to harass individuals and having the Internal Revenue Service examine the tax records of businesses reluctant to contribute to his campaign; and (3) disobeying legal orders from the House by withholding and concealing information. When the committee learned that tapes made secretly of White House conversations about the Watergate affair had been tampered with, it voted to recommend to the House of Representatives that Nixon be impeached.

Faced with dwindling political support and a lengthy trial in the Senate, Nixon resigned in August 1974. Since his vice president Spiro T. Agnew had already been forced to resign in October 1973 in an unrelated scandal, Gerald R. Ford, whom Nixon had appointed to replace him, became president. In September 1974, President Ford pardoned Nixon for any crimes he might have committed in office. Nixon spent most of his time thereafter writing books and giving advice on American foreign policy.

See also Anticommunism; Impeachment. *For events during Nixon's administration, see* Kent State Incident; OPEC Oil Crisis; *Roe v. Wade;* Space Program; Vietnam War; Watergate.

For further reading: Barbara Silberdick Feinberg, *Watergate: Scandal in the White House* (New York: Franklin Watts, 1990).

BARBARA SILBERDICK FEINBERG

NLRA
See National Labor Relations Act.

NORTH ATLANTIC TREATY ORGANIZATION

In order to strengthen ties between the United States and the nations of Western Europe, the North Atlantic Treaty Organization (NATO) was founded in April 1949. Besides the United States, the original members included France, Great Britain, Belgium, Italy, the Netherlands, Luxembourg, Norway, Denmark, Portugal, Canada, and Iceland. Several other nations, the most important being West Germany, were later admitted. The purpose of NATO was to maintain a force capable of meeting a possible attack by the Soviet Union. All members committed troops to a NATO army, but most of the soldiers and an even larger percentage of the money needed to arm and maintain them were supplied by the United States.

Although the commitment to a combined response to any possible attack was reassuring to the Western nations, the creation of NATO led directly to the creation of a similar organization of communist nations, the Warsaw Pact. On balance NATO probably intensified the cold war. With the ending of the cold war, the reunification of Germany, and the breakup of the Soviet Union, the Warsaw Pact was dissolved. But NATO continues to exist, although its purpose is now unclear.

See also Cold War.

NORTHWEST ORDINANCE

After the American Revolution had been won in 1781, the newly independent states ceded their claims to land west of the Appalachian Mountains to the central government. It became necessary to decide how the land should be sold or granted to settlers and how the region should be governed. The Land Ordinance of 1785 established the principle that the land should be sold at auction at a minimum price of one dollar an acre. How the new territory was to be governed was determined in the Northwest Ordinance of 1787. It provided that the region north of the Ohio River, south of the Great Lakes, and east of the Mississippi River was to be divided into at least three but no more than five territories.

Until the number of men of voting age in a territory reached five thousand, it was to be run by a governor and three judges appointed by Congress. At that point the voters could elect a territorial legislature and send a nonvoting delegate to represent them in Congress. Then, when the population reached

sixty thousand, the territory could draft a constitution and become a state "on an equal footing" with the already existing states. The only limits on the type of government the people could create were that it must be a republic, guarantee freedom of religion and trial by jury, and prohibit slavery.

This system sped western development by providing some government for the earliest pioneers and guaranteeing them that when enough people had arrived their state would be admitted to the Union with full powers.

NOW
See National Organization for Women.

NUCLEAR ENERGY

Nuclear energy is the force contained in the core, or nucleus, of every atom of matter. That force is released when nuclei are (1) made to split apart (fission) or (2) compelled to combine (fusion). Either way, the force set loose is enormous. Temperatures at the heart of a nuclear chain reaction—one that keeps going until fission or fusion is complete—can equal temperatures at the sun's center. The chain reaction may be explosively fast, as in a nuclear bomb, or slow and controlled, as in a nuclear power plant. Always, it gives out radioactive rays and particles that are known to cause injury or illness, even death.

Military Uses
By the 1930s, scientists knew that nuclear chain reactions occur in nature, although they had yet to start one in the laboratory. American nuclear research got a boost in 1939, when the physicist Albert Einstein

warned President Franklin D. Roosevelt that Germany, about to launch World War II, was working to develop an atomic bomb. By the time America entered the war against Germany in 1941, U.S. scientists were prepared to start work on the top-secret Manhattan Project. Their goal: producing the bomb ahead of Germany.

Manhattan Project scientists created the first manmade nuclear chain reaction in 1942. In July 1945, under the direction of J. Robert Oppenheimer, they exploded a fission bomb at a New Mexico test site. Some who witnessed the blast, including Oppenheimer, were so horrified at its destructiveness that they urged President Harry S. Truman not to use the weapon against Germany's ally Japan (Germany had already surrendered). But eager to end the war, Truman approved the dropping of a nuclear bomb on the Japanese city of Hiroshima on August 6 and a second one on Nagasaki three days later. About 170,000 civilians died in the attacks, some in the explosions, others from burns and radiation sickness. Illnesses caused by radiation from the bombs are still appearing in Japan.

Until 1949, the United States was the only country to have the nuclear bomb. Then scientists in the Soviet Union tested a device of their own, and the nuclear arms race began. The idea behind it was called Mutual Assured Destruction (MAD)—the notion that if each side had enough weapons to be sure of destroying the other after an attack, neither would dare strike first. To stockpiles of fission-based bombs were added far more powerful weapons based on fusion. Submarines were powered by nuclear energy and carried nuclear arms. Missiles, some capable of crossing continents, others of short or medium range, were equipped with one or more warheads each. Other nations—England, France, China, Israel, and India—learned

how to build the bombs and joined the "nuclear club."

While contributing to the nuclear arms race, nations also tried to control it. Treaties to limit testing of the bombs were signed in 1963 and 1974. Agreements to build fewer ones came in 1972 and 1979. The 1968 Non-Proliferation Treaty, adopted by 130 nations, aimed to halt the weapons' global spread. In 1987 and 1991, U.S. and Soviet leaders agreed to begin dismantling all their medium- and short-range weapons and 30 percent of their long-range missiles. By 1993, the breakup of the Soviet Union and an easing of U.S.-Soviet tensions had resulted in further agreement on disarmament. But still of concern was the threat of more countries learning how to build the bomb and acquiring the means of doing so and the possibility of terrorists acquiring the weapons.

Civilian Uses
Nuclear energy has several civilian uses, in science, medicine, food preservation, and, most important, in generating electricity. America's first nuclear power plant opened in 1957, amid promises that the technology would provide limitless amounts of safe, clean energy. Yet thirty-five years later, 111 plants were producing only about 20 percent of the nation's electricity.

A nuclear power plant operates much like one using fossil fuels—coal, oil, or natural gas. Steam-driven turbines run generators that produce electricity and send it over wires to the plant's customers. The difference is that in most nuclear plants, the steam is heated by the fissioning of an element called uranium in the plant's nuclear core. Workers watch the fission reaction carefully, speeding it up or slowing it down by raising or lowering specially designed control rods to manage the rate at which nuclei split. To keep radiation from escaping, the core is housed in a reactor vessel with thick steel walls surrounded by concrete. The vessel and other radioactive parts of the plant are enclosed in a three- to five-foot-thick structure.

Nuclear power plants have advantages over fossil-fuel plants. One ton of uranium fuel produces as much energy as 3 million tons of coal, 16.1 million barrels of oil, or 41.3 million cubic feet of natural gas. Such efficiency means relatively low fuel shipping and handling costs, and lower costs mean lower electric rates for consumers. Furthermore, using uranium helps conserve oil. That's very important, since the world's supply of oil, if we go on using it at the present rate, is expected to run out in the next century. Some experimental plants, called "breeder reactors," actually produce, or "breed," new nuclear fuel—plutonium—as they fission uranium. But partly because of its enormous expense, the U.S. government has stopped supporting breeder reactor research. Finally, fission does not pollute the atmosphere with soot and smoke as fossil fuels do, particularly coal.

Despite their advantages, nuclear plants have drawbacks. They produce much more extra heat than fossil-fuel plants. Part of this heat is carried off by water and ends up in rivers, lakes, and oceans, making them warmer, which can harm water life. To fission efficiently, uranium must be "enriched," increasing its concentration of fissionable material. Enrichment is an expensive process. Adding to nuclear power costs are plant shutdowns for routine maintenance or when equipment fails. And nuclear plants are costlier to build than other power plants, thanks to the elaborate containment and safety systems—meant to prevent accidental radiation releases—required by the Nuclear Regulatory Commission (NRC), the federal agency that monitors the industry.

But public safety concerns pose the greatest threat to the future use of civilian nuclear power. For one thing, under NRC rules, plants regularly release small amounts of radioactivity. Occasionally, larger amounts escape. No one can say definitely what effect repeated releases will have on public health. Another worry is that an earthquake, storm, or other disaster could damage a plant's containment structure. Reactor accidents are a third concern. Human error helped cause an accident at the Three Mile Island plant in Pennsylvania in 1979. In 1986, an explosion and fire destroyed a Soviet nuclear plant. Thirty-one people were killed, and hundreds injured. A large amount of radioactivity was released, which poisoned many acres of land, making it unsafe for people and for growing food. Yet another worry is that scientists have not figured out what to do with used reactor parts and fuel, some of which will remain radioactive for thousands of years. Throughout the world, nuclear wastes wait in temporary storage, with no permanent disposal system in sight.

Unless these problems can be solved, civilian nuclear energy may never fulfill its earlier promise of clean, safe, limitless power.

See also Cold War; Manhattan Project; Oppenheimer, J. Robert.

For further reading: Ann E. Weiss, *The Nuclear Arms Race: Can We Survive It?* (Boston: Houghton Mifflin, 1983); Ann E. Weiss, *The Nuclear Question* (New York: Harcourt, 1981).

ANN E. WEISS

NULLIFICATION CONTROVERSY

"The Constitution," Article VI states, "shall be the supreme law of the land," but the meaning of the Constitution is not always crystal clear. If the U.S. Congress passes a law that a state considers unconstitutional, can the state legally prevent it from being enforced within its borders by passing an ordinance nullifying it? Throughout early American history, beginning with the Virginia and Kentucky Resolutions denouncing the Alien and Sedition Acts of 1798, this question was hotly debated.

The leading defender of the idea of nullification was John C. Calhoun. In 1828, while serving as vice president, Calhoun wrote the "South Carolina Exposition and Protest," which argued that since the states existed before the United States and had appointed the men who had drafted the Constitution, and therefore established the Union, the states were the final judges of the meaning of the Constitution. In 1832, believing that a new tariff on manufactured goods passed by Congress was unconstitutional, the legislature of Calhoun's state, South Carolina, passed an Ordinance of Nullification, banning the enforcement of the tariff in the state after a certain date.

A national crisis resulted. President Andrew Jackson prepared to use the army to enforce the law if the ordinance was actually put into effect. To prevent a possible civil war, Congress then passed a new tariff law reducing the duties on manufactured goods. South Carolina then repealed the Ordinance of Nullification. The idea of nullification, however, remained both logical and just to many southerners. The whole issue of nullification was not finally settled until the victory of the North in the Civil War.

See also Virginia and Kentucky Resolutions.

NUREMBERG TRIALS

The trial of top Nazi leaders began in November 1945, shortly after the end of the Second World War. Held in Nuremberg, Germany, it was conducted by an international military tribunal of the American, British, French, and Russian Allies.

The accused were charged with crimes against peace (waging aggressive war), war crimes (including murder, looting, and destruction of property), and crimes against humanity (enslavement, torture, and extermination of civilian populations, especially the Jews).

Three of the leaders most responsible for these crimes—Adolf Hitler, Nazi propaganda minister Josef Goebbels, and Heinrich Himmler, who masterminded the "Final Solution"—had committed suicide after Germany's defeat. But twenty-four other high-ranking Nazis stood trial.

All the defendants pleaded not guilty, claiming they had simply carried out Hitler's orders. The prosecution argued that they were entirely responsible for their actions: "If you were to say of these men that they are not guilty, it would be as true to say that there had been no war, there was no slain, there had been no crime." Twenty-one of the twenty-four were convicted; of these, twelve were sentenced to be hanged and the remainder were sent to prison.

Many people condemned the trials as an act of vengeance by the victors, claiming that since atrocities are committed in every war by both sides, it was not justice to consider the conquerors morally superior to the conquered. President Franklin D. Roosevelt, however, asserted that "the German people as a whole must have it driven home to them that the whole nation has been engaged in a lawless conspiracy against the decencies of modern civilization."

See also World War II.

Nazi defendants at the Nuremberg trials. The headphones they wore provided translations of the proceedings, which were conducted by an international tribunal. The highest-ranking Nazi to be tried for "crimes against humanity" was Hermann Goering, who appears in the third row at the far left in the light-colored suit. Goering was founder of the Gestapo and masterminded the German air force. At one point Adolf Hitler named him as his successor, but he later fell out of favor. Sentenced to hang, he committed suicide by taking poison two hours before his scheduled execution.

O'CONNOR, SANDRA DAY

(1930–) Associate justice, U.S. Supreme Court.

Born in El Paso, Texas, O'Connor went first to Stanford and then the Stanford Law School, from which she graduated in 1952 third in her class. She was, however, unable to find a job with a private law firm because she was a woman. She therefore accepted a posi-

Sandra Day O'Connor, the first female justice of the Supreme Court.

tion as a deputy county attorney in Arizona.

After service as an assistant attorney general of Arizona, O'Connor was elected as a Republican to the state senate. Thereafter, in 1974, she became a state trial court judge and was later appointed by Governor Bruce Babbitt, a Democrat, to the state's court of appeals. In 1981 she was nominated by President Ronald Reagan to the Supreme Court and, after Senate confirmation, became the first woman to serve on that Court. The principal controversy at her confirmation hearings involved her refusal to indicate her views about the 1973 decision *Roe* v. *Wade* that established constitutional protection for abortion.

O'Connor has been, with some exceptions, a member of the Court's conservative bloc, especially in such areas as criminal justice, the right of a state government to be free from federal regulation, and the use of race as the basis of so-called affirmative action. She wrote the opinions for the majority in *Croson* v. *City of Richmond* (1989), striking down a minority-preference program in the award of public contracts, and in *Shaw* v. *Reno* (1993), which called into question the common practice of states' taking race into account when drawing political boundary lines for legislative districts.

The most important deviation of O'Connor from the conservative bloc has undoubtedly involved her general willingness to protect women's rights, including her providing the crucial fifth vote in a 1992 case that affirmed the abortion rights of women at least against "undue burdens."

See also Supreme Court.

SANFORD LEVINSON

O'KEEFFE, GEORGIA

(1887–1986)   *Artist.*

A pioneer in modern American art and one of the first to express a woman's viewpoint, O'Keeffe is best known for her paintings of flowers and desert scenes. Her work, though often controversial, earned her a place among the most important of American modernists.

O'Keeffe was born on her father's farm in Wisconsin. Her formal education in art included a year at the Art Institute of Chicago and another at the Art Students League in New York. With a solid foundation in traditional technique, she worked briefly as a freelance illustrator and taught in the schools of Texas and North Carolina. But O'Keeffe had an independent nature and in her twenties began to find her own artistic style. In 1915 she came to the attention of the influential photographer and gallery owner Alfred Stieglitz, who recognized her talent and introduced her to the art world. Encouraged by Stieglitz, she gave up teaching, moved to New York, and devoted herself to painting.

O'Keeffe's first solo exhibition, in 1923, was a sensation. The enlarged details of her sensual flower paintings suggested sexual organs to many critics, and her career was launched on a wave of scandal that never completely disappeared. Stieglitz promoted her career shrewdly and in 1924 persuaded her to marry him. He presented her in annual solo shows until his death in 1946.

During the 1920s, she painted cityscapes of New York in an abstract geometric style. Later O'Keeffe turned to the American Southwest for subject matter. Her mystical desert landscapes, often including sun-bleached animal bones, have a mysterious feeling that contributed to her reputation for capturing the female spirit in art. She moved to New Mexico in 1946 and continued painting with undiminished vigor until her death at ninety-eight. O'Keeffe seldom signed her work, explaining that if there was a personal quality in it, that was signature enough—an accurate assessment, given her unmistakable style.

See also Painting and Sculpture; Stieglitz, Alfred.

For further reading: Beverly Gherman, *Georgia O'Keeffe: The "Wideness and Wonder" of Her World* (New York: Macmillan, 1986).

DENNIS WEPMAN

OLYMPIC GAMES

For nearly a century, the modern Olympic Games have been the foremost athletic event in the world. Although they have been used by countries politically since their beginning, for athletes the Games have a unique appeal—an Olympic gold medal means that one is the best in the world in one's sport. Pierre de Coubertin of France founded the modern Games, which first took place in Athens, Greece, in 1896. (Athens was the site of the original Olympic Games over 2,500 years ago.)

Focused at first on track and field events—different kinds of running, jumping, and throwing—the Games soon added soccer, horseback riding, and rowing (1900), boxing and free-style wrestling (1904), figure skating (1908), and later basketball (1936) and volleyball (1964), as well as a host of minor sports.

Women, whose participation was controversial, first competed in the Games as early as 1908, in the new Olympic sport of figure skating. By the next Games, there were women's events in swimming and diving; they entered in fencing in 1924 and in track and field in 1928.

Individual Stars

Particularly fine achievements by individuals have always taken on a special aura. Athletes with style and flair, such as the African-American runners Florence Griffith-Joyner (two golds in 1988) and Jackie Joyner-Kersee (golds in the long jump and heptathlon), become celebrities as well as winners. In 1912, for example, the American Indian Jim Thorpe won the ten-event decathlon, earning him the title of "best athlete in the world." In 1924 the American swimmer Johnny Weismuller won three gold medals; he later went on to star in numerous movies as Hollywood's Tarzan. In 1932, the finest female athlete of her time, perhaps of the century, Babe Didrikson, All-American basketball player and later professional golfer, set world records and won gold medals in hurdles and the javelin throw and a silver medal in the high jump. And in 1972 American swimmer Mark Spitz captured an unprecedented seven gold medals.

The Winter Olympics began in 1924, in Chamonix, France, and incorporated skating, ice hockey, skiing, and bobsled—later the biathlon and luge. Norway's Sonja Henie won gold medals in figure skating in three consecutive Olympics (1928, 1932, and 1936) and raised her sport to a new level. She too went on to a successful career in Hollywood.

Political Events

The Berlin Olympics of 1936 surpassed all others of the period in size, lavishness, and political controversy. Adolf Hitler intended the Games to demonstrate the cultural and athletic superiority of Nazi Germany. Although Americans considered boycotting the Olympics to protest Nazi anti-Semitism, they ended up competing. The hero that year was the African-American track star Jesse Owens, who made Olympic history by winning four gold medals, dramatically refuting Hitler's claim of Aryan racial supremacy.

During the cold war the United States and the Soviet Union saw the Olympics as a political as well as an athletic competition. When the eighteen-year-old Cassius Clay defeated a Russian boxer to win the light heavyweight gold medal at the 1960 Rome Games, he was asked by a Russian reporter about racial prejudice in the United States. Clay, who later changed his name to Muhammad Ali and became a vigorous critic of the government, replied, "To me, the U.S.A. is still the best country in the world, counting yours."

Later, the issue of black rights worldwide became a source of Olympic controversy. Two American sprinters, John Carlos and Tommie Smith, gave a defiant black power salute during their awards ceremony in Mexico City in 1968. Though they were promptly thrown off the team and shipped home, they became international heroes for their striking, dignified protest. African countries focused attention and pressure on the apartheid regime of South Africa, resulting in that country's expulsion from the Olympics in 1970. Then in 1972 in Munich, an Olympic version of the Middle East conflict horrified the world, as a Palestinian terrorist group seized, held hostage, and then murdered the eleven-member Israeli Olympic team.

Financial Issues

Once the television networks brought their

Jesse Owens, winner of the gold medal in the broad jump during the 1936 Olympic Games in Berlin, Germany. All but Owens and bronze medalist Naosto Tajima of Japan are giving the Nazi salute. Adolf Hitler had planned to demonstrate the superiority of the Aryan race at the Olympics. Jesse Owens's magnificent performance, however, made a mockery of Hitler's racist notions.

broadcast and entertainment expertise to the Olympics, the Games became a riveting and lucrative spectacle. The ABC network paid $1 million for rights to the 1964 Games and $25 million in 1976; NBC paid $401 million for rights to the 1992 Games in Barcelona. Cities compete to host the Games. Corporations buy sponsorships and use the Olympics as a worldwide billboard for products such as clothing, beer, cameras, and soda.

The powerful forces encouraging national victories and commercial success led American Olympic authorities to erase the narrow line between amateur and professional athletes. Nearly all Olympic athletes now receive some kinds of subsidies or payments—either from their governments or from companies for product endorsements—so they are in effect professionals. But as a result, the finest athletes in the world can compete in the Olympics.

Although, like many spectator sports, the Olympic Games are a mixture of political interests and commercial entertainment, they consistently produce gripping, beautiful, superb athletic competition.

See also Ali, Muhammad; Owens, Jesse; Sports, Spectator; Thorpe, Jim; Zaharias, Babe Didrikson.

For further reading: William S. Jarrett, *Timetables of Sports History: The Olympic Games* (New York: Facts on File, 1990).

WARREN GOLDSTEIN

O'NEILL, EUGENE

(1888–1953)   Dramatist.

Most critics call Eugene O'Neill America's greatest playwright. Four of his works earned Pulitzer Prizes, and in 1936 he became the only American dramatist to win a Nobel Prize for literature.

O'Neill opened a new era in the American theater. Before him, the stage had been dominated by melodramas—action stories with lovely ladies, manly heroes, and fiendish villains. His father, James O'Neill, was a famous actor in such plays, especially *The Count of Monte Cristo.*

Thus Eugene's life was rooted in theater from the beginning. He was born in a New York hotel room near where his father performed and spent much of his childhood backstage. But his parents' travels made boarding school a hated necessity. He later recalled one especially bitter Christmas vacation spent alone at school because his parents were away on tour. Even family times at home were painful, however. His brother was an alcoholic who never recovered. And perhaps the most horrible moment of Eugene's youth came when he discovered that the mother he idolized was a drug addict.

After some alcohol-hazed years as a sailor and beach bum overseas, O'Neill returned to America to become a playwright. Instead of writing melodramatic fantasies, he gave his characters realistic problems that often reflected the unhappy events of his own life or those he saw around him: racial strife, drug abuse, alcoholism, and crippling family secrets.

Though some find weaknesses in O'Neill's writing, his plays grip many people powerfully. To anyone who has been alone and afraid, the quiet despair of his characters can seem strangely familiar. Solitary even in crowds, clinging to "pipe dreams," as he used to say, these characters wait for happy endings that will never come, often with heartbreaking courage.

His four Pulitzer Prize plays are *Beyond the Horizon, Anna Christie, Strange Interlude,* and *Long Day's Journey into Night.* His trilogy, *Mourning Becomes Electra,* is based on the *Oresteia,* a cycle of ancient Greek tragedies, which he transformed into the unhappy story of a nineteenth-century New England family. Two others of interest are *The Iceman Cometh* and *The Emperor Jones.* His most lighthearted play, *Ah, Wilderness!,* is probably a young person's best introduction to O'Neill's works.

See also Theater.

JAN CHARLES HALUSKA

OPEC OIL CRISIS

In October 1973 the festering hostility that marked the relations of Israel and its Arab neighbors erupted in another war. This led the Organization of Petroleum Exporting Countries (OPEC) to cut off oil shipments to the United States, Western Europe, and Japan. Since OPEC was by far the largest supplier of petroleum to these nations, they suffered an immediate shortage, and an economic crisis of major proportions resulted. More important, when the boycott was finally lifted the next spring, OPEC raised the price of its oil from $3.00 a barrel to $11.65.

Oil is used not only for heating purposes and as a fuel for automobiles, but in the manufacture of plastics, fertilizers, synthetic fabrics, and dozens of other products. The sudden rise in its price caused the price of almost everything else to soar. The effects were especially serious in the United States, which was by far the largest and most wasteful user of petroleum products of all kinds. For example, Americans were driving large and powerful "gas guzzlers," and traveling more than a trillion miles a year. When the price of gasoline doubled, the drain on motorists' pocketbooks was enormous.

The government responded by stockpiling petroleum, trying to increase American production, and encouraging the use of other sources of energy. To encourage conservation, a national speed limit of 55 miles per hour was established and laws were passed to encourage manufacturers to make lighter, more fuel-efficient automobiles. Nevertheless a long period of double-digit inflation disrupted the economy.

OPEN DOOR POLICY

In the late nineteenth century all the industrial nations were interested in exploiting the enormous Chinese market. Since China was weak and unable to resist foreign pressure, Japan and the major European powers took over what were known as "spheres of influence" along China's east coast. This alarmed Secretary of State John Hay, who was eager to preserve American business interests in China. But establishing an American sphere of influence in China would have caused protests by people who objected to the United States becoming a colonial power. In 1899, therefore, Hay sent diplomatic notes to Great Britain, France, Germany, Italy, Russia, and Japan asking them to agree to respect the trading rights of all other nations in their spheres of influence—that is, not to give special advantages to their own nationals and to treat the merchants and ships of all nations equally.

Most of the answers to Hay's "Open Door Notes" were at best vague. Nothing was really changed by his effort. But Hay calmly an-

nounced that the powers had "accepted" his suggestions. Then, after the United States had joined in an international expedition to rescue foreigners during the Boxer Rebellion of 1900, Hay sent off another round of Open Door Notes, this time extending the idea of equal treatment to all of the Chinese Empire not merely to the foreign spheres of influence. Hay's strategy seemed to succeed; American merchants were not discriminated against in the spheres. But there was no way the United States could make the powers respect American rights if they did not wish to do so.

OPPENHEIMER, J. ROBERT

(1904–67)   *Physicist.*

Oppenheimer led the World War II project to build the first atomic bomb. Born to a wealthy New York family, he graduated from Harvard and studied in Europe. In 1929, he became a professor at the University of California, Berkeley, and the California Institute of Technology. Sometimes temperamental, he nonetheless had devoted students and friends.

In the 1930s, physicists learned how to split uranium atoms, which releases enormous amounts of energy. This process is known as nuclear fission. The U.S. government during World War II assigned Oppenheimer and others the task of using nuclear fission to create a powerful bomb. Appointed a leader of the Manhattan Project, as it was called, Oppenheimer organized and ran laboratories in Los Alamos, New Mexico.

At the time, federal investigators questioned his loyalty to the United States because his wife and brother had been Communists and he had belonged to left-wing groups. He was too important to the project to be dismissed, however.

Oppenheimer supervised successful atomic bomb tests in 1945 and pushed for using the bomb against Japan. After two bombs were dropped, however, he had regrets because of the enormous destruction of life and property they caused.

After the war Oppenheimer headed the Institute for Advanced Study, an academic foundation at Princeton University. He also chaired an advisory committee to the U.S. Atomic Energy Commission. Then a wave of anticommunism hit the nation. Some of his critics claimed that Oppenheimer had tried to block the building of a nuclear fusion, or hydrogen, bomb, after the war. Actually, he had endorsed the project.

In 1954, the Atomic Energy Commission held a hearing on whether Oppenheimer should be allowed to continue working for the commission. Some scientists who disliked him testified against him, and he admitted misleading investigators during the war. The commission concluded that Oppenheimer had not been disloyal. But it decided that he was a "security risk" and therefore should no longer have access to secret government research.

Many people at the time believed he was treated unfairly, and he was later honored by the government for his service.

See also Anticommunism; Manhattan Project.

For further reading: Rebecca Larsen, *Oppenheimer and the Atomic Bomb* (New York: Franklin Watts, 1988).

REBECCA LARSEN

A long wagon train of settlers on the Oregon Trail, a route that stretched from Independence, Missouri, to the Willamette Valley in Oregon. The journey took an average of six months.

OREGON TRAIL

The Oregon Trail was the route followed by the settlers who flocked to the Oregon country in the early 1840s and 1850s. The first wagon train of settlers reached Oregon by way of the trail in 1842. The next year came the "great migration," during which about a thousand people followed the trail west.

It was not a road, or even a well-worn path, but a series of key points. How any particular group got from one point to the next might vary considerably.

Most caravans set out from Independence, Missouri, and proceeded up the Kansas and Platte rivers past Fort Kearny and on to Fort Laramie, in what is now southeastern Wyoming. From there they passed over the Continental Divide (beyond which rivers flow west to the Pacific) by way of South Pass. Then the trail veered northwest to Fort Hall on the Snake River and followed the Snake to the Blue Mountains. The travelers' next goal was Fort Walla Walla on the Columbia River, which they followed to trail's end in the Willamette Valley. Both the eastern and western ends of the route had been blazed by Lewis and Clark on their expedition, but much of their route ran far to the north.

It took five months or more of extraordinarily hard traveling to get to the Willamette from Independence. Most families brought everything they owned, both livestock and their furniture and personal possessions, usually in horse- or oxen-drawn vehicles, the famous Conestoga covered wagons, which in effect became portable homes. There was much to see and more to learn about pioneering along the way, but the travelers who were disappointed when they reached their destination must have been rare indeed.

See also Pioneers and Frontier Life.

OSTEND MANIFESTO

After California and the rest of the Southwest were added to the Union as a result of the Mexican War, many Americans believed that the era of territorial expansion had ended. The spirit of manifest destiny, the belief that the United States was destined to take over the continent, did not disappear, however.

The idea of annexing the Spanish colony of Cuba was always a temptation, especially among slave owners. Cuba's sugar cane crop was well suited to slave labor. In 1854, although President Franklin Pierce and Secretary of State William L. Marcy were northerners, they gave serious thought to buying the island. Marcy ordered the American minister to Spain, Pierre Soulé, to meet in Ostend, Belgium, with the American ministers to France and Great Britain, John Y. Mason and James Buchanan, to work out a strategy for persuading Spain to sell Cuba.

In October the three diplomats met and drafted the Ostend Manifesto, which took the form of a confidential dispatch to Secretary Marcy. It declared that American possession of Cuba was essential if slavery was to be preserved in the United States. Every effort should be made to persuade Spain to sell the island. But if Spain refused, "the great law of self-preservation" decreed that the United States would be "justified in wresting it from Spain" by force.

The tone of the manifesto was so aggressive that Marcy repudiated it and forced Soulé, who was responsible for it, to resign. The only beneficiary of the incident was James Buchanan, whose ambition to become president was much advanced by the southern backing that his support of the Ostend Manifesto generated.

See also Expansion, Territorial; Manifest Destiny.

OWENS, JESSE

(1913–80)   Track and field athlete.

Voted by sportswriters the outstanding track and field athlete of the first half of the twentieth century, African-American Jesse Owens gained international fame by making a mockery of Adolf Hitler's notions of Aryan supremacy at the 1936 Olympic Games in Berlin.

The grandson of slaves, James Cleveland "Jesse" Owens was born in Alabama, the tenth child of sharecroppers who moved to Cleveland in the 1920s as part of the Great Migration of African Americans from the rural South. In high school Owens was a sprinter, hurdler, and long-jumper. At the 1933 national high school championships he tied the *world record* in the 100-yard dash. At Ohio State, Owens, an extremely graceful athlete, captured a record eight individual NCAA championships. At the Big Ten Conference Championship in 1935, he tied or set world records in the 100-yard dash, long jump, 220-yard dash, and 220-yard low hurdles—all within two hours. His long jump, 26 feet, 8¼ inches, remained unbeaten for a quarter of a century.

Owens's greatest triumph came the following year, at what became known as the Nazi Olympics. Hitler had planned to use the Berlin Games to showcase Aryan racial and physical supremacy. German newspapers sneered at the ten African-American athletes (on a team of sixty-six), calling them the "Black Auxiliaries." Although Germany did win more medals than any other country, what made headlines was Owens's brilliant individual performance. He won four gold medals, tying the Olympic record in the 100-meter dash and setting new records in the 200-meter dash, long jump, and 400-meter relay. Some of those records stood until 1960.

Following his Olympic triumph Owens tried to cash in on his fame, but with little success; he eventually declared bankruptcy. He prospered in the 1950s and 1960s, however, by working in public relations for corporations. His modesty, patriotism, and sincerity made him an excellent public speaker, much in demand. Owens remained America's most popular and famous track and field athlete until his death from cancer in 1980.

See also Olympic Games; Sports, Spectator.

WARREN GOLDSTEIN

P

PACIFISM
See Conscientious Objectors.

PACT OF PARIS
See Kellogg-Briand Pact.

PAINE, THOMAS

(1737–1809)   *Political writer.*

The author of numerous pamphlets and newspaper articles, Thomas Paine was perhaps the most influential writer of his time. His importance lay in the power of his ideas and his ability to speak effectively to readers of all backgrounds and levels of education.

Growing up in England, Paine developed a hatred for governments controlled by a king and aristocracy. He moved to Philadelphia in 1774 and, in January 1776, published *Common Sense,* the first pamphlet to call for American independence. *Common Sense* outlined Paine's basic ideas: democracy was superior to monarchy, all citizens should enjoy equal rights, and the American Revolution would inspire the spread of liberty throughout the world. "We have it in our power," Paine wrote, "to begin the world over again." Written in simple, direct language and addressed to a broad audience, *Common Sense* sold 150,000 copies in 1776.

For the next several years, Paine threw himself into the cause of independence. He wrote *The American Crisis,* a series of essays that aroused support for the war. The first began with the famous words, "These are the times that try men's souls."

Paine returned to Europe in 1787. He soon entered the political debate caused by the French Revolution. His *Rights of Man* defended the revolution and advocated political democracy in England and government assistance to the poor. The British government, which felt threatened by the French Revolution, attempted to arrest Paine. He fled to France and was elected to the National Convention, only to be jailed for opposing the execution of King Louis XVI. After his release, Paine published *The Age of Reason,* which proclaimed his belief in God but attacked organized religions, including Christianity. His last great pamphlet was *Agrarian Justice,* which insisted that every person has a natural right to own land.

After his return to the United States in 1802, Paine was largely forgotten. Only six mourners attended his funeral seven years later. But his writings are still remembered by those who believe in political democracy and social equality.

See also Revolution.

ERIC FONER

PAINTING AND SCULPTURE

The arts in America, like the country's other institutions, in the beginning reflected the European traditions from which they came.

The colonists brought with them the styles, techniques, and subjects of their original homes. But distinctively American strains came to distinguish the new country's painting and sculpture, and in time an identifiable American art emerged.

Colonial Art

In the eighteenth century, the fusion of Spanish and Indian cultures in the American Southwest generated an elaborate folk art, especially of religious paintings and church decoration. But it was the matter-of-fact painting style of the English colonies in the Northeast that was to define the nation's art.

Most of the paintings produced in colonial New England were done by untrained artists. In an era before photography, the favorite art form was portraiture. The formal likenesses of colonial faces were often the anonymous work of traveling craftsmen. By the middle of the eighteenth century, however, American painters were the equal of the British professionals they imitated, and a few even attained international reputations. Philadelphia-trained Benjamin West traveled to Italy to complete his education and went on to settle in England, where he became president of the Royal Academy of Arts. The most prominent colonial artist was Boston's John Singleton Copley, whose sharply observed portraits reflect the direct, realistic style that was typical of American portraiture. Silversmith and later revolutionary war hero Paul Revere, who sat for a portrait about 1765, was one of many Bostonians whose faces Copley preserved for history.

Copley was a loyal subject of England and moved there to enjoy a successful career before the American Revolution. His most important successor, and perhaps the best portraitist of the time, was Gilbert Stuart, whose likeness of George Washington (1796) is on the dollar bill. Stuart captured the spirit of the young democracy in his simple, forthright depiction of the citizen-president with no insignia of rank or office. Another artist known for his portraits of Washington as well as other national leaders was Charles Willson Peale, who opened a portrait gallery in Philadelphia in 1782. Peale, his four sons, his brother James, and two of James's daughters were all distinguished painters and became the first important family of American artists.

By the end of the eighteenth century, however, the straightforward style of American art was beginning to give way to the romanticism then popular in Europe. Paintings depicting historical events became fashionable, and such idealized canvases as John Trumbull's *The Battle of Bunker's Hill* (1789) and *The Declaration of Independence* (1794) glorified the American experience.

Nature as Subject Matter

More important to the history of American art, however, was the growing attention to the local scene. The populace had become prosperous enough to appreciate the beauty and grandeur of nature. American artists still looked to Europe for inspiration and training, and some devoted themselves to classical styles and scenes, but many were beginning to turn to the landscapes and daily lives of their own world for subjects.

The wildlife of the New World inspired such artists as John James Audubon to create a record of the birds of the Continent published in his collection of engravings, *Birds of North America* (1827–38). Pictures showing ordinary life in America became popular at this time. William Sidney Mount produced vivid paintings like *Bargaining for a Horse*

(1835) that captured the folkways of Long Island farmers, and George Caleb Bingham created poetic scenes of fur trappers and river boatmen.

At the same time, a taste for art celebrating the majesty of the natural scene and giving it symbolic importance developed. Nature became a subject in itself. The paintings of the period employed European techniques, but their emphasis on untamed wilderness was distinctively American. In the 1820s there formed a group of artists who specialized in landscapes untouched by civilization. Thomas Cole, Asher Durand, and others worked in the Catskill Mountains and along the Hudson River and so came to be called the Hudson River school. Their works had a higher purpose than mere decoration or documentation of the scenery; they often had a philosophical message beyond the visual drama. Cole, the leader of the group, created series of canvases like *The Course of Empire* (1836) to make a patriotic statement about the growth of the nation.

Not all the new landscape artists limited themselves to Hudson River settings. Cole's pupil Frederick E. Church painted great natural wonders like *Niagara Falls* (1857) and traveled as far as South America in search of subjects. Albert Bierstadt did sensational panoramas of the Rocky Mountains, and George Catlin went to the western frontier to paint the vanishing world of the Indians. The dramatic atmosphere as well as the American subject matter of these idealized paintings was different from what was being produced in Europe at the time; it was a distinctly American art.

Although theatrical in composition, the nature paintings of the mid-nineteenth century were precise in style and continued to appeal to America's taste for literal accuracy.

Realism was to reach a peak a few decades later in the work of such illusionists as William Harnett and John F. Peto, whose still lifes were so exact in lighting and detail as to seem like real objects.

Along with the growing technical mastery shown by American artists, folk art continued to be popular. The self-taught craftsman Edward Hicks, a Quaker preacher and sign painter, produced charming landscapes and allegorical scenes like *The Peaceable Kingdom,* of which he painted many versions in the 1830s and 1840s. They illustrate the biblical prophecy of God's kingdom on earth, showing wild and domestic animals at peace together, often in real settings from Hicks's native Pennsylvania.

Sculpture

American sculpture, almost exclusively a folk art in the seventeenth century, came into its own in the eighteenth. The first important sculptor was the Philadelphian William Rush, who carved monumental wood and marble figures in a classical style during the first decade of the century. Other major workers in stone were Augustus Saint-Gaudens and Daniel Chester French, most famous for their large, formal public works. More popular and characteristically American, however, was the work of John Rogers, who executed realistic scenes of everyday home life in bronze. At the end of the century, Frederic Remington, who had followed Catlin in illustrating the Far West in oil and pencil, captured the vitality of the frontier in dynamic bronze figures of cowboys, soldiers, and Indians.

Twentieth-Century Artists

Probably the most successful American artist at the beginning of the twentieth century was

James McNeill Whistler, who worked in France and England for most of his career. The elegant, almost abstract design of his portraits made him an important forerunner of modernism. Equally international were John Singer Sargent, a fashionable society artist whose brilliant technique was much admired, and Mary Cassatt, the only American to be identified with the French impressionists. Childe Hassam and others followed, forming a group of American impressionists typically more realistic than the French.

Three artists, however, stand out as the most unmistakably American masters at the end of the nineteenth century. Winslow Homer produced rugged marine paintings with a power uniquely his own. Albert Pinkham Ryder was a visionary whose dreamlike seascapes showed an imagination that was almost mystical. The most influential of the three was Thomas Eakins, a methodical realist of great psychological penetration whose unsentimental honesty was shocking to many.

Early in the twentieth century, in a characteristically democratic rebellion against the refined subjects and styles of the times, a group of young American artists focused on the commonplace, even sordid, life of American cities. Robert Henri, John Sloan, and others became known as the Ashcan school because of their harshly realistic depictions of slums, barrooms, and boxing rings as part of American culture. No less powerful in his urban scenes was Edward Hopper, who captured the loneliness of cities in his brooding compositions. The Great Depression of the 1930s introduced more specific social commentary into American art with the social realists, who used poverty and injustice as themes.

The depression years also saw a movement toward regionalism in American art. With government support, such painters as John Steuart Curry, Thomas Hart Benton, and Grant Wood, known as the Triumvirate of the West, created vivid renderings of rural midwestern scenes and earned critical acceptance for American subjects in their work. Wood's 1930 *American Gothic,* an ironic, stylized portrait of farm folk in his native Iowa, was both a critical and a popular success.

Modernism

The radically new modern art of Europe reached America in 1913 at an exhibition at New York's Sixty-ninth Regiment Armory. Known simply as the Armory Show, it introduced the most extreme modernism to both the public and the artists of the United States. The works puzzled and even angered many, but they had a profound impact on American art. Painters and sculptors soon incorporated many of the techniques of modernism into their work.

In the 1940s New York replaced Paris as the laboratory of experiment in art. The abstract expressionists, a group of artists including Jackson Pollock, Willem de Kooning, Mark Rothko, and Franz Kline, developed original techniques and styles and formed the first American movement to influence European artists. Typically American in their energy and freedom from convention, the abstract expressionists took such liberties as dripping paint at random on canvas.

Sculpture too underwent radical change in the twentieth century. Although realistic statuary continued to be created, new forms began to appear. Louise Nevelson combined fragments of household furniture and scrap lumber into rhythmic patterns in wall hangings and free-standing pieces, and David Smith created severely abstract sculpture of geometric forms in welded metal. In the 1930s Alexander Calder introduced movement to sculpture with his mobiles, delicately poised abstract constructions of sheet metal wired together to move in the wind. Huge outdoor constructions called earthworks, erected by engineering methods and forming part of the natural environment, were created by Robert Smithson and others in the 1960s and 1970s as a statement against private ownership of art.

A reaction against the complete freedom of modernism set in during the 1960s with the development of pop art, which took its images from popular culture. Andy Warhol copied soup-can labels, Roy Lichtenstein replicated comics, and Claes Oldenburg made fabric statues of fast-food items—all as mocking comments on contemporary society. Again an American art movement had a profound international influence, as did other new styles that followed.

Since World War II, the United States has been the undisputed leader of world art, by reason of both its economic power as a market and its dynamic and diverse culture as a source of creative inspiration.

See also Abstract Expressionism; Armory Show; Ashcan School; Pop Art. Also see biographies of individual painters and sculptors and, for illustrations, the color insert following page 628.

DENNIS WEPMAN

PANAMA CANAL

The isthmus of Panama, only about fifty miles wide at its narrowest point, first attracted the attention of the United States in the 1840s, when settlers and gold seekers from the East began to make the long and difficult trek across the continent by land. To reach the West Coast by sea required sailing around the southern tip of South America. This was more comfortable but took about three months even for a speedy clipper ship. If a canal could be built across Panama, that time would be greatly reduced. But Panama was mountainous and densely forested. A French company attempted to build a canal in the 1880s, but failed to make any progress.

American interest in an isthmian canal slackened after the building of the transcontinental railroads made it cheaper and easier to cross the continent by land. But during the Spanish-American War, the military importance of a canal was highlighted when the battleship *Oregon,* stationed in the Pacific, took two months to steam around South America on its way to join in the attack on Cuba. Shortly after the war, President William McKinley was eager to get a canal constructed.

A New Panama Canal Company had meanwhile taken over the older French company, but it was no more successful. After considerable negotiation, President Theodore Roosevelt, who took office after McKinley was assassinated, agreed to pay the company $40 million for its rights. Since Panama was part of the Republic of Colombia, he then negotiated a treaty with that nation, giving the United States a ninety-nine-year lease on a strip of land wide enough to construct a canal.

The Colombian Senate, however, refused to sign this treaty. This led Panama, encouraged by the United States, to revolt and declare itself independent. It quickly signed a new treaty with the United States. In 1906 construction of the canal was begun. A gargantuan engineering project, it cost well over $300 million and involved the excavation of 240 million cubic yards of earth. Work on it had been hampered by the devastations of tropical disease, so that Col. William Gorgas's eradication of yellow fever and malaria was a vital contribution. In 1914 the canal, forty miles in length, was opened to traffic.

The commercial value of the canal was enormous both to the United States and to all nations involved in international trade. But as time passed the people of Panama came to resent the fact that because of its need to protect the canal the United States maintained a large number of troops in their country and dominated both its economy and their government. Finally in 1977 the United States under President Jimmy Carter signed new treaties increasing the benefits paid to Panama and agreeing to turn the canal over to Panama at the end of 1999.

See also Expansion, Territorial.

PARIS, TREATY OF (1783)

After the brilliant American-French defeat of Lord Cornwallis's British army at the Battle of Yorktown in October 1781, the British government gave up hope of regaining control of its American colonies. In 1782 three American commissioners, John Adams, Benjamin Franklin, and John Jay, met with British negotiators in Paris to work out peace terms.

The discussions were complicated but friendly. Most of the difficulties were caused by the French foreign minister, the Comte de Vergennes, who did not like the idea of the United States becoming too friendly with France's enemy, Great Britain.

The most significant aspect of the treaty from the American point of view was that it acknowledged the United States "to be free, sovereign and independent States." Almost equally important, Britain ceded to the new

nation all its territory in America south of the Great Lakes and east of the Mississippi River. The treaty also gave Americans the right to fish in British-controlled waters off Newfoundland and to dry and cure their catch on British territory in Canada. In addition, the British agreed to remove all their troops from the posts and forts they still held in the Great Lakes region and the Ohio Valley. The United States for its part promised to "earnestly recommend" to the individual states that they return the property of Loyalists that had been confiscated during the Revolution. Many Anglo-American problems remained, but the Revolution had ended and independence had been won.

See also Revolution: The War for Independence.

PARKS, ROSA

(1913–   )   *Civil rights activist.*

Often called "the mother of the freedom movement," Rosa Parks in 1955 refused to give up her seat on a bus in Montgomery, Alabama, to a white man—and sparked a historic movement among African Americans for social and political equality.

Born in Tuskegee, Alabama, young Rosa grew up with a deep awareness of racial injustice. From her mother, who was a schoolteacher, and through her own childhood in the segregated South, she learned firsthand about racial prejudice. In 1932, she married Raymond Parks, a barber and civil rights activist. Several years later, Rosa Parks became one of the first women to join the Montgomery chapter of the National Association for the Advancement of Colored People (NAACP).

While riding home from her job in downtown Montgomery on December 1, 1955, Parks was seated in the front of the "colored"

Rosa Parks fingerprinted at the Montgomery, Alabama, police station after she and more than a hundred other civil rights protesters were indicted on charges relating to the Montgomery bus boycott of 1956.

section—the rows of seats in the back of the bus restricted to black passengers. When a white passenger could not find a seat in front, the driver told Parks and the other black passengers in her row to move back. Rosa Parks refused. The driver summoned the police, who carted Parks off to jail.

Within days, Montgomery's black community organized a mass boycott against the city's transit system—walking, hitching rides, or car-pooling to avoid riding on segregated city buses. The bus boycott lasted until December 20, 1956, when the Supreme Court ordered city officials to integrate Montgomery's buses.

After this victory, blacks across the South organized a movement to end segregation in all public facilities, including schools and libraries, and in the voting booth, where most blacks had been denied the right to vote. Parks, like other civil rights activists, was the target of vicious harassment. After losing her

job, she and her husband moved to Detroit, Michigan, in 1957, where she continues to work for civil rights. She remains a towering example of courage and commitment to social justice.

See also Civil Rights Movement.

For further reading: Rosa Parks, *My Story* (New York: Dial Books, 1992).

HARRIET SIGERMAN

PARTY CONVENTIONS

American political parties long used conventions to pick their candidates for election to offices at all levels of government. Convention delegates, who were chosen by party members, also usually adopted a *platform*, which set forth the party's position on current issues and appointed committees to manage party affairs. The conventions served to promote unity and arouse enthusiasm in preparation for the campaign to come.

Development of the System

Before the creation of the convention system, parties relied on their members in the state legislatures to nominate candidates for statewide offices, such as governor. This type of meeting was called a legislative *caucus*. At the national level, U.S. congressmen who belonged to the Democratic-Republican Party (the party of Presidents Thomas Jefferson, James Madison, and James Monroe) met in caucus to endorse presidential and vice-presidential candidates. The practice was abandoned after 1824, in part because the party was destroyed by internal divisions.

The caucus system was replaced by conventions, which some states had tried earlier. The first national convention was held by the short-lived Anti-Masonic Party, which originated in New York in 1827 to demand the out-lawing of the Masons, a secret fraternal order. Delegates met in Baltimore on September 26, 1931, and nominated William Wirt of Maryland for president and Amos Ellmaker of Pennsylvania for vice president.

Two major parties also held national conventions in Baltimore to prepare for the 1832 election. The National Republicans, soon to become the Whig Party, convened in December 1831 and named Henry Clay of Kentucky as their presidential nominee. The Democrats met in May 1832. Because it was generally accepted that President Andrew Jackson would run for a second term, the main purpose of the meeting was to choose a vice-presidential candidate. With Jackson's blessing, Martin Van Buren of New York was selected.

Convention Routines
Over the next few decades the national party conventions followed rituals that persisted down to the mid-twentieth century. A *keynote speaker* opened the proceedings with a rousing speech designed to promote harmony and taunt the opposition party. Then the platform would be debated and adopted.

Members of the Louisiana delegation at the Democratic National Convention of 1992 engaging in typical convention hoopla: sporting badges and hats, waving posters and parasols representing Louisiana's Southern charm, clapping and shouting, and in general working themselves into a frenzy.

Next came long-winded nominating speeches, followed by boisterous demonstrations staged by the supporters of each nominee.

Meanwhile, influential party figures would be engaged in backroom negotiations to shape the convention's decisions. The most famous of these meetings occurred during the 1920 Republican convention when party leaders, puffing away on cigars, gathered in a "smoke-filled room" outside the main hall and picked Warren G. Harding as their presidential candidate. Political figures operating in "smoke-filled rooms" has become a popular image to indicate politicians deciding on issues among themselves in private without input from citizens.

The climactic event of the convention was the balloting, when each state was called upon to announce its vote. About half of the time, a single ballot produced the victor, but other times several ballots were needed. The Democrats in 1924 had to ballot 103 times before nominating John W. Davis in the lengthiest of all conventions. When preconvention favorites became deadlocked, the delegates sometimes compromised and selected a *dark horse*. This was a man who was not so well known, who hadn't been mentioned much as a nominee up to that point, and whose views were more or less acceptable to all sides. Such was the case in 1844 when the Democrats settled on the little-known James K. Polk.

The adoption of party platforms occasionally produced bitter controversies over such issues as slavery, monetary policy, the tariff, and civil rights. Three conventions failed to resolve internal problems. In 1860, just before the Civil War, the Democrats divided over the slavery question into northern and southern wings, with each going its own way. The Republicans split apart in 1912, with one faction endorsing William Howard Taft for reelec-tion and another forming the Bull Moose Party and backing ex-president Theodore Roosevelt. The Democrats split again in 1948 when the convention platform endorsed some civil rights for blacks. The party nominated Harry S. Truman who backed the platform, and southern senators walked out. They formed the Dixiecrat Party and nominated Strom Thurmond.

Decline of Conventions

The importance of national conventions declined after World War II. The presidential primary (introduced in some states in 1912 but of minor importance until the 1950s) enabled party members to vote for delegates pledged to particular candidates. Increasingly after 1952, state primaries determined which candidate would get the most votes in the convention. Since that year, all nominees have been selected on the first ballot.

Conventions are now tailored to television. Key events are designed for prime-time audiences, fewer candidates are put in nomination, demonstrations are kept short. Until Franklin D. Roosevelt flew to Chicago to accept the 1932 Democratic presidential nomination, candidates did not appear at conventions. Now the high point of the meetings is the presidential candidate's acceptance speech.

Conventions to choose candidates for state and local offices have given way to the direct primary system. Party voters in primary elections, held months before the general election, select the nominees they want without the intervention of a convention. Although the national conventions survive, they bear little resemblance to those colorful meetings that dominated national politics for more than a century.

RICHARD P. McCORMICK

PATTON, GEORGE S.

(1885–1945)   *General.*

"Hit hard, soon," was the motto of Patton, one of the most colorful American generals of this century. His courage and dash in battle earned him the nickname "Old Blood and Guts." But his personality sometimes got him into trouble.

Born in San Gabriel, California, Patton graduated from West Point in 1909. He had been especially interested in studying Civil War generals like Jeb Stuart and Philip Sheridan—cavalrymen who stressed speed and aggression in battle. Now he himself became a cavalry officer, joining Gen. John J. Pershing's expedition against Pancho Villa in 1917. But the days of horse cavalry were drawing to a close, and he was chosen to train one of America's first tank brigades in techniques of fast, violent attack. He led the unit in World War I until wounded in 1918.

At the start of World War II Patton's reputation for rapid action made him the choice to lead American troops in the North African campaign. Later his Seventh Army helped clear Sicily of Germans in a little over a month. But now Patton's warlike nature caused a crisis. He struck a private who had been hospitalized for combat fatigue, thinking to cure what he called the man's "cowardice" through shame. Gen. Dwight D. Eisenhower, commander of Allied troops in Europe, ordered him to apologize publicly. Thus Patton himself was shamed, and he became desperate to clear his name.

His chance came soon after the 1944 Normandy invasion, and Patton made the most of it. His new Third Army charged across France with a speed that bewildered the enemy and made headlines at home. Only a shortage of fuel halted it. He added to his fame in the Battle of the Bulge, when German forces slammed through the American line to his north. Within hours Patton had spun his army around to lunge into the enemy rear at Bastogne, ending German hopes of victory forever. Gen. Omar Bradley called it "one of the most astonishing feats of generalship of our campaign in the West."

After Germany's defeat, Patton made a statement that seemed sympathetic toward the Nazis, and he was removed to a minor post. But shortly after, in December 1945, he died of injuries from an auto accident.

See also World War II.

JAN CHARLES HALUSKA

PAUL, ALICE

(1885–1977)   *Suffragist and women's rights activist.*

One of Alice Paul's earliest memories was accompanying her Quaker parents to woman suffrage meetings in the homes of neighbors in Moorestown, New Jersey. She grew up believing as a matter of course that women and men were equal in all things. It did not occur to her until after she had graduated from Swarthmore College in 1905 that women would have to fight to secure their rights.

Intending to become a social worker, Paul went to London on a scholarship. While there, she joined a radical suffragette organization, picking up many tactics that she would eventually use in the United States. As a suffragette, Paul picketed Parliament and demonstrated against the British government. She was also imprisoned and participated in hunger strikes in protest. She left England with the conviction that the suffragettes were correct in demanding their rights rather than meekly asking for them.

After returning to America, Paul spent the next ten years pursuing women's suffrage. She founded the National Woman's Party and campaigned against Woodrow Wilson in 1916, because neither he nor the Democratic Party supported a woman suffrage amendment to the Constitution. When World War I began in 1917, Paul continued to picket the White House. Arrests and imprisonments resulted, but did not deter her or the Woman's Party. When it became clear that the women would not stop their protests, President Wilson in 1918 asked Congress to pass a federal suffrage amendment. In 1920, the Nineteenth Amendment was ratified.

Securing the right to vote was only a first step for Paul. In 1923, she proposed the first Equal Rights Amendment. Although she worked for women's rights for the rest of her life, both at home and abroad, Paul never achieved the amendment she desired. But today millions of women who may never have heard of Alice Paul are nevertheless indebted to her.

See also Equal Rights Amendment; Feminist Movement to 1919; National Woman's Party; Voting.

CHRISTINE A. LUNARDINI

PEACE CORPS

In his 1960 presidential campaign against Vice President Richard M. Nixon, Senator John F. Kennedy proposed a Peace Corps in which American volunteers could work for the good of the people in Africa, Asia, and Latin America. The Peace Corps, Kennedy said, would promote world peace and friendship by helping developing countries meet their needs for trained workers, by furthering a better understanding of the American people on the part of the people served, and by increasing America's understanding of other people.

Candidate Nixon ridiculed the idea of the Peace Corps, calling it "superficial" and "conceived solely for campaign purposes." After his election, however, President Kennedy gave top priority to this new kind of national service. On March 1, 1961, only six weeks after taking office, he created the Peace Corps by executive order and asked Congress to make it a permanent government program. Within a few months Congress passed a Peace Corps Act by a large majority.

Peace Corps Activities

Moving swiftly, the Peace Corps had put five hundred volunteers at work in nine African, Asian, and Caribbean countries by the end of 1961. At the peak of the Peace Corps' growth in 1966, almost sixteen thousand volunteers—mostly young college graduates—were serving in fifty-nine countries. The American people were intensely interested in what the volunteers were doing overseas. Newspapers, magazines, and television carried frequent human interest stories about their activities. One story told how a volunteer in Pakistan led a thousand villagers in building dams and culverts that saved several village rice crops. Another story recounted how a few volunteers in the Philippines organized a month-long summer camp called Camp Brotherhood for six hundred poor boys.

Such stories were true, but they did not represent most Peace Corps experience. Over half of all volunteers taught English, mathematics, and science, usually in isolated rural schools. Others worked in such jobs as village community development and nurses' training in country hospitals. Their jobs were sometimes dull, often frustrating. Loneliness and occasionally physical hardship were problems. Some volunteers resigned before their two-year assignments were completed, but most stayed on the job and made good friends in the country they were serving.

During the 1970s and 1980s the Peace Corps declined to five thousand or six thousand volunteers a year as public attention turned elsewhere and the Vietnam conflict caused many Americans to question U.S. involvement in world problems. Yet every president after Kennedy, including Richard Nixon, retained the Peace Corps as part of his administration.

New Missions in the 1990s

The Peace Corps entered the decade of the 1990s with strength and vigor. Volunteers work in seventy countries in Africa, Asia, and Latin America, and the total number of volunteers is soon expected to reach ten thousand. In a new initiative, the Peace Corps responded favorably to the request of Poland, Hungary, Romania, and other formerly communist countries of Eastern Europe for volunteers to teach English, help with environmental projects, and assist in the development of private enterprise. In 1992 and 1993 volunteers began similar work in several countries of the former Soviet Union, including one hundred small-business development volunteers in Russia.

The Peace Corps today is still fulfilling its original mission of providing needed skills while teaching people of other countries about America and giving Americans the opportunity to learn about other cultures. Volunteers are carefully selected from thousands of applicants and serve two-year assignments. They receive about ten weeks of intensive training in the language and culture of the country to which they will be assigned. Education is still a major Peace Corps activity. Since 1961 over 5 million students in developing countries have been taught by Peace Corps volunteers.

There are some notable differences between the early Peace Corps and the Peace Corps of the nineties, however. In 1961 the average Peace Corps volunteer age was about twenty-four. Today it is about thirty-one, and one in ten volunteers is fifty-five or older. The reason for the age change is that receiving countries increasingly want volunteers with experience in technical fields such as small-business development, forest and watershed management, and primary health care systems. In the sixties most Peace Corps volunteers were men. Today men and women volunteers are about equal in number.

"Come back and educate us," President Kennedy said to the first volunteers sent overseas. Since 1961 more than 130,000 volunteers have served in more than one hundred countries. Thousands of returned volunteers have made teaching their careers and have brought a special knowledge of other countries into the classroom and other kinds of public service.

Although President Kennedy did not live to see the full flowering of the Peace Corps, many people believe that it will always be thought of as his finest accomplishment.

See also Kennedy, John F.

For further reading: Brent Ashabranner, *A New Frontier: The Peace Corps in Eastern Europe* (New York: Cobblehill Books/ Dutton, 1994).

BRENT ASHABRANNER

PEARL HARBOR, ATTACK ON

During the 1930s, Japanese-American relations went steadily from bad to worse. Japan invaded first Manchuria and then in 1937, China. Under the American neutrality acts, the Japanese therefore were prohibited from buying American arms, gasoline, and scrap iron. Finally, President Franklin D. Roosevelt froze Japanese assets in the United States and banned all trade.

In 1941 the Japanese sent negotiators to America who offered to stop seizing new territory in Asia if the United States would stop helping China and lift its restrictions on the sale of goods to Japan. But while they were negotiating, the Japanese were sending a fleet

At 7:55 on the morning of December 7, 1941, Japanese planes launched a surprise attack on Pearl Harbor in Hawaii. Within two hours the planes had sunk or destroyed numerous American battleships and aircraft. More than two thousand sailors and soldiers and more than sixty civilians were killed. The United States declared war on Japan the next day.

of aircraft carriers and support ships toward the Hawaiian Islands. On December 7, 1941, they launched an all-out air attack on Pearl Harbor, the main American naval base in the islands.

The attack was a total surprise and caused enormous damage to the American Pacific fleet. Eight battleships, three cruisers, and three destroyers were sunk or heavily damaged. Most of the navy's planes were destroyed on the ground, and more than 2,300 servicemen were killed.

Japan had struck without declaring war. This was unprecedented and had much to do with the bitter enmity most Americans felt toward Japan during the war. Already existing racial prejudice against Asians was reinforced. The Japanese were seen as dishonorable sneaks and ruthless murderers who must be exterminated at all costs. On December 8, 1941, the United States declared war on Japan.

See also World War II.

PEI, I. M.

(1917–   )   *Architect.*

The son of an important Chinese family, Pei came to America in the 1930s to study architecture. He took seminars at Harvard in the 1940s with one of the creators of modern architecture, Walter Gropius. In 1948 Pei went to work for the big-time developer William Zeckendorf. Pei's skill at creating sleek, elegantly detailed apartment complexes in the modern style brought him government jobs in urban renewal—designing new housing or other uses for run-down city neighborhoods—in the 1960s. He planned Boston's Government Center (1959–63) and that city's Christian Science Church headquarters

Architect I. M. Pei standing in front of the Louvre in Paris in 1985. He points out the future site of his controversial glass pyramid, which would serve as an entrance to the world-famous museum.

(1968–73). (Impressive as these projects are, many people now wish they had not demolished the existing neighborhoods so drastically.) Other prestigious commissions followed.

The buildings of Pei's design firm are always monuments—great abstract shapes that are both simple and dramatic. Luxury materials in a few restrained colors make them seem cool and elegant. This is true whether the buildings are museums like the National Gallery East Wing in Washington, D.C. (1978), or office towers like Boston's Hancock Building (chiefly by Pei's partner Henry Cobb, 1975).

Pei's treating each building as an abstract sculpture has led to some criticism. The Hancock was called inhuman because of its great size and mirror-glass materials. Pei's master plan for the Louvre in Paris (1989), centering around a new main entrance in the form of a glass pyramid in a courtyard, has been both praised as a breathtaking solution and damned as an insult to the museum's ancient stone buildings.

Pei's designs expose one of modernism's greatest problems. His buildings as buildings always stand out. But can talents like his be used to create buildings that fit modestly into existing neighborhoods? Not all buildings have to be unique masterpieces. Where digni-fied modern masterpieces are wanted, how-ever, Pei is indeed a master.

See also Architecture.

M I L E S   D A V I D   S A M S O N

PENN, WILLIAM

(1644–1718)   Founder of Pennsylvania.

William Penn was born in London, the son of a wealthy naval officer. When he was twen-ty-two, Penn joined the religious sect called the Quakers, or the Friends. At that time, the Quakers in England were scorned, ridiculed, and often imprisoned for their beliefs. Penn was jailed several times, but he continued preaching and writing about the Quaker faith.

Edward Hicks's painting Penn's Treaty with the Indians. *Penn, standing at center, established friendly relations with the native inhabitants of his colony, Pennsylvania. His respect and sense of justice toward them (he had deal-ings with the Delawares, Tuscaroras, Shawnees, and Miamis) are apparent in a 1682 letter: "I have already taken care that none of my people wrong you, by good laws I have provided for that purpose." He signed it, "your Loveing Freind [sic], Wm Penn."*

In 1681, King Charles II granted Penn a colony in North America in repayment of a debt the king owed to Penn's father. This wilderness territory, with an area of more than fifty thousand square miles, was called Pennsylvania (meaning "Penn's woods"). Penn welcomed to his colony members of all religions as well as those who had no religion.

Several thousand people seeking religious freedom and cheap land flocked to Pennsylvania from England, Wales, Germany, and the Netherlands. Penn drew up a frame of government that gave the settlers an elective assembly and council. Soon after he visited his colony for the first time in 1682, Penn made his first treaty with the Indians. His dealings with them were so fair that peaceful relations were maintained for almost seventy years.

Penn sailed back to England in 1684. In his pursuit of religious tolerance, he had supported King James II of England, who granted pardons to Quakers and other religious prisoners. After the king was overthrown in 1688, Penn was accused of treason and forced to give up his colony in 1692. Two years later the charges against him were dismissed, and he regained Pennsylvania.

In 1699, Penn returned to his colony, which he called a "holy experiment." He learned that many colonists were unhappy because they did not play a large role in making policies and felt that their government leaders were incompetent. So Penn granted a new charter creating a one-house elected legislature with greater power. Pennsylvania remained a colony held by the Penn family until it gained statehood during the revolutionary war.

See also Colonial America; Quakers.

EDMUND LINDOP

PENTAGON PAPERS

By 1964 Secretary of Defense Robert S. McNamara had become increasingly concerned about the way the war in Vietnam was going. Thousands of American soldiers had been killed and billions of dollars spent, but no real progress toward winning the war had been made. After much thought he decided to organize a huge research project aimed at discovering how the United States had become so involved in a war in a relatively unimportant country on the other side of the world.

The result was the Pentagon Papers. When completed in 1968 they consisted of about seven thousand pages of documents and commentaries. They revealed step by step how American commitment to the war had grown steadily over the years. And each step had been taken not just in hopes of winning the war but to avoid anyone's having to admit that the lives and money already invested had been wasted.

In 1969, after Richard M. Nixon became president, a handful of copies were printed, but no announcement was made and the report remained secret. Daniel Ellsberg, however, a researcher who had access to the papers, made copies of them and distributed them to newspapers. Their publication further stimulated the antiwar movement in the country and infuriated President Nixon and members of his administration. Ellsberg was charged with theft and spying. But the case was thrown out of court when it came out that government agents had broken into the office of Ellsberg's psychiatrist in hopes of finding material that would discredit Ellsberg.

The courts also affirmed the right of the newspapers to publish the report under the

First Amendment—another matter that the government had challenged.

See also Vietnam War.

PEOPLE'S PARTY

The problems faced by American farmers in the 1880s and early 1890s led them to form Farmers' Alliances and run candidates for political office. The difficulty was that northern farmers tended to vote Republican but southern farmers were Democrats. Both groups found it difficult to support a candidate of the "enemy" organization. One result of their prejudices was the formation of a new People's, or Populist, Party, which held its first nominating convention in Omaha, Nebraska, in 1892.

The Populists nominated Gen. James B. Weaver for president. Their party platform called for national ownership of railroad, telegraph, and telephone companies, a federal income tax, and a "subtreasury" plan that would allow farmers to borrow money from the government. The loans were to be secured by the borrowers' crops, and the crops stored in government warehouses. When and if farm prices rose, the crops could be sold and the loans paid back.

In 1892 General Weaver received more than a million popular votes. He carried five states with twenty-two electoral votes—a good showing. Two years later in local elections, the Populists did still better. In 1896, however, their party convention decided to back the Democratic candidate for president, William Jennings Bryan, who supported most of their platform. After Bryan was defeated, the People's Party ceased to be an important political force. Many of the reforms it had proposed, however, were eventually enacted into law.

See also Farmers' Alliance; Populism.

PERKINS, FRANCES

(1880–1965)   *Secretary of labor (1933–45), the first female member of a presidential cabinet.*

Born in Boston, Frances Perkins graduated from Mount Holyoke College and Columbia University. In 1910 she became secretary of the New York Consumers' League. After she witnessed the 1911 Triangle Shirtwaist Company fire in New York in which 146 young immigrant women died, she became a firm advocate of factory safety standards and enforcement. She served on state investigating committees and lobbied the state for labor legislation.

After Alfred E. Smith became governor of New York in 1919, he appointed Perkins to the New York State Industrial Commission, the group that oversaw labor laws. When Franklin D. Roosevelt became governor of New York in 1929, he named her industrial commissioner, the highest post then held by a woman in the state.

Four years later Roosevelt became president and appointed Perkins secretary of labor, the first woman to sit in a president's cabinet. This capable woman played a major role in some of the century's most important legislation. She headed the committee that wrote the Social Security Act of 1935. Old age pensions, unemployment insurance, aid to dependent children, assistance to handicapped persons—all owe a great debt to her leadership. Three years later, she promoted the Fair Labor Standards Act that established minimum wages and maximum hours and abolished child labor across the nation.

Frances Perkins, secretary of labor under Franklin D. Roosevelt, visits the Carnegie Steel plant in Pittsburgh, Pennsylvania. The first female cabinet member in U.S. history, Perkins distinguished herself as an advocate for social reform.

During World War II, men headed the commissions that oversaw labor matters, although Perkins continued to serve as secretary of labor until Harry S. Truman succeeded Roosevelt in 1945. Truman appointed her to the U.S. Civil Service Commission. After 1953, she taught at Cornell University and other colleges.

See also New Deal.

LOIS SCHARF

PERSHING, JOHN J.

(1860–1948) *World War I general.*

While growing up in the little town of Laclede, Missouri, Pershing never planned on becoming a soldier. As a young man, what he most wanted was simply a good education, but he could not afford college. So he took an examination for entrance to the U.S. Military Academy and was accepted. Thus, he got his education free by agreeing to become a soldier.

Pershing graduated in 1886 as a second lieutenant in the army. Over the next twenty-five years he fought in wars against the Apache Indians of New Mexico, the Spanish army in Cuba, and the Moro people of the Philippine Islands. He became known as an officer who believed in hard discipline, but he dealt fairly with the men he led. Because he once commanded a regiment made up entirely of black soldiers, he became nicknamed "Black Jack."

John Singleton Copley,
Paul Revere *(c.1768–70)*

Edward Hicks, The Peaceable Kingdom *(c.1834)*

Frederic E. Church, Twilight in the Wilderness *(1860)*

Thomas Eakins,
The Gross Clinic
(1875)

Winslow Homer, Breezing Up (A Fair Wind) *(1876)*

Mary Cassatt, The Bath *(1891)*

George Bellows, Stag at Sharkey's *(1909)*

Top left: Georgia O'Keeffe, Single Lily with Red *(1928)*

Top right: Grant Wood, American Gothic *(1930)*

Bottom left: Jacob Lawrence, The Migration of the Negro #11 *(1940-41)*

Bottom right: Andrew Wyeth, Christina's World *(1948)*

Jackson Pollock,
No. 34 *(1949)*

Mark Rothko,
Magenta, Black, Green on Orange *(1949)*

Roy Lichtenstein,
Masterpiece *(1962)*

General John Pershing leading the unsuccessful, eleven-month-long manhunt in 1916–17 for Pancho Villa, the Mexican revolutionary who had led unprovoked and bloody raids against Americans. President Woodrow Wilson ordered him captured, dead or alive, but Villa was never caught.

In 1916 a large force of Mexican bandits led by Pancho Villa crossed the border and raided the town of Columbus, New Mexico. Pershing, now a general, led the small army that was ordered into Mexico to punish them. This made him a popular hero throughout America. At that time, World War I was raging in Europe between the Allies—France, Britain, and several other countries—and Germany, Austria, and Turkey. When the United States entered the war on the Allies' side in 1917, Maj. Gen. "Black Jack" Pershing was chosen to command the American army.

Arriving in Europe, Pershing found that the French and British leaders felt that his troops were too inexperienced. They wanted to mix his soldiers into *their* armies under their command. Pershing refused. Pounding his fist on a table, he barked that American soldiers would fight only in an American army! Pershing slowly and carefully built up and trained the American force and led it to victories that helped win the war. When he returned home in 1919, Congress promoted him to the highest rank an American general had ever held until then, general of the armies.

Pershing retired from the army in 1924, and during the course of his lifetime served in a number of honorary positions on government committees and missions.

See also Army; World War I.

TOM McGOWEN

PERSONAL LIBERTY LAWS

During the first half of the nineteenth century, many northern states sought to get around the clause of the Constitution requiring them to return captured runaway slaves by passing personal liberty laws. In New York and other states, these laws required slave owners and their agents to obtain search warrants before seizing a black, and they guaranteed accused fugitives a trial by jury. When laws of this type were declared unconstitutional by the U.S. Supreme Court, Massachusetts passed a law preventing state officials from helping to capture fugitives. This practice was blocked by the federal Fugitive Slave Act of 1850, which provided for the fining and imprisonment of citizens who refused to help in the capture of fugitives when ordered to do so by a federal marshal.

Later, the Supreme Court of Wisconsin declared the Fugitive Slave Act of 1850 unconstitutional, but the U.S. Supreme Court overruled the Wisconsin court in 1859. Nevertheless, personal liberty laws (and the public feelings that led northern states to pass these measures) made the capture and return to slavery of fugitives extremely difficult. Between 1850 and the outbreak of the Civil War only about three hundred fugitives were captured and returned to their owners.

See also Abolitionist Movement; Slavery.

PHILADELPHIA CONVENTION
See Constitution, The Making of the.

PHILIP (KING PHILIP)

(c. 1637–76)   *Chief of Wampanoag Indians.*

"Philip" was the name used by the white settlers of New England to refer to Metacom, the grand sachem, or chief, of the Wampanoag tribe, who lived on the coast of what is today Massachusetts and Rhode Island. Philip was the son of Massasoit, the sachem who had made peace with William Bradford and the Pilgrims in 1621. Philip resented the way the English, once dependent on his father's protection and goodwill, had grown numerous and haughty toward all Indians. After three of his tribesmen were hanged for murder on flimsy evidence, both Philip and the English started preparing for war.

What came to be called "King Philip's War" broke out in June 1675. Philip's men hid in forests and swamps, attacking outlying settlements and spreading terror throughout New England. Philip tried to persuade other tribes to join him, but the English had more success than he did in winning over Indian allies. Philip spent the winter of 1675–76 near Albany, New York, far away from his native region. While he was there, he tried to bring the

King Philip, or Metacom (his Indian name), was a Wampanoag chief who led a long battle (1675–76) to drive away English settlers. Twelve frontier towns were destroyed in the bloody fighting. Philip was eventually caught and beheaded.

powerful Mohawk tribe into the war on his side, but they attacked his band of men instead as a favor to the governor of New York.

Reeling from this defeat, Philip nonetheless headed back into Massachusetts in the spring. His forces dwindled, however, and the English closed in on him, capturing his wife and child. Finally, Philip was killed by a shot from an Indian serving with the whites. His body was cut up and his head publicly displayed, which was the usual English punishment for those considered traitors. His family members, like many of his fellow tribesmen, were sold into slavery in the island colonies of the Caribbean. The descendants of the Wampanoag live today in the area of Martha's Vineyard.

See also Indian-White Relations; Pilgrims.

THOMAS COLE

PHILIPPINES, ACQUISITION OF

One cause of the Spanish-American War was opposition in the United States to the brutal way Spain was attempting to suppress the rebellion going on in the Spanish colony of Cuba. The first actual fighting in the war, however, took place on the other side of the globe in the Spanish-held Philippine Islands, where the American Asiatic fleet commanded by Commodore George Dewey destroyed a Spanish fleet in Manila Bay on May 1, 1898. Occupation of Manila by land forces soon followed.

After the war the question of what to do about the Philippines caused controversy, partly because they were so far from the United States, partly because they were populated by dark-skinned "natives," and partly because of an ingrained American anticolonialism dating back to the Declaration of Independence and the Revolution. A nationalist insurrection by Philippine patriots, who had expected that after driving out Spain the Americans would depart in peace, further complicated the situation.

In the end, however, the economic possibilities involved in controlling a base in East Asia and the desire to "plant the flag" in distant shores carried the day. In the peace treaty ending the war Spain ceded the Philippines to the United States. In February 1899, the Senate ratified the treaty by a vote of fifty-seven to twenty-seven. But only after a bloody guerrilla war that raged for three years had been quelled by U.S. troops did peace come to the islands.

The United States granted the Philippines their independence in 1946.

See also Spanish-American War.

PHOTOGRAPHY

Photography was invented in France by Joseph Niepce sometime in the 1820s, and popularized there about 1840 by Louis Daguerre. Within a few years the "daguerreotype" portrait (a silvery image on a copper plate) had become all the rage among Americans. Boston daguerreotypists Albert Southworth and Josiah Hawes counted among their subjects poet Henry Wadsworth Longfellow, novelist Harriet Beecher Stowe, and former president John Quincy Adams. In one year alone, ten thousand American photographers made 3 million daguerreotypes.

A daguerreotype from around 1850. This early form of photography was popular throughout the world from about 1840 to 1860. The daguerreotype captured images in exquisite detail and was primarily used for portraiture. Its shortcoming, however, was that it produced only a single, nonreproducible image.

By the 1850s the one-of-a-kind daguerreo-type was supplanted by the wet-plate negative process, in which liquid chemicals were applied to a glass plate in a darkroom and the picture taken and processed immediately. Many prints could be made from one of these negatives.

With the wet-plate negative the stage was set for the first great era of American photography—the documentation of the Civil War. Cameramen such as Mathew Brady, Alexander Gardner, and Timothy O'Sullivan followed the conflict from battlefield to battlefield. They photographed the death and devastation of war with a brutal honesty never before seen.

Growth of Photography

When the American frontier moved west after the Civil War, photographers followed it with their ungainly wet-plate equipment. O'Sullivan documented three important government explorations through rugged wilderness. On John Wesley Powell's 1871 exploration of the Grand Canyon, the heavy camera gear was dangerous to transport down the Colorado River, but it was essential to the expedition's success. William Henry Jackson was the first man to photograph the area of Yellowstone National Park. In fact, it became a park in 1872 largely because of the impact of his photographs.

By the 1880s photographers made their negatives with store-bought ready-to-use dry plates. And a dry-plate maker named George Eastman sold a camera preloaded with roll film. "You press the button," was his slogan, "we do the rest." That original Kodak camera brought photography to the masses.

The turn of the nineteenth century saw

A stereograph of the 1906 San Francisco earthquake. Stereographs were double images seen through a special viewer called a stereoscope, which produced a three-dimensional effect. Stereographs often featured exotic foreign scenes as well as news events, and viewing them at home was a popular pastime in nineteenth-century America.

what had been a largely documentary medium become a form of artistic expression. Alfred Stieglitz was famous for his gritty images of New York and portraits of his wife, the painter Georgia O'Keeffe. Edward Steichen made powerful portraits of the rich and famous—the sculptor Rodin, millionaire J. Pierpont Morgan, and dancer Isadora Duncan. Gertrude Käsebier photographed women and children in a lush, idealized manner.

Alfred Stieglitz's The Steerage *(1907), which he considered his finest photograph, captures the atmosphere of a voyage. The gangway divides the composition, emphasizing the differences between those below in steerage, the cheapest form of travel, and those on the upper deck. Stieglitz, considered the father of modern American photography, led the movement to change the widely held attitude that photography was merely a technical craft rather than an art form. Photography, according to Stieglitz, was not simply a method of recording facts but a means of interpreting emotion and experience, as powerful as painting.*

Paul Strand found hard-edged beauty in ordinary people caught unawares on the street.

At the same time, American photographers pioneered the use of the camera as a tool of social conscience. Jacob Riis used the newly invented flash powder to shed literal and figurative light on the dismal lives of the urban poor. Lewis W. Hine's pictures of youngsters working in gloomy factories helped secure America's first child-labor laws.

Photography as a tool of social conscience continued throughout the twentieth century. Dorothea Lange made classic images of the Great Depression of the 1930s. After World War II, W. Eugene Smith traveled the world photographing the helpless and the abandoned. In the 1970s Bruce Davidson portrayed the people of Harlem. For twenty-five years Mary Ellen Mark has sensitively recorded the lives of the disfranchised.

Photography as a News Medium

Mass-circulation magazines such as *National Geographic, Life,* and *Look* made photographic feature stories extremely popular from the 1930s through the mid-1970s. American photojournalists scoured the world with their compact 35mm cameras. Alfred Eisenstadt, Margaret Bourke-White, W. Eugene Smith, and Gordon Parks were among the most famous.

Robert Capa was the Mathew Brady of his day, bringing the Spanish Civil War and World War II home to Americans. He died in Indochina in 1954 when he stepped on a land mine. David Douglas Duncan covered the twin miseries of the Korean War and the Vietnam War.

The photographer covering one-time news events also made an impact. In 1910 William Warnecke caught the image of a New York mayor who had just been shot—stumbling, bleeding, dazed. Sam Shere and others captured the explosion of the zeppelin *Hindenburg.* Joe Rosenthal shot the raising of the American flag on Iwo Jima in 1945. Weegee (Arthur Fellig) prowled New York for pictures of events bizarre or criminal.

Expanding Subjects for Photographers

Meanwhile, the beauty of nature was being pursued by American photographers, especially in the West. Edward Weston and his son Brett made detailed and sensual photographs of wild California. Ansel Adams traveled the country for half a century. He produced what are probably the most famous and popular of all American landscapes. Other prominent nature photographers include Imogen Cunningham, Minor White, and Harry Callahan. Until Eliot Porter, nature photography was a black-and-white medium. He proved that color could be used with the same rigor and richness.

American photographers also displayed a knack for innovation. In the 1880s Eadweard Muybridge produced numerous series of photos that showed people and animals in motion. The surrealist Man Ray (Emmanuel Rudnitsky) made startling images with special darkroom techniques. In 1931 a scientist and photographer named Harold E. Edgerton invented the strobe light. And in 1947 another American scientist, Edwin Land, created Polaroid film. This film produced photographic prints in the camera almost instantly, without need of darkroom processing.

American fashion and celebrity photography reached its zenith in the decades after World War II. Some of its most famous practitioners include Richard Avedon, Irving Penn, and Annie Leibowitz.

At the same time, others were exploring the darker aspects of life. Lisette Model and Robert Frank found barrenness and pessimism on the American scene. Lee Friedlander depicted the clutter and ugliness of urban landscapes. And Diane Arbus produced harsh portraits of people outside "normal" society—midgets, nudists, transvestites.

Photography continues to have the power to arouse, particularly when it challenges accepted views. In the early 1990s Robert Mapplethorpe's erotic images unleashed a firestorm of controversy about what sort of art ought to receive government funding. Sally Mann's photography touches upon another sensitive area. Should a mother documenting her children's lives make and display nude photographs of them?

As American photography enters the twenty-first century, many technical changes are in store. Photographers routinely scan their images into computers and retouch them on video monitors. Pictures are recorded on compact disks for viewing on an ordinary television screen. Cameras are available that use computer disks, not film, to record images.

See also Bourke-White, Margaret; Brady, Mathew; Eastman, George; Steichen, Edward; Stieglitz, Alfred.

D. R. MARTIN

PIERCE, FRANKLIN

(1804–69)   *Fourteenth president of the United States (1853–57).*

Pierce was accused of being a "doughface," a northern Democrat who supported the South's position on the question of slavery in the territories. A doughface was said to be as easy to mold as a lump of dough. President

Pierce, however, was simply keeping his party's campaign promise to carry out compromise measures passed by Congress in 1850, which contained concessions to the South.

Pierce, the son of a New Hampshire governor, was educated at Bowdoin College, where he formed a lifelong friendship with the author Nathaniel Hawthorne. He studied law before serving in the state legislature for four years. He moved on to the U.S. House of Representatives and the Senate where he served from 1833 to 1842. Pierce then resigned his Senate seat and returned home because of a drinking problem, but he remained active in local politics. During the Mexican War (1846–47), he fought under the command of Gen. Winfield Scott.

Pierce received the Democratic Party's nomination for president in 1852, breaking a deadlock among better known candidates. (Hawthorne wrote Pierce's campaign biography.) In the election, he defeated the Whig Party candidate, General Scott, but the victory turned out to be bittersweet. Two months before his inauguration, Pierce and his wife were in a train wreck that killed their young son, Benjamin. The new president was heartbroken at the swearing-in ceremonies.

Pierce was a loyal Democrat, devoted to maintaining party unity, but unable to cope with the bitterness of the sectional tensions, he failed to keep the northern and southern wings of his party together. They split over the controversial Kansas-Nebraska Act of 1854, which let territorial residents decide whether or not to permit slavery. This angered northerners because of the possibility of its extending slavery into western territories where it would previously have been banned under the Missouri Compromise of 1820. Settlers, both proslavery and antislavery, poured into Kansas from the South and the North, turning the new territory into a bloody battlefield.

In foreign affairs, the president welcomed the arrangements negotiated by Matthew Perry to open Japan to western traders. He also sent James Gadsden to purchase parts of New Mexico and Arizona from Mexico in 1853. After his divided party refused to nominate him for a second term, Pierce returned to New Hampshire.

See also Democratic Party. *For events during Pierce's administration, see* Bleeding Kansas; Gadsden Purchase; Kansas-Nebraska Act.

BARBARA SILBERDICK FEINBERG

PILGRIMS

The persons who were to become known in America as Pilgrims had been farmers and craftsmen living in and near the English village of Scrooby in the early 1600s. As ardent churchgoers their dissatisfaction with the rituals and requirements of the Church of England had led them to form their own "separatist" congregation. This action, combined with their somewhat righteous and disdainful attitude toward others, provoked ridicule and disfavor from officials and neighbors alike.

Plans to Emigrate
In 1607, despite laws prohibiting emigration without permission from the government, the desire to live, worship, and educate their children in a better atmosphere led these devout individuals to do just that. After repeated difficulties, the congregation gratefully resettled in the Dutch city of Leyden.

By 1619, however, war with Spain threatened the Netherlands and within their own

A painting of Pilgrims on their way to church.

community the Pilgrims feared that their carefully brought-up children were becoming "too Dutch." When Pilgrims John Carver and Robert Cushman succeeded in obtaining a patent (permission to settle in America) from the Virginia Company, about half the congregation decided to leave Leyden for life in the New World.

Thirty years later Governor William Bradford of the so-called "Plimoth Plantation" wrote, "So they left [Leyden] that goodly and pleasant city which had been their resting place near twelve years; but they knew they were pilgrims, and . . . lift[ed] up their eyes to the heavens, their dearest country, and quieted their spirits." It is because of his description that, years later, they began to be known as Pilgrims.

Upon returning to England the Pilgrims were joined by other individuals who wished to go to America, although not necessarily for religious reasons. Soon the expedition included more "strangers," persons who went in the hope of financial success, than "saints," persons of religious conviction.

Despite careful planning there were delays, quarrels, and difficulties. It was harder than expected to raise enough money to buy supplies and equipment, and some persons who had promised to lend them money threatened not to do so.

Under these circumstances it was agreed that shares in the company might be purchased on behalf of four young but illegitimate children belonging to a landowning Shropshire family. In exchange for the much needed money, the children would be taken on the voyage and placed with leading Pilgrim families by whom they were to be cared for and educated. When they grew up they would become owners of land in the New World. The other side of this arrangement was that the family was conveniently freed of the awkward possibility that these illegitimate children might grow up to inherit the family's large estate in England.

Finally, too late in the sailing season to assure a safe crossing, the two ships engaged by the Pilgrims were able to set forth. Sadly, the *Speedwell* proved unseaworthy, so that they had to return to port twice. These delays, and the eventual decision not to use the faulty vessel, led some individuals to change their minds about going. Even so, the *Mayflower* was seriously overcrowded when, on September 6, 1620, she began the historic voyage.

The small square-rigged ship carried 102 people, of whom only 41 (including 17 children) were Pilgrims, and all of their goods, books, and provisions. The ship was assailed by heavy Atlantic Ocean storms making the crossing rough. Diet was poor, many individuals fell ill, some persons died, and a baby was born.

Although the land the Pilgrims reached was strange and new to the them, it had been previously explored and even crudely mapped. Cape Cod, for example, had been given its name long before the Pilgrims made their first landing there, and when they decided to seek a better location, one of the sailors suggested a harbor that he had visited on an earlier voyage.

Establishing a Colony

While still anchored off Cape Cod the Pilgrims had signed the historic Mayflower Compact establishing their own government and describing themselves as "a civill body politick." Then, five weeks after first dropping anchor in the New World, the travelers reached their final destination and began to establish Plimoth Plantation, the settlement now known to us as Plymouth, Massachusetts.

Although spring came early in 1621, the first winter had already ravaged the colony. Nearly half its members died. As might be expected of any group of people exposed to physical, emotional, and environmental hardship, some Pilgrims proved brave beyond measure, while others—even some of the religious members of the community—faltered and had to be disciplined. If it is not surprising that some survivors went back to England when they could, it is inspiring that most stayed on, and that new families came.

Although the Pilgrims are traditionally represented as a unified community of firm religious beliefs, there are many indications to the contrary, including some passages in *Of Plimoth Plantation* written by Governor Bradford near the end of his long life.

Contrary to the view fostered by popular opinion and many history books, even in its time the colony at Plymouth was neither the first nor the only New World settlement on the eastern seaboard. Jamestown preceded it by more than a decade and the patent (rights) to all of the present state of Maine were soon to be granted to a single individual! In 1630 John Winthrop established the Puritan colony that was to become the city of Boston and before the end of the 1600s Plymouth itself had given rise to a number of smaller and newer communities such as Salem and Scituate.

See also Bradford, William; Colonial America; Mayflower Compact; Puritans.

JOAN W. BLOS

PINKERTONS

The Pinkerton National Detective Agency was founded in 1850 by Allan Pinkerton, a Scottish immigrant and the first detective to serve on Chicago's police force. The term "private eye" is believed to stem from the Pinkerton trademark—a picture of an eye above the motto "The Eye That Never Sleeps." The first nationwide detective agency, the Pinkertons aided local police departments in catching criminals and guarded trains against robberies.

One of the Pinkertons' most famous cases was the "Baltimore Plot"—a conspiracy to murder President-elect Abraham Lincoln on his way to Washington for the inauguration. The Pinkertons engineered a secret nighttime detour of Lincoln's route. His train sped undetected through Baltimore—the planned site of the assassination—at 3:30 A.M., and Lincoln arrived safely in the capital at dawn.

During the Civil War, Pinkerton served as a spy under Union Gen. George B. McClellan, assuming the alias "Maj. E. J. Allen." He and his men, who included fugitive slaves, infiltrated Confederate lines to gather information. The Pinkerton spies, however, grossly exaggerated the strength of Gen. Robert E. Lee's troops, estimating 200,000 Confederates when Lee had at most 88,000 men.

The Pinkertons continued to guard railroads and stagecoaches after the war, pursuing such infamous bandits as Jesse James. They also helped break up strikes, which often resulted in bloody confrontations. The most notorious of these was the Homestead strike in July 1892 during which nine strikers and seven Pinkertons were killed. The Pinkertons collected a large file of criminal records, the only such files until the establishment of the Federal Bureau of Investigation. A scaled-down version of the agency, called Pinkerton's Inc., still exists.

See also Homestead Strike.

PIONEERS AND FRONTIER LIFE

From the time of the French and Indian War (1754–63) until the closing of the frontier in 1890, streams of people journeyed to the West seeking new homes and opportunities. Although some established villages and others became ranchers, lumbermen, or miners, the greatest number sought cheap or free land on which to farm. Some had been humble peasants in Europe or the British Isles. Others, known as indentured servants, had worked in America for up to seven years to pay for their ocean passage; when freed of their obligations many "headed for the tall timber." Still others already lived in the colonies or after the Revolution in the settled states but headed west to make a new start.

Detective and Civil War spy Allan Pinkerton (left) with Abraham Lincoln and General McClernand at Antietam.

Making the Trip

The journey west was always difficult. Pioneers crossing the Appalachian Mountains at

Cumberland Gap often walked while a pack horse or two carried their worldly belongings. Some advanced west along the rivers, down the Allegheny, the Monongahela, or the Ohio to other rivers leading north or south into the new country. Some people, such as those headed for Colorado, California, or Oregon, followed trails in covered wagons pulled by oxen, mules, or horses. By the 1870s many pioneers were able to go west on the new railroads.

Usually they did not travel alone. A religious congregation might leave for the new country, or a group of neighbors agree to travel and settle together. Sometimes friends had gone on before them, so the pioneers knew where they were going. Men bound for the goldfields after they were discovered often grouped together for protection and sociability.

Whatever their means of transportation, the men, women, and children carried with them the essential items necessary to start a new life on the frontier. In the wooded region east of the Mississippi these included a rifle, gunpowder and lead, an ax and other tools, seed, salt, chickens, hogs, a horse or oxen, a spinning wheel, cooking utensils, bedding, and clothing. Similar necessities were carried into the prairies and plains of the Middle West, to the mining camps of Colorado and California, and to Oregon.

The New Home

Land was acquired in a variety of ways. If the family had advanced beyond an area already surveyed, it might "squat" on it, simply settling on the land without paying for it. When the crews surveying the public domain— lands owned by the federal government— reached a squatter's farm, the settler would have to purchase the land at an auction.

Sometimes poor squatters were outbid and lost their land and all the improvements they had made on it. Some pioneers purchased land from railroads. Others acquired their acreage from land companies or from the state in which they settled. After passage of the Homestead Act of 1862 many pioneers could settle free on public land that became theirs after they had registered their claim, made certain improvements, and worked the land for five years.

Once the site was selected, the pioneer family was confronted with many tasks. If the land was wooded, the trees were burned or cut down and "snaked," or dragged, away with the help of horses or oxen; in this new field a first crop of corn and beans was planted. Meanwhile the family, who had been living in their wagon (if they had one) or a lean-to, set about building a crude cabin. The pioneer prepared the site and assembled and cut to size the necessary logs. Now the word was spread throughout the neighborhood that a house raising was to take place. On the designated day neighbors appeared, the men to erect the cabin and the fireplace and the women to cook the "vittles." Even the children helped in such ways as caulking the spaces between the logs with mud mixed with hog bristles. A barrel of potent corn whiskey was likely to be present. By nightfall the pioneer family had a crude dwelling in which to live.

Usually a settlement existed within a half day's horseback ride from the farmer. Villages were built where a fort had been located, at a crossroads, or at a ford in a river. If Indian troubles arose, families might take refuge in a nearby fort. Farmers traveled to their local village to attend court; participate in a militia drill; sell their produce, animal skins, honey, and hams; see a banker, lawyer, or doctor;

The Byington family takes a rest while traveling along a pioneer trail in Utah in the late 1860s.

make a payment at the land office; or buy the few things, like needles or salt, that they could not produce themselves at home.

Cultural events included church services by a circuit-riding preacher, a man who served as minister for several churches, riding from one to another on a regular schedule. Churches also held religious camp meetings. Much appreciated was the presence of an itinerant (traveling) teacher who would spend three to seven months teaching the children their three R's—reading, writing, and 'rithmetic. Politics arrived early on the frontier. Rallies offering speeches, food, and drink were heavily attended. Quilting bees, square dances, and singing evenings were other popular ways for neighbors to get together. Life was not easy and people worked extremely hard. But they did find ways to enjoy themselves.

On the prairies and plains where there were few trees, most pioneers lived in sod houses or tar paper shacks. Here they demonstrated their ingenuity in learning to cope with the new problems created by dry land and little wood. Some of the Great Plains became a ranchers' frontier and parts of the Rockies and the Sierras a miners' frontier; a lumbermen's frontier existed across Wisconsin, Minnesota, and the Pacific Northwest. In all of these regions the development of communities from crude settlements to complex societies was similar.

The Frontier's Importance

In the view of Frederick Jackson Turner, a young history professor at the University of Wisconsin, the frontier experience molded the American character. It made Americans act and think the way they do. Noting that the U.S. Bureau of the Census declared the frontier at an end as of 1890, he published an essay entitled "The Significance of the Frontier in American History." In it, he maintained that it was the continuing existence of free land and the recurring creation of new communities and new states that made Americans different and therefore better people. Some historians have disagreed with him. But whether he was right or wrong, no one can deny the importance of the pioneer and the frontier experience in overall American history.

See also Boone, Daniel; Cody, Buffalo Bill; Cowboys; Crockett, Davy; Gold Rushes; Homestead Act; Oregon Trail; Pony Express.

RICHARD A. BARTLETT

PLATT AMENDMENT

The United States entered the Spanish-American War in 1898 to free Cuba from Spanish control, not to make the island an American colony. This objective was made clear by the Teller Amendment to a joint resolution of Congress. After the Spanish surrendered the island, however, something close to anarchy existed there. The economy was in a shambles, schools were closed, the streets of Havana littered with garbage and the bodies of dead horses.

President William McKinley responded to this situation by appointing a military governor. But civilian authority was gradually restored and in November 1900, the Cubans drafted a new constitution and American troops were withdrawn. The Cuban Constitution, however, contained an amendment drafted by U.S. Senator Orville H. Platt. This Platt Amendment gave the United States the

right to intervene in Cuba to preserve the nation's independence and to protect "life, property, and individual liberty." Cuba also had to allow the United States to maintain naval bases on its soil. But only once, in 1906, were American troops sent back to Cuba, and then at the request of the Cuban government in order to help put down a revolution. Nevertheless, the existence of the amendment made Cuba a kind of American colony. It gave the United States tremendous influence in the island, which the Cuban people deeply resented. Finally, in 1934, Cuba and the United States signed a treaty canceling the Platt Amendment. Yet American influence in Cuba did not end until Fidel Castro overthrew the government of Fulgencio Batista in 1959.

PLESSY V. FERGUSON

After federal troops were withdrawn from the South in 1877 at the end of the Reconstruction era, the white-controlled governments of the region soon began to undermine the rights that had been guaranteed to blacks by the Fourteenth and Fifteenth Amendments and the Civil Rights Acts of 1866 and 1875. Blacks were prevented from voting by threats and outright violence. At the same time strict segregation of the races was imposed by state laws. Separate schools, hospitals, hotels, prisons, even cemeteries, were created. In theaters and on trains and riverboats, blacks were forced to sit in separate sections, always inferior to the facilities reserved for whites.

In a series of cases, the U.S. Supreme Court found nothing unconstitutional in southern segregation laws. In the *Civil Rights* Cases (1883) it accepted segregation in private businesses, such as theaters, hotels, and restaurants.

Then, in 1896, the Court dealt with the complaint of Homer Plessy, a black man who had refused to sit in a railroad car reserved for blacks while traveling on a train in Louisiana. Railroads were government-owned or regulated places of "public accommodation," like schools, and the Fourteenth Amendment provided that a state government could not deny "any person . . . the equal protection of the laws."

Louisiana law required railroads to provide "equal but separate accommodations" for blacks and whites. This the Court ruled was constitutional. The Fourteenth Amendment did require "equality of the races before the law," but so long as the facilities provided for blacks were similar to those enjoyed by whites, no violation of the Fourteenth Amendment had occurred. In short, separation did not mean inequality.

The *Plessy* case is notable today mostly for the dissenting (disagreeing) opinion of Justice John Marshall Harlan. "Our Constitution is color-blind," Harlan declared. Racial segregation was "a badge of servitude." In 1896, however, Harlan spoke in vain. The *Plessy* decision was not overruled until the *Brown* v. *Board of Education* case in 1954.

See also Brown v. Board of Education; Racism.

POCAHONTAS

(1595?–1617)   *Indian "princess."*

An American Indian who played an important role in the history of Virginia, Pocahontas was a charming woman who served as an emissary between the Native Americans and the English colonists.

Pocahontas was the daughter of Powhatan, chief of the Powhatan Confederacy. Her name, meaning "playful one," was appropriate, for when the settlers first saw her in 1607, she was turning handsprings and frolicking in a Jamestown marketplace.

In 1608, Capt. John Smith was captured by her father. As he was about to be executed, Pocahontas intervened on his behalf and saved his life. Although the accuracy of this famous story has been questioned, there is no doubt that Pocahontas was instrumental in arranging a truce between the Indians and

A portrait of Pocahontas, looking more like an English aristocrat than an Algonquin chief's daughter. The portrait was painted in England, where Pocahontas traveled in 1616 with her husband, the prominent Virginia colonist John Rolfe, their baby son, and an entourage of Indians. As the inscription indicates, she had converted to Christianity and given up her Indian name of Matoak[a]—Pocahontas was actually a nickname—and had been baptized Rebecka.

the settlers. Hostilities between the two groups, however, continued.

Five years later, Pocahontas was taken hostage by the settlers and brought to Jamestown where she was baptized into the Christian faith, taught to speak English, and renamed Rebecka. Soon after, an English tobacco planter named John Rolfe fell in love with her. In 1614, permission for the two to marry was granted by the Virginia governor and Powhatan, in the hope that their union would promote peace between the settlers and the Indians.

Pocahontas sailed to England with her husband in 1616 where she was presented at court and treated with the honors due a princess. She charmed her hosts and persuaded them to take a more benevolent attitude toward her fellow Indians, encouraging the possibility of a peaceful coexistence between them and the white settlers.

Seven months later Pocahontas became ill and died. She was buried in Gravesend, England. Although technically she was not a princess, she was granted the title because of her status as a chief's daughter and the gracious way she intermingled with the English.

See also Indian-White Relations; Smith, John.

JOANN BIONDI

POE, EDGAR ALLAN

(1809–49)   *Short-story writer, poet, and critic.*

Poe's parents were actors who died when he was two years old. He was adopted by John Allan, a wealthy Richmond, Virginia, merchant. They quarreled frequently and Poe left home in 1827, determined to seek literary fame. He tried to make a living as a poet and almost starved.

Hoping to inherit his foster father's money, he made his peace with Allan and obtained an appointment to West Point in 1830. Another quarrel with Allan plunged him into bitterness, and he deliberately flunked out of the military academy the next year. His classmates financed the publication of a book of his poems containing some of his best lyrics, such as "Israfel" and "The Doomed City." But the book was barely noticed.

Poe became an editor of the Richmond-based *Southern Literary Messenger* in 1835. But he began drinking heavily and lost the job. In 1836, he married his cousin, Virginia Clemm, and moved to Baltimore with her and her mother. For the next several years he wrote poetry and stories such as *The Narrative of Arthur Gordon Pym* (1838), a tale of shipwreck in the South Seas. He also worked as an editor for various magazines, where he wrote harsh criticisms of the work of other writers.

Single-handedly, he invented the detective story with "The Murders in the Rue Morgue" and "The Gold Bug" (1843). In 1845 he published "The Raven," a gloomy poem that made him famous. Despite his fame and several prizes he won for his short stories, he still earned only four dollars for an article and fifteen for a short story. Tormented by poverty, Poe watched his wife die of tuberculosis. He began taking opium and attempted suicide.

In 1849, he swore off liquor and drugs and tried to rehabilitate himself. He became engaged to one of his boyhood sweethearts in Richmond. But a trip to Baltimore led to a fatal drinking bout. Poe's artistry somehow survived his impulse to self-destruction. From the cool rationalism of his detective stories to the dark mysticism of his poems and his tales of horror and the supernatural, his style was always perfectly attuned to his subject. His writings are still admired around the world, especially in France.

See also Literature.

THOMAS FLEMING

POLICE DEPARTMENTS

During the colonial years, the nightwatch—men who walked the streets at night watching for fires and crime—was the only police force in American cities. Poor and uneducated, the watchmen generally could not get any other job and were looked down upon by most residents. In 1808 a New Orleans newspaper said that the nightwatch was "composed principally of the most worthless part of the community."

In the 1830s and 1840s after a number of riots in American cities, citizens demanded better police forces to deal with the violence. As a result, major cities created police forces that patrolled both day and night. In the 1850s the largest cities also set about making the police more like the military. Policemen were required to wear uniforms and adopted military titles like captain, lieutenant, and sergeant.

During the late 1800s, however, many people became critical of the police. Too many policemen got their jobs by helping whichever political party, whether Democratic or Republican, was in power. Some policemen accepted bribes from gamblers and thieves, and corrupt politicians made sure these dishonest policemen were not fired.

By the early 1900s, reformers wanted to make the police more honest and less in-volved in politics. These people favored the "professionalization" of the police. In other words, they wanted the police to be better educated and respected, like doctors or lawyers. Therefore, a number of cities required people who wanted to be police officers to take examinations, and police training schools were set up. The first such school was founded in Berkeley, California, in 1908. The police now became more scientific as well, and laboratories to examine fingerprints and other evidence were founded.

In the 1950s and 1960s, however, many people were still critical of the police. Some pointed out that the police often treated people too roughly. Suspects were questioned by the police for many hours, with officers shining bright lights in their eyes. Sometimes they beat accused persons to make them confess. During the questioning, the accused were not allowed to talk to a lawyer or anyone except the police.

In the 1960s the Supreme Court forced the police to stop this form of questioning. It declared in the *Miranda* decision that persons accused of a crime must have their lawyer with them during questioning. The police also had to tell the accused that they did not have to answer questions—they could not be forced to confess.

African Americans were especially angry about cases of police brutality. They felt that white police officers too often beat up blacks and treated them unfairly. In response to black demands, city police departments hired more African-American police officers. But even in the 1990s some people said that the police were still too violent and unfair in their treatment of African Americans. Los Angeles police officers, for example, were accused of beating up a black man named Rodney King. This incident won nationwide attention and stirred renewed criticism of the police.

See also Miranda v. Arizona.

JON C. TEAFORD

POLITICAL PARTIES

See Constitutional Union Party; Democratic Party; Federalist Party; Free-Soil Party; Greenback Party; Know-Nothing Party; Liberty Party; National Woman's Party; Party Conventions; People's Party; Progressive Parties: 1912, 1924, 1948; Republican Party; Whig Party.

POLK, JAMES K.

(1795–1849)   *Eleventh president of the United States (1845–49).*

Polk put in twelve to fourteen hours a day as president, explaining, "I prefer to supervise the whole operations of the Government myself." Although born into a wealthy farming family, he had learned the values of hard work and self-discipline from his mother. He graduated from the University of North Carolina before practicing law in Tennessee.

In 1825, Polk entered the U.S. House of Representatives where he supported President Andrew Jackson's policies. The Democratic congressman served for fourteen years, holding the powerful post of Speaker from 1835 to 1839. He served as governor of Tennessee from 1839 to 1841.

Polk, in 1844, won the Democratic presidential nomination on the ninth ballot, breaking a deadlock with help from Jackson. He received the former president's backing because both men wanted the nation to ex-

pand westward and objected to President Martin Van Buren's refusal to support the annexation of Texas. Polk won the election over the Whig candidate, Henry Clay. The election results were the first to be reported by the newly invented telegraph.

As president, Polk methodically carried out the promises he had made during his campaign. In 1840, he signed the Independent Treasury Act, which ended the practice of keeping public funds in private banks, and the Walker Tariff Act, which lowered duties charged on imported foreign-made goods. In 1846, he negotiated a treaty with Great Britain establishing the northern boundary of the disputed Oregon Territory without conflict. The president provoked a war with Mexico (1846–48) that resulted in adding California and much of the Southwest to the United States. Polk thus acquired more land for the nation than any president other than Thomas Jefferson.

James Polk was not a candidate for a second term. He died just a few months after leaving office, perhaps because his self-imposed work load had ruined his health.

See also Manifest Destiny. *For events during Polk's administration, see* Expansion, Territorial; Independent Treasury; Mexican War; Wilmot Proviso.

BARBARA SILBERDICK FEINBERG

POLLING
See Public Opinion Polling.

POLLOCK, JACKSON

(1912–56)   *Painter.*

Pollock was a pioneer of the "New York school" of art, whose work is nonrepresentational (without images) and spontaneous. He was born in Cody, Wyoming, to a Scotch-Irish farm family. His mother was artistic but had little schooling. His father lost so many farms that he had to leave his family to find work. Jackson was a poor student and dropped out of high school. He joined an older brother in New York and in 1930 came under the wing of the regionalist painter Thomas Hart Benton at the Art Students League.

During the Great Depression Pollock found some work in the New Deal Federal Art Project. In 1943 he had his first one-man show, in New York. By this time he was inventing a revolutionary new kind of painting. His method was to pour and drip paint on a canvas placed not on an easel but flat on the floor. Sometimes he used a kitchen baster to squirt paint or sticks dipped in paint, which he then flicked onto the canvas. He did no preparatory drawing and might add pebbles, sand, even a cigarette butt to a painting.

This breakthrough abstract art was attacked by traditionalists and laughed at by the public. ("A five-year-old could do that" was a typical reaction.) But people open to revolutionary developments in the arts understood what Pollock was producing. The critic Clement Greenberg, for instance, called the work abstract expressionism, or "action painting." Many younger artists were also impressed, among them Lee Krasner. She became Pollock's wife in 1945.

In 1946 the Pollocks moved to East Hampton, New York, where they turned a barn into a studio. In it Pollock was able to do very large paintings, as well as work on the canvas from all four sides. These paintings had neither beginning nor end—they extended right to the edges of the canvas. To some people Pollock's action painting seemed a form of doodling or free association. But Pollock

Jackson Pollock at work on a painting in 1950. His revolutionary drip technique involved laying a large canvas on the ground and using a stick or other object instead of a paintbrush to splatter and drip paint onto its surface. He often stood on the canvas, as pictured, working with an intuitive, almost trancelike concentration that produced paintings of power, energy, and expressiveness. Pollock remarked, "When I'm working, working right, I'm in my work so outside things don't matter—if they do, then I've lost it."

insisted he was working directly from his unconscious mind.

In his lifetime Jackson Pollock earned international fame but little money, though today his works are worth very large sums. His life was a struggle against financial need, alcoholism, insecurity, and psychological depression. He died in an automobile accident in East Hampton.

See also Abstract Expressionism; Painting and Sculpture.

JEFFREY POTTER

PONTIAC

(d. 1769)   *Ottawa chief.*

Historians disagree today over the exact role of the warrior named Pontiac, but not over the importance of the conflict between Indians and whites in which he fought. That signaled the beginning of a new chapter in the history of the early American West.

Before the French and Indian War (1756–63; also called the Seven Years' War), the French had claimed the part of North America that lay between the Appalachian Mountains and the Mississippi River. The Indians of that region enjoyed independence under the French, for that nation lacked the means to dominate them. In the French and Indian War, however, France lost its possessions in North America to the British. In comparison to that of France, the British Empire in America was larger, richer, and more populous. Its representatives saw the tribes of that region as subordinate nations within British territory, not as independent powers whom they had to respect.

Pontiac suspected, and the French had warned him, that the British would not simply trade with his people, as the French had done, but would try to take the Indians' land as well. Even though the British tried to keep white settlers out of the newly acquired territory, Pontiac's people and others went to war in 1763–64 to counter this new threat to their livelihood and their ability to govern themselves. They drove the British out of almost all their western forts. Pontiac participated in a siege of the fort at Detroit, and outlying settlements as far away as western Pennsylvania were attacked before their movement disintegrated. This war marked the beginning of fifty years of conflict for control of the Old Northwest (what is today western Pennsylvania, Ohio, Indiana, Illinois, Michigan, and Wisconsin).

Because so little is known of Pontiac's life, his story belongs as much to legend and literature as to history. In 1766, Robert Rogers, an American, published a drama in verse entitled *Ponteach.* In Rogers's play, Pontiac is a bloodthirsty rabble-rouser. In his book *The Conspiracy of Pontiac,* nineteenth-century historian Francis Parkman argued that it was Pontiac himself who had the chief role in organizing and leading the tribal uprising.

See also Colonial America; Indian-White Relations; Seven Years' War.

THOMAS COLE

PONY EXPRESS

The Pony Express was established in the early 1860s to transport mail by horseback between St. Joseph, Missouri, and San Francisco, California. It not only delivered mail faster than other methods then in use but became one of the most colorful parts of the Wild West legend.

Railroads delivered mail throughout the eastern section of the country, but at that time their tracks extended only as far as Missouri. From there wagon trains and stagecoaches carried mail farther west. It took stagecoaches an average of twenty-two days to make the journey to California. The Pony Express, however, managed the trip in less than half the time. Riders, with mail pouches strapped to their horses, crossed rough terrain unfit for a stagecoach. At breakneck speed, a rider covered thirty-five to seventy-five miles before handing over the mail to the next rider, who was ready with a fresh horse. This relay race across the American West—passing through 190 way stations and using

An illustration of a rider for the Pony Express, which in its heyday delivered mail in the West at about twice the speed of any other method. As the rider gallops by, he tips his hat to workers raising the poles and stringing the wires of the first transcontinental telegraph. Once the telegraph was completed in 1862, it immediately outstripped the Pony Express as the fastest way to transmit messages.

about seventy-five horses—covered nearly two thousand miles in about eight to ten days.

Riders traveled through dangerous country, often encountering wild animals and natural disasters. The Pony Express attracted the adventurous, including such Wild West heroes as Buffalo Bill Cody and Wild Bill Hickock. An advertisement recruiting riders read:

Wanted: Young, skinny, wiry fellows not over eighteen. Must be expert riders, willing to risk death daily. Orphans preferred.

Despite its fame, the Pony Express never made a profit and lasted less than two years, from April 1860 to October 1861. It could not compete with the invention of a new method of transmitting information: the first transcontinental telegraph in 1861, which conveyed messages almost instantaneously.

See also Pioneers and Frontier Life.

POOR RICHARD'S ALMANACK

Among Benjamin Franklin's many accomplishments was the compilation of *Poor Rich-*

ard's *Almanack,* which he published annually in Philadelphia between 1732 and 1757. It outsold all other almanacs, becoming the second most popular book in the colonies after the Bible. It offered a treasury of practical information on the weather, tides, eclipses, and farming as well as poems, jokes, and recipes. Franklin presented the almanac as the collected wisdom of a fictional character, "Richard Saunders, Philomath" (a lover of learning). Many of the almanac's proverbs and sayings are still familiar more than two centuries later:

> Early to bed and early to rise makes a man healthy, wealthy, and wise.
> God helps them that help themselves.
> No gains without pains.
> Haste makes waste.

Franklin's most famous sayings advocate plain living and hard work, but his devilish humor surfaces in some of the lesser-known ones:

> Fish and visitors stink in three days.
> A learned blockhead is a greater blockhead than an ignorant one.
> God heals, and the doctor takes the fees.
> Three may keep a secret if two of them are dead.

See also Franklin, Benjamin.

POP ART

Pop art—cheeky, disrespectful, occasionally hilarious—emerged in the 1960s. It celebrated materialism and consumer culture, and looked for its inspiration to the world of advertising, fast food, slick magazines, and anything crassly commercial. Andy Warhol, the most famous of the pop artists, painted careful copies of Campbell soup cans. Roy Lichtenstein made huge blow-ups of comic strips. Jasper Johns featured American flags, and Claes Oldenburg made gigantic sculptures of hamburgers. Art, the pop artists claimed, should no longer be worshiped in hushed tones as in the past. And it should not be difficult to understand, reserved only for the trained minds of critics and connoisseurs. Pop art thumbed its nose at the masterpieces that had come before it, asserting they were stuffy and pretentious: art should be funny and loud and friendly, and available for everyone to enjoy. Critics dismissed the movement as superficial nonsense; admirers felt it raised challenging questions about what constitutes a work of art.

See also Johns, Jasper; Painting and Sculpture; Warhol, Andy.

POPULAR SOVEREIGNTY

As used in nineteenth-century America, the term *popular sovereignty* meant that Congress should not try to control whether slavery would exist in new territories in the West. Instead, that decision should be left to the actual settlers of each territory.

Originally the national government had made this decision. For example, the Northwest Ordinance of 1787 banned slavery in the region that became the states of Ohio, Indiana, Illinois, Michigan, and Wisconsin. But slavery was permitted in the new states south of the Ohio River. The growing sectional conflict over slavery, however, made it extremely difficult for Congress to reach agreement when territories in the border areas between freedom and slavery were involved. Popular sovereignty seemed a democratic way to deal with the problem. It had the added virtue of allowing congressional politicians to avoid making tough decisions.

Popular sovereignty was applied to Utah and New Mexico Territories when they were organized by Congress after the Mexican War. But few people lived in those regions, and there was little likelihood that slave owners would move there in large numbers. When the Kansas-Nebraska Act of 1854 applied popular sovereignty to those territories, the basic flaws in the system quickly came to light. *When* should the settlers of a territory make the crucial decision about slavery? The struggle between pro- and antislavery groups in Kansas Territory resulted in the preview of the Civil War known as "Bleeding Kansas."

See also Bleeding Kansas; Douglas, Stephen A.; Freeport Doctrine.

POPULISM

The largest mass movement in American history, populism, as embodied in a political party—the People's Party—carried the hopes of millions of farmers in the South and Great Plains in the last decade of the nineteenth century. Nowadays, people use the term *populism* to mean almost any movement that arises outside of the major cities and seems to care a lot about "the people." But the populism of a century ago was an upsurge among particular people, mainly farmers, who were being devastated by the crushing economic system of the day.

Hard Times on Farms
The Civil War had laid waste to southern society and agriculture. Especially for small white farmers and the newly freed slaves, life was hard and unpredictable. When Reconstruction ended in 1877, those who had governed the slave South came back to power.

African Americans were at the mercy of the former slave owners.

Poor white farmers, too, came under the control of southern merchants and landowners through the "crop-lien system." Farmers borrowed money from the "furnishing merchants" who "furnished" them with goods—food, clothing, seed, tools—until the cotton harvest. Then the farmer would pay off the merchant, who had first rights (a lien) to his crop. Unfortunately, the price of cotton was so low throughout these years and the merchants charged such high interest on their loans that the farmers couldn't pay off their debts. Each year, they sank deeper into debt to the merchants, who often ended up taking their land as payment. Throughout the South, African Americans called the furnishing merchant the "furnishin' man," or, more simply, "the man."

In states such as Kansas, Nebraska, and North and South Dakota, farmers of the Great Plains grew wheat and corn. They found themselves controlled by the exorbitant storage rates charged by grain elevator companies and freight rates by the railroads.

Farmers' Alliances
Farmers fought back against this system by organizing what they called "Farmers' Alliances," or clubs to protect farmers' interests. They formed "cooperatives," which were groups of farmers who combined their resources and bought large quantities of goods for lower prices, and sold them together—independently of the merchants. This idea spread like wildfire in the late 1870s and early 1880s. Thousands of small, county-based Alliances formed statewide Alliances and sent "lecturers" and organizers throughout the South.

The problem was that the merchants still

had most of the ready cash, and they and their allies ran most banks and businesses, as well as local governments. So although farmers were, through their cooperatives, occasionally able to get out from under the thumbs of the merchants and raise some of their own capital, by and large they could not escape their debt.

After much study and debate at conventions and camps across the southern and plains states, these poor, uneducated farmers, along with their leaders, developed a plan to change the country's economic system so that it would work for the common people instead of against them. Their plan, which they named the "Subtreasury System," called for the U.S. Treasury to lend farmers the money they needed until the harvest came in, and to do so at fair rates, so that farmers had a chance of selling their crop at a fair price and getting out of debt.

The People's Party

In order to make this happen, though, the farmers had to win control of the government. So in 1892 they formed the People's Party and ran candidates for president and Congress, as well as for state and local offices. After a good bit of success in 1892 and again in 1894 (which astounded many big-city politicians and journalists, who could not believe a "bunch of hayseeds" had organized a political movement), they set their sights on the presidency in 1896.

Their political success was short-lived, however. Their presidential standard-bearer that year, the magnificent orator William Jennings Bryan, had had little to do with the cooperative movement. He had also first been nominated by the Democratic Party, which throughout the South was hostile to the populists. In fact he did not even attend the People's Party convention. Republican William McKinley, his campaign funded by banks, railroads, and other corporations, won by only 600,000 popular votes (out of 13.5 million cast), but crushed Bryan in electoral votes, 271–176. The People's Party was effectively dead at the national level, though it continued to have some life in towns across rural America even after the turn of the twentieth century.

Nonfarmers at the time, and historians for many years, thought that populism was simply a movement to try to put more currency, mostly silver, into circulation so that farmers could pay their debts more easily. But the populists stood for much more. They tried to change the American economy so that it would work more cooperatively and less competitively, for farmers and industrial workers. They insisted that ordinary Americans had the right to self-respect and decent treatment by politicians, journalists, and the wealthy.

They were defeated by powerful factors. First, too many Americans remained in the grip of their loyalties during the Civil War, so it was hard for northerners and southerners to cooperate effectively, as the populists were asking. Second, populist efforts to build bridges between black and white farmers ran into entrenched racism North and South, so these natural allies could do little together. And finally, through their sheer political and economic power, the corporations and banks persuaded millions of citizens that the populists were dangerous, un-American radicals who could not be trusted. Still, the populist legacy survived, particularly in the Midwest, where it helped support the Socialist Party of the early 1900s.

WARREN GOLDSTEIN

PORTER, COLE

(1893–1964) *Songwriter.*

Porter's witty lyrics and lilting tropical rhythms have entertained both sophisticated theatergoers and mass audiences. Unlike most of the popular music of his day (1930s–1950s), Porter's songs were clever and exciting, rather than romantic or sentimental. In 1944, however, a friend gave him the title "I Love You" and bet that he could not write a simple love song using ordinary, commonplace words. Of course, Porter won the bet.

The grandson of a millionaire, Porter grew up in Peru, Indiana. His doting mother encouraged him to study and write music. She even arranged to have his "Bobolink Waltz" published when he was just ten years old. As a student at Yale University, he wrote two enduring football songs, "Bingo Eli Yale" and "Bulldog." He left Harvard Law School in 1914 to pursue a musical career, but his first show, *See America First* (1916), flopped on Broadway. Undaunted, he contributed songs to other shows, writing his first hit, "Let's Do It," in 1928.

Porter was an international socialite as well as a successful songwriter, and his music reflected his sophisticated, carefree attitude toward life. Then, in 1937, a horseback-riding accident left him with two crushed legs, requiring thirty operations. Despite constant pain which he suffered for the rest of his life, he continued to create lighthearted, sometimes satirical, musical comedy scores.

Among the many memorable show tunes Porter wrote are "Night and Day," for *Gay Divorce* (1932), "You're the Top," for *Anything Goes* (1934), "Begin the Beguine," for *Jubilee* (1935), "It's De-Lovely," for *Red, Hot and Blue* (1936), "Wunderbar," for *Kiss Me Kate* (1948), "I Love Paris," for *Can-Can* (1953), and "All of You," for *Silk Stockings* (1955). A number of Porter's shows were made into movies, and he contributed songs to other films as well, including "Easy to Love" for *Born to Dance* (1936) and "I Concentrate on You" for *Broadway Melody, 1940*. He also composed original scores for the films *High Society* (1956), featuring the hit song "True Love," and *Les Girls* (1957).

See also Music.

BARBARA SILBERDICK FEINBERG

POTSDAM CONFERENCE

In the summer of 1945, shortly after the end of World War II in Europe, President Harry S. Truman, Premier Joseph Stalin of the Soviet Union, and Prime Minister Winston Churchill of Great Britain met at Potsdam, outside Berlin, to settle the fate of defeated Germany. After the Labour Party won the British elections in the course of the conference, Churchill was replaced by Clement Atlee.

The Allied leaders agreed to continue running their zones of occupation in Germany separately but established an Allied Control Council to deal with problems common to all. They also decided to try the Nazi leaders as war criminals, and they made plans for the future economic organization of Germany. They also agreed to transfer part of Eastern Germany to Poland and to demand the unconditional surrender of Japan.

During the conference President Truman received word of the successful testing of the atomic bomb. He shared this information with Churchill but not with Stalin.

See also World War II.

POUND, EZRA

(1885–1972)   *Poet and critic.*

Called "the stormiest literary hurricane of the twentieth century," Pound was a controversial writer who changed the course of modern English and American poetry through both his own work and his influence on other authors. His unconventional verse was never popular with the public, but it had a profound impact on the thought and work of many of his fellow poets.

The poet Ezra Pound at age seventy-five, reading his work aloud in public for the first time. Pound had a profound influence on modern poetry, but with his literary genius came a difficult and eccentric personality and, more regrettably, an outspoken antisemitism and fascism. Ernest Hemingway once remarked, "Of course Ezra is an ass, but he has written damned lovely poetry."

Pound was born in Idaho and educated in Pennsylvania, where he received an M.A. in Romance languages. Dissatisfied with the cultural life of the United States, he went to Europe in 1906 and spent the next thirty-seven years there. In London, where he lived first, he soon formed a circle of literary friends and admirers. In Venice in 1908 he printed his first volume of poetry, *A Lume Spento* ("With Tapers Quenched"), at his own expense, but these verses in traditional style earned neither money nor prestige. Two collections of his poetry published in London the next year impressed critics with their originality, however, and he began to be recognized as a bold new voice.

Pound also translated works from ancient and modern languages and wrote criticism of art, music, and literature, but his main concern was with poetry, his own and that of others. He led several literary movements and helped such important modern authors as the novelist James Joyce and the poets T. S. Eliot and William Butler Yeats, both of whom later won the Nobel Prize.

Pound's principal poetic work was *The Cantos*. In it he criticized Western society severely, blaming the banking system of England and the United States for most of the world's problems. Difficult to read because of its obscure language and many references to foreign literature and history, it runs over eight hundred pages but was still incomplete at his death.

When World War II broke out, Pound was living in Italy, and he decided to support its Fascist government rather than the United States. He made numerous anti-Semitic and pro-Fascist radio broadcasts during the war. When Italy surrendered, U.S. forces arrested him on suspicion of treason. He was judged insane, however, and was confined for thirteen years in a mental hospital in Washington, D.C. He continued writing and publishing poetry until his release and after.

See also Literature.

DENNIS WEPMAN

POVERTY AND HOMELESSNESS

Because of its vast natural resources and energetic people, the United States has always been a wealthier country than most other nations. Yet there have also been many poor people in America. Ways of caring for these unfortunates developed early.

Help in Early America

In colonial times local authorities often helped out widows, orphans, the old, and the sick. In the 1640s, for example, John Mott, an elderly citizen of Portsmouth, Rhode Island, was unable to support himself. The town therefore gave one of its citizens forty bushels of corn a year to feed and house Mott. The town continued to pay for Mott's upkeep until he died.

This system was based partly on the colonists' religious beliefs. The Bible says that the poor will be always be with us, and religious leaders taught that it was the duty of those who were better off to give to those in need. As the colonies grew, larger towns, such as New York and Boston, built poorhouses for their widows, orphans, and others who could not earn a living. Poor people from other towns and local citizens who seemed capable of working were turned away.

"All men are created equal," the Founders said in the Declaration of Independence. This meant not that all were thought to be the same at birth but that all should have an equal chance to succeed. Many Americans argued that any healthy person who was poor must simply must be lazy. The way to end poverty was to make these "lazy" people work. In an attempt to do this, many states and cities built workhouses, where able-bodied persons who claimed to be unable to support themselves were forced to do hard tasks like chopping firewood in return for food and shelter.

Nineteenth-Century Poverty

Yet poverty did not end—as the country grew larger the problem actually got worse. During the 1800s, millions of immigrants flooded into the United States. Some became farmers, but many crowded into cities to seek work in shops and factories. Wages were low and jobs sometimes hard to find. Many could not support themselves when times were hard.

Life was particularly difficult for orphans and the children of the poor. In 1852 there were 10,000 children living on the streets of New York City. They slept in hallways and cellars, and lived off scraps and what they could beg. In 1853 Charles Loring Brace, a social worker, founded New York's Children's Aid Society. Brace believed that homeless children should be cared for in families outside the city. The society sent groups of orphans to small towns, where local people were employed to care for them. Over the years the society helped about 100,000 children in this way.

As time passed, most people who supported the Children's Aid Society and similar organizations began to question the idea that poverty was caused by laziness. Low wages, depressions during which even skilled hardworking people lost their jobs, lack of educational opportunities, and similar circumstances were the real causes, they believed. The Progressives, as they were called, argued that the government should take steps to deal with the poverty problem.

Economic conditions improved in the early 1900s, and many of the poor were able to live better. But poverty persisted. Recent immigrants, especially, and thousands of southern blacks who moved to the big cities of the North to escape the near slavery conditions on southern farms had trouble finding work.

The Great Depression

Then in the early 1930s the Great Depression struck. As businesses closed, millions lost their jobs and then their homes. In Chicago, one woman pleaded, "I am without food for myself and my child. I got only $6.26 to last me from the tenth to the twenty-fifth [of the month]. . . . Please give us something to eat. I cannot stand to see my child hungry."

Only the federal government had the resources and power to deal with this disaster. In 1932 Franklin D. Roosevelt was elected president. He persuaded Congress to adopt a series of reforms known as the New Deal. A Federal Farm Bankruptcy Act kept farmers from losing their land, and the Agricultural Adjustment Act cut back on farm production so that the price of their crops would rise. The Social Security Act provided for old age and unemployment insurance. Millions of people were put to work building post offices, courthouses, roads, and other public facilities.

The outbreak of World War II ended the Great Depression. With war production soaring, nearly everyone capable of working could find a job. When the war ended in 1945, millions of Americans had money in their pockets, and they spent it freely. The econo-

my boomed. Workers could afford automobiles, new homes, and all kinds of other goods. The "American way of life" was the envy of the world.

Poverty in the 1960s and After

Yet poverty had not disappeared. In the 1960s Americans were shocked to read in Michael Harrington's book *The Other America* that millions of people were still living below the poverty line. Few children were actually starving, but many were not getting enough milk, vegetables, and other foods necessary for a healthy existence.

In the early 1960s President Lyndon B. Johnson introduced the War on Poverty as part of his Great Society program. The government spent billions of dollars to provide the poor with better housing, health care, and education. In many ways Johnson won his War on Poverty. The number of Americans living below the official government poverty line dropped from 39 million in 1959 to 23 million in 1973. But this was still far too many.

Many people believed that the programs had not worked very well and that, in any case, they had been far too expensive. In 1980, Ronald Reagan, running for president as a Republican, argued that government spending on such programs should be cut sharply. Taxes could then be reduced. That would leave taxpayers with more money to spend and invest productively, which would create more jobs that poor people could fill and thereby emerge from poverty on their own. Reagan was elected on this platform by a large margin. Congress swiftly put his program—known as "supply side economics" because it stressed increasing the production of goods—into effect.

For a time the economy boomed. But lower taxes increased the income of people already rich far more than the income of poor and middle-class individuals. The gap between rich and poor increased, and when the boom ended, poverty and homelessness were worse than they had been in the 1960s. Despite the wealth of the United States, in the 1990s, millions of its citizens remained poor, and many thousands lived on city streets.

See also Depressions and Recessions; Ghettos; Great Society; New Deal; Settlement House Movement; Unemployment; Welfare and Public Relief.

ABIGAIL JUNGREIS

POWELL, COLIN

(1937–) *First black national security adviser and first black and youngest chairman of the Joint Chiefs of Staff.*

Powell was among the first American military advisers to be sent to Vietnam in the early 1960s. During two tours, he was wounded once and saved fellow passengers in a helicopter crash. He was awarded eleven medals, including a Purple Heart and two Bronze Stars.

After Vietnam, Powell graduated from the National War College, achieved the rank of general, and alternated between duty in the field and desk jobs, including various positions at the Pentagon. Impressing his superiors, he continued to move up through the ranks and in 1987 was named national security adviser by President Ronald Reagan. In this position, he oversaw the invasion of Panama to arrest President Manuel Noriega, a supporter of drug smuggling into the United States.

After receiving his fourth general's star from departing President Reagan, Powell was appointed chairman of the Joint Chiefs of Staff by Reagan's successor, George Bush. In this position, he supervised the Gulf War with Iraq in early 1991. Without publicly making his objections known, he obeyed his commander in chief, President Bush, and halted the drive into Iraq before its president, Saddam Hussein, was toppled.

When Bush's successor, Bill Clinton, announced that he would end the military's ban on gays, however, Powell objected publicly. A career "good soldier," he did not oppose the president outright. But he did object to the frequently made argument comparing anti-gay discrimination with antiblack discrimination in the military five decades earlier. He retired in 1993.

For further reading: Jim Haskins, *Colin Powell: A Biography* (New York: Scholastic, 1992).

JIM HASKINS

PRESIDENCY

The presidency, as created by the Constitutional Convention, was chiefly the design of James Wilson of Pennsylvania. Although the delegates assumed that George Washington would be the first president, the question of how to choose a chief executive was fully aired. The task was finally assigned to an electoral college to be selected by the state legislatures. The length of the president's term was fixed at four years. The president was made commander in chief of the armed forces and charged with making sure that the laws of the nation are faithfully executed.

The president is now also by custom the head of his political party and the chief architect of foreign policy. Congress, moreover, has conferred other powers not mentioned in

UNITED STATES PRESIDENTS

No.	Name	Born–Died	Years in Office	Political Party	Home State
1	George Washington	1732–1799	1789–1797	None	Va.
2	John Adams	1735–1826	1797–1801	Federalist	Mass.
3	Thomas Jefferson	1743–1826	1801–1809	Republican*	Va.
4	James Madison	1751–1836	1809–1817	Republican	Va.
5	James Monroe	1758–1831	1817–1825	Republican	Va.
6	John Quincy Adams	1767–1848	1825–1829	Republican	Mass.
7	Andrew Jackson	1767–1845	1829–1837	Democratic	Tenn.
8	Martin Van Buren	1782–1862	1837–1841	Democratic	N.Y.
9	William Henry Harrison	1773–1841	1841	Whig	Ohio
10	John Tyler	1790–1862	1841–1845	Whig	Va.
11	James K. Polk	1795–1849	1845–1849	Democratic	Tenn.
12	Zachary Taylor	1784–1850	1849–1850	Whig	La.
13	Millard Fillmore	1800–1874	1850–1853	Whig	N.Y.
14	Franklin Pierce	1804–1869	1853–1857	Democratic	N.H.
15	James Buchanan	1791–1868	1857–1861	Democratic	Pa.
16	Abraham Lincoln	1809–1865	1861–1865	Republican	Ill.
17	Andrew Johnson	1808–1875	1865–1869	Republican	Tenn.
18	Ulysses S. Grant	1822–1885	1869–1877	Republican	Ill.
19	Rutherford B. Hayes	1822–1893	1877–1881	Republican	Ohio
20	James A. Garfield	1831–1881	1881	Republican	Ohio
21	Chester A. Arthur	1830–1886	1881–1885	Republican	N.Y.
22	Grover Cleveland	1837–1908	1885–1889	Democratic	N.Y.
23	Benjamin Harrison	1833–1901	1889–1893	Republican	Ind.
24	Grover Cleveland	1837–1908	1893–1897	Democratic	N.Y.
25	William McKinley	1843–1901	1897–1901	Republican	Ohio
26	Theodore Roosevelt	1858–1919	1901–1909	Republican	N.Y.
27	William Howard Taft	1857–1930	1909–1913	Republican	Ohio
28	Woodrow Wilson	1856–1924	1913–1921	Democratic	N.J.
29	Warren G. Harding	1865–1923	1921–1923	Republican	Ohio
30	Calvin Coolidge	1872–1933	1923–1929	Republican	Mass.
31	Herbert Hoover	1874–1964	1929–1933	Republican	Calif.
32	Franklin D. Roosevelt	1882–1945	1933–1945	Democratic	N.Y.
33	Harry S. Truman	1884–1972	1945–1953	Democratic	Mo.
34	Dwight D. Eisenhower	1890–1969	1953–1961	Republican	Kans.
35	John F. Kennedy	1917–1963	1961–1963	Democratic	Mass.
36	Lyndon B. Johnson	1908–1973	1963–1969	Democratic	Tex.
37	Richard M. Nixon	1913–1994	1969–1974	Republican	Calif.
38	Gerald Ford	1913–	1974–1977	Republican	Mich.
39	Jimmy Carter	1924–	1977–1981	Democratic	Ga.
40	Ronald Reagan	1911–	1981–1989	Republican	Calif.
41	George Bush	1924–	1989–1993	Republican	Tex.
42	Bill Clinton	1946–	1993–	Democratic	Ark.

*The Republican party of the third through sixth presidents was not the modern party, which was founded in 1854.

the Constitution upon the president, ranging from authority over trade relations to the management of labor disputes.

From the beginning, the selection of presidents has riveted public attention. The early chief executives were chosen by the electoral college, as the Constitution specified, although the election of Thomas Jefferson in 1800, for lack of a majority in the college, had to be decided in the House of Representatives. By 1800 loosely organized political factions (which were like modern political parties although not fully developed yet), through their leaders in Congress, were assembling in meetings called caucuses and selecting the presidential candidates. After 1825, when John Quincy Adams won an election that was also thrown into the House of Representatives for decision, "King Caucus" gave way to nominating conventions composed of popularly chosen delegates. By 1832, the major parties were nominating their presidential candidates in national conventions.

Development of the Presidency

Andrew Jackson, a military hero famous on the frontier, was elected in 1828. He created a new kind of presidency, increasingly responsive to public opinion. The death in 1841 of William Henry Harrison, the first president to die in office, settled the problem of immediate presidential succession. Vice President John Tyler's insistence that he was not merely an "acting president" but a full-fledged president prevailed.

The election of Abraham Lincoln in 1860, which caused the Southern states to secede (that is, leave the Union) and brought on the Civil War, opened yet another presidential era. Lincoln's Republican Party, recognized as the savior of the Union, became for generations the party of the presidents. Between

1860 and 1932, only Grover Cleveland (in 1884 and 1892) and Woodrow Wilson (in 1912 and 1916) carried the Democratic banner to victory. But the Great Depression, which led in 1932 to the election of Franklin D. Roosevelt, a Democrat, not only shattered the spell of the Republicans but also once more altered the character of the office. Under Roosevelt, it became a dynamo of energetic social experimentation. The Second World War, which broke out in the middle of FDR's unique four-term presidency, gave the office immense prestige as the very voice of democracy and of the free world.

By then presidents were elected following campaigns of nationwide barnstorming, after the pattern set by William Jennings Bryan, the Democratic candidate in 1896. In 1932 radio became a major means of reaching the public, and since 1948 television has been the chief medium of electioneering. Recently candidates have used television talk shows to establish direct contact with the people.

The Modern Presidency

The long cold war that ended with the collapse of the Soviet Union in the late 1980s was a triumph in part of presidential patience and determination. Yet in the same period the presidency itself had not flourished uniformly. John F. Kennedy was assassinated in 1963 (the fourth assassination in the history of the office, the others being Lincoln in 1865, James A. Garfield in 1881, and William McKinley in 1901), and Lyndon B. Johnson's presidency (1963–69) was devastated by the nation's growing opposition to the war in Vietnam.

Richard M. Nixon's tenure (1969–74) was terminated by his resignation (the only one in White House history), when he was about to be impeached on charges growing out of the Watergate affair. Nixon's vice president,

Spiro T. Agnew, had been forced to resign under threat of indictment for income tax evasion, and Nixon replaced him under the terms of the Twenty-fifth Amendment by appointing Representative Gerald R. Ford of Michigan. When Ford became president upon Nixon's departure, he in turn named Nelson A. Rockefeller to be vice president, thus giving the country for the first time in its history an unelected chief executive and an unelected number-two man.

The election in 1976 of Jimmy Carter of Georgia, in 1980 of Ronald Reagan of California, and in 1992 of Bill Clinton of Arkansas—all men whose main experience had been their governorships—seemed to show a popular desire to have a president from outside the "intrigues" of Washington, D.C. On the other hand, in 1988, when George Bush was elected, the public seemed to be seeking not only a continuation of the prosperity of the 1980s but also a person well acquainted with the ways of the national capital. Time and again, the electorate has chosen their chief executive because of his battlefield triumphs. Each victorious war has produced a hero who became president, and the Civil War yielded a series of them.

In recent years, presidents have had to wrestle with questions that used to be dealt with on the city and state levels but today reach the White House for solution. Consequently, the president must rely on many specialized advisers. The cabinet, which came into existence in 1791, is the president's "official family." It originally consisted of the heads of the Departments of State, Treasury, and War, and the Office of the Attorney General; today fourteen departments are represented.

Many of the amendments to the Constitution have affected the presidency, although not its powers. The Twelfth Amendment (1804) provided that the president and vice president be chosen on separate ballots. The Twentieth Amendment (1933) moved up Inauguration Day from March 4 to January 20 and provided that if the president-elect fails to qualify by that day, the vice president–elect then becomes president. The Twenty-second Amendment (1951) declared that no person may be elected president more than twice. The Twenty-fifth Amendment (1967) specified the procedure to be followed in case of presidential disability. The line of succession to the presidency after the vice president was established by an act of Congress in 1947. Now in its third century, the presidency remains the richest political prize in the world and is pursued like no other.

See also Assassinations, Presidential; Cabinet; Elections (table); Electoral College; First Ladies; Impeachment; Vice Presidency. *And see biographies of individual presidents.*

HENRY F. GRAFF

PRESIDENTIAL ELECTIONS
See Elections.

PRESLEY, ELVIS
(1935–77)   *Singer and actor.*

Presley, one of the greatest single influences on rock, country, and popular music, is called the king of rock 'n' roll. Although he died in 1977, his record sales still surpass those of most other performers.

Born in Tupelo, Mississippi, Presley began singing in a church choir and at the age of twelve taught himself to play the guitar. After moving to Memphis, Tennessee, in 1953, he cut his first record and immediately after signed a multirecord recording contract. The raw energy and driving beat of his delivery

Rock 'n' roll's mass appeal began with Elvis Presley, who came to be known as "the King." His stellar rise, career tribulations, and untimely death made him an American icon.

made several of these records national hits. When he appeared on the Ed Sullivan television show, his gyrating-hips performance created an international sensation, earned him the title "Elvis the Pelvis," and established him as a superstar who left teenage girls screaming with excitement.

In 1958 Presley's career was interrupted when he was inducted into the U.S. Army. Two years later he resumed his recording career and starred in a series of movies including *Love Me Tender* and *Jailhouse Rock*. In 1967 he married Priscilla Ann Beaulieu, and a daughter was born one year later. The two divorced in 1972.

Some of Presley's best and most popular records include *All Shook Up, Hound Dog, Jail House Rock, Blue Suede Shoes, It's Now or Never,* and *Burning Love.* Presley, a white man who performed what was often called black music, is noted for crossing racial barriers and bringing this so-called black music to mainstream white audiences. He also starred in over thirty movies. Although his professional success was enormous, his personal life was often troubled. His mother's death in 1958 left him severely depressed, and later in his life he suffered from drug addiction, overeating, and violent mood swings. His death from a heart attack induced by a drug overdose at the age of forty-two shocked and saddened the world. Graceland, his mansion in Memphis, is now a museum that attracts thousands of visitors a year.

See also Rock Music.

JOANN BIONDI

PRIMOGENITURE

Primogeniture was an English system of inheritance dating back to medieval times. Under primogeniture a person left all the land he owned to his oldest male child. The purpose was to prevent large properties from being broken down over the generations into smaller, uneconomical units. Primogeniture was established in some of the American colonies, but it was relatively unimportant because land was abundant and cheap and labor relatively scarce. Younger sons could obtain land easily, and few persons could command enough labor to make owning extremely large properties practicable.

Primogeniture affected the colonies indirectly by causing many younger sons in England to seek their fortunes in America. Even so, the abolition of the system was one of the social and economic results of the American Revolution.

See also Colonial America.

PRISONS

There are 1.25 million persons locked up in American prisons and jails, more people than live in the cities of Dallas or Detroit, a number greater than the population of fourteen states. It is as though everyone who attended the last fifteen Superbowls was put behind bars. No other democratic nation has so many people imprisoned; it is our national disgrace. Tragically, the number of inmates grows each year.

What makes this number so shocking is that our nation was founded in large measure by people determined to escape the dungeons and prisons of Europe, where people could be unjustly locked up indefinitely for minor crimes or simply for being poor. English judges often gave defendants a choice between going to America or jail. The colony of Georgia at first was populated in part by convicts.

The Constitution and Bill of Rights contain a number of provisions that make imprisonment difficult. There are prohibitions against double jeopardy (being tried twice for the same crime), passage of an ex post facto law (which makes an action a crime *after* it has happened), illegal searches and seizures (those made without a court order called a warrant), as well as cruel and unusual punishments. Persons can be imprisoned only by due process of law: they must be informed of their rights, represented by an attorney, and offered a trial by jury.

Punishment in Earlier Times

From the beginning, colonists built some types of jails, but they tried to use them as little as possible. There was such a severe labor shortage it made no sense to keep an able-bodied person locked up. Alternative punishments were found. An offender was publicly whipped or placed in *stocks,* wooden frames that held fast the hands and feet. Both methods held the person up to public ridicule. On the other hand, authorities imposed the death penalty for what today would be considered relatively minor offenses, such as theft.

Over time, as the population grew, so did the size of jails and the number of people in them. In the late 1700s and early 1800s, Quakers sought to ease the harsh conditions in prisons and to reform the inmates. Two schemes developed. In the Pennsylvania System prisoners were kept in individual cells and required to work at carpentry and such. They were allowed out only an hour a day. Reformers believed solitary confinement would encourage reform by inducing repentance. Most European prisons were modeled after this system. The Auburn System came to be most widely used in the United States. It was an attempt to change behavior. Prisoners worked in groups, but in total silence. Any effort to speak or communicate, even by moving the lips or giving hand signals, was punished by flogging. The idea behind this system was that prisoners would learn to work, yet silence would prevent their learning about crime from one another, then believed to be the major cause of crime.

The modern era of prisons began in 1876 at Elmira, New York, with the opening of the first *reformatory* for prisoners aged sixteen to thirty. They were given meaningful work and paid for it, the money being set aside for their release. They received educational, physical, and military training and were supervised by parole officers upon their release. By the 1920s these methods had been expanded to include all prisoners.

Punishment Today

All the earlier ideas about punishment and prisons have influenced American thinking throughout the country's history. Stocks and public ridicule were replaced first by making prisoners wear striped suits; today they are issued other prison uniforms. Hard labor and silence took the form of chain gangs with convicts marching in lockstep. Then chain gangs were abolished, and prisoners were isolated in individual cells. Overcrowding, however, has led to two or more inmates confined in cells designed for one. Death seen as suitable punishment led to vigilantes and lynch mobs (people operating outside the law and killing someone without a trial). Today the death penalty is the subject of an ongoing national debate, with some holding that it deters crime and others opposed to it on practical and moral grounds.

As in the past, reformers still complain that the prison system is self-defeating. Almost no one has anything good to say about it. It is not only wasteful but futile, worsening the very problem it is intended to correct.

Two armed guards stand on either side of a trio of prisoners who have been sentenced to serve on a chain gang. The guards have enlisted the prisoners to help them hunt down an escaped prisoner.

Americans read or hear that someone has been sent to prison and perhaps feel safer because another criminal is off the streets. They should not, however, because eventually the person will have served his or her sentence and will be released—usually angrier and more bitter than ever. More than 40 percent of those released are *recidivists*—that is, they end up back in prison after committing a new crime.

Little learned in prison prepares people to lead a better, more productive life when they are freed. The convict enters a society unlike any other in America, dominated by violence, a human jungle governed by survival of the strongest. The prison society has rules of conduct and morality found nowhere else. The inmate surrenders privacy and nearly all personal decision making. Life is regimented. Skills learned in prison industries, such as furniture refinishing, laundering, and license plate making are not in much demand on the outside.

This futile, self-defeating system of corrections came to exist and persists today because of two beliefs. One is the idea of *justice:* criminals must pay for their crimes. Everyone, including even some convicts, believes crime should be punished by imprisonment. The question is for how long? In Britain, there is no death penalty and sentences of longer than five years are seldom imposed. Yet the crime rate there is lower than here.

The second idea is that punishment *deters* crime. If a person knows a crime will lead to prison and prison is an unpleasant place, goes the argument, the crime will not be committed. This may be true for law-abiding citizens, but it obviously is not for the 1.25 million in prison. The average term for violent crime tripled between 1975 and 1989 without making so much as a dent in the crime statistics. For all our prisons and prisoners we have more, not less crime.

Repeated studies have indicated that the best way to reduce violence and crime is through prevention rather than imprisonment. Programs to create jobs and alleviate poverty, improve public schools, make more affordable housing available, and provide alcohol and drug treatment programs, as well as counseling and educational campaigns to show the futility and waste of crime, may be more effective deterrents than prisons.

ROBERT A. LISTON

PROCLAMATION OF 1763

After France ceded its colonies in North America to Great Britain in the peace treaty ending the French and Indian War in 1763, English colonists began to move west across the Appalachian Mountains into the Ohio Valley. This quickly led to trouble with the Indian tribes of the region. Pontiac, a chief of the Ottawas, organized a formidable resistance. After much bloodshed, peace was restored. The British then stationed fifteen regiments of Redcoats in the area. To prevent future trouble, the government also issued the Proclamation of 1763.

The proclamation established a temporary ban on the migration of settlers beyond an imaginary line drawn along the peaks of the Appalachian Mountains. Colonists and indeed the colonial governments were forbidden even to buy land beyond the proclamation line. Only licensed fur traders could have any business dealings with the tribes.

The proclamation was deeply resented by many colonists, especially land speculators who wanted to buy up huge tracts of western land cheaply and then sell them in small units to settlers. George Washington, for example, called the proclamation an "expedient to quiet the minds of Indians."

As a temporary policy, necessary to restore order in the West, the proclamation was probably a good idea. But the British never canceled it. As time passed it was resented more and more, and became one of the causes of the American Revolution.

See also Colonial America; Seven Years' War.

PROGRESSIVE PARTIES: 1912, 1924, 1948

There have been three third-party movements that took the name "Progressive." All were liberal movements seeking to achieve political, economic, or social changes that, according to the progressives, the major parties seemed unable or unwilling to deal with.

In 1912, after he failed to win the Republican presidential nomination, ex-president Theodore Roosevelt ran as the candidate of the **first Progressive Party,** popularly known as the Bull Moose Party. He called for dealing with large corporations by regulating them rather than by breaking them into smaller units under the antitrust law. He received more than 4 million popular votes and eighty-eight electoral college votes, but lost to the Democrat, Woodrow Wilson, by a large margin.

The **second Progressive Party** was led by a former member of the first one, Senator Robert M. La Follette of Wisconsin. In 1924, when both the major parties nominated conservatives for president, La Follette, with outside support from the Socialist Party, entered the race. His platform called for nationalizing the railroads, the direct election of the president,

and other reforms. He received only thirteen electoral votes and a much smaller percentage of the popular vote than Roosevelt had received in 1912.

The **third Progressive Party** nominated ex-secretary of agriculture Henry A. Wallace for president in 1948. Wallace was principally motivated by his fear that the major parties were likely to cause another world war because of their anti-Soviet policies. Wallace received barely 1 million popular votes.

PROHIBITION AND TEMPERANCE

Since the earliest years of their history, many Americans have believed that alcoholic beverages were essential to their pursuit of happiness. Many others, however, have feared that the unrestrained use of these beverages threatened the future of the nation. In Thomas Jefferson's time, probably most of his fellow citizens knew drunkenness—their own or someone else's—as a common experience. Jefferson himself believed in "temperance"—he hoped that people would stop drinking so much whiskey and rum and instead learn to drink moderate amounts of less alcoholic wine and beer. A few years later James Madison asked young people, for the "good of the country," to stop drinking any beverage that could be intoxicating. And in 1842, Abraham Lincoln urged people to see that the thoughtless use of "intoxicating liquors" was bringing tragedy to almost every American family.

The Drive for Prohibition
At the same time a Maine businessman named Neal Dow was discovering that where "grog shops" were competing to sell strong drink, such competition encouraged people to get drunk, and that among his friends, rel-

atives, and neighbors he could measure the sad results in the bloody workplace accidents that occurred almost daily, in poverty, in crime, and in the number of men who physically abused their wives and children. Preaching to people about the wisdom of "temperance," Dow said, did not change anything. He called instead for the state government to pass a law that would "prohibit" both the manufacture and the sale of all intoxicating liquors. This "Maine Law" became the first state prohibition law in 1851. Many people agreed with Dow, and by 1855 thirteen of the thirty-one states had such laws.

In states where the legislatures repeatedly refused to pass prohibition laws, many women joined organizations that promised to find other ways to abolish the grog shops, which after the Civil War were called "saloons." In the 1870s it was not uncommon for women to parade through the streets from a church meeting to a saloon—interrupting traffic as they marched—where shoulder to shoulder they sang and prayed against what they called the evils of the "liquor traffic" and the "drunkard-making business." Although these women were often insulted and ridiculed and even physically harassed, their absolute seriousness caused saloon customers to feel extremely uncomfortable. As they turned away from the angry women, some saloonkeepers actually did close their doors.

These women knew, however, that to close all saloons they would have to confront their lawmakers, and they sought help from such organizations as the Woman's Christian Temperance Union (WCTU). Its president, Frances Willard, was a former college dean who sought political solutions to social problems such as drunkenness, poverty, crime, and ignorance. Willard urged American women to support lawmakers in their states who favored "home protection and saloon destruc-

tion" and to demand that they pass state laws that would make saloons illegal. Those who opposed such laws were then called the "wets," and those who favored them became the "drys." Political leaders could not escape being labeled "wet" or "dry," and the number of dry states continued to grow. By 1916, twenty-one states had banned saloons.

The Eighteenth Amendment

By then, too, voters had sent to Washington, D.C., a Congress in which the drys outnumbered the wets by two to one. This first dry Congress wanted a federal prohibition law that would cover the entire nation, and it approved the Eighteenth Amendment to make unconstitutional any "manufacture, sale, or

Federal agents smashing beer barrels during Prohibition, the period from 1920 to 1933 when the sale and manufacture of alcoholic beverages were prohibited in the United States.

transportation of intoxicating liquors." In 1919 it was ratified by the states and became part of the Constitution. To spell out what the Eighteenth Amendment meant, Congress passed the National Prohibition Act—often called the Volstead Act—that took effect in January 1920. The law required that all distilleries, breweries, and wineries in the United States must close and that anyone who sold alcoholic beverages thereafter could be charged with a federal crime.

For several years probably most Americans supported the law, believing that it would contribute to the security and prosperity of the next generation. They were pleased by reports that public drunkenness was declining and that the incidence of illnesses associated with the excessive use of alcohol was dropping. But many people who had never wanted to manufacture or sell alcoholic beverages fully intended to continue drinking them, and drinking was not prohibited by the Constitution. These people presented enormous problems to federal prohibition agents, and most of these problems were unsolvable. Congress had no plan, for example, to stop the illegal movement of alcohol into the United States by land or sea. Any such plan to police the immensely long seacoasts and borders would have required raising huge armies and navies at a cost in tax dollars that was simply out of the question.

Those who moved shipments of liquor across the country's borders were often called "rumrunners." Those who sold liquor by the bottle in the towns and cities were called "bootleggers." And in places where the authorities were lukewarm toward Prohibition, saloons called "speakeasies" operated openly. Although many of those defying the law were arrested and sent to prison, most were not. Especially in the larger cities, their presence became so obvious that almost anyone could

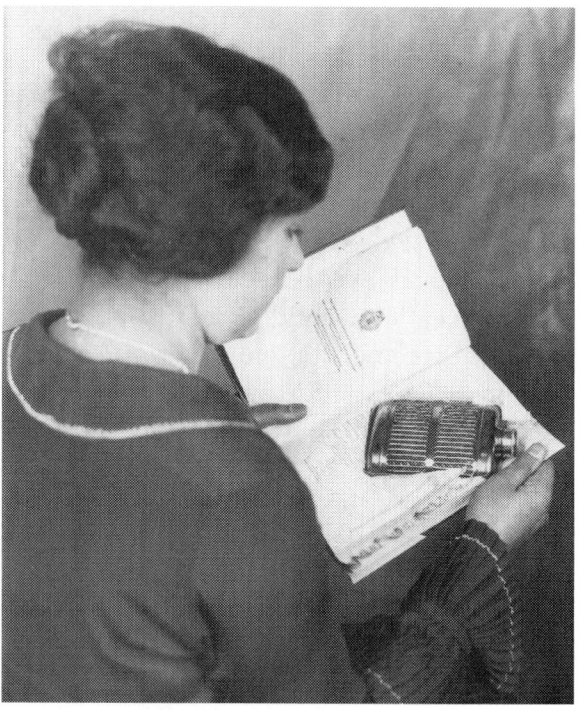

One ingenious example of how liquor was hidden during Prohibition—the pages of a book have been cut out in order to fit a flask, which is undetectable when the book is shut.

see that the Volstead Act was not in fact prohibiting. Some people came to fear that the failure of the act was so widespread it might undermine respect for the Constitution and for law and order generally. Yet even if they had grave doubts about the Volstead Act, most nevertheless agreed with Herbert Hoover who, in his successful presidential campaign in 1928, supported Prohibition, calling it "a great social and economic experiment."

But when the Great Depression struck in 1929, many citizens refused any longer to support the continuation of the "experiment." They decided that legalizing liquor would supply steady jobs for the unemployed in the manufacture and sale of alcohol and that a renewed liquor traffic would bring in much needed tax revenues. Other critics hoped to see the federal government stop trying to control what people drank and return the country to its traditional personal freedoms. An organization called the Association Against the Prohibition Amendment proposed a Twenty-first Amendment to repeal the Eighteenth, and this group found eager supporters. Their work brought about the ratification of the Twenty-first on December 5, 1933—the only time an amendment to the Constitution has been repealed. The matter of liquor control returned to the states. Today state laws—as in 1851—demonstrate wide differences.

See also Anti-Saloon League; Drugs; Nation, Carry.

NORMAN H. CLARK

PROTESTANTS

One of the important events in American history occurred *before* Europeans arrived in the New World. In 1517 a Catholic priest named Martin Luther nailed his Ninety-five Theses to the door of All-Saints Church in Wittenberg, Germany. These were a list of abuses that Luther believed had crept into the Roman Catholic church. He "protested" the luxurious life-style of the popes in Rome—they were living as kings, he said, not as men of God—and the sale of indulgences. The church taught that for a sum of money a person could purchase forgiveness of sins. To Luther, it looked like people could buy their way into heaven.

Luther's protest quickly spread throughout Europe. Although he had no intention of founding a new religion (he wanted only reform of the Catholic church, which ultimately did occur), he had launched Protestantism. It took root in England, Switzerland, and northern Europe, as people sought to free themselves from Catholic dogma and papal authority. The movement further splintered into sects, as individuals and groups read their own meaning into the Bible and exercised their newfound freedom to protest.

Protestants in America

So devoted were Protestants to their beliefs that they endured hardship and oppression from state-authorized, or established, religions. As early as 1607, certainly by 1620, Protestants came to the New World, seeing it as a haven. There might still be hardships, but at least they could practice their religion according to their beliefs. And come they did—Anglicans (Episcopalians today), Puritans (today's Congregationalists or United Church of Christ), Calvinists (Presbyterians), Anabaptists, Mennonites, Quakers, Lutherans, French Huguenots, and many more. Catholics came, too, to avoid Protestant oppression in some countries.

The United States would be a far different place today had not Protestants come in such numbers. Given their belief that individuals, or congregations of like-minded individuals, must make their own way to God and salvation, Protestants fostered the idea of individual liberty—the hallmark of what it means to be an American. Freedom to worship as an individual pleases was written into the Constitution as the First Amendment of the Bill of Rights: "Congress shall make no law respecting the establishment of religion, or the free exercise thereof." Nothing is more sacred to an American, and Protestants brought the idea to these shores. The First Amendment protects not only Protestants but Jews, Catholics, Muslims, Buddhists, and members of other religions, as well as nonbelievers—atheists and agnostics.

Today the United States is the most populous Protestant nation on earth—roughly 80 million adherents out of 330 million worldwide. It is difficult to exaggerate their importance in American history and culture. All presidents have been Protestant, save one, John F. Kennedy, who was Catholic. Protestant beliefs in the sanctity of the individual, self-reliance, the right to dissent from authority, are ingrained in the American character. This is what makes us such a difficult people to govern. It is also what makes us a democracy.

Because Protestants often disagree, there are hundreds, maybe thousands of sects, some consisting of a single church or a meeting of believers. Congregations have split over dislike for a minister, some item of dogma or ritual, lack of agreement over a proposed reform. In 1860 the Free Methodists broke away from the Methodists because they objected to a dress worn by a bishop's wife.

Kinds of Protestants

There are today four main types of Protestants in the United States. The *mainstream* Protestants are the oldest sects; they are, in order of size, the Baptists, Methodists, Lutherans, Presbyterians, Episcopalians, Congregationalists, and Christian Church–Disciples of Christ. Most American Protestants belong to one of these denominations. Differences between them for the most part involve their rituals. All believe that the way to God lies not in a quick, emotional experience but a steady life of faith, worship, prayer, good works, and moral behavior. Members often move between denominations, sometimes for social reasons.

Where mainstream Protestants view the Bible as a historic guide subject to interpretation, *fundamentalists* believe it is the precise word of God and must be accepted as literally true if the person is to escape punishment in this life or avoid "hellfire and brimstone" in the afterlife. *Evangelists* believe in and practice *saviorism*—that is, a person will lead a good life now and in the hereafter if he or she is saved by accepting Jesus Christ and his teachings and becoming a Christian. Evangelists seek to save as many people as possible by aggressively proclaiming their beliefs, often via radio and television programs. *Pentecostals* go a step further, believing that someone's being saved through accepting Jesus is manifested by a variety of emotional experiences such as *glossolalia*—speaking in tongues in which a person renders the word of God in an obscure or unknown language.

Protestantism in America has sometimes been marked by intolerance of other beliefs leading to discrimination and even violence, by bizarre cults, and by swindlers who take advantage of the gullible (as the writer H. L. Mencken half-jokingly put it, "The quickest way to get rich in America is to start a religion"). But it has also expressed itself in individualism, love of liberty, hard work, charity, morality, and patriotism.

See also Church and State, Separation of; Graham, Billy; Great Awakening; Hutchinson, Anne; Mather, Cotton; Pilgrims; Puritans; Quakers; Salvation Army; Shakers; Williams, Roger.

ROBERT A. LISTON

PUBLIC OPINION POLLING

Public opinion polling seeks to discover how large populations feel about a person, a product, or an issue. If it is done right, a poll of 1,200 individuals around the country accurately reflects the attitudes of all 185 million U.S. adults.

In its crudest form, the idea of *sampling*—judging the whole of something by closely examining a small part of it—is ancient. A king might have consulted his advisers before going to war. But although this survey would have revealed how the men around him felt, it would have said little about what ordinary people thought. Early U.S. polls were nearly as uninformative. In 1824, newspaper reporters in Wilmington, Delaware, asked some 500 passers-by who would win the coming presidential election. But since the reporters did not check to see whether those they questioned were likely to vote, nor compare their answers with results from polls in other parts of the state or country, their findings were too incomplete to be useful in predicting the election's outcome. Later polls were larger and more sophisticated. By 1912, newspapers in thirty-seven states were collecting and pooling information about voter attitudes. *Literary Digest* magazine correctly predicted all five presidential winners between 1916 and 1932. Market research surveys began enabling businesses and manufacturers to identify their customers' needs and demands.

Scientific and Random Sampling

In 1936 came *Literary Digest*'s biggest-ever poll. The magazine mailed mock ballots to 10 million Americans whose names appeared in telephone books and on automobile registration lists. Two million people returned their ballots, "voting" overwhelmingly for President Franklin D. Roosevelt's challenger, Alfred Landon. Yet Roosevelt beat Landon— overwhelmingly. What had gone wrong?

Independent pollsters like George Gallup and Elmo Roper knew. The *Literary Digest* sample was what is called *biased*. In 1936, America was in the middle of a serious depression, and millions of its people were too poor to own either a car or a telephone. Ignored in the sample, these people's preference was not known until Election Day. Most of them supported Roosevelt. Only if they, and all other types of voters, had been represented in the poll would its results have been accurate.

How to be sure of including them? Again, Gallup and Roper had the answer. Choose the sample scientifically, by quota. If 20 percent of Americans are farmers, 20 percent of the sample must be farmers, and so on. Quotas seemed to work. The accuracy of polls improved, and they were used more and more often. In 1941, as World War II threatened, government surveys indicated Americans' feelings about entering the conflict. Professional interviewers asked soldiers how they felt about their food, equipment, and uniforms. After the war, market research became increasingly useful to business.

Pollsters' confidence now soared. But a few

Pollsters predicted that Harry S. Truman would lose the 1948 presidential election to Thomas E. Dewey. So certain seemed Truman's defeat that the Chicago Daily Tribune printed an edition of the paper ahead of time announcing Dewey's victory even though all the election returns had not been counted. It was an embarrassing blunder—Truman in fact won the election. Here the triumphant president displays the erroneous headline.

days before the 1948 election, they predicted defeat for President Harry S. Truman. Truman's surprise victory destroyed their faith in quota-based samples. So pollsters turned to *random sampling,* using the mathematical rules of probability. Gallup explained how this could work in selecting a sample of 10,000 Americans representative of all Americans. First, list every adult in alphabetical order. Second, divide the total number of adults by the number you want in your sample—in this case, 10,000. In 1990, that came to 18,500. You then divide the total list into sections of 18,500 people each. Next, pick any number under 18,500—say, the number 5,000. Then the 5,000th person in each section becomes a member of your sample. For practical reasons, random samples are usually chosen according to more elaborate formulas. But if the basic principle is observed, and every individual in the population is given an equal chance of being in the sample, results will be remarkably accurate.

There is always a degree of *sampling error,* however. Sampling error is the extent to which the results of interviewing everyone in the sample would differ from the result of interviewing everyone in the total population. Leading public opinion research firms, including those established by Elmo Roper, George Gallup, and Daniel Yankelovich, report a sampling error of plus or minus 3 percent for their customary 1,200- or 1,500-member samples.

Polls and Democracy

At their best, polls represent democracy in action. They may inform politicians by telling them which issues are important to voters, or they can help government agencies pinpoint public needs and design effective social programs. Polls can help business, too.

Market researchers claim success rates of up to 89 percent in predicting which new products consumers will buy. The entertainment industry depends upon polling to develop movies and television programs that people will like.

Yet polls are far from perfect, democratically or scientifically. Efforts to lower costs or speed up the results may mean improperly selected samples. Questions may be worded carelessly, which can lead to biased answers. A hurried or hostile interviewer might alienate respondents (those in the sample). Respondents sometimes answer incompletely or untruthfully.

More seriously, polls may be misused, particularly in politics. Some politicians read the polls first and *then* decide where they stand on the issues. Others pay for surveys deliberately designed to bolster their positions. Many in the news media sensationalize polls, turning elections into mere "horseraces." Occasionally, polls create a "bandwagon effect": voters eager to back the winning candidate abandon one who the polls suggest may be losing. Exit polls—which ask voters as they leave the balloting place whom they voted for—have been singled out for special criticism. When their results are released before voting ends, the trailing candidate's discouraged supporters may decide not to vote at all. Such polling abuses are bad for democracy.

For further reading: Ann E. Weiss, *Polls and Surveys: A Look at Public Opinion Research* (New York: Franklin Watts, 1979).

ANN E. WEISS

PUBLIC TRANSPORTATION

No city in the world before 1825 had a public transportation system—vehicles operating regularly along a planned route, with a set schedule, for one price. In the United States, people paid to ride on horse-drawn carriages called hackneys for short trips, and for longer ones, they took stagecoaches.

The Omnibus

The first transportation system anywhere was developed in Nantes, France, in 1826. A retired army officer set up a short stage line to carry people from the center of town to his public baths on the edge of town. But he discovered that many boarded his vehicles to travel to points along the way, and he changed his service. His new *omnibus,* or "bus for all people," combined the roles of the hackney and the stagecoach. Word of his success spread quickly.

In the United States, omnibus service began in 1829, when Abraham Brower started a route along lower Broadway in New York City. Others took the idea to Philadelphia in 1831, Boston in 1835, and Baltimore in 1844. Usually the city government granted a private company sole rights to operate horse-drawn omnibuses along a given street.

The omnibus was an obvious improvement over walking, but its unpadded bench-

A horsecar in New York City in 1901, followed by a trolley, which would soon put the horse-drawn trolley out of business.

es, poor air circulation, and slow speed provided an uncomfortable ride, and the bumpy condition of city streets added to the difficulties. It was no surprise that few city dwellers were passengers. Even in New York City, which had the largest system, only about one resident in twenty-five used the omnibus on a daily basis in 1850.

The Horsecar

Placing the omnibus on iron rails was the next major change. In 1832 John Mason developed a streetcar drawn by horses on regular railroad tracks in Manhattan. Called the horsecar, it combined the low cost, flexibility, and safety of animal power with the efficiency, smoothness, and all-weather utility of railway lines. After 1852, horse-drawn railways became more common when Alphonse Loubat developed a rail that lay level with street pavement. This was an important improvement because earlier rails, which stuck up six inches above street level, seriously interfered with traffic.

The horsecar on rails provided a much smoother ride than the omnibus, and its speed of six to eight miles per hour was twice as fast. Its lower friction allowed a single horse to pull a thirty-to-forty-passenger car that had more room inside, an easier exit, and more effective brakes than the omnibus. These advantages lowered operating costs, and the price of a single ride fell from fifteen cents on the omnibus to ten cents on the horsecar. Only the driver's ride was not improved. He sat unprotected from the weather on an open platform. It was believed that if the platform were enclosed, the driver might not be as alert. By the mid-1880s, there were 415 street railway companies operating over six thousand miles of track and carrying 188 million passengers per year.

The Cable Car

In 1867, Charles T. Harvey developed a passenger car that was connected overhead to a constantly moving cable. First tried in Manhattan, it eventually failed, but then Andrew Smith Hallidie, a Scottish immigrant and wealthy manufacturer, copied the English mining method of moving cars by large cables. Passenger cars ran along tracks like those of the horse railways, but the power came from giant steam engines that moved the cable. These cable cars were more suited to the broad, straight avenues of American cities than the narrow, winding streets of European metropolises. They worked especially well on steep hills like those in San Francisco, where they were introduced in 1873. By 1890, cable transportation had reached its peak with five hundred miles of track in twenty-three cities carrying 383 million passengers per year.

Cable car construction costs, however, were much higher than those of the horsecar. Thus, cable operations had to be limited to those routes that were most heavily traveled and would provide enough income to recover the investment. Not surprisingly, the popularity of cable systems soon declined, and most cities continued to use the horsecar. Only San Francisco has kept Hallidie's invention as a reminder of the past and as a tourist attraction.

The Steam Railroad

The first American railroads were designed for long-distance trips rather than local travel. But they looked for passengers wherever they could find them and very early built stations whenever their lines passed through villages on the outskirts of larger cities. In New York, passengers began traveling to work on steam railroads in 1832, and over the next decades, the establishment of regular service by several railroads allowed people to live some distance from the cities in which they worked. Population growth along these lines increased substantially. By 1898 the three major passenger lines to the north of New York City alone carried 118,000 daily commuters, and by 1900 railroad commuting was also well established in Philadelphia, Boston, and Chicago.

Railroad travel, however, was expensive and time consuming. Steam engines were difficult to start and stop, and they gained speed slowly. The result was that railroad suburbs developed like beads on a string outside the central city. The towns were connected by the railroad line, but they had to be located at least a mile or two from each other.

The Electric Streetcar

The trolley, or electric streetcar, was born in the United States. This type of transportation was first used in Baltimore in 1885. Two years later Frank Julian Sprague expanded the idea in Richmond, Virginia, by moving many cars at the same time via an overhead electric wire. By the turn of the century, half the streetcar systems in the United States were equipped by Sprague, and 90 percent were using his patents.

The typical trolley had metal wheels, open platforms front and rear, and large windows all around. About half the size of a modern bus, it swayed and clanged down small railroad tracks installed in the street. With its humming motor controlled by a driver in a glassed-in compartment, the vehicle had no front or back because it could not be turned around at the end of the line.

The pollution-free electric-powered trolley had many advantages. Faster than either the cable car or the horse-drawn streetcar, it raised the speed of city travel to twenty miles per hour and could go even faster outside built-up areas. It was also cheaper. It required neither the vast underground equipment of the cable car nor the great expense in animals, feed, and stables of the horsecar, and the average fare dropped from a dime to a nickel.

Americans welcomed the trolley enthusiastically. In 1890, there were 5,700 miles of horsecar track, 500 miles for cable cars, and 1,260 for the trolley. By the end of 1903 America's 30,000 miles of street railways were 98 percent electrified. It was one of the most rapidly accepted changes in the history of technology. The quickness of the American adoption of the trolley was especially striking in comparison with other nations. In 1890, for example, the number of passengers carried on American street railways was over 2 billion per year, or more than twice that of the rest of the world combined.

Rapid Transit

Because the streetcar could not avoid traffic jams on the streets, transit experts turned early to the idea of an unobstructed path for their busiest lines. Two methods were possible—trains overhead and subways underground. The elevated train was the older method, the first line in New York having opened in 1870. Faster but more expensive than the horsecars with which it competed at first, the "els" were noisy, unattractive, and dirty, even after electrification began to replace the small steam engines after 1900.

A better solution was underground transportation, which became necessary when the elevated structures themselves obstructed the smooth flow of traffic. The first American subway opened in Boston in 1897, long after London's (1863). But New York City, after its first underground line opened in 1904, became the world model for two reasons—its vast size and its technologically new methods. New York's competing transportation companies built new lines and extended old ones with unmatched energy. By 1937, the region had 308 route miles (and more than 700 track miles) of rapid transportation service and was handling 4.2 million passengers per day, not including bus and streetcar passengers. As designed by Chief Engineer William Barclay Parsons, New York's subway was the first in the world with a coordinated express and local system. Parsons's underground became a model for the construction of rapid transportation elsewhere.

The Twentieth Century

The public transportation system of the United States was easily the best in the world in 1900. But in the following decades, it slipped badly. By 1920, it had been overtaken by the government-sponsored systems of Germany, France, Holland, and Britain. The number of American streetcar riders hit a high in 1923, but then declined steadily until by 1990, the clang of the trolley bell could be heard on only a few lines in Boston, New Orleans, Pittsburgh, Philadelphia, and Newark. At first, the streetcars were replaced by gasoline-powered buses, but they proved unable to compete with the private automobile. In the 1990s, America's public bus lines offered poor service at high prices in comparison to transportation systems elsewhere.

The steam railroad survived automotive competition better than the trolleys and subways did. Indeed, the golden age of railroad travel was the 1920s, when every major city benefited from frequent rail service. The depression years saw a sharp drop in customers, but the end of the once magnificent passenger railroad system did not come until the 1950s. Bankruptcy and declining service were the inescapable results of a national transportation policy that supported air and automobile travel and taxed the railroads. By 1994, only a handful of cities—including New York, Boston, Chicago, and Philadelphia—could boast of impressive railroad passenger traffic.

Meanwhile, the private automobile became the leading form of transportation in the United States. Automobile registrations climbed from 1 million in 1913 to 10 million in 1923. Kansas alone had more cars than France or Germany, and Michigan had more than Great Britain and Ireland combined. By 1927, the United States was building about 85 percent of the world's automobiles, and there was one motor vehicle for every five people in the country.

The success of the private automobile was greatly helped by federal policy. Unlike European governments, Washington treated public transportation as if it were a private business but supported the motor car with public funds. Between 1945 and 1980, 75 percent of government expenses for transportation went for highways, and only 1 percent went to public buses, trolleys, or subways. By 1993, the United States had the world's best road system and very nearly its worst public transportation service.

See also Automobiles; Aviation; National Road; Railroads.

KENNETH T. JACKSON

PUBLIC WORKS ADMINISTRATION

The Public Works Administration (PWA) was created under the New Deal National Industrial Recovery Act of 1933. It is often confused with another New Deal agency, the Works Progress Administration (WPA). Both were established to handle the high unemployment that characterized the Great Depression of the 1930s.

The Public Works Administration was part of the Department of the Interior, headed by Harold L. Ickes. Its purpose was to construct public works, such as highways, dams, public housing, post offices, airports, even warships. Although all PWA projects were required to use labor rather than machinery "whenever possible," their nature involved spending large amounts of money on materials rather than on labor. Thus their effect on unemployment, though significant, was smaller than the projects of Harry Hopkins's WPA, which were largely tasks like repairing roads, clearing slums, and various conservation projects.

See also New Deal.

PUERTO RICO, ACQUISITION OF

After the United States declared war on Spain in 1898, its troops "freed" Puerto Rico as well as the primary object of the war, Cuba. Spain formally ceded the island to the United States in the Treaty of Paris in December 1898. The government established for Puerto Rico by Congress closely resembled the intermediate stage of government through which mainland territories passed on the way to becoming states. The Puerto Rican people elected the lower house of the legislature, but the president named the governor of the island as well as the members of the upper house of the legislature. In addition, Congress exer-cised the right to place tariffs on Puerto Rican products imported into the United States. The constitutionality of these duties, which would have been illegal if applied to the products of a mainland territory, was upheld by the Supreme Court in 1901.

In 1917 Puerto Ricans were granted American citizenship. This meant that they could move freely to the United States, as many thousands have done over the years. Congress made the island a commonwealth in 1952. Thereafter it has had its own constitution and is self-governing so far as local affairs are concerned.

See also Expansion, Territorial.

PULITZER, JOSEPH
(1847–1911)   *Journalist.*

Pulitzer ranks among the major American journalists. His investigative reporting skills, creative use of the English language, and dedication to the pursuit of truth and justice created a standard of excellence that today's journalists still aspire to.

Born in Hungary, Pulitzer came from a modest family and left his country for America in search of adventure when he was seventeen. Like most immigrants he spent his first years in the United States working at menial jobs, until 1868 when he was hired as a reporter for a German-language newspaper in St. Louis. Covering politics, corruption, and injustices of government, he quickly established himself as an outstanding newsman. He then moved on to become a newspaper owner.

In 1878 Pulitzer bought the *St. Louis Dispatch* and in 1883 the *New York World*. Four years later he founded the *Evening World*. He made his papers prosperous and popular by adding illustrations, cartoons, and dramatic news stories. Although the papers fell into decline because of the competition with newspapers owned by his rival, William Randolph Hearst, they remained an influential force in America. They also made Pulitzer a very rich man.

Pulitzer was also a lawyer active in politics, first as a Republican and later as a Democrat. In 1885 he was elected as a New York congressman. In 1903 he announced his intention to found a school of journalism in connection with Columbia University.

When he died, he left the money to create the school, as well as the scholarships and prizes for journalism and other forms of writing that bear his name and are meant to encourage public service and education. The annual Pulitzer Prizes are among the most prestigious awards in America. And the establishment of Columbia University's School of Journalism led to the growth of many other journalism schools throughout the country.

See also Magazines and Newspapers.

JOANN BIONDI

PULLMAN STRIKE

In 1894, in the midst of a serious economic depression that was hurting his business, George Pullman, inventor and manufacturer of the railroad sleeping car, discharged a large number of his workers and reduced the wages of those remaining by 30 percent. He did not, however, reduce the rents on the homes of these workers in his company-owned town, Pullman, Illinois. When a delegation of the workers asked him to lower their rents, he refused and fired three of their leaders.

The workers then went on strike. Since some of them belonged to the American Railway Union, its president, Eugene V. Debs, ordered all members of the union to refuse to handle trains to which Pullman cars were attached anywhere in the nation. Rail traffic in and out of Chicago ground to a halt. Since this affected trains carrying mail, President Grover Cleveland sent federal troops to the area. When Debs defied a federal injunction ordering the strikers back to work, he was jailed for contempt of court and the strike was broken. The American Railway Union soon collapsed.

See also Debs, Eugene V.; Labor Movement.

PURE FOOD AND DRUG ACT

Throughout the late nineteenth century, meat was an important American export, and at times, questions were raised by foreign nations about its quality. In the 1880s several European nations banned American pork when some uninspected pork was shown to be diseased. A federal meat inspection law was then passed, and the Europeans allowed American meat products to again be imported. Enforcement of the law was poor, however. During the Spanish-American War, an "embalmed beef" scandal erupted about the condition of food exported for consumption by the American troops fighting in Cuba.

Then, in 1906, Upton Sinclair's description of unsanitary conditions in the Chicago stockyards in *The Jungle* brought the issue to a head again. President Theodore Roosevelt sent inspectors to the yards. He did not release their report on the ground that it was so shocking it would cause foreign nations to ban American meat again.

Public reaction was one of unanimous outrage. The meat packers, popularly known as "the Beef Trust," were seen as public enemies. Congress responded by passing a stronger meat inspection law and (more important) the Pure Food and Drug Act of 1906. This measure made manufacturing, selling, or falsely labeling any food or drug product illegal. Patent medicines making extravagant claims to be able to cure all kinds of diseases and containing alcohol and even cocaine or other narcotics could now be seized, their producers fined or thrown in jail. This was the first of many American consumer protection laws.

See also Jungle, The.

PURITANS

In 1630 a company of Puritans quite different from the Plymouth Pilgrims set sail from England for America, carrying with them a charter signed by the king permitting them to establish a colony in Massachusetts. These people were not escaping from persecution. Rather, they disliked the elaborate ceremonies of the official Church of England. Mainly well-to-do farmers and merchants, they sold their lands and businesses to follow leaders who were possessed by a dream. These Puritans planned to create in the New World a society that would serve as a model for all the world to see, a community of God-fearing people living and worshiping with the simplicity and purity of the early Christians. They believed that while living in strict accordance with the word of God as revealed in the Bible, they could still make a living.

Settling in Salem and Boston, under their elected governor, John Winthrop, the colonists prospered from the beginning. Ships bringing new immigrants arrived every few weeks. They did not suffer the devastating illnesses that had plagued the Plymouth colony, and they had had the foresight and the money to bring with them the tools and livestock that would carry them through the first difficult months.

A Difficult Life

Still, life was hard and the work unending. Each householder had first to clear a place in the forest, felling the great trees and wresting from the ground the stones that would make a foundation for a house. With his broadaxe he had to hew posts and clapboards, for the Puritans did not build log cabins but insisted on the frame houses they had known in England. Neighbors lent willing hands for the house-raising, and when the roof beams were finally set in place, men, women, and children joined in one of the few celebrations these earnest people allowed themselves.

Life was hardest of all for the children, who were expected to share the labor of the household and to do so respectfully and soberly. They were given little time for playing. Swimming and games were forbidden, and running, jumping, or even giggling could bring a stern rebuke or worse.

There is a story told of Judge Sewell of Boston who one day discovered in his rainspout a ball belonging to his son. He sent for the minister, and they held a long session with the boy, explaining to him that he must constantly fight against the powers of darkness that tempted him to such mischief.

Puritan parents were not unkind. Early letters and diaries show homes filled with affection, even laughter. But danger was ever present, and more than they feared Indians or starvation they feared Sin. Prodded by the warnings that their ministers thundered from the pulpit every Sabbath, parents were constantly alert for the cunning devices of Satan. Even three-year-olds were required to memorize the Young Child's Catechism, which contained such warnings as:

Question: What must become of you if you are wicked?

Answer: I shall be sent down to everlasting Fire and Hell among wicked and miserable creatures.

Puritan Laws and Schools

It had seemed to the first settlers that if people followed their own individual consciences, guided by the Bible, there would be no need of laws. But they soon realized that Satan had pursued them across the ocean. And as time passed, many newcomers were not Puritans. Many laborers and farmers came to the New World not for religious reasons but to make a better living for themselves and their children. Most of them were loyal to the Church of England, and though they were compelled to attend Puritan churches, they did not always understand the Puritans' zeal for "righteousness." The many fines imposed upon them for minor misdemeanors must have bewildered them.

The clergy, who were considered best fitted to set penalties, often found it difficult to find in the Bible the exact penalty to fit each crime. What about the man who allowed his pigs to wander into his neighbor's vegetable patch? Or the woman who, reprimanded for wearing a bow on her bonnet, appeared the next Sabbath adorned with two bows?

As the towns multiplied there was popular demand for a uniform code of laws. In 1641 a bill known as the Body of Liberties was adopted by the General Court. The Body of Liberties did not bring about democracy, but it was a step in that direction.

Another important step had already been taken toward the goal of education for all children. It was assumed that parents would teach their children to read, and many children could do so by the age of three. From their A B C's they went directly to the Bible, since for Puritans, reading the Bible was after all the main purpose of learning to read. For most children—and for all girls—schooling ended when they could spell out words. Further learning was considered unnecessary for girls. Boys at the age of six or seven went on to the grammar schools that by 1649 were required in every town of one hundred families. There, sitting on narrow benches in icy rooms where in winter the meager fire often could not thaw out the ink wells, they struggled with Latin and Greek, a task too difficult for many. Serious scholars went on to Harvard College, which had been established in 1636 for the purpose of training future leaders and clergy for the growing communities.

Stern and stiff-backed these Puritans seem to us today. But from such homes and schools came people of strength and resolution, with keen minds and a strong sense of vision, ready when the time came to forge a new republic of free citizens.

See also Colonial America; Pilgrims; Winthrop, John.

ELIZABETH GEORGE SPEARE

P W A
See Public Works Administration.

Q

QUAKERS

There are only about 100,000 Quakers in the United States, yet this small group has had a great influence on American history. When their correct name is used—the Society of Friends—it is easy to understand why. They are *Friends* to all, offering brotherhood, charity, and peace to the world, especially the oppressed and deprived.

Early History

Friends do not call themselves Quakers. For a long time it was a derogatory term, believed to have originated during a trial in England when members were said to have "trembled" at the Word of God. Today, however, the term *Quaker* is widely used, having lost its scornful overtones.

Quakerism was founded in England in the 1600s by George Fox as a protest against the church hierarchy, domination of the church by the state, and elaborate rituals in services. From the outset believers were subjected to imprisonment, mob violence, and loss of property.

Quakers were among the earliest colonists in America, but they found no relief from persecution here. The Puritans banished them from Massachusetts. If they returned, their ears were cut off. If they returned a second time, they were put to death. But Quakers did find a safe haven when William Penn, himself a Quaker, founded Pennsylvania in 1681.

Beliefs

Why the persecution? In part it was because they were different. In those days Friends wore "plain" clothes. For women this was a simple gray dress and bonnet. Men wore black suits without lapels, decorative buttons, or neckties. They also wore broad-brimmed black hats and practiced "hat honor." This meant wearing the hat indoors and out, even to church, and taking it off only when praying. Plain dress and hat honor are no longer observed.

Then there was "plain" language. Friends did not use the word *you* when addressing a person, substituting *thee* and *thou* as in the Bible. Names of the days of the week and months of the year were not used because they derive from names of early pagan gods. Quakers numbered them instead, speaking of *First Day* instead of *Sunday* and *First Month* instead of *January.* Plain speech has also been abandoned today, except at worship or in the privacy of some homes.

Another problem for outsiders was the Quaker form of worship. Even today they have no spoken or written creed. Their faith is that people can approach and experience God directly without a priest or minister. Experiencing God is called *Inward Light,* and it instructs and transforms a person's conscience and guides all thought and action.

The Friends' church service is called a *meeting* and has no ritual, program, sacrament, or clergy. Friends gather at an appointed time and sit silently, awaiting the Inward Light. Out of their silent waiting may come spiritual messages, vocal prayer, Bible reading, or ministry by a member. At the end,

worshipers shake hands with their neighbors and depart. Non-Quakers who have attended meetings describe them as calming and uplifting.

Early Quakers also got into trouble over their refusal to take an oath in court or other civil proceedings. They believe that an oath should be given only to God. Besides, since

A painting of a Quaker meeting, which, unlike other church services, was not a formal religious ceremony and was not led by a clergyman or a single speaker. Members of the congregation moved to speak—feeling an "inward light" or "Christ within"—shared their religious thoughts with the others. The painting depicts a man who stands and addresses his fellow Quakers. Below him one man seems to be nodding off, and the Quaker next to him is either in a deep meditation or sound asleep.

telling the truth is part of being a Quaker, there is no need to swear that one will do so. In consideration of this Quaker belief, the Constitution permits a person to *affirm* or *attest* to the truth rather than *swear* to it. Herbert Hoover, the only practicing Quaker president, used the word *affirm* when he took the oath of office at his inauguration in 1929.

The biggest early problem but ultimately the Quakers' greatest contribution to America came from what is called *Quaker Witness.* To Quakers, religion is not just a First Day observance. It is part of the fabric of their lives. Thus, Quakers have always opposed war. Being pacifists, they have refused to fight. Nonetheless, many have served gallantly in American wars as medics and other noncombatants.

Quaker Witness has also meant opposition to slavery and racial segregation. They are against the death penalty and favor prison reform, kind intelligent treatment of the mentally ill, equality for women, and a more just economic and social system.

The Society of Friends has not merely advocated these beliefs but worked hard to put them into practice. In 1947, the American Friends Service Committee was awarded the Nobel Peace Prize for its efforts.

See also Conscientious Objectors; Penn, William.

ROBERT A. LISTON

QUARTERING ACTS

After the rioting and destruction in the colonies that followed the passage of the Stamp Act, the British stationed large numbers of Redcoats in the principal colonial towns. To accommodate them, Parliament in 1765 passed a Quartering Act requiring the various colonial governments to provide barracks to house the troops and to supply them with food and other necessities. If adequate barracks were not available, the act provided that public inns and stables, even private barns and other unoccupied dwellings, were to be used.

In New York, the colonial assembly offered in 1766 to provide some of these items, but not enough to cover the needs of the large number of soldiers. When the British objected, the New York assembly refused to supply anything at all. This led the British to suspend the right of the assembly to pass laws of any kind until the colony obeyed the Quartering Act. In 1767 the assembly finally allocated three thousand pounds to house the Redcoats.

The problem arose again in 1773 after the Boston Tea Party. To punish the Patriots for that incident, Parliament, in addition to the Coercive Acts, passed a new Quartering Act that provided for housing soldiers in private homes as well as in unoccupied buildings. The depth of the colonists' anger over the Quartering Acts can be seen in the Declaration of Independence, which lists the king's "quartering [of] large bodies of armed troops among us" as one of his actions that were "foreign to our constitution" and a reason for rebellion.

See also Revolution: The War for Independence.

QUEBEC ACT

In 1763, in the treaty ending the Seven Years' War, France ceded all its North American possessions to Great Britain. Thus the province of Quebec, populated by French-speaking Catholics, became part of the British Empire. To establish a new government for this colony, Parliament passed the Quebec Act in 1774. This law extended the territory of Quebec to include the land north of the Ohio River. It provided that while English criminal law would now apply to Quebec, French civil law, including suits "relative to Property and Civil Rights," should remain in effect. In addition, the Quebec Act declared that it was "inexpedient" to set up an elected legislature. The colony was to be governed by a council appointed by the king. Finally, it guaranteed toleration to French Catholics.

A leading American historian has called the Quebec Act "one of the most enlightened pieces of colonial administration in the history of European colonial expansion." But the American colonists of that time found it as "intolerable" as the Coercive Acts passed in the same year. In effect it made permanent the Proclamation of 1763 and turned the region they had won in the French and Indian War back to people who considered themselves French. Since most of the American colonists were Protestants, they feared and despised the Catholic religion, still another reason they disliked the Quebec Act.

See also Colonial America.

R

RACE RIOTS

Racial rioting often accompanied the movement of large numbers of African Americans to big cities. Thus, during the nineteenth century, when the majority of blacks lived in the rural South, such urban disorders were rare. Nevertheless, riots protesting the antislavery movement struck several cities beginning in the 1830s, and Cincinnati's neighborhoods of free blacks were assaulted by whites in 1829 and 1841. The worst violence against blacks in this era occurred during the New York City draft riots of 1863, in which more than a hundred blacks died.

After the Civil War, southern cities suffered most immediately from racial rioting. First, violent outbreaks in Memphis and New Orleans during 1866 gave evidence of southern whites' desire to maintain white supremacy after the emancipation of the slaves. Second, southern cities were often the first destination for blacks fleeing the countryside. The result was a string of riots closely associated with the movement of blacks to the cities and with the rise of Jim Crow (the system of legalized segregation) around 1900. Riots in Wilmington, North Carolina, in 1898, in New Orleans in 1900, and in Atlanta in 1906 were typical.

The mass migration of southern blacks to the urban North made racial rioting a national phenomenon. New York suffered more disturbances in 1900, and even Abraham Lincoln's hometown of Springfield, Illinois, endured a white assault on its black community in 1908. This last incident contributed to the creation of the National Association for the Advancement of Colored People (NAACP) as many whites and blacks reacted against the rising tide of violence.

Wartime Tensions and Riots

The presence of black soldiers in the military during World War I sparked deadly clashes between local authorities in southern training camps and African-American soldiers unwilling to accept second-class treatment—as in Houston in 1917. Wartime tensions also contributed to the violence against blacks taking part in the Great Migration of 1914–18, as African Americans sought work outside the South. A riot in East St. Louis, Illinois, in 1917, for example, saw whites, unrestrained by police and at times even helped by them, kill at least forty blacks.

The worst violence, however, came during the so-called Red Summer of 1919. Between May and September of that year, riots broke out in Charleston, Washington, D.C., Chicago, and Omaha. The Chicago riot was the most deadly. Twenty-three blacks and fifteen whites were killed in what amounted to an interracial war in miniature. Closely related to the growth of Chicago's black ghetto, that riot was embedded in an era of house bombings and small-scale violence that reached into the 1920s.

The massive movement of people, the expansion of cities, and racial competition for jobs, votes, and services led to riots again during World War II. The summer of 1943 witnessed a string of riots similar to that of 1919. The violence flared first in small southern towns and military encampments. Then major disorders broke out in Mobile, Alabama; Beaumont, Texas; Los Angeles; Detroit; and New York. The Los Angeles riot involved large numbers of military personnel and Chicanos as well as blacks, and the Detroit upheaval (thirty-four killed, hundreds injured) most closely approached the level of violence suffered in 1919. The eruption in New York's Harlem, rather than being an interracial battle, consisted primarily of black assaults on white-owned property within segregated black neighborhoods. It was similar to an earlier 1935 Harlem outbreak and was repeated in the ghetto rebellions that dominated the 1960s.

Riots after 1960

The heightened black expectations arising from the civil rights movement and the public reaction against the Vietnam War contributed to a series of "long, hot summers" between 1964 and 1968. Riots during those years resulted in nearly two hundred deaths (mostly blacks), twenty thousand arrests, and hundreds of millions of dollars in property damage. Beginning in New York's Harlem and in the Bedford-Stuyvesant section of Brooklyn (1964), continuing through Watts in Los Angeles (1965), and most devastatingly in Detroit and Newark (both in 1967), violent black protests against ghetto conditions led to onslaughts against white-owned property and confrontations with the police in dozens of cities. The riots brought a flurry of public attention to inner-city problems, but also a longer lasting conservative reaction that cut short attempts at reform.

More recent riots, too, such as those in Miami in the 1980s and the Los Angeles "Rodney King" riot of 1992, were sparked by charges of discrimination and by confrontations with police. But these explosions also involved more than white-black disputes. Increasingly, Hispanics and Asians, the newest immigrants to urban America, have been drawn into such conflicts, whether as police officers, property owners, or ordinary citizens. Urban disorder is thus likely to remain an issue in American life for some time to come.

See also Draft Riots of 1863; Ghettos.

ARNOLD R. HIRSCH

RACIAL SEGREGATION
See African Americans: 1877–1945; Segregation.

RACISM

From the time of the first European settlement, racism—judging people inferior on the basis of the color of their skin—has been common in North America. People have tried to justify this attitude with both religious and economic arguments. When the first Europeans encountered American Indian cultures, such as the Aztecs in Mexico, the Powhatans in Virginia, and the Pequots in Massachusetts, they viewed the Native Americans as heathens (not Christians) and therefore did not hesitate to take their land or enslave them. Indians did not prove to be good slaves, however, for they died by the thousands from harsh treatment and diseases brought from the Old World. The Europeans then began to import black slaves from Africa. Africans were not willing slaves, either, but there was a seemingly unending supply from the vast continent thousands of miles to the east.

Racist Attitudes

The African slave trade was already well known to the first European settlers in America, the English and Spanish. They justified this trading in human life by maintaining that Africans were not Christians and were uncivilized. Therefore they were suited only to hard labor.

The first Africans brought to the British colonies in North America were, like many of the first white settlers, indentured servants, who had signed contracts to work a certain period of years in exchange for passage to the New World and eventual freedom. But before the middle of the seventeenth century it became clear that they would be treated differently than white indentured servants. In 1642 a Virginia judge sentenced two white indentured servants to an additional year of service as punishment for running away, while sentencing a black servant to labor for the rest of his life for the same offense.

With the settlement of southern colonies whose soil and climate allowed for large-scale cultivation of rice, tobacco, and cotton, the demand for a large labor force increased, and slavery became entrenched and legal. As justification for slavery, southerners cited the Bible: Africans were eternally cursed by God as the descendants of Noah's son Ham, who had fathered a child in the Ark. They also created new "scientific" reasons to explain their practice—that various physical characteristics, from the size of Africans' heads to their apparently greater ability to withstand extreme heat, uniquely equipped them to be

slaves. Although southerners went to what now seem laughable extremes to justify slavery, it should be pointed out that nearly all whites believed that black people were inferior, and so even free African Americans had a difficult time of it. Many areas had laws designed to keep free blacks from living in them.

The abolitionist movement, which gained strength in the mid-nineteenth century, aimed at ending slavery. Abolitionists, however, did not necessarily want to treat blacks as equals. In fact, many supported the idea of sending them back to Africa and helped found the colony of Liberia there. Some free blacks did emigrate, but most African Americans, slave and free, were not interested. They believed that their rightful home was, for better or worse, the United States.

Although the issue of slavery in the South was the root cause of the Civil War, there was no real commitment after it ended to integrating the freed people into American society. The idea of black inferiority was so widespread that the North turned a blind eye to the South's eventual solution of semislavery through the sharecropper system. Black Codes, lynchings, and other forms of intimidation kept blacks "in their place" in the South. At the same time, segregation by custom, rather than by law, in housing, education, and employment effectively did the same in other regions.

The European immigrants who arrived in waves before and after the Civil War were greeted with hostility by many Americans who were already here, but after a few generations, most were able to assimilate into the larger society. Among the first American attitudes that many of the newcomers adopted was antiblack racism because it made them feel better to think that another group was lower than they were and because both groups, being on the lower rungs of the social ladder, had to compete for jobs.

Other nonwhite groups have faced racism, also, notably Chinese Americans, Latinos, and Japanese Americans, the latter particularly during World War II. Latinos have faced special problems because of language differences.

Countering Racism

The civil rights movement of the 1950s and 1960s ironically used the same religious

The ugliness of racism is plainly visible on the face of a young white girl who jeers and shouts at Elizabeth Eckford. She and other black students bore vicious insults and abuse the first day they tried to attend the formerly segregated Central High School in Little Rock, Arkansas, in 1957. One person shouted, "No nigger bitch is going to get in our school! Get out of here!" Elizabeth, who was fifteen at the time, recalled, "I tried to see a friendly face somewhere in the mob. . . . I looked into the face of an old woman, and it seemed a kind face, but when I looked at her again, she spat on me."

and economic arguments that had long justified slavery and unequal treatment of blacks to push for greater equality. It was largely a church-led movement in the early days, with Dr. Martin Luther King, Jr., and others appealing to the basic goodness they believed most Americans possessed. At the same time they refused to buy merchandise from white-owned stores and carried out other forms of nonviolent protest. Although King's dream of racial harmony has never been fully realized, the tactics of the civil rights movement achieved many gains for blacks, and they have since been used by other groups, among them American Indians, Latinos, and Asian Americans.

Judging by the fighting between Catholics and Protestants in Ireland and Serbs and Muslims in Bosnia, to name just two examples, many people seem to need to be against somebody else in order to know who they themselves are. Hostility between people of different races is an unfortunate fact of human life, certainly of American life. But the American experience has in some ways been different. The United States was founded on the idea that "all men are created equal" (the Declaration of Independence) and has a Constitution and a Bill of Rights that provide legal safeguards against anyone's being denied his or her rights. These safeguards have not always worked, but they have stood as ideals to strive for. Also, except for American Indians, no ethnic group has been here for more than four hundred years, and from the beginning, different groups have had to live and work with one another. The American experience, for all its flaws and failures, has shown that people of many races and religions can live together in a largely peaceful and productive fashion.

See also African Americans; Asian Americans; Civil Rights

Movement; Free Blacks before Emancipation; Hispanics; Indian-White Relations; Japanese Americans, Internment of; Ku Klux Klan; Lynching; Reconstruction; Segregation; Slavery.

JIM HASKINS

RADIO AND TELEVISION

Since the invention of movable type made reading matter available to everyone, nothing has so influenced the way people think and behave as the transmission of the human voice, and later of images, through the air. When Italian physicist Guglielmo Marconi developed the first practical wireless telegraphy in 1895, he started a chain of technological advances that have profoundly altered our lives in many ways.

Radio

Marconi's invention permitted the sending of messages by a code of dots and dashes. In the next twenty years, developments by Sir Ambrose Fleming, Reginald Fessenden, Lee De Forest, and Edwin Armstrong created the technology of modern radio. Its use for military broadcasting during World War I gave it further impetus but prevented its commercial exploitation until 1919, when many amateur stations were founded. In 1912, the U.S. Department of Commerce took charge of assigning wavelengths, and in 1927 Congress created the Federal Radio Commission (later the Federal Communications Commission, or FCC) to license and regulate stations.

The first professional radio station, KDKA in Pittsburgh, Pennsylvania, was licensed in 1920 and broadcast music, sports, and reports of the 1920 presidential election. Other stations followed rapidly, and in 1922 alone the government licensed more than five hundred. At first stations sold radio sets to finance their operations. The first radio commercial—a ten-minute announcement costing the sponsor fifty dollars—appeared on station WEAF in New York City in 1922. Soon the sale of air time for advertising was radio's principal source of revenue.

With the advent of the first networks of stations—NBC in 1926 and CBS in 1927—radio became an almost universal part of everyday life. Originally relying on live music to fill air time, the industry began to include vaudeville comedy acts in the 1920s. In 1930, "Amos 'n' Andy," the most popular program on the airwaves, claimed an audience of over forty million. Many plays were adapted or written for radio, including children's adventures and daytime serial dramas with domestic themes, directed at housewives. These were called "soap operas" because they were sponsored by soap companies.

The coming of World War II in 1939 prompted networks to develop extensive news departments with teams of correspondents providing on-the-spot coverage. Radio became as important as a source of information as it was of entertainment. It has strongly influenced political and social opinion, and it remains a pervasive force in popular culture. In 1985, an estimated 99 percent of American homes had at least one radio set, and many had far more.

Television

As radio technology and programming advanced during the 1940s, a potentially even more popular medium was emerging. Although the idea of television, the transmission of visual images, had been explored as far back as the 1880s in Europe, it was the work of Vladimir Zworykin and Philo T. Farnsworth in America in the 1920s that created the electronic television in use today. A workable system was demonstrated at the New York World's Fair in 1939, and President Franklin D. Roosevelt appeared on a public transmission. But the popularity of radio and the competition for wavelength frequencies delayed the commercial development of television.

In 1944, the FCC assigned twelve very high frequencies (VHF) and seventy ultra-high frequencies (UHF) as television channels, and the industry began to take off. There were six thousand television sets in operation in U.S. homes in 1946; by 1951, the number had grown to 12 million. Radio's popularity plunged. The audience ratings of Jack Benny's comedy show, 26.5 percent in New York in 1948, fell to less than 5 percent in 1951, for example.

For the first ten years of its history, all television shows were "live," seen at the same time as they were being produced. It was not until 1956 that a method for recording televi-

A family watches the first televised presidential debate, between John F. Kennedy and Richard M. Nixon, on September 26, 1960. Many believe that one of the reasons Nixon lost the election was his poor performance on television. Compared to the photogenic Kennedy, Nixon appeared pale and grim.

sion on tape was developed by Ampex, the company that had produced the first audio-tape for recording sound. This permitted programs to be edited and broadcast at different times in different places. Color transmission was perfected in the 1950s but was not compatible with the receiving sets then in use and was not widely used until the next decade.

Other technical advances were quick to follow. Equipment for playing filmed television material became available in the 1960s but was not successful. In 1975, Sony marketed a videocassette recorder (VCR) that used tape instead of film and was capable of recording from television. Sales of prerecorded videocassettes soared in the 1980s, and their production and distribution has become a major industry. Hollywood, once threatened by the loss of its audience to television, has turned to the VCR to sell its motion pictures. They appear on cassettes almost as soon as they do in theaters. Videotape is also proving increasingly useful in education. Interactive video, which permits the viewer to participate by making choices, has become an important tool in military and industrial training.

Cable television, which transmits signals by a special electric cable rather than through airwaves, originated in 1949 for areas with poor reception. The national Cable Act of 1984 ended local control over cable rates, and the industry expanded widely. Communications satellites have made hundreds of specialized cable channels possible, including Cable Network News (CNN), Music Television (MTV), and all-movie, sports, religion, pornography, and even weather channels. Home Box Office (HBO), a pioneer in cable television, not only presents new movies but produces many of its own.

The Media's Impact

In 1985 it was reported that 98.1 percent of American homes had television sets, and that the average viewer watched seven hours a day. Like radio, it is a powerful molder of public tastes and thought. Naturally, media with such social, political, and intellectual influence have generated considerable controversy. On the one hand, television has been applauded for educating children and keeping them out of trouble; on the other, it has been condemned for corrupting them and keeping them out of school and bed. Critics have charged that shows contain too much sex and violence and that viewers become passive "couch potatoes."

Radio and television have been blamed for manipulating public thought, hypnotizing their audiences into buying unnecessary products, and turning political elections into stage-managed contests of showmanship. Above all, they are accused of aiming at the lowest common denominator intellectually. The industries defend their programming as reflecting "cultural democracy" and "giving the public what it wants." The debate raises the profound and troubling question of how much control a free society should exercise on the artistic and moral standards of its media.

See also Federal Communications Commission.

DENNIS WEPMAN

RAILROADS

In the early 1830s several American cities were impressed by the success of the new railroads in England. Baltimore and Charleston in 1830, Albany in 1831, and Boston in 1834 began building railroads. Small locomotives, some made in England, passenger cars built like stagecoaches, and four-wheeled freight cars started to serve the public. Doctors warned of the "excessive" speed of the new mode of transportation, and canal and turnpike owners hated the competition. But the opposition did not last long.

Early Growth

Most of the mileage built in the 1830s was in the New England and Mid-Atlantic states, with much less in the South and West. The 2,800 miles operating in 1840 far exceeded the 1,800 miles found in all of Europe, and mileage tripled during the 1840s. In 1847 Daniel Webster claimed that railroads were the greatest invention of the age.

In 1850 freight revenue far exceeded passenger revenue. The typical freight train consisted of a dozen eight-wheeled cars, each of about ten-ton capacity. Longer passenger cars with seats for forty or fifty had replaced the earlier stagecoach design. Most trains were drawn by wood-burning American-type locomotives bright with paint and brass.

The rail network had grown to 30,000 miles by 1860 and reached to the frontier west of the Mississippi. During the 1850s mileage in the Northeast had doubled, that in the South had increased fourfold, and that in the West had grown eightfold. Most northern lines were built with the standard English 4-foot-8½-inch gauge (the distance between the parallel rails of track). Most southern roads were built with a 5-foot gauge.

Merchants and shippers welcomed the year-round rail service, which was fast, cheaper than turnpikes, and more direct than steamboat and canal packets. Most of the railroads were owned by private companies, though many states and cities gave them some aid. The dozens of new lines in Ohio,

AMERICAN RAILROAD MILEAGE AND EMPLOYMENT

Year	Mileage	Employment
1840	2,800	6,000 (est.)
1860	31,000	80,000 (est.)
1880	93,000	419,000
1900	193,000	1,018,000
1916	254,000	1,701,000
1933	246,000	991,000
1965	212,000	655,000
1987	163,000	247,000

Indiana, and Illinois strengthened economic and political ties between the agricultural West and the industrial East by the eve of the Civil War in 1861. That war was the first conflict in which railroads played a major role. Since most of the fighting was in the South, the weaker and inferior Confederate rail lines were in a shambles by 1865.

Postwar Events

After the war the Union Pacific and the Central Pacific companies built a line from the Missouri River to California, one building from the east, the other from the west. It was opened in a "golden spike" ceremony in Utah in May 1869. It was called this because the final spike uniting the two lines was a golden one. These western roads were aided by generous federal land grants. Between 1850 and 1871 about 19,000 miles of track were laid in the West, and the lines received a total of 131 million acres of federal land. Since all land-grant roads charged lower rates for government traffic, the savings to the government were about equal to the value of the land grants.

Rail mileage grew nearly fourfold between 1870 and 1900. Four Granger lines (roads

A photograph commemorating the meeting of the eastern and western railroads in 1869. Heading toward the west was the Union Pacific Railroad, which laid track starting in Nebraska. It employed a crew made up largely of Civil War veterans and Irish immigrants. The Central Pacific Railroad built eastward from Sacramento, California, and its crew included many Chinese immigrants. Although the Central Pacific had a shorter distance to travel, the Sierra Mountains stood in its way. The two railroads met at Promontory Point, Utah, on May 10, 1869. The final spike to be hammered into the unified track was made of gold.

serving farmers) were built in the northern central plains. Additional roads to the Pacific were completed in the 1880s and 1890s. During the depressions of 1873 and 1893 many railroads went bankrupt. Labor trouble—the railroad strike of 1877 and the Pullman strike of 1894—also followed each depression. Railroad labor lost both strikes since the workers, except for the Big Four Brotherhoods (engineers, conductors, firemen, and trainmen), were not well organized.

In the last decades of the century the use of heavier steel rails, larger, more powerful engines, bigger freight cars, steel passenger coaches, airbrakes, automatic couplers, and better signals improved both freight and passenger service. Standard time was adopted in 1883, and standard or uniform gauge in 1886. Freight rates had declined steeply. National markets had been created for Chicago-packed meat, New England shoes, Twin City flour, and Pittsburgh steel.

But the last years of the century were also years of railroad corruption and discrimination. "False front" construction companies like the Crédit Mobilier, railroad pooling, free passes, and much freight discrimination angered western farmers, shippers, and the general public. Grange-sponsored regulation in the 1870s and 1880s was followed by the Interstate Commerce Act of 1887. And still more severe federal regulation was passed between 1903 and 1916. These were the same years that highways, airplanes, and pipelines created new competition for the railways. Even so, in 1916 American railroads were carrying 77 percent of all intercity freight and 98 percent of passenger traffic.

Decline of Railroads

Because of equipment shortages and severe winter weather, the federal government operated the railroads during World War I and a short time after (December 1917–March 1920). The Transportation Act of 1920 returned the railways to their owners, but strong federal regulation continued. Stiff competition from trucks, automobiles, and pipelines increased during the 1920s. By 1930 railroads had lost a quarter of their freight and a third of their passenger traffic. Rail traffic, wages, and profits all dropped sharply during the Great Depression of the 1930s. By 1938 nearly a third of the nation's rail mileage was bankrupt or in severe financial trouble. The railroads during World War II, with a great cooperative effort, avoided federal operation and provided a freight and passenger service well above that of World War I. Their wartime prosperity permitted the railroads to pay off a fifth of their debts.

In the postwar years the acceptance of the diesel locomotive was the most important technical advance. The new type of power was cheap to operate and easy to maintain; it provided long hours of service. By 1957 nearly all passenger, freight, and switching service was performed by diesel units. New types of freight cars, longer trains, heavier rail, and the use of radio all helped to upgrade freight service. The use of "piggyback" service, mechanized track maintenance equipment, and better communication helped slow the decline in freight traffic. Many lines also improved their passenger service with new streamliners and slumber coaches, but this did little to stop the sharp drop in rail passenger traffic. By the 1980s railroads were providing about 37 percent of the intercity freight traffic and only 3 percent of the passenger service.

In 1971 Congress created Amtrak passenger service over a 24,000-mile network. This action ended nearly all other rail passenger service. Five years later Congress set up Conrail to give freight service on several bankrupt northeastern lines. Both Amtrak and Conrail received government subsidies. Amtrak was soon paying two-thirds of its way, however. Conrail was making a small profit by 1981 and was sold to private interests in 1987. In 1980 Congress passed the Staggers Rail Act, which reduced much federal rail regulation. By the mid-1980s railroads had a rate of return of about 5 percent, well above the 2 or 3 percent of earlier decades. Railroad managers still complained about some of the union work rules, but they had to admit that labor's productivity in moving freight was doubling every fifteen to twenty years. In the 1990s the American railroad system still remained a useful and reliable mode of transportation.

JOHN F. STOVER

RAILROAD STRIKE OF 1877

This strike began in Martinsburg, West Virginia, after the Baltimore and Ohio Railroad cut its workers' wages by 10 percent. It spread quickly, first to Baltimore, then to Pennsylvania, finally to most of the major eastern and western lines. Eventually about two-thirds of the railroad mileage of the nation were paralyzed. More seriously, when state militiamen were called in to break the strike, fighting often followed. Trains were overturned, freight cars and barns set afire. In Pittsburgh, rioters, not all of them striking railroad workers, roamed the streets unchecked for days.

For several weeks the strike wore on. Sympathy strikes by workers in other industries added to the confusion. Finally President Rutherford B. Hayes called out army units to restore order. The troops were rushed from place to place, wherever trouble developed.

When order was finally restored, the strike collapsed. Rarely has conflict between American workers and their employers been more bitter. The fact that the federal government had come to the aid of the employers added further to the workers' anger.

See also Labor Movement.

RANDOLPH, A. PHILIP

(1889–1979)   *Labor leader.*

A. Philip Randolph was born in Crescent City, Florida, where his father was a minister in the African Methodist Episcopal tradition. Randolph spent most of his childhood years in Jacksonville, Florida. He attended a Methodist school and was always encouraged to read at home. Blacks were segregated and had virtually no political power at this time. Randolph decided to pursue politics in order to fight this situation.

He left Jacksonville for Harlem, the center of black life in New York City in the early 1900s, arriving there in 1911. By 1917, when the United States entered World War II, Randolph had become a socialist. He encouraged blacks to stay home and fight for their civil rights rather than join the war effort. His views appeared increasingly in socialist magazines, such as the *Messenger*. He also participated in elected activities, becoming secretary of state of New York in the 1920s.

In 1925, Randolph joined the Brotherhood of Sleeping Car Porters' union that represented workers on railroad cars, who were mostly blacks. He enlisted the support of the two major black organizations of the time—the NAACP and the Urban League—and formed alliances with other organizations in order to fight on behalf of the black workers. Through Randolph's efforts, the porters won higher wages and better working conditions. Randolph also formed alliances with international labor organizations to fight against discriminatory practices globally.

Organizing marches on Washington was one of Randolph's major achievements. A first march, in search of better job conditions and an end to discrimination against blacks in the growing defense industry, was planned for July 1, 1941. It was canceled when President Franklin D. Roosevelt, feeling the pressure of the threatened march, issued an executive order against discrimination. A second March for Jobs and Freedom, however, did take place in 1963 during the civil rights movement. Randolph introduced the speakers at this march attended by some 200,000 Americans committed to the struggle for equal rights and justice. Martin Luther King's I Have a Dream speech was delivered at this march.

Throughout his life Randolph believed in nonviolent protest as the best way to bring about change in the lives of American blacks. He worked tirelessly to this end until his death. In his honor, the A. Philip Randolph Institute was created in Washington, D.C.

See also African Americans; Labor Movement.

LAYN SAINT-LOUIS

RANKIN, JEANNETTE

(1880–1973)   *First woman elected to the U.S. Congress and activist for peace and women's rights.*

Rankin was born on a ranch near Missoula in Montana Territory, the oldest of seven children. The area was part of what we now call the Wild West. She grew up hearing stories of bloody conflicts between settlers and American Indians. According to her sister, those tragic stories were responsible for Rankin's lifelong devotion to peace.

Rankin graduated from the University of Montana, studied social work, and moved to Seattle, Washington. There she joined the drive to grant Washington women suffrage (the vote). In 1914 Rankin returned home to Montana to lead the fight there. Male voters were convinced, and Montana women were granted suffrage in November.

The victory made Rankin a well-known political leader. In 1916 she ran for the House of Representatives as a Republican. Her platform called for national women's suffrage, laws to protect children, and world peace. Her election made international headlines. Before the excitement died down, however, Rankin was faced with a difficult decision. In April 1917, President Woodrow Wilson wanted the United States to enter World War I, which had broken out in Europe in 1914. German submarines had sunk American ships in the Atlantic, and popular feeling ran high against the Germans. Women's suffrage leaders worried that if Rankin opposed entering the war, men would claim that women were

weak and unpatriotic. Even Rankin's brother urged her to cast "a man's vote" for war. But she refused, declaring, "I want to stand by my country, but I cannot vote for war."

Instantly unpopular, Rankin lost her bid for reelection in 1918. She spent the next twenty years working for world peace. That stand became more acceptable after the outbreak of World War II in 1939. Once again Rankin ran for Congress, promising that she would work to keep the country out of the war. Once again she was elected. Then, on December 7, 1941, Japanese planes attacked U.S. forces in Hawaii. The next day, President Franklin D. Roosevelt asked Congress to declare war on Japan. Every member voted yes—except Rankin, who thus became the only member of Congress to vote against U.S. entry into both world wars.

Montanans again were angry with her decision, and she was defeated when she ran for reelection in 1942. Afterward, she traveled abroad, exploring ways to keep the peace. In 1968 the United States was fighting another war, this time in Vietnam. Rankin, now eighty-seven years old, led the Jeannette Rankin Brigade in a demonstration against the war in Washington, D.C. When she died five years later, she was praised for sticking to her beliefs, regardless of the cost.

See also Conscientious Objectors; Feminist Movement; Voting.

ABIGAIL JUNGREIS

REAGAN, RONALD

(1911–   )   *Fortieth president of the United States (1981–89).*

Born in Tampico, Illinois, Reagan grew up in Dixon, Illinois. After graduating from Eureka

College in 1932, he landed jobs at two Iowa radio stations as a sports announcer. A Hollywood screen test in 1937 won him a contract at Warner Brothers studio. During his acting career he appeared in more than fifty movies, including *The Santa Fe Trail, Knute Rockne, All-American,* and *King's Row.*

Following World War II army duty, Reagan served six years as president of the Screen Actors Guild. As his acting career faded, he turned to politics. In 1966 he successfully ran for governor of California as a conservative Republican. Two four-year terms as governor made Reagan a national political figure. In 1980 he ran for president against the incumbent Democratic president Jimmy Carter and Independent candidate John Anderson. "Are you better off than you were four years ago?" Reagan asked voters. On Election Day, he won by a huge margin.

At sixty-nine Reagan became the oldest person ever elected president. His conservative economic program, called "Reaganomics" by critics, created jobs by slashing government spending and cutting taxes, but it also greatly raised the national debt.

In 1984 Reagan won reelection by defeating former Democratic vice president Walter Mondale. During his second term, Reagan and Soviet Union president Mikhail Gorbachev negotiated the intermediate-range nuclear forces treaty, calling for the destruction of hundreds of American and Soviet nuclear missiles.

Reagan, who survived an assassination attempt in March 1981, was regarded by many as one of America's most popular presidents. At the end of his presidency, he retired to California.

For events during Reagan's administration, see Cold War; Iran-Contra Affair.

For further reading: Zachary Kent, *Ronald Reagan* (Chicago: Childrens Press, 1989).

ZACHARY KENT

President Ronald Reagan (right) and Soviet leader Mikhail Gorbachev laugh and shake hands at a 1985 summit meeting in Geneva, Switzerland.

RECONSTRUCTION

In American history, Reconstruction refers to the process by which the divided nation was brought together after the Civil War. Reconstruction lasted from the end of the war in 1865 to 1877 and remains one of the most controversial periods in American history. For many years it was seen as a time of misgovernment, caused, some said, by granting the right to vote to black men. Today it is viewed more favorably, as an attempt to extend American democracy to the former slaves.

President Abraham Lincoln announced his plan of Reconstruction in 1863, midway through the Civil War. He offered a pardon to any Confederate, except high-ranking officials, who pledged to support the Union and accept the end of slavery. When 10 percent of a state's voters (all of whom were white) took this oath, the state would be permitted to form a new government.

As the war progressed, many Republicans came to believe that the federal government had a responsibility to protect the liberty of the former slaves. Radical Republicans went further, insisting that Reconstruction could not be secure unless blacks were given the vote. Their commitment to equality for the former slaves had an impact on Lincoln. In a speech shortly before his assassination in April 1865, he endorsed the idea of giving some African Americans the right to vote.

Presidential Reconstruction

Lincoln's successor, Andrew Johnson, was a former Democrat from Tennessee. Johnson was ill-suited for the responsibilities he now assumed. A man intolerant of criticism and unable to compromise, he held deeply racist views. In May 1865, Johnson announced his plan of Reconstruction. Essentially, he offered the white South a free hand in creating new governments.

But even as Johnson put into effect a Reconstruction for whites only, African Americans were seeking to give meaning to their new freedom. Throughout the South, former slaves left plantations in search of better jobs, family members from whom they had been separated by sales, or a taste of personal freedom. They withdrew from churches dominated by whites, establishing congregations that laid the foundation for the modern black church. Former slaves pooled their resources to start schools and hire teachers. Adults as well as children poured into these schools, seeking the education denied them as slaves. The former slaves also insisted that freedom entitled them to equal rights as American citizens.

The governments established during this period—called Presidential Reconstruction (1865–67)—turned a deaf ear to black demands. New state laws called the Black Codes required blacks to sign year-long labor contracts; those who refused could be arrested. The Black Codes, one Republican complained, seemed to be aimed at "getting things back as near to slavery as possible."

When Congress met in December 1865, the Republican majority concluded that Johnson's program needed to be changed. Early in 1866, Congress passed two bills to offer protection to the former slaves. One extended the life of the Freedmen's Bureau, an agency established in 1865 to assist blacks in the transition from slavery to freedom. Another, the civil rights bill, declared that African Americans were citizens of the United States, entitled to the same legal rights (except the vote) as white persons. Johnson vetoed both measures. In April, the Civil Rights Act became the first major bill in American history to receive a two-thirds vote of Congress and become law over a president's veto.

Radical Reconstruction

Congress now moved to implement its own program, which was called Radical Reconstruction (1867–77). First, it approved the Fourteenth Amendment to the Constitution, requiring each state to guarantee all citizens, regardless of race, "equal protection of the laws." In 1867, the Reconstruction Act temporarily divided the South into military districts and gave black men there the right to vote. The Fifteenth Amendment, ratified in 1870, decreed that no state could discriminate

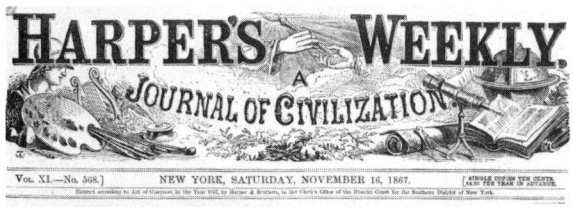

The right to vote was granted to African-American men during Reconstruction. This 1867 engraving from Harper's Weekly *shows a black artisan (note the tools in his pocket) casting his first vote. A well-dressed businessman and a soldier are lined up behind him— the three are symbols of black leadership.*

among voters because of race. These measures established equality before the law, enforced by the national government, as a fundamental right of all American citizens.

In 1868, the House of Representatives voted to impeach President Johnson—that is, ordered him tried by the Senate for "high crimes and misdemeanors." At the trial, Republicans fell one vote short of the two-thirds needed to remove Johnson from office.

During Radical Reconstruction, blacks held major offices at the national and state levels. Sixteen African Americans sat in Congress, and hundreds more served in southern legislatures and in other state and local positions. Some of these officeholders had been born free, but a majority were former slaves who had earned leadership positions by serving in the Union army or engaging in political and church work.

The southern Republican Party also brought to power new groups of whites. "Carpetbaggers," recent arrivals from the North, were generally army officers, teachers, and businessmen. "Scalawags," white Republicans who had been born in the South, were mostly poorer farmers who had remained loyal to the Union during the Civil War.

The governments of Radical Reconstruction established the South's first state-supported public school systems, as well as numerous hospitals and asylums for orphans and the insane. They enacted sweeping civil rights laws, making it illegal for railroads, hotels, and other institutions to discriminate on the basis of race. They also took steps to promote the South's economic recovery.

The former slaves, however, were disappointed that the governments did little to assist them in acquiring land. To African Americans, freedom meant economic independence. But most emerged from slavery without property and were forced to seek employment from southern whites. Many white farmers, too, found it impossible to escape from poverty. Reconstruction brought a political revolution to the South, but not an economic revolution to accompany it.

Opposition to Reconstruction

Many white southerners vowed to do everything in their power to overturn the new governments. Corruption in some states angered many, as did the rising taxes needed to pay

A group portrait of the first black senator (H. R. Revels of Mississippi, at the far left) and congressmen. A total of sixteen blacks served in the House and Senate during the Reconstruction years.

for schools and other new public facilities. The basic reason for opposition to Reconstruction, however, was that few southern whites could accept the idea of former slaves voting and holding office.

In many areas, Reconstruction's opponents resorted to violence to secure their ends. Secret societies sprang up, intent on terrorizing blacks and preventing them from voting and on assassinating local Republican leaders. Most notorious was the Ku Klux Klan, which committed some of the most brutal acts of violence in American history. In Meridian, Mississippi, in 1871, for example, some thirty blacks were murdered in cold blood, along with a white Republican judge.

When the new southern governments proved unable to restore order, the federal government stepped in. President Ulysses S. Grant, who had succeeded Johnson, sent federal marshals to arrest Klansmen throughout the South in 1871. Despite this response to terrorism, however, many northerners came to feel that the South should solve its problems without interference from Washington. When, in the mid-1870s, violence again reared its head, the Grant administration showed no desire to intervene. One by one, Republican governments were toppled.

In 1876, Republicans nominated Ohio governor Rutherford B. Hayes to succeed Grant. His Democratic opponent was Samuel J. Tilden of New York. The election was so close that whoever won Florida, Louisiana, and South Carolina—which both parties claimed to have carried—would become the next president.

After much uncertainty, a compromise was reached. The Republican Hayes became president, but he promised to recognize Democratic control of the entire South. He ordered federal troops, who had been helping to keep the last Republican governors in office, to return to their northern barracks.

The bitter era of Reconstruction was over. In the next decades, the white South nullified (or overturned) the civil and political rights of the former slaves. By the early twentieth century, virtually no black could vote anywhere in the South. Not until the civil rights movement of the 1950s and 1960s—a period often called the Second Reconstruction—was the nation again ready to accord African Americans the rights set forth in the laws and constitutional amendments enacted during Reconstruction.

See also African Americans; Black Codes; Carpetbaggers and Scalawags; Compromise of 1877; Freedmen's Bureau; Impeachment; Ku Klux Klan; Lynching; Redeemers.

ERIC FONER

RECONSTRUCTION FINANCE CORPORATION

By the beginning of 1932, the Great Depression had been worsening for more than two years. Many of the nation's banks had failed and still more were in danger. Since there was no government insurance of bank deposits at this time, ordinary citizens were in danger of losing their savings. This led many depositors to take their money out of the banks, which further injured already shaky institutions.

To deal with this problem, in 1932 Congress created the Reconstruction Finance Corporation (RFC) to make "emergency loans" to banks, insurance companies, and railroads in danger of failing. President Herbert Hoover, who in general opposed government aid to private businesses, approved of the RFC. He argued that the loans were sound business deals, not government handouts. The troubled companies the RFC helped had valuable assets, which were used as security in case the loans were not repaid.

During the New Deal years the RFC continued to operate. It also played a role in stimulating the building and operating of defense plants during World War II. By the time it was phased out after the war, it had lent about $12 billion, nearly all of which was eventually repaid.

See also Depressions and Recessions.

RED CROSS
See American Red Cross.

REDEEMERS

After the Civil War the federal government forced many political and social changes on the states of the defeated Confederacy. The purpose of these changes was to protect the newly freed blacks from exploitation, to help them obtain a decent education, and to improve their economic prospects. These changes were resented by many southern whites. When federal military control of the South ended in the mid-1870s, these whites organized politically and sought to get rid of them and "redeem" (reclaim) their old way of life.

The Redeemers were a loose political coalition, not a well-organized national party. Basically conservative, they sought to lower government spending as well as keep the blacks down. When they controlled a legislature they reduced expenditures on public education, on salaries of government workers, and on aid for the badly run-down southern railroads. They also enacted poll taxes designed to keep blacks from voting. In the long run, the Redeemers injured every southern interest, their own included.

See also Reconstruction.

RED SCARES
See Anticommunism.

REFORM
See Civil Rights Movement; Feminist Movement; Great Society; Muckrakers; New Deal; Populism; Prohibition and Temperance; Social Legislation.

REHNQUIST, WILLIAM
(1924–)   *Chief justice, U.S. Supreme Court.*

Born in Milwaukee, Wisconsin, and educated at Stanford and Harvard, Rehnquist graduated in 1951 from the Stanford Law School. His achievements won him a coveted position as clerk to Supreme Court Justice Robert Jackson.

After his clerkship, Rehnquist practiced law in Phoenix, Arizona, and became active in Republican politics. When Richard M. Nixon became president in 1969, Rehnquist returned to Washington to work in the Justice Department. In 1971, Nixon unexpectedly nominated Rehnquist to the Supreme Court. In the Senate hearings regarding his nomina-

tion, senators focused much of their attention on a memorandum he had written as Jackson's clerk supporting the constitutionality of so-called separate-but-equal racially segregated public schools. The Court (including Justice Jackson) rejected this view in the *Brown* v. *Board of Education* decision of 1954. Rehnquist insisted that the memorandum did not reflect his own views, and the Senate confirmed his nomination.

He was the most conservative member of the Court headed by another Nixon appointee, Chief Justice Warren Burger. One thread of his philosophy was doubts about claims of individual rights being overridden by state regulation. Thus, he was, with Justice Byron White, one of the two dissenters in *Roe* v. *Wade,* the 1973 case that extended to women the right to have an abortion. Another thread was sympathy for states objecting to what they deemed overregulation by the national government. This was reflected in *National League of Cities* v. *Usery* (1976), in which the Court struck down an act of Congress that applied federal minimum wage laws to state and city employees. (This decision was later overruled by the Court in 1985 over Rehnquist's sharp dissent.) Finally, Rehnquist was hostile to any claims by persons accused or convicted of criminal conduct.

After Burger's resignation in 1986, President Ronald Reagan nominated Rehnquist to be chief justice. He was confirmed by the Senate after heated debate. The Rehnquist Court, bolstered by several other justices appointed by Reagan and President George Bush, became markedly more conservative, especially in limiting the rights of persons accused of crimes and in upholding the death penalty. It also expressed doubt about the legality of so-called affirmative action programs based on race.

With President Bill Clinton's election and the likely replacement of several of the justices in the 1990s, it remained to be seen whether Rehnquist would continue in the majority or, once again, become a conservative dissenter.

See also Supreme Court.

SANFORD LEVINSON

RELIGION
See Catholic Church; Christian Science; Church and State; Jews; Mormons; Protestants; Quakers; Shakers.

REMINGTON, FREDERIC

(1861–1909)   *Painter and sculptor.*

Remington was the most important documentary artist of the American western frontier. He is best known for the swift action and accurate detail of his portrayals of cowboys, Native Americans, soldiers, and horses.

Remington was born in New York State and attended the Yale School of Fine Arts for two years. At the age of nineteen he made a trip to Montana, working as a cowboy and scout and sketching scenes of a pioneer life that was fast passing into history. In 1883 he bought a sheep ranch in Kansas and lived there for a year.

Remington moved to New York City in 1885 and attended the Art Students League for a time while he sought a career in commercial art. He soon became the leading illustrator of western scenes for magazines and books. In 1895 he illustrated articles by Theodore Roosevelt for *Century* magazine and two years later produced a series for Henry

Frederic Remington's bronze statue The Bronco Buster, *the first and most popular of his sculptures.*

Wadsworth Longfellow's poem *Song of Hiawatha*. His 1892 illustrations for Francis Parkman's *Oregon Trail* were also to become classics. Honored internationally, his work was exhibited by the National Academy and won a medal at the Paris Exposition of 1889.

In 1895 Remington began modeling his subjects in clay, and although he had no formal training in sculpture, he quickly mastered the medium. The action-filled bronze *Bronco Buster* (1895), cast from his model, is probably the best-known statue of the American West.

Remington served in Cuba during the Spanish-American War of 1898 as an artist and correspondent for newspapers. But his favorite subject remained the western frontier. He wrote and illustrated nine books of fiction and nonfiction about the open plains and many articles about his experiences there. In his paintings, sculpture, and illustrations, he left an exciting visual record of a vanishing scene and way of life.

See also Painting and Sculpture.

For further reading: Ernest Raboff, *Frederic Remington* (New York: HarperCollins, 1988).

DENNIS WEPMAN

REPUBLICAN PARTY

The Republican Party is one of two major U.S. political parties. It was founded in 1854 over the issue of slavery, then legal in the South. In February of that year midwesterners opposed to the westward extension of slavery began meeting to protest a bill opening the Kansas and Nebraska territories to slavery. The meetings became a movement and on July 6, the Republican Party was formally established. It adopted the structure of the already existing Democratic Party, with organizations on the local, state, and federal levels and the nominating conventions and campaign politicking we know today. The party's 1856 presidential candidate, John C. Frémont, ran on a strict antislavery platform and lost. Republicans responded by broadening their appeal, downplaying the slavery issue somewhat while advocating western settlement and business growth. On this platform, Abraham Lincoln won the presidency in 1860. Eleven southern states then seceded from the Union, and the Civil War began.

Post–Civil War Policies
As president, Lincoln's overriding goal was to crush the rebellion and preserve the Union. He succeeded, but his plans for postwar national reconciliation were never implemented. After his assassination in 1865, congressional Republicans amended the U.S. Constitution to abolish slavery and confer citizenship and voting rights upon the former slaves. The party's stand on slavery and civil rights won it generations of black support.

Backed also by its original constituents—northern farmers and businessmen—and facing little effective opposition from southern Democrats, the GOP, or Grand Old Party as Republicans had dubbed themselves, dominated national politics for the remainder of the century. Republican lawmakers offered federal land free to farmers and placed high tariffs (taxes) on imported goods, giving U.S. industry a competitive advantage. The nation grew in size and wealth.

The first drawing of the Republican Party symbol, the elephant, created by the political cartoonist Thomas Nast.

But with growth came problems. For working people, factory hours were long and wages low. As a party, Republicans resisted efforts to improve conditions. Party policy also favored the wealthy by condoning *trusts*. A trust is a business monopoly, which, because it is the only producer of a given item or service, can keep its price artificially high. Other problems surfaced, too. Black Americans faced increasing discrimination. Government was corrupt. And in the 1890s the nation suffered a severe depression. Although some Republicans urged reform, it was not until 1901, when Theodore Roosevelt became president, that the party changed course.

Rise and Fall of Progressivism

Roosevelt called the presidency a "bully pulpit." From it, he steered the party—and the nation—toward a more progressive path. He demanded a "square deal" for American workers and set about "trust-busting," breaking up several competition-stifling monopolies. He enlarged the role of the federal government, promoting the regulation of interstate commerce, signing the nation's first pure food and drug law, and doubling the number of national parks. More of an internationalist than earlier Republicans, he intervened in Latin American affairs and urged the building of the Panama Canal through Central America. Roosevelt was succeeded in 1909 by a less activist Republican, William Howard Taft. In 1912, Roosevelt challenged Taft for the presidency, running under the banner of his own Progressive Party, or Bull Moose Party, as it was popularly called. This split the Republicans and allowed a Democrat to become president for only the third time in over forty years.

The 1912 split deprived the Republican Party of its progressive elements, and the Republicans who occupied Congress and the White House from 1921 to 1933 harbored the pro-business, antilabor views of the past. Such policies satisfied most Americans, enjoying as they were the prosperity of the Roaring Twenties. But in 1929, the economy collapsed, plunging the country into depression. Republicans, generally blamed for the hard times, lost the White House in 1932.

Not until 1952, with the depression only a memory and the country fresh from victory in World War II, did Americans elect another Republican president, war hero Dwight D. Eisenhower. Generally partial to business interests, Eisenhower nevertheless extended some social programs, like tax-funded pensions for retirees (Social Security), initiated by the Democratic administrations of the depression years. He was reelected in 1956, and the next year, ordered U.S. army troops to enforce school racial desegregation laws in Little Rock, Arkansas. Such policies and positions alienated more conservative Republicans, as did Eisenhower's attitude toward communism and the Soviet Union. After World War II, Soviet leaders had imposed communist governments on much of Eastern Europe. Now they threatened to do the same in Africa, Asia, and Latin America. Although Eisenhower, who was certainly opposed to communism, resisted these threats, he was never as fervent in his rhetoric as were such GOP stalwarts as Senator Joseph McCarthy and his own vice president, Richard M. Nixon.

Conservatives Take Power

Nixon ran unsuccessfully for president in 1960. Over the next eight years, he and other conservatives tightened their grip on the party. In 1968, Nixon ran again and won. As president, he pursued American involvement in the Vietnam War, undertaken during the administrations of Democrats John F. Kennedy and Lyndon B. Johnson to resist the spread of communism in Southeast Asia. On the domestic front, Nixon took a get-tough approach to street crime, while only half-heartedly enforcing civil rights laws. These policies brought many conservative southern Democrats into the Republican camp. Yet Nixon reached out to moderates, too, visiting Communist China in 1972, pulling out of Vietnam a year later, and establishing the Environmental Protection Agency. Nixon's presidency ended in scandal. Both he and his vice president, Spiro T. Agnew, were forced to resign from office—the latter for income tax evasion, and Nixon because he tried to conceal crimes committed by his staff during his 1972 reelection campaign.

But while Nixon left Washington in disgrace, his party remained relatively unscathed. A Democrat was elected president in 1976, but four years later, the GOP made a dramatic comeback. It did so with the help of ultraconservative Ronald Reagan. One of this country's most popular presidents, Reagan attracted Republican faithfuls, midwestern farmers, and big business with promises of "less government"—lower taxes and reduced social programs. Conservatives applauded his zealous anticommunism, his willingness to intervene militarily on behalf of U.S. interests worldwide, and the massive increases he ordered in defense spending. Many white middle-class voters approved his disdain for civil rights legislation and his denunciations of affirmative action programs intended to promote the interests of traditionally disadvantaged groups like minorities and women. Reagan also won support from a new constituency, the "Religious Right," conservative Christians intent upon outlawing abortion,

making Christian prayer mandatory in public schools, and the like. He was reelected by a landslide in 1984 and was succeeded by his vice president, George Bush, in 1988.

Bush continued Reagan's policies, but by 1992, Americans were becoming restive. The tax reductions of the 1980s, combined with lavish military spending, had left the country a record $3.5 trillion in debt. The economy was weak, with millions jobless. Cuts in social welfare programs meant less government help for the needy. Moderate Americans were dismayed by the demands of the Religious Right. Even the communism issue no longer served Republicans, for the Soviet Union had fallen apart in 1991. President Bush lost his 1992 reelection bid to Bill Clinton.

See also Party Conventions; Progressive Parties. And see biographies of Republican presidents listed in table under the entry Presidents.

ANN E. WEISS

RESERVATIONS
See Indian Reservations.

REVERE, PAUL

(1735–1818)   Silversmith, industrialist, and American Revolution figure.

Revere is mostly remembered as the hard-riding hero of Longfellow's poem ("The Midnight Ride of Paul Revere"), but he was even more significant as a skilled craftsman. His father, the French Huguenot silversmith Apollos Rivoire, had been sent to America alone at the age of ten to escape religious persecution in France. When he died, nineteen-year-old Paul took over the family business in Boston. During the next twenty years, he became one of the greatest American gold-smiths—a term that included every aspect of working with precious metals. Besides silver bowls, utensils, pots, and flatware (many of which are museum pieces today), Revere and his workers produced many engravings: pictures, calling cards, bookplates, tradesmen's billheads, and even musical scores. As a sideline, he practiced a primitive form of dentistry. Revere also served as an artilleryman in the French and Indian War.

As a member of the Freemasons and the Sons of Liberty, Revere worked with Samuel Adams to secure American independence, serving primarily as a messenger to other colonies and as an engraver of propaganda pictures. The highlight of his revolutionary activities came the night of April 18–19, 1775, when he crossed the Charles River and rode to Lexington, Massachusetts, to warn Samuel Adams and John Hancock that British troops were coming and planning to arrest them. Once the Revolution started, Revere again served in the artillery, though without distinction, particularly during a failed expedition to Castine, Maine.

After the war, Revere developed a profitable foundry and hardware business, establishing the nation's first successful sheet-copper mill. The navy could now copper-bottom its ships, including the new USS *Constitution*, with American-rolled copper. Revere later became grand master of the Masonic Grand Lodge, organized Boston's first successful mutual fire insurance company, served as Suffolk County coroner, and was the first president of the Boston Board of Health.

See also Revolution: The War for Independence.

For further reading: Esther Forbes, *Paul Revere and the World He Lived In* (Boston: Houghton Mifflin Co., 1962).

HILLER B. ZOBEL

REVOLUTION: THE WAR FOR INDEPENDENCE

The Seven Years' War, called the French and Indian War in the colonies, ended in triumph for Great Britain in 1763. But it had been very expensive, and the British believed that the colonies in America, which benefited from the victory, should shoulder some of the costs. The English people were already paying far higher taxes than the colonists did. Parliament passed the Revenue (or Sugar) Act of 1764, placing a new tax on sugar. The funds raised were to be used to pay the expenses of a British army stationed in America to defend the colonists on the frontier. But Americans were angered. Because they had no representatives in Parliament, they declared that "taxation without representation is tyranny!"

Tensions Increase

The following year Parliament passed another tax, the Stamp Act. The wave of colonial protests that followed forced Parliament to repeal the legislation. But England's financial problems remained, and in 1767, Parliament tried again. The Townshend Acts taxed luxuries: paper, paint, glass, lead, and tea. Again there were protests, and again Parliament backed down. It repealed all the taxes except that on tea, which it kept because it wanted to save face.

Meanwhile, units of the army that was supposed to protect colonists on the frontier were stationed in New York and Boston. Parliament passed another law requiring the colonists to house the soldiers. This Quartering Act was another kind of taxation without representation. What was more, the professional soldiers living in the cities were not welcome. They were rough men—notoriously heavy drinkers who swore, ha-

George Washington (standing at right) and the French general, the Marquis de Lafayette (left) at Valley Forge, the site in Pennsylvania where American forces camped from December 19, 1777, to June 19, 1778. It was a severe winter and the troops lacked food, clothing, and supplies. Many soldiers died; others deserted. Washington, Lafayette, and the Prussian general Steuben endured the winter with the troops. By spring, Steuben had organized the men into a disciplined and well-trained army.

rassed women, got into fistfights, and committed petty thefts. Mobs of boys, servants, and laborers fought with them in New York and Boston. After many minor clashes, a company of soldiers killed five civilians in the so-called Boston Massacre on March 5, 1770. After that, the British removed the troops from the city.

There was no further trouble for almost five years. Then the tea tax became an issue. A group of colonists, in an act of protest, tossed a ship's cargo of tea overboard into Boston Harbor. Parliament looked upon the Boston Tea Party as a criminal act and passed the Co-ercive Acts as punishment. Troops were sent back into the city, and Gen. Thomas Gage was ordered to confiscate all stockpiles of weapons and military supplies in the region.

The War Starts

On April 18, 1775, Gage sent eight hundred British troops on a night march to Concord to arrest leaders of the colonial rebels and confiscate weapons in the town. (This was the occasion of Paul Revere's famous ride to warn the colonists, "The British are coming.") In the morning, they found seventy American Minute Men mustered on Lexing-

Major Events of the Revolutionary War,

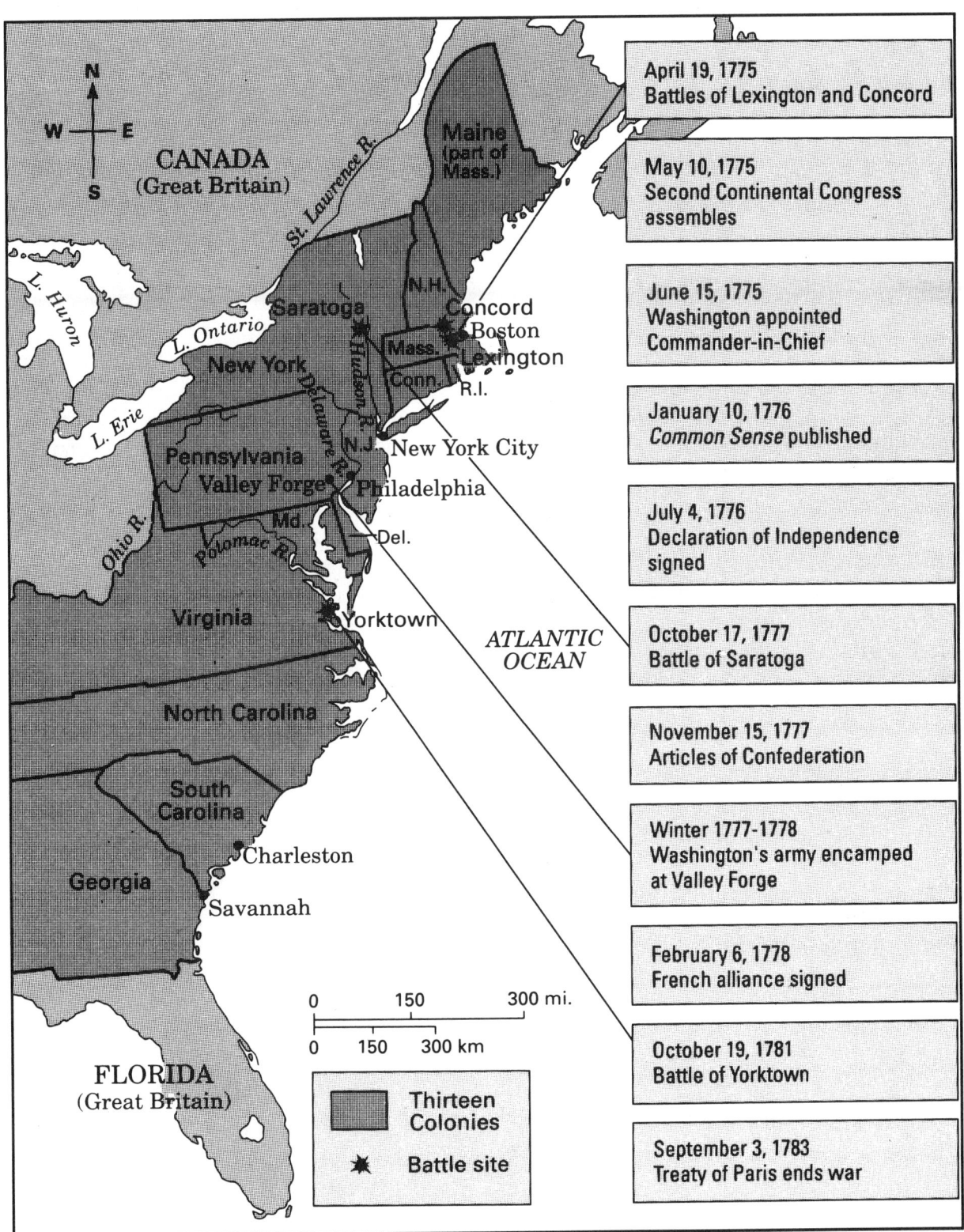

April 19, 1775
Battles of Lexington and Concord

May 10, 1775
Second Continental Congress
assembles

June 15, 1775
Washington appointed
Commander-in-Chief

January 10, 1776
Common Sense published

July 4, 1776
Declaration of Independence
signed

October 17, 1777
Battle of Saratoga

November 15, 1777
Articles of Confederation

Winter 1777-1778
Washington's army encamped
at Valley Forge

February 6, 1778
French alliance signed

October 19, 1781
Battle of Yorktown

September 3, 1783
Treaty of Paris ends war

Thirteen
Colonies

Battle site

ton Common barring their way. The war began on that spot when shots were fired. In the battles fought at Lexington and Concord almost four thousand American militiamen forced the British to retreat to Boston. The Americans then settled in around the city and laid siege to it.

Two weeks later, the Continental Congress appointed the Virginian George Washington as commander in chief of the American army. Before he could join his troops in Boston, they fought an impressive action on June 17 at the Battle of Bunker Hill. By this time their force had grown to 10,000, but only 1,600 were at the small fortification they had built on the heights when the British attacked. Outnumbered two to one, the Americans could not hold the position. But they inflicted heavy casualties on their attackers before withdrawing, much to the surprise of the British.

For the next year, the American army under Washington kept an eye on the British in Boston while another American force unsuccessfully attempted an invasion of Canada. At the same time a mixed force of North Carolinians and Virginians forced the British to evacuate Norfolk, Virginia, although they burned the town before they left. The British evacuated Boston on March 17, 1776.

In July, Congress issued the Declaration of Independence, hoping to bring other European nations into the war on the colonial side. Meanwhile, the British moved to New York City, which became their new base of operations. Despite American resistance at the Battles of Long Island and Fort Washington, the city was under British control by the end of the summer. Washington's troops were forced to retreat into New Jersey. Finally, in December 1776, Washington launched surprise attacks on isolated British garrisons at

Trenton and Princeton. At last the Americans had won a victory.

The British planned a grand strategy for 1777, hoping to end this embarrassing colonial war before France and Spain, England's traditional enemies, decided to become involved. The grand plan envisioned three armies converging in New York to isolate New England from the other colonies. The British general, Sir William Howe, succeeded in capturing Philadelphia in September and Washington was unable to retake it. His troops eventually went into winter quarters at Valley Forge, where with insufficient clothing and supplies, they suffered terribly during the cold months. There was a ray of hope, however, in American successes farther north. A campaign in New York ended in disaster for the British at the Battle of Saratoga in October. Actually, the rugged country in upstate New York, coupled with fierce small-scale attacks by the Americans, had virtually destroyed the British force before it even reached Saratoga. But the formal surrender of the remnants of his army by Gen. John Burgoyne to the American general Horatio Gates impressed the Europeans. In 1778, France and Spain entered the war on the side of the colonies.

England now faced serious military danger around the world. The British could not afford to carry on the fight that had escalated to include the major powers. They began to look for ways to end the war diplomatically.

Independence Is Won

Meanwhile, the focus of military operations moved to the South where vicious if small-scale actions eroded British strength in the Carolinas. The British general, Lord Cornwallis, then marched into Virginia and took a stand at Yorktown. At this point, French warships and troops gave George Washington the edge he needed to organize a complex land-sea operation. Cornwallis was besieged at Yorktown in October 1781 and was forced to surrender. The war was over.

After two years of negotiation, Great Britain and the United States signed the Treaty of Paris, which became effective on January 20, 1783. It was a triumph for the American diplomats Benjamin Franklin, John Jay, Henry Laurens, and John Adams. In the treaty England recognized American independence and ceded all claims to territory east of the Mississippi. This enormous expanse doubled the size of the new nation.

See also Boston Massacre; Boston Tea Party; Coercive Acts; Committees of Correspondence; *Common Sense;* Continental Congresses; Declaration of Independence; Minute Men; Paris, Treaty of (1783); Proclamation of 1763; Quartering Acts; Quebec Act; Seven Years' War; Sons of Liberty; Stamp Act; Sugar Act; Townshend Acts.

LINDA GRANT DE PAUW

REVOLUTION: POLITICAL AND SOCIAL IMPACT

The Americans who fought the War for American Independence were not fighting for change. They were fighting to resist changes they thought the English were trying to force on them. But the war brought political and social changes no one had foreseen.

New Political Arrangements
The most obvious change after the war was the elimination of monarchy. All the major European powers had kings. History seemed to show that republican government could work only in very small political units. Some Americans never did give up the idea that only a monarchy would be stable; some

wanted George Washington to become king of the United States. But with the Revolution, Americans rejected all kings, not just tyrants.

For government at the federal level, Americans adopted the Articles of Confederation. The Articles provided for a permanent alliance between the individual states. The Continental Congress was the chief governing authority, and the president was merely an officer who presided over congressional meetings.

During the war, all the states except Connecticut and Rhode Island wrote new constitutions. The two exceptions continued to use their seventeenth-century charters as the basis of government, merely cutting out references to the British monarch. All the new state constitutions strengthened the representative legislatures that had the power to tax and to pass other laws. Most states kept two houses in the legislative branch and weakened the powers of the governor. Many of the new constitutions also included a Bill of Rights, specifying the rights of individuals that no legislation could take away. The general law of the land continued to be the common law of Great Britain.

All the new state constitutions allowed more people to vote. For a few years New Jersey even enfranchised unmarried women and free blacks who owned property. The new constitutions also lowered property qualifications for voting. Many poor men had risked their lives as soldiers during the war. Their willingness to sacrifice had been as great as that of those with fortunes to protect.

The Social Impact
Before the war, about 10 percent of the population consisted of white indentured servants. These people were not much freer than black slaves, except that their terms of service had a

limit. After the war, this class shrank. (Many servants were felons, sent from England to America as punishment. After the Revolution, England sent its criminals to Australia.) Simultaneously, the early stages of the Industrial Revolution made owning servants less profitable than hiring free laborers who could be fired when they grew old or sick or when business was slack. The number of poor free persons had begun growing even before the war, but the war accelerated the trend.

A substantial number of the wealthiest men in the colonies remained loyal to England. Many of them left America. The men serving in the state legislatures after the war owned only about half as much property as those serving in 1775. They were likely to be modest farmers or craftsmen rather than large landowners or merchants.

The emphasis on freedom and equality that inspired the Revolution made slavery less acceptable. The first antislavery society in America had begun to organize just as the war was starting. The service of black soldiers in the military reinforced antislavery arguments. Almost every state that recruited black soldiers either freed them outright or gave them freedom after the war. Eleven of the states either prohibited buying and selling slaves or taxed the slave trade heavily. Massachusetts, New Hampshire, Connecticut, and Rhode Island outlawed slavery entirely, and Pennsylvania adopted a program of gradual emancipation.

Women had also proved their patriotism during the war. Those remaining at home made gunpowder and cartridges for the army. Others were active as espionage agents. A surprising number served as combat soldiers, sometimes disguising themselves with a male name, but sometimes merely putting on a uniform. In addition, as many as twenty thousand women accompanied the Continental army during its campaigns and served in combat support roles. But the status of women fell after the war.

The British common law placed many limitations on women, but under the rough conditions of the early colonial settlements, Americans had ignored them. There were few lawyers or law books, so the settlers made their own rules, including allowing divorce by mutual consent. As society developed, the common law became a real burden. Abigail Adams wrote to her husband, John, when he was in Congress urging him to put limits on

• •

For further information on the American Revolution, see the biographies in this book of the following men. All were leaders or participants in the events surrounding America's drive for independence.

ADAMS, JOHN

ADAMS, SAMUEL

ARNOLD, BENEDICT

ATTUCKS, CRISPUS

BURR, AARON

FRANKLIN, BENJAMIN

HAMILTON, ALEXANDER

HANCOCK, JOHN

HENRY, PATRICK

HUTCHINSON, THOMAS

JAY, JOHN

JEFFERSON, THOMAS

JONES, JOHN PAUL

MADISON, JAMES

MONROE, JAMES

MORRIS, ROBERT

PAINE, THOMAS

REVERE, PAUL

WASHINGTON, GEORGE

the absolute power the law gave the male head of the family. He only laughed. Women's rights were not an issue for another half century.

See also Abolitionist Movement; Articles of Confederation; Bill of Rights; Constitution; Continental Congresses; Voting.

LINDA GRANT DE PAUW

RFC
See Reconstruction Finance Corporation.

RICKEY, BRANCH

(1881–1965)   *Major league baseball executive.*

Rickey graduated from Ohio Wesleyan University in 1906. Attracted to baseball, he became a major league catcher with the Cincinnati Reds in 1904. But because of injuries and his refusal to play on Sundays for religious reasons, his playing career ended quickly.

Rickey took a law degree in 1911 at the University of Michigan, where he also coached baseball. Deciding to be a baseball executive, Rickey started as manager of the St. Louis Browns and assistant to the owner. To help the Browns compete with wealthier clubs, he created a farm system—arrangements with minor league teams to take on their players as these teams developed them. Then he became manager and president of the other St. Louis team, the Cardinals. There he perfected the farm system and became rich on his share of the money the Cardinals made by selling surplus "farm hands" to other teams.

Rickey left the Cardinals for the Brooklyn Dodgers in 1945, becoming president and general manager and then a co-owner. The new farm system he created came quickly to include black and Latin American players.

Rickey had made up his mind to breach the racial barrier in organized baseball. He carefully selected and groomed Jackie Robinson, an outstanding athlete from the University of California at Los Angeles, assigning him in 1945 to a Dodger farm team, the Montreal Royals of the International League. Rickey promoted Robinson to Brooklyn in 1947, where after a struggle overcoming the racism of fans and other players, Robinson established himself as a baseball great.

In 1950 Rickey left the Dodgers for the Pittsburgh Pirates. Failing to build there yet another championship team, he was dismissed in 1955. Rickey then headed the short-lived Continental League, which aimed to bring big-league baseball to cities lacking a franchise. A brilliant baseball innovator, Rickey is remembered best as the Man Who Emancipated Baseball by hiring Jackie Robinson. Their mutual effort helped stimulate the modern civil rights movement.

See also Baseball; Robinson, Jackie.

HENRY F. GRAFF

RIOTS
See Draft Riots; Race Riots.

ROBBER BARONS

This term was used by critics of the rich and powerful industrialists, bankers, and railroad presidents who dominated the American economy in the late nineteenth century. The name combined the charge that these men used illegal methods to obtain their wealth (robber) with the conviction that they ruled over their enterprises the way a medieval lord of the manor controlled the serfs who labored in his fields (baron).

The robber barons benefited from the rapid expansion of the American economy after the Civil War and from the many important technical advances of the period. They drew upon plentiful supplies of labor and rich sources of raw materials. The fact that there were no income taxes and capital gains taxes made it possible for them to accumulate wealth quickly.

Some of these men, such as John D. Rockefeller of Standard Oil and Andrew Carnegie, kingpin of the steel industry, became fabulously rich by what today seem unscrupulous means. But Rockefeller and Carnegie were also excellent business executives. They reinvested their profits and expanded production. Others, such as the stock market manipulator Jay Cooke, the railroad investor Daniel Drew, and the mining tycoon William A. Clark, fully deserved the title robber baron. They were greedy, crude, and utterly materialistic. Clark, for example, built himself a mansion with more than a hundred rooms on Fifth Avenue in New York City.

A famous remark of William H. Vanderbilt captures what seems worst about both types of robber baron — "The public be damned!"

See also Carnegie, Andrew; Morgan, J. P.; Rockefeller, John D.; Vanderbilt, Cornelius.

ROBESON, PAUL

(1898–1976)   *Actor, singer, and radical black activist.*

Robeson played several roles in the course of his long, controversial life. He was first a black man who made every effort to cooperate with the white community and play by its rules. The son of a clergyman who had been born a slave, he graduated from Rutgers (where he was an all-American football player and class valedictorian) and Columbia University Law School. Facing extreme racial discrimination, he never really practiced law, but turned to the stage. Roles for blacks were scarce, and public opinion was often hostile to black actors playing opposite white actresses, even in such well-established roles as Othello. Robeson received his big break in 1924 when he won the support of Eugene O'Neill to play in *All God's Chillun Got Wings* and a revival of *The Emperor Jones.*

Hurt and angered by hostile notices, as well as slights in hotels and restaurants,

Paul Robeson plays Othello in 1959 at the Stratford Shakespeare Memorial Theatre in England.

Robeson became politically active. He joined the National Association for the Advancement of Colored People (NAACP) and expressed sympathy for the Communist Party. He turned increasingly to acting in films and giving folk concerts. Filmmakers cast him in roles that degraded blacks, but with his magnificent singing Robeson made a major impact. Touring Europe, he discovered European modernists who were reevaluating folk music. They encouraged him to turn his attention to both Africa and America for suitable material.

Robeson publicly supported the Soviet Union, where he had been well received, and refused to criticize its excesses. After Germany invaded Russia in World War II, an American could be pro-Soviet without being criticized. After the war that was no longer possible, but Robeson refused to retract his leftist statements. He became the object of persecution by the FBI and numerous less official groups. He never actually joined the Communist Party but supported blacks all over the world in their efforts to throw off imperialist domination and overcome discrimination.

ROBERT M. CRUNDEN

ROBINSON, JACKIE

(1919–72)   *Baseball player.*

Robinson was the first African American to play major league baseball in the twentieth century. Proud of his talents and his blackness in a segregated world, Robinson fought

Brooklyn Dodgers second baseman Jackie Robinson (right) attempts to steal home.

fiercely against racism his entire life. At UCLA he lettered in football, track, basketball, and baseball and also won trophies in swimming, golf, and tennis. During World War II he served in the army and was court-martialed (though later acquitted) for refusing to go to the back of an army bus because he was black.

When Branch Rickey of the Brooklyn Dodgers decided to break baseball's unwritten rule against hiring African Americans, he approached Robinson, who was then playing for the Negro League Kansas City Monarchs. Robinson accepted Rickey's offer, along with his one condition: not to fight back when people abused him for being black.

Robinson thrived on the pressure. In his first game in white baseball (April 18, 1946, with the Dodgers' top farm club), he was up five times and hit three singles and a three-run homer, stole two bases, and scored four times. Promoted to the Dodgers the next year, Robinson quickly became one of the most exciting, aggressive players in the game, despite a torrent of abuse, including death threats. He was named Rookie of the Year in 1947 and Most Valuable Player in 1949. According to his manager, Leo Durocher, "This guy didn't just come to play. He come to beat ya." Responding to Robinson, African Americans filled ballparks to watch him play.

Robinson kept his promise to Rickey for two years, but then became an outspoken advocate for civil rights. He criticized baseball for moving too slowly in hiring other African Americans and urged teams to use their power to change segregated practices in southern hotels and ballparks.

Robinson continued his struggle for racial justice after his retirement in 1956, and in his last public appearance, told a national television audience, "I'd like to live to see a black manager." The Reverend Jesse Jackson, preaching at his funeral, said, "When Jackie took the field, something reminded us of our birthright to be free."

See also Baseball; Rickey, Branch.

WARREN GOLDSTEIN

ROCKEFELLER, JOHN D.

(1839–1937)   *Industrialist and philanthropist.*

Rockefeller was the primary force behind the establishment of the Standard Oil Company and thus, really, of the entire American petroleum industry. Always active in the Baptist church, Rockefeller began early to make substantial charitable contributions. In the final decades of his long life he gave away an estimated $550 million to worthy causes.

Rockefeller was born in Richford, New York. The family moved to Cleveland, Ohio, where he finished high school in 1855 and began his business career as a bookkeeper-clerk.

Oil was first successfully drilled for in western Pennsylvania in 1859, and Rockefeller realized that Cleveland, being nearby, was ideally situated to exploit this new resource. He built his first refinery in 1863 in partnership with others.

The early oil business was chaotic and hazardous. During the 1860s, the price per barrel rose as high as $13.75 and fell as low as 10¢. But Rockefeller, a brilliant manager, kept his firm consistently profitable and growing. In 1870 he, Henry Flagler, and others formed the Standard Oil Company, with Rockefeller owning 26.7 percent of the stock. Taking advantage of such then-legal tactics as railroad rebates and predatory pricing (pricing something below what it cost to produce in order to drive a competitor out of business), Standard Oil steadily increased its hold over the American oil industry, until by 1880 it controlled fully 90 percent of it.

The corporate structure of this quickly expanding enterprise had become unwieldy, however. Individual state incorporation laws made it difficult to operate as a nationwide company. In 1882, the Standard Oil Company's lawyers devised a way around the problem, which became known as the trust form of organization. Standard Oil thus became both the first and the largest of the "trusts," one of the great bogeymen of American politics ever since.

As such, it became a major target of reformers. But though he played the game hard, Rockefeller never operated outside the law or sought an absolute monopoly. Rather, he wanted Standard Oil to be just large enough to enforce "order" in the oil business and prevent any return to the chaos that had marked the industry's early years. Nevertheless, despite Standard's near-monopoly position, the price of oil and oil products fell drastically in the thirty years between 1870 and 1900.

In 1883, Rockefeller moved the company's headquarters to New York. As Rockefeller's resources grew, so did his philanthropy. He had largely retired from Standard Oil by 1897 and devoted much of his energy to looking for creative ways to give his money away. He was often guided by the Baptist ministers among others, and he established an organization to investigate prospective recipients carefully before giving them money. Once he made up his mind, however, he gave with unprecedented generosity. In 1889 he gave $600,000 to establish the University of Chicago (the family would ultimately give it more than $80 million). Later he established the Rockefeller Institute, the General Education

Board, the Rockefeller Foundation, and the Laura Spelman Rockefeller Memorial Foundation.

See also Robber Barons.

JOHN STEELE GORDON

ROCK MUSIC

Rock music is characterized by a heavy, danceable beat and repetitive patterns. It is usually played by three to five musicians with a few electrically amplified instruments—particularly electric guitars—rather than the full orchestra normally required to be loud enough for dancing.

Rock's Early Days

Rock is one of the few kinds of music originally created in the United States. Its beginnings can be traced to black churches in the South and group-music sessions called ring shouts, where a song leader sang a line, which the congregation then repeated. This musical style was called "rocking and reeling," from which we may have derived the term *rock*. Alan Freed, a disk jockey (someone who plays records, or "disks" on the radio), first popularized the term *rock and roll.*

Rock was quickly embraced by young people, but many parents disliked it. Some dubbed it "the Devil's music," claiming the repetitive beat and sometimes suggestive lyrics were an unwholesome influence. Parents and school groups held record-burning parties, circulated petitions to get rock music banned, and organized pledge drives to get teenagers to agree not to listen to it. Their efforts, however, only seemed to increase rock's popularity. The music became both a means and a symbol of rebellion among teenagers.

Rock 'n' roll took shape as an original

American music form in the 1950s, when singers began combining elements of country, blues, and western swing into a style often called "rhythm and blues." The most widely accepted of these singers was Memphis-based Elvis Presley, a white singer who performed in the style of black musicians. Because most white-owned radio stations wouldn't play songs by black performers, many white artists "covered" (re-recorded) black musicians' hits.

In 1955, former western swing musicians Bill Haley and His Comets recorded the first original white rock 'n' roll hit, "Rock around the Clock," which was introduced to many Americans through the movie *The Blackboard Jungle.* An important early black rock musician was Chuck Berry, who wrote a se-

Jerry Lee Lewis was an early star of rock 'n' roll. In the 1950s conservative eyebrows were raised at his piano-pounding hits, like "Whole Lot of Shakin' Goin' On" and "Great Balls of Fire," and at his scandalous private life, making him rock 'n' roll's original Bad Influence.

ries of parts, called "licks" or "riffs," for electric guitar. These licks formed the basis of many rock songs and are still widely copied today.

During the late 1950s and early 1960s, vocal styles became more important than instruments in rock music. Groups such as the Platters, the Drifters, and the Beach Boys featured as many as five vocalists. The Everly Brothers introduced traditional country harmony to rock 'n' roll with a distinctive vocal sound that influenced such later groups as the Byrds and the Beatles.

Groups from England began to be popular in the United States in the early 1960s. Although most of the music was heavily influenced by Americans such as Chuck Berry and the Everly Brothers, the English groups had a unique style of dress and performance that set them apart. Beginning in 1964, this period was called the "British Invasion," because groups from England had taken over the lists, or charts, of best-selling records. The most popular group from this period was the Beatles: at one point in 1965, eight of the top ten songs on the charts were theirs. Other popular British groups of this period were the Rolling Stones, the Who, and Herman's Hermits.

The early sixties also saw the emergence of soul, a secular outgrowth of predominantly black church music. Combining the powerful styles of gospel music with the messages and accessibility of rock, artists such as Ray Charles, James Brown, and Percy Sledge demonstrated the continuing influence of early black music on rock 'n' roll and paved the way for later artists like Aretha Franklin.

In the 1950s and early 1960s, most rock songs like earlier popular music were about boy-girl relationships. By the midsixties, the Byrds, Bob Dylan, and the Beatles were performing songs that asked meaningful questions about life, peace, and complex social issues such as poverty, racial discrimination, and the Vietnam War. Peter, Paul, and Mary's "Blowin' in the Wind," written by Dylan, was sung at the 1963 March on Washington and became an anthem of peace.

New Styles Emerge

A new sound, typified by groups like the Jefferson Airplane and the Grateful Dead, began to emerge on the rock scene in the late 1960s. Called psychedelic, it used new recording technology to create unusual sounds. The most notable psychedelic artist was Jimi Hendrix, who pioneered the use of distortion and special effects with the guitar. Although he recorded only a handful of albums before his death in 1970, they continue to sell millions of copies a year.

The psychedelic music of the late sixties paved the way for the sophisticated "art-rock" period of the early seventies. Bands, including the Moody Blues, Electric Light Orchestra, and Pink Floyd, began experimenting with combining classical music

The Grateful Dead emerged from San Francisco's psychedelic subculture in the 1960s, experimenting with rock and blues in an improvisatory style. Loyal fans of two generations— "Deadheads"—continue to make the Dead the most enduring live rock band.

styles with rock 'n' roll. The piano and the newly invented synthesizer competed with the electric guitar as the most important instrument.

As rock became more popular, concerts moved out of small clubs and into giant stadiums and outdoor festivals. One of the most notable was the Woodstock Music and Art Fair held for three days in 1969 near Bethel, New York. It was attended by over 300,000 young people.

By this point, rock had become big business. But it had been created by and for young people, and the audiences rebelled against what they considered the selling-out of rock 'n' roll. The result was two new styles of rock that appeared in the midseventies: punk/new wave and disco. Punk and new wave were both popularized by musicians who felt alienated from the world in general and the big business of music in particular. Punk began as a political and musical revolt: groups like the Ramones, the Sex Pistols, and the Clash scorned the fashions and life-styles of famous rock stars while demonstrating that rock could be expressive without expensive equipment or sophisticated technique. New wave groups like Devo, Roxy Music, and the Residents, in contrast, used synthesizers and unusual singing styles to sound as different as possible from traditional rock.

Disco brought dance back to rock. The term *disco* is short for *discotheque,* a type of nightclub that offered music from albums, or "disks," instead of a live performance. Songs by artists such as Donna Summer, K.C. and the Sunshine Band, and the Village People emphasized a consistent, heavy beat ideal for dancing while eliminating the meaningful lyrics—or in many instances, *all* lyrics—that had characterized rock in the sixties. Disco fashions and life-styles gained wide popularity through the movie *Saturday Night Fever.*

Music videos, in the form of M T V, brought enormous changes to rock. For the first time, a cable channel was devoted to visual presentations of rock music. Physical appeal had always been an important part of rock and roll, but suddenly the presentation of the music became as important as the music itself. This gave rise to new types of performers like George Michael, Prince, Madonna, and Michael Jackson, all of whom combined the musical and visual sides of rock effectively enough to become celebrities as well as multimillionaires.

The problem, as in the seventies, was that young audiences felt that many rock performers had sold out. And again, in the late 1980s and early 1990s, a backlash created new strains of rock: rap, a black music and dance style, combined elements of disco and rock with relevant spoken lyrics and a hard urban edge. While rap has not enjoyed the universal acceptance of disco, artists such as Hammer, Salt 'n' Pepa, and DJ Jazzy Jeff and the Fresh Prince have found a wide audience. Grunge, metal, and thrash are all variations of an angry, hard-edged sound played by artists such as Nirvana, Pearl Jam, Metallica, and Anthrax. Like punk, these types of rock have moved from the underground music scene to become major rock styles.

See also Berry, Chuck; Dylan, Bob; Music; Presley, Elvis; Sixties, The; Woodstock.

TED REYNOLDS
GEORG W. TURNER

ROEBLING, JOHN
ROEBLING, WASHINGTON

(John: 1806–69; Washington: 1837–1926)
Engineers and bridge builders.

As a young engineer, born and educated in Germany, John Roebling developed a keen interest in constructing bridges—especially those in which the roadways were suspended from chains. In 1831, he immigrated to the United States and settled near Pittsburgh, Pennsylvania. The construction of canals was then at its height, and Roebling worked on some canal projects, mainly building dams and locks. He was troubled by the weakness and high cost of the thick hemp ropes used to haul the loaded boats up and down slopes. So he invented and began manufacturing stronger and cheaper cables made from twisted metal wire.

In 1846, Roebling completed his first suspension bridge, built to carry a road over the Monongahela River at Pittsburgh. His first suspension bridge that was strong enough to

The Brooklyn Bridge under construction in 1881. John Roebling had just begun directing the building of the suspension bridge in 1869 when he was injured in an accident and died. His son, Washington, took over the massive project and saw it completed in 1883.

carry railroad cars was constructed at Niagara Falls between 1851 and 1855.

Roebling was appointed chief engineer to direct the building of the Brooklyn Bridge, a spectacular structure that would soar 1,595 feet across the East River and connect Brooklyn to Manhattan. Just as work was about to begin in 1869 on the bridge—America's greatest engineering marvel of the nineteenth century—a ferryboat smashed into the pilings on which Roebling was standing and crushed some of his toes. Tetanus set in, and he died a short time later.

His son, Washington Roebling, who was also an engineer, promised to finish the project that his father had started. But in 1872 he developed a crippling illness while working in a compressed-air chamber used for underwater construction. From that time until the bridge was completed eleven years later, he directed its construction from his house overlooking the site. He watched the work through a telescope set at his window, and then his wife, Emily, would carry his instructions to the crews.

Amid huge bursts of fireworks, the Brooklyn Bridge was opened on May 24, 1883. The tolls at that time were a penny for a pedestrian, two cents for a sheep, and ten cents for a horse and carriage.

EDMUND LINDOP

ROE V. WADE

Abortion was legalized in 1973 when the Supreme Court decided *Roe* v. *Wade*, one of its most controversial cases. In that case a pregnant woman from Texas wanted to terminate her pregnancy but could not legally do so because in that state abortion was a crime unless it was necessary to save the life of the pregnant woman. *Roe* v. *Wade* was a class action suit. This means that it was brought not just in the name of one woman but on behalf of all women in a similar situation.

The Court declared that having an abortion is part of a woman's right to privacy. This right is not absolute. It differs according to the stage of pregnancy. The justices divided pregnancy into three three-month parts, or trimesters. In the first trimester a woman has the right to make the abortion decision with her doctor and without interference from the government. During the second trimester the government can regulate abortion procedures but only in order to protect the health of a pregnant woman. But in the third trimester, after the fetus reaches viability—the point at which it can survive outside the woman's body—the government can ban abortions except if they are necessary to save the life or health of the woman. The Court justified this by arguing that the state does have an interest in protecting potential life and that that interest outweighs a woman's privacy rights in the third trimester of pregnancy.

See also Abortion.

ROMAN CATHOLIC CHURCH
See Catholic Church.

ROOSEVELT, ELEANOR

(1884–1962)   Social reformer, Democratic politician, and First Lady (1933–45); recognized as the most influential woman of her time.

Eleanor Roosevelt struggled to overcome an anguished childhood and a sheltered upper-class background. The daughter of wealthy New York socialites, she was a timid child whose mother told her, "You have no looks,

so see to it that you have manners." By the time she was ten, both of her unhappy parents were dead. She was reared by relatives, who sent her to an exclusive girls' finishing school in England. The headmistress, Marie Souvestre, recognizing in Eleanor special qualities of mind and spirit, encouraged the shy young student and became a lifelong influence.

In 1905 Eleanor married her distant cousin, Franklin D. Roosevelt, an aspiring politician. She settled down as a respectable society matron in an era when a woman's life was ruled by her husband's interests and needs. When Franklin was stricken by polio in 1921, Eleanor agreed to act as his political stand-in while he recuperated. Hesitantly at first, then with growing confidence and skill, she became a political power in her own right, working for the women's division of the Democratic Party and forging a unique political partnership with her husband when he

First Lady Eleanor Roosevelt (foreground) sits with soldiers at a party on the White House lawn.

became governor of New York in 1929 and president in 1933.

During her years in the White House, Eleanor Roosevelt transformed the role of America's First Lady. She became the first president's wife to have a public life and career. Though she held no official position, she had a powerful impact on public opinion. Through her newspaper columns, press conferences, lectures, radio broadcasts, and endless travels throughout America, she publicized her views on social justice, civil rights, equality for women, and world peace. Behind the scenes, she urged her husband to support causes she believed in. The most outspoken of First Ladies, and the most controversial, she became a passionate advocate for the weak and disadvantaged in American society.

When she attended a conference in the segregated South in 1939, she was told that blacks and whites were not permitted to sit together in the auditorium. They were required by law to sit on opposite sides of the auditorium's center aisle. The First Lady refused to obey the segregation order and sat on the blacks' side. Informed by the police that she was violating the law, she had a chair placed in the middle of the center aisle and sat there.

After her husband's death in 1945, Eleanor Roosevelt continued her activities on a global scale, serving as an American delegate to the United Nations, where her work on behalf of human rights earned her the title "First Lady of the World." Her unfailing energy and curiosity were legendary, and her continued popularity with the American people astonished politicians in both parties. Polls consistently named her the most admired woman in the world. Through her extensive travels, lectures, and writings, and by personal example, she championed her beliefs until her death,

exerting a lasting influence on the course of American democracy and on the social attitudes of the twentieth century.

See also Roosevelt, Franklin D.

For further reading: Russell Freedman, *Eleanor Roosevelt: A Life of Discovery* (New York: Clarion Books, 1993).

RUSSELL FREEDMAN

ROOSEVELT, FRANKLIN D.

(1882–1945)   Thirty-second president of the United States (1933–45).

During his twelve years in the White House, Roosevelt faced not just one national crisis but two. He led the country through the Great Depression of the 1930s. Then, as commander in chief, he guided the nation to victory during the Second World War.

Roosevelt was an only child who enjoyed a privileged boyhood on his parents' Hudson

President Franklin D. Roosevelt greets a crowd in Warm Springs, Georgia.

River estate at Hyde Park, New York. Educated at Harvard College and Columbia Law School, he married Eleanor Roosevelt, a distant cousin, went into politics, won election to the state senate in 1910, and served as assistant secretary of the navy during the First World War. In 1921 he was struck down by polio. Although he regained robust health in every other respect, his legs remained paralyzed and useless. Encouraged by his wife to continue his political career, he proved his fitness in 1928 by campaigning across New York State and won the governorship. In 1932 Roosevelt defeated Herbert Hoover for the presidency.

Roosevelt took office during the darkest days of the Great Depression. Millions of families were in desperate need, and the economy seemed about to collapse. The nation was shrouded in pessimism and gloom. The new president acted swiftly to restore confidence. He declared that it was the duty of government to regulate the economy and expand the choices available to the poor and powerless. During his administration, the national government, for the first time, made itself responsible for the welfare of those Americans who suffered economic hardship through no fault of their own.

Roosevelt's approach was frankly experimental. If a program failed, he dropped it and tried another. Some of the lasting reforms introduced by his New Deal include unemployment insurance, the Social Security program for the elderly and disabled, bank deposit insurance, and federal guarantees of the right to join a union. Roosevelt's opponents charged that he was strangling free enterprise and turning the nation into a gigantic welfare state, but his policies won a huge following. In 1936 he was overwhelmingly reelected.

When Roosevelt first came to office, isolationism was strong in America. Isolationists felt that the United States should concentrate on its own affairs and not worry about other countries. But with the rise of German and Japanese aggression during the 1930s, the nation under Roosevelt's leadership took on the responsibilities of a world power. After the country entered World War II, he proved a popular and effective commander in chief. He led the nation in the huge mobilization of manpower and resources needed to fight a war on two fronts and traveled to war zones despite his disability. In his meetings with other wartime leaders, he helped create the United Nations and the framework of the postwar world. When he died in 1945, the war was almost over and the United States had become the most powerful nation in history.

Roosevelt occupied the White House longer than anyone else. The only president to be elected to a third term, he served part of a fourth term as well. He was so active and projected such a buoyant optimism that people forgot that he could not walk, or even stand up, without help. No president has had a greater impact on that office or done more to change the relationship between ordinary citizens and their government.

See also Presidency; Roosevelt, Eleanor. *For events during Roosevelt's administration, see* Atlantic Charter; Civilian Conservation Corps; D-Day; Depressions and Recessions; Dust Bowl; Federal Theatre Project; Federal Writers' Project; Four Freedoms; Good Neighbor Policy; Hundred Days; Japanese-Americans, Internment of; Labor Movement; Lend-Lease Act; Liberty League; Manhattan Project; Marches on Washington; National Labor Relations Act; National Recovery Act; Neutrality Acts; New Deal; Pearl Harbor, Attack on; Public Works Administration; *Scottsboro* Case; Sit-Down Strikes; Tennessee Valley Authority; Works Progress Administration; World War II; Yalta Conference.

For further reading: Russell Freedman, *Franklin Delano Roosevelt* (New York: Clarion Books, 1991).

RUSSELL FREEDMAN

ROOSEVELT, THEODORE

(1858–1919)   *Twenty-sixth president of the United States (1901–09).*

Teddy Roosevelt's zest for life and his many accomplishments made him one of the most popular presidents in American history.

Roosevelt, born into an old New York family, was a rancher in the Dakota Territory, a historian of note, and a heroic commander of the Rough Riders during the Spanish-American War. He was also an explorer and big-game hunter. More important, he was perhaps the best field naturalist of his time and the nation's greatest conservation president.

Roosevelt graduated from Harvard in 1880 and two years later won election to the New York State Assembly. By the end of his third term he had become the leader of the reform Republicans. Distraught over the death of his wife in childbirth in 1884, he went to Dakota's Badlands to run cattle. He returned and lost a campaign for mayor of New York City in 1886. He then married his childhood friend, Edith Carow, and they had five children.

In 1889 Roosevelt joined the U.S. Civil Service Commission and soon became its head. By the time of his resignation in 1895 he had transformed it into an effective agency. As president of the Board of Police Commissioners of New York City from 1895 to 1897, he modernized the force and reduced graft. He became assistant secretary of the navy in 1897 but resigned after a year to organize the Rough Riders. Elected governor of New York after the end of the war with Spain, he drove numerous progressive measures through the legislature and was "kicked upstairs" to the vice presidency by conservative Republicans. He became the youngest president in U.S. history upon William McKinley's assassination in September 1901.

The famous quotation from one of Theodore Roosevelt's early speeches—"speak softly and carry a big stick"—has often been used to characterize his aggressive foreign policy.

As president Roosevelt strove both to balance and advance the interests of farmers, workers, and industrialists. He early won a reputation as a "trust buster" by destroying some of the most obvious monopolies, although he preferred simply to regulate the trusts. Following election in 1904 to a term in his own right, he became more progressive. He supported regulation of the railroad, food, and drug industries, and he called for income and inheritance taxes. Meanwhile he created 150 national forests and 51 bird preserves. "Is there any law that will prevent me from declaring Pelican Island a Federal Bird Reservation?" he asked. Told that there was none, he replied: "Very well, I so declare it."

A fervent nationalist, Roosevelt fostered his country's foreign interests. "I took Panama," he boasted. He was happy to shoulder the burdens of world power. In the Roosevelt Corollary to the Monroe Doctrine, he assumed the right of the United States to intervene in the affairs of Latin American states. In 1906 he won the Nobel Peace Prize for facilitating mediation of the Russian-Japanese war.

Roosevelt's growing commitment to an expanded regulatory and welfare program (called the New Nationalism) made conflict between him and his successor, William Howard Taft, almost inevitable. He could not prevent Taft from receiving the Republican nomination in 1912, so he ran on the Progressive, or Bull Moose, Party ticket. He outpolled Taft but lost to Democrat Woodrow Wilson. Roosevelt strongly supported American participation in the First World War, but opposed the League of Nations as conceived by Wilson.

See also New Nationalism; Progressive Parties; Spanish-American War. *For events during Roosevelt's administration, see* Antitrust Movement; Brownsville Affair; Conservation and Environmental Movements; Muckrakers; Panama Canal; Pure Food and Drug Act; Roosevelt Corollary.

WILLIAM H. HARBAUGH

ROOSEVELT COROLLARY

When President James Monroe declared in his Monroe Doctrine that the age of colonization in the Western Hemisphere was over, the European powers did not take the statement seriously. But with the growing power of the United States, especially after the Spanish-American War, Great Britain, Germany, and other imperialist-minded nations began to realize that their interests in the region could best be protected by letting the United States act as a "big policeman" there.

This was the situation in 1904 when the European powers were considering intervening in the Dominican Republic, which had defaulted on debts owed to some of their citizens. In a message to Congress, President Theodore Roosevelt announced that though the Monroe Doctrine prohibited such intervention, "chronic wrongdoing" in Latin American countries might require the United States to exercise "international police power" in the offending nations. As he said in another message to Congress in 1905, "We do not intend to permit the Monroe Doctrine to be used by any nation . . . as a shield to protect it from the consequences of its own misdeeds." These statements are known as the Roosevelt Corollary, or logical deduction from the Monroe Doctrine.

See also Monroe Doctrine.

ROSENBERG CASE

In 1950, during the height of the postwar red scare and concern about possible communist spying in the United States, Klaus Fuchs, a British atomic scientist, was discovered to have provided Soviet officials with information about the making of atomic bombs. It came out that several Americans were also involved, among them Julius Rosenberg, a machine shop operator, and his wife, Ethel. The Rosenbergs maintained they were innocent, but they were convicted of providing vital secret information to the Soviets and sentenced to death.

No one claimed that the Rosenbergs were professional spies or that they had done anything more than pass on information obtained by others. They appealed the death sentence to the Supreme Court. By a vote of six to three, the Court upheld the sentence,

Ethel and Julius Rosenberg after they were convicted for espionage in 1951. They became the first U.S. citizens to receive the death sentence for wartime spying.

and on June 19, 1953, they were executed. The Rosenberg execution remains controversial. Many people feel that the two were victims of anticommunist hysteria—that even if they were guilty they did not deserve the death penalty.

See also Anticommunism.

RUTH, BABE

(1895–1948)   *Baseball player.*

Ruth, who played with the Boston Red Sox (1914–19), New York Yankees (1920–34), and Boston Braves (1935), was the greatest and most famous player in baseball history. A beloved popular hero, he was one of the most appealing celebrities of the 1920s and 1930s.

Babe Ruth (born George Herman Ruth) learned to play baseball in St. Mary's Industrial School for Boys, where his parents placed him at the age of seven. His father, a Baltimore saloonkeeper, used to beat him brutally, and young George got into a lot of trouble. At St. Mary's he played the game so well that while still a teenager he was signed to pitch for the International League Baltimore Orioles. When his manager, Jack Dunn, walked out on the field with the young prospect, one of the Orioles said, "Here comes Dunn and his new Babe"—and Babe Ruth received his lifelong nickname. By the end of the year Babe had been promoted to the Boston Red Sox in the American League.

Babe Ruth's baseball accomplishments were unique. He was the only player in history to master both pitching and hitting. Even though he is known mostly as a hitter, he might have been elected to the Hall of Fame even if he had stayed a pitcher. Ruth was already a superstar when he astounded the baseball world in 1920 by hitting not only more home runs than any previous player, but more than any other *team* in the American League.

Before Ruth, baseball strategy had been built around scoring runs one at a time through "scientific" batting (bunts, hit-and-run plays, place hitting), stolen bases, and the complicated scheming called "inside baseball." By showing how power hitting could be at the center of baseball offense, Ruth helped transform the way baseball was played for the rest of the twentieth century.

Fans loved watching Babe Ruth play. His home run hitting for the New York Yankees in 1920–21 helped take fans' minds off the upsetting "Black Sox" betting scandal of 1919. When the new Yankee Stadium opened in 1923, it was called "The House That Ruth Built" because of all the fans he attracted.

Babe Ruth in 1935 during his season with the Boston Braves. Nicknamed the "Bambino" and the "Sultan of Swat," Ruth is considered by many to have been the greatest baseball player of all time.

Ruth's incredible baseball skill, and the ease with which he played the game, amazed his fellow players and still astonishes historians. He held the record for the most career home runs for nearly forty years, until Hank Aaron broke it in 1974. Baseball has always been such a difficult game that fans think of those few who play it well and joyfully and gracefully—Ruth and Shoeless Joe Jackson and Willie Mays, for example—as almost enchanted.

Ruth's fame spread beyond baseball and around the world. He was large, jovial, and easygoing. Boys loved him and Ruth returned the feelings. Known everywhere and by everyone as "the Babe," Ruth himself seemed an oversized child in how he played the game and lived his life.

Babe Ruth was the first athlete to have a press agent who arranged public appearances for a fee. Like modern athletes, he made thousands of dollars from endorsements. His appetite was a legend too. He could eat enormous quantities of food—several dozen hot dogs at a time—and drink quarts of soda and beer.

See also Baseball.

WARREN GOLDSTEIN

S

SACAJAWEA

(1787?–1812?)   *Native American guide and interpreter for the Lewis and Clark Expedition.*

President Thomas Jefferson commissioned Meriwether Lewis and William Clark to ex-

plore the vast unknown northwestern region that America acquired in the Louisiana Purchase of 1803. The two assembled a party of fifty men to map the area and report on its natural resources. They set out from St. Louis, Missouri, in 1804. When they reached what

A painting by N. C. Wyeth of Sacajawea, the Shoshone Indian who was a guide and interpreter on the Lewis and Clark Expedition. Her name means "bird woman."

is now North Dakota that winter, they paused to build a fort and hired a French-Canadian trader named Toussaint Charbonneau as a guide for the rest of the expedition. His wife, a member of the Shoshone tribe, was named Sacajawea (pronounced SAC-uh-juh-WE-uh; also spelled Sacagawea). She came along to speak for them in case they met native tribes along the way.

The crew often ran into difficulties in the wilderness, and Sacajawea repeatedly kept them from becoming lost on their journey. Her greatest service came when they entered Shoshone territory in the Rocky Mountains. There the explorers met a band of suspicious Indians who challenged their further passage—until it was discovered that their chief was Sacajawea's brother. She was able to communicate between the two groups and succeeded in persuading the tribe to give the explorers horses.

Little is known of the life of Sacajawea, whose name means Bird Woman, before or after the time of the Lewis and Clark Expedition. But when the explorers reached the Pacific Ocean in 1805, they acknowledged that they would probably have failed to complete their mission without her help. Sacajawea's intelligence, cooperation, and skill provided much valuable information to the new nation.

See also Indian-White Relations; Lewis and Clark Expedition.

DENNIS WEPMAN

SACCO-VANZETTI CASE

In April 1920 a paymaster and a guard at a Massachusetts shoe company were murdered by two robbers. The next month Bartolomeo Vanzetti, a fish peddler, and Nicola Sacco, a

Nicola Sacco (right) and Bartolomeo Vanzetti (left) in handcuffs. In 1921 they were convicted of robbery and murder and eventually executed. The evidence supporting conviction was slim, and many felt that the fact that they were Italian immigrants and anarchists prejudiced the court against them. The case made worldwide headlines. In 1977, on the fiftieth anniversary of their execution, they were officially declared innocent.

shoemaker, were arrested, charged, and convicted of the crime. The two men were Italian immigrants and also anarchists. The trial judge, Webster Thayer, made it clear from the start that he was convinced they were guilty. Unprejudiced persons who followed the proceedings were convinced that the accused men had not received a fair trial and had been convicted only because they were foreigners and radicals. The dignified behavior of the accused and Vanzetti's moving declaration of his innocence roused widespread sympathy. Extensive efforts were made to get them a new trial.

After long delays, however, Judge Thayer sentenced them to death. On August 23, 1927, they were executed. Later studies of the marks left on bullets fired from a gun owned by Sacco have persuaded some modern historians that he, at least, was guilty. But the case is still controversial, mainly because the unreasoning prejudice of the authorities made a fair trial of the accused impossible.

SAINT-GAUDENS, AUGUSTUS

(1848–1907)   *Sculptor.*

Born in Dublin, the son of a French shoemaker father and an Irish mother who immigrated to New York when he was an infant, Saint-Gaudens became world-renowned for his idealistic, heroic-sized statues. At nineteen, after training as a shell and stone cameo cutter and studying drawing at Cooper Union and the National Academy of Design in New York City, young Gus sailed for Paris to complete his artistic education at the Ecole des Beaux-Arts under François Jouffroy. When the Franco-Prussian War broke out in 1870, Saint-Gaudens went to Rome where he modeled his first large sculpture, *Hiawatha,* which was executed in marble and is now in Saratoga, New York.

Returning to New York, Saint-Gaudens plunged into sculpting full-length statues of Adm. David Farragut for Madison Square in New York and merchant privateersman Robert Richard Randall for Sailors' Snug Harbor, Staten Island. His largest body of works consists of public monuments that memorialize Civil War heroes including Abraham Lincoln (Chicago), Robert Shaw (Boston), and Gen. William Tecumseh Sherman (New York). His beautiful *Diana* (his only nude) graced the top of the original Madison Square Garden for thirty years. At the request of President Theodore Roosevelt, he modeled *Liberty* in

an Indian headdress for the twenty-dollar gold piece and other U.S. coins. His finest work is perhaps an enigmatic hooded bronze figure he sculpted for the Adams Memorial in Rock Creek Cemetery, Washington, D.C.

"A terrific worker" (his own words), who often pushed himself to his emotional and physical limits, Saint-Gaudens advised those who would excel in any field: "Conceive an idea. Then stick to it. Those who hang on are the only ones who amount to anything."

In Cornish, New Hampshire, Saint-Gaudens's country estate named Aspet (for his father's village in France) is now a National Historic Site. The sculptor's house, studios, and gardens are open to the public.

See also Painting and Sculpture.

PATRICIA CONDON JOHNSTON

SALEM WITCH TRIALS

Most colonists in late-seventeenth-century New England believed in witches. Charges that one or another person was under the spell of the devil and his witches, and were bent on bringing destruction to the community, were commonplace. But by far the greatest number of these accusations occurred in Salem Village, Massachusetts, in 1692. A group of teenaged girls (who had participated in fortune telling and had probably been influenced by tales of witchcraft and voodoo) began experiencing spectacular fits, during which they thrashed about, wincing and shrieking. They accused a number of local residents of being witches who had cast spells on them. They pointed their fingers at mostly middle-aged women, but also accused men and even a four-year-old child. Mass hysteria ensued, and the accusations snowballed. Ar-

The trial of two suspected witches in Salem, Massachusetts, in 1692.

rest followed arrest until hundreds had been charged. Many were found guilty on the basis of "spectral evidence"—testimony based on ghostly visions or voices. Twenty-seven people stood trial, and nineteen were hanged. One victim of the witch-hunt frenzy, Giles Corey, was crushed to death by heavy stones.

Few colonists dared to question the proceedings lest they too be accused of keeping company with the devil.

By the end of the year, however, the community had grown uneasy as the charges became more and more outrageous. Doubts set in, especially when some of Salem's most upstanding citizens were accused of practicing witchcraft. The trials ceased and the remaining prisoners caught up in the Salem witch-hunt were released. Accusations of witchcraft decreased dramatically thereafter throughout New England.

See also Colonial America.

SALINGER, J. D.

(1919–) *Writer.*

Although he has published only one novel and a handful of short stories, New York–born Jerome David Salinger has become one of the most popular American authors. His novel *The Catcher in the Rye* (1951), a portrait of a sensitive teenage boy, was a best-seller and has remained one of the defining works of its time.

Salinger wrote some conventional stories for magazines during the early 1940s, but it was with "A Perfect Day for Bananafish," the story of a young intellectual's suicide published in *The New Yorker* in 1948, that he first attracted the attention of serious readers.

Three years later, *The Catcher in the Rye* appeared and created a sensation. It is the story of Holden Caulfield, a perceptive sixteen-year-old so distressed by the hypocrisy of the people around him that he runs away from his boarding school. His experiences in New York City further confuse and disgust him and finally lead to a nervous breakdown. Salinger's command of adolescent speech and insight into the mind of his unhappy hero struck a responsive chord among high school and college students. Holden's revolt against "phoniness" made him a symbol for the youth of his generation.

Salinger's three other books are all collections of short stories. *Nine Stories* (1953) reprinted "A Perfect Day for Bananafish," which introduced the Glass family, the subjects of all his later stories. *Franny and Zooey* (1961) and *Raise High the Roofbeam, Carpenters* and *Seymour: An Introduction* (1963) continue the chronicle of these brilliant, troubled young people. Lacking in plot but rich in psychological and philosophical content, the four long stories that make up these two volumes were admired by many but criticized by some reviewers as obscure and pretentious.

Salinger has published nothing since 1963 except for one short story in the *New Yorker* in 1965. An intensely private man, he withdrew from the larger society in the 1960s and lives in seclusion in a small New Hampshire town.

See also Literature; Literature, Children's and Young Adult.

DENNIS WEPMAN

SALK, JONAS

(1914–) *Developer of first polio vaccine.*

Salk won international fame and the gratitude of millions of parents in 1955 when he created the first vaccine for polio (short for *poliomyelitis*). This disease had killed or crippled thousands of children and adults. Polio is caused by a virus, an organism much smaller than a bacterium. The illness struck chiefly in summertime. In public places where many children shared the water in a swimming pool or used the same play equipment, the polio virus could spread easily. In the late 1940s and early 1950s each summer brought a new epidemic of polio. Some victims died from the disease; others were paralyzed for life, unable to breathe without the help of an "iron lung," a mechanical breathing machine in which the victim lay with only his or her head exposed. Millions of other victims were temporarily or permanently crippled, and desperate parents tried everything they could think of to keep their children from contracting the disease.

Polio could also attack adults; Franklin D. Roosevelt contracted polio in 1921 and was permanently crippled by the disease. In 1937, as president, Roosevelt set up the National Foundation for Infantile Paralysis (another name for polio) to raise money for research. Its annual "March of Dimes" campaign supported Salk's research in the late 1940s.

Salk was born in New York City; his mother disapproved of his original desire to study law, so he selected medical research as his second choice. He proved to be exceptionally gifted in medicine and was known in his medical school class for his extraordinary ability to diagnose illnesses.

At the time, medical authorities believed that it was not possible to create a vaccine to immunize people against viral diseases. Salk thought otherwise, and he proved that he was right. After creating the influenza vaccine (his first viral vaccine), he moved to research on polio, ultimately developing the polio vaccine. The Salk vaccine was declared safe and effective by medical authorities at a press conference held on April 12, 1955. Next, he founded the Salk Institute for Biological Sciences in La Jolla, California. Today it is one of the world's most important medical research centers.

In 1984 Salk began work on an AIDS (acquired immune deficiency syndrome) vaccine. It is designed as a *treatment* vaccine for those already infected, rather than as a *preventive* vaccine to protect those who have not yet been infected. This unusual approach was criticized at first and then endorsed (and in some cases adopted) by other researchers. Salk's research may result in significant advances in our understanding of AIDS and in the ability to control its spread.

See also Epidemics; Medicine.

LYDIA BRONTE

SALVATION ARMY

The Salvation Army is an international religious and charitable organization based on Christian principles but not connected with any formal church. Its goal is to lead people to God by means of various social services, which it provides equally to all races and religions. Its programs include emergency disaster services, free meals for the homeless, help for alcoholics and drug addicts, day care for the children of working mothers, clubs and residences for the elderly, summer camps for the poor, family counseling, and assistance to prison inmates and parolees.

The Army was founded in England in 1865 by William Booth, a Methodist minister who worked with poor people and social outcasts in London. Originally called the Christian Mission, it was given its present name in 1878, when Booth reorganized it on military lines. Ministers of both sexes serve as officers holding military rank, and members, who provide voluntary service to the Corps, are its soldiers. By 1890 the Army had divisions in Europe, Australia, India, and North America.

Salvation Army work began in the United States in 1880. In 1904 the founder's daughter, Evangeline Booth, became the U.S. commander, with her main office in New York

City. She held that post until 1934, when she became the general of the international Army, headquartered in London.

Training for officers includes a two-year course in special Salvation Army schools and a period of fieldwork in the Army's community centers. A graduate holds the rank of lieutenant and is also an ordained minister, authorized to perform marriages. Although officially a religious body, the Salvation Army stresses practical human services, and the training of its officers emphasizes the psychological and sociological needs of the people it helps.

The Salvation Army was created to appeal to those who are not members of any church, and it has always avoided the formality of traditional Christian church services. Its public meetings, often conducted on city sidewalks, include the music of its brass bands and singing groups as an essential part of its ministry.

DENNIS WEPMAN

SANGER, MARGARET

(1879–1966) *Pioneer birth-control advocate.*

From the early part of the twentieth century to her death, Sanger devoted her life to educating people about birth control. Even though it cost her many personal sacrifices, she refused to give up the struggle for the right of a woman to plan the size of her family for the sake of her own health and her family's standard of living. Today the right to practice birth control has been established by the U.S. Supreme Court. It is hard to believe that Margaret Sanger went to jail nine times to win this right.

Born in Corning, New York, to Anne and Michael Higgins, Sanger grew up in a poor Irish family of eleven children. Her mother died of hard work and tuberculosis as Margaret was finishing high school. Sanger came to believe that without the burdens of such a large family, her mother's life would have been much better. While training to be a nurse in New York City, Margaret married William Sanger, an architect. When their three children had begun school, she returned to nursing, taking only childbirth cases on the Lower East Side. The tenements there were crowded with the immigrant poor. Pregnancy was almost a permanent condition for the wives of these working families.

Many of the women wanted to stop having more babies, but they didn't know how or the methods they heard of didn't work. Desperate, they often turned to illegal abortions, ending up injured or dead. It was illegal in the United States then to advocate or discuss birth control openly, since many people be-

Margaret Sanger (right) and her sister Ethel Byrne, during their 1916 trial for establishing a birth control clinic in Brooklyn, New York. Providing birth control or information about it was at that time illegal.

lieved that the practice was "unnatural" or against the will of God and that talking about it was somehow obscene. But appalled by what she was seeing, Sanger was determined to make doctors and the public face the facts. She gave speeches, wrote articles and pamphlets, and organized public demonstrations to break the wall of silence and fear that surrounded the issue.

She founded a birth-control magazine and a group that was the forerunner of today's Planned Parenthood Federation, with birth-control clinics throughout America and the world. She often traveled in Europe, looking for simpler, safer, and cheaper methods of contraception (another word for "birth control"). By the 1930s her long campaign had won not only popular agreement but the backing of the medical profession, which had not always supported her.

Margaret Sanger stood up to relentless persecution and frequent jailing. And she made her message prevail: that human beings should be allowed to control their own lives, and that with this independence they would raise society to a new level of dignity.

See also Birth Control.

For further reading: Milton Meltzer (with Lawrence Loder), *Margaret Sanger: Pioneer of Birth Control* (New York: Crowell, 1969).

MILTON MELTZER

SANITARY COMMISSION

This organization was set up to care for sick and wounded Union soldiers during the Civil War. Although privately financed, it was officially authorized by President Abraham Lincoln in 1861 to inspect army camps and hospitals and to supply nurses, ambulances, and other medical services for the troops. Its work sometimes conflicted with that of the regular Army Medical Bureau and also with the private Christian Commission, which provided food and other nonmedical supplies for soldiers and sailors. Members of the Christian Commission believed that the Sanitary Commission was at times more interested in providing high-profile "war work" for its upper-class members than in caring for the medical needs of ordinary soldiers and building their morale.

Whatever the motives of some of its leaders, the Sanitary Commission did much good work during the war. It was therefore popular with the general public and had considerable influence on Congress, which it encouraged, for example, to promote younger, more progressive army surgeons. In the long run it demonstrated the importance of private philanthropy. By working as nurses and in other jobs, many women became interested in taking a more active role in public affairs. Numbers of postwar feminists worked for the Sanitary Commission during the war.

See also Civil War.

SCALAWAGS
See Carpetbaggers and Scalawags.

SCANDALS
See Corruption and Scandals in Government; Iran-contra Affair; Teapot Dome Affair; Watergate.

SCANDINAVIAN AMERICANS

Many Americans trace their ancestry back to the Scandinavian countries of Denmark, Finland, Iceland, Norway, and Sweden. Scandinavians were the first Europeans to arrive in

America, establishing colonies in Newfoundland and perhaps other places over five hundred years before Columbus.

Those settlements disappeared, but in 1638 (eighteen years after the *Mayflower* arrived in America) Scandinavians returned, this time to the land around the Delaware River. Swedes built a settlement there, which they called New Sweden. Some Finns were even more adventurous, heading straight into the woods where the Delaware Indians used slash-and-burn farming and loved sauna baths—just as the Finns always had. They got along especially well.

Later Scandinavian-American settlements tended to be like New Sweden: small farming communities on permanently cleared land. Most sprang up in the 1800s, a time of poor economic conditions and overpopulation in Scandinavia. One location was the Fox River valley in Illinois. Another was the rolling Wisconsin prairie where Norwegian mountaineers brought the first skis to the New World.

As the century went on, Scandinavian Americans settled more generally across the country. But they tended to stay in small, fiercely independent groups whose religious, cultural, and language differences divided them even from one another. That sometimes made other Americans suspicious. During World War I, when distrust of other nationalities deepened, some states passed laws forcing newspapers printed in Scandinavian languages to stop publishing temporarily.

In the face of such attitudes, later generations of Scandinavian Americans began to feel uncomfortably isolated. Many chose not to learn the languages of their parents, deciding just to "melt" into mainstream American society. Still, enough others maintained the old customs to keep their heritage alive;

towns like California's Solvang are centers of Scandinavian crafts and festivals. Popular humorist Garrison Keillor has entertained readers and radio audiences with stories of Scandinavian American life in mythical Lake Wobegon, Minnesota.

Notable Scandinavian Americans in this century have included the actresses Greta Garbo and Ingrid Bergman, aviation pioneer Charles Lindbergh, and Supreme Court Justices Earl Warren and William Rehnquist.

JAN CHARLES HALUSKA

SCHOOLS
See Education: Elementary and High School; Education: Universities and Colleges; Education, Women's.

SCIENCE AND TECHNOLOGY

In the early days of colonial settlement, American scientists were untrained amateurs, few and scattered, with almost no books, instruments, money, or even encouragement from others. They could do little more than gather data about the natural world around them and send the information to Europe for study. By 1700, however, Boston, which pioneered in education and had ties with European scientists, had developed a small scientific community. After 1720, as America grew, other towns followed suit, especially Philadelphia, New York, and Charleston. A few libraries, colleges, and newspapers appeared. Communication improved. Americans, most notably Benjamin Franklin, began contributing scientific ideas as well as data. But since most Americans were small farmers who made their own equipment, they added little to technology other than improving wooden implements such as ax handles.

Science in the New Nation

In the 1760s friction with England stirred the pride and ambition of American scientists. The Revolution (1775–81) disrupted their work, but the winning of independence challenged them to prove that freedom nurtured science. Museums, journals, societies, and colleges sprang up. During the next half century the rise of mechanized industry in England, the fast-growing American market for goods, and the immigration of British engineers, mechanics, and craftsmen also stimulated American technology. The very size of the new nation created a demand for improved transportation. Steamboats, canals, and eventually railroads were built by inventors and by engineers trained in American technical schools.

Meanwhile President Thomas Jefferson fostered the study of nature by backing the Lewis and Clark Expedition and the Coast Survey. By 1830 states were setting up geological surveys, colleges were hiring scientists as teachers, and the public was taking an interest. The army undertook scientific exploration of the vast western territory acquired in the 1840s. This prolonged the American tendency to gather data on natural history rather than do long-term research and thinking.

Nevertheless, modern American science

An N. C. Wyeth painting shows a twenty-two-year-old Cyrus McCormick in 1831, striding behind his ground-breaking invention, the first successful mechanical reaper. This horse-drawn device helped gather and cut grain, making harvesting faster and easier, and reducing costs for farmers and consumers.

took shape between 1846 and 1876. It followed the lead of Europe in professionalism, specialization, graduate education, governmental and philanthropic support, and organizations of scientists. An inner circle of leading scientists, who jokingly called themselves the "Lazzaroni," or "beggars," because of their continual need to seek funds, promoted all this and fought against sloppy science. They led in establishing the American Association for the Advancement of Science (AAAS) in 1847. One of them, Joseph Henry, headed the new Smithsonian Institution, which collected data and encouraged research. The Lazzaroni also campaigned for universities like those in Germany, which gave professors time and money for research. By 1876, when the Johns Hopkins University was founded with an emphasis on research, several colleges were awarding Ph.D.s in science.

To win public support, scientists claimed that technology depended on science. That was not generally true until the end of the century. But technologists were adopting the scientists' research methods and following their example in developing journals, professional associations, and higher education.

Progress after the 1860s

Like the Revolution, the Civil War (1861–65) hurt American science by drawing scientists into military service, distracting them, and diverting resources to war purposes. Societies like the AAAS were suspended, others were weakened, and some died out. Southern science, weak even before the war, was devastated by military operations and financial collapse. Neither side tried seriously to develop new weapons, expecting the war to be short. But because southerners, who had previously blocked federal aid to science and technology, had left Congress, the war made possible the establishment of the Department of Agriculture, the system of federal land grants to finance scientific and technological colleges, and the National Academy of Sciences, eventually important as an adviser to the government.

In the half century after the Civil War, inventors and engineers like Thomas A. Edison and Alexander Graham Bell raised America to world leadership in technology. Some, from Edison to Henry Ford, created elaborate technological systems. Tools of great precision and speed made mass production possible on an unprecedented scale. By the start of the twentieth century giant corporations like General Electric and AT&T were setting up major research laboratories, and colleges were training large numbers of professional engineers.

By 1900 the fast-growing state universities were following private institutions in supporting scientific research. They also stimulated science in the Midwest and Far West. The U.S. Army sponsored western scientific explorations and won a famous victory over deadly yellow fever in Cuba and Panama. Beginning in the 1880s the Department of Agriculture conducted important researches on plants, animals, and insects. So Washington, D.C., became a major scientific center. Other centers emerged when the vast new private fortunes of the time endowed great research foundations. And the scientific community formed its own power centers as the AAAS revived and grew, the National Academy enlarged its role, and specialized national associations were formed in fields like chemistry.

Twentieth-Century Developments

As the twentieth century began, American scientists gained ground on Europeans, winning their first Nobel Prizes in 1907 and 1914.

The dreams of the Lazzaroni came true with more basic theory, more long-range strategy, less insistence on quick payoffs, more independence in research, and better balance among scientific fields. The growing interdependence of science and technology enriched and strengthened both. Medicine became more scientific, thanks in part to the rise of bacteriology and foundation-backed research. Americans made major contributions to the understanding of genetics.

World War I (1914–18) aroused government interest in applying science and technology to war. America's part in the war was too brief for the resulting government agencies to achieve much. But some survived afterward, and one ultimately evolved into the National Aeronautics and Space Administration (NASA) in 1958. During the 1920s private support grew in importance. Foundations increased their funding, the federal Commerce Department promoted industrial research, and physics developed strong ties with industry.

American technology captivated the mind of Europe, especially Henry Ford's assembly-line techniques and Frederick Winslow Taylor's principles of "scientific management." But Europe influenced American science, too. Albert Einstein's revolutionary ideas inspired American physics, which in the 1930s moved toward "big science"—huge projects carried out with massive and costly equipment. And in that decade the rise of the Fascists and Nazis enriched American science, as brilliant European refugees like Einstein, Enrico Fermi, and others fled persecution and totalitarianism.

After the 1930s Americans led in winning Nobel science prizes. During World War II, the government put American scientists to work on weapons development, mostly at universities. The most notable new weapons—radar, the proximity fuse (in which a tiny radar device detonated the projectile at the most effective distance from the target), the atom bomb—sprang from prewar research. It was applied technology, the stupendous production of weapons, that won the war. But the atom bomb convinced the nation that science could win, or better yet prevent, the next war.

The cold war rivalry with the Soviet Union led to a massive government research and development (R&D) program. The National

The blastoff of the Space Shuttle Discovery.

Education Defense Act of 1958 strengthened the educational underpinnings of science and led to NASA and the moon landing of 1969. Federal wealth supported a new age of big science not only in high-energy physics but also in astronomy and biomedicine. And big technology armed science with space vehicles, computers, lasers, and other wonders.

Computer Revolution

Americans led in the postwar computer revolution, which was created jointly by scientists and technologists and gave both groups an immensely powerful tool. Though European mathematicians had laid much of the theoretical foundation, Americans conceived and produced the first large-scale automatic digital computer (1937–44) and the first all-electronic, general-purpose computer (1943–45). They also formulated and led in achieving basic objectives such as stored programs, random-access memories, and conditional branching. American advances in solid-state technology, notably the transistor, greatly reduced size and cost and increased reliability and speed. The scope and power of these new instruments accelerated not only technology and most sciences but also industry, transportation, economics, and business. They even entered the home in entertainment equipment and appliances.

With all these triumphs, American science and technology still faced problems. The weight of government tended to unbalance science, tilting it toward certain fields like physics, microbiology, and weapons development. It also cramped scientists by imposing politics and secrecy on their work. Most people admired and respected science, but some did not, such as creationists, environmentalists, and believers in the supernatural. Ameri-

For biographies of men and women prominent in American science and technology, see the following entries:

BANNEKER, BENJAMIN
BELL, ALEXANDER GRAHAM
CARSON, RACHEL
CARVER, GEORGE WASHINGTON
EDISON, THOMAS A.
EINSTEIN, ALBERT
FORD, HENRY
FRANKLIN, BENJAMIN
FULTON, ROBERT
HENRY, JOSEPH
McCLINTOCK, BARBARA
McCORMICK, CYRUS HALL
MITCHELL, MARIA
MORSE, SAMUEL F. B.
OPPENHEIMER, J. ROBERT
WHITNEY, ELI
WRIGHT, ORVILLE AND WILBUR

can science still led the world, but its lead was narrowing. And in applying technology, the Japanese, Germans, and others pulled ahead in some areas. As the third millennium drew near, Americans could be proud but not complacent.

See also Automobiles; Aviation; Industrial Revolution in America; Lewis and Clark Expedition; Medicine; Nuclear Energy; Railroads; Smithsonian Institution; Space Program; Television and Radio.

ROBERT V. BRUCE

SCLC

See Southern Christian Leadership Conference.

SCOPES TRIAL

In 1925, a high school teacher named John T. Scopes was arrested in Dayton, Tennessee, for teaching the theory of evolution to his biology class—the theory that humans gradually evolved over millions of years from lower forms of life. Scopes was charged with violating a state law that prohibited the teaching in public schools of any theory that conflicted with the biblical story of the Creation. The case was nicknamed the "Monkey Trial" because religious fundamentalists were outraged by the suggestion that human beings were not the descendants of Adam and Eve but had evolved from the likes of monkeys.

The Scopes case, which received national attention, was the first jury trial brought to the public by live radio broadcasts. Hordes of spectators converged on Dayton, which took on a carnival-like atmosphere with vendors selling Bibles, toy monkeys, and hot dogs and lemonade.

During the trial William Jennings Bryan, a three-time presidential candidate famous for his eloquent speeches, argued Tennessee's case against Scopes. Clarence Darrow, a renowned trial lawyer known for taking on difficult cases, defended the schoolteacher and his right to teach evolution.

The case became a battle between science and religion. Darrow called only one witness to the stand—Bryan himself. In his testimony, Bryan insisted that every word in the Bible was true, exactly as it was written. He claimed that Jonah had been swallowed whole by a whale, that Eve had literally been made from Adam's rib, and that in 2348 B.C. the world had been flooded and all living things perished except the animals in Noah's ark. In a courtroom, such pronouncements sounded especially out of place, and Bryan

The famous courtroom lawyer Clarence Darrow arguing his case during the Scopes trial of 1925. He defended John T. Scopes, who was arrested for teaching the theory of evolution in his high school biology class. State law prohibited any teachings that conflicted with the Bible, even in a biology class where science was the focus, not religion. Darrow considered Scopes's arrest a violation of academic freedom and declared to the court: "Scopes isn't on trial, civilization is on trial. The prosecution is opening the doors for a reign of bigotry equal to anything in the Middle Ages. No man's belief will be safe if they win."

appeared foolish and shallow. By the time Darrow finished with him, he seemed less a pious defender of the Bible than a buffoon.

Nevertheless, the jury found Scopes guilty. He had, after all, broken the law, even if it was clear to most that it was an unjust law that among other things violated the First Amendment rights of free speech and freedom of religion. The judge fined him one hundred dollars. But religious fundamentalism had been dealt a severe blow by the trial; a real victory had been won for progressive ideas and the advances of science. The law against teaching evolution remained on the books, but it was never again enforced, and evolution continued to be taught in Tennessee schools.

See also Bryan, William Jennings; Darrow, Clarence.

SCOTTSBORO CASE

The *Scottsboro* case involved nine black youths, aged thirteen to twenty-one, who were charged with raping two white women aboard a freight train in Alabama on March 25, 1931. Although the evidence was flimsy, an all-white jury found the "Scottsboro boys"

The Scottsboro defendants with their lawyer, Samuel Leibowitz, in March 1933. Haywood Patterson, sitting next to Leibowitz, remarked after the first of several blatantly racist trials they would endure, "The courtroom was one big smiling white face."

guilty, and they were sentenced to the electric chair. The U.S. Supreme Court overturned the convictions in 1932, ruling that the defendants had been denied their constitutional right to a fair and impartial trial. But an Alabama court again found them guilty, even though one of the women who accused them admitted to lying. Public outrage increased with each trial, condemning the blatant racism that the South passed off as justice. The Supreme Court reversed the convictions yet again in 1935. In a third trial (1936–37), charges against four of the defendants were dropped, but the other five were sentenced to long prison terms. One remained in jail until 1950.

SCOUTING

Scouting is an internationally organized movement for young people dedicated to developing good character, physical fitness, service to others, and loyalty to God. There are over 22 million members in more than a hundred countries, with 7 million in the United States alone. Scouting is divided into two groups, Boy Scouts and Girl Scouts.

Origins of Scouting

The history of Scouting dates back to the late 1890s when Lord Baden-Powell, a British lieutenant serving in South Africa, decided to help his troops adjust to military life by writing a book explaining scouting and mapmaking skills. When he returned to England, he rewrote the book for young boys interested in the outdoors and in 1907 organized the first English Scout troop. In 1909 Baden-Powell teamed up with William D. Boyce, an American businessman, who founded the Boy Scouts of America in 1910.

The national headquarters of the Boy Scouts of America is in Irving, Texas, and the organization hosts a national jamboree in a different state every four years. Boy Scout uniforms resemble the military uniform worn by Baden-Powell when he served in South Africa—shorts, shirt, scarf, and hat. Their slogan, "Be Prepared," also came from the British military.

In 1911, Juliette Gordon Low of Savannah, Georgia, became acquainted with Scouting while living in Scotland, and with the encouragement of Baden-Powell, she founded the Girl Guide troops in England. Upon her return to the United States in 1912, she organized the first American Girl Guides in Georgia. In 1913, the name was changed to Girl Scouts.

The national headquarters of the Girl Scouts of the U.S.A. is in Washington, D.C. The emblem representing Girl Scouts, a silhouette of three girls' faces inside a three-leaf clover, symbolizes the organization's commitment to girls, cultural diversity, and the three parts of the Girl Scout Promise—"On My Honor, I will try: To serve God, my country and mankind." Although the word "God" remains an integral part of the Girl Scout Promise, in an effort to acknowledge the growing ethnic diversity of the Girl Scouts, in 1993 the organization voted to allow girls to substitute the words "Allah," "the Creator," or any religious term they wish.

Principles and Programs

The principles of the Boy Scouts and the Girl Scouts are similar. Both are dedicated to enabling children and young adults to become active participants in society. They seek to develop leadership skills, self-esteem, consideration for others, respect for nature, healthy living habits, appreciation of the arts, physical fitness, career goals, awareness of other cultures, pride in their heritage, and loyalty to God and country.

Camping has always been an important part of Scouting. Both groups offer regular camping trips that include nature study, fire-building, cooking, first aid, hiking, swimming, and life-saving.

The Boy Scouts of America consists of three groups: (1) Cub Scouts, boys eight to ten; (2) Scouts, boys eleven and older; and (3) Explorers, boys and girls fourteen and older. The Girl Scouts of the U.S.A. program consists of four groups: (1) Brownies, girls six to eight; (2) Juniors, girls nine to eleven; (3) Cadettes, girls twelve to fourteen; and (4) Seniors, girls fourteen to seventeen. Each group has an internal ranking system that requires task-oriented activities for advancement. Badges representing proficiency at a skill or accomplishment of a task serve to set goals. Scouts often take pride in showing off their badges at group meetings. Children of all races, religions, nationalities, and economic backgrounds are welcome to join.

Both groups are governed by adult volunteers who serve as leaders, national and council board members, and advisers. The training program for Scout leaders is one of the largest adult education programs in America. Meetings are held in various locations including churches, schools, and community centers. Activities usually take place in small groups, usually called troops, under the guidance of an adult supervisor. Membership dues are minimal.

International Scouting

Although Scouting programs throughout the world have their own individual uniforms and programs, they share the same philosophy as the American organizations. All are nonpolitical and emphasize belief in some form of God, devotion to country, service to others, and love of the outdoors.

The World Scout Bureau in Geneva, Switzerland, coordinates international Scouting programs for boys. A World Scout jamboree for boys is held in a different country every four years. The Girl Scout World Association has four major centers located in India, England, Mexico, and Switzerland. In some countries the organization is called Girl Guides rather than Girl Scouts.

JOANN BIONDI

SCULPTURE
See Painting and Sculpture.

SDS
See Students for a Democratic Society.

SECESSION

Secession in American history refers to the withdrawal of eleven Southern states from the Union in 1860–61. Almost from the beginning of the Republic, groups had challenged national authority. In 1798, the Virginia and Kentucky Resolutions declared that the Constitution was a compact of states that had voluntarily formed the Union and asserted that the Alien and Sedition Acts recently passed by Congress were unconstitutional.

On three occasions before the Civil War the Union seemed threatened by secession: in 1820, in 1832, and most seriously in 1850 over a group of questions centering on slavery.

Background of Secession
Dramatic events during the 1850s stirred strong emotions and divided Northerners and Southerners. Throughout the decade the nation went from one crisis to another. Repeal in 1854 of the Missouri Compromise of 1820 prohibiting slavery in the northern part of the Louisiana territory inspired formation in the North of the Republican Party to oppose further expansion of slavery in the western territories. Southerners then threatened to secede if a candidate of the new party was elected president. The Supreme Court in the *Dred Scott* case declared in effect that the Republican policy was unconstitutional. The abolitionist John Brown tried to bring about a slave rebellion in Virginia. The struggle between pro- and antislavery settlers for control of Kansas became so murderous that the area was called "Bleeding Kansas."

Differences in ideas further widened the gap between the two sections. The North argued that no constitutional right to secede existed; the South asserted that it did. Northerners came to believe that a "Slave Power" threatened the Republic's future and that slavery was morally wrong. Southerners argued that slavery was a proper condition for blacks. They feared Northern interference with what historians have called their "peculiar institution" and distrusted the industrializing, urbanizing, growing North.

During the presidential election of 1860 Southerners uttered repeated threats of secession if a Republican won. Already badly divided, the nation further split when the Democratic Party broke apart, and North-

A political cartoon during the 1864 presidential campaign shows President Abraham Lincoln and Confederate president Jefferson Davis tearing apart the Union while Gen. George B. McClellan attempts to hold the country together. The cartoon is biased in favor of McClellan, who was running against Lincoln for the presidency on the Democratic ticket. What the cartoonist does not indicate is that Lincoln was in fact determined not only to abolish slavery but to preserve the Union as well.

erners and Southerners in the party nominated their own candidates. The Republicans nominated Abraham Lincoln, who had said, "A house divided against itself cannot stand," and had condemned slavery as immoral.

The South Secedes

Lincoln's election by a purely Northern vote sparked secession in the Lower South. South Carolina, long the storm center of secession, seceded December 20, 1860, invoking the compact theory outlined in the Virginia and Kentucky Resolutions and charging that the

North had broken the compact by failing to return fugitive slaves. Since states had entered the Union voluntarily, they could withdraw voluntarily, went the argument. Fear of emancipation gave further momentum to the secession movement.

South Carolina's example propelled six more states—Mississippi, Florida, Alabama, Georgia, Louisiana, and Texas—to withdraw. They formed the Confederate States of America a month before Lincoln's inauguration. While the new nation prepared for war, outgoing president James Buchanan watched

The Divided Nation—Slave and Free Areas, 1861

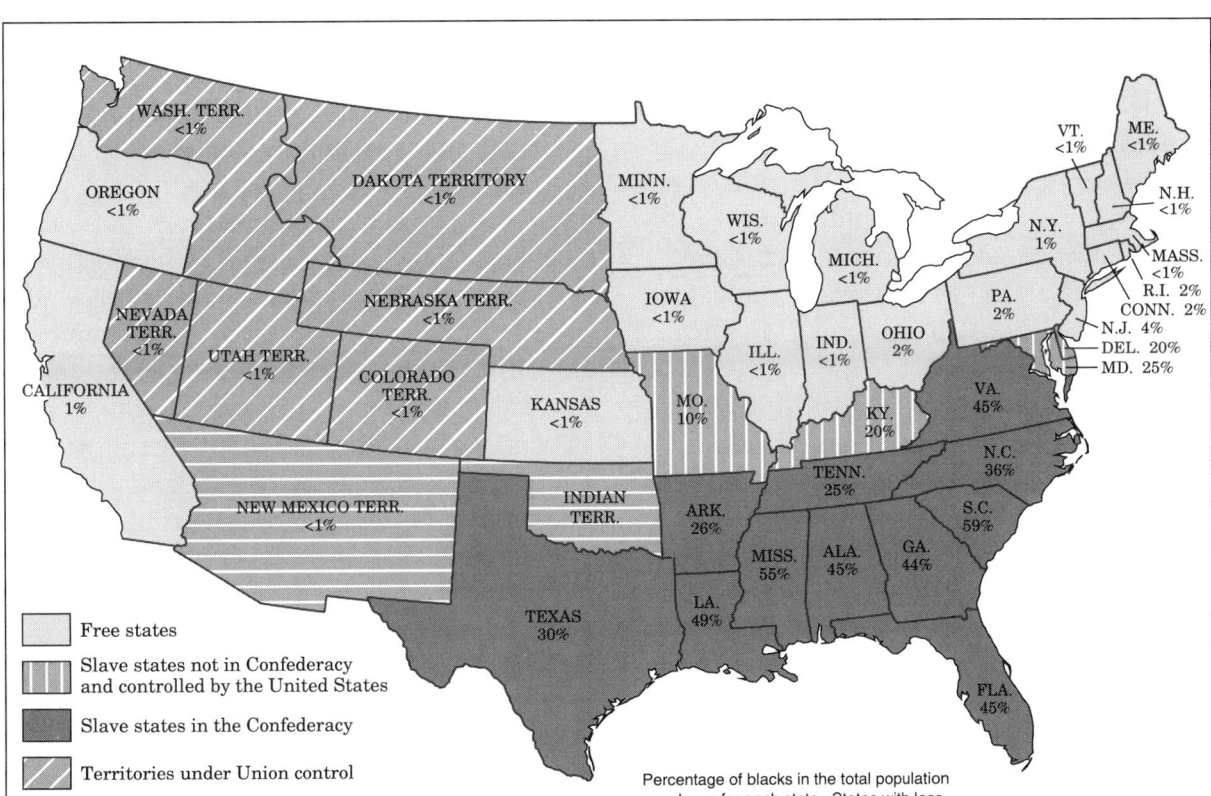

Percentage of blacks in the total population are shown for each state. States with less than 1% of blacks are shown as <1%

Legend:
- Free states
- Slave states not in Confederacy and controlled by the United States
- Slave states in the Confederacy
- Territories under Union control
- Territories aligned with the Confederacy

helplessly, saying secession was unconstitutional but that he was powerless to do anything about it.

Some in Congress attempted to reach a compromise. The major effort, sponsored by Senator John J. Crittenden of Kentucky, proposed to draw a line at 36° 30' latitude dividing the western territories between freedom and slavery. Republican congressmen, privately advised by President-elect Lincoln, refused to back down on their stand to allow slavery no further expansion in the territories.

When Lincoln took office he tried to assure Southerners that he would not interfere with slavery in the states. But he insisted that he would not allow it to spread in the territories,

and he rejected the idea that secession was legal. Misunderstanding marked both sides, Northerners believing Unionism stronger in the slave states than it was, and Southerners believing the North would not fight.

The War Starts

A crisis simmered in the harbor of Charleston, South Carolina, where the Union garrison at Fort Sumter was running out of supplies. After receiving conflicting advice and much deliberation, Lincoln determined not to surrender the fort. Giving advance notice to the Confederates, he sent a provision ship. But the Confederates opened fire on Fort Sumter before the ship arrived, and the Union force surrendered. Lincoln promptly declared that a state of insurrection existed, and on April 15 he called out 75,000 militiamen.

Lincoln's call to arms inspired a rush to enlist in the North and a fresh wave of secession in the South. Four more slave states—Virginia, Arkansas, Tennessee, and North Carolina—seceded and joined the Confederacy. The rebel nation thus expanded from 5 million to a little under 9 million, including the black population. Four slave states—Delaware, Maryland, Kentucky, and Missouri—remained in the Union.

Secession followed a pattern—seven Lower South states seceding before Lincoln's inauguration; four Upper South states seceding after Lincoln called for arms; and four border states remaining in the Union. The timing of decisions to secede related to the proportions of slaves, of plantations, of members of three leading churches—Methodist, Baptist, and Presbyterian, each of which split from the North over slavery—and of members of the Democratic Party. These elements, waning in strength the farther north one went, tended to unite Southerners into a community that fought for four years until secession was defeated by force of arms. The question was laid to rest by the Civil War. No serious attempt at secession has occurred since.

See also Civil War; Confederate States of America; Virginia and Kentucky Resolutions.

JAMES A. RAWLEY

SEGREGATION

Segregation is the physical separation of types of people, most commonly on the basis of sex, race, religion, or social class. It can be enforced by law (in which case it is referred to

by the Latin term *de jure*) or can be the result of custom (in which case *de facto* is used). Although the word normally suggests an involuntary situation, segregation can also be voluntary. In American history, the term usually refers to the treatment of blacks.

Pre–Civil War Segregation

Before the Civil War, blacks in the North and in southern cities were more likely to be segregated than those in the southern countryside. In the mid-1800s in the North, an increasing number of immigrants came from Europe and more white men were allowed to vote. The competition for jobs, and prejudice on the part of the new voters, brought an end to a period of relatively good race relations. Segregation became common in schools and other public places, at the same time that blacks lost jobs to whites and were prevented from voting. Blacks responded to segregation by founding their own churches and social organizations. Although growing segregation in housing was partly due to the desires of blacks, segregation in general was mostly the result of white hostility. For example, blacks prevailed upon the Massachusetts legislature in 1855 to abolish segregated schools and had some success in desegregating trains, but even in that state they lost other challenges to segregation.

In southern cities, white fears of slave rebellions and what were called "uppity" free Negroes produced a slightly different situation. Although black sections of town were beginning to take shape, most slaves lived behind their masters' houses. Some free Negroes and slaves organized independent black churches, but most were segregated within white congregations. Blacks also had segregated access to some theaters, but total exclusion was the general rule.

Reconstruction Practices

After the Civil War the Thirteenth, Fourteenth, and Fifteenth Amendments to the U.S. Constitution abolished slavery, made blacks citizens with equal rights before the law, and prohibited racial discrimination in voting. The Civil Rights Act of 1875 banned discrimination in public accommodations. Yet Reconstruction governments in the South generally tried to replace the old policy of total exclusion with a new one of two separate but equal systems. Except in New Orleans, schools were segregated, as were poorhouses, institutions for the blind, deaf, dumb, and insane, cemeteries, and most prisons. Segregation also existed in militia units, and on most trains, boats, and streetcars.

Segregation thus became the rule throughout most areas of the South. Nevertheless, blacks and their white Republican allies viewed it as an improvement—segregated facilities were better than total exclusion. Meanwhile blacks were forming their own associations. Former slaves established their own churches. They left their quarters behind their former masters' houses and built communities with other blacks on the outskirts of cities.

Rise of Jim Crow

With the return of the former Confederates to power in the South during the 1870s, and the ending of northern determination to protect their rights, conditions for southern blacks deteriorated. The new post-Reconstruction governments accepted the shift from exclusion to segregation, but abandoned all but the pretense of equal treatment.

Then beginning in the late 1880s, the region's race relations worsened still more. Amid increased lynchings and antiblack feeling, a coalition of planters, merchants, and agrarian radicals kept blacks from voting and passed state and local "Jim Crow laws" that extended segregation to cover even such things as phone booths and water fountains and legalized discrimination in public accommodations. In 1890, for example, Atlanta's new zoo was housed in a single building but had aisles on either side of the row of cages—one for blacks, the other for whites. "There is no communication between them," the *Atlanta Constitution* assured its white readers.

In *Plessy* v. *Ferguson* (1896), a case that grew out of a Louisiana law requiring segregation on the state's railroads, the Supreme Court held that such separation was constitutional as long as both races received equal treatment. That rarely occurred, but the courts refused to intervene even when confronted with blatantly inferior provisions for blacks. Only in *Buchanan* v. *Warley* (1917), a decision that declared legally enforced residential segregation unconstitutional, was any form of segregation successfully challenged in court.

By the turn of the century the policy of separate but *unequal* treatment of the races had become entrenched in the South. Blacks sat, or if white passengers needed more seats, stood in the back of streetcars and buses. They attended dilapidated schools in which they studied out-of-date textbooks. They were confined to filthy sections in theater balconies and rode elevators labeled "For Colored People, Freight, etc." When they died, often following treatment in inadequate segregated hospitals, they were buried in "colored sections" of the local cemetery.

Southern blacks could only try to make the best of a bad situation. During a widely publicized speech at the Cotton States and International Exposition in Atlanta in 1895,

Booker T. Washington, a prominent black leader, urged blacks to accept rather than protest discrimination. In what came to be known as the Atlanta Compromise, he proclaimed to his segregated audience: "In all things that are purely social we can be as separate as the fingers, yet one as the hand in all things essential to mutual progress." But long before this, a new middle class of black ministers, teachers, and businessmen had developed with a vested interest in segregation. Until the middle of the twentieth century, most black leaders simply attacked instances of exclusion or unequal separate treatment.

Northern Segregation

Reconstruction posed a greater challenge to segregation in the North where, down to the 1890s, a new black vote was often crucial. The Civil Rights Act of 1875 was declared unconstitutional in 1883, but northern state governments passed their own civil rights legislation. Although segregation persisted in many places, it was now against the law.

But increased migration of blacks northward after the turn of the century and post–World War I competition with immigrants and white veterans for jobs and housing led to the creation of large-scale black urban ghettos with their own schools, community institutions, and businesses. Conditions for blacks in the North and South came to resemble each other more closely, especially with regard to the centrality of segregation.

Prior to the 1950s, northern blacks were more likely than their southern counterparts to challenge segregation. But during the civil rights movement of the mid-twentieth century the federal government ended discrimination partly in response to demands for change from southern and northern blacks and white liberals and partly out of concern

Segregated water fountains, marked "white" and "colored." This example serves as a demonstration of how "separate but equal" facilities for the races involved flawed and dishonest reasoning. Note that the fountain for whites is clearly the larger and more modern one—blacks were left with the inferior facility. Segregated facilities were separate and anything but equal: whites always received the better schools, restaurants, public transportation, theaters, hotels, hospitals, and housing. As Justice John Marshall Harlan said in protest of the "separate but equal" clause, "The thin disguise of 'equal' accommodations . . . will not mislead anyone."

for world opinion. The North's de facto segregation, however, proved more difficult to overcome than the South's law-based system. Today, legal segregation is a thing of the past, but in many areas, especially housing and public education, custom-based segregation persists in the nation's cities and suburbs.

See also African Americans: 1877–1945; Ghettos; *Plessy v. Ferguson*; Racism; Reconstruction.

HOWARD N. RABINOWITZ

SENATE

The U.S. Senate is the upper house of Congress, the legislative branch of the federal government. The lower house is the House of Representatives. The idea of upper and lower houses grew out of a dispute among the delegates who wrote the U.S. Constitution in 1787. Delegates from large populous states wanted a legislature based on population—the more people in a state, the more lawmakers they would send to Congress. Those from smaller states demanded equal representation for all. The compromise solution: a House of Representatives, with membership determined by each state's population, and a Senate, with two members from each state regardless of size. The first Senate had twenty-two members. Today's has a hundred, two from each of the fifty states.

Senators' Requirements and Duties

Envisioning the Senate as a place for more thoughtful debate than the larger House, the Framers of the Constitution made other distinctions between them. Senators must be slightly older than representatives, a minimum thirty years of age instead of twenty-five. They must have been U.S. citizens for nine years, not seven as in the House. Senate terms are for six years; House terms, just two. And while all representatives must retire or seek reelection at the same time every two years, senators have staggered terms—only one-third expire at a time. Thus, the Senate is a "continuing body" and has a sense of stability lacking in the House. Finally, since House members represented *people,* they were to be elected directly by them. Senators—who represented *states*—were to be selected by each state's legislature. (In 1913, the Constitution was amended to allow the direct popular election of senators.) Originally all white and all male, the Senate has come to include blacks and members of other racial and ethnic minorities. A Native American and a record seven women were sworn in as senators in 1993.

The Senate's chief responsibility, like that of the House, is considering proposed federal laws. Also like the House, it may investigate aspects of public life, including alleged wrongdoing in the executive (presidential) branch of government. Federal officials who have been *impeached*—charged with "high crimes and misdemeanors" in office—go on trial in the Senate. Beyond that, the Senate shares power with the president in ways the House does not. Two-thirds of the Senate must approve any treaty the president makes with another nation. Presidents must also win Senate approval of their choices for ambassadors, executive department heads, federal judges, and Supreme Court justices.

The Senate at Work

According to the Constitution, the U.S. vice president serves as president of the Senate. But since the vice president may vote in the Senate only to break a tie, he is rarely present unless a close vote is likely. Various temporary presidents preside over day-to-day Senate affairs. The Senate also elects a permanent temporary president. Traditionally, the temporary president is the longest-serving member of whichever political party, Republican or Democratic, holds the majority of Senate seats.

In fact, it is around the two political parties that the Senate is, for practical purposes, organized. In the January of odd-numbered years, when each two-year session of Congress begins, Democratic and Republican senators *caucus* (meet) separately to select their leaders. The majority party chooses the *majority leader;* the minority party, the *minority leader.* In addition, each party elects a *whip,* whose job is to make sure members are present for important votes. The caucus also makes committee assignments.

Typically, a senator serves on four of the Senate's sixteen *standing* (permanent) *committees*. The majority party holds the majority of seats on each committee. The committee chair is also of the majority party—customarily, its most senior member on the committee. Each standing committee is responsible for considering bills (proposed legislation) in a particular area—banking, foreign relations, armed services, and so on. Each is divided into a number of specialized subcommittees. It is at subcommittee meetings that senators hear expert testimony for and against the bills before them. It is also where they discuss bills and decide whether to recommend them for passage.

Only a few hundred of the ten thousand–odd bills submitted during each session get a recommendation. Those go to the majority leader, who schedules them for debate by the full Senate. Bills that the majority leader and his party favor generally make it to the Senate floor quickly. Those they oppose may never get there. But powerful as the majority is, the minority has a counterforce—the *filibuster*.

A filibuster is a long speech. Unless senators agree in advance to limit debate on a bill, they may speak as long as they wish. Filibustering senators simply talk and talk and talk, hoping to wear down their opponents and get them to drop a bill—or change it. The filibuster was used in earlier years mostly by southern senators to kill measures aimed at improving the treatment of blacks in the South. Otherwise, it was rarely resorted to before 1970. By the 1990s, it had become almost a weekly affair, employed by senators trying to prevent action on bills they oppose—especially when they expect to lose if the bill is voted on. The only way to stop a filibuster is for three-fifths of the Senate to vote *cloture*, an end to debate. Three-fifths is a proportion of votes so large it is hard to come by. Sometimes the mere threat of a filibuster is enough to produce compromise legislation.

A bill *enacted* (passed) by the full Senate must also be passed in the House before going to the president. He either signs it into law or *vetoes* (refuses to sign) it. Vetoed bills can become law if they are passed again by a two-thirds majority in both houses, an action that is called *overriding a veto*.

The Senate in History

Sharing power as they do, the Senate, the House, and the president have long struggled for dominance. President George Washington was surprised when senators insisted upon taking time to examine a treaty he proposed before approving it. But during most of its first thirty years, the Senate acted cautiously. Ambitious politicians, like Founding Father and president-to-be James Madison, preferred to serve in the livelier House.

In the 1820s, the Senate entered its "Golden Age." The issue of the day was slavery and whether it should be legal not only in the South but in the new western states then joining the Union. In a series of compromises, the Senate agreed that for every new state that permitted slavery, there would be a new one that did not. Such compromises held the nation together until 1861, when the Civil War began. Three years after it ended, in 1868, the Senate became the setting for the impeachment trial of President Andrew Johnson. Johnson, the only U.S. president ever impeached, was acquitted.

Throughout this century, the Senate has continued its role of checking and balancing the power of the president. In 1919, it refused President Woodrow Wilson's request to agree to a treaty that would have brought the United States into the League of Nations, an international peacekeeping organization. Twenty-six years later, it did approve U.S. entry into the United Nations. In 1973, a special Senate committee launched an investigation into illegal activity by members of President Richard M. Nixon's staff in the Watergate scandal. Partly as a result of that investigation, Nixon became the first president to resign from office.

Senators, like representatives, are often criticized for their high salaries ($129,500 a year in 1993) and abundant privileges. Many Americans also fault the Senate for maintaining its tradition of the filibuster, which allows a minority to delay or prevent the passage of legislation favored by the congressional majority.

See also House of Representatives; Impeachment; Watergate. *And see biographies of the following senators:* Calhoun, John C.; Clay, Henry; Douglas, Stephen A.; McCarthy, Joseph R.; Sumner, Charles; Webster, Daniel.

ANN E. WEISS

SENECA FALLS CONVENTION

In July 1848 a group of women's rights advocates, led by Lucretia Mott and Elizabeth Cady Stanton, met at Seneca Falls, New York, to draft a Declaration of Sentiments. The gathering was attended by 240 people, 40 of whom were men. The Declaration of Sentiments was based on the Declaration of Independence and stated that "all men and women" are created equal. It went on in imitation of Thomas Jefferson's long list of woes inflicted on the colonies by King George III to describe the "injuries and usurpations on the part of man toward woman, having in direct

Elizabeth Cady Stanton addressing the first women's rights meeting at Seneca Falls, New York, on June 19-20, 1848. She, Lucretia Mott, and several other women drafted a Declaration of Sentiments that included the following: "The history of mankind is a history of repeated injuries and usurpations on the part of man toward woman, having in direct object the establishment of an absolute tyranny over her....[Man] has endeavored, in every way that he could to destroy her confidence in her own powers, to lessen her self-respect, and to make her willing to lead a dependent and abject life."

object the establishment of an absolute tyranny over her."

Eleven resolutions were also adopted by the convention. These included statements that "woman is man's equal," that all laws restricting the rights of women had "no force or authority," that "the same amount of virtue, delicacy, and refinement" expected of woman "should also be required of man," and that women should have the right to vote. All of these were adopted unanimously except the resolution about voting. It was approved by a majority, but some of the delegates considered it too extreme.

The Seneca Falls Convention was the first significant public meeting in the United States dealing with women's rights. Thereafter similar gatherings took place every year.

See also Feminist Movement to 1919.

SERRA, JUNÍPERO

(1713–84) *Missionary priest.*

Serra founded nine religious communities called missions in California. He was beatified by the Roman Catholic church in 1988. Beatification is a step toward being declared a saint.

The son of peasants in Majorca, an island off Spain, Serra was christened Miguel José. As a teenager he joined the Franciscans, a Catholic religious order, and called himself Junípero after a follower of Saint Francis of Assisi. For eighteen years, Serra taught at a convent on Majorca and then decided to become a missionary. In 1749, he sailed for Mexico. After arriving in Vera Cruz, Serra chose to walk to Mexico City rather than travel by horseback. Along the way, local people fed and housed him. An insect bit Serra's foot during the trek, and the bite became infected. The sores he developed troubled him for the rest of his life.

Serra went first to missions in the Sierra Gorda, a rugged mountain area. His main goal was to convert Indians to the Catholic faith. These converts also farmed and built churches for the priests, who were called friars. Some historians believe the Indians were treated like slaves at the missions. Certainly, many died of disease and rough treatment. Others claim that the mission friars protected the Indians from cruel soldiers and settlers and that Serra himself was a defender of Indian rights. This argument came to a head when Serra was beatified and is still unsettled.

In 1768, Serra was sent to run the missions of Baja California. A year later, he joined Spanish soldiers in exploring Alta California, which is now the state of California. After traveling by mule for months despite his painful leg, he founded Mission San Diego de Alcala in July 1769, the first Spanish settlement in California.

Serra sailed north the next year with soldiers and other friars to Monterey Bay to start another mission, San Carlos Borromeo de Carmelo, which became his headquarters and his favorite mission. After that, he founded missions up and down the coast of California—San Antonio de Padua, San Gabriel Arcangel, San Luis Obispo de Tolosa, San Francisco de Assis, San Juan Capistrano, Santa Clara de Assis, and San Buenaventura. It is estimated that he baptized six thousand Indians in his lifetime.

REBECCA LARSEN

SETTLEMENT HOUSE MOVEMENT

The settlement movement originated in England in the late nineteenth century. It was part of a broad effort to improve the lives of poor people and develop a sense of community in the slums of industrial cities. The idea was for well-educated people to "settle" in the slums. There they would not only help relieve poverty and despair but also learn something about the real world from those who lived in the inner city.

The Movement in America

The settlement idea spread quickly to the United States. The first American institution was the Neighborhood Guild founded on the Lower East Side of New York in 1886. The most famous American settlement house was Hull-House, founded in Chicago by Jane Addams and a college classmate, Ellen Gates Starr, in 1889. By 1900 there were one hundred settlements in the United States, and by

1910 over four hundred, most of them in large cities. Settlement residents organized clubs and classes, music schools, theaters, recreation programs, and other activities to serve their neighbors. Working with recent immigrants to ease their adjustment to the new country and act as their advocate in the city and the nation became a primary function of most of the settlements.

Still they had an impact on only a small percentage of the immigrants and an even smaller proportion of the black community. Although Hull-House and the other settlements helped establish separate institutions for black neighborhoods and worked for equality in American society, blacks were not usually welcome at the major settlements in the period before World War I (1914–18).

To improve living and working conditions in their neighborhoods, settlement residents made careful surveys of the social problems. In addition, they often moved beyond their local area to study conditions at the city, state, and national levels. Because of their concern for children, they became leaders in the anti–child labor movement and joined efforts to establish kindergartens and improve the schools. They also worked to improve housing and build parks and playgrounds. They had faith that if they could provide better schools and living conditions for the immigrant poor, they could help a whole generation escape poverty.

In the early years of the movement the settlements were financed entirely by donations, and the residents often paid for their own room and board. Jane Addams, Lillian Wald, and some other leaders spent a lifetime in the same settlement house, but many of the young residents came for a year or two before moving on to other careers.

Especially for young, unmarried women,

A pottery class for children at Hull-House in 1937.

the settlement provided an acceptable alternative to living alone or with their family. To live like the poor was never their objective. Instead they chose to live in a middle-class style in a poor section and thus teach by example. Most settlements had maid service and a community dining room, which freed residents from housekeeping tasks. But more important, the living arrangements often provided stimulating companionship and personal friendships and encouraged cooperative reform efforts. For many women the settlement was a training ground for a later career in government, industry, or education.

Change to Neighborhood Centers

In the 1920s settlements began to change as social work became more professionalized. Shifting populations and urban renewal in the period following World War II (1939–45) forced out many of the settlements. Most became what they called "neighborhood centers," and all gave up the requirement that settlement workers live in the house. The settlements were no longer leaders in a national movement for social justice, but as centers, many still provided needed services to senior citizens, disadvantaged youths, and battered women and children. In many cities they represented a measure of hope in a time of despair.

See also Addams, Jane.

ALLEN F. DAVIS

SEVEN YEARS' WAR

Unlike earlier European wars involving the English colonies in North America, the Seven Years' War, also known as the French and Indian War, grew out of a strictly colonial conflict. In 1754 French and English colonists and their Indian allies clashed over control of the Ohio Valley. Although the English greatly outnumbered the French, the early victories in the war were won by the French. This was true because most of the Indians in the region sided with the French. The crushing defeat of British and colonial forces led by Gen. Edward Braddock in July 1755 and other setbacks resulted in the war spreading to Europe in 1756, with Great Britain and Prussia opposing France and Austria.

The tide continued to run toward the French until 1757, when William Pitt became prime minister of Great Britain. Pitt counted on Prussia to do most of the fighting in Europe; he concentrated British troops and supplies in America. Then, one by one, British and colonial forces captured the French forts in the Ohio region, including Fort Duquesne, site of present-day Pittsburgh. In 1759 and 1760 Quebec and Montreal, the last important French strongholds in Canada, were captured. Other French colonies in the Caribbean Sea and in Asia were also taken over by British naval units.

The war was ended in 1763 by the Peace of

Paris. In this treaty France ceded all its possessions on the North American continent to Great Britain. Actually the Peace of Paris was more a truce than the end of fighting. Britain and France were again at war during the American Revolution and remained so almost continually until 1815.

SHAKERS

Of the many religions that have flourished in America, one of the most distinctive is the United Society of Believers in Christ's Second Appearing, commonly known as the Shakers.

Early History

Shakerism began in England around 1747 when two ex-Quakers, James and Jane Wardley, founded their own religious group. Although similar to the Quakers, the new group featured much physical activity at their religious services. After a brief period of meditation, worshipers would begin to tremble, shout, sing, and dance. They came to be known as "Shaking Quakers" or simply "Shakers."

In 1758, a young woman named Ann Lees (later changed to Lee) joined the Shakers. Although she never attended school and held only simple jobs, Mother Ann, as she came to be known, shaped the Shaker system of beliefs and eventually became leader of the movement.

Because of their beliefs and their style of worship, the Shakers soon came into conflict with the official Church of England and suffered persecution. So, in 1774, Mother Ann and seven other Shakers left England to settle in America. The period from the American Revolution to the Civil War was a time of religious revivalism—an interest in intense reli-

A Shaker religious service, which provided worshipers with emotional release through singing, dancing, speaking in tongues, falling into trances, and trembling—thus the name "Shakers."

gious experience and expression—and experimentation in new forms of communal living. Shakerism offered these features, as well as security and a decent living during periods of economic difficulties when people could not find jobs and whole families ended up on the streets. Shakerism eventually died out in England, but in America, it attracted a large number of followers. By the middle of the nineteenth century, there were about six thousand Shakers living in twenty communities in the East and Midwest.

Beliefs

Although Shakerism belongs to the Protestant branch of Christianity, certain characteristics set it apart. Unlike most other Christians, the Shakers consider Jesus to be a human being who was adopted as the son of God. Their official title, the United Society of Believers in Christ's Second Appearing, reflects their belief that the second coming of Christ means the active presence of Christ's spirit within the Shaker movement. The Shakers were also unique, at least until recently, in that they have treated men and women exactly the same way. There is no established ministry or priesthood, and women as well as men serve as leaders of the community. God is often addressed as "Mother and Father."

A number of Shaker practices can be found in other religions, but in a more limited way. All Shakers are celibate—they do not have sexual relations. Shakers live in their own communities, separate from the world, and all property is held in common. In these respects, the Shakers are similar to communities of monks and nuns.

Some Shaker beliefs have at times gone against general public attitudes. Shakers have practiced racial equality from the very beginning, sometimes purchasing slaves in order to free them. Although the Shakers opposed slavery, their pacifism prevented them from fighting in the Civil War. They became the first officially recognized conscientious objectors in the United States when President Abraham Lincoln exempted them from the draft. The Shakers have also at times refused to pay specific taxes that were earmarked for purposes contrary to their beliefs.

Shaker Life

At their high point, the Shaker communities were actual villages made up of communal houses. In each house, men and women lived apart. When an entire family joined the group, its members would separate, and the children would be cared for by the community as a whole.

Shaker villages supported themselves by selling farm products and household goods. Shakers were responsible for a number of innovations we now take for granted, such as the flat broom and the selling of flower and vegetable seeds in packets. The motto "hands to work and hearts to God" reflects the Shaker belief that all work is holy, and this is apparent in the quality of the things they produced. Although their guiding principle always was how useful an object was, the Shakers have had a lasting influence on American artistic taste. The furniture they built is widely sought after and copied for the simple elegance of its design. Shaker hymns have become symbolic of traditional American music. Their architecture is greatly ad-

mired for its modern quality of "form following function": each element in a building's design—a door or roof or window, for example—is built to best fulfill that element's purpose. Nothing is added simply for decoration.

Shakers dress modestly and live quiet lives, but unlike the Amish (with whom they are sometimes confused), they do not reject modern technology. In fact, many inventions are credited to Shakers, including the circular saw and an improved washing machine, and in this century, electricity and automobiles could be found in Shaker villages.

Since Shakers were celibate, they did not produce children to carry on their faith. The movement could receive new members only through conversion. But after the Civil War, the number of converts began to drop. The opportunities for jobs provided by modern industrial society, along with a decline in revivalism, contributed to a decreasing membership. One by one, the villages closed down, and many now are only museums. At Sabbathday Lake, Maine, however, there is still an active Shaker community, which in recent years has been attracting new members.

For further reading: Flo Morse, *The Story of the Shakers* (Woodstock, Vt.: Countryman Press, 1986).

WALTER PETROVITZ

SHAYS' REBELLION

During the depression following the American Revolution many farmers suffered badly. In Massachusetts the situation was particularly serious because during the 1780s the state legislature raised property taxes steeply in order to pay off the state's revolutionary war debts. At the same time bad weather reduced the size of the farmers' harvests, and the depression was causing the prices they received for their crops to fall. Many farmers, caught in this squeeze, lost their land because they could not pay their taxes. Some who could not pay their debts were thrown into debtors' prison.

In 1786 angry Massachusetts farmers led by Daniel Shays, a revolutionary war veteran, marched on Springfield and prevented the court there from meeting. This blocked the legal proceedings involved in seizing farms for nonpayment of taxes. But when Shays' twelve-hundred-man "army" tried to take over the Springfield armory early in 1787, it was driven off by the state militia. Shays fled to Vermont, which had not yet been admitted to the Union. The rebellion collapsed.

The legislature, however, then provided some tax relief to the farmers and peace was restored. As Thomas Jefferson said, Shays' rebellion was only a minor uprising that served as a "medicine necessary for the sound health of government." But it also pointed up the weakness of the national government, which had been unable either to check the rebels or to do anything to ease their problems. It was therefore an important reason many prominent leaders in other parts of the country demanded that the national government be strengthened. It encouraged the movement for revising the Articles of Confederation that resulted in the drafting of the Constitution.

SHERMAN, WILLIAM TECUMSEH

(1820–91)   *Union Civil War general.*

At age sixteen Sherman entered West Point, graduating sixth in his class, after which he

served in several military positions. Most of his service was in southern states, and he developed a fondness for the South and its people.

Sherman was so well regarded that when the Civil War came, he was offered a high commission in the Confederate army. He turned it down because he believed that the "Union and its Government must be sustained, at any and every cost."

At Bull Run, Shiloh, and other battles, Sherman showed he could organize and lead troops. Photographs show a man with a stern expression, fierce dark eyes, and a face etched with lines. He could strike fear in his men, but officers closest to him remembered his animated conversations and deep loyalty. Ev-

A photograph of Union general William Tecumseh Sherman in 1865, the year following his famously brutal March to the Sea. After burning much of Atlanta, Georgia, he set his army marching toward the seaside city of Savannah, destroying everything in his way.

eryone noted his energy and physical courage. At Shiloh, he had four horses shot out from under him while rallying his men.

In September 1864, Sherman's army captured Atlanta, a victory that helped Abraham Lincoln win reelection. He immediately set out with his army on his famous "March to the Sea." "We are not only fighting hostile armies," Sherman said, "but a hostile people, and must make old and young, rich and poor, feel the hard hand of war." His troops destroyed everything of military value, including farms. They lived off the land as they went, seizing crops and farm animals for food.

After capturing Savannah, Sherman went north and brought his concept of total war to the Carolinas. The hardships to the people and land were so severe that even friends criticized his tactics. But when the Confederate forces surrendered, he drew up lenient peace terms—and found himself criticized for that, too.

After the war, Sherman was appointed head of the army (1869) and applied the same harsh tactics of warfare against Native Americans in the West. Sherman was a complex man, one who wanted peace so badly he used savage methods to attain it.

See also Civil War.

JIM MURPHY

SINATRA, FRANK

(1915–) *Popular singer and actor.*

Born in Hoboken, New Jersey, Sinatra was the child of Italian immigrant parents. Although he had no early musical training, he displayed a talent for musical phrasing and improvisation that made him immensely popular as a singer of jazz arrangements and ballads.

Sinatra began his career at the age of nineteen singing on the radio. In 1939, he performed in New York with a swing band led by Harry James and then spent three years (1940–42) with the Tommy Dorsey Orchestra. Sinatra's early reputation rested on his solo singing and his sex appeal, and he was among the most popular male interpreters of standard ballads of the 1940s. He became famous for the hordes of bobby-soxers screaming and swooning at his appearances. (Teenage girls were called "bobby-soxers" in those years because they wore "bobby socks," another term for "ankle socks.") He toured extensively and recorded for Columbia Records during this period.

By the early 1950s, many critics felt that Sinatra (now nicknamed "Old Blue Eyes") had passed his prime as a singer because the years and the demands of his performing schedule had taken their toll on the quality of his voice. But his appearance as an actor in the 1953 film *From Here to Eternity* established him in a new field and earned him an Academy Award.

After his initial film success, Sinatra returned to singing, this time with more emphasis on his skills as a jazz interpreter in live performances and recordings with Capitol Records. At the peak of this phase of his career, Sinatra appeared in a number of important films, including *Guys and Dolls* (1955) and *The Man with the Golden Arm* (1955). He remained an important force in popular music in the 1960s, even as rock, soul, and the "British Invasion" of such groups as the Beatles and the Rolling Stones captured the attention of young audiences.

In 1971, Sinatra announced his retirement, but he did not remain out of the public eye for long. By 1973, he had resumed a busy concert schedule in the United States and abroad. He toured with Woody Herman's Orchestra and has maintained an active performing schedule since the mid-1970s. In 1985, President Ronald Reagan awarded him the Presidential Medal of Freedom.

Frank Sinatra's importance lies in his ability to interpret the text of a song. His singing has been described as clear and direct, with excellent diction. A "natural" singer, his success has inspired many imitators.

See also Jazz; Music.

BARBARA L. TISCHLER

SIT-DOWN STRIKES

Because of New Deal labor legislation, especially the Wagner Labor Relations Act, by 1936 many large manufacturing corporations had been unionized, and the Congress of Industrial Organizations (CIO) had established locals in many of the largest and most important industries in the nation. In their efforts to exact concessions from their employers, militants in the automobile industry in 1936 and 1937 adopted a tactic recently developed by French workers. Instead of "going out" on strike, they "sat in" the factories, refusing to leave until their demands were met. This was very effective, because the employers hesitated to try to drive workers from their plants for fear that valuable machinery and other property might be destroyed or damaged in the process.

In December 1936 a General Motors factory in Cleveland was taken over by the workers. Early in 1937 GM's important Fisher body plant in Flint, Michigan, was occupied. When they tried to get the strikers out, local police were met with a shower of pop bottles, plates, and small tools.

The federal government refused to act against the strikers, and the governor of Michigan, Frank Murphy, was openly sympathetic to them. To end the occupations, General Motors gave in and granted most of the workers' demands. The sit-downs spread to other GM factories and to those of other manufacturers. By the end of 1937 about 400,000 workers had engaged in sit-down strikes, and most of them had won significant gains from their employers.

Eventually, however, the Supreme Court declared such strikes illegal, and the movement died out rapidly.

See also Labor Movement.

SITTING BULL

(c. 1834–90)   *Hunkpapa Sioux leader.*

Because the Hunkpapas lived in Dakota territory, north of the western travel routes of the pioneers, Sitting Bull had little contact with whites until 1864. After resisting an attack by soldiers at Killdeer Mountain that year, he resolved to guide his people away from the white man's world. With other leaders he took the Hunkpapas westward to the Powder and Yellowstone river valleys. He soon became an ally of Red Cloud of the Oglalas in driving soldiers from those rich hunting grounds.

In 1873 when surveyors came to lay out the route for the Northern Pacific Railroad, Sitting Bull led war parties against the invaders. In one skirmish he almost captured Lt. Col. George Armstrong Custer, who was commanding a cavalry escort.

Sitting Bull, whose Indian name was Tatanka Yotanka, or Sitting Buffalo, was chief of the Hunkpapa Sioux. He became famous among whites after defeating Gen. George Custer at the Battle of Little Bighorn and later as a member of Buffalo Bill's Wild West Show. Because of his courageous resistance against the U.S. government, Sitting Bull is considered by many historians to have been one of the most capable as well as visionary of the Indian leaders.

Three years later the two met again at the Little Bighorn River in Montana. By this time Sitting Bull's influence as a holy man had brought him recognition on the northern Plains as the leader of tribes who refused to live on reservations. After his warriors defeated and killed Custer and all his men at the Battle of Little Bighorn, he was forced by a vengeful pursuing army to flee to Canada.

In 1881 Sitting Bull returned to the United States and surrendered. For two years he was

kept prisoner at Fort Randall, South Dakota Territory. Then he was given permission to live as a reservation Indian at Standing Rock. In 1885 Buffalo Bill Cody arranged for him to travel with his Wild West Show.

Upon his return to Standing Rock, Sitting Bull strongly opposed U.S. Indian policies and fell into disfavor with the government. He refused to use his influence to stop the new Ghost Dance religion, which was spreading among Indians throughout the West. It taught that all white people would soon disappear and the Indians' ancestors would return to earth. Although the movement was nonviolent, its message and the frenzied dancing that was part of its ceremonies alarmed some white settlers. Government authorities, hoping to halt it, decided to imprison Sitting Bull.

When Indian police were sent to arrest him on December 15, 1890, Sitting Bull was killed in the ensuing struggle outside his cabin.

See also Cody, Buffalo Bill; Custer, George Armstrong; Indian Reservations; Indian-White Relations.

DEE BROWN

SIXTIES, THE

No decade in American history is more talked about than the 1960s. And everyone seems to agree on what is meant by "the sixties"—it serves almost as a shorthand for a list that includes rock and roll, beards and long hair, student protests against everything, drugs, tie-dyed shirts, hippies, and the sexual revolution.

But our image of this extraordinary decade comes more from its second half than from its first five years. It may help to think of the sixties as two distinct periods, the first half dominated by public hope about America's future, the second more by despair, anger, and conflict over the very possibility of America's survival in the world.

Hopeful Years

The hope of the earlier years came partly from the widely held opinion that the election of forty-three-year-old John F. Kennedy in 1960 was going to "get the country going again," after what many people felt to be the dull stagnation—economic and spiritual—of the Eisenhower years. Kennedy's fresh, quick-witted, youthful, and athletic style; his young, fashionable, and beautiful wife; his small children—all contrasted favorably in public opinion with the grandfatherly golf-playing president Dwight D. Eisenhower.

But this feeling of hope came too from the remarkable nonviolent struggle being waged by the civil rights movement led by the courageous and eloquent Rev. Dr. Martin Luther King, Jr. Inspired by the success of the Montgomery, Alabama, bus boycott of 1955 and 1956, African Americans and their white supporters had begun trying to integrate schools, lunch counters, public transportation, and the voting booths of the racially segregated South. Although these brave people used the theory and practice of nonviolence, they met tremendous resistance, much of it violent. Marchers and demonstrators were beaten and set upon with police dogs and fire hoses; their homes and churches were bombed; some were assassinated. Still, their valiant, moral, and resolutely nonviolent approach earned the admiration of millions of people around the world. As they insisted on following federal laws opposing segregation, they ended up forcing the federal government to

protect them and eventually got Congress to pass the Voting Rights Act of 1965.

The most important speech of the decade may have been King's I Have a Dream speech, delivered in front of 250,000 supporters (with millions more watching on television) at the March on Washington on August 28, 1963. That speech was probably the hopeful, nonviolent high-water mark of the sixties. The rest of the decade seems to have been defined as much by violence—at home and abroad—as by anything else.

Mounting Violence, Protests

The hopes of the civil rights years began to fade as the cities' black ghettos erupted in flames of anger and despair: Watts in Los Angeles (1965), Newark and Detroit (1967). The goal of integration itself seemed to recede in the face of Malcolm X's eloquent demand for black separatism and the rise of the movement known as "black power."

And then there were the assassinations: President Kennedy (1963), Malcolm X (1965), King (1968), Senator Robert F. Kennedy (1968). These men had carried the hopes of millions; their deaths seemed to signal a public world gone crazy.

But the most violent saga of the decade and dominating the second half was the war in Vietnam. Though never a declared war, the conflict lasted longer than any other American war; it claimed over 58,000 American lives and over a million Vietnamese. At the height of American troop strength in 1968, there were over 500,000 soldiers in Vietnam. Though low-level American involvement in the country had begun in the 1950s under Eisenhower, the number of what at first were called "military advisers" grew steadily, reaching 16,000 by the time President Kennedy was killed. But when Congress passed the Gulf of Tonkin Resolution (August 1964) in response to a fabricated North Vietnamese "attack" on American destroyers, President Lyndon B. Johnson began the enormous military buildup that turned what had been a relatively low-level conflict into a full-scale war.

The Vietnam War had a powerful effect on American society and culture. Because a series of military and civilian leaders had been predicting victory against a nationalist and Communist guerrilla force for so many years (since the Eisenhower days), but no matter how many troops were sent to Vietnam, victory seemed no closer, the war began to look irrational, weird, even a little crazy: one general said in all seriousness, "We had to destroy that village in order to save it." Because television news came of age in the 1960s, Americans saw close up a war that made little sense every night on television. As casualties mounted, protest against the war did, too, particularly by the young men who were at risk of being drafted to fight it.

The protests, which began in 1965, had grown more widespread by the time of a 1967 march on the Pentagon and had become truly massive by 1969. The movement drew people from all elements of society, from clergy to homemakers, but it was the students who gave protests their popular image. Long-haired men and women shouted angry slogans and sang the John Lennon song "Give Peace a Chance." At times demonstrations resembled rock concerts (and rock musicians played at protest marches). Both could have an energetic carnival-like atmosphere in which participants wore tie-dyed T-shirts, listened to the Rolling Stones, and puffed on marijuana cigarettes.

Partly because of the enormous opposition to the war, President Johnson withdrew

A particularly flamboyant hippie, circa 1967.

from his 1968 reelection campaign and began peace negotiations with North Vietnam. His successor, Vice President Hubert Humphrey, was nominated at a tumultuous Democratic convention in Chicago, marked by massive confrontations in the streets between hippies and peace demonstrators, on one hand, and Chicago police, on the other. Humphrey narrowly lost the election to Richard M. Nixon, who began withdrawing troops from Vietnam, substituting increased bombing in the north. American casualties dropped; North Vietnam was devastated, but an American victory remained out of reach.

Cultural Changes

Although most Americans did not join demonstrations or smoke marijuana, many began to question their leaders as never before during this period. While the war hung over much of the decade, the economic boom of the 1960s gave many the freedom to experiment with new ideas, new work, new kinds of relationships. Hippies and flower children appeared in 1967 and 1968. Young men and women dropped out of the "rat race" of climbing career ladders, some banding together in communes.

A new feminism also began during this decade, as more women (and men, for that matter) attended college than ever before. When birth-control pills became widely available, many middle-class Americans, especially young people, began trumpeting a "sexual revolution"—even though women still carried most of the risks of this "revolutionary" behavior. And rock music came of age in the 1960s, as the Beatles, Rolling Stones, Bob Dylan, Janis Joplin, Jimi Hendrix, Aretha Franklin, the Supremes, the Band, and the Jefferson Airplane, among others, transformed popular music.

See also Birth Control; Chicago Seven; Civil Rights Movement; Drugs; Feminist Movement since 1919; Kent State Incident; Marches on Washington: 1941, 1963; Rock Music; Students for a Democratic Society; Vietnam War; Woodstock. *And see biographies of the following major figures of the sixties:* Johnson, Lyndon B.; Kennedy, John F.; King, Martin Luther, Jr.; Malcolm X; Nixon, Richard M.

WARREN GOLDSTEIN

SLAVERY

Slavery is a very old institution, mentioned in the Bible and practiced by Greeks and Romans. In the United States slavery differed from older systems: it enslaved a single race and was hereditary—a slave's child was born a slave.

Slavery in the Colonies
The colonies' transatlantic trade in slaves, with the Portuguese, Dutch, French, and English participating, began when a Dutch ship brought the first Africans to British North America in 1619. Virginians looked down on Africans because they were black and not Christians. In Virginia and Maryland, the first colonies to have many slaves, blacks were denied rights enjoyed by whites. By the early eighteenth century slaves were living under a separate set of laws, suffering heavier penalties than whites for the same offenses.

Replacement of white workers by black slaves resulted from the growing cost of white labor and the profitability of producing tobacco in the Chesapeake and rice in South Carolina. Some Africans proved valuable because, unlike their masters, they knew how to cultivate rice from their lives in Africa. Within about a quarter of a century after its

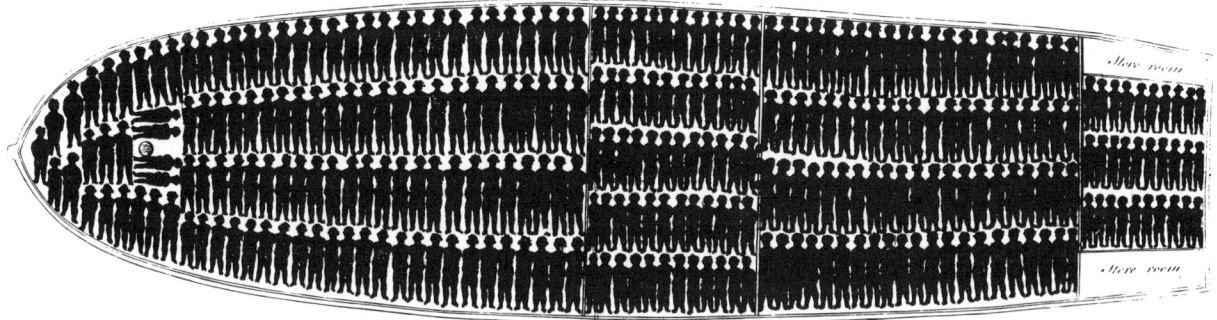

A plan for loading a slave ship, which has packed its human cargo into every possible space on the ship.

founding, South Carolina had a black majority, toiling in unhealthful swampy fields.

In the eighteenth century a quarter of a million Africans were brought to British North America before the American Revolution. English merchants were the main sellers of slaves. American slave traders, principally Rhode Islanders, sold their black cargoes mostly in the West Indies, many to be transferred north later. All thirteen colonies had slaves, but the majority of them lived in the region stretching from Chesapeake Bay through Georgia. Slaves accounted for much of the South's agricultural prosperity. In northern colonies they often worked in cities as domestics and craftsmen.

Post-Revolution Slavery

The Revolution, breathing ideals of freedom and equality, nourished the first antislavery movement. Northern states passed measures abolishing slavery—though in some cases only gradually—and the central government prohibited slavery in the old Northwest Territory (Ohio, Indiana, Illinois, Michigan, Wisconsin). By 1800 slavery had become a southern institution and the nation had been divided between free and slave states. The Constitution made possible suppression of the foreign slave trade after 1807, while providing for the return of fugitive slaves to their owners and allotting to the states congressional representation for three-fifths of their slave populations.

After the Revolution, slave traders resumed their interrupted business supplying the southern labor market. Congress prohibited further importation after 1807, but during the next half century traders smuggled in about 1,000 slaves each year. In the whole period of importing, an estimated 600,000 Africans arrived in the United States.

SLAVE POPULATION, 1790–1860

Year	Total Population
1790	697,624
1800	893,602
1810	1,191,362
1820	1,538,022
1830	2,009,043
1840	2,487,355
1850	3,204,313
1860	3,953,760

Source: A Century of Population Growth: From the First Census of the United States to the Twelfth, 1700–1900 (Baltimore: Genealogical Publishing Co., 1970).

The invention of the cotton gin in 1793 made it possible to grow cotton more economically. The expanding "cotton kingdom" employed most of the unfree blacks. In Mississippi, Alabama, Louisiana, Arkansas, and Texas the harshness of their servitude increased as western planters intent on making fortunes drove the workers hard. But a higher birthrate and less deadly working conditions than in the West Indies caused rapid population growth on the mainland. The slave population shot up from about 700,000 in 1790 to 4 million in 1860 on the eve of the Civil War.

As slaves grew in numbers, adding to the political power of the slave states (because of the three-fifths representation provision), many northerners became alarmed over the expansion of slavery into the new western territories. Some also believed that slavery anywhere was wrong. A crisis occurred when Missouri sought admission as a new slave state, which would upset the balance between free and slave states in the Union. The Missouri Compromise of 1820 eased the tensions and banned expansion of slavery north of latitude 36°30′ west of Missouri.

Slave Life

Slaves most commonly worked on plantations. Planters organized them into gangs, assigning tasks to be done under the supervision of an overseer, who was sometimes himself a slave. The slaves lived in rude cabins and received rations of food and clothing. They sometimes tended their own vegetable gardens with the privilege of selling the surplus. Discipline could be severe; slaves who were unruly or who fled and were caught usually suffered harsh penalties. The severity, however, varied with the master, the work, and the region. Some masters were kind, and some even offered incentives for jobs well done. The ultimate reward was freedom; by 1860, 250,000 free blacks lived in the South, over half of them in Virginia and Maryland. But most slaves lived in fear of harsh punishment or of seeing their families divided and sold. They were kept illiterate and usually could worship in church only under white observation.

Many slaves lived in urban communities, which offered a measure of freedom. Some were hired out, occasionally keeping part of their wages. Other slaves worked as craftsmen, domestics, and industrial laborers. A few won distinction. Phillis Wheatley, born in Africa and sold in Boston, startled the world when she published a book of poems. Richard Allen, a Delaware slave, purchased his freedom and founded the African Methodist Episcopal church, which became the leading black religious organization. Frederick Douglass escaped bondage and became a renowned orator and writer.

Slave rebellion was uncommon in the United States, compared with Latin America. A slave revolt at Stono, South Carolina, in 1739 took the lives of about twenty-five whites and four times as many blacks before it was put down. The most famous rebellion occurred in 1831 when Nat Turner, a slave preacher, and his band killed fifty-seven whites in Southampton County, Virginia. The militia captured Turner and quelled the revolt. In many parts of the South white patrols kept vigil at night to prevent escapes or rebellions. Fear was an emotion shared by white and black.

Flight was another form of rebellion, though overdramatized by writers like Harriet Beecher Stowe and exaggerated in numbers. Some escaped slaves like Douglass worked in the abolition movement. Others like Harriet Tubman helped fugitives flee to the North through a loosely organized network called the Underground Railroad.

But most slaves endured life with little hope for anything better in this world. The law afforded scant protection against injustices piled on to their captivity; for cruelty there was virtually no redress. Marriages were not recognized by law; slave testimony was not accepted by courts; women toiled alongside men in the fields; and education as well as freedom lay beyond their grasp.

Several generations of slaves on a southern plantation.

With the growth of an abolitionist movement in the North and expanding prosperity in the South, the lot of the slave probably became increasingly harsh. The Fugitive Slave Law was made more severe in 1850. The national government in the 1850s abandoned the 1820 Compromise and permitted slavery to expand in the territories. The Republican Party was organized to halt this expansion. Its success in electing a president, Abraham Lincoln, in 1860 led to southern states leaving the Union, civil war, and emancipation. The death of slavery, effected in part by 190,000 black soldiers in the northern army, came in 1865 with ratification of the Thirteenth Amendment abolishing slavery in the United States.

For further reading: William Loren Katz, *Breaking the Chains: African-American Slave Resistance* (New York: Atheneum, 1990).

JAMES A. RAWLEY

SMITH, JOHN

(1580–1631)   *Soldier, explorer, and historian.*

John Smith grew up in England, but left his native land as a youth to serve as a soldier in the Balkan Mountains of southeastern Europe. After many colorful adventures he returned to England in 1604. He spent the rest of his life exploring, promoting, and writing about the colonies of Virginia and New England.

Smith was a member of the first party of colonizers sent by the Virginia Company in 1607. The little group suffered from disease and conflicts even before it landed at the site of Jamestown. Its members could not cooperate enough even to raise food for themselves and relied on corn that they begged or stole from the surrounding Powhatan Indians.

Exploring the Chesapeake Bay, Smith obtained provisions from the people living along its shores. He was captured and held prisoner by the Powhatans long enough to learn some of their language and observe their customs, which he described in his later writings about Virginia. He also told how Pocahontas, the chief's daughter, begged her father to spare Smith's life.

Elected president of the Jamestown colony in 1608, Smith showed his skills as a leader by demanding, for example, that each man work as many hours in the day as he himself did. The colonists survived the winter without great loss of life. But after an injury forced Smith to return to England the next year, they neglected their work and almost starved to death.

Smith wrote of Virginia in three books. The last and longest of them was the *Generall Historie of Virginia, New-England, and the Summer Isles* (1624), which tells also of his exploration of the coast of New England. He is always the hero of his own tales, but historians suppose him to be generally reliable when describing the people and lands of North America.

See also Colonial America; Pocahontas.

THOMAS COLE

SMITH, JOSEPH

(1805–44) *Founder of the Church of Jesus Christ of Latter-day Saints (Mormon).*

Born in Vermont, Smith was reared in a poor but ambitious family who lived on farms in southern Vermont and New Hampshire. When he was ten, they moved to Palmyra, New York. Along with working on farms and in village shops, young Joseph read the Bible and attended religious revivals.

When Smith was fourteen, he knelt to pray in the woods and had a vision of "Divine Beings" who comforted him and responded to his earnest questions by expressing disapproval of the teachings of existing churches. He was instructed to tell his parents of the vision and to keep a pure heart. When he was seventeen he reported a nighttime experience during which an angel named Moroni told him about a sacred history engraved on gold plates that were hidden on a nearby hill. The history, the angel said, gave an account of the historical and religious experiences of early inhabitants of America, who had migrated thousands of years ago from the Near East.

After marrying Emma Hale, a schoolteacher, Smith obtained the plates, he said, and, under inspiration, dictated to his wife and other local scribes his interpretation of the writings on the plates. Six hundred pages in length, the manuscript, known as the *Book of Mormon,* was published in 1830, when Joseph was twenty-five. It is regarded by many scholars as the most unusual religious work produced in America.

Shortly after the book's publication, Smith gathered a few friends and believers in his new Christianity from the Manchester and Fayette, New York, areas, and organized the Church of Christ (later called the Church of Jesus Christ of Latter-day Saints). Claiming he had received them from God, Smith revealed additional doctrines and practices and eventually established settlements for believers in northeastern Ohio, western Missouri, and western Illinois.

Because of their different religious beliefs, their vigorous preaching and baptizing, and their group practices, his followers, called Mormons because of their belief in the *Book of Mormon,* were regarded as undesirable. Driven out of their homes in Missouri, they moved to Hancock County in western Illinois, where they built Nauvoo, at one time the largest city in Illinois. On June 27, 1844, an anti-Mormon mob, including many members of the Illinois state militia, raided the jail in Carthage, Illinois, where Joseph and his brother were being held on a trumped-up charge and killed the two men. Smith was only thirty-eight.

As a leader, Smith was a good organizer. He laid out cities, built temples, founded a university, and established a woman's auxiliary, the Women's Relief Society. Because of his claims of heavenly instruction and his rejection of other religions, he was subjected to lawsuits, kidnappings, tarrings and featherings, and threats on his life. Nevertheless, he attracted and retained the loyalty of a large, diverse, and talented group of associates. There were 35,000 members of his church at the time of his murder.

His followers fled Illinois after his death, walking and riding in covered wagons to the Valley of the Great Salt Lake in Utah, where the church he had founded continued to grow.

See also Mormons; Young, Brigham.

For further reading: George Q. Cannon, *A History of the Prophet Joseph Smith for Young People* (Salt Lake City, Utah: Deseret, 1957).

LEONARD J. ARRINGTON

SNCC
See Student Non-Violent Coordinating Committee.

SOCIAL GOSPEL

The growth of city slums in the late nineteenth century and the plight of the poor people who inhabited these squalid neighborhoods led many ministers to try to understand the relation between poverty and crime, corruption, and disease. They soon concluded that the poor were victims of these conditions, not weak or sinful people whose misdeeds and lack of sound moral character caused poor neighborhoods to deteriorate.

They preached a social gospel. The way to save souls, they argued, was to apply Christian principles to social problems. They therefore sought to improve living conditions rather than to persuade slum dwellers to change their habits and seek salvation in prayer. Before the poor could be expected to lead pure lives, they must have decent places to live, healthy food, and proper medical care. Instead of denouncing immoral behavior and warning of the eternal punishment that awaited sinners, they attacked corrupt big-city politicians, counseled laborers to join unions, and called for the construction of parks, public housing projects, and better schools. Some became convinced that capitalism was the underlying cause of slum conditions and joined the Socialist Party.

The best known of the social gospel preachers were Washington Gladden, a Congregational minister in Columbus, Ohio, whose book *Applied Christianity* (1887) was a kind of social gospel bible, and Walter Rauschenbusch, a professor of church history and author of *Christianizing the Social Order* (1907).

SOCIAL LEGISLATION

The term *social legislation* refers to laws intended to protect the rights and well-being of those people—children, members of racial or ethnic minorities, women, the unemployed, elderly, ill, physically or mentally disabled—who might be unable to care for themselves because of forces beyond their control. Such forces include discrimination, economic changes, and prejudice.

The United States has thousands of pieces of social legislation at all levels of government. There are workplace safety laws, welfare programs, Social Security pensions, civil rights measures—even income tax laws, called "progressive," that require richer Americans to pay at a higher rate than poorer ones. Nearly all are controversial to some extent.

The controversy is rooted in history. When Europeans began settling in America in the early 1600s, they found a huge continent teeming with natural resources. Almost anyone could earn a decent living and many prospered. By the 1800s, the country was seeing its first self-made millionaires. Their rags-to-riches stories seemed to prove that in this land of opportunity anyone, however poor or disadvantaged, could succeed simply through hard work. With that idea came another: that people who do not succeed in life fail because they are lazy. They have only themselves to blame and deserve little help from society.

Early Inequities

Among those who believed that hard work brings success were the millions of immigrants who poured into America during the nineteenth century. But the country had changed. The United States was becoming an industrialized nation. Instead of limitless opportunity, many immigrants found only low-paying factory jobs. In 1859, men in the shoe factories of Massachusetts were working sixteen-hour days for three dollars a week. Women worked the same hours for a dollar a week and children as young as eight or ten for pennies. Others who found that hard work did not necessarily bring material success were blacks. Though slavery was abolished in the 1860s, racial prejudice kept most blacks from getting an education, voting, or finding good jobs.

By the end of the century, some Americans were trying to correct such injustices. Several states passed laws to limit the working hours of women and children. In 1916, the first federal child labor law was passed. But it, along with state labor laws, was overturned by the Supreme Court. In addition, the Court had overturned a progressive income tax law in 1895. (In 1913, the Constitution was amended to permit a progressive tax.) Moreover, the Court upheld racial segregation in 1876, 1884, and 1896.

Social Measures Enacted

It took a catastrophe to bring about desperately needed social change. In 1929, the U.S. economy collapsed. By 1933, when Franklin D. Roosevelt became president, millions of Americans were jobless, homeless, and hungry. Roosevelt promised them a New Deal. At his urging, Congress enacted emergency bills to give jobs, money, and food to the poorest.

Yet although Roosevelt knew the emergency aid was essential, he was determined to keep it temporary. Permanent relief for the needy leads to "spiritual and moral disintegration," he warned in 1935. He asked Congress to help working Americans protect themselves against the possibility of future need. Under his Social Security plan, workers would pay into a fund that they could later draw upon for unemployment benefits and retirement pensions.

It was soon clear that the Social Security Act of 1935 was not broad enough to help all who needed assistance. Among those whom it left unprotected were unemployed widows, members of the clergy, and agricultural and domestic workers. Over time, the law was rewritten to include all these and others. Aid to

Dependent Children (now called Aid to Families with Dependent Children, or AFDC) was enacted. Public health clinics were opened. Congress set a federal minimum wage for workers. In a switch, the Supreme Court upheld the growing patchwork of social legislation.

With time, new pieces were added to the patchwork. Harry S. Truman, president from Roosevelt's death in 1945 until 1953, championed black civil rights. President Dwight D. Eisenhower (1953–61) extended Social Security. President John F. Kennedy saw little of his New Frontier program enacted before his assassination, but his successor, Lyndon B. Johnson (1963–69), had better luck with his Great Society. Food stamps for the hungry, Head Start for preschoolers from low-income families, Medicare to provide health care for the elderly, and Medicaid to provide it to the needy were among its provisions. Johnson also signed two major civil rights acts and promoted programs of affirmative action to increase educational and employment opportunities for blacks, women, and others discriminated against in the past. At the same time, states and cities were enacting social legislation of their own.

Controversy Grows

With the new programs came objections to them. One concerned fairness. Affirmative action laws, in particular, were singled out as unfair to white men. Civil rights laws were also attacked as favoring some groups over others.

Another criticism had to do with money. Minimum wage and workplace safety laws cost industry too much, business leaders claimed. Wealthy Americans complained about progressive taxation. But what most outraged many Americans was the soaring cost of welfare programs like AFDC. In 1955, the country spent $621 million on AFDC. In 1970, it spent $4.1 *billion*. Even allowing for years of rising prices, that was an enormous increase. For some families, welfare seemed to be not temporary but a permanent way of life. Or so a number of politicians, including Ronald Reagan, charged.

Reagan, elected president in 1982, pledged to cut social spending. During his two terms, food stamp and AFDC spending was reduced almost 20 percent. (Nevertheless, AFDC cost taxpayers over $20 billion in 1991.) Reagan also signed a less progressive income tax law and reduced enforcement of civil rights and affirmative action measures.

Reagan's policies, combined with bad economic times, took their toll. As the 1990s be-

• •

For descriptions of specific social problems and legislation or programs to deal with them, see the following entries:

gan, over 35 million Americans—13 million of them children—were living in poverty. Eight million were jobless; 37 million had no health insurance. Estimates of the number of homeless Americans ranged upward to 3 million. Racial tensions led to big-city riots, including one in Los Angeles in 1992 that left fifty-two people dead.

Like every modern president, Bill Clinton, who entered the White House in 1993, had to decide how to balance the needs of poor and disadvantaged Americans against the national spirit of independence and self-sufficiency. His administration seemed committed to civil rights, affirmative action, progressive taxation, worker safety, and so on. But problems loomed. Clinton promised to reform welfare by limiting the length of time a person could receive benefits. Other presidents tried to do that—and failed. He also promised a program to provide health insurance for every American, and a debate continues over its provisions.

For further reading: Ann E. Weiss, *Welfare: Helping Hand or Trap?* (Hillside, N.J.: Enslow, 1990).

ANN E. WEISS

SONS OF LIBERTY

After the passage of the Sugar Act of 1764, informal groups of colonists opposed to British tax policies began springing up in various American towns. Members frequently called themselves Sons of Liberty. When Parliament passed the hated Stamp Act of 1765, these groups began to get in touch with one another to discuss how to persuade Parliament to repeal the law and, if Parliament refused, how to prevent the stamps from being distributed

and sold. The name Sons of Liberty was adopted by all of the groups at this time.

Most of the "Liberty boys" were respectable, middle-class people. They claimed to be loyal subjects of the king, and they rarely advocated violent demonstrations or other illegal acts. But they frequently collaborated with more radical individuals and sometimes participated in and even organized violent demonstrations. In Boston, for example, they joined mobs that broke into the homes of the lieutenant governor and the man appointed to sell the stamps.

The Sons stopped their activities after the repeal of the Stamp Act, but the movement sprang to life again after the passage of the Townshend Acts in 1767 and continued until the outbreak of the Revolution. Sons of Liberty joined enthusiastically in the Boston Tea Party.

See also Revolution: The War for Independence.

SOUTHERN CHRISTIAN LEADERSHIP CONFERENCE

The Southern Christian Leadership Conference (SCLC) was led by the Reverend Dr. Martin Luther King, Jr., and was the backbone of the civil rights movement of the 1950s and 1960s. In 1957 following the Montgomery, Alabama, bus boycott (1955–56), which resulted in the desegregation of buses in that city, sixty black ministers from ten states met in Atlanta to form the organization. They elected King, one of the boycott's leaders, as SCLC's first president, and the Reverend Ralph Abernathy treasurer.

The SCLC followed the nonviolent tactics of civil disobedience, which King adopted from the Indian nationalist leader, Mahatma Gandhi. As King expressed it, "I had come to see early that the Christian doctrine of love operating through the Gandhian method of nonviolence was one of the most potent weapons available to the Negro in his struggle for freedom."

The organization took a leading role in the Freedom Rides, which challenged segregation on southern buses and other public accommodations In the 1963 March on Washington, which gathered together over 200,000 peaceful protesters, King delivered his famous I Have a Dream speech. The march publicized blacks' struggle for civil rights and demanded that the country wake up to the racial inequities in American society. The SCLC also took part in the 1964 Freedom Summer program to register rural Mississippi blacks to vote. The group conducted demonstrations in southern cities to fight discrimination and focus attention on racism. The demonstrations the SCLC set up in Selma, Alabama, and the segregationists' violent response to them helped persuade Congress to approve the Voting Rights Act of 1965, which eliminated local laws and practices that prevented blacks from voting.

Although the SCLC played a major role in the civil rights movement, it lost influence as the movement continued. Many blacks, especially younger ones, rejected the nonviolent tactics that King and the SCLC preached and resented what they perceived as King's willingness to compromise with whites. After King's assassination in 1968, the SCLC leadership was deeply divided over the organization's future. Nevertheless, led by King's family and friends, the SCLC has continued fighting discrimination.

See also Civil Rights Movement; King, Martin Luther, Jr.

SPACE PROGRAM

Soon after the end of World War II, in 1945, scientists working for the U.S. government literally began trying to produce "spaceships." During the late 1940s and early 1950s, pilotless rocket-powered vessels were sent higher and higher, finally reaching the edge of space. By 1955, rocket scientists felt they would soon be able to put a small craft filled with instruments into orbit around the earth—an artificial satellite. It would collect information about conditions in space and send it back to earth. Confident in the superiority of their science and technology, Americans calmly waited for this great accomplishment.

But suddenly, on October 4, 1957, Americans were shocked to learn that they had been beaten! A satellite called *Sputnik* was whizzing around the earth in orbit, but it had been put there by America's great rival, the Soviet Union.

President Dwight D. Eisenhower quickly launched an all-out program to catch up with Russia, and on January 31, 1958, a tube-shaped satellite called *Explorer I* was shot into orbit from Cape Canaveral, Florida. Later that year, an organization known as the National Aeronautics and Space Administration—NASA—was created by the government and made responsible for the U.S. space program.

The Moon Program

In 1961, newly elected president John F. Kennedy announced the goal of landing an American astronaut on the moon by 1970. A "space race" then developed between the United States and the Soviet Union. The Russians forged ahead in 1961 by sending the first human being (Yuri Gagarin) into space in an orbiting vessel. But during the next eleven months, American astronauts Alan Shepard, Jr., and Virgil Grissom made nonorbiting trips into space. Then on February 20, 1962, John Glenn became the first American to go into orbit, circling the earth three times in four hours and fifty-five minutes. The Soviet Union scored another "first" in 1963, however, by putting the first woman into space: cosmonaut Valentina Tereshkova.

Meanwhile, attempts were made to learn as much as possible about the moon before anyone went there. Beginning in 1961, a series of remote-controlled vessels called *Rangers* were sent to the moon to take close-up pictures of the surface, test the soil, and collect other information. The first six *Rangers* failed, but *Ranger 7*, launched in July 1964, sent back by television the first close-up pictures of the surface of the moon, showing things never before seen by human eyes.

Scientists working on the program to put a person on the moon knew it might sometimes be necessary for an astronaut to go outside a ship while in space. They had to find out if a human could do such a thing without having physical or mental problems. In 1965 both the United States and the Soviet Union conducted "space walks," with men wearing special space suits floating outside their orbiting vessels, to which they were attached by lifelines. The first U.S. space walk was made by astronaut Edward White on June 3, 1965. The space walks proved that humans could function outside a vessel in space without any ill effects.

The next step in the moon program was to solve the problem of "linking up"—making one spacecraft connect to another, so that astronauts could move from one to the other. This was accomplished on March 16, 1966, when *Gemini 8* crewed by Neil Armstrong and David Scott, slid its barrel-shaped nose into the flared cone at the rear of an *Agena* spacecraft while both vessels were orbiting at a speed of about 18,000 miles an hour.

By 1969 all was ready for the assault on the moon. First, in March, two vessels orbiting above the earth practiced linking up, unlinking, and then linking again, as spacecrafts would have to do above the moon. In May, three astronauts made a practice run, flying a ship to within eight miles of the moon and returning to earth. Then, on July 20, while the spacecraft *Columbia*, piloted by Michael

Astronaut Edwin "Buzz" Aldrin about to take his first step on the moon. The photographer was Neil Armstrong, already having taken his "giant leap for mankind."

Collins, orbited around the moon, a smaller craft, *Eagle*, manned by Neil Armstrong and Edwin ("Buzz") Aldrin, unlinked from *Columbia* and dropped to the moon's surface. Armstrong became the first person to walk upon the moon, leaving footprints that are still there.

Other Space Projects

Work was also going on to explore the other planets of the solar system. In 1965, the remote-controlled spacecraft *Mariner 4* provided the first pictures of the surface of Mars, and in 1967, *Mariner 5* gathered information about the planet Venus. Launched to go into orbit around Mars in 1971, *Mariner 9* sent back more than seven thousand astounding pictures, showing such features as a giant volcano and an enormously long canyon.

In 1973, NASA launched *Skylab 1* into orbit. This was a "space laboratory," in which astronauts could live and work for months at a time. *Skylab*, however, was damaged in launching, and the first crew sent up had to fix it before anyone could live in it. During the next nine months three different crews stayed in *Skylab*, doing important scientific work that could be done only in space. But *Skylab*'s orbit gradually dropped toward earth, and in 1979 the empty vessel entered the atmosphere, where it burned up.

In the meantime, the exploration of the solar system continued. In 1973, *Mariner 10* sent back the first pictures of the surface of Mercury. *Pioneer 10*, which had been launched in 1972, flew past Jupiter in 1973 and provided amazing pictures. In 1976, a robot landing craft dropped onto the surface of Mars, where it took pictures and made tests of the soil in an inconclusive attempt to find out if life exists on the Red Planet. The vessels called *Voyagers* were launched in 1977, and three years later *Voyager 1* produced the first

awe-inspiring glimpses of distant Saturn and its moons.

In 1981, the space shuttle *Columbia* went up, the first of the kind of spacecrafts now in use. They are launched into orbit by huge rockets, and when their mission is completed, they actually glide back down to earth. Thus, they can be used again and again. Throughout the 1980s and early 1990s there were many shuttle missions, with several kinds of satellites and the Hubble Space Telescope carried up and put into orbit by the shuttle crews. In 1983, Dr. Sally Ride became the first American woman in space, and Col. Guion Bluford the first black American astronaut, when they served on the crews of shuttles that year. Dr. Taylor Wang became the first Asian American to go into space in 1985, and a year later Dr. Franklin Chang-Diaz was the first Hispanic American to go on a shuttle flight. Ten days after Dr. Chang-Diaz's shuttle landed, another shuttle, the *Challenger*, was launched, and in a horrifying tragedy it exploded, killing the entire crew.

In the 1980s, *Voyager 2* sped past Saturn and then far-off Uranus and Neptune, providing pictures that vastly increased knowledge of the solar system. For the future, NASA is planning more shuttle missions, a two-year study of Jupiter by a remote-controlled craft, and construction of a space station in orbit around earth. And sometime in the twenty-first century, human beings will probably fulfill the dream of exploring Mars.

See also Armstrong, Neil; Glenn, John; Science and Technology.

TOM MCGOWEN

SPANISH-AMERICAN WAR

Victory in the brief Spanish-American War of 1898 won the United States world-power status and brought with it responsibilities that America has borne, often unwillingly, to the present day.

The war with Spain came at the close of a half century of rapid industrialization and westward movement. Proud of their country's growth, many Americans called for further territorial expansion. The expansionists argued that colonies would provide markets and raw materials for American industry, and win the United States the respect of the European colonial powers. Expansionism also satisfied a missionary impulse in the American character: a belief that the United States had the moral obligation to "civilize the backward peoples" of the world.

Cuba, Spain's island colony ninety miles south of Florida, became the immediate focus of the expansionists' ambitions. The United States had repeatedly tried to buy Cuba, but Spain, determined to save the remnant of its once mighty empire in the Americas, rejected the American offers and brutally suppressed a Cuban independence movement. When the patriot Máximo Gómez led a revolt in 1895, the Spanish authorities forced more than a million country folk into concentration camps where an estimated 400,000 died of hunger and disease.

The suffering in Cuba brought an outcry in the United States. President William McKinley demanded reforms in Cuba's government and dispatched the battleship *Maine* to Havana, the colony's capital, as a demonstration of American resolve. While lying at anchor in the harbor on February 15, 1898, the *Maine* was torn apart by an explosion that killed over two hundred of its crew. Within a day, American newspapers published lurid accounts of the disaster. Rival newspaper publishers William Randolph Hearst and Joseph Pulitzer created a war hysteria by blaming the explosion on an underwater mine.

While American and Spanish investigators probed the cause of the disaster, expansionists in the U.S. government did not wait for their findings. Instead they seized on the incident as an excuse to prepare for war. Assistant Secretary of the Navy Theodore Roosevelt readied the Atlantic fleet for an invasion of Cuba and ordered the navy's Far Eastern squadron outfitted for an attack on the Philippine Islands, Spain's restless colony in the Pacific. In Roosevelt's expansionist thinking, the Philippines represented an ideal opportunity for the United States to join the imperial competition with a prosperous colony that would provide a secure base for a Pacific fleet and a bridge to the world's largest potential market: China.

Spanish investigators concluded that coal in one of the *Maine*'s storage bunkers had kindled by spontaneous combustion, touching off ammunition stored nearby. American investigators sided with the mine theory, although they could not identify who was responsible. (Seventy-eight years later, American naval engineers would review the evidence and conclude that the Spaniards had been correct.)

The War Comes

Under pressure from the American press and public, McKinley demanded independence for Cuba. Spain refused, and on April 19, 1898, Congress gave McKinley permission to use force. Spain responded with a declaration of war.

Executing Roosevelt's orders, Commodore George Dewey set sail with his Far Eastern squadron for Manila, the capital of the Philippines. On May 1, Dewey's warships destroyed the Spanish fleet in the Battle of Manila Bay. Dewey anchored to await the arrival of an American army, while the Spanish government continued to hold Manila, and a large army of rebels under Gen. Emilio Aguinaldo surrounded the city. Aguinaldo declared a republic on June 12, but the Americans refused to recognize Philippine independence.

In the Caribbean, American plans for an attack on Havana hit a snag when a wily Spanish admiral, Pasqual Cervera, slipped through the American blockade to anchor his small squadron in the fortified harbor of

Santiago de Cuba on the island's southeastern coast. Overestimating the danger that Cervera's ships represented, American military planners redirected the invasion fleet. On June 22, an army of sixteen thousand American soldiers under Gen. Rufus Shafter landed east of Santiago. Among the army's regiments was the First Volunteer Cavalry, nicknamed the Rough Riders by its second in command, Lt. Col. Theodore Roosevelt, who

Col. Theodore Roosevelt (in spectacles and bandanna just left of center) and the Rough Riders, a colorful and legendary group of soldiers made up of cowboys, football players, miners, eastern bluebloods, and other adventurers. They are posed at the top of San Juan Hill in Cuba after its capture in July 1898.

had resigned his desk job to get into the fight.

Under heavy fire the army assaulted Santiago's outlying defenses along the San Juan Heights on July 1. Roosevelt, who had succeeded to command of the Rough Riders, led the attack on Kettle Hill (not the San Juan Hill of popular legend). With the Americans holding the heights and the besieged city facing starvation, Santiago's commander asked Havana for permission to surrender. On the morning of July 3, Cervera's little squadron sacrificed itself for Spain's honor in a running fight with the American fleet. Santiago surrendered on July 17, bringing the war in Cuba to a close.

While Shafter's army suffered through a deadly epidemic of yellow fever in Cuba, a fresh army landed in Puerto Rico, advancing toward the capital of San Juan against light opposition. A third American army arrived in the Philippines, giving Dewey the means to take Manila on August 13. What Secretary of State John Hay called the "splendid little war" was over.

Results of the War

Spain and the United States signed a peace treaty in December 1898. Spain gave up any claim to Cuba, and the United States supervised the formation of a new Cuban government, promising independence in two years. Spain also ceded Puerto Rico and the Pacific island of Guam to the United States and accepted a token payment of $20 million for the Philippines. America thus became a colonial power at the risk of its democratic principles.

Returning home a hero, Roosevelt was elected governor of New York and then vice president, succeeding to the presidency when McKinley was assassinated in 1901. Under Roosevelt, the United States built a large navy, began digging the Panama Canal, and as-sumed a major role in international affairs. But the experience of war and his new responsibilities cooled Roosevelt's expansionist passions. Prominent Americans, including industrialist Andrew Carnegie, author Mark Twain, and former president Grover Cleveland, formed the Anti-Imperialist League in a successful campaign against further expansionist activity.

America's brief adventure in imperial expansionism had enduring consequences. The Filipinos waged a bloody rebellion against American rule that cost the lives of four thousand American soldiers, twenty thousand rebels, and two hundred thousand civilians between 1899 and 1902. Cubans bitterly resented decades of interference by the United States in their internal affairs, and American meddling and economic exploitation also created deep hostility elsewhere in Latin America.

See also Dewey, George; Expansion, Territorial; McKinley, William; Philippines, Acquisition of: Puerto Rico, Acquisition of; Roosevelt, Theodore.

For further reading: Alden R. Carter, *The Spanish-American War: Imperial Ambitions* (New York: Franklin Watts, 1992).

ALDEN R. CARTER

SPIES
See Espionage.

SPOCK, BENJAMIN
(1903–)   *Pediatrician and peace activist.*

As a college student, Spock won a gold medal in the 1924 Olympic Games in Paris while rowing with the Yale University crew team. He was the first person to become both a pediatric doctor and a child psychiatrist. He taught medicine and child psychiatry, did research, and wrote many magazine columns on child care.

After practicing medicine for ten years, Spock began writing a manual of advice for parents, *Baby and Child Care.* Published in 1946 and selling for twenty-five cents, the book was an instant success because it gave parents a lot more sensible information than earlier books had.

Over the years, *Baby and Child Care* has sold some 40 million copies, more than any other American book except the Bible, and has been translated into thirty-nine languages. Spock revolutionized modern child care by teaching many generations of parents to understand their children better. He encouraged parents to be flexible and to trust their own instincts.

In the 1960s, Spock became an active opponent of the United States' involvement in the Vietnam War. He devoted himself to peace efforts and was a popular speaker at antiwar rallies. In 1968, a federal court convicted him of counseling men to evade the draft, but his conviction was overturned the next year. Spock was nominated in 1972 as a presidential candidate by the People's Party and ran an unsuccessful campaign on a platform of peace and equality for people all over the world.

See also Family Life; Medicine.

For further reading: Benjamin Spock and Mary Morgan, *Spock on Spock* (New York: Pantheon, 1989).

LEDA BLUMBERG

SPORTS
See Baseball; Basketball; Boxing; Football; Golf; Gymnastics; Hockey; Horseracing; Olympic Games; Sports, Popular Participation in; Sports, Spectator; Tennis.

SPORTS, POPULAR PARTICIPATION IN

Americans have nearly always participated in some sort of games and physical recreation, though they have not always called such activities sports. How much time and effort Americans devoted to their leisure depended on where and when they lived, and to which class they belonged.

Colonial Sports
Northern colonists in the 1600s and 1700s, for example, rarely thought about play or exercise as an end in itself. Their world was overwhelmingly rural. Clearing land, plowing, harvesting, building, performing household chores—these kept people so physically active that they never felt the need for exercise. They and their children, however, did feel the need for play and celebration, and they organized such activities mainly around useful occasions: house-raisings, corn-husking parties, election days, militia musters, and spinning and quilting bees.

Puritan men, like their English forebears, used such events to engage in shooting, wrestling, and running contests, as well as combat sports like sword-fighting. In the winter ice skating and sledding were common. They also sang, played ball games, conducted plowing and tree-cutting contests, and hunted and fished. Most rural peoples throughout history have combined the work of their lives with occasional revelry. Hunting and fishing, for example, were both useful and pleasurable.

From their earliest days, the southern colonies were more open to sports and games. Soon after the founding of Jamestown in 1607, Capt. John Smith worried that for too many, "4 hours each day was spent in worke, the rest in pastimes and merry exercise." Later in the century, planters modeled themselves on English gentlemen and played their sports: cockfights and horse races, cardplaying and the hunt. Although southerners, especially small farmers and African slaves, worked just as hard as northern farmers, they put much more value on leisure, and public sporting displays became a major part of southern life. Increasingly over the seventeenth and eighteenth centuries, how a man acted in play and sport—whether he was competitive, whether he was willing to risk a lot of money on a horse race or cockfight, whether he knew how to defend his "honor"—determined how he was viewed by his fellows.

Children, of course, North and South, engaged in all sorts of games and physical activities. "I spent my time," John Adams, the second president, recalled in his *Autobiography,* "driving hoops, playing marbles, playing Quoits, Wrestling, Swimming, Skaiting and above all in shooting."

Sports in the Cities

City people often felt they needed more exercise, and this helps explain why participant sports became more popular as cities grew more numerous and larger in the nineteenth century. The Reverend Sylvester Graham, inventor of the graham cracker, wrote and lectured widely in the 1830s on the benefits of a good diet, fresh air, and exercise. German immigrants introduced gymnastics to America in the decades before the Civil War. Many people seem to have become more conscious of the value of physical activity. Crowds of fifty thousand ice skaters jammed the lakes of New York's Central Park while it was still being built.

Cities were also home to saloons, which frequently put on cockfights and bare-knuckle prizefights in the early nineteenth century. Many young working-class men joined volunteer fire companies and volunteer militias, which combined much physical competition with lots of alcohol and occasional brawling. There were no organized sports leagues at the time, but there were occasional, well-attended sports contests—prizefights, horse races, "pedestrian" (foot) races, and rowing matches—in the New York metropolitan area throughout the first half of the nineteenth century.

Baseball began to sweep the Northeast in the late 1850s, and was already being called the "national pastime" before the Civil War. Thousands of young clerks and craftsmen, as well as middle-class sportsmen, joined the new baseball clubs. The Civil War contributed greatly to the interest in sports. Soldiers usually had little to do between battles and organized sports contests to keep occupied. They also taught each other their regional sports, thereby spreading baseball across the United States.

Postwar Changes

Following the war the United States experienced its first real boom in participant and spectator sports. The upper classes brought tennis (1875) and golf (1890s) to this country from England and Scotland.

But baseball led all other sports in popularity and participation. Editors commented on "baseball fever" in the 1880s and 1890s, as young people made the game a truly national sport. The children of Irish and German immigrants flooded into the professional game, and every town in the country, it seemed, had its local team. Even women took up the sport, though they had to buck substantial public disapproval to do so.

Through most of American history, women were prohibited from engaging in the more active physical sports. In the 1830s, reformers such as Catharine Beecher had tried to improve women's overall health by persuading women to take more exercise. But hers was a minority voice. In the 1890s, however, middle-class women simply flooded out of doors, walking, hiking on nature trails, and riding bicycles, which quickly became highly popular.

American football and basketball joined the sporting "big three" in the 1890s. Football became a hugely popular, though extremely violent, college participant and spectator sport, while basketball, invented in 1891 at Springfield College, was quickly adopted by urban youth, male and female, across the country.

The twentieth century has seen several major developments in participant sports. Organized sports moved into public schools following World War I and became part of the required curriculum and central to school life. At the same time, formerly elite sports such as tennis and golf spread throughout the society. Women's sports underwent a revolution in the 1960s and 1970s, producing many millions more female athletes than there had been even a generation earlier. So did the sporting experience of African Americans, who finally leaped over most remaining racial barriers in participant sports. And finally, there was the immense, ever-present impact of television—which poured billions of dollars into sports leagues, associations, athletic salaries—and the dreams of young people. Nowadays, too, as Americans have become more concerned about their health than at any time in history, sports—particularly aerobic exercise, running, and walking—have become immensely popular throughout the society.

See also Sports, Spectator.

WARREN GOLDSTEIN

SPORTS, SPECTATOR

Games have been around for thousands of years. Native Americans played all sorts of games—fighting and wrestling contests, hunting and shooting matches, ball games like lacrosse. Europeans also played countless games. The English during the years when they were colonizing the Americas were famous for their love of play. Some of their pastimes we would recognize today, such as horse racing, or simple ball games. But some—like cudgeling (fighting with sticks) or animal baiting (where trained dogs were set against bulls or bears)—would seem strange to us.

Games Become Sports

Games and sports are cousins, not identical twins. For example, children playing baseball in the street are engaged in a game; when professionals play in a stadium, the game becomes a sport. Games are informal: when, where, and by whom they are played changes all the time; the rules bend according to who is playing; no large amounts of money hinge on the outcome. Sports, on the other hand, are much more formal: players are professionals or trained amateurs; massive amounts of money are spent; rules are spelled out by organizations like the National Football League or the National Basketball Association; paying fans attend regularly scheduled contests in stadiums.

By this definition, sports have been with us for only a little over a hundred years. American have always played games, but not until the late nineteenth century have they been familiar with sports. Children and adults in the colonies played marbles and rounders, a forerunner of baseball. President John Quincy Adams loved to swim, and he owned a billiard table. During the Civil War, Union and Confederate soldiers held informal boxing matches and baseball games. But only since the last third of the nineteenth century have there been baseball leagues, championship prizefights, and regular football matches between rival colleges. In fact, it was not until the 1880s that a separate sports section appeared in newspapers, and only in the 1890s was the sport of basketball even invented!

Before the Civil War, harness racing (where horses pulled men riding in carriages) was the closest thing to a modern sport in America. Tracks held regularly scheduled contests, horses were timed, and racing organizations made sure that rules were enforced. During the 1850s, countless amateur baseball clubs were formed. In northern cities, running races (called pedestrian matches) occasionally attracted thousands of fans, and in the South, horse racing and cockfighting were highly popular. But the most important milestones on the way to creating modern sports were the founding of baseball's National League in 1876, which made teams into businesses that played in their own cities with their own players, and the legalization of boxing in the 1890s, when boxers wearing gloves first fought championship matches. By the beginning of the twentieth century, countless teams and athletes were competing in playground basketball programs, on college football teams, in country-club tennis matches, and in a variety of other organized sports.

Why did Americans suddenly grow interested in sports around the beginning of the twentieth century? Technology offers one answer. Electric lights now could brighten an indoor arena; trains could transport fans and teams; printing presses could cheaply produce thousands of newspapers to publicize

Mickey Mantle at bat in a game against the Philadelphia Phillies in 1963. Mantle, who played center field for the New York Yankees, was one of the all-time great home run hitters.

events. More important, Americans, with more money and more free time, looked for ways to spend their leisure hours.

Some of the strictness of the earlier times began to loosen up, too. When leagues were first organized in the 1870s and 1880s, baseball players were often thought of as men who gambled, drank, and swore too much, men who played when they should be working. By the twentieth century, some people still said such things, but now ball players were more often thought of as heroes, celebrities whose talent, fame, and money were to be admired. Sports were becoming part of what historians call the consumer culture.

Biases in Sports

American sports historically have been dominated by men; women were largely kept out. Rough sports like boxing had been at the center of male, urban street life. Baseball clubs encouraged all-male camaraderie. College football, it was said, made leaders out of men. Through sports, young men were taught to

Althea Gibson at the Wimbledon tennis championships in England on July 2, 1957, where she won the singles title. She was the first black athlete to play Wimbledon as well as the U.S. grass court championship at Forest Hills, New York.

value certain "manly" traits—strength, courage, speed, toughness, ferocity, the will to win. Until around 1950 or so, men kept this masculine world to themselves by systematically excluding women. Yet as we now know, sports such as tennis, basketball, track, and field reveal the great athletic talents of women, and despite some continuing discrimination, their participation as fans and athletes grows with every passing decade.

In terms of ethnic groups, too, sports have a checkered history. Sports idealize equality—"may the best man win" expresses the ideal that athletes compete under conditions in which talent alone determines the outcome. But not only does "may the best *man* win" exclude the female half of the population; sports have rarely been open to *all* men. After Moses Fleetwood Walker's career as a major league catcher ended with the 1880s, sixty years passed before another black man—Jackie Robinson of the Brooklyn Dodgers—was allowed to play in the big leagues. Boxing champions, including John L. Sullivan in the 1880s and Jack Dempsey in the 1920s, refused to fight black opponents, probably out of fear they would lose their titles. Professional and even amateur sports continue to offer few opportunities to African Americans and Hispanics in management positions.

It is true that there has been a sort of ladder effect—ethnic groups arrive from impoverished lands, and their progress (and assimilation) can be measured by their success in sports. Thus, first the Irish, then Jews, next Italians, followed by African Americans, Hispanics, and Koreans have done well in the prize ring. But this ignores the fact that men in these groups entered the ring out of the desire to rise economically. It was a means of social mobility, which the larger society denied.

Media's Impact

The most important changes in spectator sports have been related to the mass media. Radio first demonstrated the possibility of reaching new audiences, when as much as half the country listened to events like the Dempsey-Tunney fights in the 1920s. But television, beginning in the 1950s, came increasingly to dominate sports. Television generated incredible revenues, used to provide enormous player salaries and owner profits. Big money, though, altered relationships among athletes, fans, and teams. Rules have been changed to improve the way the games are seen on the small screen. Even our perceptions of sports have been affected. For example, sitting in a football stadium, fans can watch all the receivers' patterns and the defenders' coverage. But television is more likely to show just the quarterback and the interior linemen. Viewers do not really get the full complexity of the play as it unfolds; they do not see the receivers' patterns and the defensive alignments.

How people play, then, is very much grounded in particular times and places. American sports have a history that grew out of the larger American past, and the study of sports reveals to us much about our character as a nation.

See also Olympic Games; *entries on individual sports:* Baseball; Basketball; Boxing; Football; Golf; Gymnastics; Hockey; Horse Racing; Tennis; *and entries on individual sports figures:* Ali, Muhammad; DiMaggio, Joe; King, Billie Jean; Louis, Joe; Mays, Willie; Owens, Jesse; Rickey, Branch; Robinson, Jackie; Ruth, Babe; Thorpe, Jim; Zaharias, Babe Didrikson.

ELLIOTT J. GORN

STAMP ACT

After passing the Sugar Act of 1764, Parliament continued its efforts to raise money to meet what it called "the necessary expenses of defending" the colonies by passing the Stamp Act of 1765. This law required that all printed material issued in America bear stamps of various denominations. It applied to newspapers, legal documents such as wills, deeds, and contracts, liquor and marriage licenses, advertisements, and even playing cards. These stamp duties were quite high—five shillings for a will, for example, twenty for a liquor license. The stamps were printed

The Stamp Act was the first direct tax imposed on the colonies by the British Parliament. Tax stamps were required on all pamphlets, newspapers, and a wide variety of documents. The colonists were outraged that they were taxed without their consent—"taxation without representation." The Pennsylvania Journal and Advertiser *designed a stamp of its own in protest—a skull and crossbones.*

in England and shipped to stamp masters, men appointed by the British who were supposed to put them on sale.

These were direct taxes, not like those imposed by the Sugar Act related to the regulation of trade. Reaction in the colonies was angry and so unanimous that it proved impossible to put the stamps on sale, let alone collect a penny. The slogan "taxation without representation is tyranny" was heard everywhere. Some of the stamp masters resigned. Others went into hiding to avoid being attacked by rioting colonists. When the New York stamp master made a show of carrying out his duties, a mob broke into his house and smashed his furniture. A Stamp Act Congress representing nine of the thirteen colonies met in New York and petitioned Parliament to repeal the law. Organizations of merchants pledged not to import any British goods until this was done.

Totally frustrated, Parliament did repeal the Stamp Act. But it then passed a law stating that it had the power to tax the colonies, a statement that had just been proven to be untrue.

See also Revolution: The War for Independence.

STANTON, ELIZABETH CADY

(1815–1902)   *Women's rights activist.*

Born in Johnstown, New York, on November 12, 1815, Elizabeth Cady was raised by parents who, like others of that time, believed in providing a classical education for their son but only domestic training for their five daughters. Even so, Elizabeth attended Troy Female Seminary and studied law with her attorney-father, though she knew she would never be allowed to practice before the bar.

At twenty-five, she married Henry Stanton and lived briefly in Boston before moving to Seneca Falls, New York, a small town not far from her childhood home. It was there that Cady Stanton came to resent the great inequity she saw between her role in life and that of her husband, who enjoyed rights and freedoms denied her and other women. She drew up a Declaration of Sentiments, a statement of rights modeled on the Declaration of Independence, but substituting "all men and women are created equal" for Thomas Jefferson's "all men are created equal." She read the declaration at the Woman's Rights Convention, which she helped organize. That convention, held in Seneca Falls in July 1848,

launched the nineteenth-century women's rights movement.

From that point on, Elizabeth Cady Stanton, a woman of boundless energy, juggled the care of her seven children with her work for women's rights. In 1851 she found a kindred spirit in Susan B. Anthony, who became her lifelong friend and fellow crusader. In 1869, when the Fifteenth Amendment gave the vote to black males but not to women of *any* race, Cady Stanton and Anthony formed the National Woman Suffrage Association, and for the next twenty-one years Cady Stanton served as its president.

Upon her death at age eighty-six in 1902, Elizabeth Cady Stanton was praised as a learned and courageous leader of the fight for women's rights. Her influence lived on, and in 1920, eighteen years after her death, the Nineteenth Amendment, giving women the right to vote, became the law of the land.

See also Feminist Movement to 1919.

For further reading: Linda Peavy and Ursula Smith, *Dreams into Deeds: Nine Women Who Dared* (New York: Scribner's, 1985).

LINDA PEAVY
URSULA SMITH

STATUE OF LIBERTY
See National Monuments.

STEFFENS, LINCOLN

(1866–1936)   *Journalist and reformer.*

Steffens was one of the most famous radicals of his generation. *The Autobiography of Lincoln Steffens* (1931) was an enormous popular success, and Steffens even now remains in American history a kind of self-made myth about how a person can lead a life of both excitement and social relevance.

Born into a wealthy family, Steffens was something of a playboy at the University of California and during a period of study in Germany. He liked beer and pretty girls at least as much as he liked German psychology and urban planning. When his father finally stopped supporting him, he returned to America and a journalistic career based usually in New York. He worked first for the *New York Post* but disliked its moralistic editor, E. L. Godkin, because of Godkin's contempt for workers and immigrants. Then, with Jacob Riis, he studied the New York City that Riis was portraying in his famous book, *How the Other Half Lives* (1890). Compared to the German cities Steffens remembered, New York and other American cities were social disaster areas. He spent his most productive years trying to discover why, and what could be done to improve them.

He made his reputation working for *McClure's Magazine,* writing muckraking articles that appeared there and in book form. *The Shame of the Cities* (1904) made the strongest impression on his readers. His work stressed the guilt of such individuals as "honest" businessmen who cooperated with criminals and corrupted politicians. He was eager to support reform mayors and governors who would provide responsible leadership.

Steffens, however, eventually became disillusioned with moralistic progressive reform and sought alternatives. He sampled Freudian ideas regarding repression and psychoanalysis, studied Karl Marx's and other radicals' alternatives to democracy, and took a serious look at Benito Mussolini and Fascist Italy after World War I. A late marriage to Ella Winter, a leading radical of the next generation, pushed him almost to the edge of embracing communism in the years just before his death.

See also Muckrakers.

ROBERT M. CRUNDEN

STEICHEN, EDWARD

(1879–1973)   *Photographer.*

Steichen, who was born in Luxembourg, became America's most celebrated and highest paid photographer. His career spanned three-quarters of a century and embraced two radically differing styles: impressionism and hard-edged realism. Elevating photography to an art form, he created a breathtaking gallery of perceptive portraits, landscapes, still lifes, theater scenes, and war pictures.

Three years old when he immigrated with his parents to Michigan, Steichen bought his first camera when he was sixteen. Experimenting with impressionistic photography, he sometimes bathed his lens in water or jiggled the tripod as he tripped the shutter to achieve a misty effect almost as if the picture had been painted rather than photographed. In 1899 his soft-focus print *The Lady in the Doorway* attracted national attention at the second Philadelphia Salon exhibition.

Steichen subsequently studied painting and photography in Paris, producing a portrait photograph of sculptor Auguste Rodin that won first prize in a competition at The Hague, Holland. When he returned to New York in the early 1900s, he helped Alfred Stieglitz establish the Photo-Secession galleries on Fifth Avenue to exhibit avant-garde photography. During World War I, he performed important aerial camera work with the American Expeditionary Force, sent to fight in that war.

After the war, Steichen became chief photographer for Condé Nast Publications. His slick portraits of stage and screen stars appeared regularly in *Vanity Fair* magazine, and his sophisticated fashion photography graced *Vogue*. He also did work for the J. Walter Thompson advertising agency. His income soared, and he charged a thousand dollars for private portraits.

Reenlisting during World War II, Steichen supervised all navy combat photography. He produced the film *The Fighting Lady*, wrote and illustrated the book *The Blue Ghost*, and mounted two war photo exhibitions for the Museum of Modern Art in New York. The museum named him director of its photography department in 1947, a position he held until 1962, and it later established the Edward Steichen Photography Center.

See also Photography.

PATRICIA CONDON JOHNSTON

STEIN, GERTRUDE

(1874–1946) *Author.*

Stein was one of the most original and best-known American writers—though perhaps the least widely read—of the first half of the twentieth century. Born in Allegheny, Pennsylvania, and raised in Oakland, California, she studied psychology and philosophy with her mentor William James at Harvard and medicine at Johns Hopkins before deciding to embark upon a career as a writer.

Although fascinated by the American language and always thinking of herself as profoundly American, she moved to Paris in 1903, where she lived for the rest of her life. In the French capital she became known for her forceful personality and for the weekly salon at which she played hostess to writers, artists, and intellectuals from all over the world. Among her friends and regular visitors were Henri Matisse and Pablo Picasso, artists whose genius she recognized and whose paintings she bought long before they were world-famous; and the American writers Sherwood Anderson, F. Scott Fitzgerald, and Ernest Hemingway, members of what she called the "lost generation." These writers readily admitted that their work had been influenced by her imaginative use of language, her disregard for conventional rules of grammar and punctuation, and her employment of repetition for effect, as in the famous line "rose is a rose is a rose."

Although Stein's experimental writing was recognized as an important influence, she had great difficulty in finding a publisher or public for her own work. It was often obscure and difficult to understand, and she was frequently ridiculed by outraged readers and critics. In 1933, however, she finally achieved popular success with the publication of a best-seller, *The Autobiography of Alice B. Toklas*. Despite its title, which refers to Toklas, who was Stein's lifelong companion and secretary, the book—witty, charming, and easily understood—is in fact Stein's own autobiography.

See also Literature.

HOWARD GREENFELD

STEINBECK, JOHN

(1902–68) *Author.*

Before becoming a writer, Steinbeck worked as a rancher, road worker, cotton picker, painter, caretaker, surveyor, and fruit picker.

These jobs taught him firsthand about the problems ordinary people suffer, and he wrote with compassion about their hardships. The heroes of his books are migrant workers, minorities, the elderly, the underprivileged, and the poor.

Steinbeck's first book, *Cup of Gold,* about the pirate Sir Henry Morgan, was published in 1929 when he was twenty-seven years old. Although this book was not particularly successful, he kept writing and had his first popular success in 1935 with *Tortilla Flat,* a sensitive story about Mexican Americans in Monterey, California. Steinbeck grew up in California, and many of his novels, short stories, and plays take place there.

In 1939 he wrote *The Grapes of Wrath,* a moving novel about poor farmers who leave the Dust Bowl region of the Great Plains during the depression of the 1930s and migrate to California to find work. It won the Pulitzer Prize for fiction and was produced as a classic movie in 1940.

Several other stories Steinbeck wrote have been made into plays and films. *Of Mice and Men,* written as a play-novel, was produced on Broadway in 1937 and then filmed in 1939. The story tells about two farm workers whose dream of obtaining their own farm is shattered by tragedy. *Travels with Charley,* written in 1962, is a charming account of a trip across the United States he took with his dog, Charley.

In a letter written to his publisher in the 1930s, Steinbeck stated, "My whole work drive has been aimed at making people understand each other." His dramatic portrayals of American life did just that. In 1962, he won the Nobel Prize for literature.

See also Literature.

LEDA BLUMBERG

STEINEM, GLORIA

(1934–)   *Feminist activist and writer.*

Steinem, who was born in Toledo, Ohio, had a difficult childhood. By the time she was ten, Steinem was living on the edge of poverty and was the sole caretaker of her mentally ill mother. But in 1952 she won a scholarship to Smith College. After spending four happy years there, she started writing and by 1960 was supporting herself as a free-lance journalist. She often wrote pieces about famous people and occasionally the sort of articles male editors considered appropriate for a woman reporter—for example, a long piece on textured stockings, or on tropical vacations.

It was not until 1968 when Steinem became a founding editor of *New York* magazine that her work as a journalist and her political interests began to combine. While covering an abortion hearing before a state commission that consisted of fourteen men and a nun, Steinem decided to become a fighter on behalf of women's rights. The feminist movement was just beginning to gain momentum, and Steinem emerged as one of its leading voices. When magazines refused to publish her openly feminist articles, she went on the road as a public speaker. To counter the popular assumption that feminism was a white middle-class women's movement, she was often accompanied by a black woman speaker.

In 1972 Steinem helped found *Ms.,* a nationally circulated feminist magazine. Many essays originally published in *Ms.* are collected in her 1983 book, *Outrageous Acts and Everyday Rebellions.* In 1992, Steinem published the best-selling *Revolution from Within: A Book of Self-Esteem,* in which she explains how unequal treatment destroys self-esteem and how women can fight back. She has

Gloria Steinem, wearing a "Women Against Reagan" button, denounces the Republican Party platform at a rally in 1980.

shown that the insidious forces of oppression not only foster public injustice in our communities but also destroy self-esteem in individuals. Therefore, for equality to exist, there must be both political and personal change.

In addition to her work as a feminist leader, Steinem has been active in political campaigns and in the civil rights and peace movements. Her humor and intelligence have made her a popular media figure. She has worked hard to make America a country that lives up to the words of the Pledge of Allegiance—a place where there's "freedom and justice for all."

See also Feminist Movement since 1919.

For further reading: Sondra Henry and Emily Taits, *One Woman's Power: A Biography of Gloria Steinem* (Minneapolis: Dillon Press, 1987).

LAURIE LINDOP

STEVENS, THADDEUS

(1791–1868)   *Political leader.*

As a member of Congress before and during the Civil War and Reconstruction, Stevens was an eloquent defender of political and economic rights for black Americans.

Born in Vermont, Stevens as a young man moved to Lancaster, Pennsylvania, where he practiced law and worked as an iron manufacturer. He served several terms in the state legislature, where he was a leading advocate of free public education. As a member of the convention that drafted a new state constitution in 1838, Stevens unsuccessfully opposed a clause taking the right to vote away from Pennsylvania's black citizens.

Stevens served in Congress from 1849 to 1853 and again from 1859 until his death. He was a blunt speaker and a master of debate. Even his opponents respected his honesty, and everyone feared his quick wit. As Republican leader in the House of Representatives, Stevens controlled the division of speaking time. He once introduced an opponent with the comment "I now yield the floor to the honorable gentleman, who will make a few feeble remarks."

Stevens hoped that Reconstruction after the Civil War would create a "perfect republic" based on equality for all, regardless of race. He strongly opposed President Andrew Johnson's plan to restrict the right to vote in the South to whites. Stevens was a prime mover in the unsuccessful attempt in 1868 to remove Johnson from office.

Stevens was closely identified during Reconstruction with a plan to divide land of former slaveholders among the former slaves. But this was never enacted. He considered many Reconstruction measures too moderate, but voted for them anyway, remarking, "I live among men, not among angels."

Before he died, Stevens directed that he be buried in one of Pennsylvania's few cemeteries that served both blacks and whites. He hoped, he wrote, to illustrate in death the principle that had guided his life: "Equality of Man before his Creator."

See also Abolitionist Movement; Reconstruction.

ERIC FONER

STIEGLITZ, ALFRED

(1864–1946)   *Photographer, art gallery proprietor, and patron of the arts.*

Born in Hoboken, New Jersey, in a wealthy German-Jewish family, Alfred was raised to appreciate the arts. In 1881, when he was seventeen, the Stieglitzes moved to Germany, where Alfred studied mechanical engineering at the Polytechnikum in Berlin. Bored with his studies, one day on impulse he bought a camera and began teaching himself photography. In 1888 he took first prize in a prestigious London competition; by 1899, now a world-renowned photographer, he had won more than 150 medals in England, Germany, France, and America.

Stieglitz believed strongly that photography should be recognized as the artistic equal of painting and sculpture. In New York in 1902 he organized the Photo-Secession, a group of creative photographers who shared his views. From 1903 until 1917, to promote their work, he arranged exhibitions and edited and published *Camera Work*. One of the most beautiful and important art magazines of all time, *Camera Work* encouraged excellence in photography and kept readers abreast of current trends in art, literature, and criticism in America and Europe.

In 1905, with Edward Steichen, Stieglitz organized the Little Galleries of the Photo-Secession at 291 Fifth Avenue to exhibit art photography. Soon he was also showing avant-garde paintings, drawings, and sculptures. By 1908, "291," as the gallery became known, was the most progressive center for fine arts in America. Here, in 1911, Pablo Picasso had his first one-man show anywhere. Here, Paul Cézanne, Henri Matisse, Auguste Rodin, and Henri de Toulouse-Lautrec made their American debuts. American modernists whose work Stieglitz showcased included John Marin, Arthur G. Dove, Marsden Hartley, and Georgia O'Keeffe (whom he married in 1924). Without Alfred Stieglitz and 291, American painting would not have developed as it did.

See also O'Keeffe, Georgia; Photography.

PATRICIA CONDON JOHNSTON

STIMSON, HENRY L.

(1867–1950)   *Statesman.*

This wealthy graduate of Harvard and Yale served in cabinet-level positions under three presidents, most notably as secretary of war from 1940 to 1945 under Franklin D. Roosevelt. The one-time protégé of Theodore Roosevelt left his mark on American national security policies. A believer in the citizen's obligation to perform national military service, Stimson attended the famous Plattsburg military training camps before American entry in World War I and then saw action as an artillery colonel in France during the war. He supported selective service legislation in both world wars. As secretary of state for President Herbert Hoover, he issued the Stimson Doctrine under which the United States refused to recognize Japan's conquest of Manchuria in 1931–32.

When Germany's blitzkrieg victories in 1940 caused President Roosevelt to appoint Republicans Stimson and Frank Knox to head the War and Navy Departments, it signaled bipartisan support for American participation in World War II. Scrupulously honest and dignified (though somewhat hot-tempered), the aging secretary oversaw creation of the huge U.S. Army and Air Forces that eventually defeated Germany, Italy, and Japan. With "the door that was always open" between their adjoining offices, Stimson ensured harmonious civil-military relations with the army chief of staff Gen. George C. Marshall. As President Harry S. Truman's senior adviser on the military use of atomic energy, Stimson made the deciding recommendation to drop the atomic bombs on Japan in 1945. "My chief purpose was to end the war in victory with the least possible cost in the lives of the men in the armies which I had helped to raise," he later wrote. In his last cabinet meeting in September 1945, Stimson advocated a direct approach to the Soviet Union to reach an agreement on the international control of nuclear weapons. After retirement, he continued to support the cold war policies of his wartime associates.

See also Roosevelt, Franklin D.

J. GARRY CLIFFORD

STOWE, HARRIET BEECHER

(1811–96) *Author.*

Lyman Beecher, Stowe's father, was an outstanding clergyman, who has been called the "father of the most brains in America." Harriet's older sister, Catharine, became an educator who promoted education for women, and of her six brothers all but one became ministers, including Henry and Edward, both strongly opposed to slavery.

Her mother died when Harriet was four, and the girl grew up in a household governed

A photograph of Harriet Beecher Stowe. Her novel, Uncle Tom's Cabin, *was the first one to present African-American characters in a humane light. She meant the book "to awaken sympathy and feeling for the African race" and to persuade readers to "feel right" about the issue of slavery.*

by her sternly moral and intellectual father, who encouraged his children not only to serve God but also to be achievers. Though a stepmother arrived two years after her mother's death, Harriet always turned to her father for help and was close to two African-American servants. Harriet gained her education, which was heavily religious, partly at home and partly in Connecticut schools, one of which sister Catharine operated. She listened carefully to her father's sermons and long remembered his denunciation of the slave trade.

The family moved to Cincinnati in 1832 when the father became president of Lane Theological Seminary, a center of antislavery feeling. Harriet began to write, winning a literary prize, and in 1836 married a faculty member and clergyman, Calvin Stowe, who encouraged her writing. Living just across the Ohio River from the slave state of Kentucky, she became familiar with slavery and the Underground Railroad—the slaves' means of escape to freedom. By 1850 she had given birth to seven children and postponed her literary career.

Congress as part of the Compromise of 1850 passed the strict Fugitive Slave Law that led to mob action in the North against efforts to return fugitives to slavery. When Harriet in that year moved her family to Maine, where her husband had taken a new job, she heard angry words from many persons including brother Edward when she stopped off in Boston.

Harriet, inflamed with the horrors of the slave system, began to write a story that was published serially in an antislavery newspaper in Washington. "I feel as if I had written some of it almost with my heart's blood," she said. Published in 1852 in book form *Uncle Tom's Cabin* struck a responsive chord among

readers. Within a year it sold 300,000 copies; published abroad it sold 1.5 million copies in England and was translated into many languages. Untold millions of people followed the narrative in stage adaptations.

Her story centers on the good and pious Uncle Tom, a Kentucky slave owned by a kindly master who, in need of money, sells him South where in time he becomes the property of Simon Legree, a brutal master in Louisiana. Harriet was a skillful creator of characters; Uncle Tom became, unfairly, a term for a black who submits to whites, and Simon Legree, not unfairly, a name for cruelty. Other memorable characters are the light-skinned Eliza and her baby, who escape being sold South by fleeing across the frozen Ohio

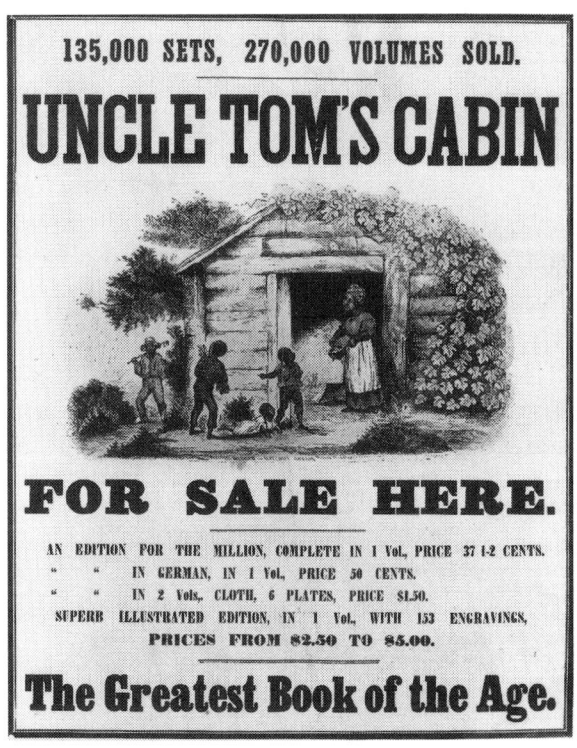

A poster advertising the sale of Uncle Tom's Cabin. *Published in 1852, it sold 300,000 copies in the first year and eventually about 7 million throughout the world.*

River and, helped by her husband, George, follow the Underground Railroad to freedom in Canada. Little Eva, an angelic child, who dies, and the little black girl, Topsy, who says she was never born but just "growed," furnish sadness and comedy. Uncle Tom becomes a martyr, whipped to death by the wicked Legree.

Harriet could hardly have anticipated the reception given her book. In the North it excited a growing sense of outrage about slavery. During the Civil War when Harriet met President Abraham Lincoln, he is reported to have said to her, his eyes twinkling, "So you're the little woman who wrote the book that made this great war." In the South her book was savagely attacked.

The powerful moral tale was the great achievement of her long life. She wrote many articles and books, including a defense of *Uncle Tom's Cabin*. She traveled abroad where she was enthusiastically greeted. After the war, in which her son was wounded, she and Calvin moved to Florida. There she continued to write, started a chapel for the freedpeople, and began a career as a lecturer. After her husband died she declined in health and moved back North where she died. An extraordinary woman, she deserves a prominent place in the annals of American literature and the Civil War.

See also Abolitionist Movement; Beecher, Catharine; Civil War; Fugitive Slave Law; Slavery.

For further reading: Robert E. Jakoubek, *Harriet Beecher Stowe* (New York: Chelsea House, 1989).

JAMES A. RAWLEY

STRIKES

A strike is the refusal by a group of workers to continue working until a specific set of demands is met. Throughout American history, the strike has been one of the main weapons workers have used to promote their interests. Disputes over wages have been the most common cause of strikes, but workers have walked off their jobs for many reasons. There have been strikes to shorten the workday, to win or keep benefits such as health insurance, to protest the firing of workers, and to force companies to recognize and negotiate with a union. Occasionally strikes have been called to keep particular workers—for example, African Americans—from getting jobs in a specific trade.

Early Strikes

The first strike by American workers that we know of took place in 1786, just ten years after the signing of the Declaration of Independence. A group of Philadelphia printers left their jobs when their employers tried to lower their wages. "Turn-outs" or "stand-outs" (as strikes at first were called) typically began when a group of craftsmen, such as printers, shoemakers, or carpenters, decided on a scale of "prices" for their labor. They pledged not to work for any employer paying less. Often employers gave in because in any town or city there was only a limited supply of workers skilled in a particular trade.

To fight strikes employers turned to the courts. Starting in 1806 workers in several cities were charged with the crime of conspiracy for forming unions, holding strikes, or refusing to work with nonunionists. Only over the course of many years did workers win the clear legal right to strike.

Nonetheless, in the decades before the Civil War, the labor movement grew and strikes became more common. In the 1820s, women workers and workers in factories (which were just starting to be built) began to strike. In 1850 two New York tailors were killed by police dispersing a crowd of strikers. They were the first Americans to die in a strike. Since then hundreds, possibly thousands, of people have died in clashes between strikers and company guards, police, or scabs (men or women continuing to work during a strike).

Post–Civil War Strikes

After the Civil War, as cities grew and transportation improved, unions found it increasingly difficult to prevent employers from recruiting scabs. As a result, many strikes were lost. To avoid strikes most unions stopped setting wage scales and working hours by themselves. Instead they began meeting with employers to negotiate written contracts. Some unions rejected strikes altogether. But strikes continued, with or without union backing.

During the severe economic depression that began in 1873, textile workers, coal miners, and railroad men waged long, bitter strikes to resist wage cuts. In 1877 a strike of 100,000 workers paralyzed the railroad system. It began in West Virginia and soon spread to Baltimore, Pittsburgh, Chicago, and St. Louis. When local militiamen refused to attack the strikers, state and federal troops from other regions were brought in. Violent battles between troops and strike supporters led to over a hundred deaths and contributed to the defeat of the walkout.

The number of strikes soared during the mid-1880s. In 1886 over half a million workers took part in strikes. During the next three decades, as the volume continued to grow, strikers introduced new tactics. These included mass picket lines (parades by large groups of workers around struck factories to keep anyone from entering) and strike meetings conducted in many languages, so that immigrants could participate.

The wave of strikes peaked in 1919. That year 4 million workers, one-fifth of the nation's work force, went on strike. In Boston, policemen struck; in New York, garment workers and actors; in New England, textile workers and telephone operators. In Seattle, a general strike—a walkout by workers from many different industries—paralyzed the city for five days.

In an effort to counter the national unrest, employers enlisted the aid of government troops to break the strikes. They also began a red scare, claiming that the strikes were really an effort by foreign-born communists to make a revolution. These measures helped defeat the most important strike of the era, a walkout by over 300,000 steel workers.

Strikes in Hard Times

During the 1920s the labor movement was in retreat and strikes were infrequent. But strikes again rocked the nation during the 1930s. Workers were suffering another devastating economic depression. The 1932 election of President Franklin D. Roosevelt, who was sympathetic to unions, and the passage by Congress of prolabor legislation encouraged many workers to join unions. In 1934 striking Toledo auto workers, Minneapolis truckers, and West Coast longshoremen won important concessions after surviving attacks by police and private individuals opposed to their demands. These strikes helped persuade Congress to pass the National Labor Relations Act, which made it easier for unions to organize.

In 1937 workers at General Motors—the largest manufacturing company in the world—held a successful six-week sit-down strike to force recognition of their union. In a sit-down strike, workers stop working but do not leave their workplaces. They eat, sleep, and live in them until the strike is settled. The victory of the General Motors strikers gave the labor movement an enormous boost. It also popularized sit-downs until they were declared illegal by the Supreme Court in 1939.

Decline of Strikes

In 1946 more workers went on strike than in any other year in the country's history, but during the 1950s the number of strikes decreased, as unions and employers grew used to settling disagreements through negotiations. The number rose briefly again during the 1960s, when many strikers were government employees, such as teachers, transit workers, and post office employees. Until then government workers had rarely taken part in walkouts.

During the 1970s and 1980s strikes became less common. Among the reasons were a severe economic recession which made workers fear for their jobs, declining union membership, and a more conservative political climate. Shortly after taking office in 1981, President Ronald Reagan fired more than ten thousand air traffic controllers who went on strike in spite of a law forbidding their doing so. Many businesses took similarly tough stands against strikers. Strikes in the copper-mining, meat-packing, airline, and intercity bus industries were defeated when companies hired scabs. Although workers became more reluctant to take part in strikes, they nevertheless continued to use this powerful if risky weapon when unable to find alternatives.

See also Homestead Strike; Labor Movement; National Labor Relations Act; Pullman Strike; Railroad Strike of 1877; Sit-Down Strikes. *And see entries on labor leaders and unions listed under* Labor Movement.

JOSHUA B. FREEMAN

STUDENT NON-VIOLENT COORDINATING COMMITTEE

The Student Non-Violent Coordinating Committee (SNCC) was an organization of black student activists that was to become one of the more radical branches of the civil rights movement. The dominant civil rights organization at the time was the Southern Christian Leadership Conference (SCLC), led by Martin Luther King, which some felt was out of touch with younger blacks who wanted faster progress on the road to black equality. So SNCC (pronounced *snick*) was founded in 1960 to give students their own role in the movement.

Members took part in some of the most courageous and dangerous acts of the movement, including directing many of the black voter registration drives in the South. The

Strikers picketing outside a construction site.

civil rights movement as a whole believed in nonviolence and civil disobedience, but SNCC was impatient and argued for aggressive, direct action. The group fought racism head on when it helped to integrate lunch counters in the South. A group of SNCC members would sit at the counter, waiting to be served. White waitresses nervously ignored them until the police arrived to arrest them and haul them away. Immediately, another group would take the empty places at the counter.

Members also participated in the Freedom Rides, which sought to integrate interstate buses. Desegregation on buses was the law but not the practice in the South. Blacks who ignored the racist codes of the Deep South risked beatings and even death. The groups participating in the Freedom Rides sent black passengers into "whites only" sections of the buses, rest rooms, waiting rooms, and restaurants of bus terminals between Washington, D.C., and New Orleans. The first bus was set on fire by angry whites, and other buses with Freedom Riders also met with violence.

In 1966 Stokely Carmichael was elected head of SNCC. He popularized the term *black power*, which characterized the new principles of the movement: black self-reliance and violence as a legitimate means of self-defense. The group grew increasingly more militant, but internal conflict eventually caused it to be disbanded.

See also Civil Rights Movement.

STUDENTS FOR A DEMOCRATIC SOCIETY

Founded in 1960, Students for a Democratic Society (SDS) was a radical student group that supported the civil rights movement, protested the Vietnam War, and attacked America's indifference to social injustice. In 1962 the organization met in Port Huron, Michigan, where it drafted the sixty-three-page Port Huron Statement, which condemned the empty values of the so-called Affluent Society that made up mainstream America, and that it felt mindlessly worshiped materialism and wealth. The key to change, the statement proposed, was student activism.

For the remainder of the decade, SDS organized mass demonstrations and eventually achieved a level of power and prominence unprecedented for a student organization. It was especially effective in organizing large-scale protests of the Vietnam War. Its most dramatic action became one of the enduring images of sixties' activism: the takeover of the administrative offices of Columbia University. To protest Columbia's participation in war-related research and its plans to build a gymnasium on a site where a public park stood, students took over the president's office as well as others. Not until police arrested 712 students, injuring over 200, did the occupation end. Similar occupations spread to some forty other campuses across the country.

The organization grew increasingly revolutionary, but disagreements within its ranks resulted in its collapse in June 1969.

See also Sixties, The.

SUFFRAGE
See Voting.

SUGAR ACT

After the French and Indian War ended in 1763, the British government was faced with a large national debt and the need to raise money to govern and protect its expanded empire in North America. It seemed to Lord Grenville, the British prime minister, that it was only fair to make the American colonists pay for at least part of these costs. The Sugar Act was the result. It placed import duties on foreign sugar, coffee, wine, cloth, and other products in common use in America. Regulations aimed at preventing smuggling were stiffened.

Although Parliament had taxed foreign imports many times, earlier laws had been designed to make foreign products so expensive that they would not actually be imported. The Sugar Act taxes, however, were specifically designed to raise money. For example, the Molasses Act of 1733 had levied a tax of sixpence a gallon on French molasses. This tax made French molasses more expensive than molasses produced by British producers. The hope was that none would be imported into America. The tax on molasses was reduced to three pence a gallon by the Sugar Act. This lowered the price enough so that molasses from the French West Indies could compete effectively with molasses from the British islands. The three-penny tax would, the British expected, be actually collected.

The colonists disliked the Sugar Act. More important, they began to grumble about being taxed at all by Parliament, a legislature in which they were not represented. As James Otis put it in a pamphlet, a person should be "free from all taxes" by legislatures in which he is not represented.

See also Revolution: The War for Independence.

SULLIVAN, LOUIS H.

(1856–1924) *Architect.*

While he was growing up in Boston, Sullivan was thrilled by buildings, bridges, and the powerful men who created them. He studied architecture at Massachusetts Institute of Technology and the Ecole des Beaux-Arts in Paris, but he hated being trained—as all architects were in the nineteenth century—to copy ancient styles instead of inventing new ones. After moving to Chicago and becoming the partner of architect and engineer Dankmar Adler, Sullivan worked to create a style reflecting the forces of the modern American city.

Sullivan invented the rules for the skyscraper as a type of architecture. In its scale, materials, and purely economic purpose, the multistory steel-frame office building (which first appeared in Chicago in the mid-1880s) made all the rules of past styles worthless. Sullivan's Wainwright Building in St. Louis (1890) daringly made the building's steel skeleton itself the main visual feature. Until then,

Architect Louis Sullivan's Carson, Pirie, Scott Building (1899) in Chicago. Sullivan designed the first steel-skeleton skyscraper and was one of the originators of modern design.

exposing the structure of a building would have been considered ugly; earlier architects deliberately camouflaged the structure with decorative elements. Sullivan also exaggerated the vertical girders in the façade to dramatize the building's great height.

The Wainwright Building illustrates Sullivan's famous slogan, "form follows function": what something looks like (its form) should reflect its purpose (function). But Sullivan did not stop with the structural and economic purposes of a building—he *dramatized* them. In so doing, he showed architects—including his assistant and pupil, Frank Lloyd Wright—that they did not need to hide modern building types and materials behind styles taken from other times and places.

Sullivan spent his last twenty-five years crusading against the older styles most architects stuck to. But he got fewer and fewer jobs, and his personal life collapsed; he died poor. Nevertheless, his insistence that architecture starts with function, not decoration, made him a founder of modern architecture.

See also Architecture.

MILES DAVID SAMSON

SUMNER, CHARLES

(1811–74)   *U.S. senator and antislavery leader.*

Sumner was born in Boston, Massachusetts, graduated from Harvard, and earned his law degree at Harvard Law School. While a practicing attorney, he became involved in reform movements, including the abolition of slavery, improving prison conditions, and outlawing war.

Sumner was elected to the Senate in 1851 by a Free-Soil–Democratic coalition that was opposed to the extension of slavery into newly acquired territories. In 1854, he helped organize the Republican Party and was reelected to the Senate as a Republican three times. Sumner strenuously argued against southern efforts to extend slavery into Kansas, and in May 1856 he strongly denounced Senator Andrew P. Butler of South Carolina for his support of slavery. A few days later, Congressman Preston Brooks, a relative of Butler's, assaulted Sumner on the Senate floor, beating him mercilessly with a cane. The Massachusetts senator was so severely injured that he could not return to Congress for three and a half years.

After the Civil War broke out in 1861, Sumner urged President Abraham Lincoln to expand the North's war goals to include, besides the preservation of the Union, the abolition of slavery. Following the war, Sumner became a leading spokesman for the Radical Republicans, who believed that the Reconstruction programs proposed by Lincoln before his assassination and later by President Andrew Johnson were too lenient toward the defeated South. He demanded that the freed slaves be given all civil rights, including the males' right to vote, before the southern states could reenter the Union. When Johnson was tried on impeachment charges in 1868, Sumner was among the president's most ardent opponents.

As chairman of the Senate Foreign Relations Committee, Sumner was accused of trying to dictate foreign policy to President Ulysses S. Grant and Secretary of State Hamilton Fish. His differences with the Grant administration led to his removal from the chairmanship of the committee in 1872, but he continued serving in the Senate until his death.

See also Abolitionist Movement; Free-Soil Party; Reconstruction; Republican Party.

EDMUND LINDOP

SUPREME COURT

The Supreme Court is the nation's highest court of law. According to the U.S. Constitution, "The judicial power of the United States shall be vested in one Supreme Court, and in such inferior courts as the Congress may . . . establish." That puts the Supreme Court at the top of the judiciary, one of the three branches of the federal government. But it is Congress, the legislative (law-making) branch, that has the power to organize the federal judiciary. And the men who wrote the Constitution in 1787 gave the president, head of the executive branch, the right to choose Supreme Court justices (members) and other federal judges. The president's choices must be approved by the Senate, one of the two houses of Congress. This sharing of authority among the branches of government is part of our constitutional system of checks and balances. The system is intended to keep any one branch from seizing too much power.

Congress acted promptly to establish the federal court system. The Judiciary Act of 1789 called for a six-member Supreme Court. (Congress later changed the number of justices. Since 1869, there have been nine, a chief justice and eight associates.) During his two terms as president, George Washington appointed, and the Senate confirmed, ten justices, including two chief justices. In 1801, President John Adams named John Marshall to head the Court.

The Marshall Court

Marshall served as chief justice until his death in 1835. Among the first cases to come before the Marshall Court was *Marbury* v. *Madison.* (The *v.* stands for *versus,* Latin for "against.") The case was complex and involved the Judiciary Act of 1789. But the Court's 1803 decision was simple. It said that one section of the Judiciary Act violated (went against) the Constitution. In that section, Congress had given itself more power over the Court than the Constitution allowed. That part of the law was therefore *unconstitutional* and could not be enforced. This ruling established the Court's right of *judicial review,* the right to examine laws, compare them to the Constitution, and decide whether they are valid. Today, nearly two hundred years later, ruling on the constitutionality of local, state, and federal legislation remains the Court's major task.

The Marshall Court made other landmark decisions. In 1810, it ruled for the first time that a *state* law was unconstitutional. Nine years later, it permitted Congress to establish a federal bank. Although the Constitution does not say outright that Congress may create a bank, the justices decided that it implies that Congress may do so. The idea that Congress has *implied powers* beyond those specifically listed in the Constitution strengthened both Congress and the federal government itself. So did an 1824 decision that allowed Congress to pass laws regulating trade among the states.

The Court at Work

Along with making decisions and defining the role of the Court, its early justices began establishing the work routines still in use today. Most cases are heard on appeal. Appeals come from those who have lost a case in a lower court and believe that according to constitutional law, they should have won. Because the Court's work load is so heavy—thousands of cases a year—the justices take only those cases they consider most important.

When the justices do agree to hear a case, lawyers from both sides meet at the Supreme

Court building in Washington, D.C., to present written and oral arguments. During the oral arguments, the justices question the lawyers, interrupting them if necessary to be certain they understand the points being made. Later, they discuss the case privately among themselves, with the chief justice directing the discussion. Then they vote. A simple majority wins. In important cases, though, chief justices try to get a unanimous or near-unanimous decision because it sounds more authoritative. After the vote, one of the justices on the winning side writes the *majority opinion,* explaining the legal reasoning behind the ruling. A justice on the minority side (if there is one) writes a *dissenting opinion,* outlining that position. Occasionally, a justice who has voted with the majority or minority, but disagrees with it on some point of law, writes a *concurring opinion.* All the opinions are made public, so everyone, including the lower court judges, knows exactly where the Court stands on constitutional issues. Lower courts must follow Supreme Court rulings.

The Court in History

Once the Court has taken a position, it is slow to change. But it has done so. In 1857, for example, Chief Justice Roger B. Taney ruled in the so-called *Dred Scott* case that Congress could make no law to stop the spread of slavery, legal in the South, throughout the United States. This ruling dismayed and angered antislavery Americans. It helped bring about the Civil War four years later.

Even after the war ended, and slavery had been abolished and the rights of citizenship granted to blacks, the Court upheld state laws that made it difficult or impossible for blacks to vote. In 1883 and 1896 it found racial segregation constitutional. Blacks could be kept separate from whites in hotels, railroads, and other places of public accommodation, it decreed. Not until 1954, in *Brown* v. *Board of Education,* did the Court begin putting an end to legal segregation. Similarly, during the late 1800s and early 1900s, the Court consistently sided with business and industry, overturning laws aimed at forcing employers to protect the lives and health of their workers, many of whom were children. Finally, in 1937, the Court began reversing itself.

Opposition to the Court's rulings against racial and economic justice came from John Marshall Harlan, who wrote dissenting opinions in the 1883 and 1896 civil rights cases, and Oliver Wendell Holmes, Jr., and Louis D. Brandeis, who dissented in a number of probusiness rulings.

The Modern Court

Starting in the 1920s, the Supreme Court heard several cases involving laws that limited Americans' individual liberties, including the First Amendment right to freedom of speech. Gradually it removed some limits. Its pace quickened with the 1953 appointment of Earl Warren as chief justice. Under Warren's leadership, the Court not only promoted racial integration and protected freedom of speech but also ruled in favor of greater freedom of religion and enhanced the legal rights of people accused of committing crimes.

Although many Americans admired the Warren Court's apparent pursuit of liberal social reform, others felt that it had gone too far. After Warren retired in 1969, President Richard M. Nixon named a more conservative chief justice, Warren Burger. Yet Burger and two other Nixon appointees joined in the controversial 1973 opinion that guaranteed a woman's right to have an abortion (*Roe* v. *Wade*). Still, the trend was away from liberalism. Between 1981 and 1990, conservative presidents Ronald Reagan and George Bush appointed a total of six justices including Chief Justice William Rehnquist and the Court's first female associate, Sandra Day O'Connor. During those years, the court reversed several Warren Court decisions, particularly those having to do with the rights of suspected criminals.

In 1992, the election of a more liberal president, Bill Clinton, and the expected retirement of several justices suggested the possibility of a new direction for the Court.

See also Brown v. *Board of Education of Topeka*; *Dred Scott Case*; *Marbury* v. *Madison*; *Miranda* v. *Arizona*; *Plessy* v. *Ferguson*; *Roe* v. *Wade*. *And see biographies of justices whose names are starred in the accompanying table.*

A N N E. W E I S S

THE SUPREME COURT

Chief Justices

Chief Justices	Term of Service[†]	Years of Service	Life Span
John Jay*	1789–1795	5	1745–1829
John Rutledge‡	1795	—	1739–1800
Oliver Ellsworth	1796–1800	4	1745–1807
John Marshall*	1801–1835	34	1755–1835
Roger B. Taney*	1836–1864	28	1777–1864
Salmon P. Chase	1864–1873	8	1808–1873
Morrison R. Waite	1874–1888	14	1816–1888
Melville W. Fuller	1888–1910	21	1833–1910
Edward D. White	1910–1921	11	1845–1921
William H. Taft*	1921–1930	8	1857–1930
Charles E. Hughes*	1930–1941	11	1862–1948
Harlan F. Stone	1941–1946	5	1872–1946
Fred M. Vinson	1946–1953	7	1890–1953
Earl Warren*	1953–1969	16	1891–1974
Warren E. Burger*	1969–1986	17	1907–
William H. Rehnquist*	1986–	—	1924–

*This encyclopedia includes biographies of the justices who are starred.
†Term of service refers only to years as chief justice. Any previous service as associate justice appears in the next columns.
‡Appointed and served one term, but not confirmed by the Senate.

Associate Justices

Associate Justices	Term of Service	Years of Service	Life Span
John Rutledge	1789–1791	1	1739–1800
William Cushing	1789–1810	20	1732–1810
James Wilson	1789–1798	8	1742–1798
John Blair	1789–1796	6	1732–1800
Robert H. Harrison	1789–1790	—	1745–1790
James Iredell	1790–1799	9	1751–1799
Thomas Johnson	1791–1793	1	1732–1819
William Paterson	1793–1806	13	1745–1806
Samuel Chase	1796–1811	15	1741–1811
Bushrod Washington	1798–1829	31	1762–1829
Alfred Moore	1799–1804	4	1755–1810
William Johnson	1804–1834	30	1771–1834
Henry Brockholst Livingston	1806–1823	16	1757–1823
Thomas Todd	1807–1826	18	1765–1826
Joseph Story	1811–1845	33	1779–1845
Gabriel Duvall	1811–1835	24	1752–1844
Smith Thompson	1823–1843	20	1768–1843
Robert Trimble	1826–1828	2	1777–1828
John McLean	1829–1861	32	1785–1861
Henry Baldwin	1830–1844	14	1780–1844
James M. Wayne	1835–1867	32	1790–1867
Philip P. Barbour	1836–1841	4	1783–1841
John Catron	1837–1865	28	1786–1865
John McKinley	1837–1852	15	1780–1852
Peter V. Daniel	1841–1860	19	1784–1860
Samuel Nelson	1845–1872	27	1792–1873
Levi Woodbury	1845–1851	5	1789–1851
Robert C. Grier	1846–1870	23	1794–1870
Benjamin Curtis	1851–1857	6	1809–1874
John A. Campbell	1853–1861	8	1811–1889
Nathan Clifford	1858–1881	23	1803–1881
Noah H. Swayne	1862–1881	18	1804–1884
Samuel F. Miller	1862–1890	28	1816–1890
David Davis	1862–1877	14	1815–1886
Stephen J. Field	1863–1897	34	1816–1899
William Strong	1870–1880	10	1808–1895
Joseph P. Bradley	1870–1892	22	1813–1892
Ward Hunt	1873–1882	9	1810–1886
John M. Harlan*	1877–1911	34	1833–1911
William B. Woods	1880–1887	7	1824–1887
Stanley Matthews	1881–1889	7	1824–1889
Horace Gray	1882–1902	20	1828–1902
Samuel Blatchford	1882–1893	11	1820–1893
Lucius Q.C. Lamar	1888–1893	5	1825–1893
David J. Brewer	1890–1910	20	1837–1910
Henry B. Brown	1890–1906	16	1836–1913
George Shiras, Jr.	1892–1903	10	1832–1924
Howell E. Jackson	1893–1895	2	1832–1895
Edward D. White	1894–1910	16	1845–1921
Rufus W. Peckham	1895–1909	14	1838–1909
Joseph McKenna	1898–1925	26	1843–1926

Associate Justices	Term of Service	Years of Service	Life Span	Associate Justices	Term of Service	Years of Service	Life Span
Oliver W. Holmes*	1902–1932	30	1841–1935	Harold H. Burton	1945–1958	13	1888–1964
William R. Day	1903–1922	19	1849–1923	Tom C. Clark	1949–1967	18	1899–1977
William H. Moody	1906–1910	3	1853–1917	Sherman Minton	1949–1956	7	1890–1965
Horace H. Lurton	1910–1914	4	1844–1914	John Marshall Harlan*	1955–1971	16	1899–1971
Charles E. Hughes*	1910–1916	5	1862–1948	William J. Brennan, Jr.	1956–1990	34	1906–
Willis Van Devanter	1911–1937	26	1859–1941	Charles E. Whittaker	1957–1962	5	1901–1973
Joseph R. Lamar	1911–1916	5	1857–1916	Potter Stewart	1958–1981	23	1915–1985
Mahlon Pitney	1912–1922	10	1858–1924	Byron R. White	1962–1993	31	1917–
James C. McReynolds	1914–1941	26	1862–1946	Arthur J. Goldberg	1962–1965	3	1908–1990
Louis D. Brandeis*	1916–1939	22	1856–1941	Abe Fortas	1965–1969	4	1910–1982
John H. Clarke	1916–1922	6	1857–1945	Thurgood Marshall*	1967–1991	24	1908–1993
George Sutherland	1922–1938	15	1862–1942	Harry A. Blackmun	1970–1994	24	1908–
Pierce Butler	1923–1939	16	1866–1939	William H. Rehnquist*	1972–1986	14	1924–
Edward T. Sanford	1923–1930	7	1865–1930	Lewis F. Powell, Jr.	1972–1987	15	1907–
Harlan F. Stone	1925–1941	16	1872–1946	John P. Stevens	1975–	—	1920–
Owen J. Roberts	1930–1945	15	1875–1955	Sandra Day O'Connor*	1981–	—	1930–
Benjamin N. Cardozo	1932–1938	6	1870–1938	Antonin Scalia	1986–	—	1936–
Hugo L. Black*	1937–1971	34	1886–1971	Anthony M. Kennedy	1988–	—	1936–
Stanley F. Reed	1938–1957	19	1884–1980	David Souter	1990–	—	1939–
Felix Frankfurter*	1939–1962	23	1882–1965	Clarence Thomas	1991–	—	1948–
William O. Douglas	1939–1975	36	1898–1980	Ruth Bader Ginsburg*	1993–	—	1933–
Frank Murphy	1940–1949	9	1890–1949	Stephen Breyer	1994–	—	1938–
James F. Byrnes	1941–1942	1	1879–1972				
Robert H. Jackson	1941–1954	13	1892–1954				
Wiley B. Rutledge	1943–1949	6	1894–1949				

T

TAFT, WILLIAM HOWARD

(1857–1930) *Twenty-seventh president of the United States (1909–13) and tenth chief justice of the U.S. Supreme Court (1921–30).*

Taft was a talented administrator but an inept politician. Educated at Yale University and Cincinnati Law School, he became a federal appeals court judge in 1892. The respected Ohio Republican was appointed civil governor of the Philippines in 1901 and helped persuade the Filipinos to accept American rule. In 1904, he served as secretary of war under President Theodore Roosevelt and efficiently supervised the construction of the Panama Canal. With Roosevelt's support, Taft easily defeated Democrat William Jennings Bryan in the election of 1908. The new president was so huge—he weighed three hundred pounds—that a special bathtub had to be brought to the White House for his use.

Unlike Roosevelt, Taft wanted to limit presidential power. He was unwilling to pressure Congress to keep his campaign promise to lower tariff rates (fees charged on foreign-made goods coming into the country). He demonstrated his lack of political savvy first by praising the Payne-Aldrich Tariff's higher rates (1909) and then by dismissing Roosevelt's activist Chief Forester Gifford Pinchot, a popular conservationist (1910). To his credit, Taft brought more antitrust suits (to break up companies that controlled entire industries) than even Roosevelt, who is famous for being a "trustbuster." Although Taft believed in international law as a means of settling disputes between nations, he supported a program of "dollar diplomacy," using military power and U.S. diplomacy to protect American business interests in China and in the Caribbean.

When Roosevelt's newly formed Progressive Party, also called the Bull Moose Party, split the Republican vote in 1912, the president lost his bid for reelection to Democrat Woodrow Wilson. Taft became a professor of law at Yale (1913) and served as joint chairman of the War Labor Board in World War I (1918). His lifelong wish was granted when he was appointed chief justice of the Supreme Court in 1921, the only former president to head the nation's highest court. In addition to his judicial work, Taft modernized the federal court system. He wrote enthusiastically, "I don't remember that I ever was president."

See also Panama Canal; Philippines, Acquisition of; Progressive Parties: 1912, 1924, 1948; Supreme Court. *For events during Taft's administration, see* Antitrust Movement; Ballinger-Pinchot Controversy; Dollar Diplomacy.

BARBARA SILBERDICK FEINBERG

TAFT-HARTLEY ACT

After the Republicans gained control of Congress in the 1946 elections, they passed the Taft-Hartley Labor Relations bill of 1947, a measure designed to reduce the power of labor unions. It was named after its sponsors, Senator Robert A. Taft and Representative Fred Hartley, Jr.

The law banned closed-shop union contracts, which forced new employees to join the union before they could be hired. Secondary boycotts by unions were also made illegal. If in the opinion of the president of the United States a strike threatened the national interest, he could seek a court order forcing the union to postpone striking during an eighty-day "cooling-off period." During this time a fact-finding board was to investigate the situation and make recommendations aimed at settling the dispute.

President Harry S. Truman vetoed the Taft-Hartley bill, but Congress passed it over his veto. He made effective use of what he called an antilabor law in his successful campaign for reelection in 1948. Nevertheless, the president took advantage of the cooling-off provision on a number of occasions. Although the AFL and CIO denounced the Taft-Hartley Act, it had few harmful effects on unions. It outlawed the closed shop, but it did not prohibit open-shop contracts, which required new workers to join the union after they were hired.

See also Labor Movement.

TANEY, ROGER B.

(1777–1864)   *Chief justice, U.S. Supreme Court.*

Taney (pronounced TAW-ney) began his political career as a leader of the Federalist Party in the Maryland legislature. A strong proponent of states' rights, he joined the new Democratic Party in the 1820s and was elected at-

torney general of Maryland in 1826. President Andrew Jackson named him U.S. attorney general in 1831.

Taney helped draft Jackson's veto of the renewal of the Second Bank of the United States, a major bone of contention between economic nationalists (who supported the Bank) and their state-oriented opponents. Thereafter, Taney was nominated to be secretary of the treasury, but the Senate refused to confirm his nomination. Taney returned to Baltimore to practice law. In early 1835 Jackson nominated Taney to be an associate justice of the Supreme Court, but again the Senate rejected the nomination. Jackson was successful, however, when he nominated Taney months later to succeed John Marshall, and Taney became the fifth chief justice of the United States.

Taney is best remembered as the author of the *Dred Scott* v. *Sanford* opinion (misspelled *Sandford* in the court papers), in which the Court held that blacks, whether slave or free, could not be citizens of the United States. Blacks, wrote Taney, "had no rights which the white man," as a matter of law, "was bound to respect." Moreover, he in effect declared unconstitutional the political platform of the newly emerging Republican Party insofar as it wanted to prohibit the movement of slaves into U.S. territories. Although they could, upon becoming states, choose to prohibit slavery, Congress could not, according to Taney, make that decision for the territories. Abraham Lincoln, unsuccessfully running for the U.S. Senate in Illinois in 1858, denounced *Dred Scott* and accused Taney of being part of a pro-slavery conspiracy.

Taney remained chief justice into the period of the Civil War. Sitting as a circuit judge, he wrote an angry decision denouncing Lincoln's suspension of habeas corpus, which allowed the military to arrest persons and refuse to bring them before courts to test the basis of their arrest.

See also Dred Scott *Case; Supreme Court.*

SANFORD LEVINSON

TAYLOR, ZACHARY

(1784–1850)   *Twelfth president of the United States (1849–50).*

Taylor, who was raised on a southern plantation, never received a formal education. He was commissioned a second lieutenant in the Regular Army in 1808 and saw service fighting Indians on the frontier. When the Mexican War broke out, he was a major general commanding troops along the border. Taylor became a national hero by winning the Battles of Monterrey (1846) and Buena Vista (1847), although his men were outnumbered by the enemy. His troops nicknamed him "Old Rough and Ready" because he wore comfortable clothes instead of a uniform and suffered the same hardships they did. He was fearless under fire but was not a brilliant strategist.

In 1848, the Whig Party nominated Taylor as their presidential candidate, despite his lack of political experience. He had never held public office or even voted in elections. Northerners admired his military record, and southerners supported him because he was by this time a prosperous slaveholder with plantations in Louisiana and Mississippi. In the election he defeated the Democratic candidate, Lewis Cass.

The new president's reliance on his own judgment despite his inexperience led him to oversimplify difficult problems. For example, Taylor angered the South by insisting that the territories of California and New Mexico, acquired from Mexico after the war, apply for admission to the Union as two free (rather than slave) states. He claimed that the climate was unsuitable for plantations and slavery. That the two areas should be admitted as free states was one element of the Compromise of 1850, a plan that was being worked out in Congress to solve the problem of how the new territories should be governed. He also offended moderates in Congress because he stubbornly refused to accept other elements of the compromise that they favored. Several southern leaders met privately with Taylor in February 1850 and threatened to secede, or leave, the Union if he did not back down. He retorted that he would lead the army against them if they did. He may have been a slaveholder, but he was also loyal to the Union.

Politicians were still debating the status of the new territories when Taylor participated in ceremonies at the Washington Monument on a sweltering Fourth of July. He suddenly took sick that afternoon and died five days later.

See also Mexican War. *For events during Taylor's administration, see* Compromise of 1850; Gold Rushes.

BARBARA SILBERDICK FEINBERG

TEAPOT DOME AFFAIR

During World War I an oil-rich area in Wyoming known as Teapot Dome and a similar area in California, Elk Hills, were set aside as reserves for the U.S. Navy. In 1921, however, Secretary of the Interior Albert B. Fall persuaded Secretary of the Navy Edwin Denby to transfer these reserves to his department.

Fall then leased the reserves to private oil companies. Elk Hills went to the Pan-Ameri-

This political cartoon shows the Republican Party elephant tied to the Teapot Dome Scandal. The harder he tries to rid himself of the scandal, the more noisily it clanks behind him. On the sidelines, the gleeful Democrats delight in the Republicans' embarrassment—"The first good laugh they've had in years."

can Petroleum Company, controlled by Edward L. Doheny, and Teapot Dome to the Mammoth Oil Company, owned by Harry F. Sinclair. When he was criticized for disposing of the reserves in this way, Fall explained that drillers on adjoining properties were draining off the reserved oil; better to lease the oil than to have it lost.

This explanation did not satisfy critics, and in 1923 the Senate ordered an investigation, managed by Senator Thomas J. Walsh of Montana. The investigation revealed that in return for the leases Doheny had secretly "lent" Fall $100,000 and that Sinclair had given him $300,000 in cash and securities, a direct bribe. Fall resigned, and when put on trial he was convicted, fined $100,000, and sentenced to a year in prison. The leases were

canceled and the reserves returned to government control.

The Teapot Dome affair was the most spectacular of the scandals that disgraced the administration of President Warren G. Harding.

See also Corruption and Scandals in Government.

TECHNOLOGY
See Science and Technology.

TECUMSEH

(1768?–1813)   *Native American leader and warrior.*

Sometime after Tecumseh, a Shawnee Indian, was born near present-day Xenia, Ohio, village chieftains gave him his name, which means "Man Who Waits Like the Crouching Panther or the Shooting Star."

The fierce Shawnee Indians in the late 1700s resisted the advance of white pioneers into the Ohio River valley. As a young man Tecumseh declared that chieftains who signed away land in treaties with the whites had no right to do so. Gaining a reputation as a leader, Tecumseh vowed to defend the rights of his people. His younger brother Lalawethika, a *shaman,* or medicine man, helped him by preaching pride in Native American traditions. As his fame spread, Lalawethika became known as "The Prophet." Tecumseh and his brother established a village called Prophet's Town along the banks of Tippecanoe Creek in Indiana.

During 1810 and 1811 Tecumseh traveled through the Midwest and South. In emotional speeches he urged the divided Indian nations to join against their common enemy.

But Gen. William Henry Harrison took advantage of Tecumseh's absence from Indiana. On November 7, 1811, Harrison and a thousand militiamen at Tippecanoe Creek defeated five hundred Indians commanded by The Prophet. Harrison's victory set back Tecumseh's plans for united Indian resistance against the whites.

Tecumseh then chose to join the British in fighting the Americans in the War of 1812. Parties of Wyandot, Chippewa, Sioux, Sauk, Fox, and Winnebago Indians soon entered Tecumseh's camp ready for battle. The Indians ambushed columns of American troops along the Michigan-Canada border, and in August 1812, Tecumseh and his British allies captured Detroit. On October 5, 1813, the Indians and British fought an American army at the Battle of the Thames in Ontario, Canada. "Be brave! Be brave!" Tecumseh shouted to his warriors. The Indians fought furiously, but Tecumseh was killed.

The dream of a united Indian nation died with this great Shawnee leader. Within the next twenty years most of Tecumseh's Indian allies had surrendered their homelands and trudged westward to reservations across the Mississippi River.

See also Indian-White Relations; War of 1812.

For further reading: Zachary Kent, *Tecumseh* (Chicago: Childrens Press, 1992).

ZACHARY KENT

TELEVISION
See Radio and Television.

TEMPERANCE
See Prohibition and Temperance.

TENNESSEE VALLEY AUTHORITY

During World War I the government had built a dam at Muscle Shoals on the Tennessee River to make electricity needed to power factories making explosives for the armed forces. After the war, efforts to develop the site by either private or public interests failed. In 1933, however, in the early days of the New Deal, Congress created the Tennessee Valley Authority (TVA) to build dams and power plants and sell the electricity and fertilizers thus produced to local communities and private companies. A board (the authority) was set up to manage these projects and to carry on flood control and soil conservation.

The TVA proved to be one of the most successful of all New Deal agencies. It brought electricity to thousands of farms. Its conservation measures were of great importance. And by producing and selling electricity at cost, it provided a yardstick by which the fairness of private utility prices could be measured. The dams it built on the Tennessee created lakes on which fishing and boating and other recreational activities flourished.

See also Conservation and Environmental Movements; New Deal.

TENNIS

Tennis, known for many years as lawn tennis, started as a sport for country estates and upper-class clubs. To this day, despite its popularity in public parks, the rarity of grass courts in most of the world, and the recent rise of big-money professional tournaments, tennis keeps some of its snobbish, lawn-party image.

The French were batting balls back and

forth with their hands as early as the thirteenth century, and rackets appeared in the sixteenth century, but tennis as we know it was invented by Walter Clopton Wingfield, a retired British officer. He introduced it to friends at an estate in Wales in December 1873. It spread to the United States in the next year—the date, site, and players of the first game on American soil are subjects of debate.

America's best early player was Richard Sears, who won the first national singles title at Newport, Rhode Island, in 1881, and then won six more in a row. He is credited with being the first American to develop the volley, in which he worked his way to the net and hit the balls before they bounced. In the same period he and James Dwight won five doubles titles.

From the beginning, tennis was acceptable recreation for girls and women. Mary Outerbridge saw the game being played in Bermuda and brought rackets, balls, and a net home to Staten Island, New York, in October 1874. Ellen Hansell, playing in a long dress more suitable for a prom, won the first U.S. women's singles title at the Philadelphia Cricket Club in 1887.

Tennis has been a part of eleven Olympic Games, but the most important nation-versus-nation event is the annual Davis Cup tournament for men. It was the brainchild of a wealthy young Harvard graduate, Dwight Davis, who donated the silver bowl that bears his name. At the start, in 1900, it was just the United States against Britain, but other countries soon jumped in. America has played Davis Cup matches against thirty-one countries and, led by such stars as John McEnroe, Stan Smith, and Bill Tilden, has won the trophy thirty times.

America has women's teams, too, but the Wightman Cup (United States against Brit-

William "Big Bill" Tilden during a tournament at Forest Hills in 1926. Tilden was the top-ranked tennis player in the 1920s and 1930s and a sports idol. In addition to his magnificent performance on the tennis court, Tilden led a stylish life, socializing with Hollywood stars and writing plays and novels (none, however, had much literary merit). Tilden's glamorous image helped transform tennis into the major spectator sport it is today.

ain, which started in 1923) and the multination Federation Cup (1963) have not caught the public's fancy as the Davis Cup has.

For more than ninety years, tennis was mostly Caucasian and upper-crust, but slowly the game became more democratic. Pancho Gonzalez, a Mexican American from the playgrounds of Los Angeles, won the U.S. singles title at Forest Hills, New York, in 1948 and 1949. Althea Gibson, an African-American woman from Harlem, won at Forest Hills in 1957 and 1958. Arthur Ashe was a pioneer for black men, being the first black to win the U.S. singles title (1968) and the Wimbledon singles title (1975). He also served as Davis Cup captain (1981–85).

For many years, too, the game was considered to be primarily for amateurs. Professionals were barred from the Davis Cup competition and the prestigious Grand Slam tournaments: the national championships of America, Australia, France, and Britain (the tradition-encrusted event known as Wimbledon). The few pros had to settle for annual head-to-head cross-country tours—Tilden versus Ellsworth Vines in 1935, Gonzalez versus Jack Kramer in 1949, and many more.

Wimbledon, the world's most important tournament almost since its start in 1877, admitted pros to its well-manicured lawns in 1968, and that opened the floodgates, not to mention the bank vaults. The men's Association of Tennis Professionals (ATP), organized four years later, started its own tour in 1990, and in 1993 had eighty-seven tournaments in thirty-four countries on six continents (played on grass, concrete, clay, and indoor carpets, and worth millions of dollars in prize money). The Women's Tennis Association (WTA) started in 1973, led by champion player and rebel Billie Jean King. By 1990, more than thirty women had earned at least $1 million in prize money.

As the pro tours got bigger and more powerful, so did the rackets. The rules don't limit the size of rackets, which for about a century were made of wood. In 1974, Wilson, a sporting-goods giant, came out with a racket of steel tubing. Rival Spalding countered with one of aluminum: The Smasher. Manufacturers began to use fiberglass, graphite, and combinations of woods, metals, and plastics. Because of the light weight and super strength of these space-age materials, designer Howard Head in 1976 was able to bring out rackets with much larger heads than the older ones.

They looked weird and unwieldy, but they were surprisingly effective, allowing accuracy along with incredibly hard shots. Today it is the old wooden, small-head rackets that are

novelties. Sweden's Bjorn Borg, who won five straight Wimbledon singles (1976–80) before retiring, tried a comeback in the early nineties with his old wooden weapon. He quickly switched after he realized that he was using a slingshot against laser guns.

See also King, Billie Jean; Sports, Spectator.

JOE JARES

TENURE OF OFFICE ACT

Under the Constitution, important officials such as cabinet ministers, ambassadors, and the members of various boards and commissions are chosen by the president. But they cannot take office until their appointments have been confirmed by the Senate. The Constitution says nothing, however, about removing such officials, and until after the Civil War, the right of a president to discharge an appointee on his own authority was not challenged. In 1867, however, Congress passed the Tenure of Office Act, which provided that members of the cabinet could not be discharged "during the term of the President by whom they may have been appointed" without the consent of the Senate.

The law was passed over the veto of President Andrew Johnson, at whom it was directly aimed. Johnson had succeeded President Abraham Lincoln after his assassination in April 1865. The Republican majority in Congress bitterly resented Johnson's resistance to their Reconstruction policies. Some of the cabinet also agreed with these Reconstruction policies, especially Secretary of War Edwin M. Stanton, who had been appointed by Lincoln. The Tenure of Office Act was intended to prevent Johnson from firing Stanton.

Johnson believed that the act was unconstitutional. To test it he discharged Stanton, and the House of Representatives promptly impeached him. In the trial before the Senate, Johnson's lawyers argued that the law was unconstitutional and that in any case it did not apply to Stanton because he had been appointed by Lincoln in 1862. Johnson was acquitted by the margin of a single vote. Thereafter the Tenure of Office Act was a dead letter, and it was repealed in 1887.

See also Johnson, Andrew.

TERRITORIAL EXPANSION
See Expansion, Territorial.

TET OFFENSIVE

In late 1967 during the Vietnam War American and South Vietnamese troops seemed to be in solid control of most South Vietnamese cities. They were also gradually extending their hold on rural areas. But in January 1968, on Tet, the Vietnamese New Year's Day, North Vietnamese and Viet Cong units suddenly attacked most of the cities in South Vietnam, all of the American bases, and thirty-nine of the forty-four provincial capitals of the country.

At first these massive surprise attacks created almost total chaos. Viet Cong soldiers actually broke into the grounds of the American embassy. To drive them out of Saigon, the capital of South Vietnam, the defenders had to level whole neighborhoods. The communists held the city of Hue, far to the north, for nearly a month, and when they withdrew, they left much of the city a smoking ruin.

American officials claimed that the Tet of-

fensive was a failure because the communists had suffered enormous losses and had been driven from all the towns and cities they had attacked. This was true, but Tet was a terrible psychological setback for the United States. It made the possibility of ending the war seem more remote than ever. When Gen. William Westmoreland, the American commander, requested an additional 200,000 troops, his appeal was turned down. Criticism of the entire American war effort mounted.

See also Vietnam War.

TEXAS REVOLUTION AND ANNEXATION

Most Americans know at least one thing about the Texas Revolution against Mexican rule—brave men fought to the death at the Alamo. But the rebellion's results should be remembered, too. Texas lived for a number of years as an independent nation before joining the United States. When it surrendered that independence, it changed America forever.

Texas under Mexican Rule
Mexico, after gaining its own independence from Spain in the 1820s, welcomed foreign settlers to Texas, part of its land at the time. Led by Stephen F. Austin and other colonizers, over twenty thousand Americans had moved there by 1834. Most settled along the Brazos and Colorado rivers and in eastern Texas. They soon outnumbered the local Mexicans, known as Tejanos.

Though they had been provided with generous land grants, many Americans became unhappy with the Mexican government. Some believed that the United States had established a claim to Texas when it bought the

Louisiana territory from France, and many felt that their land would be more valuable if America controlled Texas. Mexico angered settlers when it began to withdraw privileges it had earlier granted them, such as freedom from import taxes. Slavery caused trouble, too. Many Americans believed that Texas, with its vast lands and relatively few people, could prosper only if black slaves were imported to grow valuable crops like cotton and sugar. But Mexican authorities passed various antislavery measures. In 1830, Mexico, alarmed at the rapid growth of the American population and the immigrants' independent ways, passed laws to slow settlement. The laws upset Texans, and the government, weakened by political conflict, had a hard time making people obey them. This fact points to a more basic problem. The Mexican government demanded too much and delivered too little to suit settlers and many Tejanos. Nineteenth-century Americans had grown up with certain understandings about the proper role of government. These clashed with Mexican practices, which allowed the government more say in economic, social, and even religious matters than Americans were used to. In Texas the Mexican military was permitted to interfere in what Americans took to be nonmilitary or private affairs—trade, legal proceedings, slaveholding. At the same time, Mexico, a new and unstable nation, could not provide the things Americans *did* expect of government such as speedy justice and trial by jury.

By 1835, many already troubled Texans were becoming alarmed as Gen. Antonio López de Santa Anna won increasing power over Mexico. They imagined that their liberties and property (including their slave "property") would be endangered either by a stronger central government or by continued political disturbances. Santa Anna's triumph also seemed to dash many Tejanos' hopes for a more dynamic, democratic Mexico. In the summer of 1835, after a dispute with soldiers at Anahuac, Texans resisted when authorities demanded that troublemakers be turned over to the military. When large numbers of Mexican reinforcements arrived in Texas, many concluded it was time to take up arms.

The Revolution Starts

The rebellion was confused and disorganized. Fighting occurred at Gonzales and around San Antonio long before the rebels officially declared independence (at first, they called only for a separate state government for Texas within Mexico). Texan leaders quarreled among themselves and failed to create a disciplined military organization. Volunteers remained at the Alamo in San Antonio, for instance, despite orders to the contrary from Gen. Sam Houston.

The creation of a new government and a single military command after Texas declared independence on March 2, 1836, did not immediately improve the situation. Houston's small army had to retreat, causing a panicked fleeing of settlers known as the "Runaway Scrape." But Santa Anna had grown overconfident and Texans even more angry after the massacre of their soldiers at the Alamo (March 6) and Goliad (March 27). On April 21, Houston's men surprised and defeated a Mexican army at San Jacinto, capturing Santa Anna.

Texas had suddenly become independent, but independence was not what many Texans really wanted. Voters elected Houston president, but also declared their support for Texas joining the United States. Presidents Andrew Jackson and Martin Van Buren refused to annex Texas, however, fearing diplomatic and political trouble. Slavery, now entirely legal, was growing rapidly in Texas. But Americans had become increasingly divided over slavery. Differences over admitting a large slaveholding territory to the nation could threaten the unity of the Democratic and Whig parties, each of which had both northern and southern supporters. As a result, for nearly ten years the Republic of Texas struggled on alone, deep in debt and menaced by an unhappy Mexico.

Joining the Union

By the early 1840s some Americans had grown less cautious about Texas annexation. Many southerners were eager to expand American slavery westward. But that could be prevented if Britain, as expected, attempted to make Texas's independence permanent and to promote the abolition of slavery there. For Secretaries of State Abel Upshur and John C. Calhoun the welfare of the South and the preservation of slavery was more important than maintaining party unity. And since the president they served, John Tyler, was unpopular with both parties, he did not much care if the Texas issue divided them as long as it brought him new supporters.

To many it seemed that America's growing enthusiasm for national expansion and opposition to British meddling in Texas might cancel out northern concerns over the annexing of slave territory. In the contest for the 1844 presidential nominations, however, Tyler trailed Whig Henry Clay and Democrat Martin Van Buren. Both opposed immediate annexation. A treaty admitting Texas as a territory failed in the U.S. Senate. In the meantime, though, southern Democrats blocked Van Buren's nomination, opening the way for the nomination of expansionist James K. Polk, who called for U.S. control of both Texas and Oregon (which was expected to remain free territory). Taking Polk's narrow victory over Clay as a sign of support for annexation, Congress voted to admit Texas as a state in early 1845.

With the annexation of Texas, America took a big step toward civil war. Annexation helped start the Mexican War, which brought America even more southwestern land. Afterward, northerners and southerners disagreed ever more violently over whether these and other territories should be slave or free. The political parties found it harder to resolve these differences because Texas and later controversies had divided them, too. In 1861, the slavery issue led Texas to leave the Union it had been so eager to join a few short years before and cast its lot with the Confederate States of America.

See also Alamo; Austin, Stephen F.; Houston, Sam; Mexican War; Polk, James K.

PATRICK G. WILLIAMS

THEATER

Before movies, television, or video existed, there was theater. Over two thousand years ago the ancient Greeks filled large amphitheaters to see performers act out dramas on stage. In America, live theater began before the American Revolution when groups of English actors traveled about the colonies. By the early 1800s drama had become commonly seen, particularly in large towns such as New York and Philadelphia. Most actors still came from England, but America began to produce some of its own stars, such as Charlotte Cushman and the muscular Edwin Forrest.

Nineteenth-Century Theater

What was it like to go to the theater in the nineteenth century? In cities you would find large theaters with balconies and a stage that projected out into the audience. Theaters were dark and evil smelling, being lit in this preelectric age mainly by candles or later by gas lamps. They were also firetraps, and a number of terrible theater fires occurred. A modern visitor attending a pre–Civil War theater would be amazed at the noise of the audience. Frequently audiences would hiss a performer who displeased them, shout out their approval for one they liked, demand that a favorite song or scene from a play be performed again, and on occasion break out in such a riot that the show had to come to a stop. One famous theater riot in New York City in 1849 led to the deaths of over twenty people. Away from cities, theatrical performances took place in a strange assortment of places: meeting halls, dining rooms, barns, tents, or river flatboats called showboats.

Actors lived lives of adventure and hardship in the nineteenth century. Most actors belonged to what were called stock companies: a permanent group of actors attached to a theater who staged various plays. But stock company actors would also frequently tour across America. Their experiences "on the road," in small towns and out-of-the-way places, were often fascinating. Occasionally a member of the audience, perhaps never having seen a play before, became so wrapped up in the drama that he would leap onto the stage to "save" the heroine. Actors on tour also had to endure endless coach and later train rides, fleabag hotels, cold dressing rooms, as well as other discomforts. Except for a few stars, actors also had to put up with low pay and long stretches of unemployment. Making matters even worse, many Americans looked down upon the theater and its performers. (This condition was further worsened when an actor, John Wilkes Booth, assassinated President Abraham Lincoln during a theater performance in 1865.)

Popular Entertainments

What did nineteenth-century audiences watch? A great variety of things. Of course there were comedies, tragedies, histories, and most popular of all—melodramas. Melodramas were action-packed plays in which heroes and heroines fought villains, and in the end good always triumphed over evil. Although most plays were written by Europeans (Shakespeare being the most famous), plays on American themes increasingly came to be staged: *Metamora,* about a noble Indian chief; *Uncle Tom's Cabin,* based on Harriet Beecher Stowe's famous novel about slavery; and *Davy Crockett* and *Rip Van Winkle,* dramas about real or legendary American figures. Often, before the play and between acts there would be songs, orchestral pieces, dances—even trained animal acts. Afterward, a short comedy sent the audience home laughing.

In addition to plays of the legitimate theater, nineteenth-century theatergoers enjoyed two types of entertainment developed in America. Minstrel shows, in which white men blacked their faces, sang songs, and told jokes in a crude imitation of African Americans, were very popular for several decades beginning in the 1840s. These minstrel shows influenced American music. Stephen Foster's songs about plantation life, for example, were written for minstrels.

Vaudeville, another form of theater, appeared in the 1870s and remained hugely popular into the 1920s. Vaudeville shows presented a series of acts (repeated several times during the day) that ranged from comedy sketches to love songs to gymnastic exhibitions to strange novelty acts such as the "human lizard." The coming of motion pictures finally killed vaudeville in the 1930s, but the fast-paced action of vaudeville has shaped radio and television programming down to the present.

The Twentieth-Century Stage

In the early twentieth century, theater was at its height in America. Hundreds of touring companies set out from New York City to crisscross America each year. Stars such as William Gillette (the stage's first Sherlock Holmes), Maude Adams (who was famous as Peter Pan), and Ethel Barrymore (a member of the most famous acting family in American history) enjoyed a wealth and influence unknown before. Moreover, they now acted in theaters equipped with much brighter electric lighting and in front of audiences that seldom disturbed their performances (except to applaud).

But the twentieth century also brought new competition from the movies, and by the

Mary Martin, playing Peter Pan, flies down to the deck of Captain Hook's pirate ship.

1920s movies had replaced live theater as mass entertainment. Fewer theatrical companies left New York to tour the nation. Professional theater, though never disappearing from larger cities, became associated with visiting New York's Broadway theater district.

Although theater was now seen by fewer people, it continued to develop in new directions. American drama entered its golden age. Playwrights such as Eugene O'Neill, Tennessee Williams, and Arthur Miller wrote powerful dramas on American themes. Musicals, sometimes considered America's greatest contribution to theater, took on their modern form after World War I. *Showboat* (1927) and *Oklahoma* (1943) combined wonderful music with interesting plots in ways not done before and influenced later musicals. Theater has also found new attention outside of Broadway. Many colleges now have theater departments to train students in theatrical arts. In addition, thriving community theaters have shown that productions do not have to have professional actors or directors in order to produce high-quality drama. Communities often have children's theaters, where young people perform in plays geared for youthful audiences, such as *The Secret Garden, Cinderella*, or *The Wizard of Oz*.

Live theater cannot duplicate the close-ups, fast-paced editing, or other special effects of motion picture and video. Unlike movies or television, a stage production cannot be seen by millions of people simultaneously across the nation. But these limitations are also theater's strength, because only on stage do flesh-and-blood actors make drama come alive. Each performance is slightly different from the one before, depending on how the actors approach their roles and on their interaction with one another and with the audience. This quality gives theater a magic that cannot be matched by any other medium.

See also biographies of playwrights Miller, Arthur; O'Neill, Eugene; *composers for the musical stage* Berlin, Irving; Bernstein, Leonard; Porter, Cole; *actor-singer* Robeson, Paul; *and stage producer* Ziegfeld, Florenz.

BENJAMIN MCARTHUR

THIRTEENTH AMENDMENT

See Emancipation Proclamation and Thirteenth Amendment.

THOREAU, HENRY DAVID

(1817–62)   *Writer and naturalist.*

Thoreau was one of four children born to John and Cynthia Thoreau. Schooled at Concord Academy and Harvard College, he returned home to study nature and literature. His ways of earning a living were many: schoolmaster, surveyor, carpenter, gardener, handyman, lecturer, pencil-maker. He was a friend of Concord's many famous writers—Emerson, the Alcotts, Hawthorne—as well as of its ordinary citizens. His massive *Journal,* which he kept for twenty-four years, records his exploration of nature and his thoughts on the place of individuals in society. The *Journal* provided the raw material for his superb essays, lectures, and books.

Thoreau's masterwork is *Walden,* written while he lived in a cabin he built on Walden Pond near his hometown of Concord, Massachusetts. Published in 1854, it is the account of his two-year adventure there and his philosophy of living the simple life. It has influenced the life of many a reader. A leading example of literary nonfiction, it is a permanent classic in world literature as well.

Besides *Walden,* the only other book to appear during his brief life (he died of tuberculosis at forty-four) was *A Week on the Concord and Merrimack Rivers.* Later, editors compiled volumes of his journal, poetry, correspondence, and travels in Maine and on Cape Cod.

Thoreau, with his family, helped shelter fugitive slaves fleeing the South. To protest the Mexican War, which he believed was fought to extend slave territory, he refused to pay his poll tax and was briefly jailed. Out of that experience came his influential essay "Civil Disobedience," in which he urged his readers to resist evil by nonviolent means. Its message inspired both Mohandas K. Gandhi (also called Mahatma Gandhi) in his campaign against British rule in India and Martin Luther King, Jr., in his drive for civil rights for blacks in the South. Both men adopted his philosophy of nonviolent resistance as a moral obligation.

In 1859, John Brown, an antislavery crusader, was arrested while raiding an armory at Harpers Ferry, Virginia, to obtain arms for a slave uprising. When Thoreau received news that Brown had been sentenced to be hanged, he summoned the people of Concord to the town hall to hear his passionate "Plea for Captain John Brown," which is considered one of the great speeches in American history. Thoreau's appeal for freedom of conscience still inspires readers today.

See also Brown, John; Civil Disobedience; Conscientious Objectors; King, Martin Luther, Jr.; Literature.

For further reading: Milton Meltzer (with Walter Harding), *A Thoreau Profile* (New York: Crowell, 1962).

MILTON MELTZER

THORPE, JIM

(1888–1953)   *Olympic and professional athlete.*

Thorpe was probably the greatest male athlete of his time. Born in Oklahoma of mostly Native American descent, he attended the Carlisle Indian School in Pennsylvania. His great athletic skill led him to national star-

Jim Thorpe was of Potawatomi, Sauk, Fox, French, and Irish descent. His Indian name was Wa-tho-huck, which meant Bright Path. Thorpe excelled at football, baseball, and especially track. He was voted by the Associated Press the greatest athlete of the first half of the twentieth century.

dom on Carlisle's collegiate track and football teams. For a couple of summers Thorpe, like many college athletes, played minor league baseball for pay in the Eastern Carolina League.

Thorpe came to international attention in the 1912 Olympics, where he put on a display of athletic prowess that had never been seen before. He won a gold medal in the pentathlon by winning four of the five events outright. His overpowering victory in the ten-event decathlon led King Gustav V of Sweden to say to him, "You, sir, are the greatest athlete in the world." "Thanks, King," Thorpe replied.

But the following year a newspaper reported Thorpe's two seasons of professional baseball. Although he had never concealed the facts (and had played under his own name, unlike most other collegians), the American authorities revoked Thorpe's amateur status, and the International Olympic Committee took away his medals.

In 1913 Thorpe turned to both professional football and professional baseball and became the foremost star of the early chaotic years of pro football. He served as the first commissioner of the new National Football League in 1920, and coached and played for a number of NFL teams in the 1920s. He also played six seasons as a part-time outfielder for the New York Giants and Cincinnati Reds but never became a superstar. He was said to have two weaknesses—for curveballs and whiskey.

After retiring from football in 1928, he lived a hard life, working as a laborer and actor until he died. Shortly before his death, Thorpe said, "It'd be great to be a young buck again, just for a season. That was the best time of my life." In 1982, after years of appeals, the International Olympic Committee returned Thorpe's Olympic medals to his family.

See also Baseball; Football; Olympic Games.

WARREN GOLDSTEIN

TOBACCO

When Christopher Columbus arrived in the New World, he saw the Native Americans using the leaves of a strange new plant—tobacco—for smoking, chewing, and inhaling as snuff. The Arawak tribe of the Caribbean smoked cigars and used a soapstone pipe called a *tobago*, the source of the word *tobacco*. Smoking quickly became popular in Europe, and tobacco became one of the world's most important crops.

Its commercial cultivation began in the Jamestown colony in Virginia in 1612. Within ten years tobacco was so valued it was used as money in the American colonies, accepted for the payment of taxes and the salaries of public officials. In 1619, shipments of tobacco to England totaled 20,000 pounds; within eight years, exports totaled 500,000 pounds, and in 1639 Jamestown sent 1.5 million pounds to the mother country.

Cigarette Smoking

Native Americans smoked tobacco wrapped in corn husks or stuffed into hollow reeds. It was not until the nineteenth century that the cigarette as we know it was born. During the Crimean War in 1856, the French and English saw soldiers in the Turkish army smoking paper-wrapped tobacco and introduced the custom to the Western world. In a short time, cigarettes became the most popular form of tobacco.

In 1864 the first American cigarette factory

opened and produced almost twenty million cigarettes that year. The invention in 1880 of a machine to produce and wrap cigarettes sped up production and made the James B. Duke Company of Durham, North Carolina, the leader of the industry. In 1913, however, Richard J. Reynolds of Winston-Salem, North Carolina, developed a blend of Turkish and American tobaccos that soon dominated the market.

Although tobacco is grown in over a hundred countries, the United States continues to be the world's leading producer, accounting for more than one-sixth of the six million tons produced annually. Tobacco is the fifth largest in cash value among American farm crops and one of the country's major exports. There are more than 180,000 tobacco farms in the United States, and the economies of six southern states depend largely on the crop. Heavily taxed from the beginning of the industry, it is a major source of revenue for the federal government, especially in the form of cigarettes.

Tobacco has been controversial since it was introduced into Europe. Penalties were imposed on its use in England by James I in the early 1600s and later by the governments of Russia and Turkey. Smoking, like gambling or drinking, was often seen as a vice that could lead to the moral downfall of those who indulged in it. Nevertheless, the habit spread steadily throughout the world. Almost exclusively a man's practice at first, smoking became fashionable among women in the 1920s. From 1930 to 1980 the average number of cigarettes smoked per person in America increased from less than a thousand to nearly three thousand a year.

The Dangers of Smoking

Scientific studies made in the United States during the 1950s established that among the more than 4,700 compounds contained in cigarette smoke, forty-three cause cancer. In response, the U.S. Public Health Service appointed a committee to study the dangers of smoking. Surgeon General Luther L. Terry issued a report in 1964 announcing that almost all American deaths from lung cancer were caused by cigarette smoking and implicating tobacco in such other illnesses as bronchitis, emphysema, and heart disease.

It is estimated that now nearly half a million Americans die annually from smoking, and many more are disabled. Recent research suggests that another fifty thousand Americans a year may die from "passive smoking"—inhaling the smoke of other people's cigarettes—and "passive smoke" has been listed as the third largest preventable cause of death in America, after smoking and alcohol. Evidence has also shown that smoking by pregnant women may be harmful to their unborn children.

Cigarette manufacturers deny the danger of smoking and have attempted to counteract the influence of the bad publicity they have received. The introduction of filter tips to remove much of the tar from tobacco and adding "fresh-tasting" menthol flavoring were efforts to provide a healthier image for smoking. Massive advertising campaigns have tried to link smoking cigarettes with a vigorous, youthful lifestyle.

In recent years, however, all cigarette packages and advertisements have had to carry a health warning, and in the 1970s commercials for tobacco products were banned on radio and television. Smoking has been prohibited in many public places such as restaurants and stores, and it is unlawful to carry lighted tobacco in elevators. Since the 1980s, U.S. airlines have not permitted smoking on domestic flights. But although a massive campaign against smoking has brought about a reduction in tobacco consumption, an estimated fifty million Americans continue to smoke because tobacco is such a highly addictive drug. In fact, it can be so hard to give up the habit once one has started smoking that doctors and others—including older smokers themselves—increasingly urge young people not to start at all.

See also Drugs.

For further reading: Robert Stepney, *Tobacco* (New York: Franklin Watts, 1987).

DENNIS WEPMAN

TOWNSEND PLAN

As time passed in the mid-1930s without the New Deal reforms bringing an end to the Great Depression, more drastic proposals began to be suggested. One of these was the brainchild of Dr. Francis Townsend, a retired California physician. Townsend's Old Age Revolving Pensions scheme called for paying every person over sixty who was unemployed or who would agree not to work two hundred dollars a month provided that they spent the money within a month. The money was to be raised by a 2 percent federal sales tax.

Townsend argued that the resulting increase in national spending would stimulate production and thus create thousands of new jobs. The public response was overwhelming. Townsend Clubs sprang up everywhere; soon half a million people had enrolled. A newspaper, the *Townsend National Weekly,* had a circulation of more than 200,000.

The plan, however, was quite impractical. Ten million Americans were eligible for the pensions; their annual cost would have been

$24 billion, half the national income. Its popularity, like that of Huey Long's Share-Our-Wealth scheme and the National Union for Social Justice founded by Father Charles E. Coughlin, was symptomatic of the failure of the New Deal to make much headway in the fight to reduce unemployment and put an end to the Great Depression.

See also Depressions and Recessions.

TOWNSHEND ACT

In 1767 Charles Townshend, the British chancellor of the exchequer, or finance minister, persuaded Parliament to pass a law taxing the importation into the colonies of glass, lead, paint, tea, and paper. The law stated plainly that the purpose of these taxes was to raise money. It was thus a direct challenge to those in the colonies who claimed that Parliament did not have the power to tax them. Townshend argued that while the Stamp Act of 1765 had been a direct tax, the new measures were indirect taxes like the Sugar Act of 1764, which the colonists, with some grumbling, had accepted.

The colonists, however, reacted against the new taxes almost as unanimously as they had against the Stamp Act. The fact that the British also strengthened their efforts to prevent smuggling in America further angered the colonists. Merchants swiftly organized a boycott of all British imports, not merely the newly taxed items. The boycotts soon reduced imports from the mother country by about half.

When they realized that they could not raise money in America by taxing imports, the British repealed all the Townshend taxes except the three-penny tax per pound on tea.

The tea tax, Townshend insisted, was kept on the books as a matter of principle to demonstrate that Parliament had the right to tax the colonists. The colonists then lifted the boycott, but they refused to import British tea.

See also Revolution: The War for Independence.

TOYS
See Games and Toys.

TRAIL OF TEARS

The Trail of Tears was the route that U.S. troops forced fifteen thousand Cherokee In-dians to march in the winter of 1838–39. They were evicted from their homeland of Georgia and made to resettle in Indian Terri-tory (present-day Oklahoma).

In 1791, a U.S. treaty had recognized Cher-okee Territory in Georgia as independent, and the Cherokee people had created a thriv-ing republic with a written constitution. But the land owned by Indian tribes in the South-east (the Choctaw, Chickasaw, Creeks, and Cherokee) grew increasingly attractive to whites. The prevailing attitude of the day— that the white man was superior to the Indian and entitled to whatever property he wanted, whether Indian-owned or not—was to win

A painting of the Trail of Tears by Robert Lindneux shows the Cherokees on their forced march to the West. The Su-preme Court ruled in favor of the Cherokees and against the state of Georgia, which wanted to take over the Cher-okees' land. Chief Justice John Marshall had stated that the "acts of Georgia are repugnant to the Constitution. . . . They are in direct hostility with treaties [that] solemnly pledge the faith of the United States to restrain their citi-zens from trespassing on [Cherokee territory]." But President Andrew Jackson and Georgia officials nevertheless eventually forced the Cherokees off their land.

out. In 1830, President Andrew Jackson signed the Indian Removal Act, which was to force all tribes east of the Mississippi River to leave their homelands and take up territory in the West. The Choctaw, Chickasaw, and Creeks reluctantly complied with the authorities, but the Cherokee resisted. The Supreme Court backed the Cherokees' claim to their land, declaring the Indian Removal Act unconstitutional (*Worcester* v. *Georgia*, 1832). But the national and state harassment of the Cherokee did not stop. Finally, in 1838 U.S. troops used force to expel the Cherokee from Georgia.

The Indians had to abandon their property, livestock, and ancestral burial grounds. In the midst of severe winter weather, they were marched over eight hundred miles to Indian Territory. An estimated four thousand people—about 25 percent of the Cherokee Nation—died along the trail. A private in the army who witnessed the march remarked: "The trail of the exiles was a trail of death. They had to sleep in the wagons and on the ground without fire. I have known as many as twenty-two of them to die in one night of pneumonia due to ill treatment, cold, and exposure."

The Trail of Tears became a national monument in 1987, serving as a symbol of the suffering and injustice American Indians received at the hands of the U.S. government.

See also Indian-White Relations.

TRANSPORTATION
See Public Transportation.

TREATY OF PARIS (1783)
See Paris, Treaty of (1783).

TREATY OF VERSAILLES AND LEAGUE OF NATIONS

The Treaty of Versailles was drawn up at the Paris Peace Conference in 1919 between the victorious Allies and the defeated German Empire to end World War I and establish the first international organization of nations. (Versailles is a great palace just outside of Paris, France.)

In 1918, American president Woodrow Wilson had proposed "Fourteen Points," as goals for which the Allies (the United States, Britain, France, Italy, and others) were fighting. These included disarmament, freedom of the seas, removal of obstacles to free trade, a ban on secret treaties, readjustment of national boundaries to match ethnic populations, and the establishment of an international association to settle disputes between nations. At war's end, Germany agreed to accept the Fourteen Points as the basis for a peace settlement.

Provisions of the Treaty
The leaders of the major Allies—Vittorio Orlando of Italy, David Lloyd George of Britain, Georges Clemenceau of France, and President Wilson—met in Paris to draw up the treaty. They refused to let Germany participate in the negotiations and imposed severe penalties on the defeated nation. The European statesmen had already made secret arrangements to divide up the German Empire despite Wilson's noble goals. Germany's colonial possessions were distributed among Britain, France, and Japan. The provinces of Alsace and Lorraine were returned to France, northern Schleswig went back to Denmark, and Belgium was enlarged. Poland, which had been wiped off the map of Europe for a century, was reconstructed from German ter-

ritory, isolating East Prussia from the rest of Germany.

To prevent future threats to the hard-won peace, the Allied leaders forced Germany to disarm by reducing the size of its army, outlawing submarines and military aircraft, forbidding the purchase or manufacture of weapons, and dismantling military installations. In addition, they inserted a "war guilt" clause in the treaty, blaming Germany for starting World War I. They required that nation to pay billions of dollars in reparations for wartime damages suffered by civilian populations.

Although the Germans signed the document in the Hall of Mirrors at Versailles, they complained that the peace treaty had been dictated to them and that it violated the Fourteen Points. Their continued resentment of the settlement paved the way for the Nazis to come to power in Germany during the 1930s.

The League of Nations

At the peace conference, President Wilson had reluctantly agreed to the European leaders' territorial demands in order to win their support for his fourteenth point, the establishment of the League of Nations. He refused to compromise, however, when members of the U.S. Senate, led by Henry Cabot Lodge, chairman of the Senate Committee on Foreign Relations, threatened to vote against the treaty unless changes were made in the League. Isolationist senators wanted the United States to avoid further involvement in European affairs. Other senators argued that the League would violate America's sovereignty—its right to make its own decisions in the national interest. Most of the treaty's opponents were alarmed by Article 10 of the League Covenant, or charter, requiring each member of the organization to pledge to protect the existing borders of other member states. They feared this would involve the United States in another war without its consent.

The senators offered Wilson a series of amendments, or changes to the treaty, that would have allowed the United States to join the League with certain reservations. He turned them down, claiming that the amendments would make the League weak and useless. In September 1919, the determined president went on a nationwide speaking tour to urge the public to support his position. A month later, while still on tour, he suffered a stroke that left him an invalid. In November 1919, the Senate voted to reject the Treaty of Versailles, and the United States never became a member of the League.

Nevertheless, the League began meeting in January 1920 in Geneva, Switzerland. Sixty-three nations eventually joined the organization, which was made up of four main bodies. In the *Assembly,* representatives from all member nations discussed international problems. The *Council* negotiated disputes and recommended actions to keep the peace. The major powers were permanent members of the Council, and other nations were elected to rotating membership by the Assembly. The *Secretariat* managed the daily operations of the organization, and the *Permanent Court of International Justice* ruled on legal disputes between states. Another League organization, the *Permanent Mandates Commission,* supervised the welfare of inhabitants in the former German colonies. Among other activities, League agencies helped refugees, promoted world health, and tried to improve conditions for working people.

The League successfully settled some disputes between smaller nations, but it could not halt the German, Italian, and Japanese conquests that led to World War II. The Assembly met for the last time in 1939 when it voted to expel Russia for attacking Finland. The League was formally dissolved in April 1946 and was replaced by the United Nations.

See also Fourteen Points; Wilson, Woodrow; World War I.

BARBARA SILBERDICK FEINBERG

TRIANGLE SHIRTWAIST FIRE

On March 25, 1911, a fire broke out in the factory of the Triangle Shirtwaist Company.

The New York Fire Department attempts to extinguish the blaze at the Triangle Shirtwaist Company in 1911.

The factory was located on an upper floor of a New York City sweatshop. When the young women who worked there tried to escape, they discovered to their horror that all the exits were locked. There were no fire escapes. Many of the women leaped out of the windows in a desperate effort to escape the flames only to die when they struck the sidewalk far below. All told, 146 workers were killed.

The tragedy resulted in the passage of many improved municipal building codes and the enactment of stricter state factory inspection acts. The International Ladies' Garment Workers Union, which had earlier tried to organize the Triangle Company workers, and the Women's Trade Union League used the Triangle fire in their efforts to recruit members.

See also Labor Movement.

TRIANGULAR TRADE

All the American colonies had great need for manufactured products that they were not yet able to produce. These goods could be had in England and elsewhere in western Europe. The southern colonies had no trouble importing them because their own agricultural products, such as tobacco and rice, could not be grown profitably in the cool climate of northern and western Europe. The products of northern farmers, such as wheat and fish, however, were produced in adequate amounts in Europe. There was no market for them in that region. So northern merchants and shippers had to engage in indirect trade to get the things they and their customers wanted. A Massachusetts merchant, for example, might ship flour or salted fish to the West Indies, trade it there for sugar, and ship the sugar to England, where it could be exchanged for manufactured goods that in turn could be brought back to Massachusetts. When plotted on a map, this exchange took the form of a triangle.

Many of the exchanges were even more complicated and some did not include Europe at all. One of the most famous involved selling northern farm and forest products in the West Indies in exchange for molasses, which was then manufactured into rum in Rhode Island. The rum was shipped either to Africa where it was traded for slaves who were sold in the West Indies or the mainland colonies, or to Europe where rum was a popular drink.

See also Colonial America.

TRUMAN, HARRY S.

(1884–1972) *Thirty-third president of the United States (1945–53).*

Truman got up early every morning to take a brisk walk, challenging reporters to keep up with him, for he never forgot the habits he had developed as a farm boy in Independence, Missouri. He could not afford to attend college but educated himself by reading histories, something he enjoyed all his life. The scrappy, outspoken Democrat was a World War I veteran who rose from Missouri county public works commissioner to U.S. senator. During World War II, he headed a special Senate committee to investigate the awarding of contracts in the defense industry. His work attracted favorable national attention, which led to his nomination and election as Franklin D. Roosevelt's vice president in 1944.

Truman, who was never consulted on government matters before Roosevelt's death in 1945, was unprepared for his sudden eleva-

tion to the presidency. He said later that when he was told of FDR's death, he felt as if "the moon, the stars, and all the planets had fallen on me." Nevertheless, the new president proved himself capable and decisive. In one controversial decision, he ordered atomic bombs dropped on Japan, ending World War II (1945), because he was convinced that would shorten the war and save American lives. The arrival of the nuclear age led him to modernize and reorganize the defense establishment (1947). He realized that America now had international responsibilities and responded to the threat of Soviet expansion with the Truman Doctrine (1947), under which military supplies and other aid was sent to Greece and Turkey; the Marshall Plan (1947), which rebuilt war-torn Western Europe; and the Berlin airlift (1948), which flew supplies into the Western half of the isolated German city when the Soviets cut off ground access to it. He backed the North Atlantic Treaty Organization (NATO; 1949), which promised protection to Western Europe in the event of a Soviet attack. He sent American troops along with other U.N. units to defend South Korea (1950) after Communist forces invaded from the North. He also ended racial segregation in the armed services (1948), recognized the new state of Israel (1948), and started the Point Four program (1949), which offered technical aid to developing nations.

During his 1948 presidential campaign, he made "whistle-stop" train trips, appealing directly to the voters for support. He criticized what he called the "Do-Nothing" Eightieth Congress for blocking his Fair Deal programs, including national medical insurance and low-income housing. Despite universal predictions of an overwhelming defeat, Truman triumphed over Republican Thomas E. Dewey.

His second term was dominated by the Ko-

President Harry S. Truman on his famous 1948 whistle-stop train campaign. Stopping in towns along the railroad on his cross-country trip, Truman gave fiery speeches that helped get him reelected. Here he holds up a wooden paddle that reads, "For use on Republicans only!"

rean War, during which he fired the popular Gen. Douglas MacArthur for defying the president's orders, reminding critics that under the Constitution the president is commander in chief of the armed services. The rise of the postwar red scare, aggravated by Senator Joseph McCarthy's charge that Truman and members of his administration were pro-Communist, hurt much of the president's domestic program. The charge was untrue, but many believed it. The senator's reckless accusations and the seemingly endless war contributed to Truman's unpopularity at the time he left office. His accomplishments, however, have become more appreciated in the years since his death, and his reputation has risen.

For events during Truman's administration, *see* Anticommunism; Berlin Blockade; Cold War; Fair Deal; Korean War; Marshall Plan; North Atlantic Treaty Organization; Nuremberg Trials; Potsdam Conference; Progressive Parties; *Rosen-*

berg Case; Taft-Hartley Act; Truman Doctrine; World War II.

For further reading: Barbara Silberdick Feinberg, *Harry S. Truman* (New York: Franklin Watts, 1994).

B A R B A R A   S I L B E R D I C K   F E I N B E R G

TRUMAN DOCTRINE

This policy, announced by President Harry S. Truman in a speech to Congress in March 1947, requested American economic and military aid for Greece and Turkey. Greek communist guerrillas, aided by communists from other Balkan countries and probably backed by the Soviet Union, were threatening the existing Greek government. Great Britain had been supporting that government, but in February British leaders had informed Truman that, given England's postwar financial crisis, they could no longer afford to do so. Truman feared that if Greece went communist, Turkey and other Middle Eastern nations might also be taken over, thus greatly expanding Soviet power and influence. He therefore asked Congress to provide $400 million to help Greece and Turkey resist communist pressure. "It must be the policy of the United States to support free peoples who are resisting . . . outside pressures," he said. Congress appropriated the money and the communist threat was checked.

The Truman Doctrine marked a turning point in post–World War II international relations. Its success led to American aid to Western Europe through the Marshall Plan and to the global competition between the United States and the Soviet Union known as the cold war.

See also Cold War.

TRUTH, SOJOURNER

(c. 1797–1883)   *Evangelist, abolitionist, and feminist.*

Although Sojourner Truth had no formal schooling, she raised her eloquent voice in support of the abolition of slavery, the welfare of the freedpeople after abolition, and the rights of women. Tales are told of her powerful dramatic style on the lecture platform. Once when an audience questioned her womanhood because of her aggressive manner, she bared her breasts and challenged her hecklers with "Ain't I a woman?"

Sojourner Truth was the first black woman to reach large audiences with her abolitionist and feminist messages. Her speech to the Ohio Women's Rights Convention in 1851 was powerful and direct: "Then they talk about this thing in the head, what's this they call it? [Intellect, someone responds.] That's it, honey. What's that got to do with women's rights or Negroes' rights? If my cup won't hold but a pint, and yours holds a quart, wouldn't you be mean not to let me have my little half-measure full?"

Truth was six feet tall, had a powerful voice, and was driven by deep religious faith. Harriet Beecher Stowe, author of *Uncle Tom's Cabin,* wrote that she had never talked to a more powerful personality. Truth was born of slave parents in New York. Details of her early life remain cloudy. We know, however, that her name was Isabella and she served a household in New Paltz, New York, from 1810 to 1827, where she bore five children by a fellow slave. At least two daughters and one son were sold away from her during these years.

Isabella escaped from slavery in 1827, one year before the final emancipation of slaves in New York State. She fled to a Quaker family and later moved to New York City, where she worked as a domestic. During these years Isabella worked for moral reform, became a visionary evangelist, and started her street-corner preaching career. In the 1840s in Massachusetts she worked with William Lloyd Garrison and his group of abolitionists. For several years she lived in a utopian community in Northampton, Massachusetts. A popular platform figure, she told stories and sang gospel songs that instructed and entertained. She adopted the name "Sojourner Truth" in 1843, when she became a traveling orator. In the mid-1850s she settled permanently in Battle Creek, Michigan.

During the Civil War, Truth collected food and clothing for black regiments. In 1864 she met with Abraham Lincoln at the White House and labored as a teacher of domestic skills and as a distributor of relief supplies among the freedpeople. During Reconstruction, Truth used her talents in support of women's rights, especially the right to vote. She developed strong ties to women's rights leaders such as Elizabeth Cady Stanton and Lucretia Mott. Until the end of her life Truth preached godliness and cleanliness to blacks;

but she also initiated a petition drive demanding land for ex-slaves.

Perhaps Truth's most important legacy is the tone and substance of her language. On behalf of ex-slaves, she would say, "Give 'em land and an outset [a start in life], and hab teachers learn 'em to read. Den they can be somebody." Always she fought racism. Once when she was brutally knocked off one of Washington's segregated streetcars, she declared, "It is hard for the old slaveholding spirit to die, but *die* it must." When she herself died, her funeral in Battle Creek was the largest that town had ever seen. Sojourner Truth was a leader who led with her voice, her physical determination, and her moral courage.

See also Abolitionist Movement; African Americans; Feminist Movement.

For further reading: Margaret Washington, ed., *Narrative of Sojourner Truth* (New York: Vintage, 1993).

DAVID W. BLIGHT

TUBMAN, HARRIET

(1820?–1913)   *Abolitionist and Civil War spy.*

Growing up on a plantation in Dorchester County, Maryland, Harriet was known by the name Araminta. She was one of eleven children born to slave parents, Harriet Green and Benjamin Ross. As a young girl, she was rebellious and suffered many whippings from the whites who owned her family. Once when she tried to help a slave friend in trouble, the plantation overseer became angry and threw a lead weight at her, which knocked her out and left a permanent dent in her forehead. She was unconscious for several days and unwell for several months. From that day forward she was determined to seek her freedom.

At the age of twenty-three she married

Harriet Tubman was a Civil War spy and nurse as well as the most famous "conductor" on the Underground Railroad. She grew up a slave in Maryland, forced to bear beatings by her master and endure back-breaking fieldwork. When her owner died and it seemed likely she would be sold out of state, she escaped to Philadelphia.

John Tubman, a free black. In 1849, when her master died, she decided to escape rather than be sold. She left her family, made her way to Philadelphia, and took the name Harriet Tubman. She met a number of abolitionists, people working to free the slaves, and joined what was known as the Underground Railroad—those who helped escaped slaves make their way secretly to freedom. Tubman and others were breaking the law, but they believed that blacks deserved the same rights as all Americans. Tubman earned a reputation as a fearless leader: she made many trips back into slave territory, risking her own freedom to help others escape (including her family).

Tubman moved to Canada in 1852, but came back to the United States when the Civil War broke out. She had earned the nickname "General Tubman" during her service as a "conductor" on the Underground Railroad, but after 1861 she contributed directly to the military effort. She worked at Fortress Monroe in Virginia before being sent to Beaufort, South Carolina, where she led raids during 1863 to liberate slaves on Confederate plantations along the Combahee River. Nearly eight hundred African Americans found their way behind Union lines with her assistance. She also served as a spy for the Union cause.

Tubman received only three hundred dollars for her two years of military service, and her commanding officers, Col. James Montgomery and Maj. Gen. David Hunter, lobbied unsuccessfully to secure a Union pension for her after the war. She retired to Auburn, New York, and opened a Home for Indigent and Aged Negroes. She died in 1913, penniless and alone, an unsung heroine for the cause of black freedom.

See also Abolitionist Movement; Civil War; Free Blacks before Emancipation; Slavery; Underground Railroad.

For further reading: Ann Petry, *Harriet Tubman: Conductor on the Underground Railroad* (New York: Crowell, 1955); Dorothy Sterling, *Freedom Train: The Story of Harriet Tubman* (New York: Scholastic, 1987).

CATHERINE CLINTON

ginia. The institution of slavery dominated his entire life. Although he escaped at one time, he returned voluntarily nearly thirty days later, believing that he had a duty to educate and free the other slaves.

Turner learned to read and write, which was unusual for slaves. Reading the Bible played an important role in his spiritual development. He came to realize that slavery was wrong and believed that he was a special messenger of God sent to end the institution. The Bible inspired him to encourage other slaves to revolt. He taught them that they were all God's children and were not meant to live under such conditions.

Nat Turner's rebellion began early in the morning of August 22, 1831, in the town of Southampton, located in southeastern Virginia. Turner planned the rebellion with about six followers, and another sixty to eighty slaves joined along the way. The actual rebellion lasted only one day, during which the slaves went from farm to farm and massacred about fifty-five whites. All of the white Southampton community lived in terror thereafter, a fear that did not diminish until Turner was captured on October 31. Convicted of insurrection, he was executed on November 11 along with seventeen other slaves. Innocent blacks were also killed, and many were sold into slavery elsewhere as a result of the rebellion. Nat Turner's rebellion failed, but it forced many Americans to take a closer look at the institution of slavery.

See also African Americans: to 1865; Slavery.

LAYN SAINT-LOUIS

TURNER, NAT

(c. 1800–31)   *Religious and slave rebellion leader.*

Turner grew up on the plantation of Benjamin Turner in Southampton County, Vir-

TVA
See Tennessee Valley Authority.

TWAIN, MARK

(1835–1910) Author.

"Mark Twain" was the pen name of Samuel Langhorne Clemens. This was what a sailor on a riverboat, measuring the depth of the Mississippi, called out when his lead line showed that the water was two fathoms (about twelve feet) deep. Throughout his life Mark Twain clung with more than ordinary fondness to his boyhood memories of life on the Mississippi. He grew up in Hannibal, Missouri, a sleepy village, which he always remembered through a golden haze of nostalgia. "It was," he recalled, "a heavenly place for a boy."

His father's death in 1847 meant the end of formal schooling for young Sam, and he was apprenticed to a printer. Since Benjamin Franklin's time print shops had been known as the "poor boy's college." Equipped with a trade that was always in demand, he left Hannibal in 1853 to make his way in the world as a printer. For the next seventeen years he lived the restless life of a wanderer, traveling as far east as Boston and as far west as the Sandwich Islands (now Hawaii). In addition to setting type, he piloted riverboats on the Mississippi, prospected for silver in Nevada, and served briefly as a soldier.

Failing to make his fortune at these occupations, he at last struck it rich by turning his experiences into novels and travel books and, as his fame increased, into public readings and lecture tours. His first popular success was a short story, the comic masterpiece "The Celebrated Jumping Frog of Calaveras County" (1865), a tall tale recounted in the racy speech of the frontier.

In 1870 Mark Twain married Olivia Langdon of Elmira, New York. The marriage crowned a two-year courtship in which the gifted roughneck from the Wild West sought and gained the approval of this refined woman and her wealthy family. The couple settled in Hartford, Connecticut, and during the next twenty-five years Olivia bore four children while her husband tried with mixed success to accommodate himself to eastern manners and customs. Chiefly he worked at his writing, growing in maturity and self-confidence as book followed book.

In 1884, Twain published *The Adventures of Huckleberry Finn,* his dazzling tale of the journey of an orphan boy and a runaway slave down the Mississippi River. His realistic

Mark Twain claimed that a good story "must be written with the blood out of a man's heart." Twain wrote one of the greatest American novels, The Adventures of Huckleberry Finn. *In his last years, he made this prediction: "I came in with Halley's Comet in 1835, and I expect to go out with it." Twain was right: Halley's Comet reappeared in 1910, the year he died.*

picture of American society in the mid-nine-teenth century is unforgettable, and his brilliant re-creation of everyday speech changed the course of American literature. *Huckleberry Finn, Tom Sawyer,* and Twain's vivid memoir of his river days, *Life on the Mississippi* (1883), are the three works that assure his place as one of the giants of world literature.

Mark Twain watched with growing dismay, however, as his streak of good luck ran out. His beloved wife died in 1904 after a terrible illness and only one of his four children survived him. Always a gambler addicted to get-rich-quick schemes, he lost large sums of money in chancy business ventures and exhausted himself paying off his creditors. Beneath the mask of the genial and witty Mark Twain, who had made the world laugh with his books and lectures, his closest friends, like fellow writer William Dean Howells, saw Sam Clemens, a bitter and disillusioned man. Readers of such dark later works as "The Man Who Corrupted Hadleyburg" (1899) could only guess at the demons haunting the author. The depth of his despair was revealed long after his death with the publication of such works as *The Mysterious Stranger* (1916) and *Letters from the Earth* (1962).

See also Literature.

CHARLES BOHNER

TWEED RING

The Tweed ring was a group of corrupt New York City politicians headed by William Marcy Tweed who controlled the government of the city after the Civil War. Tweed was the

One of political cartoonist Thomas Nast's many depictions of the corrupt Tweed ring. The caption asks, "Who stole the people's money? Do tell." The response shows a ring of Boss Tweed's men each pointing the finger of blame at the next man, claiming: "'Twas him."

boss of Tammany Hall, the local Democratic machine. Unlike most nineteenth-century political bosses, Tweed held a number of important elected offices, including a term in the U.S. House of Representatives from 1853 to 1855. In the late 1860s and early 1870s he dominated the state Democratic Party as well as Tammany Hall. He and his close associates in the ring collected millions of dollars in the form of kickbacks from companies supplying the city with everything from bricks and sewer pipe to printing services. In addition, companies doing business in New York City paid bribes disguised as legal fees merely to be left alone. Tweed supervised the construction of a new courthouse that cost the city $12 million, about three times what the building was actually worth.

When bankruptcy threatened the city because of the ring's corruption, reformers led by *Harper's Weekly* and the *New York Times* began an investigation. The cartoons of Thomas Nast of *Harper's Weekly* held Tweed up to ridicule. Tweed was eventually convicted of graft and thrown in jail. The total graft collected by the Tweed ring is unknown; estimates range from $30 million to $200 million.

See also Corruption and Scandals in Government.

T Y L E R , J O H N

(1790–1862) *Tenth president of the United States (1841–45).*

Tyler was known as "His Accidency" because he was the first vice president to complete the term of a president who had died in office. The son of a Virginia governor, Tyler came from a family of aristocratic planters and was educated at the College of William and Mary. His career in politics included service as a state legislator (1811–16, 1823–25), U.S. congressman (1817–21), governor of Virginia (1825–27), and U.S. senator (1827–36). He resigned from the Senate and shifted allegiance from the Democratic to the Whig Party because he objected to Democratic President Andrew Jackson's policies. In 1840, he was elected vice president under William Henry Harrison and became president when Harrison died a month after the inauguration.

Tyler set an important precedent by refusing to be treated as an "acting president." Instead he insisted on exercising the full powers of his new office unconditionally: "I can never consent to being dictated to. . . . I, as President, shall be responsible for my administration." He clashed with the nationalist Whigs in Congress and vetoed their bill to establish a national bank because he was committed to states' rights, the belief that a too-strong central government posed a threat to the power of individual states. The Whig cabinet, originally appointed by Harrison, resigned in protest, so Tyler replaced them with southern Democrats, who were more in line with his own views. Secretary of State Daniel Webster, however, remained long enough to complete the Webster-Ashburton treaty (1842), which established the present-day border between Maine and Canada.

Just before the strongly proslavery president left office, he pushed the United States' annexation of Texas (1845) through Congress to ensure that the Lone Star republic would not ally with Great Britain. Since that country was opposed to slavery, Tyler feared that such an alliance would lead to abolition in Texas. The annexation led to the Mexican War, however.

After failing to be nominated for reelection as president, Tyler retired to his Virginia plantation. During the secession crisis in 1860, he headed an unsuccessful peace convention of North and South. He reluctantly voted for Virginia's leaving the Union but died soon after winning election to the Confederate Congress.

See also Texas Revolution and Annexation; Whig Party.

B A R B A R A S I L B E R D I C K F E I N B E R G

U

UNCAS

(c. 1606–c. 1683) *Mohegan chief.*

Uncas was born into the Pequot tribe in what is today the state of Connecticut. Sometime before the arrival of English settlers in the area, he led a rebellion of the western Pequot, who were called the Mohegan once they achieved their independence.

Beginning in 1629, the Puritans began arriving from England in Massachusetts Bay and settling in the region. When war broke out between the English and the Pequot in 1637, Uncas joined the English against his old tribe. The English also had the help of the Narragansett tribe, who were old enemies of the Pequot. The war ended with the massacre of a Pequot village and the sale of captured Indians into slavery.

The Narragansett chief, Miantonomi, was horrified at the way the English made war, but Uncas saw them as powerful potential allies. He made it a policy to cultivate the goodwill of the English. He signed a peace treaty and received support from them in some of his quarrels with other tribes.

Uncas captured Miantonomi in 1643 and received permission from the Commissioners of the United Colonies to kill him. Miantonomi had tried to enlist Uncas in a multitribal alliance to resist the English. Uncas, however, was more concerned with eliminating a rival than uniting against a common enemy and had the death sentence against

Miantonomi executed. The Mohegans were the only tribe in the region who were still intact after King Philip's War in 1675–76. Even so, their numbers declined over the eighteenth century. Their descendants today live in Connecticut and Wisconsin.

The novelist James Fenimore Cooper created a character named Uncas, whom he called "the last of the Mohicans." In the book he is a young brave, son of a chief, but he is not based on the actual Uncas. The "Mohicans," in fact, are also a fiction. Cooper arrived at the name by combining *Mohegan* with *Mahican*, the name of a New York tribe.

See also Indian-White Relations; Philip (King Philip); Puritans.

THOMAS COLE

UNDERGROUND RAILROAD

Beginning in the 1830s, a secret network of people helped slaves from the South escape to Canada or to northern free states. Simply reaching a free state, however, did not guarantee a slave freedom: the Fugitive Slave Act demanded that runaway slaves be captured even in free states. The Underground Railroad operated mainly in the North, with "conductors" smuggling runaway slaves from "station" to "station," providing food and hiding places until they reached areas considered safe from bounty hunters.

Harriet Tubman (far left) with some of the slaves she helped free on the Underground Railroad. Herself an escaped slave, she made at least nineteen trips back into slave territory to rescue hundreds, determined that "my people must go free."

Before hooking up with the Underground Railroad, however, runaway slaves had to make the first and most dangerous part of the escape on their own. Fleeing the plantation, slaves hid in swamps or woods, inching their way through the southern slave states until they connected with the Railroad in the north.

The Underground Railroad was run by white abolitionists and free blacks, with blacks engineering most of the rescues. One of its most famous conductors was Harriet Tubman, herself an escaped slave who guided three hundred fugitives to freedom. The Underground Railroad was not as highly organized as the many stories circulating about its heroic rescues claimed, and it in fact helped free only a small fraction of the slave population. But reports of its successes, whether real or exaggerated, infuriated proslavery forces and fueled northern sympathy for the plight of slaves. The Underground Railroad became a powerful symbol for the abolitionists' cause, each escape seeming to chip away at the institution of slavery.

See also Slavery; Tubman, Harriet.

UNEMPLOYMENT

Unemployment has long been an extremely significant problem in the United States. For more than a century, it has been a source—perhaps the most important source—of poverty and economic hardship; it has raised questions about the health of the economy and the fairness of our economic system; it has also had a major impact on elections.

Unemployment, however, has not always been a part of the American landscape. As a social problem, it appeared in the United States with the triumph of an industrial free-enterprise economy during the first half of the nineteenth century. Only when large numbers of working people became *employees,* rather than self-employed farmers or artisans, was it possible for large numbers of people to become unemployed; they could be laid off only if they worked for someone else in the first place. The word *unemployed* acquired its modern definition—to be out of work and needing or wanting to work—between 1850 and 1880. The term *unemployment* first appeared in print in 1887.

Prevalence of Unemployment

Once it had arrived, the problem of unemployment quickly became widespread: during the economic depression of the 1870s, there were jobless workers throughout the Northeast and the Midwest, and by the depression of the 1890s unemployment was clearly a national issue. From the Civil War until World War II, the national unemployment rate (the average percentage of labor force members who are unemployed at any one time) ranged from roughly 4 or 5 percent in the most prosperous years to more than 15 percent during the worst depressions. But this figure tells only part of the story: an unemployment *rate* of 5 or 6 percent generally meant that roughly 20 percent of all working people were unemployed at some point during the year (because there was always turn-

over in the unemployed population). Indeed, in the course of an *average* year about 20 to 25 percent of all working Americans experienced some unemployment with the average spell lasting for three months. During depressions (which occurred at least once every decade), the toll was higher, but even during good years millions of Americans were jobless for months at a time. Only in wartime when all-out production of war goods became vital was it possible for all able-bodied workers to find jobs.

Nonetheless, unemployment became a public policy issue—a problem on the government's agenda—only gradually. In the late nineteenth century, workers and their unions tried to develop solutions to the problem (such as shortening workers' hours of

Robley D. Stevens, thirty years old, wears a desperate sign on a Baltimore sidewalk in 1931.

labor so that more workers would be needed), but these invariably ended in failure. They also demanded relief and public works projects from city, state, and federal authorities, most visibly in 1894 when Jacob Coxey led an "army" of the unemployed to Washington to demand aid from the national government. These efforts too bore few fruits. Mainstream politicians, supported by prevailing economic theories, maintained that government could not and should not interfere with the market to reduce unemployment levels or help the unemployed. As a result, the only aid came from unions, private charities, or traditional local "poor relief" agencies.

Government Steps In

These ideas began to change early in the twentieth century. But it took the crisis of the Great Depression of the 1930s—when unemployment rates zoomed to 25 percent and remained high for the entire decade—to produce new national policies and institutions. Massive public works and relief programs were created as a part of President Franklin D. Roosevelt's New Deal, and after years of debate, an unemployment insurance system was authorized by the Social Security Act of 1935.

Without question, the decade of the 1930s constituted a turning point in the history of unemployment. Thereafter both major political parties recognized that minimizing unemployment levels was an important task for the national government. The period after the 1930s, then, can be thought of as one of "managed" rather than "uncontrolled" unemployment. Moreover, the relatively low unemployment rates after World War II, coupled with the popularity of new economic theories, led many economists and public fig-

ures to conclude, in the 1950s and 1960s, that the problem of unemployment would soon be solved.

Unfortunately, the picture has looked less rosy since the early 1970s. The unemployment rate crept upward in that decade, and in 1982 it exceeded 10 percent for the first time since the 1930s. In the late 1980s and early 1990s, the unemployment rate stayed persistently in the neighborhood of 7 or 8 percent. And rates were even higher for teenagers, African Americans, and employees in particular industries (such as automobiles) or regions (such as Texas and Louisiana in the late 1980s or California in the 1990s). To make matters worse, changes in the unemployment insurance system meant that by 1990 less than half of the unemployed were receiving any benefits from the system created in 1935.

Indeed, by the early 1990s the optimism about unemployment that had been so

Masses of unemployed men wait on a breadline in New York City during the Great Depression.

strong after World War II had all but vanished. The statistical record suggested that the problem of unemployment might, in the long run, be growing more rather than less severe. And few analysts had promising solutions to offer. As a result, more than a century after the term first appeared in print, unemployment has remained a haunting social and economic problem.

See also Coxey's Army; Depressions and Recessions; Labor Movement; Poverty and Homelessness.

ALEX KEYSSAR
WITH NATALIE KEYSSAR

UNIVERSITIES
See Education: Universities and Colleges.

URBAN GROWTH

The first cities of the United States grew from colonies planted by Dutch, British, French, and Spanish settlers. Looking at New Amsterdam (New York), Boston, Detroit, and Los Angeles, one can see that while each group of colonists arrived with slightly different ideas about where and how to lay out a settlement, in general they created an open space with public buildings and some dwellings surrounding it, and garden and farm lots just beyond.

In 1790, the largest cities included about the same number of people as an average suburb has today. New York boasted 33,131 residents, Philadelphia 28,522, Boston 18,320, Charleston 16,359, and Baltimore 13,503. All were seaports, with wharves, warehouses, and ships, bankers and merchants, sailmakers and ropemakers, tightly clustered together. Sometimes called "walking cities," they rarely stretched more than a mile or two from the waterfront. Residents, rich and poor, lived and worked in the same neighborhoods, sometimes in the same building.

Nineteenth-Century Changes
During this period the United States was a rural society trading for European manufactured goods through its ports. As the nineteenth century progressed, increasing industrial development brought large numbers of workers to expanding urban centers. The old ports developed their natural resources and transportation networks such as canals and railroads and became major centers of production. By 1850, New York housed over half a million people, and the next five largest cities, all located in the East, held over 100,000 each. (At this time, Chicago and Los Angeles were still little towns.)

To accommodate the rush of new residents and businesses, Manhattan in 1811 was laid out in a grid of streets fronted by narrow lots, even though much of it was still undeveloped land. By the second half of the century the grid was filling with factories and tenement houses, and the urban area was spreading.

Immigrant workers rented whatever quarters they could find, usually cramped tenements, which were six- or seven-story apartment buildings with little plumbing and many tiny windowless rooms. Horsecars and later electric streetcars rushed through streets congested with wagons and private carriages, creating a chaotic scene. Factory owners and workers now lived in different districts of the city, and the contrast between rich and poor was sharp. Racial segregation was common, and ethnic groups—the Irish, German, eastern Europeans—often clustered in distinct neighborhoods. In the immigrant districts men, women, and teenagers worked long hours to help the family get by. Beggars and homeless people, including many children, endured the life of the streets.

City Improvements

The crowded industrial city was gradually made bearable by the advance of sanitary reforms. Clean drinking water was brought in from distant reservoirs by aqueducts, and en-

gineers designed water-carried sewage systems. By the late 1800s, social reforms were being promoted by the organizers of settlement houses—community centers located in poor districts and offering classes, child care, playgrounds, and other social services. Jane Addams became famous as the leader of one called Hull-House in Chicago.

The urban parks movement in the middle

LARGEST CITIES BY POPULATION, 1700–1990

	1700		1790		1850	
	City	*Population*	*City*	*Population*	*City*	*Population*
1.	Boston	6,700	New York	33,131	New York	515,547
2.	New York	4,937[a]	Philadelphia	28,522	Baltimore	169,054
3.	Philadelphia	4,400[b]	Boston	18,320	Boston	136,881
4.	—	—	Charleston	16,359	Philadelphia	121,376
5.	—	—	Baltimore	13,503	New Orleans	116,375
6.	—	—	Northern Liberties, Pa.[c]	9,913	Cincinnati	115,435
7.	—	—	Salem, Mass.	7,921	Brooklyn[d]	96,838
8.	—	—	Newport, R.I.	6,716	St. Louis	77,860
9.	—	—	Providence, R.I.	6,380	Spring Garden, Pa.[e]	58,894
10.	—	—	Marblehead, Mass.	5,661	Albany, N.Y.	50,763

	1900		1950		1990	
	City	*Population*	*City*	*Population*	*City*	*Population*
1.	New York[f]	3,437,202	New York	7,891,957	New York	7,322,564
2.	Chicago	1,698,575	Chicago	3,620,962	Los Angeles	3,485,398
3.	Philadelphia	1,293,697	Philadelphia	2,071,605	Chicago	2,783,726
4.	St. Louis	575,238	Los Angeles	1,970,358	Houston	1,630,553
5.	Boston	560,892	Detroit	1,849,568	Philadelphia	1,585,577
6.	Baltimore	508,957	Baltimore	949,708	San Diego	1,110,549
7.	Cleveland	381,768	Cleveland	914,808	Detroit	1,027,974
8.	Buffalo, N.Y.	352,387	St. Louis	856,796	Dallas	1,006,877
9.	San Francisco	342,782	Washington	802,178	Phoenix	983,403
10.	Cincinnati	325,902	Boston	801,444	San Antonio	935,933

[a] Figure from a census taken in 1698.   [b] Philadelphia population includes suburbs.   [c] Annexed by Philadelphia in 1854.   [d] Consolidated with New York in 1898.   [e] Annexed by Philadelphia in 1854.   [f] Population is for New York and its boroughs, consolidated in 1898.

of the century helped ease congestion by providing landscaped green spaces for public recreation. New York's Central Park and Boston's Franklin Park were designed by Frederick Law Olmsted, a leading landscape architect.

Meanwhile buildings were growing taller around these open spaces, made possible by the new elevator and advances in structural framing. By the end of the nineteenth century, skyscrapers began to define the skyline, housing offices that were concentrated in city centers and separated from manufacturing facilities. In the 1930s, the Empire State Building in Manhattan reached a hundred stories. (As a result of excess office space and the Great Depression, it could not be leased easily, and was nicknamed the "Empty State Building" for a while.)

Along with the skyscrapers came other new urban buildings, such as department stores. New kinds of jobs attracted thousands of workers to downtown districts, including clerical work and sales jobs for women, as well as opportunities for engineers, architects, lawyers, and their assistants, who were almost always men. New forms of middle-class housing, like the apartment house, contributed to more thickly settled cities. The large public high school emerged in this era, as teenagers stayed in school longer.

Cities in the West

The growth of Chicago and Los Angeles differed from that of the eastern cities. Chicago developed as a market for the cattle, hogs, and agricultural products of the Midwest and West, as well as a railroad and industrial center. By 1900 it was the second largest city in the United States with 1,698,575 people. Los Angeles boomed in the 1880s when the transcontinental railroad reached the town and rate wars brought fares down. Starting with citrus groves, vineyards, and cattle ranches, the city grew even more rapidly as the price of real estate rose and oil was discovered in the 1890s.

The labor force in Los Angeles differed from that of New York and Chicago. Those two cities drew immigrants mostly from Europe. Los Angeles's workers were Native Americans and immigrants from Mexico, China, and Japan, as well as from the East, the South, and Europe. African Americans flocked to the northern and western cities from the South after 1890.

Coming of Suburbs

Although it seemed at one point as if the big city and its high-rise downtown might grow larger forever, the twentieth century saw a different kind of urban growth owing to the automobile and the shift of the economy toward mass consumption. The streetcar had created "streetcar suburbs" in the late nineteenth century, and the private car accelerated the process. Suburban areas drew housing, economic activities, and jobs from the city centers, and their growth was limited only by the length of the daily commute people were willing to undertake. By 1990, Los Angeles's metropolitan area, for example, stretches over 34,000 square miles, with a population of almost thirteen and a half million.

In the post–World War II era, federal government subsidies for veterans' mortgages and the building of the interstate highway system brought additional economic advantages to the suburbs. Because of racial segregation, African Americans were concentrated in the old city centers, along with poor people. Some public housing was built, but often in a shoddy way. Inner-city "urban renewal" destroyed many stable working-class neighborhoods that then became commercial and highly profitable real estate, such as Boston's

West End and Los Angeles's Bunker Hill. The inner city's job base eroded and unemployment became common.

By the late twentieth century, American cities were in crisis not simply because of hasty development and overcrowded conditions but because of decades of poor government policy at the federal level, often matched by the greed and cynicism of local officials and real estate interests. A new kind of urban renewal, based on equal treatment of all citizens, and the provision of employment and housing, schools and pleasant public spaces, are the challenges for the next century of urban growth.

See also Automobiles; Big-City Bosses; City Government; Ghettos; Housing; Levittowns; Public Transportation; Settlement House Movement.

DOLORES HAYDEN

U-2 AFFAIR

On May 1, 1960, an American high-altitude U-2 reconnaissance plane flying over the city of Sverdlovsk, in Russia, was shot down by Soviet antiaircraft fire. When the Soviets announced this without describing the plane, the American State Department assumed that the pilot of the plane had been killed in the crash. Thinking that the Soviets had not realized what the plane was doing, the State Department said merely that a weather observation plane based in Turkey had veered off course. The Soviet leader, Nikita Khrushchev, then announced that the pilot, Francis Gary Powers, had parachuted safely to earth and had confessed that he had been photographing Soviet military installations. An embarrassed president Dwight D. Eisenhower then admitted that he had known about the flight.

Khrushchev made a show of being shocked by what had happened, and a summit meeting between the two men planned for two weeks later was canceled. The Russian leader accused the United States of "piratical" acts of aggression and threatened atomic war unless such aerial spying was stopped. Coming at a time when cold war pressure seemed to be easing, the incident was a blow to American prestige.

See also Cold War; Espionage.

V

VAN BUREN, MARTIN

(1782–1862) *Eighth president of the United States (1837–41).*

Van Buren was known as the "Little Magician" in recognition of his skills in organizing voters and making political deals. He was the first professional politician to serve as president.

Van Buren was a New York state senator from 1812 to 1819, and served as state attorney general from 1816 to 1819. He founded the "Albany Regency," a powerful political machine that enabled him to control New York politics even after he went to Washington as a U.S. senator (1821–28). He helped Andrew Jackson win the presidential election of 1828.

Van Buren was elected governor of New York in 1828, but he resigned to become President Jackson's secretary of state and trusted adviser in 1829. He enthusiastically supported the president's use of the "spoils system," the practice of replacing holdovers from the previous administration with loyal Democrats. With Jackson's approval, he manipulated the entire cabinet into resigning after a series of embarrassing political disagreements in 1831. The grateful president appointed him minister to Britain, but the Senate rejected the nomination.

In 1832, Van Buren was elected vice president. He was widely regarded as Jackson's political successor and easily won the presidential election of 1836 in a field of five candidates. In his inaugural speech, Van Buren proudly stated that he was the first president born after America became independent in 1776.

During the panic of 1837, a severe economic downturn, the new president took a hands-off approach to the economy. Unwilling to let the government intervene in the crisis, he simply cut federal spending instead. Eventually, he persuaded Congress to pass the Independent Treasury Bill (1840) that separated the management of federal funds from the private banking system. President Van Buren refused demands to annex the Republic of Texas into the Union because he opposed the extension of slavery (slavery was legal in Texas) and was fearful of provoking a war with Mexico, which was against the annexation. His stand on Texas split the Democratic Party and cost him reelection in 1840 and the renomination in 1844. He ran as the Free-Soil Party's candidate for president in 1848, but lost. Out of office, he continued to oppose slavery until his death.

See also Free-Soil Party. *For events during Van Buren's administration, see* Depressions and Recessions; Independent Treasury; Texas Revolution and Annexation.

BARBARA SILBERDICK FEINBERG

VANDERBILT, CORNELIUS

(1794–1877) *Steamboat and railroad owner.*

Born on Staten Island, New York, Vanderbilt, at age sixteen, borrowed a hundred dollars from his mother and purchased a small sailing vessel to carry produce and passengers to Manhattan, across New York Bay. Before long he owned a fleet of sailing ships that operated as far afield as Virginia and the Carolinas.

Recognizing the potential of steam, Vanderbilt sold his vessels and took a job as captain of a small steamboat. He soon owned his own vessels and by the 1830s was the greatest shipowner in the country. It was at this time that a newspaper began calling him Commodore, a title he has been known by ever since.

Vanderbilt was always honest in his business dealings, although he was merciless if double-crossed. He succeeded by charging the lowest rates and operating his ships much more efficiently than his competitors did. But he never cut corners when safety was concerned. In an era when steamboats did "a wholesale business in human slaughter," as one writer put it, Vanderbilt never lost a ship to fire, explosion, or shipwreck. After the discovery of gold in California, he personally pioneered a route to the gold fields across Nicaragua that was shorter, cheaper, and safer than the Panama route the gold rushers had been taking, and he reaped millions from it.

In the 1860s Vanderbilt sold his ships and moved into railroads, buying their stock in Wall Street, where he proved himself a master of the dog-eat-dog tactics of the day. He soon controlled the Hudson River and Harlem railroad lines out of New York City. In 1869 he became president of the New York Central.

Whenever Vanderbilt took control of a railroad, it became much more profitable (and the value of its stock soared) because of his relentless insistence on efficiency. By the time of his death in 1877, he controlled forty-three hundred miles of railroad, stretching as far west as Chicago. He left a fortune of $105 million, making him by far the richest self-made man in the world.

An 1879 political cartoon showing William Henry Vanderbilt, the son of the tycoon Cornelius Vanderbilt, running the railroad empire his father started. He is pictured as a greedy giant, straddling the railroads of America and manipulating the reins. Two lesser railroad owners, Jay Gould to the right and Jim Fisk on the left, stand at Vanderbilt's feet, controlling the little bit of remaining action.

Vanderbilt's reputation suffered after his death at the hands of historians who were often careless with the facts. His obituary in the *New York Times* tells what his contemporaries thought of him: "His one foible of opposition was an immense boon to the public, for wherever his keen eyes detected a monopoly he pounced down upon the offenders. . . . His principle of low rates was never violated, so that in every way the public were the gainers."

See also Robber Barons.

JOHN STEELE GORDON

VICE PRESIDENCY

The vice president of the United States is something like a reserve quarterback on a football team. His principal duty is to be ready to take over in case the president dies, resigns, or is impeached. His chief constitutional duty is to preside over the meetings of the Senate. As Theodore Roosevelt wrote shortly before running for vice president in 1900, it is "a most honorable office, but for a young man there is not much to do."

The Founding Fathers nevertheless expected vice presidents to be experienced and talented men. They provided that in each election the candidate receiving the second largest number of electoral votes for president should become the vice president. In 1796, the first closely contested presidential election, the Federalists nominated John Adams and Thomas Pinckney. The Democratic-Republican candidates were Thomas Jefferson and Aaron Burr. Adams was elected president with seventy-one electoral votes to Jefferson's sixty-eight. But some of the Federalist electors did not vote for Pinckney. Since Jefferson got more votes than Pinckney, he became vice president.

An Evolving System

Four years later Jefferson and Burr were again the choice of the Democratic-Republican Party. In this election, party lines held firm. Jefferson defeated Adams seventy-three electoral votes to sixty-five. But Burr also re-

ceived seventy-three votes. When Burr refused to agree to become vice president, the tie had to be resolved by the House of Representatives, who chose Jefferson as president. To avoid this situation in the future, the Twelfth Amendment was passed in 1804. It provided that the electoral college should vote separately for president and vice president.

Running separate candidates did not mean that second-rate men quickly took over the second spot. From Adams and Jefferson to John C. Calhoun and Martin Van Buren, men of character and ability were nominated and elected. But as the country grew larger, the custom of using political office to reward loyal supporters changed the way vice-presidential candidates were selected. In 1836 the Democrats nominated Richard Mentor Johnson for vice president. Johnson's chief claim to fame was that he had killed the great Indian chief Tecumseh during the Battle of the Thames in 1813. But he had been a loyal supporter of retiring president Andrew Jackson, and Jackson rewarded him by arranging for his nomination.

In 1840, the Whig candidate William Henry Harrison was elected president. John Tyler was his vice president. Only a month after his inauguration Harrison died. The question immediately arose: was John Tyler now president of the United States or merely acting president? Many people argued the latter case. But Tyler took the oath required of presidents by the Constitution and the question was settled.

Successors, 1850–1901

Between 1850 and 1901 four more presidents died in office. A historian has described Millard Fillmore, who succeeded upon the death of Zachary Taylor in 1850, as "bland in man-

VICE PRESIDENTS OF THE UNITED STATES

Vice President	Born–Died	Served Under*
John Adams	1735–1826	George Washington
Thomas Jefferson	1743–1826	John Adams
Aaron Burr	1756–1836	Thomas Jefferson
George Clinton	1739–1812	Thomas Jefferson
		James Madison
Elbridge Gerry	1744–1814	James Madison
Daniel D. Tompkins	1774–1825	James Monroe
John C. Calhoun	1782–1850	John Quincy Adams
		Andrew Jackson
Martin Van Buren	1782–1862	Andrew Jackson
Richard M. Johnson	1780–1850	Martin Van Buren
John Tyler	1790–1862	William Henry Harrison
George M. Dallas	1792–1864	James K. Polk
Millard Fillmore	1800–1874	Zachary Taylor
William R. King	1786–1853	Franklin Pierce
John C. Breckinridge	1821–1875	James Buchanan
Hannibal Hamlin	1809–1891	Abraham Lincoln
Andrew Johnson	1808–1875	Abraham Lincoln
Schuyler Colfax	1823–1885	Ulysses S. Grant
Henry Wilson	1812–1875	Ulysses S. Grant
William A. Wheeler	1819–1887	Rutherford B. Hayes
Chester A. Arthur	1829–1886	James A. Garfield
Thomas A. Hendricks	1819–1885	Grover Cleveland
Levi P. Morton	1824–1920	Benjamin Harrison
Adlai E. Stevenson	1835–1914	Grover Cleveland
Garret A. Hobart	1844–1899	William McKinley
Theodore Roosevelt	1858–1919	William McKinley
Charles W. Fairbanks	1852–1918	Theodore Roosevelt
James S. Sherman	1855–1912	William Howard Taft
Thomas R. Marshall	1854–1925	Woodrow Wilson
Calvin Coolidge	1872–1933	Warren G. Harding
Charles G. Dawes	1865–1951	Calvin Coolidge
Charles Curtis	1860–1936	Herbert Hoover
John Nance Garner	1868–1967	Franklin D. Roosevelt
Henry Wallace	1888–1965	Franklin D. Roosevelt
Harry S. Truman	1884–1972	Franklin D. Roosevelt
Alben W. Barkley	1877–1956	Harry S. Truman
Richard M. Nixon	1913–1994	Dwight D. Eisenhower
Lyndon B. Johnson	1908–1973	John F. Kennedy
Hubert H. Humphrey	1911–1978	Lyndon B. Johnson
Spiro T. Agnew	1918–	Richard M. Nixon
Gerald Ford	1913–	Richard M. Nixon
Nelson A. Rockefeller	1908–1979	Gerald Ford
Walter F. Mondale	1928–	Jimmy Carter
George Bush	1924–	Ronald Reagan
J. Danforth Quayle	1947–	George Bush
Al Gore, Jr.	1948–	Bill Clinton

*The following presidents served without a vice president for at least part of their term(s): John Tyler, Millard Fillmore, Andrew Johnson, Chester A. Arthur, Theodore Roosevelt, Calvin Coolidge, Harry S. Truman, and Lyndon B. Johnson.

ner, loyal to party, and a natural compromiser." Andrew Johnson who became president in 1865 after John Wilkes Booth assassinated Abraham Lincoln, was chosen because he was a Democrat from a slave state, Tennessee, who had stayed with the Union when his state seceded. Chester A. Arthur, who became president after James A. Garfield was assassinated in 1881, was a New York political boss who had never even run for an elective office before being nominated for vice president.

In 1900 Theodore Roosevelt, the governor of New York, was picked as President William McKinley's running mate in his campaign for a second term only because McKinley's first vice president, Garret A. Hobart, a New Jersey politician, had died in 1899. If the party leaders who engineered Roosevelt's nomination had thought that McKinley might die in office they would never have selected him. They considered him radical and unstable. By "kicking him upstairs" into the powerless office of vice president, he would be forced out of New York politics, where he might, in their opinion, do damage.

Twentieth-Century Practices

In the twentieth century, three more presidents, Warren G. Harding, Franklin D. Roosevelt, and John F. Kennedy, died in office. They were succeeded by Calvin Coolidge, Harry S. Truman, and Lyndon B. Johnson, respectively. A fourth, Richard M. Nixon, was forced to resign in disgrace and was succeeded by Gerald R. Ford. Though the power and influence of presidents increased steadily during those years, both the Republicans and the Democrats continued to select their vice-presidential candidates without much thought of what kind of president they would make.

Nowadays most states select presidential candidates in primary elections. The national party nominating conventions take place, but usually the decision has already been made before they open. The choice of a running mate, however, is still left to the person who wins the presidential nomination. When nominating conventions were important, party leaders had to consider how the delegates would react to the person selected. Often there were real contests for the vice-presidential nomination. After nominating Harding for president, the delegates at the 1920 Republican convention rejected Senator Irvine Lenroot of Wisconsin, who had been chosen by the leadership, and nominated Calvin Coolidge. After Franklin D. Roosevelt was nominated without opposition for a fourth term as president in 1944, he consulted at length with delegates from key states before agreeing to the election of Harry S. Truman as his running mate.

Replacing Vice Presidents

On many occasions vice presidents have died or otherwise left office during their terms. Vice President John C. Calhoun resigned in 1832, and after the deaths of Vice Presidents William R. King in 1853, Henry Wilson in 1875, Thomas A. Hendricks in 1885, Garret A. Hobart in 1899, and James S. Sherman in 1912, the office stood vacant until the next presidential election. To deal with this problem, in 1967 the Twenty-fifth Amendment was added to the Constitution. It requires the president to nominate a successor "whenever there is a vacancy in the office of the Vice President."

As a result, when Vice President Spiro T. Agnew resigned in 1973 after being forced to admit that he was guilty of tax evasion, President Nixon chose Ford as vice president. The next year Nixon resigned to avoid being impeached because of his role in covering up the Watergate affair. Ford then became presi-

dent, and he appointed Nelson Rockefeller vice president. For the next two years, both the president and the vice president were appointees rather than elected officials! This is not likely to happen again. But the Twenty-fifth Amendment gives the force of law to the principle that presidents have the right to name their successors.

Leaving the choice to the presidential candidate is both undemocratic and illogical. In practice it has sometimes resulted in a president selecting a person he dislikes or disagrees with. (This happened in 1960, when candidate John F. Kennedy picked Lyndon B. Johnson of Texas in order to win southern votes in the election.)

The primary system is a good way of finding out which candidates for president the voters prefer. To win popular support the candidates have to explain what they intend to do if elected. But they never say whom they want as running mates until after they have been chosen. Given the frequency with which vice presidents have become presidents, the current system makes little sense.

JOHN A. GARRATY

VIETNAM WAR

France ruled Vietnam for many years as a colony, much as England ruled America before the American Revolution. In 1950 the United States began giving weapons and other aid to France to help fight a group in Vietnam called the Vietminh. The Vietminh leader was a gray-haired man named Ho Chi Minh (many of his people called him Uncle Ho). Ho and his followers were popular because they wanted to end French control of their country.

Americans understood that the people of Vietnam wanted to be free, but U.S. leaders did not think that Ho Chi Minh believed in freedom. As a communist, Ho wanted to force rich landowners to turn their property over to poor farmers. He also was friendly with the Soviet Union and China, communist countries that were enemies of the United States in the 1950s. For these reasons, the United States decided to help France fight the Vietminh.

A Divided Country

France's war did not go well. The Vietminh were good fighters and had the support of many Vietnamese. In 1954, after Ho's army defeated French troops in a major battle at a place called Dien Bien Phu, France decided to end the war. At a conference in Geneva, Switzerland, an agreement was made to divide the country. North Vietnam would be ruled by the Vietminh. French troops would remain in South Vietnam until 1956, when an election would decide on one government for all of Vietnam. That election, however, was never held.

The United States disliked the election plan because it feared that the popular Ho would win. The Vietnamese leader who opposed Ho was a shy man named Ngo Dinh Diem. With the help of money and advice from the United States, Diem set up a government in South Vietnam and became its president. France then withdrew its troops, leaving only the United States to assist Diem's new government.

By 1961, many people in South Vietnam had come to oppose Diem's rule. Some wanted Ho Chi Minh to lead Vietnam, and others thought Diem did not care about the people. With the help of North Vietnam, a force in the South began to fight against Diem. These soldiers were guerrillas, who fought in small groups and used ambush and surprise tactics. They called themselves the National Liberation Front, but Diem and the Americans called them the Vietcong. President John F. Kennedy sent sixteen thousand U.S. soldiers to South Vietnam to help Diem's army.

Despite this assistance, the government of South Vietnam grew weaker. Diem was a Catholic, and most people in Vietnam were Buddhists. Diem became afraid that the Buddhists were plotting against him, and he attacked their places of worship. Some Buddhist leaders, called monks, protested by burning themselves to death on the streets of Saigon, South Vietnam's capital. South Viet-

The Vietnam War

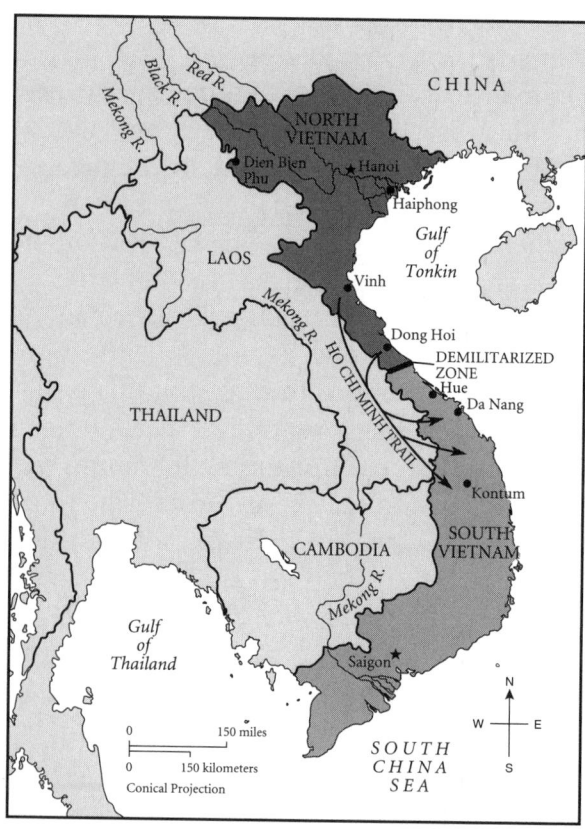

namese army officers, who were mostly Buddhists, decided that Diem had to be removed as president. On November 1, 1963, these officers began a coup, or military takeover of the government. Diem was killed the next day in this struggle for power.

American Efforts Increase

Three weeks after the coup, President Kennedy was assassinated, and President Lyndon B. Johnson had to decide what to do in Vietnam. Diem's death had made the government in Saigon even weaker, and the Vietcong seemed to be growing stronger. Johnson did not want the United States to fight a major war, but he believed that he had to increase the number of American soldiers in Vietnam or else he would be blamed for letting South Vietnam be taken over by North Vietnam.

In August 1964, Johnson received reports that North Vietnam's navy had attacked U.S. Navy ships in the Gulf of Tonkin near North Vietnam's coast. Although the facts about the attack were unclear, Johnson sent planes to bomb navy bases in North Vietnam. With almost every member voting yes, the U.S. Congress passed the Gulf of Tonkin Resolution, which gave the president permission to use military force in Vietnam.

In July 1965, American leaders decided that South Vietnam's army could not defeat its enemies unless the United States took over most of the fighting. Johnson, still unhappy about expanding the war, nevertheless was determined not to lose in Vietnam. He sent 300,000 U.S. soldiers to South Vietnam, and he kept increasing these forces until by 1968 they numbered over 500,000. Also, from 1965 to 1968 Johnson ordered more tons of bombs dropped on North and South Vietnam than the United States had dropped during all of World War II.

A medic with a head wound crawls to the aid of other injured men during heavy shelling in the Vietnam jungle. A medical evacuation helicopter attempts to land in the background.

Antiwar Protests

Despite this gigantic effort, North Vietnam and the Vietcong continued fighting. As casualties mounted in Vietnam, some Americans began to protest that the United States should not be in the war at all. In January 1968 during the Vietnamese New Year's celebration called Tet, the Vietcong attacked cities and military bases all over South Vietnam. A growing number of Americans now doubted their government's claims that the enemy was nearing defeat, and increasingly demonstrations were mounted, calling for a change in U.S. policy. Johnson became so unpopular that he announced that the United States would begin peace talks with North Vietnam and the Vietcong and that he would not run again for president.

In 1969, President Richard M. Nixon started trying to arrange what he called a "peace with honor." He reduced the number of U.S.

soldiers in Vietnam but increased the bombing until he had ordered more bombs dropped than Johnson had. He also sent U.S. troops into Cambodia, a neutral country next to Vietnam, to search for the enemy, eliciting even more protests. In one terrible incident, four college students were killed at Kent State University in Ohio when soldiers in the Ohio National Guard fired their rifles at demonstrators.

After secret talks with North Vietnam and more U.S. bombing, Nixon's chief adviser, Henry A. Kissinger, signed a peace agreement with North Vietnam on January 27, 1973. The remaining U.S. troops left Vietnam, and North Vietnam released its American prisoners of war. Fighting continued, however, until April 1975, when North Vietnam captured Saigon, renamed it Ho Chi Minh City, and united the country under its rule.

More than 58,000 Americans had died in Vietnam in this country's longest war. Looking back, many Americans agreed that the war was a sad mistake and that the United States should never have fought it.

See also Cold War; Gulf of Tonkin Resolution; Kent State Incident; Kissinger, Henry A.; Tet Offensive.

For further reading: Elizabeth Becker, *America's Vietnam War: A Narrative History* (New York: Clarion Books, 1992).

DAVID L. ANDERSON

VIRGINIA AND KENTUCKY RESOLUTIONS

The restrictions on freedom of speech and the press imposed by the Alien and Sedition Acts of 1798 caused Thomas Jefferson and James Madison to draft papers challenging the constitutionality of such measures. Jefferson's resolutions were adopted by the legislature of the new state of Kentucky in November 1798, Madison's by the Virginia legislature the next month. The actual authors of the resolutions were not announced at the time.

In the Kentucky Resolution Jefferson argued that because the separate states had created the Constitution, each had "an equal right to judge for itself" when Congress had passed a law it considered not authorized by the Constitution. It could therefore prevent such laws from being enforced within its borders.

Madison's Virginia Resolution insisted that the states "have the right and are duty bound" to "oppose every infraction" of the rights of citizens "not delegated by the Constitution." It declared the Alien and Sedition Acts in violation of constitutional guarantees of freedom of speech and the press and therefore illegal.

Neither state, however, attempted actually to prevent the enforcement of those laws. The chief significance of the resolutions is that the argument they advanced was used in the nineteenth century by John C. Calhoun and other defenders of states' rights to justify nullification and eventually secession.

See also Alien and Sedition Acts.

VOTING

Voting is one way members of a group choose their leaders and make other decisions. The right to participate in free elections is so fundamental to American democracy that we have come to use voting methods to make all sorts of everyday choices. We vote for president of the United States—and for prom king and queen. We vote in schools, clubs, and churches. Yet ingrained as voting is in our society, millions of Americans were not allowed to exercise the *franchise* (the right to vote in political elections) until well over halfway through the twentieth century. Some still find it difficult or impossible to vote. And of the 190 million Americans who could have voted in the 1992 presidential election, only about 101 million—about 53 percent—bothered to do so.

Voting in Early America

The English settlers who began colonizing America in the early 1600s did not think of voting as a right. To them, it was a privilege to be bestowed upon only a few members of each community. Which members? Those the colonial authorities regarded as trustworthy enough to share their governing power. Not surprisingly, that meant voters who closely resembled the authorities themselves: white men who owned property—land or money—and worshiped in the colony's officially established church. Women, Native Americans, and blacks (free blacks as well as slaves) were considered intellectually incapable of voting wisely. Men who failed to accumulate property, or refused to attend the "right" church, were deemed too irresponsible to help direct public life.

As people of different nationalities and religions began arriving in America, attitudes changed. Tolerance grew, and as it did, some voting restrictions were eased. After 1690, most property-owning Protestant men were *enfranchised* (given the right to vote). So, over the next century, were many Catholics and Jews. Property requirements became less strict.

By 1790, the United States had won its independence. The U.S. Constitution, adopted in 1789, left it up to each state to write its own

voting laws. Basically, all the states followed a similar pattern, continuing to deny the vote to blacks and women, but abolishing most remaining religious and property requirements. There were exceptions. Until 1841, Rhode Island men had to own $134 worth of property in order to vote and New Hampshire Catholics did not win the franchise until 1851. New Jersey women *could* vote until an 1807 law stopped them. In some northern states, free blacks voted. Most states did require that a man live in a place for one or two years before voting there. Residency was assumed to demonstrate a voter's commitment to the community.

States also adopted the practice of printing and issuing election *ballots* bearing the names of candidates for voters to mark in secret. In early colonial times, voting was done orally (out loud). Later, voters were required to sign their ballots. The secret ballot is essential to democratic government.

Extending the Franchise

In 1848, women's rights leaders Lucretia Mott, Elizabeth Cady Stanton, and others issued a call for woman *suffrage* (voting rights). Their demand was largely ignored. Black men would be the next to win the vote—in theory, at least.

In 1861, the Civil War began, partly over the issue of slavery. After the war ended in 1865, Congress passed and the states ratified (agreed to) three amendments to the Constitution. The Thirteenth Amendment abolished slavery. The Fourteenth made blacks citizens. The Fifteenth ensured their right to vote.

Few white southerners, however, had any intention of honoring the Fifteenth Amendment by giving their former slaves a voice in public affairs. Although seven blacks were elected to Congress from the South in 1872, white racists, many of them members of the Ku Klux Klan, launched a terrorist campaign that used violence to keep blacks away from the *polls* (voting places). In the 1890s, southern legislators legalized black disfranchisement by requiring voters to pay a poll tax and take a literacy test. Few blacks (or poor whites) could afford the tax. Literacy tests were deliberately made so tricky even the best-educated would fail. Whites did not have to take the tests. In the North, literacy tests were sometimes used to prevent newly naturalized American citizens, many of them from eastern Europe and Asia, from voting.

Meantime, women pressed on with their suffrage movement. Suffragist Susan B. Anthony voted in the 1872 presidential election.

She was arrested and fined. In 1878, a constitutional amendment to give women the vote was introduced in Congress, but it failed to pass. Reintroduced in every session of Congress for the next forty years, it became part of the Constitution in 1920. Women, many of whom had been jailed, mistreated, and ridiculed for wanting to vote, finally had the franchise.

The Franchise in the Twentieth Century
Four other amendments related to voting have been added to the Constitution in this century. The Seventeenth Amendment, ratified in 1913, allowed the direct popular election of U.S. senators. Before that, senators were elected indirectly, chosen by each state's elected legislature. The Twenty-third Amend-

Women suffragists in 1912 display a banner demanding the right to vote. The banner makes reference to the fact that some western states had already granted women the vote, a right they urged be extended to the eastern states. It was not until 1920, with the passage of the Nineteenth Amendment, that women's suffrage became nationwide.

ment (1961) gave residents of the District of Columbia, the nation's capital, the right to vote in presidential elections. Since many who live in the district are black, this was a boost for black civil rights. The Twenty-fourth Amendment (1964) stopped states from imposing poll taxes in federal elections. (A 1966 Supreme Court decision banned poll tax laws in state and local elections as well.) The Twenty-sixth Amendment (1971) lowered the voting age from twenty-one to eighteen.

In 1965, Congress passed the strongest-ever federal voting rights law. The Voting Rights Act made the provisions of the Fifteenth Amendment, ratified ninety-five years earlier, reality at last. It outlawed literacy tests and required ballots to be printed in two languages in parts of the country where much of the population is not fluent in English. Ballots in largely Hispanic areas, for example, must be available in Spanish as well as English. The law also gave federal authorities the power to supervise elections around the country to make sure the rights of blacks and members of other minorities are observed. The Voting Rights Act is currently valid through the year 2007.

Besides extending the franchise, federal lawmakers have tried to increase the percentage of eligible citizens who actually vote on election day, a percentage that is considerably lower in this country than in many other democracies. Under a 1993 federal law, Americans can register to vote when they obtain or renew a driver's license (hence the law's nickname, motor-voter law), apply for welfare or disability benefits, or enlist in the military. The law also standardizes the process of reg-

istering by mail throughout the country. State laws, however, continue in varying degrees to keep some convicted felons and some individuals judged to be mentally incompetent from voting.

See also Civil Rights Movement; Feminist Movement to 1919; Reconstruction; Voting Rights Act of 1965.

ANN E. WEISS

VOTING RIGHTS ACT OF 1965

This law was enacted by Congress in direct response to the suppression of southern civil rights groups, especially the brutal police attacks on black and white protest marchers at Selma, Alabama, in March 1965. It outlawed state poll taxes, literacy tests, and other devices used to discriminate against blacks. It also provided for the appointment of federal examiners to supervise voter registration districts where fewer than half the persons of voting age had registered or voted in the last presidential election. When state regulations were nullified as a result of the law, new state regulations had to be approved by federal authorities before they could go into effect. A panel consisting of three district court judges was appointed to determine when and if supervision by federal examiners was no longer needed to ensure that all citizens were able to vote. In addition, criminal penalties were provided for officials "who denied any qualified voter the right to vote." As a result of this measure, southern efforts to prevent blacks from voting practically ceased.

See also Civil Rights Movement.

W

WADE-DAVIS BILL

This measure, introduced in July 1864 by Senator Benjamin F. Wade of Ohio and Representative Henry W. Davis of Maryland, was an attempt to limit the power of President Abraham Lincoln over the readmission of the seceded states after the Civil War. Lincoln had proposed admitting these states when 10 percent of the voters had sworn loyalty to the United States. His argument was that other southerners would "rally round" this "nucleus" and thus speed the reconstruction of the Union.

The Wade-Davis bill proposed much tougher terms for admitting the Confederate states after the war. It provided that a majority of each state's white male citizens had to take a loyalty oath before the state could be readmitted. It also prohibited anyone who had "held or exercised any office, civil or military," under the "rebel" government from voting.

The bill passed both houses of Congress, but Lincoln vetoed it. Since the war had not yet ended, the bill was of no immediate importance. Its historical significance lies in the fact that it was an early sign of the conflict that was to develop between those northerners who favored admitting the seceded states on easy terms and those who put punishing the Confederates and granting political rights to the blacks above returning the country to normal. It was also the start of a struggle between Congress and the chief executive for control of Reconstruction policy.

See also Reconstruction.

WAGNER ACT
See National Labor Relations Act.

WALKER, ALICE

(1944–)   *Writer and civil rights activist.*

Walker was born in Eatonton, Georgia, the youngest of eight children. Her father, a sharecropper, earned $900 a year, and her mother worked as a maid. Her parents were both fine storytellers, and Alice began to write stories of her own when she was eight years old. Through her personal experience of poverty and through the lives of the people around her, she became profoundly aware of the struggles of African Americans in the South.

When Alice was ten, she lost the sight of her right eye in an accident with a BB gun. In 1961 she won a scholarship for handicapped students and entered Spelman College in Atlanta. In 1963 she transferred to Sarah Lawrence College in Bronxville, New York. Encouraged by poet Muriel Rukeyser, one of her teachers at Sarah Lawrence, she began to write seriously. Her first book of poems, *Once,* was published in 1968.

During and after college, Walker was deeply involved with the African-American civil

Alice Walker is author of the Pulitzer Prize–winning novel The Color Purple *(1982) and other works focusing on the lives of black women.*

rights movement. She worked briefly as a social worker in New York City and for several years taught black studies at Jackson State University in Mississippi. Wherever she lived, whatever job she held, she continued to write.

Walker's first novel, *The Third Life of Grange Coveland,* appeared in 1970, followed in 1973 by a collection of short stories, *In Love and Trouble.* Her novel *The Color Purple* (1982) won the American Book Award and the Pulitzer Prize in 1983 and was made into an Oscar-winning movie. *The Color Purple* tells the story of two sisters, separated as teenagers. One survives the poverty and racism of the rural South while the other gains an education and becomes a missionary in Africa. Walker's other works include *In Search of Our Mothers' Gardens,* a series of essays (1984), and *Possessing the Secret of Joy,* a novel (1992).

An abiding concern with the harsh realities faced by African Americans is the driving force behind Walker's poetry and fiction. She is especially eloquent when she writes about the hardships endured by black women. "I'm really paying homage to people I love," she explained in an interview, "the people who are thought to be dumb and backward but who were the ones who first taught me to see beauty."

See also Literature.

DEBORAH KENT

WALLACE, DEWITT

(1889–1981)   *Magazine and book publisher.*

Suppose, back in 1922, long before television, that you were a busy person who wanted to know what was going on in the world but didn't want to read long, boring articles full of hard words and complicated ideas. Suppose that someone offered to go through hundreds of magazines for you, pick the most interesting stories, boil them down into short, lively reports in everyday English, and every month put thirty-one of them—one to read each day—into a mini-magazine that you could stick in your pocket for twenty-five cents. Would you be interested? DeWitt Wallace bet that you would, and he won. His "little wonder," the *Reader's Digest,* launched one of the most successful publishing companies in history.

Wallace grew up in Minnesota, believing in religion, patriotism, self-improvement, and community service. He had begun a successful career selling educational materials when World War I changed his life. He enlisted and was badly wounded in France in 1918. During long weeks of recovery in a hospital he got his idea for the *Digest*. When one publisher after another turned down his sample copy, he and his wife, Leila Acheson Wallace, scraped together enough money to pay for a small first printing.

It was an immediate hit. By 1929 the *Digest*'s circulation (number of copies sold) was 216,000 and climbing. Millions of Americans, living in a fast-moving age of automobiles, radio, and movies, were ready for its tasty tidbits of popular science, history, and politics, sprinkled with jokes and glimpses of life in a United States painted as generally kindhearted and fair-minded.

The Wallaces guessed that there were *Digest*-minded readers in countries all over the world and were right about that, too. In 1938 they started a successful British edition and after that versions in other languages. By the middle of the 1950s, the *Digest*'s "articles of lasting interest" were being read in sixteen languages by over 30.5 million people.

When he died in 1981, DeWitt Wallace was a giant of the age of mass-produced popular journalism.

See also Magazines and Newspapers.

BERNARD WEISBERGER

WALLACE, GEORGE

(1919–)   *Alabama governor and four-time candidate for president of the United States.*

Wallace began his political career as a racial "moderate" in the 1940s and early 1950s. But when he lost his first run for the Alabama governorship in 1958 at the hands of a white

supremacy candidate, he switched his position. He won election in 1962 by pledging to maintain "Segregation now! Segregation tomorrow! Segregation forever!"

In June 1963 he "stood in the schoolhouse door," as he put it, at the University of Alabama in an effort to block the enrollment of two black students in the all-white school. Although he backed down when President John F. Kennedy called out the National Guard to enforce court-ordered integration, the nationally televised confrontation gained Wallace national attention.

In 1964 he entered the Democratic presidential primaries in Wisconsin, Indiana, and Maryland and opposed the civil rights measures endorsed by Kennedy's successor, Lyndon B. Johnson. Even though Wallace failed to prevent the passage of the Civil Rights Act, he surprised many by drawing from 30 to 43 percent of the vote in these three nonsouthern states.

In 1968, he formed the American Independent Party and ran on a campaign of continued opposition to civil rights. His party won 14 percent of the nation's vote, half of it from outside the South.

His political strength as a national figure peaked in the spring of 1972 when he abandoned his third-party effort and ran in a dozen Democratic presidential primaries. He called for "law and order," supported prayer in the schools, and bitterly attacked the federal courts for ordering the busing of schoolchildren in order to end racial segregation. Wallace won decisively in a number of southern presidential primaries. He also came in first or second in a series of northern states, including Indiana, Pennsylvania, Wisconsin, and Michigan.

His campaign for the presidency ended on May 15, when an emotionally unstable twenty-two-year-old named Arthur Bremer gunned him down at a Laurel, Maryland, campaign rally. Wallace survived, but he was paralyzed from the waist down.

Although he was finished as a national candidate, the voters of Alabama elected him governor through most of the 1970s and 1980s. After 1972, Wallace renounced his earlier support for segregation and successfully appealed to black voters in his state. But he will always be remembered as the man who led the backlash of white Americans who were opposed to civil rights for African Americans.

See also Civil Rights Movement.

DAN T. CARTER

WAR HAWKS

The War Hawks were a group of congressmen who favored declaring war on Great Britain in 1811 and 1812. They had no formal organization or official policy but tended to vote together on key issues. Henry Clay, the Speaker of the House of Representatives, was the most prominent War Hawk.

Although their main criticism of Great Britain concerned British violations of American rights on the high seas, especially the impressment of American sailors by British warships, most War Hawks were from western and southern states, far from the Atlantic Ocean where the British attacks took place. They were primarily superpatriotic expansionists who hoped that a war with Great Britain would lead to the annexation of British Canada and perhaps also to the seizure of Spanish-controlled Florida and the lower Mississippi River valley.

War Hawk denunciations of Great Britain helped mobilize support for war among the general populace. When the war actually broke out, however, they and their followers proved they were far more effective speakers than fighters. In Congress they resisted appropriating money to build up the American navy, and western military units were repeatedly routed by Canadian forces in the fighting along the frontier.

See also War of 1812.

WARHOL, ANDY

(1928?–87)   *Pop artist.*

Andy Warhol's painting of a Campbell's soup can, the most famous image of pop art, seems commonplace today. But when it was first exhibited in 1962, the public was scandalized: how could this crassly commercial subject, requiring little imagination (or effort) on the part of the "artist," pretend to be serious painting? A gallery near where Warhol first exhibited decided a joke was in order: they arranged a few actual Campbell's soup cans in their display window and posted the sign, "Get the real thing for 20 cents." Their message: why waste money at an art gallery when you can get a real can of soup at your local supermarket for next to nothing?

Warhol was discovered by the art world overnight, becoming the most famous of the 1960s pop artists. His paintings portrayed everyday items (Coke bottles and Brillo pads) and celebrities (Elvis Presley and Marilyn Monroe). Warhol's art mirrored a superficial, money-driven, image-conscious consumer society. Yet it was hard to tell from his paintings whether he was celebrating this world or condemning it. His studio was called the Factory—the name implied a place where art was mass produced, much like everything else in America.

Warhol was adored by Manhattan's avant-garde and underground—though with his silvery hair, pasty-pale skin, and whispery voice he was a ghostlike figure who seemed an unlikely celebrity. It was he who made the much-quoted prediction, "In the future, everyone will be world-famous for fifteen minutes." Fame and wealth were not reserved for those with special talent, Warhol implied. If he could make a can of Campbell's soup famous—and himself into a superstar—then anything or anyone might follow suit.

Andy Warhol's Campbell's Soup *(1965), one of many versions in which he immortalized this supermarket product. Warhol typically repeated his images over and over again, seeing little importance in originality. His art deliberately echoed the consumer society around him, in which everything is mass produced or a cheap imitation.*

Warhol remained deliberately mysterious. "If you want to know all about Andy Warhol," he said, "just look at the surface of my paintings and films and me, and there I am. There's nothing behind it." Was he really as shallow and naive as he claimed to be? Or was his art making a shrewd comment on the materialistic, celebrity-hungry world he lived in? Although no longer shocking or revolutionary today, Warhol's work continues to raise provocative questions about the nature of art.

See also Painting and Sculpture; Pop Art.

For further reading: Andy Warhol, *The Philosophy of Andy Warhol: From A to B and Back Again* (San Diego, Calif.: Harcourt Brace Jovanovich, 1990).

BORGNA BRUNNER

WAR
See Barbary Wars; Bay of Pigs Invasion; Civil War; Gulf War; Indian-White Relations; Korean War; Mexican War; Revolution; Spanish-American War; Vietnam War; War of 1812; World War I; World War II.

WAR CRIMES TRIAL
See Nuremberg Trials.

WAR OF 1812

The War of 1812 pitted a young United States against its former ruler, Great Britain. The conflict resulted in no material gain for either side, but it had far-reaching consequences for the history of North America.

Background of the War
For Britain the war was a distraction from its titanic struggle with France that began in the late 1700s after the French Revolution. By the early 1800s Emperor Napoleon I of

France had conquered most of continental Europe, while Britain, protected from Napoleon's armies by the English Channel, ruled the sea with its mighty navy. Ignoring American protests, Royal Navy boarding parties routinely searched American merchant vessels for war materials and deserters. British captains used the searches to "impress" thousands of American sailors into service aboard their short-handed warships.

By law and custom, neutral warships were exempt from such searches. But on June 22, 1807, a British warship made an unprovoked attack on the American frigate USS *Chesapeake*. President Thomas Jefferson demanded an apology and recognition of America's rights as a neutral. The British government refused, ordering its warships to seize any neutral ship failing to dock in a British port for inspection. Jefferson retaliated by convincing Congress to pass the Embargo Act of 1807, which banned trade with Europe. But the embargo hurt the American economy more than Britain's, and Jefferson's successor, James Madison, lifted it. When Britain refused to compromise the two nations' differences, however, Madison reimposed a ban on the importation of British goods. Between 1810 and 1812, Royal Navy warships seized hundreds of American vessels.

There was also friction in the Old Northwest, the wilderness region adjoining the Great Lakes. The United States accused British authorities in Canada of encouraging the Shawnee chief Tecumseh in his attempts to organize an Indian confederation to resist white settlement in the area. In November 1811, Indiana's territorial governor, William Henry Harrison, a future president, broke Tecumseh's confederation at the Battle of Tippecanoe. Tecumseh retreated to Canada, vowing to rebuild his confederation under British protection.

Congress waged a bitter debate in the winter of 1811–12. Led by Speaker of the House Henry Clay, the "War Hawks," who were members of Madison's Democratic-Republican Party, demanded the conquest of Canada. The opposition Federalist Party, strongest in the Northeast, which was highly dependent on foreign trade, argued for continued negotiations. Madison resisted the pressure for war until Britain undercut negotiations by insisting that American vessels apply for British licenses. Faced with this new challenge to American sovereignty, Madison reluctantly signed a declaration of war on June 18, 1812.

Early Setbacks in the War

The United States was woefully unprepared for war. Any hope of a quick American victory depended on conquering Canada before Britain could send reinforcements to North America. But British general Sir Isaac Brock frustrated the American strategy by capturing Detroit and defeating an American invasion at Queenstown, Ontario, in a battle that cost him his life.

Both sides rushed to build fleets on Lakes Erie and Ontario. On September 10, 1813, Commodore Oliver Hazard Perry destroyed the British squadron on Lake Erie. Perry's fleet then ferried Governor Harrison's army across the lake, where it crushed a British and Indian army at the Battle of the Thames on October 5. Tecumseh died in the fighting, and the United States secured a permanent hold on the Old Northwest. In the East, however, American commanders fumbled the chance to follow up Harrison's victory, and the war along the border settled into a bloody stalemate.

The war at sea opened well for the United States. American privateers (armed merchant ships commissioned by the government to operate against the enemy) captured hundreds of British merchant ships, while the navy's superb warships—most notably the USS *Constitution*, nicknamed "Old Ironsides"—won a stunning series of victories against Royal Navy frigates and brigs. But by late 1813, the arrival of British naval reinforcements bottled the American navy in port. British landing parties raided towns along Chesapeake Bay almost at will.

In Europe, Napoleon surrendered in the spring of 1814, and the British turned their full attention to the war in America. On August 24, 1814, a British army routed American militia at Bladensburg, Maryland, and marched into Washington, D.C. British soldiers burned the government's buildings, including the White House, only hours after Madison and members of his cabinet fled the capital.

The Tide Turns

In the crisis following the burning of Washington, a startling reversal in American fortunes saved the United States from having to beg for a humiliating peace. The people of Baltimore erected massive earthworks that stymied a British land attack on the city. The Royal Navy tried to blast its way into the port, but Fort McHenry in the harbor entrance held out against the furious bombardment. (The sight of the American flag still flying over the fort at dawn on September 14 inspired Francis Scott Key to write the "Star-Spangled Banner.")

More good news arrived soon after from upstate New York, where a British army had been advancing south along the shores of Lake Champlain toward the Hudson River valley and New York City. On September 11, Lt. Thomas Macdonough, commander of the American naval squadron on the lake, de-stroyed the British fleet in a trap at Plattsburgh Bay. Its supply line broken, the British army abandoned its invasion.

Pressured by its people, who were sick of war, Britain revived the peace talks under way in Ghent, Belgium. With the end of the Napoleonic Wars, free trade and impressment were no longer significant issues, and British and American negotiators quickly agreed to restore the prewar boundaries in North America.

The Treaty of Ghent was signed on December 24, 1814, but news of the peace arrived too late to prevent a tragic battle at New Orleans, Louisiana. On January 11, 1815, a British army charged the American defenses south of the city. Holding steady under the command of Gen. Andrew Jackson, a future president, a ragtag army of townspeople, frontier militia, regulars, free blacks, and bayou pirates slaughtered some of Britain's finest infantry.

Results of the War

Although hardly a glorious page in American military or diplomatic history, the War of 1812 marked a crucial stage in the forging of a stronger, more unified nation. Following the war, Britain and the United States adopted an edgy policy of mutual toleration. The breaking of Tecumseh's confederation ended meaningful Indian resistance east of the Mississippi and opened the Old Northwest to rapid settlement by whites. The United States abandoned ambitions for the conquest of Canada, allowing both countries to pursue peaceful development.

Despite its ineffective handling of the War of 1812, the Democratic-Republican Party became the dominant party for a generation. In the Era of Good Feelings, the Democratic-Republicans adopted many sound Federalist ideas to strengthen the nation's economy and political institutions. Of profound influence was the memory of President Madison's steadfast adherence to the U.S. Constitution, even in the darkest days of the war. A confident, prosperous people began viewing themselves not so much as citizens of rival states as Americans sharing a common future. In combination, these developments greatly strengthened the Union established by the Constitution.

See also Clay, Henry; Embargo Act of 1807; Federalist Party; Hartford Convention of 1814; Impressment Controversy; Key, Francis Scott; Madison, James; Tecumseh; War Hawks.

For further reading: Alden R. Carter, *The War of 1812: Second Fight for Independence* (New York: Franklin Watts, 1992).

ALDEN R. CARTER

WAR OF INDEPENDENCE
See Revolution.

WAR ON POVERTY
See Great Society.

WARREN, EARL

(1891–1974)   *Chief justice of the U.S. Supreme Court.*

Born in Los Angeles, the son of a railroad car repairman, Earl Warren served in public office in California for thirty-four years. A Republican, he was elected attorney general of California in 1938, and four years later he became governor. Twice reelected, the popular governor won the Democratic as well as the Republican nomination in 1946.

Warren made two unsuccessful bids for

national political office. In 1948, he ran for vice president on the losing Republican ticket with Governor Thomas E. Dewey of New York, and he briefly sought the Republican nomination for president in 1952. He later threw his support to the victorious candidate, Dwight D. Eisenhower. In 1953, President Eisenhower appointed Warren chief justice of the Supreme Court, even though he had never served as a judge.

Warren brought to the bench outstanding leadership ability, which helped the Supreme Court play a dynamic role in protecting and extending the rights of ordinary people. The chief justice and his colleagues affirmed repeatedly that the Court must be guided by social, economic, and political realities, not merely by legal precedents (decisions that courts had made in the past).

This activist philosophy of the Warren Court was demonstrated in its most famous decision, *Brown* v. *Board of Education* (1954). More than a half century earlier, the Supreme Court had upheld the "separate but equal" doctrine by which blacks could be legally segregated from whites in the use of public facilities. The *Brown* case arose when black children were denied admission to neighborhood public schools because of their race. The Supreme Court unanimously declared that this practice was unconstitutional and ordered the integration of all public schools.

The Warren Court took bold steps to safeguard the provisions expressed in the Bill of Rights and the Fourteenth Amendment. It defended the rights of people to make unpopular statements and to gather in peaceful demonstrations. In accord with the constitutional principle requiring the separation of church and state, the Court banned prayer and Bible reading in public schools. This provoked fierce controversy and led some of the chief justice's critics to call for his impeachment.

The Court during Warren's term also vigorously protected the rights of persons accused of committing crimes. In landmark decisions, it forbade prosecutors to use illegally seized evidence in trials and required states to provide a lawyer for a poor defendant who could not afford to hire one. In *Miranda* v. *Arizona* (1966), the Court set down rules to protect arrested persons from incriminating themselves.

The issue of voting equality came before the Warren Court when some states refused to redraw electoral districts after changes had occurred in the size of the districts' population. In a series of decisions based on the principle of "one person, one vote," the Court ruled that all the electoral districts within a state must have approximately the same number of people.

While serving on the Court, Warren headed the commission that investigated the assassination of President John F. Kennedy in 1963. When Warren resigned from the Supreme Court in 1969, scholars generally ranked him alongside John Marshall as one of the two most influential chief justices in American history.

See also Supreme Court.

EDMUND LINDOP

WASHINGTON, BOOKER T.

(1856–1915) *Educator.*

Across the landscape of the most difficult period of American race relations, the age of Jim Crow (1895–1915), strode the self-confident and influential Booker T. Washington. He was the most important black educator, power broker, and institution builder of his time. In 1881 he founded Tuskegee Institute, a black school in Alabama devoted to industrial education, the training of public school teachers, and the building of moral character. From his southern small-town base, he created a nationwide network of schools and newspapers, as well as the National Negro Business League (1901).

In response to the wave of racial segregation laws that swept the South toward the end of the nineteenth century, Washington offered the doctrine of "accommodation," the idea that blacks should seek economic independence rather than social and political equality. He believed that to strive for civil rights rather than economic self-determination was to begin at the wrong end of achieving social uplift and a secure future for black people.

Born a slave on a farm in Virginia, Washington was nine years old when the Civil War ended in 1865. His upbringing was humble and stern. He worked in a salt furnace when he was ten and served as a houseboy for a white family. Washington was educated at Hampton Institute, one of the earliest "freedmen's schools" set up to educate the newly freed slaves. At Hampton the pupils received training in industrial arts and moral education (character building) rather than in intellectual pursuits. Hampton was the model upon which Washington based his school at Tuskegee.

Washington's philosophy about race relations and his network of influence won him widespread support among wealthy white northern philanthropists and great recognition among blacks. In a speech delivered in 1895, known as the Atlanta Compromise address, he declared the doctrine of accommodationism in its most famous terms. Washington urged blacks to work hard wherever they found themselves rather than strive to achieve positions closed to them. "Cast down your buckets where you are," he said. To whites who were listening he announced, "In all things that are purely social, we can be as separate as the fingers, yet one as the hand in all things essential to mutual progress." These antidemocratic views stood for many years as an endorsement of segregation.

Washington retained his position of leadership by sometimes using ruthless methods against those blacks who differed with him. At times he practiced a brand of boss politics, intimidating other black leaders into silence if they disagreed with his philosophy. In fact, black newspaper editors and intellectuals risked isolation and unemployment if they fought for equality rather than accept Washington's accommodationism. Such a dispute was the famous debate between Washington and W. E. B. Du Bois over the aims of "industrial" as opposed to "classical" education for blacks.

Growing black and white opposition to Washington's silence as blacks were increasingly denied their rights of citizenship led to the formation of the Niagara Movement (1905–09) and the NAACP. Both organizations worked for civil and political rights as well as against lynching. In secret Washington also labored against racial violence and Jim Crow laws. He wrote letters of protest in code names and sometimes protected blacks from lynch mobs, but these efforts were generally not known at the time.

Washington was more interested in the practical outcome of his actions than in theoretical ideas. He would deliberately act in ways that maintained white recognition of his leadership and brought him international fame, believing this was essential for black

progress in a segregated society. He served as an adviser to Presidents Theodore Roosevelt and William Howard Taft. His autobiography, *Up from Slavery* (1901), stands as a classic example of stories by American self-made men and is still widely read today. Although his control of black institutions did not long survive his death, his practical ideas about economic self-reliance remain one of the deepest and most controversial elements in African-American life.

See also African Americans; Du Bois, W. E. B.; National Association for the Advancement of Colored People; Niagara Movement; Segregation.

DAVID W. BLIGHT

WASHINGTON, GEORGE

(1732–99)   *First president of the United States (1789–97).*

It is hard to think of a better way to describe George Washington than as the "Father of His Country"—a tired phrase, but a true one. He was commander in chief of the Continental army during the Revolution as well as the first president. His image is sculpted in stone on Mount Rushmore and engraved on the one-dollar bill. But behind the legendary figure was a real man—ambitious, energetic, impulsive—whose strengths had a profound effect upon his country's destiny.

Washington was born into a planter family in Virginia. No aristocrat, he did not benefit from wealth or a good education. His schooling was only elementary, but he never stopped learning from living. In his early teens he taught himself the surveyor's skills and practiced them on the frontier as new lands were acquired to replace worn-out tobacco farms.

As a young major in the colonial militia,

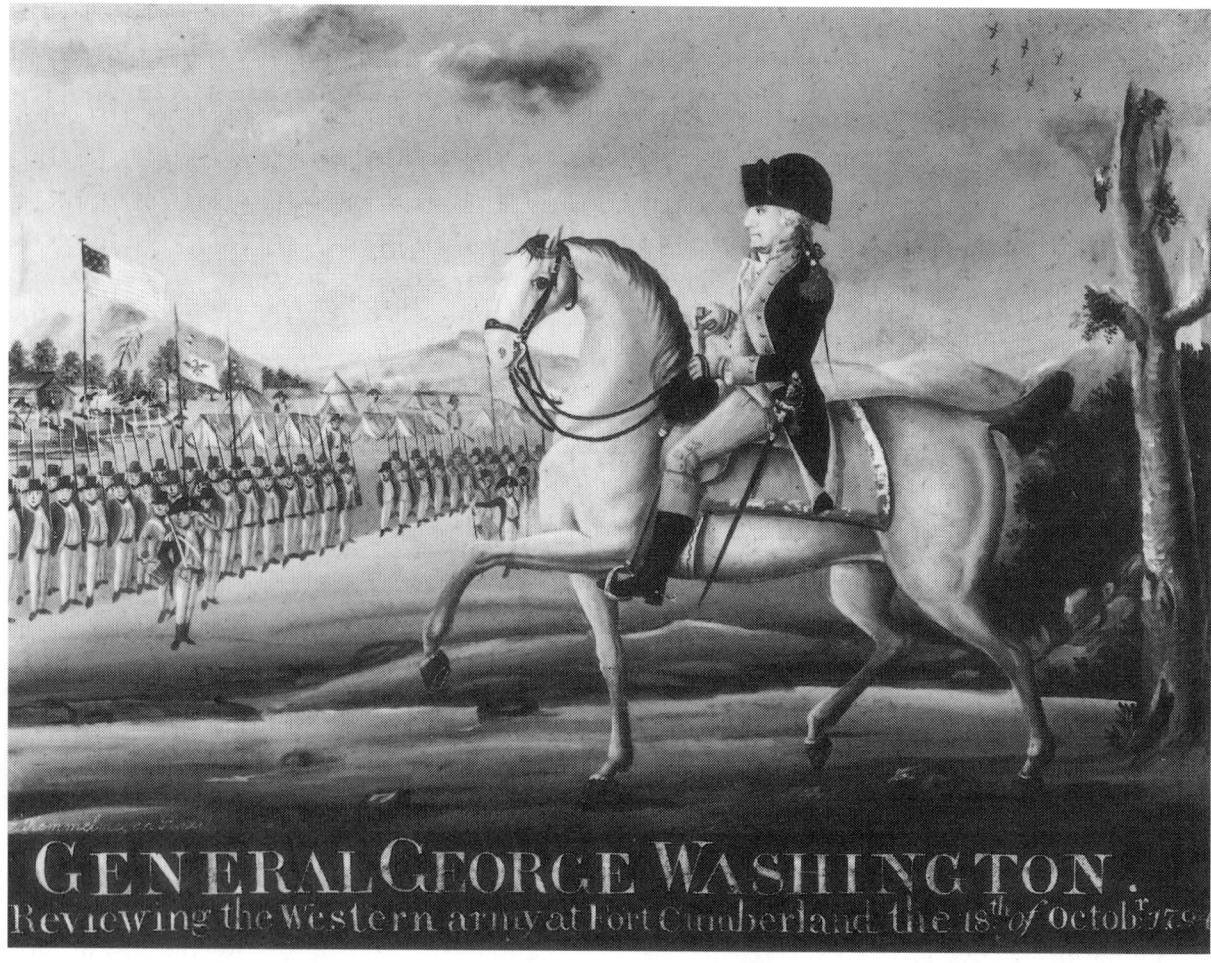

President George Washington reviewing the militia, which he had called together to suppress the Whiskey Rebellion of 1794. This uprising by Pennsylvania farmers against a proposed federal tax on whiskey was the first major test of the new government's power. Washington organized nearly thirteen thousand militiamen against the farmers, which was a greater number than he had commanded during the Revolution. The rebellion crumbled without any fighting taking place. The United States' government, less than two decades old, had demonstrated its authority to enforce its laws.

Washington had a commanding personality. He stood well over six feet tall and was a superb horseman. He first tasted combat on a military mission into the Ohio country to spy out French forces contending for control of that territory. When a skirmish with French troops followed, the bloodshed set off the French and Indian War. In this battle, Washington ignored good advice from Indian allies and suffered a disastrous defeat at the hands of a superior French force. Nevertheless, he was hailed as a hero after his return to Virginia. When the British refused him a commission in their regular army, he resigned from service.

In 1759 Washington married Martha Custis, a wealthy young widow with two small children, and they went to live on his estate at

Mount Vernon. He raised tobacco, invested in slaves, improved his holdings, and speculated in western lands. An excellent manager, he found time for fox hunting, fencing, shooting, and horse racing. He enjoyed the theater and dancing, too, read widely, and was a generous host.

In 1758 Washington was elected to the Virginia legislature, where he was soon playing a role in the rising revolt against Britain. When the king's forces and the colonials clashed at Lexington, open war began. The Continental Congress unanimously chose Washington to be the American commander in chief.

Washington led a long hard war to win independence from Britain. Many losses, many mistakes, many bitter disappointments. But his devotion to duty and his love of freedom held the Americans together until victory came at Yorktown.

After eight years in the field Washington wanted only peaceful retirement at Mount Vernon, but he was called to preside over the Constitutional Convention at Philadelphia. His commanding presence helped the fifty-five contentious delegates compromise their differences, and the result was a masterpiece of practical statecraft.

If the new government was to survive, everyone agreed that Washington should head it. In the nation's shaky first years he led the country as he had led its army, with quiet strength and profound good sense. He made difficult decisions in domestic and foreign affairs and won the respect of Europe and the devotion of his people. In his farewell address he urged Americans to avoid both partisan squabbles and "permanent entangling alliances" with foreign nations. In 1797 he returned to Mount Vernon, where he died two years later at the age of sixty-seven.

See also Constitution, The Making of the; Continental Con-

gresses; Federalist Party; Revolution. *For events during Washington's administration, see* Bank of the United States; Bill of Rights; Jay's Treaty.

For further reading: Milton Meltzer, *George Washington and the Birth of Our Nation* (New York: Watts, 1986).

MILTON MELTZER

WATERGATE

During the 1972 presidential campaign, a group of burglars was caught breaking into Democratic Party headquarters in the Watergate, an office building in Washington, D.C. They belonged to a group known as "the plumbers" that had been appointed a year earlier by President Richard M. Nixon to conduct political espionage and engage in "dirty tricks" aimed at ensuring Nixon's reelection.

Nixon went on television to insist that he had not authorized the burglary. After the election the burglars were convicted, but one of them, James McCord, charged that high Republican officials had been involved in the break-in. A resulting investigation revealed that this was true and also that the burglars had committed many other crimes during the campaign. After their arrest they had been paid by the White House to keep quiet and accept all the blame for the incident.

Nixon continued to deny that he had known about the break-in, but he refused the request of a Senate committee that he hand over tapes made of White House conversations between the president and his advisers.

Eventually, however, he was forced by the Supreme Court (and by the threat of impeachment if he refused) to make the tapes available. They revealed clearly that he had lied when he told the nation he was not involved and that he had tried to obstruct justice after the scandal became known. When it became clear that he would be impeached if he stayed in office, he resigned as president on August 9, 1974.

His successor, Gerald R. Ford, then pardoned him for "any crimes he might have committed while in office." There was a great national outcry over the pardon. Most people assumed it was in exchange for Nixon's having appointed Ford vice president (and therefore his possible successor) when Spiro T. Ag-

new had to resign from the vice presidency earlier over unrelated corruption charges. Many high officials in Nixon's administration served sentences in prison for their roles in the break-in or the cover-up, including his closest White House assistants, H. R. Haldeman and John Ehrlichman, and his attorney general, John Mitchell.

See also Corruption and Scandals in Government; Nixon, Richard M.

Garry Trudeau's comic strip Doonesbury *satirized the Watergate scandal. Here a reporter questions Ron Ziegler, press secretary under President Richard M. Nixon, who loses his temper at the mere mention of Watergate. The White House felt that the constant media attention was keeping Nixon from doing his job and that the president's enemies were behind it. Trudeau's strip expressed the outrage of those who felt the president was hiding something and owed it to the people to come clean.*

WAYNE, JOHN

(1907–79)   *Movie actor.*

One of the best-known leading men in American movies, John Wayne became the screen embodiment of both the western frontier hero and the patriotic American soldier. In a Hollywood career spanning some fifty years, Wayne appeared in more films than any other star.

Wayne, who was born Marion Michael Morrison in Iowa, started in the movies while still a student at the University of Southern California, acting as an extra during his summer vacations. An athlete at college, he first performed before a camera (in *Brown of Harvard* in 1926) as a stunt man. He was working as an assistant prop man at Universal in 1928 when he blundered onto the set during the filming of *Four Sons.* The director, John Ford, was impressed by his appearance and began giving him bit parts in his films. Wayne's rugged good looks brought him to the attention of other directors, and in 1930 he was cast for the lead in Raoul Walsh's western *The Big Trail,* the first film in which he was credited as John Wayne. Although well received, the film did not bring him much professional attention. He was never without work, but for the next nine years he received no important

John Wayne in the 1969 movie True Grit. *Wayne made more than eighty cowboy films and became the symbol of the American tough guy with a heart of gold. In 1930 one of the first directors to hire Wayne, Raoul Walsh, offered this formula for stardom: "To be a cowboy star, you've got to be six-foot-three or over, have no hips, and a face that looks right under a sombrero." Wayne fit the bill.*

parts. It was Ford's award-winning film *Stagecoach* (1939) that made Wayne a star. His complex, larger-than-life role as an escaped murderer in this relatively sophisticated drama established his reputation. Like the characters he portrayed, Wayne was a confirmed individualist and a devoted patriot, and he became well known for his conservative political views.

Wayne made more than 150 movies, many of them directed by his friend John Ford. More than half were westerns, but he was also very successful in such war films as *The Sands of Iwo Jima* (1949), *They Were Expendable* (1952), and *The Green Berets* (1968), which he

also directed. Other notable non-western movies in which he starred include *The Long Voyage Home* (1940) and *The Quiet Man* (1952), a romantic comedy in which he played a genial ex-boxer. Wayne won an Academy Award for his performance of a gruff, aging gunslinger in *True Grit* (1969).

See also Movies.

DENNIS WEPMAN

WEAPONS
See Guns and Gun Control; Nuclear Energy

WEBSTER, DANIEL

(1782–1852)   *Statesman, lawyer, and orator.*

Born on a New Hampshire farm and educated at Dartmouth College, Webster became a stirring orator and promising lawyer while in his early twenties. At the age of thirty, partly because he opposed the War of 1812, which was unpopular in New England, he was elected to the House of Representatives from New Hampshire.

After serving four years in the House, Webster moved to Boston, where he gained national acclaim as a brilliant constitutional lawyer. Before the Supreme Court, he argued successfully such landmark cases as *Dartmouth College* v. *Woodward, McCulloch* v. *Maryland,* and *Gibbons* v. *Ogden.* These cases greatly strengthened the authority of the federal government over the states.

In 1823, Webster returned to the House of Representatives, this time as a Massachusetts congressman, and served there until 1827, when he was elected to the Senate. When Sen. Robert Y. Hayne of South Carolina asserted in 1830 that a state could refuse to obey federal laws to which it objected, nationalist Webster replied that Hayne's states' rights theory could lead only to civil war. The Massachusetts senator concluded his speech with these famous words, "Liberty *and* Union, now and forever, one and inseparable!"

Webster served as secretary of state under presidents William Henry Harrison, John Tyler, and Millard Fillmore. During the Tyler administration, he negotiated the Webster-Ashburton Treaty (1842), which settled the boundary dispute between Maine and New Brunswick and helped avoid a war with Great Britain.

In 1836, 1840, and 1852, Webster was an unsuccessful contender for the Whig Party's nomination for the presidency. Webster's funeral occurred four days after the 1852 election in which Democrat Franklin Pierce defeated Whig candidate Winfield Scott. But more than sixteen hundred Massachusetts voters paid a final tribute to their beloved leader by writing the dead Webster's name on their ballots.

See also Webster-Hayne Debate; Whig Party.

EDMUND LINDOP

WEBSTER, NOAH

(1758–1843)   *Author of the first dictionary of American English.*

Noah Webster was an educator and the father of American language study. His many textbooks and his dictionary were the first books to distinguish the speech of the new nation from that of England and were responsible for the standardization of American spelling and pronunciation.

Webster was born in Hartford, Connecticut, to an old American family that included two New England colonial governors. He attended Yale from 1774 to 1778, interrupting his schooling to serve in the revolutionary war, and then studied law while making a living teaching. Noting that children's textbooks used examples from European history, he began to write his own, beginning with *The American Spelling Book,* published in 1783. This "Blue-Backed Speller," drawing on usage in the New World, is still in print, with sales estimated at over 100 million copies.

Webster went on to produce grammars, readers, and pamphlets defending his belief that the rules of language are based on living speech rather than artificial principles. He also wrote on medicine, economics, weather, farming, and politics. As there was then no protection for authors' work, he became a successful lobbyist for a national copyright law.

The climax of Webster's life work was the dictionary to which he devoted more than twenty years. First published in 1806, *A Compendious Dictionary of the English Language* contained over five thousand more words than any other English dictionary, including many Americanisms. In 1828, he published an expanded version, *An American Dictionary of the English Language,* in two volumes. With seventy thousand entries and nearly forty thousand new definitions, it revolutionized American language study. Although many of its word origins were wrong, this often-reprinted and revised work remains the basic authority on American speech and is perhaps the greatest dictionary ever produced by a single author. Webster's name is still so closely associated with dictionaries that many use "Webster's" in their title even though they have no connection with Noah Webster's original work.

DENNIS WEPMAN

WEBSTER-HAYNE DEBATE

This exchange between Senator Daniel Webster of Massachusetts and Senator Robert Y. Hayne of South Carolina took place between January 19 and January 27, 1830. The immediate issue involved a bill restricting the sale of government land. This was opposed by westerners eager to obtain land at low prices. On January 19 Hayne attacked the measure, suggesting that southern and western legislators should combine behind a policy of cheap land and low tariffs on foreign-made manufactured goods. Daniel Webster then attacked Hayne, arguing that his policy would be a threat to the Union.

Hayne responded to Webster's attack with a defense of states' rights. He came close to warning that if federal policy displeased them, the southern states had the right to secede from the Union. Webster's "second reply to Hayne" was an all-out attack on this states' rights position. Today his speech is interesting more for its tone than for the argument Webster advanced. It was full of patriotic rhetoric. (He referred to the Stars and Stripes as "the gorgeous ensign of the Republic.") Webster ended his two-day oration with the famous line: "Liberty *and* Union, now and forever, one and inseparable!"

See also Webster, Daniel.

WELFARE AND PUBLIC RELIEF

One job of government is to make sure that people can meet their basic needs—food, clothing, shelter, and health care. The United States has a variety of programs to accomplish this. Some give direct help to people in need. These are called relief programs because they *relieve* immediate suffering. Others, such as the Social Security system, provide services to all Americans.

History of Public Relief in America

In the eighteenth and nineteenth centuries, the poor were provided for by private charity. Wealthy people often donated money for "good works." Neighbors helped neighbors; friends helped friends. This arrangement worked fairly well for those who had generous friends and neighbors. But it left many others with no help at all.

The Industrial Revolution brought masses of immigrants flooding into the nation's cities. Many lived in terrible poverty. Those who had jobs worked ten to twelve hours a day under unhealthy and often dangerous working conditions. In return, they got barely enough to keep their families alive. Sick or injured workers lost their jobs. They and their families were often thrown into the streets, joining those who had never found jobs at all.

In the mid-nineteenth century, thousands of small charitable groups began to spring up across America. Most were local organizations designed to meet specific needs. Some, like the Belgian Benevolent Society, helped members of a particular immigrant group. Others tackled specific problems like alcoholism or joblessness. Settlement houses in slum neighborhoods encouraged people to work together to solve their problems. The best known was Hull-House in Chicago, founded by Jane Addams in 1889.

The largest nineteenth-century charity was the Salvation Army. Founded in England, it opened its first American branch in New York City in 1880. Before long, it had more than 20,000 "soldiers" waging war on poverty in cities across America.

Government Attitudes toward Welfare

For almost 150 years, the federal government did little to relieve the sufferings of the poor. Most officials believed that helping poor people would rob them of the desire to work hard and make a success of themselves. In reality, of course, most poor people were already working hard. They just couldn't make enough to lift themselves out of poverty.

European governments had a different attitude. Many of them had been involved in poor relief of various kinds for years. In 1880, Germany established the first modern welfare system. Worried by growing unrest among German workers, Chancellor Otto von Bismarck created an insurance system for those who lost their jobs and pensions for retired workers. These "social insurance" programs gave German workers financial security and made them more productive. Other countries soon followed Germany's lead. By 1911, every European nation had a government-paid insurance program for its workers. Many had other welfare programs as well.

The New Deal

The United States resisted the idea of government-supported welfare until the 1930s, when the Great Depression threw millions of Americans out of work. With no unemployment insurance, thousands lost their homes. Armies of homeless families camped out in fields and shantytowns. Some states set up emergency relief agencies, and at least one—Wisconsin—started an unemployment insurance program. But state efforts were not enough. It was a national problem.

In 1933, President Franklin D. Roosevelt launched the New Deal, a series of experimental government programs. Agencies like the Civilian Conservation Corps and the Works Progress Administration gave jobs to the unemployed. The Federal Emergency Relief Administration gave money to the states to provide food and other immediate help to the poor. Critics still complained that government "handouts" were bad for people in the long run. But as one New Dealer pointed out, "People don't eat 'in the long run.' They eat every day."

One of the most important New Deal measures was the Social Security Act of 1935, America's first social insurance program. It provided limited unemployment insurance, old-age pensions for workers and their families, and immediate help for the elderly poor. These benefits were paid for by contributions from both workers and their employers.

Later acts expanded Social Security to cover other groups and provide new benefits. The most important additions came under President Lyndon B. Johnson in 1965. They were Medicaid, which helps poor people pay their medical bills, and Medicare, which does the same for the elderly.

The Modern Welfare System

The American welfare system has continued to expand. In general, Democratic presidents have encouraged the development of new and bigger programs, and Republicans have tried to limit the system's growth. President Ronald Reagan tried to shrink the system as a whole by eliminating some programs and reducing the benefits provided by others. But welfare costs continued to climb even under the Reagan administration.

Today's welfare system is both enormous and complex. It includes more than seventy programs sponsored by the federal government, as well as hundreds run by state or local governments. Among the most important current welfare and relief programs are the following:

◆ *Supplementary Security Income* (SSI) provides cash payments to blind, elderly, and disabled people who have little or no money of their own.

◆ *Aid to Families with Dependent Children* (AFDC) is a joint federal and state program that provides money for poor families with young children. Almost 8 million children, about nine out of ten of whom live with a single parent, receive help under this program.

◆ The *Women, Infants, and Children* (WIC) program supplies supplementary food to over 4 million low-income mothers and children each month.

◆ The *Federal School Lunch Program* provides meals for almost 12 million children on school days.

◆ The biggest of all the government food programs is *food stamps,* which provides low-income people of all ages with coupons they can exchange for food.

◆ *Head Start* prepares children from low-income families for school.

Such programs pay out more than $175 billion in benefits each year. About three-quarters of that money comes from the federal government, the rest from state and local governments. Roughly 50 percent goes to individuals in the form of cash, food stamps, or housing assistance; 40 percent pays for medical care; and most of the rest goes to educational and job-training programs. Despite this enormous expense, however, many of the 33.5 million poor people in America still do not receive the help they need to escape poverty.

See also Addams, Jane; Civilian Conservation Corps; Day, Dorothy; Great Society; Medicare and Medicaid; New Deal; Poverty and Homelessness; Public Works Administration; Salvation Army; Settlement House Movement; Social Legislation; Unemployment; Works Progress Administration.

For further reading: Michael Kronenwetter, *Welfare State America: Safety Net or Social Contract?* (New York: Franklin Watts, 1993).

MICHAEL KRONENWETTER

WELLES, ORSON

(1915–85) *Actor and director.*

Born in Wisconsin, Welles began his acting career in Ireland. Although only a teenager, he talked himself into a job with a famous Dublin theater company by convincing the managers that he was an experienced actor in America. He was a success and returned home in triumph.

While still in his early twenties, Welles in 1937 cofounded the Mercury Theatre Company in New York with the producer John Houseman. In only a few years, he helped stage and perform several productions that are still remembered among the most imaginative in theater history. He also created a series of memorable radio dramas, including on Halloween night 1938 a version of H. G. Wells's story about an invasion of the earth by creatures from Mars. "The War of the Worlds" was presented as if it were an emergency news bulletin about something that was really happening. Listeners who tuned in too late to hear the opening announcement that it was only a play were taken in by its realism and became panic-stricken. Hundreds called the police or ran into the streets.

At the age of twenty-five, Welles directed, produced, starred in, and helped write his first movie, *Citizen Kane* (1941). It is still considered one of the greatest films ever made. Because he used many innovative film techniques, it won Welles a reputation as a "boy genius." Unfortunately, he also got a reputation for being "difficult." Hollywood studios were reluctant to trust him despite his brilliance. He directed only a handful of other movies over his long career, many of them made in Europe. Among them were *The Magnificent Ambersons* (1942), *Touch of Evil* (1957), *Othello* (1951), and *Chimes at Midnight* (1966). They were of varying quality, since he was constantly plagued by studio interference and a lack of money.

Welles was in greater demand as an actor than as a director. He played handsome leading men with dark pasts in such classic movies as *The Third Man* (1949) and *Jane Eyre* (1944). But he became hugely fat in middle age, and after that, he specialized in character parts that allowed him to use his enormous bulk to good advantage. Among his juiciest character roles were those in *The Long Hot Summer* (1958) and *Compulsion* (1958). The American Film Institute honored him with a Lifetime Achievement Award in 1975.

See also Movies.

MICHAEL KRONENWETTER

WELLS-BARNETT, IDA B.

(1862–1931)   *Civil rights and women's rights activist and journalist.*

Born a slave in Mississippi, the daughter of Jim Wells and Lizzie Warrenton was the oldest of eight children. Ida was barely three when the Civil War ended in 1865. Her parents believed ardently in education, and Ida remembered vividly her mother accompanying the children to a freedmen's school and remaining with them so that she, too, could learn to read and write. When a yellow fever epidemic claimed the lives of both parents and a brother in 1878, the teenager assumed responsibility for the younger children. She

taught school in Mississippi before accepting a better-paying position in Tennessee.

On a train trip in 1887, Ida was ordered to move to a segregated car. When she refused, she was bodily thrown off the train. Ida sued the railroad and was awarded five hundred dollars. Even though the ruling was later overturned by a higher court, the experience taught Ida that people could fight back against racism.

Ida B. Wells-Barnett was an eloquent crusader against lynching, which she defined as a peculiarly American crime. Her writing aimed to "disclose to the world that degree of dehumanizing brutality which fixes upon America the blot of a national crime. Whatever faults and failings other nations may have . . . no other civilized nation stands condemned before the world with a series of crimes so peculiarly national. It becomes a painful duty of the Negro to reproduce a record which shows that a large proportion of the American people avow anarchy, condone murder, and defy the contempt of civilization."

A few years later, Wells-Barnett was offered the editorship of a weekly newspaper. It was, she knew, the chance to reach many more people than she could through teaching. Thus began her career as a journalist. Over the years, Wells-Barnett wrote for several newspapers, including the *New York Age* and the *Chicago Conservator,* concentrating at first on issues related to education.

Then in March 1892, three of her friends in Memphis were lynched—that is, murdered by mobs. At the time, many people including Wells-Barnett believed that lynchings usually involved cases where African-American men were accused of attacking white women. But her friends had been lynched simply because a competing white businessman, jealous of their success, had accused them of conspiring against him. The incident launched Wells-Barnett on an antilynching campaign that made her an outcast in the South for many years and involved her in other causes including woman suffrage and the founding of black women's clubs devoted to reform.

Wells-Barnett married the owner of the *Chicago Conservator,* Ferdinand Barnett, in 1895, and the couple had four children. She was an imposing figure with flashing eyes. People paid attention when Wells-Barnett spoke. When she died in 1931, Wells-Barnett was among the most influential African-American women of her day. Her courage and integrity made her a role model for those who followed.

See also African Americans; Lynching; Voting.

CHRISTINE A. LUNARDINI

WEST, THE
See Cowboys; Gold Rushes; Oregon Trail; Pioneers and Frontier Life; Pony Express.

WESTWARD EXPANSION
See Expansion, Territorial.

WHARTON, EDITH
(1862–1937) *Author.*

Born Edith Jones into upper-crust New York society, Wharton spent much of her childhood in Europe. She married Edward Wharton in 1885, came into substantial inheritances, and started writing seriously. In 1907, after the success of her second novel, *The House of Mirth,* she moved to Paris and, welcomed in French and British literary circles, decided she belonged there.

Although she lived in France, Wharton's close friend Henry James, the American author, urged her to *"do New York."* In her books, she described America, especially her own convention-bound, moneyed class. The strange twists of love and the traps of marriage are dominant themes in her stories.

Wharton refused to leave France during World War I and set up relief projects for poor seamstresses, refugees, war orphans, and French soldiers suffering from illness. The French government awarded her the Legion of Honor for her work.

After the war Wharton bought two estates where she entertained the cream of the literary and art worlds. She traveled frequently and produced at least one novel or collection of stories or essays a year—plus writing many thousands of letters. Wharton was one of the most eminent American writers of her time. She earned great amounts of money and collected such honors as the 1921 Pulitzer Prize for her novel *The Age of Innocence* and an honorary degree from Yale University.

Like the character Ethan Frome in one of her books, she was locked in an unhappy marriage until her divorce in 1913 after twenty-eight years. Her one passionate love affair, in middle age, brought her as much anguish as happiness. But Wharton's countless friends and admirers, her riches and honors, and her astonishing energy never failed her. She died at seventy-five in her home near Paris, an "incorrigible life-lover" to the end.

See also Literature.

ELSA MARSTON

WHIG PARTY

The Whig Party was one of two major political parties that competed for power during the years 1834 to 1854; the other was the Democratic Party. Both parties had supporters in all regions of the United States. The most famous leaders of the Whig Party were Henry Clay, John Quincy Adams, and Daniel Webster; all were opponents of President Andrew Jackson, who led the Democrats. The Whig Party elected two presidents, William Henry Harrison in 1840 and Zachary Taylor in 1848, but unfortunately both men died in office after serving only a short time.

The Whig Party in America was formed to resist President Andrew Jackson, who was seen as wanting too much power. The name "Whig" traditionally meant one who resisted the power of the English king. (During the American Revolution those who had supported American independence had sometimes been called Whigs.) In contrast to President Jackson, or "King Andrew," as his critics scornfully called him, the Whigs supported a national bank owned jointly by the federal government and private investors. They also advocated a protective tariff (a tax on goods imported from other countries that made it

easier to sell articles produced by American companies, which did not have to pay the tax) and spending government money on internal improvements for better transportation (canals, highways, and railroads). In those days the United States was largely agricultural, and these policies were intended to encourage manufacturing and economic diversification. Such policies made the Whig Party attractive to businesspeople. The opposing party, the Democrats, charged that they would chiefly benefit people who were already prosperous.

The Whig Party was also attractive to certain reformers. The Whigs supported public schools, the reform of mental hospitals and prisons (where the inmates could be improved instead of just confined), and controls on the abuse of alcohol. Sometimes they even tried banning alcoholic drinks altogether. The party wanted to sell the public lands in the West instead of giving them away to settlers, so the government could use the money for public education and internal improvements. The Whigs interpreted the Constitution to provide for a stronger federal government that could implement its economic and reform programs. The Whig Party opposed taking away the lands of the Indians to give to white people; it also opposed the war against Mexico. On both of these issues, however, it was unsuccessful.

The Whig Party came to an end in the 1850s, when its members divided over the slavery question. Most of the northern Whigs joined the new Republican Party, which was opposing the extension of slavery into the territories in the West.

See also Adams, John Quincy; Clay, Henry; Harrison, William Henry; Taylor, Zachary; Webster, Daniel.

DANIEL WALKER HOWE

WHITE SUPREMACISTS
See Ku Klux Klan.

WHITMAN, WALT
(1819–92) *Poet, editor, and journalist.*

As a young adult, Whitman spent several years teaching, but he eventually became a writer and an editor. He particularly enjoyed writing about America, and in *Democratic Vistas* (1871) he celebrates the American way of life. Whitman wrote about both the good and the bad of American society. People who were used to reading about tame topics were shocked by his frank approach to subjects like sex, crime, and war.

Whitman's main contribution to American literature was his poetry. In 1855 he published a collection, *Leaves of Grass,* which contained a new form of poetry. People in Whitman's time expected poems to rhyme, to be divided into stanzas, to have a predictable rhythm, and to make points about how life should be lived. Whitman wrote free verse—poetry that does not follow standard rules. His poems do not rhyme, they are not divided into regular stanzas, they do not follow a predictable rhythm, and they celebrate life without trying to tell readers how to live their own. Because of Whitman's influence, poets since his time have felt freer to experiment in form and subject, and most poetry is now written in free verse.

During the Civil War Whitman cared for wounded soldiers. His experiences inspired a series of powerful Civil War poems, *Drum Taps* (1865). These poems reveal the tragic, personal nature of the war.

Whitman lived his life as freely as he wrote his poetry. He was content to be different

Whitman's poetry was exuberant and raw—in his own words, a "barbaric yawp."

from other people, and he challenged others to live life in their own ways. Because his ideas were controversial, few important people of his own time liked him. But his life and work have inspired many writers to live and write with the kind of freedom that democracy celebrates.

See also Literature.

DAVID C. SMITH

WHITNEY, ELI
(1765–1825) *Inventor and manufacturer.*

Born on a farm in Massachusetts, young Eli Whitney enjoyed puttering around his fa-

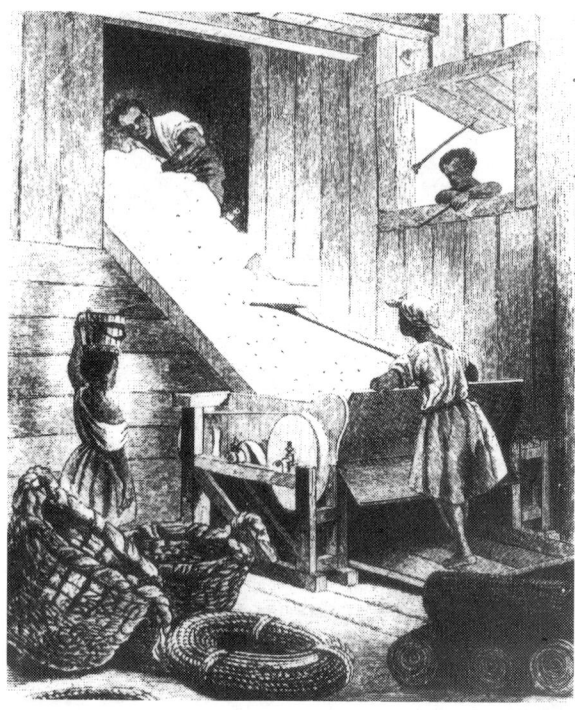

Eli Whitney's cotton gin in action. Before it was invented, the seeds from cotton balls had to be removed by hand. With a cotton gin, fifty times as much cotton could be cleaned in a day. "Gin" was short for engine.

ther's shop and became a skillful mechanic. When he was only fifteen, he began making nails, which were in great demand during the Revolutionary War.

After graduating from Yale College, Whitney traveled south to Georgia. There he saw why the South could not produce enough cotton to meet the needs of Britain's newly invented spinning and weaving machines. Separating the cotton from its sticky seeds by hand was so time-consuming that it took a worker one whole day to obtain a pound of marketable cotton. Whitney decided to figure out a way to do the job more quickly. In 1793, he invented the cotton gin, a machine that separated the cotton from its seeds so rapidly that one person could do the work of fifty.

The production of cotton rose dramatically, and cotton exports from the United States increased from 2 million pounds in 1794 to 1,768 million pounds in 1860, with three-fourths of it going to Britain's mills. As its cotton industry expanded, the South needed many more slaves. With more and more of its money invested in slaves and as cotton production grew so profitable, the region became more determined than ever to keep its slaves.

Whitney never profited financially from his revolutionary invention. He patented the gin, which meant that he was supposed to receive a payment each time someone made or sold one. But his machine was based on such simple principles that others could readily copy it, and many did so without paying Whitney. The lawsuits he brought in defense of his rights ate up most of his earnings.

Meanwhile, Whitney turned to another invention. In 1798, the federal government gave him a contract to build ten thousand muskets. Until that time guns had been hand-made one by one and no two were precisely the same. Whitney designed a machine that could manufacture parts exactly alike. Thus, a part could fit any number of guns rather than only the one it was made for. This use of interchangeable parts in manufacturing became one of the foundation blocks of the modern industrial system of mass production.

Ironically, while his cotton gin had helped the South to prosper, Whitney had laid the groundwork for the production of weapons with interchangeable parts that would contribute to the South's defeat in the Civil War.

See also Industrial Revolution in America.

EDMUND LINDOP

WILLIAMS, ROGER

(1603?–83) *Colonial religious and political leader.*

Williams was born in London and educated for the ministry at Cambridge University. He became increasingly opposed to some of the practices of the Church of England and migrated to Massachusetts in 1631. He believed that in the New World he could fulfill his quest for complete religious freedom. Williams was offered a post in a Puritan church in Boston, but he turned it down because its members had not separated, or broken away, from the Church of England. In 1633, in defiance of the Massachusetts General Court (the legislature), he accepted a ministry at a church in Salem.

Williams refused to soften his views to please the Puritan leaders. Insisting upon the complete separation of church and state, he opposed the Puritan principle in which government officials exerted authority in religious matters. He also insisted that the king of England had no right to take the lands of Indians without paying for them. In 1635, the Massachusetts General Court banished him from the colony, and he fled south into the wilderness.

The next year, Williams and a few followers founded the first settlement in what is now the state of Rhode Island. Grateful for his successful escape from Massachusetts, Williams called the settlement Providence. There he put into practice his ideas about religious liberty, generous land policies for the settlers, and friendly relations with the Indians. For example, he insisted that the Narragansett Indians be paid for the land they provided for the new colony.

To protect the colony from the claims of Massachusetts, Williams traveled to England in 1643 and obtained a charter for the Providence Plantation. Then he returned to the colony he had founded and continued to be active in its affairs. Williams's greatest contribution to American democracy was his unshakable belief in religious freedom and the complete separation of church and state.

See also Church and State, Separation of; Colonial America; Puritans.

EDMUND LINDOP

WILMOT PROVISO

After the Mexican War broke out in 1846, American military and naval units overran much of northern Mexico, what is now the southwestern section of the United States. Their successes raised the question of the future of slavery in territories that might be added to the United States when the war ended. Representative David Wilmot of Pennsylvania was a Democrat who, though he was not strongly opposed to slavery, was resentful of the extent to which southern politicians were dominating the administration of President James K. Polk. Wilmot in August 1846 introduced an amendment to a bill appropriating money for negotiating a peace treaty with Mexico. The amendment provided that "neither slavery nor involuntary servitude shall ever exist" in any territory acquired from Mexico.

The Wilmot Proviso passed the House of Representatives but was defeated in the Senate. It became apparent that no such rule could ever get through both houses of Congress. But the issue of the future of slavery in the western territories was central to the complex negotiations leading to the Compromise of 1850 and to the crisis precipitated by the passage of the Kansas-Nebraska Act in 1854.

See also Compromise of 1850; Kansas-Nebraska Act.

WILSON, WOODROW

(1856–1924)   *Twenty-eighth president of the United States (1913–21).*

Wilson began his career as a lawyer in Atlanta, Georgia. But he disliked practicing law, and in 1886 he obtained a Ph.D. at Johns Hopkins University. From 1885 to 1892 he taught political science, first at Bryn Mawr, a women's college, and then at Wesleyan University and Princeton. He was a brilliant teacher, so popular with students that there was never an empty seat in his classes. He was also a productive scholar, author of several important books on government.

In 1902 Wilson was appointed president of Princeton. At first he was as successful and popular as a college administrator as he had been as a teacher. He reformed the Princeton curriculum and brought in many first-rate young scholars to teach the courses. But by 1910 his reforms had angered the Princeton board of trustees and he was forced to resign. By then, however, he had attracted a national reputation as a reformer, and he was persuaded to run for governor of New Jersey on the Democratic ticket. Despite his lack of political experience he was triumphantly elected.

As governor Wilson persuaded the New Jersey legislature to enact a number of progressive reforms including workers' compensation, public utility regulation, and the direct primary. Two years later he was elected president of the United States, defeating President William Howard Taft, the Republican candidate, and ex-president Theodore Roo-

sevelt, who ran on the Progressive "Bull Moose" ticket.

As his biographer Arthur S. Link has written, "Wilson transformed the presidency . . . by his strong leadership in foreign affairs, his command of public opinion, and his leadership of [his] party in Congress." In two years he obtained a major reform of the tariff; the creation of the Federal Reserve banking system; the establishment of a Federal Trade Commission with power to outlaw unfair business practices; and the Clayton Antitrust Act strengthening the government's ability to break up monopolistic corporations.

When World War I broke out in Europe in 1914, Wilson tried to protect American interests but also to remain neutral. He offered repeatedly to mediate between the warring powers. He was reelected president in 1916 partly because of these peace efforts. But in 1917 because of German submarine attacks on neutral ships, Wilson called on Congress to declare war.

While accepting the need to fight, Wilson also hoped to "make the world safe for democracy" after the war was won. He drafted a Fourteen Point program designed to achieve a fair and just peace. After the war ended in November 1918, he went personally to the peace conference in Paris. There a treaty was drafted to establish the League of Nations, which Wilson believed would be able to prevent the outbreak of wars in the future.

The U.S. Senate hesitated to join the League unless guarantees protecting the right of Congress to decide whether or not to declare war were added. Wilson, however, refused to compromise, probably because his judgment had been impaired by a serious stroke suffered in the middle of the fight over joining. The Senate must ratify the treaty as it was, he insisted. The Senate refused and as a result the United States did not join the League of Nations. Wilson died a few years later, a bitterly disappointed man.

For events during Wilson's administration, see Antitrust Movement; Federal Trade Commission; Fourteen Points; New Freedom; Prohibition and Temperance; Treaty of Versailles and League of Nations; World War I.

JOHN A. GARRATY

WINTHROP, JOHN

(1588–1649) *Leader of the Massachusetts Bay Colony.*

Member of a landed family in Suffolk, England, Winthrop became attracted to Puritan thought as a young man. He practiced law in London and in 1627 joined the Massachusetts Bay Company, formed by Puritan merchants to settle in New England.

Winthrop saw this not as a way to abandon an England that he believed wicked and ripe for punishment by God but as a chance to create a new, perfect society. In this society people would lead good, industrious lives, obey God's laws, and try to overcome evil in themselves and their community. It would serve as a model for a reformed church and England.

Elected governor of the company, Winthrop organized and led the first group of Puritans to Massachusetts in 1630, settling around what is now Boston Harbor. Winthrop's faith that God favored this experiment kept the colony going through the first hard winter. He also concerned himself with the community's economic stability, to be achieved by trade in furs and fish. In the next few years about twenty thousand settlers arrived to join the colony.

Less rigid than other Puritan leaders, Winthrop soon found that his main challenge was to prevent the colony from splintering into separate churches, which he feared would invalidate its unique "commission" from God. Individuals with dangerously divisive ideas, such as the charismatic Roger Williams and Anne Hutchinson, were forced to leave.

Believing that good government depended to a certain extent on the consent of the ruled, Winthrop allowed virtually all adult male church members to vote annually for deputies who in turn elected governing officers from a small elite group. These men, in Winthrop's view, were best suited to rule— preferably little hampered by legislation. Winthrop served as governor for most of the colony's first nineteen years, leading it as close to the "Godly kingdom on Earth" as could have been hoped.

And as good Puritans should, Winthrop highly valued his family life. His first son, John, became governor of Connecticut. Winthrop lived until March 1649, still recording God's approval of life in his Massachusetts.

See also Colonial America; Hutchinson, Anne; Puritans; Williams, Roger.

ELSA MARSTON

WITCHCRAFT
See Salem Witch Trials.

WOBBLIES
See Industrial Workers of the World.

WOMEN AND THE WORK FORCE

Women in the United States have always worked. Whether in offices, on farms, in factories, or in homes, their labors have helped sustain our society from the beginning. Until recently, jobs were divided on the basis of sex, a result of beliefs about the way society should be organized that the colonists brought with them. Women, they felt, should be subordinate to men. As in England, colonial women were denied political rights and excluded from positions of power. Nevertheless, the rigors of life in the colonies meant that although women were politically second-class citizens, the work they performed was of first-class importance.

Women were expected to be homemakers, fulfilling the varied and endless needs of their families. From sun-up to sun-down a colonial woman was a whirlwind of activity. She would cook, clean, wash clothes, feed livestock, milk cows, plant vegetables, make soap and candles, spin yarn, weave cloth, sew it into clothing, knit, watch over and teach her children. She would also assist her husband in his work whether he was a farmer, shop owner, or tradesman. On the frontier, it wasn't unusual for a woman to sling a gun over her shoulder and go out to hunt for food.

Slave women were expected to serve as homemakers for their own families as well as work for their owners. When laboring for their masters, their physical strength was more important than their sex in determining the type of jobs they'd perform. Some strong slave women worked alongside men plowing the fields. Older women or children were more likely to be found working as domestic servants.

Women's Work in the 1800s

During the early 1800s, poor women helped support their families by spinning and weaving for merchants who paid them with either cash or goods. But by the middle of the century technological advancements made it more profitable for manufacturers to hire women to work in factories that were being built around the Northeast. Young women from the surrounding communities left their parents' farms to work in the growing mill towns. Although the work was hard, earning their own wages gave them newfound economic and social independence unknown to their mothers' generation.

During this period of rapid industrial expansion, the home was seen as the "woman's sphere," an idealized place of stability and moral refuge separate from the world of commerce. Only the poorest women and black women tended to work outside their homes after marriage. Because discrimination kept black men from securing good-paying jobs, most married black women sought employment as domestic servants to help support their families. A few worked in factories but only at the most menial tasks, such as sweeping floors.

Factory work had become more difficult by midcentury. Increased competition led mill owners to demand that their workers labor more intensely for less pay. Many factory girls sought work elsewhere and were replaced by impoverished immigrant women who had few choices. At the turn of the century only 3 percent of women factory workers belonged to unions. Middle-class groups like the Women's Trade Union League began to help female workers fight for protective legislation that was designed to improve working conditions. The actual outcome of the legislation was mixed. The laws did protect women's health, increase their wages, and limit their hours, but at the same time they narrowed their employment opportunities by keeping them out of jobs that could be deemed injurious to their health, morals, or reproductive capacity. Fortunately, at the same time as these laws were limiting women's options, the expanding economy presented qualified women with many new white-collar jobs as office clerks, stenographers, and switchboard operators.

By the turn of the century, the most skilled, highest paying jobs were reserved for white men, but a few trailblazing women succeeded in establishing themselves in traditionally male professions: The first woman lawyer was admitted to the bar in Iowa in 1869, and by 1910 there were almost nine thousand licensed women physicians. More and more women were attending college, and the vast majority of graduates became teachers, librarians, social workers, and in smaller numbers, academics.

The Impact of War

During both world wars women were expected to adapt their labors to the needs of the country. When men left their jobs to fight

Telephone operators working the switchboard in about 1915.

overseas, women, both married and single, were encouraged to show their patriotism by filling in for them. Bans against women in heavy industry were lifted as millions of women entered the defense industry doing everything from riveting airplanes to assembling machine guns. By 1945 one out of every four married women worked for wages. Sexism and racism combined to keep black women working at low-paying domestic jobs; they were not permitted to work in the defense industry unless there was no white woman or black man interested in the same job.

The infiltration of women into traditionally male jobs during the world wars was short-lived, however, and did not foreshadow a significant shift in opinion about the role of women in society. At the end of both wars, the government wanted to ensure that women would give their jobs back to the returning soldiers and conducted propaganda campaigns glamorizing motherhood and urging women to once again become homemakers. During the Great Depression of the 1930s women had been told it was their duty to let male breadwinners have even their low-paying jobs. But after that, more and more married women began to participate in the labor force. By the late 1950s middle-class families were learning that a second income was helpful, even necessary. The advertising industry had emerged as a powerful force, and families were spending more money on cars, household gadgets, and furnishings. Young people were also attending colleges in greater numbers than ever before, and a woman's paycheck could help families make ends meet, a pattern that continues today.

The Situation Today

The 1960s and 1970s were decades of feminist activism. In 1964 a law was passed that prohibited discrimination in employment on the basis of race and sex. For the first time, women could sue companies that did not give them equal access to jobs. On the other hand, though the 1963 Equal Pay Act specified that companies pay men and women equal wages, serious discrepancies still exist: in 1970 women were paid about 45 percent less than men for the same jobs; in 1985 about 35 percent less.

Today, educated women have far more options than ever before, and they are moving into positions of power. Between 1972 and 1983 the number of women managers doubled to 3.5 million. The majority of businesswomen in corporate America, however, find that they hit what has been called a "glass ceiling" that keeps them from being promoted to the top positions. Currently, women hold only 4 percent of the twelve thousand

A woman working on railroad tracking.

directorships in America's top companies. Further, women in every field still find it difficult to mediate between the demands of their families and the demands of their jobs. In the 1990s men and women continue to advocate for more and better child care and parental leave, and greater health-care coverage for all Americans. Resolving these issues will bring women one step closer to achieving true equality in the workplace.

See also Feminist Movement; Labor Movement; Slavery; Women's Trade Union League.

LAURIE LINDOP

WOMEN'S EDUCATION
See Education, Women's.

WOMEN'S MOVEMENT
See Feminist Movement.

WOMEN'S TRADE UNION LEAGUE

In 1903 a group of settlement house workers and other progressive social reformers joined with officials of unions employing women to found the Women's Trade Union League. Their objectives were to encourage working women to join unions and to lobby for state and national minimum-wage and maximum-hours legislation and for other laws protecting women workers. The league also organized women pickets during strikes, provided economic aid to female strikers, and publicized the cause of women workers.

The president of the league from 1907 to 1922 was Margaret Dreier Robins, who worked for women's suffrage and other reforms as well as for organized-labor issues. In 1914 Robins persuaded the league to establish a special school to train female labor organizers. The league passed out of existence in 1950 after having announced that all its objectives had been achieved.

See also Labor Movement.

WOODHULL, VICTORIA
(1838–1927)   *Social reformer.*

Victoria Claflin was born in Homer, Ohio, the seventh in a boisterous, eccentric family of ten children. The major influence in her life was her mother, who was a follower of spiritualism—the belief that the living can communicate with the dead. Victoria traveled throughout the Midwest with her family's fortune-telling and medicine show, selling a concoction called the Elixir of Life. At fifteen Victoria married Dr. Canning Woodhull, but she continued to travel with the family show. She was divorced in 1864 and two years later married a Civil War veteran, Col. James Blood.

In 1868 she announced that the ancient Greek orator Demosthenes, with whom she claimed to speak regularly, advised her to go to New York. With her husband and her sister, Tennessee, she moved to New York City, where she made considerable money on the stock market. She and her sister opened the first female brokerage house on Wall Street.

In 1870 the sisters began publishing the *Woodhull and Claflin Weekly,* a paper that championed equal rights for women. The *Weekly* condemned marriage as female slavery and aired public scandals to show the hypocrisy of people in high places.

Outspoken and flamboyant, Woodhull was a controversial figure wherever she went. She proved an eloquent speaker for women's suffrage—the right of women to vote. At a suffrage meeting in 1871 she declared, "We are plotting revolution! We will overthrow this bogus republic and plant a government of righteousness in its stead!" In 1872 Woodhull became the first woman to run for president of the United States, with the newly formed Equal Rights Party, though as a woman she herself could not vote.

By 1877, her marriage to Blood at an end, Woodhull moved to England. Six years later she married John Biddulph Martin, the son of a wealthy banking family. She remained in England for the rest of her life, writing and lecturing on women's rights.

See also Feminist Movement to 1919.

DEBORAH KENT

WOODSTOCK

The Woodstock festival (August 15–18, 1969) has become the world's most famous rock concert and a symbol of the youth movement of the sixties. More than 400,000 young people, most between the ages of fifteen and twenty-five, made their way to Bethel, New York, near the artists' colony of Woodstock. The concert featured some of the decade's best rock musicians: Jimi Hendrix, Jefferson Airplane, the Who, Blood, Sweat and Tears, Joe Cocker, Carlos Santana, and Crosby, Stills, Nash, and Young, among others. For three days they camped in an endless sea of mud and rain, and tried to live up to the sixties' creed of peace, love, and "doing your

Citizens of the "Woodstock Nation."

own thing." The style was love beads, long hair, bell-bottoms, and occasional nudity; the drugs of choice were marijuana and L S D; and the political climate was anti-Nixon and overwhelming opposition to the Vietnam War.

Abbie Hoffman, probably the most famous of the yippies (a hippy intensely involved in politics), struggled to describe the mood of this massive event in his book *Woodstock Nation*: "God, how can you capture the feeling of being with 400,000 people and everyone being stoned on something? Were we pilgrims or lemmings? Was this really the beginning of a new civilization or the symptom of a dying one? Were we establishing a liberated zone or entering a detention camp?" An award-winning documentary of the concert is still in circulation and serves as a telling record of the sixties counterculture, which is sometimes referred to as the Woodstock generation.

See also Rock Music; Sixties, The.

WOOLWORTH, FRANK

(1852–1919)   *Merchant.*

Woolworth wanted a career in business from early childhood, when his favorite game was "playing store." Born on a farm in Rodman, New York, he spent two terms in a business college and at the age of nineteen accepted an unpaid job clerking in a grocery store for the experience. Two years later he moved up to $3.50 a week in another store. Never a very successful salesman, he worked on and off as a shop clerk in Watertown, New York, until 1878, when he heard of a store with a counter at which only goods selling for five cents apiece were offered. He persuaded his employer, W. H. Moore, to lend him three hundred dollars to open a five-cent store in Utica.

Woolworth's first store failed in three months. Convinced that he had not offered a large enough selection of goods, he talked Moore into supporting a second venture, this time in Lancaster, Pennsylvania, in 1879. This one was a success. When he added a line of ten-cent merchandise, the business grew so rapidly that he began to open stores in other cities. To increase the range of merchandise he could offer for five or ten cents, Woolworth had items especially manufactured for his stores.

Other chains of five- and ten-cent stores were created by former partners of Woolworth's during the next few years, but one by one the F. W. Woolworth Company acquired them as well, along with the stores of his former employer, W. H. Moore. When he died in 1919, Woolworth owned more than a thousand "five-and-dime" stores in the United States and Canada.

From 1909 to 1913, Woolworth fulfilled a childhood dream by erecting, in New York City, the sixty-story Woolworth Building, the world's tallest structure until 1930, for which he paid $13.5 million in cash. One of the most successful self-made businessmen in American history, Woolworth became the director of many banks and amassed a personal fortune of over $65 million.

DENNIS WEPMAN

WORK
See Child Labor; Labor; Slavery; Women and the Work Force.

WORKS PROGRESS ADMINISTRATION

One of the major achievements of the New Deal was its provision of work for millions of unemployed people. In March 1933 the Civilian Conservation Corps was established and in June came the Public Works Administration, designed to put unemployed people to work constructing roads, public buildings, airports, and similar projects. Then, between November 1933 and March 1934, the Civil Works Administration put some 4 million jobless people to work.

Finally, in April 1935, a more permanent agency, the Works Progress Administration (WPA), headed by Harry Hopkins, was created. Needy people who were unable to work were made the responsibility of state agencies. Finding jobs for those able to work was the task of the WPA.

During the next eight years many millions of jobless people, skilled and unskilled, young and old, were employed by the WPA not only constructing roads and public buildings but also performing countless other activities. The object was to put the jobless to work doing whatever they had done when they were employed. They were paid at regular wage rates, which varied, of course, with the type of work involved. But the number of hours a person could work was held to about thirty a week so as to spread the jobs as widely as possible.

Among the most innovative WPA programs were the Federal Theatre Project, the Federal Art Project, the Federal Writers' Project, and the National Youth Administration, which found work for students. By the time the WPA was disbanded in 1943, more than 8.5 million persons had been on its payroll.

See also New Deal.

WORLD WAR I

Also known as the Great War, this major conflict was fought mostly in Europe from 1914 to 1918 and involved many nations of the world.

America's Entry into the War

In August 1914, the Allies (Britain, France, Russia, and associated states) and the Central Powers (the German and Austro-Hungarian empires and other states) went to war. The United States took no sides at first but was gradually drawn into the Allied camp when Germany repeatedly violated its neutrality. Contrary to international law, German submarines attacked merchant ships without first providing for the safety of passengers and crews. Although Germany warned neutrals not to board ships going into war zones, President Woodrow Wilson refused to limit Americans' freedom to travel. After the 1915 sinking of the British liner *Lusitania*, with a loss of 128 American lives, and the 1916 torpedoing of the French ship *Sussex*, injuring more Americans, the United States threatened to break off diplomatic relations with Germany. In response, Germany issued the "Sussex Pledge," promising to warn those on board a ship to be attacked so that they could abandon ship beforehand.

In January 1917, the British turned over to President Wilson an intercepted message from the German foreign secretary Arthur Zimmermann to the German ambassador in Mexico. It said that if the United States entered the war, Mexicans should be encouraged to join the Central Powers and be offered the chance to recover New Mexico, Texas, and Arizona from the United States. Americans realized that the war was not just a European conflict.

On January 31, 1917, Germany broke the Sussex Pledge in the belief that the Central Powers would soon be victorious. The U.S. government responded by arming American merchant ships and on April 6, 1917, by enter-

American soldiers saying goodbye as they prepare to depart for France in 1917.

ing the war. Since Russia had just overthrown Czar Nicholas II, the president now claimed that the United States was fighting to "make the world safe for democracy."

Progress of the War

All along the western front, the opposing armies had dug in, occupying narrow trenches separated by a no-man's-land. When they emerged and charged each other's defenses, they would gain only a few yards of territory at a tremendous cost in lives. In 1917, however, the Germans planned a surprise offensive to break the stalemate. Four divisions of American "doughboys" (nicknamed for the shape of the buttons on their uniforms) arrived in France in May and awaited reinforcements. Gen. John J. ("Black Jack") Pershing,

commander of the American Expeditionary Force, coordinated his growing forces with those of the French marshal Ferdinand Foch.

After the Germans launched their offensive along the western front in May 1918, American troops helped drive them back across the Marne River at Château-Thierry, fifty miles from Paris. In June, they fought at Belleau Wood. A month later, 85,000 doughboys joined in a counterattack against the German armies in the Second Battle of the Marne. In September, 550,000 Americans successfully reduced a large concentration of German troops at Saint-Mihiel near Verdun in just a few days. From late September to early November, 1.2 million American soldiers were sent to the Argonne Woods to take the city of Sedan and cut off lines between

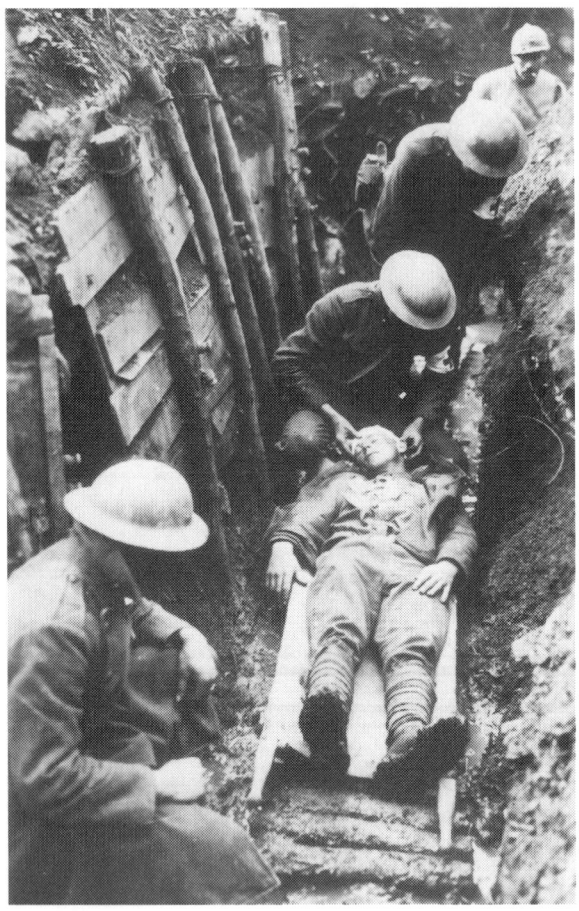

A wounded American soldier lying in a trench in France in 1918. Combat on the western front of World War I was characterized by trench warfare. Each side attacked by throwing grenades and firing rifles and machine guns from trenches, which offered some protection. Trench warfare was static—that is to say, little ground was gained or lost by either side for more than four years. Yet the casualties were enormous.

there and Metz. Despite heavy casualties, the American army gained thirty miles of territory and captured many prisoners and supplies. Meanwhile, British, French, and Belgian armies attacked the crumbling German defenses along the rest of the front.

On November 11, 1918, the Germans signed an armistice ending the war. The Americans had fought for only a short time, but they made a vital difference to the Allies. Of the 4.7 million Americans who served, more than 100,000 died and 200,000 were wounded.

On the Home Front

America had geared up for war by drafting men into military service and building training camps and barracks to house them. To pay for the war effort, the government raised taxes and borrowed money by selling war bonds. New agencies were set up to regulate the economy. Among them were the War Industries Board, which oversaw manufacturing, and the Food Administration, headed by future president Herbert Hoover, which was charged with assuring adequate food supplies for civilians and the military. The War Labor Board settled labor disputes; the Railroad Administration operated the nation's trains under a single system; and the Fuel Administration supervised coal and oil production.

The Committee on Public Information mobilized public opinion to support the war effort and issued anti-German propaganda statements. The public reacted by lashing out against German Americans, destroying their property and rejecting all things German—from music and literature to dachshund dogs and pretzels. Others believed to be radicals (political extremists), such as pacifists and socialists, were also mistreated, especially after the Espionage Act was passed in 1917. It fined and imprisoned those convicted of interfering with the draft or encouraging "disloyal" acts. The 1918 Sedition Act penalized individuals who obstructed war bond sales or military recruiting or who spoke or published statements criticizing the American government or showing disrespect for the flag. Under these laws, over fifteen hundred people were arrested, many of whom were innocent.

Aftermath of the War

At war's end, most people in the United States wanted to "return to normalcy," to go back to simpler times. Many people resented the thousands of immigrants coming from southern and eastern Europe and urged the passage of restrictive laws to keep them out. Some even condemned workers striking for higher wages as un-American. During the red scare of 1920, some six thousand people, including many labor union leaders, were arrested on flimsy charges as suspected communists.

Some Americans, however, did not want a return to "normalcy." During the war, hundreds of thousands of African Americans had flocked to the North to work in factories. They were not welcomed and were crowded into run-down ghettos. Returning black veterans, resentful of having served in segregated units, joined them in demanding their rights as citizens. In 1919, twenty-six race riots took place in northern cities. Lynchings increased in the South, and membership in the Ku Klux Klan rose.

Although they had been barred from military service, some forty thousand women had turned from homemaking to jobs in the war industries. In peacetime, American women insisted on ending their exclusion from national politics, and in 1920, they finally won the right to vote.

A new generation of young adults, the "lost generation," also emerged from World War I, looking for excitement and rejecting many of the values of their parents. Thus postwar Americans could not simply return to the past.

See also Treaty of Versailles and League of Nations.

BARBARA SILBERDICK FEINBERG

WORLD WAR II

Germany and the Soviet Union invaded Poland in September 1939, touching off World War II. It became a global conflict between the Allies—the United States, Great Britain, France, the Soviet Union (after 1941), China, and forty-five other nations—and the Axis powers—Germany, Italy, Japan, the Soviet Union (until 1941), and six other countries.

Disillusioned by World War I, the United States did not want to become involved in European conflicts and pursued an isolationist policy. At first it remained officially neutral, though the government helped the Allies with money and arms through the Lend-Lease Act. Then Japanese planes launched a surprise attack on the American naval base at Pearl Harbor, Hawaii, on December 7, 1941. In less than two hours, the raid killed 2,400 servicemen, badly damaged the U.S. Pacific fleet, and destroyed hundreds of American planes. The next day, Congress declared war on Japan. Japan's partners, Adolf Hitler's Nazi Germany and Benito Mussolini's Fascist Italy, then declared war on the United States. By this time, Germany had invaded and conquered most of continental Europe, including Denmark, Norway, France, Belgium, Holland, Greece, and Yugoslavia, among other countries.

The War in Europe

America and British planners decided on a "Europe First" strategy. Hitler had signed a nonaggression pact with Joseph Stalin in 1939, but he turned on Stalin and sent German armies storming into the Soviet Union in June 1941. The Allies were not yet strong enough to land troops in western Europe to relieve the German pressure on the Soviet Union. Instead, they launched heavy air at-

German soldiers assembled at a rally in Nuremberg, Germany, to hear a speech by Adolf Hitler.

tacks on German military and industrial targets.

In November 1942, American troops under Gen. Dwight D. Eisenhower invaded North Africa. After the "Desert Fox," Gen. Erwin Rommel, and his German tank corps had been defeated in the spring of 1943, the Allies controlled the southern and western Mediterranean region.

In July 1943, the Americans invaded the Italian island of Sicily. By September, the city of Naples on the Italian mainland had fallen. The troops then slowly inched their way north through the rugged Italian peninsula against stiff resistance. They did not capture Rome until June 4, 1944.

Operation Overlord, the invasion of Occupied France, took place two days later, on June 6, called D-day. Under Eisenhower's overall command, 3 million men, 11,000 aircraft, and countless ships crossed the English Channel in bad weather to land in Normandy. At the end of July, Gen. George S.

Patton's Third Army drove the Germans from Brittany. In August, the Allies liberated Paris.

The advance toward Germany was held up for a time by a German counterattack at the Battle of the Bulge in Belgium, but the Allies repulsed the assault and drove on into Germany. In March 1945, Soviet armies advancing from the east linked up with American troops at the Elbe River. The victorious Allied armies liberated survivors of the Nazi death camps. At Auschwitz, Treblinka, and other concentration camps, between 5 and 7 million Jews were systematically killed by the Nazis, as were Gypsies and others. Their plan of genocide is known as the Holocaust. On May 7, with the capital, Berlin, in ruins, Hitler committed suicide and Germany surrendered.

The War in the Pacific

Meanwhile Japanese forces had occupied many of the islands of the Pacific Ocean. American troops in the Philippines were penned up on the Bataan Peninsula and forced to surrender in 1942. On President Franklin D. Roosevelt's orders, their commander, Gen. Douglas MacArthur, escaped to Australia where he assumed supreme command of the Allied forces. The victorious Japanese sent off the captured American troops on a "Death March" to prison camps.

A long and bitter naval war then developed in the Pacific. A Japanese invasion of New Guinea was turned back by the Americans at the Battle of the Coral Sea in May 1942. In the decisive Battle of Midway Island in June, carrier-based American planes severely crippled a huge Japanese fleet, sinking four aircraft carriers. In August, American and Australian forces fought their way onto the island of Guadalcanal in the Solomon Islands. After long and bitter fighting, the Japanese surrendered the island in February 1943.

The United States dropped an atomic bomb on Nagasaki, Japan, on August 9, 1945; three days earlier an A-bomb had been dropped on the city of Hiroshima. The enormous devastation of the nuclear attack caused Japan to surrender.

The Allies pursued an island-hopping strategy, advancing from the Solomon Islands to the Gilberts to the Marshalls. Each victory brought them closer to Japan. In October 1944, MacArthur returned to the Philippines at the head of an army, and the navy won a major victory over a Japanese fleet at the Battle of Leyte Gulf. Between February and June 1945, the Japanese islands of Iwo Jima and Okinawa were captured, but at the cost of eleven thousand American lives.

On August 6, the United States dropped the first atomic bomb on the Japanese city of Hiroshima, killing eighty thousand people and leveling four square miles of the city. A second bomb was dropped on Nagasaki three days later. Only then did the Japanese admit defeat. On V-J Day, September 2, 1945, they signed an official surrender on the battleship *Missouri*.

By war's end, 16 million Americans had served in the armed services. Some 300,000 had lost their lives, and another 671,000 had been wounded.

The War's Effects on Americans

During the war, life changed for many groups of Americans. Under pressure from African Americans, President Roosevelt set up a Fair Employment Practices Committee to end discriminatory hiring in war plants. Black and white officer candidates attended the same training schools, and in 1945, a few military units were desegregated. Indians, however, were not segregated in the armed forces, and women were finally permitted to serve in the military, though as noncombatants. Far more than in World War I, women (6.5 million) found jobs in war plants between 1941 and 1945.

On the other hand, forty-five thousand Japanese Americans, men, women and children, were evacuated from the West Coast and forced into internment camps. Not one

For biographies of World War II leaders, see the following entries:

BRADLEY, OMAR

EISENHOWER, DWIGHT D.

KING, ERNEST

MACARTHUR, DOUGLAS

MARSHALL, GEORGE C.

NIMITZ, CHESTER

PATTON, GEORGE

ROOSEVELT, FRANKLIN D.

TRUMAN, HARRY S.

of these people was proved to have been disloyal. The action against them was based solely on their ancestry. Many Japanese Americans served valiantly in the European theater during the war. The 442nd Infantry unit, made up of Japanese-American volunteers, became the most decorated unit in American military history.

Victory in World War II was won by the efforts of many nations, but American military force and techniques of mass production were crucial. Shielded from attack by two oceans, no American city or factory was ever bombed. Tanks, ships, and aircraft lost in battle were quickly replaced. The United States thus emerged at war's end an economic as well as a military superpower.

See also Atlantic Charter; D-Day; Four Freedoms; Holocaust, Response to; Japanese Americans, Internment of; Lend-Lease Act; Manhattan Project; Marches on Washington; Neutrality Acts; Nuremberg Trials; Pearl Harbor, Attack on; Potsdam Conference; Yalta Conference.

BARBARA SILBERDICK FEINBERG

WOUNDED KNEE MASSACRE

The Wounded Knee massacre on December 29, 1890, was the last military encounter between American Indians and whites and represents one of the most shameful episodes in American history. A vastly outnumbered and for the most part unarmed group of 150

The burial of the dead at the massacre of Wounded Knee in 1891.

Hunkpapa Sioux—the majority of them women and children—were slaughtered by the U.S. Seventh Cavalry near Wounded Knee Creek, South Dakota.

The massacre took place at a time when American Indians were profoundly demoralized: the U.S. government had by then defeated the Indians in battle after battle and forced them off their lands. Indians lived in poverty on reservations, dependent on whites for handouts, and were continually under pressure to give up their Indian ways. It became grimly certain that Indian culture was in danger of extinction.

A source of hope came with the emergence of a new religion, the Ghost Dance, founded by Wovoka, a Paiute Indian. Wovoka promised that if Indians lived good, productive lives and performed the ritual Ghost Dance, the whites would disappear, the Indians' ancestors would return to earth, and the world would become a paradise where Indians could live in peace and happiness. The religion spread rapidly to various reservations, and alarmed whites saw it as defiant and threatening. It was in this charged atmosphere of distrust—Indians certain that whites were bent on their destruction and whites skittish about the reemergence of Indian pride and solidarity—that led to the atrocities at Wounded Knee.

The U.S. Seventh Cavalry intercepted a band of starving and sick Ghost Dancers near Wounded Knee Creek, South Dakota, and ordered the Indians to surrender their guns. The Indians, fearing that without their few remaining weapons they would be defenseless, refused. The soldiers became uneasy. A single shot fired in the air by an Indian set off the 500 cavalrymen, who opened fire on the 150 Indians with guns and even cannons. In less than an hour almost no Indians were left standing. Some of the women managed to run as much as three miles before they were overtaken and shot by the soldiers. Frozen bodies littered the scene of this senseless show of military might by a government that had already stripped the Indians of their land and their strength, and seemed determined to destroy any of their remaining pride.

See also Indians.

W P A
See Works Progress Administration.

WRIGHT, FRANCES
(1795–1852)   *Feminist and reformer.*

Born in Scotland, Wright read widely in philosophy while still a teenager and published her first work at age eighteen. Inspired by the egalitarian ideas of the American Revolution, she set sail for New York in 1818. After returning to Britain, she wrote *Views of Society and Manners in America* (1821), the first serious account of the United States by a British woman. The book won her the admiration of the aging Marquis de Lafayette, and in 1824, she accompanied him on a tour of America. She ended up staying in the United States for most of the rest of her life.

By this time, Wright had taken an interest in the ideas of the British utopian socialist Robert Owen and in the American antislavery movement. Using a large portion of her inheritance, she established a community experiment, Nashoba, in Tennessee, where she planned to help slaves earn their freedom. The experiment soon collapsed after scandalizing Americans, not least because it encouraged sexual and racial equality.

Undaunted, Wright joined forces with

Owen's son, Robert Dale Owen (who had established a socialist community in New Harmony, Indiana) and moved with him to New York City in 1829. Here she won her greatest fame as an electrifying radical writer and lecturer—the first woman of importance to address the general public in such ways. She discussed the touchiest of themes, attacking slavery, revealed religion, and economic inequalities. Above all, Wright denounced traditional marriage and the legal subjugation of women. Wright was an early advocate of free love, the idea that women as well as men ought to be able to express their passions without interference from the church or the state. For this she gained a small but intense following—and suffered abuse from mainstream and conservative writers who dubbed her "the Red Harlot of Infidelity." A dazzling performer, she gave as good as she got.

Even at the height of her fame, Wright endured many hardships: the sudden death of her sister in 1831, followed by a loveless marriage to a fellow radical, along with continual attacks from the press. Yet she continued with her work, a steadfast champion of women's rights. When she died, she was largely forgotten, but her fearless example encouraged later reformers and rebels who fought for the equality of women.

See also Feminist Movement to 1919.

SEAN WILENTZ

WRIGHT, FRANK LLOYD

(1867–1959)   *Architect.*

One of the most important and original architects of the twentieth century, Wright was a founder of modern building design. An innovator in both style and methods of construction, he changed the appearance of private houses and public buildings.

Wright was born in Wisconsin and studied engineering at the University of Wisconsin before moving to Chicago in 1887. He worked briefly as a draftsman in an architect's office and later was hired by Louis Sullivan, the most progressive architect in America at the time. In 1893 Wright lost his job because he supplemented his modest salary by doing outside work, and the next year he opened his own office.

Wright began immediately to create a new kind of house, different from the highly ornamented Victorian homes then in fashion. Believing that the nation required its own form of architecture, using native materials and expressing original ideas, he designed low, extended residences with terraces that fitted naturally into their surroundings. During his first twenty years of work, he built almost a hundred private homes, which he called "prairie houses," in the Midwest. But his style was unpopular among those with more conservative tastes, and he was seldom called on to design public buildings.

Always inventive, Wright pioneered many innovations in lighting, heating, structural materials, and plumbing. He was the first to design an office building using plate-glass doors, metal furniture, wall-hung toilets, and air conditioning (the Larkin Building in Buffalo, New York, 1904), and the first to employ poured concrete for a public building (Unity Temple Church in Oak Park, Illinois, 1905). In 1915 he accepted a commission to build the Imperial Hotel in Tokyo, Japan, which had to resist the earthquakes common in that country. The huge building, finished in 1922, contained an original system of concrete supports made flexible by being set in a foundation of soft mud. A structural success, it was undamaged by the severe earthquake that destroyed much of Tokyo in 1923.

Determined to avoid European influences, classical decorations like columns, and artificial surfaces, Wright developed an organic style of building fitted to its natural setting. The Kaufmann House, in Bear Run, Pennsylvania (1936–37), was built over a waterfall and incorporated its environment into its design so harmoniously that it is difficult to tell where the building begins and the landscape ends.

The next year Wright built the first of what he called his "Usonian" homes, named for his ideal of a democratic America. These were medium-sized, inexpensive houses with the same solid construction, efficient design, and elegantly simple style as the custom-built residences for which he was becoming famous. The buildings had an important influence on suburban architecture.

As his reputation grew, Wright was employed to create buildings all over the world, including the grandiose Civic Auditorium in Baghdad, Iraq (1957), and the revolutionary Guggenheim Museum in New York (1959). The museum contains a six-story spiral ramp ascending around an open central space that permits a view of galleries from above and below.

Wright was a poet and a philosopher of architecture, who never failed to bring something original to his work. He believed, as he once wrote, that "man takes a positive hand in creation whenever he puts a building upon the earth beneath the sun."

See also Architecture.

For further reading: Wendy Murphy, *Frank Lloyd Wright* (New York: Silver Burdett Press, 1990).

DENNIS WEPMAN

WRIGHT, WILBUR
WRIGHT, ORVILLE

(Wilbur: 1867–1912; Orville: 1871–1948)
Aviation pioneers.

Wilbur and Orville early displayed mechanical skills. While Orville was still in high school, they built a printing press and began publishing a newspaper. In 1892, they opened a bicycle sales and repair shop and then began manufacturing bicycles. Encouraged as children to pursue intellectual interests, they studied aeronautical literature. By 1896, Wilbur had concluded there were design flaws in the glider being used by Otto Lilienthal in Germany. Wilbur's ideas proved tragically correct when Lilienthal was killed flying that August. Now determined to achieve powered flight themselves, the brothers decided to conduct glider flights and to focus their efforts on a means of controlling flight in three dimensions.

With U.S. Weather Bureau help, the brothers chose as the site for their experiments the sand dunes at Kitty Hawk, North Carolina. During the winter of 1901–02, the Wrights constructed a six-foot-long wind tunnel at home to observe wind effects on wing shapes (a device on display at the Air Force Museum in Dayton). Next the brothers constructed a small gasoline engine. On December 17, 1903, Orville flew first, traveling 120 feet in 12 seconds. Wilbur then flew a distance of 852 feet in 59 seconds. They did not release the now-famous "first flight" photograph, taken at Kitty Hawk.

During 1904 and 1905, the brothers built and flew three powered aircraft from a field near Dayton and dickered with U.S. and foreign government agencies, winning a War Department contract in 1908. That same year, *Collier's* magazine sent photographer Jimmy

The first powered airplane flight was made by the Wright brothers at Kitty Hawk, North Carolina, on December 17, 1903. Orville Wright (lying down) is seen operating the plane while his brother Wilbur runs along at right.

Hare to witness new flights at Kitty Hawk. The first photograph seen by the public of a Wright plane in flight appeared in the magazine's May 30 issue. On August 8, Wilbur made a short flight from a racecourse at Le Mans, southeast of Paris, France. Before an audience of awed European air pioneers, he flew again for an hour and twenty minutes at Le Mans on December 31, drawing headlines the world over.

In 1912, Wilbur died of typhoid fever. Three years later, Orville sold the Wright Company to a group of investors. He died in 1948, a widely acclaimed figure in aviation.

See also Aviation; Science and Technology.

For further reading: John Evangelist Walsh, *One Day at Kitty Hawk: The Untold Story of the Wright Brothers and the Airplane* (New York: Crowell, 1975).

WILLIAM WELLING

WRIGHT, RICHARD

(1908–60)   *Writer.*

Born to a poor family in the rural South, Wright had little formal education but became the most important African-American author in the country. His writing changed the way Americans viewed black people and earned him the respect of intellectuals around the world.

Wright decided at an early age to become a writer and published his first short story in 1924 before he had finished junior high school. He never stopped studying as he worked at low-paying jobs to support himself. At the age of nineteen he moved to Chicago, where he wrote poems, stories, and articles for magazines.

Angry at the discrimination he encountered, Wright became involved in liberal organizations in order to work for racial equality. In 1932 he joined the Communist Party and five years later went to New York to become a contributing editor of a party magazine. But he found the Communist philosophy increasingly hard to accept, and he quit the party in 1942 after an argument over what he should and should not say in his writing.

Wright's harsh view of the life of African Americans was a revelation to white America. His first book, a collection of short fiction called *Uncle Tom's Children* published in 1938, won him high praise, and his 1940 novel *Native Son* became a classic portrayal of racial oppression. This brutally honest story of a ghetto dweller driven to crime and then cruelly punished by a society he cannot understand was a best-seller and was made into a hit play.

Driven always by the belief "that Negro life was a sprawling land of unconscious suffering," Wright published twelve more books of fiction, autobiography, travel pieces, and social criticism. His was one of America's most eloquent voices calling for racial justice.

See also African Americans; Literature.

For further reading: Joan Urban, *Richard Wright* (New York: Chelsea House, 1989).

DENNIS WEPMAN

X Y Z

XYZ Affair

During the 1790s France and Great Britain were at war. The United States had made an alliance with France during the War of Independence, but in 1793 President George Washington issued a neutrality proclamation. This angered the French, as did Washington's signing the Jay Treaty with Great Britain.

As neutrals, American merchants sought to trade with both sides. As a result both France and Great Britain seized many American vessels on the high seas—about six hundred in 1793 and 1794 alone. Hoping to end French attacks in 1797, President John Adams sent three diplomats to Paris to negotiate a settlement. They were met by three agents who told them they must pay a bribe of $250,000 to Foreign Minister Charles Maurice Talleyrand before negotiations could begin. The Americans flatly refused. "No, no, not a sixpence," one of the Americans, Charles Pinckney, told them.

The three Americans then returned home. Their report, which identified the French agents as X, Y, and Z, was published in April 1798. It caused a sensation. War seemed imminent. Congress voted to establish a cabinet-level Navy Department and appropriated money to build about fifty warships. Pinckney's refusal to pay a bribe was "translated" as "Millions for defense, but not one cent for tribute!" A two-year "quasi-war" with France

followed as American privateers attacked French merchant ships. Damage on both sides was heavy. Peace did not come until 1800 when Adams sent a new team of diplomats to Paris. There the political climate had changed, and they were able to negotiate a peace treaty without bribing anyone or being asked for a bribe.

Yalta Conference

In February 1945, when the defeat of Germany was almost certain, President Franklin D. Roosevelt, Prime Minister Winston Churchill of Great Britain, and Premier Joseph Stalin of the Soviet Union met at Yalta, a resort in the Crimea, to decide the future of Europe. They agreed to demand the unconditional surrender of Germany and to divide it into four zones, to be occupied by their three nations and France. They also agreed to meet again in April in San Francisco to draft a charter for an international organization, the United Nations.

These decisions were reached without argument and were carried out without difficulty. More controversial and far less successful was the attempt of the three leaders to settle the future of the countries of Eastern Europe that had been overrun by Germany and were currently occupied by the victorious Red Army. The Soviets were determined

British Prime Minister Winston Churchill (left), President Franklin D. Roosevelt (center), and Soviet premier Joseph Stalin (right) meet at the Yalta Conference.

to protect their western border from any future attack by establishing governments they could control in Hungary, Romania, and especially Poland, the country across which Hitler's armies had marched when they invaded the Soviet Union. The trouble with this was that the people of these nations, and again especially the people of Poland, were strongly anti-Russian.

Roosevelt and Churchill agreed to allow Stalin to annex the eastern part of Poland, but they insisted that he allow free elections in the rest of the country. Stalin promised to do so, but he never did; postwar Poland was run by an unelected pro-Soviet government. This became a source of resentment in the United States and a major cause of the cold war.

See also Cold War; World War II.

YMCA/YWCA

The Young Men's Christian Association is an international volunteer organization intended to promote physical, mental, and spiritual welfare. Although originally focused on young Christian men in England, it now serves both men and women of all ages and religions in over ninety countries. The Y M C A offers recreational facilities, health programs, senior citizens' activities, academic education, vocational training, and residential and hotel accommodations. Its symbol, an inverted triangle, represents the Y's triple objective: development of mind, body, and spirit.

The Y M C A was founded in London in 1844 to provide young shop clerks from the countryside with a place to study the Bible and to find respectable lodgings. Six years later, associations with the same name and purpose opened in Boston, Massachusetts, and Montreal, Canada. Local Y's belong to the National Council of Young Men's Christian Associations of the United States of America (Y M C A–U S A), headquartered in Chicago and affiliated with the World Alliance of Y M C A's.

Public gymnasiums became an important part of the American Y M C A soon after it was founded. The organization's first swimming pool opened in 1856 in Brooklyn, New York. In 1891, basketball was invented at a Y M C A in Springfield, Massachusetts, and four years later a physical education instructor at the Holyoke, Massachusetts, Y invented volleyball.

The San Francisco Y M C A admitted women in 1874, and women and girls now compose about 25 percent of the membership of the American association. A separate organization, the Young Women's Christian Association (Y W C A), was organized in London in 1855. It came to the United States as the Young

Ladies' Christian Association in 1858 and is now the world's largest organization of women. The American YWCA has more than 4 million members.

The YMCA–USA provides some 1,400 gyms and pools, 2,600 handball courts, 1,000 tennis courts, 275 camps, and 250 residences. In 1993 its membership numbered nearly 13 million.

DENNIS WEPMAN

YOUNG, BRIGHAM

(1801–77) *Mormon leader, western colonizer, and Utah's first governor.*

Born in southern Vermont, Young was the ninth of eleven children. His family moved to western New York when he was three. After his mother died in 1815 he left home to make his living as a carpenter, cabinetmaker, painter, and landscape gardener.

Young was baptized a member of the Church of Jesus Christ of Latter-day Saints (Mormon) in 1832 and became a preaching missionary. He soon moved his family to northeastern Ohio, where he did carpentry work and continued missionary endeavors in New England and Canada. He was ordained an apostle in 1835 and directed missionary work, migration and settlement, and construction projects for the church. He was a missionary in Great Britain in 1840–41 and upon his return was placed in charge of business operations. When Joseph Smith, founder of the church, was assassinated in 1844, Young was chosen to succeed him and continued as leader of the Mormons until his death in 1877.

Between 1846 and 1852, Young directed the migration of sixteen thousand Mormons from Illinois to the Salt Lake Valley, and over the years shepherded another eighty thousand Mormon converts from Great Britain, Scandinavia, and continental Europe to the American West. He also organized the colonization of 350 settlements in the mountain states and California.

Young supervised the erection and operation of a twelve-hundred-mile telegraph line that connected Mormon settlements with Salt Lake City, and then helped construct the Union Pacific and Central Pacific railroads and connecting branch lines that provided an efficient transportation network for western communities.

Young, a popular leader, kept informed by frequent travel and wrote thousands of letters giving counsel and advice. He advocated fairness in dealing with Native Americans. Builder of the famous Mormon Tabernacle and Theater in Salt Lake City, he also began the erection of the Salt Lake Temple. He founded many industries in Utah and several colleges and universities, including Brigham Young University and the University of Utah.

See also Mormons; Smith, Joseph.

For further reading: Olive Burt, *Brigham Young* (New York: Messner, 1956); Barbara Williams, *Brigham Young and Me, Clarissa* (Garden City, N. Y.: Doubleday, 1978).

LEONARD J. ARRINGTON

YOUNG ADULT LITERATURE
See Literature, Children's and Young Adult.

ZAHARIAS, BABE DIDRIKSON

(1911–56) *Athlete.*

Mildred Didrikson acquired her nickname "Babe" as a young girl: she hit so many home runs playing baseball with friends, they said she was "just like Babe Ruth," and the nickname stuck. Her extraordinary athletic ability, zest for life, and competitive drive appeared early. Growing up in a poor neighborhood in Beaumont, Texas, Babe was much given to rough-and-tumble sports. Never much of a student, she dropped out of school in 1930.

In those days, there were few opportunities for women athletes, but many businesses sponsored women's sports teams to compete in Amateur Athletic Union (AAU) games. Babe was recruited by a company as a typist and player for the firm's teams. She made her mark immediately. Chosen an All-American

Babe Didrickson Zaharias clowning with Babe Ruth. She had been nicknamed "Babe" after the baseball star because of her own baseball talents.

basketball player in 1930, 1931, and 1932, she led her team to a national championship in 1931. In the AAU's national track and field meet in 1932, she was the sole member of her team and won the meet *by herself,* scoring 30 points; the next best team had twenty-two members who *together* scored only 22 points.

Babe then went to Los Angeles for the 1932 Olympics. There she won two gold medals and set world records in the 80-meter hurdles and the javelin, breaking the javelin record by an astonishing 11 feet. She tied for first place in the high jump, setting another world record, but judges ruled against the way she made one jump and awarded her the silver medal.

Her performance at Los Angeles made national headlines. She became a favorite with reporters, who loved her colorful quips, high-spirited personality, and competitive zeal. She then traveled the country, making money and winning competitions in basketball, softball, tennis, swimming, diving, bowling; she even pitched in a few major league baseball exhibition games. In 1938 she and George Zaharias, a wrestler, were married. She became friends with the famous, including Amelia Earhart and even President Dwight D. Eisenhower.

In the meantime, Babe was mastering golf. She won eighty-two tournaments in the 1940s and 1950s, including a record seventeen consecutive tournaments in the mid-1940s. Spectators cheered her smashing drives. (She won a bet with Babe Ruth and embarrassed Ted Williams in public contests by driving golf balls farther than they did.) In 1947 she became the first American to win the prestigious British Ladies Amateur Championship. Chosen Woman Athlete of the Year six times, she was named Woman Athlete of the Half Century in 1950 by the Associated Press.

Babe was stricken with cancer in 1953 and underwent radical surgery. But only a year later, she was back on the links and won the U.S. Women's Open by twelve strokes, a record never broken. The cancer returned, however. When she died in September 1956, President Eisenhower opened a press conference by saying, "I should like to take one minute to pay a tribute to Mrs. Zaharias, Babe Didrikson. She was a woman who won the admiration of people all over the world. Everyone of us feels sad that finally she had to lose this last one of all her battles."

See also Olympic Games; Sports, Spectator.

For further reading: R. Rozanne Knudson, *Babe Didrikson: Athlete of the Century* (New York: Puffin Books, 1986); William R. Sanford, *Babe Didrikson Zaharias* (New York: Crestwood House, 1993).

CECILE RHINEHART WATTERS

ZENGER TRIAL

One of the earliest American tests of the principle of freedom of the press came about as a result of a petty quarrel over the amount of back salary owed a politician. In 1733 William Cosby, governor of the colony of New York, claimed that money was owed to him, but his claim was rejected by Judge Lewis Morris. Angered at the verdict, Governor Cosby then fired the judge.

To get back at him, Morris and his political allies founded a newspaper, the *New-York Weekly Journal,* edited and printed by John Peter Zenger. The paper began running articles charging Cosby with undermining the independence of the courts and stressing the right of people to criticize public officials. Cosby reacted swiftly. He arrested editor Zenger, charging him with seditious libel.

Zenger was held in jail for ten months incommunicado, meaning he was not allowed to communicate in any way with anyone outside the prison. His wife kept his paper going while he awaited trial in April 1735. Under the interpretation at that time of seditious libel, the truth of what was said or printed about an official was no excuse for printing unpleasant material about him. But Zenger's lawyer, Andrew Hamilton, argued that if an injurious statement about an official was indeed true, then it should not be considered libelous. The court refused to admit evidence of the truthfulness of the paper's remarks about Cosby, but the jury nonetheless acquitted Zenger. The case became a precedent. Today it is accepted that truth is an adequate defense against the charge of libel.

See also Freedom of the Press.

ZIEGFELD, FLORENZ

(1869–1932) *Theatrical producer.*

During the first two decades of the twentieth century, Ziegfeld made the revue, a series of musical skits, a popular form of American stage entertainment. His *Ziegfeld Follies* were noted for their artistry, lavish costumes, and exquisite show girls. The productions were extravagant reflections of American prosperity.

Ziegfeld launched his show business career by hiring musicians for the World's Columbian Exposition of 1893 in Chicago. He also managed Eugene Sandow, a famous strong man, who appeared at the Chicago fair and then toured the nation. Ziegfeld introduced French star Anna Held to American audiences in his show *A Parlor Match* (1896), using advertisements to publicize her many

The butterfly chorus in Florenz Ziegfeld's 1920 production of Sally. *His lavish productions represented the height of American show business and symbolized an America that was happy and prosperous.*

charms. He married her in 1897 and cast her in many of his productions. They divorced in 1913, and the next year he wed actress Billie Burke (who later played Glinda, the good witch, in the movie *The Wizard of Oz*).

He staged the first of twenty-one editions of the *Ziegfeld Follies* during the summer of 1907. Wanting to "glorify the American girl," he personally selected a chorus line of glamorous women to appear in each show and dressed them in highly ornate costumes. He idealized tall, slender young women, and they soon replaced the ample, full-figured female as a symbol of beauty in the popular culture.

His revues presented comedy sketches, songs and dances, and specialty acts. They were showcases for the leading performers of the day, including Fanny Brice, Eddie Cantor, Will Rogers, and Ed Wynn. The *Follies* featured the music of such well-known composers as Irving Berlin, Jerome Kern, and Victor Herbert. Among the popular songs Ziegfeld stars introduced were "A Pretty Girl Is Like a Melody," "Shine On, Harvest Moon," and "My Blue Heaven." Each production was more spectacular and elaborate than the previous one. Ziegfeld also produced some memorable Broadway shows, such as *Showboat* (1927) and *Bittersweet* (1929), before his death in 1932.

See also Theater.

BARBARA SILBERDICK FEINBERG

APPENDIXES

Map of the United States
The States
Population of the United States
The Declaration of Independence
The Constitution of the United States

CONTRIBUTORS

ILLUSTRATION CREDITS

INDEX OF CONTRIBUTORS

GENERAL INDEX

The United States

CANADA

ATLANTIC OCEAN

PACIFIC OCEAN

Gulf of Mexico

MEXICO

BAHAMAS

CUBA

N E S W

States and capitals

MAINE — Augusta
N. H. — Concord
VERMONT — Montpelier
MASS. — Boston
RHODE ISLAND — Providence
CONN. — Hartford
NEW YORK — Albany
NEW JERSEY — Trenton
PENN. — Harrisburg
DELAWARE — Dover
MARYLAND — Annapolis
W. VA. — Charleston
VIRGINIA — Richmond
Washington, D. C.
Chesapeake Bay

NORTH CAROLINA — Raleigh
SOUTH CAROLINA — Columbia
GEORGIA — Atlanta
FLORIDA — Tallahassee
Lake Okeechobee

OHIO — Columbus
IND. — Indianapolis
MICHIGAN — Lansing
KENTUCKY — Frankfort
TENNESSEE — Nashville
ALABAMA — Montgomery
MISS. — Jackson
Ohio R.

WISCONSIN — Madison
ILLINOIS — Springfield
IOWA — Des Moines
MINNESOTA — St. Paul
MISSOURI — Jefferson City
ARKANSAS — Little Rock
LOUISIANA — Baton Rouge
Mississippi R.
Missouri R.

Lake Superior
Lake Michigan
Lake Huron
Lake Erie
Lake Ontario

NORTH DAKOTA — Bismarck
SOUTH DAKOTA — Pierre
NEBRASKA — Lincoln
KANSAS — Topeka
OKLAHOMA — Oklahoma City
TEXAS — Austin
Platte R.
Arkansas R.
Red R.
Rio Grande

MONTANA — Helena
WYOMING — Cheyenne
COLORADO — Denver
NEW MEXICO — Sante Fe
IDAHO — Boise
UTAH — Salt Lake City
ARIZONA — Phoenix
NEVADA — Carson City
CALIFORNIA — Sacramento
WASH. — Olympia
OREGON — Salem
Missouri R.
Snake R.
Columbia R.
Great Salt Lake
Colorado R.
Lake Powell
Gila R.

San Francisco Bay
Monterey Bay

500 miles
500 kilometers
250
250
0
0
Albers Equal-Area Projection

HAWAII
KAUAI
OAHU
Honolulu
MOLOKAI
MAUI
HAWAII
100 miles
100 kilometers
0

ALASKA
Juneau
KODIAK I.
Gulf of Alaska
ALEUTIAN IS.
Bering Sea
ARCTIC OCEAN
400 miles
400 kilometers
0

The States (Including the District of Columbia)

State	Capital	Year of Statehood	Order of Admission	Population*	Reps. in Congress†	Total Area (Sq. Mi.)	Largest City
Alabama	Montgomery	1819	22	4,040,587	7	52,423	Birmingham
Alaska	Juneau	1959	49	550,403	1	656,424	Anchorage
Arizona	Phoenix	1912	48	3,665,228	6	114,006	Phoenix
Arkansas	Little Rock	1836	25	2,350,725	4	53,182	Little Rock
California	Sacramento	1850	31	29,760,021	52	163,707	Los Angeles
Colorado	Denver	1876	38	3,294,394	6	104,100	Denver
Connecticut	Hartford	1788	5	3,287,116	6	5,544	Bridgeport
Delaware	Dover	1787	1	666,168	1	2,489	Wilmington
District of Columbia				606,900	0	68	Washington
Florida	Tallahassee	1845	27	12,937,926	23	65,758	Jacksonville
Georgia	Atlanta	1788	4	6,478,216	11	59,441	Atlanta
Hawaii	Honolulu	1959	50	1,108,229	2	10,932	Honolulu
Idaho	Boise	1890	43	1,006,749	2	83,574	Boise
Illinois	Springfield	1818	21	11,430,602	20	57,918	Chicago
Indiana	Indianapolis	1816	19	5,544,159	10	36,420	Indianapolis
Iowa	Des Moines	1846	29	2,776,755	5	56,276	Des Moines
Kansas	Topeka	1861	34	2,477,574	4	82,282	Wichita
Kentucky	Frankfort	1792	15	3,685,296	6	40,411	Louisville
Louisiana	Baton Rouge	1812	18	4,219,973	7	51,843	New Orleans
Maine	Augusta	1820	23	1,227,928	2	35,387	Portland
Maryland	Annapolis	1788	7	4,781,468	8	12,407	Baltimore
Massachusetts	Boston	1788	6	6,016,425	10	10,555	Boston
Michigan	Lansing	1837	26	9,295,297	16	96,810	Detroit
Minnesota	St. Paul	1858	32	4,375,099	8	86,943	Minneapolis
Mississippi	Jackson	1817	20	2,573,216	5	48,434	Jackson
Missouri	Jefferson City	1821	24	5,117,073	9	69,709	Kansas City
Montana	Helena	1889	41	799,065	1	147,046	Billings
Nebraska	Lincoln	1867	37	1,578,385	3	77,358	Omaha
Nevada	Carson City	1864	36	1,201,833	2	110,567	Las Vegas
New Hampshire	Concord	1788	9	1,109,252	2	9,351	Manchester
New Jersey	Trenton	1787	3	7,730,188	13	8,722	Newark
New Mexico	Santa Fe	1912	47	1,515,069	3	121,598	Albuquerque
New York	Albany	1788	11	17,990,455	31	54,475	New York City
North Carolina	Raleigh	1789	12	6,628,637	12	53,821	Charlotte
North Dakota	Bismarck	1889	39	638,800	1	70,704	Fargo
Ohio	Columbus	1803	17	10,847,115	19	44,828	Columbus
Oklahoma	Oklahoma City	1907	46	3,145,585	6	69,903	Oklahoma City
Oregon	Salem	1859	33	2,842,321	5	98,386	Portland
Pennsylvania	Harrisburg	1787	2	11,881,643	21	46,058	Philadelphia
Rhode Island	Providence	1790	13	1,003,464	2	1,545	Providence
South Carolina	Columbia	1788	8	3,486,703	6	32,007	Columbia
South Dakota	Pierre	1889	40	696,004	1	77,121	Sioux Falls
Tennessee	Nashville	1796	16	4,877,185	9	42,146	Memphis
Texas	Austin	1845	28	16,986,510	30	268,601	Houston
Utah	Salt Lake City	1896	45	1,722,850	3	84,904	Salt Lake City
Vermont	Montpelier	1791	14	562,758	1	9,615	Burlington
Virginia	Richmond	1788	10	6,187,358	11	42,769	Virginia Beach
Washington	Olympia	1889	42	4,866,692	9	71,303	Seattle
West Virginia	Charleston	1863	35	1,793,477	3	24,231	Charleston
Wisconsin	Madison	1848	30	4,891,769	9	65,503	Milwaukee
Wyoming	Cheyenne	1890	44	453,588	1	97,818	Cheyenne

*U.S. Bureau of the Census, 1990 figures.

†This column lists the number of members of the House of Representatives for each state; as provided in the Constitution, each state has, in addition, two senators.

POPULATION OF THE UNITED STATES BY CENSUS YEAR

Census Year	Population	% Change from last Census	Census Year	Population	% Change from last Census
1790	3,929,214	—	1900	75,994,575	20.7
1800	5,308,483	35.1	1910	91,972,266	21.0
1810	7,239,881	36.4	1920	105,710,620	14.9
1820	9,638,453	33.1	1930	122,775,046	16.1
1830	12,866,020	33.5	1940	131,669,275	7.2
1840	17,069,453	32.7	1950	151,325,798	14.5
1850	23,191,876	35.9	1960	179,323,175	18.5
1860	31,443,321	35.6	1970	203,211,926	13.3
1870	39,818,449	26.6	1980	226,504,825	11.5
1880	50,155,783	26.0	1990	248,709,873	9.8
1890	62,947,714	25.5			

THE DECLARATION OF INDEPENDENCE

July 4, 1776

THE UNANIMOUS DECLARATION OF THE THIRTEEN UNITED STATES OF AMERICA

When in the course of human events, it becomes necessary for one people to dissolve the political bonds which have connected them with another, and to assume, among the powers of the earth, the separate and equal station to which the laws of nature and of nature's God entitle them, a decent respect to the opinions of mankind requires that they should declare the causes which impel them to the separation.

We hold these truths to be self-evident: That all men are created equal; that they are endowed by their Creator with certain unalienable rights; that among these are life, liberty, and the pursuit of happiness; that, to secure these rights, governments are instituted among men, deriving their just powers from the consent of the governed; that whenever any form of government becomes destructive of these ends, it is the right of the people to alter or to abolish it, and to institute new government, laying its foundation on such principles, and organizing its powers in such form, as to them shall seem most likely to effect their safety and happiness. Prudence, indeed, will dictate that governments long established should not be changed for light and transient causes; and accordingly all experience hath shown that mankind are more disposed to suffer, while evils are sufferable, than to right themselves by abolishing the forms to which they are accustomed. But when a long train of abuses and usurpations, pursuing invariably the same object, evinces a design to reduce them under absolute despotism, it is their right, it is their duty, to throw off such government, and to provide new guards for their future security. Such has been the patient sufferance of these colonies; and such is now the necessity which constrains them to alter their former systems of government. The history of the present King of Great Britain is a history of repeated injuries and usurpations, all having in direct object the establishment of an absolute tyranny over these states. To prove this, let facts be submitted to a candid world.

He has refused his assent to laws, the most wholesome and necessary for the public good.

He has forbidden his governors to pass laws of immediate and pressing importance, unless suspended in their operation till his assent should be obtained; and, when so suspended, he has utterly neglected to attend to them.

He has refused to pass other laws for the accommodation of large districts of people, unless those people would relinquish the right of representation in the legislature, a right inestimable to them, and formidable to tyrants only.

He has called together legislative bodies at places unusual, uncomfortable, and distant from the depository of their public records, for the sole purpose of fatiguing them into compliance with his measures.

He has dissolved representative houses repeatedly, for opposing, with manly firmness, his invasions on the rights of the people.

He has refused for a long time, after such dissolutions, to cause others to be elected; whereby the legislative powers, incapable of annihilation, have returned to the people at large for their exercise; the state remaining, in the mean time, exposed to all the dangers of invasions from without and convulsions within.

He has endeavored to prevent the population of these states; for that purpose obstructing the laws for the naturalization of foreigners; refusing to pass others to encourage their migration hither, and raising the conditions of new appropriations of lands.

He has obstructed the administration of justice, by refusing his assent to laws for establishing judiciary powers.

He has made judges dependent on his will alone, for the tenure of their offices, and the amount of payment of their salaries.

He has erected a multitude of new offices, and sent hither swarms of officers to harass our people and eat out their substance.

He has kept among us, in times of peace, standing armies, without the consent of our legislatures.

He has affected to render the military independent of, and superior to, the civil power.

He has combined with others to subject us to a jurisdiction foreign to our constitution and unacknowledged by our laws, giving his assent to their acts of pretended legislation:

For quartering large bodies of armed troops among us;

For protecting them, by a mock trial, from punishment for any murders which they should commit on the inhabitants of these states;

For cutting off our trade with all parts of the world;

For imposing taxes on us without our consent;

For depriving us, in many cases, of the benefits of trial by jury;

For transporting us beyond seas, to be tried for pretended offenses;

For abolishing the free system of English laws in a neighboring province, establishing therein an arbitrary government, and enlarging its boundaries, so as to render it at once an example and fit instrument for introducing the same absolute rule into these colonies;

For taking away our charters, abolishing our most valuable laws, and altering fundamentally the forms of our governments;

For suspending our own legislatures, and declaring themselves invested with power to legislate for us in all cases whatsoever.

He has abdicated government here, by declaring us out of his protection and waging war against us.

He has plundered our seas, ravaged our coasts, burned our towns, and destroyed the lives of our people.

He is at this time transporting large armies of foreign mercenaries to complete the works of death, desolation, and tyranny already begun with circumstances of cruelty and perfidy scarcely paralleled in the most barbarous ages, and totally unworthy the head of a civilized nation.

He has constrained our fellow-citizens, taken captive on the high seas, to bear arms against their country, to become the executioners of their friends and brethren, or to fall themselves by their hands.

He has excited domestic insurrection among us, and has endeavored to bring on the inhabitants of our frontiers, the merciless Indian savages, whose known rule of warfare is an undistinguished destruction of all ages, sexes, and conditions.

In every stage of these oppressions we have petitioned for redress in the most humble terms; our repeated petitions have been answered only by repeated injury. A prince, whose character is thus marked by every act which may define a tyrant, is unfit to be the ruler of a free people.

Nor have we been wanting in our attentions to our British brethren. We have warned them, from time to time, of attempts by their legislature to extend an unwarrantable jurisdiction over us. We have reminded them of the circumstances of our emigration and settlement here. We have appealed to their native justice and magnanimity; and we have conjured them, by the ties of our common kindred, to disavow these usurpations, which would inevitably interrupt our connections and correspondence. They, too, have been deaf to the voice of justice and of consanguinity. We must, therefore, acquiesce in the necessity which denounces our separation, and hold them, as we hold the rest of mankind, enemies in war, in peace friends.

We, therefore, the representatives of the United States of America, in General Congress assembled, appealing to the Supreme Judge of the world for the rectitude of our intentions, do, in the name and by the authority of the good people of these colonies, solemnly publish and declare, that these United Colonies are, and of right ought to be, FREE AND INDEPENDENT STATES, that they are absolved from all allegiance to the British crown, and that all political connection between them and the state of Great Britain is, and ought to be, totally dissolved; and that, as free and independent states, they have full power to levy war, conclude peace, contract alliances, establish commerce, and do all other acts and things which independent states may of right do. And for the support of this declaration, with a firm reliance on the protection of Divine Providence, we mutually pledge to each other our lives, our fortunes, and our sacred honor.

John Hancock

NEW HAMPSHIRE

Josiah Bartlett

William Whipple

Matthew Thornton

MASSACHUSETTS

John Adams

Samuel Adams

Robert Treat Paine

Elbridge Gerry

NEW YORK

William Floyd

Philip Livingston

Francis Lewis

Lewis Morris

RHODE ISLAND

Stephen Hopkins

William Ellery

NEW JERSEY

Richard Stockton

John Witherspoon

Francis Hopkinson

John Hart

Abraham Clark

PENNSYLVANIA

Robert Morris

Benjamin Rush

Benjamin Franklin

John Morton

George Clymer

James Smith

George Taylor

James Wilson

George Ross

DELAWARE

Caesar Rodney

George Read

Thomas McKean

MARYLAND

Samuel Chase

William Paca

Thomas Stone

Charles Carroll of Carrollton

NORTH CAROLINA

William Hooper

Joseph Hewes

John Penn

VIRGINIA

George Wythe

Richard Henry Lee

Thomas Jefferson

Benjamin Harrison

Thomas Nelson, Jr.

Francis Lightfoot Lee

Carter Braxton

SOUTH CAROLINA

Edward Rutledge

Thomas Heyward, Jr.

Thomas Lynch, Jr.

Arthur Middleton

CONNECTICUT

Roger Sherman

Samuel Huntington

William Williams

Oliver Wolcott

GEORGIA

Button Gwinnett

Lyman Hall

George Walton

THE CONSTITUTION
OF THE UNITED STATES

Preamble*

We the people of the United States, in order to form a more perfect union, establish justice, insure domestic tranquility, provide for the common defense, promote the general welfare, and secure the blessings of liberty to ourselves and our posterity, do ordain and establish this Constitution for the United States of America.

Article I
Legislative Branch

SECTION 1. CONGRESS

All legislative powers herein granted shall be vested in a Congress of the United States, which shall consist of a Senate and House of Representatives.

SECTION 2.
HOUSE OF REPRESENTATIVES

1. Election and Terms of Members.   The House of Representatives shall be composed of members chosen every second year by the people of the several States, and the electors in each State shall have the qualifications requisite for electors of the most numerous branch of the State Legislature.

2. Qualifications.   No person shall be a Representative who shall not have attained to the age of twenty-five years, and been seven years a citizen of the United States, and who shall not, when elected, be an inhabitant of that State in which he shall be chosen.

3. Number of Representatives per State.   Representatives and *direct taxes* shall be apportioned among the several States which may be included within this Union, according to their respective numbers, *which shall be determined by adding to the whole number of free persons, including those bound to service for a term of years, and excluding Indians not taxed, three-fifths of all other persons.*† The actual enumeration shall be made within three years after the first meeting of the Congress of the United States, and within every subsequent term of ten years, in such manner as they shall by law direct. The number of Representatives shall not exceed one for every thirty thousand, but each State shall have at least one Representative; *and until such enumeration shall be made, the State of New Hampshire shall be entitled to choose three, Massachusetts eight, Rhode Island and Providence Plantations one, Connecticut five, New York six, New Jersey four, Pennsylvania eight, Delaware one, Maryland six, Virginia ten, North Carolina five, South Carolina five, and Georgia three.*

4. Vacancies.   When vacancies happen in the representation from any State, the Executive authority thereof shall issue writs of election to fill such vacancies.

5. Special Powers.   The House of Representatives shall choose their Speaker and other officers, and shall have the sole power of impeachment.

SECTION 3. SENATE

1. Number, Term, and Selection of Members.   The Senate of the United States shall be composed of two Senators from each State, *chosen by the Legislature thereof,* for six years; and each Senator shall have one vote.

2. Overlapping Terms and Filling Vacancies.   Immediately after they shall be assembled in consequence of

---

* The titles of the Preamble, and of each article, section, clause and amendment have been added to make the Constitution easier to read. These titles are not in the original document.

†Parts of the Constitution have been italicized to show that they are not in force any more. They have been changed by amendments or they no longer apply.

the first election, they shall be divided as equally as may be into three classes. *The seats of the Senators of the first class shall be vacated at the expiration of the second year, of the second class at the expiration of the fourth year, and of the third class at the expiration of the sixth year,* so that one-third may be chosen every second year; *and if vacancies happen by resignation, or otherwise, during the recess of the Legislature of any State, the Executive thereof may make temporary appointments until the next meeting of the Legislature, which shall then fill such vacancies.*

3. *Qualifications.*   No person shall be a Senator who shall not have attained to the age of thirty years, and been nine years a citizen of the United States, and who shall not, when elected, be an inhabitant of that State for which he shall be chosen.

4. *President of the Senate.*   The Vice President of the United States shall be President of the Senate, but shall have no vote, unless they be equally divided.

5. *Other Officers.*   The Senate shall choose their other officers, and also a President pro tempore, in the absence of the Vice President, or when he shall exercise the office of President of the United States.

6. *Impeachment Trials.*   The Senate shall have the sole power to try all impeachments. When sitting for that purpose, they shall be on oath or affirmation. When the President of the United States is tried, the Chief Justice shall preside: and no person shall be convicted without the concurrence of two-thirds of the members present.

7. *Penalties.*   Judgment in cases of impeachment shall not extend further than to removal from office, and disqualification to hold and enjoy any office of honor, trust or profit under the United States: but the party convicted shall nevertheless be liable and subject to indictment, trial, judgment and punishment, according to law.

SECTION 4.
ELECTIONS AND MEETINGS

1. *Election of Congress.*   The times, places and manner of holding elections for Senators and Representatives shall be prescribed in each State by the Legislature thereof; but the Congress may at any time by law make or alter such regulations, except as to the places of choosing Senators.

2. *Annual Sessions.*   The Congress shall assemble at least once in every year, *and such meeting shall be on the first Monday in December, unless they shall by law appoint a different day.*

SECTION 5.   RULES OF PROCEDURE

1. *Organization.*   Each house shall be the judge of the elections, returns and qualifications of its own members, and a majority of each shall constitute a quorum to do business; but a smaller number may adjourn from day to day, and may be authorized to compel the attendance of absent members, in such manner, and under such penalties as each house may provide.

2. *Rules.*   Each house may determine the rules of its proceedings, punish its members for disorderly behavior, and, with the concurrence of two-thirds, expel a member.

3. *Journal.*   Each house shall keep a journal of its proceedings, and from time to time publish the same, excepting such parts as may in their judgment require secrecy; and the yeas and nays of the members of either house on any question shall, at the desire of one-fifth of those present, be entered on the journal.

4. *Adjournment.*   Neither house, during the session of Congress, shall, without the consent of the other, adjourn for more than three days, nor to any other place than that in which the two houses shall be sitting.

SECTION 6.
PRIVILEGES AND RESTRICTIONS

1. *Pay and Protection.*   The Senators and Representatives shall receive a compensation for their services, to be ascertained by law, and paid out of the treasury of the United States. They shall in all cases, except treason, felony and breach of the peace, be privileged from arrest during their attendance at the session of their respective houses, and in going to and returning from the same; and for any speech or debate in either house, they shall not be questioned in any other place.

2. *Restrictions.*   No Senator or Representative shall, during the time for which he was elected, be appointed to any civil office under the authority of the United States, which shall have been created, or the emoluments whereof shall have been increased during such time; and no person holding any office under the

United States shall be a member of either house during his continuance in office.

SECTION 7. MAKING LAWS

1. Tax Bills.   All bills for raising revenue shall originate in the House of Representatives; but the Senate may propose or concur with amendments as on other bills.

2. Passing a Law.   Every bill which shall have passed the House of Representatives and the Senate, shall, before it become a law, be presented to the President of the United States; if he approve he shall sign it, but if not he shall return it, with his objections to that house in which it shall have originated, who shall enter the objections at large on their journal, and proceed to reconsider it. If after such reconsideration two-thirds of that house shall agree to pass the bill, it shall be sent, together with the objections, to the other house, by which it shall likewise be reconsidered, and if approved by two-thirds of that house, it shall become a law. But in all such cases the votes of both houses shall be determined by yeas and nays, and the names of the persons voting for and against the bill shall be entered on the journal of each house respectively. If any bill shall not be returned by the President within ten days (Sundays excepted) after it shall have been presented to him, the same shall be a law, in like manner as if he had signed it, unless the Congress by their adjournment prevent its return, in which case it shall not be a law.

3. Orders and Resolutions.   Every order, resolution, or vote to which the concurrence of the Senate and House of Representatives may be necessary (except on a question of adjournment) shall be presented to the President of the United States; and before the same shall take effect, shall be approved by him, or being disapproved by him, shall be repassed by two-thirds of the Senate and House of Representatives, according to the rules and limitations prescribed in the case of a bill.

SECTION 8.
POWERS DELEGATED TO CONGRESS

1. Taxation.   The Congress shall have power to lay and collect taxes, duties, imposts, and excises, to pay the debts and provide for the common defense and general welfare of the United States; but all duties, imposts and excises shall be uniform throughout the United States;

2. Borrowing.   To borrow money on the credit of the United States;

3. Commerce.   To regulate commerce with foreign nations, and among the several States, and with the Indian tribes;

4. Naturalization and Bankruptcy.   To establish a uniform rule of naturalization, and uniform laws on the subject of bankruptcies throughout the United States;

5. Coins and Measures.   To coin money, regulate the value thereof, and of foreign coin, and fix the standard of weights and measures;

6. Counterfeiting.   To provide for the punishment of counterfeiting the securities and current coin of the United States;

7. Post Offices.   To establish post offices and post roads;

8. Copyrights and Patents.   To promote the progress of science and useful arts by securing for limited times to authors and inventors the exclusive right to their respective writings and discoveries;

9. Courts.   To constitute tribunals inferior to the Supreme Court;

10. Piracy.   To define and punish piracies and felonies committed on the high seas, and offenses against the law of nations;

11. Declaring War.   To declare war, *grant letters of marque and reprisal,* and make rules concerning captures on land and water;

12. Army.   To raise and support armies, but no appropriation of money to that use shall be for a longer term than two years;

13. Navy.   To provide and maintain a navy;

14. Military Regulations.   To make rules for the government and regulation of the land and naval forces;

15. Militia.   To provide for calling forth the militia to execute the laws of the Union, suppress insurrections and repel invasions;

16. Militia Regulations.   To provide for organizing, arming, and disciplining the militia, and for governing such part of them as may be employed in the service of the United States, reserving to the States respectively the appointment of the officers, and the authority of training the militia according to the discipline prescribed by Congress;

17. National Capital. To exercise exclusive legislation in all cases whatsoever, over such district (not exceeding ten miles square) as may, by cession of particular States and the acceptance of Congress, become the seat of government of the United States, and to exercise like authority over all places purchased by the consent of the Legislature of the State in which the same shall be, for the erection of forts, magazines, arsenals, dockyards, and other needful buildings; and

18. Necessary Laws. To make all laws which shall be necessary and proper for carrying into execution the foregoing powers, and all other powers vested by this Constitution in the government of the United States, or in any department or officer thereof.

SECTION 9.
POWERS DENIED TO CONGRESS

1. Slave Trade. The migration or importation of such persons as any of the States now existing shall think proper to admit shall not be prohibited by the Congress prior to the year one thousand eight hundred and eight, but a tax or duty may be imposed on such importation, not exceeding ten dollars for each person.

2. Habeas Corpus. The privilege of the writ of habeas corpus shall not be suspended, unless when in cases of rebellion or invasion the public safety may require it.

3. Special Laws. No bill of attainder or ex post facto law shall be passed.

4. Direct Taxes. No capitation, or other direct, tax shall be laid, unless in proportion to the census or enumeration herein before directed to be taken.

5. Export Taxes. No tax or duty shall be laid on articles exported from any State.

6. Ports. No preference shall be given by any regulation of commerce or revenue to the ports of one State over those of another; nor shall vessels bound to, or from, one State be obliged to enter, clear, or pay duties in another.

7. Regulations on Spending. No money shall be drawn from the treasury, but in consequence of appropriations made by law; and a regular statement and account of the receipts and expenditures of all public money shall be published from time to time.

8. Titles of Nobility and Gifts. No title of nobility shall be granted by the United States; and no person holding any office of profit or trust under them, shall, without the consent of the Congress, accept of any present, emolument, office, or title, of any kind whatever, from any king, prince, or foreign State.

SECTION 10.
POWERS DENIED TO THE STATES

1. Complete Restrictions. No State shall enter into any treaty, alliance, or confederation; grant letters of marque and reprisal; coin money; emit bills of credit; make anything but gold and silver coin a tender in payment of debts; pass any bill of attainder, ex post facto law, or law impairing the obligation of contracts, or grant any title of nobility.

2. Partial Restrictions. No State shall, without the consent of the Congress, lay any imposts or duties on imports or exports, except what may be absolutely necessary for executing its inspection laws; and the net produce of all duties and imposts laid by any State on imports or exports, shall be for the use of the treasury of the United States; and all such laws shall be subject to the revision and control of the Congress.

3. Other Restrictions. No State shall, without the consent of the Congress, lay any duty of tonnage, keep troops, or ships of war in time of peace, enter into any agreement or compact with another State, or with a foreign power, or engage in war, unless actually invaded, or in such imminent danger as will not admit of delay.

Article II
Executive Branch

SECTION 1.
PRESIDENT AND VICE PRESIDENT

1. Term of Office. The executive power shall be vested in a President of the United States of America. He shall hold his office during the term of four years, and, together with the Vice President, chosen for the same term, be elected as follows:

2. Electoral College. Each State shall appoint, in such manner as the legislature thereof may direct, a number of electors, equal to the whole number of Senators and Representatives to which the State may be entitled in the Congress; but no Senator or Representative, or person holding an office of trust or profit under the United States, shall be appointed an elector.

3. Election Process. *The electors shall meet in their respective States, and vote by ballot for two persons, of whom one at least shall not be an inhabitant of the same State with themselves. And they shall make a list of all the persons voted for, and of the number of votes for each; which list they shall sign and certify, and transmit sealed to the seat of the government of the United States, directed to the President of the Senate. The President of the Senate shall, in the presence of the Senate and House of Representatives, open all the certificates, and the votes shall then be counted. The person having the greatest number of votes shall be the President, if such number be a majority of the whole number of electors appointed, and if there be more than one who have such majority, and have an equal number of votes, then the House of Representatives shall immediately choose by ballot one of them for President; and if no person have a majority, then from the five highest on the list the said house shall in like manner choose the President. But in choosing the President, the votes shall be taken by States, the representation from each State having one vote; a quorum for this purpose shall consist of a member or members from two-thirds of the States, and a majority of all the States shall be necessary to a choice. In every case, after the choice of the President, the person having the greatest number of votes of the electors shall be the Vice President. But if there should remain two or more who have equal votes, the Senate shall choose from them by ballot the Vice President.*

4. Time of Elections. The Congress may determine the time of choosing the electors, and the day on which they shall give their votes; which day shall be the same throughout the United States.

5. Qualifications. No person except a natural-born citizen, *or a citizen of the United States at the time of the adoption of this Constitution,* shall be eligible to the office of President; neither shall any person be eligible to that office who shall not have attained to the age of thirty-five years, and been fourteen years a resident within the United States.

6. Vacancies. In case of the removal of the President from office, or of his death, resignation, or inability to discharge the powers and duties of the said office, the same shall devolve on the Vice President, and the Congress may by law provide for the case of removal, death, resignation, or inability, both of the President and Vice President, declaring what officer shall then act as President, and such officer shall act accordingly,

until the disability be removed, or a President shall be elected.

7. Salary. The President shall, at stated times, receive for his services a compensation, which shall neither be increased nor diminished during the period for which he shall have been elected, and he shall not receive within that period any other emolument from the United States, or any of them.

8. Oath of Office. Before he enter on the execution of his office, he shall take the following oath or affirmation:—"I do solemnly swear (or affirm) that I will faithfully execute the office of President of the United States, and will to the best of my ability, preserve, protect and defend the Constitution of the United States."

SECTION 2.

POWERS OF THE PRESIDENT

1. Military Powers. The President shall be commander in chief of the army and navy of the United States, and of the militia of the several States, when called into the actual service of the United States; he may require the opinion, in writing, of the principal officer in each of the executive departments, upon any subject relating to the duties of their respective offices, and he shall have power to grant reprieves and pardons for offenses against the United States, except in cases of impeachment.

2. Treaties and Appointments. He shall have power, by and with the advice and consent of the Senate, to make treaties, provided two-thirds of the Senators present concur; and he shall nominate, and by and with the advice and consent of the Senate, shall appoint ambassadors, other public ministers and consuls, judges of the Supreme Court, and all other officers of the United States, whose appointments are not herein otherwise provided for, and which shall be established by law: but the Congress may by law vest the appointment of such inferior officers, as they think proper, in the President alone, in the courts of law, or in the heads of departments.

3. Temporary Appointments. The President shall have power to fill up all vacancies that may happen during the recess of the Senate, by granting commissions which shall expire at the end of their next session.

SECTION 3.   DUTIES

He shall from time to time give to the Congress information of the State of the Union, and recommend to their consideration such measures as he shall judge necessary and expedient; he may on extraordinary occasions, convene both houses, or either of them, and in case of disagreement between them with respect to the time of adjournment, he may adjourn them to such time as he shall think proper; he shall receive ambassadors and other public ministers; he shall take care that the laws be faithfully executed, and shall commission all the officers of the United States.

SECTION 4.   IMPEACHMENT

The President, Vice President and all civil officers of the United States, shall be removed from office on impeachment for, and conviction of, treason, bribery, or other high crimes and misdemeanors.

Article III
Judicial Branch

SECTION 1.   FEDERAL COURTS

The judicial power of the United States shall be vested in one Supreme Court, and in such inferior courts as the Congress may from time to time ordain and establish. The judges, both of the Supreme and inferior courts, shall hold their offices during good behavior, and shall, at stated times, receive for their services, a compensation which shall not be diminished during their continuance in office.

SECTION 2.
AUTHORITY OF THE FEDERAL COURTS

1. *General Jurisdiction.*   The judicial power shall extend to all cases, in law and equity, arising under this Constitution, the laws of the United States, and treaties made, or which shall be made, under their authority;—to all cases affecting ambassadors, other public ministers and consuls;—to all cases of admiralty and maritime jurisdiction;—to controversies to which the United States shall be a party;—to controversies between two or more States;—*between a State and citizens of another State;*—between citizens of different States;—between citizens of the same State claiming lands under grants of different States, and between a State, or the citizens thereof, and foreign states, citizens or subjects.

2. *The Supreme Court.*   In all cases affecting ambassadors, other public ministers and consuls, and those in which a State shall be party, the Supreme Court shall have original jurisdiction. In all the other cases before mentioned, the Supreme Court shall have appellate jurisdiction, both as to law and fact, with such exceptions, and under such regulations as the Congress shall make.

3. *Trial by Jury.*   The trial of all crimes, except in cases of impeachment, shall be by jury; and such trial shall be held in the State where the said crimes shall have been committed; but when not committed within any State, the trial shall be at such place or places as the Congress may by law have directed.

SECTION 3.   TREASON

1. *Definition.*   Treason against the United States shall consist only in levying war against them, or in adhering to their enemies, giving them aid and comfort. No person shall be convicted of treason unless on the testimony of two witnesses to the same overt act, or on confession in open court.

2. *Punishment.*   The Congress shall have power to declare the punishment of treason, but no attainder of treason shall work corruption of blood, or forfeiture except during the life of the person attainted.

Article IV
Relations among the States

SECTION 1.   OFFICIAL RECORDS

Full faith and credit shall be given in each State to the public acts, records, and judicial proceedings of every other State. And the Congress may by general laws prescribe the manner in which such acts, records, and proceedings shall be proved, and the effect thereof.

SECTION 2.
PRIVILEGES OF THE CITIZENS

1. *Privileges.*   The citizens of each State shall be entitled to all privileges and immunities of citizens in the several States.

2. *Return of a Person Accused of a Crime.*   A person charged in any State with treason, felony, or other crime, who shall flee from justice, and be found in another State, shall on demand of the executive authority of the State from which he fled, be delivered

up, to be removed to the State having jurisdiction of the crime.

3. Return of Fugitive Slaves.   No person held to service or labor in one State, under the laws thereof, escaping into another, shall, in consequence of any law or regulation therein, be discharged from such service or labor, but shall be delivered up on claim of the party to whom such service or labor may be due.

SECTION 3.
NEW STATES AND TERRITORIES

1. New States.   New States may be admitted by the Congress into this Union; but no new State shall be formed or erected within the jurisdiction of any other State; nor any State be formed by the junction of two or more States or parts of States, without the consent of the Legislatures of the States concerned as well as of the Congress.

2. Federal Lands.   The Congress shall have power to dispose of and make all needful rules and regulations respecting the territory or other property belonging to the United States; and nothing in this Constitution shall be so construed as to prejudice any claims of the United States, or of any particular State.

SECTION 4.
GUARANTEES TO THE STATES

The United States shall guarantee to every State in this Union a republican form of government, and shall protect each of them against invasion; and on application of the Legislature, or of the executive (when the Legislature cannot be convened) against domestic violence.

Article V
Amending the Constitution

The Congress, whenever two-thirds of both houses shall deem it necessary, shall propose amendments to this Constitution, or, on the application of the Legislatures of two-thirds of the several States, shall call a convention for proposing amendments, which, in either case, shall be valid to all intents and purposes, as part of this Constitution, when ratified by the Legislatures of three-fourths of the several States, or by con-

ventions in three-fourths thereof, as the one or the other mode of ratification may be proposed by the Congress; provided *that no amendments which may be made prior to the year one thousand eight hundred and eight shall in any manner affect the first and fourth clauses in the ninth section of the first article; and* that no State, without its consent, shall be deprived of its equal suffrage in the Senate.

Article VI
General Provisions

1. Public Debt.   All debts contracted and engagements entered into, before the adoption of this Constitution, shall be as valid against the United States under this Constitution, as under the Confederation.

2. Federal Supremacy.   This Constitution, and the laws of the United States which shall be made in pursuance thereof; and all treaties made, or which shall be made, under the authority of the United States, shall be the supreme law of the land; and the judges in every State shall be bound thereby, anything in the Constitution or laws of any State to the contrary notwithstanding.

3. Oaths of Office.   The Senators and Representatives before mentioned, and the members of the several State Legislatures, and all executive and judicial officers, both of the United States, and of the several States, shall be bound by oath or affirmation to support this Constitution; but no religious test shall ever be required as a qualification to any office or public trust under the United States.

Article VII
Ratification

The ratification of the conventions of nine States shall be sufficient for the establishment of this Constitution between the States so ratifying the same.

   Done in Convention by the unanimous consent of the States present the seventeenth day of September in the year of our Lord one thousand seven hundred and eighty-seven and of the independence of the United States of America the twelfth. In witness whereof we have hereunto subscribed our names.

George Washington, President and Deputy from Virginia

DELAWARE

George Read

Gunning Bedford, Junior

John Dickinson

Richard Bassett

Jacob Broom

MARYLAND

James McHenry

Daniel of St. Thomas Jenifer

Daniel Carroll

VIRGINIA

John Blair

James Madison, Junior

NORTH CAROLINA

William Blount

Richard Dobbs Spaight

Hugh Williamson

SOUTH CAROLINA

John Rutledge

Charles Cotesworth Pinckney

Charles Pinckney

Pierce Butler

GEORGIA

William Few

Abraham Baldwin

NEW HAMPSHIRE

John Langdon

Nicholas Gilman

MASSACHUSETTS

Nathaniel Gorham

Rufus King

CONNECTICUT

William Samuel Johnson

Roger Sherman

NEW YORK

Alexander Hamilton

NEW JERSEY

William Livingston

David Brearley

William Paterson

Jonathan Dayton

PENNSYLVANIA

Benjamin Franklin

Thomas Mifflin

Robert Morris

George Clymer

Thomas FitzSimmons

Jared Ingersoll

James Wilson

Gouverneur Morris

AMENDMENTS
TO THE CONSTITUTION

Amendment I (1791)*
Basic Freedoms

Congress shall make no law respecting an establishment of religion, or prohibiting the free exercise thereof; or abridging the freedom of speech, or of the press; or the right of the people peaceably to assemble, and to petition the government for a redress of grievances.

Amendment II (1791)
Weapons and the Militia

A well-regulated militia being necessary to the security of a free State, the right of the people to keep and bear arms shall not be infringed.

Amendment III (1791)
Housing Soldiers

No soldier shall, in time of peace, be quartered in any house, without the consent of the owner, nor in time of war, but in a manner to be prescribed by law.

Amendment IV (1791)
Search and Seizure

The right of the people to be secure in their persons, houses, papers, and effects, against unreasonable searches and seizures, shall not be violated, and no warrants shall issue, but upon probable cause, supported by oath or affirmation, and particularly describing the place to be searched, and the persons or things to be seized.

Amendment V (1791)
Rights of the Accused

No person shall be held to answer for a capital or otherwise infamous crime, unless on a presentment or indictment of a grand jury, except in cases arising in the land or naval forces, or in the militia, when in actual service in time of war or public danger; nor shall any person be subject for the same offense to be twice put in jeopardy of life or limb; nor shall be compelled in any criminal case to be a witness against himself, nor be deprived of life, liberty, or property,

---

* The date beside each amendment is the year that the amendment was ratified.

without due process of law; nor shall private property be taken for public use without just compensation.

Amendment VI (1791)
Right to a Fair Trial

In all criminal prosecutions, the accused shall enjoy the right to a speedy and public trial, by an impartial jury of the State and district wherein the crime shall have been committed, which district shall have been previously ascertained by law, and to be informed of the nature and cause of the accusation; to be confronted with the witnesses against him; to have compulsory process for obtaining witnesses in his favor, and to have the assistance of counsel for his defense.

Amendment VII (1791)
Jury Trial in Civil Cases

In suits at common law, where the value in controversy shall exceed twenty dollars, the right of trial by jury shall be preserved, and no fact tried by a jury shall be otherwise reexamined in any court of the United States, than according to the rules of the common law.

Amendment VIII (1791)
Bail and Punishment

Excessive bail shall not be required, nor excessive fines imposed, nor cruel and unusual punishments inflicted.

Amendment IX (1791)
Powers Reserved to the People

The enumeration in the Constitution of certain rights shall not be construed to deny or disparage others retained by the people.

Amendment X (1791)
Powers Reserved to the States

The powers not delegated to the United States by the Constitution, nor prohibited by it to the States are reserved to the States respectively, or to the people.

Amendment XI (1798)
Suits Against States

The judicial power of the United States shall not be construed to extend to any suit in law or equity, commenced or prosecuted against one of the United States by citizens of another State, or by citizens or subjects of any foreign state.

Amendment XII (1804)
Election of the President and Vice President

The electors shall meet in their respective States, and vote by ballot for President and Vice President, one of whom, at least, shall not be an inhabitant of the same State with themselves; they shall name in their ballots the person voted for as President, and in distinct ballots the person voted for as Vice President, and they shall make distinct lists of all persons voted for as President, and of all persons voted for as Vice President, and of the number of votes for each, which lists they shall sign and certify, and transmit sealed to the seat of government of the United States, directed to the President of the Senate;—The President of the Senate shall, in the presence of the Senate and House of Representatives, open all the certificates and the votes shall then be counted;—The person having the greatest number of votes for President shall be the President, if such number be a majority of the whole number of electors appointed; and if no person have such majority, then from the persons having the highest numbers not exceeding three on the list of those voted for as President, the House of Representatives shall choose immediately, by ballot, the President. But in choosing the President, the votes shall be taken by States, the representation from each State having one vote; a quorum for this purpose shall consist of a member or members from two-thirds of the States, and a majority of all the States shall be necessary to a choice. And if the House of Representatives shall not choose a President whenever the right of choice shall devolve upon them, *before the fourth day of March next following,* then the Vice President shall act as President, as in the case of the death or other constitutional disability of the President. The person having the greatest number of votes as Vice President shall be the Vice President, if such number be a majority of the whole number of electors appointed; and if no person have a majority, then from the two highest numbers on the list, the Senate shall choose the Vice President; a quorum for the purpose shall consist of two-thirds of the whole number of Senators, and a majority of the whole number shall be necessary to a choice. But no person constitutionally ineligible to the office of President shall be eligible to that of Vice President of the United States.

Amendment XIII (1865)
End of Slavery

SECTION 1.   ABOLITION

Neither slavery nor involuntary servitude, except as a punishment for crime whereof the party shall have been duly convicted, shall exist within the United States, or any place subject to their jurisdiction.

SECTION 2.   ENFORCEMENT

Congress shall have power to enforce this article by appropriate legislation.

Amendment XIV (1868)
Rights of Citizens

SECTION 1.   CITIZENSHIP

All persons born or naturalized in the United States, and subject to the jurisdiction thereof, are citizens of the United States and of the State wherein they reside. No State shall make or enforce any law which shall abridge the privileges or immunities of citizens of the United States; nor shall any State deprive any person of life, liberty, or property, without due process of law; nor deny to any person within its jurisdiction the equal protection of the laws.

SECTION 2.
NUMBER OF REPRESENTATIVES

Representatives shall be apportioned among the several States according to their respective numbers, counting the whole number of persons in each State, excluding Indians not taxed. But when the right to vote at any election for the choice of Electors for President and Vice President of the United States, Representatives in Congress, the executive and judicial officers of a State, or the members of the Legislature thereof, is denied to any of the male inhabitants of such State, being twenty-one years of age, and citizens of the United States, or in any way abridged, except for participation in rebellion, or other crime, the basis of representation therein shall be reduced in the proportion which the number of such male citizens shall bear to the whole number of male citizens twenty-one years of age in such State.

SECTION 3.   PENALTY FOR REBELLION

No person shall be a Senator or Representative in Congress, or Elector of President and Vice President, or hold any office, civil or military, under the United States, or under any State, who, having previously taken an oath, as a member of Congress, or as an officer of the United States, or as a member of any State Legislature, or as an executive or judicial officer of any State, to support the Constitution of the United States, shall have engaged in insurrection or rebellion against the same, or given aid or comfort to the enemies thereof. But Congress may by a vote of two-thirds of each house, remove such disability.

SECTION 4.   GOVERNMENT DEBT

The validity of the public debt of the United States, authorized by law, including debts incurred for payment of pensions and bounties for services in suppressing insurrection or rebellion, shall not be questioned. But neither the United States nor any State shall assume or pay any debt or obligation incurred in aid of insurrection or rebellion against the United States, or any claim for the loss or emancipation of any slave; but all such debts, obligations, and claims shall be held illegal and void.

SECTION 5.   ENFORCEMENT

The Congress shall have power to enforce, by appropriate legislation, the provisions of this article.

Amendment XV (1870)
Voting Rights

SECTION 1.   RIGHT TO VOTE

The right of citizens of the United States to vote shall not be denied or abridged by the United States or by any State on account of race, color, or previous condition of servitude.

SECTION 2.   ENFORCEMENT

The Congress shall have power to enforce this article by appropriate legislation.

Amendment XVI (1913)
Income Tax

The Congress shall have power to lay and collect taxes on incomes, from whatever source derived, without apportionment among the several States, and without regard to any census or enumeration.

Amendment XVII (1913)
Direct Election of Senators

SECTION 1.   METHOD OF ELECTION

The Senate of the United States shall be composed of two Senators from each State, elected by the people thereof, for six years; and each Senator shall have one vote. The electors in each State shall have the qualifications requisite for electors of the most numerous branch of the State Legislatures.

SECTION 2.   VACANCIES

When vacancies happen in the representation of any State in the Senate, the executive authority of such State shall issue writs of election to fill such vacancies: Provided, that the Legislature of any State may empower the executive thereof to make temporary appointments until the people fill the vacancies by election as the Legislature may direct.

SECTION 3.   EXCEPTION

This amendment shall not be so construed as to affect the election or term of any Senator chosen before it becomes valid as part of the Constitution.

Amendment XVIII (1919)
Ban on Alcoholic Drinks

SECTION 1.   PROHIBITION

After one year from the ratification of this article the manufacture, sale, or transportation of intoxicating liquors within, the importation thereof into, or the exportation thereof from the United States and all territory subject to the jurisdiction thereof for beverage purposes, is hereby prohibited.

SECTION 2.   ENFORCEMENT

The Congress and the several States shall have concurrent power to enforce this article by appropriate legislation.

SECTION 3.   RATIFICATION

This article shall be inoperative unless it shall have been ratified as an amendment to the Constitution by the Legislatures of the several States, as provided in the Constitution, within seven years from the date of the submission hereof to the States by the Congress.

Amendment XIX (1920)
Women's Suffrage

SECTION 1.   RIGHT TO VOTE

The right of citizens of the United States to vote shall not be denied or abridged by the United States or by any State on account of sex.

SECTION 2.   ENFORCEMENT

The Congress shall have power to enforce this article by appropriate legislation.

Amendment XX (1933)
Terms of Office

SECTION 1.   BEGINNING OF TERMS

The terms of the President and Vice President shall end at noon on the twentieth day of January, and the terms of Senators and Representatives at noon on the third day of January, of the years in which such terms would have ended if this article had not been ratified; and the terms of their successors shall then begin.

SECTION 2.   SESSIONS OF CONGRESS

The Congress shall assemble at least once in every year, and such meeting shall begin at noon on the third day of January, unless they shall by law appoint a different day.

SECTION 3.
PRESIDENTIAL SUCCESSION

If, at the time fixed for the beginning of the term of the President, the President-elect shall have died, the Vice President-elect shall become President. If a President shall not have been chosen before the time fixed for the beginning of his term, or if the President-elect shall have failed to qualify, then the Vice President-elect shall act as President until a President shall have qualified; and the Congress may by law provide for the case wherein neither a President-elect nor a Vice President-elect shall have qualified, declaring who shall then act as President, or the manner in which one who is to act shall be selected, and such persons shall act accordingly until a President or Vice President shall have qualified.

SECTION 4.
ELECTIONS DECIDED BY CONGRESS

The Congress may by law provide for the case of the death of any of the persons from whom the House of

Representatives may choose a President whenever the right of choice shall have devolved upon them, and for the case of the death of any of the persons from whom the Senate may choose a Vice President whenever the right of choice shall have devolved upon them.

SECTION 5.   EFFECTIVE DATE

Sections 1 and 2 shall take effect on the 15th day of October following the ratification of this article.

SECTION 6.   RATIFICATION

This article shall be inoperative unless it shall have been ratified as an amendment to the Constitution by the Legislatures of three-fourths of the several States within seven years from the date of its submission.

Amendment XXI (1933)
End of Prohibition

SECTION 1.
REPEAL OF EIGHTEENTH AMENDMENT

The eighteenth article of amendment to the Constitution of the United States is hereby repealed.

SECTION 2.   STATE LAWS

The transportation or importation into any State, Territory, or Possession of the United States for delivery or use therein of intoxicating liquors, in violation of the laws thereof, is hereby prohibited.

SECTION 3.   RATIFICATION

This article shall be inoperative unless it shall have been ratified as an amendment to the Constitution by conventions in the several States, as provided in the Constitution, within seven years from the date of submission thereof to the States by the Congress.

Amendment XXII (1951)
Limit on Presidential Terms

SECTION 1.   TWO-TERM LIMIT

No person shall be elected to the office of the President more than twice, and no person who has held the office of President, or acted as President, for more than two years of a term to which some other person was elected President shall be elected to the office of the President more than once. *But this article shall not apply to any person holding the office of President when this article was proposed by the Congress, and shall not*

prevent any person who may be holding the office of President, or acting as President, during the term within which this article becomes operative from holding the office of President or acting as President during the remainder of such term.

SECTION 2.   RATIFICATION

This article shall be inoperative unless it shall have been ratified as an amendment to the Constitution by the Legislatures of three-fourths of the several States within seven years from the date of its submission to the States by the Congress.

Amendment XXIII (1961)
Presidential Votes for Washington, D.C.

SECTION 1.   NUMBER OF ELECTORS

The District constituting the seat of government of the United States shall appoint in such manner as the Congress may direct:

A number of electors of President and Vice President equal to the whole number of Senators and Representatives in Congress to which the District would be entitled if it were a State, but in no event more than the least populous State; they shall be in addition to those appointed by the States, but they shall be considered, for the purposes of the election of President and Vice President, to be electors appointed by a State; and they shall meet in the District and perform such duties as provided by the twelfth article of amendment.

SECTION 2.   ENFORCEMENT

The Congress shall have the power to enforce this article by appropriate legislation.

Amendment XXIV (1964)
Ban on Poll Taxes

SECTION 1.   POLL TAXES ILLEGAL

The right of citizens of the United States to vote in any primary or other election for President or Vice President, for electors for President or Vice President, or for Senator or Representative in Congress, shall not be denied or abridged by the United States or any State by reason of failure to pay any poll tax or other tax.

SECTION 2.   ENFORCEMENT

The Congress shall have the power to enforce this article by appropriate legislation.

Amendment XXV (1967)
Presidential Succession

SECTION 1.
VACANCY IN THE PRESIDENCY

In case of the removal of the President from office or of his death or resignation, the Vice President shall become President.

SECTION 2.
VACANCY IN THE VICE PRESIDENCY

Whenever there is a vacancy in the office of the Vice President, the President shall nominate a Vice President who shall take office upon confirmation by a majority vote of both houses of Congress.

SECTION 3.
DISABILITY OF THE PRESIDENT

Whenever the President transmits to the President pro tempore of the Senate and the Speaker of the House of Representatives his written declaration that he is unable to discharge the powers and duties of his office, and until he transmits to them a written declaration to the contrary, such powers and duties shall be discharged by the Vice President as Acting President.

SECTION 4.   DETERMINING
PRESIDENTIAL DISABILITY

Whenever the Vice President and a majority of either the principal officers of the executive departments or of such other body as Congress may by law provide, transmit to the President pro tempore of the Senate and the Speaker of the House of Representatives their written declaration that the President is unable to discharge the powers and duties of his office, the Vice President shall immediately assume the powers and duties of the office as Acting President.

Thereafter, when the President transmits to the President pro tempore of the Senate and the Speaker of the House of Representatives his written declaration that no inability exists, he shall resume the powers and duties of his office unless the Vice President and a majority of either the principal officers of the executive departments or of such other body as Congress may by law provide, transmit within four days to the President pro tempore of the Senate and the Speaker of the House of Representatives their written declaration that the President is unable to discharge the powers and duties of his office. Thereupon Congress shall decide the issue, assembling within forty-eight hours for that purpose if not in session. If the Congress, within twenty-one days after receipt of the latter written declaration, or, if Congress is not in session, within twenty-one days after Congress is required to assemble, determines by two-thirds vote of both houses that the President is unable to discharge the powers and duties of his office, the Vice President shall continue to discharge the same as Acting President; otherwise, the President shall resume the powers and duties of his office.

Amendment XXVI (1971)
Voting Age

SECTION 1.   RIGHT TO VOTE

The right of citizens of the United States, who are eighteen years of age or older, to vote shall not be denied or abridged by the United States or by any State on account of age.

SECTION 2.   ENFORCEMENT

The Congress shall have power to enforce this article by appropriate legislation.

CONTRIBUTORS

TYLER ANBINDER teaches at the University of Wyoming. His book about the Know-Nothing Party, *Nativism and Slavery,* was awarded the Avery O. Craven Prize of the Organization of American Historians.

DAVID L. ANDERSON is an award-winning teacher of American history at the University of Indianapolis. He is the author of *Trapped by Success: The Eisenhower Administration and Vietnam,* and the editor of and principal contributor to *Shadow on the White House: Presidents and the Vietnam War.*

LEONARD J. ARRINGTON, professor of western history emeritus at Brigham Young University, is the author of a score of books that deal with Mormon and western American history.

BRENT ASHABRANNER, former deputy director of the Peace Corps and Ford Foundation official, has written widely for young readers on American social history and complex social issues. Among his award-winning books are *Always to Remember: The Story of the Vietnam Veterans Memorial* and *Dark Harvest: Migrant Farmworkers in America.*

DORE ASHTON is the author of some twenty-five books on the various arts, many dealing with modern American art. She is a professor of art history at Cooper Union. She has received numerous prizes and honors, including Guggenheim and Ford grants and the College Art Association Prize for art criticism.

BETH BAILEY teaches history and American studies at Barnard College, Columbia University. She is the author of *From Front Porch to Back Seat: Courtship in Twentieth-Century America* and, with David Farber, *The First Strange Place: The Alchemy of Race and Sex in World War II Hawaii.*

RANDALL BALMER teaches religion at Barnard College, Columbia University. His weekly commentaries on religion are distributed nationally by the New York Times Syndicate, and he was nominated for an Emmy Award or his PBS documentary, *Mine Eyes Have Seen the Glory.* He lives in New York City with his two sons.

LOIS W. BANNER, a professor of history and gender studies at the University of Southern California, has written *American Beauty* and *In Full Flower: Aging Women, Power, and Sexuality.* She is a past president of the American Studies Association and the American Historical Association, Pacific Coast Branch.

RICHARD A. BARTLETT, professor emeritus of history at Florida State University, is an authority on western American exploration. Among his books are *Great Surveys of the American West* and *The New Country: A Social History of the American Frontier.*

BERNARD W. BELL, professor of English, American, and African-American literatures at the University Park campus of Pennsylvania State University, is the author of more than fifty scholarly articles and reviews and three books, including the prize-winning *The Afro-American Novel and Its Tradition.*

IRA BERLIN is professor of history and dean for undergraduate studies at the University of Maryland. He is the author of *Slaves without Masters: The Free Negro in the Antebellum South* and editor of *Freedom: A Documentary History of Emancipation.*

RICHARD B. BERNSTEIN teaches legal history at New York Law School and is assistant editor of the Papers of John Jay, Columbia University. His books include *Are We to Be a Nation? The Making of the Constitution* (with Kym S. Rice), *Amending America* (with Jerome Agel), and *Of the People, By the People, For the People* (with Jerome Agel).

JOANN BIONDI is a freelance journalist and travel book author. She teaches tourism and cultural geography at Miami-Dade Community College.

DAVID W. BLIGHT teaches American history and black studies at Amherst College. He is the author of *Frederick Douglass' Civil War: Keeping Faith in Jubilee* and editor of a teaching edition of *Narrative of the Life of Frederick Douglass, an American Slave,* and *When This Cruel War Is Over: The Civil War Letters of Charles Harvey Brewster.*

JOAN W. BLOS, well-known writer of children's books, was the 1980 recipient of the Newbery Medal. Her books include three works of historical fiction and two picture books on historical subjects. A lecturer and critic, for many years she taught children's literature. Her husband is Peter Blos, Jr.

PETER BLOS, JR., M.D., is a psychiatrist and psychoanalyst who works with children, adolescents, and adults with mental illnesses. He has written on the subject and taught others in the field for more than thirty years. From 1992 to 1994 he was president of the Association for Child Psychoanalysis, an international organization.

LEDA BLUMBERG is the author of *Pets, Breezy, The Horselover's Handbook* and, with Rhoda Blumberg, *The Simon and Schuster Book of Facts and Fallacies* and *Lovebirds, Lizards and Llamas.* She writes and takes photographs for magazine articles, teaches horseback riding, and is completing a graduate degree in psychology.

RHODA BLUMBERG, historian for young people, has received many awards, including a Newbery Honor in 1986 for *Commodore Perry in the Land of the Shogun,* the Golden Kite Award in 1989 for *The Incredible Journey of Lewis & Clark,* and the California Library Association Beatty Award in 1990 for *The Great American Gold Rush.*

CHARLES BOHNER teaches at the University of Delaware. Among his books is the novel for young readers *Bold Journey: West with Lewis and Clark.*

JULIAN BOND teaches at American University in Washington, D.C., and at the University of Virginia in Charlottesville. He was active in the southern civil rights movement of the 1960s and served twenty years in the Georgia General Assembly. He speaks and writes extensively about race relations and politics.

ALAN BRINKLEY is professor of history at Columbia University. He is the author of *Voices of Protest: Huey Long, Father Coughlin, and the Great Depression; The Unfinished Nation: A Concise History of the American People;* and the forthcoming *Transformation of New Deal Liberalism.* He is also coauthor of *American History: A Survey,* a widely used college textbook.

DAVID BRODY is professor emeritus of history at the University of California, Davis. He is coauthor of a major college text, *America's History,* and of a number of books on American labor history, including most recently *In Labor's Cause: Main Themes on the History of the American Worker* (1993).

LYDIA BRONTE is the author of *The Longevity Factor* (1993) and coeditor with Alan Pifer of *Our Aging Society: Paradox and Promise* (1986).

DEE BROWN is the author of several books on the American West and the Civil War, including *Bury My Heart at Wounded Knee, Hear That Lonesome Whistle Blow,* and *When the Century Was Young.* Before his retirement he was a librarian at the University of Illinois.

RICHARD D. BROWN, professor of history at the University of Connecticut, is the author of *Revolutionary Politics in Massachusetts: The Boston Committee of Correspondence and the Towns, 1722–1774* and the editor of *Major Problems in the Era of the American Revolution, 1760–1791.* His interest in the history of communications is manifest in his book *Knowledge Is Power: The Diffusion of Information in Early America, 1700–1865.*

ROBERT V. BRUCE, professor emeritus of history at Boston University, is the author of *Lincoln and the Tools of War, 1877: Year of Violence, Bell: Alexander Graham Bell and the Conquest of Solitude,* and *The Launching of Modern American Science,* which won the 1988 Pulitzer Prize in history.

BORGNA BRUNNER is a senior editor at Houghton Mifflin specializing in history. She received a B.A. from Vassar College and an M.Phil. from Trinity College, Dublin.

JEAN M. BURKS was curator of recreational artifacts at the Strong Museum, Rochester, New York. She has held curatorial and research positions at Canterbury Shaker Village, Winterthur Museum, the Philadelphia Museum of Art, and the Cooper-Hewitt

Museum. Her publications include *The Complete Book of Shaker Furniture* and *Birmingham Brass Candlesticks.*

ALDEN R. CARTER's many nonfiction books for young readers include *The War of 1812: Second Fight for Independence, The Spanish-American War: Imperial Ambitions,* and *China Past—China Future.* Four of his novels, including *Up Country* and *Sheila's Dying,* were named ALA Best Books for Young Adults. His latest novel is *Dogwolf.*

DAN T. CARTER, Kenan Professor at Emory University, is a specialist in twentieth-century American history and the history of the South. He is the author of *Scottsboro: A Tragedy of the American South* and *When the War Was Over: The Failure of Self-Reconstruction in the South.*

NORMAN H. CLARK is the author of *The Dry Years,* a book about the prohibition movement in the state of Washington, and *Deliver Us from Evil,* a book about the prohibition movement across the nation. He lives in Tumwater, Washington.

J. GARRY CLIFFORD is a professor of political science at the University of Connecticut in Storrs. He is the author of *The Citizen Soldiers: The Plattsburg Training Camp Movement, 1913–1920* and, with Thomas G. Paterson, *American Foreign Relations: A History.*

CATHERINE CLINTON has taught at Brandeis University, Harvard University, and Brown University. She is the author of *The Plantation Mistress, Portraits of American Women,* and, most recently, *Divided Houses: Gender and the Civil War,* which is dedicated to her two sons, Drew and Ned Colbert.

THOMAS COLE received his B.A. from Vassar College and M.A. and Ph.D. from Johns Hopkins University. He has taught history at several colleges and universities in the United States.

HAMILTON CRAVENS is professor of history at Iowa State University, in Ames, Iowa, where he teaches undergraduate and graduate courses in American cultural history and the history of science and technology. Among the books he has published are *The Triumph of Evolution* (1978, 1988), *Ideas in America's Cultures* (1982), and *Before Head Start* (1993). He is currently working on a history of American culture from 1900 to 1920.

ROBERT M. CRUNDEN is professor of history and American civilization at the University of Texas at Austin. His most recent books are *Ministers of Reform: The Progressives' Achievement in American Civilization, 1889–1920* and *American Salons: Encounters with European Modernism, 1885–1917.*

NOBLE E. CUNNINGHAM, JR., is the Curators' Professor of History at the University of Missouri, Columbia. Among the seven books he has written are *In Pursuit of Reason: The Life of Thomas Jefferson, The Process of Government under Jefferson,* and *Popular Images of the Presidency from Washington to Lincoln.*

ROGER DANIELS is professor of history at the University of Cincinnati. His most recent books are *Prisoners without Trial: Japanese Americans in World War II* (1993) and *Coming to America: Immigration and Ethnicity in American Life* (1993).

ALLEN F. DAVIS is a professor of history at Temple University, Philadelphia, Pennsylvania. He is the author of *Spearheads for Reform: The Social Settlements and the Progressive Movement, American Heroine: The Life and Legend of Jane Addams,* and coauthor of *One Hundred Years at Hull-House.*

ANDREW DELBANCO is professor of English at Columbia University in New York City, where he lives with his wife and two children. He has written and edited many books and articles about American literature and history, including a short selection of the writings of Abraham Lincoln, *The Portable Abraham Lincoln.* His most recent book is *The Death of Satan: The Idea of Evil in the American Imagination,* to be published in 1995.

LINDA GRANT DE PAUW is professor of history at George Washington University. She is the author of numerous books, including two prize-winning histories for young adults: *Founding Mothers: Women of America in the Revolutionary Era* and *Seafaring Women.*

ROBERT S. DESOWITZ, professor of tropical medicine and medical microbiology at the University of Hawaii, is an expert on parasitic diseases, particularly malaria. He has written three books on infectious diseases for the general reader. His most recent book, *The Malaria Capers,* made the short list for the 1993 Rhone-Poulenc Prize.

ROBERT ELLSBERG is editor in chief of Orbis Books. He was managing editor of the *Catholic Worker* from 1976 to 1978 and has edited several books, including *Dorothy Day: Selected Writings* and *Fritz Eichenberg: Works of Mercy*.

BARBARA SILBERDICK FEINBERG received a doctoral degree in political science from Yale University. She is the author of books for young people about American history and politics, including *Harry S. Truman*, *Words in the News: A Student's Dictionary of American Government and Politics*, and *American Political Scandals Past and Present*.

JEREMY R. FEINBERG, son of Barbara Silberdick Feinberg, is a student at Columbia Law School. A former sports editor of the *Columbia Daily Spectator*, he has written for *New York Newsday* and interned at *Sports Illustrated*. He wrote *Reading the Sports Page* (1992).

GILBERT C. FITE is professor of history emeritus, University of Oklahoma and University of Georgia, and a specialist in agricultural and economic history. His books include *American Farmers: The New Minority* and *Cotton Fields No More: Southern Agriculture, 1865–1980*. He lives with his wife, June, in Bella Vista, Arkansas.

THOMAS FLEMING is a novelist and historian, whose books include *1776: Year of Illusions* and *Time and Tide*. Among his books for young readers are *One Small Candle*, the story of the Pilgrims' first year in America, and *First in Their Hearts*, a biography of George Washington.

ERIC FONER, DeWitt Clinton Professor of History at Columbia University, is the author of numerous books and articles on nineteenth-century American history. He received the Bancroft and Parkman prizes for *Reconstruction: America's Unfinished Revolution* (1988). In 1993–94 he served as president of the Organization of American Historians.

PAULA FOX won the 1974 Newbery Medal for *The Slave Dancer* and the Hans Christian Andersen Medal in 1978 for her contribution to children's literature. She has published twenty-one books for young people and six other novels.

RUSSELL FREEDMAN received the 1988 Newbery Medal for *Lincoln: A Photobiography*. His books for young readers also include *Franklin Delano Roosevelt* and *Eleanor Roosevelt: A Life of Discovery*, which received a 1993 Newbery Honor.

JOSHUA B. FREEMAN is associate professor of history at Columbia University. He is the author of *In Transit: The Transport Workers Union in New York City, 1933–1966* and coauthor of *Who Built America? Working People and the Nation's Economy, Politics, Culture, and Society*, Vol. 2.

MARLENE GERBER FRIED is a professor of philosophy and the director of the civil liberties and public policy program at Hampshire College. She teaches and writes about public policy, law, and ethics related to reproductive rights and health. She is the editor of *From Abortion to Reproductive Freedom: Transforming a Movement*.

RICHARD A. GARCIA, professor of ethnic studies at California State University, Hayward, is the editor of *Chicanos in America, 1540–1974* and the author of *Chicano Ideology: A Comparative Study of Three Chicano Organizations* and *The Rise of the Mexican American Middle Class, San Antonio, 1929–1941*.

JOHN A. GARRATY, professor emeritus of history and former chairman of the Department of History at Columbia University, is the editor of this encyclopedia and of *The Reader's Companion to American History*. His other publications include *The Story of America*, a textbook for eighth graders; *The American Nation*, a similar work for college students; and *1001 Things Everyone Should Know About American History*.

JAMES CROSS GIBLIN is an author, editor, and lecturer in the field of children's literature. Many of his books deal with historical topics, including such recent titles as *The Riddle of the Rosetta Stone*, *George Washington: A Picture Book Biography*, and *Be Seated: A Book about Chairs*. He lives in New York City.

WARREN GOLDSTEIN teaches American studies at the State University of New York/College at Old Westbury. He is the author of *Playing for Keeps: A History of Early Baseball* and, with Elliot J. Gorn, *A Brief History of American Sports*.

ELAINE and WALTER GOODMAN received a Christopher Award for their book on the Supreme Court, *The Rights of the People*. Ms. Goodman is a New York artist. Mr. Goodman, the author of several books on the American scene, is a television critic for the *New York Times.*

JOHN STEELE GORDON writes a regular column in *American Heritage* magazine on American business history and is a frequent commentator on "Marketplace," National Public Radio's daily business news show. He is the author of *The Scarlet Woman of Wall Street,* a history of Wall Street in the 1860s.

ELLIOT J. GORN teaches history and American studies at Miami University, Oxford, Ohio. He is the author of *The Manly Art* and, with Warren Goldstein, of *A Brief History of American Sports.* He also coedited *Constructing the American Past* and the *Encyclopedia of American Social History.* He is currently working on a biography of Mother Jones.

HENRY F. GRAFF, professor emeritus of history and former chairman of the Department of History at Columbia University, is a specialist on the presidency and the foreign relations of the United States. His publications include a number of widely used American history textbooks, among them *America, the Glorious Republic* (for tenth and eleventh graders) and *This Great Nation* (for seventh and eighth graders).

HOWARD GREENFELD, an editor and publisher for many years, is the author of several books, for both young people and adults. Among these are *The Hidden Children, The Devil and Dr. Barnes, Books: From Writer to Reader,* and introductory biographies of the painters Marc Chagall and Paul Gauguin.

ROBERT L. GRISWOLD teaches history at the University of Oklahoma. He has written *Fatherhood in America: A History* and *Family and Divorce in California, 1850–1890.* His publications also include articles on nineteenth-century women, law, and family life.

RICHARD GRISWOLD DEL CASTILLO teaches Mexican-American history at San Diego State University, San Diego, California. He is the author of *The Los Angeles Barrio: A Social History, 1850–1890; La Familia: Chicano Urban Families in the Southwest; The Treaty of Guadalupe Hidalgo: A Legacy of Conflict;* and, with Richard A. Garcia, the forthcoming *Sacrifice and Struggle: The Life and Times of Cesar Chavez.*

ALLEN GUTTMANN teaches at Amherst College. His biography of Avery Brundage, *The Games Must Go On* (1984), was named Book of the Year by the U.S.

Olympic Committee. *Women's Sports* (1991) won the annual prize of the North American Society for Sport History. His most recent book is *Games and Empires: The Diffusion of Modern Sports and the Question of Cultural Imperialism* (1994).

JOY HAKIM, a former teacher and newspaper editor, is the author of a ten-volume American history entitled *A History of US.*

JAN CHARLES HALUSKA, Ph.D., teaches English at Southern College of Seventh-day Adventists. A former flight instructor and jazz band leader, he has been an educator at the high school and college levels for twenty years. He has coedited two secondary literature texts and has twice won Zapara Awards for classroom excellence.

JOYCE HANSEN is a teacher and the author of books and stories for young people. Her historical novel *Which Way Freedom* received honorable mention, the Coretta Scott King Award. Her nonfiction book *Between Two Fires: Black Soldiers in the Civil War* was selected as a Notable Children's Trade Book in the Field of Social Studies for 1994.

WILLIAM H. HARBAUGH is Langbourne M. Williams Professor of History Emeritus at the University of Virginia. His *Power and Responsibility: The Life and Times of Theodore Roosevelt* was a History Book Club selection in 1961. His *Lawyer's Lawyer: The Life of John W. Davis* was a finalist for the National Book Award in 1974.

NEIL HARRIS, Preston and Sterling Morton Professor of History at the University of Chicago, specializes in the evolution of American cultural institutions and the study of the built landscape. His books include *The Artist in American Society, Humbug: The Art of P. T. Barnum,* and *Cultural Excursions.*

JIM HASKINS is professor of English at the University of Florida and lives in New York City. Author of more than one hundred books for children, young adults, and adults, he has received the ASCAP–Deems Taylor, Carter G. Woodson, and Coretta Scott King awards, as well as other recognition for his writing.

ELLIS W. HAWLEY teaches American history at the University of Iowa. He is the author of *The New Deal and the Problem of Monopoly, The Great War and* the Search for a Modern Order, and other works on the 1920s and 1930s.

DOLORES HAYDEN is professor of architecture, urbanism, and American studies at Yale University and the author of several books on housing and urban history, including Seven American Utopias, The Grand Domestic Revolution, Redesigning the American Dream, and Storytelling with the Shapes of Time.

ARNOLD R. HIRSCH is a professor of history and a specialist in urban affairs and race relations at the University of New Orleans. He is the author of Making the Second Ghetto and coeditor of Creole New Orleans and Urban Policy in Twentieth-Century America.

ARI and OLIVE HOOGENBOOM are historians who live in Brooklyn, New York. She is an associate editor of American National Biography, and he teaches at Brooklyn College and the Graduate Center of the City University of New York. His most recent book is a biography of Rutherford B. Hayes, nineteenth president of the United States.

DANIEL WALKER HOWE is Rhodes Professor of American History at Oxford University in England. He is the author of The Political Culture of the American Whigs and other writings on American history.

KENNETH T. JACKSON is the Jacques Barzun Professor of History and the Social Sciences at Columbia University. His books include Crabgrass Frontier: The Suburbanization of the United States; The Ku Klux Klan in the City, 1915–1930; and Silent Cities: The Evolution of the American Cemetery. He is also editor in chief of the forthcoming Encyclopedia of New York City.

JOE JARES is the author of six books on sports. In addition to freelance work for the New York Times and many magazines, he has been a staff writer for UPI, the Los Angeles Times, Sports Illustrated, and the Los Angeles Daily News.

PATRICIA CONDON JOHNSTON writes widely on American history and art subjects. Her latest book is The Shape of Things: The Art of Francis Lee Jaques (1994). The founding editor of the Afton Historical Society Press, she is married to artist and photographer Charles Johnston; they live in Afton, Minnesota.

ABIGAIL JUNGREIS is the author of Know Your Hometown History and has won an Edpress Award for

her work at Scholastic Inc. Pakistan coordinator for Amnesty International U.S.A., she is a former reporter for the Anchorage Daily News and is presently a social studies editor at Houghton Mifflin.

DEBORAH KENT grew up in Little Falls, New Jersey. She earned a bachelor's degree at Oberlin College and a master's at Smith College School for Social Work. She began her writing career while living in San Miguel de Allende, Mexico. She has written more than a dozen young-adult novels, including Belonging and Why Me? Her children's nonfiction includes Benjamin Franklin: Extraordinary Patriot, The Story of Jane Addams and Hull House, and numerous books about the states in the series America the Beautiful.

ZACHARY KENT grew up in Little Falls, New Jersey, and attended St. Lawrence University. After college, he worked at a New York City literary agency for two years before launching a career as a freelance writer. He has published more than forty books of American history and biography for young people.

ALEXANDER KEYSSAR is a professor of history at Duke University. His many publications include the prize-winning Out of Work: The First Century of Unemployment in Massachusetts. His daughter NATALIE KEYSSAR, age ten, reads a lot, likes history, and helps her father write for young readers.

MICHAEL KRONENWETTER is a freelance writer and columnist and the author of more than twenty highly regarded books for young readers. Among them are Welfare State America: Safety Net or Social Contract?, United They Hate, Cities at War: London, Taking a Stand against Human Rights Abuses, and Prejudice in America.

HAROLD D. LANGLEY, Ph.D., is the curator of naval history at the Smithsonian Institution's National Museum of American History. He is the editor of So Proudly We Hail: The History of the United States Flag, published in 1981.

REBECCA LARSEN is the author of several young-adult biographies of important Americans, including Paul Robeson, Franklin D. Roosevelt, Robert Oppenheimer, and Richard Nixon. Her biography of Robeson won the 1990 Carter G. Woodson Award from the National Council for the Social Studies. Larsen is a longtime journalist and editor with the Marin Independent Journal in Novato, California.

THOMAS C. LEONARD is professor and associate dean at the Graduate School of Journalism, University of California, Berkeley. He is the author of *The Power of the Press: The Birth of American Political Reporting* and other works on the media in the United States.

SANFORD LEVINSON teaches law at the University of Texas Law School. He is the author of *Constitutional Faith* (1988), awarded the 1989 Scribes Award by the American Society of Writers on Legal Subjects, and is coeditor, with Paul Brest, of *Processes of Constitutional Decisionmaking* (3d ed. 1992).

BLANCHE LINDEN-WARD has taught history, American studies, and women's studies at Brandeis University and elsewhere after receiving her doctorate from Harvard in 1981. She is research associate professor in the Center for the Humanities at the University of New Hampshire and associate editor of the *Encyclopedia of New England Culture.* Her publications include *American Women in the 1960s: Changing the Future* (1993), coauthored with Carol Hurd Green, and essays on Kate Millett and President John F. Kennedy's Presidential Commission on the Status of Women.

EDMUND LINDOP taught in middle schools and high schools for thirty-eight years and trained history teachers at two universities. He has written twenty-nine historical trade books and textbooks for young readers. His recent books include *Presidents by Accident, Assassinations that Shook America,* and *Presidents versus Congress.*

LAURIE LINDOP, formerly in the editorial department at St. Martin's Press, is a staff writer for the Massachusetts Department of Education. Her writings have appeared in such publications as *Iowa Woman,* the *Beloit Fiction Journal,* and *Writer's Digest.* She was a speaker at the 1993 Virginia Woolf International Conference.

ROBERT A. LISTON is the author of more than forty books for young readers, including titles on censorship, prison reform, comparative religion, conscription, and other American social and political issues. A native of Ohio, he now lives in Santa Barbara, California.

GUY LOGSDON, a research associate at the Smithsonian Institution, is an independent scholar funded by a grant from the National Endowment for the Humanities to compile a biblio-discography of the songs of Woody Guthrie. He has gained international recognition for his scholarship and writings about Woody Guthrie, cowboy songs/poetry, and country music.

PRISCILLA LONG is the author of *Where the Sun Never Shines: A History of America's Bloody Coal Industry.* She is an independent scholar and writer who publishes poetry and short fiction as well as scholarly work on American history. She lives and writes in Seattle.

CHRISTINE A. LUNARDINI, Ph.D., is a freelance writer who resides in New York. Currently, she is working on a book on milestones in women's history.

EDWARD LURIE teaches American history at the University of Delaware and is the author of *Louis Agassiz: A Life in Science.*

ELSA MARSTON writes for young people and specializes in both fiction and nonfiction about the Middle East, where she has lived on several occasions. Her New England heritage also appears in her work. She lives in Bloomington, Indiana.

D. R. MARTIN is a writer and photojournalist who has been published in scores of regional and national publications, including *American Heritage* and *Reader's Digest.*

BENJAMIN MCARTHUR teaches American history at Southern College of Seventh-day Adventists in Tennessee. Author of *Actors and American Culture, 1880–1920,* he has also written history articles for *American Heritage* and other publications. His children, Emily and Mills, enjoy history stories at bedtime.

RICHARD P. MCCORMICK, University Professor of History, Emeritus, Rutgers University, specializes in American political history. Among his several books are *The Second American Party System: Party Formation in the Jacksonian Era* and *The Presidential Game: The Origins of American Presidential Politics.*

TOM MCGOWEN is the author of more than forty books for children and young adults, including both fiction (chiefly fantasy) and nonfiction, in the areas of science and history. He was the recipient of the 1990 Children's Reading Round Table Annual Award for outstanding contributions to the field of children's literature.

JAMES M. MCPHERSON is George Henry Davis 1886 Professor of American History at Princeton University, where he has taught since 1962. A specialist in the American Civil War, he has published eight books, including *Battle Cry of Freedom: The Civil War Era,* which won the Pulitzer Prize for history in 1989.

MILTON MELTZER is the author of nearly ninety books for young people and adults. Among his many honors have been five nominations for the National Book Award. He has also written for newspapers, magazines, radio, television, and films. He lives in New York.

JIM MURPHY has written more than twenty books for children. *The Boys' War: Confederate and Union Soldiers Talk about the Civil War* and *The Long Road to Gettysburg* each received the SCBWI Golden Kite Award for excellence in nonfiction. He lives in New Jersey with his wife, Alison, and son, Michael.

PAUL L. MURPHY is Regents' Professor of American History at the University of Minnesota where he specializes in constitutional and legal history with an emphasis upon the history of civil liberties and civil rights in the United States. His publications particularly explore the history of the speech and press clauses of the First Amendment.

RODERICK FRAZIER NASH is professor of history and environmental studies at the University of California, Santa Barbara. A founder of the new field of environmental history, he has written *Wilderness and the American Mind* (1982), *The Rights of Nature* (1989), and *American Environmentalism* (1990).

JUDY NORSIGIAN is a coauthor of *Our Bodies, Ourselves* and *The New Our Bodies, Ourselves* as well as codirector of the Boston Women's Health Book Collective. She speaks frequently on a wide range of women's health concerns and has appeared on numerous national television and radio programs, including *Oprah, Donahue, The Today Show,* and *Good Morning America.*

ALEX OBERWEGER is a graduate of Columbia University and the S. I. Newhouse School of Public Communications at Syracuse University. He was a member of Columbia's hockey team and in 1991 was voted the MSG network college sportscaster of the year.

LINDA PEAVY and URSULA SMITH, independent scholars who have been writing women's history for a dozen years, are coauthors of two collective biographies for young readers, *Women Who Changed Things* and *Dreams into Deeds,* and of *Women in Waiting in the Westward Movement: Life on the Home Frontier.*

WALTER PETROVITZ teaches English as a second language at St. John's University in New York City.

JEFFREY POTTER's biography of Jackson Pollock, *To a Violent Grave,* is to be a film starring Barbra Streisand and Robert De Niro. Potter is a high school dropout, a handicap which he does not recommend.

HOWARD N. RABINOWITZ is professor of history at the University of New Mexico. He is the author of *Race Relations in the Urban South, 1865–1890; The First New South, 1865–1920;* and *Race, Ethnicity, and Urbanization* and editor of *Southern Black Leaders of the Reconstruction Era.*

JAMES A. RAWLEY is professor emeritus of history at the University of Nebraska, Lincoln, and former chairman of the department of history and interim dean of the University of Nebraska, Lincoln, Libraries. A specialist in the Civil War and the foreign slave trade, he is the author of *Race and Politics* and *The Transatlantic Slave Trade: A History.*

TED REYNOLDS and GEORG W. TURNER are writers and musicians living in Chattanooga, Tennessee. Reynolds is the former editor of *Southern Jam,* an Atlanta-based music magazine. Turner is a published playwright finishing work on his first novel.

JAMES I. ROBERTSON, JR., is Alumni Distinguished Professor in History at Virginia Tech. His many books include *Civil War! America Becomes One Nation,* which received the American Library Association's 1993 Best Book for Young Readers Award.

LAYN SAINT-LOUIS, originally from Haiti, is a doctoral and law student at Howard University specializing in African studies and international law, respectively. He has been a teaching fellow in the Afro-American Studies Department at Harvard University and an instructor at Wellesley College. His most recent publications were on the American Colonization Society and Edward Wilmot Blyden.

MILES DAVID SAMSON teaches the history of art and architecture at Worcester Polytechnic Institute, Worcester, Massachusetts. His field of interest is architecture and American society, and in 1990–91 he held a fellowship at Columbia University's Buell Center for the Study of American Architecture.

LOIS SCHARF teaches American history at Case Western Reserve University. She is the author of *To Work and to Wed: Female Employment, Feminism and the Great Depression;* and *Eleanor Roosevelt: First Lady of American Liberalism.*

RICHARD B. SEWALL, emeritus professor of English at Yale, won the National Book Award for *The Life of Emily Dickinson* in 1974. His other publications on Dickinson include *The Lyman Letters: New Light on Emily Dickinson and Her Family* (1965) and *Emily Dickinson: A Collection of Critical Essays* (1963).

HARRIET SIGERMAN is the author of *An Unfinished Battle* and *Laborers for Liberty,* two volumes in the Young Oxford History of Women in the United States. She has a Ph.D. in American history from the University of Massachusetts at Amherst.

DAVID C. SMITH teaches English and chairs the Department of English and Speech at Southern College of Seventh-day Adventists. He specializes in nineteenth-century American literature and is completing a book on Thoreau: *The Transcendental Saunterer: Thoreau and the Search for Self* (1994).

ELIZABETH GEORGE SPEARE is an author of historical novels for young people, for two of which, *The Witch of Blackbird Pond* and *The Bronze Bow,* she received the Newbery Medal.

R. CONRAD STEIN was born and grew up in Chicago. He attended the University of Illinois, where he earned a degree in history. Stein is the author of more than fifty history books for young readers. One of his recent books is *The Mexican Revolution, 1910–1920.*

JOHN F. STOVER, professor emeritus of history at Purdue University and a fellow in the Society of American Historians, received a Senior Achievement Award in Railroad History from the Railway and Locomotive Historical Society. His books include *American Railroads, Iron Road to the West,* and *History of the B & O Railroad.*

STERLING STUCKEY is the author of *Slave Culture: Nationalist Theory and the Foundations of Black America* (1987) and *Going Through the Storm: The Influence of African American Art in History* (1994). He is professor of history and religious studies at the University of California at Riverside.

JON C. TEAFORD is professor of history at Purdue University. His most recent book is *Cities of the Heartland: The Rise and Fall of the Industrial Midwest.*

ATHAN G. THEOHARIS, professor of history at Marquette University, Milwaukee, Wisconsin, is a specialist on federal surveillance policy and twentieth-century America. He wrote, with John S. Cox, *The Boss: J. Edgar Hoover and the Great American Inquisition* and edited *From the Secret Files of J. Edgar Hoover.*

EDMUND R. THOMPSON, major general (ret.), former assistant chief of staff for intelligence, U.S. Army, is the editor and a principal author of *Secret New England: Spies of the American Revolution.*

BARBARA L. TISCHLER teaches history and American studies at Columbia University, where she is the director of admissions and financial aid at the School of General Studies. She is the author of *An American Music: The Search for an American Musical Identity* (1986) and the editor of *Sight on the Sixties* (1992). Her current research interests include American music and twentieth-century wartime culture.

CLIFFORD E. TRAFZER, who is of mixed Wyandot Indian heritage, is professor and chair of ethnic studies and director of Native American studies at the University of California, Riverside. His books include *The Kit Carson Campaign: The Last Great Navajo War, Renegade Tribe,* and *Earth Song, Sky Spirit.* His new work is entitled *Death Stalks the Yakima: A Social and Cultural History of Death on the Yakima Indian Reservation, 1888–1964.*

MELVIN I. UROFSKY is professor of constitutional history at Virginia Commonwealth University and the author of biographies of Louis Brandeis and Felix Frankfurter.

THEODORE VRETTOS taught English at Salem State College and until 1991 was writer-in-residence at Simmons College. He is the author of four novels and a nonfiction book.

SUSAN WARE teaches history at New York University. She is the author of *Still Missing: Amelia Earhart and the Search for Modern Feminism,* as well as several other books on women in twentieth-century America.

HARVEY WASSERMAN helped form the Clamshell Alliance against the Seabrook nuclear plant in New Hampshire and has worked for more than two decades for a renewable solar-based economy. He is a senior adviser to Greenpeace and the author of *Harvey Wasserman's History of the United States.*

MARGARET M. WATERS was born in Brooklyn, New York, and studied American and Irish history at Yale University and Irish literature at Trinity College, Dublin. She is a writer who lives in Cambridge, Massachusetts.

CECILE RHINEHART WATTERS, an editor and writer, in mid-career became interested in American history. She returned to college and received a degree in American history and civilization from Boston University. She specialized in editing books in the field.

BERNARD WEISBERGER has taught United States history in universities, written books for all ages and audiences, consulted on historical film and television projects, and is a columnist for *American Heritage.* After forty years of it, he still loves the subject and enjoys sharing his enthusiasm with young people everywhere.

ANN E. WEISS is the author of nearly thirty books for children and young adults. Her topics range from bioethics, welfare, and prisons to word derivations, lies and deceptions, and the business of sports. She lives in Maine with her husband and has two grown daughters.

WILLIAM WELLING received the Gold Quill Award from the Aviation/Space Writers Association (1988); the Frank Luther Mott Research Award from the University of Missouri Journalism Scholarship Society for his history of early American photography (1978); and a citation for Distinguished Service to Aviation from the National Committee to Observe the 50th Anniversary of Powered Flight (1953).

DENNIS WEPMAN has taught English at the University of Miami, Florida, and the City University of New York. He has published eleven volumes of history, biography, and art criticism.

SEAN WILENTZ is professor of history and Cotsen Fellow at Princeton University. He writes widely on American history, but his major interests lie in the period from the American Revolution to the Civil War. His books include the award-winning *Chants Democratic* (1984) and, with Paul E. Johnson, *The Kingdom of Matthias* (1994).

PATRICK G. WILLIAMS has received degrees from Columbia University and the University of Texas and writes about the history of Texas and the American South in the post–Civil War period. He lives in northwest Arkansas.

NANCY WOLOCH teaches history and American studies at Barnard College, Columbia University. She is the author of *Women and the American Experience* and *Early American Women: A Documentary History, 1600–1900,* and the coauthor of *The American Century* and *The Enduring Vision,* a textbook in American history.

ROBERT WOOSTER teaches history at Texas A&M University, Corpus Christi. He is the author of several books, including *The Military and United States Indian Policy, 1865–1903* and *Nelson A. Miles & the Twilight of the Frontier Army.*

GWENDOLYN WRIGHT teaches the history of architecture and urbanism at Columbia University. She is the author of *Building the Dream: A Social History of Housing in America* and other books on related subjects.

Judge HILLER B. ZOBEL of the Massachusetts Superior Court wrote *The Boston Massacre* and (with L. Kinvin Wroth) edited the three-volume *Legal Papers of John Adams,* which won the American Historical Association's Littleton-Griswold Prize in 1966. He has published numerous articles on law, trial courts, and colonial and legal history.

PICTURE CREDITS

INDEX OF CONTRIBUTORS

GENERAL INDEX

Page numbers in **boldface type** refer to the major article for an entry. Page numbers in *italics* refer to illustrations.

Prevention of Lynching (ASWPL), 510
Astaire, Adele, 59
Astaire, Fred, **59–60**
Astley, Philip, 150
Astor, John Jacob, **60**
Atkins, Chet, 206
Atkinson, Ti-Grace, 308
Atlantic Charter, **61**
Atlantic Monthly magazine, 411, 514
Atlee, Clement, 652
Atomic energy. *See* Nuclear energy
Atomic Energy Commission, 608
Atomic weapons, 28, 172, 266, 287, **597–98,** 724, 738, 790, 823, 887. *See also* Hiroshima and Nagasaki; Manhattan Project; Nuclear energy
Attucks, Crispus, **61,** 103
Audubon, John James, **61–62,** 612
Augustine (saint), 188
Austin, Moses, 62
Austin, Stephen F., **62–63,** 809
Autobiography of Malcolm X, The, 516
Automobiles, **63–65,** 674. *See also* Ford, Henry; Suburbia
Autry, Gene, 206
Avedon, Richard, 634
Aviation, **65–67.** *See also* Earhart, Amelia; Lindbergh, Charles A.; Wright, Orville; Wright, Wilbur

Babbitt (Lewis), 492
Babbitt, Bruce, 602
Babcock, Orville, 363
Baby and Child Care (Spock), 778
Bacon, Henry, 579
Bacon, Nathaniel, 68
Bacon's Rebellion, **68**
Baden-Powell, Lord, 741
Baez, Joan, 572
Bailey, James A., *74,* 74, 151
Bailey v. *Alabama,* 411
Baker, Ella, *68,* **68–69**
Bakke, Allen, 16
Balanchine, George, **69–70,** *70,* 218
Baldwin, James, **70–71**
Ballet, 217, 218–19. *See also* Balanchine, George
Ballinger, Richard A., 71
Ballinger-Pinchot controversy, **71**
Ballou, Hosea, 387
Baltimore and Ohio Railroad, 555, 692–93
Band, the, 763

Banks of the United States, 37, **71–72,** 198, 302, 422, 439, 442, 803
Banneker, Benjamin, *72,* **72–73**
Bannerman, Martin, 179
Barbary wars, **73,** 521, 587
Barkley, Charles, 80
Barnard College, 264
Barnburners, 331
Barnett, Frederick, 869
Barnum, Phineas T., **73–74,** *74,* 150–51, 496
Barron v. *Baltimore,* 526
Barry, Comm. John, 436
Barrymore, Ethel, 813
Barrymore, Lionel, 366
Bartholdi, Frédéric Auguste, 581
Bartók, Béla, 358
Barton, Clara, 36, **74–75,** *75*
Baseball, **75–77,** 372, 530–31, 711, 714, 725–26, 779, 780, 781
Basie, Count, 314
Basketball, **77–80,** 372, 780, 895
Batista, Fulgencio, 641
Battles. *See names of specific places and conflicts*
Bauer, Catherine, 409
Bay of Pigs invasion, **80,** 137, 172
Báz, Farouk el-, 46
Baziotis, William, 365
Beach Boys, 716
Beanes, Dr. William, 470
Beat generation, 350–51, 470
Beatle Bailey (Walker), 181
Beatles, 86, 572, 716, 758, 762
Beauregard, Gen. P. G. T., 286
Beauvoir, Simone de, 307
Bechet, Sidney, 451
Beecher, Catharine, **80–81,** 408, 779–80, 790
Beecher, Edward, 790, 791
Beecher, Henry Ward, 790
Beecher, Lyman, 80–81, 790
Beecher, Mary, 81
Beers, Clifford, 543
Belgian Benevolent Society, 865
Belknap, William W., 363
Bell, Alexander Graham, *81,* **81–82,** 737
Bell, John, 198
Bell, Melville, 81
Belles-lettres, 500
Beloved (Morrison), 559
Belushi, John, 255
Benedict, Ruth, **82–83**
Bennett, Floyd, 118

Bennett, James Gordon, 514
Benny, Jack, 688
Benton, Thomas Hart (painter), 614, 646
Benton, Thomas Hart (senator), 332
Benz, Carl, 63
Berbick, Trevor, 33
Bergman, Ingrid, 735
Bering, Vitus, 294
Berkeley, Busby, 219
Berkeley, Sir William, 68
Berkman, Alexander, 353, 354
Berlin, Irving, 60, **83–84,** 455, 571, 899
Berlin blockade, **84,** 171, 823
Berlin Wall, 172
Bernadotte, Count Folke, 116
Bernstein, Leonard, **84–85,** 571
Berry, Chuck, **85–86,** 572, 716
Bessemer process (steel making), 125
Bethel Methodist church, 34
Bethune, Mary McLeod, *86,* **86–87**
Biddle, Nicholas, 72
Bierstadt, Albert, 613
Big-city bosses, **87–88,** 204, 566, 829–30
Billings, William, 569
Bill of Grievances (AFL, 1906), 484
Bill of Rights, 43, **88–91,** 94, 116, 133, 147, 196, **327–28, 328–30,** 391, 396, 513, 514, 616–27, 667, 799, 857
Billy the Kid, 212
Bingham, George Caleb, 613
Birds of North America, The (Audubon), 62, 612
Birney, James G., 494
Birth control, **91–93,** 132, 297, 308, 353, 524, 733–34, 762. *See also* Abortion
Birth of a Nation (Griffith), 366, 529, 564
Bismarck, Otto von, 866
Black, Hugo, **93–94,** 323
Black Codes, **94–95,** 156–57, 457, 685, 696
Black Hawk, 95, **951–96**
Black Hawk War, 95
Black Legionnaires, 516
Black Manhattan (Johnson), 458
Black Muslims (Nation of Islam), 24, 32, 516
Black nationalism: and civil rights movement, 23–24, 349; before emancipation, **96–97**
Black Panther Party, 24
Black power, 349, 761, 795
Blacks. *See* African Americans
Black Sox scandal, 76
Blackwell, Elizabeth, **97–98**

Hughes, Charles Evans, 378, **411–12**
Hughes, Langston, 380, *412,* **412–13,** 414
Hull-House, 12–13, 375, 752, 836, 865. *See also* Settlement house movement
Human Rights for Women, 308
Humphrey, Hubert H., 595, 762
Hundred Days, **413**
Hunter, Maj. Gen. David, 827
Hurston, Zora Neale, 380, **414**
Hutchinson, Anne, **414–15,** *415,* 875
Hutchinson, Thomas, 103, 104, **415–16**
Hyde Amendment, 5
Hydrogen bomb, 7. *See also* Atomic weapons; Nuclear energy
Hyer, Tom, 106

Iacocca, Lee, 436
Ice hockey, **392–93**
Ickes, Harold, 21, 675
Illness. *See* Disease; Medicine
Immigration, **417–20;** and architecture, 407–8; colonial, 175–76, 584–85; and nativism, **584–87;** quotas in, 55, 418–19, 586; and racism, **685–86;** and religion, 131–32; sources of, *419* (table); and urban growth, 835; during World War II, 397. *See also* Know-Nothing Party; Nativism; Settlement house movement
Immigration Act (1965), 146
Immigration Restriction League, **420**
Impeachment, 404, **420–21,** 749
Imperialism, 518. *See also* Expansion, territorial
Impressment controversy, 281, **421–22,** 853, 855
Improvisation. *See* Jazz
Indentured servitude, 141, 143, 175, 638, 685, 709–10
Independence Day (Fourth of July), 394, *394*
Independent treasury, **422**
Independent Treasury Act (1840), 422, 645, 839
India: civil disobedience in, 154; immigrants from, 55
Indian Removal Act (1830), 820
Indian Reorganization Act (1934), 432
Indian reservations, 211, 288, **422–24,** 430–32, 461–62
Indian societies and cultures, **424–29;** and architecture, 46, 407; and assimilation, 423; and Columbian Exchange, 176; and conservation, 191; and Dawes

Severalty Act, **221–22;** and epidemics, 283; and family life, **295–96;** and games, 780; games in, 338; map of, *429*
Indian-white relations, 289–90, 343–44, **430–32,** 442–43, 759–60, 805–6, 819–20, 888–89
Industrialization: and child labor, 144; and economic inequalities, 769; and law, 110–11; and medical hazards, 375–76; and poverty and homelessness, **654–55,** 865. *See also* Labor movement
Industrial Revolution, **432–33**
Industrial Workers of the World (IWW), **433,** 570
Industry. *See* Automobiles; Industrialization; Industrial Revolution; Iron and steel industry; Labor movement; Lowell system; Textile industry; Tobacco
Influenza, 283, 732
"In God We Trust," 148
Inheritance of property, 660–61
Integration. *See* African Americans: since World War II; Civil rights movement; Segregation, racial
Internal combustion engines, 63, 319
International Business Machines (IBM), 45
International Committee of the Red Cross, 36, 75
International Council of Women, 40
International Geophysical Year (1957–58), 119
International Ladies' Garment Workers Union, 822
International Typographical Union, 482
International Woman Suffrage Alliance, 40
Interstate Commerce Act (1887), 167, 692
Interstate highway system, 67
Intolerable Acts. *See* Coercive Acts (1774)
Intolerance (Griffith), 366
Inventions. *See* Patents; Science and technology
Invisible Man (Ellison), 279
Iran-contra affair, 135, 137, **434**
Iran hostage crisis, 128, **434–35**
Iran-Iraq War, 45
Iraq, 155. *See also* Gulf War
Irish immigrants, 131–32, 243, 387, 418, **435–36**
Iron and steel industry, 125, 400
Isabella (queen of Spain), 176, 177
Isolationism, 35, 589, 722

Israel, 266, 823. *See also* Arab-Israeli conflict
Italian immigrants, 132, **436**
Ives, Charles, 200, **437**
Ivy League, 78
Iwerks, Ub, 237
Iwo Jima, battle of, 522
IWW. *See* Industrial Workers of the World

Jackson, Andrew, *438,* **438–39;** and annexation of Texas, 810; assassination attempt on, 58; and banking reform, 72, 422, 439, 442; and Battle of New Orleans, 856; and Democratic Party, 228, 618; in elections, 10, 123, 166, 203, 228, 270 (table), 406, 439, 442, 618, 658, 839; and Indian removal, 820; Kitchen Cabinet of, 120, 439; and preservation of the Union, 409; and tariffs, 123, 442, 600. *See also* Jacksonian Democracy
Jackson, Jesse, 24, **439–40,** *440,* 714
Jackson, Michael, 718
Jackson, Robert, 700
Jackson, Shoeless Joe, 726
Jackson, Gen. Thomas J. ("Stonewall"), 162, **441**
Jackson, William Henry, 632
Jacksonian Democracy, 228, **441–43**
Jagger, Mick, 251
Jahn, Friedrich Ludwig, 371
James, Frank, 212, 444
James, Harry, 758
James, Henry, 411, **443–44,** 869
James, Jesse, 212, **444–45,** 638
James, Will, 503
James, William, 234, 443, **445,** 786
Jamestown colony, 637, 766–67, 816
Japan: immigrants from, 55, 342; U.S. trade with, 311, 635
Japanese Americans, internment of, 55, **445–47,** 887
Jay, John, 194, 196, 302, **447–48,** 616, 709
Jay's Treaty, **448–49,** 894
Jazz, 277–78, 314–15, 358, **449–51,** 570, 571
Jazz Singer, The (film), 564
Jefferson, Blind Lemon, 100, 450
Jefferson, Martha Wayles Shelton, 451
Jefferson, Thomas, **451–52;** and architecture, 46–47, 451, *insert following* 52; and banking reform, 198, 374–75; and Barbary wars, 73; on Declaration of Independence committee, 226, 324,